THE DISORGANIZED PERSONALITY

THE DISORGANIZED PERSONALITY Second Edition

George W. Kisker

Professor of Psychology, University of Cincinnati

McGRAW-HILL BOOK COMPANY

New York   St. Louis   San Francisco   Düsseldorf
Johannesburg   Kuala Lumpur   London   Mexico
Montreal   New Delhi   Panama   Rio de Janeiro
Singapore   Sydney   Toronto

THE DISORGANIZED PERSONALITY

Library of Congress Catalog Card Number 75-172656

07-034874-X

234567890MURM798765432

This book was set in Helvetica by Black Dot, Inc., printed by The Murray Printing Company, and bound by Rand McNally & Company. The designers were Howard Leiderman and J. E. O'Connor; the drawings were done by John Cordes, J. & R. Technical Services, Inc. The editors were John Hendry and David Dunham. Peter D. Guilmette supervised production.

CONTENTS

PREFACE TO THE SECOND EDITION

The revision of a textbook is undertaken for several reasons. First, and perhaps most obvious, is the fact that new developments in theory and new experimental findings make it necessary to update the book. At the same time, material that has been superseded or has lost its usefulness must be weeded out.

A second objective in revising a textbook is to reflect the broader changes in thinking and philosophy related to the particular field of study. For example, in the period since *The Disorganized Personality* was first written, there has been a growing dissatisfaction with the view that mental disorder is an illness or disease. While the disease model still has a firm grip on the thinking of many members of the medical profession, most psychologists, psychiatrists, and other behavioral scientists are more inclined to view personality disturbance as a learned reaction pattern. The second edition of this book reflects this change in thinking. Even though the essentially biological orientation of the first edition is retained, the book deemphasizes personality disturbance as a disease and places greater importance on the role of learning. Another major trend in thinking in the field of abnormal psychology has been the growing concern with humanism. More attention is being placed on the self and the person. This significant shift in emphasis is also recognized in the present edition of this book. Perhaps the most important

change in the field of abnormal psychology has been the continuing decline in the influence of psychoanalytic concepts and theories. This decline sharply accelerated during the period between the writing of the first and second editions of this book. At the same time, the behavior approach has become increasingly important. Consequently, this edition of *The Disorganized Personality* places less emphasis on the Freudian point of view and considerably more emphasis upon behavior shaping in the causation of mental disorders and upon behavior modification in the treatment of them.

A third objective of a textbook revision is to make changes that will improve the book as a teaching device and make it a more rewarding experience for students. Feedback from teachers and students can be a great help. Sometimes, however, this feedback appears to be contradictory. Some of the users of the first edition felt there was too much emphasis on organic factors in personality disturbance; others felt that too much weight was given to Freudian psychology. These opposite points of view suggest that organically oriented psychologists did not find the book organic enough and that psychoanalytically oriented psychologists did not find it Freudian enough.

These contradictory views are evidence that one of the primary aims of the book has been met, namely, that it present a balanced point of view. An introductory textbook should not be an instrument for selling a theoretical orientation to the beginning student. He should be presented with a variety of approaches, and he should be allowed to develop his thinking according to his individual interests and inclinations. The first course of abnormal psychology is not the place for a one-sided presentation of the psychoanalytic position, the biological position, psychoanalysis, behavior theory, or humanism. Obviously, each of these approaches has an important contribution to make. Biases, prejudices, and theory-bound thinking have a way of taking over soon enough.

The plan of this edition of *The Disorganized Personality* is similar to that of the first edition. Chapter 1 is an introduction to the field of abnormal psychology and shows how the subject relates to other professional fields and to the problems of everyday life. A new emphasis has been given to the impact of our rapidly changing society on personal adjustment. The second chapter deals with the history of the subject. The major change in this chapter is the introduction of the revised system of classification adopted by the American Psychiatric Association in 1968. The next three chapters discuss the roles of organic, psychological, and cultural factors in the causation of personality disorganization. Chapter 3 introduces new material on behavioral genetics, and chapter 4 emphasizes more heavily the role of learning in the development of personality disturbances and behavior disorders. Psychoanalytic concepts have been deemphasized. Chapter 5 discusses sociocultural influences in personality disorganization.

Chapters 6 through 12 are concerned with the clinical types of psychological disorders. In addition to the tape-recorded clinical interviews which accompanied these chapters of the first edition and of this new edition as well, a supplementary set of recorded interviews is available. The clinical chapters are followed by three chapters dealing with diagnosis and treatment. Chapter 13 has been expanded to include electrophysiological techniques that are used to supplement psychodiagnosis. Here the student is also introduced to the concept of computer-assisted diagnosis. Chapter 14, dealing with medical treatment, has been somewhat simplified, and surgical techniques have been deemphasized. Chapter 15 has been reorganized to permit a more detailed discussion of behavior therapy. While some authorities are inclined to view behavior therapy as a subdivision of psychotherapy, I consider the differences between them to be great enough to discuss them as separate treatment approaches. Chapter 15, which concludes this edition, discusses selected topics of experimental and innovative psychopathology.

Special acknowledgments for this edition of *The Disorganized Personality* are made to John Hendry, Basic Book Editor of the McGraw-Hill Book Company, whose perceptive and conscientious editing has been of inestimable value to me; to my secretary, Mrs. Irene Giessl, whose skill and efficiency contributed in a very substantial way to the completion of the book; and to my wife, Florence Ray Kisker, who encouraged me when I needed it most, and to whom this book is gratefully dedicated.

George W. Kisker

PREFACE
TO THE FIRST
EDITION

The Disorganized Personality is a book dealing with the troubled mind. The volume was written in response to the need for an introductory textbook which would reflect the dramatic changes which have been taking place in the field of mental health and illness. Recent advances in this field have had greater impact and significance than the combined developments of the previous half century. The present book is designed to make available to students and to instructors a work that is at once readable and teachable, authoritative, and scientifically accurate.

It is recognized that even the most objective survey of any field must reflect some of the interests and inclinations of the author. This book is no exception. The reader will not fail to sense the essentially biological orientation of the work. The nervous system, and particularly the brain, is one of the most intriguing structures to be found in the physical world. Its development has made it possible for man to move from mere brutishness to an early phase of humanity. Interference with the smooth functioning of the nervous system— whether a result of stress, disease, or damage— sets the stage for personality disorganization.

In recent years there has been something of a revolution in thinking with reference to the problems of personality disturbance. As a result of the influence of Sigmund Freud early in the present century and the subsequent development of the psychogenic point of view, there was a much-needed emphasis on psychological factors in mental illness. Physical factors, which in the nine- teenth century had been overemphasized, came to be relatively neglected. The most recent trend, and the dominant orientation and philosophy of this book, has been in the direction of a more reasonable balance of physical, psychological, and social factors.

It is important to remember that there is no basic conflict between the biological, psychological, and cultural points of view. It is not a question of which approach is correct or more desirable. It is merely a matter of emphasis and interest. If we know anything at all about mental illness, it is that its causes are many-sided. Few illnesses can be explained in terms of simple causation. Every disturbance of the personality involves the total person and grows out of the most complex kind of physical, psychological, and sociological interaction. The present book emphasizes this multidisciplinary aspect of the problems of mental health and illness.

The book follows a plan of development in which Chapter 1 introduces the reader to the field of abnormal psychology and shows its relevance to other scientific disciplines as well as to some of the everyday aspects of the world in which we live. The second chapter places the subject matter in a broad historical perspective. Chapters 3, 4, and 5 discuss in some detail the organic, psychological, and cultural factors contributing to the causation of personality disorganization. Chapters 6 through 12 take up in turn the various clinical types of personality disturbance. The order of presentation is from the most minor and temporary disorders brought about almost entirely by external stress to the most serious and irreversible conditions involving organic changes of the nervous system.

Following the clinical chapters, there are three chapters dealing with diagnosis and treatment. Chapter 13 surveys the field of psychodiagnosis, Chapter 14 deals with physical treatment methods, and Chapter 15 introduces the reader to the nature and techniques of psychotherapy. The book concludes with a chapter on experimental psychopathology, the content of which forms a bridge to the future for the student.

It will be noted that the book follows the American Psychiatric Association's classification of personality disturbances. The author is well aware of some of the shortcomings of this classification. However, as much as one might wish to introduce a more dynamic and imaginative system, the fact remains that the APA classification is the only one which has found wide acceptance. Moreover, this system is the backbone of the official statistical reporting to the National Institute of Mental Health, and is the only means of intelligent and consistent communication between clinics, hospitals, and other agencies and institutions concerned with mental health and illness.

In presenting case material, *The Disorganized Personality* introduces an entirely new method. More than forty cases described in the book, ranging from the mildest to the most serious conditions, are brought into the classroom by way of tape-recorded interviews made by the author on the wards of a mental hospital and in the psychiatric clinic of a juvenile court. This method of presentation makes it possible for the student to read about a patient in the book and then to hear the author's interview with that same patient. While some schools are located in areas where it is possible to make occasional visits to psychiatric hospitals, most schools are not able to have their students observe actual cases. Even where hospital visits can be made, it is impossible to observe a wide range of cases showing classic symptoms.

The recorded interviews accompanying this book have been designed to demonstrate particular symptoms and to bring out as vividly as possible the full range of characteristics of the various disorders. Since the interviews were primarily diagnostic rather than therapeutic, it was possible to "test the limits" in some cases in a deliberate attempt to determine frustration tolerance, anxiety level, degree of hostility, and similar factors. The recorded case reports bridge the gap between the classroom and the hospital and add an entirely new dimension to the study of personality disturbances.

Written as a textbook to the introductory course in abnormal psychology, this book will be equally useful as a text or as supplementary reading in psychiatry, psychiatric social work, psychiatric nursing, mental hygiene, special education, and other courses concerned with the problems of mental health and illness. The book also has relevance for the teacher, clergyman, lawyer, business executive, and indeed for all those men and women who seek to understand their own personality problems and those of others with whom they live and work.

I would like to express my appreciation to the many distinguished authorities in psychology, social science, psychiatry, internal medicine and other specialized fields for their comments and suggestions; to my colleagues at Longview State Hospital, Behavioral Science Associates, and the Hamilton County Juvenile Court for reviewing the galley proofs; and to my students in abnormal psychology who read and commented on various sections of the book prior to publication.

Special acknowledgement is made to Dr. Elizabeth R. Miller and Professor William C. Wester II for their constant support, advice and assistance; to Fred Sway for his perceptive photographs used in Chapters 4, 7, 13, 14, 15, and 16; and to Mildred Hazlewood who served as secretary and research assistant with a degree of efficiency and dedication without which the book could not possibly have been completed. Both Dr. Miller and Miss Hazlewood also contributed in a substantial way to the development of the Instructor's Manual which accompanies this book.

George W. Kisker

TO THE STUDENT

This is a textbook written for *you*—the student. Every phase of its planning and its development to completion had you in mind. The book reflects the author's experience of more than twenty-five years of teaching in the field of abnormal and clinical psychology, and an equal number of years of almost daily contact with children, adolescents, and adults showing behavior problems, personality disturbances, and mental illness. While the style and organization make the book easy to read and study, its value to you will be increased considerably if you will keep a few points in mind.

As with any new field of knowledge, it is important to start with a comprehensive picture of the field. You will want to know its scope and its limits and boundaries. One way of acquiring this general "feel" for the subject is to study carefully the Table of Contents of the book. See how the book is organized, and what it contains. Later, when you begin to read the text, the material will be more meaningful to you because it will be seen as part of a larger pattern.

You will find that there are a number of new and unfamiliar technical terms. Usually these terms are defined at their first appearance. In instances where this is not the case, the sense of the word is clearly evident from the way it is used. If you cannot remember the meaning of a word when it recurs in the text, consult the Glossary at the back of the book. Remember that the mastery of any new technical subject is largely a matter of learning the specialized *language* of the subject. If you ignore the unfamiliar terms, you will soon find yourself lost completely. Words and concepts are like building blocks; if they are not placed securely in the foundation, the entire structure—in this case your knowledge of abnormal psychology—will become increasingly precarious.

Students are frequently dismayed by the many unfamiliar names of people to be found in a textbook. Even when an author takes special care (as here) to eliminate less relevant names, the number remains substantial. Obviously, all authorities would not agree on the relative importance of the people mentioned. However, the names of some men and women, because of a special contribution to the field of abnormal psychology or because of a significant influence on the culture of their time, should be familiar to every student of the subject. In this book, names accompanied by dates of birth and death should be given special attention.

The problem of dates is of a somewhat similar nature. While most instructors would not insist that you know very many specific dates in this course, it is helpful to know the approximate time of an event or the period during which an important individual lived and worked. Such knowledge lets you place the developments in the field of abnormal psychology in a more meaningful historical perspective.

The book in general will be more valuable to you if you will read each chapter, outline it, and list unfamiliar words and important names. Since the entire book, as well as each chapter, follows a logical and carefully developed pattern, you will find it relatively easy to outline the material for study. Discussing the content of a chapter with fellow students will also help you to understand and retain its important points.

Recommended readings are footnoted in each chapter. You will notice that for the most part these books have been limited to those published in recent years. No one will expect you to read all these books. Yet here or there you may become intrigued by some special phase of the course. When this happens, take advantage of the recommended readings by exploring the subject further.

Do not neglect the case reports—an important feature of chapters 6 through 12. These reports give the actual circumstances of the development and expression of personality disorganization. Students sometimes hurry through this material, or skip it completely, feeling that it is not something the professor is likely to use in a quiz. This attitude is unfortunate because the very heart of a book of this type is the case material. All patients

described in this book were examined personally by the author in his work at the psychiatric hospital and the juvenile court. Every case has been selected to illustrate a particular symptom or combination of symptoms.

One of the most unusual features of your book is its accompanying series of *tape-recorded interviews* with children, adolescents, and adults. The author, who has recorded hundreds of interviews with patients over a period of years, selected many of the most dramatic and illustrative cases for you to hear in the classroom. Listen carefully to these recorded case reports. Long after the details of the textbook are forgotten, the memory of the cases should remain vividly in mind.

I hope you will get as much pleasure out of reading this book as I got from writing it. I certainly hope that you will enjoy the course as a whole—and I further hope that some of you will begin to seriously consider a career in one of the mental-health professions.

THE DISORGANIZED
PERSONALITY

1 CHANGING CONCEPTS OF NORMALITY

Abnormal psychology is a subject of the most direct and immediate interest to large numbers of people. The hundreds of thousands of patients in mental hospitals, the even larger number being treated privately or in clinics, and the millions more who are troubled, anxious, discontented, fearful, and unhappy bring the problems of emotional disturbance close to the door of every family.

The study of abnormal psychology is a means

of understanding, to some degree, the strange and seemingly incomprehensible actions of others and frequently the anxiety-provoking thoughts and feelings of ourselves. Such understanding is one of the ways by which an individual is able to protect himself from many minor emotional upsets and personality disturbances. More important, when these minor upsets are avoided, the chances of developing more serious personality problems are decreased.

It is a peculiarity of man that each person is inclined to feel that he is the only one who is tense, anxious, fearful, and unhappy. He looks with envy at his friends and acquaintances, begrudging them their apparent happiness and freedom from concern. The truth is that most people have their full share of problems. A Yale University psychiatrist said flatly, "Almost everybody—far from being happy—is actually unhappy most of the time" (Havemann, 1960).

At this point, a word of advice is in order. Many students find themselves imagining they have the very symptoms about which they are reading. It is not at all unusual for medical students and nurses in training to suspect that they are the victims of the diseases they study. In the same way, students of abnormal psychology run the danger of becoming overly subjective and alarmed about their impulses, their emotions, and their thoughts. These ideas disappear as the student becomes more knowledgeable and sophisticated in the field.

A knowledge of abnormal psychology is of value to the individual in ways other than self-understanding. It is one of the most important avenues to the understanding of others, particularly to behavior which is odd, strange, unusual, different, and seemingly inexplicable. Anyone who takes the trouble to keep up with the news events of his community is faced with the daily reminder that personality disorganization is the concern of everyone. The headlines of the newspapers and the news stories on radio and television underline the frequency and puzzling nature of abnormal behavior.

WAVE OF TEEN-AGE SUICIDES BY FIRE

Paris, Jan. 24—A 17-year-old girl set fire to herself in a Roman Catholic high school in an exclusive district of Paris. Then she leaped four floors to her death in the street. She was the fifth teen-age suicide by fire within a week. The series began in the city of Lille when a 16-year-old boy doused himself with gasoline and set himself on fire on the school playground. A few days later a 19-year-old burned himself to death in a schoolyard. He left a note saying, "I did it because I cannot adapt myself to this world. I did it as a sign of protest against violence and to see love again."

POLICE SEEK PHANTOM FOOT KISSER

New Haven, Conn. Feb. 15—A mysterious attacker with the penchant for kissing the feet of coeds has been haunting the stacks of the Sterling Memorial Library at Yale University. On at least four occasions coeds studying in isolated sections of the library have been accosted. The young man approached his victims, dropped to his knees and began kissing their feet. One coed commented, "I've had some pretty weird passes made at me, but nothing like this!"

SCHOOLBOY KILLS PRINCIPAL WITH SHOTGUN

Tomah, Wis. Oct. 3—A 14-year-old boy walked into a junior high school office and opened fire with a shotgun, killing the principal. Police said the boy entered the office late in the lunch hour and fired four times, "apparently in a fit of anger."

Unfortunately, most of us do not need to turn to newspapers to find examples of personality disorganization. We are confronted daily with living examples of the troubled personality, sometimes in members of our families, our fellow students at the university, our colleagues at work, and our friends and associates.

These conditions do not develop haphazardly and without reason. There is a cause for everything the human being does, thinks, feels, and imagines. Sometimes the cause is clear, even to the individual himself. Sometimes the cause is hidden from the individual but is clear to others. In the most serious cases, the causes are frequently complex and obscure, both to the individual and to others.

The implications of personality disorganization extend well beyond the individual. In fact, it is impossible to consider many of the problems of abnormal psychology without considering the cultural matrix in which they are embedded. The social situation frequently has an important, and sometimes critical, influence on the emergence and the pattern of a personality problem. Moreover, abnormal psychology has important implications for family life, for the local and national community, and for international relations.[1]

SOCIAL CHANGE AND NORMALITY

We live today in what probably is a time of the most rapid social change in the history of the world. Such phrases as *the new morality* and *enlightened ethics* are used to describe the social ferment in which we are living. A new permissiveness has been sweeping our world, and it is at once a heady and a troubling experience. We see this permissiveness in the dissent and rebellion of teen-agers, in the violence of young adults on our streets, in sexual behavior and erotic expression, and in the erosion of traditional religious values and rituals.

The eruptions of discontent and dissatisfaction among teen-agers and young adults, as well as among members of minority groups of all kinds, frequently are signs, or *symptoms,* of the difficulty in coping with the demands of the world in which we live. Revolt and defiance have reached epidemic proportions because young people are caught up in change in a way that would not have been possible earlier in our century.

Even under the most ideal conditions, life is difficult. We must adjust to our constantly changing and often harsh physical environment, to the people around us, and even to ourselves. We feel ourselves under constant physical, social, and psychological pressure. Psychologists use the word *stress* to describe this feeling of pressure which everyone has to some degree or other. And the way we react to this stress, the way we handle it and what we do about it, determines to a considerable degree whether we are reasonably well-adjusted (normal) or whether we are maladjusted or disorganized (abnormal).

Radio, television, communication satellites, motion pictures, the automobile, and the jet plane have destroyed the time and space barriers which protected people in the not too distant past. Technological change not only has made possible immediate involvement in the lives and frustrations of millions of others, it has made it necessary and inevitable. The result is a psychological overload which contributes to the personality problems which develop in so many people.

A rapidly changing society generates high levels of stress, especially in those of us who are caught up in the midst of the change. This is why the present decade is such an important one for mental health. It is also the reason that we are going to begin our study of abnormal psychology by taking a look at some of the stress-provoking aspects of the world in which we are living.

PROTEST AND REBELLION

Many observers of the social scene tell us that there has always been a gap between the generations and that we must therefore look elsewhere to explain the behavior ferment observed among young people. These observers fail to realize that recent technological advances have given a completely new meaning to the "generation gap." More than one-half of the population of the United States is under thirty years of age, and the percentage is increasing. A United Nations report predicted that before the end of the 1970s, the conflict between generations "will assume proportions not previously imagined."

One of the most visible expressions of protest and rebellion in recent years has been the hippie movement among young people. Sandals, beads, flowers, and flowing hair have become the symbol of all of the stored-up disaffection and disillusion-

---

[1]A nontechnical approach to the overall problems of mental health is found in Mike Gorman's *Every Other Bed* (World Publishing, 1956); *Popular Conceptions of Mental Health: Their Development and Change* (Holt, Rinehart and Winston, 1961) by Jum C. Nunnally, Jr.; and **Americans View Their Mental Health** (Basic Books, 1960) by Gerald Gurin, Joseph Veroff, and Sheila Field.

Figure 1.1 *The violence of student confrontation. (Reprinted with permission from the Chicago Daily News. Photography by Perry Riddle.)*

ment of youth. While the causes of the resentment and defiance are complex, the hippie movement gives a common philosophy, a sense of security, and a feeling of identity. Young people by the tens of thousands, in this country and abroad, defy parents and the entire adult establishment to take up the cause of peace, love, and "doing your own thing." A new subculture has been born.

To many adults, the most disturbing consequence of the hippie movement has been the casual acceptance and almost ritualistic use of drugs. The fact that the drugs are strange and exotic hallucination-inducing substances rather than the hard drugs of the conventional addict does nothing to lessen the anxiety of parents,

school officials, and the police. Marijuana, LSD, and amphetamines are used with increasing frequency and with little regard for their inherent dangers.

Paralleling the hippie movement, and sometimes growing out of it, a number of more militant protest groups have become part of the scene. The Yippies, the Crazies, the Weathermen, the Black Panthers, and similar groups lean on the adult establishment. At first the frightened and confused adults attempted to maintain social equilibrium by yielding to the many pressures and demands. Later a reaction set in, and the adult world adopted a harder line and a tougher policy. But the smoldering unrest remains as strong as it ever was, and violent and even murderous actions occur whenever the stress becomes too much to handle.

POLICE CLUBS SMASH HARVARD STUDENT DEMONSTRATION

Cambridge, Mass. (UPI)—Club-swinging, riot-garbed police cleared a path through 500 demonstrating students at Harvard University's administration building Thursday and arrested dissidents who had seized the building to protest military training at the school. Students later declared a three-day strike.

Similar headlines and news stories appeared in the nation's press calling attention to the unrest on campuses in every part of the country:

STUDENT REBELS SEIZE PRESIDENT'S OFFICE AT COLUMBIA

STUDENTS DEMONSTRATE AT PURDUE

POLICE JAIL 100 MEMPHIS STATE STUDENTS

ARMED STUDENTS ROAM CORNELL CAMPUS

STUDENT VIOLENCE THREATENS DARTMOUTH

TEAR GAS USED TO CONTROL STANFORD STUDENTS

Rioting has not been limited to our campuses. A report by Brandeis University's Lemberg Center for the Study of Violence underlined the rapid spread of urban disorders in the late 1960s. In one month (April, 1968) there were street riots reported in 172 cities. The number of people arrested and the property damage during that one month exceeded the figures for the twelve months of the previous year.

Our contemporary society is characterized by an escalation in the climate of violence in which we live. While crimes of violence, assassinations, and torture have been part of the history of mankind, the acceptance of such behavior today, and indeed the apparent pleasure so many people get out of it, can be explained in part by the gradual desensitization of millions of men, women, and children, by motion pictures and by television. Constant exposure can eventually deaden one's reaction to even the most unimaginable horrors. The thinking, feelings, and behavior of people

can be influenced in profound ways by the nature of the information input.

THE SEXUAL REVOLUTION

The changes in attitudes toward sexual behavior can be observed in the increasing permissiveness in matters of public nudity, in the wide availability of written and pictorial pornography, in the greater acceptance of premarital sexual relationships, in the more relaxed attitudes toward marital infidelity, in the trend toward the legalization of abortion, and in the casual acceptance of homosexuality and other nonconforming types of sexual behavior.

By 1970 both male and female nudes were part of the everyday scene. *Playboy* and similar magazines glorified the unclothed girl-next-door, the Dancers Workshop in San Francisco presented a nude ballet, a nude girl appeared on television in the Netherlands, male and female nudes were used in magazine advertisements, and nude scenes in motion pictures became commonplace. The off-Broadway theaters offered full-front nudity as well as simulated sexual intercourse on the stage.

Another indication of a dramatic shift in sexual attitudes is seen in the ready availability of pornographic material. Only a few years ago tourists to Europe smuggled back copies of *My Secret Life* by Frank Harris, *Tropic of Cancer* and *Tropic of Capricorn* by Henry Miller, and other "forbidden" books. Today these same books, and dozens like them, can be bought at the corner drugstore, the local newsshop, and even the college bookstore. Truly hard-core pornography is now openly sold in many cities across the country.

The acceptance of nonconforming types of sexual behavior is another characteristic of the changing morality. In novels, films, and plays, there has been a preoccupation with male homosexuality and female lesbianism. While such themes are not new in literature, they had never been pictured with such stark realism until brought to the off-Broadway stage and later to the motion picture screen. Scenes depicting masturbation and oral sexuality are on view in a number of plays and films.

The liberal attitude toward sexual expression

Figure 1.2 *Nudity on the stage as an example of changing concepts of morality. (United Press International photo.)*

is also reflected in the lifting of social restrictions on college campuses. Coed housing, the abolition of the curfew, and freer visiting hours are being introduced at many universities. It is not unusual for coeds to be permitted to invite their boy friends to their rooms.

A more dramatic example of the sexual revolution in our colleges is the pattern of behavior known as *student cohabitation*. One or more unmarried couples simply live together off campus. The parents and college officials may or may not be aware of the arrangement. Such behavior is more common in colleges located in large metro-politan areas because it is less conspicuous than it would be in a smaller community.

The change in sexual standards is reaching well into the younger adult group. The underground newspapers carry hundreds of ads of men and women seeking sexual relationships without marital ties. Both normal and nonconforming sexual activities are sought and offered. Group sexual encounters are mentioned frequently. Among married people, adultery with the consent of one's mate is an emerging pattern, while "wife swapping" is an accepted pattern of behavior among young and middle-aged "swingers." In such a

Figure 1.3 *Group sex is another indication of the relaxed social and moral norms of our time. (Elliot Gould, Natalie Wood, Robert Culp, and Dyan Cannon in a scene from* Bob & Carol & Ted & Alice, *a Frankovich Production from Columbia Pictures.© 1971 by Columbia Pictures, Inc.)*

climate of permissiveness, it should not be surprising that when a high school in New York graduated seventy girl students, eleven of them were pregnant.

While not all—or even most—people are part of the revolution in sexual behavior, the widely publicized permissiveness can be a source of conflict and confusion for many individuals. The knowledge that a relatively high degree of sexual freedom has been reached, if only in a limited segment of the population, can be frustrating and stressful even to those men and women who are not directly involved.

THE CRISIS IN RELIGION

The swift and dramatic changes which have been taking place in connection with religious beliefs and values are another source of conflict and con-

fusion in the contemporary world. The open questioning, and even defiance, of traditional religious concepts by religious leaders themselves has served to weaken and undermine faith and long-held beliefs, and has added to personal insecurity and to the lack of meaning and direction in life.

The Reverend Malcolm Boyd shocked many members of his audience when he declared, "God isn't up there any more. Nothing but clouds are up there. Religion is still laced with superstition and magic and the manipulation of God." Whatever virtue there may be to the "God is dead" issue, some psychologists believe that the impact on many people in this generation has been emotionally unhealthy.

Changes in the traditional forms of religious worship, the challenge of vows of celibacy, the liberalization of dress, participation in militant causes, the defiance of the bishops, the questioning of religious dogma, and the increasing move away from religious vocations by men and women, are but a few of the signs of ferment in the church. The National Association for Pastoral Renewal reported that more than 700 priests quit their religious vocations in 1966 and 1967, and that at least a hundred of these men had been priests for fifteen years or more. A Jesuit sociologist at Harvard asserted that the report was an underestimate and did not reveal the true extent of the problem.

The question is not whether religious belief as we have known it is ultimately desirable or undesirable. In either case, attacks on the religious establishment, however well intentioned, serve to erode further the already precarious psychological foundations of millions of people.

The result of the unrest, uncertainty, and insecurity generated by the rapid social change has been reflected in the search for security and stability. The wave of interest in astrology, the success of such pseudoscientific systems as *Scientology,* the "inner seeking" through transcendental meditation and similar cults, the preoccupation with sensory contact and encounter groups, and similar movements, show the extent of the inner psychological and emotional emptiness of modern man. That many young people cannot cope with the stress of their lives is indicated by the fact that suicide has become the second most frequent cause of death among college students, and third among high school students.

THE MYTH OF NORMALITY

Who is normal? Most people like to think of themselves as being normal. They are convinced that they act normally and do things in a normal way. They even believe they are more normal than their friends and neighbors. Yet in spite of the widespread insistence on being considered normal, there are authorities in psychology who are not so sure that normality is such a desirable state.

A distinguished expert on mental health once said, "To be normal seems shockingly repellent to me. I see neither hope nor comfort in sinking to that low level" (Menninger, 1930). Another authority assures us that "Only a fool would continue to wish to be normal after he discovered what it would be like." (Seabury, 1934). And the head of one of America's most famous private mental hospitals commented that all the normal people in any city could be housed in its city hall.

Robert Louis Stevenson, in the novel *Markheim,* wrote a line about that character which fits a great many people: "While one portion of his brain was alert and cunning, another trembled on the brink of lunacy." George Santayana said that even the most intelligent man "holds a lunatic in leash." Bertrand Russell, another distinguished philosopher, wrote: "I do not believe that there is, or can be, anywhere, any normal person. We all have something queer about us." And the *Glossary of Psychiatric Terms,* published by the American Psychiatric Association, does not even list the word "normal."

How is it possible to reconcile the popular desire to be normal with the opinion of these established authorities who scoff at the very notion of normality? The answer, in part, is to be found in the confusion and general lack of clarity associated with the words "normal" and "abnormal." Such words have a wide range of meaning and imply different things to different people. It is extremely difficulty to define abnormality in a generally meaningful way. On the surface, it would appear to be a simple matter. Anything not normal must therefore be abnormal. The difficulty is in trying to decide what is normal.

The word *normal* comes from the Latin *norma,* which means a carpenter's square. A *norm* therefore became a rule or pattern or standard, and it was in this sense that the word was introduced into the English language. The word *abnormal,* with its prefix *ab* ("away from"), means a variation from the normal. Human behavior and experiences which are strange, unusual, or merely different are often considered abnormal. The exact way in which such behavior has been defined, however, varies in many respects.

One of the perplexing difficulties with definitions of normality and abnormality is the assumption that these concepts are qualities possessed by the organism. Actually this is not the case. The concepts are abstractions and do not refer to measurable dimensions of the organism. Normality and abnormality can be determined only through the use of *value judgments,* and these judgments are never open to scientific verification. For this reason, it is quite impossible to arrive at a truly scientific definition of these terms.

Another serious objection, particularly to the word "abnormal," is that it has acquired an *emotional loading.* "Abnormal" arouses feelings and emotions which make it difficult, if not impossible, to use the word and at the same time maintain an objective and scientific attitude. Sometimes the emotional impact of a word becomes so detrimental to its use in science that the word must be discarded. "Insanity," "feebleminded," and "pervert" are examples of other words which have lost their scientific usefulness, and which are avoided by careful writers. Albert Einstein referred to this emotional loading when he said, "Although words exist for the most part for the transmission of ideas, there are some which produce such violent disturbance in our feelings that the role they play in the transmission of ideas is lost in the background" (Einstein, 1954).

Some writers attempt to avoid the problem by substituting the term *psychopathology,* meaning the systematic investigation of morbid mental conditions, for *abnormal psychology.* However, the problem cannot be solved simply by eliminating the words "normal" and "abnormal." Since they are an important part of our general language, and are not specialized technical terms, it is unlikely that they could be eliminated. Moreover, to avoid the words and to retain the impeding attitudes would be useless and unrealistic. It is more important to accept the fictional nature of the concepts and to use them with the necessary caution and reservation.

THEORETICAL MODELS OF NORMALITY

How do we decide whether or not a person is normal? Think about some of the people you know. You can probably rank them from the most normal to the least normal. How do you do it? Upon what do you base your judgment?

Ordinarily we arrive at our decision by means of *theoretical models* or patterns which serve as standards against which we measure the behavior of people we know or hear about. *Descriptive models* emphasize the criteria used in determining whether or not behavior is abnormal; *explanatory models* are based upon the assumed processes underlying abnormal behavior.

DESCRIPTIVE MODELS

These models seek to describe abnormal behavior in terms of external criteria. Some type of standard is adopted, and behavior is considered normal or abnormal to the extent that it adheres to the standard or deviates from it. Models of this type include the subjective model, normative model, statistical model, and cultural model.

The Subjective Model

In the subjective model, normality is a personal judgment on the part of each individual. The judgment is made by establishing oneself as the standard of comparison. If other people are similar to ourselves, we are likely to consider them normal. If they are sufficiently different from ourselves by deviating in their patterns of action and thinking, it is probable that we would consider them abnormal.

> Everyone is queer
> Save thee and me,
> And sometimes I think
> Thee a bit queer, too.
>   Quaker proverb

The subjective model insists that people are either normal or not normal. There is no overlapping, and there is no transition from one to another. "Once a thief, always a thief" is a popular belief that applies equally well to mental disorders. "You can't change human nature" is an idea rooted deep in the thinking patterns of the great majority of people. This view assumes a qualitative difference between those who are normal and those who are not. It implies that people who are not normal are of a completely different kind.

The Normative Model

In the normative model, an ideal of behavior is established, and those who most nearly approach the ideal are considered the most normal. Complete normality, according to this view, is perfection.

The great religious leaders of the world, including Buddha, Confucius, Mohammed, Moses, and Christ, ordinarily are regarded as the most ideal of all personalities. Many men aspire to

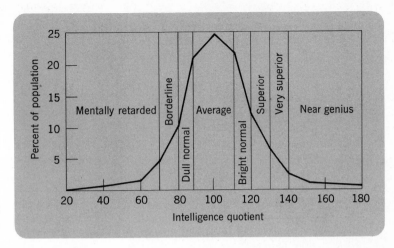

Figure 1.4 *The normal distribution curve. (Adapted from L. M. Terman,* Measuring Intelligence, *1937.)*

emulate the selfless behavior of these eminent historical figures. The monastic life, and the lives of the saints, are vivid examples of the efforts of some men and women to attain the ideals of human perfection. A rare few manage to reach degrees of perfection far beyond anything attained by the masses of people. These few become idealized, and serve as models of behavior to which other men aspire. The great philosophers, members of nobility, and creative geniuses also have been regarded from time to time as models of normality.

The weakness in the normative model is that seemingly ideal personalities, when examined closely, reveal a full share of human frailties and shortcomings. A more fundamental flaw in the normative model is that it is based ultimately on the idea of "what ought to be." Such a concept has no place in scientific investigation. Science is not concerned with what ought to be or what should be. It is concerned only with the world as it exists.

The Statistical Model

The statistical conception of normality says that the "average" is normal. There is an average weight, height, hat size, shoe size, and clothing size. The closer the average is approached, the more normal the person is considered to be. A man would not be normal if he wore a size ten hat, or a size fourteen shoe.

The statistical model is best illustrated by the normal distribution curve. This curve is derived

by plotting cases along a base line, with the number of cases indicated on the vertical axis. The bell-shaped appearance of the curve is due to the fact that most cases fall in the middle of the distribution, with fewer and fewer cases trailing off at the lower and upper ends. According to the statistical model, cases falling around the middle of the distribution most closely approximate normal cases. As cases fall farther and farther toward the ends of the distribution, the degree of abnormality increases.

The statistical criterion of abnormality is illustrated clearly in the case of intelligence. When intelligence test scores are plotted along a base line, the majority of the scores fall into the middle section of the distribution; that is, most people have average intelligence. Relatively few people have high intelligence, fewer have very high intelligence, and a rare few are geniuses having an extraordinary capacity for imaginative creation, original thought, invention, or discovery. Similarly, some people have low intelligence, fewer have very low intelligence, and a relatively small number are mentally retarded. For this reason, fewer and fewer cases are plotted as the ends of the distribution are approached. When large numbers of cases are involved, the typical bell-shaped curve appears. Individuals with abnormally high intelligence and abnormally low intelligence are at either end.

Unfortunately, this approach does not lend itself conveniently to the analysis of the personality. While the statistical model is an adequate means of portraying relatively uncomplicated traits and of representing simple biological measurements, it cannot reflect the subtle complexities of a total personality. The difficulty is not in the nature of the model, but in the present inability of science to formulate personality variables in a way in which they can be handled meaningfully by statistical techniques. The inability to isolate and quantify the variables of personality makes the statistical model largely ineffective in the field of personality disturbance at the present time.

Another difficulty with the statistical model is that the frequent occurrence of a given type of behavior is not necessarily healthy, desirable, or normal. Many physical conditions, such as tooth cavities, hardening of the arteries, high blood pressure, and defective vision, are so frequently encountered that they are average in the statistical sense. Similarly, millions of people are anxious, worried, fearful, guilt-laden, depressed, and emotionally unstable. Yet the mere frequency of these conditions does not make them normal in terms of mental health.

The Cultural Model

The cultural model is based on the assumption that normality is the standard approved by the greatest number of people. If enough people adopt a hairstyle, article of clothing, type of dance, manner of speech, or way of behaving, it is assumed to be normal. The cultural view was expressed by Ruth Benedict, an American anthropologist, who said, "Normality, within a very wide range, is culturally defined. It is primarily a term for the socially elaborated segment of human behavior in any culture; and abnormality is a term for the segment that that particular civilization does not use." The cultural view also is expressed in the following comment by a psychiatrist: "Whenever we try to give a definition of what mental health is, we simply state our preference for a certain type of cultural, social, and ethical order" (Szasz, 1956).

There are many examples of the cultural determination of normality and abnormality. Homosexuality is frowned upon and considered abnormal in our society. But at other times and in other places, such behavior has been considered quite acceptable and normal. The severe view of this type of behavior in the Old Testament is indicated by the admonition: "If a man also lieth down with a man as he lieth with a woman, both of them have committed an abomination. They shall verily be put to death. Their blood shall be upon them." However, in ancient Greece, sexual love among members of the same sex was looked upon favorably, and even encouraged. Plato said: "They [speaking of homosexuals] act in this way because they have a strong soul, manly courage, and a virile character" (Jowett, 1953). Today, in our culture, homosexual behavior is neither an abomination nor a sign of strong character. It is looked upon as an expression of a personality problem. Here, then, are three sets of attitudes toward the same behavior. Each attitude is a function of the culture in which the behavior occurs.

Changes in attitude toward what is acceptable and "normal" are seen clearly in the relaxation of restrictions on "obscene" language in literature. When the movie version was made of Tennessee Williams' play *A Streetcar Named Desire,* the producers were required to eliminate the last three words from the line "I would like to kiss you softly and sweetly *on the mouth.*" And Norman Mailer had to invent the word *fug* to give the flavor of profanity to his war novel *The Naked and the Dead.* But with the publication in 1969 of Philip Roth's *Portnoy's Complaint,* all barriers to erotic realism in acceptable literature were demolished.

This shift in values and attitudes is highlighted by an incident at Hunter College for women in New York City. An issue of *Envoy,* the Hunter student newspaper, did not appear because one of the girl reporters used the word *fuck* shouted frequently by Yippies in Chicago during the 1968 Democratic convention disorders. The female editor backed up the reporter, and both were supported in the use of the word by the female Dean. But the commercial shop that printed the paper refused to set the word in type. What is "normal" for girls at Hunter is still "abnormal" for the older generation of male printers.

The legal concept of abnormality is a special form of the cultural model. The view assumes that normal behavior is that which is consistent with the codified regulations of society, while abnormal behavior is inconsistent with the rules of society. The difficulty with the legal criterion of abnormality is that it measures behavior in terms of rules, regulations, ordinances, and laws, many of which have been established arbitrarily, with little consideration for the complexities of human behavior.

Furthermore, the legal world is still burdened to some extent by the archaic concept of determining "insanity" by the test of whether an individual knows right from wrong. The assumption is that if this distinction can be made, the individual is "sane"; if the distinction cannot be made, the individual is "insane." Nothing could be more incorrect.

While the legal concept has been modified in some states, the continuing use of the ability to distinguish between right and wrong as a measure of mental competency is completely without justification. Serious forms of personality disorganization are found in some men and women who would have little trouble in making such a distinction, while the distinction cannot be made by many antisocial individuals who have never shown any symptoms of personality disturbance (see Chapter 7).

EXPLANATORY MODELS

While descriptive models are convenient for the thinking of the layman, the professional worker in the field of mental health is more concerned with the underlying processes leading to abnormality than in how abnormal behavior differs from normal behavior. He wants to know *why* deviation in behavior occurs. To help him in his thinking, he uses explanatory models. The principal models of this type are the disease model, the psychodynamic model, the learning model, and the stress model.

The Disease Model

The traditional model of mental disorder has been a medical one in which personality disturbance is looked upon as an illness. This point of view has a long history reaching back to the time of Hippocrates and ancient Greek medicine. It is not surprising that this view has maintained a firm hold on the thinking of psychiatrists, psychologists, and other professionals working in medical settings. For a number of centuries—and until less than a hundred years ago—the interest in mental disturbances was limited to patients in mental hospitals and asylums. No one questioned the accepted view that the inmates were mentally ill as a result of some type of disease.

Today the disease model of abnormal behavior is under severe attack. The validity of the concept is being challenged by a growing number of psychologists and psychiatrists who are convinced that personality disturbances can no longer be regarded as illnesses in the traditional medical sense. Even in those cases in which abnormal changes in the personality accompany demonstrable organic disease in patients who are physically ill, the disturbed personality is not the illness or disease. It is merely an indication of the underlying abnormal physical condition.

In rejecting the idea of mental illness it is argued that individuals are considered mentally ill only because of the way in which society defines what is psychologically healthy and psychologically "sick." The situation is quite different in the medical field, where a diseased kidney is a diseased kidney regardless of what other people say or think. But behavior standards are established in an arbitrary manner by social definition, and variations in behavior can be judged only in terms of this definition. Such reasoning, which has much to say for it, is difficult for many people to accept because it runs counter to what appears to be the "commonsense" view that abnormal behavior is somehow an indication of an illness.

The Psychodynamic Model

The first important departure from the concept of mental disorder as a disease occurred at the beginning of the present century when psychiatrists began to study and treat the personality disturbances of people who were not in hospitals or other institutions. When it became clear that most personality disturbances develop in individuals who are physically healthy, the traditional view that mental disorder is due to some type of underlying disease process had to be reexamined. Even more important, a new explanatory concept was required. This new explanatory model was provided by the Austrian physician Sigmund Freud (1856–1939) and his colleagues and followers, who developed the psychodynamic model.

The psychodynamic model seeks to explain abnormal behavior and mental disorder in terms of psychological processes taking place at the hidden levels of the personality. The concept of unconscious mental activity is used to describe these processes which ordinarily are beyond the range of the individual's awareness. This view emphasizes unconscious motivation, unconscious conflict, and an unconscious struggle to rid ourselves of the conflict. When this inner drama is unsuccessful, the symptoms of personality disturbance appear. The form these symptoms take is determined by a combination of inborn, developmental, and learned factors.

The psychodynamic approach has certainly been one of the most important developments in the history of abnormal psychology. It has shaped the thinking of many psychiatrists and other professionals in the mental health field. It has had an even more extensive impact on the cultural climate of our time. But while the psychodynamic model of abnormal behavior has tended to weaken the hold of the disease model, it has by no means replaced it.

The Learning Model

The most recent challenge to the view that mental disorder is a disease has come from those psychologists and psychiatrists who see the disturbed personality as a pattern of learned behavior. Here the emphasis is on the way in which life experiences have shaped the behavior of the individual. This view seeks to explain abnormal behavior in terms of the established laws of conditioning and other forms of learning. In addition to rejecting the idea that mental disorder is an illness, the learning model suggests that many of the psychodynamic explanations can be replaced by more simple and verifiable principles of learning theory.

While the full impact of the learning model was not felt in the field of abnormal psychology until the 1960s, the principles upon which this approach is based were introduced at the beginning of the twentieth century by the Russian neurophysiologist Ivan P. Pavlov (1849–1936) and the American psychologist Edward Lee Thorndike (1874–1949).

The Stress Model

This explanatory model of abnormal behavior holds that personality disturbance is a response to stress or pressure which the individual is unable to handle satisfactorily. The stress may be due to physical, psychological, or social pressures, alone or in combination. The symptoms of personality disturbance grow out of the individual's struggle to maintain balance or equilibrium in the face of stress. An important advantage of the stress model is that it can be readily reconciled with the learning model, the psychodynamic model, and even the disease model.

The word *stress* has been used in psychology in at least two different ways. Some writers use the word to mean a state of psychological upset or disequilibrium in an individual. In this meaning, stress is a characteristic of the organism. More properly, stress should be regarded as a class of stimuli which threaten the individual in some manner and produce disturbances in behavior and inner experience. The stress is not the disturbance itself but the strain and pressure leading to the disturbance. A stress situation ordinarily is inferred as a result of the disorganized behavior or the disorganized experience of the patient.

Stressful situations may be organic, psychological, or cultural. At the organic level, injury and other physical stresses result in an increase in the blood level of pituitary and adrenal hormones. Psychological stress also raises the level of these hormones in the blood. Similarly, social pressures which have a psychological impact upon the individual are reflected in one or another form of disturbance of behavior or experience.

Everyone is faced many times each day with minor stress situations. The alarm fails to go off in the morning, there is not enough hot water, the toast is cold, traffic is heavy, and the student is late getting to the campus for class. At noon the cafeteria is crowded, and it is necessary to stand in line. A professor criticizes the student's work during class. A low grade is received on an examination. That evening, the blind date turns out to be a complete disappointment. Such situations are common to everyone and are an unwelcome part of everyday existence. At the time, the individual is annoyed and irritated. He may become angry. But the incident is soon forgotten.

In addition to the minor stress situations faced each day, most people now and then are faced with stress situations of a much more serious nature. A severe illness of a member of the family, a dangerous surgical operation, a failure in a course that makes it necessary to postpone graduation, a poor record on an important job, bills that pile up beyond one's income, a physical handicap, marital discord, and similar situations frequently are threats which cannot be ignored or shrugged off. Such stress situations are often capable of bringing about behavior disorders and personality disturbances which may last for prolonged periods.

Whether or not a given situation is a stressful one depends ultimately upon the behavior of the individual. Some people are able to handle the most threatening situations without too much difficulty. Other people break down under relatively mild stress. A stress situation for one person may not be a stress situation for another. There are wide individual differences in ability to handle threatening stimuli.

Limitations of Explanatory Models

Each of the explanatory models of abnormal behavior has been criticized by opponents and praised by advocates. An objective view of the problem suggests that each of the approaches has a degree of validity when applied to the appropriate behavior. The disturbed thinking of the patient with brain syphilis is most certainly a symptom of disease even though it is not the disease itself; but the young man who exposes his penis to women in public places might very well be reacting to internal conflicts of a psychodynamic nature; and those individuals plagued by abnormal fears could have learned that pattern of behavior. Moreover, in all three of these instances it is quite possible that the abnormal behavior is a response to stress. A well-balanced approach to explanation in abnormal psychology does not attempt to fit all forms of disorder to a preconceived model but seeks to find the model which most readily handles the facts of the individual case.[2]

APPROACHES TO PERSONALITY DISORGANIZATION

Now that we have knowledge of the various models on which normality is based, we can turn to some of the more common approaches to the disorganized personality. These approaches are (1) historical, (2) etiological, (3) descriptive, (4) clinical, and (5) experimental.

THE HISTORICAL APPROACH

A full appreciation of any field of study depends upon an understanding of the forces that have shaped it. Abnormal psychology is no exception. If anything, the historical approach is even more important in this subject than in many other fields because it is a meeting point of the physical, psychological, and social sciences. It is possible, of course, to plunge headlong into the present state of things in psychopathology. Students are frequently anxious to do just this. It is more important, however, to come to the present by way of the past. To do so ensures a more solid understanding of present-day concepts and techniques.

The historical approach does more than place a profession in a more meaningful perspective; it also increases professional efficiency. A knowledge of past efforts warns of avenues to avoid and suggests other avenues that might be followed to better advantage. It is a remarkable fact that so few people, even professionals, know that many of the so-called "new developments" in the field of mental health are merely the elaboration of ideas advanced in the past. It is only the rare genius who is able to produce a truly original idea. For the most part, "new" ideas and developments are refinements and distillations of the wisdom of the years.

The historical development of abnormal psychology is an intriguing story and one with which

---

[2]Books dealing with the complex problem of the definition of mental disturbance include *The Definition and Measurement of Mental Health* (U.S. Department of Health, Education, and Welfare, 1968) edited by S. B. Sells; and two throught-provoking and controversial volumes by Thomas S. Szasz, *The Myth of Mental Illness* (Hoeber, 1961) and *The Manufacture of Madness: A Comparative Study of the Inquisition and the Mental Health Movement* (Harper and Row, 1970).

every educated and cultured man and woman should be familiar. This story is told in Chapter 2.

THE ETIOLOGICAL APPROACH

The word *etiology* refers to the study of the causes of an abnormal condition. Basically there are three major sets of etiological factors leading to the disorganized personality. The first of these sets of factors consists of organic conditions, the second involves psychological conditions, and the third is made up of social or cultural conditions.

Causes which grow out of the physical nature of the organism are known as *physiogenic* or *somatogenic*. Many forms of personality disorganization are the result of such physical factors as hereditary variations, disturbances of the body chemistry, glandular disorders, toxic states, injuries to the brain, and similar conditions. In such cases, the personality deviation exists primarily because of the alteration in the organic structure of the body, particularly of the brain and the nervous system. The organic causes of personality disturbances are covered in Chapter 3.

Psychological, or *psychogenic,* factors are also important in the development of disorganized patterns of behavior. The motives, conflicts and frustrations, feelings of guilt and anxiety, and personality defenses designed to handle such feelings play an important role in many behavior disorders and personality disturbances. When the symptoms of personality disorganization are psychologically determined, the condition is called *functional* to differentiate it from conditions having an organic cause. Chapter 4 explores the ways in which psychological stress results in personality problems.

Cultural, or *sociogenic,* factors are also involved in the development of personality disturbances. While these factors cannot operate independently of the organic and psychological organization which constitutes the individual, social forces exert a powerful influence in the determination of certain types of disorganized personality. Such factors as marital status, place of residence, race, nationality, age, sex, occupation, socioeconomic level, and cultural background are related in-

directly, and sometimes directly, to the incidence of personality breakdown and to the form it takes in individual cases. These cultural factors are discussed in Chapter 5.

THE DESCRIPTIVE APPROACH

The descriptive approach to personality disorganization deals largely with the signs, or symptoms, of the various conditions. In the most general sense, it involves the study of the clinical features of the various forms of disorganized personality. The descriptive approach is one in which interest is focused on the types of personality disorganization. Psychological disturbances, like physical illnesses, are of many kinds and are characterized by more or less distinctive groups of symptoms known as *syndromes*.

Though only the most highly trained specialist in the field would be expected to have a detailed knowledge of the many syndromes, the beginning student in abnormal psychology must have a working knowledge of the clinical categories. The descriptive approach is designed to bring order and meaningfulness to what might at first appear to be a vast number of vague and unrelated symptoms. Moreover, a knowledge of the descriptive approach is necessary before one can consider the applied problems of diagnosis and treatment. Without a knowledge of the major clinical types of personality disturbance, the entire range of applied psychopathology would remain closed to the student.

In the descriptive approach, all personality disturbances are divided into (1) mental disorders associated with organic brain disease and (2) mental disorders occurring without brain tissue changes. Chapters 6 to 12 cover the various forms of psychogenic and organic disorders.

THE CLINICAL APPROACH

The clinical approach focuses on the particular case and is concerned only with the individual patient. The method is directed toward diagnosing a condition and attempting to treat it. Diagnosis involves the identification of an abnormality from the symptoms or from other information such as the origin and course of the disturbance. It is a matter of describing the various clinical conditions and recognizing their similarities and differences. Diagnosis means differentiating among personality disturbances. It requires the skill to make fine clinical discriminations of conditions within the major diagnostic categories. The diagnostic approach goes a step beyond history, etiology, and clinical description, and moves into the applied problems of medical psychology. The relationship of diagnosis to abnormal psychology is discussed in Chapter 13.

Therapy is the treatment of the various forms of personality disorganization. Depending upon the condition, and especially upon the etiological factors involved, treatment may be medical or psychological. Medical treatment involves training in anatomy, physiology, neurology, pharmacology, endocrinology, and similar areas basic to medicine. Such treatment makes extensive use of drugs, electric shock, controlled fever, brain surgery, vitamin therapy, and other physical methods. These techniques are discussed in Chapter 14.

The treatment of personality disorders by psychological methods is based on suggestion, emotional support, various forms of learning and relearning, and the exploration of nonconscious mental activity. This form of treatment is reviewed in detail in Chapter 15.

THE EXPERIMENTAL APPROACH

The experimental approach is one of establishing the basic facts related to the disorganized personality. It begins by obtaining a knowledge of the field, suggesting hypotheses, testing them experimentally, formulating theories, and eventually establishing laws that can be used to facilitate the understanding, the diagnosis, and the treatment of personality problems. While psychologists and psychiatrists for many years have undertaken experimental studies in the field of personality disturbance, the specialty known as *experimental psychopathology* is a relatively recent development. Chapter 16 is concerned with this approach.

THE EXTENT OF THE PROBLEM

How important is the problem of abnormal behavior? The statistics tell the story. Over 40 percent of the nation's hospital beds are occupied by patients with personality disturbances; a third of the people in our country suffer symptoms of depression; at least five million people are alcoholics; hundreds of thousands are dependent upon drugs; and probably more than fifty thousand people will commit suicide this year. The statistics are so staggering that we run the risk of becoming insensitive to their meaning.

It is probable that more than 20 million people in the United States have some form of psychological disturbance needing treatment. There are about a half million people in mental hospitals at any given time, with more than a million men, women, and children admitted each year to the more than 500 public and private mental hospitals. Another 1.5 million people are being treated in approximately 2,500 mental health clinics and by psychiatrists and psychologists in private practice (NIMH, 1970).

The number of nonhospitalized mental patients is sufficiently large to make the use of hospital statistics of limited value. A survey in Maryland

Figure 1.5 *Trends in mental illness: number of resident patients, total admissions, net releases, and deaths, in state and county mental hospitals in the United States, 1950–1968. (From* Mental Health Statistics, Current Facility Reports, *National Institute of Mental Health, 1969.)*

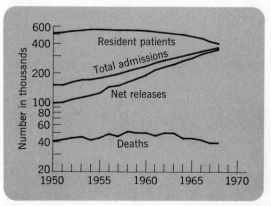

showed that for every four persons in a mental hospital, there was one person outside the hospital who was mentally disturbed but had never been admitted to a hospital (Tietze et al., 1942). A similar survey in Tennessee revealed that there was one mentally disturbed person who had never been admitted to a hospital for every patient actually admitted to a mental hospital from the community (Roth and Luton, 1943).

Military statistics also underline the extent of the problem of personality disorganization. During World War II, 15 million inductees were examined for military service. Of these, nearly 2 million men, or about 12 percent, were rejected because of personality disturbances (Hadley et al., 1944). The manpower loss to our Armed Forces in World War II because of personality disturbances was larger than the total number of men the Army sent to the Pacific theater of operations during the entire war.

An analysis of hospital statistics over a period of years indicates that there has been a dramatic increase in the total overall number of hospital admissions. The United States population has increased approximately 10 percent every ten years. However, the admissions to mental hospitals have increased about 40 percent every ten years. In 1840, there were only 2,500 patients in mental hospitals. By 1880, this number had risen to 40,000. Ten years later, in 1890, it was 75,000. By 1923, the number had risen to more than a quarter of a million, and it passed the half million mark by the middle of the present century (Malzberg, 1959).

Figure 1.6 *The decline in patients hospitalized for mental illness, as reflected by statistics for California State Hospitals, 1960–1970. (California Department of Mental Hygiene 1–10, November 23, 1970, p. 8.)*

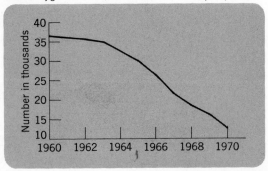

While these figures suggest a steady rise in the occurrence of personality disturbance, there is very good evidence that the rates for most conditions are the same today as they were a hundred years ago. A study of the statistics of mental hospital admissions in the state of Massachusetts for a hundred years, beginning with 1840, indicated that the apparent increase can be accounted for in terms of the admission of patients older than age fifty (Goldhamer and Marshall, 1953). Below this age, there has been very little change in admission rates. The significance of this finding is that personality disturbances requiring hospitalization, with the exception of those conditions related to the later years of life, have not increased significantly during the past century.

In 1955, the Biometrics Branch of the National Institute of Mental Health reported that the resident mental hospital population of public mental hospitals in the United States had declined for the first time. This decline was due largely to an increase in the discharge of hospital patients as a result of the development of new mental health programs and treatment facilities both in the hospital and in the community. Even though admissions continue to mount, the discharges outnumber the admissions, with the result that the hospital population has been decreasing.

By 1970 there were approximately 150,000 fewer patients in our public mental hospitals than in 1955 when the downward trend began. If the old pattern of increase had continued in an uninterrupted way, there would have been about 300,000 *more* patients than was actually the case in 1970 (NIMH, 1970).

In recent years there have been marked differences in trends in specific clinical categories. There has been a sharp increase in diseases of old age, due primarily to the increasing age span of our population. There also has been an increase in the admission of alcoholics and of children and adolescents. On the other hand, the number of admissions of patients with syphilis of the brain and other infectious disorders has fallen off sharply due to the development of antibiotics and other more effective treatment methods.

Among the factors which play a role in the overall increase in diagnosed cases of personality disturbance are the population growth of the country, the lengthening age span, increased urbanization, a more tolerant and accepting attitude toward personality problems and hospitalization, and public information campaigns designed to encourage people with personality disturbances to seek professional help. The increase in the number of hospitals and hospital beds also makes possible a larger total number of institutionalized patients.

Whatever the causes of the increase in hospital admissions, the economic loss associated with personality disturbances has reached staggering heights. Between 1950 and 1970 the total expenditure for mental health more than tripled, and it is likely to increase steadily in the future.

In 1970 the estimated total cost of personality disturbance was slightly over 20 billion dollars per year. About 80 percent of this cost was due to the decreased productivity of the afflicted. Most of the remaining amount reflected the cost of treatment services, of which 1.5 billion dollars was required to operate public mental hospitals (NIMH, 1970).

There are many other statistics that reflect situations which are the soil out of which personality disorganization develops. At least 10 percent of the public school children in the United States are emotionally disturbed and need psychological counseling or therapy. Among college students, emotional difficulties are relatively common. About 10 to 15 percent of the students on the average campus are disturbed enough to need professional help.

The problem of emotional instability is reflected also by the trends in marriage and family life. The divorce rate has risen to a point where about one of every three marriages ends in a divorce action. In California, the rate is close to one divorce for each two marriages.

Family life is further complicated by the rapidly increasing rate for children born out of wedlock. In 1950, about 4 percent of the children born in the United States were illegitimate. By 1970, the national figure had reached 10 percent, with the rates considerably higher in some cities. In New York City the illegitimacy rate is about 20 percent (USPHS, 1970).

Also important in any consideration of the mental health of the nation are the 20 million Americans above the age of 65. While this group of citizens makes up 10 percent of the population,

---

Mental Health Profile of a Community

The extent of the problem of impaired mental health can be brought more sharply into focus by visualizing an average community of 150,000 citizens. This population is about the size of the catchment areas being served by the new community mental health centers which are being established in various parts of the country. If we project the characteristics of the entire United States population to our average community, we come up with some startling facts.

Our average community will have 600 seriously disturbed mental patients; tens of thousands suffering depression; nearly 4,000 alcoholics, 3,000 homosexuals, 50 known hard drug addicts, and over 1,000 college students who have used marijuana or LSD; and 400 mentally disturbed children—nearly a hundred of them in mental hospitals. Each year, 2,000 citizens will be the victims of serious crimes, and 1,000 children will be marked as juvenile delinquents; 150 residents will attempt suicide; 225 illegitimate children will be born, over 6,000 students will drop out of high school; and 140 draftees will be rejected from military service because of mental or emotional disorders.*

*Based on National Institute of Mental Health Statistics, 1970.

Some Facts about Crime and Delinquency

About 4.5 million serious crimes were recorded in 1968.

The crime rate rose 99 percent between 1960 and 1968, while the population increased by only 11 percent.

Juvenile arrests for serious crimes increased 78 percent during the same period.

Armed robberies rose 113 percent.

Daytime burglaries of residences rose 247 percent.

There are 1.3 million offenders under correctional supervision.

Of all offenders released in 1963, 43 percent were rearrested within one year, and 63 percent were rearrested within five years.

The monetary cost to the nation of crime and delinquency is estimated at more than 20 billion dollars per year.*

*U.S. Federal Bureau of Investigation, 1970.

it accounts for 24 percent of all first admissions to state mental hospitals, and occupies 30 percent of all public mental hospital beds. There is a high incidence of depression, suicide, and withdrawal in older people. The mental health aspects of aging are therefore most important (NIMH, 1970).

The statistics on crime and delinquency also have important implications for mental health. Millions of serious crimes are committed each year, with the rates for adult crime and for juvenile delinquency increasing in an alarming way. The monetary cost to the nation—including expenses related to law enforcement, administration of justice, correctional efforts, and damage caused by offenders—reaches many billions of dollars. Even more important, in terms of mental health, is the psychological damage inflicted upon countless numbers of innocent people—parents, wives, husbands, children, and others—whose lives are disturbed in numerous ways by delinquency and criminal activity.

These statistics indicate why personality disturbance is considered the most important public health problem of the present time. While it is true that the middle of the present century has been marked by the beginning of a new revolution in the care and treatment of many of the more serious mental conditions, the rapidly changing social and physical world in which we live has been responsible for a sharp increase in personal tensions and anxieties which are leaving less obvious, but no less real, scars on modern man.[3]

ABNORMAL PSYCHOLOGY AND THE PROFESSIONS

An effective understanding of the field of abnormal psychology must include a clear idea of how this branch of psychology fits into the broader field of general psychology and how it is related to other professions concerned with the problems of mental health. Most professional psychologists define psychology as the science of behavior and they point out that this science, similar to the others, is made up of a wide range of specialties.

Child psychology studies the behavior and experience of childhood; genetic psychology is concerned with the development of behavior and experience over a period of time; industrial psychology directs itself to the human aspects of business and industry; social psychology is concerned with groups and the individuals who are group members; educational psychology deals with motivation, learning, remembering and forgetting, and other phenomena related to the school situation; and comparative psychology turns its attention to the similarities and differences between the behavior of man and the lower animals.

Abnormal psychology is that phase of psychology which studies deviations in behavior and experience. The field is oriented toward the description of personality disturbances, the development of theories to explain the observed conditions, and the use of experimental techniques in the attempt to validate hypotheses and theories. As such, abnormal psychology is not in itself an applied field. It is more concerned with providing the raw material for other scientists who are interested in finding applications for this knowledge.

The applied fields making use of the data of abnormal psychology include (1) clinical psychology, (2) psychiatry, (3) psychiatric social work, and (4) psychiatric nursing. In addition, abnormal psychology is of considerable practical importance in the fields of education, law, business, and religion.[4]

---

[3]The following books deal with the incidence, economics, and manpower problems in the field of mental health: *Applications of Mental Health Statistics* (World Health Organization, 1969) by Morton Kramer; *Manpower for Mental Health* (Aldine, 1969), edited by F. N. Arnhoff, E. A. Rubinstein, and J. C. Speisman; and Rashi Fein's *Economics of Mental Illness* (Basic Books, 1958).

[4]*Mental Health Digest* A nontechnical and readable publication designed to reflect the entire range of mental health and to present a broad sampling of subject matter and professional points of view. The magazine presents news items, reports, comment, and digests of articles. Published by the National Clearinghouse for Mental Health Information. National Institute for Mental Health, 5454 Wisconsin Avenue, Chevy Chase, Maryland 20203.

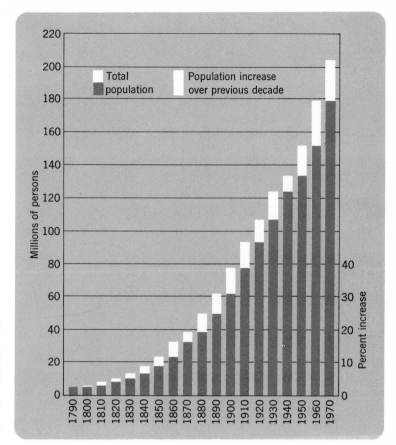

Figure 1.7 *The population trend in the United States, 1790–1970. The population was about 100 million as recently as 1920. It doubled to 200 million by 1970 and, at the same rate of increase, would be more than 300 million by year 2000. (U.S. Census Bureau, 1970.)*

CLINICAL PSYCHOLOGY

The clinical psychologist is a professionally trained person concerned with the problems of the diagnosis and treatment of personality disturbances, particularly those of a nonmedical nature. The personal problems which most people face are not problems of traditional medicine. Microscopes, laboratory analyses, and electrical readings throw little light on feelings of guilt and anxiety or on the psychological dynamics which protect people from being overwhelmed by these feelings. Nor can traditional medicine tell us much about many other symptoms and processes of personality disorganization.

While the clinical psychologist is not a physician, he is trained, both in theory and in practice, to a degree of proficiency and technical skill which is quite comparable to that of his medical colleagues. Such a psychologist is likely to be found in a university, a community mental health center, a child guidance clinic, a psychiatric hospital, a juvenile court clinic, or a correctional institution. Increasingly he is to be found in management consulting and in private practice.

The role of the clinical psychologist in mental health programs has developed more rapidly than that of any other professional group. When the first psychological clinic was established at the University of Pennsylvania in 1896, the primary function of the clinical psychologist was to administer psychological tests. Today, the special contribution of the clinical psychologist is to be found in his training in the broad principles of human behavior and in the relation of these principles to the origin and development of behavior disorders and personality disturbances. The three major functions of the clinical psychologist are diagnosis, therapy, and research. In large mental health centers and psychiatric hospitals, teaching is a fourth function.

Historically, the clinical psychologist made his earliest contributions in the area of diagnostic procedures. Later, his interests shifted noticeably to the problems of treatment. More recently, the clinical psychologist has concerned himself with basic and applied research. The problems of basic research are largely in the area of the causes of personality disorganization. Applied research directs itself to the improvement of techniques used in diagnosis and treatment.

The emphasis upon one or the other of the major functions of the clinical psychologist depends to a considerable extent upon the setting in which

the psychologist works. In some hospitals and clinics, the psychologist serves primarily in the role of diagnostician. Less frequently, his primary function is that of a therapist with individuals or groups of patients. More often, he combines his role of diagnostician and therapist. The degree to which he engages in research depends upon the availability of time and facilities and upon the encouragement which he receives from the institution.

In the area of diagnosis, the clinical psychologist has been trained in the use of special testing techniques and interpretive skills for evaluating behavior and personality. He is equipped to make objective studies of intelligence, aptitudes, interests, and personality traits. He is trained also to

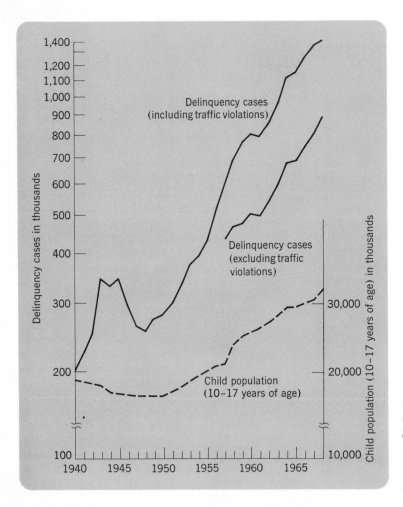

Figure 1.8 *Trends in juvenile court delinquency cases and child population ten to seventeen years of age, 1940–1968. (Juvenile Court Statistics, U.S. Office of Juvenile Delinquency and Youth Development, 1970.)*

Figure 1.9 *Students observing a diagnostic interview through a one-way mirror. (Department of Psychology, Longview State Hospital.)*

use a variety of highly specialized psychological techniques for exploring the deeper levels of personality functioning.

The role of the clinical psychologist in treatment has not been clearly defined. While many university programs include training in both the theory and practice of psychotherapy, the training is seldom enough to allow the psychologist to deal competently with the risks and responsibilities of psychotherapy. Most clinical psychologists gain their skill in psychotherapy as a result of supervised training at the postdoctoral level.

While some physicians are firmly opposed to the idea of the psychologist engaging in psychotherapy, there is rather general agreement among enlightened medical men that adequately trained clinical psychologists can and should participate in individual and group therapy. The important issue is the extent to which the clinical psychologist should practice psychotherapy independently of medical supervision.

In addition to his role as a diagnostician and therapist, the clinical psychologist has a research function. In the field of diagnosis and treatment, the psychologist ordinarily serves in a subsidiary capacity. His diagnostic work is largely for the benefit of the physician, and his treatment activities usually are under medical supervision. In the area of research, the story is quite different. The clinical psychologist, by the nature of his training, has a thorough grounding in research methodology. His knowledge of research problems and research techniques is superior to that of all but the very few physicians who have received advanced research training. For this reason, the clinical psychologist is in a position to make his most unique contribution to mental health through the utilization of his special research skills. In this field, his training and competence mark him as a leader rather than a follower.[5]

The traditional areas of research for the clinical psychologist have been psychological evaluation, or psychodiagnosis, and the study of the effectiveness of various forms of psychological and physical treatment methods. There has also been an increasing interest in man's ability to withstand stressful situations. This emphasis grew out of the problems of military psychology starting with World War II and was accelerated sharply in the

[5]Students planning careers in clinical psychology and related mental health fields will find the following books of interest: David Shakow's *Clinical Psychology as Science and Profession* (Aldine, 1969), and *Manpower for Mental Health* (Aldine, 1969), edited by F. N. Arnhoff, E. A. Rubinstein, and J. C. Speisman.

early 1960s by developments in manned space flight.

That the role of the psychologist in research in the field of personality disturbance is dominant is shown by the fact that in the several hundred research projects supported by the National Institute of Mental Health in a recent year, the principal investigator in 53 percent of the projects was a psychologist. Psychiatrists were the principal investigators in 23 percent, and the remaining projects were undertaken by social workers, anthropologists, biochemists, educators, biologists, physiologists, neurologists, pediatricians, and other specialists.

The rapidly increasing demand for clinical psychologists in diagnostic work, treatment, and research in mental health has resulted in a critical shortage which has existed since World War II. In spite of the fact that there were more than 20,000 psychologists working in the mental health field by the early 1970s, many hospitals, and a large number of clinics and other mental health agencies, do not have psychological services of any kind because of the personnel shortage.

The Joint Information Service of the American Psychiatric Association and the National Association for Mental Health, which issues continuing reports on the personnel needs in the field of mental health, has estimated that the number of clinical psychologists now available meets about 83 percent of the need in public mental hospitals according to existing standards. These standards, however, are recognized as being unrealistic in view of the many new services being demanded of clinical psychologists in the mental hospital. It is probable that no more than 60 to 70 percent of the need is being met in an adequate way. Current training facilities are not sufficient to meet this growing demand, and while many universities have been expanding training facilities as rapidly as time and staff allow, it is likely that the personnel needs in clinical psychology will continue to exceed the supply for a number of years.

THE PSYCHIATRIST

Many otherwise informed people, including some physicians, are unable to differentiate clearly between the clinical psychologist and the psychiatrist. The most fundamental difference is that the clinical psychologist receives research training and holds the nonmedical degree of Doctor of Philosophy, whereas the psychiatrist is medically trained and holds the degree of Doctor of Medicine. The psychiatrist, being a physician, is qualified to diagnose and treat the more severe mental disorders and those of an organic nature. However, his primary interests may be either in the physical aspects of personality disturbances or in the psychological problems involved in such conditions.[6]

The psychiatrist is ultimately responsible for examining and interviewing hospitalized patients and for prescribing the types of treatment to be carried out. When the treatment program has been decided upon, the psychiatrist supervises the treatment. When he feels that patients are ready to leave the hospital or to terminate treatment, he makes the necessary recommendations. Within the limits of available time, he supervises and participates in individual and group therapy. The psychiatrist is also likely to be involved in research studies, training functions, hospital and clinic administration, and community relations.

A psychiatrist ordinarily is consulted when the personality breakdown is severe, when it is suspected that the condition has an organic cause, when the disorder is so serious that hospital care is needed, and when commitment to a hospital is required by the courts. A psychiatrist is also consulted in most cases of alcoholism, drug addiction, and personality changes associated with physical illnesses, convulsions, and other organic symptoms.

The psychiatrist who makes use of physical methods of treatment in his practice is known generally as a *neuropsychiatrist;* the psychiatrist who limits his treatment to psychological methods is

---

[6]*Psychiatric News* Published each month in tabloid form, this official newspaper of the American Psychiatric Association is a comprehensive and up-to-the-minute review of the field of psychiatry. Articles, news items, editorials, job openings, and general comments make this paper well worth reading. Published by the American Psychiatric Association, 1700 18th Street, N.W., Washington, D.C. 20009.

called a *psychotherapist*. The relationship between clinical psychology and psychiatry sometimes seems confused because there are many personality disturbances which do not have an organic basis and which appear to be completely nonmedical. The result is that, in practice, both the clinical psychologist and the psychiatrist engage in psychotherapy. A *psychoanalyst* is a psychotherapist who uses the methods and theories of Sigmund Freud in his work. In the United States, most psychoanalysts are psychiatrists, although in other countries there are many nonmedical analysts called *lay analysts*.

The personnel shortage in psychiatry is more serious than it is in clinical psychology, even though the overall number of psychiatrists in the United States has increased each year from about 5,000 in 1950 to nearly 25,000 in the early 1970s. More than 50 percent of the psychiatrists in the United States are located in five states: California, Illinois, Massachusetts, New York, and Pennsylvania; and there are no psychiatrists at all in two-thirds of the counties in the United States (American Psychiatric Association, 1970).[7]

Although the general practitioner in medicine does not specialize in personality problems, the long-range objectives of mental health require such physicians to interest themselves in the problems of abnormal psychology and psychiatry. Fortunately, there has been a gradual trend in this direction. Many physicians realize that while their primary skills and interests are in other directions, their success depends to a considerable degree upon their ability to establish effective emotional relationships with their patients. The physician must understand the personality problems of his patient and of himself. Patients are not the only ones who become emotionally upset during physical illness. Very often the physician himself becomes tense and anxious. He needs to understand his emotional reactions and the effect his behavior has on his patients.

The increase of psychiatrists in private practice has had a damaging effect upon the availability of psychiatrists for service in mental hospitals and psychiatric clinics. The public has come to realize that most minor personality disturbances can be treated effectively in the community and without hospitalization. As a result, the young psychiatrist finds little difficulty in establishing an active private practice. Since the financial rewards of private practice are likely to be superior to those of most public clinics and hospitals, mental health institutions and facilities are hard pressed to maintain even minimally adequate staffs.

The training problem is more critical in psychiatry than in clinical psychology, because training is restricted to the approved medical schools in the United States, and these schools cannot begin to supply the demand for specialists in this field. Each medical school is limited, in terms of staff, physical space, and training facilities, in the number of psychiatrists it can train.

While the need for psychiatrists is pressing in the United States, Canada, England, and the countries of Western Europe, the need in other parts of the world is staggering.[8]

THE PSYCHIATRIC SOCIAL WORKER

The field of psychiatric social work is one in which social workers with special interest and training in the problems of personality undertake the study of personality disorganization as an expression of the social milieu. The psychiatric social worker is a social case worker who functions in a psychiatric setting. The basic preparation is the same as

[7]*Hospital & Community Psychiatry* A monthly journal published for psychiatrists and others who work in mental hospitals, clinics, and community mental health centers. The journal contains relatively nontechnical articles, news items, book and film reviews, and other information of general interest. Available from the American Psychiatric Association, 1700 18th Street, N.W., Washington, D.C. 20009.

[8]Premedical students and others wishing to know more about the field of psychiatry are referred to A. A. Rogow's *The Psychiatrists* (Putnam, 1970); *Careers in Psychiatry* (Macmillan, 1968), edited by Clair Burch and others; and Walter Freeman's *The Psychiatrist: Personalities and Patterns* (Grune & Stratton, 1968).

for that of every social case worker, although the psychiatric social worker must have a more thorough knowledge and a deeper understanding of abnormal psychology, as well as of diagnosis and treatment. This type of social worker contributes to the care and treatment of mental patients by serving as a link between the patient and his home and between the hospital and the community. He provides social, economic, and environmental information to the psychiatrist and to others who form part of the treatment team.

When the patient is admitted to the hospital, the psychiatric social worker helps him to adjust to the new situation and to understand the facilities available to him for treatment. Moreover, the psychiatric social worker helps the family understand the problems of the patient. He strives to reduce the stresses and strains arising in the family as a result of the patient's personality problems.

The psychiatric social worker seeks not only to assist the patient in the hospital but also to keep him functioning effectively when he returns to his home and community. At the time of discharge from the hospital, the patient may return to his home or may go to a foster home as part of the treatment. In either case, the social worker is the key to the effective solution of the problem. He makes sure that the home environment is adequate. If a foster home is required, it is his responsibility to find one. The psychiatric social worker continues to supervise the patient in the home and assists him in reestablishing himself in the community.

In many mental hospitals, and particularly in public and private mental hygiene clinics and other social welfare agencies, the psychiatric social worker undertakes individual and group treatment under the direction of a supervising psychiatrist. However, only a small number of state hospitals in the United States meet the minimum standards of the American Psychiatric Association for the number of psychiatric social workers on their staffs. While there has been a gradual expansion of training facilities in this field, the expansion has not been rapid enough to keep up with current needs.

In addition to psychiatric social work, the field of abnormal psychology contributes in a substantial way to such specialized areas of social work as criminology and penology. The understanding of the juvenile delinquent and the adult criminal is facilitated by a knowledge of motivation and conflict and, more importantly, by an appreciation of personality defenses and the way they break down or become distorted.

PSYCHIATRIC NURSING

The nurse who intends to make a career of psychiatric nursing has the same need for a basic understanding of abnormal psychology as does the clinical psychologist, the psychiatrist, and the psychiatric social worker. Her work brings her into daily contact with the entire range of personality disturbances. She must have a thorough knowledge of the different types of personality disturbances, diagnostic procedures, and treatment methods if she is to be an effective and successful member of the mental health team.

The psychiatric nurse functions as the immediate assistant to the psychiatrist. It is her job to manage the psychiatric ward, and she is responsible for other ward personnel assisting with the care of patients. The psychiatric nurse is also the major observer of the changes in the patient's condition. She aids the psychiatrist and cooperates with other professional staff members, in developing plans for the care and treatment of the patient.

The psychiatric nurse is expected to provide the best possible therapeutic climate for her patients. The mental hospital ward is a highly specialized environment and one which must be managed with considerable skill and understanding. The extent to which the psychiatric nurse participates directly in treatment varies with the policies and needs of different hospitals. In an emergency, she is expected to provide support for patients in stress situations. In some cases, she takes part in occupational and recreational therapy activities.

Unfortunately, a relatively small number of nurses graduating each year find their way into psychiatric hospitals or clinics. While more than 50 percent of the hospital beds in the United States are occupied by psychiatric patients, few graduate nurses work in psychiatric hospitals.

Nurses in other specialties also need to understand personality disturbances. Physical illness and the prospect of surgery are stress situations which cause fear, worry, depression, and, in many instances, emotional disturbances of a more serious nature. Similarly, the problems of nursing care associated with chronic illness and old age require, in almost every case, an appreciation of the personality factors involved in illness and disability.

The nature of· the relationship between patient and nurse is a critical one. The nurse assumes the role of the mother, even to the most elderly patient, and becomes the symbol of security and protection. Her understanding of the psychological dynamics of the emotional relationship between herself and her patients may mean the difference between quick recovery and prolonged illness. In many instances it means the difference between life and death.[9]

THE PSYCHIATRIC AIDE

The psychiatric aide is the modern version of the mental hospital attendant. Underpaid and often unrecognized, the psychiatric aide is a key person in the treatment of hospitalized patients because he is on the ward with the patient on an hour-after-hour basis. This close and continuing contact with the patient can make the difference between success and failure in the treatment program. A sensitive and dedicated psychiatric aide often can do more for the patient than any other member of the mental health team. Increasingly the training of aides is being upgraded, and the work is being made more attractive and rewarding. However, most psychiatric hospitals have much to do in these respects.

THE TEACHING PROFESSION

A knowledge of abnormal psychology is of the greatest importance to teachers, particularly in the primary and elementary grades. It is the classroom teacher who must detect the early signs of personality disorder and take the responsibility for pointing out the danger signals to the school administration. Where psychological or psychiatric services are not available, the teacher should have some idea of how to handle the problem and when and where to make a referral.

Every teacher sooner or later is confronted with personality problems among her students. Mental retardation, hostile and aggressive behavior, sexual acting out, vandalism and destructiveness, seclusiveness and withdrawal, and similar symptoms are frequent. Her job is made far easier when she has some conception of the conditions with which she must deal.

Teachers are in a unique position to observe signs of personality disturbance in their young pupils. Parents seldom notice these changes unless the deviant behavior is very pronounced. Moreover, parents usually lack the necessary training, and it is difficult for them to be objective about their own children. The teacher is the first professional person to observe the young child for an extended period of time. While some children are seen by a pediatrician, or child specialist, he sees them for a short period and is concerned primarily with physical symptoms. The teacher, from nursery school to the higher grades, has the best opportunity to discover the early signs of emotional disturbance. If she has a knowledge of abnormal psychology, she can serve a valuable function in promoting the cause of mental health.

■ **AN EMOTIONALLY DISTURBED SCHOOLBOY**

Richard R. was a somewhat quiet eight-year-old boy in the third grade. In the schoolyard he did not participate in games with other children, but rather stayed to the side and watched silently. Most of the time he preferred to remain in the classroom to "help the teacher." During class, this boy was never any trouble. He remained quiet, did what he was told, and never created a disturbance. Because of his quiet ways and passive attitude, the boy was well liked by the teachers in the first and second grades. However, the third-grade teacher was troubled by his passivity. His failure to communicate with the other children, his preference for remaining close to the teacher, and his lack of inclination to participate in group activities caused this teacher to refer the child for psychological

---

[9]Students considering mental health careers in the field of psychiatric nursing are referred to J. L. Audrey's *A Study of Psychiatric Nursing* (Williams and Wilkins, 1961).

study. When the suggestion was made at a teachers' meeting, the first- and second-grade teachers expressed annoyance that this "perfect little boy" should be considered a problem case. Nevertheless, when the school psychologist examined the youngster, there was evidence that the boy was in the early stages of a serious emotional illness. The parents were incensed when it was suggested to them that their child needed psychological help. It was only after considerable persuasion that they agreed to send the youngster to a clinic for treatment. Within a few months, the boy's behavior showed marked changes. He began to smile and laugh, he learned to enjoy group activities, and he became interested in his environment. The teacher's alertness to the signs of mental ill health probably saved the youngster from a serious personality disturbance.

The emotional damage to schoolchildren in the primary and elementary grades can be very great indeed. A first-grade boy, caught whispering by the teacher, was made to sit the rest of the morning in a wastepaper basket, with arms and legs dangling over the hard metal rim. Another teacher encouraged her pupils to chant, "Jimmy is a baby! Jimmy is a baby!" when a youngster broke his crayon. Other teachers gratify deviant and often unrecognized needs through cruel and excessive demands upon their students.

Teachers at the junior and senior high school level also need to be knowledgeable about personality difficulties. Because of the nature of adolescence and the transition from the dependency of childhood to the relative independence of adult life, many personality difficulties are seen first during the adolescent years. Difficult problems of social adjustment, conflict with parents, and relations with members of the opposite sex are rich sources of stress leading to emotional disorders of many kinds.

Teachers at the college level are frequently faced with the need to identify and understand the various forms of personality disturbance. The disturbances seen on the campus are roughly comparable to emotional problems observed in outpatient psychiatric clinics in the community.

Many colleges and universities offer psychological and psychiatric services in the form of psychological clinics, counseling centers, and other mental hygiene services. Most professors, particularly those in psychology, are likely to be consulted from time to time by students with personality problems. A random selection from the files of the author shows students who were referred because they could not concentrate or pay attention during classes, others who were having difficulty with their parents and many who were concerned about more serious problems. A freshman girl was so depressed that she had gone to the roof of her dormitory with the intention of jumping off. The greatest number of students complained of feelings of inadequacy and inferiority. The competition of college had revealed to these students that they were neither as capable nor as popular as they had come to believe. This realization is always a disturbing one and one that has far-reaching consequences for personality integration.

■ AN EMOTIONALLY DISTURBED COLLEGE STUDENT

Jane R. is an attractive 19-year-old sophomore who was referred to the author by the president of her sorority. The immediate problem was that several of Jane's sorority sisters had reported that she had been "taking things" that did not belong to her. The girls in the sorority recognized that Jane had something of an emotional problem, and it was agreed that the sorority president should talk to her and insist that she receive professional help.

When Jane was first seen, she was somewhat defensive and hostile. However, she was willing to talk about her problem, most of which she blamed on other people. Jane's classwork had become progressively worse, and she complained of not being able to concentrate or to pay attention. After several interviews, she began to talk about her difficulties with other girls. She admitted she was not popular and that many of the girls actually disliked her. She was inclined to explain her lack of popularity in terms of jealousy on the part of the other girls. However, she admitted also that while boys seemed to be attracted to her at first, they soon lost interest in her. It was obvious that Jane was a demanding, irritable, and rather unpleasant person, and her lack of popularity was easy to understand.

When the matter of "taking things" from the other girls was mentioned, Jane became belligerent and vehemently denied the accusations. Later, she admitted them and said that her actions were impulsive and that she had no explanation for them. It became clear, however, that the stealing was an attempt to "get even" with the other girls. Further interviews brought to light that Jane also had been involved in a series of unhappy and unfortunate love affairs and recently had been troubled by thoughts of suicide. Psychological treatment was continued until Jane left college to take a job in another city.

An important area of conflict at the college level is that of sexuality. Heterosexual relationships are frequently initiated at this time, and the guilt associated with such behavior is a serious threat to personality stability. Homosexuality is another form of behavior which often is precipitated during the college years. Since sexuality in all forms is rigidly controlled in our society, even the most minor excursions into heterosexual or homosexual realtionships are likely to cause emotional difficulties. A study of students who were seen by the Division of Student Hygiene at Yale University showed that 39 percent had emotional difficulties connected with sex. Of the freshmen who sought help, 21 percent had sexual difficulties, with the rate rising to 35 percent for seniors, and to 55 percent for graduate and professional students (Ross and Mendelsohn, 1958).

Occasionally, students fear they might be victims of more serious personality disturbances. More than likely, this is not the case. However, from time to time, the student is correct, and there are unmistakable signs of the early stages of one of the more serious mental disorders. In most instances, prompt psychological or psychiatric treatment prevents the emotional condition from becoming critical.[10]

THE LEGAL PROFESSION

There has been a noticeable increase in the realization that psychiatry and other mental health specialties can make a contribution to the legal field. Increasing numbers of medicolegal cases are being referred to hospitals and clinics for examination and expert opinion. Moreover, courts have been increasingly ready to seek psychiatric treatment for certain classes of offenders. In some universities, such courses as "Psychiatry and the Law" are being introduced as a joint undertaking of the medical school and the law school.

In criminal actions, both the prosecution and the defense attorneys must be aware of the role of possible psychological disturbance in the defendant. Sometimes hostile and aggressive acts of a most serious kind are committed as a result of emotional stress or of physical changes in the brain itself. Other delinquent and criminal acts are associated with toxic conditions brought on by drugs and alcohol. Occasionally people find themselves in court as a result of impulsive sexual misbehavior based on more serious emotional disturbances.

The lawyer needs a knowledge of abnormal psychology to help him understand some of the deviant motives of his clients and of witnesses in the courtroom. Another problem is the validity of testimony by psychiatrists, psychologists, and other experts in the field of mental health. Expert testimony often presents difficulties in the courtroom because of the restrictions placed upon the witness. Psychiatric testimony is probably the most precarious and uncertain of all expert testimony.

During the trial of Sirhan Sirhan for the assassination of Robert Kennedy, the nature and quality of psychiatric testimony came in for sharp and deserved criticism. The man on trial was described by two psychiatrists and six clinical psychologists as being the victim of assorted emotional damage during childhood, fantasies of persecution, and psychological problems. One psychiatrist claimed that Sirhan murdered Kennedy while in a hypnotic "trance." A clinical psychologist described Sirhan in words taken without acknowledgment from a recently published book.

The lawyer must also have a knowlege of abnormal psychology because certain forms of personality disorder lend themselves to being

---

[10]The relation between personality problems and the schools is developed in some detail in *Emotional Problems of the Student* (Appleton-Century-Crofts, 1961) by G. B. Blaine, Jr., and others; the second edition of Harold W. Bernard's *Mental Hygiene for Classroom Teachers* (McGraw-Hill, 1961); the controversial, if not somewhat explosive, *The Mentally Disturbed Teacher* (Chilton, 1961) by Joseph T. Shipley; and *The Role of Schools in Mental Health* (Basic Books, 1962) by Wesley Allinsmith and George W. Goethals.

expressed through lawsuits and litigation. At least 10 percent of the clients of legal aid societies are borderline psychiatric cases. Many attorneys find themselves involved unwittingly in cases initiated by men and women with serious personality disturbances.

A mature woman working on a graduate degree failed to attend many of the class sessions and was not given credit for the course. The student protested violently and went so far as to threaten physical harm to the professor. Her next step was to hire an attorney to bring action against the university. When the attorney contacted the university, the situation was explained to him and he withdrew from the case. Since that time, the same incident has been repeated with four other attorneys. The student was the victim of a personality disturbance whose chief symptoms are suspicion and ideas of persecution.[11]

PSYCHOPATHOLOGY AND BUSINESS

The study of abnormal psychology is of considerable importance to business and industry, particularly in the areas of industrial relations and personnel administration. A knowledge of the role of inner conflict is helpful in dealing with many problems related to the selection and upgrading of employees, to the handling of problem employees, to executive evaluation and development, to employee grievances, and to similar matters. While the diagnosis and treatment of personality disturbances must be left to trained professionals, a knowledge of abnormal psychology enables the businessman to be more sensitive to the human problems of his organization.

Mental health is industry's most costly health problem. Every business and industry has problem employees. White collar, blue collar—laborers, skilled workers, and executives—all are threatened by emotional disturbances and personality problems. These problems add up to an estimated 10 billion dollar loss to American business and industry each year.

Absenteeism due to personality problems costs business 5 billion dollars annually. Accidents, of which an estimated 85 percent are caused by mental or emotional disturbance, account for another 3 billion dollar loss. Excessive drinking and alcoholism adds another billion. The final billion is charged to physical illness, since half of all medical and surgical cases involve a mental or emotional disturbance complication, and to worker inefficiency and turnover, where it has been found that 70 percent of those dismissed for inefficiency are actually suffering from personality disturbances (NAMH, 1970).

It is not enough for the foreman, the manager, or the executive to know the problems of costs, production, sales, marketing, and other business matters. He must also have the deepest possible knowledge of human beings. He must know something of the inner workings of the individual and the effects of one individual on another.

Business and industry are based on a complex series of human relationships which is subject to intrapersonal, as well as interpersonal, disorganiation. A knowledge of abnormal psychology makes it possible to avoid some of the difficulties and to minimize the damaging effects of others. Among the more common types of emotional disturbance in the work situation are the frustration of not being recognized for the job one does, conflicts of personality among employees, marital or financial difficulties which reach into the job situation, and damaging attitudes such as overaggressiveness or pronounced passivity.

■ AN EMOTIONALLY DISTURBED EMPLOYEE

Beula M. was a forty-four-year-old single woman who had been employed for sixteen years as a secretary-bookkeeper in the office of a small company. Her employer consulted the author about certain changes in her behavior which were upsetting to the other employees. The employer had come to depend heavily

---

[11]Prelaw students and others interested in the legal aspects of mental health should look at A. S. Watson's *Psychiatry for Lawyers* (International Universities Press, 1968); *Mental Impairment and Legal Incompetency* (Prentice-Hall, 1968) by R. C. Allen and others; *Orthopsychiatry and the Law* (Wayne State University Press, 1968), edited by Morton Levitt and Ben Rubenstein; and Sheldon Glueck's *Law and Psychiatry* (Johns Hopkins Press, 1962).

upon this woman, and she had taken increasing responsibility so that most of the routine office matters were handled by her. However, over a period of months, she had become increasingly irritable, dictatorial, and uncooperative. Several new employees left the company after a few weeks, complaining that they were not able to work with her. Because of her efficiency and knowledge of the business operations, the employer had been reluctant to talk with her about the complaints. However, he found that he was beginning to be afraid to make comments and suggestions about his own company.

When the employer finally confronted his employee with the matter, she became hostile and even somewhat threatening. It was at this point that the employer decided to seek professional advice. The recommendation to the employer was that he should encourage his secretary to seek psychological help. When this suggestion was bitterly rejected by the secretary, it became necessary to discharge her.

If the employer had had some degree of insight into personality disorders, it would have been possible for him to spot this serious mental disorder many months before the symptoms became pronounced. It might have been possible for him to persuade his secretary to seek help at a time when she might have been accepting of it. By the time he became aware of the seriousness of the disturbance, it was much too late to help matters.

An important trend in psychology has been the application of the clinical approach to the problems of business and industry. Traditionally, the personnel psychologist evaluated the worker in terms of external criteria. Major attention was paid to educational level, previous work history, and scores earned on psychological tests. The clinical psychologist in industry, on the other hand, attempts to study the worker from the inside. He wants to know how the employee thinks, what

forces are motivating him, and what areas of conflict might lead to job inefficiency.[12]

As early as 1916, a business organization hired a psychiatrist to assist with problems of human relations, while a model psychiatric setup was established in the 1920s by one of the largest department stores in New York City. An early survey showed that 62 percent of discharged employees had been discharged because of personality difficulties rather than occupational incompetence (Anderson, 1929). World War II saw a rapid expansion in recognition of the importance of the mental health problem in industry. Since that time, an increasing number of American business and industrial organizations have made use of the services of part-time or full-time psychologists and psychiatrists.

That much remains to be done, however, is shown by a 1967 survey of mental health programs in a random sample of 250 leading corporations. More than 70 percent did not consider their company as having a formal mental health program. Twenty-one companies said they had an informal program, but only three reported what could be considered a comprehensive program for the mental health of their employees.[13]

PSYCHOPATHOLOGY AND RELIGION

There has been a growing interest in the relationship between religion and psychopathology, particularly in connection with the treatment process. With the possible exception of magic, religion is the oldest form of psychological treatment. Throughout the centuries, the religious adviser has performed a therapeutic role. He gives emotional support to men and women who are

---

[12]*Occupational Mental Health Notes* A publication directed to the scientific and professional community interested in occupational mental health, and to executives in management and labor. Each issue contains abstracts of current literature and reports on recent developments in the field. Published at irregular intervals. Available from the National Institute of Mental Health, 5454 Wisconsin Avenue, Chevy Chase, Maryland 20015.

[13]The following books are suggested as supplementary reading for students interested in mental health problems in business and industry: A. N. Schoonmaker's *Anxiety and the Executive* (American Management Association, 1969); Harry Levinson's *Emotional Health: In the World of Work* (Harper & Row, 1964); and *Mental Health in Industry* (McGraw-Hill, 1958) by A. A. McLean and G. C. Taylor.

discouraged, depressed, frightened, and guilt-laden.

In a national mental health survey, it was found that of the people who had sought professional help for personal problems, 42 percent went to a clergyman, 29 percent to a physician, 18 percent to a psychiatrist or psychologist, and 10 percent to other private practitioners or social agencies (Gurin et al., 1960).

For the most part, religious counseling has been on an intuitive basis. More recently, the priest, the rabbi, and the minister have reached into the field of abnormal psychology for facts about emotional disturbance and into the fields of psychiatry and clinical psychology for techniques to improve their religious counseling. Clergymen and mental health experts are in agreement that there are a number of areas in which the clergyman needs to be better informed in order to perform his function more effectively. These areas include the stresses of divorce and broken homes, premarital problems, the plight of the aged, the alcoholic and his family, and the problem of suicide.

The increasing rapprochement between religion and the mental health field has come about in a number of ways. The earliest step was one in which the individual minister, rabbi, or priest took the initiative to inform himself about the ways in which abnormal psychology could be of assistance in his religious counseling. A second approach was the development of programs at state psychiatric hospitals for informing local clergymen about the procedures of commitment, treatment, and the return of the patient to the community. A third form of relationship has been the high-level conference involving experts in theology and psychiatry who get together to exchange views in this field. The value of conferences of this kind is found in the fact that these meetings help to establish favorable attitudes in both professions. The fourth type of program for bringing religion and psychiatry into closer rapport has been workshops and seminars conducted by experts for the benefit of clergymen who have had little formal education in the field of mental health.

The organized interest of clergymen in the clinical problems of mental health was expressed as early as 1925, when the Council for Clinical Training of Theological Students was established. The purpose of this organization was to provide internships in psychiatric hospitals for pastors in training. Since that time, a number of mental health programs have been undertaken by clergymen, church groups, and religious organizations.

One of the best examples of the cooperation between psychiatry and religion is the Menninger Foundation program at Topeka, Kansas. This organization extends psychiatric training facilities to members of the clergy, teaching them viewpoints and skills helpful in carrying out their pastoral work. The Foundation also looks to the clergy for help in dealing with patients in mental hospitals, in marriage counseling situations, and in the many phases of outpatient care and inpatient aftercare. Each year the Foundation holds a series of conferences which include psychiatrists, psychologists, and theologians of all faiths.[14]

PSYCHOPATHOLOGY AND THE ARTS

One of the richest and most rewarding means of gaining insight into the deep nature of human conflict and emotional disturbance is the study of the fine arts. In most matters, the creative artist, on the basis of his special sensitivity and intuitiveness, has anticipated the psychologist and the psychiatrist. The revolutionary formulations of modern psychology were implicit in the dramatic works of the playwrights of ancient Greece, and they appeared later in the plays of Shakespeare in the sixteenth century and in a wide range of contemporary art forms including literature, painting, music, and the dance.

The arts are of interest at several different

---

[14]Books dealing with the relationship between religion and mental health include *Psychiatry, the Clergy, and Pastoral Counseling* (St. John's University Press, 1969), edited by D. L. Farnsworth and F. J. Braceland; Edgar Draper's *Psychiatry and Pastoral Care* (Prentice-Hall, 1966); and *The Churches and Mental Health* (Basic Books, 1962) by R. V. McCann.

levels. Some artistic productions, particularly literature, present extraordinary intuitive demonstrations of the clinical types of personality disturbance. Artistic productions may also be demonstrations of psychological dynamics, including nonconscious factors in motivation, the influence of childhood events on later behavior, and the importance of symbolism. Or there may be in an artistic creation expression of the hidden needs and conflicts of the artist.

The earliest and most important psychological dramas were products of ancient Greece. Beginning with the Homeric legends and culminating with the tragedies of Aeschylus, Sophocles, and Euripides during the classical Greek period, these dramas reveal the most profound insights into the human personality. Only occasionally, in the many intervening centuries, has a writer appeared who has been able to match the intuitive knowledge of the early Greek dramatists.

The Greek drama is important not only for its portrayal of emotional conflict at a heroic level, but also because of its frequent depiction of personality disturbance. While the Greek writers did not have a correct interpretation of the causes of personality disturbance, they were well aware of the objective symptoms of such disorders and did not hesitate to use mental disorder freely in their characters.

With the writings of William Shakespeare in the sixteenth century, mankind once again was treated on a grand scale to a profound understanding of the disturbed personality. The plays of Shakespeare, no less than those of the Greek dramatists, were based upon an extraordinary grasp of the inner life and deep motivations of man. Shakespeare's work contains a wide range of sharply etched portrayals of emotional disturbance.

Modern drama, from Henrik Ibsen to The Theater of the Absurd, is another rich source of material for the student of abnormal psychology. The dramatist, perhaps more consistently than any other literary artist, concerns himself directly with problems of motivation and conflict and with the impact of distorted motives on the subsequent lives of the characters in the play. Among motion pictures, the film *Last Year at Marienbad* is a beautifully artistic example of the admixture of fantasy and reality, dream and waking, madness and sanity, and even life and death. Both technically and artistically this film represents one of the high points in the contribution of motion pictures to an understanding of the workings of the deeper levels of the human mind.

Turning to the novelists, the work of such subjective writers as Feodor Dostoevski, D. H. Lawrence, Thomas Wolfe, James Joyce, Virginia Woolf, Franz Kafka, and Marcel Proust probes deeply into the motivations, conflicts, and personality defenses of their characters. When Philippe Pinel, the French pioneer in modern psychiatry, was asked by a young student to recommend a good textbook, Pinel's immediate answer was, "Read *Don Quixote*."[15]

The importance of poetry to abnormal psychology is found in the fact that through the poetic image we are brought close to the deeper layers of the personality. Just as the dream reveals an unknown and forbidden part of the dreamer, so the poem reveals something of the inner life of the poet. William Shakespeare, in *A Midsummer Night's Dream,* said:

The lunatic, the lover and the poet
Are of imagination all compact.

For many poets, imagery is spontaneous and relatively uncensored. Sometimes the poetic imagery has all the seemingly chaotic quality of the dream. Many years ago, an eminent professor of psychology said, "Every true poet contributes more to the advance in psychology than a hundred scientists and a thousand laboratories."

The student who wishes to study poetry for the light it throws on the inner experience of man

---

[15]Students of abnormal psychology should read the work of contemporary writers who explore the borderlands of human thinking, emotions, and behavior. Some suggested novels of this type are John Fowles' *The Magus* (Little, Brown, 1965); Brigid Brophy's *In Transit* (Putnam, 1969); John Barth's *Giles Goat-Boy* (Doubleday, 1966); Vladimir Nabokov's *Ada* (McGraw-Hill, 1969); Philip Roth's *Portnoy's Complaint* (Random House, 1967), and *One Hundred Years of Solitude* (Harper & Row, 1970) by Gabriel Garcia Marquez.

Figure 1.10 The Juggler *by Marc Chagall. The artist often has an intuitive sense of the world of dreams and fantasy. (Art Institute of Chicago.)*

should turn to the work of the emotionalists, the intuitivists, and the symbolists. Stéphane Mallarmé, Paul Válery, Arthur Rimbaud, W. B. Yeats, and others are important because of their emphasis upon the unreal and the imaginative. These poets, and the writers they influenced in a variety of fields, sought to explore new dimensions of human experience. They created an art form based on the subjective outpouring of the poet's inner life.

The entire range of graphic and pictorial arts offers another rich source of experience and understanding of the disorganized personality. In painting, the artist is free to modify and distort the world of reality and to use symbols and the images of the dream as a means of expressing his creative urge. The paintings of Hieronymus Bosch, Odilon Redon, Vincent Van Gogh, Georgi

de Chirico, Salvador Dali, Marc Chagall, Paul Klee, and Pablo Picasso are pictorial representations of deep-hidden fantasies.

Music is another art form contributing to an appreciation of the disorganized personality. It is a common observation that music springs from the deepest layers of the human personality. The composer reveals his needs, his conflicts and frustrations, and his tensions and anxieties through the formal as well as the emotional characteristics of his compositions. Just as literature and painting tell us something about the writer and the artist and about life experience in general, music also is revelatory. Music appeals to the deep inner parts of the personality. While the student of abnormal psychology will find it more difficult to verbalize the insights provided by fine music, his understanding of the private experiences of man will be enriched intuitively.

Finally, through the study of the history of dance from primitive to modern times, a deeper insight can be gained into the problems of tension and emotional relief. More important, the dance is an outstanding example of the taming and socialization of sexual and aggressive impulses which are threatening to the individual and to the group. The psychological impact of the dance is conveyed in widely divergent ways by such dancers as Nijinski, Isadora Duncan, Paul Draper, Katherine Dunham, Agnes de Mille, and Merce Cunningham. In spite of the contrasting and dissimilar

Figure 1.11 *The dance as a form of emotional expression, as suggested by* Dance, 1909, *by Henry Matisse. (Collection, Museum of Modern Art, New York. Gift of Nelson A. Rockefeller.)*

forms, the dancing in each of these cases is emotionally expressive and psychologically revealing.

In these many ways, an appreciation of the various art forms contributes to an understanding of some of the more subtle and ephemeral problems of abnormal psychology. It is through the windows of the fine arts that one often gets the first glimpse of what the human personality is really like at its deeper levels.[16]

SUMMARY

1. We are living in a time of very great social and technological change. Dissent and rebellion, violence in the streets and on the campuses, permissive sexual behavior, and the decline of traditional religious values are indications of changes which subject individuals of all ages to heavy stress.

2. Abnormal psychology is the study of the behavior disorders and personality disturbances that grow out of the physical, psychological, and social stresses of life. However, the word "abnormal" must be used with caution because of the difficulty in defining it, the dangerous assumption that it is a quality possessed by the individual rather than a value judgment about behavior, and the fact that the word has acquired a negative "emotional loading."

3. Normality and abnormality can be viewed in terms of *theoretical models* of behavior. *Descriptive models* deal with the definition of abnormal behavior, while *explanatory models* seek to get at the cause of such behavior. The major descriptive models are the *subjective normative, statistical,* and *cultural* models. The principal explanatory models are the *disease, psychodynamic, learning,* and *stress* models.

4. The conventional approaches to the disorganized personality are *historical, etiological, descriptive, diagnostic, therapeutic,* and *experimental.* The historical approach is concerned with the early forces that helped shape the field of abnormal psychology. The etiological approach is concerned with the causes of mental illness, while the descriptive approach deals with symptoms and clinical categories. The diagnostic approach involves the identification of abnormality, the therapeutic approach is concerned with treatment, and the experimental approach seeks to establish the basic facts and principles of personality disorganization.

5. The problem of personality disturbance is one of vast proportions. It has been estimated that as many as 20 million people in the United States need treatment for some form of emotional disturbance. Approximately 1 million patients are in mental hospitals, with about 0.8 million receiving treatment outside hospitals. Relatively large numbers of men, women, and children need treatment but do not get it. With the exception of the personality disturbances of old age, the rates for mental disorders today are roughly similar to those of a hundred years ago. The total number of patients has increased dramatically, but the rate per unit of population has remained about the same in most of the diagnostic groups.

---

[16]For students interested in the literary and artistic approach to abnormal psychology, the following books will be of interest: *Psychiatry and Art* (Karger, 1969), edited by Irene Jakab; L. Y. Rabkin's *Psychopathology and Literature* (Chandler, 1966); *The Abnormal Personality through Literature* (Prentice-Hall, 1966), edited by A. A. and S. S. Stone; and V. W. Grant's *Great Abnormals: The Pathological Genius of Kafka, Van Gogh, Strindberg, and Poe* (Hawthorn, 1968).

6. Abnormal psychology is a subject of particularly great interest since it concerns so intimately both the individual and society. Most individuals are involved because few families are untouched by emotional disturbance. Moreover, a knowledge of abnormal psychology contributes to self-understanding and to the understanding of the actions of our friends, neighbors, and associates. Abnormal psychology also has implications for the society in which we live. Not only are the symptoms of personality disturbance determined to some extent by our culture; they also contribute to social disorganization by making it difficult or impossible to respond to social controls.

7. The facts and theories of abnormal psychology are basic to such applied mental health fields as clinical psychology, psychiatry, psychiatric social work, and psychiatric nursing. Abnormal psychology is also of practical importance in education, law, business, and religion.

8. There is a close relationship between abnormal psychology and the pictorial arts, literature, music, and the dance. Some of the earliest insights into the deeper levels of the personality were given to the world through the sensitivity and intuition of the creative artist.

AUDIOTAPES

These tapes are recommended as useful supplements to Chapter 1.

Motives of Rebellion
Dr. Frederick Wyatt presents a forty-eight-minute talk on the crisis of authority among students. The discussion examines the relationship between unrest on the campuses and the political and social problems of our times. Recorded in 1968. Sound Seminar 75511, *McGraw-Hill Book Company*.

The Myth of Normality
Dr. Thomas S. Szasz presents a thirty-nine-minute lecture on his theory that mental illness is merely a disguise for moral and psychosocial problems of living. Recorded in 1968. Sound Seminar 75562, *McGraw-Hill Book Company*.

The Development of Clinical Psychology
Dr. Lawrence E. Abt discusses problems related to the establishment of clinical psychology as a science and profession. Twenty-six minutes. Recorded in 1967. Sound Seminar 75700, *McGraw-Hill Book Company*.

2 THE HISTORY OF MENTAL DISORDER

The concept of personality disturbance is not a new one. Such disturbances have been recognized, in one form or another, since the beginning of recorded history. The roots of abnormal behavior are to be found in the early prehistory of man and possibly in the prehuman stages of animal development.

Based on our knowledge of the behavior of primitive tribes, it is probable that early man paid little attention to illness of any kind, physical or mental. The elderly, the handicapped, the invalids, the misfits, and the maladjusted were killed off or left to die of exposure. It is unlikely that tender emotion was a mark of the primitive mind. It was probably relatively late in the development of mankind that the necessary intelligence and sentiments emerged to make it possible for men to be concerned about physical illness and mental disorder.

ANIMISM AND THE ANCIENTS

The earliest attitudes toward personality disturbances grew out of the primitive concept of *animism,* or the belief that the world is controlled by spirits, gods, and other kinds of supernatural beings. Primitive man believed that the winds blew, streams flowed, stones rolled, and trees grew because of spirits residing within the objects. He explained in the same way all behavior he was not able to understand.

The early history of every ancient culture is characterized by animistic thinking. In the medical writings of the Hindus, the idea of animism was prominent in the form of demon possession. In the medicine of ancient Egypt, the concept of possession by evil spirits played an important role. Elaborate temple rites were developed to assist in the treatment of the physically and emotionally ill. Songs, hymns, and religious ceremonies of various kinds were used. In some temples, patients were covered with fragrant blossoms in order to appease the angry spirits.

The primitive belief in animism not only served as an explanation of the cause of mental illness; it also did much to determine the direction of treatment. Since the spirits responsible for mental illness were regarded generally as being evil, punitive, and uncooperative, it seemed necessary to drive them out by drastic means. Victims were flogged, starved, burned, and otherwise tortured.

Even a primitive form of head surgery was undertaken as a result of the belief in animism. In the late nineteenth century, a large number of ancient skulls with small holes cut through the bone were discovered in Peru. While in some cases the skulls have fracture lines suggesting the holes had been cut for therapeutic purposes, in most instances the skulls are intact. It is not unlikely that the purpose of the holes was to allow demons, devils, spirits, and other supernatural beings to escape from the head of the patient.

NATURALISM AND THE CLASSICAL PERIOD

The influence of Greek thought in medicine, particularly in connection with mental disorder, began during the Homeric period, approximately three thousand years ago. The belief was that man became mentally disturbed because angry gods took his mind away. People were treated by prayer, charms, and sacrifice in order to appease the gods who had taken possession of the victim. It was believed that if those who were possessed participated in the mysteries of Hecate at Aegina, or in the rites of the Corybantes, the god responsible for the disorder might be persuaded to leave the body of the sufferer.

There were relatively few developments of importance to psychopathology between the Homeric period and the time of Hippocrates, some five hundred years later. However, in the sixth century B.C., Alcmaeon established the fact that the sense organs are connected with the brain and suggested that the human faculty of reason is located in the head. During the same century, Pythagoras, the philosopher-physician of Samos, developed some of the first principles of mental and physical hygiene. It was his idea that the primary concern of the physician should not be the cure of disease, but rather the prevention of it.

A most important change in the tradition of animism, spirit possession, and temple medicine came about with Hippocrates (460–367 B.C.). This physician and his followers developed a revolutionary point of view in medicine. This new and daring approach was *naturalism,* which held that disorders of any kind, mental or physical, are the result of natural causes. Hippocrates had the courage and vision to challenge the beliefs that had been accepted almost without question since man first started to think about the problem. He denied the influence of spirits, gods, and demons as a cause of disease in his treatise, *The Sacred Disease.* Hippocrates wrote, "If you cut open the head, you will find the brain humid, full of sweat, and smelling badly. And in this way you may see that it is not a god which injuries the body, but disease."

Hippocrates viewed man as a miniature embodiment of the four principal elements of the universe—earth, water, fire, and air. It was his belief that each of these elements was represented in the body by a *humor,* or fluid. The yellow bile of the body was derived from the dryness of the earth, the black bile from moisture, the blood from heat, and the mucous, or phlegm, from cold air. Each of the body humors was thought to be related to a corresponding temperament. Those people in whom there was an excess of yellow bile were considered to be *choleric,* or angry and irritable, while too much black bile was characteristic of the *melancholic.* When blood was the dominant humor, the person was *sanguine,* or hopeful and confident; when mucous was dominant, the temperament was *phlegmatic,* or cold and self-possessed. Disturbances in behavior, according to this view, were the result of an imbalance of the body humors.

Hippocrates, who was above all else a clinician, was deeply interested in the symptoms of his patients. His writings include remarkably accurate descriptions of such conditions as sensory disorders, migraine headache, convulsions, paralysis, and alcoholic delirium. He listed the clinical signs of cerebral hemorrhages, or strokes, and described the distinguishing neurological effects of such conditions.

The treatment recommended by Hippocrates and his followers grew out of the theory that illness has natural causes. Venesection, or bloodletting, was a common practice. Incisions were made in various parts of the body, and veins were opened in the arms and legs and at the temples of the head. In addition, a variety of physical measures, such as exercise, controlled diet, and the avoidance of all excesses, were recommended.

The ideas of Plato (429–347 B.C.) were in direct contrast with the naturalistic views of Hippocrates. Plato retained the popular belief that certain forms of disturbed behavior were due to the intervention of the gods. While accepting the theory of body humors for some conditions, Plato insisted that the "delirium of the prophets" was caused by Apollo, the "delirium of the poets" by the Muses, and the "delirium of the lovers" by Aphrodite and Eros.

In giving the weight of his authority to the concept of divine and revelatory madness, Plato undermined the naturalistic medicine of Hippocrates and profoundly influenced the thinking of the early Christian era.

Plato's distinguished pupil, Aristotle (384–322 B.C.), accepted the humoral theory of Hippocrates but maintained that reason, due to its immortal nature, could not be attacked by illness. Aristotle rejected psychological causes in the development of behavior disturbances and consequently retarded the development of a naturalistic psychopathology.

In ancient Rome, the early period was marked by animism, a concept later replaced by the belief in divine intervention. The Greek gods were adopted by the Romans and given Latin names. Here and there, however, the naturalistic views of Hippocrates and his followers were taken over and elaborated by a few Roman physicians. One of the first of these physicians was Asclepiades, who anticipated the modern view that personality problems are often due to emotional disturbance. He discussed such matters as disturbances of thinking and disorders of perception as problems of medicine. In keeping with his naturalistic approach, his treatment procedures included music, baths of controlled temperature, and suspended beds. He believed that the gentle swaying motion of such beds had a sedative effect on disturbed patients. Moreover, he opposed placing mental patients in cells and dungeons and spoke out sharply against the prevalent practice of bloodletting.

Another important figure in Roman medicine who concerned himself with mental disturbance was Aretaeus of Cappadocia. This physician observed the recurrent nature of certain depressions and described the clinical symptoms of such conditions as cerebral hemorrhage and convulsive disorders. Other physicians of ancient Rome included Celsus, the encyclopedist of ancient medicine, who recommended enforced fasting, intimidation, mechanical restraint, and corporal punishment, and Caelius Aurelianus, who advanced a theory of vital forces as the source of human motivation and was an important Latin commentator on earlier medical writings dealing with personality disturbances.

By far the most influential figure of the Roman

period was Galen (ca. 130–200 A.D.), a Greek physician born at Pergamon in Asia Minor, who accepted and extended the humoral pathology of Hippocrates and carried out important work in the area of animal dissection. His most outstanding original contributions were made in connection with the anatomy of the nervous system. Galen also developed a rational psychopathology and advocated a treatment program that was substantially medical, physical, and psychological. He regarded excitement as due to an inflammation of the brain, while holding that melancholia was the result of stomach disorder.

While Galen considered the brain to be the center of psychological functions, he believed that there were two irrational souls. The word *irrational* at that time meant substantially what we mean today by the word *emotional*. Galen thought that the heart was the center of the irascible, energetic, or male soul, while the liver was the seat of the sensual female soul. He associated the quality of thinking with the quality of the substance of the brain and said: "The keenness of the mind depends upon the fineness of the brain substance. Slow thinking is due to its heaviness . . . its firmness and stability produce the faculty of memory. The shifting of opinions is produced by the mobility of the brain."

MADNESS AND THE MIDDLE AGES

While ancient history is ordinarily divided from medieval history by the fall of Rome to the barbarians in the fifth century, the decline of medicine began with the death of Galen in 200 A.D. Roman physicians, with the notable exceptions of Alexander Trallianus in the sixth century and Paulus Aegineta in the seventh century, reverted to popular superstition and, later, to demonology and sorcery.

Alexander Trallianus followed the ideas of Galen and gave many excellent clinical descriptions of personality disorganization. More important, he was among the first to emphasize the possibility of inborn, or constitutional, factors in personality disturbances. He suggested, for example, that people with dark hair and slim body builds are more likely to develop melancholia

Figure 2.1 St. Anthony Tormented by Demons, *a fifteenth-century German engraving by Martin Schongauer. (Philadelphia Museum of Art.)*

than people with light hair and heavy build. Such thinking anticipated by many centuries the problems of typology and constitutional medicine which play an important role in abnormal psychology today.

Paulus Aegineta also advocated a return to the ideas of Hippocrates and Galen. But, unfortunately for medical psychology, the general trend of medicine in its larger aspects, and in relation to personality disturbance particulary, was one of rapid and almost incredible deterioration. The naturalistic approach of Hippocrates and Galen came to be discarded completely in the Christian world. The ideas of Plato and Aristotle, with emphasis on a mind divorced from the body, and the Judeo-Christian concept of demons and devils struggling for possession of the body led to a preoccupation with magic, sorcery, satanism, and finally witchcraft. The medical treatment of the mentally disturbed was abandoned because such conditions were no longer looked upon as natural disorders, but rather as signs that the victims were possessed by devils or demons.

During the medieval period, the only survival of naturalistic medicine was in Arabia where the writings of Paulus Aegineta were preserved by such eminent Arabian physicians as Rhazes (860–930) and Avicenna (980–1037). While Arabian medicine brought little that was original to the care and treatment of the mentally disturbed, it was refreshingly free from the demonological theories which were sweeping over Europe.

In the Christian world, the only link between the ancient and the medieval schools of medicine

Figure 2.2 Tom o'Bedlam, *an old print. (New York Academy of Medicine.)*

was maintained by the Benedictine monastery at Monte Cassino in Italy. Interest in the medical literature of classic Greece and Rome was kept alive, however feebly, in this church community. Eventually, the medical studies at this monastery attained great prominence, and a school of medicine was established. After flourishing for some time, this school gave way to a new one at Salerno. This medical center was situated in the province of Naples, and Greeks and Arabs came to it from Sicily, bringing with them the medical lore which had been preserved in Arabia. During the tenth century, Constantinus Africanus brought the Arabian medical manuscripts back to the Western world, and Salerno became the most important medical center of the eleventh century.

In the thirteenth century, there were signs that the human intellect was reawakening. It was in this century that medical men were first called *doctors* and small hospitals were opened. It was at this period also that the great universities were established. The University of Paris, which opened about 1250, was followed by medical schools at Padua, Naples, Oxford, Cambridge, Lisbon, and other cities.

Nevertheless, the major intellectual developments of the time, such as the scholastic psychology of St. Thomas Aquinas (1225–1274), neglected the problems of psychopathology. Men and women who were mentally disturbed continued to be looked upon with fear and suspicion. The few physicians who concerned themselves with the problem struggled to reconcile the traditional views of ancient Greece and Alexandria with the astrology, alchemy, and demonology of their own time. Occasionally there was emphasis upon a naturalistic approach. Roger Bacon insisted that mental disorders were due to natural causes. However, since he was an imprisoned monk, his opinions carried neither spiritual nor medical authority. Here and there a voice echoed Bacon's belief, but these voices were rare indeed.

It is not surprising that the first institutions for mental patients were developed in the non-Christian countries where physicians continued to be influenced by the ideas of Hippocrates. In Baghdad, a large building called the House of Grace was used to detain mental patients until they recovered. Magistrates visited the institution from time to time and released those who seemed to be well. Similar institutions were common among the Moors, and as a result of their influence the first mental hospital in Europe was opened in Spain in the early part of the fifteenth century. This hospital, or asylum, was established at Valencia in 1410 and received the support of Pope Benedict XIII. Fifteen years later, an asylum was opened at Sargossa, followed by one at Seville. The asylum at Granada was established in 1452 by King Ferdinand and Queen Isabella.

The most famous of all historic institutions for mental patients, Bethlehem Royal Hospital in London, was established in 1547 after Henry VIII had seized various church properties. The institution had been founded 300 years earlier by Simon Fitzmary as a priory and received a few "lunatics" as early as 1400. After the institution became a mental hospital, the name was corrupted to "Bedlam." Applications for admission were so numerous that most patients were released before they were cured. Some of the inmates were permitted to roam the countryside begging for alms. These demented beggars were identified by foxtails hanging from their hats, and frequently they carried long sticks with many-colored ribbons. Shakespeare referred to this practice in *King Lear* when he wrote:

> The country gives me proof and precedent
> Of Bedlam beggars, who, with roaring voices,
> Strike in their numb'd and mortified bare arms
> Pins, wooden pricks, nails, sprigs of rosemary;
> And with this horrible object, from low farms,
> Pour pelting villages, sheep-cotes, and mills,
> Sometimes with lunatic bans, sometimes with
>   prayers,
> Enforce their charity.

The true nature of mental disorder was obscured at the time by ignorance and superstition. Since evil spirits were believed to be responsible for mental disturbance, certain saints were thought to have special power in the exorcism of these spirits. Mental patients by the thousands were taken to religious shrines where it was believed they might be cured. One of the best known was the shrine of St. Dymphna at Gheel, Belgium. At St. Nun's pool in England, the mentally ill were plunged backwards into the water and dragged back and forth until their emotional excitement ceased. The Glen-na-galt, or "valley of lunatics" in Kerry, Ireland, had two famous wells. The men-

tally ill were brought to drink the waters which were thought to have supernatural powers in curing madmen. Special prayers, incantations, the touching of relics, sanctified ointments, and mystical potions were used in an almost endless variety.

Visits to sacred shrines were the mildest form of treatment during the Middle Ages. More frequently the mentally disturbed individuals were burned, starved, flogged, immersed in painfully hot water, and otherwise tortured in an effort to rid them of the evil spirit that had taken possession of them. In most places they were confined in filthy and evil-smelling dungeons where they received little, if any, attention.

At many institutions, the patients were exhibited to visitors on Sundays and holidays. A fee was charged, and people visited the cells of the mental patients just as one might today visit the zoo. The practice continued for several hundred years, and as late as the eighteenth century, as many as ninety thousand visitors paid admission each year to see the mental patients at Bethlehem Hospital in London. At the same time, patients were displayed in cages on the continent of Europe. Only a hundred years ago, the public paid admission to stare at inmates at the Hospital of St. Andre in Lima, Peru.

During the fifteenth century, the belief in demon possession reached its most virulent form. Prior to that time, two types of possession had been recognized. The first type was *unwilling possession;* in it the victim was seized against his will by the devil as a punishment by God for sins committed. Mental patients were considered to be of this type. The second type was *willing possession;* the possessed in this case were witches who were the willing followers of Satan. Gradually the distinction between the two types of possession was lost, and mental patients also came to be regarded as witches. In 1484, a statement issued by Pope Innocent VIII urged the clergy to do everything possible to detect witches and stamp out the practice of witchcraft.

Two Dominican monks in Germany, Johann Sprenger and Heinrich Kraemer, became the leaders of a movement for the extermination of witches. With the publication of their infamous book *Malleus Maleficarum* (The Witch Hammer), a campaign to rid the world of witches got under way in earnest. This treatise confirmed the existence of witches, described the signs by which they could be detected, and prescribed the legal form for examining and sentencing them. Over the years, this work came to be regarded as almost divinely inspired, both in Catholic and Protestant countries. The result was two hundred years of witch-hunting and the torture and violent death of hundreds of thousands of mentally ill men, women, and children.

During these terrible years, even the most serious and respected physicians were convinced that witches existed. Ambroise Paré (1510–1590), the distinguished pioneer of modern surgery, believed that the devil caused women to become witches and that they should be destroyed, not treated as sick people. And Felix Plater (1536–1614), who lived for a time in the dungeons with mental patients, and who developed an important classification of mental disorder, nevertheless accepted

Figure 2.3 *Paracelsus, 1493–1541. He reintroduced clinical observation and experimental methodology into European medicine. (Collection Viollet, Paris.)*

the idea that the underlying cause was demon possession.

While mental patients were burned at the stake by the tens of thousands, isolated voices here and there were raised in protest against the ignorance and superstition of the times. One of the earliest influences in the reappearance of scientific questioning in Europe was Paracelsus (1493–1541), who heralded the return of the Hippocratic emphasis on clinical observation and the experimental methods of Galen. Paracelsus, whose real name was Aureolus Philippus Theophrastus Bombastus von Hohenheim, was a strong-minded and unconventional physician who was seldom in favor with his colleagues. He shocked the scholarly world by lecturing and writing in the vernacular rather than in Latin, and he struck out angrily at the physicians of his day. Once he said, "They go around the art of medicine like a cat around hot porridge." Paracelsus insisted that the great psychological epidemics of the Middle Ages were a disease and were not caused by demon possession. His ideas were two hundred years ahead of his time and disturbingly unconventional for the period in which he lived. As a result, he was hounded and persecuted, and his works were burned by the church.

It is difficult to evaluate the contribution of Paracelsus because his prolific writings contain many confusing and esoteric trends. He was very much interested in the influence of the stars and planets on physical and mental health, and he was intrigued by the strange phenomenon which was later to become known as hypnosis. Paracelsus was of great importance in the development of abnormal psychology because he helped to reintroduce the naturalistic point of view.

Johann Weyer (1515–1588), often called the father of modern psychiatry, spent his life fighting the superstitions and practices associated with witchcraft. His great work, *De Praestigiis Daemonum,* was an attempt to refute the contentions of the *Malleus* and to repair the damage caused by that fanatical book. Weyer's treatise was, in reality, the first textbook in psychiatry. Not only did it contain refutations of arguments supporting witchcraft and demonology, but also it included a great number of sharply etched clinical descriptions of mental illness.

Weyer was the first physician interested primarily in mental disorder. As such, he anticipated the specialty of psychiatry as a part of medical practice. He was a skilled clinician whose accounts of mental illness are superb examples of descriptive psychiatry. More important, Weyer played a major role in divorcing abnormal psychology from theology. At the time of the publication of Weyer's book, there were few men to applaud his efforts. Most of his colleagues criticized and abused him, and his book was listed in the *Index Librorum Prohibitorum*.

During this same period, Jean Bodin (1530–1596), a French lawyer, published a work on demonology that set back science in a serious way. His book went far to confirm the public belief in the theologistic doctrines of the time. He described how people possessed of the devil could cough up pieces of wood, pins, and other objects and how they were able to speak in strange and unknown tongues and to discuss matters with which they were unacquainted. Bodin believed that demons could enter the body on the order of a sorcerer and that they could be expelled from men, animals and houses by the same method. Bodin also attacked Weyer, saying that only "a very ignorant or a wicked man" could write such a book as *De Praestigiis*. Since Bodin admitted that Weyer was not ignorant, he accused him of being wicked and described him as a "protector of witches." As a result of Bodin's work, the legal profession supported the religious point of view, and Weyer remained under attack for more than a hundred years.

St. Vincent de Paul (1576–1660) was another early voice raised against the current beliefs in demonology. At the risk of his life, he wrote: "Mental disease is no different from bodily disease. Christianity demands that the powerful must protect, and that the skillful must relieve, one condition as well as the other." St. Vincent was one of the first men in France to show a humane interest in mental patients. In 1632, he founded the Maison de St. Lazare in Paris. This religious asylum used a combination of isolation, intellectual work, and prayer in the treatment of the inmates. A number of other religious asylums were patterned after this institution during the seventeenth and eighteenth centuries. The monks of the Order of St. John of God founded at least ten, and others were established by the Order of St. Francis, the Order of the Cordeliers, and the Friars of the Christian School.

In England, Reginald Scot (1538–1599) was an outspoken opponent of the superstitions of the time. In 1584, he published *The Discoverie of Witchcraft,* an exposition of the fallacies of witchcraft and demonology. This book, along with Scot's other writings, was ordered burned by King James I, who wrote a personal refutation of it and a reassertion of demonology. Scot, however, devoted his entire life to his fight against the belief in demon possession.

The laws against witchcraft were not repealed until the eighteenth century. As late as 1768, the eminent Protestant clergyman John Wesley declared, "The giving up of witchcraft is in effect the giving up of the Bible." And in America, where thirty-two witches had been put to death over the years, an official trial for witchcraft took place in New England in 1793.[1]

THE RETURN TO REASON: EIGHTEENTH AND NINETEENTH CENTURIES

The great changes generated by the Renaissance, in the form of the reappearance of scientific method, emphasis on individual dignity, and the political belief in liberty and the rights of man,

---

[1]Fascinating nontechnical accounts of the history of abnormal psychology are Walter Bromberg's *The Mind of Man: A History of Psychotherapy and Psychoanalysis* (Harper & Row, 1959) and Robin McKown's *Pioneers in Mental Health* (Dodd, Mead, 1961). An outstanding classic which should be read by every serious student is Gregory Zilboorg's *A History of Medical Psychology* (Norton, 1941). Other general accounts of the historical development of abnormal psychology and psychiatry are *The History of Psychiatry: An Evaluation of Psychiatric Thought and Practice from Prehistoric Times to the Present* (Harper & Row, 1966) by F. G. Alexander and S. T. Selesnick; *Psychiatry and Its History* (Thomas, 1970) by George Mora and J. L. Brand; *Madness in Society: Chapters in the Historical Sociology of Mental Illness* (University of Chicago Press, 1968) by George Rosen; and A. A. Roback's *History of Psychology and Psychiatry* (Greenwood Press, 1969).

Figure 2.4 *Philippe Pinel, 1745–1842, the great French psychiatrist humanitarian. (National Library of Medicine, Washington, D.C.)*

were reflected in the latter part of the eighteenth century in an emerging concern for mental patients. By the late 1700s, the return to the naturalistic approach of Hippocrates was well under way. Emphasis was placed once again on anatomy and physiology, and the physical treatment of mental patients was stressed by physicians.

In France, the writings of Montaigne at the end of the sixteenth century and of Voltaire in the middle of the eighteenth century were important milestones in returning to a naturalistic, nontheological interpretation of mental disorder.

It remained for a French physician, Philippe Pinel (1745–1826), to apply a new social and political philosophy to the problems of mental illness. Pinel became the most important figure in the history of mental disorder in France, if not in the entire world. His importance began in 1793 when he was chosen for the position of physician-in-chief to the Bicêtre Hospital for the Insane in

Paris. The hospital was recognized as a disgrace to the nation, with patients chained to posts, walls, and beds. On Sundays and holidays, the attendants charged a fee for allowing sightseers to visit the cells and to tease and taunt the patients. Pinel found that while some progress had been made over the years in clinical observation and in the collection of data, the individual patient had been neglected to a most shameful degree.

One of Pinel's first actions was to demand the removal of the chains from some of the patients. After considerable difficulty, permission was obtained to undertake this daring plan. Most of the officials considered Pinel to be as mad as his patients for even contemplating it. However, Pinel selected forty men for the experiment, and within a few days their chains were removed. The results were sensational. Even the most excited and maniacal patients became easier to handle. Patients who had been chained for twenty or more years and who had been considered extremely dangerous, strolled about the hospital in camisoles or restraining jackets. They showed no inclination to harm anyone. Noise and excitement decreased, and the discipline of the hospital improved remarkably. Pinel had demonstrated in a most dramatic way the value of his radical theory of nonrestraint.

In 1795, Pinel left the Bicêtre and became head of the Salpêtrière, a large general hospital established for the care of the poor in the city but also required to care for mental patients. Pinel reorganized the hospital in the same way he had reorganized the Bicêtre. Chains were removed, cells were disinfected, and personnel were transferred or replaced. Additional improvements were made by segregating the agitated patients and by establishing separate wards for different types of mental patients.[2]

While Pinel is usually credited with being the first psychiatrist to strike the chains from mental patients, this observation is not completely accurate. Physicians in several other countries had already liberated their patients. However, progress in the care and treatment of mental patients was to be a long and slow process in spite of the efforts

---

[2]Two books of considerable interest dealing with the life and influence of Pinel are *Philippe Pinel, Unchainer of the Insane* (Watts, 1968) by Bernard Mackler and Walter Riese's *The Legacy of Philippe Pinel: An Inquiry into Thought on Mental Alienation* (Springer, 1969).

of the more concerned and enlightened physicians. J. E. D. Esquirol (1772–1840), a pupil of Pinel and later his assistant, became chief physician of the asylum at Charenton in 1826. He was one of the first clinicians, if not the first, to give lectures in psychiatry. His major work, *Des Maladies Mentales,* was published in 1838. Esquirol described the state of mental patients early in the nineteenth century:

> I have seen them naked, or covered with rags, and protected only by straw from the cold damp pavement upon which they were lying. I have seen them coarsely fed, deprived of fresh air, or water to quench their thirst, and of most of the necessary things for life. I have seen them delivered and abandoned to the brutal supervision of veritable jailers. I have seen them in squalid, stinking little hovels, without air or light, chained in caves where wild beasts would not have been confined. These unfortunate beings like the criminals of the state, are cast into dungeons, or into dark cells into which the eye of humanity never penetrates. There they remain to waste away in their own filth under the weight of chains which lacerate their bodies. Their faces are pale and emaciated; they await only the moment which will end their misery and conceal our disgrace. They are exhibited to the public gaze by greedy keepers, who make them appear as wild beasts. They are huddled together in a disorderly manner with no known means of maintaining order among them, except terror. Whips, chains and dungeons are the only means of persuasion employed by keepers who are as barbarous as they are ignorant (Esquirol, 1838).

The conditions described by Esquirol were typical of those found throughout Europe and the United States. In many parts of the world, the plight of the mental patient was far worse. It was not unusual to confine a mentally disordered man or woman in a hole dug in the floor with a grid fitted over the top. The patient sat or crouched in the hole, received his food, excreted his wastes, and finally, sometimes after many years of such confinement, died in his cramped and filthy quarters.

In England, the modern era in the care and treatment of mental patients began with William Cullen (1712–1790). This physician sought to establish a psychological basis for mental disturbance, advocated more liberty and privileges for patients, and urged less drastic measures of physical restraint. However, Cullen also favored

the use of fear and physical punishment for patients who were difficult to handle.

The interest in mental patients in England and the need for reform in their care and treatment were accelerated in the late eighteenth century by the mental condition of King George III. From age twenty-seven to age seventy-two, the King had intermittent attacks of excitement that made it necessary to place him in the charge of keepers or attendants. The dramatic events of the King's illness brought the problem forcibly to the attention of the English people.

Another influence of great importance in the humanitarian reform in England was the interest taken in the condition of mental patients by William Hack Tuke (1732–1822), a prominent tea

Figure 2.5 *An etching by Ambroise Tardieu depicting a patient at Charenton Hospital. From* Des Maladies Mentales *by Jean Etienne Esquirol. (Philadelphia Museum of Art.)*

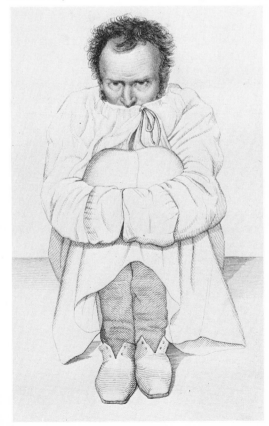

and coffee merchant and a member of the Society of Friends. After observing a group of pauper lunatics in a workhouse, Tuke recorded the following comments:

> I cannot describe my feelings and astonishment when I perceived that the poor women were absolutely without any clothes. The weather was intensely cold, and the evening previous to our visit, the thermometer had been sixteen degrees below freezing. One of these forlorn objects lay buried under a miserable cover of straw, without a blanket or even a horse-cloth to defend her from the cold (Tuke, 1882).

From that time, Tuke devoted himself to the cause of bettering the condition of mental patients. He started to raise funds for a home for mental patients in which chains would be unknown. In 1796, he founded the York Retreat. This Quaker hospital played an important role in improving the lot of mental patients in England and in other countries of the world.

In spite of initial advances in the care and treatment of mental patients in various countries, the general level of hospital care was deplorable. Rooms were crowded, wards were wet and poorly ventilated, and patients were forced to sleep in straw beds which were filthy and crawling with vermin. At one hospital, patients were chained to their cribs from Saturday night until Monday morning in order to give keepers the weekend off. Then, on Monday, the filth-covered patients were cleaned with mops and buckets of cold water. There was no change of clothing, the patients stood naked in summer and winter while waiting for their clothes to be washed and dried. There was no medical officer in residence, and the only treatment was strong purgatives.

During a parliamentary inquiry into the condition of mental patients in England in 1859, a witness said:

> Patients are seized and thrown with reckless violence on the stone floor, or across an iron bedstead, and they are then kneaded with the knee on the chest, at the risk of breaking their ribs; then they are seized by the throat until the eyes start out of the socket, and the blood comes out of the mouth. They are also taken by the neckcloth and their heads thumped against the floor or banged against the wall. That is the normal treatment, I fear, of the patients in the refractory wards generally throughout the country (Perceval, 1860).

Among the restraints used for mental patients in the 1800s were chairs with boards in front of the patient's face so he could not spit at the attendant, gloves without fingers, jackets with long sleeves which could be tied behind the patient, spring straps which allowed the patient to move slowly but not to run or kick, cushioned masks to stop screaming, and wire face masks to stop spitting and biting. The Aubanel bed was a padded bed inside a coffin-like box with holes or slats to give ventilation.

John Conolly (1794–1866), a native of Scotland who became Professor of Medicine in the University College of London, and later Superintendent of Hanwell Hospital, introduced the nonrestraint system into the English asylums. He published several controversial works which were the beginning of a movement that gradually brought about a marked reduction in the use of mechanical restraints in hospitals throughout the world.

The growing interest in the mental patient was not confined to France and England. In Germany, Johann Christian Reil (1759–1813), a contemporary of Pinel, was a widely recognized clinician and research worker in the medical field. While his first work was on the anatomy of the brain, he emphasized psychological factors in the treatment of mental disorders. Johann Heinroth (1773–1843), a contemporary of Esquirol, occupied an equally outstanding position in German psychiatry. He was made Professor of Psychical Medicine when the chair was founded in the University of Leipzig. He considered moral factors to be of greater importance than any others in the origin of personality disturbance.

Wilhelm Griesinger (1817–1868) wrote the first modern textbook on psychiatry. This book, *Mental Pathology and Therapeutics,* helped to free psychiatry from its long bondage to metaphysical and theological speculations Griesinger was the first physician to urge the establishment of special psychiatric clinics, and he developed the concept of the psychopathic hospital for the active treatment of early cases. As a result of his work in Germany, the first hospital of this type in the United States was established at the University of Michigan in 1909.

The wave of reform in Europe was paralleled

Figure 2.6 Psychopathic Ward, *a lithograph by Robert Riggs. (Philadelphia Museum of Art.)*

in colonial America, where the Pennsylvania Hospital in Philadelphia opened its doors to mental patients in 1752. Modern psychiatry, however, began in the United States in 1783 when Benjamin Rush (1745–1813) joined the staff of the Pennsylvania Hospital. Rush had graduated from New Jersey College (now Princeton University) at the age of fifteen and took his doctoral degree at twenty-two at the University of Edinburgh. While at Edinburgh, he studied under William Cullen, British pioneer in the field of mental disturbances.

When Rush became a member of the medical staff of the Pennsylvania Hospital there were twenty-four patients who had been admitted as "lunatics." Little was known about the cause of such conditions, and less was known about how to cure them. As a result, the patients were confined to damp and poorly ventilated cells which were cold in the winter, hot in the summer, and always smelly.

Rush objected strenuously to these conditions, pointing out that nearly every patient "took cold" after a few weeks confinement and that bronchitis and pneumonia were common. The Board of Managers of the hospital admitted that the conditions were very bad but insisted that no money was available for improvements. Rush took the matter to the people of Philadelphia through newspaper articles, speeches, and personal influence. Finally, after thirteen years, a separate ward for mental patients was established in 1796. Rush continued to push for enlightened treatment of these patients, insisting that they be given interesting work as well as recreation and amusement. Later he advocated separate wards for men and women and isolation buildings for noisy and disturbed patients. He kept detailed notes on his patients and in 1812 published *Medical Inquiries and Observations upon Diseases of the Mind*. This book was the first to be published on mental illness in the United States.

In spite of almost insurmountable difficulties in the form of lack of adequate funds, untrained hospital personnel, misconceptions and prejudice on the part of the public, and indifference on the part of most of the medical profession, the nineteenth century saw the beginning of trends which were to revolutionize the care and treatment of the mental patient. These trends included expansion of mental hospitals, the aftercare movement, the family care system, the open-door policy, and the mental hygiene movement.

MENTAL HOSPITALS

The first asylum in America for the care of mental patients was established in Mexico in 1566 by missionaries from Spain, where the first asylums in Europe were located. It was two hundred years before mental patients were received in a hospital in the United States. Although the Pennsylvania Hospital received mental patients as early as 1752, it was not until 1773 that the first separate public mental hospital was opened at Williamsburg, Virginia.

The growth of the mental hospital movement in the United States was vigorous during the early part of the nineteenth century. The Friends' Asylum was opened at Frankford, near Philadelphia, in 1817, to be followed in 1818 by the McLean Asylum in Massachusetts, by the Bloom-ingdale Asylum in New York in 1819, and by the Retreat at Hartford, Connecticut, and the Lexington Asylum in Kentucky in 1824. Other early hospitals for the mentally ill were the Massachusetts State Hospital at Worcester (1833), the Vermont State Asylum (1836), and the Ohio State Asylum (1838). By 1840, there were fourteen mental hospitals in the United States, with a total population of 2,500 patients (Hall et al., 1944).

In 1844, a group of thirteen physicians, all superintendents of hospitals for the mentally disturbed, met at Philadelphia to form the Association of Medical Superintendents of American Institutions for the Insane. Later this organization came to be called the American Medico-Psychological Association, and today it is known as the American Psychiatric Association.

The year 1844 also saw the first issue of the *American Journal of Insanity* (now the *American Journal of Psychiatry*). This publication was the first in the English language to be devoted to the problem of mental disorder. Four years later, the *Journal of Psychological Medicine and Mental Pathology* appeared in England, and the *Journal of Mental Science* appeared in England in 1853. The second American journal devoted to mental disorder was founded in Cincinnati, Ohio, in 1853. This periodical was called the *American Psychological Journal*. In 1867, the *Quarterly Journal of Psychological Medicine and Medical Jurisprudence* was published in New York.[3]

THE AFTERCARE MOVEMENT

One of the extensions of the state hospital program was the *aftercare movement* to give assistance to mental patients following their release from the hospital. The first aftercare association was founded in Paris in 1841. This organization operated a "convalescent home" where patients could

---

[3]Excellent accounts of the history of various aspects of abnormal psychology and psychiatry in the United States can be found in *Psychiatry and the Community in Nineteenth-century America* (Basic Books, 1969) by Ruth and Gerald Kaplan; *Psychoanalysis in America: Historical Perspectives* (Thomas, 1966), edited by M. H. Sherman et al.; and Nina Ridenour's *Mental Health in the United States: A Fifty Year History* (Harvard University, 1961). Similar histories of the subject in Great Britain are the classic *Chapters in the History of the Insane in the British Isles* (Kegan Paul, 1882) by Daniel Hack Tuke; and Denis Leigh's *The Historical Development of British Psychiatry: Eighteenth and Nineteenth Centuries*, vol. 1 (Pergamon, 1961).

Figure 2.7 *A traditional psychiatric ward. (Photograph by Jerry Cooke.)*

remain for several weeks while looking for work and becoming adjusted to the problems of living outside the hospital. Moreover, the home held weekly reunions to which recently released patients returned, often with husbands or wives as well as children, for a day of hospitality and chapel services. In England, an After-care Association was organized in 1879, and a system of helping discharged mental patients existed prior to 1900 in Switzerland. Patients were given advice, financial assistance, and help in finding suitable jobs.

The problem of aftercare in the case of a patient who has been in the hospital for a long period is a particularly difficult one. He has lost his job skills, he may no longer be in touch with his family and former friends, and he finds the community a confusing and alien place. Patients of this type often prefer to remain in the hospital because they are more comfortable and secure there.

The importance of aftercare facilities and services cannot be overemphasized. Even under the most favorable conditions, many people who have experienced emotional and personality problems requiring hospital treatment find it difficult to make a satisfactory adjustment when hospitalization is no longer necessary. The problem is a particularly serious one among younger people who have been hospitalized.

A study of 100 persons 17 to 41 years of age who had been discharged 8 to 23 years earlier showed that only 34 percent were leading "normal" lives according to such criteria as a stable marriage, regular employment, and being happy and content. Sixty-one percent showed some degree of maladjustment ranging from marginal and "peculiar" lives to chronic mental illness and institutionalization (Roche, 1968).

Very considerable advances in the aftercare of mental patients have been made in Russia, where patients are visited at home by psychiatrists. In the United States the usual pattern is for the psychiatrist who treated the patient at the hospital to lose contact completely at the time of the patient's discharge. The typical Russian psychiatrist makes at least twenty visits a month to his patients who have returned to the community (American Psychiatric Association, 1968).

An important development in helping patients meet the difficult problems of adjustment after leaving the mental hospital has been the *halfway house*. This term has been used for a variety of plans and projects. A common feature is that the released patient does not return immediately to his home but lives for a period of time in a small community center where he can gain confidence and receive various kinds of support and help when needed. In this way the stress on the recently released patient is lessened, and he has a better chance to make an adjustment at his own pace and without the pressures that might otherwise delay his full recovery.[1]

FAMILY CARE

The *family care system,* another major development in the treatment of mental patients, began many years ago at Gheel, Belgium. For centuries the mentally ill had been brought by relatives to the shrine of St. Dymphna, but the colony was not established until the seventeenth century. At first, patients who were not cured during the festival of St. Dymphna were left with the villagers of Gheel to wait for the next festival. In this way, a system of family care came into operation.

The families, or "caretakers," of the patients were not permitted to take more than two patients, and these had to be of the same sex. The caretaker was required to provide a room, and meals were to be the same as those taken by members of the household. Clothing was furnished by the administrators of the colony. The patients were given complete freedom and were encouraged to help with the housework, assist in the preparation of meals, look after the children, and otherwise make themselves useful.

When patients became physically ill, excited, or unmanageable, families were permitted to return them to the local infirmary. Moreover, the families were paid for each patient under their care, with the amount being determined by how dirty the habits of the patients were. Families were paid 60 centimes a day for clean patients, 70 centimes for patients with slightly dirty habits, and 75 centimes for patients with very dirty habits.

In 1858, Belgian government physicians assumed administration of the Gheel colony, which was divided into sections, each under the supervision of a specialist in mental disorders. The foster homes were carefully selected and regularly inspected. Small charges were made to those patients able to afford them.

Today, 1,800 of Gheel's 30,000 inhabitants are mental patients, most of whom are cared for by normal families in the town. One in seven families is responsible for the care of one or two mental patients, and the parents and grandparents of 85 percent of these families also took care of patients in their homes. Though the program originally was designed for long-term care, about half of the patients in the program today are able to return to their home communities after about sixteen months. While in the foster home at Gheel, a nurse visits each patient every two weeks and a physician looks in once a month. Because of the use of tranquilizing drugs, there has not been a serious outburst of violence for many years.

The family care treatment of mental patients spread to other countries in the last half of the nineteenth century. Patients who were considered harmless, easily managed, or incurable but not dangerous were boarded out to private homes. While the system had the advantage of making

---

[1]The following books discuss the problems of the mental patient in making an adjustment after being released from a psychiatric hospital: *The Psychiatric Halfway House* (Thomas, 1966) by N. D. Rothwell and J. M. Dorniger, and *The First Year Out: Mental Patients after Hospitalization* (Johns Hopkins Press, 1969) by W. W. Michaux et al.

more room in the hospitals for acutely disturbed cases and for those patients who might respond to intensive treatment, it had the disadvantage of being open to many abuses by greedy and sometimes cruel people who were more interested in the money paid them by the state than in the care or rehabilitation of the patient. Nevertheless, the advantages outweighed the disadvantages.

The growth of family care as a kind of substitute for being in the hospital has evolved into a concern for the adjustment problems faced by patients when they return to their homes, jobs, and communities after having been hospitalized. Even today most of us continue to look with some uneasiness, if not suspicion, upon the person who has been treated in a psychiatric hospital. The discharged patient must make an adjustment to relatives, employers, friends, and fellow workers, just as they must learn to adjust to him.

THE MENTAL HYGIENE MOVEMENT

In the United States, the objectives of all humane efforts in behalf of mental patients came to be embodied in the *mental hygiene movement*. Historically this movement began with the efforts of Dorothea Lynde Dix (1802–1887), a Massachusetts schoolteacher who became interested in the plight of mentally disturbed men and women confined in jails, prisons, and almshouses. In 1841, Miss Dix began a forty-year crusade to improve the condition of mental patients. Directing her efforts primarily toward the need for special hospitals for mental patients, she pointed out the widely prevalent brutality toward mentally disturbed individuals and the neglect of patients in almshouses and jails. She emphasized statistics which tended to show that most mental patients could be cured if sent to hospitals during the early stages of the disorder. Meeting a degree of success, she was encouraged to carry her investigation to other parts of the United States and eventually to England and Scotland. Her work was an important factor in awakening public consciousness to the needs of mental patients.

However, the uncritical acceptance of the idea that cures could be brought about merely by placing patients in hospitals resulted in a somewhat unrealistic "cult of curability." During this period in the 1800s, the heads of mental hospitals claimed recovery rates from 90 to 100 percent of recent cases. When it became apparent that such cures were exaggerated, public opinion reacted against psychiatry and the mental hospital.

The term *mental hygiene* first appeared in 1843 (Sweetser, 1843). However, the term was used in a somewhat special manner to refer to the relationship between emotions and physical illness. By 1878, the concept of mental hygiene was in more or less general use and was accepted as referring to the prevention of personality disturbances and the promotion of mental health. The mental hygiene movement gained momentum in 1880 with the organization of the National Association for the Protection of the Insane and the Prevention of Insanity. While this organization existed only a few years, it was the first important organized effort to prevent mental disability and promote mental health.

MENTAL HEALTH AND THE TWENTIETH CENTURY

The mental hygiene movement, as we know it today, started with a man and a book. The man was Clifford W. Beers (1876–1943) of Connecticut, and the book was his autobiography, *A Mind That Found Itself*. After graduating from Yale in 1897, Beers started on a business career. However, he experienced an emotional disturbance in 1900, at which time he attempted suicide. For the next several years he was in three different mental hospitals. While in these hospitals, he was the victim of a variety of brutalities, and he observed his fellow patients being subjected to indifference, lack of consideration, humiliation, and inhuman restraints.

Beers wrote to many officials, including the Governor of Connecticut and the President of the United States, demanding an investigation of conditions in mental hospitals. Since he was himself a patient, his letters were disregarded. Nevertheless, he continued to make detailed notes on his observations, and five years after leaving the hospital he published his explosive autobiography in 1908.

The book exposed existing evils and suggested ways in which these unfortunate conditions could be corrected. The volume was an immediate success and was read widely and quoted extensively. Soon after publication of the book, the Connecticut Society for Mental Hygiene was founded; and Beers was made executive secretary. The state society was so successful that in 1909 a National Committee for Mental Hygiene was established in New York City. Beers was appointed secretary and held the position for thirty years. The official journal, *Mental Hygiene,* was founded in 1917.[5]

In 1950, the National Committee for Mental Hygiene merged with the National Mental Health Foundation and the Psychiatric Foundation to form the National Association for Mental Health. The goals of this organization include the promotion of mental health, the prevention of mental and nervous disorders, and improved care and treatment of the mentally disturbed and the mentally retarded. By 1970, there were approximately one thousand local mental health associations in the United States.

At the international level, the National Committee for Mental Hygiene organized in 1930 the first international congress dealing with this problem. The meetings generated worldwide interest. As a result of the congress, the International Committee on Mental Hygiene was established in 1931. The purpose of the committee was to promote work for mental health in various countries of the world.

The activities of the International Committee on Mental Hygiene led to the formation of the World Federation for Mental Health in London in 1948. This organization has become the most important single mental health organization operating at the international level. The purpose of the Federation has been to continue and to expand the work of the International Committee by bringing together in one organization the mental health societies of various countries. Through the Federation, it has been possible for associations of anthropologists, educators, nurses, psychiatrists, psychologists, sociologists, and social workers to become involved in international work for mental health.

The Federation publishes a quarterly journal, *World Mental Health,* and maintains a close relationship with the United Nations and various specialized agencies. The Federation is on the register of the Secretary-General of the UN as an organization to be consulted by the Economic and Social Council (ECOSOC), and it maintains a consulting status with the United Nations Educational, Scientific and Cultural Organization (UNESCO), the International Labor Organization (ILO), the United Nations Children's Fund (UNICEF), and the World Health Organization (WHO).

The World Health Organization, through its Mental Health Unit, is another important force in the promotion of mental health on a worldwide basis. The unit is assisted by an expert advisory panel on mental health, made up of experts from a number of countries. Various types of expert committees are drawn from the ranks of this advisory panel.[6]

With all the advances in our attitudes toward the mental patient and in our upgrading of psychiatric hospitals, there continue to be reports of abuses and injustice. In 1968 a patient who had been confined to the Matteawan (New York) State Hospital for the criminally insane for more than fourteen years was awarded 300,000 dollars in damages by a New York judge who described practices at the hospital as "incredible." In his legal opinion, the judge said, "He (the plaintiff) was struck, kicked and beaten by attendants. After a beating he was stripped and placed in a small dark room without toilet facilities, without water, and without a bed or mattress. He was kept in the

---

[5]*Mental Hygiene*   A relatively nontechnical quarterly journal for physicians, lawyers, educators, nurses, social workers, public officials, and students of social problems. Contains original articles, reports of surveys, new methods of prevention and treatment, and items of general interest. All students preparing for careers in mental health should be familiar with this professional journal. Published by the National Association for Mental Health, 1800 North Kent St., Rosslyn, Va. 22209.

[6]Books dealing with key personalities in the history of mental hygiene include Clifford Beers' classic *A Mind That Found Itself* (Longmans Green, 1908); Helen E. Marshall's *Dorothea Dix: Forgotten Samaritan* (University of North Carolina, 1937); *The Autobiography of Benjamin Rush* (Princeton University, 1948); Nathan G. Goodman's *Benjamin Rush: Physician and Citizen, 1746–1813* (University of Pennsylvania, 1934).

room for about eight days on bread and water, and with a full meal once every three days." The damages were awarded for the brutality and for the lack of meaningful psychiatric care.

Was this merely an isolated case of the abuse of a mental patient? Unfortunately not. In 1969 the state legislature of New Jersey investigated charges that female patients at the state's largest mental hospital had been abused sexually by hospital employees. Girls were smuggled out of the wards by attendants for acts of prostitution. The attendants received ten dollars each time a girl was smuggled out, and the girl received a bar of candy or a coin. The activity came to light when the parents of a teen-age girl complained to the hospital authorities that she was pregnant.

Perhaps the most dramatic and shocking revelation of brutal and inhuman treatment of mental patients is seen in the documentary film *Titicut Follies,* filmed at the Bridgeport Hospital for the Criminal Insane in Connecticut. A Boston judge of the Superior Court described the film as "a nightmare of ghoulish obscenities." He then ordered the producer of the movie to surrender all prints and negatives of the film because it "exceeded the public's right to know" about conditions in mental institutions such as Bridgewater. Eventually the film was released to audiences throughout the United States and Canada.

It is an unfortunate fact that the conventional mental hospital environment literally teaches patients to remain sick. Endless hours and days of boredom, inactivity, and lack of stimulation are combined with little treatment, or none at all, and a complete lack of meaningful human contact. Even the best-intentioned hospital finds itself overwhelmed by the large numbers of patients and the relatively few staff members. The use of volunteers from the community helps ease the situation to a slight degree, but the basic and de-pressing aura of the institution cannot be erased from the minds of the patients. The result is a gradual giving in to the psychologically damaging influence of institutional life.

The degrading and dehumanizing character of the mental hospital is seen in the lack of privacy, lack of a place for personal belongings, lining up for meals at appointed times, absence of free communication by mail and phone, restricted visiting procedures, lack of beds for naps, ward odors, and similar frustrations. While many hospitals try to offset these negative aspects of hospital life by providing programs of resocialization and remotivation, most institutions eventually become victims of their own lethargy.[7]

COMMUNITY MENTAL HEALTH

As a result of the growing recognition that the conventional psychiatric hospital cannot solve all the problems of mental disorder, there has been a rapidly accelerating movement toward community mental health programs. Most American communities cannot provide comprehensive mental health services. It was to help provide these services that the national Community Mental Health Centers Program was established.

The community mental health movement has taken place in the years since Congress passed the National Mental Health Act in 1946. From that time there has been an extraordinary amount of clinical, applied, and administrative research, and in planning, implementing, and expanding preventive and remedial mental health programs.

Another event of importance was the passage of the Mental Health Study Act by Congress in 1955, which established the Joint Commission on Mental Illness and Mental Health. Its purpose was to analyze and to evaluate needs and resources

---

[7]The role of the mental hospital in the history of psychiatry and the changing concepts of the importance and function of the hospital are explored in *Asylums: Essays on the Social Situation of Mental Patients and Other Inmates* (Doubleday, 1961) by Erving Goffman; *Life and Death of a Mental Hospital* (University of Washington Press, 1965) by E. Stotland and A. L. Kobler; D. J. Vail's *Dehumanization and the Institutional Career* (Thomas, 1966); *Hospitalization and Discharge of the Mentally Ill* (University of Chicago Press, 1968) by R. S. Rock and others; *Methods of Madness: The Mental Hospital as a Last Resort* (Holt, Rinehart and Winston, 1969) by B. M. Braginsky and others: and *The Desegregation of the Mentally Ill* (Routledge, 1969) by J. Hoenig, and M. W. Hamilton.

of mentally disturbed individuals as a basis for making recommendations for a national mental health program. The joint commission issued a final report and recommendations in 1960 *(Action for Mental Health,* 1961).

The report prompted President John F. Kennedy to deliver a presidential message to Congress on the subject of mental health. He called for a national government-backed program to help plan, build, and staff a network of community mental health centers. The "necessary services" to be provided by these centers were to include in-patient and outpatient care; part-time hospitalization on a day or night basis; emergency services; consultation, diagnostic, and rehabilitation functions; training; and research.

This message led to the passage by Congress in 1963 of the Mental Retardation Facilities and Community Mental Health Centers Construction Act. Another milestone was reached in 1965 when Congress passed legislation providing funds for meeting the initial cost of staffing these centers. These various forms of legislation provided considerable impetus to the rapid development of community mental health facilities and to the training of the necessary professional staff.[8]

The goal of the community mental health centers program is to improve the organization and delivery of mental health services with the objective of making the most effective mental health care available to all the people of the nation. It seeks to reduce suffering and costly disability and to deploy resources so that greater progress can be made toward preventing personality disturbances.

Approximately two thousand community mental health centers are needed in order to serve adequately the national population. A total of 218 million dollars in federal funds awarded from the inception of the program in 1965 through the fiscal year 1968 enabled communities throughout the country to develop 331 new community mental health centers. These centers, when fully operational, will serve over 51 million people. The diversity of the areas served by these 331 centers is remarkable. They range from the very poorest counties in Appalachia to the affluent urban-suburban fringes of our major cities. Fifty-seven

of the centers have been funded in population areas of 500,000 or more. One hundred and sixty-five will serve smaller cities, and 109 centers are being established in small towns and communities which will serve large rural areas where mental health services have previously been virtually unavailable (NIMH, 1970). Despite the relative newness of the community mental health centers program, it is already demonstrating its effectiveness by bringing mental health services to people who previously had no access to them.

In a number of urban ghetto areas across the country, community mental health centers have taken the leadership in developing innovative and imaginative services, utilizing a wide variety of professional and of paraprofessional personnel. A significant number of educational institutions, inspired by the leadership of the community mental health movement, have implemented educational programs to provide formal training for new career personnel.

Community mental health centers have also provided a mechanism through which exciting new therapeutic concepts and techniques are being developed and put into practice, including aftercare and partial hospitalization. Day care engages a patient in a treatment program during the day, permitting him to return to his family at night and for weekends. Night care assists those who are able to function in a job or at home but who require more intensive supervision than can be provided on an outpatient basis.

Community mental health centers are providing valuable direct services to persons in need and are having a constructive impact on the traditional care-giving institutions in our society. Their continued growth and development and the extension of services to the large population still unserved depends upon continued federal assistance (NIMH, 1969).

While the general objectives of the community mental health centers are similar, the form and functions of the center are determined by local resources and needs.

Temple University in Philadelphia developed a program for 200,000 residents of an area bearing the deep scars of poverty. The consultation and

---

[8]*Community Mental Health Journal*   A bimonthly publication devoted to emergent and innovative approaches to mental health research, theory, and practice as they relate to the community. Available from Behavioral Publications, Inc., 2852 Broadway, New York, New York 10025.

Center for Metropolitan Problems

As part of its effort to focus attention on mental health problems of national importance, the National Institute of Mental Health established the Center for Metropolitan Problems. This center coordinates activities concerned with the impact of urban development on human well-being. To fulfill its mission, the center offers research grants and contracts, training grants, fellowships, and consultations with private, state, and local agencies. Typical research programs have been a study of urban, social, and political processes from the perspective of ethnicity; a study of racism as a historical and social science concept; and a project to identify problems confronted by the inner-city black in working for the "white establishment."

---

education units of the center conduct in-service training programs for police, public health nurses, and poverty program representatives in forty neighborhood areas. The center also has a number of research activities designed to provide follow-up evaluation studies of the effectiveness of the diagnostic, treatment, prevention, and consultation services. This community health center program illustrates how the resources of a large medical center can be channeled into a comprehensive health effort.

A quite different type of community mental health center has been developed by the Methodist Hospital in Pikesville, Kentucky. This center serves four counties, among which are two of the poorest counties in the United States. Because of the very limited mental health resources available in the area, several scattered general hospitals supply emergency and short-term services. Each of these hospitals has a direct telephone line manned twenty-four hours a day by professional consultants. In this way the outlying hospitals are in immediate touch with the center. Groups of professionals make weekly visits to remote mountain communities to advise local service teams made up of a social worker, psychiatric nurse, and physician. "Family houses" staffed by volunteers having phone contact with the community mental health center serve as rehabilitation centers for county residents who earlier would have been placed in the alien environment of a state psychiatric hospital.

A third example of the community mental health center movement in action is the Golden State Community Mental Health Center in Los Angeles County. This center serves a catchment area of 165,000 citizens in four adjoining but quite different communities. These areas include rural and urban living patterns, affluent and impoverished groups, as well as Mexican-American and black populations. The center receives active support from all community-related organizations within the service area. Growing out of what originally was a child guidance clinic, the center is now affiliated with a county hospital, a private hospital, two health department clinics, and a number of voluntary aftercare and rehabilitation services. The center demonstrates the way in which the resources of a community can be mobilized to provide a wide range of services previously unavailable to many people.[9]

MODERN ORIGINS OF ABNORMAL PSYCHOLOGY

Many trends have combined to form the present-day concept of mental disorder. Some of these trends had their roots in the medicine of Hippocrates and in the philosophy of Plato and Aristotle. Other trends have been of more recent origin. In any case, three major approaches can be identi-

---

[9]Books related to the preventive, treatment, and rehabilitative potential of community mental health programs include *Mental Health and the Community: Problems, Programs, and Strategies* (Behavioral Publications, 1969) edited by M. F. Shore and F. V. Manning; *Handbook of Community Mental Health Practice* (Jossey-Boss, 1969), edited by H. R. Lamb et al.; *The Treatment of Mental Disorders in the Community* (Baillière, 1968), edited by G. R. Daniel and H. L. Freeman; *Community Life for the Mentally Ill: An Alternative to Institutional Care* (Aldine, 1969) by G. W. Fairweather et al.; *The Community Mental Health Center: An Interim Appraisal,* published by the Joint Information Service of the American Psychiatric Association, 1969; and *Community Psychology and Community Mental Health* (Holden-Day, 1970), edited by P. E. Cook.

fied: (a) the emphasis on classification, (b) the emphasis on organic conditions, and (c) the emphasis on psychological factors.

THE CLASSIFICATION APPROACH

Long before there was any real understanding of the causes or nature of mental disorder, men observed and classified symptoms. One of the first important classifications was proposed by Hippocrates, who described three personality disturbances: (1) *mania,* (2) *melancholia,* and (3) *dementia.* Then, as now, mania referred to overactivity, excitement, and violence. Dementia was reserved for patients who behaved in strange and incomprehensible ways. There is some question, however, about whether Hippocrates limited melancholia to depression, as is done today. It seems likely that he included a much wider range of symptoms.

In addition to the three basic mental disorders

Figure 2.8 *Emil Kraepelin, 1856–1926. German clinician and classifier of mental illness. (Permission of Robert A. Becker, Inc.)*

mentioned by Hippocrates, a fourth condition, known as *hysteria,* was recognized by the ancient medical writers. At that time, the disorder was not regarded as a personality disturbance. It was considered to be a disease of women, having its origin in the disturbed activity of the uterus. The Greek word for uterus is *hysteron,* hence the term *hysteria.*

The classifications of Aretaeus, Caelius Aurelianus, and Galen were very slight modifications of the categories suggested by Hippocrates. With the exception of melancholia, the terms used to designate the various forms of personality disturbance were descriptive of the symptoms observed. In the case of melancholia, which was believed to be due to a disturbance of the body humors, the classification was based on etiology, or causation.

Following the death of Galen in 200 A.D., the classification of Hippocrates was lost along with the rest of naturalistic medicine. More than a thousand years later, his classification appeared again, in various elaborated forms. In the sixteenth century, classifications distinguished between congenital (inborn) and acquired conditions. In the eighteenth century, there was a marked renewal of interest in the classification of mental disorder. Diseases were grouped in classes, orders, and genera in the same way that plants and animals were being grouped by the natural scientists.

By the middle of the nineteenth century, there was a tendency to consider every symptom a new disease. Abnormal psychology was filled with Latin and Greek terms. Among the melancholias alone, there were *furens, misanthropica, erotica, attonita, errabunda, simplex, religiosa, catacriseothobia,* and *oneirodynia.* There were nearly as many classifications as there were writers dealing with abnormal mental conditions.

An important development in classification occurred when the course of the disorder as well as the symptoms became the basis of the classification. The most outstanding example of this classification approach was developed by the German psychiatrist Emil Kraepelin (1856–1926). In the development of his system, he consolidated the many other systems that had been presented and then developed a new classification which soon became the most widely accepted scheme for grouping personality disturbances. The first presentation of Kraepelin's classic work was a *Compendium,* or outline of psychiatry, published in 1883. By the time the work reached the fourth edition in 1893, it had become a *Lehrbuch* (textbook) and was the most comprehensive presentation of psychiatry written up to that time.

Kraepelin's classification made use of the existing terms *neurosis* and *psychosis.* A neurosis was looked upon as a relatively mild personality disturbance in which the patient remained in touch with reality and did not require hospitalization. A psychosis, on the other hand, was viewed as a severe personality disorganization, marked by a break with reality and requiring hospitalization. In addition, Kraepelin considered all forms of personality disorganization to be either *functional* or *organic.* The functional disorders were those in which physical pathology could not be found, and the assumption was that such conditions were psychogenic, or of psychological origin. The organic disorders were those in which physical pathology could be shown to account for the disturbed behavior of the patient.

Adolf Meyer (1866–1950), an eminent American psychiatrist who became dissatisfied with the classification system of Kraepelin, preferred to think in terms of reaction types, or patterns of behavior, rather than specific disorders. He called these reaction types *ergasias,* and he established a classification based on them. While this classification was never published, it has infiltrated the literature to some extent through the writings of Meyer's students.

Sigmund Freud and the psychoanalysts also were opposed to the static nature of Kraepelin's system and proposed a classification based on the dynamic processes involved in mental disorder. This classification, like that of Adolf Meyer, had little practical impact on the day-to-day work of the practicing psychiatrist and clinical psychologist.

During and following World War II, there was a rapid deterioration in the classification of mental disorder. In most institutions, the traditional Kraepelinian classification was in use. However, the Armed Forces and the Veterans Administration were forced to develop new classifications because there was no way to classify many of the relatively minor personality disturbances not seen ordinarily in the public mental hospitals. In some hospitals and clinics, locally designed categories were used. As a result, it became quite impossible to collect meaningful statistics on incidence and treatment.

It was not until the early 1950s that the confusion was halted. A new and more stable classification system was introduced. This system grew out of a number of years of work by a committee of the American Psychiatric Association and was published in 1952 in the form of a diagnostic manual. This manual became the basis for diagnosis and for the statistical handling of diagnostic data. While the system of classification outlined in the manual was not without its faults, it represented a distinct advance over anything previously available.

A revision of the American Psychiatric Association's Diagnostic Manual appeared in 1968. This revision is a more flexible and progressive system which makes it easier to describe people in the zones between clear-cut mental disorder and socially unacceptable behavior. A major addition is a diagnostic category to handle the behavior disorders of children and adolescents. On the basis of the 1968 classification system it is possible to place all behavior disorders and personality disturbances under eight major headings:

1. Transient situational disturbances
2. Personality disorders
3. Neuroses
4. Psychophysiologic disorders
5. Psychoses not attributable to physical conditions
6. Psychoses associated with organic brain disorder
7. Mental retardation
8. Behavior disorders of childhood and adolescence

The revised classification, by detailing the symptoms of a number of relatively minor conditions, makes it possible to talk about them in a more meaningful way and to assure a higher degree of clinical understanding in diagnosis, treatment, and research.

Transient situational disturbances refer to those disorders that occur in individuals without any apparent underlying mental disorder,

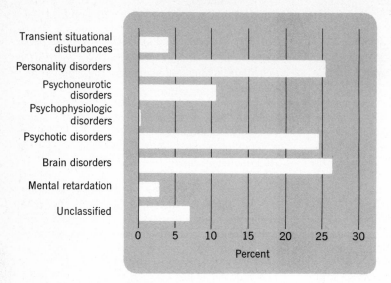

Figure 2.9 *Distribution of first admissions to public mental hospitals in the United States. (From data furnished by the National Institute of Mental Health, 1970.)*

and as an acute reaction to overwhelming environmental stress. If the individual has good capacity for adaptation, the symptoms gradually disappear as the stress decreases. If the symptoms persist after the stress has been removed, some other type of disturbance is indicated.

Personality disorders are conditions marked by deeply ingrained maladaptive patterns of behavior. Generally, these are lifelong patterns that can often be recognized during childhood or adolescence. The disorders are more or less fixed in the personality and are usually difficult to change. Some of the personality patterns seen in this group of conditions are the inadequate and immature, the suspicious, the withdrawn and isolated, the passive and aggressive, the explosive, the compulsive, and the antisocial. Also included here are the alcoholics, sexual deviates, and those who are dependent upon drugs.

Neuroses are conditions characterized by anxiety. It may be felt and expressed directly, or it may be controlled unconsciously by any one of a number of psychological mechanisms. Generally these mechanisms produce symptoms experienced as feelings of stress from which the individual desires relief. For the most part, the neuroses do not show gross distortion or misinterpretation of external reality, nor gross personality disorganization. Neurotic patients,

no matter how serious the handicap, are aware that their mental functioning is disturbed.

Psychophysiologic disorders are marked by physical symptoms that are caused by emotional factors and involve a single organ system, usually a system under the influence of the autonomic nervous system. The physiological changes involved are those that normally accompany certain emotional states, but in these disorders the changes are more intense and longer lasting. The individual may not be consciously aware of his emotional state.

Psychoses refer to conditions in which the mental functioning of the patient is impaired sufficiently to interfere grossly with his capacity to meet the ordinary demands of life. The impairment may result from a serious distortion in the capacity to recognize reality. There may be disturbances in perception, language, memory, thinking, and mood. Ordinarily patients who are psychotic require treatment in a hospital setting.

The *organic brain syndrome* is a basic mental condition resulting from diffuse impairment of brain tissue function. The most common symptoms are impairment of memory, orientation, judgment, and intellectual functions such as comprehension, calculation, knowledge, and learning. There is also likely to be emotional instability. The brain syndrome may be the only disturbance present, or it may be associated with other personality disturbances and behavior disorders.

Mental retardation refers to subnormal general intellectual functioning which originates during the developmental period. The retardation is associated with impairment of learning and social development, with impaired maturation, or with both conditions.

Behavior disorders of childhood and adolescence include conditions that are more stable, internalized, and resistant to treatment than the transient situational disturbances but less resistant than psychoses, neuroses, and personality disorders in children and adolescents. This intermediate stability is attributed to the greater fluidity of all behavior at this age. Characteristic manifestations include such symptoms as overactivity, inattentiveness, shyness, feelings of rejection, overaggressiveness, timidity, and delinquency.

There has been a growing feeling that this conventional system of classification of abnormal behavior is ineffective and lacking in vitality. This criticism is not completely unjustified. But the system cannot be discarded without something more suitable to replace it. Thus far critics of the present classification system have not been able to offer a more satisfactory and generally acceptable alternative.

Even though the present system is imperfect in many ways, it does represent a thoughtful and serious attempt to come to some common agreement on terminology. No matter how much we might prefer a more dynamic and imaginative system, the standard classification is by far the most widely used and accepted diagnositc framework.

THE ORGANIC APPROACH

Emphasis on the physical organism had its origins in the naturalistic views of Hippocrates and his followers in ancient Greece and Rome. After the death of Galen, the organic concept of mental disorder disappeared from view and was not to return until the scientific reawakening in the sixteenth and seventeenth centuries. Even then, the organic viewpoint was presented cautiously and

tentatively and in the face of fanatical opposition from the clergy.

There have been three major lines of development in the organic approach: (1) the study of the brain in its relation to behavior, (2) the investigation of the physical causes of mental disorder, and (3) the use of physical methods of treatment.

While there were efforts to understand the role of the brain as early as the golden age of Greek medicine, the ancient physicians were blocked by their limited knowledge of the nervous system and its functions. Then, for many centuries, the Church forbade the dissection of the human body. It was not until the middle of the fourteenth century, when the bans on dissecting were lifted, that the anatomy of the brain and nervous system itself began to be studied.

One of the most important influences in the development of interest in the brain was the introduction, early in the nineteenth century, of Franz Josef Gall's theory of *phrenology*. Gall (1758–1828), who was born in the Grand Duchy of Baden, became intrigued with the functions of the brain while he was in medical school. After a number of years of study and observation while practicing medicine in Vienna, he began to deliver lectures on his new theory, which maintained that character

Figure 2.10 *The dissected human brain. A woodcut from the* De Humani Corporis Fabrica *of Andreas Vesalius. (Courtesy of* Scientific American.*)*

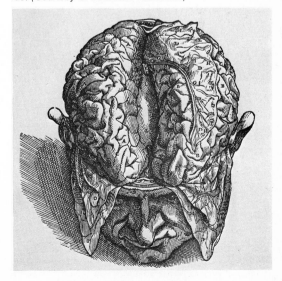

traits are localized in thirty-seven different regions, or "organs," of the brain. He concluded that these organs in turn exerted an influence on the shape of the skull. He came to believe that the personality of an individual, both in mental health and in mental disorder is revealed by the physical geography of the skull. In short, an overdevelopement of a particular psychological characteristic would lead to an enlargement of that area of the brain, with a consequent change in the contour of the skull. Gall believed it was possible to localize each mental disturbance to a specific area of the brain (Gall, 1825).

Figure 2.11 *A phrenological model, with a skull map of brain areas alleged to correspond to psychological abilities and characteristics. (Courtesy of Talon, Inc.)*

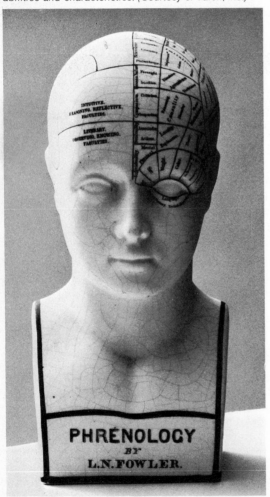

Gall's lectures were attended by many influential people, including members of the Emperor's staff. However, strong opposition to the lectures developed, principally from the Emperor's physician and from the clergy. In 1802, the Austrian government issued an edict banning all private lectures unless special permission was obtained. Although Gall and his friends sought permission for him to continue with his lectures, it was not granted. As a result of the action of the government, Gall and a colleague by the name of Johann Gasper Spurzheim (1776–1832) began a lecture tour and eventually settled in Paris. Here again, there was considerable opposition. But in 1809 the two German physicians published a comprehensive work with the imposing title *The Anatomy and Physiology of the Nervous System in General, and of the Brain in Particular: with Observations upon the Possibility of Ascertaining Several Intellectual and Moral Dispositions of Man and Animals, by the Configuration of Their Heads.*

For a time, Gall and Spurzheim collaborated, but later Spurzheim split with Gall and struck out on his own. He traveled to the United States in 1832, where he gave a series of lectures and was received with honors at both Yale and Harvard. More than fifty phrenological societies were established in the United States during the 1840s. Many prominent citizens, including James A. Garfield, Walt Whitman, Edgar Allan Poe, Clara Barton, and the eminent psychologist G. Stanley Hall, became enthusiastic advocates of the new "science." In England and on the Continent, such distinguished followers as Queen Victoria and Prince Albert, Bismarck, Karl Marx, Charles Baudelaire, Honoré de Balzac, and George Eliot lent their prestige to the movement.

In spite of the unbridled enthusiasm of many prominent scientists, educators, physicians, and literary figures for the doctrines of phrenology, there was much objection to the new theory. The clergy was generally opposed to it because of its materialistic implications. Oliver Wendel Holmes was sarcastic in his appraisal of the pseudoscience, and John Quincy Adams commented that he could not see how two phrenologists could look each other in the face without bursting into laughter.

Gall's major contributions to the history of abnormal psychology were his protest against the metaphysical thinking that had preceded him and his emphasis on the functions of the brain. His work, and that of his followers, attracted wide attention, and its controversial nature stimulated considerable interest in the brain. While Gall was serious in his efforts to base personality disturbances on physical disorders of the brain, his work was obscured by the extravagant claims of his followers.

The modern emphasis on the role of the brain in mental disorder was largely the work of German psychiatry. Wilhelm Griesinger, who published an influential textbook in psychiatry in 1845 when he was twenty-eight years old, took the position that mental disorders were diseases of the brain and that the causes were always physiological. He made no distinction between organic and functional disorders. He wrote, "Psychiatry and neuropathology are not merely two closely related fields, they are the same field in which only one language is spoken and the same laws rule" (Griesinger, 1845).

In 1869, a series of experiments by F. L. Goltz in Germany called attention in a dramatic way to the relationship of the brain to behavior. Goltz showed that when the brain of a frog is removed he can hop, swim, jump out of hot water, and adjust himself to external conditions. However, the same frog will sit and starve to death, making no effort to seek food. Later, Goltz succeeded in removing the brains of two dogs and keeping the animals alive for periods of fifty-seven and ninety-two days. The third and most famous of Goltz's dogs lived eighteen months and was shown at various medical meetings throughout Europe (Goltz, 1892).

Interest in the relationship of the brain to behavior was also aroused in 1870 by two German investigators who made studies of soldiers with brain injuries during the Franco-Prussian war. They discovered that if parts of the exposed cerebral cortex are stimulated, a motor response in the form of a muscular movement takes place (Fritsch and Hitzig, 1870). This observation set off a new wave of interest in the cerebral localization of function.

The first electrical stimulation of the brain of a human subject took place in Cincinnati, Ohio, in 1874. A mentally retarded girl was dying of a malignancy of the scalp, and a physician obtained her consent to insert wires into the part of her brain which was exposed by the disease. It was found

Figure 2.12 Bumpology, *a caricature of phrenology by George Cruikshank. (National Library of Medicine, Washington, D.C.)*

that when current was applied, muscular contractions occurred in the right arm and leg. The arm jerked, the fingers were extended, and the leg came forward. Various other observations were made over the course of several days (Bartholow, 1874).

It became increasingly clear that the nervous impulse was related to electrical energy and that under certain circumstances electric current could be used to stimulate nerve elements. This knowledge was used in investigating functional relationships between the brain and the various areas of the body musculature. It was found that when current was applied to small areas of the exposed human brain a wide variety of clinical symptoms was produced. These symptoms ranged from simple motor reactions, such as muscular twitching, to more complex subjective experiences. It was also observed that the symptoms bore a consistent relationship to the area of the cortex stimulated. By 1900, the stage had been set for the coming emphasis on the use of electricity in the field of mental disorder. Many diagnostic, treatment, and research techniques found their beginning in the scattered investigations which took place before the turn of the century.

A major advance in the understanding of brain function in relation to personality disorganization was made by the German investigator Hans Berger in the early part of the present century. Berger discovered that the brain generates electrical impulses which can be amplified and recorded graphically. Moreover, he found that these impulses are produced in a rhythmical fashion and are influenced by various internal and external conditions of the organism (Berger, 1929). The discovery of these electrical brain waves led to

Figure 2.13 *Friedrich Anton Mesmer, 1734–1815, the founder of "mesmerism," which later developed into scientific hypnosis. (Collection Viollet, Paris.)*

Frédéric, Antoine, Mesmer

né à Weiler près Constance le 23 Mai 1734.

Lith. de Langlumé

the development of the field of *electroencephalography,* a technique widely used to assist in the diagnosis of certain forms of behavior disorder and personality disturbance.

A second line of support to the organic point of view has been the interest in the physical causes of personality disorganization. It has been a matter of common observation that many physical conditions are related both directly and indirectly to psychological disturbances. The problems of heredity, constitution, infection, drugs, alcohol, metabolic disturbances, endocrine disorders, nutritional deficiencies, brain injuries, brain tumors, and similar clinical conditions have kept alive a sharp interest in the organic foundations of psychopathology. These matters are discussed in detail in Chapter 3.

The third major line of development contributing to the organic approach has been the use of physical methods of treatment. Drugs and medications based on folk medicine were among the earliest treatment techniques. Similarly, bloodletting had a long history, reaching from ancient times to the present century. Surgery and, more recently, electricity have also had periods of popularity in the treatment of mental disorder. Physical methods of treatment are discussed in Chapter 14.

THE PSYCHOLOGICAL APPROACH

While the philosophy of Plato and Aristotle and the theological ideas of the Judeo-Christian ecclesiasts did much to shape the early conception of psychological factors in mental disorder, the modern psychological approach to mental illness began with the work of Franz Anton Mesmer (1734–1815), a Viennese physician who was interested in the theory of magnetic medicine advanced in a treatise, *De Medicina Magnetica,* which suggested that a vital magnetic force resides both within and outside the body (Maxwell, 1679).

While in Vienna, Mesmer learned that a Jesuit priest was performing remarkable cures by placing a steel magnet on the painful part of the patient's body. Mesmer became interested in this work and cooperated with the priest in his experiments. The medical profession in Vienna opposed the method, and Mesmer came in for sharp criticism. Mesmer's observations led him to believe that the magnet itself was not necessary to the treatment and that the important factor was some form of animal magnetism. Mesmer reasoned that all human beings are under the influence of the stars and that this influence is brought about through a constant flow of magnetic fluid which fills the universe. He said that it is the harmony, or balance, of this fluid within the individual which protects him from physical and mental disorder (Mesmer, 1781).

As a result of the growing opposition to his work in Vienna, Mesmer moved to Paris in 1778. He busied himself immediately with the task of making his presence known to the most important people. He maintained a luxurious suite on the Place Vendôme where he treated his patients by placing them in a trance-like state, then suggesting that their symptoms had vanished. The Marquis de Lafayette, along with other statesmen, men of letters, and members of the aristocracy, were among his patients. Mesmer was protected by Marie Antoinette, and the King proposed to establish a clinic and to pay him an annual retainer. In 1781, the Society of Harmony was founded to study and use Mesmer's methods. The members of the society were sworn to secrecy, and mesmerism—called *hypnosis* fifty years later—became a cult.

The dramatic nature of Mesmer's work brought him immediate fame, and patients crowded into his consulting rooms. He became so successful, in fact, that members of the medical profession of Paris insisted that the curative effects of magnetism be investigated. However, Mesmer refused to cooperate with such an investigation. Eventually the Academy of Science petitioned the King of France to appoint a committee to look into the claims of Mesmer and his followers. The committee was appointed in 1784 and included among its members such men as Benjamin Franklin, who was the U.S. Ambassador to France, Antoine Lavoisier, the discoverer of oxygen, and Joseph Guillotin, the man who invented the beheading device. When the investigating committee submitted a report unfavorable to Mesmer, he was denounced as an imposter and charlatan and was forbidden to practice in France. He left the country and settled in a village outside Zurich, Switzerland, where he remained until his death.

ANIMAL MAGNETISM— The Operator putting his Patient into a Crisis.

Figure 2.14 *A late eighteenth-century Dodd engraving showing an "animal magnetizer" putting his patient into a trance. (National Library of Medicine, Washington, D.C.)*

The departure of Mesmer from Paris did not take place, however, until after the influence of his work had taken firm root both in England and in France. In England, the development of mesmerism was due largely to the work of James Braid, John Elliotson, and James Esdaile.

James Braid (1795–1860), a physician and surgeon of Manchester, was present at a public performance of mesmerism in 1841. Feeling certain that it was a fraud, and wishing to expose such demonstrations, Braid went about collecting data for his proof. In the course of his investigations, he found that he could produce the same trance-like states he had observed in the public demonstration. As a result, he prepared a scientific paper with the title *Neurypnology, or the Rationale of Nervous Sleep,* and offered it to the British Medical Association, but the paper was rejected. Later, it was published privately. It was in this technical paper that the term *hypnotism* first was used (Braid, 1843).

John Elliotson (1791–1860), a physician at London's St. Thomas Hospital, was an open-minded and progressive man who was one of the first to use a stethoscope, even though he was greeted with ridicule. In 1837, when mesmerism was demonstrated in England, Elliotson became interested in its possible therapeutic uses. He experimented with the method and lectured about his results (Elliotson, 1843). Despite his status as a senior physician at the hospital, he was criticized severely. In the following year, the Council of the University College banned the use of mesmerism, and Elliotson resigned his position.

A group of men sympathetic to Elliotson's views began to publish *The Zoist,* a professional journal devoted to mesmerism. In the first issue, Elliotson wrote: "The science of mesmerism is a new physiological truth of incalculable value and importance." Despite the fact that *The Zoist* exerted a marked influence on contemporary

Figure 2.15 *Jean Martin Charcot, 1825–1893, the founder of modern neurology and the director of a world-famous clinic in Paris. (Collection Viollet, Paris.)*

thought and was responsbile for the opening of clinics in England, Scotland, and Ireland, the ideas expressed found little favor with most members of the medical profession. The journal owed its success to the fact that the recognized medical journals refused to accept papers on any phase of mesmerism, and a publication was needed to meet the demands of the increasing interest in hypnosis. Many members of the more conservative element of the medical profession outwardly opposed mesmerism but maintained a private interest in the subject, especially since *The Zoist* carried numerous accounts of surgical operations performed with hypnosis as the anesthesia.

The third English physician to play a key role in the development of mesmerism was James Esdaile (1808–1859), a surgeon employed by the East India Company. In 1845, he read about the use of hypnosis to relieve pain during surgery, and he used the method in an operation that ordinarily was extremely painful. The anesthesia was so successful that the patient did not know for several hours that the surgery had already been performed (Esdaile, 1850). Lord Dalhousie, the Governor-General of India, was so impressed by the demonstration that he set aside a special hospital in Calcutta for Esdaile's use. In all, more than 250 surgical operations were performed using hypnosis as the anesthesia. The discovery of drug anesthesia, however, soon brought an end to the interest in hypnosis as an anesthetic.

The importance of Mesmer's work was not in his technique and was even less in his theory. Mesmer himself had no idea of what he was doing or why he obtained his cures. His work was of lasting importance because it focused attention on psychological processes which before that time were not known to exist. Mesmer was important also because his work was the first tentative step toward a psychology of the abnormal. Until that time, psychology had been rooted in the philosophies of the past, and those philosophies for the most part dealt with the normal mind.

During the middle and latter part of the nineteenth century, the major progress in psychopathology continued to take place in France, primarily as a result of the work of Jean Martin Charcot (1825–1893). Charcot's early background was in research in general pathology, but by 1875 he had developed a clinical science of neurology.

In 1881 he was chosen by the University of Paris to occupy the first chair of clinical neurology ever to be established. His clinic at the Salpêtrière attracted students and physicians from all parts of the world.

As a neurologist, Charcot thought primarily in terms of the nervous system. When hypnosis was introduced in his laboratory, he was interested in the method only as a means of studying changes in the brain and nerves during hypnotic states. Nevertheless, the clinical studies carried out by Charcot and his students set off a storm of controversy concerning the fundamental nature of hypnosis. Believing hypnosis to be a special kind of neurotic reaction, Charcot made the following observation in D. Hack Tuke's *A Dictionary of Psychological Medicine:* "This neurosis has, under the name of hypnotism, been evolved, in an immense majority of cases, on a soil prepared by hysteria, with which it has so many points in common" (Charcot, 1892).

An opposite view was taken by A. A. Liébault (1823–1904) of Nancy, France, who maintained that hypnosis is simply a matter of suggestion. The importance of the Nancy Clinic reached its height when Hippolyte Marie Bernheim (1837–1919), who had read Charcot, went to Nancy to study Liébault's technique. Identifying himself with the Nancy School, Bernheim published a series of articles in which he declared hypnosis to be artificial sleep, with no morbid aspects (Bernheim, 1889). He stressed the psychological importance of the problem and immediately met with the opposition of the Charcot group. In this way, two opposing schools of thought, one centered at Paris and the other at Nancy, became crystallized. Eventually the views of the Nancy group prevailed.[10]

THE DISSOCIATIONISTS

Pierre Janet (1859–1947) began his career in the field of philosophy. At twenty-two, he was Professor of Philosophy at the LeHavre Lycée. However, he was interested in science and turned his attention to the problems of dream life, sleepwalking, loss of memory, and dual personality. Janet began his research at a local mental hospital, but his brilliance was soon recognized by Charcot, who brought him to Paris. A psychological laboratory was established for him there at the Salpêtrière. In 1895, he was appointed Professor of Psychology at the Collège de France. He remained at the Salpêtrière and at the Collège de France until his retirement.

Janet believed that many personality disturbances are the result of an inborn weakness of the nervous system. He emphasized the importance of heredity and, like Charcot, adhered closely to the tradition of neurological-physiological thinking. He believed that the mind is a synthesis built up of the varied and innumerable experiences (sensations, perceptions, images, etc.) which come to us daily. He used the term *dissociation* to describe the pathological condition brought about by the breakdown of this synthesis.

This theory held that at any particular moment an individual possesses a quantity of psychological energy which enables him to reach a certain level of psychological achievement. If energy is high, one is capable of reasoning, reflection, and the organization of ideas. If the level of energy is lowered, the personality synthesis becomes weakened, and the individual falls into a state of mental ill health.

The factors which lead to dissociation are partly hereditary and partly the result of toxic states, fatigue, shock, or persistent emotion. In this way, Janet associated pathological psychological reactions with physiological states. He viewed the mind as a balanced system of forces, a delicate equilibrium between inherited and acquired tendencies. Any disturbance of this equilibrium is reflected in a disturbance of attention with conflict between reflective thought and more deep-seated tendencies within the personality (Janet, 1925).

While there are serious defects in the psychological theories of Janet, the richness of his clinical experience and the detailed accuracy of

---

[10]Three books appropriate to this part of the history of abnormal psychology are *Franz Anton Mesmer: A History of Mesmerism* (Doubleday, 1934) by Margaret Goldsmith; *Franz Anton Mesmer, Physician Extraordinaire* (Garrett, 1967); and Georges Guillain's *J. M. Charcot: His Life—His Work* (Hoeber, 1959).

his observations have been of major importance in the development of our understanding of psychopathology.

One of the most important followers of Janet was the American physician Morton Prince (1854–1929). Following his graduation from Harvard Medical School in 1879, he took his mother to Charcot's clinic in Paris for treatment. As a result of this experience, he became interested in psychopathology and devoted the rest of his life to its study. Prince carried out a wide variety of clinical experiments in abnormal psychology and published a number of books and a great many articles and monographs. He founded the *Journal of Abnormal Psychology* in 1906. Prince was particularly interested in such problems as dreams, automatic writing, and hypnosis. In addition to his published observations of abnormal behavior, Prince is important because of his efforts to integrate the field of abnormal psychology with that of neurology and general psychology.

Other men who were influenced by the work of Janet were the French psychologist Alfred Binet (1857–1911) and the American philosopher and psychologist William James (1842–1910). Binet wrote on such topics as psychological anesthesias, automatic writing, sleepwalking, and dual personality. The work of James was an important force in bringing Janet's theories to the attention of psychologists in the United States.

The Psychoanalysts

More than any other single influence, the work of Sigmund Freud (1856–1939) brought to full maturity the psychological approach to personality disorganization. Freud's contribution to psychopathology, both in personality theory and in psychological treatment, was of great importance during the first half of the present century.

Freud was born at Freiburg, Moravia, and received his medical training at the University of Vienna. As a young physician, he worked in the laboratories of such distinguished men as Ernst Brücke and Theodore Meynert. In 1885, he went to Paris to study under Charcot. At the Charcot clinic Freud had many occasions to observe the cure of *psychogenic,* or psychologically determined, paralyses and other conditions by means of suggestion and hypnosis. These early observations in Paris served as the basis for the later development of his theory and technique of psychoanalysis.

When Freud returned to Vienna after a year with Charcot, he continued his interest in psychopathology and used hypnosis as his method of treatment. While he was not strikingly successful as a hypnotist, he noted that under hypnosis it was possible for patients to remember intense emotional experiences of earlier life. It was at this time that Freud became associated with Josef Breuer (1842–1925), a physician who had discovered that emotional disturbances have meaning and purpose and that they are likely to be related to the events of earlier life. Freud began to treat his patients by having them relive their earlier experiences through a process of "talking out," at first with the help of hypnosis. Later, he

Figure 2.16 *Sigmund Freud, 1856–1939, the founder of psychoanalysis. (Collection Viollet, Paris.)*

discarded hypnosis as unnecessary to the treatment.

In order to explain the success with his revolutionary new method of treating patients, Freud developed his theory of psychoanalysis. This theory started with a relatively simple concept and evolved, as a result of a lifetime of effort, into the most comprehensive theory of personality ever developed. Freud's original assumption was that emotional disturbances grow out of traumatic, or shocking, experiences which occur early in childhood and which involve sexual experiences. Because of the sexual nature of these early experiences, the child is filled with guilt, and the experiences are pushed out of consciousness into the deep and relatively inaccessible parts of the personality. These hidden experiences are the cause of emotional difficulties later in life. During psychoanalytic treatment, the experiences are brought to the surface of consciousness, and their relevancy to the symptoms of personality disturbance is explained and understood. In this way the patient is relieved of his symptoms.

To support this fundamental assumption, Freud devoted his life to the formulation of theories of motivation, conflict and frustration, psychosexual development, guilt and anxiety, and personality defenses to protect the patient against guilt and anxiety. These ideas, many of which underwent revision during Freud's lifetime, make up one of the most important theories of normal and pathological personality processes. While only the most orthodox Freudian would accept the Freudian theoretical model in its totality, many of the ideas have influenced the thinking of psychologists, psychiatrists, and social workers.

The first interest in psychoanalysis in the United States was reflected in the lectures of William James at Harvard in 1894. Early in the 1900s, several psychiatrists from the United States and Canada went to Europe to study psychoanalysis. When they returned, the new theory and technique was introduced. In 1909, the Department of Psychology at Clark University invited Freud to come to America to present a series of lectures. This visit was the only one Freud ever made to the United States. Two years later the American Psychoanalytical Association was organized in Washington, D.C.

The Freudian Dissidents

While the work of Sigmund Freud was an important influence in shaping the modern psychological approach to personality disorganization, there were other influences, not as extensive perhaps, but nevertheless of considerable significance.

Among Freud's early medical colleagues were Carl G. Jung (1875–1961) and Alfred Adler (1870–1937), both of whom later came to object to certain aspects of Freudian theory. Eventually a split occurred, and Jung and Adler developed theoretical approaches of their own.

Jung, who founded the school of *analytical psychology* in 1912, began by reinterpreting certain Freudian concepts and stripping them of their all-pervasive sexual nature. Jung disagreed with Freud primarily on the role of sexuality as a factor in personality development and disorganization. Whereas Freud regarded sex as the most powerful source of human action, Jung preferred to

Figure 2.17 *Carl Gustav Jung, 1875–1961, the founder of analytical psychology. (Photograph by Yousuf Karsh.)*

Figure 2.18 *Alfred Adler, 1870–1937, the founder of individual psychology. (The Bettmann Archive.)*

look upon sex as merely one of the many expressions of a more fundamental life force.

Jung also regarded psychological processes in a somewhat different way than Freud. Jung accepted the Freudian idea of hidden motivation, but he described the inner life of man in new and elaborated ways. He introduced a somewhat mystical and metaphysical dimension to man's psychological life and stressed aspects which Freud had only touched upon or had completely neglected.

Adler split with Freud in 1911 and developed the school of *individual psychology*. He suggested that thwarted self-assertion, rather than the blocking of the sexual instincts, is responsible for personality maladjustment. According to Adler, the basic conflict in life is the struggle to overcome feelings of inadequacy and inferiority.

Another Freudian dissident who had an important influence on the direction of psychological

theory in relation to mental illness was the lay analyst Otto Rank (1884–1939). It was Rank's belief that the experience of birth is not only one of physical stress for the infant but also one of intense psychological stress. He gave the name *birth trauma* to this initial emotional shock and suggested that it creates an inner anxiety that is the pattern for the anxiety aroused by all later separation situations. Anxiety is aroused in the young child each time the mother leaves the house, when the child leaves home to go to school, when the young man or woman leaves the family to marry, and finally when death approaches. The uneasiness in each of these situations, according to Rank, has its roots in the traumatic experience of birth (Rank, 1929).

The Neo-Freudians

In addition to Freud and the Freudian dissidents, the psychological approach to mental disorder was extended by a group of psychologists and psychiatrists who did not reject Freudian theory but altered and modified it to bring it more in line with their own ideas. The members of this group are sometimes called the neo-Freudians, and they include such authorities as Karen Horney, Harry Stack Sullivan, and Erich Fromm.

Karen Horney (1885–1952) came to the United States from Germany in 1932 and spent a number of years as an orthodox Freudian psychoanalyst. Eventually she moved toward theoretical ideas at odds with the traditional doctrines. She found it particularly difficult to accept some of Freud's theories in the field of motivation and his views of feminine psychology. Horney believed that the roots of personality disturbance are in the interpersonal relations of childhood, especially in hostile impulses which are in conflict with the need for dependence and socialization. These hostile impulses, which according to Horney are learned rather than inborn, become particularly strong when parents are rejecting or when they lack emotional warmth (Horney, 1950).

The ideas of Harry Stack Sullivan (1892–1949) have been referred to as *interpersonal theory* because he placed primary emphasis upon the interpersonal relationships the patient has with the "significant others" in his life. They are the people who are most intimately concerned with rewarding him and punishing him. Sullivan believed that a person's conception of himself is obtained from the evaluations made by these significant others. A child may come to look upon himself as strong and capable if his parents consider him so. Similarly a perception of oneself as a weak and dependent person grows out of such an evaluation by others. The individual, as a result of disturbed interpersonal relations during early life, develops a distorted set of perceptions of other people. As a result of his misconception of others, he develops an unrealistic view of their evaluations of himself. Consequently, he has a distorted self-perception (Sullivan, 1953).

Erich Fromm (1900–   ) is a nonmedical neo-Freudian whose early training was in the social sciences and humanities. After receiving his Ph.D. degree in Germany from Heidelberg University in 1922, he was trained in psychoanalysis in Munich and later at the Psychoanalytic Institute in Berlin. Fromm visited the United States in 1933 as a lecturer at the Chicago Psychoanalytic Institute and then became an American citizen. His importance lies in the fact that he has reformulated certain aspects of psychoanalytic theory, much as Horney and Sullivan have done. He has been concerned particularly with the impact of moral and ethical values on the behavior of man (Fromm, 1947).

Psychobiology

While Freud and his followers played a significant role in the development of the dynamic approach to personality disorganization, the less dramatic school of psychobiology, under Adolf Meyer, has had an important influence in shaping applied psychiatry, especially in the United States.

Adolf Meyer (1866–1950), whose work in the classification of mental disorder was mentioned earlier, was a native of Switzerland. He came to the United States in 1892 and was a pathologist in various state psychiatric hospitals. In 1910, he became a professor of psychiatry at Johns Hopkins University. Although he wrote little, his leadership and influence through teaching brought him to a position of eminence in the field.

The psychobiological point of view insists that all aspects of the life of an individual must be taken into consideration in diagnosing and treating personality disturbances. Organic, psychological, and cultural factors must be analyzed and then synthesized. Meyer stressed the continuity of psychology with natural science. He emphasized, above all else, the importance of understanding the individual as a whole, and in his total life situation. Meyer said of his system: "Psychobiology starts not from a mind and a body, or from elements, but from the fact that we deal with biologically organized units and groups and their functioning" (Meyer, 1957).

The theory of psychobiology holds that man is the indivisible unit of study and that this study can be approached from a variety of levels of integration. The highest level of human integration is the activity of man as a psychobiological unit. It is with this level that the psychiatrist is concerned. Not only does the patient need to be studied as a whole, but he must be studied as a part of society. The psychobiological approach is deceptively simple. It is, as Meyer himself described it, a "commonsense" psychiatry. As such, it has had an exceptionally beneficial effect upon American psychiatry.

Figure 2.19 *Adolf Meyer, 1866–1950, the founder of psychobiology. (Courtesy of Merck & Co., Inc.)*

HUMANISM AND EXISTENTIALISM

One of the most important developments in the recent history of abnormal psychology has been the movement of thinking in the direction of humanism and existentialism. These approaches, which had their origins in philosophy rather than science, emphasize the person and his concept of himself. Major attention is focused on human values, the uniqueness of the individual, and the individual meaning of life and destiny. Serious questions are being raised about every aspect of abnormal behavior—cause, diagnosis, treatment, and even the validity of the concept of mental disorder.

The humanistic and existential emphasis in psychology came about largely through the work of Ludwig Binswanger, Medard Boss, Viktor Frankl, and others of European origin. The approach has been given prominence in the United States by Rollo May and Carl Rogers and by Ronald D. Laing in Great Britain. Without the advantage of the perspective of time, it is difficult to say which of the many psychologists and psychiatrists cur-

Figure 2.20 *Ivan Pavlov, 1849–1936, the founder of reflexology and a pioneer in behavior modification. (Courtesy of Don Carlos Peete, M.D.)*

rently identified with this movement will eventually take a significant place in the history of abnormal psychology.

This approach in part has been a reaction against the strong biological orientation which has characterized American psychology throughout the century. The new movement has also tended to reject psychoanalysis and its psychodynamic concepts on the basis that they are too pessimistic and rigidly determined. While some of the more enthusiastic advocates of humanistic psychology see a forthcoming revolution in psychological concepts and orientation, it is more likely that the humanistic approach will serve as a leavening process which will add in an important and positive way to the evolution of thinking in normal and abnormal psychology.

THE BEHAVIOR APPROACH

Paralleling the emphasis placed on the humanistic and existential approach in abnormal psychology during the 1950s and 1960s, a somewhat different —though no less important—movement developed in the direction of what has come to be known as *behavior theory* and *behavior therapy*. This approach has its roots in the learning theories of Ivan P. Pavlov (1849–1936) in Russia and Edward Lee Thorndike (1874–1949) in the United States.

Pavlov's most important impact on the field of abnormal psychology grew out of his development of experimental techniques related to the induction of behavior disorders in animals. During his classic conditioning experiments, he observed that animals frequently developed behavior disorders under certain conditions. As a result of this work, Pavlov and his associates, and later his followers in other countries, showed the exact conditions under which behavior disorders could be elicited. More importantly, they suggested methods by means of which these disorders could be alleviated (Pavlov, 1928). In spite of the ever-present dangers involved in making analogies from the behavior of lower animals to that of man, the work of Pavlov must be regarded as one of the most significant landmarks in the history of abnormal psychology.

During the same period that Pavlov was working in his laboratory in Russia, the American psychologist E. L. Thorndike was studying animal learning from a different point of view at Columbia University. His observations of the trial-and-error learning of animals in mazes and puzzle boxes convinced him that learning is strengthened, or reinforced, by reward and by punishment. This reinforcement of learned behavior is looked upon today as a special form of conditioning called *instrumental* and *operant* conditioning to distinguish it from the *classical* conditioning described by Pavlov. These two forms of conditioning, as they apply to our understanding of the cause and treatment of abnormal behavior, will be discussed in Chapter 15. It is sufficient to note here that the work of these two pioneers laid the groundwork for highly important current developments in abnormal psychology.

As in the case of the humanistic and existential movement, we are too close to the events taking place to predict which of the behavior theory advocates will achieve a lasting place in the history of abnormal psychology. The most influential figure has been B. F. Skinner (1904–   ) of Harvard University, whose work in the 1930s paved the way for an increasingly large number of investigators in the United States and abroad.

It must be remembered that the various approaches discussed in this chapter are merely theoretical models to help us in our thinking about the problems of personality disturbance and behavior disorders. The specialized vocabulary of the several approaches makes it possible to communicate ideas more precisely. Seeming contradictions between approaches frequently turn out to be difficulties in translating the concepts of one theoretical model to that of another model. Moreover, it should not be disturbing to find real contradictions existing. Our knowledge of abnormal psychology is in an early stage of development. It is not unlikely that most of our present-day theoretical formulations will undergo extensive revision before the many problems of mental disorder will have been solved.[11]

SUMMARY

1. The phenomenon of mental disorder has been recognized for a great many centuries. *Animism* was the earliest explanation of disturbed behavior. With the emergence of the concept of *naturalism* in medicine, mental disorder came to be regarded by Hippocrates and his followers as the result of natural causes. This naturalistic view

---

[11]Students interested in the psychodynamic approach are referred to Sigmund Freud's *Collected Papers* (Hogarth, 1946), *The Collected Works of C. G. Jung* (Bollingen, 1966), and *The Individual Psychology of Alfred Adler* (Basic Books, 1956), edited by H. L. and R. R. Ansbacher. Books by the neo-Freudians include Karen Horney's *Neurosis and Human Growth* (Norton, 1950), Erich Fromm's *The Heart of Man* (Harper & Row, 1964), and *The Interpersonal Theory of Psychiatry* (Norton, 1953) by Harry Stack Sullivan. The psychobiological point of view is advanced in the *Collected Papers of Adolf Meyer* (Johns Hopkins Press, 1951), edited by E. E. Winters.

Books dealing with the development of the humanist-existential approach include *Existence: A New Dimension in Psychiatry and Psychology* (Basic Books, 1958), edited by Rollo May and others; *Humanistic Viewpoints in Psychology* (McGraw-Hill, 1965), edited by F. T. Severin; *Challenges of Humanistic Psychology* (McGraw-Hill, 1967), edited by J. F. T. Bugental; and the second edition of *Existential Psychology* (Random House, 1969), edited by Rollo May. Other important books include *On Becoming a Person* (Houghton Mifflin, 1961) by Carl Rogers, and R. D. Laing's *The Divided Self: An Existential Study in Sanity and Madness* (Penquin Books, 1965).

Recommended books dealing with the behavior approach and emphasizing the importance of learning include *Science and Human Behavior* (Macmillan, 1953) by B. F. Skinner; O. H. Mowrer's *Learning Theory and Personality Dynamics* (Ronald Press, 1950); *Principles of Behavior Modification* (Holt, Rinehart and Winston, 1965) by Albert Bandura; and *Pavlovian Approach to Psychopathology: History and Perspective* (Pergamon Press, 1970) by W. H. Gantt and others.

was carried over to ancient Rome by the physician Galen. Following the death of Galen, and for the next fifteen hundred years, disturbed personality once again became a matter of superstition. The most prevalent idea was that of *demonology*. Gradually, with the scientific reawakening in the seventeenth and eighteenth centuries, mental and emotional disturbances were once again considered to have natural causes.

2. Some of the most important reforms in the care and treatment of mental patients took place in France in the late eighteenth and early nineteenth centuries. Parallel advances were made in England, Germany, the United States, and other countries. The progress took the form of the *expansion of mental hospitals,* the *aftercare movement,* the *family care system,* the *open-door policy,* and the *mental hygiene movement.* The *community mental health center program* has been the most significant development of the present century.

3. The major trends leading to the present-day concept of mental disorder have included the emphasis on *classification,* on *organic conditions,* and on *psychological factors.* The classification approach began in ancient Greece when personality disturbances were divided into *mania, melancholia,* and *dementia.* This classification, in terms of the symptoms of the patient, remained the basis of classification for two thousand years.

4. Emil Kraepelin, in the late nineteenth and early twentieth centuries, developed a classification system which was based on the course of the disorder as well as on its symptoms and causes. The system remained in use until 1952, when the American Psychiatric Association introduced a new system which was adopted by most hospitals in the United States. A 1968 revision of this system classifies all abnormal behavior under eight major headings: *transient stress disorders, personality disorders, psychoneurotic disorders, psychophysiologic disorders, psychotic disorders, brain disorders, mental deficiency,* and *behavior disorders of childhood and adolescence.*

5. The second line of emphasis leading to the modern concept of mental disorder has been the organic approach. This approach has included the study of the brain and its relation to behavior disorders, the investigation of physical causes of mental illness, and the use of physical methods of treatment.

6. The third approach, which emphasizes psychological factors, had its origins in the philosophical speculations of the ancient Greeks and the later Judeo-Christian theology. The modern psychological emphasis began with the interest in *mesmerism* in the late eighteenth century. While mesmerism prepared the way for the development of a psychological approach to mental disorder, the Freudian theories and techniques of *psychoanalysis* dominated the psychological approach during the first half of the present century and were the most significant influence in this direction. The psychological approach was also influenced by the Freudian dissenters, of whom the major figures were Jung and Adler, who split with Freud early in the present century and developed their own psychological systems, and by the neo-Freudians (Horney, Sullivan, and Fromm), who modified orthodox Freudian theory by placing more emphasis on social and cultural influences. Non-Freudians, such as Pierre Janet, who emphasized the theory of dissociation; Adolf Meyer, who developed the school of *psychobiology;* the *humanists* and *existentialists* such as Carl Rogers, Rollo May, and R. D. Laing; and the *behavior approach* beginning with Ivan Pavlov in Russia and Edward L. Thorndike in the United States, also contributed in substantial ways to the psychological conception of abnormal behavior.

3 PHYSICAL STRESS AND PERSONALITY DISORGANIZATION

The theory of the organic origin of personality disturbance goes back to the naturalistic medicine of ancient Greece, when Hippocrates declared that the body fluids, or "humors," were responsible for mental disorder. Since that time, except where superstition and demonology have been prevalent, there has been a persistent belief that the physical condition of the body plays an important part in personality disorganization. While this belief disappeared with the death of Galen, it emerged again at the time of the scientific reawakening in the seventeenth and eighteenth centuries.

By the early 1800s the physical causes of personality disturbance were believed to include such a variety of conditions as deformities of the skull, convulsions in infancy, brain congestion, old age, syphilis, typhoid fever, rheumatism, organic disturbances of the heart, lung disease, intestinal worms, menstrual disorders, alcoholic drinks, excessive tobacco, mineral poison, intense heat and cold, and blows and falls upon the head. A medical report in the 1860s stated that mental disorder is the result of a "diseased condition—a physical lesion—of the brain" and that "all causes are sooner or later physical" (Tuke, 1892).

At that time, the theory of *neuropathic taint* was widely accepted. This theory advanced the idea that most mental disorders have the same predisposing causes and the same hereditary background and arise from the same source. It was believed that there is an abnormal family condition out of which personality disturbances develop. This theory was prevalent for many years and is reflected to the present time in a modified form by the thinking of psychologists and psychiatrists who emphasize the role of inborn weakness, or *constitutional predisposition,* in the development of certain forms of abnormal behavior.

During the first half of the present century the emphasis shifted away from the organic causes of mental disorder and focused on psychological causes. This change was due in part to the impact of Sigmund Freud and his theories of unconscious motivation. Today we have a more balanced view of the causes of personality disorganization and recognize the possibility of a combination of physical, psychological, and social factors as contributing in equally important ways to the development of personality disturbances and behavior disorders. In the modern view, the common factor in causation is *stress,* no matter what its source. The disturbed behavior may be learned, or it may appear as a result of disease or damage to the nervous system. In either case the stress triggers the chain of events which culminates in clinical symptoms.[1]

THE NATURE OF PHYSICAL STRESS

To understand the dynamics of the organic origin of personality disturbance, it is important to appreciate how physical stress unleashes the chain of events which culminates in the clinical symptoms. The most important impetus to stress theory was given by the classic work of Hans Selyé (1907–   ), the University of Montreal scientist who developed the concept of the *general adaptation syndrome* (Selyé, 1952). This theoretical model

Figure 3.1 *Hans Selyé, 1907–   , the University of Montreal medical research scientist whose work demonstrated the importance of stress in physical and mental health. (Courtesy of Dr. Selyé.)*

---

[1]Interest in physical factors determining both normal and abnormal behavior is reflected in a number of nontechnical and extremely readable books. Students are referred to the reprint of Eugene Marais' *The Soul of the Ape* (Atheneum, 1969); *The Naked Ape* (McGraw-Hill, 1967) and *The Human Zoo* (McGraw-Hill, 1969) by Desmond Morris; *The Human Animal: The Mystery of Man's Behavior* (Putnam, 1970) by H. Haas; and Gustav Eckstein's *The Body Has a Head* (Harper & Row, 1970).

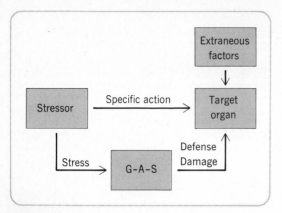

Figure 3.2 *The G-A-S model. All stressor agents (physical, psychological, social) produce both stress and specific actions. The specific actions affect the target organ in a variety of ways. Stress, which acts only through the General Adaptation Syndrome, causes defense and damage. Factors extraneous to the G-A-S (heredity, constitution, diet, previous exposure to stress, etc.) can condition the responses. The reaction of any target organ depends upon a combination of the specific action of the stressor, the effects of the G-A-S, and extraneous conditioning factors. (Adapted from Hans Selyé The Physiology and Pathology of Exposure to Stress. Montreal: Acta, 1950, p. 791.)*

states that there are various types of internal and external stress in the form of injuries, infections, poisons, hormones, diet, and similar factors, which mobilize a system of defensive reactions. One of the most important features of the general adaptation syndrome is that the major response to stress depends upon two main channels. The first is a nervous system reaction, primarily through the activation of the autonomic centers in the hypothalamus. The second is an endocrine reaction through the production of hormones of the pituitary and adrenal glands. It is through this very complex excitation, involving both the hypothalamus and the pituitary, that the symptoms of personality disorganization make their appearance. The excitation involves the body through activity of the glands and the autonomic nervous system, and it involves the brain through a process of feedback. Excessive or prolonged stress is capable of producing confusion, disturbed thinking, distorted perceptions, and other symptoms.

In considering the development of personality disturbances, it is important to remember that environmental pressures often lead to internal stress. A difficult situation in school, at work, or in the home creates stressful conditions within the body which are capable of triggering organic changes of an important kind. Even though the environmental pressure does not appear to be excessive, the long continuance of stress-provoking conditions can bring about alterations in body functions which ultimately may result in irreversible tissue changes.

The impact of environmental stress has been shown dramatically in animal experiments. A series of rats were subjected to stress situations including brilliant flashes of light, loud music, a cat walking around the cage, and being threatened with pincers. The rats showed signs of irritation almost at once, but the stress was maintained from 12 to 105 days. The rats were then killed, and the pituitary bodies and the adrenal glands were removed, weighed, and fixed. There was some enlargement of the pituitary gland with clear enlargement of the adrenal glands, particularly in the adrenal cortex (Naatahan and Jankata, 1954).

The stress-theory model helps us to understand how a wide variety of stress situations can result in tension and anxiety or, in more severe cases, in the organic-like symptoms of psychosis. Moreover, it helps to explain the puzzling effectiveness of the many widely differing and nonspecific treatment procedures ranging from bloodletting to protein therapy, shock treatment, psychosurgery, and the tranquilizing drugs. The common therapeutic factor appears to be the triggering of body defenses which are physically and psychologically beneficial.

Another important concept is one which holds that complex living organisms have two environments: (1) a general environment which is external to the organism and surrounds it, and (2) an internal environment made up of the living elements of the body itself. According to this view, cells make continual and automatic adjustments in their efforts to remain in a *constant state* even though they are subjected to changing internal and external stress (Bernard, 1865).

The term *homeostasis* was introduced by Walter B. Cannon (1871–1945) to describe this self-adjusting nature of the internal environment (Cannon, 1932). Cannon, a Harvard physiologist,

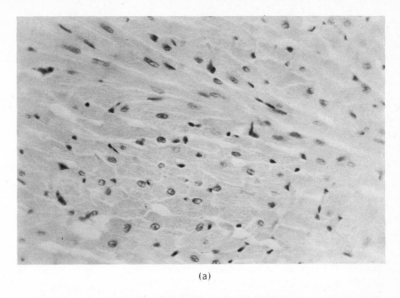

(a)

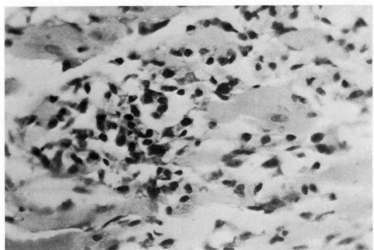

Figure 3.3 *Photomicrograph showing the effect of stress on body cells: (a) before exposure to stress, and (b) after exposure. (Courtesy of Ciba.)*

(b)

said that homeostasis is the capacity of the organism to maintain a constant state in spite of the vast number of changes which take place both outside and within the body. The maintenance of this steady state, through the operation of a number of intricate self-regulating operations, is one of the most intriguing accomplishments of living organisms.

Homeostasis is the process by which many different activities of the body are controlled and integrated. One of the most obvious examples is

temperature regulation. The body temperature remains relatively constant in spite of extreme variations in the temperature of the environment. When an individual leaves his warm house to step out into subzero weather, his body temperature does not go down. Instead, it maintains a constant and steady state. Many other biochemical and neurophysiological mechanisms are similarly self-regulating.

The mechanism of homeostasis depends largely upon the principle of *feedback*. In a conventional

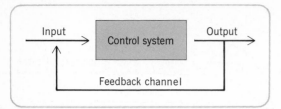

Figure 3.4 *A simple feedback model in which the nature of the input is influenced by the output.*

feedback system, a message is transmitted from a receptor to a controlling component which relays the message to a responding system. Feedback implies that the activity of the response system is monitored back to the receptor system, so that the entire system is self-regulating. Feedback is basic to the action of the thermostat, to the activity of self-propelled missiles which seek out the target, and to a large number of self-regulating mechanisms of the living organism.

The assumption that certain types of mental disorders are related to brain changes associated with homeostatic disturbances is one of the most important aspects of the organic approach. While the evidence, with several notable exceptions, is scattered and inconclusive, there is a persistent and growing impression that the solution to some of the more serious mental disorders will one day be found in our increasing knowledge of the physical response of the human body to various forms of stress.[2]

THE NERVOUS SYSTEM AND THE BRAIN

All human activities, whether implicit or overt, are dependent upon the nervous system. It is only through the nervous system that we become aware of our environment and can respond to the world in which we live. The nervous system, in its simplest form, is a system for receiving impressions from the external environment, integrating these impressions, and organizing them in such a way that the body makes a response. The degree of biological adaptation of the organism depends upon the efficiency with which external stimuli are received, coded, and transmitted to the muscles and glands so that a response may be made.

It will be recalled from elementary psychology or biology that the human nervous system is made up of the central nervous system and the peripheral nerves. The central nervous system, in turn, has a *somatic division,* including the brain and spinal cord, and an *autonomic division.* Both divisions are of considerable importance to the understanding of the nature of personality disorganization.

The somatic division is concerned primarily with adaptation and adjustment to the external environment. Through the sensory nerves, leading from the sense organs (eyes, ears, tongue, skin, nose, etc.), the individual receives information about energy changes in the environment. This information, in the form of electrical changes in the *neurons,* or nerve cells, is carried to the brain or spinal cord, where there are elaborate connections with other nerve cells. Motor nerves leading to the muscles and glands make it possible for the individual to respond to those energy changes.

The autonomic division is more concerned with the integration and regulation of the internal environment of the organism. It is related to the control of such basic life processes as heart rate, blood pressure, body temperature, fluid balance, respiration, and a wide range of complex biochemical and neurophysiological processes. The autonomic system is related intimately to our emotional life and in this way is of critical importance in many forms of abnormal behavior.

While an understanding of the entire nervous system is essential in abnormal psychology, it is particularly desirable to have a clear picture of the major aspects of the structure and function of the brain. Some of the more serious personality

[2]The following books are technical presentations of clinical, theoretical, and experimental developments related to the physical aspects of personality disorganization: *Higher Cerebral Functions and Their Clinical Disorders: The Organic Basis of Psychology and Psychiatry* (Grune & Stratton, 1962) by Benno Schlesinger; *Physiological Correlates of Psychological Disorder* (University of Wisconsin Press, 1962) by Robert Roessler and N. F. Greenfield; and *Recent Advances in Biological Psychiatry* (Grune & Stratton, 1960) edited by Joseph Wortis.

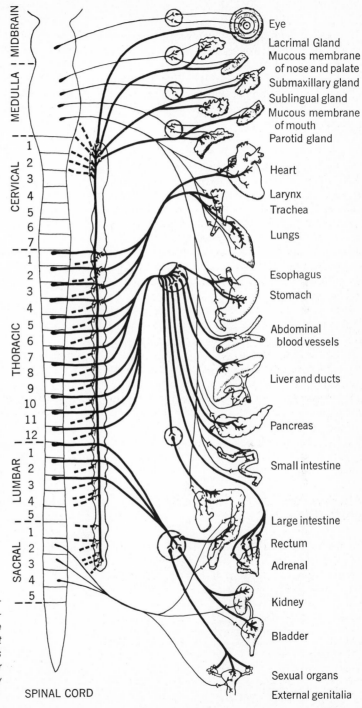

Figure 3.5 *The autonomic nervous system, showing the parasympathetic branches arising from the brain and sacral vertebrae (light lines) and the sympathetic branches arising from the thoracic and lumbar vertebrae (heavy lines). (Courtesy of* Scientific American.)

disturbances are associated with damage to the brain tissue.

The human brain, encased in the skull, is merely an enlargement of the spinal cord. At maturity, the brain is made up of three parts: the *forebrain,* the *midbrain,* and the *hindbrain.* The forebrain consists of the *cerebrum* and the *diencephalon.* The cerebrum is the largest and, in terms of our species development, most recently developed part of the human brain. It is a two-lobed structure growing as an extension of the brain stem. The lobes (hemispheres), which are connected by a broad band of tissue, fill out most of the cranial cavity. The great mass of the cerebrum is made up of supportive tissue and connecting fibers called the *white matter.* The outer layer of the cerebrum, or the *gray matter,* is called the *cortex.* This part of the brain is a thin but tightly packed network of highly specialized nerve cells. It has been estimated that the cortex alone contains about twelve billion nerve cells. These nerve cells are connected in pairs, in threes, in fours, and in many other combinations. It is entirely possible that the human cortex is one of the most complex structures in the entire universe.

There are three major functional areas of the cerebral cortex: (1) the *sensory areas,* (2) the *motor areas,* and (3) the *association areas.* The sensory areas are those parts of the cortex which receive incoming signals from the sense organs and translate these signals into patterns of sensory experience. The motor areas control the major conscious movements of the body. The association areas have reached the highest level of evolutionary development and are responsible for the intellectual differences between man and the lower animals. Reasoning, planning, foresight, problem solving, imagination, memory, and similar high-level intellectual activities involve, but are not completely dependent upon, the association areas.

While the cerebral cortex plays a major role in various aspects of abnormal behavior, other cerebral areas have equally important, though less well understood, implications for personality disorganization. The most important of these areas is the *limbic lobe,* or *visceral brain.* This lobe is made up of a ringlike convolution around the base of the cerebral hemisphere, together with certain subcortical nerve centers. The limbic system, which has also been called the *rhinencephalon,* the *paleocortex,* and the *olfactory brain,* is situated in a strategic way for receiving and integrating oral, visceral, sexual, and basic sensory sensations. The system involves a primitive cortical area, and it serves functions quite

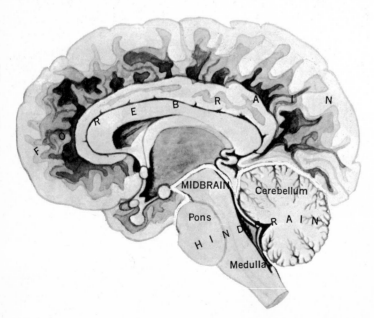

Figure 3.6 *Midsagittal view of the right cerebral hemisphere, showing the relative position of the forebrain, midbrain, and hindbrain. (Courtesy of Mary Lorenc, Harold E. Himwich, and the Wallace Laboratories.)*

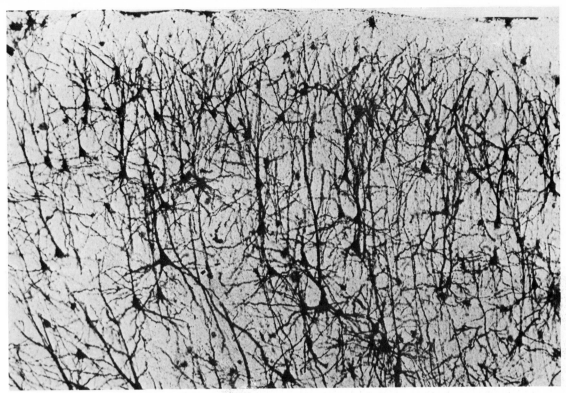

Figure 3.7 *A photomicrograph of a cross section of the cerebral cortex. Only 1.5 percent of the neurons are made visible by staining. (Courtesy of University College, London.)*

different from those related to the more highly developed parts of the brain. It is concerned with the physical expressions of emotion, such as trembling, quickened heart beat, alterations in facial expression, and similar physical changes. "Emotional coloring" is added to higher cortical processes by means of the limbic system.

The limbic system has important implications for abnormal psychology. Interference with the system in experimental animals results in over-sexuality and bizarre sexual behavior. Surgical removal of portions of the limbic system causes wild animals to become tame. There is also evidence that the system might play a role in the control of blood pressure. Other studies show that stimulation of this area results in changes in gastric secretions.

The second major part of the forebrain is the *diencephalon,* connected in front with the hemispheres and behind with the midbrain. Among its

important centers are the *thalamus* and the *hypothalamus.*

The thalamus is a structure made up of two egg-shaped lobes, one on each side just above the midbrain. It is embedded in the tissue of the cerebral hemispheres. The various nuclei of the thalamus serve as sensory centers, are involved in emotional behavior, and play a part in the sleep mechanism. The thalamus also serves as a relay center for the transmission of impulses to higher brain centers. Lesions of the thalamus cause a wide range of sensory disturbances and, in some cases, a loss of emotional expression.

The hypothalamus is located deep in the brain below the thalamus and just above the major integrating gland (the pituitary) of the body. Within the boundaries of the hypothalamus are masses of cells referred to as the *hypothalamic nuclei.* These nuclei are of critical importance to a number of very basic human functions. They are concerned

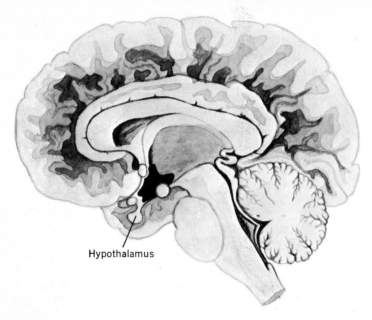

Hypothalamus

Figure 3.8 *Midsagittal view of the right cerebral hemisphere, showing the location of the hypothalamus. (Courtesy of Mary Lorenc, Harold E. Himwich, and the Wallace Laboratories.)*

with the maintenance of the water balance of the body, carbohydrate metabolism, temperature control, sweat secretion, blood pressure regulation, control of appetite, and the sleep-waking mechanism. The hypothalamus also plays a critical role in the emotional life of an individual. Various types of emotional changes are induced when this area of the brain is stimulated artificially. These changes range from apathy to excitement. Electrical stimulation of one part of the hypothalamus produces violent rage in experimental animals. This rage builds up to the point where the animal will attack the observer, but the behavior rapidly disappears when the stimulus is removed.

The midbrain and hindbrain, which are the oldest parts of the brain in terms of the development of the species, are concerned with the regulation of some of the most basic life processes and have traditionally been of limited interest to the student of abnormal psychology. Recent discoveries, however, of the importance of the *reticular formation* transversing the hindbrain and the midbrain have made these lower brain areas a source of lively interest to everyone who is concerned with brain function and its relationship to behavior.

The reticular formation is made up of a large mass of brain stem cells which are not part of the conventional sensorimotor system. This forma-

tion of cells, which is richly supplied with input and output connections to other parts of the nervous system, sends nerve fibers to the cortex, the hypothalamus, the cerebellum, and various other brain areas. This area appears to play a vital part in arousal from sleep and in maintenance of alertness in the waking state. As a result of recognition of the "arousal" function of the reticular formation, this part of the brain is known also as the "reticular activating system" (RAS).

As an anatomical structure, the reticular formation has been described for many years. As early as 1897, Sir Charles Sherrington, the noted British neurophysiologist, commented on these fibers by saying that they probably have "functions by which they take part in our psychical life, functions for which the words neither motor nor sensory are fitting" (Sherrington, 1897). While Sir Charles did not know the exact function of these cells, his intuitive feeling about them proved to be correct. The reticular activating system is neither sensory nor motor in the classic sense. Its functions are related to the general arousal from sleep to waking and to general alerting or attentiveness.

When the reticular formation of an experimental animal is stimulated directly, there are electrical changes in the brain identical to those observed when human subjects awaken from sleep. There is a shift from the high-voltage slow waves associated with sleep to the low-voltage fast waves of wakefulness. Such findings suggest that through the study of the reticular activating system it may become possible to solve some of the problems related to disturbances of consciousness.

The many new variables introduced by the increasing knowledge of the reticular activating system have made necessary a complete reevaluation of our concepts of the functions of the human nervous system. The first neurological view was a mechanistic theory based on simple reflex action. Eventually it became clear that a more dynamic approach was necessary. Today the complex functions of the brain are described in terms of reverberating circuits involving various forms of feedback. However, this new conception of brain function extends and supplements, rather than replaces, the more conventional viewpoints.[3]

THE INFLUENCE OF HEREDITY

An understanding of the role of heredity in personality disorganization must start with the realization that psychological characteristics in themselves are not inherited. What is inherited is physical material which, under given conditions, is able to determine or to influence psychological characteristics. Mental disorders are not passed on from generation to generation. What is transmitted is a combination of physical variations which make it difficult, if not impossible, for the patient to meet the demands of his environment. This is what Henry Maudsley meant many years ago in his book *The Pathology of Mind* when he said: "A person does not inherit insanity, but a predisposition or tendency" (Maudsley, 1879).

Long before the genetic discoveries of the Austrian monk Gregor Mendel in 1860, there was a general conviction that mental disorder was in some way passed on from one generation to another. While it is known today that few conditions are inherited in a simple manner, there remains a reasonable likelihood that some personality disturbances develop only because the soil has been prepared by a highly complex hereditary pattern.

In the late part of the nineteenth century, Sir Francis Galton underlined the growing interest

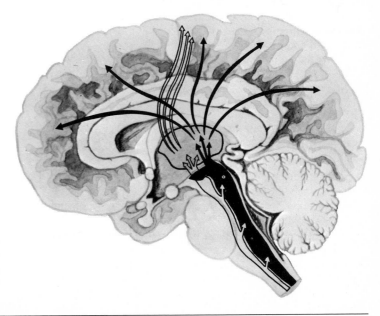

Figure 3.9 *The pathways of the ascending sensory system (white) and the reticular activating system (black). (Courtesy of Mary Lorenc, Harold E. Himwich, and the Wallace Laboratories.)*

---

[3]Nontechnical books dealing with the brain and nervous system include W. Grey Walter's *The Living Brain* (Norton, 1953); John Pfeiffer's *The Human Brain* (Harper & Row, 1955); *The Senses of Man* (Crowell, 1969) by Joan Wilentz; Gustav Eckstein's *The Body Has a Head* (Harper & Row, 1970); and *The Brain* (Putnam, 1970) by C. U. M. Smith.

in the problems of the inheritance of psychological characteristics with his book *Inquiries into Human Faculty and Its Development* (Galton, 1883). Galton showed how the study of twins could throw light on investigations in the field of inheritance and suggested the use of the statistical method in the study of the heredity of mentally disordered persons.

As a result of the rediscovery of Mendel's work in 1900, the scientific literature of the early part of the present century was flooded with studies of heredity in relation to physical and psychological characteristics. The greatest single factor in the United States for promoting the study of the psychological aspects of heredity was the establishment in 1909 of the Eugenics Record Office at Cold Spring Harbor, New York. This unit was set up for the purpose of systematically collecting and organizing data relative to human inheritance. In England, the Eugenics Laboratory was established with similar objectives at the University of London.

The early studies on the inheritance of mental disorder were concerned with the idea that there is a common underlying inherited weakness, or neuropathic constitution, that expresses itself in a variety of abnormal conditions (Tuke, 1882). The first important blow to the belief that the neuropathic constitution was a separate genetic entity was the result of a series of German studies which indicated that the incidence of "hereditary taint" was not much different in normal families than in the families of mental patients (Rudin, 1916). By the early 1920s, the idea of neuropathic constitution had been abandoned by most investigators, and genetic studies were focused on the possible inheritance of specific clinical conditions.

For the next thirty years, many studies were made of mental disorder in close relatives of individuals who behaved abnormally. Attempts were made to isolate genetic characteristics and to demonstrate the operation of hereditary factors in the families of mental patients. However, the complexity of the problem of human inheritance and the limited understanding of underlying genetic mechanisms combined to prevent any substantial increase in the knowledge of the inheritance of personality disturbances.

The first important breakthrough in this area came with the great advances made in the field of molecular biology in the 1950s and 1960s. These advances came about largely from the discovery that the DNA (deoxyribonucleic acid) molecule, thought to be the carrier of genetic information, has a rather simple shape in the form of a pair of strands twined together in a helix, something similar to a spiral staircase. From this model it became possible to determine how information is encoded in the DNA molecule by a combination of four different kinds of chemical subunits called *nucleotides*. The basis for all characteristics of living matter appears to be contained in the arrangement of the nucleotides in the DNA molecule.

The two major strands of the DNA molecule are sugar-phosphate units which are repeated over and over again. The "stairs" of the spiral are made up of four base compounds. These base units are A (ademine), T (thymine), G (guamine), and C (cytosine). The order in which these base units occur along the strands make up the *genetic code*.

The location of genetic information in a specific molecule has led to the possibility of influencing heredity by chemically manipulating the DNA. Such genetic engineering has even been suggested as a means of increasing intelligence and preventing certain types of mental disorder and mental retardation. The advances in genetics have been so dramatic that it is possible that within a few years biologists will be able to produce identical copies of mammals from a single original. Also the genetic manipulation of human heredity will probably occur before the end of the present century.[4]

---

[4]Nontechnical introductions to developments in the molecular biology of genetic material can be found in *Threads of Life; Genetics from Aristotle to DNA* (Natural History Press, 1970) by A. E. Klein, Lawrence Lessing's *DNA: At the Core of Life Itself* (Macmillan, 1966), and *The Double Helix* by J. D. Watson (Atheneum, 1968). More advanced discussions can be found in E. J. DuPraw's *DNA and Chromosomes* (Holt, 1970), *The Principles of Human Biochemical Genetics* (American Elsevier, 1970) by Harry Harris, and David Rosenthal's *Genetic Theory and Abnormal Behavior* (McGraw-Hill, 1970).

METHODS OF INVESTIGATION

The information available on the role of inheritance in mental illness is a result of three major procedures: (1) the *family history method,* (2) the *method of statistical prediction,* and (3) the *twin study method.*

The fact that behavior disorders and personality disturbances appear to run in families was observed from the time of Hippocrates, who considered epilepsy to be the most familial of all diseases. More than two thousand years later Esquirol believed that at least 85 percent of his cases were due to family inheritance. In 1838 he wrote, "Of all diseases, mental alienation is the most markedly hereditary, and the most likely to run in families" (Esquirol, 1838). One of the earliest family studies was made in 1877 (Dugdale, 1877) and continued thirty-five years later (Estabrooks, 1916). The study was made of the Juke family, particularly the descendants of mentally deficient sisters. Nearly three thousand cases were studied, with a large number judged as having been mentally defective and emotionally unstable. The most famous family case study was made in 1912 by an American psychologist (Goddard, 1913). This study involved two lines of descendants of Martin Kallikak, a code name given by Goddard to a soldier who had fought in the American Revolutionary Army. The line of descendants starting with Martin Kallikak and a mentally deficient girl contained a large number of mental deficients and persons with other types of behavior disturbances.

The dangers involved in studies such as those of the Jukes and Kallikaks are very great. It is risky business to attempt personality evaluations and diagnoses of men and women who have been dead for many years and about whom the most meager records exist. A second objection is to the conclusion that such studies prove physical inheritance. Social inheritance, in terms of cultural influences, might be an equally valid explanation. The family history method very obviously has a limited application. It is effective only in those conditions accompanied by relatively constant physical symptoms that can be readily traced through a number of generations.

In the method of statistical prediction, the rates of mental disorder for representative samples of blood-related and nonrelated groups of individuals are compared. In this way it is possible to determine the degree of frequency with which a condition expresses itself in blood relatives as opposed to the general population. The higher the rates among blood relatives, the greater the likelihood of hereditary influences.

In the twin study method, the rates of mental disorder are compared for siblings, fraternal twins, and identical twins. If a genetic factor is present, rates for siblings and for fraternal twins should be similar with much higher rates for identical twins.

While a number of twin studies suggest the strong possiblity of hereditary influences in several forms of severe mental disorder, other twin studies fail to substantiate these findings. The genetic hypothesis is by no means unfailingly established by twin studies, although the weight of evidence appears to support the probability that hereditary influences frequently are as important as, if not more important than, psychological factors and cultural stress.

HEREDITY AND THE CLINICAL CONDITIONS

The exact manner in which hereditary factors influence the development of abnormal behavior is not understood. The investigation of heredity in the various clinical types of personality disturbance has been limited largely because of methodological difficulties, not the least of which is the problem of diagnosing these conditions in a consistent way. While an exact diagnosis is often possible in organic disorders, the problem becomes more difficult in conditions in which tissue changes cannot be demonstrated. For these reasons, studies of heredity in personality disturbances have met with indifferent success.

In connection with the transient mental stress disorders, it is probable that the effects of heredity operate in the area of individual resistance. It has been established that resistance to stress varies from one individual to another. Some people break down emotionally under very slight stress conditions, while others manage to maintain the integrity of the personality under the most trying circumstances. This individual difference in resistance to stress is due to a combination of inborn and learned factors. The inborn factors, by definition, would be open to hereditary influences.

The situation in connection with the personality disorders is somewhat more problematical than that of the stress reactions. At least part of the difficulty grows out of the fact that the personality disorders include a wide range of conditions of very diverse etiology. Moreover, few of the conditions grouped under the personality disorders have been studied carefully to determine the role of genetic influence.

The antisocial personality has been one of the few personality disorders subjected to genetic investigation. Studies have indicated that criminality rates vary from about 14 percent in twins of opposite sexes to 54 percent in fraternal twins of the same sex to 66 percent in identical twins (Rosanoff et al., 1934). These figures suggest that the influence of unfavorable environmental influences, as well as basic personality traits, is important in the etiology of criminality.

Wide interest in the relation between antisocial personality and genetic makeup was aroused in the 1960s when it was found that some men with chromosome abnormalities had a history of antisocial behavior. The first publicity was given to this relationship when a prostitute was found strangled in Paris in 1965. A thirty-one-year-old man surrendered himself to the police and confessed to the crime. When his guilt feelings led to a suicide attempt, a complete medical examination was ordered by the court. During the tests it was found that the man had a chromosome abnormality in the form of two, rather than one, Y chromosomes. The Y chromosome is known as the male chromosome because women do not have Y chromosomes in their cells. The Frenchman was classified as an *XYY variant,* a genetic deviation which occurs in about one out of every 2,000 men.

Since the time of the classic case in France, there has been additional evidence that men showing XYY abnormalities tend to be overly aggressive. Moreover, there is a tendency for these men to be tall and intellectually dull, to suffer from acne, and to have a somewhat bizarre sexual history. Richard Speck, who massacred eight Chicago nurses in 1966, fits this discription and is an XYY deviant. However, sex chromosome aberrations are present in a very small percentage of the total population of emotionally disturbed individuals.

While there is some question as to whether or not an extra Y, or male, chromosome inclines a man to mental dullness and crime, the YY chromosome pattern produces a clear increase in aggressiveness in male killifish. By using carefully timed doses of sex hormones to produce chromosomal changes, it has been possible to develop male killifish which are superior in the battle for the opportunity to mate with females. In 155 tests, YY males won 137 contests, and XY males were superior in only 18 cases (Hamilton, 1969).

In the case of psychoneurotic disorders, hereditary factors are difficult to assess, and the available data are of a most limited and questionable kind. There have been suggestions over a period of years of genetic influences in these conditions. Such impressions, however, have seldom had experimental, or even clinical, justification.

A British study involved a series of objective tests given to twenty-five pairs of identical twins and twenty-five pairs of fraternal twins. A statistical analysis was carried out, and a neuroticism factor was extracted. The results suggested that 80 percent of the individual difference in the neuroticism factor is due to heredity and 20 percent to environmental influence. The study suggests the possibility of an inheritable organic factor underlying at least some forms of neurotic behavior (Eysenck and Prell, 1951).

In the psychophysiologic disorders, an heredity factor may play a role in certain of the allergic disorders, such as asthma and eczema, and in such cardiovascular disorders as arterial hypertension, or high blood pressure. It is possible that there are genetic factors combining to produce a nonspecific reaction to stress. These factors may influence the onset, if not the particular form, of the psychophysiologic disturbance.

Investigation of the genetics of the psychotic disorders has been carried considerably further than the investigation of the genetics of transient mental stress disorders, personality disorders, psychoneurotic disorders, and psychophysiologic disorders. Several psychotic reactions (schizophrenia and the manic-depressive psychoses) have been studied carefully in terms of possible hereditary factors, and there is evidence that at least some psychotic conditions are due primarily to hereditary tendencies, with physiological factors contributing in varying degrees (Rosenthal, 1970).

Manic-depressive psychosis, in which mania and depression occur in the same individual, appears to be linked to the female sex chromosome and may be caused by one or more defective genes. It has been observed for many years that moods and changes in energy level seem to run in families. Some families appear to be consistently elevated in mood while other families are consistently low.

In the brain disorders, heredity appears to play an important part in the primary convulsive disorders and in a variety of relatively rare neurological conditions (Huntington's chorea, paralysis agitans, Friedreich's ataxia) which are characterized more by sensory and motor disabilities than by deviant emotional life or altered thinking. Inheritance is also a factor in the development of certain types of brain tumors and in the mental diseases of old age. In the latter conditions, hereditary influences seem to affect the rate at which an individual ages and to contribute indirectly to the length of life.

Several relatively rare forms of mental retardation appear to be related directly to genetic factors, while the more common types of retardation seem to involve more general inheritance factors. Direct inheritance is seen more frequently in conditions with demonstrable neurological or biochemical defects. Most cases of mental retardation are due to an unfortunate combination of inferior genes rather than to the influence of specific dominant or recessive genes.

CONSTITUTIONAL FACTORS

Any consideration of the organic factors in personality disorganization must take into account the problem of constitution and constitutional types. An individual's constitution includes the physical traits transmitted through the genes plus the effects of any traumatic incidents before or at the time of birth, as well as life experiences at a very early age. This constitution is relatively fixed throughout life and is extremely resistant to modification by any means.

Constitution may be regarded as the total psychobiological make-up of an individual. One definition says that constitution is "the sum total of the morphological, physiological and psycho-logical characters of an individual, with additional variables of race, sex, and age, all in great part determined by heredity but influenced in varying degrees by environmental factors" (Tucker and Lessa, 1940). Another outstanding authority in the field of constitutional medicine looks upon constitution as depending entirely upon genotypical, or inborn, factors (Bauer, 1947). A more usual view, however, regards constitution as a combination of inherited factors as they are modified by the early environment (Draper, 1944).

In a sense, an individual's constitution is the *gestalt,* or pattern, of inherited factors. In a musical composition, the individual notes played separately have little meaning. They are merely the notes of the scale. But played together as a unified composition, these same notes take on a unique and unmistakable aspect. The total composition is considerably more than the sum of the notes. Similarly, each individual is more than the mere sum of isolated inherited factors.

The importance of constitutional influences in behavior is shown in the selective breeding of strains of rats that are high or low in learning ability. It has been demonstrated that it is possible to breed *maze-bright* and *maze-dull* rat strains (Tryon, 1940). While it is probably true that we are not dealing with a simple matter of breeding intelligent and nonintelligent rats, the mere fact that animals showing such marked behavioral differences can be developed through selective breeding is important evidence for constitutional differences.

It has also been demonstrated that through selective breeding it is possible to obtain animals that have a very high resistance to stress and others that have quite a low resistance. The importance of constitutional factors in stress is also shown in studies of audiogenic seizures with inbred strains of mice. Mice with one strain are highly resistant to sound-induced convulsions, while those of another strain are extremely susceptible to them.

In view of these animal studies it seems quite probable that similar strengths and weaknesses develop in human families as a result of chance selection. The conditions in the uterus of the mother may have an effect on the mental health of the developing child.

Research scientists at the National Institute of

Mental Health studied identical twins in which one twin remained normal and the other developed a mental disorder. The mentally disordered twin was usually lighter in weight at the time of birth and in some cases had a less active thyroid gland. The investigators suggested that unfavorable conditions in the uterus, possibly in the form of a poorer position or nutritional differences, may trigger a genetic potential for mental disorder in the less favored twin. Following birth this disadvantage may be aggravated by the parents who treat the less mature twin as being less competent (Pollin and Stabenau, 1967).

The importance of constitution in personality disorganization is best shown in connection with the study of human body types. From the time of early Greek medicine, there have been attempts to relate body types and physical characteristics to personality disturbances.

The founding of a school of clinical anthropology in Italy in 1885 marked the first serious attempt to define constitutional differences in *anthropometric* terms, that is, through the measurement of physical

Figure 3.10 *Ernst Kretschmer, 1888–   , German psychiatrist and biotypologist. (Courtesy of Dr. Kretschmer.)*

characteristics (Di Giovanni, 1919). This early work influenced the thinking of Cesare Lombroso (1836–1909), whose major contributions were in the study of the delinquent and the criminal and the relation of criminality to psychopathology (Lombroso, 1911). Lombroso believed that the difference between the mental patient and the criminal was one of degree rather than quality. He came to the conclusion that the criminal is midway between the patient and the savage and that he represents a special type in the human race. Lombroso regarded this type as *atavistic,* that is, marked by characteristics of earlier races and lower species. The psychopathic criminal, according to this outmoded theory, is a regressive phenomenon of the human species produced independently of environmental forces.

THE KRETSCHMERIAN HYPOTHESIS

One of the greatest single influences on the study of the constitutional basis of mental disorder has been the work of Ernst Kretschmer (1888–   ), who developed a system of *biotypology,* or classification of body types and related psychological characteristics. This German psychiatrist described three primary types: (*a*) the *pyknic,* or stout and compact, (*b*) the *athletic,* or muscular, and (*c*) the *asthenic* or *leptosomic,* a tall, thin, relatively weak body type. A fourth type, the *dysplastic,* includes unusual and atypical body structures found associated with glandular disturbances.

The most important part of the Kretschmerian hypothesis is that each of the body types has psychological and behavioral correlates. According to this theory, the asthenic and athletic types are more likely to exhibit *schizoid* patterns of behavior, while the pyknic type is inclined toward *cycloid* behavior. Schizoid personalities are quiet, reserved, and unsociable. They are frequently sensitive people who are inclined to be shy and timid. They live much within themselves; and while they appear to others to be silent and indifferent, actually they are tense and excitable. The cycloid pattern is characterized by sociability, general friendliness, and a cheerful outlook. Such people are likely to be good-natured but softhearted and easily depressed.

Kretschmer found that of the cases diagnosed

as having a manic-depressive illness, two-thirds had a pyknic body type. Of those diagnosed as schizophrenic, two-thirds were athletic or asthenic. On the basis of these clinical observations, he commented that there is a "clear biological affinity between psychic disposition of the manic-depressives and the pyknic body build and between the psychic disposition of the schizophrenes and the bodily disposition characteristics of the asthenics, athletics, and certain dysplastics" (Kretschmer, 1925). He concluded that mental disorder is the result of a traumatic episode superimposed upon predisposing constitutional factors.

Kretschmer's work is important because it emphasized the possible relationship between body build and mental disorder and stimulated a vast amount of research interest. However, his work has been open to many serious criticisms. His original observations were based on a small series of cases, his sample was limited in terms of race, and he failed to make objective measurements or to establish quantitative indices. Nor were the data classified according to age, sex, intellectual level, social status, and similar variables which might have influenced the findings.

SHELDON'S SOMATOTYPES

A different approach to the problem of biotypology was undertaken by William H. Sheldon (1899–   ) of Harvard University, who did not believe that body types exist as separate entities in the sense used by Kretschmer. Instead, he attempted to type the human body in terms of basic variables derived from the embryonic development of the individual. These variables were: (1) *endomorphy,* or rounded fatness, (2) *mesomorphy,* or square muscularity, and (3) *ectomorphy,* or fragile linearity.

In addition to the three primary components, Sheldon studied such secondary factors as (1) *dysplasia,* or disharmony between different regions of the body, (2) *gynandromorphy,* or bisexuality of the physique, (3) *texture,* or fineness or coarseness of the structure, and (4) *hirsutism,* or hairiness of the physique.

Sheldon arrived at his somatotypes, or body types, by photographing his subjects from three views and then taking measurements from the pictures. Seventeen measurements were needed to determine a somatotype and to differentiate it adequately from other somatotypes. A system was developed for describing each individual in numerical terms. A scale from 1 to 7 indicates the relative amount of each of the three variables. The somatotype for any physique is a three-digit number describing the variables. For example, a somatotype of 5-2-1 would describe a body type predominantly endomorphic and small mesomorphic and even smaller ectomorphic components.

Sheldon believes that somatotypes remain easily recognizable throughout adult life, except in the case of glandular disorders, paralysis, or muscle-wasting disease. He is of the opinion that the body type is established before birth and that it is relatively inalterable. "It seems probable that the physical constitution at the morphological level is rather rigidly determined before birth and that it cannot be perceptibly changed during the course of a lifetime" (Sheldon, 1940).

Sheldon's most important contribution to abnormal psychology has been his attempt to correlate his somatotypes with psychological processes and personality disturbances. He came to the conclusion that individuals who are predominantly endomorphs have a personality pattern he called *viscerotonic,* that mesomorphs are *somatotonic,* and ectomorphs are *cerebrotonic.* The viscerotonic temperament is one in which relaxation, sociability, conviviality, and love of comfort are dominant. It is a personality type dominated by the digestive system. The somatotonic temperament is expressed through exertion, exercise, and vigorous physical self-expression. The cerebrotonic personality type is more inclined toward intellectual pursuits.

In considering the relationship of constitution to mental disorder, Sheldon studied 3,000 young schizophrenics and 300 manic-depressives. He found that dysplasia, or disharmony between different regions of the same physique, is more prevalent than any other somatotype in schizophrenia. There is also evidence that the type of dysplasia bore some relation to the clinical type of schizophrenia. The manic-depressives were dominantly endomorphic and mesomorphic (Sheldon, 1940).

The role of biotypology has not been determined in relation to personality disturbances and behavior disorders. However, if a valid relationship could be established between body type and temperament, it would have important mental-hygiene implications. It would mean that children and adolescents of a particular body type could be observed more carefully for signs of early mental disorder. The establishment of such a relationship might also extend our knowledge of genetic factors in mental illness.

While the weight of the evidence suggests that constitutional factors may play an important part in one's susceptibility to emotional disturbance and mental disorder, a clear relationship between biotypes and clinical syndromes has not been established. Where such relationships appear to exist, the variables of age, nutritional patterns, physical habits, and similar matters can account for most of the findings.

HORMONES AND NEUROHORMONES

The human organism is made up of a complex network of body systems, including the skeleton, the muscles, the nerves, the blood vessels, the glands, and other specialized parts of the body. Of these body systems, the nervous system and the glandular system are most closely related to the onset and course of personality disorganization.

The glandular system consists of (1) duct glands and (2) ductless, or *endocrine,* glands. The duct glands are those whose product is secreted to the external or internal surface of the body by means of a duct or canal. Tear glands and sweat glands are examples of duct glands. For the most part, glands of this type are relatively unimportant in psychopathology. The endocrine glands, however, frequently play a critical role in the development and form of personality disturbance. These glands produce chemical substances called *hormones* and secrete them directly into the blood stream. These substances have a powerful regulatory effect on various functions of the body.

The origins of modern endocrinology are found in *organ magic,* a set of beliefs which has formed an important part of the folk medicine of many primitive people. The essence of organ magic was that one could reinforce his own virtues by consuming the organs of men killed in combat or animals taken in chase. The warrior who wanted to add to his own courage would eat the heart of a brave enemy. For the same reason, the hunter would eat the heart of a lion.

The naïve belief in organ magic eventually was transferred, in a more sophisticated form, to orthodox medical practice. It was thought by ancient physicians that diseases of various kinds were caused by lack of substances in body organs and that cures could be brought about by remedying the deficiency. Patients with heart disease were advised to eat hearts, liver disorders were treated by a diet of liver, and kidneys were prescribed for illnesses involving that organ. Eventually, this system of treatment came to be called *opotherapy.*

The earliest direct relation between endocrine dysfunction and psychological disorder was the recognition, by Felix Plater in the sixteenth century, of mental retardation in cases of thyroid disturbance. In 1603, a work by Paracelsus (who had died sixty-two years earlier) remarked on a possible relation between the thyroid gland and mental disorder. In the eighteenth century, Théophile de Bordeu, physician to the court of Louis XV, suggested that each gland, as well as each organ of the body, manufactured specific substances which were carried to other parts of the body by the blood. He believed that these substances in some way participated in the integration of the functions of the body as a whole. This theory was intuitively correct, and it anticipated the modern science of endocrinology.

The first actual demonstration of the physiological nature of endocrine function was the discovery that sugar stored in the liver in the form of glycogen is released as dextrose directly into the blood stream and not through ducts as in the case of ordinary glands. This work definitely established the concept of ductless glands and set the stage for more exact knowledge about the endocrine glands and their secretions (Bernard, 1865).

HORMONAL INFLUENCE

It is generally accepted that the organization of personality is dependent, in more or less direct ways, on the hormones of (1) the pituitary gland, (2) the adrenal glands, (3) the thyroid glands, (4) the tissue of the pancreas, and (5) the sex glands (gonads). In a less direct way, the parathyroid glands, the thymus, and the pineal gland are related to behavior disorders and personality disturbance.

The Pituitary

The pituitary gland (hypophysis) is situated in a small bony structure at the base of the brain. The gland is made up of two lobes, the *anterior* and the *posterior.* While each of these two lobes produces a number of hormones with different functions, the anterior pituitary is of greater interest in abnormal psychology. This part of the endocrine gland secretes a growth hormone, overproduction of which leads to giantism, underproduction to dwarfism. More important to personality integration is the fact that the anterior pituitary also secretes a series of hormones which exert a powerful influence over the hormones produced by the other endocrine glands.

The anterior pituitary hormones form a major integrating system of the body, second only to the nervous system. For this reason, the pituitary has frequently been called the "master gland." However, relatively little work has been done in the analysis of anterior pituitary functions in mental disorder. The reason, in part, is that methods for investigating the hormones of the anterior pituitary lobe are not so far advanced as the methods used for studying thyroid and adrenal cortical hormones.

The Adrenals

The adrenals are a pair of glands located adjacent to the kidneys. Each gland is made up of two parts, the *adrenal cortex* and the *adrenal medulla.* The cortex is the external portion of the gland, and the medulla is the inside core. Both the cortex and the medulla produce hormones important to the maintenance of personality organization.

There has been a substantial amount of work showing that there are important disturbances of adrenocortical functioning in mental disorder. One evidence of this pathological functioning is the abnormality in the urinary excretion of many patients. However, normal adrenocortical functioning is found in many mental patients, and for this

reason adrenal disorder cannot be regarded as a necessary causative factor.

The secretion of adrenocortical hormones is facilitated by one of the anterior pituitary hormones (ACTH). When there is a deficiency of ACTH or when the adrenal cortex is injured, there is likely to be an underproduction of adrenocortical hormones, resulting in a condition known as *hypoadrenocorticism.* The major syndrome is Addison's disease, marked by weakness, faintness, coma, and a dark pigmentation of the skin. It has also been observed that personality disturbances develop in some patients treated with ACTH. In most instances, an impairment of consciousness is involved, with the basic personality pattern of the patient determining the content of the disorder.

In a series of detailed studies involving ACTH, investigators at the Worcester (Massachusetts) State Hospital observed that two-thirds of the schizophrenic patient group showed an impaired biochemical response to ACTH (Pincus and Hoagland, 1950). There is evidence that some type of deficiency of the adrenal cortex itself, or an anterior pituitary failure which may be related to hypothalamic dysfunction, is involved. The psychological disturbances brought on by the administration of ACTH are identical to those resulting from treatment with cortisone. However, serious personality disorganization occurs in only a small percentage of patients receiving ACTH. One possible explanation of personality disorganization associated with ACTH and cortisone is that a toxic condition interferes with the normal action of the nervous system. Another is that the substances trigger psychopathology latent in the personality of the patient.

Another hormone, 17-hydroxycorticosteroid (17-OHCS) represents the major metabolic breakdown product of the primary adrenalcortico-hormone *cortisol,* which is secreted in increased amounts when a person is under heavy physical or environmental stress. Possibly there is a connection between an elevated level of this stress hormone and the suicidal drive. There is evidence that suicidal tendencies are associated with an excess of the hormone when compared to the level in nonsuicidal individuals (Fawcett and Kerste, 1968).

The adrenal medulla secretes an entirely different set of hormones, the most important of which is *adrenalin (epinephrine).* This hormone is intimately involved in the maintenance of personality organization, since all emotional reactions result in a release of adrenalin, which in turn influences the sympathetic nervous system. When adrenalin is released, there is a rise of blood pressure, an increase in the level of sugar in the blood, and a more rapid blood coagulation. Each of these changes is an adaptive response of the organism to an emergency. The rise in blood pressure brings

Figure 3.11 *A case of congenital hypothyroidism. (Courtesy of the Columbus State School.)*

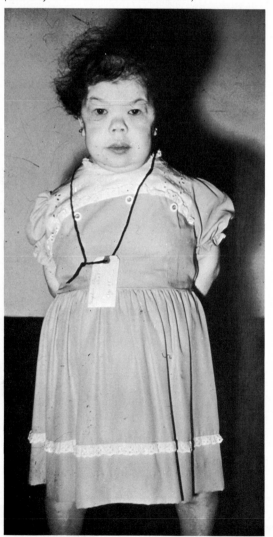

more blood to the muscles; the release of sugar into the blood from the liver supplies the organism in case it is wounded in fight or flight.

The Thyroids

The thyroid glands consist of a pair of organs joined together one on each side of the neck just below the larynx. The principal hormone *(thyroxine)* influences cell metabolism, cell organization, and body growth and maturation. Along with the pituitary and the adrenals, the thyroid glands play an important part in maintaining the equilibrium of the personality.

The relation between the thyroid glands and emotional behavior was reported nearly 150 years ago. Ten years later a classic monograph on *hyperthyroidism,* or thyroid overactivity, was published in which the author attempted to establish a relationship between thyroid functioning and neurotic behavior (Graves, 1835).

The action of the *thyrotrophic,* or thyroid-stimulating, hormone of the anterior pituitary influences the size and the secretory activity of the thyroid glands. A relation also exists between the thyroid glands and the hypothalamic centers of the brain. In this way, the thyroid glands have a critical impact on the nervous system.

Thyroid overactivity can be caused by many conditions, including a defect of the thyroid glands, increased stimulation by the nervous system by way of the hypothalamic centers of the brain, and action of the thyrotrophic hormone of the anterior pituitary. Whatever the cause, tension and irritability are seen frequently, along with such physical symptoms as weakness, loss of weight, and increased sensitivity to temperature changes. The majority of studies of hyperthyroid patients point to a close relationship between the endocrine disturbance and personality problems.

An underactive thyroid, or *hypothyroidism,* may be due to defects in the thyroid glands, to a deficiency of the thyroid-stimulating hormone of the anterior pituitary, or to a lack of raw materials to manufacture thyroxine. Whatever the reason for the deficiency, the patient becomes lethargic, apathetic, and sluggish, with a general slowing down of thinking and psychomotor processes. The condition is marked by feelings of fatigue, headache, irritability, lack of sexual potency in men, menstrual irregularity in women, vague pains, and emotional instability. Where there is a serious hypothyroidism during embryonic development, mental retardation is a common symptom. When a severe thyroid deficiency develops later in life, the psychological symptoms often include depression, and mental disorder is not unusual.

Knowledge of thyroid function has been increased substantially by the development of more advanced laboratory methods and the use of radioactive isotopes to study the iodine uptake of the thyroid glands (Cranswick, 1955). These studies suggest that a disturbance of thyroid functioning plays an important role in at least some of the major mental disorders. The findings are supported by the fact that there have been scattered reports of improvement in certain mental conditions following treatment with thyroid hormones.

The Pancreas

While the pancreas itself is not an endocrine gland, tissue embedded within the pancreatic mass secretes the hormone *insulin*. Through the production of insulin, the sugar metabolism of the body is kept in balance. And since the oxidizing, or burning, of sugar is one of the chief sources of body energy, the maintenance of an optimal sugar balance is of critical importance to the organism.

When there is an underproduction of insulin, the sugar content of the body rises to levels higher than normal. The body has an excess of sugar in the blood and in other organs. The result is a physical disorder called *diabetes,* in which there is physical weakness, excessive thirst, frequent urination, and eventual damage to the blood vessels if the condition is allowed to go untreated. Patients with this disorder must control the body sugar by means of diet or by taking in additional insulin to help oxidize the excess sugar.

While excessive body sugar is medically important, personality disturbances are more likely to be associated with *hypoglycemia,* or a deficiency of sugar. In these cases, too much insulin is produced, and the relatively large amount of this hormone burns the sugar to a point where there is not enough for ordinary body needs. In short, there is too much insulin and too little sugar.

There are many psychological symptoms when blood sugar dips below its normal level. The more common symptoms include apathy, anxiety, fatigue, restlessness, and irritability. As the hypoglycemia deepens, the patient becomes confused, excited, disoriented, and delirious. False perceptions and distorted ideas and beliefs are not uncommon. If the deficiency is not corrected, the patient becomes stuporous, goes into a coma, has convulsions, and eventually dies. However, the progress of this disturbance can be checked at any point, even during the stage of convulsions, through the administration of sugar in the form of glucose.

Because of the complex endocrine interrelationships of the human body, hypoglycemia can be caused by a variety of conditions. In addition to true hyperinsulinism, in which there is a primary disorder of the insulin-producing mechanism, an overproduction of insulin can be caused by anterior pituitary insufficiency, adrenocortical insufficiency, or severe hypothyroidism. On the other hand, sugar deficiency can be caused by such nonendocrine conditions as liver disease affecting the storage of glycogen.

The Gonads

The sex glands (gonads) are related to the development of secondary sex characteristics in men and women and to the female menstrual cycle. The male sex hormones are produced in the *testes,* while the female sex hormones are derived from the *ovaries.*

The major female sex hormone, or estrogen, is *estrone.* It is produced by the ovaries from the fetal period until the menopause and steers development in the direction of femininity. At puberty, it is responsible for the appearance of secondary sex characteristics, including the development of the breasts, the pattern of fat distribution on the body, and the typical female pattern of hair distribution. A second ovarian hormone, called *progesterone,* is produced only during the active reproduction years. The purpose of this hormone is to modify the inner surface of the uterus for the implantation and maintenance of the embryo.

The principal male sex hormone, or androgen, is *testosterone.* In early life, this hormone determines the development of masculinity. During adolescence, it is responsible for the male voice change, fat distribution, and hair pattern.

An example of the relation of endocrine changes to personality in everyday behavior is the tension, irritability, and depression experienced by a great many women before the onset of menstruation. There is likely to be an outburst of physical and mental energy at this time. Activity also runs high at the time of ovulation but without the other symptoms associated with premenstrual tension.

In most mammalian species, the males fight more than the females. The male sex hormones *(androgens)* have been implicated as a cause. In studies at Stanford University it has been found that male hormones must be present at birth if a rat is going to display characteristically male fighting behavior as an adult. Animals castrated at birth show feminization and a relatively weaker fighting response. According to one theory of sexual development, the male hormones present at birth physically organize the brain into a male pattern, while the absence of these hormones creates a female brain pattern. From that time the action of sex hormones, whether male or female, is regulated by this fundamentally established pattern (Conner, 1968).

Adult female mice given a single injection of a male gonadal hormone *(estradiol benzoate* or *testosterone propionate)* showed a marked increase in spontaneous aggression. During mating, the aggression rose to a point where the females often attacked, wounded, and, in one case, killed the male (Bronson and Desjardins, 1968).

In an experiment in England, male prisoners convicted of sexual offenses, most of them against children, underwent a painless operation under local anesthesia in which a small pill of synthetic female hormone was inserted under the skin of the buttocks. Observations over a two-year period showed a marked decline in the abnormal tendencies of the men who received the treatment.

NEUROHORMONES

The neurohormones are chemical mediators in the transmission of the nerve impulse and are distributed in characteristic patterns in the nervous system. The chemicals are released from storage areas in the body as a result of some form of stimulus. Once released, they play a role in neural transmission and then are destroyed when they have served their purpose.

The importance of the neurohormones in the transmission of nerve impulses was first shown in 1921 when it was demonstrated that, following the stimulation of the vagus nerve of a frog's

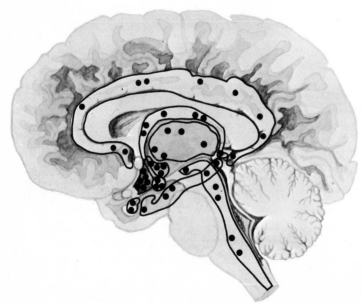

Figure 3.12 *The principal neurohormone depots of the brain. (Courtesy of Mary Lorenc, Harold E. Himwich, and the Wallace Laboratories.)*

heart, a compound appeared which, when transferred to a second isolated heart, produced an effect similar to vagus stimulation (Loewi, 1921). The substance responsible for this stimulation was later identified as *acetylcholine*. While the first interest was in the relation of this substance to the action of the nerve impulse at the synapse, in the 1950s interest was extended to the role that acetylcholine plays in abnormal behavior.

Under normal conditions, this neurohormone has a stimulating effect on synaptic transmission. Excessive amounts of acetylcholine appear to decrease resistance at the synapse and to exaggerate the transmission of nerve impulses. In this way, pathological mental activity might be induced as a result of the lessening of normal synaptic control.

While acetylcholine is not normally present in the cerebrospinal fluid, it is found in the majority of patients with convulsions, particularly in patients who had frequent seizures. It is also possible to induce convulsive seizures in man by injecting acetylcholine into the veins. Similarly, there have been reports linking acetylcholine with various other types of mental disorder.

Histamine is a neurohormone which was first synthesized in 1907 and is found in many parts of the body, including the nerve tissue. The importance of histamine in abnormal psychology grew out of the observation, first reported in the 1930s, that the brain changes in certain mental patients resemble changes found in animal brains after histamine intoxication. There is also an indication that certain mental patients have an unusually high tolerance for histamine (Jodrey and Smith, 1959).

A third neurohormone is *noradrenalin,* or *norepinephrine.* The important difference between noradrenalin and adrenalin is that the neurohormone is present in the brain, particularly in areas concerned with the regulation of the autonomic nervous system.

The possible role of noradrenalin in personality disorganization is suggested by the action of its breakdown products. These unstable chemical substances, such as *adrenochrome* and *adrenolutin,* result in psychological changes which are difficult to measure. However, there is a possibility that these chemicals play a role in certain types of mental disturbance. The first evidence of this kind was an observation by an anesthetist that psychological disturbances followed the use of deteriorated adrenalin solution which was found to contain adrenochrome. When experimental subjects were injected with adrenochrome, the development of psychotic-like symptoms was also observed.

Serotonin is a neurohormone distributed in various amounts in the different parts of the brain. Although the presence of serotonin as a substance in the body had been known for more than a hundred years, it was not until the 1950s that the function of serotonin and its role in behavior became known (Wooley and Shaw, 1954). When this neurohormone, which causes constriction of the smooth muscle of the blood vessels, is injected into the brain of an experimental animal, the result is drowsiness, lethargy, and an unwillingness to perform normal movements (Abramson, 1960). Another evidence for the role of serotonin in the activity of the brain is that many of the new psychotherapeutic drugs influence the action of serotonin while ridding the patient of the mental symptoms.

The importance of the neurohormones cannot be understood without reference to their *structural analogs,* or *antimetabolites.* These chemical compounds are shaped to resemble the neurohormone, but they have minor structural differences. Since the antimetabolite is very similar to the neurohormone, it can occupy the space of the neurohormone; but because of the slight difference in structural detail, it cannot perform the same function. Moreover, by occupying the space, it prevents the normal entry of the neurohormone. The situation is similar to that of a key and a lock. While only one key is cut so that it will operate the lock, similar keys can be inserted even though they cannot perform the function of the original key. Moreover, as long as the wrong key is in the lock, the right key cannot do its work.

In the case of serotonin, there are several naturally occurring structural analogs. Among these are the harmala alkaloids (*harmine* and *reserpine*) and the ergot alkaloids (*ergotamine* and *lysergic acid*). *Bufotenine,* another derivative of serotonin, occurs widely in nature, with its main source being the narcotic mushroom *Amanita muscaria*. This mushroom produces marked psychological disturbances when eaten and has been used for many years by Siberian tribes of the Kamchatka Peninsula. It is also used in the United States and abroad as part of the growing drug subculture among students and other young people.

The study of the action of the neurohormones and their structural analogs has opened one of the newest and most exciting chapters in the understanding of the subtle interrelationships involving the endocrine system, the nervous system, and personality disturbances.

NUTRITION AND MENTAL HEALTH

There is increasing evidence that nutritional deficiency is an important factor in the development of certain types of personality disturbance. While it is probable that this type of deficiency brings about its effects in a number of subtle and as yet unknown ways, it is clear that at least two major types of deficiencies are involved. These two types are (1) general nutritional deficiencies and (2) vitamin deficiencies.

NUTRITIONAL DEFICIENCIES

Although the importance of nutrition in physical and mental health has been recognized for many centuries, the precise role of nutritional deficiencies in behavior disorders and personality disturbances has been relatively neglected. But it is known that the tissue of the brain, spinal cord, and peripheral nerves depends in a very critical way upon a variety of nutritional elements. Iron, sodium, and potassium are needed for tissue respiration and to maintain the electrolytic balance. In a similar way, fats and proteins are essential to the effective functioning of the nerve cells.

Among lower animals diet has a pronounced influence on behavior. Chickens lacking a proper diet become irritable, and young rats brought up on a magnesium-deficient diet show excitability. They may become apprehensive and fearful and may finally develop convulsions. The common saying "feeling your oats" reflects the fact that horses fed too heavily on oats become extremely high-spirited.

An example of a behavior disorder due to a nutritional deficiency is the disease called *enzootic ataxia* found in sheep in Australia and England. The young lambs of ewes which feed in pastures deficient in copper show paralysis, lack of coordination, and in some cases blindness. The brain of the abnormal lamb is smaller than that of the normal newborn, and there are marked changes in the frontal sections of the brain. The cortex is thin and the convolutions are flattened and poorly defined. The severe brain damage is due to the copper deficiency, and the disorder among lambs is reduced or eliminated when the pregnant ewes are fed copper.

Observations on the behavioral effects of nutritional deficiencies in human subjects have been less common. Arctic explorers have reported restlessness, short temper, and inability to adjust to ship routine by sailors on inadequate diets (Mercier, 1916). During World War II, psychological changes associated with nutritional deficiencies were observed in persons who had been in concentration camps (Merzbach, 1941). The onset of the illness was insidious and usually appeared gradually over a period of several days to a few weeks. The behavior was marked by suspicion, irritability, and querulousness. However, relatively little is known about the relation of specific deficiencies to personality disorganization. In the case of salt depletion and a low blood chloride, the patient shows such clinical symptoms as restlessness, insomnia, dizziness, and depression. In many cases there is trembling and other signs of tension and anxiety. As soon as the salt deficiency is corrected, the symptoms disappear (Ocko, 1959).

A low level of sugar in the body leads to irritability, negativism, indecision, and loss of initiative. More severe sugar deficiency results in stupor, coma, and convulsions, often with psychotic symptoms. Lack of iron in the diet results in anemia and indirectly cuts down on mental activity. Calcium deficiency causes irritability, and sodium deficiency can result in delirium and psychotic conditions.

Magnesium depletion also has important behavioral and psychological effects since this element is indispensable to the efficient functioning of the neuromuscular system. In magnesium deficiency in animals, the symptoms are bizarre involuntary muscle activity, trembling of the limbs, twitching of the face, and, in more serious cases, convulsions. In man, these neurological symptoms are combined with delirium, confusion, distorted perceptions, and pathological thinking (Suter et al., 1958).

There is good reason to believe that inadequate nourishment of the brain during infancy and early childhood has lasting effects on both the physical and psychological development of the individual. When it is realized that by 1970 there were about 300 million malnourished children under five in the world and that 60 percent of preschool children lack sufficient protein food, the implications for physical and mental health are very grave indeed.

A South African physician reported on an eleven-year study of forty children in Cape Town. Twenty of the children had been virtually starved during the first year of life. They were the most grossly undernourished children that could be found. These children were matched with twenty other children from a similarly poor background but who were not underfed. The differences in mental capacity and head size between the two groups of children were striking. The food-deprived children averaged 1 inch less in head circumference than other children. The overall intelligence of the undernourished group was significantly lower. Sixty percent of the undernourished fell below the level of even the lowest adequately fed child. Even though thirteen of the undernourished children were subsequently moved to better homes, they never caught up in mental development (Stock, 1967).

The effect of nutrition on behavior has also been demonstrated by the Institute of Nutrition of Central America and Panama. In a study of two matched pairs of villages in Guatemala where 50 percent of the children die before the age of five, and the average life span is only 37 years, inhabitants of one village received an enriched and supplemented diet at a nutrition center. As many as 90 percent of the villagers from two months to sixty years old received a morning ration of nonfat dry milk, bananas, a high-protein gruel, and a sweet bread containing eggs. In the villages where the enriched diet was available, the general lassitude of the villagers disappeared, and the children became more talkative, friendlier, and more alert (SKF Psychiatric Reporter, 1968).

A study of 150 selected children from homes in South Memphis, Tennessee, revealed that 40 percent had irreversible mental and physical damage, most of which was due to inadequate diet during the first year of life. This finding demonstrates the damaging effects of malnutrition on young children raised in poverty-stricken urban ghettos.

Malnutrition can lead to deficiencies in RNA (ribonucleic acid) and to impaired enzyme action during the developmental period—conditions which contribute to physical and mental retardation. These biochemical disturbances are as important as those caused by inborn errors of metabolism and other factors. Many of the defects of the developmental period could be avoided if the nutritional condition of parents could be assured at the time of conception; if appropriate nutrition and diet could be maintained during the pregnancy of the mother; and if proper nutrition could be ensured following birth.

Undernutrition involves a deficit in calories, proteins, and vitamins. Lack of protein is ordinarily the most serious problem, although vitamin deficiencies are also important. Since grains are the principal source of protein throughout much of the world, individuals without sufficient grain foods in their diets frequently do not obtain the essential amino acids. It is possible to have an adequate caloric intake from low-cost foods and still be undernourished.

Many mental patients lack the correct amount of vital substances that ordinarily are present in the body. These vital substances include the vitamins, certain amino acids, and fatty acids. When the brain does not have the proper concentrations of these substances, its function is impaired. The deficiency can result from a genetic defect or it can be due to a diet having improper quantities of the substance (Pauling, 1968).

Another indication of the possible role of nutrition in personality disorganization is the finding that gluten-like protein in cereal may be a factor in the production of mental disorder in those with hereditary susceptibility to it. It was noted that a marked improvement in mood and behavior occurred in patients when wheat, rye, barley, and oat products were removed from their diets. It was also observed during World War II that there was a decrease in admissions for schizophrenia when there was a reduction in wheat and rye consumption.

To test this possible relationship, patients in a mental hospital were placed on a program of strict food control in a locked ward. The number of days a patient was required to remain in the locked ward was used as an index of improvement. The rate of release of patients on the cereal-free diet was about twice that of patients assigned to a high-cereal diet. The study was controlled in such a way that psychological factors were not the cause of the more rapid release of the patients on the restricted diet (Dohan, 1968).

Animal experimentation also indicates that diet and nutrition are critically important in the early stages of growth and development. On a diet no worse than that of millions of people in some parts of the world, animals develop central nervous system abnormalities. There is consistent and clear brain damage in many species as a result of early protein deficiency. Man's brain is also susceptible to protein deficiency, especially during the growth spurt in the last few weeks of pregnancy and the first six months following birth.

It is probable that nutritional deficiencies are the direct cause of psychological disorders in some cases. On the other hand, personality disturbances from other causes tend to interfere with food intake and in this way produce secondary deficiencies which reinforce the damaging cycle.

VITAMIN DEFICIENCIES

In 1892 a scientist in Germany observed that chickens fed on polished rice developed a disease similar to *beriberi*—a condition known for centuries in the Orient and marked by degeneration of the nerves. This observation led to experiments culminating in the extraction, in 1911, of a crystalline substance from rice polishings which could prevent beriberi. This substance was named a *vitamin*. Since that time more than twenty different vitamins have been isolated and identified.

The vitamins play a variety of complicated roles in body chemistry. For example, they are involved in the process of energy transformation. The principal source of energy for the nervous system is sugar in the form of glucose, which is broken down progressively within the cell until it is reduced to carbon dioxide and water. The vitamins enter the process at various stages of the breakdown, assisting in the release of energy.

The major impact of the vitamins on the personality is through *avitaminosis,* or vitamin deficiency. Such deficiencies are brought about in a number of ways. A faulty or improperly balanced diet may furnish the body with inadequate amounts of a vitamin, or there may be an incomplete absorption of the vitamins from the alimentary canal. It is possible also that the vitamin storage may be defective, the cells may be unable to use the vitamins made available to them, or vitamins may be used up at an excessive rate due to stress.

Of the various vitamins, those in the B group have the most immediate implications for personality disorganization. *Thiamine,* or vitamin B_1, was the first of this group to be identified. A deficiency in thiamine results in neurological changes and in a variety of circulatory symptoms. The deficiency also brings about a neurotic-like reaction characterized by lack of appetite, sleep disturbances, irritability, and increased feelings of fatigue. Patients are likely to have many vague physical complaints. Psychologically, they are forgetful, find it difficult to think in an orderly way, and are unable to concentrate. Occasionally, there are ideas of persecution. In more serious forms of thiamine deficiency, there is severe depression with loss of memory, confusion, distorted thinking, and perceptual disorders.

A study at the Mayo Clinic was made of the effects of vitamin B_1 deficiency on behavior. A group of women with no history of nutritional disturbance or of physical or psychological disorder was placed on a thiamine-restricted diet. The intake was roughly the average found in the poor diets of many city wage earners. After several weeks of the restricted diet, the women became irritable, quarrelsome, fearful, and depressed. Several developed confused memory, and all complained of weakness and fatigue. Most of the women were unable to continue with work they had been doing satisfactorily before the experiment began. After three to six months, the subjects developed anemia, nausea and vomiting, and a lowered basal metabolism. When the diet was supplemented with thiamine, gradual relief was obtained, and over a period of several weeks the deficiency symptoms disappeared.

Our present knowledge of vitamin functions and vitamin deficiencies suggests that there is no causal relationship between vitamin lack and specific clinical conditions. However, because of the intimate and diffuse functions of the vitamins in the biochemistry of the body, any significant lack of these substances might be expected to be reflected in a variety of psychological symptoms.

VARIETIES OF BRAIN DAMAGE

Some of the most striking personality disturbances grow out of physical damage to the brain in the form of infection, toxic conditions, injuries, neoplasms (brain tumors), and similar organic disturbances. Each of these conditions is a stressful situation in the body. The nervous system is affected, and its functioning is impaired. The result may be a personality disturbance. The severity of the symptoms depends on the location, extent, and persistence of the damage.

INFECTION

Infectious disease has been recognized as a source of personality disturbance for many years. Sometimes the psycholgical effects result from the direct action on the nervous system by the microorganism of a disease, and sometimes the effects are a result of secondary factors in the form of elevated body temperature, disordered water balance, deficient oxygen consumption, or other homeostatic disturbances. In either case, there is always the possibility of organic changes which may interfere with the function of the nervous system, resulting in psychological symptoms of various kinds.

Clinical reports of mental changes during the fever and toxic phases of infectious disease have been a part of the medical literature for many centuries. It was not until the early 1800s, however, that medical knowledge was sufficiently advanced and concern with mental disturbances sufficiently strong to draw serious attention to the problem. At that time, considerable interest was aroused by

what appeared to be a relationship between pulmonary tuberculosis and mental disorder.

Renewed interest in the problem of infection was generated in 1875, when a British psychiatrist reported recoveries from mental disorder following the extraction of infected teeth. While the full significance of this finding was not realized at the time, similar reports in Europe and the United States began to appear early in the present century. As a result, the theory of *focal infection* was introduced (Cotton, 1921). This theory held that personality disturbances grow out of a variety of chronic infections with the teeth, sinuses, tonsils, colon, and appendix receiving most of the blame. Treatment consisted of removing the site of infection by excision, cauterization, washing, and draining. Following the removal of the site, patients were treated with vaccines. Eventually, the theory of focal infection was placed in a more realistic perspective as a result of a study of patients under rigid experimental conditions. The physical examinations were sharp enough to detect all areas of infection, and standard laboratory techniques were used. In the cases selected for operation, the rule of radical surgical removal was followed. The experiment proved convincingly that focal infection is not a causative factor in mental illness (Kopeloff, 1941).

In the early part of the present century, several investigators also claimed to have isolated a *Bacillus epilepticus* from the intestinal tracts of patients with convulsive disorders (Reed, 1916). It was assumed that this microbe was the cause of the convulsions. However, the theory that convulsions are caused by specific microorganisms in the intestinal tract has not been substantiated, and in the light of our increasing knowledge of these conditions, such a theory is highly unlikely.

Similarly, there has been a suspected relationship between schizophrenia and tuberculosis. A number of early studies reported an abnormally high incidence of the tuberculous microorganism in schizophrenia, but later studies showed that this relationship did not exist. Nevertheless, the belief that there is some connection between schizophrenia and tuberculosis has persisted. It has also been suggested that certain mental patients harbor in the nasal passages, in pulpless teeth, and sometimes in the blood various types of streptococci-producing neurotoxins which have an affinity for various structures of the brain and which contribute in this way to the development of mental disorder (Rosenow, 1947).

The clearest example of the role of infection in personality disturbance is in connection with syphilis of the brain. It was established beyond question early in the present century that the microorganism of syphilis is responsbile for the wide range of psychological symptoms that had been observed for several centuries in certain cases of mental illness. Systemic infections such as malarial fever, influenza, pneumonia, smallpox, scarlet fever, and typhoid fever also result in temporary, or sometimes permanent, changes in the personality of the patient. During the acute phases of the disease, the symptoms include restlessness, irritability, dazed and stuporous conditions, confusional states, perceptual distortions, and delirium. The acute symptoms usually clear once the organic disease process subsides. In some instances, however, there are permanent changes in the nervous system, and the patient continues to show the symptoms of personality disorganization.

INTOXICATION

The effect of intoxicating beverages and other toxic substances on the behavior of man and animals has been observed for many centuries. Naturalists have observed that woodpecking birds become intoxicated from drinking fermented sap, that the behavior of ants becomes disorganized when they eat the exudations of certain beetles, and that European thrushes occasionally develop a craving for certain berries which eventually cause paralysis and death. It has also been observed that sheep and goats in the pastures of certain parts of Africa become intoxicated and aggressive from eating the beans of the coffee plant. Cattle, sheep, and horses contract serious nervous disorders from feeding on the loco weed found in the western plains of the United States. The taste for this plant develops into an addiction which sometimes leads to death. In the eastern states, cattle acquire the "trembles" from eating the white snakeroot plant.

In man, the principal intoxicant is alcohol. Of the many different kinds of alcohols, the type found in most intoxicating beverages is ethyl alcohol. While this substance affects nearly every tissue of the human body, it has a particularly toxic action upon the tissues of the central nervous system. Alcohol is essentially a physiological depressant, although some of the effects are psychologically stimulating. Characteristically, the more delicate shades of feeling are blunted, the cares of life are minimized, and the tongue is loosened. Typical behavior patterns, determined in part by the fundamental personality type, are released in the form of affectionate advances, maudlin sympathy, or hostility and aggression. Finally, the patient shows increasing signs of physical and psychological disorganization. The usual sequence is confusion and disorientation, incoordinate speech and movements, and finally sleep and unconsciousness.

When alcohol reaches the brain in toxic concentrations, it influences autonomic regulation through its effects on the medulla and the vagus nerve. Both heart action and respiration are influenced in this way. Similarly, the effects of alcohol on the cerebellum lead to postural and coordination difficulties. Emotional behavior is influenced through the thalamic centers, speech through the frontal lobe, and drowsiness and sleep through the hypothalamus.

Unlike most foods, alcohol is absorbed into the blood stream without digestion. A relatively small part of alcohol taken into the body goes into the blood stream from the stomach; most of it passes into the small intestine and is there absorbed rapidly into the blood. The alcohol, whether absorbed from the stomach or the small intestine, is held in the body tissues until it can be broken down, or oxidized, by the liver and eliminated.

While a certain amount of alcohol is lost through urine and perspiration, the most part must be oxidized in the liver. With heavy or constant drinking, the rate of oxidation cannot keep up with the alcohol being supplied to the cells, and the drinker remains in a a prolonged state of intoxication. Eventually the chronic intoxication leads to organic changes within the body. These changes at first are reversible and disappear when drinking is stopped. In the most serious cases, the organic changes become irreversible and are seen as cirrhosis of the liver, impairment of the peripheral nerves, and brain damage.

Table 3.1   *The effects of alcohol: a scale of toxic symptoms*

ALCOHOL IN THE BLOOD (MG PER CC)	SUBJECTIVE STATES AND OBSERVABLE CHANGES IN BEHAVIOR UNDER CONDITIONS OF HEAVY SOCIAL DRINKING	ALCOHOL IN THE BLOOD (MG PER CC)	SUBJECTIVE STATES AND OBSERVABLE CHANGES IN BEHAVIOR UNDER CONDITIONS OF HEAVY SOCIAL DRINKING
0.10	Clearing of the head. Freer breathing through nasal passages. Mild tingling of the mucous membrane of the mouth and throat.		on his past exploits. "Can lick anybody in the county," but has observable difficulty in lighting a match. Marked blunting of self-criticism.
0.20	Slight fullness and mild throbbing at back of head. Touch of dizziness. Sense of warmth and general physical well-being. Small bodily aches and fatigue relieved. Not fretful about the weather or worried concerning personal appearance. Quite willing to talk with associates. Feeling tone of pleasantness.	0.70	Feelings of remoteness. Odd sensations on rubbing the hands together, or on touching the face. Rapid strong pulse and breathing. Amused at his own clumsiness or rather at what he takes to be the perversity of things about him. Ask others to do things for him. Upsets chair on rising.
0.30	Mild euphoria, "everything is all right," "very glad I came," "we will always be friends," "sure I will loan you some money," "it isn't time to go home yet." No sense of worry. Feelings of playing a very superior game. Time passes quickly.	1.00	Staggers very perceptibly. Talks to himself. Has difficulty in finding and putting on his overcoat. Fumbles long with the keys in unlocking and starting his car. Feels drowsy, sings loudly, complains that others do not keep on their side of the road.
0.40	Lots of energy for the things he wants to do. Talks much and rather loudly. Hands tremble slightly, reaching and other movements a bit clumsy; laughs loudly at minor jokes; unembarrassed by mishaps, "you don't think I'm drunk do you, why I haven't taken anything yet." Makes glib or flippant remarks. Memories appear rich and vivid.	2.00	Needs help to walk or to undress. Easily angered. Shouts, groans, and weeps by turns. Is nauseated and has poor control of urination. Cannot recall with whom he spent the evening.
0.50	Sitting on top of the world, "a free human being," normal inhibitions practically cut off, takes personal and social liberties of all sorts as impulse prompts. Is long-winded and enlarges	3.00	In a stuporous condition, very heavy breathing, sleeping and vomiting by turns. No comprehension of language. Strikes wildly at the person who tries to aid him.
		4.00	Deep anesthesia, may be fatal.

SOURCE: *Adapted from H. Emerson,* Alcohol and Man. *New York: The Macmillan Company, 1932, p. 259.*

Less widespread than alcoholism, but no less important to abnormal psychology, are the toxic conditions brought on by addiction to drugs. The psychological distortions of reality produced by drugs have been observed for many centuries. The modern clinical psychologist and psychiatrist are familiar with the special effects of the sedatives and hypnotics, the opiates, cocaine, marijuana, and, most recently, the tranquilizers, antidepressants, and hallucinogens.

Each drug, or group of drugs, produces a more or less unique effect on the human organism, depending upon the particular pharmacodynamic action of the drug. Excessive use of sedatives and hypnotics may result in prolonged states of delirium. The opiates induce distortions in visual perception, cocaine results in disturbed body sensations, and marijuana interferes with the perception of time. The hallucinogens produce complicated psychological states bearing a strong resemblance to the more serious mental disorders. Prolonged drug intoxication can result in chronic brain damage.

Much less frequent than alcoholism and drug addiction are cases in which metal poisons produce personality disturbances. The toxic effects of lead on the nervous system have been recognized for centuries. Paul of Aegina referred to convulsions caused by lead poisoning, and Dioscorides described delirious states produced by this same metal. By the nineteenth century, the effects of lead on the nervous system were fully recognized.

The early symptoms of lead intoxication consist of headache, disturbed sleep, and terrifying dreams. There are also likely to be sensory disturbances involving flashes of light and ringing in the ears. Thinking slows down, and the patient becomes depressed. As the condition progresses, delirium develops, particularly during the night. As the lead intoxication increases, maniacal behavior is seen, accompanied by marked visual distortions and speech disturbances. Eventually the patient may develop convulsive behavior (Jenkins and Mellins, 1957).

Within recent years there has been a renewed interest in lead poisoning and its effects on central nervous system activity. This interest has been brought about by the increasing number of young children who have become the victims of the disorder by licking and chewing on toys, window sills, woodwork, and plaster walls coated with lead-based paint. The symptoms include irritation, lethargy, abdominal pain, vomiting, disturbances of balance, and convulsions.

It is not only young paint-eaters who are in danger of lead poisoning. In some cities the lead intake of inhabitants approaches—or exceeds—dangerous levels as a result of air pollution from auto exhaust. The problem is so serious that federal legislation has been enacted to require automobile manufacturers to take steps to control the danger. Another example of potential metal poisoning is the finding of dangerously high levels of mercury in certain fish. It is possible that the increasing environmental pollution will have a more damaging physical and psychological effect on people than has yet been realized.

BRAIN INJURY

Personality disorganization also occurs as a result of injuries to the head and brain. In most cases, such injuries show neurological changes as the primary symptoms, but it is not unusual for psychological symptoms to be present as well. It is a commonplace observation that injuries of this type result in personality change. Such everyday expressions as "He fell on his head" and "He must have fallen out of the cradle when he was a baby" are evidence of the popular acceptance of the role of head injury in personality disturbance.

The earliest account of head injury appears in the Edwin Smith papyrus of the seventeenth century B.C. This document refers to three classes of head injuries, including superficial lacerations in which the bone of the skull is uninjured, injuries in which the bone is perforated and the patient unable to turn his head, and injuries in which both the bone and the brain tissue are wounded. Treatment consisted merely in sewing the skin of the scalp and dressing the wound with lint, honey, and grease. A fifteenth-century physician who wrote about personality changes in patients after head injury observed peculiarities in sexual habits and eating.

The symptom picture varies in different forms of cerebral trauma, depending upon the extent and location of the damage. However, the initial and most frequent symptoms include fluctuating impairments of consciousness, ranging from mild confusional states to deep stupor. Another early symptom of brain damage is a defective memory. Such defects range from brief lapses to a complete loss of memory. In more serious cases of head injury, the patient may experience illusions, visual and auditory perceptual disturbances, and disordered thinking. In addition, irrelevant and incoherent speech is often part of the symptom picture.

One evidence of the impact of brain trauma on personality organization is found in brain surgery for the purpose of alleviating mental illness. These operations indicate that it is possible to damage the frontal lobes extensively without any detrimental effect upon intellectual ability. However, patients who have had this type of operation show a loss in initiative, an inability to plan for the future, and a lack of concern for responsibility.

Subcortical lesions are also capable of producing insidious psychological changes. Lesions in the basal ganglia, hypothalamus, or brain stem may result in various types of alterations of consciousness. The symptoms are most likely to take the form of emotional instability, anxiety, depression, and apathy.

While brain injuries may result in personality disturbances of varying degrees of severity, it is interesting that rather dramatic injuries sometimes result in relatively little change in behavior and personality.

A fifty-one-year-old bacteriologist was robbed and beaten on the street. When he regained consciousness, he took a taxi to his hotel. The next afternoon he went to a physician because of "a little headache." When x-rays were taken, it was found that there were five bullets in his head. Under the bruises and clotted blood on the face, small holes were found below the left eye, at the corner of the right eye, under the nose, in the roof of the mouth, and in the top of the head. While any one of the bullets could have been fatal, each went precisely to a safe place in the head and brain. The only remarkable symptom was a partly paralyzed tongue that made speaking and swallowing difficult. The patient had no memory of the shooting. It was believed that the robbers shot him out of frustration upon learning that he had very little money in his pockets (Fournier, 1968).

Another dramatic example of brain injury without pronounced psychological effect is the classic case of Phineas Gage. This man worked on a railroad construction job where he used a crowbar to force dynamite charges into holes bored into the rock during the blasting for a roadbed. One of the charges accidentally exploded, and the crowbar crashed into the side of his jaw and into his brain. A large portion of the brain was destroyed. Nevertheless the workman survived the explosion and the brain damage, and it became possible to observe his behavior over a period of time. Other than being somewhat more irritable

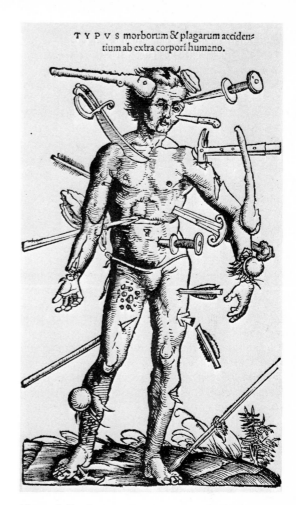

Figure 3.13 *The wound man. An old print showing the types and sites of the most common injuries. (Courtesy of Dr. Cyril B. Courville.)*

and having less control of his temper, little change was noticed in his personality.

The surgical removal of half the brain (hemispherectomy) also demonstrates how it is possible to alter large parts of the brain with relatively little effect on personality and behavior. This radical type of brain surgery has been used with patients having massive brain tumors and also in the case of the *Sturge-Weber syndrome* in which babies show a huge birthmark on the face and neck. The birthmark is caused by excessive growth of blood vessels in the skin, and there is a similar overdevelopment of blood vessels under the scalp and on the surface of the brain. Babies with such a mark ordinarily develop disabling seizures and convulsions. The treatment in the past was with drugs, but the dosage had to be so heavy that youngsters were in a continuous state of grogginess. Today it is possible to treat such cases by removing the entire half of the brain. When the surgery is performed during infancy or early childhood, the psychological damage is minimal or nonexistent. In fact, such children are usually much better adjusted following the removal of the brain tissue than they were before.

EXPERIMENTAL BRAIN DAMAGE

The study of brain damage in animals and man has been one of the classic lines of development leading to the modern science of experimental psychopathology. Most of the experimental work has involved the measured removal of brain tissue, although several other techniques have been used to damage the different areas of the brain. The application of drugs, localized cooling, experimental concussion, and similar techniques have contributed to our understanding of the effects of brain damage on behavior.

Some of the earliest work on the functions of the brain was undertaken in 1875 by a British neurologist who described behavior changes in monkeys following the experimental removal of the frontal lobes (Ferrier, 1876). Later in the nineteenth century in Germany, the behavioral effects of the decerebrate dog were observed (Goltz, 1892). In the United States, extensive studies were made of human patients in whom parts of the brain were damaged (Franz, 1905).

The interest in behavior changes in animals following the experimental removal of various brain areas and patients with naturally damaged brain areas was accelerated sharply in the late nineteenth and early twentieth centuries. This increased interest resulted from greater knowledge of the nervous system and the development of more advanced surgical techniques which made such research possible. In man, studies were restricted for the most part to brain disease, accidental brain damage, and surgical intervention. Among animals, it was possible to extend the investigations to more or less controlled removal of brain tissue.

Much of the research directed toward the localization of function in brain areas has been concerned with the frontal lobes. Not only are the frontal lobes more readily accessible, but there has also been a general assumption that the frontal brain is more closely associated with the advanced developmental stages of man. However, in spite of the large amount of attention given to the frontal lobes, there is little agreement on the psychological functions which are affected as a result of traumatic or surgical damage to this area. Some authorities ascribe intellectual functions to the frontal area; others relate the frontal area to motivation, foresight, capacity for prolonged attention, and the like.

Among the symptoms observed after the removal of the frontal lobes of experimental animals are a loss in the ability to delay responses, disturbances in learning, and overactivity. In man, the frontal lobes appear to have only a most indirect relationship to conventionally measured psychological functions. It is possible to remove large portions of the frontal lobes without any observable change in the intellectual functioning or personality characteristics of the subject (Rylander, 1943).

Some of the most significant research related to the functions of the frontal lobes in man has been undertaken in connection with the use of psychosurgery. This operation, which involves a substantial portion of the prefrontal pathways, has surprisingly little effect on the behavior of patients. The most frequently observed symptom is a loss in planning capacity and a lack in the ability of the patient to project himself into the future. However, there are relatively few changes in intellectual ability, memory, problem solving, and similar psychological functions (Kisker, 1944).

Important landmarks in research on the effects of brain damage on behavior were reports to the London meetings of the Second International Neurological Congress in 1935 (Fulton and Jacobsen, 1935) and to the 1937 meetings of the American Physiological Society (Klüver and Bucy, 1937). The London report, dealing with the effects of frontal lobe damage on the behavior of frustrated animals, contributed to the development of the psychosurgical technique of prefrontal leucotomy. The report described the symptoms seen in monkeys following the removal of both temporal lobes of the brain. These two major research efforts were key factors in stimulating further interest in brain-behavior research.

When regions of the brain other than the frontal lobes are considered, the most consistent findings are that patients with lesions of the left hemisphere are likely to be poor at verbal tasks, while lesions of the right hemisphere seem to be associated with deficiency in practical tasks, particularly those involving space and time-space relationships. The dominant hemisphere (usually the left) ordinarily governs language functions, while nonlanguage tasks are more likely to be related to the nondominant hemisphere.

Findings with reference to the temporal lobes are inconsistent. Part of the difficulty is the relative inaccessibility of this part of the brain and the inability to determine the extent of temporal brain pathology. An important development was the finding that memory functions may be related to the temporal lobes. It has been shown, by means of electrical stimulation of the exposed cortex, that memory functions are in some way related to this part of the brain (Penfield, 1959). In the case of the parietal and occipital lobes, the major conclusions are that damage to the parietal lobe is likely to produce impairment in functions involving space relationships, while damage to the occipital lobes is reflected in visual disturbances.

Some of the more recent work on subcortical structures has dealt with the brain stem reticular formation. Since this brain area appears to be essential for consciousness, attention, and possibly learning, it has been the center of an increasing amount of research. Similarly, the limbic system has been found to be an important part of the neural substrate for motivation, emotion, learning, and memory. Consequently it has received a substantial share of research attention.

An intriguing avenue of brain research is the use of the split-brain technique in experimental animals. It will be recalled that the two hemispheres of the brain are interconnected by a broad band of nerve fibers. When this band is cut, there is surprisingly little disturbance of behavior. It is even possible for animals with split brains to learn tasks independently with each half of the brain. Of even greater interest is the fact that when one hemisphere of the brain has been trained to do one thing and the other trained to do the opposite, there is little evidence of conflict in the

animal. It appears that when one hemisphere begins to dominate behavior, the output of the other hemisphere is inhibited by lower brain centers (Glickstein and Sperry, 1960).

A number of techniques other than surgery have been used to induce brain damage in animals. The purpose of these studies has been to observe the nature and degree of the resulting behavior disorganization. Among the research methods are cerebral implantations, experimental concussion, freezing, and centrifugation. By means of cerebral implantations it is possible to produce chronic recurrent convulsive seizures of various types in animals. The motor cortex of an anesthetized animal is exposed, and a small, round linen disc containing a chemical substance is placed flat on the brain surface. The membranes of the brain are then sutured firmly over the disc to hold it in place, and the incision in the scalp is closed. In most animals in which seizures develop, the attacks occur three to eight weeks after the operation. When such a disc is placed on the temporal cortex of an experimental animal, restlessness and increased sexual behavior may be observed. When the disc is applied to the occipital cortex, animals frequently show an increase in irritability, continual pacing, and a peculiar visual attentiveness suggestive of possible hallucinatory experiences (Kopeloff et al., 1942).

In other experiments, a catatonic-like state has been induced through the introduction of heavy water (deuterium oxide) into the cerebrospinal fluid. The heavy water produces a state of catalepsy which develops within a few minutes and lasts for several hours. Complete recovery eventually occurs in the animals (Hermann and Barbour, 1937). The injection of suspensions or extracts of brain tissue has also been found to produce behavior similar to certain forms of mental disorder seen in human subjects. Early studies showed that paralysis in rabbits could be obtained by injecting them with human brain tissue (Hurst, 1932). In a later study of the effects of the intramuscular injection of brain extract in monkeys, inoculations of an emulsion of rabbit brain were given to a series of monkeys for a period varying from four to thirteen months. A progressive condition characterized by symptoms of widespread involvement of the central nervous system was observed in all animals. Unnatural position of the head, ataxia, tremors, and spastic paralysis were the most frequent symptoms (Ferraro and Jervis, 1940).

Neurological and behavior disorders in animals have also been produced experimentally by concussion. As early as 1874, it was found that animals could be killed by repeated small blows on the head without there being any evidence of structural damage to the brain (Tuke, 1892). Other experiments showed that convulsive disorders could be produced in animals by blows on the frontal area of the skull and that cerebral concussion could be induced by the measured blow of a hammer to the occipito-parietal area. When the subconcussive blows are delivered in a short period, one impact after another one minute apart, injury affecting nerve cells and nerve fibers is a consistent finding (Tedeschi, 1949).

In a different type of experiment, it has been found that freezing limited areas of the cerebral cortex of an animal causes convulsions after several hours, followed by death some time later. If the frozen tissue is removed immediately, no symptoms result unless the area is in the motor cortex. Transplantation of the frozen tissue to the brain of a healthy animal causes convulsive symptoms and death (Speransky, 1935).

Body rotation also results in behavior disturbances. Mild degrees of rotation bring about decreased movement in rats; but, as the speed of rotation is increased, the animals become overactive. At very high rotation rates, convulsive seizures occur. These seizures are frequently followed by death. Postmortem examinations of the brains of animals subjected to the rotation experiments show swelling and hemorrhages (DeJong, 1945).

BRAIN TUMORS

Brain tumors, or *neoplasms,* are another source of personality disorganization. Such tumors result in psychological symptoms in about 50 percent of the cases. In the other 50 percent, the neoplasm is in one of the "silent areas" of the brain where important tissue changes can take place without external signs of the process. In cases where symptoms are present, they are likely to be in the form of convulsions and other neurological disturbances, as well as memory impairment, confusion, and delirium. The nature and extent of psychological symptoms are determined by the increase in intracranial pressure, the structural damage caused by the proliferation of brain cells, the edema, or swelling of the tissue, and the location of the growth. In tumors of the frontal lobes,

Figure 3.14 *Brain atrophy and dilatation of the ventricles with aging: (a) coronal view of the normal brain of a young adult and (b) the same view of an aging brain, showing severe atrophy of the tissue and enlargement of the ventricular spaces. (Courtesy of Dr. J. A. N. Corsellis, London.)*

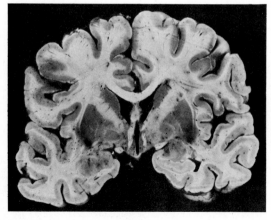 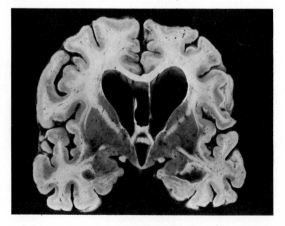

(a)   (b)

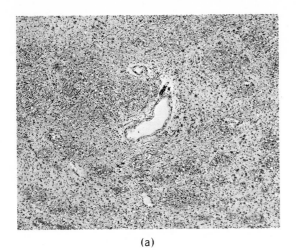

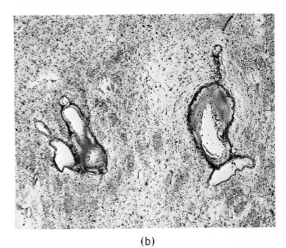

(a)   (b)

Figure 3.15 *Degenerative changes in blood vessels accompanying the aging process: (a) small group of normal blood vessels in the area of the thalamus and (b) the same brain area in an aging patient. Note the degenerative changes and the effect of the degeneration on the surrounding tissue. (Courtesy of Dr. J. A. N. Corsellis, London.)*

it is quite possible to have large masses of pathological tissue with few signs of personality disorganization, or none at all.

DEGENERATIVE CHANGES

The degeneration of tissue due to aging is also a factor in the development of mental illness. In every living organism, there are normal structural changes which take place with aging. These changes are related to the regulation of blood and tissue chemistry, the maintenance of uniform body temperature, basal metabolism, alimentary absorption and digestion, the processes of excretion, and resistance to injury and disease. In a similar way, sensorimotor changes take place in the normal aging process. Vision, hearing, reaction time, and other perceptual and motor functions are altered in significant ways. The physical cost of maintaining the complex mechanisms of adjustment increases as the individual ages.

As the cells of the body grow older, their capacity to adapt decreases, and they become more vulnerable to environmental stress. During old age, the entire brain shrinks in size. The convolutions on the surface of the brain become flattened, and the *sulci,* or crevices, which separate the convolutions, become widened. The membranes covering the brain are likely to be thickened, and many cells within the brain deteriorate and disappear.

In the older tissues of the body there is an increase in the amount of inert material such as filbrin and collagen. Since these substances surround many cells, there is an interference with the diffusion of oxygen and foodstuffs. In this way, the metabolic processes of the cells are impeded. Another condition prevalent during old age is the increase of calcium and cholesterol within the capillary walls.

Scientific interest in the problems of the mental disturbances of later life is relatively new. For one reason, these disturbances have loomed suddenly as one of the most important, if not the most important, problems of modern life. Not many years ago, the age span was so short that few people attained an advanced age, and consequently the mental disorders of later life were not emphasized. Today, however, with rapidly increasing numbers of men and women living to advanced ages, the problem of mental illness during the later years has become one of increasing urgency and importance.

NEUROCHEMISTRY AND MENTAL DISORDER

The neurochemistry of personality disturbance has been a matter of research interest for the greater part of the present century. This interest was intensified in the 1950s by the development of a wide range of *psychoactive* drugs.

While the gap between brain chemistry and emotional life is still too great to correlate behavior with specific chemical changes in most cases, modern science is moving in this direction and with steadily increasing acceleration. Every personality disorder, no matter how mild or how severe, must eventually be represented in the neurochemistry of the body. Research into brain biochemistry may lead to the solution of some of the more elusive problems associated with personality disorganization. However, there are very difficult methodological and other problems to be solved in research of this type, and extreme caution must be exercised in interpreting the findings. The research in this field has centered on blood chemistry, water metabolism, urinary constituents, analysis of the cerebrospinal fluid, the relation of brain enzymes and coenzymes to personality disorganization, and similar problems.

A number of studies have been made of the cholesterol level in personality disturbances. Cholesterol is a crystalline solid, insoluble in water, which is a part of all animal cells. The brain and spinal cord, as well as the adrenal glands, contain relatively large amounts of the substance. In the blood, cholesterol is distributed equally between the red blood cells (erythrocytes) and the plasma. Generally, the variability has been so great that cholesterol levels cannot be used for diagnostic purposes. However, it is significant that the range of variability in severe personality disturbances is about twice as great as the variability among normals (Harlow and Woolsey, 1958).

Other investigations have suggested that the blood serum and cerebrospinal fluid of psychotic patients possess characteristic properties. An Italian investigator in the late nineteenth century found that the blood of psychotic patients, when injected into experimental animals, caused death. He came to the conclusion that death was due to toxic substances present in the blood of the patients (Keup, 1954). More recently it has been established that the blood serum of certain mental patients kills tadpoles, while tadpoles survive in normal serum (Fischer, 1953); that the patient serum inhibits the germination of plant seed (Macht, 1950); that it is toxic to the larvae of certain insects (Fischer, 1953); and that it is toxic to certain molds and fungi (Fedoroff, 1956). Other experiments have shown that the injection of blood plasma from certain psychotic patients produces a disorganizing effect in rats which interferes with their performance (Winter and Flataker, 1958).

In one series of experiments, rats were trained to climb a vertical rope approximately five feet high. The rats were induced to climb by the incentive of a dish of food on a platform at the top of the rope and a mild electric shock applied to their feet through a wire grid on the floor of the cage. After intensive training, the rats learned to climb the rope in about four seconds after the stimulus was applied. The climbing time delay was highly significant in the case of rats injected with plasma from schizophrenic patients. In addition to the objectively measured delay in climbing time, the animals showed marked changes in their cage behavior. They huddled in the back of the cage and became quiet and withdrawn. Climbing was clumsy; and when the animals reached the feeding platform, they refused to eat.

At Tulane University, plasma from mental patients was injected into the veins of normal prison inmates who volunteered for the study. All volunteers receiving plasma from patients developed symptoms which persisted for fifteen to forty-five minutes. While the reactions were not severe, the subjects described symptoms of personality disturbance. Control subjects receiving plasma from normal donors did not show these symptoms (Heath et al., 1958).

The relation of water metabolism to mental disorder has also been a matter of interest since the physicians of ancient Greece and Rome observed that the brains of patients with convulsive disorders were "unusually moist." This clinical observation, made more than two thousand years ago, foreshadowed the present knowledge that the water balance in convulsive patients is more unstable than in normal persons. When human subjects or experimental animals take in excessive amounts of water, there is a sharply increased susceptibility to convulsive seizures (Rowntree, 1926).

Another line of biochemical investigation is related to the urinary constituents in mental disorder. One research group, studying the day-to-day variation in the excretion of aromatic compounds, was able to show that there are marked differences between the urinary excretion of psychotic patients and normal subjects (McGeer et al., 1957). Other studies have indicated that animals injected with extracts from the urine of patients react in a pathological manner, while animals injected with normal extracts do not exhibit similar changes (Meduna and Vaichulis, 1948). Similarly, pathological changes occur in the electrical brain waves accompanying injections of urinary extracts from psychotic patients, while those changes do not occur with normal extracts (Wada and Gibson, 1959).

An additional area of interest in the neurochemistry of personality disturbances is related to the cerebrospinal fluid. This fluid is in part formed by the action of the choroid plexuses in the ventricles and in part is a product of an exchange between the blood and the nervous system. Since the cerebrospinal fluid maintains a homeostatic relationship with the blood as well as with other fluids of the central nervous system, it is sensitive to disease processes involving the brain and spinal cord. The cerebrospinal fluid has been analyzed in terms of proteins, enzymes, amino acids, carbohydrates, lipids, pigments, electrolytes, and other constituents. While significant changes have been observed in connection with neurological diseases, most of the work related to mental illness is of a contradictory nature. Even in those cases where there is general agreement on the findings, the significance, in terms of personality disorganization, is generally obscure (Bogoch, 1958).

The relationship of brain enzymes, or chemical regulators, to personality disorganization is in an early stage of investigation. There is evidence, however, that much of our future knowledge of certain mental disturbances will grow out of our increased knowledge of the effects of enzyme systems.

Enzymes are members of the protein family, and they serve to speed virtually all chemical reactions within the body. There are more than 1,000 individual enzymes known to be involved in the body's biochemistry. These enzymes trigger reactions that furnish energy for breathing, heart pumping, digestion, and nerve transmission. The first enzyme to be synthesized artificially was *ribonuclease* (1968). The function of ribonuclease is to destroy RNA (ribonucleic acid), the cell's carrier of genetic information, after it has been used.

While specific relationships cannot be established between enzyme levels and clinical disturbances, there is a wider variation of the enzyme *cholinesterase* in psychiatric patients than in normal patients (Mutrux and Glasson, 1947). In a study of *carbonic anhydrase,* the lowest values for this enzyme are obtained where there has been injury to the brain. Some mental patients show a relatively low level of carbonic anhydrase activity compared with normals (Ashby, 1950). The findings suggest a biochemical involvement in at least some categories of mental illness.

A number of factors must be taken into consideration in the interpretation of biochemical studies of mental illness. Among the possible sources of error are the accuracy of the diagnosis, the effect of institutionalization on diet and exposure to infection, the influence of treatment with various drugs, emotional stress, and the bias of the investigator.

Suggested additional readings related to the neurochemistry of personality disorganization are *The Chemical Basis of Clinical Psychiatry* by A. Hoffer and H. Osmond (Thomas, 1960); T. L. Sourkes' *Biochemistry of Mental Disease* (Hoeber, 1962); and *Psychochemical Research in Man,* edited by A. J. Mandell and M. P. Mandell (Academic Press, 1969).

SUMMARY

1. The organic approach to personality disturbances began with Hippocrates and his followers, who believed that a disorder of the body humors, or fluids, caused personality disturbance. From that time, physicians interested in natural causes of mental disorder emphasized a wide range of organic factors. By the nineteenth century, the theory of *neuropathic taint* was established. This theory, which came to be widely disputed, held that there is a common physical basis for all abnormal mental conditions.

2. One of the most important factors in the development of personality disturbance is *stress*. The stress, which may be physical, psychological, or social, triggers a chain of events which may result in clinical symptoms. The most important theoretical model of stress theory has been advanced by Hans Selyé, who introduced the concept of the *general adaptation syndrome*. Stress theory makes it possible to understand how a wide variety of nonspecific stress situations can result in the symptoms of personality disorganization. Among the more recent, and less controversial, concepts contributing to the organic approach have been those of the *internal environment*, *homeostasis*, and *feedback systems*.

3. The organic basis of personality disturbances cannot be understood without a clear conception of the nervous system and its functions. The central nervous system is made up of a *somatic division*, including the brain and spinal cord, and an *autonomic division*, concerned with the integration and regulation of the internal environment. The human brain consists of the *forebrain*, the *midbrain*, and the *hindbrain*. The most important parts of the forebrain are the outer layer called the *cortex*, the *limbic system*, and the *diencephalon*, including the thalamus and hypothalamus. The midbrain and hindbrain have been of relatively limited interest in abnormal psychology. However, the discovery of the *reticular activating system*, a mass of cells important in psychological arousal and alerting, has focused increasing attention on the structures of the lower areas of the brain.

4. Hereditary factors also play a part in the etiology of mental disorder. While only a few relatively rare conditions are inherited in a Mendellian sense, indirect genetic influences probably play an important role in predisposing individuals toward one or another kind of personality disturbance. Most of the investigations of the genetics of abnormal behavior have been carried out by the *family history* method, the method of *statistical prediction*, or the twin study method. The twin study method appears to be the most valid approach.

5. Constitutional factors also seem to be related to personality disturbance. Constitution refers to the total psychobiological organization of the individual as determined by his heredity and by his early environment. It determines to some extent the degree of tolerance an individual has for stress or the point at which he will break down and the form the disturbance will take. The most important studies of constitution have been those of Ernst Kretschmer, who described the *pyknic, athletic,* and *asthenic* types of body build. He believed that each of these biotypes is related to a characteristic temperament. The pyknic type is supposedly inclined toward *cycloid* behavior, while the asthenic and athletic types are more likely to show schizoid behavior. A second major approach to biotypology is that of William H. Sheldon, who described three somatotypes called *endomorphy, mesomorphy,* and *ectomorphy*. Like Kretschmer's biotypes, each of these somatotypes is supposedly related to a temperamental type.

Sheldon believed that endomorphs have a *viscerotonic* personality pattern, meso-morphs are *somatotonic,* and ectomorphs are *cerebrotonic.*

6. The endocrine system, which is structurally and functionally connected with the nervous system by way of the hypothalamus, exerts its influence on the body through the action of the hormones. The endocrine glands most closely related to personality disturbance are the *pituitary,* the *thyroids,* the *adrenals,* the *gonads,* and the *tissue of the pancreas.* The *neurohormones,* substances which play a role in the transmission of the nerve impulse, are also important in abnormal psychology. These neurohormones have structural analogs, or antimetabolites, which are chemical compounds resembling the neurohormone but having minor structural differences. The antimetabolites can occupy the space of a neurohormone without carrying out its normal function. There is evidence that the neurohormones and their structural analogs are involved in at least some forms of abnormal behavior.

7. Body nutrition plays a role in personality disturbances through general malnutrition and specific vitamin deficiencies. In both cases the lack of proper nutritional substances can result in physical and psychological damage. The most serious damage occurs when the malnutrition takes place during infancy and early childhood.

8. Personality disturbances are related to physical damage to the nervous system. This damage may take the form of infection, toxic conditions, injuries, brain tumors, and other physical conditions. The severity of the personality disturbance depends upon the location, extent, and persistence of the damage.

9. Abnormal behavior may also arise from a disturbance of the neurochemistry of the body. Studies of the blood, urine, spinal fluid, water metabolism, and the enzyme systems suggest that biochemical imbalance is a contributing, if not causative, factor in a number of conditions.

OTHER AUDIOTAPE

Stress and the General Adaptation Syndrome

Dr. Hans Selyé presents an introduction to his "stress concept" as it applies to medicine and the formulation of a biologically sound way of life. Twenty-three minutes. Recorded in 1964. Sound Seminar No. 75901, *McGraw-Hill Book Company.*

4 PSYCHOLOGICAL STRESS AND PERSONALITY DISORGANIZATION

While organic stress in personality disturbances must not be underestimated, it is equally true that it is relatively unimportant in some forms of personality disturbance. By definition, the psychogenic disorders are those in which organicity cannot be demonstrated. For this reason, it is necessary to examine the way in which psychological stress leads to personality disorganization.

Man, from the beginning of his existence, has speculated on the forces that drive him to action. Primitive man explained behavior in terms of animism, and most ancient civilizations accepted the notion of influence by various types of divinity. The philosophers of the eighteenth and nineteenth centuries emphasized the role of *life forces* in human behavior. Today, the behavioral sciences offer a variety of theoretical models of motivation.

THE NATURE OF MOTIVATION

Motivation refers to those energies, or force systems, within an organism which drive it to action. All animal forms, from the protozoa to man, are moved to action in order to seek an optimal balance of their energies. It is necessary that a chemical steady state be maintained within the body and that a constant internal environment be in balance with the shifting external environment. To maintain this balance, the basic tissue needs of the organism must be satisfied.

Most lower animals are motivated entirely by the demands of their tissues. These tissue needs, or organic drives, determine the types of activity in which the animal will engage and when the activity will take place. Among the basic biological drives are the need for food, water, oxygen, the elimination of waste products, the relief of sexual tension, rest, and exercise.

Man, in common with the lower animals, must satisfy these tissue demands. But, unlike the lower animals, man is seldom able to satisfy his organic drives in a direct or immediate way. No matter how imperative the need, with the exception of the intake of oxygen through breathing, satisfaction is likely to be delayed and expressed under more or less rigidly prescribed conditions.

While much of the behavior of man can be explained in terms of his attempts to satisfy his fundamental biological urges, this phase of human motivation is but a small part of the total picture. It is also necessary to consider social needs. These needs include a wide range of behavior which is acquired through social conditioning. Men and women do not need to learn that the body requires food, fluids, oxygen, exercise, and other physical conditions necessary to the maintenance of body equilibrium. They do learn the need to be with other people, to gain power and prestige, to acquire possessions, to love and be loved, to have religious faith, and to have other motives which are not inborn.

A number of theories have been advanced to account for the forces that drive men to action. These theories fall into three major groups: *behavior* theories, *cognitive* theories, and *psychodynamic* theories.

Behavior theories state that drives are generated by various needs which are satisfied through learning. Behavior that is reinforced (rewarded) tends to be repeated, leading to the establishment of habitual actions. The cognitive approach places major emphasis upon more or less conscious and thought-out plans and purposes. Psychodynamic theories focus upon impulses and forces of which the individual is largely unaware. It is assumed that the most important motivating forces are buried deep within the personality and are not open to direct observation or to conscious control.

THE ROLE OF THE UNCONSCIOUS

Each individual carries within himself a vast and powerful system of energies and forces of which he is usually completely unaware. This system represents the *unconscious* level of human experience. For the most part, conscious activity and unconscious activity flow along together, but the amount of conscious activity is very small indeed compared with the unconscious activity that goes on at the same time. Conscious life is a mere fragment of the total psychological life.

While the concept of the unconscious is merely an hypothesis, it is needed to explain the facts of consciousness. The same is true in astronomy when a star system is entered on a celestial map even though there is no direct evidence that the stars exist. No one has ever seen them. However, the behavior and activity of stars and planets that can be seen indicate that something additional must be at a certain place in space in order to explain their behavior. A similar situation in psychology made it necessary to postulate unconscious motivation.

The idea of unconscious motivation reaches far back into the history of philosophical psychology. Socrates, in Plato's *Republic,* anticipated the modern concept of the unconscious when he said: "In all of us, even in good men, there is a lawless, wild-beast nature, which peers out in our sleep." This same inborn nature of man, dram-

Figure 4.1 The Sleep of Reason Produces Monsters, *an etching and aquatint by Francisco Goya taken from the first issue of the* Caprices, Madrid, 1797. *The picture is a self-portrait showing the influence of deeply buried impulses of vanity, pride, greed, gluttony, lust, cruelty, and similar characteristics. The artist anticipated intuitively the findings of modern psychopathology. (Philadelphia Museum of Art.)*

atized in the doctrine of original sin, is emphasized in the writings of St. Paul, St. Thomas Aquinas, and the Protestant reformers.

One of the earliest scientific references to unconscious motivation in personality disturbances is found in the work of Paracelsus in the sixteenth century, who referred to the inner fantasies of mentally disturbed children. The importance of the unconscious was also anticipated by Blaise Pascal, in the seventeenth century, whose classic sentence, "The heart has reasons which the reason knows not of," is an exceptional phrasing of a problem which was not to be solved until two centuries later.

In a somewhat different direction, Gottfried Wilhelm Leibnitz (1646–1716) affirmed the existence of ideas of which we are not conscious and emphasized their vast importance in determining the behavior of men. Leibnitz referred to these unconscious ideas as *petites perceptions,* or ideas of too low an intensity to affect consciousness. The present-day concept of unconscious motivations was also anticipated in the writings of Immanuel Kant (1724–1804) and Arthur Schopenhauer (1788–1860); in the "unconscious sensations" of Gustav Theodor Fechner (1801–1887); and in the "nonconscious ideas" of Johann Friedrich Herbart (1776–1841). In 1863, Eduard von Hartmann published his monumental work *The Philosophy of the Unconscious,* which summarized knowledge about the subject up to that time.

The modern views of unconscious motivation have grown out of the work of Freud. He showed that the unconscious life of man is not a mere storehouse of odd bits of information, images, memories, and assorted experiences, but a dynamic system of primitive needs and urges seeking expression. Yet many of these unconscious drives are expressed only under certain conditions, while others remain hidden throughout one's lifetime. To fit these clinical findings into a theory, Freud created a theoretical model made up of three layers: (1) *conscious* mental activity, (2) *preconscious* (or *foreconscious*) activity, and (3) *unconscious* activity. Conscious activity was considered to be immediate experience; preconscious activity was regarded as psychological events outside consciousness, but readily available through the process of memory; and unconscious activity was assumed to be made up of psychological events that could enter consciousness only with considerable difficulty, if at all.

In order to explain the manner in which unconscious activity is kept in check, Freud assumed the presence, at the preconscious level, of an *intrapsychic censor.* This censor (or *process* of censorship) makes certain that unwanted, disturbing, embarrassing, and other undesirable unconscious strivings do not reach the level of conscious thought. The process of censorship serves to protect the individual from the consequences of his deep, unconscious, and often socially unacceptable yearnings and strivings.

The result of the censorship process is that many insistent and powerful urges are *repressed,* or held back from consciousness. Freud believed that these repressions, the most important of which, he held, are related to early childhood experiences of a sexual nature, are the primary cause of personality disorganization. His technique of treatment grew out of his conviction that the cure of certain forms of mental illness could be brought about only as a result of the discovery and ventilation of unconscious repression systems.

In addition to the concept of the unconscious, the related terms *subconscious* and *coconscious* appeared frequently in the psychological literature of the early part of this century. The idea of the subconscious has been used in several ways. Pierre Janet and writers in the tradition of the French school used "subconscious" as being synonymous with "unconscious." Others reserved "subconscious" to refer to impressions in the margin of attention. Today, the term "subconscious" is used relatively little in abnormal psychology and psychiatry.[1]

THE CLINICAL VALIDATION OF UNCONSCIOUS PROCESSES

The clinical and experimental evidence to support the general theory of unconscious motivation is of considerable weight. The very facts of remembering and forgetting, intuition and the sudden emergence of solutions, and creative thinking and artistic expression underline the reality of psychological processes outside the range of immediate awareness, or consciousness. More dramatic evidence of unconscious activity is to be found in symbolism, dream life, sleepwalking, automatic writing, multiple personality, and hypnosis.

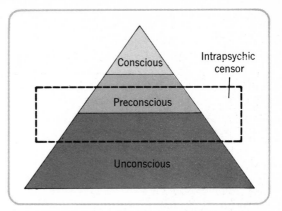

Figure 4.2 *A simple model of the Freudian concept of the conscious, preconscious, and unconscious. Note the approximate area in which the censorship process operates.*

Ordinary remembering and forgetting is the most obvious and direct indication that psychological activity takes place outside the field of immediate awareness. When an individual is asked his name, his type of work, or other commonplace information, he is able to give it without difficulty unless there are emotional or organic factors which prevent it. Moreover, he is able to produce the information in a great variety of forms and combinations, indicating that unconscious mental activity is not a mere static process of storing information, but a dynamic process in which information is sorted, selected, classified, worked over, altered, and, in the case of the mental patient, often twisted and distorted.

Similarly, it is not unusual to have ideas and solutions emerge suddenly and in complete form. Sometimes it happens in dreams; more often there is a sudden emergence during waking life. Suddenly everything is clear, and the individual knows what he is going to do and how to do it. It may be a problem in school, at home, in

[1]For a further understanding of the role of unconscious processes in abnormal behavior, it is suggested that the student begin with L. L. Whyte's very readable *The Unconscious before Freud* (Basic Books, 1960). The serious student of the historical development of the idea of the unconscious is referred to Eduard von Hartmann's monumental *Philosophy of the Unconscious* (Harcourt, Brace & World, 1931). More psychological treatments of the subject are James G. Miller's *Unconsciousness* (Wiley, 1942), and *The Discovery of the Unconscious* (Basic Books, 1970) by H. F. Ellenberger.

business, in the creative arts, or a personal problem during psychological treatment. In any event, there is sudden insight, as if all the pieces somehow were put together without the individual's conscious knowledge. It is probably not an exaggeration to say that unconscious mental and emotional activity are the sources of most philosophical speculation, religious experience, and artistic creation.

Unconscious Motivation in Daily Life

The evidence for unconscious motivation in ordinary day-to-day behavior is found in the way in which guilt, anxiety, hostility, jealousy, selfishness, egotism, and other unhealthy attitudes are expressed. An example of such behavior is the slip of the tongue in which a person says one thing when he means something else. These slips are not without unconscious meaning. A host, in saying farewell to a departing guest, said, "So glad you are leaving so early" instead of "So sorry you are leaving so early." When someone says the wrong thing, it often means that deep down he has feelings consistent with what he says. Even though he would not admit to himself that he has such feelings, they exist at the unconscious level.

Many people have had the embarassing experience of calling someone by the wrong name. Switching names is not accidental. It is usually unconsciously determined, just as are errors in writing, misaddressing envelopes, and failing to enclose a check or money order in payment of a bill. Gestures and movements may also be motivated unconsciously. Very often, without knowing it, an individual may smile, frown, or appear sad. The cues for such outward emotional expression are internal. The facial changes, and even alterations in posture, are determined by mental and emotional activity at the unconscious level.

When walking along the sidewalk, some people seem to have difficulty keeping to a straight line. They nudge and bump into their companions, forcing them gradually toward the street or toward the buildings. While such behavior might be explained occasionally in terms of perceptual or neurological disturbance, there is clinical evidence that sometimes it is a symbolic act of aggression. Unconsciously, the individual might like to push his companion off the curb or perhaps through the glass of a shop window.

A somewhat different form of unconscious motivation is seen in misplacing and losing objects. In many cases, the misplaced or lost object will be something that the individual did not want in the first place. In other cases, the loss has a symbolic meaning. One does not need a high degree of psychological sophistication to comprehend the hidden meaning of losing an engagement ring or, more often, a wedding band.

Another dramatic example of unconscious motivation is the *purposive accident*. Except where mechanical failure is involved, there is growing evidence that deep-seated psychological needs and emotional attitudes may play a role in determining the time, place, and type of accident. In brief, many accidents do not merely happen; they are determined by powerful psychological forces.

Accidents also may be a disguised form of suicide. When people allow themselves to be run down by automobiles, to fall out of windows, or to fall overboard and drown, they may be satisfying an unconscious urge to do away with themselves. The accidental nature of the act disguises and modifies the true purpose and intention.

Dream Life

The powerful forces of unconscious motivation are demonstrated vividly in our dreams. From the very earliest times, the dream has intrigued men, and there is a vast literature on the nature and meaning of dreams. The major theories on the origin of dreams have included (1) the supernatural, (2) the meaningless, (3) the psychophysiological, and (4) the psychodynamic.

The supernatural theory of dreams is expressed in beliefs ranging over many centuries and many different cultures. Primitive man, the ancient Orientals, the holy men of the Bible and the Talmud, the philosophers of classical Greece and Rome, and the religious scholars of the Middle Ages in one way or another supported the idea of the dream as something supernatural. Many primitive tribes have held the belief that the dream is an experience of the spirit which has left the body during sleep.

Figure 4.3   *The dream of the primitive, as suggested by Henri Rousseau's painting* The Dream. *(Collection, Museum of Modern Art, New York. Gift of Nelson A. Rockefeller.)*

When the supernatural theory of dream life was discarded, it came to be believed that the dream is essentially meaningless. Cicero, in his poem *On Divination,* expressed the opinion that "dreams are not entitled to any credit or respect whatever." The dream was regarded merely as a chaotic rumbling of the brain, without direction and without reason. It was looked upon as a series of meaningless, purely accidental images which at most were remnants of the impressions of the previous day.

The psychophysiological view says that dreams result from perceptual experiences of the day, organic changes within the body during sleep, and a variety of psychological conditions of an emotional and ideational kind. Aristotle was one of the first to point out that dreams may be caused by inner physiological changes which are not noticed in the waking state. He suggested that these changes are smothered by our waking impressions, but during sleep the slight changes of the internal organs are translated into dream images.

Lucretius, in *De Rerum Natura,* also suggested that dreams deal with daytime occurrences or with bodily needs which are satisfied in the dream. Galen said, "A dream indicates the condition of the body." St. Thomas Aquinas, while convinced that some dreams are sent by God, believed that bodily processes are revealed by the symbols of the dream and that these internal processes can be discovered through dream interpretation. Robert Burton, in his *Anatomy of Melancholy,* said: "The gods do not send our dreams; we make our own." He believed that troublesome dreams are the symptoms of melancholy men, who can rid themselves of these disturbing dreams by following a proper diet. Thomas Hobbes supported the view that all dreams are the result of bodily stimuli, and Immanuel Kant

Figure 4.4 *The dream fantasy, as suggested by Marc Chagall's painting* I and the Village. *(Collection, Museum of Modern Art, New York. Mrs. Simon Guggenheim Fund.)*

argued that the most important factor in dream life is a disordered stomach.

The psychodynamic model of the dream combines many of the features of earlier dream theory. Here the dream is viewed not as a special phenomenon of sleep but as unconscious activity that continues uninterruptedly during both sleep and waking. The dream is merely an expression of unconscious mental activity during sleep. The so-called dream material is present during waking as well, but it does not break through to conscious life because of the increased preoccupation with environmental stimuli. According to this theory, unconscious psychological activity flows on in an uninterrupted way. A student may doze off in the classroom during a lecture and in

a matter of moments experience fragmentary dream material. During any lapse of attention, dream images may appear. The dream has no necessary connection with sleep. It is only that during certain phases of sleep there is optimal opportunity for dream material to come to the surface.

Sleepwalking

Unconsciously motivated behavior is demonstrated clearly in sleepwalking, or *somnambulism*. While dreams are limited to sight, sound, and other sensory images, there is the addition of bodily movement in sleepwalking. Somnambulists are likely to show the same pattern over and over again. The walking occurs at the same time during the night, the same path is followed, and the same kind of behavior occurs. Sometimes this behavior is of a most complicated kind. The sleepwalker may go down the stairs, play the piano, bake a cake, drive the family car around the block, or mow the lawn.

Contrary to popular belief, the somnanbulist does not have supernatural powers when he walks in his sleep. He cannot do anything that would be physically impossible for him were he awake, but he sometimes does things he would not risk doing while awake. This is the case when a sleepwalker climbs out on the roof and walks perilously along a small ledge or gutter. He is less likely to fall because of his intense concentration and his enhanced ability to balance himself. His attention is focused more sharply, and he is less influenced by distractions in his environment.

When a person walks in his sleep, he may be escaping from reality. He may be fulfilling a repressed wish, and his actions very often are symbolic. A young married woman got out of bed almost every night and searched her room thoroughly for a "package." This episode occurred so frequently that her family insisted that she seek psychological help. It was found in treatment that the package symbolized a child and her constant searching represented her frustrated wish to be a mother. Shakespeare described the nocturnal wanderings and symbolic actions of guilt-ridden Lady Macbeth.

Sleeptalking, or *somniloquy*, is another indication of unconscious motivation. One of John Wesley's assistants would get out of bed and preach his sermons while asleep. A college girl returned from a date, and her sorority sisters were eager to know what had happened. When she refused to tell, one of the girls jokingly said, "You will probably talk about it in your sleep." Later that night, when the girl had fallen asleep, she began to talk—and she talked on and on for several hours. She repeated the entire conversation that had taken place during the date.

Hypnosis

Hypnosis is one of the most dramatic examples of the influence of unconscious motivation. By means of hypnosis, it is possible to explore the deeper motivational systems of an individual, to modify existing systems, and to implant new ones. Moreover, it is possible to accomplish these alterations without the conscious knowledge of the subject.

While the early mesmerists were interested primarily in the removal of symptoms, later work indicated that the hypnotic state exerts a powerfull effect on the motivational patterns of the subject. More important, hypnosis demonstrates in vivid ways that the forces which drive men to action are often below the surface of ordinary waking conscious life.

An excellent example of the use of hypnosis in the validation of unconscious motivation is

Figure 4.5 *A student in various stages of hypnosis induced by the author (a) fully awake before hypnosis, (b) a light hypnotic sleep, (c) the involuntary raising of the hand to the head (hand levitation) is a commonly used test for depth of hypnosis, (d) the student with eyes open, but under deep hypnosis.*

(a)   (b)   (c)   (d)

Figure 4.6 *A demonstration of group hypnosis in a class of student nurses. Note the hand levitation.*

seen in connection with *amnesia*, or loss of memory. In these cases, an individual is found wandering on the streets without knowing who he is, where he lives, or how he happened to be there. Sometimes the loss of memory is merely a matter of hours; in other cases it lasts for days, weeks, or even months. When such cases are examined in the hospital, it is not unusual to find that under hypnosis the patient will remember the circumstances surrounding his memory loss. However, when the patient is awakened, he will have no knowledge of the facts he had revealed only a few minutes earlier. It is as if the individual were functioning psychologically at two different levels.

Hypnosis as an example of unconscious motivation is observed in a number of strange situations. A man was hypnotized and then induced to rob a bank on the French Riviera. The robber was apprehended while still in the hypnotic trance. Even more publicity was given in the newspaper accounts of a woman who was seduced by a friend who hypnotized her and told

her he was her husband. Incidents such as these raise the interesting problem of whether a subject under hypnosis can be forced to engage in activities which are against his morals, ethical standards, or religious beliefs. The answer to this question is not an easy yes or no. One must first know what the individual is like at the unconscious level. Many people have strong ethical and moral standards on the surface, but are willing to disregard them at the slightest excuse. This is why a most proper person might behave in a most improper manner under the influence of alcohol. Similarly, if the moral and ethical standards of a subject under hypnosis are superficial, it is possible that a suggestion given to violate these standards would be carried into action. However, if the moral and ethical standards are deeply rooted in the personality, such a suggestion given under hypnosis would not likely be put into action. The unconscious personality structure, and not the conscious structure, determines which suggestions shall and which shall not be acted upon.[2]

---

[2]Books dealing with problems of unconscious motivation include Freud's classic volume *The Psychopathology of Everyday Life* (Benn, 1956); *The Accident Syndrome* (Thomas, 1956) by Morris Schulzinger; Werner Wolff's *The Dream: Mirror of Conscience* (Grune & Stratton, 1952); and the *Handbook of Clinical and Experimental Hypnosis* (Macmillan, 1968) edited by J. E. Gordon.

CONFLICT AND FRUSTRATION

Whatever the source of motivation—biological, psychological, or social—the human organism is never able to satisfy its entire range of needs. Much of what the individual wants and desires, both at conscious and unconscious levels, cannot be attained. There are external and internal controlling processes which make it impossible to satisfy many drives and motives. The two major conditions which interfere with the satisfaction of every individual's needs are (1) frustration and (2) conflict.

The word *frustration* comes from the Latin *frustra,* meaning "in vain." Dictionary definitions ordinarily include the idea of being defeated, baffled, or thwarted. Frustration, which begins in the very earliest period of life, is a condition in which the individual seeks to attain a goal of some kind and finds that his way to the goal is blocked by a barrier.

Frustration is brought about by (1) physical barriers, (2) biological barriers, (3) psychological barriers, and/or (4) cultural barriers. The physical barriers include time, space, distance, temperature, and confinement. The prisoner is frustrated because he cannot get out of jail. The baby is frustrated because he cannot reach his toy which has fallen through the bars of his playpen. The young man is frustrated because his car breaks down and he cannot be on time for his job interview.

Biological barriers leading to frustration include physical unattractiveness, intellectual limitation, and lack of strength, energy, or skill. The athlete is frustrated because he does not have sufficient strength or skill to win his event. The young woman is frustrated because her unattractiveness interferes with her social life. The student is frustrated because he finds he does not have the necessary intelligence to enter the profession of his choice. The stagestruck girl is frustrated because she finds she is without talent.

Frustration is also created by psychological barriers. Many men and women are frustrated because their feelings of guilt make it impossible for them to do the things they would like to do. The college student is frustrated because he is

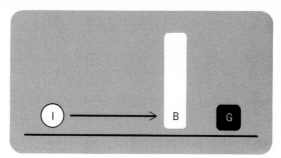

Figure 4.7 *The basic frustration model. The individual (I) is prevented by a barrier (B) from reaching the goal (G).*

not interested in the career of his choice. The young man with an ambition to become a salesman is frustrated because he does not have the required personality characteristics. An unforgettable account of the way in which frustration can gradually erode the personality of a human being is seen in Arthur Miller's play *Death of a Salesman.*

Cultural barriers are equally important as sources of frustration. The whole range of rules, regulations, and restrictions placed upon behavior by the group is a potential source of frustration. It is necessary to do things "the right way," to behave in the "proper manner"—"to obey and to conform."

In spite of the many and inevitable frustrations in life, the major problems facing man are not those involving goals blocked by barriers. Even more important are those situations in life in which a choice must be made between alternative goals. When such a choice cannot be made readily, the individual experiences the psychological state of conflict. The word *conflict* comes from the Latin *conflictus,* part of the verb meaning "to strike together." Psychological conflict involves the collision of incompatible drives and motives. It is a well-known fact that "we cannot eat our cake and have it, too." Bennett Cerf once defined conflict as the feeling you have "when you see your mother-in-law backing over a cliff in your new car."

The general model for conflict is shown in Figure 4.8. Here the individual faces a choice between two goals, or situations, of equal attrac-

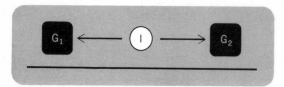

Figure 4.8 *The basic conflict model. The individual I is forced to choose between two goals (G₁ and G₂) of equal or nearly equal attraction.*

tion or repulsion. The fundamental problem in conflict is the difficulty in making a choice. Often the choice is relatively unimportant, and a decision is made automatically without our knowing that there has been a conflict. To one degree or another, however, every choice involves some degree of conflict.

Most conflicts are not clear-cut and involve a combination of biological urges, internal psychological forces, and social pressures. All kinds of situations give rise to important conflicts. The impending death of a beloved but aged and hopelessly ill parent, wanting to marry outside one's religious faith against the wishes of the parents, accepting an attractive job offer and having to give up a scholarship to graduate school—these, and countless incidents like them, create serious conflicts within us. How one learns to handle these conflicts determines whether life is to be troubled and confused, or whether it is to be reasonably calm and serene.

Whatever the form of frustration or conflict and whatever its intensity, the probablity of its resulting in a personality disturbance depends upon how completely it is resolved. Fortunately, most people learn to decrease their frustrations by recognizing the barriers and finding ways to circumvent them or, more often, by establishing substitute goals that are realistic and attainable. Similarly, conflicts are resolved through the simple expedient of making a choice and accepting it. However, it happens frequently that a choice cannot be made in a serious conflict situation, or that if it is made, it cannot be accepted by the individual. When this happens, the result may be some form of personality breakdown.

In our culture, the frustrations and conflicts most likely to result in stress are clustered around (1) sexuality, (2) hostility and aggression, (3) status and prestige, and (4) feelings of dependency.

STRESS AND SEXUALITY

The stress related to sexuality in our culture is one of the most powerful forces leading to personality disorganization. While everyone has sexual and erotic impulses to one degree or another, these impulses are more unruly and more insistent in some people than in others. What a person learns to do with these impulses depends upon his physical makeup, opportunities for sexual expression, and, most important, attitudes toward sex established during infancy, childhood, and early adolescence.

Although many people are reluctant to recognize sexuality in the young child, it is nevertheless true that early childhood is a period of intense sexual curiosity and preoccupation. A great many incorrect and inaccurate theories of conception, birth, and the sex act are learned by the child. One of the most common notions is that women become pregnant through something that is eaten. Other mistaken notions held by children are the beliefs that birth comes about through the intestines of the mother, that the female has a male sex organ, and that the sexual act is one of pain and violence. These more or less standard notions are incorporated in the thinking of every young child. As children grow older, they may forget that they ever had such ideas. But the previously learned attitudes remain buried in the unconscious and have an important effect on later thinking and the development of personal conflicts.

Another major problem of early childhood is the conflict between sexual impulses and physical immaturity. As the child grows older, sexual urges become increasingly difficult to handle. The impossibility of getting relief from the tensions of sex may result in deep frustrations which lead to emotional difficulties later in life. Sexual conflict of this type is sometimes related to the *primal scene,* a concept referring to the observation of sexual scenes or activities between parents or other adults. Such events are likely to be traumatic for the child since he is not prepared to control or understand the sudden flood of emotional excitation to which he is subjected.

Children, even very young children, ordinarily experience strong sexual urges that must be satisfied in one way or another. The infant may satisfy these urges by nursing at the mother's breast, by urinating and defecating, or by manipulating the sex organs. However, the sex urge in the child does not have the intensity or the specificity of the sex drive in the adult. It aims merely at getting pleasure from the mouth (nursing), from the anus (bowel movements), and from the sex organs (masturbation).

During infancy, sexual urges are diffuse, generalized, and undifferentiated. Obviously the infant nurses because he is hungry and not because there is a sexual urge. But when the infant sucks his thumb as a pacifier, he is no longer satisfying hunger; he has learned to obtain pleasure. Similarly, the child has a bowel movement because of organic tension, not because of the sex need. Yet nearly all children come to a point where they prolong the toilet experience. This activity is pleasurable. Later, the child learns about the pleasant sensations that are aroused when he touches his sex organs. From this time on, every normal child engages in episodic masturbation.

Another important characteristic of infantile sexuality is *narcissism,* or self-love. The young child is literally in love with himself. He is, for a short period following birth, the whole world. Gradually other people and other things become meaningful to him. As he learns about the world around him, he shifts from self-love to the love of other objects and persons. In this way, *object love* develops and matures until it culminates in marriage and in children. Yet, throughout the development of object love, each individual retains some of his original narcissism. People continue to be objects of their own love and affection. Oscar Wilde said, "To love oneself is the beginning of a life-long romance."

Narcissistic people are found in all walks of life—the trades, the professions, and the arts. But in many ways, Hollywood and Broadway are the centers of adult narcissism. Every actor and actress has an unusually large degree of self-love. This is true for all those who perform in public. Franz Liszt was the first concert pianist to turn the piano sideways during a performance; it gave him a chance to reveal his striking profile.

Narcissism is expressed in many different ways. It is sometimes the motivation for the deep-cut gowns of women on television, bikini bathing suits, and the studied "plain-ness" of well-to-do society women. A motion picture actress once had her hair cut in front of an invited audience of twenty newsmen. Another actress announced that she was insuring her bosom for fifty thousand dollars with Lloyd's of London. And Marie Laurencin, the celebrated French artist, painted dozens of self-portraits. Narcissism was also suggested in the incident of the twenty-year-old editor of a university yearbook. When it appeared, it contained more than two dozen pictures of herself. Other students were so angry that they burned the 500 copies.

Creative artists, whose intuitive knowledge of the human personality preceded, and in many

Figure 4.9 *Narcissism, as suggested by the painting* Girl in a Mirror *by Morris Hirshfield. (Museum of Modern Art, New York.)*

ways surpasses, the more exact knowledge of the psychiatrist and the psychologist, have frequently portrayed the narcissistic woman. Lucy, a character in Stephen Vincent Benet's poem *John Brown's Body,* clearly illustrates the love of a narcissistic woman for her own body, as well as her incapacity for mature heterosexual adjustment. In James Joyce's *Finnegan's Wake,* narcissism is shown by Anna Livia Plurabelle, who symbolizes the feminine principle in the universe. A classic literary example of narcissism is Emile Zola's description of Nana admiring herself in front of her bedroom mirror.

One of the important sources of stress in life is between narcissism and the necessity to relinquish at least a part of our self-love and offer it to others. In most cases, people learn to resolve this conflict to a satisfactory degree. In many cases, however, the inability to turn love from oneself to others results in an emotional disturbance. In some instances, the result is a major personality breakdown.

Freud's Theory of Psychosexual Development

Some of the most serious human conflicts related to sexuality involve the stages of psychosexual development outlined by Freud. While the theory of psychosexual development has been subjected to attack and criticism over the years, it represents a very useful theoretical model of the stages of human sexual development and their psychological implications.

The Oral Period

The initial period of psychosexual development is centered on the mouth and its activities. The phase is divided into two periods. The first, called the sucking period, covers the time of birth through about eight months. The second period lasts from the eighth to the eighteenth month and is called the biting period. During the oral sucking period there is a strong identification with the mother. The infant is emotionally and physically attached to the mother as the result of nursing and other care. For this reason, weaning comes as an important psychological shock. The time of weaning is one of serious frustration. And since the intensity of personality disorganization later in

life, according to Freud, depends largely upon earlier conflicts, these early oral experiences may become the source of personality difficulties.

The manner in which children are fed during their early months is a critical matter. Temperament may be determined by the first few months, especially by the amount of feeding and the attitudes of the mother during feeding. It is necessary to know whether feeding was difficult and whether the child was satisfied or oversatisfied. Such matters have important implications for later personality development.

Throughout later life, from childhood to old age, people behave in ways carried over from infancy. Thumbsucking, the pleasure in eating, licking the lips during a difficult problem, sucking a pencil or a pen, smoking, kissing, whistling at girls, admiring a pretty mouth, and even stuttering and stammering may be, according to Freudian theory, residual expressions of early oral pleasure. Chain-smoking, and the preference for large cigars and pipes, have been regarded as a reflection of unresolved conflict during the nursing period. The cigarette, the cigar, and the pipe are looked upon as substitutes for the mother's breast, while the smoking is an unconscious reliving of the nursing experience.

Oral sexuality is also thought to be reflected in people who get pleasure out of talking. Such talking is sometimes considered to be related to frustrations during early infancy. Teachers, actors, public speakers, and orators seem to get an oral pleasure out of their work. The extensive talkativeness of many mental patients also may be a symptom of oral needs. The constant talking day after day, from morning to night, may be the result of early oral frustrations. Similar frustrations may also be involved in the peculiar mouth movements of certain mental patients.

Biting is a more advanced stage of infantile sexuality. When the child is from eight to eighteen months old, he begins to learn that he is an independent person, that he is a "self" quite apart from other individuals in his environment. He learns to feel both love and hate for his mother. It is during this time that cruelty and aggression make their appearance. The child begins to show his hostility by biting the mother's breast or the nipple of his bottle during the nursing period. This behavior is most common during the time of weaning, when the child feels insecure, fearful, and angry. The expressions of biting are carried throughout life just as the expressions of sucking are. Children who bite their fingernails are indulging in a form of aggression that may be related to their early biting behavior. Children also bite one another, spit at one another, and stick out their tongues. Chewing the stub of a pencil or the stem of a pipe, or simply chewing gum, might be a form of delayed infantile aggression according to this theoretical viewpoint.

All biting actions are considered to be potentially hostile. The most extreme form of biting is seen in the cannibalistic rites of certain primitive tribes. Biting is also reflected in our speech and language. Debating, argument, wit, and sarcasm may be adult expressions of infantile biting. We speak of "biting remarks." Shakespeare, in King Lear, speaks of unkindness "sharp as a serpent's tooth" and a "serpent-like" tongue. The infantile biting influence also seems to be carried over to adult lovemaking, where young lovers nibble at one another's ears, noses, and chins. A common phrase is, "I love you so much I could eat you." Lovers also "devour" one another with their eyes.

The Anal Period

The next level of psychosexual development is related to the control of the bowels and the processes of elimination. During this stage of development the child derives great pleasure from his toilet activities. The pleasure is of two kinds. First, there is an erotic element, due to the close relationship in the autonomic nervous system between sexual excitement and the processes of excretion. With each act of urination and defecation, there is a certain amount of erotic stimulation. Second, these acts give pleasure because they relieve physiological tensions.

One of the earliest shocks in life is the child's realization that he must learn to control his bowels and bladder. He becomes frustrated, and strong resentments are developed. This period is ordinarily one of serious conflict between the child and the parent. It is at this time that the child realizes that he is an individual and that there are other individuals with whom he must cope.

Early childhood is marked by an absorbing interest in the toilet functions and in the products of excretion. The impulse to play with feces may be channeled into making mud pies, smearing paints, and molding clay. The smutty talk of children and "bathroom humor" among adults may be expressions of this same interest.

It was no accident some years ago that Chic Sale's The Specialist, a book that discussed the design and advantages of various kinds of outhouses, was a best seller. Gems of American Architecture was another book of the same kind. Such books are successful because they appeal to the unconscious interest people have in the processes of excretion. This interest is expressed openly during childhood, but society forces children to repress it as they grow older. Interest in the subject, however, comes to the surface in many disguised ways during everyday life.

Obscene and vulgar language is frequently related to frustrations of infancy and early childhood. When some of the pleasures of the young child are taken away (by forced toilet training) before the child is ready for it, the result may be "dirty" talk. It is for this reason that many nursery schools have occasional epidemics of vulgar and obscene language. Since such language is ordinarily under rigid control by parents and teachers, the urge to use obscene words is repressed, only to appear later in life. This delayed reaction explains the peculiar fascination the four-letter words have for so many people, even those of culture and refinement.

Many children, and certain adults, derive great pleasure from the frequent and violent expulsion of air from their bowels. Although this practice is frowned upon in our society, the pleasures growing out of this type of behavior are frequently so strong that social conventions are defied. The psychological importance of flatulence, as a revolt against authority or as an aggressive action, is demonstrated in the wide use of the "Bronx cheer," and the custom of giving people "the bird." Both noises are thinly veiled substitutes for flatulence.

It is not uncommon for anal interests to appear in direct or disguised form in literature and the arts. In Gulliver's Travels, Swift shows his fascination with the products of excretion in his description of Gulliver's urination and also of the urination of the Brobdingnagian Maids of Honor in Gulliver's presence. He was also interested in animal excrement and discussed the excrement of flies, dogs, hogs, and cows. One of his lengthy episodes concerns Gulliver's unsuccessful attempts to leap across some cow dung in the land of Brobdingnag. The height of anality in literature is found in Rabelais' *Gargantua and Pantagruel.* In one place, five-year-old Gargantua explains to his father, Grangousier, the minute details concerning his excretory and eliminative experiences.

The Phallic Period

Childhood typically involves stress related to masturbation, exhibitionism, and sexual experimentation. In early childhood, sex differences between the male and female are not recognized, or at least they are not important. Later, there is a growing recognition of sex differences. Children begin to play "house," "mother and father," and "doctor." All the while there is a growing interest and preoccupation with sex. Such interest is to be expected. There is nothing "naughty" or "sinful" in childish curiosity about sex anatomy. Unfortunately, many parents become extremely upset when the inevitable incidents of childhood occur. When this happens, parents are planting the seeds for later personality problems.

The most important conflict at this time of life has to do with masturbation. Not many years ago it was an accepted belief, among physicians as well as laymen, that masturbation would lead to mental disorder. Even today, parents become so emotionally excited upon discovering the auto-erotic practices of their youngsters that they make statements that affect the children for the rest of their lives. One mother said, "You're going to get softening of the brain, and be like Gerald" (a boy whom the children called "crazy"). Small girls are told that they will be "sick," that they will get "sores," and that "God won't like them." Little boys have the even more terrifying prospect of having "to go to the hospital to have it cut off" or "to have the policeman chop it off." One mother made the dramatic threat, "It will just rot and dry up, and you will be the only boy walking around without one."

As a result of these cruel and psychologically damaging warnings, countless numbers of men and women in our culture learn to have intense guilt feelings. As children, they were made to feel ashamed, fearful, and anxious. They were led to believe that they were being sinful. These severe guilt feelings continue to be fostered by a distressing number of parents, teachers, and others responsible for child training. One of the most important influences in the development of personal conflict in our culture can be traced directly to destructive attitudes toward this sex practice.

In young children, masturbation is universal and normal. It is also to be expected during adolescence. It is even normal among adult men and women who have no other adequate outlet for their sexual urges. This is the case for soldiers and for men and women who are segregated in prisons or confined in other institutions.

One of the most critical psychological stresses of life happens during childhood. It is the appearance of strong erotic attachments to the parent of the opposite sex. A son has romantic longings for his mother, and a daughter has similar feelings toward her father. During the childhood years, youngsters are likely to love the parent of the opposite sex intensely and to become jealous and resentful of the parent of the same sex. It is not unusual for a young boy to ask mother whether she loves him or daddy the most. The little boy may learn to love his mother so fiercely that he cannot tolerate any rivalry from his father. In some cases, this feeling is so strong in the boy that he wishes his father would die or go away. If the mother is too caressing and indulgent, the son learns to become excessively attached to her, and a lifelong resentment toward the father may be established. Freud called this relationship the *Oedipus complex.*

When this strong emotional bond is not broken and redirected, sons remain attached to their mothers, and daughters to their fathers, for their entire lives. Such relationships have been portrayed vividly in the Greek tragedies *Oedipus Rex* and *Elektra;* in the writings of D. H. Lawrence, especially his novel *Sons and Lovers;* and in Eugene O'Neill's *Mourning Becomes Electra.*

The emotional attachments of children to their parents account for a large number of men who remain bachelors and women who go through life as spinsters. In cases of strong father fixation, a daughter may never marry, or she may marry her father symbolically by marrying someone who reminds her of her father in some way. Sons who are strongly attached to their mothers spend their lives looking for mother substitutes. In a popular song of some years ago there is the line, "I want a girl, just like the girl, who married dear old dad." In other words, he wants a girl just like "dear old mom." It is no mere coincidence that this song is a sentimental favorite with male quartets.

Similarly, parents frequently become involved in pathological emotional attachments to their children. In Lesley Storm's drama *Black Chiffon*, a mother has such an intense attachment to her son that when she discovered that her son's fiancée wears a black nightgown, she is driven by unconscious forces to steal a similar nightgown from a shop. This theft was motivated by her deep-seated desire to compete with the girl for her son's affection and at the same time to be punished for her forbidden unconscious wishes.

FATHER KILLS COED DAUGHTER
ON DAY OF HER WEDDING

Wichita, Kan., June 12—Saturday was to have been the wedding day for a 17-year-old University of Wichita coed. But at 8:30 a.m. the bride-to-be was shot and killed by her father, who then killed his pet dog and himself because "the load is more than I can bear."

DAUGHTER "TOO SWEET": FATHER SLAYS HER

Los Angeles, Sept. 18—A father shot and killed his 21-year-old daughter, police said today, because she was "too sweet to leave alone in this big round world without her daddy." Then he turned the gun on himself. Police said the father left a note reading: "Don't blame anyone but myself. . . . Play the record *Irene, Irene* for me." They added that the daughter's name was Irene.

The tragedies of these two fathers and the daughters to whom they were emotionally attached are reenacted, in a more subtle way, in homes throughout the land. Many young mothers flirt with their sons and treat them as if they were their dates. Sometimes the maternal coquetry is a means for making a husband jealous, sometimes it is a device for making the mother feel young again, and sometimes it is because the mother finds qualities in her son that are lacking in her husband. One of the most brilliant portrayals of the seducer-mother is found in the novel *Portnoy's Complaint* (Roth, 1969). Here the mother continues to call her thirty-three-year-old son "Lover" in front of his father.

Parents learn to react, at an unconscious level, in rather characteristic ways. The mother is inclined to be somewhat hostile toward her daughter, and the father is likely to deprecate his son by "taking the wind out of his sails." The father knows intuitively that his son is a serious rival in the affections of his wife, and the mother realizes that her daughter is her rival with the husband. More than a few fathers have said to their daughters, "If I were a young man, I'd marry you in a minute!"

Fathers are traditionally critical of their daughter's boy friends, and "the father of the bride" is a traumatic and rejected figure. Similarly, few mothers are enthusiastic about their son's girl friends. However, mothers can seldom wait to marry off their daughters and fathers are proud and happy to see their sons marry.

The emotional bond is so powerful that the taboo against *incest*, or sexual relations with close relatives, is one of the most widely invoked restrictions in the world. This barrier is needed because incestuous urges and strivings are powerful in the unconscious lives of all men and women. The strength of the incest motive is clearly seen in dreams. During sleep, the unconscious incestuous urges come to the surface. Sometimes, the urges become so insistent that they overwhelm the individual during waking life.

Freud assumed that the Oedipal relationship is normal and universal. Other experts have taken exception to this position. The neo-Freudians consider the relationship a neurotic one and neither normal nor universal. It is looked upon as a learned attitude fostered by the parents, not an outgrowth of the child's instinctive nature. Fathers and mothers sometimes lay the foundation for the problem by allowing children to witness sex scenes, by erotically tinged caresses, and by flirtatious and seductive attitudes toward children of the opposite sex. Leo Kanner, a pioneer authority in child psychiatry, said that the relationship is something that was "imposed" by Freud and his followers and not the result of observation of children.

The Latency Period

During later childhood there is a gradual repression of sexuality. Parents, teachers, church, and society exert pressure on the child by saying "naughty, naughty!" to his sex interests and activities. His perfectly natural sexual urges and desires are crushed and forced underground. As a result of this pressure from parents and others, the child learns to avoid sexuality. A daughter becomes upset because her mother smokes, or uses too much rouge or lipstick. A son is disturbed when he sees his father ogle a female clerk in a store. Such children become extremely critical of their parents.

It would be a mistake, however, to conclude that children are without sexual strivings during this period. The strivings and urges remain active, but in a less open way. It is at this time that the most serious conflicts take place between children and their parents. Parental control, no matter how wisely undertaken, inevitably results in a measure of hostility and aggression. Moreover, the problem of rivalry between brothers and sisters becomes increasingly important at this time of life.

The Genital Period

The final level of psychosexual development is one in which there is a reawakening of physiological sex urges at the time of puberty and early adolescence. During this period there are physical changes in the form of lowering of the voice, development of a typical male or female pattern of hair distribution on the body, redistribution of body fat, and menstruation in the female. It is also a time of the revival of infantile and childish interests in sex. Kissing games, petting, necking, dirty jokes, and masturbation again become prominent. Girls have crushes on one another, and on their female teachers. Boys join gangs and clubs. But as the girls and boys grow older, there is a gradual shift in interest to members of the opposite sex, and there is the beginning of heterosexual adjustment.

The first heterosexual relationships, however, tend to be of a narcissistic nature. "Puppy love" is really self-love. During adolescence, boys and girls are not interested unselfishly in members of the opposite sex. Each is more concerned with himself in the role of lover than with the beloved. Real heterosexuality does not develop until emotional attachments are shifted from one's own body image to a member of the opposite sex.

STRESS AND AGGRESSION

As in the case of sexuality, hostile and aggressive urges must be denied and hidden in our culture. The child learns early in life that aggression invites retaliation, loss of love, and disapproval. He learns that hostility is "wrong," especially when directed toward the people he loves.

One theory is that there is an inborn urge to be aggressive both toward ourselves and toward others. This primary aggression is regarded as an unlearned pattern in the human personality. It is a deep-rooted destructive force recognized in all cultures.

Learned aggression, sometimes called secondary or compensatory aggression, grows out of the frustrations people experience in their everyday living. It serves to reinforce and strengthen whatever aggressive tendencies are a part of the basic makeup. Compensatory aggression may be a reaction to feelings of inferiority, to sexual frustration, to physical illness, to special disabilities such as deafness, blindness, or malformation of the body, or to feelings of insecurity and inadequacy.

There is considerable disagreement among experts as to the relationship between violence on television programs and aggressive acting out among children and immature adults. One view is that the watching of violence is an outlet and that viewers of TV violence are less likely to be aggressive in other ways. Another view takes quite the opposite position. It holds that TV violence stimulates fantasies of aggression which may later be acted out. It seems probable that the daily fare of TV violence helps to desensitize children and adults in a way which makes them accept violence more readily. As a result, an increasingly higher level of aggression is tolerated in our society.

Experiments indicate that violence that is witnessed serves as a model which tends to increase aggression rather than to decrease it. The viewing of aggression does not seem to act as an outlet or safety valve which helps to reduce inner aggressive impulses. Quite the contrary. The more aggression that is observed, the stronger one's own aggression becomes (Berkowitz, 1968). Such findings bring into sharp question the rather commonly held view that one can reduce aggression by experiencing it vicariously.

The idea that violence breeds violence is further supported by a study covering three generations of families with abused children. This investigation indicated that a child who has been a victim of violence early in life has an increased potential for becoming a violent member of society in the future (Silver et al., 1969).

There is a possibility that the mere witnessing of violence may affect brain chemistry. Studies at the Memorial Research Center and Hospital of the University of Tennessee showed that groups of onlooker mice observing prolonged fighting among other mice showed a marked decrease in the level of the chemical norepinephrine in the brain and a consequent increase in aggressive behavior (Welch, 1969). Norepinephrine is involved in transmitting nerve impulses and in alerting behavior.

The amount of aggression a person is permitted to express and the way that aggression is expressed are determined to a considerable extent by the culture in which he lives. Some children feel no self-blame over aggression. They fight for their rights with clubs, knives, guns, and fists. The Pilaga Indians of South America go out of their way to encourage their children in acts of aggression. In other cultural groups, such as the Zuni, the Arapesh, and the Quakers, aggression has been forbidden or frowned upon. In every society, however, people have a certain amount of hostility and aggression that must be released. This hostility is expressed in three major ways: (1) directly, (2) indirectly, and (3) vicariously, or through sharing in some other person's aggressive behavior.

Direct Aggression

Hostility of the direct type may be expressed in physical action such as a fistfight, stealing, destroying property, and setting fires, or in such verbal action as scolding, swearing, and calling names. D. H. Lawrence, H. L. Mencken, Philip Wylie, and George Bernard Shaw are known for their incisive wit, their satire, irony, parody, or caricature. Their work is "sharp" and "razor-edged." There can be no doubt that their art has an aggressive purpose. Their inner hostility is expressed in the language they use.

Aggression toward others is begun during the early days of life. The angry and frustrated infant squirms, twists, and thrashes his arms and the legs. Later, it becomes more specific and takes the form of purposeful slapping, hitting, kicking, and biting. The hostile feelings of the child toward the parent are clearly seen in the case of a young woman who confided that, at the age of twelve, she had intensely hostile feelings toward her mother. "I had a horrible desire to kill my mother. I loved her but I wanted to kill her." In another case, a high school student killed his father and his mother with a rifle as they sat in their darkened living room, watching a Sunday night television show. The boy later said, "I loved them more than anything in the world. I don't know why I did it." Aggression toward the parents is reflected in the following entry in the diary of a disturbed adolescent: "Why could not Mother die? Dozens of people are dying all the time, thousands, so why not Mother and Father too. Life is very hard."

Clinical studies of aggressive delinquents suggest that hostility toward authority may be a matter of aggression that has been shifted from the parents to parent images or to persons who remind us (because of their power over us) of our parents. Early hostile feelings toward the parents may evolve into hostility toward any figure in authority. It is a common observation that many people resent anyone in a position of power or authority. Some students are hostile toward teachers, some workers are hostile toward the employer, and many otherwise docile citizens are hostile toward policemen and public officials. On the political level, revolution is an expression of mass hostility toward authority.

Parental aggression toward the child is also frequent. When the mind of a parent is troubled and in conflict, a child in the family is likely to suffer. Since children are weak, they become the victims of parental hostility and hatred. It may be the frown of the mother or a shout of criticism by the father. It may be shown by a spanking, by locking the child in a closet, by scolding, or by sending the youngster to bed without supper. With few exceptions, these actions of resentment and hostility condition the attitudes of the child toward the parents and authority.

Unspeakable cruelty to children by parents is a problem of major proportions. An authority at the Colorado Medical Center said, "More children under 5 die every year from injuries inflicted by a parent or guardian than from tuberculosis, whooping cough, polio, measles, diabetes, rheumatic fever and appendicitis combined" (Helfer, 1969). The same authority estimates that at least 60,000 children are willfully beaten, burned, smothered, and starved each year in the United States.

> Four-year-old Jody weighed only 17 pounds when she arrived at the University of Colorado Medical Center. Her skull was fractured, one arm and both hands were broken. All her life she had been beaten, starved and neglected by her parents. She was the victim of the "battered child syndrome." When the authorities became aware of the situation she was taken from her parents and placed in the hospital. Thereafter she showed a dramatic improvement, growing six inches during the six months after leaving the hospital (*Newsweek*, 1968).

Another common arena of aggression is marriage. The nature of the marital relationship in our culture leads inevitably to the frequent spilling over of inner hostilities. Husbands and wives spend a considerable portion of their lives learning to keep their aggressive impulses from flaring up, but even their best efforts are often in vain. They show their aggression in ways ranging from subtle words and gestures to punching, kicking, slapping, and killing. In classical mythology, the fifty sons of Aegyptus married the fifty daughters of Danaus, and all except one of the newly wedded husbands were murdered by their brides on the wedding night. Since that time, an alarming number of unsuspecting husbands and wives have had their lives brought to abrupt ends by mates whose inner hostilities got out of control.

The hostility of husbands and wives toward one another sometimes lasts to the grave and occasionally beyond. The inscription on a tombstone at Old Greyfriars, Edinburgh, reads:

> Here snug in grave my wife doth lie,
> Now she's at rest, and so am I.

And finally there is this brief line of aggressive sentimentality that a wife had inscribed on her husband's tombstone:

> Tears cannot restore him, therefore I weep.

Indirect Aggression

Considering the intensity of the aggressive impulses people carry around within themselves, it might appear remarkable that such institutions as marriage and the family, as well as other more or less permanent social groupings, have been able to survive. They have done so only because people learn so many indirect and socially approved means for satisfying hostile urges.

Early in life the child turns to veiled and camouflaged aggression. He learns to disguise his aggression in teasing. His hostility becomes more indirect. In a joking way the child tells the parent, "You look like a puppy dog," or "I'm going to tie your hands and feet," or "I'll run over you with my train." One child said, "I'm going to stuff you down the toilet." The naïve mother thought this remark was very clever indeed. She would have been shocked to learn how much the child really meant what he said.

When the child is unable to direct his hostility toward members of his own family, he learns to direct it elsewhere. The aggressive impulses in children are revealed in the gruesome stories they tell and in their sadistic play with toys and dolls. One youngster wrote the following letter to Santa Claus:

> *Dear Santa:*
> *Please send me two atom bombs, a couple of pistols and a good sharp knife.*

Some men learn to release their aggression by taking up boxing, wrestling, football, hockey, soccer, and other contact sports. There are definite psychological reasons for making such a choice. Satisfaction may be derived from being able to gratify the primitive urge to inflict pain on other people. It may be an outlet for the hostility which is bottled up in day-to-day living. There is the opportunity in these activities to satisfy aggressive needs by hitting, pulling, punching, and kicking the opponents.

Few people, however, find such expression for their feelings. Most people learn to reduce their hostility through activities that disguise the aggression. It has been suggested that one reason why golf, tennis, and baseball are so popular is that these activities are more socially acceptable forms of aggression. The player takes out his feelings against a ball, rather than against people. Mastering the ball may become a substitute for mastering other people.

The primitive aggressive urge may be disguised in other ways. Hunting and fishing are extremely popular hobbies, and for some people these activities may be acceptable ways of satisfying the need to dominate, to master, and to inflict pain. Occupational therapists in mental hospitals have observed that similar needs can be satisfied in crafts where pounding, jabbing, cutting, scraping, or tearing is required. Hobbies such as sewing, carving, metalwork, and leather craft also seem at times to relieve hostile feelings.

Aggressive urges are watered down even further in card playing. Here the physical form of the aggression has been entirely suppressed. Bridge, poker, gin rummy, canasta, and other card games contain an element of psychological aggression. People sometimes play in order to dominate other people. It may be a veiled expression of the urge to be powerful and masterful.

Another indirect form of aggression is wit and humor. Since one of the easiest ways to hurt people is to play mean jokes on them, the practical joke has become an established institution in our society. A person is hostile if he can get a laugh out of pulling a chair away when someone is about to sit down, pushing a friend into the pool, giving him a hotfoot, or making him look foolish. Some people get their biggest kicks out of humor of the aggressive type. Our everyday language is filled with phrases to describe this kind of humor. We talk about "poking fun," "giving a dig," "biting" humor, "sharp" wit, and "dying laughing."

We are being aggressive whenever we laugh at the embarrassment and misfortune of others. For most people there is nothing funny about an elderly man falling down the stairs and breaking his hip; yet the daughter of a man who did just this could not control her giggles while she waited for his ambulance. Deep down, this young woman probably had a wide streak of aggression in her.

The night before Halloween, a group of children in Florida were playing "trick or treat." One neighbor had a special treat for them. She heated pennies in the frying pan, and tossed them on the floor on the front porch. The children scrambled happily for the coins, but a moment later they were screaming with pain. The tips of their fingers were swollen with blisters. The woman thought it was a great joke; but not the parents of the children. They had the jokester hauled into court the next day.

A particularly heartless example of this kind of aggression took place in Los Angeles when someone with a twisted sense of humor telephoned a number of people and gasped out stories of a sudden death to close relatives. One woman answered her phone to hear a feminine voice say, "Your husband has just been killed in a traffic crash at Sepulveda Boulevard and Sherman Way." The wife rushed to the intersection only to learn that there had been no crash. She was so distraught that she collapsed and had to be taken to a hospital. Later, she learned that her husband was safe in San Diego where he had gone on a business trip.

Aggressive humor is so widespread that novelty companies have made a fortune out of such items as exploding cigars, sneezing powder, stench bombs, and a hundred different kinds of artificial bugs, worms, mice, and snakes designed to scare the wits out of unsuspecting victims. And at conventions, water squirters and electric shockers are thought to be hilariously funny.

Teasing is another learned form of aggressive humor. Although it is usually done in a spirit of affection, deep in the unconscious teasing may have another meaning. It may mean that affection is mixed with hostility. A person sometimes teases because it is a disguised (and socially acceptable) way of releasing aggression toward others. For this reason, playful teasing often ends in an argument, a fight, or an accident in which someone is hurt.

Vicarious Aggression

The vast majority of men and women are content to satisfy their need for aggressiveness in a vicarious, or substitute, fashion. They release their aggressive impulses by watching other people being aggressive. This is one of the reasons why spectator sports are so very popular. Being a spectator makes it possible to release feelings of aggression without danger to oneself.

Boxing, wrestling, football, hockey, and other contact sports draw large crowds because they allow the fan to express his aggression in complete safety and comfort. Shouting insults at a referee or an umpire, or at members of an opposing team, is an exhilarating experience. People sometimes enjoy the opportunity to blow off steam and release their emotional tension more than they enjoy the event itself.

Any kind of fighting and aggression holds an hypnotic-like fascination. Many people thrill to see the blood pouring from the boxer's nose, they shout themselves hoarse while the fullback crashes through the line, and they squirm with pleasure as the look of agony increases on the wrestler's face. They will watch anything from a bullfight to Siamese fighting fish. And in each of these sports, the spectator is quite safe. He is not threatened by the aggression, yet he experiences it and feels himself a part of it.

One of the reasons why cartoon comedies are so successful is that there is so much aggression on the screen. The mice, cats, dogs, and ducks are forever kicking, pulling, hitting, shooting, twisting, cutting, biting, and tormenting or being tormented. Audiences roar with laughter when the villain gets hit in the face with a slamming door, when he is mangled in a cement mixer, or when he gets his tail caught in the electric fan. Similarly, the prevalence of violence on television shows is, in part, a response to the aggressive needs of the viewers.[3]

STRESS AND STATUS

Another important source of stress in our culture is the attempt to satisfy the urge to be powerful. Part of this urge grows out of the original weakness and inferiority of the child. It is a reaction and a protest against being at the mercy of the superior mental and physical prowess of the adult world. Children struggle to assert themselves, to gain recognition, to achieve, and to be successful.

Later in life these early needs are continued because the society in which we live is a highly competitive one in which the materially successful man is rewarded. Consequently, for many people life is a constant struggle to be with the "in" group, to belong to "the" club, to be "upper crust," and to be "top dog." Such an individual seeks the highest possible status in his social group. A worker in a large industrial plant struggled for several years to change his job to one that paid only 2 cents an hour more, because the new job was of a type that would give him status. When he finally landed the job, he was accepted in employee circles where previously he had been excluded.

Inferiority is first felt when the child learns that he is physically, intellectually, and socially inferior to the adults who are taking care of him. These feelings are further reinforced by teachers and others who are in a position to discipline the child. Defective organs or limbs, short stature, poor general health, sensory impairments such as deafness or blindness, birthmarks, lameness, crooked teeth, poor vision, stuttering, and similar conditions place many children at a further disadvantage.

Far more important than real physical, social, and intellectual inferiorities are imagined inferiorities. Most people feel inferior because of conditions that either do not exist or are so unimportant that they are of little interest or concern to anyone else. Many young boys feel that the sex organs they have are too small. They spend considerable time peeking at other boys in order to allay their secret fears. To one degree or another, this feeling of sexual inferiority is carried over to adult life by many men. As a result, they are inclined to worry about their capacities and to attempt in various ways to prove their masculinity.

In a somewhat related way, the young girl may develop feelings of inferiority when she

---

[3]Students interested in more detailed exploration of the problems of aggression are referred to *Aggression and Defense* (University of California Press, 1967) edited by C. D. Clemente and D. B. Lindsley, *Aggression* (University of Chicago Press, 1958) by J. P. Scott; and *On Aggression* (Harcourt, Brace, 1963) by Konrad Lorenz.

realizes that the boy has a penis and she has none. She may come to the conclusion that somehow she has been deprived of what rightfully belongs to her. In such cases, she may feel inferior to, and envious of, the male throughout her life.

The importance of status, and the prevalence of feelings of inferiority and inadequacy, are reflected in the following comments by college students:

I was recently married for a period of three months. Being a person considered by my community of sound judgment and character, I am afraid that I am being criticized for leaving my husband after so short a trial. I know in my own mind that I was right, but I fear they will consider my behavior erratic, and that I will lose a position I once held in their minds.

I am always afraid that I shall not succeed in whatever I undertake to do. I feel that what I do or say—especially what I say—is inadequate. I am afraid of possible ridicule and criticism.

I have a strong conviction of my own inferiority. This conviction may arise from being the only girl in a large family, whose other members always seemed to me to be outstanding.

My greatest fear is failure. This does not pertain to school work especially, but rather to what I shall do later. That is, I wish to do great things; but I fear I shall fail without having tried.

A variety of factors contributes to feelings of inferiority. One of these factors is the order of birth. Each time a new baby arrives in the family, the security and status of the other children are threatened. The status of a middle child is the worst, since he is threatened by his younger, as well as his older, brothers and sisters. An only child, while less likely to feel inferior in early childhood, sometimes finds it more difficult to face competition later in life.

The level of aspiration is another important source of inferiority. Many children are encouraged to adopt unrealistic goals in life. Parents often have expectations the child simply cannot hope to meet. In most cases, the parent is attempting to rid himself of his own feelings of inferiority by expecting the child to accomplish what the parent was not able to do himself.

One father expects his son to be a star athlete, another wants his son to be a business genius, a surgeon, or a lawyer. A mother hopes to see her daughter be popular, marry into a higher social group, or go on the stage. These are cases of the projection of the ambitions of the parent onto the child. Unfortunately, these projections are often made with little regard for the interests or the abilities of the child. Since the goals set by the parents are unattainable, the child is doomed to a life of failure, frustration, and inferiority.

Even under the most favorable conditions, each individual must contend with feelings of inferiority. People wish they were more popular or better looking, had more money, were better known in the community, were more highly respected, were smarter, had a larger house in a better neighborhood, drove a more expensive car, or had a better job. Feelings of inferiority are observed at every level in our society. A study showed that the majority of Harvard students were bothered by inferiority feelings in spite of the fact that as a group they were above average socially, financially, and intellectually.

People learn to handle their feelings of inferiority in different ways. Some simply give up and withdraw from competition. They avoid other people by insulating themselves from them. In this way they have no one with whom to compare themselves, and feelings of inferiority are minimized. Others learn to deal with inferiority through daydreams. The clerk dreams of marrying the daughter of his boss, the unpopular girl dreams of marrying a movie star, and the medical student imagines himself a great surgeon.

No one likes to think of himself as a Caspar Milquetoast. Yet each individual is troubled by the lurking fear that in one way or another he does not measure up, that he is less fortunate than others, or that the world has not rewarded him adequately. William Cook, one of the most vicious desperadoes of our century, had the legend H-A-R-D L-U-C-K tattooed on his knuckles.

STRESS AND DEPENDENCY

Dependency needs and the desire to be independent are other sources of psychological stress. The human infant is completely dependent upon the mother for satisfaction of such vital biological requirements as nourishment and protection from the environment. It would be unable to live without the care and support of a mother or mother-substitute. In lower animals, complete independence from the parents is frequently reached after a relatively short span of life. But the period of dependency in humans extends from birth through infancy, childhood, and adolescence. These years make up 25 percent or more of the entire life of the individual.

Because of the prolonged and necessary dependency during the first quarter of the human life span, it is not easy to overcome the attitudes and behavior patterns based upon dependency. Many men and women retain exaggerated dependency needs which influence their thinking, their feelings, and their behavior throughout their lives.

The conflict between firmly established dependency needs and the contradictory desire to be free and independent often results in serious frustration and conflict. Every individual wants to live his own life, but at the same time he has learned to depend upon others for support, approval, and assistance. It is a rare person who is able to function in a completely self-sufficient manner. And those people who insist upon their complete independence are likely to be considered eccentric or worse.

An example of the conflict between dependency needs and the desire to be independent is seen during adolescence. Boys and girls who have learned to be dependent upon their parents suddenly gain a new freedom and a measure of independence. The adolescent begins to perceive himself as an individual who is able to function on his own. Parents, however, continue to perceive the adolescent as a dependent child. The usual result is a sharp conflict between parents and their adolescent sons and daughters. Even more important is the emotional stress which builds up inside the adolescent as a result of the frustration of having the adult role postponed.

The conflict between dependency and the urge to be independent is also seen in marriage relationships. Here, individuals of widely differing temperaments, interests, attitudes, inclinations, and biological makeups must learn to make the many adjustments necessary to achieve and maintain a reasonably stable and harmonious human relationship. One of the most difficult of these adjustments is the relinquishing of independent action in the interest of marital harmony. This problem is not a critical one for men and women with strong dependency components in their personalities, since the marriage relationship encourages and reinforces dependency. However, when one or both partners to the marriage have firmly established needs to be independent, the marriage itself is likely to be threatened, or a high level of stress will be built up in the husband or wife.

One type of psychological disturbance growing out of a pattern of excessive dependency is the passive personality. While passivity itself is not abnormal, excessively passive reactions may interfere with adjustment to a considerable degree. In some cases the realization of one's own passivity leads to a compensating aggressiveness.

As in conflict generated by sexual needs, hostile and aggressive impulses, and the need for status, the problems related to feelings of dependency and the need to be independent can be important sources of psychological stress. When this stress becomes difficult or impossible to handle, the result may be some form of personality disorganization.

GUILT AND ANXIETY

As a result of the feelings of stress involving sexuality, hostility, status, and dependency, a characteristic emotional state is generated within the human organism. This emotional state consists of a generalized psychophysiological tension called *anxiety* combined with the psychological attitude of *guilt*.

ANXIETY

W. H. Auden's poem *Age of Anxiety* inspired Leonard Bernstein to write his Symphony No. 2 for piano and orchestra. Each of these sensitive geniuses was attempting to capture, one in poetry and the other in music, something of the underlying uneasiness and apprehension that pervades our modern world.

The early view of anxiety, advanced during the

1800s, was largely neurological. Anxiety was regarded as an overexcitation of the nervous centers, as the action of normal stimuli on pathologically overexcitable centers, or as the action of pathological stimuli, such as intestinal toxins, on normal centers. It was believed rather generally that a constitutionally weakened nervous system was the cause of morbid anxiety.

The psychogenic approach showed that it was not necessary to assume a damaged nervous system or pathological stimuli. It demonstrated that anxiety can be induced by the action of normal physiological stimuli on a normal nervous system. The only pathological factor, according to this view, is the way the individual perceives the social situation responsible for the stimulation.

One of the problems associated with the concept of anxiety is the necessity to differentiate it from fear. While this differentiation is not always easy or even possible, fear is a relatively well-defined response to a real or imagined danger, and anxiety is more likely to be vague, diffuse, and undefined. Fear is a learned reaction to external events. Anxiety, a more chronic state, is produced usually by the conditioning of physiological reactions.

Another problem involves the difference between normal anxiety and pathological anxiety. The first occurs when the reasons for the anxiety are obvious. The second occurs when the reasons are not apparent. When we are told that another war may be on the way, real anxiety sweeps the country. Everyone can see the threat that lies ahead. But when a person is troubled and worried and there seems to be no reason for it, he is experiencing neurotic anxiety. Most of the anxiety that grows out of unconscious conflict belongs to this latter class.

Anxiety-arousing stimuli, whether products of the external environment or inner conflict, serve as stress situations. In this way, psychological stress arouses the organism through the activity of the hypothalamus-pituitary relationship and its influence on the autonomic nervous system and the endocrine system. Since anxiety is a basic undifferentiated emotion, the physiological changes are essentially the same for fear and anger and for flight and fight. Whenever the security of the individual is threatened, the

sympathetic segment of the autonomic nervous system swings into action. It takes over from the parasympathetic system, which functions when there is no danger.

The emergency changes are of various kinds. The heart speeds up, blood pressure increases, and the pulse is quickened. In extreme anxiety palpitation of the heart and pain in the chest may be experienced. Another anxiety symptom is related to respiration. The breathing rate is increased, and there may be frequent and deep sighing. In severe cases there may be feelings of choking and suffocation and temporary cessation of breathing.

Digestion is also disturbed during anxiety. Ordinarily there is a loss of appetite, which may be complicated by nausea or vomiting and by diarrhea or constipation. Patients describe their feelings by saying that their "insides are turning over," that their stomach is "cooking," or that there is a "sinking feeling in the pit of the stomach." A change in kidney function may be reflected in frequent urination.

There are also changes in muscle activity and in the sense organs. Hands and fingers tremble, the patient shakes and shudders, or he experiences a sudden weakness which makes it difficult for him to stand or walk. He may have peculiar sensations which lead him to pick at the skin of his hands and fingers, or he may develop such nervous habits as clearing his throat, coughing, sniffing, or wrinkling his forehead. Stuttering and stammering are frequently based upon feelings of anxiety.

The glandular changes associated with anxiety are responsible for profuse sweating, for clammy hands and feet, and for alternating flashes of cold and heat. Internally, the liver secretes more sugar, and more adrenalin is released into the bloodstream. In most cases, physical symptoms are present without the individual realizing what the real trouble is. He complains simply that he is "tense," "nervous," "jumpy," or "on edge." Yet he cannot say what it is that makes him feel as he does. Anxiety permeates and influences the entire body. It is difficult for the individual to comprehend what is taking place.

On the psychological side, anxiety is closely related to everyday worry. Mild anxiety is experienced as a vague uneasiness, more intense anxiety as apprehension, and severe anxiety as dread. The psychological pattern of anxiety, like the physiological pattern, is vague, diffuse, and difficult to isolate and identify. Frequently there are feelings of depression, pessimism, gloom, inadequacy, inferiority, and helplessness.

Inability to sleep, terrifying dreams, and nightmares are other ways in which anxiety is expressed. Those who are troubled with this condition spend their nights turning and tossing, punching their pillows, living through horrible dreams, and awakening at the slightest sound. Most people have experienced nocturnal anxiety in the form of nightmares and night terrors. At puberty, when anxiety is at a high level, nightmares are extremely common. Anxiety attacks which occur during sleep consist of an incomprehensible dread or an overmastering fear and terror. Dreams of being buried alive under a huge pile of rocks, being caught in the coils of a large snake, drowning, or perishing in a fire are of this type. The dreams may be filled with wild animals, ghostly phantoms, and unearthly sounds. The victim finds himself unable to scream or to cry out; or he thinks he is screaming, but actually the only sounds are stifled moans. These nocturnal anxiety attacks seem vividly real, even after awakening.

Anxiety is aroused by physical injury, disease, change to a new environment, repeated failures, loss of love, and any situation in which the demands of the physical, emotional, social, or intellectual environment become too stressful. Birth may be the first anxiety-provoking situation because it is the first important stress the individual must learn to face. The necessity for a new and independent life, the metabolic and chemical adjustments that must be made, and the shock of separation from the body of the mother are highly stressful. While the embryo is in the uterus of the mother, it is taken care of completely. It is fed automatically, and elimination occurs through the body of the mother. The maternal uterus is a warm, pleasant, and completely comfortable "biological heaven."

At the time of birth, this security is shattered. Descending through the birth canal, the infant is squeezed, pulled, and tugged. Then the cord is cut, and he is on his own. The quiet world of the uterus has been relinquished for a world of strange noises, smells, bright lights, and temperature changes. Birth is a profound shock, both physiologically and psychologically.

While birth may very well be the first important separation in life, later separations are also profoundly stressful. Weaning, leaving the mother to take the first step, leaving home to go to school, leaving the family to marry, and finally death are forms of stress to which most people learn to react with considerable anxiety. Life may be considered a series of critical and anxiety-provoking incidents.

Anxiety plays two major roles in the dynamics of personality organization and disorganization. First, it serves as a signal; second, it is a symptom. Anxiety as a signal alerts the individual to impending danger. It enables the individual to set into motion the defensive and adjustive processes which will serve to protect him against the inner threats. Anxiety as a symptom is an expression of the breakdown of the defensive operations in the personality. In this role, anxiety becomes the basic symptom of a number of personality disturbances.

GUILT

Of the many different psychological reactions related to anxiety, guilt is potentially the most dangerous and destructive. It is a form of stress present to one degree or another in everyone. While guilt feelings are closer to the surface of consciousness in some than others, no one is completely guilt free. These feelings frequently are a product of fantasy life and grow out of an uneasy conscience.

> But they whose guilt within their bosoms lie
> Imagine every eye beholds their blame.
> William Shakespeare

Guilt feelings are portrayed in the literature and folklore of a great many different cultures. A classic example of guilt is seen in Shakespeare's *Macbeth* in which the two principal characters suffer intense guilt reactions as a result of having murdered King Duncan. Macbeth betrays his guilt feelings by his hallucinations; Lady Macbeth reveals her guilt in the sleepwalking scene in which she symbolically washes her hands to rid herself of the guilt.

In the Old Testament there are a number of examples of the symbolic nature of handwashing. In Isaiah 1:15 we read: "Your hands are full of blood. Wash ye, make you clean." And in Jeremiah 2:22: "For though thou wash thee with nitre, and take thee much soap, yet thine iniquity is marked before me, saith the Lord God." The ceremony of immersion and baptism is based on the idea of cleansing the sinner of his guilt.

Guilt feelings are learned reactions instilled by the teaching of parents, the church, the school, and the community. From the early years, children are told in one way or another that they are naughty, wicked, bad, or shameless. Everything possible is done to create guilt feelings. The idea, of course, is to curb and control the primitive animal nature of man. Sören Kierkegaard, a distinguished Danish philosopher, emphasized that guilt has constructive aspects in that it guides the individual and keeps the more violent tendencies of the personality in check.

The major source of childhood guilt in our culture is related to sexual interests. Adults react to such interests (which they themselves harbor and express in their own guilty fashion) by teaching the child to feel fearful and humiliated. They blame, condemn, find fault, become incensed, and fail to understand. And so their guilt is passed on to their children, and the children's guilt will, in turn, be passed on to their children.

In other cultures, feelings of guilt based on sexual interest are frequently much less severe, if indeed they are present at all. Among the Hopi and Navaho Indians, adults engage in sexual play with their children without embarassment. The children feel free to do the same. The result is that there is no shame or guilt connected with such behavior.

Guilt is associated with the expression of all those urges most frowned upon in our society. People learn to feel guilty not only about their sexual needs and their erotic experiences, but also about their hostile and aggressive urges and other basic impulses. The most damaging conflicts are those in which the feelings of guilt are the most intense.

Some people have little or no sense of personal guilt. There are those who, in the eyes of society, are guilty of delinquency or crime and yet have no feeling of guilt. Other people may not be guilty of anything, yet have overwhelming feelings of guilt. When a person has guilt feelings for something he has not done, it may mean that he is blaming himself for wishing he had done it. The blame is for the wish, not the deed. In Dostoevski's novel *The Brothers Karamazov,* Dmitri demands that he be punished for his father's murder, not because he was guilty of the crime but because he had wished for his father's death and therefore felt guilty.

Guilt arises in a variety of situations. Some people feel guilty whenever they enjoy themselves. Others have guilt feelings aroused simply by looking at such signs as "No Smoking" and "Keep Off the Grass." In fact, any tabooed activity is likely to arouse feelings of guilt. Reading a banned book, engaging in a forbidden affair, going on a drinking spree, cheating at cards or golf, and spending too much money are forms of behavior that may lead to loss of self-respect. When the image of one's self is threatened, guilt and anxiety soon put in their appearance.

Feelings of guilt vary in intensity from one person to another. Some people learn to live with their guilt by discounting it, others by devoting their lives to expiation. But in a great many people, guilt is a source of constant psychological irritation. Some people are not directly aware of their guilt, nor do they realize that many of their actions are attempts to rid themselves of guilt feelings.

Mourning customs are one of the ways through which people express their guilt. In our culture, mourning is more or less limited to weeping, wearing black mourning clothes, and shunning social activities. The guilt feelings are more strongly reinforced in certain other cultures, where mourning rites consist in serious personal deprivations and often in self-inflicted injuries.

Guilt is such a powerful force in our society, and is so widely recognized as such, that institutionalized means for reducing the tension and anxiety associated with guilt feelings have been devised. A well-known saying, "Confession is good for the soul," is psychologically sound—so sound, in fact, that the technique of confession is used to great advantage by such differently oriented groups and individuals as the Catholic

Church, the religious revivalist, and the psychiatrist in his consulting room.

One way in which the power and lasting effect of feelings of guilt is demonstrated is by the conscience funds that have become a part of many companies. A guilt-ridden man in Minneapolis paid $110 for a $5 ride he had taken nearly half a century earlier. He wrote the following letter of explanation to the Great Northern Railway:

Gentlemen:

Many years ago when a youngster of high school age, I stole a ride of about two hundred miles in a box-car of one of your trains. A few years later I rode your coach train one station farther than my ticket called for. This has troubled my conscience all these years (47 of them). Here is payment for the rides with 6 per cent compound interest, and asking to be forgiven for the long delay.

Some psychoanalysts believe that there is a universal unconscious urge to confess forbidden impulses. It has been suggested that this urge stems from a desire to be punished and so to relieve feelings of guilt and anxiety. For example, a young boy was in the habit of stealing a few small coins from his mother's purse in the morning before he went to school. The mother never found out about it, but the boy felt guilty about what he had done. When his report card came, he changed his high grades to low ones, so that his father would punish him. He could not bring himself to admit the stealing, so he lied about his report card in order to be punished. In this way, he attempted to rid himself of his guilt feelings.

One of the most dramatic expressions of guilt was the case of seventeen-year-old William Heirens of Chicago who, after murdering a young woman, left a message scrawled in lipstick on the mirror saying: "For heaven's sake, catch me before I kill more. I cannot control myself." A month later, he abducted a six-year-old girl and dismembered her body.

Guilt feelings are also expressed by individuals who confess to crimes they have not committed. Some years ago in California, a young model and movie extra was the the victim of a sex slaying that came to be known as the Black Dahlia murder. Since that time more than twenty-five men and women have confessed that they committed the unsolved crime.

It may also be possible to satisfy the unconscious need for punishment through hobbies and recreational activities. The best example of a self-punishing hobby is gambling. A well-known actor was a frequent visitor at a gambling establishment near Hollywood. He lost many thousands of dollars over a period of a few months. He told his friends it was just a hobby, but it was discovered that there was more to it than that. The actor had cheated a friend out of an important part in a new picture. His gambling was a form of self-punishment. The only way he could get rid of his feelings of guilt was by losing his earnings at the gambling table.

Throughout history, one of the strongest motivating forces for religious conversion and religious revivals has been an accumulating sense of guilt. From the time of Peter the Hermit to Mary Baker Eddy, the success of the religious revival has been due in large part to the revivalist's ability to bring guilt feelings close to the threshold of consciousness. The Reformation, the Puritan movement, the Wesleyan revival in England, the Great Awakening in the United States, and many similar movements were due largely to guilt feelings engendered by the culture.

Origen, one of the early Christian church fathers, mutilated himself by castration so that he could escape temptation while teaching religion to mixed classes of men and women. Another religious leader fainted while preaching a sermon. It was found that he was wearing a coarse undershirt with dozens of small fish-hooks sewed inside. These hooks were caught in his flesh, and the self-torture had caused him to faint. The mortification of the flesh had been undertaken as a form of self-punishment.

Ritual self-punishment is common in many cultures. The Skopsi of Russia was a sect founded in the middle of the eighteenth century. The men castrated themselves and beat themselves with whips. Early in the nineteenth century, the sect became popular among women. They allowed themselves to be whipped, and many had their breasts amputated so that they would be less of a temptation to men. Today, the Penitantes of New Mexico go into the canyons during the Easter season and carry out religiously motivated rites of self-punishment. Some of the cultists have themselves nailed to wooden crosses; others wear heavy chains and crowns of thorns.

The Hindu fakirs induce curious and painful self-injuries by holding a hand closed until the nails grow through the palm and out the back of the hand, by staring at the sun until they become blind, sitting or reclining on boards studded with pointed nails, scorching themselves in front of blazing hot fires, standing on one leg day and night, and performing other activities designed to rid themselves of their guilt.

Guilt feelings are frequently seen in mental patients. One patient stopped her physician in the hall every day and said, "Everybody is sick because of me. I am to blame for everything. I ought to die." Another patient asked that she be put in a furnace. She repeated over and over that she was a sinner and that she should be sent to hell to burn for her sins.

The most direct expression of self-punishment is suicide. There are more than twenty thousand successful suicides in the United States each year, and for every successful suicide there are a great many abortive attempts. While there are many possible reasons for wanting to destroy oneself, a feeling of guilt is basic to all such actions.[4]

At the beginning of the century the suicide rate was 11.3 per 100,000 population, but by 1915 it increased to 17.9, a rise of 58 percent in fifteen years. During the period surrounding our entry into World War I, the rate declined steadily, reaching a low point in 1920 of 11.5. Over the next few years the rate increased slowly, reaching 18.6—the highest in this century—during the depression year of 1932. In the later depression years the rate dropped slowly, and it continued to decrease during World War II, reaching a new low of 9.6 in 1957. From this low point it has risen slightly to about 11.0 per 100,000 population in 1970 (NIMH, 1970).

To meet the growing problem of suicide among

Some Facts about Suicide

Suicide is the tenth highest cause of death among United States adults.

It is the third highest cause of death in our peacetime army.

It is the third highest cause in the fifteen- to nineteen-year-old age group.

It is the third highest cause of death on college campuses.

The rate of suicide increases as you go west in the United States.

Suicide is more common among males than females (except on the West Coast).

Whites have a higher rate of suicide than blacks.

There were more than 100 suicide prevention centers in operation in 1970.

---

all age groups, cities throughout the nation are establishing suicide prevention centers to meet the emergencies created by suicide threats and attempts. The center in Los Angeles answered nearly 7,000 calls in one recent year from potential suicides, their families, friends, and neighbors.[5]

COPING WITH STRESS

Each individual strives continually to protect himself from his feelings of anxiety and guilt. To do this, he makes use of a variety of psychological defenses, or ways of reacting. These techniques,

---

[4]*Bulletin of Suicidology* Published by the Center for Studies of Suicide Prevention, National Institute of Mental Health. The purpose of the publication is to facilitate the exchange of information in the field of suicidology and to provide abstracts of the recent literature on suicide and suicide prevention. Available from the Superintendent of Documents, U.S. Government Printing Office, Washington, D.C. 20402.

[5]The problems of guilt and anxiety are dealt with by E. P. Levitt in *The Psychology of Anxiety* (Bobbs-Merrill, 1967); Rollo May in *The Meaning of Anxiety* (Ronald, 1950); Harold Basowitz and others in *Anxiety and Stress* (McGraw-Hill, 1955); Walter Garre's *Basic Anxiety: A New Psychobiological Concept* (Philosophical Library, 1962); and *Shame and Guilt: A Psychoanalytic and a Cultural Study* (Thomas, 1953) by Gerhart Piers and Milton Singer.

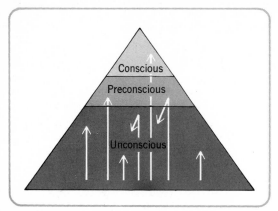

Figure 4.10 *The basic repression model in which unacceptable impulses are kept below the threshold of consciousness.*

which are largely unconscious, are used to reduce or eliminate the tension of anxiety and to allay the gnawing pangs of guilt. In addition to protecting the individual from often intolerable feelings of guilt and anxiety, the defenses permit him to maintain an internal steady state or homeostasis. This balance makes possible a continuation of adaptation to the physical world and adjustment to the psychosocial world.

The two major overt defenses are (1) fight and (2) flight. In the first of these defenses, the individual learns to control his guilt and anxiety through hostile and aggressive behavior. One way to protect oneself from the danger is to destroy the source of the danger. The individual strikes out against his environment. He seeks to overcome his anxiety by destroying its source. Much of the hostile and aggressive behavior in the world can be explained as attempts on the part of individuals, or groups of individuals, to control their anxiety.

The second form of overt defense is flight. Just as one attempts to control anxiety through fighting back, it is also possible to reduce anxiety through running away. Flight is the avoidance of guilt and anxiety by avoiding situations which arouse those feelings. People who use this defense become passive and withdrawn. At the slightest indication of conflict, they retreat from the situation arousing it. These individuals are the escapists. They are the ones who bury their heads in the sand. Excessive use of this defense has its own damaging effects upon the personality.

In addition to the overt defenses, there are a number of internal defenses which operate to protect the personality. Among the more important of these defense mechanisms are (1) repression, (2) substitution, (3) rationalization, (4) projection, (5) identification, (5) compensation, (7) reaction formation, (8) fantasy, (9) disengagement, (10) regression, and (11) sublimation.

REPRESSION

The psychological process of *repression* is one of the most important of all defenses. By means of repression, the inner conflict at the unconscious level is not permitted to reach the level of consciousness. The unconscious life of each individual is made up of troublesome urges, strivings, and impulses which are constantly seeking to be expressed. There is a critical, selective process which allows some urges to be expressed while others are held in check. At any given moment an individual does not express all the urges he carries about with him. He expresses only a select few. The rest are controlled by the powerful forces of repression.

Although repression is carried on automatically and unconsciously, there are conscious forces supporting the process. The conscious part of this controlling mechanism is the *conscience,* or set of attitudes having moral overtones. When the conscience bothers a person, he has become aware of the struggle between his unconscious impulses and the code of ethics and morals he has adopted.

Repression is particularly important as a defense mechanism in patients with personality disturbances. While it is true that all people learn to repress their impulses to one degree or another, the patient with a psychogenic emotional difficulty is probably using repression to an exaggerated degree. The basis of the difficulty in such cases is that critical experiences have been relegated to the unconscious, where they are bottled up and held in check by the process of repression. In a great many cases, the repressed experiences involve sexuality and aggression since these two phases of behavior are most likely to be regarded as unacceptable in our culture.

Suppression, which is sometimes confused with

repression, is a defensive maneuver by means of which the individual consciously attempts to push disturbing thoughts and feelings out of mind. It is not unusual for people to seek to forget their troubles and the unpleasantness of life by losing themselves in work, by becoming involved in needless activities, or by falling in love.

SUBSTITUTION

The defense mechanism of substitution is a common one and is used freely by most people in their efforts to maintain personality stability. Through substitution, the individual learns to overcome anxiety related to stress by seeking alternative goals and gratifications. Life is filled with unfulfilled longings, unrequited loves, and thwarted plans and ambitions. To protect himself from disappointment, the individual learns to seek substitute satisfactions. While substitution is used as a defense mechanism by everyone in the normal course of events, the patient with a personality disturbance is likely to distort or exaggerate this form of defense.

Among children and adolescents, substitution may be the source of such undesirable habits as nail biting, nose picking, and pulling at the skin of the hands and fingers. These actions may be substitutes for masturbation, and while the solution may seem more acceptable than the underlying problem, the behavior remains undesirable. More serious forms of substitution are found in delinquent acting-out behavior. The adolescent girl who does not find the love and affection she requires in her home is likely to seek it in sexual activity. The alarming increase in illegitimacy, particularly among teenagers, is in part a reflection of the frustration of personal needs and the attempt to satisfy these needs through sexual relationships. Many other forms of juvenile delinquency can be explained in terms of misguided attempts at substitution.

Adult personality disturbances are also based in many cases upon the unhealthy use of substitution as a defensive measure. Some young mothers attempt to reduce stress by accepting a child as an emotional substitute for the husband. Such substitutions are not unusual when the wife is thwarted in any significant way by the husband. In such cases, the emotional attachment is withdrawn from the husband and centered on the child. Substitutions of this kind are observed frequently in our culture and are damaging not only to the emotional life of the child but also to the stability of the marriage. Many of the problems of marriage are direct results of the inability of husbands and wives to seek adequate substitutions when faced with the inevitable frustrations of the marital relationship. Drugs and alcohol also may be substitute goals when real-life goals become difficult or unattainable. Similarly, criminal behavior, sexual deviancy, and other unacceptable forms of adult behavior may sometimes be substitution behavior symptomatic of underlying personality difficulties.

RATIONALIZATION

Rationalization is a defense mechanism by means of which a person reduces stress by justifying his deficiencies to himself and to others. It is a form of self-deception and mental camouflage. People make excuses and formulate fictitious arguments to convince themselves that their behavior is not so absurd and illogical as it actually is.

Aesop's fable "The Fox and the Grapes" is a good example of rationalization. In this fable, a fox who was fond of grapes one day saw some luscious grapes on a vine out of his reach. He jumped for the grapes a number of times, but he was unable to reach them. He gave up in despair, and as he walked down the road away from the vineyard he said, "They were probably sour grapes anyway. Who wants sour grapes? Certainly not I!" Another example of this mechanism was a custom in the Punjab, where a Hindu was not permitted to marry a third wife. To get around this restriction, it became customary to marry two wives and then to marry a babul tree. The next wife (through rationalization) became the fourth, and everyone was happy.

Most people spend a good deal of their time rationalizing one situation or another. The college student who has an examination tells himself that it is better to go to a movie than to study, since what he really needs is relaxation. A child fails in school, and he tells himself that the teacher was spiteful. A coed is faced with the prospect of a dull date, and she decides that she is not feeling well enough to go. People struggle to make excuses which they can believe and which they get other people to believe.

Some of the most absurd rationalizations are made in attempts to get out of trouble. A man who was arrested for stealing his twenty-ninth automobile said, "I just wanted to learn how to drive." A sixteen-year-old girl who took a tour of the United States with a young evangelist admitted that they had been intimate, but added, "I went with him because I believed he was sincere in his religion. He didn't let me drink or smoke."

Complaining about ill health is another example of rationalization. It is a way of explaining failure, inadequacy, and humiliation. If a person is sick or in pain, it is customary in our culture to excuse his poor performance. We even reward his mediocre achievements with praise which he would not earn if he were well.

The use of rationalization as a defense is carried to an extreme in cases of personality disturbance. A thirty-year-old Long Island mother of three children got up at four o'clock in the morning without disturbing her sleeping husband, went to the bedroom of her eight-year-old daughter, and strangled her. Her reason was rationalization: "The world isn't a good enough place for her to live in." And an Illinois father killed his young son because the boy "would never be able to make much of himself."

PROJECTION

In projection, which is a variant of rationalization, the individual refuses to recognize his faults and deficiencies. He disowns his weaknesses and attempts to blame them on someone else. Very few automobile accidents happen that were not "the other fellow's fault." In school the youngster projects the blame for low grades to the teacher; in business the businessman projects the blame for his failure to the ineffectiveness of his associates. The batter who strikes out will blame it on a loose cleat on his shoe; the woman who drops a stitch while knitting will say that she was distracted; the husband or wife who fails to make a success of marriage insists that the partner is to blame, or else projects the blame on interfering relatives.

"Passing the buck" is probably the best known form of projection. If the blame can be placed elsewhere, the individual is spared the pain and discomfort of feelings of guilt and anxiety. The unfaithful husband or wife is the first to suspect infidelity in his partner.

Projection is frequently behind cases in which women accuse men of misconduct. A woman in an elevator made a scene when she accused a male passenger of pinching her leg; another woman called police and complained that a man in a parked automobile was trying to flirt with her; still another accused men of making suggestive remarks to her. In every case, the men were innocent victims of the projected expression of poorly repressed sexual problems of the women.

This defense mechanism is of particular importance in abnormal psychology because it is the basic reaction in those patients who feel they are being persecuted by others. It is not uncommon for such patients to believe that they are being pursued, plotted against, and even marked for death. In extreme cases, they hear voices accusing them of misbehavior and telling them they are going to be killed. In reality, these same hostile ideas and feelings are harbored by the patient. However, since he cannot face his own hostile impulses and suspicious ideas, he projects the feelings and ideas to others. This device makes it possible for him to accuse others of attitudes which are in fact his own.

IDENTIFICATION

In identification, the individual learns to overcome his feelings of loneliness, inferiority, or inadequacy by taking on the characteristics of someone who is more important. Sometimes the identification is not with a person but with an organization, an institution, a cause, or a movement. In any case, the underlying motivation is to gain security, recognition, and importance.

Children imitate the dress, the speech, and the mannerisms of their fathers or mothers. In so doing, they gain a certain degree of satisfaction. They have a feeling of being grown up. Women quickly adopt the hairdo of a stage or screen star. They buy a certain type of coat or dress because they have seen it worn by some prominent woman. When men and women identify, they are trying to enhance themselves by adopting the characteristics of others who have attained some degree of eminence. Louis XIV of France always danced the role of the god in the court ballets.

Identification may be made on the basis of guilt feelings, the need for punishment, and strong emotional attachments. In Kay Boyle's short novel *The Crazy Hunter,* a lonely young girl identifies herself in her isolation and unhappiness with a blind horse. In Gerhart Hauptmann's *The Fool in Christ,* Emanuel identified himself so thoroughly with Christ that it finally induced a complete split in his personality.

A powerful identification is seen in a child who had a kitten the parents did not want. They got rid of the kitten, but they underestimated the extent to which the child had identified with the animal. As soon as the kitten was gone, the child refused to sit in a chair and would neither talk nor walk. From that time, the child crawled on the floor, made noises like the kitten, and had to be fed from a dish under the table. In desperation the parents got the kitten back, and the child became herself once again.

A specialized form of identification, called *introjection,* is one of the key factors involved in mourning. Many people have an unconscious tendency to take on the characteristics of someone close to them who has died recently. In certain Australian tribes, the mourners at a funeral cover themselves with white paint. In this way they identify themselves with a skeleton or a bleached corpse. Sometimes the emotional identification is so strong that when one person dies, the other takes his own life.

A socially prominent civil engineer committed suicide by diving into his swimming pool with his feet tied the day after his wife drowned during a fishing trip. And a New York man went to the funeral home where his wife's body awaited burial. He stabbed himself in the heart with a butcher knife while standing beside her coffin. In his pocket the police found a note which said: "Forever and ever, you and me. Walk slow, honey, and I will catch up."

An unusual, though not uncommon, form of identification, is the custom of *couvade.* In certain primitive tribes in South America, Africa, and the Far East, the husband of a wife who is expecting a child goes through the same routine as the wife. He will abstain from eating certain foods, rest in bed, and behave generally as if he were to have the baby. He complains of pains and morning sickness. After the baby is born and the mother is back to work, the father remains in bed. Friends of the family call and wish him a speedy recovery. In one tribe, at the end of thirty days of this symbolic illness, the husband is forcibly ejected from his bed, and the period of identification is over.

The distortion and exaggeration of identification as a defensive measure is a common characteristic of personality disturbance. In milder cases, the symptoms of dependency frequently take the form of unhealthy identifications. Attachments to other people based upon dependency needs are the precursors of later emotional problems. In more serious cases of personality disturbance, identification may be carried to the extremes of distorted thinking. Not only does the patient identify closely with another person, but he comes to believe that he is actually the other person. It is not uncommon for a mental patient to believe he is a member of a royal family or some prominent figure in the headlines. In these cases, the line between reality and unreality has been erased, and identification appears as a symptom of psychosis.

COMPENSATION

One of the most common ways in which people learn to deal with tension arising from feelings of inferiority and inadequacy is through compensation. Sometimes a person compensates for an organic inferiority which is real, but more often it is for a psychological inferiority that is a product of the imagination.

The classic example of compensation is Demosthenes, the orator and statesman of ancient Greece, who suffered early in his life from a serious speech defect. He determined to overcome his handicap and practiced public speaking. He placed pebbles in his mouth to make it more difficult to pronounce his words. This action was a deliberate and conscious attempt to compensate for a real physical defect.

Theodore Roosevelt is another excellent example of compensation. As a young man,

Roosevelt was a rather weak person, with little physical stamina. He determined to overcome his physical limitations, and he followed a rigid schedule of physical exercise. He was so successful in his compensation that he led the Rough Riders in Cuba during the Spanish-American War.

History furnishes us with numerous examples of successful compensation. Many of the ancient gods were defective. Odin had one eye, Vulcan was lame, Vidar was unable to speak, and Tyr had only one hand. In real life, Mozart, Beethoven, Bruckner, and Smetana became celebrated musicians and composers despite hearing disorders; Glenn Cunningham, who was given up for a cripple following an accident, came back to be one of the world's great track stars; Ted Shawn, a victim of polio, went on to become one of the greatest dancers; and the late Franklin D. Roosevelt compensated for his physical disabilities by becoming a President with powers far beyond those of any of his predecessors. An amazing example of compensation is the case of a man who, though without arms, paints pictures by holding the brush in his mouth. And a Florida girl, a victim of spastic paralysis, learned how to sew and type with her toes.

Psychological compensation is seen every day. The small man compensates by developing a loud voice, smoking large cigars, wearing flashy clothes, and indulging in other types of behavior to make himself psychologically "bigger." Willy Loman, in Arthur Miller's drama *Death of a Salesman*, is a classic example of the everyday compensations of an unsuccessful man. The student who is basically a cheat may compensate for this tendency by becoming scrupulously honest. The coed who is not too sure of her morals compensates by becoming excessively virtuous. Similarly, the unfaithful husband is often compelled to compensate for his infidelity by becoming overaffectionate and oversolicitous to his wife and children.

Compensation is also seen in the "he-man" novels and short stories of such writers as Rex Beach and Zane Grey. The writings of Ernest Hemingway, as well as his way of life, suggest an overcompensated masculinity. Consciously or unconsciously, such writers seem to have doubts about their own maleness.

While much compensatory behavior appears to be constructive and psychologically healthy, there are compensations which are destructive and unhealthy. The coward uses the tactics of a bully to compensate for his cowardice, and the sexually inadequate man may compensate by making advances toward children. Similarly, the insecure individual may find his compensation in drugs or alcohol. A wide range of compensations can be observed in most of the personality disturbances and mental disorders.

REACTION FORMATION

Some people learn to reduce their tension by denying the conflict. The so-called "old maid's neurosis" (the fear of finding a man under the bed) is a thin disguise of a repressed wish. Similarly, childhood prudery is a reaction against growing sexual interest. The reformer and the vice crusader are also examples of reaction formation. They are reacting in many cases against their own erotic interests and inclinations.

The Anthony Comstocks, Carry Nations, and crusading reformers in general may be attempting to control their own unruly impulses. Carry Nation, who violently attacked alcohol, nicotine, kissing, and ladies' fashions, was not above the reproach in her own personal life prior to her emergence as a champion of morals and virtue. Another vice crusader tried unsuccessfully to introduce a bill into a state legislature banning the display of lingerie in shop windows. More successful reformers have managed to have laws passed to ban drinking, gambling, and houses of prostitution. In one state, young women are prohibited by law from sitting on a man's knees while riding in an automobile; in another, couples walking or sitting on a bathing beach must be at least 6 inches apart; and still another regulation bans waitresses who are under forty years of age. The Senate of the University of Tubingen in Germany once refused a request that women be allowed to use the swimming pool for one hour a week. The request was refused on the basis that the minds of the young men swimmers would be "contaminated" by the knowledge that girls' bodies had shortly before been plunging about in the pool.

A more recent example of reaction formation as a defense strategy was the uproar created when the "Little Brother" doll was placed on the American market. Unlike most dolls, "Little Brother" had a penis. There was an immediate protest. Two women in Ohio formed a national committee to oppose the distribution of the doll. They claimed that the morals of American children were being undermined. It made no difference to the protesters that "Little Brother" was a faithful copy of Verrochio's statue of an angel in the Palazzo Della Signoria in Florence, Italy.

PREGNANT GIRL SCOUT POSTER CAUSES FUROR

New York (AP)—Court action was threatened today by the Girl Scouts of America over a new gag poster showing a smiling, golden-haired youngster in a Girl Scouts' uniform with her hands clasped above her clearly pregnant abdomen. The young mother-to-be is standing contentedly beside the motto "Be Prepared." The Girl Scouts group took "violent exception" to the poster and claimed that it "intended to impute unchastity and moral turpitude to members."

Alexander Cruden, the compiler of a Concordance to the Bible, felt it necessary to carry a sponge with him so that he could wipe off any coarse and profane chalk marks he might see while strolling through the city. A German artist was fined because he drew keyholes around photographs of a dancer undressing in her boudoir. The judge pointed out that the punishment was not for the pictures, but because the keyholes made them "unchaste." The same kind of reaction formation was behind the storm of indignation aroused at Wimbledon when tennis star Gussie Moran's skirt swirled up to reveal frilly lace panties instead of the regulation tennis shorts.

A common reaction formation is the use of euphemisms, or watered-down language, for words and phrases that are embarrassing. The pregnant woman is often referred to as "in a family way," "having a little secret," or "awaiting a blessed event." A newspaper announced that Princess Grace of Monaco had to cancel some of her activities "for a joyful reason." Life is filled with such euphemisms. The prostitute is a "lady of the evening," and a woman's undergarments become "unmentionables." In "West Side Story," the hit musical, there is a song to Officer Krupke. There was no mistaking the meaning of the final line, "Dear Officer Krupke, Krup you!" Similarly, in the John Barth novel *Giles Goat-Boy*, the repeated

phrase "Flunk you!" needs no explanation.

Don Juanism is also a reaction formation. Men who chase women excessively may be defending themselves against strong homosexual inclinations. Such men may be trying to prove to themselves that they really do not have homosexual tendencies. They are saying to themselves and to others, "See what a virile man I am." The opposite type of behavior can also be a reaction formation. Helen Arlington, an author of dog stories, and known as "The Dear Dog Lady," took a vow of chastity as a young girl. Although she married, the marriage was never consummated. Significantly, the couple lived at Mrs. Arlington's "Touch-Me-Not Ranch" in California. A similar reaction formation is seen in the remarks of a nine-year-old girl at a Juvenile Court psychiatric clinic:

> I am going to marry Captain Video when I grow up. We won't have any children. We will adopt children. Having babies is dirty. I don't want to know about it.

Reaction formations also grow out of aggressive impulses. When an individual is frightened by the force of these impulses, he is likely to react with particular violence to what appears to be cruelty and aggression. The ranks of the antivivisectionists, who oppose cutting or dissecting living animals for medical investigation or other scientific purposes, contain at least some men and women who are struggling to control their own hostile urges.

The exaggerated symptoms of certain personality disturbances may also take the form of reaction formations. Fears, obsessive thoughts, and compulsive actions can often be understood as attempts to deny a disturbing and deep-seated conflict. The thread of reaction formation runs through a large number of both minor and major personality difficulties. In most cases, however, this personality defense is merely one of a number of devices the individual has learned to use to cope with his anxiety or guilt.

FANTASY

Another way in which individuals learn to reduce stress is through daydreams, or fantasy. Such thinking is egotistical and self-centered. It is an attempt to build up a dream world more acceptable than the world of reality. Fantasy life, when carried to an extreme, is one of the key characteristics of the more serious personality breakdowns.

Fantasy is a turning-in of the mind on itself and its own problems. Ordinarily, fantasies have a concrete, pictorial quality which disregards logic and reason. They are determined by unfulfilled ambitions, motives, desires, and unconscious wishes. It is not uncommon for young girls to have fantasies of romance. Some girls mail love letters to themselves so that they may have the pleasure of reading them. Others have flowers sent to themselves. The same sort of fantasy occurs when a child talks to a doll or to toy animals. James Still, in his short story "Mrs. Razor," deals with the problem of a child's imaginary playmate. In Maxim Gorky's story "Her Lover," an ugly woman finds solace for the hardships of her life by creating an imaginary lover.

Fantasies in themselves are not abnormal or undesirable. Much of the genius of the world has grown out of fantasy life. Creative art and inventions of all kinds depend upon fantasy. The ability to see something in an unusual relationship is the essence of genius. In this respect there is a very thin line between the genius and mental disorder. Both the genius and the psychotic have a rich fantasy life. The important difference is that the genius uses his fantasy life to better advantage and in more constructive ways.

Fantasy is freely used in the various art forms. It is seen in fairy tales, cartoons, and comic strips, in the paintings of Salvador Dali, Marc Chagall, and Odilon Redon, in Shakespeare's *Midsummer Night's Dream*, in James Joyce's *Finnegan's Wake*, and in the novels of Franz Kafka and Herman Hesse. It is the essence of the legend "Beauty and the Beast," in which a household drudge is delivered into the hands of a monster who falls in love with her and is eventually revealed as a handsome prince. One of the best accounts of fantasy life in literature is James Thurber's story "The Secret Life of Walter Mitty." This story is a powerful description of the everyday fantasies of an average man.

A common fantasy many people experience is that of revenge. An employee is reprimanded by his boss. Later the employee, while sitting at his desk, begins to daydream. He dreams of meeting his boss and soundly thrashing him. Or

he may have more subtle fantasies. Perhaps the employee daydreams of stealing his employer's wife. A favorite fantasy of enlisted men and junior officers during time of war is what they will do if they meet their superior officers when the war is over. An unhappy young boy expressed his revenge fantasies by exclaiming, "If I had a locomotive I would rush down the street at 100 miles an hour, and knock everybody over in a heap."

The fantasy of death occupies the minds of most people at one time or another. Sometimes it takes the form of the "They'll be sorry when I'm dead" daydream. One man had the fantasy of being in his casket, with people gathered around and his boss sitting in the front row. Everyone was saying what a fine man he had been and how sorry they were that he was no longer there. Tears flowed profusely while the minister delivered an extravagant eulogy.

Another prevalent fantasy in our culture is the dream of power. This fantasy is expressed in a number of ways. It is the basis for such familiar American advertising themes as "They all laughed when I sat down to play the piano." It is related to the extraordinary feats of such legendary figures as Achilles, Hercules, Beowulf, Samson, Siegfried, and Paul Bunyan, and to the invincible Batman and Superman. Because of physical or intellectual power, these well-known figures always conquer their opponents and appear to be invincible and invulnerable. The power fantasy is one of the reasons why certain fairy tales enjoy such a universal appeal. "Jack the Giant Killer," for example, shows the child that he is not completely powerless against his own personal giant—the adult. The story also stimulates the power fantasies of adults who face their own giants in the forms of marriage, finances, job, and social life.

"Cinderella" also has a universal appeal because it stimulates the success fantasy. People respond immediately to the story of a family drudge (as many consider themselves) who is rewarded by having a prince fall in love with her. The fantasy is a variation of the rags-to-riches theme and is reflected in the story of the "Ugly Duckling." It is also seen in the pleasure we have when the underdog or dark horse wins. In a sense, it is the legend of David and Goliath.

Many people create fantasies in order to

overcome the drab realities of everyday life. A frustrated and unhappy woman, tired of her husband, her children, and her marriage, imagines a life in which she is wealthy, clever, and irresistibly beautiful. She imagines herself pursued by handsome men. She convinces herself that other women are jealous of her. She constructs an unreal world in which she is the center of attention. Soon it becomes difficult for her to distinguish sharply between what is real and what is imagination. One of the finest literary examples of this type of fantasy is Tennessee Williams' drama *The Glass Menagerie*.

In the case of some of the most serious mental disorders, fantasy life is carried to an extreme. The world of fantasy is substituted almost entirely for the world of reality. Such people become seclusive and withdrawn and seem out of contact with their environment. It is impossible to reach them by means of the ordinary processes of communication. They live in a dream world of their own making, preferring it to the difficult world of everyday reality. The wards of every large mental hospital are filled with men and women who prefer a fantasy world to the sometimes harsh and bitter realities of ordinary living.

DISENGAGEMENT

Disengagement or noninvolvement is another common personality defense. We reduce our anxiety by turning our backs on problems. We simply refuse to take part in any event in which we run the risk of being threatened. We avoid situations likely to cause us distress or discomfort.

An example of disengagement as a defense is the refusal of people to come to the assistance of someone in trouble. A young woman in New York was stabbed to death while more than two dozen people who saw the murder or heard the victim scream made no effort to help her. This incident was neither unusual nor isolated. It was the expression of an attitude that has become all too common in the United States.

In a three-year study of twelve-year-old children in England, Switzerland, the Soviet Union, and the United States, the children were asked what they would do if they saw one child hurting another.

The standard reaction among American children was to do nothing. This attitude was expressed less freely among the children of other nations.

The process of disengagement is also an important part of the gradual withdrawal from outside contact with increasing age. The individual who uses this defense becomes increasingly able to tolerate the idea of approaching death (Cummings and Henry, 1961).

REGRESSION

Some people learn to reduce stress through a return to earlier and more primitive forms of behavior. Each individual progresses through a series of developmental stages during his lifetime. First, there is the period during which he is relatively safe in the uterus of the mother. It is an easy and presumably anxiety-free time. Some psychoanalysts believe that it is a life to which most people secretly long to return.

Following the stress of birth, there is the period of infancy. Here, too, despite the many stresses associated with sexuality, toilet training, socialization, and the harnessing of aggression, life is easy compared to the later struggles which people must endure. Following the period of infancy, there are the characteristic stresses of childhood, adolescence, early adulthood, maturity, and finally old age.

When an individual regresses, he returns psychologically to one of the earlier periods when life was easier, when there were fewer problems, and when there was less anxiety and less guilt. Everyone at one time or another shows signs of psychological regression. When this happens, it indicates that stress has become overwhelming. It means that anxiety has become so severe that the individual is forced to retreat to an earlier level. He seeks to solve his problems by behavior that proved satisfactory earlier in life.

Regression is frequently expressed in social customs and in artistic creations. Baptism, whether it be sprinkling the head with water or total immersion of the body, symbolizes a rebirth. Regression is expressed clearly in the well-known Biblical phrase, "Except as ye become as little children, ye cannot enter the kingdom of heaven."

Figure 4.11 *A baby mandrill baboon finds the customary infant's security in thumb-sucking. (Courtesy of the Cincinnati Zoo.)*

In India, in one of the districts near Bombay, a child born under an unlucky star is placed in a bamboo vessel and reborn symbolically by being put for a moment in the mouth of a cow. In a similar way, the Indian desire for Nirvana implies a regression or return to the mother.

Regression has been an important theme in literature. In Sally Benson's short story, "Little Woman," a woman who had been pampered and admired because of her frailty as a young girl regressed to childhood as she grew older. Regression is also an important theme in D. H. Lawrence's "The Rocking Horse Winner."

The beginning of regression can be observed in young children. An infant who has learned to walk may find it so much of a problem that he will regress to crawling. Older children, when they are frustrated and unhappy, regress to crying or thumbsucking. Even animals show signs of regression. Bear cubs and young chimpanzees suck their toes and thumbs when they are scolded or neglected.

Among adults, a wide range of regressive behavior can be observed. When a grown woman displays a temper tantrum, she is trying to get her way by using a device she found successful as a child. In fact, most fits of anger are regressions. Similarly, adults show regressive behavior when they begin to cry because their problems are too much for them; or instead of crying, they may bite their fingernails, chew a pencil, or smoke incessantly. During wartime, many soldiers who are sent to training camp suffer from enuresis, or bedwetting. Their anxiety is so great that the infantile symptom returns.

Sexual behavior shows a wide range of regressions. An adult man who has anxiety over contracting venereal infection or a woman whose anxiety is related to fear of pregnancy may resort to autoerotic practices which were an earlier form of sexual satisfaction. Regressive masturbation is an escape from reality when more adequate outlets are available but not utilized. Homosexuality may also be a regression. Some homosexuals are people who have found that normal heterosexual relationships are too anxiety-provoking. Since strong attachment to members of the same sex is characteristic of the early phase of adolescence, an individual may find later in life that it is easier to adjust emotionally to this earlier level than to the level of mature sexuality where heterosexual relations are expected.

Very strong, and frequently unhealthy, emotional attachments to children may develop out of the inability to assume an adult masculine or feminine role. If a person is frightened in his relations with other adults, he may regress to an earlier and easier type of relationship with young children. It is no mere coincidence that there are so many unmarried men and women teaching in our schools. The same inner fears and conflicts that prevent marriage are sometimes responsible for the choice of a career in the world of children rather than in the world of adults.

One of the happiest solutions (for the world, if not for himself) of this dilemma over assuming an adult role was made by the Reverend Charles

L. Dodgson, known to most of the world as Lewis Carroll, the author of *Alice in Wonderland*. His inability to obtain a mature relationship with older women led to his showering his affections and his talents on young children, most of whom were girls. In less fortunate cases, emotional attachments to children become unhealthy and distorted. Newspapers are filled with accounts of sex crimes involving children. In these cases, the regressive urge usually involves adults who must love someone, yet cannot love another adult. The condition arises when normal heterosexual adjustments are physically or psychologically impossible.

Unconscious regressive desires are sometimes betrayed in sleep and dreams. It is not unusual for people to assume the fetal, or uterine, posture when they sleep. They sleep on their sides with their knees drawn up and their arms close together at the chest. They assume a ball-like, rounded position very similar to the position of the fetus in the uterus of the mother. Some psychoanalysts believe that when the fetal posture is assumed during sleep, the individual is unconsciously returning to the womb.

Regressive elements may also be involved when people dream they are children or infants, are immersed in water, or are in a dark cave or cavern. Such dreams are thought by psychoanalysts to be thinly disguised wishes to return to the security and warmth of the uterus. Even *Alice in Wonderland* has been interpreted as a symbolic regressive trip back to the mother's womb.

Regressive behavior is seen in its most unvarnished form in mental disorder. The person's behavior may be infantile or childish. He may suck his thumb, masturbate, and show keen interest in urination and defecation. He may even play with his feces and smear them on the floor and walls in the manner of a young child. Among individuals in the old-age groups, a regression to childhood patterns is not unusual. "Second childhood" is an attempt to hang on to life by regressing psychologically to one's early years.

SUBLIMATION

While the psychological process of sublimation is sometimes considered a defense, it is unlike the others in that it is not a single technique. Rather it is a term applied to the efficiency and acceptability of the overall defensive system of the personality. When an individual's efforts are channeled into socially acceptable activities, he is not likely to be looked upon as being abnormal. The vast majority of people learn to make a reasonably effective adjustment to life as a result of sublimation. Such sublimations may be through an occupation or profession, a hobby, study, sports as a participant or spectator, an interest in the welfare of others, the church and religion, or any one of a great number of other personal and group interests and activities. By definition, sublimation is positive and constructive. The clinical psychologist and the psychiatrist are seldom concerned with the individual who learns how to sublimate his unacceptable sexual and aggressive impulses. It is only when the defensive system breaks down and sublimation is ineffective that the symptoms of personality disorganization put in their appearance.

SUMMARY

1. An understanding of the psychological basis of abnormal behavior must begin with a consideration of motivation, or the forces which drive men to action. There are three major groups of theories of motivation: *behavior* theories, emphasizing the role of learning; *cognitive* theories, stressing more or less conscious planning; and *psychodynamic* theories, focusing on unconscious impulses.

2. Motivating forces operate on an unconscious as well as a conscious level. There are many forces outside the field of immediate awareness which contribute to the behavior of man. The clinical and experimental evidence which supports the general theory

of unconscious motivation includes ordinary remembering and forgetting, intuition, the sudden emergence of solutions, creative thinking and artistic expression, dream life, sleepwalking, automatic behavior, multiple personality, and hypnosis.

3. The nature of the many, and often contradictory, needs which the individual strives to satisfy makes satisfaction impossible in many cases. *Frustration* occurs when a barrier blocks the individual's goal-seeking activities. *Conflict* appears when the individual must make a choice between alternative goals. In both cases, the individual faces a stress situation. The most important conflicts in our culture center on *sexuality, aggressive urges, status,* and *dependency needs.*

4. When individuals are faced with critical conflicts and frustrations which cannot be solved readily, the result is an emotional reaction called *anxiety*. This emotion is a conditioned physiological response to any threat to the integrity of the organism. It is a carry-over of the primitive emergency response of animals to danger. Because of the nature of the conflicts, particularly when they involve sex and/or aggression, the anxiety is likely to be accompanied by feelings of *guilt*.

5. Since guilt and anxiety are unpleasant to the individual, various personality defenses have been developed to protect the individual from these feelings. The defenses include *rationalization*, or the making of excuses; *projection*, or placing blame elsewhere; *repression*, or keeping impulses buried in the unconscious; *regression*, or returning psychologically to earlier and easier levels of adjustment; *disengagement*, or noninvolvement; and *sublimation,* or channeling unacceptable impulses into socially acceptable activities.

6. When the defense structure of the individual remains intact and works efficiently, the individual is considered to be well adjusted. When the defenses become exaggerated or distorted, the individual is considered to be emotionally disturbed. When the defense mechanisms break down completely, there is likely to be a mental disorder requiring hospitalization.

OTHER AUDIOTAPES

The Nature of Hostility
Dr. Philip Worchel presents a nineteen-minute lecture on some of the problems associated with the concepts of hostility and aggression. Recorded in 1960. Sound Seminar 75938, McGraw-Hill Book Company.

The Nature of Anxiety
The late Dr. Kurt Goldstein, one of the most distinguished psychiatrists of our time, presents an eighteen-minute lecture on the fundamental nature of anxiety and the importance of the "catastrophic reaction." Recorded in 1953. Sound Seminar 75796, McGraw-Hill Book Company.

5 SOCIOCULTURAL FACTORS IN PERSONALITY DISORGANIZATION

While physical and psychological stress play a major role in the development of abnormal behavior, they are incomplete in themselves. It is necessary also to consider social and cultural factors. Social factors are those involving the life, welfare, and relations of human beings in a community. Cultural factors are the ways of living which are transmitted from one generation to another. For our purposes, it will not be necessary to make a fine distinction between the two terms. But the problems of abnormal psychology must be understood in terms of the sociocultural matrix in which personality disorganization develops and expresses itself, since some forms of abnormal behavior appear only in a well-defined social climate.

The cultural approach to the problem of personality disturbance is one important aspect of the newly emerging field of social psychiatry. In the United States, social psychiatry includes community mental health services, mental hygiene in industry, group therapy, and administrative psychiatry, as well as the impact of culture on the etiology of mental illness. Another way of viewing social psychiatry is to regard it as a meeting point of psychiatry, medical epidemiology, and social science.

The present chapter is concerned with personality disorganization as it is related to the enmeshment of the individual to the cultural fabric. The word *culture* has several meanings. In one sense, it is a general phenomenon of all human societies. All children must learn to speak, and all children must be trained by adults. Culture is a matter of the way in which these universal variables are involved in personality formation. The word *culture* is also used in the sense of cultural differences. Here the question is: What difference does it make, in terms of the developing personality, whether a child is raised a Zuñi, a Japanese, a Russian, or a Brazillian? Finally, culture can be viewed in the sense of cultural change and the effect such change has on personality organization within a single cultural group.

In mental and emotional disorders, there is the problem of what actually is determined by the culture in which the person lives. Certainly, patterns of stress are different in different cultures, and the reactions of individuals to stress are conditioned by social factors. At the very least, the surface characteristics of personality disturbance, such as the nature of the complaints and the content of disturbed thinking and perceptual disorders, are determined culturally. It is probably also true that the prevalence of organic psychoses is influenced to some degree by cultural differences in eating preferences, attitudes toward sanitation, medical treatment and hospitalization, and similar matters.

The first important contacts between psychiatry and the social sciences early in the present century were due to the convergence of the interests of a few culturally oriented psychiatrists and psychiatrically minded anthropologists. These pioneers placed emphasis upon the importance of society and culture in shaping and developing the individual personality, in influencing the interaction between the individual and his society, and in determining the form and content of psychopathology. Gradually, over the years, an increasing number of psychiatrists, psychologists, and other social scientists were attracted to the problems of the relationship between culture and mental disorder.

An influence of considerable significance in the development of the cultural approach was the insistence of the neo-Freudians on the social nature of man. They took the position that many of the emotional disturbances of man are a result of conflicting demands which a culture imposes on the individual, rather than of the unfolding of an immutable biological process. By the middle of the present century, there was a rapid development of interest in the social and cultural approach to the problems of psychopathology. An entirely new dimension was given to the views of personality disorganization which were traditionally held, and a new field of social psychiatry emerged. The study of psychiatric concepts in the framework of the social sciences has resulted in a deeper understanding of the causes of some of the more subtle and elusive forms of personality disorganization. While the ultimate causes of all behavior—abnormal as well as normal—must eventually be explained in terms of the functions of the nervous system, the practical problems of social stress and cultural conditioning can only be solved at the interpersonal level.[1]

Some of the major cultural approaches to the problem of personality disorganization involve (1) family studies, (2) cross-cultural studies, (3) the

---

[1]General discussions of social factors as they relate to problems of personality disorganization are to be found in *Social Stress* (Aldine, 1970) by Sol Levine and N. A. Scotch; *Cultural Change, Mental Health, and Poverty* (University of Kentucky Press, 1969), edited by J. C. Finney; *Social Psychiatry* (Science House, 1969), compiled by Ari Kiev; *Social Psychiatry* (Grune & Stratton, 1968), edited by Joseph Zubin and F. A. Freyhan; *The Sociology of Mental Disorders* (Aldine, 1967) edited by S. K. Weinberg; M. K. Opler's *Culture and Social Psychiatry* (Atherton, 1967); and *Issues and Problems in Social Psychiatry* (Thomas, 1966) by B. J. Bergen and C. S. Thomas.

epidemiology of mental illness, and (4) the analysis of shared psychopathology.

THE IMPORTANCE OF THE FAMILY

Early in the present century, a few psychiatrists and psychologists began to look upon mental disorder as a failure in the adjustment of the individual to his situation. This emphasis led to a consideration of the family and other social groups as factors in the development of personality disorganization. It became clear that the success or lack of success of a family member in his particular family role may be critical to the maintenance of mental health. The family experience often determines if and when a personality disturbance first appears and sometimes influences the form it takes. Recent years have seen a sharp increase in the interest in the impact of the family on the development of mental disorder, especially in connection with parental attitudes, personality characteristics, and the dynamics of family relationships.

PARENTAL ATTITUDES

The attitudes of parents are important sources of strength or weakness in the development of the personality structure of the child. Rejection, overindulgence, overprotection, domination, submission, and similar attitudes are at times responsible for failures of later personality integration. The rejecting mother is a figure depicted in literature throughout history and the source of much emotional conflict in modern times.

Investigations of families of mental patients show that the mothers and fathers in such families are likely to be unstable themselves and to have attitudes and patterns of behavior which contribute to the emotional disturbance of the mentally ill family member. While this generalization does not hold for all mental disorders, it appears to be valid for at least some of the neuroses and functional psychoses.

In a study of family interaction in mental disorder, it was found that where the disturbed child had made a good adjustment prior to his difficulties, the father was the strong personality, while the

mother was inclined to be weak and submissive (Clausen and Yarrow, 1955). In families where the child had made a poor adjustment prior to his disturbance, the mother was dominant while the father was submissive. In both cases there was a striking pattern of conflict and discord. In the normal control group, in which the child was not disturbed, there was a shared pattern of authority in the family with a minimal trend toward maternal dominance. Moreover, there appeared to be little indication of conflict between parents.

A detailed study of family attitudes in mental disorder was made at the Brooklyn State Hospital (Gerard and Siegel, 1950). The study revealed a marked contrast between the attitudes of the families of patients and the families of control subjects. The families of patients showed, among other relationships, two major attitudes existing between parents. One was an attitude of active discordance, tension, defiance, and dislike. In these families, the parents were frank and open in their hostility toward one another. A second parental attitude was one of passivity and lack of warmth. Both attitudes were marked by little affection between the parents.

It was also found in this study that the mother was the dominant figure in the home. The patient ordinarily had a heightened emotional relationship with the mother and a diminished relationship with the father. The father was inclined to be weak and passive, while the mother covered feelings of insecurity with efficiency and aggressiveness. Caught in the middle, the patient was pampered and indulged and often was the favored child. It was not uncommon for him to play a "special" role in the family group and to be exposed constantly to overprotective attitudes. An examination of the family background factors found in these patients suggests that at least some of the factors may be the result of the personality prior to the illness. For example, the pampering and indulgence, the special role in the family constellation, the overprotective attitudes, and the role of favorite sibling might be explained in terms of the conscious or unconscious realization that the youngster is constitutionally different and thus needs special attention.

In another study of family relationships in mental disorder, the mother was the dominant parent in three-fourths of the cases (Reichard and Tillman, 1950). The child was openly rejected by 13 percent of the mothers, while 63 percent of them covered feelings of rejection by means of overprotective attitudes. Maternal attitudes were marked by self-sacrifice and martyrdom, subtle and indirect domination, overprotectiveness, and overconcern with the sexual behavior of the children.

The importance of disturbed parents and the interactions between such parents and the future patient was shown clearly in a study in Denmark (Alanen, 1958). Of 100 unselected cases of disturbed children, the mother's personality was also considered to be disturbed in 84 cases. Where the mother's personality appeared more or less normal, it was considered that the father's personality was disturbed.

Another study revealed some of the parent-child interactions in families with a schizophrenic child. The parents of such a child tended to be depressed, aloof, and distant from him. Physical contacts between parents and child were rare. When contacts did occur, the purpose was to encourage the child to perform or to censure the child, and not to express warmth or emotion. The father of such a child was often better than the mother at getting the child to respond (NIMH, 1968).

Most studies of the attitudes of the parents of disturbed children indicate that these attitudes differ markedly from the attitudes of parents of normal children. Moreover, there appear to be distinguishing features in the attitudes of both mothers and fathers. The mothers are inclined to be strong, dominant, and aggressive. The fathers show a contrasting attitude of weakness and relative passivity.

FAMILY DYNAMICS

The interpersonal relationships in families in which there is a disturbed person are likely to be disturbed, since the presence of a mentally disturbed family member is usually a stress situation which threatens even the most stable family relationship. There is evidence, however, that disturbed family relationships frequently are a cause of the individual's difficulties and not merely a result of it.

In a study of family units, disturbed children were seen in intensive treatment while the parents were seen on an outpatient basis (Clausen and Yarrow, 1955). The purpose of the study was to determine the patterns of relationship in the families and to develop hypotheses about the effect of these relationships on the development of the child. It was found that in families containing mentally disturbed children, the marital relationships of all parents were grossly disturbed. In more than half the families, there was an open split between the parents. In these families, the parents frequently threatened to separate, and there were other constant difficulties. The child was not able to identify with either parent for fear of antagonizing the other.

Another study of the families of disturbed children found that not a single family was well integrated (Lidz, 1958). Most of the marriages were severely disturbed, and serious conflict existed between the two parents, with each trying to devalue the opposite parent to the children and striving to win the children to one side or the other. Insecurity and confusion, suspiciousness and distrust, and similar damaging attitudes were seen in many cases. Frequently one or the other parent would be classified as suffering from an incipient mental disturbance.

The Laboratory of Socio-Environmental Studies of the National Institute of Mental Health found that families in which either the husband or wife was hospitalized for mental disorder frequently went through a progression of disruptions and interpersonal conflicts well in advance of the patient's hospitalization. For women, the marital role itself was most often the first to show a deficit, with disruption coming through accusations of infidelity and various degrees of psychological withdrawal. The role of the wife as housekeeper was next most frequently impaired. Housecleaning, cooking, and laundry work became irregular or failed to get done. The care of the children seemed to be markedly impaired in the early stages in only one case.

By three months prior to hospitalization, about half the women were performing almost none of their household tasks. The men also had diminished their performance of household tasks, but their functions were less critical to the maintenance of the household. Most of the men were able to hold their jobs and to perform more or less adequately in them up to a month or less before hospitalization.

In almost all essential life tasks, performance was impaired at the end, although many women were able to care for their children, and many men were able to meet the requirements of their jobs, down to the last few days before entering the hospital. While extreme conflict may have been the pattern of the marital interaction for a number of months, as long as the disturbed wife was able to look after her children and the disturbed husband to hold his job, some degree of personal integration and family integration was maintained (NIMH, 1968).

As far as communication is concerned, when comparing families of schizophrenic persons with families where there are no mentally disordered members, the normal families perform significantly better (Feinsilver, 1970). Communications problems of parents affect the psychological development of the child in areas which typically are impaired in personality disturbances. These defects in communication can lead to a variety of difficulties involving the use of language, motivation, and interpersonal relations. In a study of the families of normal people as well as those of people with mental disorders, important differences in patterns of family social interaction were found. Parents of normal children tended to use direct methods of behavior control, whereas disturbed families resorted to indirect manipulation. The relative dominance of father, mother, and son differed among normal and disturbed families, as did the degree of flexibility and adaptability in communication and interaction among family members (NIMH, 1968).

Another study examined parent-child interaction in families with a withdrawn, disturbed adolescent and contrasted them with families containing antisocial adolescents. Early results showed that withdrawn children came from families in which members were relatively inaccurate at predictions of one another's behavior. Parental domination of the withdrawn child was achieved by covert methods in contrast to the overt and power-oriented techniques utilized in the families of the antisocial child. The withdrawn child viewed his parents as punitive and perfectionistic in their demands of him, whereas the antisocial child characterized his parents as practicing overt domination (NIMH, 1968).[2]

Excessive sibling rivalry, or jealous competition between children in the same family, is another example of disturbed dynamics which may lead to emotional difficulties. Young children are often jealous of a new arrival in the family even before it is born. As soon as a child hears the "news," the hostile reaction begins. At first it is vague and unformed. But as the pregnancy of the mother advances, the hostility becomes more and more apparent.

The coming of a second child creates a unique emotional conflict for the child already in the family. It makes him realize for the first time that he cannot have his mother to himself. Sometimes the hostility that is aroused inflicts a scar that is carried throughout life. A little girl of three was so jealous of her mother's attention to a younger child that she stubbornly refused to kiss her mother for more than twenty years. It was only when her mother was dying that she finally consented to kiss her.

Another little girl was so hostile toward her baby brother that she had a complete personality change. Before the new brother arrived she had been easy to manage; but as soon as her brother was born, she refused to feed herself or to dress and undress herself. She expressed her hostility by completely ignoring the new addition to the family. When anyone asked her about her baby brother, she denied that she had one. In another case, a little boy had whooping cough when his baby sister was born. The doctor told him not to cough near the baby. "If you cough near her," explained the doctor, "she will get sick and then you won't have a baby sister any more." Several times after this, the youngster's mother found him coughing in the baby's face. The mother was desperate. She tried to teach him to pat the baby's face. He did so very tenderly when his mother

---

[2]*Social Psychiatry* (available from Springer-Verlag, 175 Fifth Avenue, New York, N.Y. 10010) is a quarterly journal concerned with the effects of social conditions upon behavior and the relationship between psychiatric disorder and the social environment. Articles appear in English, French, and German. Recommended primarily for students with a serious interest in the relation of social factors to mental illness.

watched him. But when she turned her back, he slapped the baby and bit her finger.

Sibling rivalry is such a powerful force that it sometimes causes young children to commit the most aggressive crimes. A boy strangled his little sister who was still in the cradle. Another boy cut his younger brother's throat with a razor. A four-year-old girl hit her baby brother with a hammer when he was asleep. Ever since Cain killed his brother Abel, brothers and sisters have harbored intensely hostile feelings toward one another. An eighteen-year-old girl who beat her eleven-year-old brother to death told police, "My parents gave him more love than they gave me."

Another family situation of importance is that of parental deprivation, or the absence, for one reason or another, of one or both parents. The most common form of parental deprivation is the death or prolonged absence of a parent from the home. There is considerable evidence pointing to a relatively high frequency of parental death and separation during the childhoods of children who later show delinquent and antisocial behavior (Glueck and Glueck, 1950). There is also evidence, although less well established, that there is a significantly increased parental deprivation during childhood in the cases of children who later show the various forms of mental disorder (Gregory, 1958).

In a classic study by Sheldon and Eleanor Glueck, comparisons were made between 500 juvenile delinquents and 500 nondelinquent boys matched by age, intelligence, national origin, and residence in underprivileged neighborhoods (Glueck and Glueck, 1952). It was found that 60 percent of the delinquents came from homes that had been broken by separation, divorce, death, or prolonged absence of the parent. Parental deprivation was found in only 34 percent of the nondelinquents. While this finding does not mean that the broken home inevitably produces a juvenile delinquent, it does mean that there are factors inherent in the broken-home pattern which seem

to be associated with delinquency in a significant number of cases.

Relatively little attention has been paid to the effect of personality disturbance in a family member on the rest of the family group. For the most part, disturbance in one family member has a disorganizing effect upon the other members. A variety of damaging attitudes may develop among these other family members. Some feel hostile toward the person for "letting the family down." Other members may feel shamed that the family has a disturbed person among its members. Still other reactions include feelings of guilt, hopelessness, depression, tension and anxiety, and similar attitudes. While mental disorder in a family member may have occasional positive effects on other family members, such effects have not yet been studied carefully.[3]

THE EPIDEMIOLOGY OF MENTAL DISORDER

Epidemiology is the study of the occurrence and distribution of conditions such as mental disorder. The interest in the epidemiology of mental disorder grew out of studies of infectious diseases. Some of the earliest studies of this type were in connection with the great epidemics of cholera, poliomyelitis, and other disorders. Such studies, which are concerned with population groups rather than with individuals, provide information about the probable causes of illness. They do not indicate the relative importance of causal factors in individual cases. However, epidemiology today does not concern itself merely with the study of epidemics, nor is it confined to the study of physical disease.

Epidemiology makes up a significant part of the scientific foundation for public health. The emphasis on mental health epidemiology has increased because of the movement away from custodial care and because of the growing interest in the etiology and prevention aspects of

---

[3]The impact of family life on the mental health of children is discussed in *Interaction in Families: An Experimental Study of Family Processes and Schizophrenia* (Wiley, 1968) by E. G. Mishler and N. E. Waxler; *Family Dynamics and Female Sexual Delinquency* (Science and Behavior Books, 1969) edited by Otto Pollock and A. S. Friedman; and in Bruno Bettelheim's *The Children of the Dream* (Macmillan, 1969).

personality disturbance. New facilities can be efficiently planned only if the needs of the population served are known. Similarly, community programs to prevent and treat mental disorder can be properly developed only if factors leading to its occurrence have been identified. The National Instititute of Mental Health established a Center for Epidemiologic Studies in 1967 to provide unified leadership and support for a national program in the epidemiology of mental disorder and mental health.

Epidemiology as a technique in social psychiatry is concerned with the location, distribution, and statistical study of psychiatric cases. While some of the earliest studies of hospital rates of mental disorder were made in the nineteenth century, the first important epidemiological community research in the United States was a survey in 1936 of more than 50,000 persons in the Eastern Health District of Baltimore (Lemkau et al., 1942). This study was followed in 1938 by a similar survey of Williamson County, Tennessee (Roth and Luton, 1943). The most significant epidemiological study of the period, however, was the investigation of mental disorder in Chicago (Faris and Dunham, 1939).

The Eastern Health District of Baltimore, an area of about one square mile, was made up largely of residential dwellings. Of the approximately fifty-five thousand inhabitants at the time of the survey, about one-quarter were black. A large number of the white residents were of Hebrew and Czech extraction. The income of both white and black families was below the city-wide average. The study, based largely on cases known to agencies, found 3,337 active cases of mental disorder during the survey year. This rate was equal to 60.5 active cases per 1,000 population.

Williamson County, at the time of the survey, was a Tennessee agricultural area of 586 square miles and a population of 25,000. One-quarter of the population was black, and the white population was largely of English or Scotch-Irish extraction. This survey found 1,721 cases of mental illness in a population of 25,000, or a rate of 69.4 cases per 1,000. The study went a step beyond the Baltimore survey in that an effort was made to spot cases whether or not they were known to community agencies.

Because of important methodological differences, the findings in the Eastern Health District survey and the Williamson County survey are not directly comparable. There were differences in locating the cases, in computing the prevalence of mental disorder, in the classification of the diagnostic groups, and in the definition of "active" cases. However, in spite of these differences, both surveys support the view that at least 6 percent of the population of the United States suffers from some type of serious mental disorder.

The Chicago study was a classic pioneering effort in mental health epidemiology. The investigators studied a large number of cases in the Chicago area and plotted them on census maps. In this way it was possible to analyze the relationship between various types of personality disturbance and different areas of the city. Characteristic distributions were found for a number of different abnormal conditions.

The major epidemiological studies in the post-World War II period have been the work among the Hutterites (Eaton and Weil, 1955); the field studies in Stirling County, Nova Scotia (Leighton, 1961); the Texas studies (Jaco, 1960); and the Midtown Manhattan Study (Srole et al., 1962).

These various epidemiological studies are directed toward different questions. Some of the investigations have been interested in the relative incidence of mental disorder in urban and rural societies; others have been concerned with the incidence in civilized and primitive societies; some have dealt with the differential distribution of mental disorder within an urban area; while others have emphasized the problems of social stratification.

The epidemiological survey of the Hutterites was undertaken in order to study the incidence of personality disturbance in a highly stable and homogeneous rural society in the United States. The Hutterites are members of an isolated Anabaptist religious sect in which there is social harmony and economic security. The survey sought to discover all cases of mental disorder known to have occurred among members living at that time. In keeping with earlier and less systematic reports, it was found that the members of the group had a low rate of mental disorder as measured by hospital statistics. Not a single case could be found of a Hutterite in a mental hospital at the time of the survey. However, a careful screening of the entire population showed that 2.3 percent either had symptoms of mental disorder or had recovered from such a condition. Apparently even the most protective and well-integrated society provides no complete immunity against personality disorganization.

The Stirling County study was conducted by Cornell University in collaboration with the Department of Public Health of the province of Nova Scotia and with the cooperation of Acadia University and Dalhousie University. This study, under the direction of Alexander Leighton, a psychiatrist and anthropologist, was a continuing investigation of the relationship between psychiatric disorders and sociocultural factors in a community. Extensive information was gathered on psychiatric cases by means of field-work methods. The investigators drew a probability sample of the population and then tried to get all possible information from and about these people whether or not they were previously known to any physician or psychiatric agency. One of the major objectives of the project was to ascertain the true prevalence of personality disturbance, rather than the prevalence of treated cases only.

The Texas study is a survey of the incidence of psychosis during 1951 and 1952. During the period of the survey, the population of Texas was about eight million. A crude annual incidence rate of 73 psychoses per 100,000 general population was found. Only those patients who sought treatment for the first time during the study period were included. Rates were calculated specifically for age groups and for sex and for three subcultures, Anglo-American, Spanish American, and non-white. The survey is a model of its kind and was an important step in the development of epidemiological research in the field of mental disorder.

The Midtown Manhattan Study was another major undertaking in social psychiatry. The study was based on an eight-year research investigation of the midtown section of the borough of Manhattan in New York City. As in the case of the Stirling County survey, an attempt was made to determine the real incidence of personality disturbance in the population, rather than cases hospitalized or simply known to medical and social agencies.

The research plan was based on a probability sampling of adults in the Manhattan area under investigation. The study made use of a systematic

Figure 5.1 *Alexander Leighton, 1900– , a psychiatrist and anthropologist who has developed and carried out important epidemiological studies to determine cultural differences in mental disorders. (Blackstone Studios.)*

sample of blocks from all city blocks in the midtown area, a systematic sample of dwellings in the sample blocks, and a systematic sample of age-eligible occupants of the sample dwellings. Each selected individual was assigned to an interviewer, who was not permitted to accept any substitute source of information. The total sample, drawn from 110,000 adults in the area, totaled 1,911 persons between the ages of 20 and 59. Of the total sample, it was possible to interview 1,660 individuals, or 87 percent of those selected. The interviewers used a questionnaire which later was rated by project psychiatrists. The persons interviewed were classified into six levels of symptom formation ranging from "well" to "incapacitated." These levels are indicated in Table 5.1.

When the ratings were completed, 23.4 percent of those interviewed were considered to be psychologically impaired. The distribution of symp-

Table 5.1 *Mental health categories used in the Midtown Manhattan Study*

ORDINAL RATINGS	DEFINITIONS	CATEGORY OF SYMPTOM FORMATION
0	No significant symptom formation (symptom free)	Well
1	Mild symptom formation, *but* functioning adequately	Mild
2	Moderate symptom formation with *no* apparent interference in life adjustment	Moderate
3	Moderate symptom formation with *some* interference in life adjustment	Marked
4	Serious symptom formation, and functioning with some difficulty	Severe
5	Serious symptom formation, and functioning with *great* difficulty	Incapacitated
6	Seriously incapacitated, unable to function	Incapacitated

SOURCE: Adapted from L. Srole et al., *Mental Health in the Metropolis: The Midtown Manhattan Study.* McGraw-Hill Book Company, New York, 1962, vol. 1, p. 399.

tom formation in the interview sample is shown in Table 5.2.

The high rate of impaired mental health found in the Midtown Manhattan Study is at variance with certain other investigations, notably the 1957 investigation in Baltimore conducted by the Commission on Chronic Illness. The latter study, based on a drawn sample of 1,292 persons, involved laboratory tests and physical examinations of 807 individuals, or 62.5 percent of the sample. It was estimated on the basis of this study that the prevalence rate for mental disorder was 10.9 percent. It should be noted, however, that the evaluation of mental health in this study was made by physicians who were interns with varying degrees of training and interest in psychological medicine. It is entirely possible that many cases of per-

sonality disturbance went unrecognized and unrecorded.

A major study in San Francisco has been analyzing psychiatric, physical, sociological, and anthropological information about 600 elderly people living in the community and a similar number of elderly people admitted for the first time to a psychiatric ward. One finding is related to social isolation, which has long been thought of as a possible factor in personality disturbance. The investigators reported that old persons who are psychologically disturbed, whether they are hospitalized or living in the community, are far more isolated than other old people. However, the researchers also found that people who have been extremely isolated all their lives run no greater risk of being hospitalized for mental disorder in old age than people who have been socially active (NIMH, 1969).

The epidemiology of mental disorder is complicated by a number of important variables. One set of variables involves the demographic, or population, characteristics of the group being studied. Epidemiology is also concerned with the ecology, or spatial distribution, of mental disorder and with the influence of social stratification.

POPULATION VARIABLES

The major population characteristics involved in the epidemiology of mental disorder are age, sex, marital status, occupational level, urban-rural differences, educational level, religious affiliation,

Table 5.2 *Severity of symptoms found in the Midtown Manhattan Study*

CATEGORY OF SYMPTOM FORMATION	PERCENT
Well	18.5
Mild symptom formation	36.3
Moderate symptom formation	21.8
Impaired*	23.4
Marked symptom formation	13.2
Severe symptom formation	7.5
Incapacitated	2.7
(*N* = 100 percent)	(1,660)

*Marked, severe, and incapacitated combined.
SOURCE: Adapted from L. Srole et al., *Mental Health in the Metropolis: The Midtown Manhattan Study.* McGraw-Hill Book Company, New York, 1962, vol. 1, p. 138.

and race. Each of these variables is related to some extent to the occurrence of personality disturbance. While the relationship is not ordinarily of direct etiological importance, the frequency of mental disorder in a given population cannot be understood without reference to these demographic influences.

Age Differences

The relation of age to personality disturbance has been studied primarily by means of first admission rates to mental hospitals. Such studies have revealed important differences. In terms of age groups, approximately 1 percent of patients admitted to mental hospitals are under 15 years of age. About 16 percent are between 15 and 29 years of age, 45 percent are between 30 and 59, and 38 percent are over 60. Because of the increasing longevity of our population, the proportion of patients in the older age group has been increasing rapidly.

Approaching the problem in a different way, the expectancy for admission to a mental hospital changes as age increases. At age 25, the chances are 1 in 74 of being admitted to a hospital. By age 45, the chances are 1 in 25. By 65, they have dropped to 1 in 13, and by 75 the chances are 1 in 9.

The Midtown Manhattan Study found a positive relationship between mental health and age. In general, impairment was least prevalent among the 20 to 29 age group, moderately prevalent in the 30 to 39 and 40 to 49 age groups, and most prevalent in the 50 to 59 age group. Moreover, it was found that younger adults were more likely to seek psychotherapy than those in the older age groups.

Sex Differences

The question of the relative incidence of personality disturbance among men and women was of interest as early as the second century. Caelius Aurelianus came to the conclusion that women were less likely to become mentally disturbed than men, but this contention was disputed by J. E. D. Esquirol and others in the eighteenth and nineteenth centuries. However, the early observations were of little value because of the lack of adequate statistics and because of glaring errors in methodology.

The study of chronic illness in Baltimore reported a higher mental disorder rate among females than among males. Other studies show similar rates for the two sexes. The Midtown Manhattan Study emphasized the complexities of this problem and suggested that the sex factor alone is unrelated to the frequency of personality disorganization. Such a finding does not preclude the possibility of important sex differences in connection with specific types of emotional disturbances.

When the different diagnostic categories are considered, males have a higher incidence in the brain syndromes, while females show somewhat higher rates for the psychoses and neuroses. However, a reversal of this trend is seen in schizophrenia, which shows about 55 percent male admissions to mental hospitals, compared with about 45 percent female admissions. In the case of alcoholism, approximately five times as many men as women are victims of alcohol addiction. This figure is open to some question because female addicts are much less likely to be hospitalized. Similarly, in the area of sexual offenses, the frequency of such offenses among males is far greater than among females. Of the total number of such cases referred to the Psychiatric Institute in Chicago during one year, 83 percent were males and only 17 percent were females (Braude, 1950).

In the case of federal narcotic law violations, there are approximately nine men arrested to one woman. The ratio for actual drug addiction, however, probably would be somewhat less, since the federal arrests include selling and distributing narcotics, in addition to the possession and use of drugs.

In spite of the greater number of men hospitalized for mental disorder and the greater incidence of alcoholism and drug addiction among men, there is evidence that women are more likely to perceive themselves as having adjustment problems. The National Mental Health Survey found that women are more likely than men to report distress in all areas of adjustment (Gurin et al., 1960). This difference appears in general adjustment, in attitudes toward the self, in matters connected with marital and parental roles, and in specific symptom patterns. Generally, the survey showed that women are more likely to be worried, more unhappy in their marriages, more occupied with problems in their marriages, and more likely to fear a nervous breakdown. Women feel more inadequate as parents and are less accepting of themselves. Similarly, they more frequently report symptoms of emotional disturbance.

Marital Status

Marital status is another demographic factor related consistently to the incidence of personality disorder. Considering all mental disorders, the highest rates are found among divorced persons. The next highest rates are for single persons, while lower rates are found among widows and widowers. Married men and women have the lowest rates (Odegaard, 1946). The Midtown Manhattan Study revealed that there is a particularly high prevalence of personality disturbance among single men and the divorced of both sexes. When the clinical groups are considered, married people have the lowest rate of disturbance in all conditions, psychogenic and organic, except personality difficulties associated with the involutional period, or change of life. Here, the lowest rates are found among single men and women.

There are several possible explanations for marital differences in admissions to mental hospitals. It may be that a single person who develops a personality disturbance is more readily admitted to a mental hospital, or that the victims of a disturbance present certain personality traits which before its outbreak act as a marriage handicap; and finally, there may be certain stabilizing factors in married life that prevent the outbreak of mental disorder. The second explanation would appear to be the most likely of the three.

Occupational Status

Early in the nineteenth century in France, Esquirol discussed the relation of occupation to mental disorder. Since that time, the problem has been studied by a number of investigators in various countries. One of the early studies was made at the Psychiatric Clinic at Freiburg, Germany. The major finding was that the largest number of cases of psychosis occurred among laborers and factory workers. At the other extreme, professional men and public officials showed the fewest cases, with businessmen and salaried employees also having a relatively low incidence of psychosis (Stern, 1913).

In a study in Chicago, more than 12,000 cases of male first admissions to mental hospitals were classified into nineteen occupational groups (Clark, 1949). Making the necessary adjustments for age, rates were calculated for each group, and the occupational groups were ranked according to the mental disorder rate, income, and prestige. The rate was found to be lower for the high occupational prestige and income groups, and higher for the low occupational prestige and income groups.

In 1950, all patients admitted to state mental hospitals in Ohio were analyzed in terms of occupation (Frumkin, 1955). First admission rates per 100,000 population were then computed for each of twelve occupational groups. In every clinical category, the highest rates were for the unskilled occupational group, and the lowest or second lowest rates in six of the nine clinical categories were found in the managerial and professional groups. It must be remembered, however, that men who have reached the managerial and professional level are more likely to receive treatment as outpatients or in private hospitals.

The Texas epidemiological study showed that when the incidence rates were adjusted for age, sex, and subculture, the highest rates for all mental disorders were found among the unemployed. The next highest rates were for the professional and semiprofessional group, a finding in striking contradiction to a number of the earlier studies. Following the professional and semiprofessional groups, the rates, in declining order, were highest for service occupations, manual labor, clerical and sales work, agricultural work, and for the managerial, official, and proprietary occupations.

Differential patterns emerge under special cultural conditions and in connection with certain diagnostic categories. While drug addiction is found in a wide range of occupations and professions, a disproportionately large share of addicts are found among musicians, nurses, and physicians. Similarly, in the case of alcoholism, while patients seen in state psychiatric hospitals are likely to be of a low occupational level, surveys of outpatients at clinics for alcoholics show that a majority of the patients hold jobs involving special skills or responsibility (Rose, 1955).

Urban-rural Differences

During the nineteenth century, considerable attention was paid to the relative frequency of mental disorder in urban and rural districts. Generally it was observed that patients were less likely to come from agricultural areas than from manufacturing areas. This finding has been reported consistently. Almost without exception, and for all major psychotic reactions and chronic brain syndromes, the rural rates are below those of urban areas.

The rates of admissions to psychiatric hospitals also vary directly with the size of the city. In one survey, the admission rate for cities of from 25,000 to 100,000 was 54.8 per 100,000 population, while the rate for cities over 100,000 was 92.5, or almost twice as great (Landis and Page, 1939). Another study showed the importance of population density in relation to the major mental disorders. Army rejection rates for such disorders during World War II varied from 7.5 percent in areas having a population of 500 per square mile to 14.0 percent in areas having a population of 20,000 per square mile (Hyde and Kingsley, 1944).

The Yale University Center for Alcohol Studies found that the chances that a person who lives in a rural area will become a chronic alcoholic are less than half as great as those for city dwellers. The rate of chronic alcoholism per 100,000 adult population was 47.4 for communities of less than 2,500 population; for cities over 100,000 population, the rate was 97.2 (Jellinek, 1947). Suicide rates also show an urban-rural difference. Rates range from 15.9 per 100,000 population in cities of 10,000 to 25,000 population to 19.9 in cities of 250,000 to 500,000 (Schroeder and Beegle, 1955). A study of mental hospital admissions in India has indicated that the tendency for admission rates to be higher in the city than in the rural areas is not limited to the United States and Europe.

There are a number of factors that might be of importance in explaining differences in the rates of mental disorder in urban and rural areas. One possibility is that there are differences in national and racial makeup of urban and rural populations. A second possibility is that it is easier to care for mentally disturbed individuals in rural areas and that this factor affects the hospitalization rates. However, the Texas study found no evidence to support the suggestion that the differential between urban and rural areas was due to the availability of treatment facilities. It has been suggested also that the higher urban rates might be due to the migration from rural areas into urban areas by older age groups approaching retirement, or to the fact that stress in rural areas is less than in cities. Similarly, the higher urban rates might be due to the more intense striving for status in urban areas, the relative lack of security of group ties, the lack of stability in social roles, the less personal forms of authority, and the relative lack of integration of religious, occupational, and social groups. These hypotheses suggest the possibility that the degree of social integration might be the important factor, and not the degree of urbanization.

The National Institute of Mental Health has initiated a number of projects related to the study of urban-rural factors in mental disorder. In one project, a substantial decline in the incidence of social problems was observed in a rural population following the establishment of a comprehensive mental health center. Another project has focused on differences between urban and rural communities in the relationship between sociocultural disintegration and psychiatric disorder. A program of reintegration is under way in order to determine if this will alleviate the amount of psychiatric disorder in a population. A third project involves the analysis of data collected on the development and dimensions of deviant behavior. A demographic atlas of symptom frequencies has been prepared to provide an integrated data bank for more detailed and theoretically based investigations (NIMH, 1968).

Educational Level

There is a tendency for higher rates of education and literacy to be associated with higher rates of neurotic disorder. This finding is rather consistent both in studies made in the United States and Europe and in surveys in other cultures.

The epidemiological study in Texas showed only a slight correlation between educational level and the incidence of mental disorder. The most interesting finding was that both extremes of education were among the highest rate group. Those individuals with no education showed a high rate of psychosis, while those individuals with a college education showed a high rate of neurosis. In other cultures, higher admission rates are generally related to a higher degree of literacy. Among Africans in Ghana the literacy rate was about 10 percent at the time of a survey. However, the incidence of literacy among the mentally disturbed was more than 40 percent (Field, 1958).

A clue to this relationship is found in the National Mental Health Survey which showed that people with more education are likely to be introspective and more concerned about the personal and interpersonal relationships affecting their lives. The survey also indicated that people with more education experience greater feelings of inadequacy than people at lower educational levels (Gurin et al., 1960).

Religious Affiliation

A number of demographic surveys have suggested relationships between religious affiliation and emotional disorder. In terms of general religious attitudes, the National Mental Health Survey found that the more frequent church attenders report happier marriages than those who attend church less frequently. The most extreme cases of unhappiness in marriage were reported by Protestants who never attend church and by Catholics who attend only a few times a year. It is of considerable interest that the survey found that church attendance is more closely related to marital happiness than to general happiness.

A study of the religious background of patients receiving treatment at a mental hygiene clinic in New York showed that the number of Jewish patients at the clinic was double their proportionate number in the population. Protestant patients were about half their number, with Catholic patients about two-thirds their number

(Eichler and Lirtzman, 1956). A similar study of patients in Connecticut showed the incidence of psychoneurotic disorders among Jews to be two and a half times the expectation in terms of their number in the population at large (Roberts and Meyers, 1954).

The Midtown Manhattan Study found that Protestants and Catholics differ very little when standardized by age and socioeconomic status, while Jews have a lower frequency of the more severe symptoms and a higher frequency of mild and moderate symptoms. As a result, Jews are lowest in the "well" mental health category (see Table 5.3).

The high rate of Jewish patients in psychotherapy may reflect such cultural factors as the importance which they place on intellectual activities, a relatively enlightened attitude toward personality disturbances, a tendency toward excessive introspection, and a lack of conflict between their religion and the psychological theories used in psychotherapy. It is also possible that the relatively low representation of the Protestant group may be based on the cultural view that the individual is responsible for himself and must work out his own salvation.

The different religious groups show different patterns in connection with such clinical conditions as alcoholism and sex offenses. The rates for alcoholism are lowest among Jews and highest among Catholics, with the various Protestant denominations falling between these two. Within the several religious groups, however, there are marked differences (Malzberg, 1936).

Among Jews who drink, the orthodox Jew has the lowest rate for alcoholism, with the Jewish conservative group having a higher rate, the Jewish reform group a still higher rate, and the Jewish secular group the highest rate. It is also of interest that while the rates for alcoholism are lowest among the Jewish groups, there are fewer total abstainers among Jews than among Catholics and Protestants (Snyder, 1955).

In the area of sex offenses, there is a disproportionate representation of Catholics. One study showed that Catholics make up 53 percent of all sex offenders (Hirning, 1945). Generally, the rates for Catholics and Protestants are relatively high, while the rates among Jewish groups are relatively low. The disproportionate representation of

Table 5.3 *Religion and mental health in the Midtown Manhattan Study*

MENTAL HEALTH CATEGORIES	RELIGIOUS ORIGIN (PERCENT)		
	CATHOLIC	PROTESTANT	JEWISH
Well	17.4	20.2	14.5
Mild symptom formation	34.5	36.4	43.2
Moderate symptom formation	23.4	19.9	25.1
Impaired	24.7	23.5	17.2
(N = 100 per cent)	(832)	(562)	(213)

SOURCE: Adapted from L. Srole et al., *Mental Health in the Metropolis: The Midtown Manhattan Study.* McGraw-Hill Book Company, New York, 1962, vol. 1, p. 305.

Catholics among sex offenders may be due to the somewhat suppressive attitude of the Church toward sexuality. Similarly, family attitudes toward sex are generally more severe among Catholics than among Jews and most Protestant denominations.

Ethnic Differences

Groups of people having a common language, culture, or racial background are called *ethnic* groups. Studies of the incidence of mental disorder in such groups are handicapped by such variables as age, sex, degree of urbanization, marital status, and socioeconomic level.

Generally speaking, the rates for mental disorder are higher for foreign-born persons than for native-born. In addition, there are important national, if not racial, differences among the various foreign-born groups. In a study of New York admission rates for a ten-year period, Italians were found to have the lowest incidence of all foreign-born whites. The Irish and Scandinavians had the highest rates (Malzberg and Lee, 1956).

In considering the cases of mental disorder (other than psychoneurosis) among Jews, rates are generally lower than for non-Jews, with the Jewish patient more likely to develop one of the functional disorders than an organic disorder (Rose and Stub, 1955). The low rate of alcohol addiction is of considerable interest since Jews have relatively high rates for psychoneurotic disorders. Moreover, the Jews have a relatively high rate of drug addiction. During World War I, their rate of drug addiction was the highest of any ethnic group.

The rate of alcoholism among Italians also is

low, in spite of the wide use of wine. The Italian pattern of drinking is a part of everyday family life, and drinking is simply a part of eating. Alcoholism also is rare among the Chinese, where family values and community disapproval discourage drunkenness.

In a study of Irish and Italian psychotic (schizophrenic) patients matched for age, education, and intellectual level, it was found that the Irish showed more latent homosexual tendencies and a greater preoccupation with sex and guilt over sexual behavior (Opler, 1956). The primary defenses were fantasy and withdrawal. The Italians showed more overt homosexual tendencies, but there was no sex guilt and no fixed delusions. The primary defense was lack of impulse control and acting-out behavior.

The studies of ethnic differences and personality disturbance are complicated by factors of a very difficult nature. As the Midtown Manhattan Study indicated, ethnic differences tend to disappear when socioeconomic class is controlled.

ECOLOGICAL VARIABLES

The ecological analysis of mental disorder is a special case of epidemiological research. Ecology refers to the study of the distribution of people as determined by the various forces of the environment. These forces operate in such a way that distinctive patterns of distribution emerge in connection with such conditions as juvenile delinquency, crime, illegitimacy, drug addiction, alcoholism, and mental disorder.

The importance of the ecological analysis of urban areas was first emphasized by sociol-

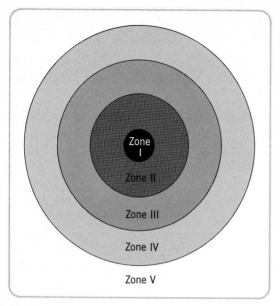

Figure 5.2 *The "natural areas" of a city. Zone I is the central business district; zone II is the area of transition in which property values are high but buildings are deteriorated and rents are low; zone III is the area of workingmen's homes; zone IV is the apartment and residential area; and zone V is the outlying commuter area. (Adapted from Park and Burgess,* The City, *1925.)*

ogists at the University of Chicago who introduced the concept of *natural areas* (Park and Burgess, 1921). By drawing a series of concentric circles stemming from the center of certain cities, it was possible to designate the central business areas, the transitional areas, and the suburbs.

A series of field studies in Chicago was undertaken to test the hypotheses related to natural areas. These ecological studies indicated that suicide rates in urban areas vary in an orderly fashion (Cavan, 1928), that the rates for delinquency and criminal behavior have a regular pattern varying from high rates in the center of the city to low rates at the periphery (Shaw et al., 1929), and that there are ecological factors determining the frequency and location of brothels (Reckless, 1933). It was also found that the ecological pattern of mental retardation resembled the pattern of juvenile delinquency (Jenkins and Brown, 1935).

Ecological analysis was applied to a study of all cases of mental disorder admitted during a twelve-year period to four Illinois state hospitals and eight private sanitariums (Faris and Dunham, 1939). The incidence rates of mental disorders per 100,000 population were plotted on census maps of the Chicago area. This ecological mapping made it possible to determine the degree of relationship existing between the various types of mental disorder and the ecological structure of the city. Mental disorder in general showed a marked concentration in the downtown areas, with the rates declining successively in all directions from the center of the city to the suburbs. The downtown rate of 499 cases per 100,000 population gradually fell off until it was only 48 per 100,000 in the outlying residential areas.

High rates for alcoholism and drug addiction were found in areas of poverty, disorganization, and transition. These cases were found in the hobo area, rooming-house area, and foreign-born slum area. The conditions were associated closely with low income level. Mental disturbance due to syphilis was especially identified with the hobo area and the rooming-house area, in which there are significant disproportions of the sexes and relatively low income. Both districts are populated heavily by single, divorced, and widowed men. There was a slight tendency for the mental disorders of old age to be associated with the central slum and black slum areas.

Studies similar to that of the distribution of mental disorder in Chicago have been made in other cities. These surveys generally support the view that the rate of mental disorders taken together declines regularly from the zone at the center of the city to the zone at the periphery of the city. The ecological research undertaken in Chicago and other cities in the ten years following the original study revealed that a number of the findings had been substantiated (Dunham, 1947).

An ecological study of psychiatric disorders in the Chinese population of Formosa, using the concentric zone theory, also showed that mental disorder occurred more frequently in the central zones of areas under study than in the peripheral zones. The pattern was identical to the one found in the study of mental disturbance in Chicago. The investigator, who was acquainted with psychiatry in Japan and the United States, as well as in Formosa, could find no significant differences in the symptoms of personality disturbance in these different cultures (Lin, 1953).

Population migration is another important ecological variable. Studies in various parts of the world indicate that first admission rates to mental hospitals are markedly higher for migrants than for nonmigrants and that rates are higher for recent migrants than for earlier migrants.

In 30,000 cases admitted to New York mental hospitals during a three-year period, rates were 7.4 per 100,000 for nonmigrants and 13.7 for migrants (Malzberg and Lee, 1956). Since migration from one state to another was associated with personality disturbance to approximately the same extent as migration from a foreign country, it seems likely that it is the migration and not the place of birth that is the important factor. A comparison of first admission rates for mental disorder of Norwegians in Norway to rates of Norwegians who had moved to Minnesota indicated that the admission rate was twice as high among the migrants as among those who had remained in their homeland (Ödegaard, 1932).

The manner in which migration influences the incidence of mental disorder was also demonstrated by a study which compared Okinawans who immigrated to Hawaii during the first half of the present century with native Okinawans at the time of the American military occupation of Okinawa (Wedge, 1952). A strikingly low rate of mental disorder was found among the natives on the island of Okinawa, but in Hawaii the rate for Okinawans was about two and a half times higher than the rate for the general population.

There are at least two possible interpretations of the findings in connection with migration and its relation to personality disorganization. The first possibility is that migration in some way triggers the onset of personality disturbance. A second view is that migration is itself a symptom of an unstable personality more prone to the development of mental disorder. The Norwegian study supports the idea that it is not the migration that is the important factor, but that a higher percentage of susceptible individuals leave their native country. Nevertheless, one cannot avoid the possibility that the act of migration, with all that

it implies in terms of change and insecurity, is a stress situation which might in itself cause an emotional disturbance.

While ecological studies of mental disorder are of great interest, the validity of the detailed findings is questionable. Many methodologically difficult problems are involved in such studies. Most of the information is derived from institutionalized cases and there is ample evidence that at least an equal number of cases have never been hospitalized. Similarly, there are difficulties in diagnosis, the accuracy of the home addresses of many patients is questionable, and the hospital

Figure 5.3 *A census map of Chicago showing the decrease in the rates of mental disorder as one goes from the center of the city to the periphery. (From Faris, R. E. L., and Dunham, H. W.,* Mental Disorders in Urban Areas, *1939.)*

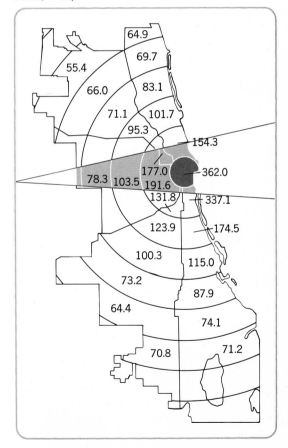

records themselves are often in error. In spite of these problems, however, there does not seem to be any good reason for doubting the validity of the general trend established in the ecological investigations.

SOCIAL STRATIFICATION

The study of the relationship of mental disorder to the socioeconomic status of the patient is another specialized form of epidemiological analysis. Early information on this subject was derived from hospital admission figures and from the analysis of men rejected from the armed services for neuropsychiatric reasons. Since World War II, studies have included patients seen by psychiatrists in private practice. All studies show a consistently increasing incidence of the more serious mental disorders as one goes down the socioeconomic scale.

In an analysis of the psychiatric rejects at the Boston Armed Forces Induction Station, the incidence of mental disorder varied from 7.3 percent in the highest socioeconomic neighborhoods to 16.6 percent in the poorest neighborhoods (Hyde and Kingsley, 1944). In addition to the increase in psychoses, the incidence of mental retardation increased from 0.9 percent in the best areas to 3.0 percent in the poorest areas. The psychoneurotic disorders, however, showed no consistent variation with socioeconomic level. Another study of more than 12,000 first admissions to public and private institutions in Chicago

Table 5.4 *The relationship of social class to the normal and psychiatric populations*

CLASS	PERCENT OF NORMAL POPULATION	PERCENT OF PSYCHIATRIC POPULATION
I	3.1	1.0
II	8.1	6.7
III	22.0	13.2
IV	46.0	38.6
V	17.8	36.8
Unknown	3.0	3.7

SOURCE: Adapted from A. B. Hollingshead and F. C. Redlich, *Social Class and Mental Illness: A Community Study.* John Wiley & Sons, Inc., New York, 1958.

supported the conclusion that high-income groups have significantly lower rates for psychosis than do the low-income groups (Clark, 1949).

One of the most comprehensive studies of social class and personality disorganization was the social stratification of the New Haven urban community by means of an "Index of Social Position" (Hollingshead and Redlich, 1958). To arrive at the level of social position, three factors were taken into consideration: (1) area of residence, (2) occupation, and (3) education. The index identified five major social class levels. The highest social level (class I) contributed only 1.0 percent of the psychiatric cases although this class was made up of 3.1 percent of the general population. At the bottom end of the social scale, class V contributed 36.8 percent of the psychiatric cases although only 17.8 percent of the normal population fell into this group. Important social class differences were also found in connection with the relative incidence of neurosis and psychosis. The highest rates for neurosis were found in classes I and II, while the highest rates for psychosis were found in classes IV and V (see Tables 5.4 and 5.5). This same relationship of an overrepresentation of neurosis among upper-class individuals and of psychosis among the lower class was found in a study of the Lebanese (Katchadourian and Churchill, 1969).

An extensive follow-up study of over 1,500 psychiatric patients in New Haven revealed that 53 percent of these patients, who were hospitalized in 1950, remained or were again hospitalized during the next ten years; 2 percent were receiving outpatient care; and 31 percent had died by 1960. An interesting association between socioeconomic class and outcome was revealed. A patient from the higher social classes had three times as great a chance of remaining out of the hospital than did a patient from the lowest social class. Upper- and middle-class ex-patients, even if they showed greater psychological impairment than lower-class ex-patients, made better social and economic adjustments than did their lower-class counterparts. Thus, membership in the higher social classes appears to confer a measure of "immunity" against hospitalization and the social and economic consequences of mental illness. The reason may be better knowledge about mental

Table 5.5 *The relationship of social class to the neuroses and psychoses*

CLASS	PERCENT NEUROTIC	PERCENT PSYCHOTIC
I	52.6	47.4
II	67.2	32.8
III	44.2	55.8
IV	23.1	76.9
V	8.4	91.6

SOURCE: Adapted from A. B. Hollingshead anf F. C. Redlich, *Social Class and Mental Illness: A Community Study.* John Wiley & Sons, Inc., New York, 1958.

health and greater tolerance of deviant behavior (NIMH, 1968).

In another study of the relationship of social class to mental disorder, 1,000 psychiatric cases in the Air Force were investigated (Lantz, 1953). The number of psychotics decreased as the socioeconomic level increased. High socioeconomic families contributed 1.9 percent of the psychotics, middle-income families contributed 4.3 percent, and low socioeconomic families contributed 10.2 percent. The findings of the Midtown Manhattan Study in this connection are presented in Table 5.6.

The finding that the probability of being admitted to a mental hospital becomes less as one's economic level increases is open to several interpretations. One is that people of higher income are able to take care of their psychological problems in ways other than commitment to a mental hospital. By being able to afford the services of psychiatrists and clinical psychologists in private practice, the higher-income family can have many personality disturbances cared for at home, in the therapist's office, or in a private nonpsychiatric hospital.

Another possibility is that the chances for recovery are less in economically deprived neighborhoods, since treatment is more likely to be of an inferior quality. Higher-social-class patients have a better chance of being selected for psychotherapy and of being treated by an experienced therapist. Lower-class patients tend to be left until they become chronic psychotics.

There is the further possibility that psychotic disorder represents a drift down the social scale as a result of incompetence. One study, however, showed that 91 percent of the patients were in the same social class as their parents, while several other studies have shown greater mobility upwards than downwards (Hollingshead et al., 1954).

A somewhat different explanation of the finding would be that increased economic status carries with it a sense of personal security. As a result of this security, stress is reduced and the individual is less exposed to tension and conflict. Such an explanation would imply that the difference in expectancy of mental illness among low-income groups and high-income groups is a real, rather than an apparent, difference.

It may also be that different cultural segments of society have different stress patterns putting pressures on the members of the segment. Other possibilities are that members of different social classes differ in their psychological defenses,

Table 5.6 *Mental health and socioeconomic status in the Midtown Manhattan Study*

MENTAL HEALTH CATEGORIES	HIGHEST STRATUM (PERCENT)	LOWEST STRATUM (PERCENT)
Well	30.0	4.6
Mild symptom formation	37.5	25.0
Moderate symptom formation	20.0	23.1
Impaired	12.5	47.3
Marked symptom formation	6.7	16.7
Severe symptom formation	5.8	21.3
Incapacitated	0.0	9.3
($N = 100$ percent)	(120)	(108)

SOURCE: Adapted from L. Srole et al., *Mental Health in the Metropolis: The Midtown Manhattan Study.* McGraw-Hill Book Company, New York, 1962, vol. 1, p. 230.

in the conflicts to which they are susceptible, and, eventually, in the type of personality disorganization.

There has been an increasing interest in mental health problems of the poor. Preliminary studies (1970) by the National Institute of Mental Health show that the negative effects on attitude and behavior of poverty and cultural deprivation are even more devastating than was suspected originally. Aggravating the problem is the fact that until the 1960s little effort was made to provide a more appropriate distribution of mental health services unrelated to economic status. The lower socioeconomic groups are being reached today through neighborhood and union facilities. In slum areas counseling centers and emergency walk-in services have been established in abandoned stores and basements. In many deprived neighborhoods, young people have been recruited and trained successfully to work with professionals to provide a variety of important mental health services to people living in these areas.

The National Institute of Mental Health's community mental health program has concentrated on the mental health aspects of the poverty cycle, including the poor person's attitudes toward society, feelings of self-esteem, family relationships, social competence, and ego-enhancing needs. Innovative methods are being tried to reach and treat the poor and culturally deprived racial and ethnic groups. In a slum area of the Bronx, a section of New York City, the psychiatric service of a public general hospital is operating a neighborhood store-front service center and is also studying the most effective ways of using neighborhood aides in a mental health program. In a very different environment, an isolated area in Appalachia, a traveling clinical team made up of a social worker and a nurse has been able to reach patients discharged from a public mental hospital and prevent their readmission (NIMH, 1969).

While the studies of the epidemiology of mental disorder are of considerable interest and importance in our understanding of abnormal psychology, they must be looked upon with caution because of the many difficulties in defining what is normal, the relative nature of deviant behavior, and similar problems.[4]

CROSS-CULTURAL STUDIES

The effect of cultural patterns upon the form of personality disorganization has been a problem of interest to the cultural anthropologist for many years. Early in the present century it was believed that the study of existing primitive tribes, relatively untouched by civilization, would make it possible to gain valuable insight into the origins of abnormal behavior. However, contemporary anthropologists ordinarily do not subscribe to the evolutionary theory of culture. The primitive tribes in the world today are no longer thought to represent "primitive" qualities in an evolutionary sense. The anthropologist is more interested in the cross-

---

[4]Among the books on epidemiology are *Psychosis and Civilization* (Free Press, 1953) by Herbert Goldhamer and A. W. Marshall; E. G. Jaco's *The Social Epidemiology of Mental Disorders: A Psychiatric Survey of Texas* (Russell Sage Foundation, 1960); *Epidemiology and Mental Illness* (Basic Books, 1960) by R. J. Plunkett and J. E. Gordon; *Mental Health and Mental Disorder: A Sociological Approach* (Norton, 1955), edited by A. M. Rose; *Mental Health in the Metropolis: The Midtown Manhattan Study* (McGraw-Hill, 1962) by Leo Srole and others; and the first volume of the Stirling County Studies *My Name Is Legion* (Basic Books, 1961) by Alexander H. Leighton.

Special problems in epidemiology are dealt with in *Social Class and Mental Illness* (Wiley, 1958) by A. B. Hollingshead and F. C. Redlich; *Family and Class Dynamics in Mental Illness* (Wiley, 1959) by Jerome K. Myers and Bertram H. Roberts; *Mental Disease in Urban Areas* (University of Chicago, 1939) by R. E. L. Faris and H. Warren Dunham; *Migration and Mental Illness* (Social Science Research Council, 1956) by Benjamin Malzberg and E. S. Lee; and *The Alcoholic Psychoses: Demographic Aspects at Midcentury in New York State* (Yale Center for Alcohol Studies, 1960) and *Mental Disease among Jews in New York State* (Intercontinental, 1960), both books by Benjamin Malzberg. Other books are *Field Studies in the Mental Disorders* (Grune & Stratton, 1961), edited by Joseph Zubin; and *Comparative Epidemiology of Mental Disorders* (Grune & Stratton, 1961), edited by Paul H. Hoch and Joseph Zubin.

cultural differences which are related to cultural change and child-rearing practices.

Anthropological research into personality disturbance in other cultures is a complicated matter. While some of the earlier cultural anthropologists were trained in psychiatry, psychiatrists with anthropological expeditions were often unskilled concerning the data and techniques of cultural anthropology. Fortunately, increasing emphasis on interdisciplinary training has made this problem less serious.

Emil Kraepelin was one of the first specialists in mental illness to interest himself seriously in the problems of comparative psychiatry. He toured a number of countries and observed forms of mental disorder in a large mental hospital in Java. He was particularly interested in learning whether the influence of climate and other tropical conditions of life modified the symptoms of mental disorder. He found that Europeans born and reared in Java presented exactly the same clinical types of mental disorder as those seen in Europe. However, Kraepelin observed symptoms among the natives that not only formed special clinical groups but also colored the character of the more common forms of mental disturbances (Kraepelin, 1896).

Freud's work in psychoanalysis, probably more than any other single force, stimulated interest in the anthropological study of personality disturbances. In his book *Totem and Taboo,* which appeared in 1912, Freud suggested that the behavior of primitive man is in many ways similar to that of the psychoneurotic. He argued that the magical practices and irrational rites which make up primitive man's system of taboos may be linked with the obsessive thoughts and compulsive actions of the neurotic patient in contemporary society. However, the validity of this hypothesis has been questioned by many social scientists.

One of the first signs of contact between anthropology and psychoanalysis was a review of *Totem and Taboo* which appeared in the *American Anthropologist* in 1920. While the reviewer remarked on the importance of psychoanalysis, he criticized Freud's belief that the Oedipus complex is the key to culture and society. He wrote: "This book is keen without orderliness, intricately rather than closely reasoned, and endowed with an unsubstantiated convincingness" (Kroeber, 1920).

Many critics of Freudian doctrine have made similar charges.

In 1924, a distinguished British anthropologist, C. G. Seligman, gave further impetus to the growing mutual interests of psychiatrists and anthropologists in the problems of culture and mental disorder when he chose the topic "Anthropology and Psychology: A Study of Some Points of Contact" as his presidential address to the Royal Anthropological Institute. Freud's book *Group Psychology and the Analysis of the Ego* had appeared in 1922, and the way was marked for field studies.

A field investigation of the South Pacific culture of Papua (British New Guinea) was made early in this century when the Papuans were considered to be at a Neolithic, or Stone Age, level. The inhabitants were found to be of an excitable and extroverted temperament with no evidence of mental disorder other than brief outbursts of maniacal excitement. The investigator favored the hypothesis, already advanced in the eighteenth and nineteenth centuries, that mental disorder is an outgrowth of cultural tensions in which economic and religious factors play an important part. He believed that true mental disorder in Papua occurred only where the natives had been disturbed by, or were in conflict as a result of, Western influence (Seligman, 1929).

A classic study of the psychoanalytic outlook applied to a primitive community was published in 1926 in the book *Sex and Repression in Savage Society.* A study was made of the natives of the Trobriand and Amphett Islands in the South Pacific. The inhabitants of the two islands were similar in race and in language, yet the Trobriand Islanders had considerable sexual freedom, while the Amphett group lived under strict prohibitions. The rate of neurotic reactions was low among the Trobrianders and high among the Amphett Islanders. This finding was viewed as evidence in support of Freud's hypothesis that sexual repression is the critical factor in the etiology of neurosis (Malinowski, 1927).

The early studies of this kind, as well as many of the more recent ones, are of interest primarily as a history of ideas. Conclusions are mostly speculative and are open to serious question. One of the obvious difficulties is the lack of standards about what should be considered an instance of psychiatric disorder. Workers in this field have many different frames of reference and degrees of competence. The result is a jumble of data which frequently permits very little comparison or generalization.

While a few studies were reported early in this century by American psychiatrists, it was not until 1920 that anthropologists began in earnest to apply theories of psychopathology to ethnological and anthropological problems. Since that time, American anthropology has been influenced to a large extent by the Freudian theory of psychoanalysis.

Ruth Benedict (1887–1948) made the first clear statement of the effects of culture upon abnormal behavior; and one of her students, Margaret Mead (1901–　　), was the first American anthropologist to organize research along psychiatric lines. Benedict showed that Melanesian society is built on traits which would be regarded as paranoid in our culture. The members of the group look upon one another as purveyors of "black magic," and the women would never think of leaving their cooking pots unguarded. The extent of the paranoid thinking is seen in the standard polite phrase of acceptance of a gift, "And if you now poison me, how shall I repay you for this present?" (Benedict, 1934).

Other anthropologists also made early contributions to social psychiatry. One investigator made a study of the Melanesian Island of Dobu and commented on the fact that the sexual freedom exercised there appeared to discourage personality disturbance having sexual content. "I did not see or hear of any one such case in Dobu. Although in the Admiralties, which has a prudish sex life without individual freedom, I both saw and heard of many. There were many aberrant persons in Dobu. But apart from pathological jealousy in a few cases, aberrations took non-sexual paths" (Fortune, 1932).

Another pioneer was a psychiatrist who did field work among the tribes of South Africa. He pointed out the importance of mythical figures in the native explanations of psychotic behavior, in the delusions of hospitalized patients, and in the dream life of normals. These figures included oversexed dwarfs, snakes lurking in the female sexual organs, and blood-eating and oversexed birds. The imagery and the interpretation of it by the natives was highly suggestive of Freudian concepts (Laubscher, 1938).

One of the most interesting contributions made by anthropologists and social psychiatrists has been the description of personality disturbances and behavior disorders which are not seen in our own culture. Early in the present century, a condition called *arctic hysteria* was observed among the natives of northern Siberia. This disorder was marked by a high degree of suggestibility which was almost hypnotic in its effect. The condition also showed symptoms in which the patient imitated the movements and actions of other people (Bogoras, 1904–1909).

Another disturbance, called *pibloktoq,* was reported among Eskimo women during Admiral Peary's expeditions (Brill, 1913). In a sudden state of excitement, the victim would begin to sing, shout, run about, and tear off her clothing. Attacks lasted an hour or two and ended in weeping and falling asleep. Sometimes there would be a loss of consciousness. The disorder was thought to be related to the insecure emotional environment of Eskimo women, who were considered the property of the male and could be acquired, exchanged, or disposed of as easily as any other property.

A similar condition has been observed in other countries in the arctic latitudes including Iceland, the Faroe Islands, and the northern extremes of Europe and Asiatic Russia. There has been an endemic prevalence of the disorder among the women of the Samoyeds, the Yakuts, and other Siberian tribes, as well as among the inhabitants of the Kamchatka peninsula in northeast Asia. The condition has also been observed among the women of the Samara district and the Kirghiz steppes in Russia (Aberle, 1952).

A special type of personality disturbance is found among the Chippewa, Cree, Ojibway, and other Canadian Indian tribes (Cooper, 1933). This condition, called *witigo (wihtigo, windigo),* is marked by the initial phase of anxiety associated with nausea, vomiting, and distaste for food. The anxiety grows out of the belief that the physical symptoms mean the victim is turning into a *witigo,* or cannibal, and that he has been bewitched. Eventually the victim becomes extremely agitated, and he sometimes asks to be killed. The oral aggressive component of the *witigo* psychosis suggests that the condition might be related to the serious problems of obtaining food encountered by these tribes.

Among the Diegueno Indians of lower California, two mental disorders are known as *kimilue* and *echul*. The dream doctor of the Indian tribe regards these conditions as types of sexual disturbance. *Kimilue* is a disorder in which the patient loses all interest in daily life, suffers a loss of appetite, is generally apathetic, and has vivid sexual dreams. *Echul,* another form of sexual disturbance, becomes acute during severe life crises such as divorce or the death of a wife, husband, or child. The condition is sometimes associated with convulsive behavior (Toffelmier and Luomala, 1936).

There has also been a persistent interest in two distinctive behavior disorders which have been reported among the Malays. The first of these conditions, called *amok,* is characterized by sudden wild outbursts of aggression. The phrase "to run amok" is derived from early reports of this behavior. The second condition, known as *lata,* is a disorder marked by extreme passivity and oversuggestibility.

A Dutch psychiatrist in the East Indies described amok as the sudden and unexpected murderous attack of the Malay man who, without any known reason, suddenly jumps up and injures or kills anyone who happens to stand in his way. Amok was regarded as an acute state of mental confusion in which the victim tries to flee from a menacing danger. At the conclusion of the attack, the individual falls into a coma. Upon awakening, there is a complete loss of memory for the preceding events. It was suggested that one factor in the etiology of the condition is the imperfect control of emotion which was felt to be common to the Malayan (Van Loon, 1927).

An anthropologist who observed his interpreter running amok on the island of Dobu described the incident in the following way:

There, just outside, was my man foaming at the mouth with contorted features, body glistening with perspiration, and spear brandished about his shoulder. . . he did not strike, though he stuffed earth into his mouth in horrid pantomime of eating me . . . still foaming, writhing, and threatening me . . . next day he was at work interpreting quite oblivious of where he had been

the day before or what had happened, except that he had felt strange on coming to from something. He could not remember what (Fortune, 1932).

The condition of *juramentado* is similar in many ways to amok. The term was used originally by the Spaniards to designate a Mohammedan Moro who after certain religious rites sought to kill others until he himself was killed. The behavior disturbance seems to be limited to men who are of the Mohammedan faith and related ethnologically to the Malays and Moros, although a similar disorder has been reported in India and Siberia (Musgrave, 1921).

A number of cases of juramentado have been reported. Sometimes it is grief, infidelity of a wife, death of a loved one, fear of disgrace, or an accusation of cowardice; or the attacks may be preceded by long periods of depression in which the patient becomes morose, gives up his work, and loses interest in life. The attacks may also be brought on by religious rites, incantations, music, dancing, and other forms of stimulation. When a sufficient frenzy is reached, the afflicted person suddenly runs into a crowded street with his *kris,* or native dagger, and kills anyone who happens to come in his way. After the attack, the patient sinks into a stuporous sleep from which he awakens in a disagreeable frame of mind.

Lata is a different type of condition. Here, a sudden fright or other strong emotion causes the Malay woman to enter a curious state in which she imitates immediately and precisely what is done before her or repeats what is said to her. All normal control of action appears to be swept away by the sudden emotion. The lata woman sometimes utters, or even shouts, highly obscene words and may express wishes which normally would be repressed. One possible explanation is that in Malay society the female is likely to be shy, colorless, and unaggressive and to live largely within the confines of the home. She is not equipped to cope with sudden, unexpected situations of an anxiety-provoking nature, and the lata reaction is her response to the threat of danger. While the Malays are particularly susceptible, the condition has also been reported in Java, Siam, China, and the Philippines. However, the disturbance does not appear to affect Europeans residing in the tropics (Yap, 1952).

DIFFERENTIAL RATES

Cross-cultural investigations are also concerned with the analysis of the relative incidence of the more conventional personality disturbances. Unfortunately, a basic confusion permeates all writing about psychiatric disorders in other cultures because the term "mental illness" and equivalent terms sometimes refer to the psychoses, sometimes to brain syndromes, sometimes only to the psychoneuroses, and sometimes to all forms of behavior disturbance. Since the etiologies of these various conditions are quite different, it is impossible to generalize from one disorder to another. As a result, the findings are often confusing and frequently misleading. Until the diagnostic categories are defined in a more explicit manner, studies of the relative incidence of mental disorder in other cultures must be interpreted with caution.

A British psychiatrist commissioned by the World Health Organization to gather data on mental illness in the Kenya Province of East Africa based his findings on more than five hundred natives admitted to the Mathari Mental Hospital at Nairobi over a five-year period (Carothers, 1948). The annual admission rate for one type of psychotic disorder (schizophrenia) was found to be 1.1 per 100,000. This low rate was compared with that of American blacks who at that time had an annual admission rate of 161 per 100,000 in Massachusetts. Detribalized natives were found to develop mental disorder more frequently than natives who did not have close contact with European civilization. While 90 percent of the natives lived on reservations and participated in the traditional primitive culture, and only 10 percent of the natives were working as laborers in the cities or on European-owned plantations, approximately 50 percent of the first admissions to the Nairobi mental hospital were drawn from the 10 percent of detribalized natives.

It was also found that there was no cerebral arteriosclerosis, or hardening of the arteries of the brain, among the natives. This finding was interpreted to mean that this disorder is an organic response to the stress of competitive living.

Another study of mental disorder among natives of West Africa investigated nonhospitalized cases on the Gold Coast (Tooth, 1950). An incidence of 96 per 100,000 was reported for all mental disturbances, with the incidence for schizophrenia being 39 per 100,000. This figure is much lower than the rate for nonhospitalized cases in Europe and America.

In a cross-cultural study of Okinawa and Guam, it was found that the incidence of personality disturbance was high in Guam but extremely low in Okinawa (Wedge, 1952). The Okinawan culture appeared to be consistent and undisturbed by internal conflict. The situation in Guam was different. There the culture was a conflicting product of native, Oriental, and Western influences. It is possible that the difference in the rate of mental disorder is related to the degree of cultural stability.

Another study analyzed admissions to mental hospitals in New Zealand for a ten-year period (Beaglehole, 1939). The admission rates for Europeans and the native Maori were compared. The rate of mental disorder was found to be 83.7 per 100,000 population for Europeans and 41.9 per 100,000 population for the Maori. This same investigator also made a study of the rate of mental disorder in Fiji. The natives of this island showed a rate of mental disorder of 16.0 per 100,000, while the Europeans had a rate of 40.5 per 100,000. In both studies, the rate for Europeans was at least double that for the natives.

Cultural factors unquestionably exert an influence on mental health. A study was made on the island of Mauritius, which lies east of the coast of Africa in the Indian Ocean. The population of Mauritius is of recent Indian or East African origin. The study was undertaken to evaluate the assertion that "unwesternized" mental patients in India and Africa recover more rapidly and more completely from psychotic episodes than do Europeans and North American patients. Results based on patients admitted to the mental hospital in Mauritius support the assertion that functional psychoses are more transitory among peoples of Indian and African origin (NIMH, 1968).

Cultural differences in psychopathology are also seen in countries with more closely related cultures. Observed symptoms in outpatient clinics in New York State have been distinctly different from observed symptoms in the Netherlands. The American patients more often exhibited agitated depression while the Dutch patients tended to show a more passive, apathetic type of depression. Psychological complaints were more common among the American patients, while Dutch patients complained more frequently of physical symptoms (NIMH, 1968).

One of the most important studies of personality disorganization in a relatively primitive African culture was undertaken in rural Ghana by a British ethnographer who took her medical degree and was trained in clinical psychiatry. When she investigated the shrine cults of Ghana, she had an unusual opportunity to observe mental disturbance among the Ashanti natives (Field, 1960). This psychiatrist established herself near a shrine where people came for help from a priest who communicated advice from a god, and she was able to obtain case histories on a number of supplicants who were mentally disturbed. Among the most important of her findings was that depression, which had been reported in earlier studies as being extremely rare, was in fact a most common symptom. Her work supports the idea that while mental disorders differ in the cultural form they take, their causes are probably very much the same from one culture to another.

It must be emphasized that cross-cultural studies of mental disturbance based on first admission rates to mental hospitals are open to serious question because of the number of uncontrolled variables. There is the question of what constitutes a first-admission case, since some hospitals list first admissions to that particular hospital while others list those who are admitted for the first time to any hospital. The lag in time between the onset of illness and the hospitalization is another variable. More important is the fact that a number of disturbed individuals are not included in state hospital records; treatment is received in general hospitals and private psychiatric hospitals and on an outpatient basis. Differences in diagnosis also play a role in giving a bias to incidence rates in different hospitals, different countries, and different parts of the same country.

CHILD-REARING PRACTICES

The cross-cultural approach is also concerned with child-rearing practices in various cultural groups. There is a large and important segment of scientific authority which maintains that personality disturbances later in life can grow out of such practices as lack of breastfeeding, a curtailed period of nursing, abrupt weaning, an overly rigid nursing schedule, premature toilet training, infrequent mothering, excessive punishment, and similar actions which operate to make the child feel unwanted, unloved, insecure, inadequate, and frustrated.

It has been shown that the suspicious and unambitious qualities so pronounced in the personality of the adult Alorese are in part a function of the way in which their infants were handled (DuBois, 1944). They were nursed at irregular intervals, their discipline was unsystematic, and there was a general lack of consistency in training. At one time an infant would be picked up and caressed if he cried; at another time, the same infant would be left to cry without the slightest attention being paid to him. The erratic and unpredictable treatment of the infant was believed to result in an adult with distinctive personality characteristics.

Among the Pilagá Indians in the Argentine of South America, there is complete sexual permissiveness from early childhood. All sexual activities within the family are carried out in full view of even the youngest children. Since there are no prohibitions placed on the sexual activities of children, they are completely free to do as they please. Both heterosexual and homosexual activities are carried out openly from early childhood. In such a completely permissive atmosphere, problems later in life seldom are related to sexual frustration (Henry and Henry, 1944).

A study of the possible effects of child rearing on later mental health was made in Okinawa. Fewer than 250 mental patients were found in a population of approximately 350,000. There appeared to be a minimum of psychosomatic disorders, and surgeons rarely reported shock reactions or fainting spells. Also, some of the organic changes due to emotional tension seen in our culture were not reported by pathologists in Okinawa. It was observed that Okinawan mothers were seldom separated from their children. The children were breast-fed whenever they were hungry or in pain, and the mothers did not force bowel training. There was no physical punishment; the infant was regarded as a human being with more rights than an adult. The investigator suggested that the emotional stability of the adult

Okinawan was to be explained by these early, satisfying life experiences (Moloney, 1945).

While the findings in connection with parental attitudes and maternal deprivation have sometimes been conflicting, work with animals has made it clear that the nature of the infant-mother relationship may have important implications for the later development of healthy and unhealthy personality characteristics. In a study of unusual interest, a University of Wisconsin psychologist raised infant monkeys with artificial mothers (Harlow, 1960). One group of monkeys was reared with wire "mothers" which were hard, cold, and unresponding. A second group of monkeys was raised with mothers made of terry cloth and foam rubber. These mothers were soft and warm, but they were also unresponding. It was found that the cloth mothers demonstrated an extraordinary capacity to instill feelings of security in the young animals. Further experiments showed that infant monkeys reared with wire mothers found it difficult later on to develop normal social and sexual companionship with other monkeys. It was not expected, however, that the monkeys raised with the terry cloth and foam rubber mothers would have this same difficulty, since these infant monkeys showed a very strong affection and attachment to this form of mother surrogate. Yet these monkeys also had difficulty in establishing normal emotional relationships with other monkeys. The findings suggest the possible critical role of the *responding* parent in the development of the well-adjusted personality.

The weight of evidence indicates that child-rearing practices may influence an individual's susceptibility to emotional disturbance. While the manner in which this influence is exerted is not clear, one of the principal impacts of child-rearing practices may be in the area of stress tolerance. An examination of various practices under experimental conditions, and in different cultures, suggests that some of these practices increase the threshold for tolerating stress, while others decrease this threshold. It is impossible, however,

to say with any degree of certainty which child-rearing practices are ultimately beneficial and which are ultimately destructive in terms of an individual's later emotional stability and mental health.

As we noted earlier, cross-cultural studies suggest that while there may be wide differences in the surface symptoms of mental disorder, the underlying processes may be very similar. This indication gives additional support to the position that there may be a physical basis for some of the more serious conditions. Since a number of the milder personality disturbances also appear universally, even though they are much more susceptible to cultural conditioning, it is also possible that there may be a constitutional basis for conditions of this type.[5]

GROUP STRESS

The story of the impact of culture on personality disorganization would not be complete without reference to the great psychological epidemics which have taken place over the centuries. From the tenth to the sixteenth centuries the Western European world was swept by a wave of epidemic behavior disorders. The year 1000 was one of particularly great stress and anxiety because the Apocalypse had predicted that at the end of a thousand years Christ would descend and preside at the Day of Judgment. In anticipation of this event, an increasing number of pilgrimages were made to the Holy Land, finally causing the opposition of the non-Christian Turks. When the pilgrims reached the Holy Land, many were robbed, beaten, and murdered. Others were not allowed to enter Jerusalem. Among those who managed to return to Europe was Peter the Hermit, a monk who was to convulse Europe with his fanatical preaching and his stories of the wrongs committed in the Holy Land.

Another important event leading to tension and anxiety was the Great Plague, or Black Death, which appeared in China in the early part

---

[5]Books concerned with cross-cultural problems include the *Ciba Foundation Symposium: Transcultural Psychiatry* (Little, 1965) edited by A. V. S. de Reuck and Ruth Porter; E. A. Weinstein's *Cultural Aspects of Delusion: A Psychiatric Study of the Virgin Islands* (Free Press, 1962); and M. J. Field's *Search for Security: An Ethno-psychiatric Study of Rural Ghana* (Northwestern University Press, 1960).

of the fourteenth century. The epidemic swept over Asia and into Europe and Africa, killing one out of every four people. The emotional stress connected with the plague precipitated a series of mass psychological disorders, including mass flagellation, the dancing mania, and the group convulsive disorders.

Flagellation, or whipping, had been considered for centuries by the Church as an appropriate punishment and atonement for sin. Horrified by the plague, people hoped to stop its progress by mortification and penance. In many parts of Europe, long lines of people, dressed in somber robes covered with red crosses, marched slowly through the streets. Twice each day the processions would halt in order to allow the marchers to do penance in the form of whipping themselves and one another until the blood streamed from their bodies. Eventually, the movement spread throughout Europe; and the Brethren of the Cross, as they came to be known, absolved one another and even took possession of many of the churches. Finally, the Church and secular authorities combined to put a stop to the Flagellants.

Another form of epidemic psychopathology was the dancing mania, or *tarantism*. This disturbance first appeared in Europe as an epidemic in Italy near the close of the fourteenth century. It was believed at first that the condition was brought on by the bite of a large spider called the tarantula. The disorder spread rapidly to other parts of Europe and lasted for several hundred years. Some of the victims experienced visual and auditory hallucinations, lost the use of speech, and were thrown into involuntary dancing movements. The only way in which the victims of tarantism could obtain relief was through music. At the sound of a flute or guitar, the victims would begin to move rhythmically, slowly at first, then faster and faster, until they fell to the ground in a state of utter exhaustion. People came to expect a cure through dancing, and this idea spread rapidly. Eventually the Festival of Tarantali was inaugurated; and a particular form of music, the *tarantella*, was developed. At the first sound of the music, the victims of the disorder rose and danced in cadence. When the music stopped, they fell to the ground in an attack of melancholy and could be roused only by the renewal of the music. The musicians

played in relays until everyone was completely exhausted. At one time more than a thousand dancers were reported at Metz and another five hundred at Cologne.

In the seventeenth century, women made an annual pilgrimage to St. Vitus's Chapel at Drefelhausen, Germany, where compulsive dancing continued for days and nights at a time. This chapel was of particular importance because St. Vitus, a fourth-century Sicilian, was afflicted with what would appear to be a neurological disorder. At the time, however, he was believed to be a victim of tarantism. As a result, his chapel became a shrine of special significance to those who were victims of the dancing mania. The disorder was still epidemic in Africa as recently as 150 years ago. Known as *tigretier,* the disturbance began by violent fever, loss of speech, and emaciation. Relatives would hire a company of musicians, and the victim would dance until he was cured.

Epidemic convulsive behavior is another form of shared psychopathology that has been observed for centuries. This type of behavior was seen in dramatic form in the eighteenth century when a rumor spread that miracles were being performed at a tomb in the St. Medard Cemetery in Paris. A visitor standing in front of the tomb was seized with convulsions, and several other people who were nearby were also stricken. This incident was the beginning of an emotional epidemic known as the *convulsionnaires*. Finally, Louis XV ordered the cemetery to be closed, but the epidemic behavior had already spread to other parts of France. It eventually spread throughout Europe and even reached to the United States.

The great religious revival movements, from Peter the Hermit to Mary Baker Eddy, are not without their implications for psychopathology. The Reformation, the Puritan movement, the Wesleyan revival in England, and the Great Awakening in America, however sincerely conceived, contained numerous examples of mass irrationality and disorganization.

The Great Awakening in America was set off in the eighteenth century by the extraordinary preaching of Jonathan Edwards. A graduate of Yale, Edwards became renowned as the pastor of the church at Northampton, Massachusetts. He was a man of tremendous earnestness, vivid imagery, and strong logical argument. His sermons terrified the members of the congregation by appealing directly to their fears and superstitions. Members of his congregation fainted, had convulsions, and showed other signs of personality disorganition.

James Davenport, a religious extremist who followed Edwards, was also noted for his power to produce agony and distress, fallings, faintings, tremblings, and shriekings. Davenport believed he had the power of discerning spirits as well as the gift of healing. Finally, he became such a nuisance that he was deported from Connecticut. Later, he was indicted in Boston, where he apologized publicly for his irrational behavior. Since that time, disorganized behavior has been encouraged by a number of organized churches, sects, or other religious bodies. The Holy Rollers, Holy Jumpers, Angel Dancers, Holy Jerkers, Shaking Quakers, and Dancing Dervishes provide examples of this form of shared psychopathology. A different form of epidemic personality disorganization occurred on a Sunday night in 1938 when Orson Welles presented a radio adaptation of H. G. Wells' *The War of the Worlds*. While the program was meant to be just another presentation of the Mercury Theater of the Air, it set off an unparalleled wave of terror and panic. A radio audience of more than six million listeners tuned in to hear that a number of hideous monsters from Mars, armed with flame throwers, had landed on a farm at Grovers Mill, New Jersey. During the course of the broadcast at least a million people were so frightened that they swamped radio stations, newspaper offices, hospitals, and police stations with frantic telephone calls, filled churches to overflowing, gathered in the streets to pray, and rushed their families into cars and fled from the advancing "monsters."

The next day the newspapers described the tidal wave of terror that had swept the continent. A man in Massachusetts took the first train out of town. He traveled 60 miles before he heard that the broadcast was only a play. College students in a midwestern university stood in line to make long-distance telephone calls to their parents to say good-bye. Hundreds of people hid in cellars. One man jumped into his car and drove halfway across Pennsylvania before he was told that he was not being pursued by Martians.

The Office of Radio Research, established at Princeton University under a grant from the Rockefeller Foundation, made an extensive study of the nationwide panic, and the major findings and conclusions, along with the script of the radio broadcast, were published in the book *The Invasion from Mars* (Cantril, 1940).

More than 250 social scientists returned a questionnaire which had asked them to point out some of the characteristics of people who were most likely to be frightened by the broadcast. The majority opinion was that women, the elderly, the uneducated, and those living in large cities would be the most upset. It was felt that emotional instability and suggestibility were the most important personality traits related to such a mass reaction. Finally, the major reasons given why people thought the broadcast was true were the war scare in Europe at the time, general intellectual immaturity, the prestige of the commentators, general emotional immaturity, the mystery of science, and personal insecurity.[6]

SUMMARY

1. Cultural and social factors combine with biological and psychological factors in triggering personality disturbance and, in some cases, in determining the form it takes. The major cultural approaches to the problem of personality disorganization include *family studies,* the *epidemiology of mental illness, cross-cultural studies,* and *the analysis of group stress.*

---

[6]There are several fascinating books dealing with epidemic psychopathology. *The June Bug: A Study of Hysterical Contagion* (Appleton, 1968) by A. C. Kerckhoff and K. W. Back, describes a modern epidemic in a mill in the South. Mentioned above was Hadley Cantril's *The Invasion from Mars* (Princeton University Press, 1940). The most complete historical account of disorganized group behavior is Charles Mackay's classic *Extraordinary Popular Delusions and the Madness of Crowds* (National Library of London, 1852).

2. The investigation of the family, as the social group most intimately involved with emotional disorder, is a major cultural approach. Family studies are usually concerned with *parental attitudes* and *family dynamics.* These studies have demonstrated the importance of such factors as consistent attitudes, stable interpersonal relationships within the family, and the personality characteristics of the parents, particularly the mother, in the maintenance of mental health among family members.

3. The epidemiology of mental illness concerns itself with the location and statistical study of psychiatric cases—the emotionally disturbed individuals in the community as well as patients who are hospitalized. One of the important aspects of epidemiology is the study of *demographic,* or population, variables. These variables include age and sex differences, marital status, occupational status, urban-rural differences, educational level. religious affiliation, and ethnic differences.

4. The *ecology* of mental disorder, a subarea of epidemiological research, is concerned with the distribution of cases in a given area. A number of important ecological studies in various urban areas suggest that there is a decline in the rate of mental disorder from the central areas of a city to the outlying residential areas. *Social stratification,* another subarea of epidemiological analysis, is concerned with the relationship of personality disturbance to social and economic variables.

5. Cross-cultural studies deal with the effect of cultural patterns upon the form of personality disorganization. The earliest studies in this field were undertaken by cultural anthropologists and later by psychiatrists with an interest in anthropology. Field studies in various parts of the world suggest that while symptom patterns may differ markedly from one culture to another, the underlying disorders are highly similar. Cross-cultural investigations also make use of hospital statistics, particularly the differential admission rates. While these rates show dramatic differences in different parts of the world, hospital statistics are not a valid reflection of the true incidence of the various mental disorders. Lack of uniformity in reporting, diagnosis, admission policies and procedures, and other factors operate to make the comparison of hospital admission rates of questionable value. The cross-cultural approach includes studies of child-rearing practices in various groups in an attempt to determine the influence of these practices on mental health later in life.

6. The study of group stress, or epidemic emotional disturbance, is also part of the cultural approach. Throughout history there have been dramatic examples of epidemic emotional disturbances. The analysis of the conditions under which these epidemics arise and the form taken by the symptoms gives valuable clues to the psychodynamic processes underlying both group and individual disorganization.

OTHER AUDIOTAPES

Social Stress and Urban Violence
Dr. Jerome D. Frank presents a twenty-two-minute analysis of the psychosocial stresses felt by blacks in urban ghettoes and relates this issue to protest activities. He discusses possible remedial measures. Sound Seminar 75586, *McGraw-Hill Book Company.*

Cultural Factors in Mental Illness
Dr. E. D. Wittkower presents a twenty-one-minute talk on the importance of cultural factors in the understanding of personality disorganization. Sound Seminar 75935, *McGraw-Hill Book Company.*

6 TRANSIENT SITUATIONAL DISTURBANCES

Many personality disturbances are of a relatively minor, and often temporary, nature. Such conditions are frequently due more to *situational* stress —that is, the stress of circumstances of shorter or longer duration—than to imperfections of the personality. These forms of personality disorganization were neglected until the present century because of the more pressing problems of the major mental disorders. Historically, cases requiring hospitalization were the first to gain attention. The chief concerns were the severely disturbed individual, those having organic disease of the brain, and the mentally retarded.

The classification system of Emil Kraepelin, and Freud's theory and techniques of psychoanalysis, shifted attention away from the institutional case and directed it to the relatively minor disturbances. These people had gone unrecognized for centuries because their problems, while serious enough, were not of the kind that made them a danger to themselves or to the community. Their personality difficulties were of a more personal and private nature.

The first half of the present century was marked by the development of our understanding of the dynamic processes of the neurotic reactions and the techniques for treating such conditions. At the same time, there was the growing realization that many other forms of personality disorganization exist and that these conditions do not fit the conventional categories of neurosis, psychosis, brain syndrome, and mental deficiency. The more subtle and obscure personality disturbances involving personal reactions to stress, the adjustment problems of critical periods of life, and deficiencies in personality patterns continued to be neglected.

With the appearance of the American Psychiatric Association's classification system in 1952, the first important step was taken to give recognition and organization to this wide range of more or less unrelated conditions. This classification system recognized a group of conditions which grow out of stressful environmental situations.

These conditions are the transient situational disturbances.

> This major category is reserved for more or less transient disorders of any severity that occur in individuals without any apparent underlying mental disorders and that represent an acute reaction to overwhelming environmental stress. . . . If the patient has good adaptive capacity his symptoms usually recede as the stress diminishes. If, however, the symptoms persist after the stress is removed, the diagnosis of another mental disorder is indicated (DSM-II, 1968).

THE IMPORTANCE OF STRESS

While each period of life has its special stresses which must be handled, other forms of stress affect people of all ages. Extremes of temperature and humidity, physical pain, hunger and thirst, and similar physical conditions are stressful at any age.

Sometimes a condition of the physical environment can be stressful without the individual's being aware of what is happening. A good example is noise. Most people find noise an unpleasant and disturbing condition. But it has been only recently that we have learned how truly stressful noise can be. Clanking garbage cans, the whine and roar of jet planes, and the assorted sounds of trucks, sirens, pneumatic drills, arguing neighbors, and rock and roll bands have a dam-

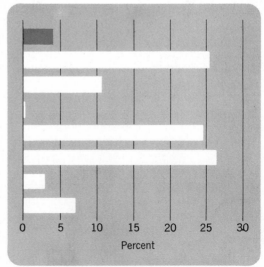

Figure 6.1 *Transient stress disorders as a percentage of total first admissions to United States public mental hospitals. (From data furnished by the National Institute of Mental Health, 1970.)*

aging effect on physical and mental health. The medical director of the American Medical Association said, "There is precious little doubt in my mind that the increasing noise levels that plague our daily lives do pose a mental health problem and contribute to a degree of emotional instability" (Barton, 1970).

Another unusual kind of stress which has grown out of the jet age has been called "time-zone stress." This reaction is due to time-zone changes accompanying long-distance air travel. The "biological clock" which regulates sleep patterns and other bodily rhythms is upset. Stress of this type has been thought to cause military officers to give incorrect orders, politicians to make wrong decisions, and business executives to be confused in their thinking. The problems of time-zone stress are so important and intriguing that a large corporation organized *Project Pegasus,* an in-depth study of physiological and psychological performance of volunteers on flights from London to San Francisco.

Even the stress of concern over the passage of time can be physically and psychologically damaging. A study showed that six times as many heart-attack deaths occurred among men who had an excessive sense of time urgency than occurred among men without this characteristic (*Roche Reports,* 1968).

While physical stress influences human behavior, psychological stress is even more important. It is not uncommon for people to feel depressed at holidays and other occasions which have special and perhaps unconscious meaning. Most psychologists and psychiatrists are familiar with the increase in complaints of depression as the Christmas holidays approach. Other individuals become depressed on their birthdays, on wedding anniversaries, and even at changes of season. These times trigger unconscious fantasies of lost happiness of the past, of the inexorable passage of time, of aging and loss of personal vigor and attractiveness, and of the deep-lying knowledge that life is passing and one's day must end.

Social factors are also responsible for generating stress. One such factor is the crowded condition of urban living. Metropolitan areas already contain most of the people in the United States, and the trend toward the cities is accelerating. By the year 2000 the population of the U.S.

is expected to reach 300 million, of which 240 million will live in urban areas. Since our cities were not designed and built for the large numbers of people and institutions that crowd them, the result has been poverty, unemployment, substandard housing, lack of recreational facilities, and other social ills characteristic of metropolitan centers.

Recognizing the mental health problems created by urban population, the National Institute of Mental Health established a Center for Studies of Metropolitan and Regional Mental Health Problems. The center deals with every aspect of mental health and has a comprehensive program for research, service, training, planning, and demonstration.

Like overpopulation, close confinement or cramped living conditions—especially when isolation is involved—can cause severe stress. A study of men isolated for many months at a remote research station at the South Pole indicates that the stress of prolonged isolation can have serious implications for personal adjustment. The men live and work where the sun is not seen for five months, where the temperature drops to more than a hundred degrees below zero, and where there is no human contact with the outside world for months at a time.

> The subjects frequently undergo severe emotional problems, extreme depression, irritability, hopelessness, inability to concentrate and insomnia. . . . Antagonisms and jealousies that normally would not surface become magnified by the enclosing walls and cause bitter conflicts, even violent fighting, as time goes on *The New York Times,* 1968).

The National Research Council Space Science Board has established a committee to study social and psychological stresses on spaceship crews. Manned space travel makes such questions as the following increasingly urgent: How will astronauts react to living in extremely close quarters on long flights in the future? What will be the effect of the knowledge that there can be no return until the mission is over, perhaps several years later? Will the prolonged stress result in a breakdown of authority? What personality changes and emotional problems are likely to occur?

Most of the stresses of life are faced and weathered without serious effects on the personality.

However, when the stress is unexpected, severe, or prolonged, and the individual is not able to cope with it, a personality adjustment reaction may result.[1]

ADJUSTMENT REACTIONS OF INFANCY

The first important stress situation in life is birth. The new individual's essentially parasitic existence within the body of the mother, when the fetus is fed and cushioned against shock, is changed radically during the birth process. When the amniotic sac bursts and the fetal head is subjected to the uterine contractions and the pressures of the pelvic canal, the physical stress is severe. Similarly, there is significant stress at the physiological and biochemical levels. While the evidence is contradictory, the possibility remains that the fetal life in the uterus of the mother and the experience of birth may have implications for the later psychological and emotional life of the individual. The stress of birth cannot be discounted completely as a source of later personality disturbance.

Other stress situations during infancy are related for the most part to adjusting to an unfamiliar environment, and to the necessity to conform to the demands of the parents. The natural impulses of the infant must be curbed. He must learn to eat according to schedule, he must be weaned from the breast or bottle, and he must be toilet-trained. These adaptations do not occur automatically or easily. Even though the infant cannot verbalize it, he is the victim of considerable stress. The tensions associated with his stress are ordinarily relieved with the help of the parents. But in some cases the stress persists to the point where lasting emotional damage occurs. In such cases the pattern of one's entire life can be affected adversely.

Most adjustment reactions of infancy, however, are a result of the infant's interaction with signifi-cant persons in his environment, or a response to the lack of such persons. The symptoms may include apathy or excitability, feeding and sleeping difficulties, breath holding, head banging, and similar disturbances. Adjustment reactions centering on the feeding problem are particularly common among infants. At least one-fourth of all infants and young children present feeding difficulties of one kind or another. These feeding problems include refusal of food, overeating, swallowing air, bringing up food and spitting it out or reswallowing it, and habitually eating substances which have no nutritional value.

A second major adjustment problem of infancy is concerned with maternal rejection in the form of lack of mothering. Infants need close bodily contact with the mother. When this contact is lacking, behavior disturbances may put in their appearance. Many hospital wards now require that an infant not only be washed and fed but also that he be picked up, petted, carried about, and otherwise mothered. There is much clinical evidence to show that the rejected infant, as well as the overprotected child, develops more than his share of undesirable personality characteristics (Chess and Thomas, 1968).

■ ADJUSTMENT REACTION OF INFANCY

Corrine M. is an eighteen-month-old infant who first came to the attention of the pediatric clinic of juvenile court in connection with a paternity action. The unwed teenage mother had little interest in the child, who was small, thin, and poorly developed. The baby slept much of the time, and was irritable when disturbed. She never smiled, showed little interest in playing, and did not respond to other people. Feeding had been a continuing problem, and it was not unusual for her to regurgitate part of her food.

When seen at the clinic, the child was listless and unresponsive. She appeared frightened when people approached her, and spent much of her time whimpering and crying. The young mother reported that the child behaved in a similar way at home. Because of the

---

[1]The key role of stress in personality disorganization is discussed in Hans Selye's classic *The Physiology and Pathology of Exposure to Stress* (Acta, 1950); H. G. Wolff's *Stress and Disease* (Thomas, 1953); *Stress Situations* (Lippincott, 1955), edited by S. Liebman; and *Stress and Psychiatric Disorder* (Blackwell, 1960), edited by J. M. Tanner; *Emotional Stress: Physiological and Psychological Reactions* (Elsevier, 1967), edited by Lennart Levi; and *The Psychology and Physiology of Stress* (Academic Press, 1969), edited by P. G. Bourne.

lack of responsiveness, it was suspected that the child was mentally retarded. However, a psychological examination revealed that this was not the case. A social service report on the home situation verified the extent to which the child had been neglected, and a foster home placement was recommended.

In her new home, the child's behavior remained unchanged for the first few days. However, the foster parents showed great interest in the child and gave her continuing attention and affection. After several days, the child began to be more interested in her surroundings. She became less of a feeding problem, and by the end of a week the child began to smile. She played with blocks, a toy doll, and a rattle. For the next two weeks the child continued to improve in her behavior and responsiveness. She smiled more often and more quickly, clapped her hands, and sought the attention of adults. She began to feed herself, and learned to stand and to walk while holding on to her crib or various pieces of furniture.

The dramatic change in the behavior of this child was due to her removal from a deprived and neglectful environment to a stimulating environment in which there was an abundance of affection. Her lack of responsiveness at home, and her seeming retardation and emotional disturbance, were attempts to adjust to an unfavorable home environment.

ADJUSTMENT REACTIONS OF CHILDHOOD

The adjustment reaction of childhood is a response to some immediate external situation or to an internal emotional conflict. The symptoms may take the form of (1) habit disturbances such as feeding problems, nail-biting, thumbsucking, stuttering, sleepwalking, enuresis, and masturbation or (2) conduct disturbances in the home, the school, or the community. Truancy, stealing, destructiveness, sexual offenses, setting fires, vandalism, and running away from home are expressions of this type of reaction.

Some of the stress situations leading to adjustment reactions of childhood include lack of affection or overaffection from the parents, early death of the mother or father, separation from the family, being an orphan, being illegitimate, divorce or separation of parents, overstrictness or overlaxness of the mother and father, being an only child,

being the only child of one sex, being markedly superior to other siblings, unusual amounts of physical illness, marked changes in family status, and early death of a sibling. The stresses of school include the hostile attitude of teachers, lack of academic or athletic success, frequent changes of schools, examination stress, and similar difficulties.

Feeding problems also continue to be observed during early childhood. The problems are likely to center on refusal to eat and overeating. The refusal to eat is related in most cases to damaging attitudes existing between the mother and the youngster. The following breakfast scene was reported by a schoolteacher father who took notes on what went on at breakfast between his five-year-old son and the mother:

Breakfast Scene

Wheaties are served at 8:15 A.M.
MOTHER: (Much coercing, yelling, threatening.)
MARTIN: (Crying, almost vomiting, refusing to eat, threatened to be put to bed.)
MOTHER: Did you get me out of bed for this? Tomorrow you can holler for your breakfast all day, but you won't get it. You are going to eat this whether you want it or not. (Pause.) Hurry up! You are going to sit here all day until you eat.
MARTIN: (Cries.) My stomach hurts. I don't want it. I won't eat it.
FATHER: (From adjoining room, to mother.) Don't start any feeding methods! The doctor said to wait until he gets well. Don't force food! Take it away. (Diverts the child's attention until he stops crying. To Martin): Your stomach has plenty of room. I'll feed it and, as you eat the Wheaties, I'll ask the stomach if it has room. Stomach says: Come on, Wheaties! . . . Thank God! (It is now 9:35. Soft boiled egg. Father leaves the dining room to listen from the adjoining room.)
MOTHER: (Pleasantly conversing with Martin.) Go on! Hurry up! Keep it up until you are finished! Don't look around until you are finished! You won't make me mad again. Don't talk to me!
MARTIN: Too much salt.
MOTHER: (Disgustedly.) Aw, you!
MARTIN: See this?
MOTHER: Watch what you are doing! Is it any wonder that you get everything all over yourself? Can't pick them up, can you?
MARTIN: I'll get 'em.
MOTHER: Come on! Hurry up! You move so slow no wonder you give it a chance to get off your spoon.

MARTIN: I get it in my tummy.

MOTHER: We gave him the works. (Egg finished at 9:47. 9:49: Chocolate milk.)

MOTHER: Go ahead! Drink it!

MARTIN: Stomach hurts.

MOTHER: Keep drinking! Go ahead!

MARTIN: My stomach.

MOTHER: (Puts her hand on Martin's abdomen.)

MARTIN: (Drinks a little. Puts glass down.)

MOTHER: Never mind massaging the stomach! You never see people rubbing stomachs in a restaurant. I'll take you back to the hospital. I'll take a blanket, wrap it around you, take a cap, and they'll straighten your stomach out.

MARTIN: My stomach is upset.

MOTHER: Pick the glass up! Pick the glass up! Pick it up! . . . Without that sour puss. Well, do you want to go outside? You have been sitting here two hours. You want to sit here another hour.

MARTIN: My stomach.

MOTHER: I don't think it's your stomach. I think you ought to have your head examined.

MARTIN: Stop hollering at me!

MOTHER: Drink it down.

MARTIN: I can't.

MOTHER: Yes, you can. You want me to put it down your throat?

MARTIN: (Crying and whimpering.) I don't want.

MOTHER: Go on! You want me to give it to you?

MARTIN: Please! Please!

MOTHER: Don't set it down so much! Pick it up! Pick it up! I said: Pick it up! (Martin cries.) That means nothing to me. I am used to seeing that mug.

MARTIN: (Tries to belch.) I can't drink it.

MOTHER: (Sarcastic.) I am so sorry. Do you want me to cry with you?

MARTIN: (Yelling.) I don't want any more.

MOTHER: Shut up! You are going to drink it. You don't want to stay here. You want to go to the hospital.

MARTIN: No! No! I don't want to go.

MOTHER: Holler a little louder so everybody can hear you!

MARTIN: (Half crying and half yelling.) I don't want any more.

MOTHER: You are going to drink. I have plenty of time. I like to see how you get all full of spasms.

MARTIN: (Hits, kicks, and pinches his mother.)

MOTHER: That's fine. I can take it. All nice boys do that. Good boys pinch, kick, and hit their mothers and daddies. (Two minutes of silence.) Do you think your cousin pinches and hits her mother? Do you think she would like it?

MARTIN: Yes.

MOTHER: I'll write her a letter and see what she says.

MARTIN: Don't write to her!

MOTHER: Well, why do you do that?

MARTIN: Because I want to. (Five minutes of silence follows. Martin sitting and milk not finished.) Go and do something and I'll drink it. You go and do your work!

MOTHER: I am going to sit right here until you drink it. You don't do what I tell you anyhow. Pick that glass up! Are you going to start all over again? Pick it up!

MARTIN: (Drinks some.) I want to take a rest.

MOTHER: How much more have you got?

MARTIN: (Wants to kiss his mother, then finishes milk. Finished at 10:15.) (Proudly.) Didn't I drink it up?

MOTHER: I won't forget that you hit your mother. Only bad little boys do that (Kanner, 1957).

While feeding problems are likely to be seen in early childhood, running away from home is observed frequently in later childhood. Children run away because they are being treated badly at home, because they are striving for a degree of independence, because they want to avoid hostile and aggressive impulses directed toward the parents, or because they are fleeing from incestuous longings. In the latter case, the boy obtains secondary gains by making his mother cry for him. Also, he imitates his father by making himself appear capable and self-reliant.

Setting fires is another way in which children act out their conflicts. While the fires usually are set in or around the home and cause little damage, they sometimes have more serious consequences. Fire-setters may show other types of behavior such as running away, truancy, stealing, aggression, and general overactivity. It is not unusual for them to show acute anxiety and to suffer from terrifying dreams.

■ ADJUSTMENT REACTION OF CHILDHOOD

Victor H. is a ten-year-old boy who has had twenty-three contacts with the police for various delinquencies. Six of these contacts resulted in referrals to a juvenile court. The boy's offenses began two years ago when he was caught stealing soft drinks and beer from the basement of a café in his neighborhood. Since that time he has been charged with fire setting, malicious destruction of property, incorrigibility, theft, assault and battery, and questionable conduct. On one occasion he set fire to a church, and later to an automobile which was entirely demolished by the fire. At another time he entered a locked building and broke most of the windows. Then he ran the elevator up and down until he was caught. He was suspended from school when he lost his temper, jumped out of a ground-floor window, and ran home. He has been involved in fights, shoplifting, stealing money from the teachers' purses, smearing tar on windows, dumping paint on stairways, stealing a peanut machine, and urinating in drinking fountains. In spite of the many delinquencies, the boy is cooperative at home, helps with the housework, and gets along well with his mother and brothers and sisters. He attends school and church regularly, although he was expelled from two schools because of his problem behavior.

Victor is a small, thin, and rather pale youngster who is friendly, polite, and ingratiating. During the psychological examination he appeared completely normal. He sat quietly, answered questions readily, and showed a normal range of emotional responsiveness. There was some anxiety, but generally he remained calm and composed. He tended to minimize his difficulties, to find excuses, and to project the blame onto others. There were no symptoms of more serious personality disturbance.

The conditions under which the family lives are most unsatisfactory. The three-room apartment is in a deteriorated area noted for its high rate of juvenile delinquency. The mother, who is divorced from her first husband and separated from her second, is a neat-appearing, narcissistic, and meticulously dressed woman. She works irregularly as a waitress, with the family supported by unemployment compensation and a small alimony from her divorced husband. The father is an unstable man who has been married six times. The mother is openly hostile toward her children and quite frankly says that she did not want any of them. The boy's brother and two sisters were born illegitimately.

The impression is that of a youngster whose numerous delinquencies grew out of a combination of stress situations including a broken home, an overtly rejecting mother, substandard living conditions, and a high-delinquency neighborhood.*

While sexual acting out is more characteristic of the adolescent years, such behavior is also seen during childhood. It will be recalled from Chapter 4 that during the Oedipal period there is an intense emotional relationship between the child and the parent of the opposite sex. When this

relationship persists and is encouraged by the parent, the child is threatened by erotic stimulation he is not able to handle or understand.

Overt incestuous activities of fathers directed toward the daughter are by no means uncommon. Similar relationships between mothers and sons are much less common, or at least are seldom reported. However, the seduction of young children by older siblings, domestic servants, and relatives is reported with some frequency.

The loss of a parent is another stressful experience faced by many children. Such a loss may occur as a result of a separation, divorce, abandonment, or death. The impact is greatest when the loss is sudden and unexpected and when there has been love for the lost parent. One youngster, who was abandoned by his parents and became a ward of the Juvenile Court, wrote the following lines:

A.L.O.N.E.

No one cares. No one wants me. I'm alone in this world. I have But few possestions and some freinds that are few. No one ecept God and some freinds care about me. They just don't care if I die, for I'm just a no one to them. If any one cares Then its few that I know. There are some freinds That at least care for me. But I will not tell. Oh, I'm left all alone, very few to love and to tell my troubles to and thats how I feel.

ADJUSTMENT REACTIONS OF ADOLESCENCE

There is a popular belief that adolescence is the most stressful period of life. While this belief is an unjustified generalization, it is true that adolescence is filled with stress situations, some of which are extensions of the stresses of childhood, while others are anticipations of the stresses of adult life. In addition, the period of adolescence, like every other period of life, has its more or less unique patterns of stress.

The most distinctive stress-provoking situation of adolescence is parental domination in the face of a growing need for independence. Many of the adjustment reactions of adolescence are expres-

---

*Case 2 of audiotape 1, "Transient Stress Disorders," in *Case Interviews to Accompany The Disorganized Personality.*

sions of the effort to achieve some degree of freedom from the parents. In some cases there are overtly expressed emancipatory strivings, while in other cases these strivings take more subtle and indirect avenues of expression. In either case, there is likely to be an unsuccessful attempt to control impulses and emotional tendencies. The most common symptoms of adjustment difficulties during the adolescent period are truancy, vandalism, running away, stealing, and sexual misbehavior.

When the aggressive strivings of the adolescent are directed toward the parents, the result may be running away from home or, less frequently, physical assault. The adolescent with inadequate emotional controls sometimes decides that his best chance for independence is to leave home. As a result, running-away behavior of this type is one of the most common reasons for referral to juvenile courts. Where emotional controls are even more poorly developed, the adolescent may seek to overpower or even to destroy the parent.

While emphasis has been placed on the lack of emotional controls of adolescents who act out by running away from home, it must be remembered that the stressful nature of many home environments is such that even the most stable adolescent might be driven away. This type of situation is seen clearly in the case of a fifteen-year-old boy who was referred to a juvenile court psychiatric clinic because he had run away from home eight times during the past two years. The examination showed the boy to be a pleasant and cooperative youngster who had average intelligence and no symptoms of emotional disturbance. The running-away behavior in this case was related to an unstable family background. The father and mother were divorced when the boy was two years old. The mother then remarried, but was murdered by her second husband when the youngster was ten years old. The stepfather then committed suicide. The boy was sent to live with his father and stepmother. The father was an alcoholic, and the stepmother did not hide her resentment of the boy. Under these circumstances, the running-away behavior is primarily a response to an intolerable home situation.

In many adolescents, the defiance of the parents is displaced to a defiance of other forms of authority. Truancy, vandalism, and stealing

Figure 6.2 *The shy and lonely child. An adjustment problem of the early years. (Rudolf Janu.)*

become expressions of the adolescent's contempt for the rules and regulations which interfere with his struggle toward independent adult status. Every secondary school has its share of problem youngsters who remain away from classes, insist on smoking on the school grounds, and adopt a defiant attitude toward the teaching staff. Similarly, the police and juvenile courts are well acquainted with the adolescent who steals or commits acts of vandalism. While it would be misleading to stamp all such cases as adjustment reactions of adolescence, it is unquestionably true that much behavior of this type is a response to stress rather than an expression of constitutionally determined character disorders.

Vandalism cost the public schools of New York City more than ten million dollars in 1969 in broken windows, damaged furniture, defaced walls,

Figure 6.3 *The aggressive behavior of adolescence. (Courtesy of Wyeth Laboratories.)*

fires, and stolen equipment. More than a quarter of a million windows were broken, and there were 300 fires. One junior high school reported 2,446 broken windows during the year, and another had 73 fires (*Annual Report, New York City Schools* 1969).

Another type of adjustment reaction of adolescence, particularly among girls, is sexual acting out. Such behavior is sometimes a defiance of parental authority, but more frequently it is related to an attempt to establish a relationship which satisfies needs for affection which are not met by the family. Every juvenile court is faced with an increasing number of teenagers referred for sexual misbehavior. While some of the girls are involved in prostitution and others are mentally retarded, the largest number of adolescents referred for sexual misbehavior are attempting to adjust to some type of situational stress.

Experiences associated with sexual promiscuity can be stressful to girls even though standards of morality have become increasingly permissive. Like other forms of stress, the guilt associated with promiscuity can produce emotional problems.

An all too common form of stress in adolescence is that facing the unwed teenage girl who becomes pregnant. A variety of damaging family attitudes may contribute to the situation. Parents may have been overly permissive, demanding and punitive, or neglectful. In any case the result is a stress situation which is often more than the girl can

handle. The result may be depression, running away, abortion, or attempted suicide. Few adolescents have the psychological strength required to live through such a stressful event without some emotional scarring.

Even in otherwise well-adjusted girls, the menstrual cycle, which begins at puberty, becomes a source of intermittent stress. Physical, psychological, and social factors are combined to create problems with which many women find it difficult to cope in a satisfactory way. Delinquency and crime rates increase markedly during the tension of the premenstrual period.

Although the adjustment reactions of adolescence take a variety of forms, the boys and girls with this form of personality disturbance are essentially normal. The personality difficulty, expressed as a form of acting out, is precipitated by an unsatisfactory environment. Under more favorable circumstances, these adolescents might very well make a satisfactory adjustment.

■ **ADJUSTMENT REACTION OF ADOLESCENCE**

Ginger M. is a fifteen-year-old girl who was seen at a psychiatric clinic following a series of adjustment difficulties. After a number of years of placement in various institutions, she had been sent to a foster home. While there she was the victim of an attempted rape, and also was "going steady" with a boy with a record of delinquency. The foster parents objected to this relationship, and as a result of the ensuing difficulties the girl was referred to the Juvenile Court. During her examination, Ginger spoke freely about her problems, volunteered information spontaneously, and revealed a degree of insight into her troubled situation. She appeared to be of average intellectual ability, showed a normal range of emotional responsiveness, and her thinking was clear and logical. She spoke coherently and showed no evidence of organic disorder or of more serious personality disturbance.

The stress situation in this adjustment reaction was the unstable family background. The father, who apparently was an emotionally unstable man, deserted the mother after several months of marriage. The mother, who recently was sentenced to a federal penitentiary on a charge of forging checks, had an illegitimate child when she was fifteen. She married the patient's father after a three-day courtship. Following her husband's desertion, she lived for several years in a common-law relationship with one man until his death. From that time she lived promiscuously with a number of other men, and has had a long history of excessive drinking.

As a result of the family situation, Ginger has been placed at various times in institutions, foster homes, and with relatives. In each case the girl has been unhappy about the placement. She hopes each time she will find what she is seeking, but never does. Under a more normal home situation and social environment it is entirely possible that Ginger could have made a completely satisfactory adjustment.*

College students, in the transition period between late adolescence and early adulthood, have many special stresses with which they must contend. Exams, grades, sex, the draft, and pressure from parents create high levels of stress. More students drop out of college for emotional reasons than because of low grades.

The typical problems of college students involve guilt and confusion over the handling of sexual impulses, concern about the expression of hostile and aggressive feelings, and worry about personal inadequacy and lack of status. Many additional problems, more or less peculiar to the college student, contribute to the forces which interfere with personality adjustment. Here are a few comments made by students:

I have no really tangible proof of my insufficiency, but my lack of confidence becomes very depressing at times. I fear that my ability is not up to the norms of the group.

I am concerned about being made to appear ridiculous. I usually attempt to conduct my affairs so as to arouse the greatest respect from my friends.

Sometimes I wonder whether life is worth the struggle. I am depressed so often that I doubt very much whether I will ever find happiness.

Sex scares me. I become uncomfortable and embarrassed whenever the subject is mentioned. I worry about it because I am afraid I am not normal.

My biggest problem is my temper. The slightest incident gets me so steamed up that I feel like blowing my top. Sometimes I do, and then I feel foolish.

The trouble with me is that I don't have any backbone. People walk all over me, and the worst part of it is that I seem to get some peculiar kind of pleasure out of it.

I am engaged, but I still place my father before and above my fiance. The transition after I am married will be hard for me.

I am a very moody person, and am particularly susceptible to depressions. Probably I am too conscientious and aware of what people think of me and say to me.

I feel that people are watching me because of my large size. I am always trying to dress in a way so that my clothes rather than myself catch the eye of others.

I lack a real sense of affection for my mother. I feel that I really should love and care for her because of all she has done for me in the past twenty years, but it seems that her demanding attitude and the fact that everything has to be done "exactly right and exactly when she wants" has destroyed my love for her.

It bothers me very much that I cannot always talk easily with people and cannot always explain myself well or express myself. I feel I am bottled up. I have many things inside that need airing, but I cannot bring them to the surface. I do not have much self-confidence.

I worry about whether I will be successful in life. I feel that I do not have self-confidence, and it bothers

---

*Case 3 of audiotape 1, "Transient Stress Disorders," in *Stress Disorders. Situational Case Interviews to Accompany The Disorganized Personality.*

me when others do better than I do, or when they seem to be able to do things more easily.

My greatest worry is of not being wanted. For example, if I don't get into medical school, I will probably leave home and move to a new city where I have no friends.

The students who made these remarks were not problem cases. They were typical young men and women. Their comments reflect their concern with themselves, with their relations with others, and with their ability to meet what the future holds for them.

People under stress frequently behave in quite unexpected ways. An Arizona State University coed admitted to her parents that she had stayed out all night with an Air Force officer she knew. The parents punished her first by withdrawing her from the university; and when she did not appear sufficiently contrite, they took the girl and her pet mongrel dog to the nearest desert where she was ordered to dig a shallow grave. The mother handed her a pistol and told her to shoot the dog as punishment for spending the night with the officer. Instead of shooting the dog, the girl killed herself by putting a bullet through her head.

Of the more than one hundred thousand college students who threaten suicide each year, about nine thousand actually attempt to kill themselves, and more than a thousand are successful in taking their lives. Excluding auto accidents, suicide is the leading cause of death among college students (NIMH, 1969).

A study at the University of California at Berkeley found that college students who killed themselves were generally above average in scholastic attainment. Such students doubted their own adequacy, were dissatisfied with their grades, and were despondent over their general academic aptitude. They set unreasonably high standards for themselves and became depressed when they failed to meet these standards. Most of the suicidal students were enrolled in humanities, with English majors topping the list.

One nineteen-year-old coed said, "I felt I was different. I just plain didn't know how to get along with other people, as if there was something missing in me. I hated my parents, and I hated myself because of them. They convinced me that I was no good, that whatever I did was nothing compared to what my two brothers did before me. I just couldn't please myself. My parents hounded me about my grades to the point where I couldn't study. They kept telling me 'You'll never make it.' By the end of the fall, I was so depressed. Failure was the worst thing in the world that could happen. I remember going home for Thanksgiving vacation, and the leaves had fallen. It was wet and cold. My midterm exams had been dreadful. I was depressed worse than ever. Then it happened. Then came 30 sleeping pills, a bottle of aspirin and a razor blade" (Sheperd, 1967).

ADULT ADJUSTMENT REACTIONS

The adjustment reactions of adult life extend from the problems of adolescence to those of old age. Because of the long span of adult years, the stress situations are of a great variety. However, most of the stress situations of adult life center on: marriage and the family; the problems of earning a living; sex, pregnancy, and the menopause; and physical health. While it is true that many stress situations of a personal nature do not fall into these groups, the problem areas suggested here will serve to illustrate the major forms of stress leading to adult adjustment reactions.

THE STRESSES OF SEX AND FAMILY

Some of the most important stress situations of adult life involve courtship, marriage, and the family. Every young adult who has been engaged, married, or a parent knows the many difficult situations which must be faced. The type of family living prescribed by our culture lends itself to a relatively high degree of stress and tension. The soaring divorce rate is merely one of the indications of the stress of modern family life. Even the most favorable marriages and family relationships must withstand periodic stresses of the greatest severity. Closely related to the problems of marriage and the family are the stresses of sex, pregnancy, and the menopause. In Chapter 4, we saw that the frustrations and conflicts in the area of sexuality constitute an important source of stress. Such stress may occur at any time throughout the range of adult life and often results in temporary adjustment problems of a more or less serious nature.

Most of the stresses of sex during the adult years concern sexual adjustments in the marriage relationship, extramarital sexual behavior, and the sexual problems of unmarried men and women. While there is no direct evidence of the frequency of sexual incompatibility in marriage, many signs point to a very high incidence of problems of this type. Similarly, the matter of extramarital sexual behavior is a problem of considerable importance. The Kinsey surveys of sexual behavior in the human male and female indicate that at least 50 percent of all married men have extramarital sexual relations at some time during their married life. Among women, the survey shows that by age forty, 26 percent of the married women also have engaged in extramarital sexual activities (Kinsey, 1953).

Pregnancy is another stressful experience; and for women pregnant for the first time, this experience is often psychologically upsetting. Even when the pregnancy has been very much desired, there are lurking fears and anxieties. Sometimes there is fear of the child being deformed or mentally retarded, of the death of the child, of the pain of childbirth, of the distortion of the body and loss of attractiveness, or of the responsibilities of being a parent.

Dependent women who have been immature in their marital lives may consider pregnancy a threat to their positions with their husbands. They may fear being displaced in the husband's affection. The pregnant woman also may wonder to what extent having a child will interfere with personal freedom and the pursuit of her personal life. More masculine women sometimes find it difficult to accept the fact of pregnancy, even under the most favorable circumstances.

A physician reported the following fears and anxieties expressed by a thirty-year-old married woman during her pregnancy:

She worried constantly about the effect of prenatal impressions on the baby. She had heard many stories about such influences; one, for example, about a child born without legs because the mother, shortly after conception, had witnessed an accident in which a child's legs were amputated. She dared not have a permanent wave because she had heard a pregnant woman might be electrocuted during it. Although she said she knew it was foolish to believe such superstitions she dared not act counter to their import. Fear of dying at childbirth, fear lest the baby die or be born "imperfect," dominated her thinking. If she felt no fetal movements she worried that the baby might be dead. Having had varied advice as to the desirability of continuing her activities, she was in severe conflict (Klein et al., 1950).

In some cases, the stress situation is the attitude of the husband rather than the wife. The woman may want the expected child very much, but her husband cannot accept the pregnancy. He may be concerned about the added economic burden, the possibility that the child will further bind him to a wife he no longer loves, or the danger of a rival for his wife's affection. Whatever the reason, he does not want the child, and his attitude and actions constitute a severe threat to the wife.

While pregnancy is a stressful experience in the life of every woman, even under the most favorable conditions, the impact of an unwanted pregnancy is far more serious. An unwanted pregnancy in a married woman generally results in a variety of mixed emotions and ambivalent attitudes. Feelings of guilt and remorse, along with blame directed toward the husband, are common. Anxiety and resentment are likely to be present at both the conscious and unconscious levels.

In the case of the unmarried woman, pregnancy is often a tragically traumatic experience. A 1970 report from the National Center for Health Statistics indicated that one-third of all first-born children in the United States from 1964 through 1966 were conceived out of wedlock.

While many illegitimate births occur in a segment of society in which illegitimacy is regarded lightly, there are many thousands of young women who are faced with severe emotional crises. In some cases, the overwhelming guilt and anxiety lead to a depression of suicidal proportions.

The experience of premature birth is another stress situation for the mother. A mother of a premature infant has an exaggerated concern following delivery about whether the baby will live and whether there is any abnormality. Such a mother sees her baby only briefly before the infant is placed in an incubator and sent to a separate nursery or perhaps to a different hospital. The baby's small size, unusual color, and unattractiveness add to the shock. Such mothers expect to hear at any moment that the child had died.

Interviews with a number of families during a two-month period following a premature birth indicate that there is a typical psychological reaction to this stressful event (Kaplan and Mason, 1960). There is a strong wish to postpone delivery as long as possible, with a fear that the premature baby will be damaged. The necessary separation from the infant also leads to anxiety and disturbing fantasies, with the mother tending to feel helpless and useless. These feelings are aggravated when the mother must return home without her baby.

Spontaneous abortion is another stress situation faced by many adult women. In a large number of these cases, there is some degree of emotional disturbance. Feelings of guilt, disappointment, inadequacy, and inferiority are observed frequently. In some cases, serious depression occurs.

The *menopause*, or the cessation of the menstrual cycle, is a time of unusual stress for many women. Some years ago it was believed that the depression and occasional mental disorder associated with menopause were due to changes in the endocrine system. Now we know that this is not the case. At least it is only a small part of the story. Far more important are the emotional implications of the so-called "change of life" in women. It is a stressful period because of what the cessation of menstruation means to the woman.

The end of the menstrual cycle is interpreted by many women as one of the great tragedies of life. Such women need to reassure themselves that they are not losing their sexual attractiveness. For this reason, there may be a burst of sexual activity as the menopause approaches and for a time after it begins. In other cases, the stress of the menopause brings on depression and personality disturbances of varying intensity and duration. There is nothing intrinsically stressful about menopause. It is a natural biological transition. The stress related to this period in life exists only in the manner in which the period is perceived by the woman who is approaching menopause.

THE STRESS OF ECONOMIC STRUGGLE

The problem of making a living in our culture is also an important source of stress during the adult years. We live in a highly competitive society in which there is a premium on economic achievement and financial security. While many people deplore the materialistic philosophy and regard it as undesirable and unimportant, the fact remains that a substantial proportion of the population struggles endlessly to maintain and to improve its financial position. Even those who scoff at the importance of money seldom turn down an economic opportunity.

The stress of financial difficulty is of greatest importance in the lower socioeconomic class. In the earlier-mentioned study of the relationship of family and class dynamics to mental illness in New Haven, it was found that 83 percent of the class V patients were seriously worried about their finances. One man said:

> Money is my main problem and worry. I don't like to be in debt, yet I always am. We owe everybody and on everything, furniture, grocery bills, and everything. As long as I'm healthy, I can work on the job, but I worry that if I get sick I'll lose my job, and then we'll really be in a bad fix. I don't get paid if I miss a day when I'm sick. I don't like my job, but I took it and have to like it and go on working because I don't have no education to get nothing better. My wife and I argue about making money. She feels I don't make enough. She hears about fellows bring home a hundred bucks a week. People like me don't bring home that kind of dough (Myers and Roberts, 1959).

Desirable or undesirable, the economic struggle is a central problem in the lives of most men and an increasing number of women. The stresses in connection with maintaining an adequate income are such that they frequently precipitate adjustment reactions.

■ ADULT ADJUSTMENT REACTION

George C. is a fifty-seven-year-old married man who was admitted to a psychiatric hospital following a series of marital crises. He has worked for many years as a barber in a downtown hotel. The patient has been married twice, and was divorced from his first wife fifteen years ago. One of his difficulties has been that a son from the first marriage has become a self-styled minister, and has been telling his father that he is living in sin because of the divorce. The son has been advising the father to break up his present home, and return to his first wife.

A second marital problem concerns the hostility of the present wife toward the patient. She is a domineering and aggressive woman who quite frankly admits that she nags her husband constantly. She has forbidden him to correct or discipline their young son, and has denied her husband any responsibility in the child's upbringing. The marital difficulties have been aggravated as a result of a marked decrease in the patient's sexual desires.

As a result of the severe marital problems, the patient became extremely tense and was unable to eat. He was placed on tranquilizing drugs by his family physician, but the constant pressure put on him by his grown son and the increasing hostility of his wife became too much for him. He was admitted to the psychiatric hospital for more intensive treatment. When seen at the hospital, the patient accepted the initial interview with considerable appreciation. He was polite and cooperative, although he showed some anxiety over his hospitalization. He was completely oriented, his thinking was logical, and his speech was relevant and coherent. Emotional reactions were within normal limits. He said that he hoped his stay in the hospital would result in a better marital adjustment and greater happiness.*

THE STRESS OF ILLNESS

Another stress situation which increases in importance during adult life is the threat of ill health. Early in the adult years, there are the more temporary stresses of acute illness and the occasional necessity for surgical operations. Later, there is the growing possibility of illness of a more chronic nature.

In the case of surgery, the site of an operation plays an important part in the degree of stress and the severity of psychological disturbance. Eye operations, with the threat of blindness and the necessity for postoperative bandaging with its consequent darkness and isolation, are particularly anxiety-provoking. Such operations sometimes lead to panic reactions of a temporary nature. The symptoms ordinarily disappear within a day or two following the removal of the bandages.

Gynecological operations are also capable of producing a very considerable psychological impact. The surgical removal of the uterus is a particularly stressful situation because the uterus is regarded as one of the most important symbols of femininity. The loss of the uterus is a threat involving nonsexual as well as sexual attitudes. By many women, the removal of the uterus is considered a loss of femininity and sexual attractiveness.

Many factors are involved in the stress associated with surgical operations. The fear of mutilation and death, the symbolic significance of a particular body organ, the fear of emotional and financial dependency, and similar factors may lead to temporary psychological disorganization.

A comprehensive study of the relationship of the surgery experience to personality disturbance was made at the Cincinnati General Hospital. In this investigation, 200 randomly selected surgical patients admitted to the hospital were subjected to psychiatric interviews between three and six months after the patient had left the hospital. The study showed that there was some form of psychiatric disorder in 86 percent of the cases (Titchener and Levine, 1960). This high rate of mental illness might be explained in part by the fact that the hospital in which the study was made draws its patients from the lower socioeconomic level of the community, and studies of epidemiology have shown that the rates for mental illness are higher in this group. While this factor probably contributed to the finding, it is also likely that the stress of the need for surgery and the surgery itself precipitated the psychiatric conditions.

At another hospital, a study was made of a group of women awaiting surgery for early breast cancer. Hormone production rates correlated significantly with the ability of the patient to handle the stress of the anticipated operation. Women who were relatively confident and optimistic had low production rates, while women who were anxious and dejected had higher rates (Katz et al., 1970).

The stress of surgical operations is also shown in a study in which 75 percent of the patients who died following kidney transplant operations suffered a sense of abandonment by their families or experienced panic and pessimism about the

---

*Case 1 ot audiotape 1, "Transient Stress Disorders," in *Case Interviews to Accompany The Disorganized Personality*.

Figure 6.4 *The loneliness of the later years. (Courtesy of the American Psychiatric Association.)*

outcome of the operation. Patients who survived the transplant operations did not have these attitudes and feelings to the same degree (Eisendrath, 1969). Patients showing a considerable amount of anxiety or depression prior to an open heart operation also have less chance of survival than other patients (Kimball, 1969).

ADJUSTMENT REACTIONS OF LATE LIFE

The later years of life have their full share of stressful situations. The elderly individual faces characteristic problems related to retirement from work, loss of family members and friends, financial insecurity, dependency upon relatives, chronic illness, and the prospect of death. These are but some of the stresses which occur frequently during the later years. The way in which the elderly person meets these stresses may mean the difference between mental health and an old age of bitterness, disappointment, and unhappiness.

Some 20 million Americans today are more than 65 years old. By the year 2000, it is estimated that 28 million will be over 65. Though medical science has increased the prospects of longevity, the complexities of modern life pose problems of adaptation, especially for older persons, far greater than those of earlier times and simpler societies.

Besides the mental health problems they share with other age groups, older people are vulnerable to specific difficulties associated with the aging process. Some of the mental impairment of many older people is related to physical aging, but the psychological reaction to the physical process makes for unnecessary impairment, as evidenced by the high incidence of depression, suicide, and other maladaptive behavior among older people. Loss of status in a youth-oriented society accelerates psychopathological reactions. Although persons over 65 constitute less than 10 percent of the population, they make up 19 percent of all first admissions to state mental hospitals, and they occupy 30 percent of all public mental hospital beds. In addition, large numbers of mentally disturbed older persons are found in such institutions as nursing homes and homes for the aging.

Some people manage to go through an entire

life with little or no physical disease or handicap. Most people, however, are faced with varying degrees of physical disability. It is apparent that the greater the degree of physical disability, the more disturbing it is to the personality. Individuals with chronic and discomforting physical disorders are generally not so likely to resist the inroads of aging as individuals who enjoy better health.

Another factor of importance is the decline in physical attractiveness, particularly among women. Much of the psychological life of a woman is built around her *body image*, or the conception she has of her own appearance. Among women, beauty and a youthful appearance are key assets in maintaining a secure position. When youth and beauty begin to fade, the change represents a threat of considerable magnitude. At first, the signs of aging are combated with cosmetics and various artificial devices. When these begin to fail, some women react with varying degrees of emotional disturbance.

Financial security is another important factor in the stress related to the later years. It is one thing to grow old with the knowledge that there is enough money to live out life without financial worry. It is quite something else to face old age knowing that it will be necessary to depend upon relatives or social agencies.

The feeling of not being wanted is also one of the critical and destructive attitudes of the later years. It is a sad but inescapable fact that many older people are not wanted, even by their families. When this attitude is felt by the older person, with or without justification, the consequences are likely to be psychologically destructive. It is not uncommon to observe a sudden increase in aging among individuals who develop this feeling. It sometimes occurs when an older person becomes a widow or widower and is required to move in with a reluctant son or daughter. It is also observed in some workers at the time of retirement. Regardless of the precipitating event, the development of the feeling of not being wanted often signals a marked weakening of the psychological defenses against aging.

■ ADJUSTMENT REACTION OF OLD AGE

Beulah M. is a seventy-three-year-old woman who was admitted to a psychiatric hospital following a clash of personality with an elderly sister with whom she was living. When seen at the hospital, the patient was friendly and cooperative. Her facial expression was animated, and she talked actively and spontaneously. Her mood was controlled, and her emotional responsiveness was within normal limits. While she said she felt very well, she admitted she was unhappy about being in a mental hospital. At times the patient was somewhat irrelevant but she did not show a flight of ideas nor was she incoherent. The patient was completely oriented as to person, place, and time; and while there was some indication of slight impairment of recent memory, remote memory appeared entirely intact.

The patient talked at length about the prominence of her family and the luxury of her early life. She showed a strong narcissistic tendency, apologizing for her present appearance and emphasizing the fact that she had been a "beauty" when she was younger. She volunteered that she was so beautiful that men could not resist her. The patient also spoke of her poetry writing, and showed great pride in the fact that she received a letter from the White House acknowledging a poem she had sent to the President.

The formal psychological examination showed that the patient was without psychological impairment beyond that to be expected for a woman of her age. The personality conflict at home apparently was a situational reaction to the stress of caring for a sister of even more advanced years. As soon as the patient was removed from the home, the stress was relieved and the patient showed a completely normal reaction. The stress of hospitalization apparently was considerably less than the problem of living in close proximity to the elderly sister.*

To determine the degree to which problems of mental impairment among residents of homes for the aged are recognized and how such problems are handled by these institutions, a psychiatrically oriented survey of such homes was conducted. As estimated by the staff of the 13 homes studied, 16 percent of the residents, on the average, were mentally impaired. By the criteria of the study

---

*Case 4 of audiotape 1, "Transient Stress Disorders," in *Case Interviews to Accompany The Disorganized Personality*.

staff, however, 60 percent were impaired. Interviews with the homes' administrators revealed that obviously impaired applicants were generally screened out even by homes that had policies permitting their admission. Usually, the higher the prevalence of mental impairment within the homes, the poorer the quality of programs for social interaction. Little attention was given to supportive measures for mentally impaired persons until a crisis occurred. When a crisis did occur, care fell almost exclusively on the medical and nursing staff members; and these generally were not well organized or did not have the proper support to deal with it (NIMH, 1968).

At Boston State Hospital, researchers from Northeastern University studied the nursing home as a community resource for aged mental hospital patients and sought to determine the factors that affect the adjustment of such people to nursing homes. Those who are suicidal, hostile, destructive, or boisterous, or who wander excessively, smoke in bed, or have severe alcoholic or drug problems, the study indicates, are not acceptable to nursing homes. On the other hand, depressed, withdrawn, confused, disoriented, hypochondriacal, and incontinent people are acceptable, as are those with sleeping and feeding problems. The presence or absence of psychiatric disturbance shortly after admission appears to be a key factor in the outcome of placement. The adjustment of nursing home patients was not inferior to that of patients of similar status still in the hospital (NIMH, 1968).

The stressful effects of radical changes during the later years of life is indicated by the fact that 24 percent of 1,000 persons placed in an old-age institution died within the first six months. The comparable death rate of elderly persons in a community setting is about 10 percent. It has also been observed that elderly persons placed in institutions have more serious physiological and psychological problems than do those who remain with their families (Lieberman, 1968). While part of this difference can be explained by the fact that the disabled elderly are more likely to be sent to institutions, at least some of the effect is due to the stress of being removed from the home.

In some societies, the older members of the group are honored and revered. They feel secure in the knowledge that they are wanted and respected. The family structure of the Chinese traditionally was such that it produced dignified, serene, and benevolent older people, particularly older men. In other cultures, including our own, the elderly members of the population have less status and less security. In still other societies, older members are discriminated against and rejected completely.

Another factor of importance is companionship during the later years. Some men and women are favored with large and loving families or have developed friendships and other associations which guarantee against loneliness. Many aging people, however, grow old in isolation. Families have drifted apart, friends have died, and no one has taken their place. Through indifference or ignorance of the consequences, they have allowed friendships to dwindle. One day these people find they are alone.

Finally, there is the stress of the realization that the end of life is approaching. The importance of this type of stress is related to the philosophy of life held by the aging individual and to the richness or barrenness of his earlier life. If that life was unproductive, uncreative, and unrewarding, the threat of death may be serious. Similarly, the individual who has not developed an effective personal philosophy of life and death is more likely to become a victim of personality disorganization during his later years.

GROSS STRESS REACTIONS

Individuals of all ages may be faced at times with extreme stress growing out of civilian disasters and military combat. These situations make extraordinary physical and emotional demands upon the individual and frequently result in *gross stress reactions*, a term used to distinguish the behavior from reactions to milder and more common forms of everyday stress.

While the impact of catastrophes on the behavior of the victim has not been subjected to extensive clinical study, there is ample evidence to indicate that various types of personality disorganization may result. Patterns of greed, aggression, selfishness, and regressive behavior are frequently observed, in addition to the more common reactions of terror and anxiety.

CIVILIAN CATASTROPHE

The most familiar forms of civilian catastrophe include tornadoes, hurricanes, and floods; fires and explosions; ship, plane, and train wrecks; and the bombing of civilians during war. In such situations, the stress is ordinarily so great that few people escape without some degree of temporary personality disorganization.

Although the advent of radar tracking and warning systems has taken the element of surprise out of the hurricane, these great storms sweep over large areas, causing injury, death, and property damage amounting to millions of dollars. Even more stressful is the tornado, which strikes suddenly and viciously with little or no advance warning. Hundreds of communities in various parts of the United States have been torn apart in a matter of minutes, with the storm leaving a path of death and destruction. The suddenness and unpredictability of the tornado makes its very possibility a source of continuing stress. No other type of storm has such personal implications.

One of the first studies of the impact of a tornado on the emotional health of a community was made by a team of research workers from the Department of Sociology of the University of Texas. In 1953, a tornado struck the small city of San Angelo, Texas, causing 11 deaths, injuring more than 150 people, and destroying or causing major damage to almost 500 homes. Following the storm, residents of the community were interviewed. A year later, a second tornado approached the area, but did not strike. Nevertheless, the violent storm caused considerable physical damage to the community. Most of the victims of the first tornado were interviewed again following their experience of the second storm.

The studies showed clearly that the emotional impact of the two disasters was more severe and more lasting than the economic implications. In the survey following the first storm,

Figure 6.5 *The stress of catastrophe, as suggested by Edward Munch's lithograph* The Shriek. *(Museum of Modern Art, New York.)*

73 percent of those interviewed reported that some family member was suffering emotionally from the tornado. Interviews following the second storm showed that over 50 percent admitted to emotional problems for the entire time between the two storms. In the families reporting emotional disturbance, the mother was involved in about 60 percent of the cases, children and adolescents in about 18 percent, and fathers in 4 percent. It was believed by 60 percent of the informants that the second storm would have undesirable emotional effects on the children of the area (Moore, 1958).

In another study of the psychological effects of a tornado, a team of psychiatrists interviewed parents, children, and community leaders a week after the storm. Special attention was paid to parent-child interactions. The major finding in this study was that a child's response to acute stress such as a tornado or similar disaster is

Figure 6.6 *The funnel of a tornado that hit Tracy, Minnesota, during the early evening of June 13, 1968. Seven persons were killed, seventy-two were injured, and more than 100 homes and business buildings were wrecked or damaged. (Courtesy of Wide World Photos.)*

determined not only by his own personality makeup but also by the nature of the family social system of which he is a part. It is not possible to consider the response of a child to stress as a phenomenon which is set apart from the reactions of others who are significant figures in his life.

One mother completely went to pieces during the tornado. Although she was in no actual danger, she wept and fainted alternately and paid no attention to the whereabouts or condition of her children, who were shopping with her in a store. Because of her own insecurity, this mother was unable to adopt the role of a supportive parent. An example of the reverse situation was the mother who gathered her children around her on the living room sofa, cuddling them and reassuring them when the roof of their home blew off. This mother seemed to be equally resourceful in day-to-day affairs, managing her household efficiently while her husband was away in the Army (Perry et al., 1956).

The stress of fires and explosions rivals the storm in precipitating personality disorganization. An eyewitness of the great Chicago fire in 1871 described the behavior of the crowds in the following words:

The danger, the excitement, the destruction, and the spectacle of the holocaust provoked a broad range of reactions. The scene was one of violent contrasts in emotion and experience, a panorama of human behavior more varied and more dramatic than the show the fire itself provided. Avarice and self-sacrifice, reason and panic, sorrow and gaiety, courage and cowardice appeared in close juxtaposition; sudden good luck in the midst of calamity, and sudden misfortune on the verge of safety, were equally common (Colbert and Chamberlin, 1871).

The damaging effects of stress on the individual personality were illustrated dramatically during the sinking of the *Titanic* on the night of April 14, 1912. In a calm sea, this transatlantic liner sank with a loss of 1,503 passengers. Some of the terror-stricken survivors of the sinking ship refused to allow other survivors to climb into their lifeboats, even though the boats were half empty. Those in the boats hit the struggling swimmers on the head with oars in order to keep them out of the lifeboats. Of eighteen lifeboats that hovered near the sinking ship, only one returned to the scene, and only thirteen survivors were picked up. Moreover, there were many small incidents revealing individual differences in reaction to stress. One young man disguised himself as an old lady in an attempt to save himself. Another man changed to evening dress. A lady refused to leave her Great Dane, and the band played *Nearer My God to Thee* as the ship went down (Lord, 1955).

A unique opportunity for a firsthand clinical observation of the psychological impact of shipwreck occurred in 1956 when the Italian luxury liner *Andrea Doria* collided in the fog with the Swedish liner *Stockholm*. Two psychiatrists, who were passengers on one of the rescue ships, took the opportunity to examine some of the survivors within a few hours of the disaster. These investigators observed that the passengers behaved as if they were under sedation. They appeared passive, compliant, and retarded, and some showed signs of loss of memory for the events. Later, the same survivors showed an intense preoccupation with the tragedy. There was a need to tell the story over and over again, dwelling on the details in an endlessly repetitious way (Friedman and Linn, 1957).

It is probable that the most stressful catastrophes of all time were the bombings of civilian populations during World War II. In the blitz bombing of London, the saturation bombing of Germany, and the atomic bombing of Japan, millions of civilians were faced with the ever-present possibility of sudden death during the air raids. The emotional impact of these bombings on the civilian population is evident in personal interviews with men and women who survived the bombings (U.S. Strategic Bombing Survey, 1947).

The mass bombings of Germany produced reactions somewhat at variance with those observed in England. The survey showed that many law-abiding middle-class Germans turned into looters when they lost their own possessions. The survey also found excessive fear among German children in the cellars and bunkers during the air raids. The study reported, "Children who had to be rescued from wrecked houses often suffered a long time and wept and cried in their sleep."

While it is not unlikely that there was looting among the British and that British children also cried in their sleep, there is evidence that the emotional effects of the bombings in Germany were more damaging than those in England. One possible explanation for this difference is that the mass bombings reached their greatest intensity at a time when the German population realized the hopelessness of the war effort. The psychological impact of bombings in a country losing a war might very well be quite different from the effect in a country confident of ultimate victory.

Perhaps the most stressful single event of modern history, if not the history of the world, was the atomic bombing of Japan toward the end of World War II. Human beings have seldom experienced death and destruction on such an immediate and massive scale. In Hiroshima and Nagasaki the devastation was of such vast proportions that it was completely incomprehensible to the population. At the time of the bombing, most survivors believed that only their immediate areas had been hit. The stress of personal injury, the mutilation and death of loved ones, and the loss of possessions were in themselves of the greatest consequence. However, when the true extent of the atomic explosion was sensed, the stress of the situation reached new, and perhaps unparalleled, heights (Siemes, 1946).

The observation of a variety of civilian catastrophes has indicated that a *disaster syndrome* made up of at least three distinct psychological phases can be expected in the reaction to gross stress situations. The *shock reaction* is the first response to the impact of the disaster. This phase is followed by the *recoil reaction* when the immediate danger is past. The third response is the *recall reaction* when the disaster victim begins to realize the wider implications of the loss and the damage (Wallace, 1956).

The shock reaction to a disaster is different for different people. About 10 to 20 percent of the survivors can be expected to behave in a cool and collected way; 70 percent are likely to become confused and bewildered, with another 10 to 20 percent showing outbursts of severe anxiety, panic, anger, and screaming. During this period of impact, there is nothing much that can be done to help the individual. He merely needs time to adjust emotionally to the situation.

The shock reaction has been described by observers of many of the major civilian catastrophes. A survivor of a severe earthquake in southern Italy described the scene by saying:

> The immediate and almost universal effect that the earthquake had on those who escaped death was a stupefaction, almost a mental paralysis. They were stunned . . . lamentation was infrequently heard except when caused by physical suffering. Tears were rarely seen. Men recounted how they had lost wife, mother, brothers, sisters, children, and all their possessions, with no apparent concern. They told their tales of woe as if they themselves had been disinterested spectators of another's loss (Hood, 1909).

A somewhat similar reaction to the San Francisco earthquake and fire is found in the following comment: "The silence which followed was almost as awesome as the dreadful sound of the quake. Survivors stood in many places 'like speechless idiots,' as one observer recalled. When they did talk, the conversation was whispered" (Bronson, 1959).

Following the bombing of Hiroshima, a number of observers remarked on the overwhelming silence of the survivors. Long lines of people moved and behaved like automatons, and walked silently away from the city. However, the shock reaction of survivors nearest the explosion was of a more frantic effort toward escape. Thousands of blinded, deafened, and physically shattered men, women, and children struggled frantically in their efforts to reach safety.

In the recoil reaction, the second phase of reaction to catastrophe, the survivor comes out of his stunned, confused, or excited state and finds that the danger is over and life must be faced. In this recoil phase, the individual may giggle or sob, or he may be forlorn or irritable. Sometimes there is anger and hostility. It is during this phase that psychological treatment is necessary. The victim must be given an opportunity to ventilate his feelings about the tragic events.

In the recall reaction, the third phase, the survivor of a disaster is tense and restless. He is preoccupied with memories of the horrifying experience, or he may blot it out of memory completely. In either case, sleeplessness, nightmares, and emotional upsets are common. This phase of the reaction is often accompanied by a variety of physical symptoms.

Civilian catastrophes sometimes precipitate regressive features in the personality. While it is true that every disaster has its stories of courage and self-sacrifice, stress situations may also release an overpowering and selfish struggle for personal survival. During the Hiroshima disaster, few survivors gave help or received help from others. The U.S. Strategic Bombing Survey showed that only 17 percent of the survivors gave help to or received help from strangers in Hiroshima on the day of the atomic bombing. In Nagasaki, only 7 percent of the survivors said that they gave aid to strangers, and not a single person interviewed in the survey said that he received help from a stranger (U.S. Strategic Bombing Survey, 1946).

While immediate personality disorganization during a catastrophe is not uncommon, the question of the frequency of long-term psychological damage has not been determined satisfactorily. Early studies, growing out of World War II experience and civilian disasters following the war, suggest that even the most terrifying stress situations seldom leave serious permanent aftereffects. A survey of 3,000 casualties of the Texas City harbor explosion in 1947 showed that long-term mental illness developed in only a few cases.

Similarly, the admission rates to mental hospitals in Great Britain during World War II indicate that the air raids of 1940 and 1941 did not lead to a rise in the number of psychiatric patients admitted to hospitals and clinics. Also, there was no increase in the incidence of suicide or alcoholic intoxication. If anything, most of the indicators of mental disorder showed a decrease rather than an increase. A Strategic Bombing Survey report on psychiatric casualties in Germany during World War II served to confirm the findings in Great Britain (U.S. Strategic Bombing Survey, 1945). German psychiatrists were in complete agreement that there was no increase in psychiatric disorders as a result of the saturation bombing of German cities.

Another bit of evidence pointing in the same direction was the absence of psychiatric casualties following the Japanese attack on Pearl Harbor on December 7, 1941. There were no psychiatric patients admitted to the hospital on the day of the attack, and during the following two weeks the number of psychiatric admissions was no greater than in the two-week period prior to the attack. Nor was there an upsurge of the more serious mental disorders as a result of the atomic bombings of Japan. A number of minor personality disturbances were reported, but long-term effects did not appear.

While it appears that long-range psychiatric disabilities growing out of civilian disasters are infrequent, the residual emotional impact of such disasters may be long-lasting and far-reaching. Relatively few victims of such disasters require hospitalization for psychiatric reasons. However, the disaster experience might very well have a long-term effect on the anxiety tolerance level of the survivors and might in this way have important mental health implications.[2]

COMBAT STRESS

Some of the most stressful situations an individual is called upon to face in life occur during time of war. The threat of war, the declaration of hostilities, induction into military service, and ultimately the experience of combat present stress situations which frequently are of such a severe nature that the individual's psychological defenses crumble and some degree of personality disorganization takes place. While these reactions to the stress of war are not reflected in the incidence rates of mental disorder, there is little question but that military service in time of war leaves emotional scars on large numbers of men.

As in all stress situations, the ultimate impact of the stressful event is determined by the individual personality. For some men, the mere expectancy of being called to military service is enough to precipitate an emotional reaction. A continuum of stress exists between the mere possibility of being inducted into service and the most terrify-

ing combat experience. The receipt of an induction notice, reporting to an induction center, being sent to a reception center, the experience in a training center, being shipped overseas, the prospect of combat, and combat itself constitute a graded series of anxiety-provoking situations which make increasingly heavy emotional demands on the soldier. Some men break down in the early stages of this sequence. Others, with stronger psychological resources, break down only under the most severe stress. Many men find it possible to withstand the most terrifying combat experiences with a minimum of emotional scarring.

Each form of combat presents its unique patterns of stress. The infantry soldier is faced with the stress of continued exposure to rifle and machine-gun fire, mines, mortar and bombardment, long-range artillery, and strafing and bombing from the air. In many respects, the infantry soldier is exposed to the greatest dangers over the longest period of time. Moreover, he is called upon to endanger himself repeatedly in a most personal way.

The air crew is subjected to an entirely different set of stresses. The lack of physical contact with the ground, flights over hostile territories in total darkness, the feeling of helplessness and insecurity while flying through the flak of anti-aircraft fire, and the danger of being forced down over enemy territory are stresses unique to air combat crews.

Submarine warfare presents still another pattern of stress. Prolonged periods of being submerged, the feeling of isolation and loneliness, the cramped living and working conditions, the danger of depth bombs, and the peril of entrapment and death at the bottom of the sea constitute severe and unusual psychological hazards.

While the stress situations in military combat are of a great variety, the emotional disturbances created by the stress are similar. Anxiety and the

---

[2]The growing interest in the psychological effects of disaster has produced several important books, including *Man and Society in Disaster* (Basic Books, 1962), edited by George W. Baker and Dwight W. Chapman; *Community in Disaster* (Harper, 1958) by William H. Form and others; *A Study of the Effect of Catastrophe on Social Disorganization* (Operations Research Office, 1952) by Leonard Logan, L. M. Killian, and Wyatt Marrs; and John Walker Powell's *The Face of Disaster: An Introduction to the Natural History of Disaster* (University of Maryland, 1954). Less technical treatments of disaster are Donald Robinson's *The Face of Disaster* (Doubleday, 1959), and Martha Wolfenstein's *Disaster: A Psychological Essay* (Free Press, 1957).

Figure 6.7 *The stress of combat. United States troops in a jungle clearing in Vietnam. (UPI photo by Shunsuke Akatsuka.)*

accompanying physical symptoms, pathological fears, and depressions are frequently observed in military hospitals. Exaggerations of such defense mechanisms as rationalization, projection, identification, and regression are also common experiences.

■ REACTION TO COMBAT STRESS

A twenty-one-year-old rifleman in Vietnam was flown directly to the hospital from an area of fighting by a helicopter ambulance. No information accompanied him, he had no identifying tags on his uniform, and he was so completely covered with mud that a physical description of his features was not possible. His hands had been tied behind him for the flight, and he had a wild, wide-eyed look as he cowered in a corner of the emergency room, glancing furtively to all sides, cringing and startling at the least noise. He was mute, although once he forced out a whispered "VC" and tried to mouth other words without success. He seemed terrified. Although staff members could approach him, he appeared oblivious to their presence. No manner of reassurance or direct order achieved either a verbal response or any other interaction from him.

His hands were untied, after which he would hold an imaginary rifle in readiness whenever he heard a helicopter overhead or an unexpected noise. The corpsman led him to the psychiatric ward, took him to a shower, and offered him a meal. He ate very little. While he began to move more freely, he offered no information.

A friend from his platoon who was on a neighboring ward described how the platoon had been caught in an ambush and then was overrun by the enemy. The patient was one of three who survived after being pinned down by enemy fire for 12 hours. Toward the end of that time the patient had developed a crazed expression and had tried to run from his hiding place. He was pulled back to safety and remained there until the helicopter arrived and flew him to the hospital.

Soon after his arrival at the hospital the patient was given tranquilizers to calm him and keep him asleep for approximately 40 hours. When he was allowed to wake, the medication was discontinued. Although he appeared somewhat dazed and subdued, his response to ward activities was dramatic. Within 72 hours after his admission to the hospital, the patient was alert, oriented, responsive, and active. Although still a little tense, he was ready to return to duty. He was sent back to his combat unit on his third hospital day (Bloch, 1969).

It is not possible to describe all the stress situations which lead to transient situational disturbances. One reason is that one cannot predict in advance what will be a stress situation for a given individual. A stressful situation which might lead to a temporary shattering of the personality in one case might have little or no disorganizing effects on the personality of another individual. It is necessary to consider not only the intensity of the situation but also how the individual perceives the situation. Even the most serious and threatening situation, unless perceived as such, will not result in a transient situational disturbance. The personality defense mechanisms discussed in Chapter 4 may change the individual's perception of a situation so that he is able to cope with it effectively.

The way in which the defense mechanisms can be used to alter the perception of a stress situation is seen in a study of the reactions of prisoners awaiting execution in the Sing Sing death house. One might reasonably expect that these prisoners would show severe depression and overwhelming anxiety, yet it was observed that this was not the case. Apparently these prisoners utilized the psychological defenses of denial, projection, and obsessive thinking in order to defend themselves from the approaching execution. Denial took the form of passing off the threat with a shrug of the shoulders, and an attitude of "So, they'll kill me." Another form of denial was the assumption that an appeal for mercy would be successful. The most extreme evidence of denial, which was found in only one prisoner, was the delusion that a pardon actually had been granted. Projection also was used as a form of defense. In these cases, the prisoners believed themselves to be persecuted and pictured themselves as martyrs rather than criminals. Finally, the defense of obsessive thinking took the form of being preoccupied furiously with other matters such as the details of their appeals, religion, and philosophy (Bluestone and McGahee, 1962).

SUMMARY

1. The transient situational disturbances are relatively minor and temporary personality disturbances due primarily to overwhelming environmental pressures. The word *stress* refers to threatening stimuli which disturb the integration and organization of the individual. It is important to note that stress can be inferred only from the changes that take place within the individual. What is stressful for one person may not be stressful for another.

2. The adjustment reactions, which grow out of the stresses characteristic of the different periods of life, are classified as adult situational reactions and the adjustment reactions of infancy, childhood, adolescence, and late life. The adjustment reactions of infancy are most likely to be centered on such problems as feeding and toilet training. The older child must deal with the stresses of going to school, making friends, and understanding sexual impulses. The adolescent faces the problems of adjusting to the opposite sex, gaining popularity, choosing a career, and breaking his dependence upon parents.

3. The adult is faced with the stresses of marriage and raising a family, earning a living, and obtaining status in his group. In late life, the individual faces the various threats of chronic illness, surgery, financial insecurity, dependency upon relatives, loss of family and friends, and the prospect of death itself. Any of these stresses, at any age level, may lead to a personality disturbance in an individual who is not equipped physically and psychologically to deal with it.

4. In addition to the more usual stress situations in everyday life, there are situations (civilian disasters and military combat) in which the stress is so severe that extraordinary physical and emotional demands are made upon the individual. In civilian life, the gross stress reaction may be observed during such traumatic experiences as severe storms, fires, explosions, and serious wrecks. The reaction of civilians to the bombing during war also falls into this category. In these cases, as in military combat,

the stress may be so great that the individual is not able to cope with it. The result is a more or less temporary breakdown in personality defenses.

5. The disaster syndrome, which is a frequent reaction to gross stress situations, has three phases: *shock, recoil,* and *recall.* The shock reaction is a response to the impact of the disaster, the recoil reaction occurs when the immediate danger is past, and the recall reaction takes place when the victim is able to comprehend the wider implications of the disaster.

7 THE PERSONALITY DISORDERS AND RELATED CONDITIONS

The transient situational disorders discussed in the previous chapter are relatively temporary conditions caused by stressful events which for the most part are external to the patient. In the personality disorders and related conditions, the critical forces responsible for the difficulty are to be found *within* the individual. These disorders have been described as "deeply ingrained maladaptive patterns of behavior. Generally, these are lifelong patterns, often recognizable by the time of adolescence or earlier" (DSM-II, 1968).

The term *personality disorder* is an unfortunate one in some respects since it is used widely in a popular and nontechnical way to mean *all* personality disturbances. More accurately, the term should be reserved for those special conditions to be discussed in the first section of this chapter.

The diagnostic group is complicated further by the somewhat unrelated nature of the conditions included in it.

A characteristic of many of the personality disorders and related conditions is the lack of concern experienced by the patient. Most patients in this group do not feel that they have personality disturbances. They come to the attention of the psychiatrist and the clinical psychologist as a result of deviant behavior which brings them into difficulty with their environment. These patients ordinarily do not seek psychological help. When they do, it is usually the result of pressure from the family or the courts.

These conditions, because of their frequency, are of considerable importance to clinical psychologists and psychiatrists, particularly those whose work is performed outside the mental hospital. The disorders range from relatively mild conditions to some of the most serious forms of behavior disturbance. The following classifications may be used: *personality disorders, antisocial personality, sexual deviations, alcohol addiction,* and *drug dependence.*

PERSONALITY DISORDERS

The personality disorders are conditions in which the person has difficulty in maintaining his emotional equilibrium and independence even under minor stress. The reason for this inability appears to be a flaw in emotional development. Some people have rigid or exaggerated character and behavior patterns, while others show a regressive reaction. The basic personality maldevelopment is the distinguishing factor in these cases.

The majority of men, women, and children with personality disorders never receive treatment for their difficulties. They do not recognize that they are disturbed, nor are they regarded by others as having personality difficulties of a serious nature. It is only when their personality characteristics lead them to overt behavior which gets them into difficulty that it is realized that they are psychologically disturbed. Since most of these people learn to live with their disturbances, they avoid serious conflicts and therefore do not come to the attention of psychiatrists and psychologists.

Some of these disturbances are relatively superficial and could be changed if treatment were undertaken. Other disturbances in this group are more deep-seated and are extremely resistant to change. In most cases the disturbances appear to be the result of developmental defects based on a combination of psychosocial and constitutional factors. The personality disorders are: the *inadequate;* the *schizoid;* the *cyclothymic;* the *paranoid;* the *passive-aggressive;* the *obsessive-compulsive;* the *antisocial;* the *hysterical;* the *asthenic;* and the *explosive* personalities.

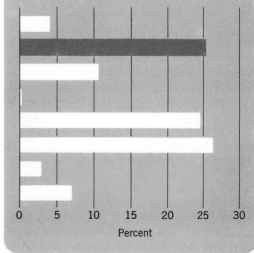

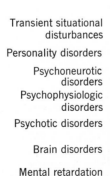

Figure 7.1 *Personality disorders as a percentage of total first admissions to public mental hospitals in the United States. (From data furnished by the National Institute of Mental Health, 1970.)*

THE INADEQUATE PERSONALITY

The inadequate personality is seen in patients who show inadaptability, ineptness, poor judgment, lack of physical and emotional stamina, and social incompatibility. Such people are neither physically nor mentally deficient, but they show inadequate response to intellectual, emotional, social, and physical demands. They are frequently found at the lower end of the socioeconomic scale, not because the low socioeconomic status leads to this type of disturbance, but because inadequate personalities tend to sink to the lower end of the scale. These individuals are the first to stand in the relief line, they wait for the doors to open at the city and state welfare offices, they make up a large proportion of the population of our city jails and workhouses, and they are the ineffective and incompetent drifters. When such people marry, the marriage is likely to be as unsuccessful as the other phases of their lives.

There are many inadequate personalities in the world. Yet in spite of their deficiencies, these individuals manage to fumble and stumble their way through life. Such people are characterized by their inadequate responses to the ordinary demands of everyday living. The cartoon character "Sad Sack," a comic-strip feature since World War II days, typifies the inefficient and inadequate personality in military service.

THE SCHIZOID PERSONALITY

The schizoid personality reaction is seen in people who are incapable of close relationships with others and who are cold, aloof, and emotionally detached. They find their satisfactions within themselves, and tend to be intellectually and emotionally independent of other people. They are the somewhat seclusive, nonsocial individuals who cannot be easily drawn into group activities. Such people are inclined to avoid both competition and cooperation, preferring to remain emotionally uninvolved.

Individuals of this type ordinarily find little satisfaction in face-to-face relationships. Sometimes such people are said to have a "shut-in" personality. They have few friends, and even these few

friends do not get to know them well. Frequently they are considered odd or peculiar. Sometimes they show exceptional intellectual ability or creative talent; but in spite of their occasional brilliance, they are likely to lead an unhappy and isolated existence.

The first signs of this rather serious personality pattern may become apparent during childhood. The child who is seclusive and withdrawn and who becomes irritable when this seclusiveness is disturbed may be beginning to build up the world of fantasy and daydreams characteristic of the schizoid personality. All children indulge freely in make-believe, and this behavior serves a useful and constructive purpose in child development. The difference between the psychologically healthy child and the schizoid child is that the schizoid finds it increasingly difficult to know what is real and what is fantasy.

One of the best descriptions of the secret world of the schizoid child is Conrad Aiken's short story "Silent Snow, Secret Snow." In Tennessee Williams' *The Glass Menagerie*, Laura is so shy and withdrawn into a world of dreams that her collection of glass animals seems more real to her than the people around her. Escape into a schizophrenic dream world is also shown in Julian Green's *The Closed Garden,* in which a young French girl takes refuge in a world of fantasy where she imagines herself to be madly in love with a perfect stranger.

Many mildly schizoid persons maintain a satisfactory adjustment throughout life. Some seek help because of difficulty in making friends, feelings of inadequacy, or general social ineptness. Hospitalization is not necessary unless a more serious mental disorder is suspected.

■ **SCHIZOID PERSONALITY**

Paul B. is a forty-four-year-old man who has had several admissions to psychiatric hospitals because of his withdrawn and somewhat peculiar behavior. His first admission was at age twenty-five when he received a psychiatric discharge from the Army. A year later the patient was convicted of forgery and was sent to the penitentiary. Upon being released from prison he was committed to another psychiatric hospital. He escaped after a few months and went to Florida, where he was involved in a series of thefts. The patient was sentenced to serve a term in the county jail, but because of his seclusive behavior he was admitted to a mental hospital. After his discharge, he was picked up by the police in another state for a minor offense. As a result of his strange behavior he was referred again to a psychiatric hospital for observation.

When seen at the hospital the patient was an effeminate-looking, slender male who appeared much younger than his age. His speech, carriage, and mannerisms were openly effeminate. While Paul denied homosexual behavior, he did admit that the patients on his ward call him by the name of Mabel. The ward attendants reported that when his real name was used, he did not answer. During the interview the patient was pleasant and cooperative. He was oriented in all areas. His speech was relevant, and his thinking was logical. He showed a normal range of emotional responsiveness, with no indication of disturbed thinking or perception, or other symptoms of more serious personality disturbance. The patient said, "I'm not sick, and I don't think anything is wrong with me. Ever since I was a kid, I was told I was abnormal. I was just quiet and didn't say anything.*

THE CYCLOTHYMIC PERSONALITY

The cyclothymic pattern is found in the extroverted individual with an outgoing adjustment to life situations. There is an apparent personal warmth, friendliness, and superficial generosity, and a ready enthusiasm for competition. Such people are subject to frequently alternating moods of elation and sadness, brought on by internal cues rather than external situations. Sometimes the person is in a persistently euphoric or depressed state, but there is no distortion of reality.

In the cyclothymic personality, the mood swings in the direction of elation or depression are not sufficiently severe to require hospitalization. Since the disturbance is in the emotional area, such people are less likely to be detected than those exhibiting the schizoid pattern, in which the disturbance is marked by social withdrawal. People are generally more likely to be tolerant of exaggerated emotional reactions than they are of peculiarities in thinking. For this reason, relatively few people are diagnosed as personality pattern disturbances of the cyclothymic type.

The cyclothymic personality whose mood tends to be elevated is even less likely to be considered a personality problem than the one whose mood is on the depressed side. The persistently elevated type of cyclothymia becomes an asset in many instances. The greater alertness, quicker thinking, and increased physical energy make such people socially attractive and occupationally valuable. The man or woman with boundless energy and enthusiasm for his work and outside projects is sought after as a committee member, campaign worker, volunteer, and organizer. The remarkable success of some people may be a result of a cyclothymic personality pattern of the elevated type.

The depressed type of cyclothymic personality, on the other hand, is ordinarily recognized more easily as a personality disturbance. Such people surround themselves with a persistent cloak of gloom, take a pessimistic view of life, and are preoccupied with the negative and less cheerful aspects of living. However, because the depression is minimal, the cyclothymic personality is usually not hospitalized and seldom receives treatment.

Just as the schizoid personality contains the germinal elements of a more serious schizophrenic psychosis, the cyclothymic personality sometimes precedes the manic-depressive psychosis. In spite of this developmental relationship, personality disturbances of these types do not necessarily evolve into full-blown psychotic behavior. Most cyclothymic personalities go through life without developing psychotic episodes which require hospitalization.

THE PARANOID PERSONALITY

The paranoid personality is marked by many of the traits of the schizoid personality, combined with a marked tendency to use projection as a defense mechanism. The result is a personality in which suspiciousness, envy, jealousy, and stub-

---

*Case 1 of audiotape 2, "Personality Disorders: Trait and Pattern Disturbances," in *Case Interviews to Accompany The Disorganized Personality*.

bornness are dominant characteristics. The reaction is relatively common in our culture. Most of us know people who are persistently suspicious. Such individuals go through life constantly questioning the motives of others. They are sure the salesclerk has shortchanged them, the grocer has cheated them, and other people are trying to get the best of them. They are likely to be stubbornly resistive to reasoning. Moreover, they find it difficult to form warm and close emotional relationships with other people. They may seek to protect themselves from the world by means of sarcasm and invective.

As with other personality disturbances, elements of paranoid thinking are found in even the most normal individuals. It is only when the paranoic trend becomes the determining factor in the behavior of the individual that the condition can be called a personality pattern disturbance.

The following letter was received from a woman with a paranoid personality:

> Dear Dr. _____:
> It looks like some people have the idea they can take what they want and give something else in return that suits their fancy. And it looks like they expect the plums while we keep the pits. A creeping petunia on our rockery—the only flower there besides myrtle—has evidently been taken by someone. I have a hunch Mrs. C. took it. It is evident she took a clump of plume grass out of our field, and all the coreopsis, too. It seems quite strange that Mrs. M. has so many double daffodils, and so many of ours are missing. And the number of iris Mrs. D. has is something to wonder about. Every time an unusual iris comes to bloom on our rockery, it is gone the next morning.
> Sincerely,

One of the best literary examples of the psychological world of the paranoid personality is Franz Kafka's novel *The Trial*. This novel, which begins with the sentence, "Someone must have been telling lies about Joseph K. . . ," is the story of a man against whom vague charges have been made. Joseph K. is told that he is under arrest, but he is not detained nor is he told what the charges are. He is required to appear before an audience in an interrogation chamber, where he protests against his unfair treatment. He believes that a "great organization" is at work and that through this organization innocent people are made to appear guilty.

During the interrogation, Joseph K. believes that he notices the magistrate making a "secret sign" to someone in the audience. He observes also that some members of the audience wear badges, and he believes that these people are in league with the magistrate. He feels that the people on the right side of the room act in a manner different from those on the left side of the room. Joseph K. also finds that many strangers and outsiders seem to know about his case. Throughout the proceedings, neither Joseph K. nor the defense counsel knows what the charges are. The novel is a masterful depiction of the inner torment of the paranoid personality.

Many paranoid personalities manage to make a marginal adjustment in spite of their symptoms. These individuals, because of their generally disagreeable nature, are likely to have few friends. Usually they prefer to live alone and either do not marry or have unsuccessful marriages. The studies of the ecology of mental disorder in Chicago showed that this type of individual was most likely to be found in rooming-house areas of the city (Faris and Dunham, 1939). Such areas contain relatively large numbers of men and women who are single, separated, or divorced. The paranoid personality not unexpectedly makes up a disproportionately large number of the members of these groups.

PASSIVE-AGGRESSIVE PERSONALITY

The passive-aggressive personality is a classification for patients who are unable to keep their emotions under control. While the cyclothymic individual also has problems with emotional control, his disturbances are limited to the dimension of depression and elation. The passive-aggressive individual has an emotional life which is erratic and unpredictable and which the expressed emotion may be exaggerated in any direction. Most patients of this type, however, are struggling with their passive and aggressive needs.

A person may handle these needs by becoming excessively passive and dependent, or he may attempt to solve the problem by resorting to a passive form of aggression. A third possible solution is the direct acting out of aggressive feelings. These three types of working out passive and aggressive needs are called (1) the passive-dependent type, (2) the passive-aggressive type, and (3) the aggressive type.

In the *passive-dependent personality,* there is a childlike clinging to other people. Such persons seek to avoid responsibility, are likely to be indecisive, and may show anxiety and ineffectual behavior in situations requiring personal initiative. This type of individual seems constantly to be seeking someone to protect and dominate him. When such a person is found, a reasonably stable adjustment is often made. Many men and women have this helpless, childlike quality and are particularly appealing to some members of the opposite sex. As one would expect, women of this type have a much better chance of making a satisfactory adjustment in our society than do men having similar dependency needs.

The passive-dependent person is usually well behaved during childhood. Frequently he is a good student; and if he has a sympathetic supervisor on his job, he may achieve occupational success of a limited kind. Because of their emotional needs, men of this kind often do not marry. If they do marry, the sexual relationship is likely to be unsatisfactory. Many men and women of this type make a reasonably good adjustment and go through life without receiving treatment. Difficulties become apparent when stress and strain become severe and the person is not able emotionally to handle the situation. Under such circumstances, the typical passsive-dependent trait becomes clear.

The passive-dependent personality is characterized both by passivity and dependency, with a complete avoidance of overt hostility. During diagnostic examinations, a person suspected of this reaction might be asked what he would do if someone were to slap his face. The characteristic answer is, "Nothing."

It is possible that, in some cases at least, the passive-dependent personality grows out of unfulfilled dependency needs during infancy and parental overprotection and domination during childhood. As such a child grows older, he accepts protection and domination as his means of obtaining attention and approval. Feelings of hostility may be repressed because of the fear that the expression of such feelings would result in rejection. The child becomes accustomed to compliance and remains excessively dependent upon authoritative figures.

The *passive-aggressive personality* is typified by the technique of rebellion through inaction and stubbornness. Such people are beyond the complete helplessness and dependency of infancy, but have not found it possible to stand on their own feet. In a sense, they are caught between a need to be dependent and the reluctance to be dominated. These people seem to seek strong and dominant individuals to lean on, but thinly disguised and indirectly expressed hostility is not unusual. The passive-aggressive personality does express aggression, but in a passive way. To be stubborn and resistive, to be mule-headed, to be sullen and spiteful, and to be negativistic is to be aggressive in a nonactive way.

The *aggressive personality* takes the attitude "Nobody's going to push me around." These are the people who carry the proverbial chips on their shoulders. They take every frustration in life as a personal affront, and they react with irritability, temper outbursts, and destructive behavior. Such people may be attempting to conceal an unconscious wish to be dominated and to be taken care of as if they were children. On the surface, however, the aggressive person spends much of his time attempting to assert himself, often in a childlike and irrelevant way.

The aggressive personality responds to the stresses and frustrations of life by acting out in a hostile way. High temper, assaultive behavior, destructive acts, and an uncontrolled striking at the object of frustration is a characteristic mode of behavior in these cases. The aggressive wife throws things at her husband, while the aggressive husband has little hesitancy about beating his wife. Similarly, aggressive parents may punish their children unmercifully. Aggressive children, in turn, are often involved in fights, vandalism, and similar behavior.

One young boy who was referred to a juvenile court was walking down the street and suddenly and impulsively struck another youngster in the face. The victim was walking along the sidewalk in the opposite direction. The boys had never seen one another before, no words had been exchanged, and, in fact, the victim had not even noticed the aggressor. The youngster who struck the boy could give no reason whatever for his behavior. In another case, a fourteen-year-old baby-sitter lashed a three-year-old boy with a leather strap. The baby-sitter became enraged after the child had broken a 10-cent ashtray. Another young baby-sitter admitted burning a two-year-old boy with a cooking fork. The girl told police she burned the child because he irritated her with his crying while she cooked his dinner.

One of the most serious cases of unprovoked aggression occurred when two teen-age boys confessed to torturing a younger boy. When the victim was found, his body was covered with lumps, bruises, cuts, and burns. He had been thoroughly beaten, and gasoline had been rubbed on his chest and ignited. His body had been cut with a knife while he screamed in terror. When asked why they did it, the boys said they "didn't know."

■ AGGRESSIVE PERSONALITY

Helen P. is a fourteen-year-old girl who was sent to a juvenile court following a runaway from home. While in the detention unit of the juvenile center, the girl's behavior became so aggressive that she was referred to the psychiatric clinic. When she entered the interview room, she shouted that she hated her mother, and would kill her if she ever had the opportunity. Throughout the stormy interview, which was punctuated by crying, cursing, and shouting obscenities, the girl variously threatened to kill her mother, herself, and the examiner. She became particularly disturbed while describing an incident involving the stabbing of a child which occurred five years earlier. The details of this incident were hazy, although the event appeared to have had a traumatic effect.

In a later interview, the youngster's mood was somewhat more depressed. On one or two occasions she came very close to tears but at no time did she cry. A few times she managed a feeble smile. She verbalized marked hostility toward her mother although she denied she would harm her. Helen admitted she had an explosive temper, especially when pressure was put on her by her mother. The aggressive personality disorder is seen in the extreme hostility toward the mother, the hostile acting out in the detention unit of the juvenile center, and the aggressive impulses directed toward the examiner during the initial clinical interview.*

THE OBSESSIVE-COMPULSIVE PERSONALITY

The individual with a compulsive personality is rigid, meticulous, and perfectionistic in his behavior. While these characteristics are found frequently in people without personality difficulties, the excessive rigidity becomes a personality disorder when the trait dominates the personality.

In terms of personality dynamics, the compulsive personality is likely to have an oversevere conscience. Such people are preoccupied with the correctness of their behavior. While many people of this type make valuable contributions to the world because of this characteristic, many more fail to achieve because the self-imposed perfectionism stands in their way. They are unable to accomplish anything because they are dissatisfied with their effort. It is not unusual for such people to strike out in many directions hoping to attain a goal. Often the compulsive personality does in fact attain a considerable degree of skill because of the demands he makes on his own behavior. Usually, however, the inflexibility and the self-critical quality of the personality make final success impossible.

One patient described her compulsive behavior by saying:

> I am incessantly concerned over the fact that I am not going to get done all I want to. I always have several lists, some very extensive, and as I do the task I cross it off. I try to make a concise list of what I plan or want for the week. During the week I will add to it, but I never cross something off as being unnecessary. Even on my day off, I get up early to do something on my list. I only wish there were more than twenty-four hours in a day.

OTHER PERSONALITY DISORDERS

In addition to the personality disorders already discussed, the 1968 revision of the Diagnostic and Statistical Manual (DSM-II) included three new categories: the hysterical personality, the asthenic personality, and the explosive personality.

---

*Case 3 of audiotape 2, "Personality Disorders: Trait and Pattern Disturbances," in *Case Interviews to Accompany The Disorganized Personality.*

The hysterical personality, which is also called the histrionic personality, is marked by excitability and a tendency to overreact to stress. Individuals showing this reaction have learned to dramatize themselves and their problems. Such people are likely to be self-centered and immature, and they revert to adolescent and even childish behavior when they are frustrated or in conflict. It is not unusual for them to be seductive in their attempts to control others and to get their own way. Their emotional life is unstable and unpredictable.

The most striking features of the asthenic personality are the low level of physical energy and the lack of enthusiasm. These individuals become easily fatigued and are usually tired and depressed. They find it difficult to meet even the ordinary demands of everyday living. Social and recreational activities to which most people would look forward are simply too much effort for the individual of the asthenic type. The capacity for enjoying life is extremely limited in such people, and they tend to be gloomy and pessimistic in their general outlook.

The explosive personality, also called the epileptoid personality, is seen in individuals who show sudden outbursts of rage and violent episodes of verbal or physical aggressiveness. The behavior of such persons is highly unpredictable. Tempers flare at the most unexpected times. No one can be quite sure when the next explosion will occur or what will trigger it. It often appears that the individual is unable to control himself. And while the word epileptoid suggests epilepsy, which is an organic disorder of the brain, the inclusion of the explosive personality among the personality disorders implies that the condition is not due to a recognizable physical problem but is a deeply ingrained personality characteristic.

One of the major difficulties with the general classification of personality disorders is that it is often difficult to differentiate these conditions from the neuroses (see Chapter 8) and the psychoses (see Chapter 10). Even though the personality disorders are described as being "characterized by deeply ingrained maladaptive patterns of behavior that are perceptibly different in quality from psychotic and neurotic symptoms" (DSM-II), these differences are not spelled out for the guidance of the clinician.

THE ANTISOCIAL PERSONALITY

Early psychiatrists were not able to accept antisocial behavior as a form of mental disorder, particularly since the more conventional symptoms are not seen in these cases. One of the paradoxes in psychopathology is that some people appear to be intellectually quite normal but at the same time quite abnormal in other personality traits. For many years there was a failure to admit this paradox. It was accepted without question that only the disintegration of reason and intellect could produce mental disorder.

Many people, however, do not show the conventional symptoms of disorientation, thinking disturbances, perceptual distortions, and other forms of pathological behavior. Philippe Pinel, in the late eighteenth century, wrote: "I had thought that madness was inseparable from delirium or delusion, and I was surprised to find many maniacs who gave no evidence of impairment of the understanding. . ." (Pinel, 1798). Other early French psychiatrists also were intrigued with the problem of mental disorder in people who appeared intellectually normal. The term *moral insanity* gradually came to be used to designate those cases in which there were serious behavior deviations but none of the usual symptoms of mental disorder. The term was introduced in England in the early nineteenth century in the following words:

> Madness consisting in a morbid perversion of the natural feelings, affections, inclinations, temper, habits, moral dispositions and natural impulses without any remarkable disorder or defect in the intellect or knowing and reasoning faculties and particularly without any insane illusion or hallucination (Prichard, 1839).

Late in the nineteenth century, the term *psychopathic personality* was introduced in Germany (Koch, 1891). He described patients who could not be classified in any of the ordinary psychiatric systems and yet who were not entirely sane.

For the next fifty years, the psychopathic personality was a prominent, though vague, classification in the field of mental disorder. Kraepelin viewed the condition as lying between normality and mental disorder. He differentiated seven types of psychopathic personalities, including the excitable, the unstable, the impulsive, the egocentric, the liars and swindlers, the antisocial, and the quarrelsome (Kraepelin, 1915). During World War I, the Surgeon General of the Army issued a classification in which there were also seven varieties of psychopathic states—inadequate personality, paranoid personality, emotional instability, criminalism, pathological lying, sexual psychopathy, and nomadism. In the 1930s, a typical classification listed sixteen types of psychopaths.

It was inevitable that the classification of psychopathic personality should become a dumping ground for all those conditions which did not qualify for the more conventional clinical categories. If a condition could not be fitted into one of the major diagnostic categories, it was called a psychopathic personality through the process of elimination. One psychiatrist said, "The only conclusion that seems warrantable is that at some time or other, and by some reputable authority, the term psychopathic personality has been used to designate every conceivable type of abnormal character" (Curran and Mallinson, 1944).

Eventually, several attempts were made to escape from the vagueness of the concept of psychopathic personality. The term *neurotic character* was introduced in an effort to emphasize the psychogenic nature of the disorder (Alexander, 1930). This term has found its widest acceptance in psychoanalysis. The term *sociopathic personality* was suggested in the same year (Partridge, 1930). This term, which includes many of the types of behaviors formerly subsumed under "psychopathic personality," emphasizes the importance of social maladjustment in these cases.

The antisocial personality presents one of the most difficult treatment problems in psychopathology. The person shows none of the symptoms of neurotic reaction or of psychosis, but at the same time he is not able to make an adequate social adjustment. His intelligence may be average. He may possess wit and charm and may have a facility for making people like him and trust him. At the same time, he is typically without scruples, without morals, and without a sense of guilt.

The antisocial personality seems always to be in trouble and does not profit from experience or punishment. Such individuals maintain no real loyalties to any person, group, or code. Very often they show marked emotional immaturity, are completely irresponsible, show lack of judgment, and have an extraordinary ability to rationalize their behavior in order to justify it. Relatively few antisocial personalities find their way to the mental hospital. Many of them are in jails, reformatories, and penitentiaries.

The antisocial reaction includes such well-known types as the pathological liar, the swindler and confidence man, the habitual criminal, and more ordinary individuals whose smoothness, glibness, lack of conscience, and general irresponsibility characterize their everyday behavior. As one British psychiatrist noted, "There are persons who indulge in vice with such persistence, at a cost of punishment so heavy, so certain, and so prompt, who incur their punishment for the sake of pleasure so trifling and so transient, that they are by common consent considered insane although they exhibit no other indication of insanity" (Henderson, 1939).

An outstanding characteristic of the antisocial personality is that these individuals seem to be completely without conscience. They are able to engage in unlawful, immoral, and unethical actions with little or no evidence of anxiety or feelings of guilt. There is a complete lack of concern and a freedom from remorse. The antisocial personality seems unable to postpone his satisfactions. Like the young child, he insists upon the immediate satisfaction of his needs. He engages in impulsive actions without thought for the future, without regard for their effect on other people, and without concern for damaging implications for himself.

An example of the impulsive behavior of the antisocial personality is the action of a New York bus driver who became bored with his route and one day drove across the George Washington Bridge and down the East Coast to Florida. When apprehended by the police, the driver explained his 1,500-mile trip by saying, "I just wanted to get away from New York."

Another type of antisocial reaction is seen in the swindler, the confidence man, and the pathological liar. Individuals of this type combine instability and imaginativeness. In most cases they are friendly and sociable people who have a way with words. Their glibness and their charm combine to create a favorable impression which often fools intelligent people. Such antisocial personalities exude self-confidence. It is not unusual for them to have an impressive, though frequently superficial, knowledge of business, the arts, science, politics, and other areas of general interest.

The antisocial personality sometimes has the knack of winning friends and worming his way into the confidence and affection of those he will eventually use and victimize. It is not uncommon for men and women who have been bilked and swindled by such individuals to come to their defense later on. A businessman who was cheated out of more than $100,000, and who never recovered a cent of his loss, could still comment, "I can't help liking that so-and-so."

Following World War II, a thirty-seven-year-old man applied to a Brooklyn hospital for a medical internship. He showed hospital authorities photostats of degrees from Scottish and German universities, and he was given a job. During the next few months he helped deliver several hundred babies. Over a period of five years, he transferred from one New York hospital to another. Finally, after he missed a payment on a car he had purchased, police found that he had never been licensed to practice medicine. Horrified officials of the hospital where he was serving as Senior Resident then learned that he had not even finished high school. In the Army he had been assigned to the Medical Corps, and he had read every medical book he could find. When the war was over, he forged credentials and references and applied to a medical placement agency as a physician. Due to the shortage of physicians, he had no trouble in finding an opening. The superintendent of the hospital where he was first hired said, "He was a very good doctor, and a nice person. He had a marvelous personality and impressed all of us at the hospital." When the self-styled "doctor" appeared in court, he found that the judge had been one of his patients at the hospital only a few weeks before. Granting that the "doctor" was quite an impressive fellow, the judge nevertheless sent him to the penitentiary for a year.

The total inability of the antisocial personality to profit from experience or to use good judgment is typified by a prisoner who thanked the warden profusely for his encouraging remarks at the time of his release from prison. However, on his way out of the office, the prisoner stole the warden's portable typewriter.

The antisocial personality is unable to establish a truly warm and meaningful relationship with other people. He is incapable of friendship based upon trust and affection. When he enters into what appears to be a friendship, it is a matter of expediency. Friends exist only to the extent that they are valuable to him. Similarly, marriage is never more than a source of narcissistic satisfaction. When the antisocial personality does not get his way, he may become dangerous and even violent. Because of his lack of conscience, he is capable of the most extreme types of behavior. Aggressive brutality, brutal sex crimes, and other acts of violence are quite within his capability.

■ ANTISOCIAL PERSONALITY

Calvin F. was admitted to a psychiatric hospital at the age of eighteen with the diagnosis of antisocial personality. Two months after admission he escaped from an attendant, but was returned by the police. The following month he escaped again by breaking a screen on a porch, and the next day he was arrested while driving a stolen car. He was transferred to a maximum security hospital where he remained for three years. At the end of this time he was returned as "improved." A month later, he escaped by sawing the iron bars on a window. Four months later he was arrested in Montana for wearing the uniform of an Army officer, and was placed on Federal probation for five years. Six months later he was arrested in Spokane, Washington, for stealing automobiles. He was hospitalized in Spokane for a short time, and was then returned to the psychiatric hospital. Two months after his return he attacked an attendant with a soft drink bottle, taped his mouth, stole his money, and escaped.

The cause of the antisocial personality is unknown. Expert opinion ranges all the way from the belief that this type of personality is a relatively unalterable constitutional defect to an emphasis on the unconscious conflicts of the person. It is probable that both constitutional and psychogenic factors are involved. Pressing psychological dynamics are more likely to work themselves out as antisocial behavior in those individuals in whom there is a constitutional character deficiency.

Center for Studies of Crime and Delinquency

This center was established in 1968 by the National Institute of Mental Health to deal with the complex problems of antisocial behavior. Among the objectives of the center are those of developing better definitions of crime and delinquency; supporting basic research on the causes and nature of law-violating behavior; developing more effective and better-coordinated community resources directed at delinquency prevention and control; intensifying the research for and utilizing a variety of community-based treatment and rehabilitation programs as alternatives to imprisonment; developing newer models for training professional and nonprofessional personnel; and pursuing a variety of concerns pertaining to the needs of mentally disordered offenders.

Antisocial conduct covers a wide range of behavior from truancy and theft to multiple homicide. The monetary cost of such deviant behavior to the nation—not only the expense of law enforcement, administration of justice, and imprisonment, but also the cost of damages inflicted by criminals—has been estimated at more than 20 billion dollars a year. The emotional and psychological consequences defy measurement.

At any given time, approximately 1.3 million offenders are under some form of supervision, with about a third of them in jails, prisons, and reformatories. Public expenditures for police, courts, and prisons are estimated at more than 4 billion dollars annually. The number of delinquency cases among youngsters between the ages of 10 and 17 has been increasing at a considerably faster rate than the number of youngsters in this age group. Recent studies have indicated that one out of five boys within this age range will at some point appear before the juvenile court. In some areas, nine out of every ten juveniles have had some contact with juvenile court authorities.

Although the 15 to 17 age group represents less than 6 percent of the population, it accounts for almost 13 percent of all arrests—the highest arrest rate of all age groups. Over half of all arrests for burglary and larceny and almost two-thirds of the arrests for auto theft are of persons under the age of 18. While juveniles predominate in these forms of offense against property, they are also becoming involved, to an increasing extent, in an offense against people—aggravated assault (NIMH, 1970).

SEXUAL DEVIATIONS

Sexual deviations are among the most important personality problems in our culture. While these cases sometimes overlap with the more serious personality disturbances, such as the neuroses and psychoses, most sexual deviations are due to personality disorganization of a less severe kind.

In the past, the sexual deviations were grouped under the heading of psychopathic personality. For this reason, the term *sexual psychopath* has been used widely in medicine, psychology, and the criminal codes. Implied in most legal definitions of the sexual psychopath are the ideas that the pattern of sexual behavior is a continual one, that there is an expression of aggression toward minors or against society, and that the action is not a consequence of alcoholism, psychosis, or mental retardation.

It must be kept in mind that not all sexual offenders, in the legal sense, are suffering from personality disturbances. Adultery, rape, and incest are criminal acts but in most instances are not committed by men and women who are sexual deviates. These acts are considered crimes, but they are "abnormal" only because of cultural conditioning.

While the concept of the sexual psychopath is found in many books and articles, the current diagnostic classification considers the sexual deviate apart from the psychopathic or antisocial type of personality disorder. Such a separation in classification is important because, while many sexually deviant acts are the result of an antisocial personality, many others grow out of personality dynamics of a quite different kind.

The sexual deviations with which the psychologist and psychiatrist are most likely to deal in clinical practice are (1) *exhibitionism,* (2) *voyeurism,* (3) *fetishism,* (4) *sadomasochism,* (5) *homosexuality* and *transvestism,* and a variety of less common conditions including *pedophilia, zoophilia, necrophilia,* and *coprophilia.*

EXHIBITIONISM

The exhibitionist obtains sexual relief by showing, or exhibiting, his body to other people. For psychodynamic reasons which are not completely clear, most of the serious cases of exhibitionism are men. Unfortunately, exhibitionism has been treated too often as a legal offense rather than as a psychiatric or psychological problem. Yet the more enlightened lawyers, police officials, and jurists are coming to the realization that this is an emotional problem which cannot be cured by a jail sentence.

The precursor of exhibitionism is seen in the inspectionism of children when they show their sex organs to one another. It is seen also in the sexual display behavior of animals, in the ceremonial dances of many different cultures, and, finally, in the erotic relationships of adult human beings. In exhibitionism, the patient's own body is the source of his gratification. The "self" is the love object.

Exhibitionism occurs both in disguised and undisguised forms. Beaches and swimming pools afford the best opportunities for thinly veiled, yet socially approved, exhibitionism. In James Joyce's *Ulysses,* the exhibitionism of Gerty MacDowell on the beach stimulates the erotic fantasies of Leopold Bloom. While this drama is reenacted every day on beaches throughout the world, the truly compulsive nature of exhibitionism is seen most clearly in those cases that come to the attention of the police or the psychologist.

The exhibitionist presents a rather typical personality pattern. Essentially he is an ambitious person whose ambitions have not been satisfied. Such individuals are basically shy and conscientious, even though it does not seem that a man who exposes his genitals in public is showing signs of shyness. In many instances, there is an unsatisfactory sexual life. While exhibitionists may be married and have children, the marriage relationship is seldom a satisfactory one.

The activity pattern of exhibitionism is fairly consistent. The exhibitionist is likely to expose himself at the same place and at the same time of of day. In fact, he seems to go out of his way to risk being caught. The executive of an advertising firm was arrested after exposing himself at his office windows to the girls who worked in the offices across the street. A man in Connecticut staged dances in the nude on moonlit residential lawns. He tapped on windows of houses to gain attention, and then he began his impromptu ballet. A trap was set by a group of husbands, and the exhibitionist was caught. To everyone's amazement, the nude dancer turned out to be the town's model policeman and the father of three children.

■ EXHIBITIONISM

George B. is a fourteen-year-old boy who was referred to a juvenile court psychiatric clinic for twice exposing himself sexually to two young girls. The boy is pleasant and cooperative, and speaks freely about his difficulties. He relates well to the examiner during the interview, and rapport is good. The youngster's thinking is clear and logical, his emotional responsiveness is within normal limits, and there are no symptoms of motor disturbances. Psychological examination shows him to be an essentially normal youngster in terms of his personality structure and development. The incidents of exhibitionism involved girls of four and five years of age. George has had no contact with girls of his own age range. During the interview the boy expresses serious doubts about his own sexual adequacy. He says that he has been concerned by the fact that he does not seem to have sexual urges as pronounced as the other boys he knows. Another factor in this case is that George was shown pornographic material by another boy just before the sexual episodes. He was told by this other boy about his relationship with a girl, and George became curious about the experience.

The following comments by an exhibitionist reveal something of the feelings, conflicts, and behavior of a man with this personality problem:

I have exhibitionistic tendencies toward women, and I am sure it will get me into difficulties. It's a peculiar thing that it is only six or seven months that I have had these impulses. I want to halt them before they get me into hot water. It's a matter of great shame. I am quite sure I can get rid of them, but I need moral support and bolstering up. If someone found out about them it would be a great disgrace. I couldn't face my wife.

The exhibitionistic tendencies really started ten years ago. I remember one incident distinctly. I used to go bathing and undress in back of some rocks and shrubbery. While I was undressing, a woman about a block away was looking at me and was interested. I made note of this interest. I couldn't help but notice that she was a member of the opposite sex and that she had an interest in my body. It made me feel important and secure. Until this experience, I had been very modest and shy about showing any part of my body. . . .

I am still not very much at ease with women. I realize that they are human beings, and I get along with them tolerably well. With my wife I am rather modest, reserved and conservative. She is the same way. I never display my body to her. . . .

Figure 7.2 *There is a bit of the voyeur in most men. It becomes a personality disorder only when carried to extremes. (Tom McCarthy)*

I have had that impulse to exhibit myself several times. To me it is such a shameful thing, I try to put it out of my mind and forget about it. It's never been toward any particular person, but it is always toward a woman my own age or younger. I can hardly bear to talk about these things. It took a lot of courage to come to talk to you.

I would have to be in a pretty secure place where no one could find out about it. It would have to be where no one knows me and with a woman who wouldn't object. It's more the thrill of anticipation. That first experience with the woman on the beach was very, very interesting. I got the impression that all women might feel the same way, and I want to experiment again to see if it is true (Henry, 1955).

There are also indirect forms of exhibitionism. Many people use indecent language on the telephone—often to strangers—and some are arrested for it. A city fireman reported that his wife received

four such telephone calls from a fifteen-year-old. A fifth call was received, and the wife was instructed to invite the caller to her home. Five minutes after the date had been made, the youth arrived (on his bicycle!) and was arrested. A similar case involved a college dean who telephoned improper proposals to more than fifty women. The man admitted calling numbers picked at random from the telephone book; if a woman answered, he would use indecent language. These "telephone seducers" use the telephone as a shield while they exhibit themselves symbolically through the use of language.

Another kind of subterfuge was used by a beatnik artist who scattered obscene verses and drawings on the streets for ten years, hoping that they would be picked up by women. He also sent his drawings to girls who were advertising for jobs in the newspapers. Otherwise he made no attempt to contact the women.

Obscene wit, or "bathroom humor," is another form of indirect exhibitionism. Jokes of this kind often use the four-letter words and deal with the most intimate body functions. People who tell such stories sometimes are attempting to satisfy exhibitionistic needs. They are exposing themselves for everyone to see. This kind of humor is a return to that earlier period of life when little boys write dirty words on the sidewalks and on the walls of buildings.

As in most psychological disorders, the dynamics of exhibitionism vary from one case to another. Sometimes it is a regressive act which repeats the experiences of infancy and early childhood. Some psychoanalysts believe it to be a frantic effort on the part of the person to deny unconsciously his castration fantasies. More commonly, exhibitionism is a response to sexual frustration. It is also possible that the exhibitionist has strong unconscious homosexual components in his personality and that the behavior is an effort to deny these feelings. In other cases, exhibitionism may be a response to impotence, an expression of narcissism, or an effort to overcome feelings of inferiority.

Voyeurism

Voyeurism, a sexual deviation also known as *scotophilia,* is closely associated with exhibitionism. In this type of behavior the patient receives his erotic satisfaction from "looking." The observation of sexually arousing situations becomes a substitute for participation in such activities.

The voyeuristic impulse is seen, in a more or less socially acceptable form, in the interest in reading "girlie" magazines, gazing at scantily clad women on beaches and athletic fields, attending stag films, reading pornographic literature, and frequenting beauty contests.

Voyeurism is responsible for a wide variety of behavior ranging from that of the frustrated youth who peeps in the windows of dormitories and sorority houses to the pathological cases of men whose only relief from sexual tension comes from watching the erotic behavior of others. One patient managed a vicarious incestuous relationship with his promiscuous daughter by encouraging her to invite young men home and then peeping at the pair during their love-making.

A fast-talking young man in Oregon worked out a novel system for satisfying his peeping urge. In the assumed role of a physician from the Portland Health Bureau, he tricked young housewives into taking examinations in the nude for a nonexistent rash. He told the women he was tracing a contagious skin rash that was spreading in the Portland area. The "doctor" even examined the husband of one of the women.

A more common trick is for a man to set himself up as a photographer and advertise in the newspapers for models or for young women to learn the photographic business. When police raided the "studio" in the home of one such "photographer," they found hundreds of photographs and negatives of women in the nude. They also confiscated note pads containing names, addresses, telephone numbers, and detailed descriptions of dozens of married and single women.

Pornography of any kind, including obscene books, pictures, and motion pictures, is based upon the compulsion to look. Many people of culture, intelligence, and social position are nevertheless fascinated by the pornographic. A banker will buy a set of "French postcards" as eagerly as a college boy. The urge to peek at what is forbidden has filled newsstands and bookshops with "art studies" and "health" and "nudist" magazines.

An extreme form of voyeurism was observed in a patient who had an urge to look under women's dresses. This man sometimes felt the impulse to such an extent that he waited for women to go into telephone booths to make calls. If a woman left the door to the booth open, he had an irresistible need to get down on his hands and knees in an attempt to see under her dress as she stood at the telephone.

The psychodynamics of voyeurism may take a variety of forms. A common psychoanalytic interpretation is that such patients are preoccupied with scenes which have aroused castration anxieties. In other cases, there is an overt sexual pleasure experienced by means of identification with one of the persons when a sex act is witnessed. Another possible explanation is in terms of the forbidden nature of the act.

FETISHISM

In fetishism, articles of clothing or parts of the body become a substitute for the entire body. The fetishist receives sexual pleasure and satisfaction from stockings, shoes, undergarments, handkerchiefs, or similar articles of wearing apparel. In other cases, the fetish object is part

Figure 7.3 *A drawing of a woman by a male patient with a hair fetish. (Department of Psychology, Longview State Hospital.)*

of the human body. The more common fetish objects of this sort are hair, hands, feet, legs, and breasts. The condition is more common among men than among women.

The study of primitive tribes reveals many instances in which an object assumes the magical power of its possessor. The system of totem and taboo is built upon this idea. In the case of the fetishist, the same principles are at work. The fetish becomes a mystical substitute for the loved one. To possess the fetish object means to possess the entire person.

There are a great number of different kinds of fetishes. "Hair snippers" are fetishists who derive pleasure out of surreptitiously clipping hair from the heads of women. A high school student cut curls from nearly a score of feminine heads before the police finally caught up with him and his scissors. He explained that he had an irresistible desire to behave as he did. As a result, he went about indiscriminately clipping the locks from redheads, blonds, and brunettes. Most of his victims were little girls. He would attract a youngster to his automobile with the offer of candy, clip her tresses, and then drive away. A search of his car revealed a pair of scissors and a large collection of curls.

A favorite haunt of the hair fetishist is the motion picture theater. Taking a seat behind a girl with attractive hair, he quietly snips a few locks for himself and then hurries away to another unsuspecting victim. If the fetishist thinks that the person is willing for him to have the lock of hair, the situation loses its attraction. Nor will he be satisfied by being given locks of hair as gifts.

The foot fetish is another relatively common distortion of the erotic impulses. A young man in Ohio telephoned a number of attractive girls and told them he was making a foot survey. He then proceeded to ask such questions as the following: "Are you more ticklish in your feet than your ribs?" "Did you ever have your feet tickled in a swimming pool?" "Can you control the movements of your feet when they are being tickled?" "Could you stand to have your feet tickled constantly for fifteen minutes?" In one case he asked, "Could I come out and see for myself whether your feet are ticklish?" The young woman said no, but a little while later the doorbell rang, and there he was. "I've come to tickle your feet," he announced.

The fetish for feet and legs is reflected in many ways in literature, art, and drama. Alfred Hitchcock, the motion picture director, gives unusual dramatic emphasis to the feet of the characters in his films. Felicien Rops, in his drawings, reveals a peculiar fascination for stocking-covered legs, and Tennyson speaks of women's feet as "sunny gems."

The fetish object may take a great many forms. One man reported that his fetish was a woman in a uniform, particularly "nurses in white, stiff, crackly uniforms" (Gillespie, 1940). Some fetishists feel compelled to steal stockings, slips, brassieres, and panties from clotheslines, laundry bundles, and even dresser drawers.

LINGERIE THIEF CAUGHT

Seattle, Jan. 11—A young airplane engineer admitted today taking more than two hundred women's panties, girdles and other undergarments from clotheslines since October. The man, a graduate of the Massachusetts Institute of Technology, was caught taking the panties from a clothesline in the laundry of the Shorewood Apartments.

■ **FETISHISM**

Richard S. was referred for treatment because his habit of stealing women's underclothing from apartment houses had brought him into difficulty with the police. He would roam through the corridors and basements of large buildings, looking for clothing he could steal. Whenever he was questioned by a janitor or tenant, he would explain that he was looking for a vacant apartment or that he had lost his way. The incident which brought him to the attention of the police was one in which he broke into the same apartment near the campus on four occasions, each time stealing an article of underclothing. One time he bought a new pair of underthings, and broke into the young woman's apartment to leave them for her. Finally, he began to telephone her and plead with her to meet him. When she finally agreed, on the advice of the police, the rendezvous included two detectives and a policewoman. The patient admitted that for a number of years he had been stealing feminine underclothing, and that his wife and two children had no idea of his activities. The judge suspended the sentence when the patient agreed to enter psychotherapy.

In some cases, behavior of this kind is learned during childhood. For example, a young boy refused to go to sleep until given some garment which had been worn by his mother. In older children, fetishism may take the form of kissing and fondling a glove, handkerchief, or other item belonging to the person to whom the strong emotional attachment has been built up. There is a displacement of sexual excitement to an object that accidentally accompanied the first sexual experiences of the child. In psychoanalytic theory, the fetish objects are substitutes for infantile sexual objects, with the selection sometimes influenced by the odor of the object.

SADOMASOCHISM

The condition of sadomasochism is made up of two components, *sadism* and *masochism,* both of which are present to some degree in most cases. Sadism refers to the expression of power urges through sexual activity, while masochism is the sexual expression of passive and submissive needs. Sadism and masochism are expressions of the same instinctual drive. However, in the case of sadism the drive is directed toward an external object while in masochism the drive is turned against oneself. In sadomasochism, the infliction of pain and suffering may be a necessary part of more conventional sexual activity, or it may become a substitute for it.

The word *sadism* comes from the name of the Marquis de Sade, whose writings are filled with cruelties. Sadism is shown in Boccaccio's exhibitionistic tales and in Zola's *Bête Humaine,* in which the sadist becomes panicky whenever he is attracted by a girl because such attraction arouses the impulse to murder her. The motion picture *The Rope* is an excellent example of sadistic impulses. In this picture, two young sadists murder their friend, hide his body in a chest, and then invite the victim's friends and relatives to a dinner party in the room to celebrate the event.

Algernon Swinburne, the British poet, whose childish conceit ended with his drinking himself to death, had strong aggressive needs. In his poetry he speaks of "the sharp and cruel enjoyment of pain," "sharp lips and fierce fingers," "fierce and bitter kisses," and the "acrid relish of suffering." Swinburne explained his impulses in the following words: "I am cruel, but so is nature. . . . The more cruel and wicked I am, the closer do I come to nature" (Hare, 1949).

A university professor described the sadistic impulses of his childhood in the following words:

> I am cruel. I was cruel even as a child. I tortured insects before I killed them. I tore the wings from flies, pierced butterflies with a needle, and fastened them alive upon the walls. I wanted to catch snakes and tear off their heads as the other boys did, but I feared they would bite me. I tweaked the cats' tails until they cried out with pain and writhed in my grasp. I would torment animals in a cage. If I tortured any animal to death, it fascinated me to watch how long it could live. My sport with earthworms was to cut them in pieces, smaller and smaller until they no longer moved. Or I would stick them with needles until they died. I would tear one or two wings and legs from an insect and take delight in watching the maimed creature trying to get away. I caught wasps, tore out their sting or laid them upon hot irons; I picked out their sting and pulled off their heads (Stekel, 1929).

A vicious case of sadistic murder took place in Long Beach, California, where a ten-year-old girl died as a result of injuries received in the home of her female music teacher. The child was found tied to a chair, with her body covered with burns, bruises, and bites. In Kansas City, a fourteen-year-old stabbed a young girl to death with a butcher knife. When arrested, he said, "I didn't want to kill anyone. All I wanted to do was to slash somebody."

MAN BEATS COLLEGE GIRLS WITH BELT

Los Angeles, Nov. 1—A 29-year-old man was taken into custody on suspicion of assault with a deadly weapon. He gained entrance to two sorority houses by posing as a Hollywood talent scout. At each sorority on the UCLA campus, he told the girls of the need for suffering in order to portray genuine emotion. He induced several of the girls to allow him to beat them with a belt in order to test their ability to register pain. In the second sorority house, one of the girls became suspicious and called the police.

Sadistic acts frequently have unmistakable sexual overtones. Fritz Hartmann, the mass murderer of Hanover, Germany, killed twenty-five young boys by biting through their windpipes. A prominent Ohio veterinarian was arrested for driving up to couples parked in lonely country lanes and throwing chemicals at them. In Atlanta, four young women were painfully burned when a young man "shot" them with a water pistol containing acid.

PHANTOM MADMAN SPRAYS GIRLS ON TROLLEY WITH ACID

Ansonia, Conn., Dec. 19—A wave of terror swept over the Naugatuck valley when it became known that at least eleven persons, mostly young working girls, had been sprayed with sulphuric acid in the last two months. Guards were placed in all trolley cars here in an effort to forestall or capture the sprayer, at least four of whose victims are reported to have suffered burns while riding in the cars. One victim suffered severe burns on her back as she walked to work. The assailant approached his victims from behind and poured acid over their clothes. By the time the acid had eaten its way through to the victim's body, the assailant had disappeared.

The term *masochism* is derived from the name of Count Leopold von Sacher-Masoch, an Austrian writer who pursued women whom he could depend upon to inflict pain on him. He would grovel at their feet and obtain the greatest erotic pleasure from his mistreatment and self-abasement. Sacher-Masoch also insisted that his wives indulge in sexual affairs with other men.

In its strict technical sense, masochism refers to the obtaining of sexual gratification through pain and punishment inflicted upon oneself. The term has come to have a wider meaning, and is sometimes used to imply suffering in general. The masochistic motive is quite apparent in Edgar Allan Poe's stories "The Purloined Letter" and "The Masque of the Red Death," in much of Joris-Karl Huysmans' writing, and in Walt Whitman's "Song of Myself." The poetry of Charles Baudelaire suggests that he suffered from masochistic impulses. Sometimes the masochistic need is more or less disguised. "Liza Jane," an Ozark mountain folksong, contains the following verse:

> I wish I was an apple
> A-hangin' on a tree
> And every time my true-love passed
> She'd take a bite of me.

Masochism is such a common compulsion that several magazines have been published containing masochistic stories, letters, historical sketches, and personal advertisements designed to put masochists in touch with one another.

The masochistic compulsion has led to all sorts of strange situations. One young man visited prostitutes and paid them to engage in an Indian war dance with him. He carried a long rubber dagger; after the dancing had completely exhausted him, he would fall to the floor, and the girl would then stab him with the dagger. There were no other intimacies. The drama was designed to satisfy a masochistic need.

GIRL USES RAZOR TO MAR BEAUTY

New York, Dec. 14—Because her fiancé complained that she was too popular, a 17-year-old girl cut fifteen deep gashes in her face, arms, and legs with a razor blade. Not until six hours after she was admitted to a hospital did she admit to police that she had inflicted the wounds herself. Previously she had insisted that she had been the victim of a hit-and-run driver.

■ MASOCHISM

Marianne S., a twenty-four-year-old schoolteacher, came for psychotherapy because of a disturbing aspect of her sexual life with her husband. While she appeared to be very much in love with her husband, she found it impossible to engage in sexual intercourse unless she had vivid fantasies of a masochistic nature. It was necessary for her husband to tell her stories of women who were slaves, forced to perform menial and often revolting tasks, and who were generally mistreated by the men who were their masters. The more masochistic the behavior of the women in the story, the more likely it was that the patient could become aroused in an erotic way. Her favorite fantasy, which her husband related to her, was that of women who were forced to perform unnatural sexual acts with strange men and against the wishes of the women. The more debasing the actions, the more stimulated the patient became. In this case, the patient experienced a vicarious form of masochism by identifying herself with the women described by her husband.

HOMOSEXUALITY

One of the most common forms of sexual deviation is homosexuality, in which the love object is a member of the same sex. Such behavior has been a favorite theme in literature. It is mentioned in the Bible, as well as in the basic religious,

Figure 7.4 *The intrinsically bisexual nature of man as suggested by a painting by René Magritte. (Collection of Mr. and Mrs. John de Cuevas. Photograph courtesy of Byron Gallery, New York.)*

artistic, and philosophical works of other cultures. Petronius discussed the problem in *The Satyricon,* and both the *Ecologues* of Virgil and the *Metamorphoses* of Ovid, written many centuries ago, contain eulogies to homosexuality.

In Greek mythology the first human beings were androgynous, or bisexual, with Zeus later separating them into two different sexes. Among the Hindus we find a similar idea. Purusha, who was alone in the world, became so lonesome that he divided himself into two beings—man and wife. The idea that gods and men were originally bisexual accounts for the word "sex," which is derived from the Latin *sexus,* akin to *secare*—to cut apart or to separate.

The basic bisexuality of mankind also has religious justification. The Talmud says that

Adam was created bisexual. God later caused him to fall asleep, and then took a little from each part of his body and created ordinary men and women. After Lilith (Adam's first wife) deserted Adam, God separated Adam into his two sexual parts by taking one of Adam's ribs and creating Eve from it.

There are many symbolic expressions of bisexuality. It is seen in Medusa, with the snakes in her hair symbolizing "maleness." It is seen also in the mermaid, who has the head and upper body of a woman and the lower body of a fish, a widely recognized male symbol. Bisexuality is illustrated clearly in the hermaphroditic dances seen in other cultures. In the Greek festival of Artemis Korythalia, the women dancers wear artificial penises. This is also true of the Nuba ceremonies of Northeastern Africa and the dances of the Altai Turks. In some cases, male dancers wear artificial breasts.

The list of eminent persons in history who have been overt homosexuals, or whose work or actions reveal the presence of strong homosexual inclinations, is an impressive one. Nero, Julius Caesar, and Alexander the Great engaged in homosexual relationships, and Emperor Heliogabalus was so effeminate that he insisted upon being addressed as "Mistress" rather than "Lord." Philip of Macedonia took castrated males with him on his war expeditions for the sexual use and pleasure of himself and his friends. Both Ludwig of Bavaria and Edward II of England received the title of "Homosexual King," while Napolean and Hitler had strong feminine components in their personalities.

The creative arts have attracted many men and women who have been homosexually inclined. Lord Byron, the English poet generally considered to be the epitome of the romantic, asked his new wife if she intended to sleep in the same bed with him on their wedding night: "I hate sleeping with any woman, but you may if you choose." Franz Kafka, the novelist, said that the sexual relationship "is a punishment inflicted upon two people who find too much happiness in being with each other" (Hoffman, 1945). Andre Gide, the French literary light, insisted that homosexuality is "indispensable to the constitution of a well-organized society" (Gide, 1950). Even on his honeymoon, Gide was preoccupied with his homosexual inclinations. He wrote later about three schoolboys in the next compartment while he was on his wedding journey with his wife:

> They had half-undressed themselves, the heat was provocative, and alone in that compartment, they simply raised hell. I heard them laugh and tussle. At each of the frequent but brief stops of the train, leaning out of the little side window which I had lowered, I could touch with my hand the arm of one of the three boys, who amused himself by leaning toward me, from the neighboring window, and lent himself to the game, laughing. I enjoyed the delicious tortures in stroking the downy amber flesh he offered to my caress. My hand slipping along his arm, rounded his shoulder. . . . I sat panting, palpitating and pretending to be absorbed in reading. Madeleine (the bride), seated facing me, said nothing, affecting not to see me, not to know me (Gide, 1951).

There are two major types of homosexuality. One is latent and unconscious, the other overt and expressed. The latent, or hidden, impulses make their appearance in a variety of ways. At a relatively superficial level, the male with this problem prefers feminine activities, reacts emotionally more like a woman, and unconsciously adopts feminine mannerisms and modes of dressing. Latent homosexuality is frequently reflected in embarrassment in undressing and taking showers in front of other people. It is not unusual for latent homosexuality to erupt into a panic reaction when a man enters military service. The necessity of living in close intimacy with large numbers of men is sometimes too much for the latent homosexual to tolerate. Some men become so anxious and disturbed that they require psychiatric treatment.

Unconscious homosexual inclinations also may create problems in sexual relationships. Some men prefer the feminine position during sexual intercourse. Other men can derive sexual pleasure only in the knowledge that the woman is also involved with another man. Persistent impotence with women may be an indication of a latent homosexual component in the personality.

A paradoxical way in which unconscious homosexuality betrays itself is in heterosexual overactivity. The Don Juan type of man is one who is preoccupied with his pursuit and seduction of women. As soon as his objective is attained, he loses interest in the woman, and the chase begins anew. Similarly, many women are seemingly insatiable in their need for men. In both cases, the frantic sexual activity may be a defense against unconscious homosexual inclinations.

An attractive twenty-five-year-old married woman with three children confessed that the only way she could achieve any degree of satisfaction in sexual intercourse was to occupy the masculine position and to have her husband assume the feminine position. Here the roles were reversed. The wife became the active and dominant partner while the husband assumed a passive female role. Such behavior, however, is deviant only when the reversed roles are always necessary to sexual satisfaction.

In some cases, jealousy has its roots in unconscious homosexuality. The emotion is based upon an erotic attraction to the rival rather than upon a concern for the apparent infidelity of the mate or lover. In Tolstoi's "The Kreutzer Sonata," the hero is tormented by the idea of his wife's in-fidelity with a musician. In spite of his jealousy, the husband encourages the musician to visit his home. It is clear that the husband has an unconscious homosexual attraction for the musician in spite of his insane jealousy. Significantly, the husband murders his wife, and not his apparent rival. In Shakespeare's *A Winter's Tale*, the jealousy of Leontes also appears to be based on an uncon-scious homosexuality.

It is probable that in any *ménage à trois*, or situation in which two men live with one woman, or two women with one man, there are strong homosexual inclinations on the part of the two members of the same sex. A classic example of such a relationship was the eighteenth-century household of William, fifth Duke of Devonshire, who lived with his wife and his mistress, Eliza-beth Foster, for twenty-seven years. The women remained inseparable friends throughout their stormy lives (Foster, 1961).

In North Dakota, a young wife reported to police that her husband tied her to a bed and forced her to have sexual relations with other men. It is not improbable that the husband was a homo-sexual who could not face his homosexuality and satisfied his homosexual inclinations in this in-direct way.

The problem of unconscious homosexuality is of considerable interest because the latent inclinations may lead to defenses which take the form of behavior disorders and personality dis-turbances. Among these pathological defenses are panic states, cruelty and destructiveness, feelings of persecution, and isolation and with-drawal.

■ SEXUAL DEVIATION

David R. is a sixteen-year-old boy who was referred to the psychiatric clinic of a juvenile court after being arrested for patting two coeds on the buttocks in a park near the university. Following his arrest, the boy ad-mitted he had made a large number of obscene tele-phone calls to women. During the initial interview David was somewhat ill at ease, but he answered questions readily and appeared willing to talk about his behavior. He could give no reason for doing what he did other than that he hoped the young women

would "have sexual relations" with him. The first incident suggesting a disturbance in the psychosexual area occurred when the boy was in the sixth grade. The parents received a letter from the school inform-ing them that their son had been expelled. No reason was given, and David insisted he did not know what it was all about. When the parents went to the principal, they were told that their son had written a note to a young woman teacher requesting sexual relations with her. The note, which was filled with obscene words, also had a crude drawing of a couple having intercourse. The boy followed the teacher to her home on several occasions and spent a number of hours near the door of her apartment waiting for her to come out. Following his examination at the juvenile court, David was sent to a psychiatric hos-pital for further study.

The psychological examination showed the boy to be functioning in the average range of intelligence, with no indication of any of the more serious forms of per-sonality disturbance. However, the examination sug-gested the possibility that David's behavior might have been due in part to latent homosexual inclinations.*

Unconscious homosexual inclinations play an important role in determining the attitudes and behavior of many people, and this form of homosexuality is a personal and social problem of considerable magnitude. The most searching study of this problem revealed that four men out of every hundred are exclusively homosexual throughout their lifetime. They have no sex drive other than homosexual urges, and they do not indulge in heterosexual relationships. They have a true *horror feminae*. The report also indicated that 8 percent of the adult male population is exclusively homosexual for a period of at least three years between the ages of sixteen and fifty-five. Moreover, half the men who remain single until they are thirty-five years old experience some kind of homosexual activity. In fact, 37 percent of all males admitted having had some kind of open homosexual experience (Kinsey et al., 1948).

■ HOMOSEXUALITY

This nineteen-year-old man had a history of strong homosexual fantasies, dreams, wishes, and desires since age 12, without any overt homosexual acting

*Case 1 of audiotape 3, "Personality Disorders: Sexual Deviations," in *Case Interviews to Accom-pany The Disorganized Personality*.

out. He had no heterosexual desires and had limited his heterosexual contacts to an absolute minimum in all areas. His initial complaint was of a strong and almost uncontrollable attraction to a university classmate, with the great temptation to approach him homosexually. He had written notes to the classmate; fortunately these were not too explicit. He had no wish to associate with girls, had no girl friends, and was motivated to get rid of his homosexual desires only because of his guilt about them. He was fearful of rejection by girls despite the fact that he was masculine in appearance, with only very minor feminine speech characteristics. He was shy and socially inept with women generally and especially anxious about mature, sophisticated older women. Unsophisticated, immature, young, and passive girls were not attractive to him but at least frightened him less.

His mother was an emotionally unstable university graduate who dominated her husband, a man described as reserved, impersonal, withdrawn, small, thin, and sexless. The father never mentioned sex and, according to the patient, the mother suggested it was for the lower classes and animals. The patient was the only child. His relationship with his mother was close, while the relationship with the father was remote and competitive (Lamberd, 1969).

■ HOMOSEXUALITY

This thirty-four-year-old man had a history of overt, exclusive homosexuality for seventeen years, with homosexual desires and fantasies since early puberty. He had been homosexually active since the age of seventeen and had no heterosexual contacts of any kind. There was a poorly remembered incident of homosexual assault at age five. At the age of seven or eight he remembers playing with dolls, and at age ten he dressed in his mother's clothes with her knowledge.

He was a pleasant, passive, unassertive man with some minor feminine traits in gesture and speech. He was popular with women socially but terrified of them sexually and frightened of obligations or responsibilities to women. He worked as a bookkeeper and was effective in his job. His homosexual contacts, which continued up to the time of therapy, were limited mostly to casual pickups, with mutual masturbation. He desired a change and looked forward to the possibility of marriage if he could change his sexual orientation. He was fond of children and had no anxiety about homosexual desires in this regard (Lamberd, 1969).

Many people were shocked when more than 90 employees were discharged from the U.S. State Department because of homosexuality and when a Senate subcommittee reported that there were nearly 4,000 homosexuals in Washington on the government payroll. But if the Kinsey report is correct (and there is little reason to doubt its major findings), for every 10,000 men in a city, there are at least 400 men who are confirmed homosexuals. A city with 500,000 males would have 20,000 men whose sexual urges were directed exclusively toward other men. In a study of 100 presumably normal freshmen at Oxford University in England, it was found that 35 percent admitted homosexual practices at some time, and 8 percent said that the practice persisted (Spencer, 1959).

Homosexuality among women, or lesbianism, while less apparent than among men, is of considerable importance to the psychologist and the psychiatrist. A survey showed that by age forty, 19 percent of the females had had some physical contact of a sexual nature with other females (Kinsey, 1953). The highest rates were found among single females and among previously married women who had been widowed, separated, or divorced. An earlier study of the sex lives of a large number of women college graduates indicated that 50 percent of the group had experienced some kind of intense emotional attachment to another woman sometime during their lifetime, and 26 percent of the women admitted having actually engaged in overt sex behavior with a member of the same sex (Davis, 1929).

Contrary to popular belief, there are no distinctive features of the homosexual physique. However, some male homosexuals are marked by what has been called *secondary gynandromorphy* (Sheldon, 1940). These secondary factors include femininity of the face, hands, and skin, the way in which the individual moves, the voice, and facial movements. Similar characteristics of a masculine nature sometimes are seen in the female homosexual.

■ HOMOSEXUALITY

Nancy S. is a fifteen-year-old girl who was referred to a juvenile court psychiatric clinic because of her involvement with a group of female homosexuals. The group was made up of three young women in their early twenties. Two of these women wore men's clothing. Nancy met them soon after she had become pregnant, although they did not know about her condition. These women introduced Nancy to various homosexual practices, and she was well on her way to becoming an overt homosexual. When she could no longer hide her pregnancy, she revealed her condition. One of the homosexual women immediately adopted the attitude of "husband" toward Nancy. When it was time for her to go to the hospital to deliver the baby, this "husband" drove Nancy to the hospital. Four days later, she appeared at the hospital and announced that she was Nancy's "husband" and that she had come for "his wife" and the baby. Nancy and the baby were released from the hospital, and were driven home by this woman dressed as a man. It was at this time that the juvenile court was notified of Nancy's relations with the homosexual group.

TRANSVESTISM

Expressing psychosexual conflict by wearing the clothing of members of the opposite sex is called *transvestism*. Such behavior has been known for many centuries and has appeared in a wide variety of cultures. Herodotus, in ancient Greece, described the Scythian illness which appeared on the northern shores of the Black Sea. In this condition, men put on women's clothing, did women's work, and behaved in a feminine way. The condition was also known in ancient Rome. Both Calig-

ula and Heliogabalus occasionally dressed as women. In Madagascar, there are transvestites called *sarombavy*. These men dress like women, do the cooking and housework, and take care of the children. Among the Chukchee people of Siberia, men are allowed to wear women's clothing, to adopt feminine mannerisms, and even to become the "wives" of other men.

Transvestism is a combination of homosexuality and fetishism. The term *eonism* has been used to refer to such cases (Ellis, 1942). The term was derived from the Chevalier d'Eon, who lived most of his life as a woman. Prior to his death in 1810, the Chevalier was accepted as a woman by everyone, including the physician who treated him during his fatal illness. The case of one of the first female physicians, Dr. Mary Walker, is a classic example of transvestism. She insisted that her profession required her to dress like a man, and she received special permission from Congress to dress in male clothing. Pictures show her in men's clothing, dressed entirely in black, and wearing a top hat.

■ TRANSVESTISM

Sonny B. is a seventeen-year-old boy who was sent to a psychiatric clinic after he used improper language on the telephone to the mother of a young girl he had called. The mother, who answered the phone, referred to him as "half-boy, half-girl." Sonny became enraged, and used obscene language in denouncing her.

Figure 7.5 *A seventeen-year-old transvestite. While not a professional female impersonator, he occasionally does a "striptease" act at private clubs and parties.*

When seen at the clinic, Sonny was a rather small, slenderly built youth with very marked effeminate features and mannerisms. He spoke in a rather high and feminine voice, and his hands fluttered about in an effeminate way as he talked. He admitted to a history of transvestite behavior for a period of years, often appearing on the street dressed as a young woman. He has appeared at private parties as a female impersonator, and has engaged in striptease acts. Sonny said that the performances are somewhat disgusting to him, since he dislikes exposing his body publicly to other males. He takes part in the shows only because he is paid for his act. He commented that while everyone tells him he looks and acts like a woman, he does not think he looks like one. He admitted, however, that deep inside he feels like a woman. He would really like to be a woman, and when he dresses in feminine clothing he feels as if he is a completely different person.

Sonny has three sisters, one of whom he described as being bisexual and having emotional attachments to both men and women. He volunteered that his second sister is a prostitute, but that his third sister is "O.K." His earliest and fondest memories are those of living in his grandmother's home where he was treated as a girl. He was permitted to play only with girls until he was thirteen, and his most cherished toys were dolls.*

A "man" who was over one hundred years old when "he" died had been known for at least fifty years by the name of Charley Howard. "He" dressed as a man, acted as a man, and engaged in a man's occupation. Not until "his" death was it discovered that Charley was really a woman. In another case, a twenty-six-year-old man posed as a woman for ten years. He worked as a waitress, a chambermaid, and even a chorus girl. Married for six years, he was arrested for a minor offense and taken to jail, where it was found that "she" was a man. The "husband" with whom he had been living for six years insisted that he was shocked to learn that his "wife" was a man. It is quite probable that in this case the two men were living in a homosexual relationship but were reluctant to admit it.

While homosexuality as a preferred form of behavior is to be considered a kind of sexual de-

viancy, every individual has some characteristics of the opposite sex. Men, to varying degrees, have feminine components in their personalities, while women have masculine components. It is not known, however, to what extent these personality components are determined biologically.

OTHER SEXUAL DEVIATIONS

While exhibitionism, voyeurism, fetishism, sadomasochism, and homosexuality are some of the more common sexual deviations resulting from the attempts to resolve unconscious conflicts, a number of other deviations are seen from time to time by psychologists and psychiatrists.

In *pedophilia*, the love object is a child, with the relationship based on either a homosexual or a heterosexual inclination. People who suffer from pedophilia are often frightened by adult sexuality. The child presents less of a threat and, because of naïveté and lack of sophistication, often becomes a willing victim. Behavior of this type is always potentially dangerous because the adult's fear of being found out sometimes leads to violence and because there is psychological damage to the child. In other cases, there is the contradictory need to love and at the same time to inflict physical punishment.

■ PEDOPHILIA

Harry E. is a fifty-two-year-old divorced man who was admitted to a hospital because of his pathological sexual behavior. The patient was having a sexual relationship with his teen-aged daughter, and at the same time was involved in a homosexual relationship with his twelve-year-old son. The patient had a history of homosexual relationships with other men, and several months before his admission to the hospital he was arrested for making suggestive remarks to two young boys.

John M. was picked up six or seven times between the ages of sixteen and twenty-three for sex offenses against children. Each time his family managed to get him off with a reprimand or a small fine. Once he was sent to jail. However, one afternoon this young man was driving along a country road when he saw a girl of

---

*Case 2 of audiotape 3, "Personality Disorders: Sexual Deviations," in *Case Interviews to Accompany The Disorganized Personality.*

nine walking home from school. He stopped and asked her if she wanted a lift. She did, and he drove her to a secluded lot where he raped her, and then, in a panic that she would identify him, crushed her skull with a rock.

Zoophilia, or bestiality, is a form of behavior in which there is sexual contact with animals. It is practiced occasionally by mentally disturbed persons and by otherwise normal adults in cases of prolonged isolation. While such actions are observed sometimes among boys and men in farm areas, indulging in this activity as a preferred pattern of sexual behavior is not common.

It is true, however, that erotic relations between human beings and animals have been socially approved at various times in the past. Among the ancient Egyptians, the goat was a symbol of sexual vigor. In the Temple of Mendes, men could have relations with a she-goat, while women were free to submit to one of the male goats. This theme is a common one in the wall decorations of the Roman baths at Herculaneum and Pompeii. Even today we refer to a frisky old man as an "old goat." In Greek legend, Pasiphae (the wife of Minos, King of Crete) gave birth to the Minotaur as a result of intercourse with a white bull. The erotic relation between animals and humans is also seen in the sculpture "Leda and the Swan" by Michelangelo and in the painting of the same subject by Correggio. It has been found that between 40 and 50 percent of the men who live on farms have had some kind of sexual contact with animals (Kinsey, 1948). As with other forms of sexual deviation, zoophilia becomes a personality disorder only when this activity becomes an end in itself and is a persistent mode of behavior which excludes more normal heterosexual satisfactions.

■ ZOOPHILIA

John D. is an eleven-year-old boy who was admitted to a psychiatric hospital from a rural foster home placement because he had been acting out in a sexually aggressive way toward the farm animals. He had been prodding the cows both rectally and vaginally with long sticks to such a degree that the cows needed medical attention. On several occasions, the boy attempted intercourse with a calf and a pig.

In *necrophilia,* a relatively rare but psychodynamically interesting condition, the patient is attracted sexually to death and dead bodies. There has always been a close connection between death and the erotic impulse. Early Greek literature indicates that among the ancient Egyptians it was not unusual for the men who embalmed and guarded the bodies of young women to have sexual relations with the corpses. In ancient Rome, the Bustuariae were women who lived in cemeteries, where they hired themselves out as professional mourners with prostitution as an important sideline. Even today, the erotic nature of death is so widely recognized that prostitutes sometimes dress themselves in shrouds and act like corpses. In a Paris brothel, prostitutes are waxed and put into a hypnotic sleep in order to give a more realistic appearance of death.

A young executive quite frankly admitted that he has erotic fantasies when he sees the corpse of an attractive young woman. A man in England who murdered a young woman in his room came back every night for eighteen nights and slept beside her body on the couch. In another case, a young woman slept in the arms of her sweetheart for several nights after he had committed suicide. A similar attraction is an important theme in the poetry of Algernon Charles Swinburne:

Yet am I glad to have her dead
Here in this wretched wattled house
Where I can kiss her eyes and head.

In terms of the dynamics of necrophilia, the passivity and utter helplessness of the corpse is important. The love object is defenseless and incapable of resisting. One case was traced to childhood experiences in which the patient had sexual relations with his sister while she was asleep. He believed that absolute quiet had to be maintained or she would awaken. The fact that she did not awaken suggests that her sleep was a defense against her feelings of guilt. At the unconscious level she probably was aware of what was happening. Later in life the brother found himself attracted to corpses. In other cases, there is a strong sadistic element. The aggressive acts can be carried out against the corpse with impunity.

Coprophilia is a form of sexual deviation involving the excretory processes and products. Some individuals receive erotic stimulation and satisfaction out of observing other individuals in the process of urination or defecation. In such cases, the stimulation is derived from strong body odors or the odor and sight of excrement. Sexual deviations of this type may be related to extreme psychological regressions to infancy and early childhood.[1]

ALCOHOL ADDICTION

The use of alcoholic beverages can be traced to the earliest period of man. Almost all people have had one or another kind of alcoholic beverage. Primitive people in widely scattered parts of the world discovered the intoxicating qualities of various fermentable materials. Honey, dates, fruits, berries, and even tree sap have been used to produce intoxicating beverages. Beer jugs identified with the Stone Age indicate that fermented beverages were well known during the neolithic period. The Egyptians had a great many different kinds of wine and beer, and hieroglyphics indicate that the priests of Osiris made laws prescribing how much the Pharaohs and the slaves could drink. The earliest known book, the Ebers Papyrus, written about 1500 B.C., contains many references to the use of beer and wine.

The dangers of excessive drinking were well known to the early Greeks and Romans. Critias described an ancient Greek drinking party by saying, "They have bowls and toasts, too. Then after their drinking they loose their tongues to tell scandalous stories and they weaken their bodies; upon their eyes a dark mist settles; memory melts away into oblivion; reason is lost completely" (McCarthy, 1959). Herodotus blamed the mental illness of Cleomenes on excessive drinking, and Hippocrates said that "if the patient be in the prime of life, and . . . if from drinking he has trembling hands, it may be well to announce beforehand either delirium or convulsion." Similarly, Plato warned of the dangers of excessive drinking.

Among the Hindus, Buddha listed drunkenness as one of the most serious forms of misbehavior. The last of his five commandments was: "Never take a strong drink." One of the early *sutras* of Buddhism offers six consequences of drinking: (1) loss of property, (2) disease, (3) discord and strife, (4) loss of reputation, (5) disturbance of temper, and (6) loss of wisdom. At one time, the Hindus decreed death for anyone making or using alcoholic beverages. Similarly, an ancient Hebrew recitative begins: "Wine is a mocker, strong drink is raging, and whosoever is deceived thereby, is not wise." And Isaiah warned, "Woe unto them that rise up early in the morning, that they may follow strong drink, that continue until night, 'til wine inflame them." King Solomon also warned the Hebrew people concerning the effects of alcohol.

Arnold of Villanova, in his thirteenth-century *Treatise on Wine,* discussed the medicinal use of various wines. He said, "No physician blames healthy people for the use of wine, unless he censures them for the quantity or for mixing it with water. If wine is taken in the right measure, it suits every age, every time, and every region. It is good for the old and for young children." Three hundred years later, a treatise appeared *On the Horrible Vice of Drunkenness* (France, 1531). Benjamin Rush wrote an *Inquiry into the Effects of Ardent Spirits,* and a book was published in 1835 with the title *Anatomy of Drunkenness* (McNish, 1835). Its author, a Scots physician, described what he

---

[1]In the field of deviant sexual behavior, the student is referred to Hervey Cleckley's extremely interesting *The Caricature of Love* (Ronald, 1957), and to such standard works as Manfred S. Guttmacher's *Sex Offenses: The Problem, Causes and Prevention* (Norton, 1951); Benjamin Karpman's *The Sexual Offender and His Offenses: Etiology, Pathology, Psychodynamics, and Treatment* (Julian, 1954); Clifford Allen's *A Textbook of Psychosexual Disorders* (Oxford University, 1962); and the now classic two-volume Kinsey reports, *Sexual Behavior in the Human Male* (Saunders 1948) and *Sexual Behavior in the Human Female* (Saunders, 1953). Books dealing with specific sex deviations are limited for the most part to the problems of homosexuality. Among recommended readings on this subject are L. J. Hatterer's *Changing Homosexuality in the Male* (McGraw-Hill, 1970); *The Gay World* (Basic Books, 1968) by Martin Hoffman; Gordon Westwood's *A Minority: A Report on the Life of the Male Homosexual in Great Britain* (Longmans, 1960); and *Homosexuality: A Psychoanalytic Study* (Basic Books, 1962) by Irving Bieber and others.

called the "spontaneous combustion" of drunkards. He asserted that the whole body is burned in a few hours by a combustion process which does not even singe the furniture surrounding the patient.

The use of alcoholic beverages is widespread in many parts of the world. In the United States, two out of three adults drink alcohol in one form or another.

Breaking the total figure of drinkers down into groups, and defining a regular drinker as one who drinks at least three times a week and all other drinkers as occasional drinkers, a study made by the National Opinion Research Center of the University of Denver found that 17 percent of the total population in the United States is made up of regular drinkers, while 48 percent are occasional drinkers. The remaining 35 percent of the total population are abstainers (Riley et al., 1948).

On the basis of several estimates, the number of alcoholics in the United States is between 4 and 6 million, and some 200,000 new cases develop each year. The vast majority of these persons are addicted to alcohol; a much smaller number have damaged nervous systems as a result of the drinking (McCarthy, 1959). The ratio of alcoholic men to alcoholic women is about 6 to 1.

These figures mean that the United States has one of the highest rates of alcoholism in the world. The effects on other family members of these 4 to 6 million alcoholics are direct and often devastating —and so perhaps 20 million people, many of whom are children, are adversely affected by alcoholism.

Alcoholics account for a large proportion of the patients known to health and social welfare agencies. For example, in recent years alcoholics have accounted for more than one-fifth of all the men admitted to state mental hospitals and to the psychiatric wards of general hospitals. Alcohol is a significant factor in almost half of all fatal motor vehicle accidents, and it is now clear that a majority of these drinking drivers are alcoholics.

In addition to the human costs, the economic losses resulting from alcoholism are great. Losses to industry from absenteeism and other problems associated with alcoholism are about 2 billion dollars annually. The President's Commission on Law Enforcement and Administration of Justice estimates that the national cost for handling

chronic alcoholics is in excess of 100 million dollars per year. Costs for hospital care and welfare costs for alcoholics and their dependents exceed 2 billion dollars per year. Thus, the total cost of alcoholism to the country is at least 4 billion dollars (NIMH, 1969).

The term *alcoholism* has been used to refer to every degree of excessive drinking from that of the party guest who drinks too much to that of the hospitalized mental patient whose nervous system has been severely damaged by alcohol. The various levels of severity have been designated by such names as *normal alcoholism, primary alcoholism, alcohol addiction,* and *chronic alcoholism.* Unfortunately, these terms are confusing, inadequately defined, and often contradictory.

Most people who drink excessively are not alcoholics in a clinical sense. Some people drink more than they should to combat boredom in their work, others to get relief from marital difficulties, and still others to reduce their tensions. Life is filled with situations which lead to excessive drinking. And while it is true that the alcoholic comes from the group of excessive drinkers, the distinction between excessive drinking and alcoholism is by no means clear.

The Alcoholism Subcommittee of the World Health Organization's Expert Committee on Mental Health has defined alcoholism as follows:

Alcoholism refers to any form of alcoholic beverage drinking which goes beyond the traditional and customary dietary use, or the ordinary compliance with the social drinking customs of the whole community concerned, irrespective of the etiological factors leading to such behavior and irrespective also of the extent to which such etiological factors are dependent upon heredity, constitution, or acquired physiopathological and metabolic influences (WHO, 1951).

For our purposes, and in keeping with the latest diagnostic classifications, there are only two major forms of alcoholism with which the clinical psychologists and the psychiatrist are concerned: (1) alcohol addiction and (2) alcoholism associated with brain damage.

In alcohol addiction, the patient uses excessive drinking as a preferred method for solving his problems. In these cases the symptoms are psychological, and there is no significant damage to the nervous system as a result of the excessive drinking. Such cases are classified as personality disorders. The second major type of alcoholism includes those cases in which the excessive drinking has resulted in reversible or irreversible damage to the nervous system and particularly the brain. These cases include a number of different conditions which are grouped together and called "brain syndromes." This form of alcoholism will be treated in detail in Chapter 11.

The point at which excessive drinking becomes alcohol addiction is dependent upon a number of factors. An individual becomes an alcoholic of the addictive type when he drinks excessively, when his drinking leads to intoxication, and, most importantly, when his drinking becomes a preferred way to solve problems. There is always a transitional period during which excessive drinking slips over into alcohol addiction. It is often difficult to say when the transition has been completed.

Whereas the social drinker takes a drink to be friendly, to feel more relaxed, to socialize with other men and women, and to gain a degree of relief from everyday tensions, the alcohol addict unconsciously drinks in order to become drunk. He does not say that this is the case. In fact, he insists that his reasons for drinking are exactly those of the social drinker. The social drinker, however, knows when to stop and is able to stop. The alcohol addict is not able to stop.

In alcohol addiction there is a more or less regular intake of alcohol of sufficient quantity to bring the drinker into conflict with his family, his friends, his employers, and sometimes the police. These are the individuals who drink steadily, or who are frequently drunk for days, weeks, or months. Physiologically, the alcohol addict is an individual whose alcohol intake exceeds the rate of alcohol metabolism for extended periods of time.

Most alcoholics get their start in the teens. One survey showed that 71 percent of the alcoholics first became intoxicated before the age of twenty, 29 percent admitted that they had "blacked out" as a result of drinking as children, 20 percent began "sneaking drinks" in their early teens, and 16 percent lost all control of their drinking while still minors (McCarthy, 1959).

In a study of 500 cases of alcoholism, it was found that about 28 percent of the alcoholics drank themselves to death either directly through increased consumption of alcohol or indirectly through injury and illness. In 20 percent of the cases, the alcoholic drank to about the same extent throughout his life, 10 percent drank with greater moderation, and 22 percent abstained during their terminal illness. It is important to note that only 11 percent of the alcoholics stopped drinking permanently (Lemere, 1953).

The alcohol addict expresses his personality disorder in various ways. The precise manner of this expression depends to a large degree upon the individual's personality structure. The alcohol has the effect of accenting preexisting personality characteristics. In some cases the drinking leads to depression and despondency; in other cases, there is a tendency to euphoria and exaltation. The drinking may also serve to release unconscious impulses. The alcoholic then shows acting-out behavior of various kinds. There may be an expression of unrestrained heterosexuality, homosexuality, assaultive actions in the form of sadomasochistic behavior, self-destructive attempts, and antisocial episodes. The form of the expressed behavior is determined by the dominant needs at the unconscious levels of the personality.

The damaging aspect of alcohol addiction, and the reason why excessive drinking may lead to a personality disturbance, is that the chronic intoxication results in the release of inhibitions, the impairment of judgment, and a loss of emotional and motor control. There may also be disturbance in self-evaluation and the creation of an unrealistic self-image. There is likely to be a deterioration of personal habits, a lack of regard for one's personal appearance, a blunting of emotional reactions, and an interference with realistic planning and foresight.

■ ALCOHOL ADDICTION

Otto A. is a forty-six-year-old man who was referred to a psychiatric hospital after an episode in which he was arrested on charges of drunkenness and refusing to pay a taxi fare. The patient was given a suspended sentence, and ordered to leave town. A few days later he was arrested again for drunkenness and refusing to pay another taxi fare. He was sentenced to the workhouse; but in view of his long history of alcohol addiction, he was sent to the psychiatric hospital.

The patient began drinking when he was eighteen years old, although his excessive drinking did not start until he was twenty-five, following his divorce from his first wife. He began drinking beer and wine, but eventually came to drink anything that was available. Most of the time the patient drinks in bars with friends. He is a "spree" drinker who manages to go for some time without touching alcohol, and then suddenly begins drinking excessively. During these bouts of alcoholism he ordinarily loses his job, and often is arrested for disorderly conduct. The episodes of excessive drinking have increased in frequency and severity over the years. The patient describes himself as the "black sheep of the family, the worst drinker in the state of Ohio, and such a great sinner that not even God will help me anymore."

Otto has a number of brothers and sisters, all of whom are well established as respected members of the community. They long since gave up in their efforts to bring an end to the patient's excessive drinking. While they continue to accept him when he is sober, they refuse to have him in their homes when he is intoxicated. During the past two years he has had very little contact with his relatives. His work history has been erratic, since he has always been able to obtain a job but can never hold one more than a few months. He has worked for numerous companies, and at one time went into business for himself. In each instance he has been unsuccessful due to his excessive drinking.*

There are at least three major factors involved in the etiology of alcohol addiction: (1) a constitutional sensitivity to alcohol, (2) a psychodynamic need for the intoxicating effects of alcohol, and (3) a permissive cultural milieu in which the excessive drinking can be expressed.

The evidence for a constitutional sensitivity to alcohol is that some individuals seem to be more resistant to the physiologic effects of alcohol than are other individuals. Men and women of this type are said to have a high tolerance and presumably are less prone to addiction than individuals who have a low tolerance to alcohol. This difference in tolerance suggests the possibility of hereditary influences, possibly in the form of inborn metabolic differences. There may be a generalized and nonspecific organic pattern which

forms a congenial soil for the development of alcoholism. There is the further possibility that alcoholism may be due to a biochemical defect in which genetic factors may lead to a failure in the production of specific enzymes. As a result of this deficiency, the patient may be unable to utilize some necessary element of nutrition. In such cases, the intake of alcohol may be regarded as a response to a tissue need.

The biochemical aspects of chronic alcohol ingestion are also in need of clarification. For example, it has frequently been speculated that the behavioral and pharmacological tolerance shown for alcohol by alcoholics might be accounted for by a more rapid rate of ethanol metabolism. A number of recent studies have shown that prolonged alcohol consumption may induce a significant increase in enzyme activity in the liver of animals. On the other hand, other studies have failed to demonstrate any differences between blood alcohol levels of alcoholics and nonalcoholics. Since disappearance of blood ethanol may not be an adequate way of measuring all steps in the degradation of ethanol, scientists have carried out a carefully controlled study on the rate of metabolism in alcoholic and nonalcoholic subjects. The data suggest that tolerance for alcohol is related to processes of adaptation in the central nervous system rather than to alterations in the rate of metabolism of ethanol.

The various organic theories of alcohol addiction suggest the possibility of the addiction occurring relatively independently of psychological and cultural factors. It is more likely that alcohol addiction occurs in a constitutionally predisposed patient in a setting of psychological stress. For this reason, the psychosocial components of alcohol addiction must be kept in mind.

At the psychodynamic level, a variety of processes have been identified in alcoholism. One of the characteristics of the male alcoholic is his overdependence upon his mother and his strong attachment to mother figures. The excessive drinking may be related to strong oral needs based upon an inadequate resolution of personal

---

*Case 1 of audiotape 4, "Personality Disorders: Addictions," in Case Interviews to Accompany The Disorganized Personality.

conflict during the oral period of psychosexual development. It has even been suggested by the psychoanalysts that alcohol is a symbolic substitute for the mother's milk.

While excessive drinking may be regression to early infantile orality in some cases, it also may be an attempt to recapture infantile feelings of importance and omnipotence or to discharge aggressions against a frustrating world. It has been suggested that people do not commit crimes because they are drunk, but rather that they get drunk in order to commit crimes. Another type of drinker may become intoxicated in order to lose himself in a state of helplessness in which he can fulfill his unconscious homosexual desires to be cared for and nursed by members of his own sex.

William James, one of America's greatest psychologists and philosophers, said that the "sway of alcohol over mankind is unquestionably due to its power to stimulate the mystical faculties of human nature, usually crushed to earth by the cold facts and the dry criticisms of the sober hour. . . . The drunken consciousness is one bit of the mystic consciousness, and our total opinion of it must find its place in our opinion of that larger whole" (James, 1938). The state of intoxication, according to this view, is one phase of the mystical experience of man and, in its own way, is comparable to the mystical experiences derived from religion.

While many different needs may be served by alcoholism, the general psychological model for excessive drinking can be stated in relatively simple terms. Alcohol is a sedative, and the ability to reduce anxiety is one of its basic properties. This anxiety reduction occurs as a result of the effects of the alcohol on the physiological mechanisms responsible for the anxiety. Since anxiety is an undesirable state, any quick and effective method of reducing anxiety is likely to meet with approval. Consciously or unconsciously, the alcoholic realizes that through excessive drinking he is able to shut out the world around him and to insulate himself from its problems, disappointments, and disillusionments. Even the Bible says, "Let him drink and forget his poverty, and remember his misery no more."

Many attempts have been made to describe the personality type most likely to become addicted to alcohol. While there is no general agreement about the overall personality of such individuals, certain traits of personality seem to be more frequent in the alcoholic. Alcoholic men and women show regressive, infantile, and oral needs in a great many cases. They tend to react with narcissistic self-gratification. While often appearing to be sociable and outgoing, these individuals have deep problems in interpersonal relations. Conflicts in the area of psychosexual development also may be prominent, with latent homosexuality not infrequently associated with the alcoholic personality pattern. Dependency sometimes appears as a characteristic trait in these cases. Finally, it is possible that at least some alcohol addicts are self-punishing individuals.

The sociological theories of alcoholism maintain that the rates of alcoholism are determined largely by the social structure. Certainly such factors as marital status, socioeconomic level, religion, education, and local and national group attitudes toward drinking combine to create a favorable or unfavorable setting for the development of alcoholism.

The consensus of informed opinion is that alcoholism results from a complex interaction of social, psychological, and biological factors. Even the most enthusiastic proponents of any specific theory of what causes alcoholism agree on the necessity of an eclectic approach to the multifaceted problems of this condition. Such an approach, if it is to be truly effective, must involve more interdisciplinary research.

In spite of the various theories of alcohol addiction, it is unlikely that there is a single explanation to account for the condition. Alcohol addiction develops in a wide range of personalities for a wide variety of different reasons. The attempt to force all alcohol addicts into a common etiologic mold is not consistent with clinical observations.

The complex nature of the causes of alcohol addiction was suggested in a follow-up of boys in the Cambridge–Somerville Youth Study. In this research, a large group of boys was given the advantages of all available medical, psychiatric, psychological, and social service facilities in the community. A matched control group of boys was allowed to grow up without these advantages. A follow-up of 255 boys in the experimental group and 255 matched controls revealed the startling and somewhat discouraging finding that 29 men from the original treatment group had become alcoholic, while only 22 had become alcoholic from the control group (McCord, 1959). There were, in fact, more alcoholics from the group of boys who had received the intensive study and help during their early years. Clearly, the intensive study and early treatment did not deter the development of alcoholism later in life. This finding supports the possibility of the importance of constitutional factors in the etiology of alcoholism, although the data are open to other interpretations.

There is no known single, most effective way to treat alcoholism. Not only are more data needed on the natural history of this illness, but prevention methods are not well developed. Trained personnel, money, and facilities are inadequate for the needs of research, treatment, and educational efforts to combat this widespread disorder. Education about alcoholism and drinking is usually weak, often unscientific, and generally not based on sound educational principles. Despite these serious problems and deficiencies, however, increasing numbers of people with alcohol problems are being treated and rehabilitated.

During the past two decades there has been a noticeable change in the view toward alcoholism. Significant advances have been made, for example, in both public and professional acknowledgment that alcoholism is a disease rather than a form of moral transgression. The contemporary approach to the study and treatment of alcoholism incorporates scientific and humanitarian goals. The courts are increasingly inclined to view the alcoholic as a psychological problem, and the legal proceedings of jailing alcoholics are in the process of being revised.

National Center for Prevention and Control of Alcoholism
The National Center for Prevention and Control of Alcoholism provides leadership in the planning and development of national programs through stimulation of research, training, educational, and service programs. Efforts are focused on developing a better understanding of the cause, natural history, and eventual cure of alcoholism through studies of the interaction of complex biological, psychological, and social factors.

As in the cases of other mental and personality disorders, rehabilitation of alcoholics is based upon development of a continuum of services including institutional programs, half-way houses, and other postinstitutional facilities, transitional employment, and appropriate job placement and follow-up.

One major roadblock to adequate treatment for alcoholics is the continuing reluctance of many general hospitals to admit them. The reluctance is based in part on the supposition that alcoholic patients require highly specialized services. This notion has now been upset by the results of a demonstration project carried out at the Massachusetts General Hospital. Investigators there have convincingly demonstrated that general hospitals can help alcoholics on an emergency basis and through follow-up care in appropriate outpatient settings. The excellence of the comprehensive care provided alcoholics by this general hospital challenges the idea that they need specialized detoxification centers and treatment units.

Teen-age youngsters are the focus of two preventive projects. In one, the children of alcoholic fathers are being studied to discover what factors are associated with successful psychological coping by the teen-agers. In the second project, consultation services are being provided by a general hospital alcoholism program to various community agencies to assist them in evolving a coordinated treatment program for fourteen- to sixteen-year-olds who appear before the court in connection with an alcohol-associated offense. The agency's involvement in the preventive activities starts with the identification of these youngsters so that there can be appropriate intervention to reduce the likelihood of development of serious drinking problems. Preliminary findings indicate that such disruptive family factors as divorce, illness, rejection, or overindulgence appear frequently in the background of these youthful offenders (NIMH, 1970).

In many parts of the country the only substantial services for alcoholics are in the state mental hospitals. There has been a steady increase in the number of alcoholics admitted to these hospitals. In over one-third of all the states more patients are admitted to mental hospitals with a diagnosis of alcoholism than with any other diagnosis. Rates of admission of alcoholic patients have increased more rapidly than those for most other psychiatric diagnoses. In the age group 45 to 54, for example, almost half of the men now admitted are alcoholics.[2]

DRUG DEPENDENCE

Dependence on drugs has many points in common with alcohol addiction.* The drug dependent individual is basically one who finds the effects of the drug to be a solution to his problems. As in the case of alcohol and the alcoholic, the drug becomes so essential to the patient that he cannot face reality without it. In drug dependence, particularly in the early stages, there is no damage to the nervous system. When damage does occur, the condition is classified as a brain syndrome rather than as drug dependence.

The World Health Organization Committee on Drugs defines drug dependence in the following way:

> A state of periodic or chronic intoxication detrimental to the individual and to society, produced by the repeated consumption of a drug (natural or synthetic). Its characteristics include: (1) an overpowering desire or need (compulsion) to continue taking the drug and to obtain it by any means; (2) a tendency to increase the dose; (3) a psychic (psychological) and, sometimes, a physical dependence upon the effects of the drug (WHO, 1961).

Whereas drug dependence in the United States has increased in recent years, drug addiction has been a problem of decreasing importance, in terms of numbers of addicts, since early in the present century. During World War I the rate of drug addiction was 1 in 1,500, while during World War II the rate fell to 1 in 10,000. The control of commerce and of the importation of narcotic drugs into the United States during World War II reduced the number of drug addicts to a minimum. Since that time, the number of white addicts has not increased significantly, although there has been a significant increase among the black, Puerto Rican, and Mexican population groups in the large cities. The total number of known addicts in the United States in 1970 was about 70,000 (NIMH, 1970).

It is probable that the number of drug addicts in the country is greater than the figures usually cited. Many addicts have never been apprehended or registered, and there is no record of them. Nevertheless, in view of the increase in the general population, the number of drug addicts represents a substantial decrease. Unfortunately, there has been a rather general increase in the number of teen-age drug addicts. In Los Angeles, for example, the number of juvenile drug arrests jumped 46 percent in a single year.

Typically, the known addict is a young ghetto dweller in a densely populated city. He is nonwhite, and he and his family are poor. These are characteristics of known addicts; that is, those known to the law-enforcing authorities. Submerged below the horizon of the law enforcement statistics are a large group who are addicted but who have not yet come to the attention of the authorities.

An unknown number of other people leading lives quite remote from the ghetto addicts also abuse drugs. While drug addiction appears to be

---

[2]A number of valuable books are available in the area of the addictions. Among the less technical ones dealing with alcoholism are Dwight Anderson's *The Other Side of the Bottle* (Wyn, 1950); Marty Mann's *Primer on Alcoholism* (Rinehart, 1950); and *Revolving Door: A Study of the Chronic Police Case Inebriate* (Free Press, 1958) by D. J. Pittman and C. W. Gordon. More technical works on alcohol addiction are *Understanding Alcoholism* (American Academy of Political and Social Science, 1958), edited by Selden D. Bacon; *Alcoholism as a Medical Problem* (Hoeber, 1956), edited by H. D. Kruse; *Origins of Alcoholism* (Stanford University, 1960) by William and Joan McCord; *Alcoholism and Society* (Oxford University, 1962) by M. E. Chafetz and H. W. Demone, Jr.; and *Drinking and Intoxication: Selected Readings in Social Attitudes and Controls* (Free Press, 1959), edited by R. G. McCarthy.

*The widespread abuse of drugs which are not addictive in the physical sense has led to the adoption of the general term *drug dependence*. The term *drug addiction* is reserved for dependence on narcotic drugs.

epidemic in our urban slums among economically deprived young people, drug dependence is an endemic problem afflicting people in every level of our society.

It is interesting to note that Great Britain, with a population of 50 million, has relatively few addicts. Drug addicts in Great Britain are treated on a psychiatric and medical basis, whereas in the United States the persisting attitude is to regard drug addiction as a criminal rather than a mental health problem.[3]

The drugs used by addicts are taken into the body in a number of ways. Some are taken by smoking, others are powdered and inserted into the nose like snuff, and occasionally drugs are taken in the form of rectal suppositories. While practically all drugs can be taken by mouth, the

Figure 7.6 *A heroin addict "mainlines" his "fix" by injecting the drug into a vein. (Bob Combs from Rapho Guillumette)*

true addict prefers to take the drug by hypodermic needle, injecting it either under the skin or directly into the vein. In this way, the drug effects are quicker and more pronounced. Since addicts frequently become careless about sterilizing their syringes and needles before using them, they may develop infections and abscesses which leave unsightly scars. These scars, together with fresh needle marks, are presumptive signs of addiction.

The drug addict does not ordinarily experience the unconsciousness typical of the alcoholic in the last stages of intoxication. He can be aroused

---

Center for Studies of Narcotic Addiction and Drug Abuse

The National Institute of Mental Health established the Center for Studies of Narcotic and Drug Abuse in 1967 to focus and coordinate programs in this critical area of concern. In addition to participating in the administration of narcotic addict rehabilitation programs, the center supports research concerning the nature and abuse of drugs of various types and supports the training of scientists in the special problems of drug abuse. For example, an intensive program has been mounted to secure answers to the many perplexing questions raised by the increased use of marijuana and by the public controversies surrounding the subject. Contracts have been awarded to secure adequate supplies of natural and synthetic *tetrahydrocannabinol* (THC—one of the active substances found in marijuana) for use in research; investigations are being conducted to learn more about absorption of these compounds, their biochemical properties, and their toxic effects. The center also supports research projects investigating the value of LSD as a therapeutic agent, as well as basic research into the mechanism of action, biological activity, and possible adverse effects of this and other hallucinogenic drugs.

---

[3]*Drug Dependence* is a journal published irregularly to facilitate the exchange of information about drug dependence and abuse and to provide abstracts of the current literature in the field. It is available from the Division of Narcotic Addiction and Drug Abuse, National Institute of Mental Health, 5454 Wisconsin Avenue, Chevy Chase, Md. 20015.

Table 7.1 *Selected drugs: their medical uses, the symptoms they produce, and their dependence potential*

NAME	SLANG NAME	CHEMICAL OR TRADE NAME	PHARMACOLOGIC CLASSIFICATION	MEDICINAL-USE	HOW TAKEN
Heroin	H., horse, scot, junk, snow, stuff, harry, joy powder	Diacetylmorphine	Depressant	Pain relief	Injected or sniffed
Morphine	White stuff, Miss Emma, M, dreamer	Morphine sulphate	Depressant	Pain relief	Swallowed or injected
Codeine	Schoolboy	Methylmorphine	Depressant	Ease pain and coughing	Swallowed
Methadone	Dolly	Dolophine Amidone	Depressant	Pain relief	Swallowed or injected
Cocaine	Speed balls, gold dust, coke, bernice, corine, flake, Star Dust	Methyl ester of benzoylecgonine	Stimulant	Local anesthesia	Sniffed, injected, or swallowed
Marijuana	Pot, grass, locoweed Mary Jane, hashish, tea, gage, reefers	Cannabis Sativa	Stimulant, depressant, or hallucinogen	None in U.S.	Smoked, swallowed, or sniffed
Barbiturates	Barbs, blue devils, candy, yellow jackets, phennies, peanuts, blue heavens	Phenobarbital, nembutal, seconal, amytal	Depressant	Sedation, relieve high blood pressure, epilepsy, hyperthyroidism	Swallowed or injected
Amphetamines	Bennies, dexies, co-pilots, wake ups, lid proppers, hearts, pep pills	Benzedrine, preludin, dexedrine, dexoxyn, methedrine	Stimulant	Relieve mild depression, control appetite, and narcolepsy	Swallowed or injected
LSD	Acid, sugar, big D, cubes, trips	d-lysergic acid diethylamide	Hallucinogen	Experimental study of mental function, alcoholism	Swallowed
DMT	Businessman's high	Dimethyltriptamine	Hallucinogen	None	Injected
Mescaline	Cactus, peyote	3, 4, 5-trimethoxy-phenethylamine	Hallucinogen	None	Swallowed
Psilocybin	Mushrooms	3 (2-dimethylamino ethylindol-4-ol) dihydrogen phosphate	Hallucinogen	None	Swallowed

USUAL DOSE	DURATION OF EFFECT	INITIAL SYMPTOMS	LONG-TERM SYMPTOMS	PHYSICAL DEPENDENCE POTENTIAL	MENTAL DEPENDENCE POTENTIAL
Varies	4 hrs.	Euphoria, drowsiness	Addiction, constipation, loss of appetite, convulsions in overdose	Yes	Yes
15 milligrams	6 hrs.	Euphoria, drowsiness	Addiction, impairment of breathing	Yes	Yes
30 milligrams	4 hrs.	Drowsiness	Addiction	Yes	Yes
10 milligrams	4-6 hrs.	Less acute than opiates	Addiction	Yes	Yes
Varies	Varies	Excitation, talkativeness, tremors	Depression, convulsions	No	Yes
1 or 2 cigarettes	4 hrs.	Relaxation, euphoria, alteration of perception and judgment	Usually none	No	?
50-100 milligrams	4 hrs.	Drowsiness, muscle relaxation	Addiction with severe withdrawal symptoms, possible convulsions	Yes	Yes
2.5-5 milligrams	4 hrs.	Alertness, activeness	Delusions, hallucinations	No	Yes
100 micrograms	10 hrs.	Exhilaration, excitation, rambling speech	May intensify existing psychosis, panic reactions	No	?
1 milligram	4-6 hrs.	Exhilaration excitation	?	No	?
350 micrograms	12 hrs.	Exhilaration, anxiety, gastric distress	?	No	?
25 milligrams	6-8 hrs.	Nausea, vomiting, headaches	?	No	?

at any time to carry out his normal activities. In fact, the drug addict can frequently work at his job without an impairment of efficiency. Even jobs requiring average motor skill may be carried out, with few signs of the influence of the drugs other than a slower rate of work. Confirmed drug addicts are sometimes able to function at their jobs better when they are under the influence of the drug than when they are not on the drug.

The drug addictions involve a number of drugs, the most common of which are the opiates, particularly morphine and its derivatives. Other drugs include cocaine, marijuana, the barbiturates, and the amphetamines. In addition, a number of exotic addictive drugs are used in special cultural settings in various parts of the world.

The addiction to raw opium is rare except in Oriental countries and in a few cosmopolitan centers where there are large Oriental colonies. In this type of addiction, the addict feels elated and carefree after smoking a number of pipes. The euphoric feeling lasts for several hours and is followed by a deep sleep. Upon awakening, the patient often experiences a feeling of malaise. The patient addicted to opium shows a number of chronic symptoms of both a physical and psychological nature. Physically, he is weak, emaciated, oversensitive to pain, and troubled by constipation. Psychological symptoms include a general apathy along with a decline in ethical values and the moral sense. There is depression, and it is not unusual for the opium addict to attempt suicide.

The most commonly seen opiate addictions involve morphine and its most important derivatives such as heroin, eudokal, and demerol. Morphine was prescribed for many years by physicians for the relief of pain, and its medical use led to many cases of addiction. There appears to be a sensitivity to morphine in certain people which makes it possible for them to become addicted very quickly. Other patients are able to take morphine over a long period of time without developing an addiction.

In 1970 the use of heroin by school-age children in New York City reached what leading officials considered to be epidemic proportions. Many of the youngsters became "hooked" inside the schools. An official of the city's Addiction Services Agency said that "an average high school can have from 5 to 100 youngsters shooting heroin—we just don't know for certain."

Many youthful student pushers have been found to be workers at "factories" and at "tables" where the heroin is cut (diluted) and placed in glassine packets. Other students buy heroin in bulk and set up their own business.

One result of the increased use of heroin by young people has been an upsurge in deaths caused by the drug among youngsters. Of 900 such deaths in New York City in 1969, 224 victims were teenagers, including twenty under the age of fifteen (The *New York Times*, Feb. 16, 1970).

The sequence of opiate intoxication is quite different from that of alcoholism. The first effects of an opiate include a temporary nausea which is followed by various body reactions such as warmth, itching sensations, feelings of pins and needles, and stomach sensations. At the same time, there is a sense of relaxation and relief from tension. It is at this time that the experience of being "high" takes place. This is a detachment from the world and its problems—a feeling of not being involved, an "out of this world" feeling in which there are no cares of worries. When the drug addict returns to his usual activities, he continues to experience these comfortable, relaxed feelings which were induced initially by the drug.

In opiate addiction, while the user is still taking relatively small doses daily or twice daily, his body develops a tissue need for the drug. This physiological addiction requires the regular and continued use of the drug and, in most cases, an increase in the amount. If the user attempts to stop his use of the drug, there are extremely distressing *withdrawal symptoms*. These include general restlessness, abdominal pains, yawning, hot and cold flashes, perspiration, increased salivation, heart palpitation, and anxiety, which increase rapidly to a marked extent. Addicts are depressed and fatigued, sleep is restless, and there may be nausea, vomiting, and diarrhea. The severity of the symptoms and their duration depend on the degree to which the person has been addicted, the length of the addiction, and the individual personality and somatic makeup. The withdrawal symptoms reach a maximal intensity after twenty-four hours and begin to subside after forty-eight to seventy-two hours.

■ DRUG ADDICTION

Norman J. is a twenty-nine-year-old narcotic addict who was referred to a psychiatric hospital after being arrested for using a false name to obtain paregoric in a drugstore. The patient has been an addict for a number of years, cooking the paregoric to obtain the narcotic residue. He has been in jail many times, and was in a federal narcotic hospital for a period of six months. While he has worked at a number of odd jobs, he has never had steady employment.

When admitted to the psychiatric hospital the patient was friendly and cooperative. His manner and voice indicated a man who was accustomed to being questioned and was willing to answer in some detail. He was fully oriented, and his thinking was clear and logical. Speech was relevant, and there was no indication of emotional disturbance. The patient claimed that he had a happy childhood, and that he started to take paregoric at age sixteen "just for the kick." While he admitted that he had become unusually upset at the time of his mother's death, and that there was difficulty in adjusting to the father's second marriage, he insisted that these stress situations had nothing to do with his addiction. He said that he did not take drugs to escape his problems, but rather for his own pleasure.

In recent months the patient has been eating and sleeping poorly, and there has been physical deterioration with a weight loss of more than twenty pounds. He was able to break the habit several times in the past, and each time experienced the usual withdrawal symptoms of sweating, abdominal pains, and heart palpitation. He has talked frequently to his younger brother about the evil effects of drugs and has attempted to frighten the brother so that he will stay away from the habit.*

Research on opiate drug dependence employs animal models of addiction, neurophysiologic studies of the effects of these drugs on various parts of the central nervous system and on the biochemical and molecular biological correlates of physical dependence and tolerance. Clinical studies with *methadone* and *cyclazocine* maintenance have been proceeding in several clinical centers. *Naloxone,* a drug which counteracts the effects of the opiates, has also been studied as a maintenance drug.

The maintenance drugs, of which methadone is the most widely used, serve as a substitute for heroin. The physiological addiction remains, but the euphoric high and severe withdrawal symptoms are not present. Also, since methadone is relatively inexpensive, the addict does not need to resort to criminal acts to obtain money to support his drug habit.

Several studies on the behavior of opiate-addicted animals seek to shed light on the behavior of human addicts. A method has been developed for inducing drug addiction in rats. This behavior survives morphine abstinence for weeks, thus pointing to a certain resemblance to the sustained drug-induced behavior of human addicts. Physiological differences among rat strains have been identified, permitting them to be classed as addiction-prone and addiction-resistant animals. This finding suggests that inherent physiological characteristics—seemingly genetically transmitted—play a part in the animal's proneness to addiction.

The problem of drug abuse is not confined to opiate addiction but embraces many classes of drugs and newer kinds of drug abusers with a pathology quite different from that of the "hardcore" addict. Americans spend 250 million dollars on tranquilizers each year, including some products with proved addiction potential. The serious increase in the use of hallucinogens, amphetamines, and marijuana among college and high school students has received national attention in recent years.

The National Institute of Mental Health has reported that between 35 and 40 percent of the total college student population has used at least one drug illegally. Of students who use drugs illegally, 73 percent have used amphetamines, 22 percent have used marijuana, and 5 percent have used LSD (NIMH, 1970).

The discovery of the sedative effects of the barbiturates led to their wide, and sometimes indiscriminate, use for the relief of tension and anxiety and for sleep disturbances. In many states, the drugs are available without prescription, and in those states where medical prescriptions are required, physicians often issue them freely. The

---

*Case 2 of audiotape 4, "Personality Disorders: Addictions," in *Case Interviews to Accompany The Disorganized Personality.*

result has been the establishment of many cases of barbital addiction. While the introduction of the tranquilizing drugs and the nonbarbiturate sedatives made the problem of barbiturate addiction somewhat less common, such cases continue to be seen in psychiatric clinics and hospitals from time to time.

The patient who becomes addicted to barbiturates is likely to be tired, mentally dull, and chronically irritable. He finds less and less satisfaction in his family and his job. Where the emotional reaction is not severe, the patient may function for a number of years with an addiction to moderate or heavy doses of barbiturates. Such individuals build up a definite physiological dependence upon the drug. While the dependence is not so pronounced as that seen in morphinism, the extended use of the drug results in a tolerance, and patients find it necessary to take larger and larger amounts to obtain the same effect.

Among other drugs, marijuana is of interest because its relatively low cost and ready availability have made it increasingly common since World War II. The drug, a resinous substance obtained from the hemp plant, has been known for centuries in the Orient under such names as *hashish* and *bhang*. The plant grows wild or can be cultivated in a great many parts of the world and under relatively adverse conditions. It has been grown in gardens and window boxes, in the strip of ground separating the lanes of expressways, and on an island in the Croton Reservoir, part of the water supply of New York City.

The leaves of the plant are dried and processed in various ways. The most common method is to use the dried leaves to make cigarettes commonly called joints or (an older term) "reefers." The drug has also been made into candy. Marijuana is called by a number of slang terms. Grass, pot, Mary Jane, weed, and other names are prevalent in various parts of the country.

Marijuana produces rather characteristic effects. There may be fear and anxiety immediately following the ingestion of the drug, but this feeling quickly turns to a sense of well-being and euphoria. There is also an increase in speech and a show of irritability in some users. Different people are affected in different ways. One feature of marijuana intoxication is the distortion of the time sense. Time intervals seem to be stretched out, and distances appear greater. This distur-

bance of the perception of time and space is the aspect of marijuana intoxication which has appealed to some jazz musicians. They feel that the distortion of time makes it possible for them to play in a faster and more distinctive style.

A thirty-two-year-old man who had been smoking two or three marijuana cigarettes every night since the age of fifteen described his experiences:

Once you smoke it, it never lets you go. It makes your mind so that it can never fail. It makes you stronger, makes you laugh a lot and makes you like everybody. It makes me very energetic to my wife so that I even got twins. There is no crime in it—it is only with alcohol that it makes you do wrong things. It is best if you smoke it with other people but if alone you can think you hear the best bands playing. Your imagination is so great that you can see someone you have not seen for a long time. But if there are other people with you, you don't see or hear anything—you just enjoy yourself. If you smoke it and go to sleep immediately you feel terrible next morning. You must have a little enjoyment and exercise before you sleep, and the next morning you feel fine (Ames, 1958).

The following description of the effects of marijuana was given by a psychiatrist who took the drug at his hospital in South Africa:

About 90 minutes after the drug had been taken some difficulty in articulation was experienced (this was not objectively demonstrable) and concurrently I became aware of an astonishing difficulty in recall, so that I could not remember events that had just occurred. This inability of recall seemed to be associated with "dips" in the level of consciousness when everything seemed rather unreal and hazy and in striking contrast to the periods when I emerged from the dip. It was like emerging from shadow into light. In addition, my concept of time was distorted so that it always seemed later than it really was and the journey down the corridor seemed eternally long.

My mood change was striking. I experienced some euphoria but to me the really striking thing was detachment. This can be illustrated by the following examples: I realized that my headache was really quite severe and yet it did not really matter and at the time I compared it to the indifference to pain apparently experienced by patients who have been leucotomized for the pain of inoperable carcinoma; when being wheeled down the corridor in full view of my patients I felt that the situation would normally have embarrassed me and I was struck by my indifference; finally after I had been taken home and was lying in bed, I could hear my children hilariously swamping the bathroom, which normally never fails to irritate me, and I was astonished at my indifference to it. Physical symptoms were not prominent. I experienced some paresthesia of hands and feet, was conscious of coldness and had a bad headache. The effect of the drug lasted for eleven hours (Ames, 1958).

In addition to the opiates, marijuana, and the barbiturates, there are several other drugs to which people become addicted from time to time. These drugs include the amphetamines, bromide, cocaine, paraldehyde, and ether.

The various forms of amphetamines have presented an increasing problem in addiction as a result of the growing use of these drugs. Such drugs are stimulants and are used to treat mild depressions and to provide psychological stimulation. The continued use of amphetamine drugs leads to a false sense of well-being which is not a reflection of the true state of the organism. It has been found that a high tolerance for this drug is developed very rapidly.

Abuse of amphetamines and barbiturates ranges from the practice of using illicitly obtained drugs to the more hidden forms of abuse represented by inappropriate usage of medically prescribed medication. Some experts would also include as an abuse the prescribing of amphetamines in programs of weight reduction. Very large quantities of these drugs are manufactured; in the case of the amphetamines, it has been estimated that fully half of the production finds its way into illegal channels.

Authorities have been particularly concerned about the upsurge in the high-dose, usually intravenous, abuse of methamphetamine ("meth," "speed," "crystal"). Increasing numbers of young people are using a hundred times the average dose in a single injection which may be repeated a number of times daily. Such a "speed freak" may exhibit impulsive, paranoid, unpredictable behavior and is a danger to himself and those around him. When this severe misuse of methamphetamine is prolonged, malnutrition, hepatitis from unsterile injection needles, brain cell damage, and disturbances of the heart rhythm become possibilities.

The bromides are no longer much of a problem in terms of addiction. Since newer sedatives and tranquilizers are readily available, few people find it necessary to use bromides over an extended period of time.

Cocaine, an alkaloid obtained from the leaves of the coca plant, has been used in medicine as a local anesthetic. Sigmund Freud studied the neuropharmacology of cocaine and was himself addicted to the drug before breaking the habit. While addiction to this drug was frequent following World War I, it is not common today.

Cocaine is usually taken by sniffing it into the nose. However, it can also be taken by means of a hypodermic. Addicts frequently use the drug in the same manner that alcohol addicts use alcohol. They go on a cocaine spree and remain on it for several days or longer. The first effects of the drug are a slight dizziness or headache. This phase is followed by a feeling of euphoria and exaltation in which there is a marked increase in psychomotor activity. Cocaine brings on a feeling of calmness, increases endurance of fatigue and hunger, and stimulates both mental and physical activity. The pleasant effects of the drug are followed by disagreeable sensations and irritability. To avoid these unpleasant sensations, some cocaine addicts also take morphine or heroin. A combination of these drugs is known as a "speed ball." While the withdrawal of cocaine does not result in the more common physiological withdrawal symptoms, the addict who does not receive the drug shows excessive fear and episodes of panic which make his behavior dangerous and unpredictable.

In a few cases, addiction to paraldehyde is observed in alcoholic patients. The symptoms are similar to those seen in chronic alcoholism, with such additional symptoms as disturbance of appetite, anemia, loss of weight, irregular cardiac action, constipation, and elevated body temperature. Because of the distinctive odor of paraldehyde, the breath of this type of addict is always characteristic. Withdrawal of paraldehyde frequently results in convulsive seizures.

Ether addiction is a rare condition restricted for the most part to men and women associated with the medical sciences. Ether results in a marked state of euphoria, a degree of excitement, and a slowing of the perceptual processes. When it is taken over a period of time, the addiction resembles the effects of alcoholism. Addiction of this type leads to serious organic changes in the form of damage to the heart, kidney, and liver.

■ DRUG AND ALCOHOL ADDICTION

Donald M. is a thirty-year-old man who was referred to a psychiatric hospital for stealing a carton of cigarettes from a drugstore. He was intoxicated at the time; and since the incident occurred only one day after being released from jail on another charge of drunkenness, hospitalization was recommended. The patient started drinking when he was eight years old, and became addicted to narcotics when he was fourteen. He was introduced to alcohol and drugs by an older brother who was a narcotic addict. Over the years, the patient has had numerous commitments to jails, workhouses, and the penitentiary on charges of stealing, intoxication, and the use of drugs. The patient's father was an alcoholic, and an uncle was a drug addict.

When seen at the hospital, the patient was a tall, well-groomed, and physically healthy man who talked quietly and expressively. He was calm and cooperative, and completely self-confident. The psychological examination showed normal thought processes, complete orientation, intact memory, and good emotional control. While judgment and insight were somewhat impaired, the patient admitted he needed professional help.*

Relatively little is known about the personality types and constitutional makeups most likely to become addicted to drugs. Such factors as the need for attention, latent homosexuality, narcissism, passive inadequacy, aggression, and similar matters have been suggested as being important in the dynamics of the addict. These factors, however, are also found in alcohol addiction. While it is impossible to specify a single personality picture for drug addicts, many addicts appear to be noncompetitive and somewhat passive individuals who use drugs to attain relief from their underlying anxieties.

Effective treatment of the narcotic addict continues to be a refractory problem. Results to date, particularly if the criterion of success is total abstinence from drugs, have been discouraging. At least part of the difficulty has been that the addict is usually treated in a hospital far from his home community and there has been no adequate program of follow-up care to assist him on his return home.

The Narcotic Addict Rehabilitation Act of 1966 was an attempt to establish a new national policy regarding narcotic addiction. The act provided for a civil commitment of narcotic addicts, including those charged with or convicted of violating federal criminal laws. With the passage of the act, Congress authorized a comprehensive medically oriented approach to the treatment and rehabilitation of narcotic addicts. The act also provided for total treatment rather than fragmented efforts. Institutional treatment, as a result, is geared more toward the supervised return of the patient to the community. For the first time, provision has been made for professionally supervised aftercare for addicts in their own community after discharge from inpatient treatment. While this approach is essential in the treatment of addiction, the high rate of recidivism has not been reduced in a significant way.

Although we do not yet understand the factors which underlie drug addiction, it is believed to be symptomatic of a personality disorder influenced by social-cultural, economic, and pharmacological factors. Drug abuse and other forms of antisocial behavior are viewed as unsuccessful efforts of individuals with poor impulse control to cope with the stresses of daily life. Current treatment efforts seek ways to support the "weak" individual and to modify his environment in such a way that he will be able to develop better coping mechanisms as alternatives to deviant behavior. Currently available methods of rehabilitating narcotic addicts have not generally been effective. The majority of addicts have relapsed soon after being discharged from hospitals or prisons. The human suffering and social disruption resulting from these disorders make it imperative that intensive research be initiated and expanded in numerous areas.[4]

---

*Case 3 of audiotape 4, "Personality Disorders: Addictions," in *Case Interviews to Accompany The Disorganized Personality*.

[4]Nontechnical discussions of drug dependence include *The Drug Beat* (Cowles, 1969) by Allen Geller and Maxwell Boas; John Kaplan's *The Marijuana Problem* (World, 1970). Also recommended is R. R. Lingeman's *Drugs from A to Z* (McGraw-Hill, 1969), a lexicon of terms from the world of

SUMMARY

1. The personality disorders and related conditions include a number of reactions which differ fundamentally from the transient situational disturbances. The cause of the difficulty in these conditions is in the nature of the individual rather than the existence of externally caused physical or psychosocial stress. The disorders are also marked to a greater extent by disturbances of behavior than by mental or emotional symptoms. The major conditions in this group are the *personality disorders* themselves and the related *sexual deviations, alcoholism,* and *drug dependence.*

2. The personality disorders are characterized by a basic maldevelopment of the personality. They include the *inadequate, schizoid, cyclothymic, paranoid, passive-aggressive, obsessive-compulsive, antisocial, hysterical, asthenic,* and *explosive* personalities.

3. The inadequate personality is neither physically nor mentally deficient but is unable to make an adequate adjustment because of his general ineptness. The schizoid personality is isolated and seclusive, while the cyclothymic experiences fluctuating moods ranging from depression to mild elation. The paranoid personality is the jealous and suspicious person, and the passive-aggressive personality struggles with his feelings of hostility. The obsessive-compulsive personality shows rigid and perfectionistic behavior; the antisocial pattern of behavior is one which brings the individual repeatedly into conflict with society. The hysterical personality shows emotional instability, excitability, and self-dramatization; the asthenic individual is easily fatigued and has a low energy level; and the explosive personality is given to outbursts of rage and verbal or physical aggression.

4. The sexual deviations include such activities as *exhibitionism,* or relieving sexual tensions by exhibiting the body; *voyeurism,* or obtaining sexual satisfaction from observing others; *fetishism,* or regarding a part of the body or article of clothing as a love object; *sadomasochism,* or obtaining sexual gratification by giving pain to others or experiencing pain oneself; and *homosexuality,* in which the love object is a member of the same sex. *Transvestism,* which is the wearing of the clothing of the opposite sex, may or may not be accompanied by overt homosexuality.

5. Alcohol addiction is also related to the personality disorders. The alcohol addict is a person whose intake of alcohol is great enough to be damaging to his personal and social functioning but which has not yet had any irreversible physical effects on the nervous system. When that point is reached, the condition becomes a brain disorder rather than a disorder of personality.

6. Drug dependence is a term used to describe the excessive use of drugs because of a psychological need or because of a physiological addiction. In both cases the condition is considered to be related to personality disorder as long as there are no long-term adverse changes in nervous system functioning. When such changes do occur, these conditions become brain disorders.

---

drug abuse. More serious approaches to the problem are found in *Drug Dependence and Aspects of Ego Functions* (Wayne State University Press, 1970) by H. Krystal and H. R. Raskin; *Narcotics and Narcotic Addiction* (Thomas, 1954) by D. W. Maurer and V. H. Vogel; David P. Ausubel's *Drug Addiction* (Random House, 1958); Thorvald Brown's *The Enigma of Drug Addiction* (Thomas, 1961); and Lawrence Kolb's *Drug Addiction* (Thomas, 1962).

8 THE NEUROSES

The neuroses are among the most common of all forms of personality disorganization. These reactions range from mild to severe, with many cases responding favorably to treatment. They are found at every age level, in every socioeconomic group, and on a worldwide basis.

This group of disorders includes reactions in which the person learns to express his anxiety in a direct way or seeks unconsciously to control it. He retains his awareness of external reality as well as the fundamental organization of his personality. Even though the symptoms may be disabling, he seldom needs to be institutionalized. Most neurotic disorders, if treated at all, are treated on an outpatient basis.

Prior to the time of Emil Kraepelin in the 1890s, the word *neurosis* had a meaning and use quite different from its present-day usage. In the late 1700s, all mental disorder from whatever cause was included in the class of *neurotica*. Because of this very general nature of the word, it was abandoned for all practical clinical purposes during most of the nineteenth century. When the word appeared again, toward the end of the century, it was used in a different sense, to refer to organic disturbances of the nervous system. The term *functional neurosis* was introduced later for those disorders of the nervous system in which an organic lesion could not be found. With the growing realization that certain conditons are psychologically determined, the word *psychoneurosis* was introduced. Today, the words *neurosis* and *psychoneurosis* are synonymous.

The symptoms of neurotic behavior fall into eight major groups: (1) anxiety, (2) pathological fears or phobias, (3) obsessions and compulsions, (4) hypochondria, (5) neurasthenia, (6) hysteria, (7) depersonalization, and (8) depression. While the underlying psychodynamic pattern is similar in all neurotic reactions, there are wide differ- ences in symptoms and in specific ways in which conflicts in the personality are worked out.[1]

ANXIETY NEUROSIS

The most basic and direct neurotic disorder is the anxiety reaction. In these cases, the individual's psychological defense system is not adequate to handle the underlying anxieties generated by his conflicts, and the anxiety comes to the surface in an undisguised and unaltered way. In its simplest form, the neurotic anxiety reaction is the presence, at the conscious level, of a disabling degree of anxiety. The following description reflects the current view of the anxiety reaction:

> In this kind of reaction the anxiety is diffuse and not restricted to definite situations or objects. It is not controlled by any specific psychological defense mechanism as in other psychoneurotic reactions. This reaction is characterized by anxious expectation and frequently associated with somatic symptomatology. The condition is to be differential from normal apprehensiveness or fear (DSM-II, 1968).

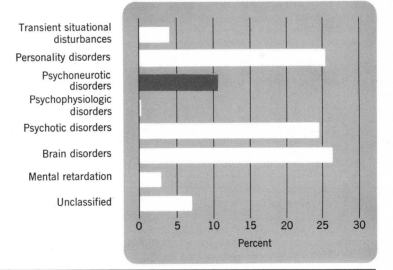

Figure 8.1 *The incidence of psychoneurotic disorders as a percentage of total first admissions to public mental hospitals in the United States. (From data furnished by the National Institute of Mental Health, 1970.)*

[1] Books dealing with neuroses in a general way are Walter C. Alvarez's *The Neuroses* (Saunders, 1951); R. Brun's *General Theory of Neuroses* (International Universities Press, 1951); Henry T. Laughlin's *The Neuroses in Clinical Practice* (Saunders, 1956); Ludwig Eidelberg's *An Outline of a Comparative Pathology of the Neuroses* (International Universities Press, 1954); and Lester Keiser's *The Traumatic Neurosis* (Lippincott, 1968).

Figure 8.2 *The anxiety reaction. (Courtesy of Mead Johnson Laboratories.)*

The mere presence of anxiety is not an indication of an anxiety reaction in the clinical sense. Even the most normal individuals will react to excessive stress situations with overt anxiety. Moreover, the nature of our culture and the times in which we live give rise to a relatively high level of anxiety in the majority of people. A survey of a residential section of New York City showed that 75.5 percent of the population reported symptoms of anxiety (Rennie et al., 1957). Depending upon the criteria used in defining the symptoms of anxiety, this percentage figure probably could be raised even higher.

A certain amount of conscious anxiety is to be expected in everyone. Many men and women who have a low tolerance for anxiety go through life in a state of constant anxiety. They are fearful, worrisome, easily fatigued, frequently complaining, unable to sleep, tense, and unhappy. In most cases in which a high level of anxiety persists, the individual does not seek treatment and is not considered to be neurotic in the conventional sense. It is only when the level of persistent anxiety reaches a point where the symptoms interfere with family life, social relations, or occupational adjustment that the condition is looked upon as a neurosis.

The typical anxiety neurotic is an excessively tense person who is filled with uncontrollable dread and apprehension. He has a tendency to a rapid pulse and elevated blood pressure and may show difficulties in breathing, frequent sighing, digestive upset, and similar physical signs of an overreacting autonomic nervous system. These physical symptoms are a reflection of the emergency measures being taken by the organism to make itself ready to meet the threat, whatever it might be. In the case of lower animals, the threat typically comes from the environment. However, in man the danger is more likely to be within the organism in the form of impulses of a dangerous or forbidden kind.

On the psychological side, the anxiety neurotic is likely to have pronounced feelings of dread and apprehension. He may be convinced that something terrible is going to happen, but he does not know what it will be, or even why it should happen. Nevertheless, he is quite sure that he is in grave danger. He lives under a cloud of impending doom, and nothing he tells himself, or is told by others, can dispel the aura of tension and fearfulness.

Anxiety reactions include acute anxiety attacks and chronic anxiety states. While these reactions may exist independently of one another, in many cases the chronic state is punctuated by acute episodes of more intense anxiety. Attacks of acute anxiety are episodic, come on unexpectedly, and may last from a few minutes to several hours. The victim of acute anxiety usually cannot account for the onset of the symptoms or for their later disappearance. Such attacks are terrifying for the victim, who not infrequently believes he is going to die. The heart begins to pound, breathing becomes rapid or difficult, the patient begins to perspire, the gastrointestinal system is upset, and there is an urge to frequent urination. The patient is thrown into a state of acute apprehensiveness without being able to verbalize what is causing it.

A woman troubled with attacks of acute anxiety described her symptoms in the following words:

It was just like I was petrified with fear. If I were to meet a lion face to face, I couldn't be more scared. Everything got black, and I felt I would faint, but I didn't. I thought, "I won't be able to hold on." I think sometimes I will just go crazy. My heart was beating so hard and fast it would jump out and hit my hand. I felt like I couldn't stand up, that my legs wouldn't support me. My hands got icy, and my feet stung. There were horrible shooting pains in my forehead. My head felt tight, like someone had pulled the skin down too tight, and I wanted to pull it away. I couldn't breathe. I was short of breath. I literally get out of breath and pant just like I had run an eight-mile race. I couldn't do anything. I felt all in, weak, no strength. I can't even dial a telephone. Even then I can't be still when I'm like this. I am restless, and I pace up and down. I feel I am just not responsible. I don't know what I'll do. These things are terrible. I can go along calmly for awhile, then, without any warning, this happens. I just blow my top (Laughlin, 1956).

Homosexual panic is a dramatic example of the acute anxiety attack. In these cases, the unconscious conflict of the patient centers around latent homosexual strivings. Whenever something in the patient's environment touches upon this unconscious problem, the patient runs the risk of being seized by an intense and uncontrollable anxiety. In one case, a young man developed a violent dislike of ballet after having attended a performance during which he was thrown into a panic. His heart pounded, he had difficulty with his breathing, and he broke into a cold sweat. As soon as he left the theater, his symptoms subsided. Later events revealed that this man had strong unconscious homosexual tendencies which he was struggling to keep from becoming conscious. He was unconsciously attracted to the male ballet dancers. His panic was a reaction to the threat that his defenses might break down and that he might reveal the homosexual component of his personality to himself or to others.

In the chronic anxiety state, the anxiety persists over a period of weeks, months, and even years. Such conditions are marked by an exaggeration of the various psychological and physiological symptoms associated with less severe states of anxiety. There is usually a persistence of autonomic symptoms of a milder degree. Frequent sighing, headache, gastrointestinal upsets, chronic fatigue, and general apprehensiveness are common complaints. Such patients often complain that they cannot concentrate, cannot keep their minds on their work, and have lost all interest in life.

■ ANXIETY NEUROSIS

Hilda J. is an eighteen-year-old girl who was referred to a psychiatric clinic because of marked anxiety centering around sexual conflicts involving her relationship with her father. The girl first came to the attention of the authorities eight months earlier when she attempted suicide. At the time she told a story of difficulties at home and of her intense fear of her father. She came to the attention of the police again later when she was arrested for drinking. She showed great

Figure 8.3 *The brain centers involved in the anxiety reaction. (1) The thalamic and hypothalamic area, (2) the limbic system, and (3) the lower level of the reticular activating system. (Courtesy of the Wallace Laboratories.)*

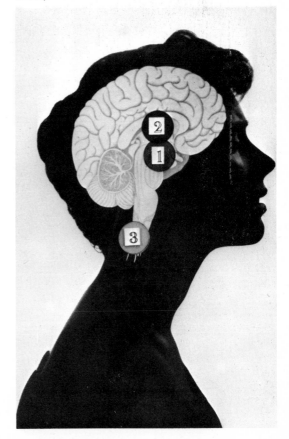

anxiety in connection with her father, and told how he beat her and her brothers and sisters, how he drank excessively, and how he attempted to molest her.

When seen at the time of the interview, Hilda was a rather small, thin, dark-haired girl who was pleasant and cooperative but who obviously was under considerable tension. At the beginning of the interview she pulled at her hands, sighed repeatedly, shifted uncomfortably in her chair, and had difficulty speaking because of her tenseness. The anxiety lessened somewhat in the face of repeated encouragement and reassurance. Eventually she told a story which revolved for the most part around her father. She said that he had told her that her mother had frustrated him sexually. At another time he kissed her, but she denied any overt sexual activities with him. She admitted having frequent dreams and nightmares, most of which involved the father. She repeated one dream in which the mother was in the kitchen making supper, and the father tried to get the patient to give him a knife so he could stab the mother. She also had dreams of old men lurking in the street.

Hilda's anxiety became so great that she insisted that her mother sleep with her. Before going to bed, she went through a ritual of barricading the bedroom door, hanging a cloth over the door knob, and forcing the cloth into the keyhole with the point of a butcher knife. She could sleep as long as her mother kept an arm over her, but she awakened and would be terrified when her mother moved her arm away. At the same time, Hilda was frightened by the mother and occasionally hesitated to eat anything the mother had prepared. The girl sometimes was so fearful that she remained awake all night in order to watch her mother.

The most striking element in this case is the dramatic demonstration of the unresolved Oedipal relationship and the anxiety it generated. The problem has been intensified by the father's seductive action toward his daughter, and by the passive reaction of the mother to the situation. The girl has deeply ambivalent feelings about both her father and her mother. In spite of her often repeated fear and hatred of the father, she is preoccupied with thoughts of him both in her waking fantasies and her dream life.*

While anxiety reactions are widely prevalent, it is well to remember that many organic states show symptoms similar to those seen in anxiety. Hyperthyroidism, organic heart disorders, disturbances of the cerebellum and the semicircular canals, toxic conditions, endocrine disorders, and numerous other diseases and dysfunctions of an organic nature may show symptoms that could readily be mistaken for anxiety.[2]

PHOBIAS

The phobic reaction is one of the most common of all neurotic conditions. The phobia, which is a pathological fear, has been described in the following way:

> The anxiety of these patients becomes detached from a specific idea, object, or situation in the daily life and is displaced to some symbolic idea or situation in the form of a specific neurotic fear. . . . The patient attempts to control his anxiety by avoiding the phobic object or situation (DSM-II, 1968).

Pathological fears were recognized as early as the time of ancient Greece. Hippocrates described a phobic reaction in his treatise "On Epidemics." And in 1700, John Locke discussed the origin of pathological fears in "An Essay Concerning Human Understanding."

Phobias are so common among children that they have been called the "normal neuroses" of childhood. Fear of the dark, ghosts and goblins, cemeteries, and bugs and animals is an everyday occurrence. Such fear reactions are

---

*Case 1 of audiotape 5, "Psychoneurotic Disorders," in *Case Interviews to Accompany The Disorganized Personality*.

[2]The classic discussion of anxiety is Sigmund Freud's *The Problem of Anxiety* (Norton, 1936). More recent approaches are *Anxiety* (Grune & Stratton, 1950), edited by Paul H. Hoch and Joseph Zubin; H. J. Eysenck's *The Dynamics of Anxiety and Hysteria* (Kegan Paul, 1957); *The Meaning and Measurement of Neuroticism and Anxiety* (Ronald, 1961) by R. B. Cattell and I. H. Scheier; and E. E. Levitt's *The Psychology of Anxiety* (Bobbs-Merrill, 1967).

particularly common when the child is four to six years old. During this period of development he learns to have fears which may influence his behavior for the rest of his life.

From ghoulies and ghosties
And long-leggety beasties
And things that go "bump" in the night,
Oh Lord, deliver us.

Cornish Prayer

Most adults also learn to have irrational fears, at times bordering on phobias. Among the common everyday fears are those of the dark, thunder and lightning, corpses and graveyards, and snakes, spiders, and creeping things. Other people are afraid of crowds, afraid to cross the street, to stand near an open window, or to cross a bridge. Still others learn to have a pathological fear of dirt, germs, and disease. It is characteristic of the phobic patient to recognize that the fear is foolish and unreasonable. At the same time he is unable to do anything about it. The fear is magnified out of proportion to the actual situation. As a result, the patient is likely to show other symptoms such as headaches, backache, stomach upset, dizzy spells, and feelings of insecurity and inferiority.

Phobias have no respect for age, intellectual level, or social position. They can attack anyone. Chopin had an intense fear of being buried alive; Arthur Schopenhauer, the German philosopher, was so frightened of razors that he singed his beard rather than shave it; Henry III of France was afraid of eggs and became terrified at the sight of them. A prominent labor leader was well known for his fear of germs. He had his New York office equipped with ultraviolet germ-killing devices, and in a handshake he used only one finger.

The phobia is in some cases a projection of the individual's anxiety to the outer world. The inner conflicts are externalized, and it becomes easier for the person to cope with the danger. External threatening situations, especially of a symbolic nature, are usually less difficult to handle than threatening conflicts buried deep within oneself. The fear of the dark, high places, men or women, animals, or sharp objects may serve as a personality defense. The disturbing nature of diffuse anxiety is avoided by focusing anxiety on a single object. In such cases, the phobic object becomes the center of all anxiety and makes it possible for the person to deal more effectively with his anxious feelings.

Psychoanalysts believe that the basic dynamic processes involved in the phobic reaction are symbolism and substitution. Through symbolism, it is possible for the phobic object to represent the real feared object in a way in which it can be more readily handled. In the classic case of Little Hans, a five-year-old boy was afraid of horses instead of his father (Freud, 1959). The boy could handle the fear of horses more effectively than the fear of his father. Similarly, the person who shows a pathological fear reaction to thunder is seldom afraid of loud noises as such. The thunder may be symbolic, as in the case of a young married woman who developed a neurotic fear of thunder during an extramarital affair. Her fear became so overwhelming that it was necessary for her to seek psychiatric help. During her treatment, it was found that at the unconscious level she associated thunder with the voice of her disapproving father. At a deeper level, the thunder might have been the voice of her conscience or even the voice of God. The phobia in this case was apparently a response to guilt feelings and a neurotic attempt to protect the woman from her misbehavior.

While phobic reactions are frequently stated in terms of psychoanalytic theory, most phobias can be explained on the basis of conditioned learning. In a classic experiment, a nine-month-old child was presented with a white rat. Each time the child reached out to pet the animal, a loud and frightening noise occurred. The child cried and retreated. After a few repetitions of this situation, the child began to show increasing fear at the mere sight of the rat (Watson and Rayner, 1920). In a somewhat similar way, phobias may be communicated to children by their parents. The mother who is afraid of lightning and thunder will ordinarily condition her children to have a similar fear. The fear of animals may be a generalization of an earlier and more specific fear of a cat or dog.

The phobia, like all neurotic reactions, may have important secondary gains for the victim. The irrational fear brings sympathy and increased attention, elicits help and assistance from others, or may be a means for dominating and controlling members of the family or other significant persons. It is for this reason that a phobic reaction may persist long after the primary need being satisfied by the phobia no longer exists. The individual learns that there are other advantages to the symptom, and consequently he is reluctant to give it up.

Most of the phobias have been given technical names. In practice these terms are seldom used, although they do appear from time to time in the literature. Some of the more common phobias are claustrophobia, or the fear of small closed places; aichmophobia, the fear of pointed objects; agoraphobia, the fear of open places; and acrophobia, the fear of heights.

The word *claustrophobia*, which first appeared in the literature in 1879, means a morbid fear of closed places. This pathological fear is probably the most common of all phobias. For its victims, the world is often a terrifying place. Airplanes, elevators, railroad cars, buses, and automobiles are all small, closed spaces. In some patients the urge to jump from a vehicle is so great that travel becomes almost impossible. A New York man who travels to work on the subway is so tense and anxious that he must get out at five or six different stations on his way to and from his job. He stands on the platform until he calms down; then he takes the next train.

Some of the most serious cases of claustrophobia are seen during a war. A soldier who was decorated for bravery in the face of enemy fire was reduced to a state of terror at the thought of being confined in a foxhole or a dugout. He preferred to lie flat on the ground out in the open even though he knew his chances of survival were lessened. "I would rather die," he declared, "than be cooped up in a hole in the ground." Similar explanations are given by other soldiers. For many of these men, the fear of battle and combat is nothing compared with their fear of being confined in a small space. When victims of claustrophobia are sent to jail, they may develop such severe physical and mental symptoms that it becomes necessary to admit them to the prison hospital. The terror of the confined prisoner is portrayed vividly in John Galsworthy's drama *Justice*.

The fear of closed spaces sometimes has a symbolic meaning. One man developed the idea that he was "in a hole" as far as his ambitions were concerned. This idea was carried over to the fear of small, enclosed spaces which unconsciously reminded him of being in a hole. It is also possible for claustrophobia to be related to death fantasies. The fear of being buried, and especially of being buried alive, is a fantasy that may start in childhood and continue into adult life. In such cases, the fear of small closed spaces may be symbolic of the grave and of burial.

Claustrophobia is also associated at times with dreams and fantasies concerning the birth experience. According to this theory, the fear of entering an enclosed space has among its ideas the one that the enclosure is the mother's body. It is assumed that the repressed memory of birth is behind the fear. Another theory advanced to explain claustrophobia is that the condition is a defense against unconscious narcissism. Being alone in small rooms, according to this view, reactivates infantile and childhood autoerotic fantasies. The phobia thus becomes a defense against the threat of sexual impulses.

In some cases of claustrophobia, the overwhelming fear can be traced back to early terrifying experiences. One youngster had been locked up in a closet as punishment at the age of five. Another child was accidentally trapped in the cellar of an old building. Still another lost his way in an abandoned mine shaft. In each of these cases, the original experience was repressed and forgotten. Later in life, however, the phobia developed as a symptom of the unconscious preoccupation with the early incident.

In *aichmophobia* the individual develops a pathological fear of sharp and pointed objects. He fears pieces of broken glass, scraps of metal, tin, nails, and scissors. Fear of this kind leads to all sorts of eccentric habits. One man must eat with his fingers because of his fear of a knife and fork. Another can eat only when he uses a blunt wooden spoon. A young woman is unable to sign her name because she is afraid of pencils and pens.

Phobias of this kind are not difficult to explain in some cases. A pointed object may represent an offensive weapon either against oneself or against some other person. It may be a means of harming and wounding. Since there are people who harbor within themselves the wish for their own destruction, this type of phobia may be a defense reaction against thoughts of suicide. If the aggression is directed toward other people rather than toward the person himself, the aichmophobia may be a reaction formation against the fear that pointed objects will be used to harm someone else. The impulse to punish and injure other people is not uncommon. When this feeling is developed to an exaggerated degree, a phobia may be the way by which such unacceptable impulses are kept under control.

The fear of pointed objects may also be interpreted in terms of its sexual symbolism. The knife may represent the male sex organ. A woman with a fear of pointed objects may have a fear of the sex relationship. She may be afraid of being harmed, injured, or mutilated during the sex act. In men, the fear of pointed objects may be a reaction formation against latent homosexuality. The fear may be one of attacking someone else on a homosexual basis or of being attacked by a homosexual.

The word *agoraphobia,* which is derived from the Greek word *agora,* meaning "marketplace," was first used in 1873. The condition refers to a pathological fear of open or public places. In such cases, the person develops sudden attacks of anxiety when he is faced with the problem of crossing a wide street or an open square. He may be afraid to go out or to leave his home. Some people remain in their houses or locked in hotel rooms for months and even years at a time.

The unwillingness to go out may have a symbolic meaning. "Going out" suggests emancipation and independence. It implies being on one's own, competing with other people, and leaving the protected environment. In this sense, the fear of going out means detachment from maternal dependence. Such people may be saying, "I am afraid to face the world alone" or "I am afraid to be separated from my mother." This type of fear is based on the idea that the world is filled with dangers and that the person is helpless to overcome them. The easiest way to solve the problem is to avoid danger by not going out. If the person does not go out, he cannot get into trouble. The fear of going out also may be a reaction formation against an underlying exhibitionism. Since some

people have a strong need to show off and to be admired, the fear of going out could serve as a protection against a deeper fear that the person might expose himself in some way. For women, the fear of going out has another possible implication. To go out on the street may arouse prostitution anxiety. The fear may be a defense against an unconscious need to prostitute oneself.

■ AGORAPHOBIA

Ellen R., a thirty-two-year-old woman, developed a severe case of agoraphobia in which she became terrified each time she attempted to leave her house. The phobia became so serious that she gave up her job and remained home at all times. When she sought psychological help, it was found that when she was in her early teens she had been sexually promiscuous with several boys in the neighborhood. The patient changed her behavior when the family moved to another neighborhood, and she entered a new school. She experienced intense guilt feelings about her behavior, and she repressed all memories for it. The phobia which developed later in her life was based on the fear that she might lose control of herself, and be led into a life of prostitution. Without realizing what had happened, the patient had reactivated the entire episode some weeks earlier when she was going through some old papers and found a group photograph of herself at the time she had been promiscuous. The chain of unconscious associations triggered by the picture was responsible for the appearance of the agoraphobia at that particular time.

Acrophobia is a morbid fear of high places; acrophobic victims are afraid to look out an open window or over a high ledge. Their knees feel weak, and they begin to tremble and shake. They may become dizzy and feel nauseated. Some people with this phobia say they are afraid they will fall; others quite frankly fear they might jump. The motivating factor in some cases of acrophobia is the defense against self-destructive impulses. The analysis of such cases suggests that in at least some people there is an underlying suicidal impulse due to repressed feelings of guilt. The person who consciously fears he might jump from a high place may be responding on the conscious level to an unconscious wish to destroy himself. Since such wishes are present in many people, it is not surprising that acrophobia is one of the more common pathological fears.

Figure 8.4 *A lithograph by Rockwell Kent suggesting the fear of falling. (Philadelphia Museum of Art.)*

OBSESSIONS AND COMPULSIONS

In the obsessive-compulsive neurotic disorder, the individual is plagued by unwelcome recurring ideas, called obsessions, which are accompanied in many cases by unwelcome repetitive actions, called compulsions. While obsessive ideas are sometimes present without the accompanying compulsive actions, the two symptoms are combined in most cases. Just as the phobia is a development of the anxiety reaction, the obsessive-compulsive reaction is a further development of the phobia. In its very nature, obsessive-compulsive behavior implies fear and anxiety and the effort to control these emotions.

The obsessive-compulsive reaction has been described in the following way:

> In this reaction the anxiety is associated with the persistence of unwanted ideas and of repetitive impulses to perform acts which may be considered morbid by

the patient. The patient himself may regard his ideas and behavior as unreasonable, but nevertheless is compelled to carry out his ritual (DSM-II, 1968).

The obsession is an idea or thought that is silly, absurd, or apparently meaningless; yet the individual is unable to get rid of it. Many people experience obsessive reactions when a catchy tune, a slang phrase, or a bit of nonsense keeps coming to mind, even though they do not want to think about it. When this happens, the individual is literally obsessed by the idea.

Compulsions are obsessions carried into action. People who suffer from compulsions repeat certain actions over and over again, even though they realize there is no sense to it. When asked why they do these things, they reply that they feel uncomfortable and uneasy if they do not do them. Some people have the compulsion to snap their fingers, tap their feet, or repeat a word or phrase. A lawyer had to make a slight bow before he could enter a door either at home or elsewhere. He managed to live with his compulsion for many years with only a few people knowing about it.

As early as 1896, Freud described compulsive behavior in a young boy:

> An 11-year-old boy had instituted the following obsessive ceremonial before going to bed. He did not sleep until he had told his mother in the minutest detail all the events of the day; there must be no scraps of paper or other rubbish on the carpet of the bedroom; the bed must be pushed right to the wall; three chairs must stand by it and the pillows must lie in a particular way. In order to get to sleep he must first kick out a certain number of times with both legs and then lie on his side (Freud, 1896).

Obsessions and compulsions occur together so frequently that ordinarily they are considered to be a single reaction. In some cases the obsessive quality is outstanding, without any overt action that could be called a compulsion. In other cases, the obsession is accompanied by compulsive actions. While it is possible for a person to show obsessive thinking without a compulsion, compulsive behavior is always based upon an obsession.

The early signs of obsessive-compulsive behavior sometimes may be seen in childhood. There are youngsters who must touch each fence post while walking down the street. A small boy could not cross a crack in the sidewalk without stepping squarely on it. If he suspected that he missed one or that he stepped on it in such a way that it ran under the arch of his foot so that his shoe did not actually touch the groove, he had to return and step on it again. Whenever his mother tried to interfere with this ritual, he flew into a violent temper tantrum.

> Step on a crack,
> Break your mother's back.
> *Children's Rhyme*

While the prognosis for obsessive-compulsive reactions is good when the disorder is seen in children, it is less favorable when the condition begins during adolescence and the adult years. Because of the disabling nature of the symptoms, some psychologists and psychiatrists are inclined to view this reaction as a link between the neuroses and the psychoses.

In terms of psychodynamics, obsessions and compulsions are bits of behavior designed, in some cases, to protect the victim from the pain of realizing how afraid he really is. The writings of Edgar Allen Poe, Thomas Wolfe, Knut Hamsun, and Marcel Proust are filled with examples of obsessive-compulsive behavior. In the case of Wolfe and Proust, the writing itself appears to be a symptom of a compulsion.

Obsessive-compulsive conditions may also serve as a protection from aggressive feelings against others. Whenever resentment and frustrations build up within an individual and unconscious feelings of aggression develop, there is a possibility that an obsession will express itself. A wife was obsessed with the idea that in some way she might poison her husband. In another case, a kindergarten teacher was obsessed each day with the idea that she would reach out and choke one of her young charges as they filed into the classroom. Another young woman could not ride in a streetcar because the thought always came to her that a man might fall under the wheels. One patient said that he could not bear to have pointed objects near his eyes. He said, "I feel I want to gouge out my eyes."

■ OBSESSIVE-COMPULSIVE REACTION

Myra Y. is a young married schoolteacher who was referred for treatment because of her disturbing thoughts about her husband. Whenever she was alone, she worried that he might have been in an accident. If she heard a siren in the distance, she began to shake and tremble, being certain that an ambulance was carrying her husband to the hospital. The symptoms became so serious that she was in an almost constant state of panic when her husband was away. In desperation she sought professional help. During her treatment she admitted that her marriage had been a failure, and that secretly she wished for her freedom. It was not difficult to show this patient that her obsession was based on her hostility toward the husband. At the unconscious level she hoped something would happen to him, and the obsession was a reaction formation against the unconscious wish.

It is not unusual for mothers to have obsessive thoughts about choking, drowning, or smothering their children, while expectant mothers are sometimes obsessed with the idea that they will somehow harm or kill their child. One woman, during

Figure 8.5 A Man in Love, *a lithograph by Paul Klee suggesting a sexual obsession. The man's head is filled with sexual symbols. (Philadelphia Museum of Art.)*

her pregnancy, began imagining she might burn her baby after it was born. Another woman was afraid she would squeeze it to death. Fortunately, such thoughts are seldom carried into action. When such obsessions are not conscious, they are frequently very close to consciousness and may be revealed in dream life.

Obsessive-compulsive behavior may also be a form of self-protection. Aggressive feelings toward oneself result in a wide variety of obsessive ideas. One man became obsessed with the idea that he would drive his car off the side of the road and over an embankment. While driving, he would grip the steering wheel so tightly that sometimes it became necessary for him to stop the car and rest. Another had the idea that he might cut his throat while shaving. Still another was obsessed with the idea that he might jump off a high place. A woman developed the idea that there might be broken glass in her food. Before she could eat, it was necessary for her to sift through everything on her plate to make certain that there was no broken glass in it. A similar case was one in which a man could not drink his coffee for fear a pin might have dropped into it. He would pour his beverage back and forth several times to make absolutely certain that a pin was not there.

Some obsessions are so powerful that the individual goes to great lengths to protect himself from what he might do to himself or to others. One man made a ceremony of locking his door every night, hiding the key, putting chairs in front of his bed, and stretching strings across the room. When asked why he did these things, he was unable to give a satisfactory reason. When he sought help, it was found that his "protective ritual" was based upon an unconscious fear that he would leave his bed while sleeping and harm his wife and children.

Other obsessive-compulsive reactions appear to be motivated by the need to get rid of guilt feelings. One of the most common compulsions of this type is the compulsion to wash, scrub, and be clean. Some people develop elaborate rituals which are learned defensive mechanisms to wipe out the guilt feelings that would result if the original impulses were satisfied. In some cases, such compulsions protect against guilt feelings connected with infantile sexuality. Compulsive washing, for example, may be a symbolic attempt to

cleanse oneself of a real or imagined "sin." Pontius Pilate typified the symbolic nature of compulsive hand-washing when he took water and washed his hands before the multitude saying, "I am innocent of the blood of this person: see ye." The hand-washing of Lady Macbeth has the same symbolic significance.

The washing compulsion was so strong in one woman that she would find it necessary to go into a drugstore and ask for a glass of water. She would then wash her fingers. Sometimes this ritual occurred as often as a dozen times during a visit to the city. Another woman covered the door handles in her house with pieces of paper to keep from becoming contaminated. Still another had to wash her hands several dozen times a day. She washed her hands over and over until the skin was red and raw. She wore gloves constantly in order to protect herself against germs on objects that other people had touched.

■ OBSESSIVE-COMPULSIVE REACTION

Linda M. is a forty-year-old married woman who was referred for psychological treatment because she felt compelled to wash her hands fifty or sixty times a day, although she was unable to give any reason why she did this. During the course of treatment, the patient revealed that she is obsessed with the idea that she will reach out and touch people on their genital areas, although she has never done this and she realizes that such behavior is unlikely.

The housecleaning compulsion is closely related to the hand-washing compulsion. One woman scrubs, cleans, and washes so much that she does not finish her housework until the middle of the night. On one occasion she was polishing the furniture at four in the morning, and her husband complained that she was still cleaning when he got up to go to work. This kind of housekeeping is a form of compulsive orderliness that is sometimes mistaken for virtue.

The compulsive doubt may also be an expression of guilt feelings. Here the guilt centers on a sense of inadequacy and personal failure. Some people are never sure of themselves. They doubt that they can do a good job, that their husbands or wives are faithful, or that they are the real children of their parents. An automobile mechanic developed the idea that he was not the father of the eight-year-old daughter he had always adored. A fashion editor was obsessed by the idea that she no longer had the necessary talent for her job, and a schoolteacher so seriously doubted her ability to teach that she had to give up her work.

Many householders suffer compulsive doubts. They insist every evening before retiring upon making sure that the doors and windows are fastened, that the water faucets, gas jets, and electric lights are turned off, and that all the children are safely tucked in bed. They think they are being cautious. Actually, their actions may point to feelings of fear and personal insecurity.

The perfectionist may also be a victim of compulsive doubt. He may hold himself in high regard but not be completely certain that he deserves it. He hesitates to place his ability, aptitude, or talent on the line. It means that his work will be compared with that of others, with the ever-present risk of criticism and possible failure. Perfectionism may be a reaction formation against the fear that one is not really as able and as competent as one believes.

In addition to obsessive-compulsive impulses directly related to conflicts in the area of sex, aggression, and guilt, there are several forms of complex behavior which satisfy multiple needs of the patient. Typical of these forms of behavior are *kleptomania, pyromania,* and *hypochondria.*

In kleptomania there is a strong, and often uncontrollable, urge to steal. The behavior is differentiated from ordinary stealing by the fact that the act is impulsive and seemingly without reason. Department store managers, judges, and bewildered relatives are faced from time to time with habitual shoplifting on the part of an individual who has been carefully brought up, who is in good financial circumstances, and who has no need for what has been stolen. When such individuals are arrested by store detectives, they are frightened and humiliated and at a loss for an explanation of their strange conduct. All they can say is that the temptation seemed to sweep over them, and that they tried to resist it but felt driven to do it in spite of themselves.

One young woman had a compulsion to go into a certain department store to see if she could get out without paying for her lunch. She kept a record of 136 stolen meals. On the 137th meal she was caught. When asked why she did it, she said, "I

don't know. There is something in me that compels me to do it. I can't explain what it is."

Compulsive stealing, and the obsessive concern with such activity, has a number of possible psychodynamic explanations. The individual who is driven to steal impulsively and without apparent reason may be expressing a reaction against authority. Such behavior is a defiance of the police and the owners of the store, both of whom may represent parental figures. It is also possible that keptomania may be an expression of a more generalized hostility and aggression within the personality. In some cases, compulsive stealing appears to be related to a need to defy convention by engaging in activity completely contrary to the moral and ethical standards under which the person was raised. This type of reaction also contains elements of hostility.

The need for punishment is an important factor in kleptomania, since most neurotics of this type are quickly apprehended. It is as if the victim desires to be caught. At the unconscious level, it may be that certain compulsive neurotics of this kind do in fact have a need to be punished. The sexual element in compulsive stealing is also present in some cases, since people not infrequently describe erotic excitement associated with the act of stealing. The dangerous and forbidden element in such behavior may be associated with fantasies of sexual activities.

The obsessive-compulsive concern with fire is called pyromania, a term first introduced in 1883. In pyromania, the individual is preoccupied with the idea of fire and may have an overwhelming urge to set fires, even though the consequences are likely to be disastrous. A fourteen-year-old Baltimore boy admitted setting innumerable fires, one of which resulted in the death of two children and another of which caused a quarter of a million dollars of damage. A pyromaniac in Seattle set fire to 130 factories, warehouses, and similar structures over a period of four years. The property damage amounted to 6.5 million dollars. In another case, six fires were started in the hallways of six different apartment buildings on Third Avenue in New York City during a two-hour period shortly after midnight.

As in all neurotic reactions, the obsessive-compulsive preoccupation with fire and firesetting is open to a variety of interpretations.

The motivation for the behavior depends upon the individual case. Among the more common reasons for this type of neurotic behavior are the defiance of authority, the expression of hostility and aggression, and the attempt to resolve unconscious sexual conflict. Pyromania as a defiance of authority is easy to understand. In these cases, the fire-setting may be directed against a specific symbol of the person's defiance, as in the case of the professor who set fire to a university building, or it may be directed against authority in general. In these cases, the defiance is usually aimed at the police in their role of father image. Pyromaniacs of this type go about setting fires indiscriminately. The building chosen is of little or no importance. The major factor is the defiant act. Similarly, pyromania as an aggressive act is relatively uncomplicated. The victim has deep inner hostilities, often of a sadistic kind, which are satisfied by setting fires and endangering lives. The obsessive ideas and compulsive actions are a means of expressing the aggressive impulses in a direct, although neurotic, manner.

At a deeper level of interpretation, there appears to be an unconscious sexual element in some cases of pyromania. Fire has always been a powerful symbol of sexuality. People speak of the "flame of love" and "the fire of passion." Men and women who are sexually excited, or excitable, are said to be "on fire" or "hot." To "play with fire" is to indulge in a dangerous or forbidden affair. When we are jealous, we are "burned up." Former girl friends are "old flames." All such expressions grow out of the unconscious acceptance of the erotic symbolism of fire.

HYPOCHONDRIA

This neurotic reaction was added to the standard classification system by the 1968 revision of the Diagnostic and Statistical Manual (DSM-II), although the term *hypochondria* has a long history in medicine. The word itself refers to the area below the ribs, the part of the body considered by the ancient Greek physicians to be the seat of the black bile which caused melancholy. Later, the term came to be used for all forms of physical complaints that were without an organic basis.

In hypochondira, a person believes he has a physical disease when there is no real evidence for such a disease. It is an extreme preoccupation with bodily functions. Marcel Proust, the French novelist, began talking about his ill health and predicting his imminent death in 1900. He died twenty-two years later. Thousands of people experience this neurotic concern over nonexistent illness.

Symptoms of almost every kind of disease are seen in hypochondria. One man said, "My troubles read like a mail-order catalog list." Cancer, diabetes, kidney and liver disease, tuberculosis, pleurisy, anemia, heart disease, rheumatism, or syphilis may be the imagined cause of the overconcern. *The Anatomy of Melancholy*, published in the seventeenth century, described the hypochondriac's symptoms as "sharp belchings, wind and rumbling in the guts, vehement gripings, suffocation, palpitation, heaviness of the heart, singing in the ears, and unseasonable sweat all over the body" (Burton, 1651).

Hypochondria is a frequent subject in literature. A classic example of hypochondria is the character Argan in Moliere's play *The Imaginary Invalid*. Similarly, Jules Romains wrote a play about an enterprising physician, Dr. Knock, who systematically set out to develop hypochondria in every man, woman, and child in his village.

Obsessive ideas and compulsive acts concerning health grow out of a wide variety of psychodynamic situations. Among the more common reasons for the adoption of neurotic symptoms of this type are the need for attention and the effort to escape life's problems through rationalization. When people find themselves losing importance and prestige, they may learn to develop attention-getting devices. Complaining about ill health is one way of getting other people to pay attention to them. They adopt the role of a sick or disabled person because they know that their families and friends will rally around them, give them more attention, and cater to their wishes. The hypochondriac grows into a household tyrant who must have special food and dress, the most comfortable chair and the best bed, entertainment as desired, and quiet when ordered.

Elizabeth Barrett Browning fell from a pony when she was fifteen years old and remained an invalid for the next twenty years. Her illness spared her competition with her brothers and sisters. Moreover, she received extra care and attention, she had a room of her own, and she fared quite well. Even as her literary career grew, she kept her symptoms. However, when she was forty, she met Robert Browning, who was six years younger. They married, and Elizabeth's symptoms promptly disappeared. At forty-one she was climbing a mountain. At forty-three, she had a child. She was no longer a hypochondriac because she no longer needed her symptoms.

A somewhat different reason for the compulsive preoccupation with health is that it becomes a way of escaping the anxiety associated with inadequacy, inferiority, and failure. In these cases the hypochondria serves as a rationalization. A young man complained of a pain in his leg after he lost a contest at school. The pain was a convenient excuse for the next twenty years. Whenever he felt he was losing a golf game or a tennis match, the pain in his leg served as a rationalization for not doing better. The hypochondriacal symptom becomes a neurotic convenience. If one is sick or in pain, poor performance is excused. Mediocre achievements may even be rewarded with praise which would not otherwise be forthcoming.

■ HYPOCHONDRIA

John M. is a thirty-one-year-old married man who was admitted to a psychiatric hospital. He had an eighth-grade education, and lived with his parents until his marriage. He worked for two years as a messenger with the Western Union Telegraph Company, but then was discharged because he was sending telegrams through the mail instead of delivering them to the homes.

The patient came from an emotionally and economically deprived environment and was hospitalized for tuberculosis for two years. Following his release from the hospital, he was referred to the Bureau of Vocational Rehabilitation where he pursued a night course in commercial subjects to prepare him for clerical work. He married a girl of extremely limited intelligence, and they have a five-year-old son. John's mother is an emotionally unstable individual, and his father has been a dependent and inadequate person who has never been able to hold steady employment. His sister, who is a patient at the same hospital, has a diagnosis of schizophrenia.

The present illness began with multiple complaints about physical health. The patient said that one day while he was playing with his five-year-old son, he suddenly felt a "jump" and he realized that his "glands were swollen and hurt." He became extremely preoccupied about this, and went from doctor to doctor insisting upon having treatments, but nothing seemed to help him. He was then referred to a psychiatrist; and since his behavior became so centered on his physical complaints that he could not work, he was sent to the hospital.

The patient is a tall, thin individual who is alert, responsive, and well oriented. He is friendly and pleasant, with a clinging, extremely docile and suggestible manner. He has a wide emotional range, expressing deep concern about his physical health and, a few moments later, flashing a friendly smile in response to a question. His thinking is clear and rational except for his preoccupation with his health. He thinks his sex glands have been infected, that he has a hernia, and that he is severely constipated. He complains of feelings of tightness and pain in his abdomen. During the interview, the patient was mildly anxious with some restlessness, but motor behavior was generally unremarkable.*

There is a general impression that the incidence of hypochondriacal reactions is rising. If such is the case, part of the explanation may be found in the various health campaigns and the preoccupation with physical illness and disability. While public health information is certainly desirable, there has been a somewhat indiscriminate publicizing of a number of diseases. The undesirable effect of confronting people with too much information about illness and disease was brought into focus by a weekly television series in Great Britain. This series consisted of ten programs, each showing the work of a different hospital in relation to a specific disease. The British Broadcasting Corporation said the purpose was to satisfy the public's "healthy interest in disease," to display the fine quality of medicine in Great Britain, and to allay fears about going into hospitals. The British Medical Association, on the other hand, accused the BBC of fostering hypochondria, pandering—by including films of surgical procedures—to a desire for sensationalism, and invading doctor-patient relationships. When the film series was put on, two viewers took their lives

---

*Case 2 of audiotape 5, "Psychoneurotic Disorders," in *Case Interviews to Accompany The Disorganized Personality.*

in the belief they had cancer, and a third viewer about to undergo a heart operation committed suicide after seeing the operation performed on television.

NEURASTHENIA

Another new category of neurosis added to the standard classification system in 1968 is *neurasthenia,* a reaction marked by lack of energy, fatigue, physical complaints, and general debility. The term neurasthenia is not a new one, although it does not have the ancient origins of hypochondria. Neurasthenia was introduced nearly a hundred years ago by an American psychiatrist in the book *A Practical Treatise on Nervous Exhaustion* (Beard, 1880). The word itself means "weakness of the nerves" and clearly reflects the now abandoned idea that the neuroses had an organic basis.

Various theories have been advanced to explain the neurasthenic reaction. The physician who introduced the term believed the condition to be due to a weakening of the nerve cells produced by overwork. Russian neurophysiologists emphasized the importance of excessive excitation of the nerve cells of the brain. Some physicians placed the blame on masturbation. Eventually the disturbance was attributed to prolonged emotional tension. Today the condition is regarded as a learned reaction to stress in individuals with inborn low energy levels.

In this neurotic condition the individual is literally in a continuing state of exhaustion. He is tired from morning until night, and even the mildest exertion causes great fatigue. In addition to the fatigue, such individuals show many bodily symptoms and complaints. Muscular pains, backaches, cramps, headaches, sleeplessness, difficulty in swallowing, and poor appetitie are only a few of the disturbances experienced by the neurasthenic.

Neurasthenia is differentiated from the asthenic type of personality disorder (see Chapter 7) on the basis of the amount of anxiety that is present.

In the personality disorders, anxiety is not an important part of the clinical picture. But in neurasthenia, as in all neuroses, anxiety is a key factor in the condition. This anxiety may be expressed at the conscious level, or it may remain partially or completely hidden.

HYSTERIA

The hysterical neurosis is one in which there is an involuntary loss or disorder of function. As in the case of all neurotic reactions, the condition is caused by psychological conflict rather than by organic disturbance. The symptoms of the hysterical neurosis, which usually begin and end in emotionally charged situations, are symbolic of the underlying conflicts.

From the time of Hippocrates, hysteria carried a broad meaning and included a great many different symptoms. Among the ancient Greeks, the disorder was thought to be a disease of women resulting from a disturbance of the uterus. This theory was held for many centuries, although in the sixteenth century it was believed that the cause of hysteria was not in the uterus but in the brain. It was argued that since this is the case, hysteria is a disorder of men as well as of women. Such an idea was extremely advanced, and the medical profession was not ready for it. It was not until 250 years later that Sigmund Freud was able to convince the world that hysteria occurs in men as well as women.

For reasons which are largely cultural, the incidence of hysterical neurosis has decreased in recent years. The dramatic acting out of inner conflicts by means of obvious symptoms of the voluntary nervous system was relatively common in Victorian society. As late as World War I, hysterical reactions were seen frequently, particularly among enlisted men. However, the incidence of such reactions during World War II was greatly decreased because of our higher level of psychological sophistication. The trend has been to the more subtle expression of neurotic symptoms through the involuntary nervous system.[3]

---

[3]The history and nature of hysteria are discussed in detail in Ilza Veith's *Hysteria: The History of a Disease* (University of Chicago Press, 1965) and in *Hysteria and Related Mental Disorders* (Wright, 1966) by D. W. Abse.

There are two major types of hysterical neurosis: (1) the conversion reaction, and (2) the dissociative reaction.

CONVERSION REACTION

Through an accident of historical development, only sensory and motor symptoms are considered to be *conversion reactions*. When the underlying psychological conflicts are converted into symptoms expressed through the autonomic nervous system, the condition is called a *psychophysiologic reaction*. This type of reaction is discussed in detail in Chapter 9.

Sensory Symptoms

The sensory symptoms of the conversion reaction may involve any one or more of the sense modalities. Disturbances of taste, smell, equilibrium, and visceral sensation are observed rather infrequently. The major sensory symptoms involve disturbances of skin sensation, vision, and hearing.

Anesthesia, or lack of skin sensation, is one of the most common conversion reactions. When anxiety becomes too great, the individual may seek to escape by drawing a "cloak of anesthesia" around himself. He no longer feels pain. It is possible to stick him with sharp objects, and he does not draw away. In some cases, a needle can be pressed under the fingernail without causing him to flinch.

The notorious "devil's claw," used during the Middle Ages as a sign of demon possession, was probably a conversion reaction. The part of the skin insensitive to pain, which was considered to be a place on the body where the Devil had laid his hand, was simply an area of localized anesthesia. Highly suggestible people, under the stress of superstition and fear, developed the type of symptom expected for them. Many hundreds, if not thousands, of men and women were put to death as witches when in fact they were showing neurotic symptoms of the conversion type.

It is not unusual to find the lack of pain sensation restricted to one part of the body. In glove anesthesia the condition involves the entire hand to the wrist, or the arm to the elbow. A stocking anesthesia covers that part of the leg ordinarily covered by a stocking. In other cases, the anesthesia involves one or the other side of the body. The psychological nature of the anesthesia is shown clearly by the fact that the areas of insensitivity follow the patient's idea of nerve supply, rather than the real nerve distribution, which is irregular and overlapping. It is also possible to have a psychological oversensitivity of the skin (hyperesthesia) or a disturbance of skin sensation (paresthesia) in which the patient experiences "tingling," "pins and needles," and "crawling" sensations.

Similarly, the emotions of man are linked very closely with vision. Sometimes a student's eyes are too "tired" to read the assignments he brings home from the university; father's eyes "hurt" so much that he postpones trying to figure out his tangled income tax return; or mother's eyes "bother" her, and she is unable to take the children to the movies. In most of these cases, there is nothing physically wrong with the eyes. The visual symptom is an unconscious rebellion against doing something unpleasant.

Visual conversion symptoms involve a variety of psychodynamic relationships. A middle-aged woman was brought to a clinic after some of the best eye specialists in the country had been unable to discover the cause of her blindness. At the clinic her story was uncovered. She had married, and her first and only child was a girl. She was disappointed because her heart had been set on a boy. The result was that she was not very kind to the little girl during the early years. When the daughter grew older she sensed her mother's dislike, and gradually she came to hate her mother because of it. The mother began to feel guilty about the way she had treated the girl, but it was already too late. The girl's hatred grew more intense each year. One day the mother suddenly went blind. She was trying not to see her daughter's hatred for her. Through psychological treatment, her vision was restored.

Some of the most dramatic examples of conversion blindness are seen during the time of war. As described in Chapter 6, the hardships and horrors of war frequently cause soldiers to break down and show severe psychological symptoms. Following the evacuation of Dunkirk during World War II, a number of acute cases of conversion blindness were seen in British

Figure 8.6   *The progressive restriction of the visual field in tunnel vision. (Courtesy of Merck Sharp and Dohme.)*

hospitals. In almost every case the blindness resulted from the patient's refusal to watch the horrors of the combat. One soldier became blind moments after he had seen a very close friend blown apart by an exploding shell. Another patient lost his sight after one glance at his own mangled leg.

In most cases, conversion reactions are limited to less serious symptoms than blindness. In *tunnel vision*, the patient manages to hang onto a tiny area of clear vision, but the area is so small that he can only see straight ahead. To see anything at either side, he must turn his head. Such patients may have the visual field so restricted that they find it difficult to read their newspapers because they can see only a few words at a time.

A young man suffered from tunnel vision for almost five years. He was examined by several eye specialists; and while they agreed that there was nothing organically wrong with his eyes, they seemed unable to find the cause. Finally the patient was told that his trouble was emotional and not physical. A psychological study of the case revealed one source of his difficulty. The condition started when the man became annoyed with the sloppy appearance of his wife. Since he was afraid to say anything about it, the tunnel vision apparently made it possible for him to be in the same room with her and yet not have to look at her unless he turned his head and looked straight at her.

Color blindness also occasionally occurs as a conversion reaction. Some people are blind for one color but not for others. One man could see all colors clearly except for red, which appeared to him as an indistinct gray. In this case it was possible to trace the difficulty to an automobile accident in which the man saw his mother covered with blood. From that time on, the color red was blotted from his memory. Functional color blindness of this type can be detected without much difficulty in most cases because the loss of the color sense usually does not correspond to the facts of color vision. Organic color blindness follows a definite pattern of color loss. When this pattern is not followed, it is likely that the color blindness is psychological.

Conversion symptoms involving hearing also are relatively frequent. It is common observation in everyday life that many people fail to hear things they do not want to hear. The child who is playing does not hear the mother calling, the young suitor fails to hear the clock, and the reluctant student does not hear the school bell. In conversion reactions, the person may become deaf so he does not hear the unpleasant things the world has to say.

A young man lost his hearing just before the war. He became so upset each time he heard the radio announcer with the war news that he used deafness to solve the problem. Unconsciously he said to himself, "If I am deaf, I will not be able to hear the bad news." During the war, especially in London and other cities exposed to bombing, cases of psychogenic deafness sometimes developed as a means of shutting out the unwelcome sounds of explosions, bells, sirens, and the screams of the injured.

Motor Symptoms

The motor symptoms of the conversion nuerosis are expressed in a variety of ways. The less serious symptoms include trembling, tic-like movements, and minor cramps and contractions of muscles. The more serious symptoms, or at least the more dramatic, involve disorders of speech, paralyzed limbs, and convulsive seizures. In many cases, the conversion symptoms closely resemble the symptoms of organic disease and disability.

One of the most common conversion reactions is *psychological tremor*, or trembling, usually of the hands. While tremors may be caused by organic conditions such as palsy and alcoholism, some people have tremors that are emotionally determined. Most people have experienced such tremors at one time or another. We tremble when we are in an accident, when we are angry, and sometimes when we are in love.

Intentional tremors are more persistent and appear when the individual is about to perform some specific movement. A person may develop a tremor of this type when he picks up a pen to write, when he takes hold of a tool he uses in his occupation, or when he is about to type, play a musical instrument, or push a button. These occupational tremors sometimes reveal inner conflict related to the work situation. If a man is not happy as a mechanic, he may tremble when he tries to handle the tools; if he is a dissatisfied musician, his hands shake when he picks up his instrument; if he is frustrated as a dentist, he trembles when he takes hold of the drill. The tremor becomes a part of the defense against the conflict and anxiety surrounding the work.

The *tic* is another motor conversion symptom. This condition is an involuntary repeated movement or twitching of the muscles of some part of the face, neck, head, or extremities. It may be a turning of the head, a winking of the eyelid, or a twitching of the corner of the mouth. Usually these movements are automatic and occur without the person being aware of them.

While it is quite possible for such movements to be based on a disorder of the nerve supply to the particular muscle group involved, it is more common for the tic to be purely psychological and to arise from an inner conflict situation. At one time it was thought that the tic movements were meaningless, but psychodynamic theory has taught us that such movements often have disguised and symbolic meaning.

Such conversion symptoms as *cramps* and *contractures* are also seen in connection with the occupational neuroses. In these conditions, the muscular disturbance may serve to protect a person from the necessity of continuing a type of work which consciously or unconsciously is uncongenial. The psychodynamics of this type of neurotic reaction are illustrated in the case of writer's cramp. Thousands of people dream of becoming writers. Some are foolish enough to announce to their friends that they are going to make a career of writing. They begin to write and send their work to magazines. To their chagrin, they find that they receive rejection slips instead of the fat checks they expected. The more they write, the more rejection slips they collect. Their friends begin to question them about their writing. They want to know when something will be published. The would-be writer finds it impossible to admit to himself, or to his friends, that there is little possibility that anything he writes will ever be bought and published. The result is that he develops a conversion symptom—a psychological cramp of the hand—that makes it impossible for him to hold a pen or pencil. Under such conditions, no one would expect him to earn his living by writing. Instead of being ridiculed, he gains the sympathy and commiseration of friends and family.

The most common conversion reactions involving the speech mechanism are *aphonia, mutism,* and certain types of *stuttering.* Aphonia is the inability to speak above a whisper. The patient can make himself heard and understood, but his voice is barely audible. Mutism is a more serious condition in which there is an inability to say anything at all. Such conditions have been recognized for many years. A case was reported in the seventeenth century in which a man was completely mute except for one hour between noon and 1 P.M.

Most people have experienced some degree of aphonia or mutism at one time or another. The child who is suddenly confronted by an irate parent may "lose his voice." He may want to say something but finds that words simply do not come. The youngster who stands up to recite his first poem in the school auditorium opens his mouth and finds that nothing comes out or that his voice is an almost inaudible whisper. Many adults face similar situations. An employee is unable to speak when he finds himself face to face with the boss; and the GI is speechless when he looks up to find the commanding general glowering at him.

The conversion paralysis is one of the most dramatic of the motor conversion reactions. The intuitive recognition of the possibiltiy of such a condition is revealed clearly in our everyday language. Such phrases as "paralyzed with fear," "scared stiff," or "glued to the spot" are merely ways of indicating that emotional conflicts have been converted into physical symptoms. In some cases, the conversion paralysis becomes a preferred way of reacting to stress. A student nurse suddenly found her arms paralyzed when she was told to scrub the operating room floor stained with blood. A soldier became paralyzed when the order was given to attack the enemy. Another soldier, who started to cry out in fear, found that after he had opened his mouth he could not close it again, nor could he withdraw his tongue. Hours later, when the attack was over, his tongue gradually withdrew and his mouth closed again. A young seaman developed a paralysis of his arms when forced to clean up the mangled bodies of his shipmates.

■ CONVERSION REACTION

Fred K. is a fifty-year-old married man who developed a marked contracture of his left hand, and a partial paralysis of his arm. He held his arm bent in front of him, as if it were in a sling, and his fingers were curled inward toward the palm of his hand. He was unable to raise his arm above the level of his shoulder, and he could move his fingers only slightly.

The symptoms came on suddenly; and before he was referred for psychological treatment, the patient had undergone medical and neurological examinations by local physicians as well as by specialists at Roch-

ester, Cleveland, Baltimore, and Boston. Various diagnoses were made, including vertebral dislocation, with the recommendation of surgery on the spine. One medical center placed the patient in an elaborate traction device "to take the pressure off a pinched nerve." Other medical treatments were tried; but the patient did not respond, and the symptoms remained unaltered.

The psychological evaluation of this patient revealed that he was a well-to-do executive, that he was married to an attractive and considerably younger wife, and that while he seemed anxious to be cured of his disorder, there was nevertheless a remarkable casualness about it, and one sensed that the patient took a certain pride in it. He displayed his hand and arm with some satisfaction, demonstrating the lack of feeling by touching his lit cigarette to the back of his hand to show he felt no pain. The attitude of the patient toward his symptom, combined with the lack of positive neurological findings, pointed to the possibility of a conversion reaction. Psychotherapy was recommended; and at the end of several treatment hours, the symptom was removed. While it returned a few days later, the psychological nature of the disorder had been proved, and psychotherapy was continued.

It was clear to the therapist that the patient had been using his neurotic symptoms to solve his problems. His young and attractive wife was fond of nightclubs, while the patient merely wanted to come home at night, have dinner, read his paper, and go to bed. The difference in age and interests resulted in serious conflict. Finally, the wife began to go out without her husband. It was at this point that the symptoms appeared.

The paralysis served a number of purposes. It gave the patient a good excuse for staying home at night. After all, who would expect a man with a paralyzed arm to go to nightclubs? It also forced the patient's wife to spend more time with him at home in the evenings. Only the most callous wife would go out and leave her paralyzed husband at home alone. Moreover, the paralysis brought the patient the sympathy and attention of friends and relatives. Previously, being a rather colorless and uninteresting person, he had been overshadowed by his attractive and vivacious wife. Now he was the center of things. Finally, because the patient was jealous of his wife, and suspected her fidelity, he used his symptom as an excuse to come home from his office at any hour of the day. Sometimes he would return home, complaining about his arm, an hour after leaving in the morning.

Interestingly enough, the eventual cure in this case was not brought about through the efforts of a psychotherapist, but rather by a policeman! The patient's suspicions about his wife had not been unfounded, and one day he awoke to find that his wife had run off with a police officer. Days later, when he was convinced that his wife would never return to him, his symptom disappeared spontaneously. It had served its unconscious purpose, and he no longer had need of it. Without his wife and the problems of living with her, the symptom served no purpose.

In one of the most serious motor conversion reactions, the symptom takes the form of a *convulsive seizure*. Superficially, the attacks resemble the epileptic convulsion. However, important differences exist. The true epileptic usually experiences a warning, known as the *aura*, just before the attack. This aura may be a flash of light, a moment of dizziness, peculiar skin sensations, buzzing or ringing in the ears, or any one of a number of other sensations. In the psychogenic convulsion, the aura is not ordinarily present. Another point of difference is the cry the true epileptic makes when he falls to the ground. The cry, which occurs when air is forced out of the lungs and through the vocal organs as a result of the involuntary contraction of the muscles of the chest, is usually absent in the psychological convulsion. Nor does the person experiencing an emotionally determined convulsion show frothing at the mouth. In addition, such a person does not bite his tongue or lips, he seldom hurts himself when he falls, he does not lose control of his bladder and his bowels, the pattern of his brain waves is normal, and he is highly suggestible during the seizure.

The psychogenic convulsion, like other conversion reactions, is essentially an escape technique. There is always some difficulty the person is trying to avoid. He is attempting to reduce his anxiety by means of the seizure. Occasionally the psychological convulsion is an acting out of some early traumatic or shocking experience. In some cases, the convulsion appears to be a dramatization of the sexual act. Many of the movements, gestures, and facial expressions during the convulsion have an unmistakable erotic quality.

The problem of diagnosis of the conversion reaction is somewhat more complicated than the diagnosis of anxiety reactions, phobias, and obsessive-compulsive conditions. In the case of conversion reactions, the symptoms must be distinguished from true organic disorders, malingering, and incipient psychotic conditions in which there may be somatic delusions. The most difficult differential diagnosis is between the conversion reaction and symptoms resulting from organic impairment of the nervous system.

A characteristic of the conversion reaction is the lack of concern the victim has for his disability. Even though the symptom is a serious handicap to the person's activites, and even though he believes his symptom is incurable, he is inclined to regard it casually and almost indifferently. It is as if the person realizes unconsciously that the symptom is not truly organic. The patient with a serious organic disability is more likely to show real concern about his symptoms. He does not treat them lightly. He is anxious and preoccupied with them. The neurotic person does not show this same concern. He seems quite willing to accept an organic interpretation of his disability and resigns himself to the fact that probably nothing can be done about it.

There are other ways in which the conversion reaction can be distinguished from a true organic disability. In some cases, the conversion symptoms do not correspond to the facts of anatomy. Skin anesthesias may show sharp lines of demarcation between areas in which pain is felt and areas in which pain is not felt. However, the distribution of pain receptors in the skin is such that sharp lines of demarcation would be highly unlikely. As noted earlier, the anesthetic areas are likely to follow the popular conception of nerve distribution rather than the actual anatomic distribution.

The onset and course of the disability is another differentiating factor. In the conversion reaction, the onset is more likely to be sudden, and the symptom disappears entirely and then recurs. In contrast, the onset of the organic symptom is usually more insidious and shows a more consistent course.

A differential diagnosis between a conversion reaction and a true organic symptom must also include a consideration of the emotional stability of the individual. In people with a history of instability, there is a greater probability that a given symptom has a neurotic basis. However, it is not unusual to find conversion reactions complicated by symptoms having an organic basis. In such cases, the organic symptoms usually were present first, with the victim learning their psychological value. He finds that the symptoms gain attention for him, make people concerned about him, bring special privileges, and are advantageous in other ways. When this situation occurs, conversion symptoms may be superimposed on the organic symptoms in order to increase the social and psychological value of the disability.

The psychodynamic view of the conversion reaction is that repressed conflicts reach consciousness by being converted into organic symptoms involving the sensory and motor functions of the central nervous system. The repressed material reaches consciousness in a disguised form. While Freud emphasized the importance of the repression of sexual experiences, it is probable that conflicts involving other needs also generate anxiety which is discharged by being converted into physical symptoms. In this way the individual gains some degree of mastery over his problems. As in the case of the phobia and the obsessive-compulsive reaction, it is easier for a person to learn to handle a circumscribed symptom than it is to handle the diffuse anxiety which permeates the entire organism.

DISSOCIATIVE REACTION

The hysterical dissociative reaction is a neurosis in which a person attempts to control his anxiety by sealing off a disturbing part of his personality and refusing to recognize it. This process of insulating the mainstream of consciousness against the less acceptable aspects of the personality involves highly complex and intriguing dynamic relationships at the deeper levels of the individual's psychological life.

Pierre Janet, early in this century, was one of the first to show that consciousness is sometimes split into a number of more or less independent streams, and that at least some forms of personality disorganization can be explained in terms of this splitting of consciousness, or *dissociation*. Such dissociation arises when deep-lying uncon-

scious impulses seek to express themselves. In some individuals, for reasons which are not completely clear, these fugitive impulses take the form of a secondary personality and assume a semi-independent existence. The hysterical dissociative reaction is the basis for a wide variety of neurotic disorders, including neurotic sleep, amnesia, automatic behavior, multiple personality, and similar conditions.

Neurotic Sleep

The psychological importance of sleep has grown out of basic biological reactions. Among the lower animals, the *still reaction* is a protective device used by many species when in danger. Animals will "play dead" or "play possum" in order to save themselves from unwelcome or dangerous situations. The most closely related condition in humans is observed among the Eskimos and the Siberian peasants. When faced with the hardships of extreme hunger and cold, these people have been known to slip into prolonged, energy-saving sleep.

The counterpart of these primitive escape reactions is seen in neurotic sleep. When we are bored or irritated, we say that people "make us tired." This expression is a reflection of the desire to withdraw and to escape into sleep, which is a widely used technique for avoiding conflicts. People who have difficulty in awakening in the morning may be saying, "If I don't awaken, I won't have to face my problems." If a person needs to be shaken, pulled, pushed, and threatened before he gets out of bed, he may be afraid of life.

Narcolepsy is a neurotic sleep attack which may last from a few moments to many years. These attacks, in at least some cases, appear to be the realization of an inner wish. They are defensive reactions dictated by unconscious needs. While such sleep is uncontrollable and untimely, it is not without purpose. Cases have been reported in which soldiers have fallen asleep during a bombardment, preachers and professors have fallen asleep while lecturing or delivering sermons, a sign painter fell asleep while on the scaffold, and a man who was having a tooth pulled fell asleep in the dentist's chair. A young woman in South Africa was in love with a man who committed suicide after her parents opposed their marriage. The girl was so overcome with grief, and felt such strong hostility toward her parents, that she fell asleep and remained asleep for thirty-three years.

CONVICTED KILLER AWAKENS FROM MYSTERY SLEEP

Los Angeles, March 19—A convicted slayer, back in a troublous world of reality, pleaded today for return to the realm of unconsciousness where she lived for 158 hours. "I want to go back where I was, away from staring eyes, fingers that point at me, crying *'You're guilty—you must pay,'* " the 31-year-old widow said after a psychiatrist coaxed her from her trance. She lapsed into the coma after she was convicted of second degree murder for the New Year's shooting of a man she said was her secret husband.

FEMININE RIP VAN WINKLE WAKENS AFTER 12 YEARS

White Pine, Tenn., May 5—Folks in this Smoky Mountain community marveled today at the constant youth of a modern feminine "Rip Van Winkle" and wondered whether 12 years sleep could do the same for them. The object of their wonder is a 52-year-old woman who lapsed into sleeping sickness a dozen years ago and awakened for the first time only a few weeks ago. Since then the white frame combination home-funeral parlor where she slept through the New Deal, Pearl Harbor and the advent of the atomic bomb has become a mecca for the curious. The woman has a new rosy, school-girl complexion. There is a spring in her walk that she lacked before. Still more puzzling, she didn't have to learn to walk again, as do most bedridden persons.

Amnesia

One of the most common hysterical dissociative reactions is *amnesia*, or loss of memory. This condition is the inability to recall events of personal identity. A person may find himself wandering in the street and be unable to remember who he is, where he lives, or whether he is married or single. When picked up by the police, the amnesia victim very often appears dazed. Sometimes he is thought to be intoxicated, but at the police station or the hospital the real trouble is likely to be discovered. In some cases, the condition lasts only a few hours or days; at other times it may be a matter of weeks or months before it begins to clear.

One type of amnesia is due to head injury. If a person suffers brain damage in a train, airplane, or automobile accident, he may lose all memory for the crash itself or for the events before or after the incident. Most cases of amnesia, however, are due to emotional conflict. Economic, marital, sexual, or social life may become so difficult that a person is driven to find a way out of the conflict. He escapes by forgetting. The amnesia is a form of "psychological suicide." One man decided to jump into the river when he lost his savings in a swindle. On his way to the river, he lost his memory and wandered through the streets until he was picked up by a policeman and taken to the hospital. Several months later his memory was restored. The real suicide he had planned had been given up in favor of the less serious psychological suicide.

A young woman found wandering along a country road was brought to the hospital by police. She knew the date and the fact that she was in Cincinnati. She said she believed she had two children and had a feeling she should "get back to them." She did not know how old she was, but she insisted, "I know I'm not over thirty." In Mississippi, a twenty-six-year-old druggist lay on a hospital bed and stared blankly at his white-haired mother, who reminded him of his boyhood in an effort to restore his memory. The druggist answered his mother's pleas by saying, "I'm sorry but I don't know you. I wish I did know you because I love you better than anything in the world." The entire family gathered around the bed, but the young man did not recognize any of his relatives.

In a study of a series of cases of amnesia in the Royal Air Force, it was found that the precipitating causes included prolonged dissatisfaction with military service, acute emotional experiences involving close relatives or girl friends, and the flight from danger and authority (Parfitt and Gall, 1944). In a sense, the amnesic patient does not forget; he simply refuses to remember.

The *fugue* is a special form of amnesia in which the patient literally flees from the difficulties he has been facing. The fugue may last from a few days to weeks or months and may take the victim to cities hundreds of miles away from his home. During the fugue state, the secondary personality appears to disregard completely the basic personality. However, the secondary personality during the period of the fugue ordinarily utilizes the previous experience of the basic personality. The patient changes his name, but usually is able to manage in a reasonably normal fashion.

The most complicated forms of behavior may be carried out during the fugue. A victim may travel great distances, purchase train or airplane tickets, take a room in a hotel, find a job, and lead a seemingly normal life in a completely different setting. A twenty-two-year-old man disappeared from his fishing boat in Florida. He was thought to be dead by his family and friends, but six years later he telephoned his brother and said that he was working as an orderly in a convalescent home in New Orleans and had suddenly remembered his name. However, he had no memory for what had happened during the six-year period.

Automatic Behavior

The hysterical dissociative type of neurotic reaction is also illustrated by *automatic behavior*. In such behavior, the individual is not consciously aware of what he is saying or doing. He may talk in an automatic way and be surprised to hear himself. In other cases, the person's hand moves involuntarily and produces automatic writing or automatic drawing. In all such cases, the personality is dissociated; and the victim is functioning in a compartmentalized way. While the conscious level of personality is the observer, the unconscious level is responsible for the behavior.

Automatic talking occurs from time to time during waking states but under ordinary circumstances is not open to clinical or experimental study. A great many people have had the experience of hearing themselves suddenly, and without conscious intention, make an exclamation or otherwise blurt out a remark or a phrase.

While relatively little emphasis has been placed on automatic writing and drawing in recent years, the technique is an excellent example of unconscious motivation. Most people have had the experience of talking on the telephone or listening to a lecture and "doodling" at the same time with a pencil on a scrap of paper.

Sometimes it is done consciously and deliberately, but more often it is done unconsciously. The results frequently come as a surprise to the person who made the drawings or designs or wrote the words.

Occasionally a very productive automatic writer is produced. Among the best-known automatic writers have been Flammarion and Sardou. Patience Worth of St. Louis wrote several novels by this method, the Reverend Stainton Moses wrote a history, Andrew Jackson Davis wrote on evolution, and Elsa Barker produced the *Letters from a Living Dead Man*. While this latter work was publicized as a series of "spirit messages," it was in reality an example of automatic writing. Gertrude Stein sometimes used automatic writing, and certain of the effects achieved by other modern writers and poets depend (with or without the writer's knowledge) upon personality dissociation.

Automatic writing appears under a variety of conditions and shows a rich variation in its expression. Very often the first words are isolated and apparently meaningless. Gradually the individual may write phrases, then sentences, and, if there are strong tendencies toward behavior of this type, the person becomes skillful in writing longer passages. In some cases, the material can be related to underlying personality conflicts.

Automatic drawing is closely related to automatic writing. Such drawing is a product of our unconscious urges and conflicts. Both Paul Klee and Vasili Kandinksy, two of the important artists of the modern school, occasionally used automatic drawing and painting to achieve their effects.

Multiple Personality

It is an easy psychological step from automatic writing, with its multiplicity of personalities, to the condition of *multiple personality*, in which the several dissociated segments of the personality exist alternately, or even concurrently, in a relatively autonomous way.

Centuries of philosophy, religion, and creative art have made us familiar with the contradictory nature of man. The inner struggle between different aspects of the self has been a subject of the most intriguing interest. Robert Louis Stevenson used the double personality as the basis for his classic story "Dr. Jekyll and Mr. Hyde." It is

Figure 8.7 *The dual personality, as suggested by Pablo Picasso's painting* Girl before A Mirror. *(Museum of Modern Art, New York. Mrs. Simon Guggenheim Collection.)*

also the theme of Dostoevski's *The Double*, E. T. A. Hoffmann's *The Devil's Elixirs*, and two stories by Gogol, "The Nose" and "Memoirs of a Madman."

Multiple personality is most likely to develop in patients who show signs of sleepwalking and sleeptalking, who are easily hypnotized, and who show a tendency toward other dissociated actions. One young woman felt herself drawn out of bed and forced to go through a series of weird dances. Another had two personalities, each of which tried to read a page in a book or magazine at the same time. Unfortunately their readings did not keep step, and one personality finished the page before the other.

The dual personality is not the same as the "imaginary" playmate that many children create

in their fantasy life. The child does not confuse himself with the product of his imagination. In neurotic dissociation, there is no projection of the additional personalities; they are not considered as being "beyond" oneself. They are more or less independent personalities struggling with one another for dominance.

Cases of multiple personality appear to be based on the repression of conflicting needs and desires. The splitting of the personality is the climax of repeated failures of personal adjustment and integration. However, the manner in which ideas and emotions are capable of breaking away from the main personality and leading a quasi-independent existence is an unsolved problem. While true cases of multiple personality are not common, they are of considerable theoretical importance when they do occur because they underline, in a dramatic fashion, the conflicting motivational systems that can be present at the unconscious level.

The following abstract of the psychiatric interview with a seventeen-year-old University of Chicago student, who received sentences on twenty-six burglaries and robberies, an assault to commit murder, and three murders, deals with a secondary personality he referred to as "George."

Q: Going back to George, how frequently did he bob up?

A: He was just a realization of mine. I just stuck him in for no good reason. Before he seemed real to me. When I went out on burglary it seemed to me that George was doing it. He seemed to be real. I cannot introduce him to anybody but he is there.

Q: Does he seem real to you now?

A: Yes, he does.

Q: Can you give us an illustration of the kind of conversation you might have had with him in the quiet of your room?

A: Usually when I had to get out I would ask him where he was going. We would talk back and forth that way. He would say, down to the lake, and I would say what are you going to do there? He said he would get some things. I would ask him why he was going and he said, because he wants to. It would be just that way. I would argue with him to stay and then I would get a headache. I would argue in every way possible with him but he always wanted to get out.

Q: When did George come into the picture?

A: He came into the picture before I started to burglarize. In the beginning I always tried to resist and after that I tried to talk to him, and later on developed writing to him.

Q: Did you write letters to him?

A: Yes.

Q: How long did you keep the letters?

A: Until I read them again, and then I would burn them.

Q: Where did you burn them?

A: In my room. When I tried to resist him, I would get a headache. It seemed like my head was a balloon filled with water. When I would lay down it would fill the balloon, and I would get a pain.

Q: When you wrote to George, how did you address the letter?

A: I would write to George, and sometimes I would write it to myself.

Q: Give us an example.

A: When I had written to myself, I would address it to Dear Bill.

Q: You wrote to George and George wrote to you? Give us an explanation.

A: He wrote about burglary. He would say that the best way to burglarize was to go in windows. He would give names of people like Mike, Joe, and Harry.

Q: What else would he write?

A: He would write about things in South America, about smuggling, and about robbery, whatever he would think of.

Q: Did he ever write to you about murder?

A: No.

Q: How did you write him?

A: I would say Dear George. On one occasion after the Degnan case, I asked him in a letter if he did it or not.

Q: Did you get a reply?

A: No.

Q: Did you ever in your letters to George discuss sexual things?

A: No.

Q: What did you write about?

A: Sometimes in the letters I would ask him for things I needed at school. I would ask him if I could borrow money from him.

Q: Anything else?

A: When this urge would come out, I would tell him there would be a letter in the drawer for him. Sometimes he would answer after I wrote and then when I would read it, it would all seem new to me. I don't remember writing the answer and would not know I had written what was written (Kennedy et al., 1947).

Occasionally the multiple personality is first recognized in connection with amnesia. A young woman was found wandering on the street; and the police took her to the hospital, where she was identified by a card in her purse which indicated that her husband should be called if she had an attack of amnesia. When examined, the patient was rather anxious and unable to give her name or any other information about herself. She did not know where she was other than in a hospital. During the course of her treatment, a distinct secondary personality emerged. The patient's real name was Sara, but the secondary personality insisted her name was Maud.

The case of Christine Beauchamp is probably the most famous of all cases of multiple personality. Miss Beauchamp, a Radcliffe student, was studied for a period of six years. During this time, three distinct personalities emerged. Prince referred to them as B1, B3, and B4. B3 was also known as Sally (Prince, 1905).

Except for amnesia, the dissociative reaction is relatively rare. It is perfectly possible to spend an entire career in the field of mental health without seeing a person who exhibits a classic dissociative reaction. When such cases do occur, the dramatic nature of the symptom picture creates wide interest. In any event, the psychodynamics of such conditions are relatively uncomplicated, even though the neurodynamics remain something of a mystery. It is possible that growing research in the field of hypnosis will clarify some of the intriguing problems related to dissociated behavior.[4]

DEPERSONALIZATION

This neurosis, which became a part of the standard classification system in 1968 (DSM-II), is a condition in which there are feelings of unreality and estrangement from the self and the environment. In such cases, the individual may begin to feel that there is something unreal about the world or to doubt his own existence. He realizes that this could not be possible, yet he is unable to free himself from the idea that he is somehow disengaged from his surroundings. He may ask himself such questions as: Is the world real or fantasy? Do I actually exist? Am I really part of what is happening?

Depersonalization may be experienced in a dramatic way by individuals under the influence of hallucination-producing drugs. Here there may be pronounced feelings of estrangement and personal isolation. The reality of one's very existence may be questioned. In such cases the altered state of consciousness is the result of drug-induced changes in the flow of nerve impulses in the brain and is not of neurotic origin.

Neurotic depersonalization by definition is not organic. It is a psychological state which the individual has learned to adopt in his effort to cope with stress and the anxiety associated with it. Like other symptoms of neurosis, depersonalization can be looked upon as an abnormal defense mechanism. The individual seeks to protect himself from his anxiety by denying the world and by doubting his own existence.

Many people have brief episodes of feelings of unreality and estrangement from the world. But these fleeting experiences are not necessarily a symptom of personality disturbance. It is only when such feelings persist and interfere with everyday activities that they become an indication of abnormal psychological functioning. Sometimes it is difficult to make a distinction between a depersonalization neurosis and the early stages in the development of a psychotic reaction. In the latter case, the feelings of unreality are likely to be more pronounced, and the individual is less likely to recognize the illusory nature of the feelings.

NEUROTIC DEPRESSION

The depressive reaction is a neurotic condition in which a person reacts to his unconscious anxiety in a defeatist, hopeless way, giving in to his feelings of dejection and depression. The disorder is characterized by a response to an external situation which would call for a normal reaction of depression. However, the depression does not disappear as would be expected. On the other hand, it does not show the additional symptoms which would cause the depression to be regarded as a psychosis. In short, the neurotic depressive reaction is a depression that is beyond the normal range but not of psychotic proportions.

In earlier systems of diagnosis, this type of reaction was called a *reactive depression,* meaning that the depressed feelings were essentially a situational reaction to some external event. This meaning is maintained in the current view of the disorder. A neurotic depressive reaction is ordinarily a response to a situation such as a death in the family, severe financial reverses, chronic illness, or some similar event.

The neurotic depressive reaction is differentiated from corresponding psychotic depressive reactions on the basis of the individual's life history, the personality structure, and the precipitating events in the environment. The differentiation is further established by the absence of malignant symptoms such as agitation, disturbances of thinking, perceptual disorders, severe slowing of

---

[4]Books dealing with hysterical dissociative states are *Amnesia* (Appleton, 1966) edited by C. W. M. Whitty and O. L. Zangwill; *The Three Faces of Eve* (McGraw-Hill, 1957) by C. H. Thigpen and H. M. Cleckley; and *The Final Face of Eve* (McGraw-Hill, 1958) by Evelyn Lancaster with James Poling.

thinking and actions, and other psychotic behavior.

Hostility is the central dynamic factor in some depressive reactions. Typically there is severe hostility toward family members or others in the environment, and this unconscious hostility results in guilt feelings. The hostility is then turned upon the self in the form of feelings of unworthiness, self-depreciation, and despondency. A twenty-one-year-old college student said, "I have great feelings of inadequacy, depression, and persecution. These feelings seem to become more severe. I am increasingly more depressed, and feel that nothing is worth doing nor is life worth living. I am actually beginning to enjoy being unhappy. I don't know how to act when things are going well."

■ NEUROTIC DEPRESSION

Virginia F. is a thirty-three-year-old married woman who is separated from her husband. She was married at the age of twenty-two and has six children. The marriage has been a disturbed one, with the husband drinking heavily and being abusive toward the patient. The children were so neglected and undernourished that it was necessary to place them in foster homes. She was admitted to a psychiatric hospital because of her severe depression. When examined she was found to be a pale, haggard, and unkempt woman who was depressed and had thoughts of suicide, but no other symptoms of mental illness. She was cooperative, and willing to talk about her family and her past life. She was pregnant, and the depression started when her husband left her. She had been living in a rundown apartment, without gas or electricity, and overrun with rats. She began to feel that it would be better to die and kill the children than to live such a life. After a short time in the hospital, and as a result of the efforts of the social service department to help her start a new life, the patient's depression lifted. The entire depressive episode was a reaction to a seemingly unbearable situation.

In commenting on neurotic depression, Carl G. Jung said:

Statistics show a rise in the frequency of mental depressions in men about forty. In women the neurotic difficulties generally begin somewhat earlier. We see that in this phase of life—between thirty-five and forty —an important change in the human psyche is in preparation. . . . he shrinks from the gray thoughts of approaching age and, feeling the prospect before him unbearable, is always straining to look behind him. . . . thoroughly unprepared we take the step into the afternoon of life; . . . but we cannot live the afternoon of life according to the programme of life's morning; for what was great in the morning will be little at evening, and what in the morning was true will at evening have become a lie. I have given psychological treatment to too many people of advancing years, and have looked too often into the secret chambers of their souls, not to be moved by this fundamental truth (Jung, 1960).

The neurotic depressive reaction is probably the least serious of all neuroses, except for the ever-present possibility of suicide. Otherwise, the prognosis for this condition is very favorable. In the majority of cases, the depression disappears as the person's situation improves or is otherwise altered. Since the *secondary gains*, or useful purposes served by the symptom, are somewhat less in this type of neurosis than in other neuroses, the spontaneous remission rate tends to be relatively high. Many of these people improve even though there is no physical or psychological treatment.

■ MIXED NEUROTIC REACTION

Ora J. is a seventeen-year-old high school girl who was admitted to a psychiatric hospital as the result of an episode in which she seemed suddenly to regress to her early childhood. She sat on the floor and played with her younger sister's dolls, and appeared not to recognize any of her other brothers and sisters. The difficulty began approximately eight weeks earlier when the patient received her report card at school. Her grades were not high enough for her to obtain a college scholarship, and she became extremely upset. She withdrew from her family and friends, did not want to go to school, and spent most of her time sleeping. She then experienced the state of temporary dissociation in which the regressive episode occurred.

The patient apparently had a normal developmental history. She began school at age five, enjoyed her school work, and made good grades. She took her studies seriously throughout the school years, and usually managed to obtain A's and B's. She would be quite disappointed if she received a C in a course. When the patient was in the sixth grade she passed entrance tests to a college preparatory school and was encouraged to attend and try for a college scholarship. However, after entering the school she became threatened by the scholastic competition. She confided to her mother that she was "scared to death" because of the high scholastic standards. Nevertheless the patient was able to maintain average to good grades until she found they were not sufficiently high to warrant a college scholarship.

The anxiety generated by the conflict over the inability to obtain the scholarship expressed itself in a variety of neurotic symptoms. These symptoms included the state of dissociation, the regressive episode, and the attacks of anxiety. There were no indications of a more serious personality disturbance.*

THE ETIOLOGY OF NEUROSIS

Anxiety, which is present to some degree in everyone, is the common source of all psychoneurotic behavior. When the underlying anxiety generated by unconscious conflict is handled adequately, neurotic symptoms are not ordinarily present. However, when this underlying anxiety is mismanaged, a neurotic reaction is, in effect, an attempt on the part of the person to cope with his anxiety. When this attempt is unsuccessful, the anxiety symptoms may express themselves in a direct fashion as an anxiety neurosis, or the anxiety may be transformed into some other type of neurotic symptom.

While each neurotic reaction grows out of a more or less unique set of conditions, the ultimate cause of neurotic behavior frequently can be traced back to three factors: (1) a constitutionally low tolerance for anxiety, (2) ineffective techniques for dealing with anxiety, and (3) precipitating experiences of a traumatic or threatening nature which sometimes occur earlier in life and the effects of which remain dormant over a period of years.

Individuals differ widely in their sensitivity to stress and in their tolerance for anxiety. This sensitivity and tolerance is dependent to a large degree upon inherited resistance within the nervous and endocrine systems. When the inherited resistance is low, the individual is likely to be overly sensitive to stress and may have a low tolerance for anxiety.

Sigmund Freud was one of the first to emphasize that neurotic behavior occurs only in predisposed individuals (Freud, 1959). He pointed out that there must be a favorable biological soil if a neurotic reaction is to flourish. He said, in effect, that inborn and constitutional factors are a necessary condition for neurotic behavior.

The second major factor in the etiology of neurotic behavior is the adequacy of the ego defense mechanisms which have been learned by the individual. Such defensive measures as rationalization, compensation, projection, identification, reaction formation, and the other techniques used to control anxiety are learned from early childhood. Some individuals develop effective and successful techniques, while others settle for less adequate defensive systems. When confronted with more than the usual amount of anxiety, the individual with an effective defense system is less likely to develop neurotic behavior than the individual with a poorly constructed defense network.

Psychoneurotic behavior tends to occur when the defense mechanisms are not able to handle the anxiety aroused by the unconscious conflicts. The pressure of the conflict may distort and exaggerate the existing defense mechanisms, or a pathological defensive system may be constructed. In either case, the underlying anxiety may break through, or it may be distorted by the defense system into some other form of neurotic symptom. The precise form of the neurosis depends upon which part of the defense system has yielded to the stress. In this way, the psychoneurotic disorders take on their characteristic symptom pictures.

A third major causal factor in the development of neurotic behavior is the precipitating experience. It is assumed that this experience, occasionally in the form of a traumatic episode in early life, remains repressed until it is triggered at a later time by some related, though perhaps minor, event. It was this idea of the repression of early childhood sexual experiences which Sigmund Freud used as one of the cornerstones of his theory.

The prevailing view is that the precipitating

---

*Case 3 of audiotape 5, "Psychoneurotic Disorders," in *Case Interviews to Accompany The Disorganized Personality.*

threat may take any one of a number of forms. In general, however, the threat centers on conflicts related to sexual impulses, aggressive tendencies, the need for status, or the conflict between needs for dependence and independence. More consciously recognized threats in the form of real or imagined physical illness, financial worries, and similar experiences are also involved in the development of neurotic reactions.

While neurotic behavior occurs during various periods of life, it is most common between late adolescence and the middle thirties. It is at this period that the threats related to social, economic, and sexual needs are likely to be most insistent. Neurotic patterns established during these years frequently pervade the personality for the rest of life.

A key element in the neurosis is the threat to the individual in the form of breaking into consciousness of unconscious conflicts which the patient is not ready to accept. The threat of the return of repressed material may create an emergency situation which activates the sympathetic segment of the autonomic nervous system.

Prolonged stress sometimes has the same practical effect as an isolated traumatic event. Continued frustration over a period of months or years may be as threatening to the personality as the memory of a repressed traumatic episode. For this reason, the cure of neurotic behavior is not always the mere uncovering of a single repressed life experience. In many cases, the improvement or cure of a neurosis can occur only when the pattern of frustration has been discovered and when the patient understands the relevancy of his frustrating experiences to the neurotic symptoms.[5]

SUMMARY

1. The neuroses, or psychoneuroses, are disturbances marked by anxiety expressed either directly or indirectly. In the *anxiety* neurosis, the anxiety is expressed directly, since the patient responds to internal and external threats by means of an overactive autonomic nervous system. The physical symptoms include a more rapid heartbeat, breathing difficulties, gastrointestinal upset, excessive perspiration, and similar bodily changes. The psychological symptoms range from vague uneasiness to apprehension and dread.

2. In neurotic disorders other than the anxiety reaction, the underlying anxiety is changed into some other symptom. One of the most common of all neurotic disorders is the *phobia*, or pathological fear, in which the anxiety becomes focused on a specific object, person, or situation. The more common phobias include the fear of closed places, pointed objects, open spaces, and heights.

3. The *obsessive-compulsive* reaction is another way in which anxiety is handled by the psychoneurotic. An obsession is an unwelcome recurring idea, while a compulsion is an unwelcome repetitive act. The two conditions frequently occur together. The more common reactions include compulsive orderliness and cleanliness and compulsive doubting.

4. The *hypochondriacal* neurosis is dominated by an overconcern with the body and the

---

[5]Although it was written some years ago, one of the most thorough and stimulating discussions of the psychodynamics of neurotic disorders is Otto Fenichel's *The Psychoanalytic Theory of Neurosis* (Norton, 1945). The learning theory of neurotic behavior is presented in *Behavior Therapy and the Neuroses* (Pergamon Press, 1960) edited by H. J. Eysenck and in *The Causes and Cures of Neurosis* (Routledge and Kegan Paul, 1965) by H. J. Eysenck and S. Rachman.

fear of disease, while the *neurasthenic* reaction is marked by complaints of chronic weakness, fatigue, and physical and mental exhaustion.

5. The *hysterical* neurosis is characterized by an involuntary and psychogenic loss of function. In the *conversion* type of this disorder, the anxiety of the patient is converted into a physical disability. The symptoms, which center on parts of the body supplied by the central nervous system, include both sensory and motor disabilities. The sensory symptoms are likely to involve vision, hearing, and skin sensation, while the motor disturbances take the form of tics and tremors, contractures and paralyses, and convulsions.

6. In the *dissociative* type of hysterical reaction, the patient unconsciously controls his anxiety by splitting his personality so that one part of the self becomes unaware of the more disturbing part. It is a process of forming a relatively independent personality system within the main personality. Dissociative reactions are expressed in the form of amnesia, automatic writing, sleepwalking, and multiple personality.

7. The *depersonalization* neurosis is dominated by a feeling of unreality and of estrangement from the self, body, or surroundings. These feelings are also seen in psychotic conditions, but the neurotic individual realizes the illusory nature of his symptoms, while the psychotic may accept them and lose complete touch with the world of reality.

8. The *depressive* neurosis is one in which anxiety is expressed as hopelessness and dejection. The condition is usually a temporary response which is self limiting. Such cases are likely to respond well to treatment, and spontaneous cures are frequent.

9. While the symptoms of neurosis vary considerably, the condition is an unsuccessful attempt on the part of the individual to cope with his feelings of anxiety. Every neurosis is a learned reaction which grows out of a low tolerance for anxiety, ineffective techniques for dealing with anxiety, and stressful experiences of a traumatic or threatening nature.

9 PSYCHOPHYSIO-LOGIC DISORDERS

In the discussion of the conversion neuroses in Chapter 8, it was pointed out that the inner anxieties of the patient are sometimes expressed as sensory and motor symptoms and sometimes as autonomic symptoms. If the symptoms are expressed through the central nervous system, the condition is ordinarily diagnosed as a conversion reaction. When the underlying emotional difficulties are expressed through body systems controlled by the autonomic system, the resulting condition is called a *psychophysiologic disorder*.

This distinction is more the result of an historical accident than of necessity. Conversion reactions have been known since the time of Charcot in the late nineteenth century and even before. The interest in psychophysiologic disorders, however, is largely an outgrowth of developments in medicine since 1930. Knowledge of the two conditions developed along more or less independent lines. When these lines came together, the distinction already had been made. In terms of causes, however, the conversion reactions and psychophysiologic disorders are similar.

> This group of disorders is characterized by physical symptoms that are caused by emotional factors and involve a single organ system, usually under autonomic nervous system innervation. The physiological changes involved are those that normally accompany certain emotional states, but in these disorders the changes are more intense and sustained. The individual may not be consciously aware of his emotional state (DSM-II, 1968).

The psychophysiologic disorders are based upon four major factors: (1) constitutional sensitivity of the autonomic nervous system, (2) learning in the form of conditioning, (3) the symbolic meaning of a particular organ system, and (4) the presence of a stress situation. Every case of psychophysiologic disorder is ultimately dependent upon one or more of these four factors. However, these factors combine in the most divergent and unique ways. The level of constitutional sensitivity varies, the learning situation takes different forms, the symbolic value of the symptom is frequently obscure, and the stress situation may be highly complex. For these reasons, it is often difficult to understand the dynamics of a psychophysiologic disorder and equally difficult to treat it.

The presence of an irritable and excitable autonomic nervous system is essential for the appearance of the symptoms of a psychophysiologic disorder. Without this constitutional sensitivity of the autonomic system, it is probable that underlying emotional conflicts will be discharged through the symptoms of other personality disturbances.

The differences in individual autonomic responses to stress are based, to a large extent, upon inborn factors. However, this inborn constitutional sensitivity is influenced by learning. A relatively weak constitutional component might be made stronger by training and reinforcement of a positive kind. Similarly, high levels of constitutional resistance might be damaged to some degree by inadequate patterns which have been learned.

While constitutional factors are of major importance in psychophysiologic disorders, the disturbance may also be a symbolic expression of an underlying conflict. The symptoms may be the end results of prolonged physiological states associated with unconscious repressed needs.

Many examples of the psychophysiologic relationship are seen among lower animals. In recent years, ethologists have shown that frustrations are likely to occur in the lives of almost all animals living in their natural surroundings. Where animals live in social groups, the frustrations are frequently caused by conflicts with

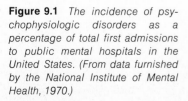

Figure 9.1 *The incidence of psychophysiologic disorders as a percentage of total first admissions to public mental hospitals in the United States. (From data furnished by the National Institute of Mental Health, 1970.)*

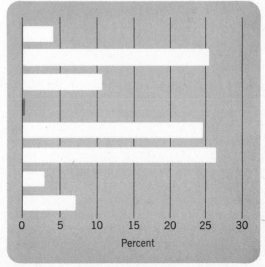

other members of the group. While these frustrations may be met by the neuromuscular response of fighting or running away, various forms of displacement are observed in which the response takes the form of a psychophysiologic disorder (Tinbergen, 1953). Some animals lose weight, while others show disturbances of breathing, heart action, or sexual drive.

Psychophysiologic symptoms are frequently seen in connection with stress situations. Some college students react to examinations by getting a headache; others develop stomach upset. Other symptoms include dizziness, accelerated heart rate, aches and pains, and similar symptoms. It is possible that earlier in life these students observed the rewarding effects of such symptoms, that is, sympathy and special treatment from others; and they learned to alter the internal body function at an unconscious level.

The critical importance of stress in psychophysiologic relationships is shown in a wide variety of unexplained sudden deaths both in animals and man. Cats whose cortical brain sections are removed are in a constant state of rage and often die in a few hours (Cannon, 1929). These animals apparently die as a result of overstimulation of the sympathico-adrenal system. In other experiments, when rats were used in stress experiments and their whiskers were clipped, there were a large number of unexplained deaths (Richter, 1957). The death reaction appeared to be related to a combination of stresses experienced in rapid succession. This stress sequence included being restrained in a bag during the trimming of the whiskers, the actual trimming of the whiskers, and immersion in a swimming jar in which the water was kept in a turbulent state. Death did not occur as a result of the restraint alone, the trimming of the whiskers alone, or immersion in the swimming jar alone, but the combination of these three stress situations in rapid sequence did produce the phenomenon.

It is interesting that the sudden death reaction was more frequent among wild rats than among domesticated laboratory rats. The reaction has also been observed among other wild animals. The European wild rabbit dies readily in captivity, mice have been known to die when handled, shrews die when restrained or exposed to sudden noises, and many birds die during banding.

The sudden death phenomenon has also been observed among humans. The phenomenon of voodoo death in man has been recorded frequently by anthropologists. Also, there have been many cases of unexplained death both in civilian and military situations. While there is a preexisting organic defect in a number of these cases, pathology cannot be shown in some cases.

Intense fear and other violent emotions can cause catastrophic disturbances of the homeostatic balance of the body. Radical changes in respiration, heart action and blood pressure, biochemistry, and other vital functions of the body sometimes lead to the sudden death of an otherwise healthy individual.

Another dramatic evidence of the psychophysiologic relationship is the "anniversary reaction," a term applied to illness of emotional origin which occurs on the anniversary of some important event in the life of the patient (Dunbar, 1946). The reaction is not unusual on the anniversaries of the deaths of parents among men and women who had strong psychological involvements with the mother or father. Anniversary reactions are also seen in connection with wedding anniversaries, as well as with birthdays, particularly during middle age and the later years of life. The birthday comes to have a special meaning in terms of declining physical attractiveness, decreased sexuality, and growing insecurity and dependency.

"Faith healing" is a further example of the powerful nature of psychological factors in influencing body systems and functions. Throughout history, and to the present day, and in a wide variety of forms, individuals, religious relics, and sacred wells and grottoes have had attributed to them the power to heal and to cure.

FAITH HEALER IN THE PHILIPPINES DRAWS DETROIT-AREA RESIDENTS

Detroit, Mich., May 22—More than a hundred residents of this area have paid six hundred dollars each to visit Antonio Agpaoa, a faith healer in the Philippines. Mr. Agpaoa has been described as a "miracle worker" by some of the thousands of people who have been "cured." Authorities take a different view. He was convicted in Manila for illegally practicing medicine, and he is under investigation by the U.S. Post Office Department and the American Medical Association.

In spite of the admitted elements of charlatanism and quackery in much that passes as faith healing, the fact remains that there have been numerous examples of dramatic improvements in physical condition which can be attributed only to changes in the attitudes of the patient. Even the most skeptical physicians are impressed from time to time by the sudden and seemingly inexplicable recovery of patients for whom hope had been abandoned.

A physician skilled in hypnosis was called to the bedside of a dying young woman. The patient's temperature had risen to 107.5, the pulse to 160, and the respiration had dropped to 60. The attending physicians said that the patient could not live more than two hours.

When I entered the room she was unconscious, her eyes were turned up so that only the white sclerotic coats were visible; she was from a medical point of view beyond the pale of hope. As I looked at the girl an inspiration came to me; I took her by the hand, learned her first name from the nurse, and said with great incisiveness: "Adele! Where are you going? You cannot die! Come back. You have work to do. Come back at once!" In answer to the summons, the upturned eyes resumed their normal angle and became riveted on mine. The voice that had for days uttered only the ravings of a delirium now spoke coherently. "It is too late," it murmured. "It is not too late. Stay where you are. Assume immediate control of your physical functions, and get well. You are going to recover." All this in an imperative, forceful tone. The directions were immediately accepted and implicitly followed. A change for the better supervened. Gradually the mental mist cleared away, the physical strength returned, and today the young lady is perfectly well and filling an important position in the musical world (Quackenbos, 1908).

While there is no longer any question about the importance of emotional factors in the development of physical illness, the matter of specific personality patterns related to specific physical illnesses is not well established. Many studies have been reported in which such personality characteristics appear to be related to one or another physical illness. However, the wide range of personality characteristics described and the questionable validity of the data from a research viewpoint cast doubt on the accuracy and meaningfulness of such relationships.

The treatment of psychophysiologic disorders is essentially psychological, although the additional attention of the internist and the medical specialist in the particular area of the physical symptom is often needed. Important advances are being made in this field, and there is every reason to believe that some of the most significant progress in medicine in future years will be in the further understanding of psychophysiologic relationships.[1]

Experiments at Rockefeller University have shown that animals can learn to control their involuntary nervous responses. Animals with electrodes implanted in the brain could learn to alter the heart rate in order to be rewarded with electrical stimulation that caused a pleasurable sensation. They eventually learned to decrease their heart rates by 20 percent in order to receive this pleasurable reward. Similarly, animals can learn to change their blood pressure, intestinal contractions, urinary excretions, and blood vessel constriction (Miller and Dicara, 1968). These findings have been of the greatest practical importance since they opened the way for the current use of conditioning techniques in the treatment of psychophysiological disorders in man.[2]

---

[1] *Psychosomatic Medicine* is a bimonthly journal devoted to technical articles and book reviews dealing with psychophysiological reactions. It is recommended to students interested in careers in medicine and nursing and is published by the Hoeber Medical Division of Harper & Row, 49 East 33d Street, New York, N.Y. 10016.

[2] An excellent and most readable nontechnical introduction to the psychophysiologic disorders is Flanders Dunbar's *Mind and Body* (Random House, 1955). The classic American work in the field is *Emotions and Bodily Changes* (Columbia University, 1946, 3d ed.) by the same author. Other technical books dealing with the subject in a general way are *Advances in Psychosomatic Medicine* (Brunner, 1961), edited by Arthur Jores and Helmuth Freyberger; *Origins of Psychosomatic and Emotional Disturbances* (Hoeber, 1962) by Charles Wenar, M. W. Handlon, and A. M. Garner; and *Psychosomatic Medicine* (Lea and Febiger, 1963), edited by John H. Nodine and John H. Moyer.

The psychophysiologic disorders are ordinarily classified on the basis of the body system through which the symptoms are expressed. The more common psychophysiologic disorders are (1) cardiovascular reactions, (2) gastrointestinal reactions, (3) respiratory reactions, (4) skin reactions, (5) genitourinary reactions, and (6) miscellaneous reactions involving such other body systems as the endocrines, musculoskeletal system, and the sense organs.

CARDIOVASCULAR DISORDERS

One of the most common of the psychophysiologic disorders is the cardiovascular reaction, in which the principal symptoms involve the heart and the blood vessels. While organic heart disease accounts for the greatest number of deaths in the United States, most heart specialists agree that a very large percentage of patients who present cardiovascular symptoms do not have an organic disease or disability. The symptoms are real enough, but the cause in such cases is emotional rather than physical. During World War II, the Office of the Surgeon General reported that nearly 50 percent of the heart cases in Army hospitals were psychological rather than physical (Lewis and Engle, 1954). The statistics are much the same for heart cases in general hospitals.

The heart invalid frequently is afraid to face the problems that are ahead of him. Among the cardiac cases is the young woman who is jealous of a prettier sister, the man with a more successful brother, the salesman who has not received his promotion, the wife who is being neglected by her husband, and the college student who cannot make good grades. For all such frustrated people, the heart symptom is a means of escape.

The body language of the heart is extensive. We "put our heart" into projects in which we are emotionally involved; we are "heartbroken" when things go wrong; we "give our heart" to our beloved; and we extend our "heartfelt sympathy" to our friends who are grief-stricken. We use such terms as "goodhearted" and "warmhearted" to indicate affection, while "hardhearted" and "cold-blooded" suggest hostility and dislike. In every instance, the heart is a prime source of emotional investment.

The nervous heart is organically sound but reacts in an unhealthy manner due to fear, worry, insecurity, or a feeling of personal inadequacy. The symptoms are real, but the basic cause is emotional conflict. One physician explained psychogenic heart disorder by saying, "A sick heart is an automobile with a defective motor. A nervous heart resembles an automobile with an excited driver."

The role of the physician as a factor in producing a psychophysiologic disorder is nowhere more important than in connection with the cardiovascular reactions. Many men, women, and children have developed psychogenic heart disorders, or have had minor heart symptoms exaggerated out of all reason, because of the careless words and attitudes of physicians. During a routine physical examination, the psychologically unsophisticated physician may make what to him is a harmless statement to the effect that, "Your blood pressure seems to be up," "You have low blood pressure," "You have a slight murmur," or some similar statement. Similarly, while listening to the heart, taking a pulse, or checking the blood pressure, the physician may find it necessary to make a recheck, or he may frown or otherwise indicate concern. The result of such behavior, verbal and nonverbal, is the establishment of an unnecessary preoccupation on the part of the patient with his heart functions. The anxiety and preoccupation, in turn, exaggerate the physical symptoms, and in this way a vicious circle is instituted.

In the past, the terms *heart neurosis* and *cardiac neurosis* were used to identify those conditions in which cardiovascular symptoms were the result of emotional stress. Various other terms have been used to indicate psychological heart disorder. *Effort syndrome* was a condition first described during the War between the States (Lewis, 1940). It was marked by fatigue, breathing difficulties, trembling, fainting, giddiness, and a fear of effort. This condition, under such names as *soldier's heart* and *neurocirculatory asthenia,* continued to be an important problem in both military and civilian medicine.

Stress situations which arouse anxiety result in an increase in heart rate, heightened blood pressure, and changes in heart rhythm. When the emotion is depression rather than anxiety, there is a decrease in heart rate and a lowering of blood pressure.

Classical techniques have been used to condition changes in blood pressure and constriction of the blood vessels (Enos et al., 1953). This work, carried out with both man and lower animals, demonstrates how anxiety can become a conditioned stimulus for the production of physical symptoms and how bodily functions may be conditioned to trigger anxiety. The work in the conditioning of autonomic reactions suggests that certain neurotic and psychophysiologic conditions might be treated effectively by reconditioning or by experimental extinction.

There is clear evidence that cardiovascular variations occur during psychotherapeutic interviews. In a study at Aberdeen University in Scotland, all subjects showed an increase in blood pressure at the start of the interview. Among normal control subjects the pressure tended to level off as the interview progressed. However, among neurotic persons there was a sustained rise in pressure, and even the resting levels after the interview did not fall as low as the resting level prior to the interview. While it is not possible to relate blood pressure changes during the interview to content in any consistent way, increased pressure is more likely to occur when new or "alerting" topics are introduced, when the subjects talk about themselves, and when verbal production is increased.

The major cardiovascular syndromes having psychophysiologic implications are (1) tachycardia, or rapid heart rate, (2) anginal syndrome, or pain in the region of the heart, (3) essential hypertension, or high blood pressure, and (4) coronary disease.

TACHYCARDIA

Tachycardia is a condition in which there is a speeded-up activity of the heart combined with an irregularity of the heart rhythm. The person, who is expressing his inner conflicts through the rapid heart rate, may also feel faint and weak and have difficulty in breathing. In severe cases, the person may go into shock. As in all psychophysiologic disorders, the emotional tension in the form of anxiety is translated into the physical symptoms.

The normal pulse is approximately 72 beats per minute. Under stress and in anxiety-provoking situations, the pulse rate may rise quickly to well over a hundred, and in extreme cases to several hundred beats per minute. When the stress situation is apparent, the normal heart soon returns to its usual level after the emergency has passed. In other cases, there is a rapid and sudden pounding of the heart without apparent reason. The attack may last only a few moments or may continue for a longer period. Eventually, and again for no obvious reason, the heart returns to its normal rate.

Attacks of tachycardia are episodic and may appear at any time and under any circumstances. It is not unusual for faintness, weakness, and respiratory difficulties, such as gasping for breath, to be associated with this disturbance. The patient with tachycardia is frequently an individual who has difficulty in competitive situations. Such individuals are basically competitive, but are afraid of competing and failing.

ANGINAL SYNDROME

The anginal reaction is characterized by sudden and severe pain in the chest. While the pain may be a symptom of organic heart disease, there are many cases in which the pain is an expression of emotional conflict. Every heart specialist is familiar with the patient who complains of anginal symptoms but has no clinical evidence of heart disease. While there is no accurate estimate of the number of cases of this type, the group forms a not inconsiderable part of the practice of the cardiologist.

The anginal symptom depends upon a combination of factors including a possible inherent weakness of the body system, social conditioning, and the need to express a conflict in a symbolic way. One patient who was a victim of an emotionally determined angina mentioned to his physician that he felt as if his heart had been "torn out of him" when his wife took up with another man. The physician was alert to the psychological implications of what the patient told him, and the patient was referred for psychological treatment after the physical findings were negative. During the treatment, it became clear that the heart symptoms began shortly after the patient learned of his wife's infidelity. While the psychological treatment served to reduce the severity and frequency of the symptoms, they did not disappear entirely until the other man went out of the picture.

In a similar case, a man described his anginal pain as a feeling of "being stabbed in the heart." Again the physical examination showed no sign of organic disturbance. During treatment, the patient related an incident in which he and his business partner engaged in a violent argument which resulted in the breakup of a partnership of many years. The patient found that his partner had been cheating him financially, and he related to his therapist that he felt as if his trusted partner had "stabbed" him. It was possible to show the patient how his feeling of being "stabbed" by his partner was related to the "stabbing" pains in his heart. When the patient began to see this relationship, he showed the first signs of improvement.

■ ANGINAL SYNDROME

Thomas M. is a fifty-six-year-old business executive who was referred for psychotherapy following extensive medical examinations which failed to reveal an organic basis for recurring chest pains. For several years the patient experienced sudden and severe pains in the region of the heart whenever he faced an unusually stressful situation. At first the patient did not see the connection between his emotional state and the heart symptoms. In fact, he prided himself upon his ability to meet and conquer difficult situations. Outwardly the patient was a hard-driving and successful businessman who gave the appearance of being in complete command of all situations. His first anginal attack occurred several years earlier following the announcement of his daughter's engagement to be married. A second attack occurred at the time of a threatened business reversal. A third attack took place following the death of his father. A number of other minor attacks also could be related to stressful events in the life of the patient. In the course of treatment, the patient began to see the significance of the pattern of his attacks, and the number and severity of

the chest pains began to diminish. After some weeks of intensive treatment, the patient was symptom-free. A few years later, in face of serious domestic difficulties, there was a recurrence of the anginal symptoms. His condition responded rapidly to further psychological treatment.

While cases of this type are relatively common, it would be a serious mistake to conclude that all anginal symptoms are emotionally based. Organic heart disease is widely prevalent, especially during the middle and later years of life. Any heart symptom should be checked carefully by a cardiologist before it is assumed that the condition is psychogenic. Some cases involve a complex combination of organic and psychological factors.

HYPERTENSION

The most important single process among the cardiovascular disorders is *hypertension,* or high blood pressure. It is estimated that at least half of all people over forty-five die of some form of cardiovascular-renal disease. Disorders of blood pressure form the largest part of the contributing causes.

The causes of hypertension are probably both psychological and physiological. No one doubts the role of the emotions in elevating the blood pressure. However, there are equally complex physiological dynamics to be considered. The exact relationship between the emotions and hypertension is yet to be demonstrated. Many normal individuals have a sharply increased blood pressure during emotional stress. Similarly, when sleep is disturbed by exciting dreams, an otherwise normal blood pressure may rise significantly (MacWilliam, 1923).

While the exact cause of hypertension is unknown, there is a possibility that the condition is related to interference with the circulatory function of the kidneys. When the kidneys are deprived of blood by a constriction of the small blood vessels or by some other factor, they release *renin,* a substance which tends to raise the blood pressure. It is also known that influences remote from the kidneys may affect their circulatory function. One such influence is the secretion of chemical substances by the adrenal glands. With the pres-

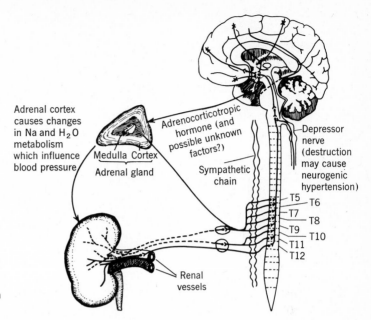

Adrenal cortex causes changes in Na and H_2O metabolism which influence blood pressure

Adrenocorticotropic hormone (and possible unknown factors?)

Medulla Cortex

Adrenal gland

Sympathetic chain

Depressor nerve (destruction may cause neurogenic hypertension)

T5 T6
T7 T8
T9 T10
T11
T12

Renal vessels

Figure 9.2 *The neurohumoral mechanism in hypertension (After Earl and Pansky,* A Functional Approach to Neuroanatomy, *1960, p. 387.)*

ent knowledge of how the emotions and glands are interconnected by way of the autonomic nervous system, it is clear that hypertension may be related to prolonged emotional upsets.

One of the common theories of the emotional origin of hypertension is that the individual has an accumulation of anger and rage. On the surface he appears calm and affable, but underneath there may be a seething volcano of anger. This inner tension elevates the blood pressure.

The personality of the hypertensive patient has been described as one in which there is a strong emotional relationship with the mother, a marked need for dependency, a tendency to use perfectionistic behavior to compensate for an underlying insecurity and lack of confidence, and a lifelong pattern of vacillation between active and passive roles. Such patients have also been described as having a tendency to brood about their difficulties or to escape through overeating or drugs (Innes et al., 1959).

While there is some question about the validity of many of the personality characteristics attributed to the hypertensive patient, there is rather general agreement that the central emotion is anger and hostility that is ineffectively expressed. These patients bottle up their anger and fail to discharge it, even indirectly. Such a situation is most likely to occur in one who has learned that aggressiveness is unacceptable and yet must function in a culture which calls for a considerable amount of aggressive behavior (Koster et al., 1970).

CORONARY DISEASE

The importance of psychological factors in heart attacks is suggested by the fact that a history of emotional stress prior to the attack is found in a number of cases. In the typical heart attack, a clot of blood forms within the blood vessel supplying the heart, causing an *occlusion,* or closing of the artery. Consequently, the muscle of the heart does not receive its proper blood supply, resulting in an area of damaged tissue.

The relationship between the heart attack and emotional stress is in the *thrombosis,* or clotting of the blood. In the discussion of the autonomic nervous system and particularly the emergency functions of this system, it was pointed out that one of the emergency changes is an acceleration of the rate of blood clotting. When the animal organism is threatened, blood coagulation is speeded up to protect the animal in the event that it is injured in flight or fight. Similarly, in man,

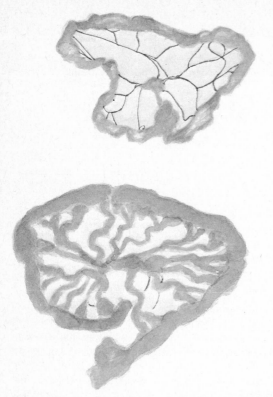

Figure 9.3 *Blood vessels of animals before and after exposure to stress. The vessels supplying a segment of the intestine of a normal rat before stress are illustrated in the top drawing. The vessels of the rat subjected to stress (bottom) are markedly thickened, leading to high blood pressure and death. (Courtesy of P. C. Constantinides and the* Scientific American.*)*

stress situations of a threatening nature result in a more rapid clotting of the blood. Anxiety, irritation, and excitement increase heart action, increase resistance to the flow of blood, and speed up blood clotting. The combination of these factors may result, particularly for an already weakened heart, in what is essentially a psychogenic coronary occlusion.

The effect of emotion on blood coagulation time was demonstrated in a study in which blood-bank donors were classified into three groups: (1) apparently calm, (2) apprehensive, and (3) frightened

and highly nervous. The blood coagulation time was 8 to 12 minutes for the apparently calm group, 4 to 5 minutes for the apprehensive group, and 1 to 3 minutes for the frightened and highly nervous group. The more anxious the donors, the more rapidly the blood coagulated (Macht, 1952).

A study of younger coronary patients revealed a distinctive personality pattern made up of extreme competitiveness, great ambition, restlessness, and a profound time-urgency. Motor behavior in the form of fist clenching, desk pounding, facial grimacing and keyed-up body movement was characteristic. The investigators suggested that these personality characteristics result in elevated blood cholesterol and speeded-up clotting time.

The relationship between certain personality types and heart attacks is strengthened by research showing that men concerned with social propriety and bothered by guilt feelings tend to have above-normal cholesterol levels. Proper, dependable, conscientious people who adhere to social norms tend to have high cholesterol levels, as do people given to passivity, self-criticism, and feelings of guilt.

The importance of stress in the production of coronary artery disease is also suggested by the fact that one death in four among physicians between ages 45 and 65 is due to this disorder. This rate is 80 percent higher than for the general population (Dublin and Spiegelman, 1947). Similarly, in studies of autopsies performed in Korea on United States battle casualties, where the average age of the men was only 22, substantial evidence of coronary disease was found in 77.3 percent of the hearts (Enos et al., 1953).[3]

GASTROINTESTINAL DISORDERS

The gastrointestinal system is one of the most common channels for the expression of unconscious conflicts and the anxiety associated with them. The processes of digestion and elimination are intimately associated with autonomic activity. Any situation within the personality which is ser-

---

[3]The psychological aspects of heart disorders are discussed in *Life Stress and Essential Hypertension* (Williams and Wilkins, 1955) by Stewart Wolf and others; Don Carlos Peete's *The Psychosomatic Genesis of Coronary Artery Disease* (Thomas, 1955); and *Psychosomatics in Essential Hypertension* (Karger, 1970) edited by M. Koster and others.

ious enough to upset normal autonomic function is capable of producing gastrointestinal disturbances, provided that this system has a constitutional weakness or is of symbolic significance.

The stomach is closely related to the emotions since it is supplied with autonomic nerve fibers which serve as the lines of communication between the brain and the viscera. By this means, unconscious forces may, with proper reinforcement, exert an influence on the tissues of the stomach and intestines.

The body language of the gastrointestinal system is rich with references denoting emotional conflict. The phrases "He makes me sick to my stomach" and "I can't stomach that" are used frequently. A common phrase in certain socioeconomic groups is, "That gripes me." The word "gripe" is a lay term for colic or abdominal pain due to spasms of the smooth muscles of the intestinal tract. Moreover, the products and processes of excretion make up a large part of the common language of derision and ridicule.

An accidental gunshot wound suffered by a hunter in the Northwest Michigan territory did much to establish our knowledge of the influence of the emotions upon the digestive tract. A physician, William Beaumont, nursed this man back to health over a long period of time in spite of the great odds against his recovery. In return for his services, the physician was permitted by the patient to make observations on his stomach, which, out of necessity, remained exposed. Observations continued for eight years, and during this time Beaumont found numerous instances when emotional changes caused changes in the flow of stomach juices (Beaumont, 1929).

Another example of the relation of the emotions to gastrointestinal activity is the case of a fifty-seven-year-old workman who at the age of nine had swallowed some scalding clam chowder with the result that his esophagus was sealed off. Attempts were made to channel a path through the stricture, but these were unsuccessful; and surgeons decided he would have to be fed through a tube directly into his stomach. The operation was interrupted suddenly when the patient almost died, and he was left with a huge gaping hole through which his surgically incised stomach protruded. From that time on, the patient fed himself through this opening, using food which he first chewed (to satisfy his taste for food) and then deposited into a funnel connected to a rubber tube to his stomach. This patient got along fairly well; but he felt he was something of a freak, and he became suspicious and secretive about his condition. He avoided doctors and managed to earn a precarious living by semiskilled labor. Finally, the constant irritation of the opening by gastric juice and the friction brought on by his work with a pick and shovel caused a blood loss which resulted in a serious anemia. After he was hospitalized, he took a job in the hospital laboratory, where he made himself available for treatment and observation. The patient's misfortune became a rare opportunity for medical scientists to study the human stomach and its reactions under a wide variety of emotional conditions (Wolf and Wolff, 1943).

The intimate relationship between gastric secretory functions and emotional life was demonstrated in a similar way in a sixty-year-old woman undergoing psychotherapy. This patient had a small gastric *fistula* (an abnormal tube-like structure with a small opening to the stomach) of fifty-two years' duration. The gastric secretions were observed regularly through the fistula for a period of two and a half years while the patient was receiving intensive pyschotherapy. For the first eight months of treatment, the hydrochloric acid secretion of her stomach remained at persistently high normal levels. At the end of eight months, when the patient became aware of her unconscious aggressive drives, and when she began to express verbally material related to these drives, the level of the hydrochloric acid gastric secretion dropped abruptly and remained at a low normal level for the next eighteen months. Whatever the psychological dynamics involved—and these dynamics can only be guessed at—the relationship between the emotions and gastric secretion was demonstrated dramatically. In some way, talking about the unconscious conflicts appeared to influence the gastric secretory functions (Stein et al., 1962).

These studies, which have permitted the direct observation of changes in the lining of the stomach and intestines during periods of stress, have made it possible for scientists to advance our knowledge of psychosomatic relationships. Ordinarily such investigations must be made on nonhuman subjects under relatively artificial laboratory conditions. While laboratory studies are often valuable, they cannot compare with the richness of observation provided by clinical research over long periods of time in more natural situations. As in so many instances in the history of science, some of our most important insights grow out of an occasional unique opportunity to make observations which ordinarily would not be possible.

The available evidence supports the view that gastrointestinal symptoms are exaggerated, if not precipitated, by stress. The relative effects of various types of stress and degrees of stress have not been demonstrated clearly. The psychoanalysts emphasize the relationship of the gastrointestinal tract to psychosexual development. They hold that disturbances of this developmental sequence may result in a variety of gastrointestinal problems. Difficulties in the digestion of food, and the consequent formation of gas, eating problems, and excessive appetite, are thought to be related to the oral phase of psychosexual development. Symptoms related to elimination, such as constipation, diarrhea, and inflammation of the lower colon, are looked upon as being related to disturbances of psychosexual development at the anal level (Engel, 1955).

While there is some clinical evidence to support such a position, the extension of the generalization to include all cases is not warranted. It is more likely that many types and degrees of stress are capable of resulting in gastrointestinal symptoms for psychologically and physiologically susceptible individuals.

Among the gastrointestinal psychophysiologic reactions are (1) loss of appetite, *anorexia nervosa,* (2) excessive appetite, *bulimia,* (3) stomach distress, *gastritis,* (4) a lesion of the mucous lining of the stomach or duodenum, *peptic ulcer,* and (5) inflammation of the colon, *colitis.* While each of these disorders may be emotionally determined, it should be kept in mind that infections, structural defects, faulty diet, metabolic disorders, and other organic conditions sometimes result in similar disturbances.

LOSS OF APPETITE

One of the most common psychophysiologic conditions is lack of appetite. People who are in conflict, grief-stricken, guilt-laden, excited, or filled with anticipation often experience a temporary loss of appetite. In its most chronic and serious form, patients must be tube-fed; and if they cannot be brought out of the condition, they may die of starvation or infection.

Anorexia nervosa was first described a hundred years ago (Gull, 1874). The disorder is marked by progressive weight loss and failure of appetite in the absence of organic pathology. The condition occurs most frequently among girls and young women and is often accompanied by such symptoms as menstrual disturbances, slow heart rate, low metabolic rate, and constipation. In spite of the emaciation, these patients sometimes show a remarkable energy and almost ceaseless activity.

Anorexia often gets its start during childhood. Children with very poor appetites are likely to have emotional problems, and most parents aggravate the emotional conflict in their children by the way in which they handle feeding problems. Anorexia may involve a long history of maternal overprotection, or it may be based on the opposite condition—maternal rejection (Lesser et al., 1960).

The disorder is most common between twelve and twenty-one years of age. Refusal of food might mean that the patient wants to make himself unattractive. It might be a defense against the possibility of marriage. It might be, at a more dynamic and analytic level, an unconscious fear of impregnation or a defense against prostitution desires (Goiten, 1942). A common fantasy of a great many children, and one that most people have repressed, is that babies are caused by something that is eaten by the mother. Among children, the refusal to eat may mean resistance to growing up. A child may have definite feelings about not wanting to grow older and meet the problems faced by his older brothers and sisters. Anorexia may also be a form of hostility. Refusing to eat may be an act of aggression against oneself or against others.

In many cases of anorexia nervosa, there are difficulties in the home, particularly involving hostility between the mother and the daughter. There may also be frustrations and disturbances in sexual adjustment. Secondary gains—benefits the patient derives from "trading on his symptoms" —are particularly important in this condition. Whatever the psychological dynamics may be, anorexia is a learned reaction designed to cope with stress.

EXCESSIVE APPETITE

Bulimia is a psychophysiologic reaction in which there is an excessive food intake, leading to obesity. The problem of obesity, once thought to be an endocrine matter, is in fact a result of glandular disturbances in relatively few cases. In most people, there are emotional reasons for the persistent overeating. The overeating may represent a substitute satisfaction of an unfulfilled need, or the obesity itself may have a defensive or symbolic value. Some obese patients show striking weight changes as their life situations improve during psychological treatment.

In the case of women, overeating is sometimes a protest against men or marriage, or it may be a substitute gratification. Food is substituted for love, for tenderness, and for attention. Other people grow fat and continue to be overweight because of the common belief that there is "security in size." The hostile nature of some forms of obesity is reflected in the popular phrase, "throwing your weight around."

Since many men and women have an unconscious desire to bear a child, overeating and obesity may be attempts to simulate pregnancy. One psychiatrist said, "Men as well as women have the longing to bear a child, and since a real child they can by no manner of means bring into their bodies, they imitate pregnancy by shaping out their bellies, and this is brought about by a symbolic fertilization of eating and drinking" (Groddeck, 1928).

According to psychoanalytic theory, the obese person is suffering from a disturbance of the oral phase of psychosexual development. The infant, during this phase, is preoccupied with the mouth and eating. If problems at this period are not adequately resolved, the oral needs of infancy may be carried to adult life (Bruch, 1957).

In the case of pregnant women, the tendency to overeat may be based on such factors as feelings of insecurity in the face of responsibilities of taking care of the expected infant, financial worries, concern over the loss of attractiveness, fear that the husband's love will be shifted to the baby, and similar problems. At a deeper level, the overeating may be an expression of unconscious death wishes against the child. The nausea and vomiting of early pregnancy, or *hyperemesis gravidarum*, also may have a psychogenic origin. The most common symbolism involved is the conscious or unconscious rejection of the fetus. However, since the nausea of pregnancy usually ceases at the third or fourth month, some authorities are inclined to believe that emotional factors are relatively unimportant. This argument is met by the suggestion that fetal movements first are felt at this time, and the mother becomes aware that the fetus is a separate individual and not something to be "thrown up" (Weiss and English, 1943).

GASTRITIS

The symptoms of gastric distress are closely associated with anger, guilt, anxiety, and other disturbing psychological stress. The most common symptoms of this generalized gastric disorder include indigestion, hyperacidity, belching, nausea, and flatulence.

Some people find that they begin to have gastrointestinal symptoms when they are faced with stressful situations. Such a reaction is not surprising in view of the fact that the gastrointestinal system is influenced to a large extent by the autonomic nervous system. When the emergency functions of the sympathetic segments of the autonomic system take over, there are important reverberations in the stomach and intestine. The problem, as in other psychophysiologic reactions, is not how the stress and emotional disturbance is translated into physical symptoms, but why it is expressed through the gastrointestinal system in one patient and not in another patient. The solution to this problem is to be found in the interplay between a basically weak body system, learned ways of reacting, and symbolism. It is not unusual for the small child to use vomiting or diarrhea as an aggressive action against the mother. Similarly, constipation among children is used as a device to manipulate the parents. Among adults, gastritis may serve as an attention-getting device, as a means of aggression against oneself or against others, or as a symbol of any one of a number of complex needs and conflicts (Alvarez, 1943).

At the least complicated level, gastritis is a direct reflection of the emergency functions of the sympathetic nervous system. In a constitutionally predisposed gastrointestinal system, the autonomic response to stress upsets the balance of the system and throws it into a state of disorganization. Digestion is upset, there is disturbance of the acidity-alkalinity balance, and stomach movements are interrupted. The result is not infrequently the chain of symptoms characteristic of gastritis.

It is also possible that a patient learns to react to stress by means of gastrointestinal symptoms. If a child is brought up in a family in which the mother or father reacts characteristically with the stomach or intestinal symptoms, the child may learn to adopt a similar pattern, particularly where the secondary gains of the symptoms are more or less apparent. If an adult receives extra care and attention and other advantages from his symptoms, a child may turn unconsciously to these same symptoms later in life. In such cases, there need be no question of an inherently weakened body system, and symbolic factors may not be involved. It is more likely a matter of conditioned learning.

As with other psychophysiologic reactions, there have been many attempts to correlate personality characteristics with the symptoms of gastritis. The factors which seem to occur most frequently in these people include a domineering parent, combined frequently with sibling rivalry and jealousy; repressed resentment and aggressive tendencies toward authority in general; and the symbolic equation of vomiting and diarrhea with rejection. While these relationships have some degree of clinical validation, it is unwise to make the sweeping generalization that all victims of gastritis show these characteristics.

PEPTIC ULCER

The peptic ulcer is an open sore situated on the lining of the stomach or, more frequently, the upper portion of the small intestine. The symptoms include pain that comes one to two hours after a meal and that can be eased by eating. There may be nausea or vomiting along with the pain. In more serious cases, there is bleeding. Peptic ulcers are frequent in modern civilized life, with an estimated 7 to 10 percent of the adult population having, or having had, the disorder. The symptoms, while very real in a physical sense,

are nevertheless the result of a complex interplay of emotional and organic factors.

The secretion of gastric juice is the most important physical factor in the production of peptic ulcers. The presence of this juice was first demonstrated at the University of Pennsylvania in 1803. It was shown that the stomach secretes a highly acid fluid, and that this fluid plays an important role in gastric digestion. The experiments showed that the gastric fluid would "digest" the leg of a frog or the ear of a rabbit (Mettler and Mettler, 1947).

There are three important components of gastric secretion: mucus, pepsin, and hydrochloric acid. The mucus protects the walls of the digestive tract from direct contact with noxious substances and helps carry away irritating agents. The pepsin is a protein-splitting enzyme essential to the process of breaking down food products and preparing them for absorption into the body. Hydrochloric acid is a powerful corrosive agent, and while it does not irritate the normal stomach or intestines, it plays an important role in the development of peptic ulcers. Almost every patient with this condition has an oversecretion of hydrochloric acid. Among physiologically normal subjects, only a small number show a similar oversecretion.

While the exact mechanism of the production of peptic ulcers is not known, it is possible that persistent emotional stress and the resulting activity of the autonomic nervous system affect the functioning of the vagus nerve, which controls both the secretion of gastric juice and the rhythmic motions of the stomach. In this way, emotional conflict exerts a direct influence on the physical state of the gastrointestinal tract.

It is also possible that the disturbed sensitivity of the walls of the stomach and intestines makes possible a greater likelihood of small irritations and lesions due to rough and irritating food products. Once such a break in the lining has been made, the abnormally large amount of hydrochloric acid begins its corrosive and destructive action.

The relation of stress to the development of ulcers was demonstrated dramatically in an experiment at the Walter Reed Army Institute of Research, where two monkeys in adjacent restraining chairs received electrical shocks, but only one monkey could prevent them (Brady, 1958). The "executive" monkey was able to avoid shocks to himself and his partner by pressing a lever. The control monkey also had a lever, but it served no function. Both monkeys received the same number of shocks, and at the same times, but only the executive monkey faced the psychological stress of trying to avoid the shock by pressing the lever.

The monkeys were placed on a schedule of shock avoidance and rest, each period lasting six hours. A red light was turned on during the avoidance periods and off during the rest periods. The executive monkey very quickly learned to press its lever at the rate of between fifteen and twenty times a minute during the avoidance periods and to stop pressing when the red light was off. While the control monkey also pressed the lever from time to time, he soon lost interest since there was no reinforcement of any kind when the lever was pressed.

After twenty-three days of the six-hour schedule, the executive monkey died suddenly during one of the shock-avoidance sessions. There had been no advance warning except that the animal had not eaten on the preceding day. Moreover, the animal had not lost weight during the experimental sessions. The autopsy showed a large perforation in the wall of the upper part of the small intestine near the point where it joins the stomach. This location is a common site of ulcers in man. The control monkey was killed a few hours later, and an autopsy revealed no gastrointestinal abnormalities. Since the control animal was not under stress, psychophysiologic changes did not occur. Additional experiments with a number of monkeys verified these findings.

Animal experiments, as well as clinical observations of patients, have led to a search for a particular type of individual susceptible to peptic ulcer. He has been described as a hard-driving individual in a highly competitive type of work. The condition is almost an occupational disease in advertising and in the radio and television industry, where competition is extremely keen. When these hard-driving men are examined psychologically, the high-pressure exterior sometimes is found to be a mask for an inner personality that is dependent and needs affection and love in an almost childlike way. The outward personality

Figure 9.4 *The executive monkey. The monkey on the left was forced to make decisions, and it was he who developed the ulcers. (Courtesy of the Medical Audio Visual Department, Walter Reed Army Institute of Research, Washington, D.C.)*

appears to be a compensation for the inner dependency. The conflict between having to make one's way in a competitive culture and the unconscious need to lean on someone else seems to be associated with the development of the ulcer. The trait of obsessive thinking has also been emphasized in the peptic ulcer case. At a more symbolic level, the source of the difficulty has been described psychoanalytically as an internalized "bad mother" who literally devours the patient from within (Garma, 1950). The existence of a general personality type prone to peptic ulcer and a psychodynamic pattern common to all patients has yet to be demonstrated.

COLITIS

Colitis is a condition in which there are multiple symptoms which may include diarrhea, constipation, lower abdominal pain, and bleeding. Colitis has been less well recognized than peptic ulcer as a psychophysiologic disorder. However, there is increasing evidence of the importance of emotional factors in the etiology of both *mucous colitis* and *ulcerative colitis*. In mucous colitis, the principal symptom is the elimination of stools containing mucous. Ordinarily the patient's appetite is poor, and he complains of indigestion. Because of the distress, he eats less in an attempt to avoid discomfort. It is not unusual to find the patient with feelings of heaviness and pain after eating, distention of the stomach, belching, flatulence, and nausea. The symptoms are frequently attributed to a wide variety of physical disturbances.

Ulcerative colitis is a condition in which there is fragility of the mucous membrane of the colon, resulting in bleeding and ulcers. The patient frequently experiences attacks of ulcerative colitis after an emotional episode. Death in the family, separation and divorce, loss of a job, and similar events have precipitated attacks of ulcerative colitis.

Attempts to relate a specific personality pattern to susceptibility to colitis suggest that these patients are likely to be average or above in intelligence but lacking the capacity for appropriate emotional experiences. When difficulties arise, these patients may respond with depression and rage accompanied by disorganization of the bowel functions. Other studies show these patients to be highly narcissistic and preoccupied with the body (Brown et al., 1938). Dynamically, they are believed to function at an immature level of psychosexual development. As early as 1910, psychoanalysts suggested that the bleeding in ulcerative colitis might be related to unconscious anal fantasies of the patient (Ferenczi, 1926).

While it would be valuable to identify a unique personality pattern related to colitis, such a pattern has yet to be demonstrated with any degree of validity. The personality characteristics usually attributed to the colitis patient are very similar to those mentioned for a number of other psycho-

physiologic reactions. The particular personality pattern is much less important than the inability to handle stress situations in an effective manner.[4]

RESPIRATORY DISORDERS

Breathing difficulties are often associated with emotional stress and fear-provoking situations. Many patients sigh excessively, gasp for breath, or experience feelings of suffocation when confronted with difficult problems or situations from which they cannot escape. The importance of emotional factors in connection with respiration is seen in our everyday language. "Breathtaking" experiences are common events. In some emotional situations, a person needs "to catch his breath." An individual with a great worry feels that he has "a weight on his chest."

At the symbolic level, emotional respiratory reactions may be related to the birth experience. A British psychoanalyst said that the experience of suffocation in stress situations is a "reenactment of the panic with which we drew our first lungful of air after being born into this world" (Fodor, 1949). According to this theory, the breathing difficulties are connected with a fear which originally occurred when the infant was cut off from the blood supply of the mother and found it necessary to start his own breathing. While interesting, the theory has little clinical or experimental support.

COMMON COLD

There is increasing clinical evidence that the common cold has important emotional components. The condition in some cases may be a reaction to frustration or irritation, neglect, need for attention, need to avoid an unpleasant situation, or any one of many other life problems. There is also indication that individuals under stress are more likely to develop colds than individuals who are not under stress (Meerloo, 1958).

---

[4]The following books deal with the psychosomatic aspects of gastrointestinal conditions: *Anorexia Nervosa* (Hoeber, 1960) by E. L. Bliss and C. H. Branch; *The Human Colon: An Experimental Study* (Hoeber, 1951) by W. J. Grace, Stewart Wolf, and H. G. Wolff; and Angel Garma's *Peptic Ulcer and Psychoanalysis* (Williams and Wilkins, 1958).

Physiologically, there are direct pathways from the autonomic nervous system to the nose, mouth, throat, and sinus cavities. During emotional states the nasal mucosa swells, a condition readily observable during weeping. As a result of the autonomic innervation of the critical head areas, emotional stress may result in tissue changes which may make the individual more susceptible to the common cold by reducing resistance to the organism causing the cold.

Psychologically, the common cold is capable of serving a variety of purposes. It may be an excuse for rest and regression, it is sometimes an instrument of hostility and aggression, and it may be a source of increased attention and concern on the part of others. One woman appeared to have frequent and prolonged colds because it made it possible for her to remain at home "close to mother." In other cases, the cold may make it unnecessary to go to school or to work, or to face some other unpleasant task or undesirable situation.

A study was made of a series of people who were being treated by psychoanalysis for other reasons, but who also were subject to repeated colds. Following treatment of these people for the primary complaints, the colds either disappeared completely or became less frequent. One woman who was subject to colds was found to be restless and anxious and to have a hypochondriacal fear of tuberculosis. She developed a cold whenever she became distressed or panicky because her intense demand for attention and affection was thwarted. It is possible that the general feeling of fatigue and loss of energy related to a cold may be a form of mild mental depression and anxiety accompanying the cold rather than the toxic manifestations of the local inflammation itself (Alexander and Saul, 1940).

RHINITIS

Rhinitis involves a congestion of the nasal mucous membrane and the blood vessels of the eyes. In most cases, there is a watery secretion from the nose combined with sneezing and itching. While rhinitis may be due to a local irritative process or to an allergy, there are cases in which the congestion apparently grows out of emotional disturbances. The specialist in diseases of the eye, ear, nose, and throat is confronted from time to time with reactions for which there do not appear to be adequate physical causes. In such cases, the possibility of a psychogenic origin for the disturbance must be considered.

Since both the nasal mucosa and the blood vessels of the eyes have a rich supply of autonomic nerve fibers, the basic connections among stress situations, the patient's emotional reaction to these situations, and the physical symptoms are established clearly. The psychological background of psychophysiologic reactions of this type must be determined for each individual case. It has been suggested that the major stress situation in rhinitis is a frustrated dependency longing directed toward the mother or the mother substitute. Psychoanalysts believe that the reaction may be related in some cases to sexual curiosity and the need to look and to smell.

A young man developed a severe attack of rhinitis following his first visit to a burlesque show. During the performance, the man noticed that his eyes began to water and that there was a congested feeling in his nose. He recalled that at the time the thought flashed through his mind that he was catching cold. The next day the rhinitis was so severe that the man consulted a physician. Some degree of relief was obtained by means of conventional treatment, but there was a tendency for the symptoms to recur from time to time. Eventually the man was referred for psychological treatment, and it was discovered that the attacks of rhinitis occurred each time the patient dated a provocative and somewhat promiscuous young woman. The further study of the case verified the relationship between the symptoms and the erotic dating experience.

HYPERVENTILATION SYNDROME

The hyperventilation syndrome is a respiratory reaction in which the person overbreathes. There is an increase in the depth and rapidity of respiration which, when continued over a period of time, results in a number of physiologic changes, with the person experiencing a variety of subjective symptoms. Dizziness, lightheadedness, numbness, and tingling of the hands and feet are frequent symptoms. Blurred vision is common, and people sometimes feel they are about to faint. There may be a sensation of air hunger and shortness of breath. Some people report a feeling of pressure in the chest or pain in the region of the heart. At the physiological level, the symptoms are caused by an oversupply of oxygen in the body cells. The reaction is ordinarily set off by acute anxiety of a situational kind. It is not unusual for these people to be able to describe the exact situations in which the hyperventilation occurs. In some cases, the hyperventilation takes place at night in connection with dreams and nightmares.

BRONCHIAL ASTHMA

Bronchial asthma is marked by difficulty in breathing due to spasms of the bronchial muscles. In addition, there may be inflammation or swelling of the bronchial mucosa, with shortness of breath, coughing, wheezing, and a sense of constriction of the chest. In many cases, the disturbance is due to a hypersensitivity to substances which are inhaled or ingested, or to the action of bacteria. In other cases, however, emotional factors appear to play an important role (French and Alexander, 1941). These factors have been recognized for centuries, and even the discovery of allergic hypersensitivity to specific substances failed to rule out the part played by psychological conflict in some cases.

A number of studies have been made of the personality characteristics of children suffering from asthma. Such children appear to be of above average intelligence, are inclined to be irritable and aggressive, and show signs of insecurity, anxiety, and a lack of self-confidence (Heuhaus, 1958). Adult victims are likely to have a deep-seated fear of separation and may show a history of strong maternal dependence (Knapp et al., 1957). Such people seem to have a need to be protected and sheltered. If they marry, it is usually late in life. Whenever these people are faced with a separation from the mother or a mother substitute an asthmatic attack may be precipitated. It is likely that there has been considerable illness in the immediate family history, that the person has marked heterosexual conflict, and that he is frequently faced with the necessity for simultaneous expression of love and hate toward the same person (Treuting and Ripley, 1948).

At the psychodynamic level, asthma may be aggression against someone else or against oneself. Simply being ill, unpleasant, and difficult to care for is sometimes an expression of aggression against other people. Asthma is commonly associated with possessiveness or retentiveness, and attacks may be associated with financial stringency. Misers are frequently described in literature as "wheezing" when they count their gold. According to one psychodynamic theory, the attack represents a repressed cry of anger and anxiety. The asthma attack has also been regarded as a cry for help and an infantile appeal not to be left alone. As in the case of much theorizing in psychodynamics, experimental validation is lacking.

■ ASTHMA

John R. is a thirty-three-year-old married man who was referred for psychological treatment in connection with his asthma. The medical specialist who had been treating the patient came to the conclusion that an important component in the case was emotional. The patient gave a history of rather severe attacks of asthma from the time he was sixteen. The first attack occurred at a summer camp where the boy had been sent while his parents were traveling in Europe. The severity of the attack was such that the camp notified the parents who cut their trip short and returned home. Another severe attack occurred while the patient was a freshman at a college in another part of the country. Once again, the attack was so serious that it was decided that it would be best if the patient were to attend the university in the city in which his parents lived. While it was not apparent at the time, the major attacks in this case occurred in connection with the stress of separation. The symptom which finally brought him to the medical specialist developed following his marriage. The attacks increased both in severity and frequency to the point that numerous medical consultations were held. The usual diagnostic and treatment procedures were of little effect, and the patient continued to suffer. It was at this time that the physician decided that psychological treatment was indicated. After a period of such treatment, the patient began to understand how his symptoms had become an effective way of protecting himself against separation from his family, particularly an overly affectionate and indulgent mother. The patient saw that prior to his marriage he was able to use the asthma attack as a device for keeping his mother near to him. He saw also that following his marriage, the device which had worked so successfully earlier in life was now of little use. The increased understanding made it possible to readjust his emotional attitudes toward his wife and his mother. From that time, the symptoms gradually disappeared.

The most suitable soil for the development of asthma appears to be a combination of a sensitive autonomic system, a tendency toward allergy, and emotional stress. When these three factors are combined, the psychological conflicts of the individual may be discharged through spasms of the respiratory system.

TUBERCULOSIS

There has been a suspicion for many years that a relationship exists between personality and tuberculosis. Medical writers suggested such a relationship as early as Greek medicine and from time to time since the eighteenth century. More recently, Thomas Mann, in his novel *The Magic Mountain*, wrote about a patient at a tuberculosis sanitarium and the role emotional factors play in this illness. This book had a remarkable influence on the thinking of the medical profession and the general public.

Tuberculosis is caused by a bacillus which results in a chronic inflammation in some part of the body, usually the lungs. It is well established, however, that emotional situations influence the resistance of the body to the disease. Patients who are about to leave a sanitarium frequently have a recurrence of their symptoms, possibly as a result of the threatened separation from their secure and familiar environment.

Among the personality characteristics that have been attributed to the tuberculosis patient are difficulties in establishing social contacts, sexual promiscuity, feelings of ambivalence, and a tendency toward a self-defeatist philosophy with accompanying ideas of suicide. Such patients sometimes show periods of depression with outbursts of hostility and aggression. It is not unusual to find uncertainty, self-doubt, and indecision in these patients, who have been described variously as sensitive, anxious, and emotionally volatile.

The personality pattern associated with the tubercular patient is probably a learned response to the illness rather than a constitutionally determined pattern. However, clinical investigations in constitutional medicine have suggested the possibility of a fundamental relationship between the asthenic body type and the susceptibility to the tubercle bacillus (Flarsheim, 1958). If such a relationship does in fact exist, and if temperamental differences can be shown to be innately related to biotypes, it is possible that at least some of the personality characteristics of the tubercular patient are determined genetically. With the present state of our knowledge, it is necessary to be extremely cautious in making generalizations concerning the relationship of personality types to specific psychophysiologic disorders.[5]

SKIN DISORDERS

The relation of skin reactions to emotional behavior has been observed for centuries. Nearly everyone is familiar with some of the ways in which the skin mirrors the emotions in everyday life. When people are embarrassed, the skin flushes, and they "blush." In severe fright or states of intense anger, the blood is drawn out of the small capillaries of the skin, and the face pales and blanches. When people are tense and upset, they may develop acne or a skin rash.

The close relationship between personality dynamics and the skin is illustrated in the use of such everyday phrases as "thin-skinned" for sensitive people; "thick-skinned" for people who are impervious to criticism; and "He is getting under my skin" for a person who is irri-

---

[5]The relationship between the emotions and the respiratory system is discussed in G. F. Derner's *Aspects of the Psychology of the Tuberculous* (Hoeber, 1953); *Psychological and Allergic Aspects of Asthma* (Thomas, 1965) edited by M. L. Hirt; and *Allergy and Human Emotions* (Thomas, 1966) by J. P. McGovern and J. A. Knight.

tating. Many other phrases reflect the unconscious realization of the psychological link between the skin and the emotions. "I burn with shame," "I blush for you," "I itch for a fight," and similar phrases constitute a body language by means of which the individual may express important psychological relationships in a deeply symbolic manner.

The skin is an unusually sensitive indicator of emotional conflict because it is so richly supplied with small blood vessels under the control of the autonomic nervous system. In this way, internal psychological threats to the individual are expressed through the activation of the autonomic system in various skin disorders.

In addition, there is an important secondary emotional factor in skin disorders which is not present in other forms of disease. This is the fact that skin disorders usually cannot be hidden, and the disease is seen by other people. To make matters worse, there is a repulsive quality to many skin diseases, based on the stereotyped idea of dirt, filth, and contagion. While most skin diseases today are not contagious, the popular idea of uncleanliness or contagion clings to skin disorders. Moreover, skin disorders strike at the body image, or the person's conception of his own appearance. A rash, acne, or other blemish on the face or hands may have an important impact on the ego as well as the emotions.

The psychological component in skin reactions has been demonstrated clinically to a greater extent than in any other of the psychosomatic disorders. In many cases it is possible to show how skin symptoms grow out of feelings of guilt, anger, hostility, resentment, inadequacy, and other damaging emotions (Obermayer, 1955).

STIGMATIZATION

The symbolic nature of certain skin reactions is shown dramatically in religious *stigmatization*. Louise Lateau, a French stigmatic of the late nineteenth century, noticed blood on the left side of her chest on Good Friday. At that time she was eighteen years old. She said nothing about it to anyone, but on the following Friday she again noticed blood at the same spot, and also on the top of her left foot. Early on the morning of the

third Friday, blood began to ooze from her left side and from both feet; by nine o'clock it flowed freely from the palms and backs of her hands. These bleedings occurred regularly for two years during which she was observed by physicians (Bourneville, 1878).

Therese Neumann of Konnersreuth, Germany, is the most famous of present-day stigmatics. For a number of years before her death in 1962, the mark of the wounds (stigmata) that Christ received during His crucifixion appeared every Good Friday on her face, hands, and feet (Hynek, 1932). She was observed by thousands of people who filed past her bed and by a number of physicians and psychiatrists. There was no question about the reality of her wounds.

Another unusual case is that of a Canadian woman, Eva McIsaac. The first stigmata occurred in 1934 in the form of a small, painful sore on the back of her right hand. Over the next three years, other wounds appeared on the palms of her hands, her instep, the soles of her feet, her side, and on her head just below the hairline. These wounds, corresponding in location to the wounds on Christ's body, began to bleed at 6 P.M. and continued to bleed until 9 P.M. The Archbishop of Toronto arranged for detailed hospital examinations by Catholic, Protestant, and Jewish physicians. A physician described the bleeding in the following words:

> Mrs. McIsaac was bright, lively and full of energy right up until late Friday afternoon. During the early part of the week she was in very good health despite the marks. . . . On Friday afternoon the marks on her body began to lose their hardness, and towards six o'clock they appeared more like fresh wounds. It was apparent that she was beginning to feel pain. . . . She appeared to lapse into a trance. . . . Her pain seemed to intensify to agony. . . . Soon a drop of blood began to form at one of the foot wounds. . . . Gradually the hands and the other wounds began to bleed. . . . Toward nine o'clock the flow of blood stopped, the pain seemed to go, and she appeared to sleep normally. . . . On Saturday morning she appeared surprisingly fresh and youthful-looking and in very good health (*Time*, 1950).

In all such cases, the flow of blood is related to some meaningful religious event. The relationship can easily be traced in such famous historical ecstatics and stigmatists as Jeanne de

Chantal, Anna Emmerich, Veronica Giuliani, Gemma Galgani, Niklutsch, and others. The inner anxiety appears to be converted into the physical expression of the intense identification with Christ or some other religious figure.

A somewhat related evidence of the effect of psychological factors on skin disorders is seen in connection with the healing of warts. The cure of warts by suggestion has been known for centuries and appears in the literature of widely scattered cultures. Various types of magical cures, prayer, incantation, bizarre rites, and other procedures have been suggested. Huckleberry Finn included dead cats, spunk water, and bloody beans among his remedies. While the clinical evidence for the effect of suggestion on warts is quite persuasive, very little controlled work has been done in this area. The apparent cures of warts by psychological methods may be instances of spontaneous improvement. Arguing against this explanation is the fact that the disappearance of warts following psychological treatment occurs within a very short period following the treatment. The probability of spontaneous improvement occurring at precisely these times would seem to be relatively slight.

NEURODERMATOSIS

The term *neurodermatosis* was introduced to describe skin disorders which seem to occur in cases of emotional instability. These disorders are revealed in a number of ways. Ring-finger dermatitis, in which the skin disorder is under the marriage band or, less frequently, under the engagement ring, is a relatively common condition. For many years, it was believed that the skin irritation was due to an allergy to the metal in the band or to soap or dirt under the ring. However, if the ring is placed on another finger, the skin irritation ordinarily does not appear at that point. In one case, removal of the marriage band appeared to represent a symbolic divorce of a woman from a marital situation which she found intolerable. When the band was removed, the skin disorder cleared (Sanger, 1959).

Another type of skin disorder which may have symbolic meaning is dermatitis of the thumb. This condition is sometimes found in immature

women who give the impression of being overwhelmed by life. Some psychoanalysts suggest that such women want to return to the security of sucking on a baby's bottle or the mother's breast. The thumb becomes a substitute for these objects, and since the woman is too big a "girl" to suck her thumb, the skin disorder protects her from the temptation of doing it. It is a provocative theory in spite of its uncertain validity.

Symbolism may also be involved in skin disorder of the external ear. *Otitis externa* is a chronic condition which often resists treatment and persists for prolonged periods. In some cases, this type of skin disorder seems to be related to the individual's fear of hearing something unpleasant. The disease of the ear appears to represent an attempt to avoid hearing the "bad news." One woman developed a skin disorder of her ear at the time her husband had his first heart attack. His condition was quite serious, and the woman was warned that another attack, possibly fatal, might occur at any time. The woman was hostile to her husband, and the hostility was accompanied by a sense of guilt and shame. The ear disease was an unconscious protection against her hostility. The disorder prevented her from hearing the news she could not admit she wanted to hear (Sanger, 1959).

Similarly, the theory has been advanced that skin disturbances of the fingers sometimes have sexual significance. According to this view, people who would like to indulge in sexual stimulation or contact but because of moral or personal reasons are unable to do so may develop a finger rash. It is believed that the dermatitis serves as a protective device, preventing the patient from engaging in erotic activities.

Skin disorders of the eyelids are also not unusual. Many cases are due to nail polish and are a form of contact dermatitis. But when physical causes have been ruled out, skin disorder of the eyelids may represent a defense against visual conflict. A woman who was no longer happy with her husband and who was "sick at the sight of him" developed a chronic dermatitis of her eyelids. It was only when the couple separated that the physical condition cleared (Sanger, 1959).

Symbolic meaning is not difficult to detect in skin disorders of the lips. Teen-age girls, who have strong needs for affection and kissing and are frustrated in these desires because of age and moral problems, occasionally develop this form of psychological skin disorder. The lip irritation prevents the person from doing what she would like to do. Moreover, the disorder serves to interrupt her preoccupation with members of the opposite sex.

Sometimes the skin reaction is related to anxiety over a future event. It is not unusual for the father of the bride or the mother of the groom to develop a skin lesion just before the wedding. One mother developed a severe eczema from head to foot when her son—"her baby"—was about to be married. The mother was distressed at the idea of the marriage and hostile toward her future daughter-in-law. In discussing her symptoms with a physician, she told of her sorrow at the thought of "losing" her son. She said she would not be able to attend the wedding because she could not get dressed, since the skin disorder had turned into a mass of oozing crusts. During the interview, the patient began to see that she was making excessive demands on her son and that life would continue to go on after he was married. She began to realize that she still had her husband, her friends, and many interests. As her insight into the situation increased over a period of time, the skin disorder began to clear.

The role of hostility and aggression in various skin disorders has also been emphasized by specialists in this field. Excessive scratching has been regarded as a displacement of the wish to be aggressive toward someone else. Instead, the individual turns the aggression on to himself. While the masochistic and self-punitive nature of such behavior seems clear, this interpretation is by no means generally accepted. Clinical support for these theories is not established firmly, and experimental evidence is completely lacking.[6]

GENITOURINARY DISORDERS

The realization that the emotional life has an important influence upon the functions of the genitourinary system is not new. The ancients were aware that both sexual and excretory processes could be excited or inhibited by emotional factors. Today, urologists and gynecologists emphasize the importance of psychological stress and conflict in disorders associated with the pelvic region and its sexual and eliminative functions. A psychiatrist at the gynecologic clinic of St. Mary's and Queen Charlotte's Hospitals in London found that 70 percent of the women attending the clinic were suffering from an illness which was entirely or mainly the result of emotional stress (Kroger and Freed, 1956).

URINARY DISTURBANCES

It is well established that at least some urinary disturbances may be caused by emotional conflict (Chapman, 1959). There are many everyday indications of the relationship between bladder function and emotional states. Since the urinary tract is richly supplied with autonomic fibers, such a relationship should not be surprising. It is not uncommon for bladder function to be inhibited in strange and unusual situations. A number of people find it difficult or impossible to urinate into a bottle when admitted into a hospital. Others cannot urinate in the presence of other people, and many women complain of a chronic frequency of urination, even though there is no apparent physiological or morphological reason for it.

In general, changes of bladder function are related to anxiety. In one experiment, it was shown that urinary frequency was associated with anxiety, aggressiveness and resentment, and overt conflict. The retention of urine was more likely to be related to emotional repression. These results were obtained by measuring bladder pressure during psychological interviews (Straub et al., 1949).

Enuresis, or bedwetting, is the most frequent urinary disturbance of childhood. Large numbers of youngsters continue to be enuretic long after toilet training has been completed. Some children continue to wet the bed until late childhood or adolescence. In such cases, the enuretic child

---

[6]M. E. Obermayer's *Psychocutaneous Medicine* (Thomas, 1955) is a comprehensive treatment of the various ways in which one's emotions influence the skin and its disorders.

is usually involved in a conflict situation. Psychological treatment of the family or manipulation of the child's environment often results in the disappearance of the symptom. Significantly, enuresis tends to recur at times of great stress. During war, enuresis is a common problem among men in military reception centers.

There is also an erotic element in urination, and the urinary disturbance may be related to sexual conflict. While the main purpose of urination is the relief of organic tension caused by the distended bladder, urination is also one of the first pleasurable experiences in infancy. The toilet functions are assoicated with sexuality in the child and adolescent, and urinary activity may be equated with sexual activity through conditioning. Many men and women have an increased frequency of urination when in the company of members of the opposite sex. Disturbances in urination in some cases may be learned in connection with problems related to early psychosexual development.

Urinary disturbances may also be an expression of hostility and aggression. Enuresis in the child or adolescent may be a learned aggressive act against the authority of adults. Every parent has been faced at times with the uncomfortable feeling that the child's lack of sphincter control is an act of revenge. It is very probable that this is the case, and that a similar element of hostility is present in some cases of urinary disturbance later in life.

MENSTRUAL DISORDERS

The onset of menstruation is especially tinged with emotion and may be one of the important precipitating factors of genitourinary disorders in women. All cultural groups show guilt over this phenomenon and try to explain it through taboos and rituals in their folklore. Some think it is a sign that a snake or some other wild animal has injured the girl, while others look upon it as a contamination that is dangerous to men. This natural phenomenon continues to be thought of today as disgusting and dirty by many people.

It is easy to see how an unhealthy concept of menstruation can be learned early in life. The child may accidentally witness the passing of blood; and, if not informed, she is forced to form her own opinion of the incident. Later, the adolescent girl may feel the hostile and unsympathetic attitude of others when she begins her menstrual flow.

Before the onset of each menstural period there is usually an emotional reaction in women which has been called *premenstrual tension*. Women often become moody, and may show anxiety symptoms of varying degrees of severity. Ordinarily the symptoms disappear at the beginning of menstruation, but in some cases they are aggravated during the menstrual period. Such symptoms may involve resentment in connection with the feminine role, or there may be a physiological basis for the disturbance.

During the premenstrual state, tension builds up gradually, with increasing restlessness, inability to concentrate, unreasonable emotional outbursts, crying spells without cause, and irritability and annoyance over trifles. These psychological changes may be accompanied by headache, backache, and insomnia. "The hair-trigger, razor-edged temper, which is usually noted by the patient herself, taxes the endurance of her family and friends" (Israel, 1959). The changes in personality during the premenstrual state can be so extreme in some women that there is a relationship between this period of the menstrual cycle and criminal offenses. In a prison survey in the United States, it was found that 62 percent of the offenses for which women were imprisoned had been committed during the premenstrual week (Oleck, 1953). In France, the premenstrual week is given official legal recognition in the form of "temporary insanity or incompetence." Some of the possible psychological reasons for premenstrual tension include unresolved Oedipal conflicts, resentment of the feminine role, hidden marital problems, and the fear of pregnancy. While most women experience some degree of premenstrual tension, the disorder is more severe in women with a neurotic constitution.

Dysmenorrhea, or the pain of menstruation, is one of the most common painful experiences of women. The menstrual period is marked by a number of physiologic changes brought about by the action of the endocrine glands. Body fluids are increased, with some women gaining as much as 5 pounds in weight. Other important metabolic and biochemical changes also occur which may be a factor in painful menstruation. There is growing evidence, however, that psychological factors play an important part in the painful experience in many women. In some cases there is a reluctance to assume the feminine role; in other women, there is an unconscious association of menstruation with injury.

One study has shown that many women with this disorder were aggressive tomboys in childhood. They made it clear they did not want to be girls. Others were found to be ailing or dependent children who were unwilling to give up their desire for dependence in adulthood. They had a strong need for sympathy and protection, and they were resentful, shy, or chronically anxious and complaining. Masculine physical characteristics were also found in a number of these cases. Another study found that dysmenorrhea was more likely to occur in young unmarried women. The disorder seemed to start when the young woman first came into contact with adult sex problems. The condition was often accompanied by fantasies that the sex act was cruel and painful (Kroger and Freed, 1956).

The importance of parental attitudes in this condition also must not be overlooked. A Scottish psychiatrist, in commenting on dysmenorrhea in young girls, said, "You will find that most of these girls have got utterly idiotic, though extremely well-meaning, mothers."

In another condition, called *psychogenic amenorrhea*, there is a decrease or complete cessation of menstruation in the absence of organic, endocrine, or nutritional disturbances. In such cases there may be situational factors of a stressful nature which precipitate the condition. Emotional shock, sexual conflict, tension created by quarreling and arguments, intense desire for pregnancy, or death of a parent, particularly the father, are a few of the conditions which have been associated with psychogenic amenorrhea. In other cases, the emotional conflict may be deeply repressed, making it extremely difficult to determine the cause.

Clinical observations have indicated that there is a relatively high rate of amenorrhea during times of war. At first it was thought that the condition was due to a dietary factor, but further studies showed that the condition appeared as frequently in well-nourished women as in undernourished women. Eventually it became clear that the menstrual disturbance was related to the lack of men, since the symptoms disappeared when the opportunity for sexual relationships was restored, even though such relationships never took place (Ekstein, 1919).

While psychogenic amenorrhea has been well established as a clinical syndrome, psychogenic bleeding also occurs. It is not unusual for a bride to begin menstruating on her wedding night, much to her surprise and embarrassment. In such cases, the protective nature of the occurrence is quite clear. The clinical observations in connection with both psychogenic amenorrhea and psychological bleeding suggest the powerful effect of the general emotional climate upon the woman and her neuroendocrine sensitivity to stress and emotional conflict.

PSEUDOCYESIS

One of the truly striking examples of the psychophysiologic relationship is seen in *pseudocyesis*, or false pregnancy. In most cases, the individual believes she is pregnant and develops all the signs of pregnancy. Such cases have been reported for many years, but it has been relatively recently that studies have been made attempting to correlate the psychological and gynecological factors.

Women with psuedocyesis may show all of the physical changes associated with the early stages of gestation. Amenorrhea, weight increase, greater frequency of urination, changes in gait, and nausea are often present. There may also be extensive mammary and uterine changes. It is not unusual to find enlargement of the breasts with darkening of the nipple, swelling of the veins, softening of the uterine cervix, enlargement of the uterus, and distention of the abdomen. In some cases, the symptoms are so pronounced that mistaken diagnoses are made. The woman goes to term and appears at the hospital with "labor pains."

Hippocrates, who reported a series of these cases, believed that the condition was due to excessive air in the womb, combined with retained menstrual fluid. Today the explanation is more likely to be made in psychogenic terms and is frequently related to an intense fear of pregnancy or to its antithesis, a strong desire for pregnancy. The false pregnancy is an attempt on the part of the body to solve an unconscious conflict. Sometimes a pregnancy is needed to appease feelings of guilt, to satisfy an unconscious desire to be like contemporaries who have children, or to attempt to save a shaky marriage. The wish for pregnancy may also be related to the unconsciously anticipated disappointment, in order to satisfy hostile and aggressive needs.

Sometimes the symptoms of pseudocyesis disappear with dramatic suddenness after a diagnosis of false pregnancy has been made. Some women who have been amenorrheic for months have a return of the menstrual cycle within a day or two following an examination. Other women who have had weeks or months of nausea and other physical symptoms are able to go back to work at once and are no longer ill.

SPONTANEOUS ABORTION

There is reliable evidence that at least some cases of spontaneous abortion are of emotional origin. It has been shown that anxiety resulting from careless remarks by the obstetrician may be effective in precipitating an abortion (Squier and Dunbar, 1946). It is also true that psychological treatment is sometimes effective in overcoming the habitual tendency to abort. In one case, a thirty-seven-year-old woman had a series of seven pregnancies, each resulting in a spontaneous abortion. Psychotherapy was then undertaken and continued until an eighth pregnancy resulted in the normal birth of a healthy infant (Sala and Salerno, 1945).

A group of habitual aborters without apparent organic basis for the disorder was compared with a group of patients with no history of spontaneous abortion. Psychological tests showed a number of significant differences. The habitual aborters, as a group, had an impaired ability to plan and anticipate, poor emotional control, great-

er conformity and compliance with the conventional, more tension related to hostile emotions, stronger feelings of dependency, and a greater tendency toward feelings of guilt. Moreover, in those habitual aborters who remained pregnant following psychotherapy, there was a significant change in scores in the direction of the control group (Grimm, 1962).

Since the uterine blood circulation and other physiological functions are regulated by the autonomic nervous system, and since the autonomic system is in turn sensitive to both internal and external stress, it is not unlikely that such stress can result in uterine disturbances which may trigger the abortion.

DISTURBANCES OF SEXUAL FUNCTION

The genitourinary reactions include a number of sexual disturbances, although some disturbances in this area are more properly classified under the psychoneurotic disorders. *Psychic impotence* and *frigidity* are the two most common psychophysiologic disorders of sexual function. In psychic impotence, the male is unable to perform and enjoy the sexual act because of emotional reasons. In the most serious cases of impotence, the patient is incapable of being aroused sexually under any condition. In the milder forms of the disorder, which are by no means uncommon, the condition is one of an occasional inability to achieve an erection.

A number of dynamic factors may play a role in this disorder. In some men, there is a dissociation of sexuality and love; in others, a conflict in love objects leads to the symptoms; in still other cases, latent homosexuality may be involved. In many cases, psychic impotence develops as a result of a lack of response in the partner. Such lack of response, often combined with damaging remarks during sexual activities, may lead to emotional interference which results in the impotency. It is not unusual for a man to be impotent with a woman for whom he has deep feelings of love, while being sexually successful with women who exert a mere physical attraction. Not a few men have been impotent with their brides, while having been previously capable of satisfactory sex relationships with prostitutes. In other cases, a man will have strong feelings of hostility toward members of the opposite sex. These feelings may involve all members of the opposite sex, based on attitudes developed during early life, or they may be restricted to one particular sexual partner. In the latter case, the hostility generally is a result of faulty interpersonal relationships between the two individuals.

A factor of great importance in psychic impotence is guilt. Our culture looks unfavorably on sexual interest and sexual expression early in life and during the adolescent years. Boys and girls are made to feel guilty about having sexual urges and particularly about giving expression to them in an autoerotic or heterosexual way. The result of these early, and often unreasonable, restrictions is to instill strong feelings of guilt in connection with any sexual activity. In adult years, during courtship and marriage, the early guilt feelings are revived, frequently making adequate sex relationships difficult and, in some cases, impossible.

The emotional nature of psychic impotence is illustrated in a case in which a man became impotent after dreaming that he had had a sexual relationship with the wife of a friend. This dream was repressed, but its implications had a profound effect on the physiology of the patient. Several years later, during psychotherapy, the dream was uncovered, its relationship to the impotence was understood, and the sexual disability disappeared.

The female counterpart of psychic impotency is frigidity. This condition, which occurs in various degrees, is one in which there is a pathological lack of sexual feeling. In some cases there is simply a diminished desire, while in the more serious forms of the condition there are local neuromuscular reactions in the form of vaginal spasms which make normal heterosexual relationships difficult or impossible.

While the dynamics of frigidity differ from one case to another, it is possible to list a number of problems and conflicts which may play a contributing role. These problems include excessive guilt feelings, fear of injury or disease, hostility toward members of the opposite sex, conflicting sexual attachments, unresolved Oedipal relationships, and latent homosexuality. Narcissistic women find it particularly difficult to relate satisfactorily in a sexual way to members of the opposite sex. Such individuals characteristically find the relief of their erotic tensions in their own bodies. They invest themselves with so much self-love that they are unable to spare any for other people. When sexual activity is carried out, the gratification of the partner is of secondary importance.

Frigidity may also be an expression of an attitude of dominance and self-sufficiency on the part of the woman. Some women find it exceedingly difficult to submit to the passive role required of them in the sexual relationship. They rebel at the implication that they are being dominated by the male. Such women find that they are frigid with masculine and dominant males, but sexually responsive to more passive males who allow themselves to be dominated. Also, it is not unusual for women to be afraid of the sexual act. This fear may be of injury, of pregnancy, or of infection and disease. When such fears are present, there is likely to be an interference with sexual responsiveness.

STERILITY

This condition is one in which normal sexual relationships take place, but pregnancy does not occur. While many such cases involve organic deficiencies on the part of the male or the female, there is a possibility that at least some cases have an emotional basis. One of the psychodynamic factors observed in some cases of psychogenic sterility among females is the feeling of inadequacy and the idea that the woman is still a little girl. It is a common observation that in many childless couples the wife is an extremely infantile individual. If the wife perceives herself as a child, it is entirely possible that there could be an interference with adult biochemical processes which permit pregnancy.

Another evidence of the relationship between sterility and the emotions is the fact that it is not unusual for a previously sterile woman to become pregnant after a decision to adopt a child. In such cases, it is probable that the decision solves the emotional problems which led originally to the sterility. While the nature of psychogenic sterility in the male is more obscure, it is possible that emotional conflict could lead to alterations of the body biochemistry which would result in sterility.[7]

OTHER PSYCHOPHYSIOLOGIC DISORDERS

The psychophysiologic reactions are not limited to the major body systems. Because of the pervasive nature of the neuroendocrine system, it is entirely possible that every organ of the body, as well as every disease and disability, has some degree of psychosomatic involvement. The endocrine system itself is extremely sensitive to emotional change, and the muscular system is frequently selected as the avenue for the discharge of emotional conflict. Similarly, the special senses, insofar as they have autonomic innervation, may show psychophysiologic reactions. Special disease syndromes, ranging from headache to carcinoma, also have important psychosomatic components.

ENDOCRINE REACTIONS

As a result of the close interrelationship between the autonomic nervous system and the endocrine system, it is not surprising that certain endocrine disturbances have a strong psychological component. While relatively little study has been given to the impact of the emotions on the endocrine system, much work has been done on the manner in which endocrine changes result in emotional states. In the early part of the nineteenth century, it was observed that sudden fright was sometimes related to overactivity of the thyroid. However, the realization that emotional states play an important role in thyroid disturbances is of relatively recent origin. In hyperthyroidism, there is frequently an emotional disturbance preceding the onset of the first typical symptom. Another discovery has been that there is a disturbance of the mother-child relationship in many cases, which appears as a fear of loss of affection and as a fear

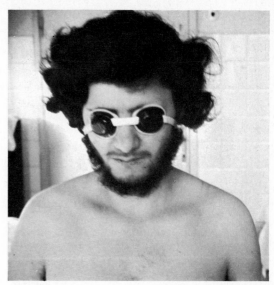

Figure 9.5 *A rare case of psychogenic hypertricosis, or excessive hair growth, in a woman. (Courtesy of Dr. Enzo Rottini, University of Perugia, Italy.)*

of the mother role. Similarly, it has been found that psychological stress often precedes the onset of the symptoms of exopthalmic goiter. It has been suggested also that overactivity of the thyroid gland is related to the release of anxiety and aggression (Dongier et al., 1956).

In the case of *diabetes mellitus,* psychological factors are important in that they increase the blood sugar level and tend to trigger the diabetic attack. While a clear personality picture has not emerged in connection with diabetes, the traits of passivity and immaturity have been emphasized. Such patients are frequently frustrated in their demands for love and attention. Dependency needs also seem to be prominent in these cases. One study of mental disorders associated with diabetes found mental depression to be the most frequent symptom described. This depression appeared to be a reaction to the loss of a love object before the onset of the diabetes in most of the cases studied. Other types of stress also played an important role in some cases (Menninger, 1935).

---

[7]The impact of the emotions on the genitourinary system is discussed in *Psychosomatic Gynecology* (Free Press, 1956) by W. S. Kroger and S. C. Freed; and A. A. Baker's *Psychiatric Disorders in Obstetrics* (Blackwell, 1967).

MUSCULOSKELETAL REACTIONS

A musculoskeletal reaction is a form of psycho-physiologic disorder in which the psychological conflicts are expressed through backache, soreness of the joints, muscular spasms, and similar conditions. As in other psychophysiologic reactions, our everyday language is evidence of the psychological factors in muscular and skeletal systems. The phrase "Oh, my aching back" was a favorite of soldiers during World War II.

■ MUSCULOSKELETAL REACTION

Julius W. is a fifty-year-old married man who was admitted to a psychiatric hospital after a number of years of chronic complaining about excruciating back pains. The patient went from doctor to doctor to seek relief, but nothing seemed to help him. The patient experienced frequent nausea and other symptoms. During one of the examinations, a physician told him his heart was slow, and the patient developed a severe nausea. From that time, he was increasingly hypochondriacal. The major symptom, however, continued to be the back pain. He often referred to being "tortured" by the pain. Much of the time the patient appeared depressed and expressed feelings of hopelessness. He was completely oriented and in contact with reality. Numerous physical and neurological examinations revealed no organic basis for the complaints.

The most common musculoskeletal psycho-physiologic reaction is rheumatic disease, one of man's oldest known chronic afflictions. This disorder is called *arthritis* when it attacks the joints and *rheumatism* when it involves the muscular tendons, ligaments, and bursae. Rheumatic disease varies from very slight pain, stiffness, or swelling to severe crippling and total disability.

Rheumatoid arthritis frequently begins, or is exaggerated, at times of emotional stress. Such stress situations as a death in the family, divorce, separation from home, loss of job, financial reverses, miscarriages, birth of a child, and similar trying events have been associated with this condition. Resentment, rebellion, anger, frustration, fear, guilt, and other damaging attitudes which generate anxiety seem to play a contributing role. There is evidence that the person with rheumatoid arthritis is a physically and intellectually active individual who is overcontrolled emotionally and who is not inclined to express his feelings in an open manner. Many of these people appear to have been raised in families where the mother was the dominant parent, with the father more passive and compliant. The victim attempts to control his inner impulses through neuromuscular activity. For example, the clenching of the hands, according to the psychoanalysts, is sometimes symbolic of holding back the impulse to strike out at a frustrating environment (Geist, 1969).

REACTIONS OF THE SPECIAL SENSES

The psychophysiologic reactions of the organs of special sense must be distinguished carefully from conversion reactions. When the symptoms are mediated by the central nervous system, the resulting disorder is a psychoneurotic conversion state. However, when the symptoms are expressed through the autonomic system, the disorder is looked upon as a psychophysiologic reaction. This difference is illustrated in the case of vision, in which amaurosis, or blindness, is a psycho-neurotic conversion reaction, but where refractive errors (nearsightedness and farsightedness), inflammation of the conjunctiva, and increased intraocular pressure are psychophysiologic reactions.

■ PHOTOPHOBIA

Rosalind G. is a fifty-six-year-old single woman who was admitted to a hospital after many years of emotional instability. The patient had worked as an office assistant to a physician for a number of years, but shortly before being admitted to the hospital she left her job, complaining that her eyes pained her. There was much hypochondriacal preoccupation, and the patient said she could not eat or sleep well. She became indifferent, would not cook or clean her home, and spent most of her time in bed listening to the radio. She ate very little, unless someone cooked her meals for her. The most consistent symptom over the years was her complaint about her eyes. She visited many eye specialists, and had dozens of pairs of glasses. She wore dark green glasses, claiming that the sunlight and electric lights bothered her. At night she remained at home with lights turned off, refusing to entertain her relatives or to visit them because of her sensitivity to light. For a number of years the patient wore dark glasses. After a time, she covered one lens completely in order to shut out the light. Later she covered the other lens. In addition, the patient wore "blinders" attached to each side of her glasses. She ordered Braille literature in order to keep up with current events since she could no longer tolerate the light.

The relationship between emotional states and refractive errors in vision is an intriguing problem, and one on which there is very little general agreement. Theoretically, it is conceivable that autonomic reactions could produce tension in the extraocular muscles, leading to an elongation or shortening of the eyeball. Under such conditions, it is possible that a psychogenic *myopia* (nearsightedness) or *hyperopia* (farsightedness) could develop.

Another condition in which a psychophysiologic reaction is sometimes involved is *conjunctival hyperemia*, in which the eyes have a bloodshot appearance. While this condition may be due to such external irritants as dust, smoke, various chemicals, and ultraviolet radiation, at least some cases are a response to emotional stress. It is not unusual for people to have an exacerbation of symptoms during times of emotional upset. Relatively little attention has been paid to the psychological aspects of this condition, and the dynamic factors are largely unknown.

A third psychophysiologic reaction involving vision, and one which has received more attention, is *glaucoma*, a condition marked by a pathologically high intraocular pressure. The disorder, known since the time of Hippocrates, takes its name from the Greek word meaning "sea green," the color of the pupil of the eye in severe glaucoma. The first observations suggesting that there is a relationship between glaucoma and the emotions were made early in the nineteenth century. Since that time, clinical evidence has confirmed the importance of stress and the emotions in this condition (Schlaegel, 1957).

There have been many reports of cases in which acute episodes of glaucoma accompanied or followed emotional crises. A busy and intelligent man in his mid-forties with chronic glaucoma experienced his symptoms every time he engaged in extramarital sexual relations; and a man in his late forties enjoyed perfect health until his daughter became engaged, at which time he began suffering constantly from glaucoma. His symptoms

disappeared after his daughter's marriage. In another case, an inventor had a severe increase in ocular tension following a stormy conference with the sponsors of his invention (Schoenberg, 1945).

In a study of a series of patients with glaucoma, it was found that every patient had a history of difficulty in personality adjustment. Mood fluctuation, excessive anxiety, and hypochondriacal tendencies were observed frequently. There were also compulsive traits such as conscientiousness, meticulousness, and perfectionism. These patients generally had unsatisfactory relationships with one or both parents, and feelings of insecurity were marked. There was also a history of difficulty in developing and maintaining satisfactory interpersonal relationships with marital partners and employers. More than half the group had consistent or transient elevations of blood pressure. The glaucoma patients usually seemed well controlled, but such emotional reactions as anger, anxiety, and depression often occurred in connection with trivial matters, while major problems were evaded (Ripley and Wolff, 1950).

In another study of patients with chronic primary glaucoma, it was found that hypnotic suggestion could bring about symptom relief. Every patient showed a significant drop in the pressure of one or both eyes. The relief in these cases was in the form of fewer headaches, less tearing, better sleeping, and a generally more relaxed condition (Berger and Simel, 1958).

It is entirely possible that similar psychophysiologic reactions are associated with hearing, taste, smell, the skin sensations, and other special sense systems. This entire field is relatively unexplored, and future investigations into the autonomic components of the special senses will probably produce important advances in our knowledge of psychosomatic relationships.

HEADACHE

The emotional component in psychophysiologic reactions is seldom so clearly illustrated as in the case of the common headache. Life is filled with anxiety-provoking situations to which we respond with head pains. Moreover, it is not unusual for us to recognize the relationship of the

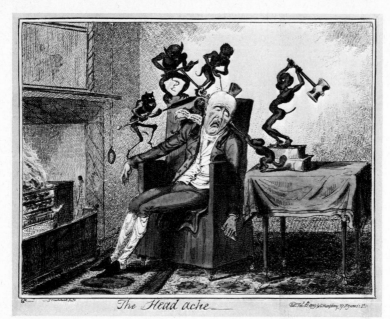

The Head ache

Figure 9.6 The Headache, *an early nineteenth-century etching by George Cruikshank. (Philadelphia Museum of Art.)*

headache to the precipitating events. Stress-induced headache is very probably the most frequently occurring psychophysiologic reaction.

The variety of headache which proves most troublesome is known as the familial, or migraine, headache. The condition appears periodically in attacks and is often accompanied by excruciating pain, nausea and vomiting, constipation or diarrhea, and urinary retention or frequency. After the attack the person may feel fatigued or overenergetic. The predisposition to this ailment is known to involve an heredity factor and is transmitted by a recessive gene. Attacks frequently occur in women at the onset of menstruation and cease with menopause; they generally appear in both sexes between the ages of fifteen and thirty-five. It is not uncommon for distinctive visual sensations, such as flickering lights, to precede the attack. Psychic disturbances, including drowsiness, anxiety, and confusion which may amount to disorientation, are found in about one-third of the cases of migraine.

In some instances the headache appears to be a product of self-inflicted punishment. The person has the headache to punish himself for being unkind to a wife, husband, or children, for cheating in business, for carrying on an extramarital affair, for being miserly, or for any other action about which he feels anxious, ashamed, or guilty. In

some cases, the migraine headache may have special symbolic meanings. One view is that migraine headaches may be an expression of hostility toward our loved ones. It may also be that the headache is due to a conflict between desire to escape from mother's influence and the fear of doing so.

A study of migraine victims revealed a characteristic constitutional type in which intelligence was outstanding while emotional make-up was retarded. The typical conflict which seemed to mark the onset of migraine was a necessity for the individual to accept independence in the form of a loss of home protection or the assumption of an adult status. Some people showed an emotional attachment to the mother which could not be resolved. Apparently the process of emotional maturity was arrested short of mature psychosexual adjustment. The headaches were found to appear in the same general pattern for each person and under similar circumstances. It was noted also that the migraine headaches were five times more prevalent among subjects suffering from hypertension than among those who were free of this illness. The same ambition, exactness, neatness, and hard drive found in hypertensive individuals appear to be prevalent in people suffering from migraine headaches. While migraine victims often are emotionally unstable, they are likely to be above average in intelligence and ambition. They are inclined to be overly conscientious and to take life too seriously. A considerable number of cases are aggravated by unhappiness, family difficulties, and sexual incompatibility (Touraine and Draper, 1934).

PERIODONTAL REACTIONS

Clinical observation indicates that extreme tension influences periodontal disease. Periodontal disease—the term being derived from the Greek words for "around" and "tooth"—is bleeding gums and infection of bones beneath gum tissue. At Hillside Hospital in New York, 50 percent of the male patients and more than 50 percent of the women reporting periodontal disease had personality profiles suggesting continued psychological disturbance. It has also been observed that students cramming for exams and men among the lower ranks in the armed services frequently suffer from Vincent's disease, commonly known as trench mouth. Canker sores may also reflect pent-up emotion (Protell, 1968).

CANCER

The problem of cancer is one of the most important in the entire field of medicine. As the age span increases and as the population grows older, this disease takes on increasing importance because it is one of the most common forms of chronic and terminal illness. Until recently, little was known about the emotional components of cancer, even though the suggestion had been made from time to time of a possible connection between personality and the disease.

The interest in the importance of personality factors in this disease goes back at least as far as Galen, who said that cancer was more frequent in melancholic women than in sanguine women. Again in the eighteenth and nineteenth centuries, physicians believed that the emotions could cause a malignant growth. Grief, disappointment, despair, and hopelessness were cited as attitudes which precipitated the malignancies. A review of the literature in the mid-nineteenth century found that there was general agreement that "women of high color and sanguineous temperament were more subject to mammary cancer than those of different constitution" (Walshe, 1846).

Today there is a renewed interest in the impact of the emotions on this disease. There are several major problems related to the possible effect of psychological factors on cancer. One deals with the problem of the development of cancer secondary to emotional disturbance. Another concerns specific types of personality in which cancer develops, while a third problem deals with the rate of growth of cancer as a function of personality characteristics.

There has been considerable interest in the relation of the onset of cancer to periods of emotional disturbance. Some authorities believe that agitated and unhappy persons contract cancer more easily than do placid persons who have something in life to depend on. While the etiological significance of viruses in some forms of cancer is becoming unmistakably clear, the virus may lie dormant for years. Something additional is needed to trigger the virus into destructive activity.

Support for the idea that there is a relationship between emotional disturbance and the development of cancer is seen in a series of Russian studies in which it was found that cancer of the internal organs develops spontaneously in dogs subjected for prolonged periods to experimental neuroses. These studies also showed that carcinogenic substances producing skin cancer in dogs and mice were effective only in animals in whom the experimental neuroses had been established (Kazansky, 1955).

As to the relation between cancer and personality variables, a survey of clinical and experimental studies indicated that there are a number of recurring themes. The first is the patient's loss of an important interpersonal relationship prior to the development of the cancer. A second common factor appears to be the inability of the cancer patient to express hostile feelings. Other factors appear to be related to the patient's unresolved tension concerning a parental figure and to disturbance in the sexual area (Leshan and Worthington, 1956).

There are several possible explanations of the apparent relationship between personality variables and the development of cancer. The two factors may be the result of different causes, and their presence together may be merely co-incidental; however, a common factor might precipitate both the physical and the emotional reactions. It may also be that a common nervous system or endocrine factor causes both the emotional disturbance and the cancer. More recent work suggests that stress may be the important factor, with the cancer developing as a result of the action of stress hormones (LaBarba, 1970).

Psychological factors may also influence the growth rate of cancer. The resistance of an individual to the spread of cancer appears to depend at least in part upon the psychological dynamics of the patient. The rate of progress in cancer may be controlled to some extent by the attitude of the victim. Cancer patients with the highest resistance to the disease seem to be those who are most successful in avoiding or reducing stress.[8]

SUMMARY

1. The psychophysiologic disorders are conditions in which the inner conflicts and the consequent anxieties of the patient are transformed into physical symptoms expressed through the autonomic nervous system. In terms of dynamics the transformation process is similar to, if not identical with, the conversion neurotic reactions. The two conditions are treated separately more as the result of an accident of historical development than because of logical or clinical necessity. There are many evidences of the close relationship in everyday life between the emotions and the autonomic nervous system. Some of the more dramatic examples of this relationship are the sudden-death reaction among both wild and domesticated animals, voodoo death, and the "anniversary reaction" in which physical symptoms coincide with the anniversary date of some significant event such as marriage or birth.

2. The most common psychophysiologic disorders are the cardiovascular, gastrointestinal, respiratory, genitourinary, and skin reactions. There are also miscellaneous reactions involving the endocrine and musculoskeletal systems, the organs of special sense, headache, and carcinoma.

3. The cardiovascular reactions are among the most frequent psychophysiologic disorders even though organic heart disease is the principal cause of death in the United States. Cardiovascular reactions which are of a psychophysiologic nature include tachycardia, or rapid heart rate; the anginal syndrome, or pain in the region of the heart; essential hypertension, or high blood pressure; and coronary disease.

4. The gastrointestinal system is particularly susceptible to psychophysiologic disorders because of its rich autonomic nerve supply. The more usual gastrointestinal psychophysiologic reactions are anorexia nervosa, or loss of appetite; bulimia, or excessive appetite; gastritis, or stomach distress; peptic ulcer, or lesions of the mucous lining of the stomach or duodenum; and colitis, or inflammation of the colon.

5. Respiratory difficulties also grow out of emotional stress and anxiety-provoking situations. The common cold; vasomotor rhinitis, or congestion of the nasal mucous membrane and the conjunctivae of the eyes; hyperventilation, or overbreathing; bronchial

---

[8]The psychosomatic aspects of some of the conditions discussed in this section of the book are emphasized in *The Psychological Aspects of Rheumatoid Arthritis* (Thomas, 1966) by Harold Geist; *Psychosomatic Ophthalmology* (Williams & Wilkins, 1957) by T. F. Schlaegel, Jr.; J. Stollzenberg's *Psychosomatics and Suggestion Therapy in Dentistry* (Philosophical Library, 1950); and H. E. Simmons' *The Psychosomatic Aspects of Cancer* (Peabody, 1956).

asthma; and tuberculosis are examples of respiratory disorders which may be entirely or in part a result of emotional disturbance.

6. The skin also has an abundant autonomic supply and readily expresses psychophysiologic symptoms. Blushing and other skin changes clearly demonstrate the close connection between the skin and the emotions. A dramatic example of this relationship is religious stigmatization, in which skin wounds caused entirely by physiologic stress are related to the Crucifixion or to some other meaningful religious event. More common psychophysiologic skin reactions include various forms of neurodermatosis, or irritation and inflammation of the skin.

7. The effect of emotional life on the genitourinary system is an everyday observation. Enuresis, or bedwetting, urinary retention, menstrual disorders, pseudocyesis, or false pregnancy, and spontaneous abortion, as well as psychic impotence, frigidity, and sterility, may have an emotional basis. In fact, psychophysiologic reactions may be seen in connection with almost any body system. There is an increasing body of evidence to suggest that endocrine and musculoskeletal reactions, disturbances of the special senses, and even cancer may have important psychological components.

8. It is not clear whether particular personality traits or reaction patterns are related to the various psychophysiologic disorders. While there is some clinical evidence pointing in this direction, the matter has not been settled. There is rather general agreement, however, that the psychophysiologic disorders are influenced by such factors as the constitutional sensitivity of the autonomic nervous system, the symbolic advantage of a particular organ system, learning in the form of conditioning, and the presence of a stress situation.

OTHER AUDIOTAPE

Psychosomatic Medicine
Dr. Franz Alexander, a former head of the Chicago Psychoanalytic Institute, presents a twenty-minute lecture on the importance of emotional factors in the production of bodily disorders. Recorded in 1953. Sound Seminar 75702, *McGraw-Hill Book Company*.

10 THE FUNCTIONAL PSYCHOSES

The psychotic disorders are among the most serious of all mental disturbances. The word *psychosis* first appeared in the literature of psychopathology early in the nineteenth century and referred to the entire range of mental disorder. In recent years, the word has taken on a more specialized meaning; now it is used to refer only to some of the more extreme conditions requiring compulsory institutionalization.

In the middle of the nineteenth century, psychotic behavior, or "insanity" as it was then called, was defined in a number of different ways. A French authority said: "Insanity, or mental alienation, is a brain disease, ordinarily chronic, and without fever, characterized by disorders of sensibility, understanding, intelligence, and will" (Esquirol, 1838). A British physician put it another way when he said: "Insanity is the impairment of any one or more of the faculties of the mind, accompanied with, or inducing, a defect of the comparing faculties" (Conolly, 1830). An outstanding

American expert of the time wrote, "Insanity is a chronic disease of the brain, producing either derangement of the intellectual faculties, or prolonged change of the feelings, affections, and habits of an individual" (Brigham, 1835).

As these definitions suggest, the term *insanity* had a wide and common usage. The word *psychosis* was rarely seen. As late as 1900, most technical books were written without mentioning the word. It remained for the immense success of Kraepelin's textbook to popularize the use of the word *psychosis* and to make it one of the central diagnostic and descriptive concepts in medical psychology. Today the term includes *schizophrenia,* the *paranoid states,* and the *affective disorders.*

> Patients are described as psychotic when their mental functioning is sufficiently impaired to interfere grossly with their capacity to meet the ordinary demands of life. The impairment may result from a serious distortion in their capacity to recognize reality. Hallucinations and delusions, for example, may distort their perceptions. Alterations of mood may be so profound that the patient's capacity to respond appropriately is grossly impaired. Deficits in perception, language and memory may be so severe that the patient's capacity for mental grasp of his situation is effectively lost. (DSM-II, 1968)

While there are many degrees of psychotic behavior, the psychosis is more serious than the neurosis because the former is a major mental disorder involving the entire personality. In the neurosis, the patient is usually able to function more or less adequately in spite of his symptoms. He is likely to know what his symptoms are, even if he does not know why they exist. The psychotic, on the other hand, is not able to view his symptoms objectively. He becomes so completely caught up in his disturbance that he loses perspective. This inability to handle symptoms is a central feature of the psychosis. It contributes in a very substantial way to the patient's loss of contact with reality.

Since the psychotic individual ordinarily is not in contact with reality, either continually or for temporary periods, he is considered to be a potential danger to himself and to others. At such times, his behavior is unpredictable and frequently uncontrollable. For this reason, any person who shows clinical evidence of psychotic symptoms is committable to a mental hospital. It does not matter whether he wants to go to a hospital or whether he agrees to go. The state assumes responsibility; and upon the proper certification by qualified psychiatrists, the court commits him to a psychiatric hospital.

The neurotic person, since he is never out of contact with reality and is able to make a reasonably adequate adjustment to his environment, cannot be committed because of his behavior. As a result, few neurotic people find their way to the public psychiatric hospitals. Sometimes there is a

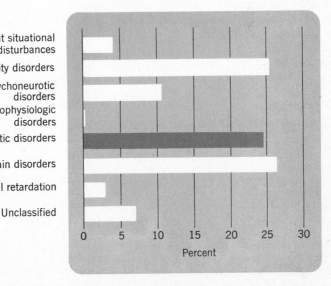

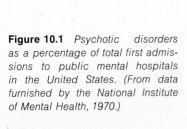

Figure 10.1 *Psychotic disorders as a percentage of total first admissions to public mental hospitals in the United States. (From data furnished by the National Institute of Mental Health, 1970.)*

question of diagnosis, and the hospitalization is ordered pending the clarification of the diagnosis, or the person himself may request commitment.

A further distinction between the neurosis and the psychosis is that the neurotic person does not deny reality but merely attempts to ignore it. The psychotic, on the other hand, flatly denies reality and attempts to substitute something else for it. In a more popular vein, someone once said that the neurotic builds castles in the air, while the psychotic lives in them.

Psychotic reactions occur when personality defenses break down completely and allow the conscious mind to be flooded with unconscious material. The neurotic, who is retreating from reality, nevertheless manages to hang on, however precariously, to the real world in which he lives. The victim of psychosis loses his contact with reality in one way or another. His world is an unreal one, made up of fantasies, fictions, and fragments of dreams. In the psychotic, the unconscious threatens to take over completely and sometimes does.

Psychotic personalities come to the attention of the police and are brought to psychiatric and psychological clinics as a result of a wide variety of bizarre actions. The police in Buffalo, New York, stopped a motorist whose car bore homemade license plates reading "Domain of the Tangible Dynamics, No. X." He astounded the police with a mystifying explanation of his "domain," which he said was beyond the dimensions of the earth. He carried papers which referred to "a resource of energy which was reached and brought to submission to mankind by John Smith, who, by virtue of the fact, locomotioned himself into the title of a conqueror."

While the psychotic disorders are considered by implication to be of psychogenic origin, it is probable that a combination of organic, psychological, and cultural factors are involved in these conditions. Some of the psychoses appear to have strong genetic and constitutional components while others may be linked to a disturbed biochemistry. The psychosis has been viewed by psychoanalysts as a disturbance in which repressed conflicts are so strong that they overwhelm consciousness in spite of the patient's frantic attempts to hang on to reality; or reality becomes so painful that the patient gives in to his unconscious impulses. Another view is that the psychosis represents a learned pattern of behavior designed to meet frustration by regression to a more primitive form of adjustment. Sociodynamic factors in the etiology of psychotic behavior also cannot be dismissed.[1]

THE SYMPTOMS OF PSYCHOSIS

The major disabling symptoms seen in the psychotic patient are:

1. Disorientation
2. Delusions
3. Hallucinations
4. Emotional disturbance
5. Disturbances of verbal communication
6. Disturbances of nonverbal communication

While many cases of incipient and borderline psychosis do not show them in a clear-cut way, every overt case of psychosis includes one or the other, and frequently a combination, of these symptoms.

DISORIENTATION

This symptom is one of the important signs indicating a psychotic break with reality. The person who is disoriented does not know who he is, where

---

[1]Students interested in acquainting themselves with the current theoretical and experimental literature dealing with the psychoses and related serious disturbances of the personality and referred to the following technical and professional journals: *The American Journal of Psychiatry* (published monthly by the American Psychiatric Association, 1700 Eighteenth St., N.W., Washington, D.C.20009); *Archives of General Psychiatry* (published monthly by the American Medical Association, 535 North Dearborn St., Chicago, Ill. 60610); the *British Journal of Psychiatry* (published quarterly by the Royal Medico-Psychological Association, 104 Gloucester Place, London W.1, England); and the *Journal of Nervous and Mental Disease* (published monthly by the Psychiatric Institute, University of Maryland, College Park, Md.).

he is, or what time of the day, week, month, or year it is. The clinician seeks to determine the degree to which the individual is oriented for *time, place,* and *person*. In some cases, the person is disoriented in only one of these areas; other people are disoriented in two or three areas.

The following material, taken from an interview with a psychotic individual, reflects a severe degree of disorientation in all areas.

Q: What is your name?
A: It is called fast colors.
Q: What is your father's name?
A: He put his head on the railroad tracks and see where he is today. He's in heaven.
Q: Do you have children?
A: How are you today?
Q: What work did you do?
A: I drove machines all around the corner.
Q: Where do you live?
A: I am not, and never was, foolish. I live in the barracks.
Q: Have you ever seen me before?
A: Well, according to your word, I will stretch it. Well, according to your word, I will stretch it. Well, according to your word, I will stretch it.
Q: What is your doctor's name?
A: Between you and me and him and the airplane.
Q: What day is it?
A: According to my brain, it is two weeks from to-morrow.
Q: What time of the day is it?
A: It's sub-noon in Egypt.
Q: How old are you?
A: Diagram.
Q: What city is this?
A: I am out of my brain today. City in mind. You're not getting any more sense out of me than out of a turnip!

The surprising flash of insight and rationality shown by the last remark is not uncommon in the psychoses. It appears sometimes that the individual is playing a game with the examiner, and to some extent this assumption is valid. It is not so much a matter of the person not knowing who he is or where he is, but of his refusing to acknowledge these facts.

Sometimes an additional dimension of orientation is used. This dimension is orientation for *situation.* Here the question is whether or not the individual realizes why he is in the hospital. This type of orientation, which is in fact a form of insight, frequently gives some indication of the patient's contact with reality. One woman who was asked why she was in the hospital replied that it had been raining outside, and she entered the hospital to get out of the rain. Another person insisted he was merely "waiting for his son." Such improbable and exaggerated rationalizations are common among psychotic patients.

DELUSIONS

A delusion, which is a belief contrary to reality, is another important symptom of psychotic thinking. Psychotics frequently hold ideas which are improbable or obviously untrue. While many people who are not mentally disturbed also cling to such ideas, they do not ordinarily continue to hold them in the face of clear evidence to the contrary. The psychotic person, however, persists in his delusional ideas in spite of rational arguments, contradictory evidence, or sheer impossibility. One man insisted that his arms and legs had been cut off, even though he was standing up and using his hands to show where his legs had been removed.

Delusional thinking has played an important role in the history of the world. *Lycanthropy,* the delusion in which men believe themselves to be wolves, appeared in one form or another for many centuries. Nebuchadnezzar, who lived more than five hundred years before Christ, was a victim of a delusion that closely resembled this condition. Virgil tells us that the daughters of Proetus believed themselves to be cows after they had been driven into the mountains by the goddess Hera. Ajax killed a flock of sheep, thinking he was attacking his enemies; and Thrasyllus of Aexone believed that he owned all the ships of the Piraeus. Philip V of Spain developed the delusion that he was already dead, and therefore he refused to eat or drink. Henry IV of Germany had the idea that the spirits of hell were trying to snatch his soul away from him. Christopher Columbus, a victim of a serious brain disorder, came to believe that he was the "ambassador of God."

In Cervantes' novel *Don Quixote,* the hero develops the romantic delusion that the windmills are giants, inns, and castles, prostitutes are great ladies, galley slaves are oppressed gentlemen, and a flock of sheep is the army of the giant Alifanfaron. Selma Lagerlof also dealt with delusions in her novel *The Emperor of Portugallia,* in which a peasant laborer had the delusion that his daughter in Stockholm had become an empress because she managed to send back money to save the farm. In the film *The Miracle,* a mentally deranged girl is seduced by a bearded vagabond whom she imagines to be Saint Joseph. Her delusion makes her a target for ridicule and abuse when she announces the "miracle" of her pregnancy.

Delusions can be classified in two ways. The first is according to the degree of cohesion or systematization of the delusional system. Delusions range from loose and unsystematic to tightly organized. The second way of classifying delusions is according to their content. The most common delusions involve ideas related to persecution, sexuality, religion, grandeur, and body changes.

The most frequently observed delusions are of the persecutory type. Here the person has the idea that he is the victim of a plot to discriminate against him, to cause him trouble, to make life difficult for him, to harm him in some physical way, or, in the more extreme cases, to take his life. The following persecutory delusions were expressed by people in a psychiatric hospital:

> The cops are after me. . . . People spit at me. . . . They are trying to steal my money. . . . The cook puts pee-pee and cat's dirt in my food. . . . They are going to horsewhip me. . . . People stick me with wires. . . . A man in the room upstairs is nailing another man's toes to the mattress. . . . Everybody I see is talking about me. . . . The communists in South America are trying to poison the beet sugar crop. . . . A gang in Washington is trying to kill me because I wanted to get in touch with the President. . . . The neighbors are saying that I am not a citizen. . . . Someone is stealing my mail. . . . The milk delivered to my apartment has been poisoned. . . . Someone down the hall is chopping little children to pieces.

Sexual ideas also are a common source of delusional material:

> My neighbors accuse me of being a pervert. . . . A man in a green convertible drives past my house at night and flashes his lights to signal that I am a prostitute. . . . The newspapers are going to release headlines saying that I am a "queer." . . . They are whispering that I am a homosexual. . . . They insinuate that I am not a man. . . . The neighbors say I have syphilis. . . . My husband made me insane so he would be free to commit adultery.

A common delusional belief, especially of emotionally disturbed women, is that certain men are in love with them. Physicians, psychologists, social workers, college instructors, clergymen, lawyers, and other professional men whose work brings them into contact with large numbers of women not infrequently find themselves the victims of this form of distorted thinking. It is interesting that these delusional ideas are relatively rare among younger women. Most cases involve mature women, usually married and often with children. Delusional thinking of this type is so common among disturbed women that a widely used rating scale for determining the seriousness of emotional disorder includes among the most critical symptoms a category called "unjustified sexual beliefs." One of the items in this category is that the woman believes without justification that certain persons have an amorous interest in her.

Delusions of power and grandeur are also observed frequently among psychotics. Patients have expressed the following ideas:

> I am the richest man in the world. . . . I am so powerful that the heads of people change when I look at them. . . . I own all the hotels in the world. . . . I have a hundred million dollars in the bank.

Similarly, religious delusions are seen in a number of people. Ideas of this kind include:

> There is a devil in my ear. . . . I am God. . . . I am the Virgin Mary. I've committed my unpardonable sin. . . . I have to shake my bed at night to get the devils out. . . . I have four devils inside me. . . . I am Jesus Christ. . . . God is my husband. . . . I went to heaven to see Jesus and to talk to the Virgin Mary.

Somatic delusions, or those involving the body are not uncommon among psychotics:

> I am sick because I swallowed a rock. . . . There are holes bored in my head. . . . My right eye is growing out of the top of my head. . . . My head is filled with cornflakes. . . . I've lost my skin. . . . I'm mangled inside. . . . I have no arms or legs. . . . My mouth is sewed closed. . . . My head has nothing in it but iodine. . . . My ears have disappeared. . . . There isn't any blood in my veins. . . . I have no heart, liver, or lungs.

A particularly interesting form of delusion is called *depersonalization.* Here the individual makes an effort to deny his existence. It is as if he were saying, "I do not exist; therefore I have no problems." One person described himself by saying, "My personality is entirely gone. It seems to me as if I had been dead for two years. The thing that exists has no knowledge of my old self." This man referred to himself as a "thing" which he compared to an empty cardboard box. He ate, but it was only the shadow of food that was conveyed to the shadow of his stomach. His pulse was only the shadow of a pulse. Another person claimed that he was not a man at all, but merely the carcass of a dead dog. Delusions of depersonalization are also expressed in such ideas as: "I don't know whether I'm dead or alive." "I feel like I am really somebody else." "The real me is dead."

HALLUCINATIONS

The hallucination, like disorientation and delusional thinking, is one of the key symptoms of psychosis. A person is said to be hallucinated when he perceives objects and events without an appropriate external stimulus. In spite of the lack of an adequate stimulus, the experience seems real to the person. Hallucinations are ordinarily classified in terms of the sensory areas involved. While visual and auditory hallucinations are the most common in psychotic disorders, it is not unusual to find hallucinations involving taste, smell, touch, and body sensations.

Hallucinations occur from time to time even in mentally healthy people during periods of emotional stress. Following the death of someone close to us, it is not uncommon to imagine that we see that person again in a favorite chair, standing in the doorway, or taking part in some familiar activity. Hallucinations are also experienced as a result of intense guilt and anxiety. A man who was stealing money from the cash register in a store was startled to "see" his father looking at him sadly. Another man "heard" his mother weeping while he was visiting a prostitute. Shakespeare's Macbeth saw a phantom dagger and later saw Banquo's ghost sitting at the table.

Many well-known historical figures, including Tasso, Schumann, Shelley, Swedenborg, E. T. A. Hoffmann, Samuel Johnson, Cromwell, Napoleon, and Joan of Arc, experienced hallucinations. Martin Luther had such a vivid hallucination of the Devil that he threw an inkwell at him. When Spinello painted the Devil in too repulsive a manner, he reported that the Devil appeared to him and complained about the way he had been painted. Christopher Columbus, on one of his voyages, heard a voice from heaven say, "Take courage. Be not afraid, nor fear. I will provide for all." On his final voyage he heard the voice again. Hallucinations are also common during periods of religious exaltation and ecstasy, when sensory input is severely limited, and when LSD or other hallucinogenic drugs are used.

The most frequently encountered hallucinations among mentally disturbed people are in the auditory area, with the victim hearing voices. Sometimes the voices are supportive and conciliatory, and sometimes they direct the individual's thoughts and activities. More often they are accusatory and disagreeable. A young man was riding on a bus and became convinced that the man in the seat behind him was carrying a hypodermic needle. Then he thought he overheard the man whisper to him, "If you want to go crazy, I'll help you." He was certain that the man was going to drug him with a needle, so he hurried off the bus at the next stop.

RADIO ANTENNA DYNAMITED
HEARD TOO MANY "VOICES"

Cincinnati, Sept. 18—A 38-year-old farmer destroyed one of the antennas of the "Voice of America" radio transmitters near Mason, Ohio, with a 50-pound charge of 40-percent dynamite. The man said he "kept hearing voices all the time." He was linked with the blast through dynamite fuse wrappers found at the scene of the blast.

"VOICES" SUMMON MAN TO HIS DEATH

Pittsburgh, Aug. 4—Strange "voices" called a 40-year-old man to his death in the Monongahela River. The victim heard the "voices" while riding a crowded trolley car across the Homestead high level bridge. He told his brother-in-law: "They're calling me—the voices down there. They want me to come down. I've got to go." He scrambled off the trolley, broke away from his brother-in-law and dived off the bridge.

**"RADIOACTIVE VOICES" BLAMED
IN MURDER OF CHILD**

Cincinnati, June 8—A screaming 8-year-old girl was
hurled to her death from the Western Hills Viaduct
by an ex-convict who had spent two years in a hospital
as a mental patient. Captured by passers-by was a
gaunt six-foot-four-inch man who blamed his act upon
"radioactivity." The strange drama unfolded near the
middle of the viaduct as horrified motorists slammed
on their brakes and jumped from their autos. The suspect, laughing and gibbering, grabbed the girl as she
stooped to tie her shoestring. He stared moodily from
deep-set eyes, and at detective headquarters he mumbled: "Radioactivity did it. They keep calling me yellow.
When I go to sleep at night they call me yellow, and when
I get up in the morning they call me yellow."

Visual hallucinations, while somewhat less
frequent than auditory experiences of this kind,
are nevertheless observed in a large number of
psychotic people. Such hallucinations are often
of a religious nature, but may involve a variety
of other images. A twenty-year-old roustabout
started a circus fire which resulted in the death
of 169 people and injury to more than 400 others.
When he was caught, he blamed his behavior on
visions of "a flaming red Indian on a fiery horse"

Figure 10.2 *The visual hallucination, as suggested
by a drawing illustrating Edgar Allen Poe's short story
"Eleanora." (Masson et Cie., Paris.)*

urging him to set the fires. The young man confessed to scores of fires from Maine to Ohio.

Lilliputian hallucinations are those in which
the person "sees" tiny figures of people or animals. One psychotic woman said that she saw a
large number of little children gathered around
her. They were so small she could take them all
in her hand. She even had names for them. One
was called Harold and another Reginald. At one
time she was heard to say, "Reginald, you must
be a good boy and not slip away through my
fingers." She would watch these children climb
down to her lap. Then, with an indulgent smile,
she would pick them up again. She complained
that Reginald gave her a great deal of trouble.

■ **HALLUCINATIONS**

Helen R. is a tall, thin, married woman of forty who was
holding both hands on the top of her head when she
entered the office. Asked about why she held her head,
she explained, "Last night while I was in bed someone
hit me with a piece of pipe. I have to hold my head to
keep my brains from oozing out." Later, she exclaimed
suddenly, "That Askerin fellow!" Asked what she
meant, she replied, "Elmer Askerin." For a time she was
reluctant to explain further, but finally she said, "Sometimes I see Elmer Askerin and his gang come over the
top of the wall and down the side of the room. I look
up, and there is Elmer and his gang. When they get
down near my bed, I hear Elmer say 'There she is. Let
her have it. Shoot her.' But he doesn't frighten me. I
tell him, 'Elmer, you get out of here and leave me
alone!' And he and his gang go back up the wall. Just
as he disappears over the top of the wall, he snaps his
fingers and says, 'Shucks, you can't fool that old
lady!' "

Another type of hallucination involves a distortion of the body image, or the mental picture the person has of himself. In *macropsia*, the
person perceives his body, or parts of his body,
as being unnaturally large. One such individual
refused to enter a hospital conference room because he said that the ceiling was not high enough
to permit him to stand upright. The opposite
condition is *micropsia*, in which the individual
feels his body, or parts of his body, to be unusually
small. Such people are afraid that they might be
trampled underfoot or come to some other harm
because of their tiny stature. A third form of dis-

torted body image occurs in *dysmegalopsia*, a condition in which the body is felt to be unsymmetrical.

Hallucinations arise from both organic and psychological causes. Organic determinants include such factors as excessive fatigue, drugs, fever, brain damage, or alcohol. Psychological determinants include, among other possibilities, the processes of projection, rationalization, wishful thinking, fantasy, and feelings of guilt.

EMOTIONAL DISTURBANCE

While disorientation, delusions, and hallucinations make up the core of psychotic behavior, there are other symptoms which reflect the severity of the personality disorganization. The psychotic person frequently shows various forms of emotional disturbance. Some people are emotionally impulsive, while others seem to have a complete lack of emotional responsiveness. Occasionally the symptom takes the form of emotional responses which are inappropriate to the situation.

The emotionally impulsive individual is completely unpredictable. It is not unusual for such people to jump up suddenly in anger or exuberance. Without apparent reason and with no warning such people may act out in an aggressive or a sexual way. Episodes of uncontrollable violence sometimes punctuate an otherwise tranquil course of psychosis. The impulsive and unpredictable emotional behavior of such people makes them a source of constant danger to themselves and others.

A complete absence of emotional responsiveness is also found in some psychotic people. Such individuals neither smile or laugh, nor do they appear depressed. They are simply without emotion, at least on the surface. During the examination of such a person, the clinician may deliberately attempt to provoke him to laughter, tears, or anger. In most cases, all such efforts fail. It is as if the person were completely incapable of expressing emotion of any kind. Inappropriate emotion is another psychotic symptom. Here the person responds emotionally in a way that is incomprehensible to anyone but him. While discussing a sad or depressing experience, the in-

dividual responds with smiles or laughter. Similarly, a humorous incident or story might call forth a feeling of melancholia or a torrent of tears. In other cases, the person may giggle or laugh without apparent reason, or he may suddenly begin to sob.

Of the several types of emotional disturbance, the absence of emotional responsiveness and inappropriate emotional responses are of the greatest diagnostic importance because these two forms of behavior are seldom seen in other classes of personality disorganization. Emotional instability, however, as we have seen in earlier chapters, is also characteristic of some of the personality disorders and neurotic reactions.

■ EMOTIONAL DISTURBANCE

Rita M. is a thirty-year-old woman who has had a number of admissions to mental hospitals. The present admission followed an incident in Florida where the patient publicly cursed a motorist who drove too close to her. She fought with the police who questioned her; and because of her marked hostility and overtalkativeness, she was sent to a psychiatric hospital.

This patient was raised in a home in which there were many children under a domineering and cruel father. When she was eleven, the patient threatened to kill her father when she saw him beating her mother. As a result, the father changed his attitude toward the mother, and the patient applied her technique of threats and belligerency toward people outside the family. At fifteen, the patient became sexually involved with a young man in the neighborhood. A year later she married this same man, but the marriage was an unhappy one because of his attention to other women. There were two children, and the patient was forced to support the family by working as a waitress in a bar. She was unable to hold a job more than a few weeks or months. The marriage ended in divorce, and four years later she married again. After three months the patient became extremely unhappy because of lack of affection on the part of the second husband. At this time, the patient began to show her first psychotic symptoms. She was convinced she was a saint, and could walk upon the water. At one time she was saved from drowning by the police who were under the impression she was trying to commit suicide.

When seen at the hospital, the patient was excitable, hyperactive, and careless about her appearance. Her voice was loud, and her manner was aggressive. She talked and walked rapidly, jumped up from her chair on numerous occasions, and frequently left the interviewing room. Sometimes she would frown in a menacing way, and other times she would laugh. Words came in an easy flow. The patient was distractible and expressed feelings of hostility toward various people. Her language was profane, and she was preoccupied with sexual matters.

DISTURBANCES OF VERBAL COMMUNICATION

Some of the most striking symptoms of psychosis are seen in connection with language. Because of his lack of contact with reality and his indifference to social conventions, the psychotic often expresses himself in highly personal ways. Since the verbal utterances of the psychotic person may be a form of self-expression rather than a means of communication with others, the language of the psychotic is sometimes strange-sounding and frequently bizarre.

Occasionally the symptoms of psychological deterioration can be detected in the writing of a creative mind in the process of disorganization. In both the poetry and letters of Ezra Pound, the development of eccentric and even bizarre thinking can be traced. The following selection is taken from his "Pisan Cantos" (Pound, 1948):

> As Arcturus passes over my smoke-hole
>   the excess electric illumination
>   is now focussed
> on the bloke who stole a safe he cdn't open
>   (interlude entitled: periplum by camion)
>   and Awoi's *hennia* plays hob in the tent flaps
>   k-lakk.....thuuuuuu
>   making rain
>   uuuh
> 2,   7,   hooo
>   der im Baluba.

While Pound was a literary genius, this selection from his work is more a symptom of a developing psychosis than an indication of his poetic gifts. Less talented people show their personality disorganization in a similar manner. The psychotic pours out a jumble of apparently meaningless and unrelated words in what has been called a "word salad."

Why nylons, autos, men city people more cancer—because more polluted meat and drinks not one single connection with cigs—never jitters from narcotics or disorganization of nervous system—"I-am-ity" Megalomania—why Napoleon had to conquer world—Hitler and Mussolini and Me Too so now that I have conquered all mystery diseases (asthma and rheumatism too/experiment any dementia case) I am going to conquer the Russians/It is just a mathematical problem/New York, Cleveland, St. Louis, Detroit, California, Miami/they have control of now pulling in Cincinnati so I won't die of cancer, or the apparent heart attack/but a couple of bullets—so KEEP my name out—Please as I know of one check upon me—mathematics they are watching me see signals in paper. Mathematics if I disappear they have me—please copy and send to Hoover—telegraphers mail men caught in net.

A relatively common language disturbance is the *neologism*, a newly made-up word having a private meaning for the individual. One woman used the word *deathenated* to mean "dead but raised alive." Another said that God is a *whoumationer*, or, as she explained, a "match for the body." Still another psychotic wrote, "Mrs. Barnes is a right-hand *bouw* of those who use the time-machine."

Neologisms are not uncommon in literature. Shakespeare, Milton, Irving, Huxley, Keats, Rabelais, and James Joyce invented words to suit their own purposes. And who has not been delighted with Lewis Carroll's word inventions in *Alice in Wonderland* and *Through the Looking Glass*? The creative artist and the psychotic person give their own meanings to their words in the same way that Humpty Dumpty did. "There's glory for you," said Humpty Dumpty, and he explained to Alice that it meant "There's a nice knockdown argument for you." Alice protested the meaning and said, "The question is whether you can make words mean so many different things." Humpty Dumpty's reply was, "The question is, which is to be master—that's all."

A classic example of the use of the neologism as a deliberate literary device is found in the writings of the Irish novelist, James Joyce. The following selection, taken from *Finnegans Wake*, is filled with neologisms:

> Hark!
> Tolv two elf kater ten (it can't be) sax.

Hork!

Pedwar pemp foify tray (it must be) twelve.

And low stole o'er the stillness the heartbeats of sleep. White fogbow spans. The arch embattled. Mark as capsules. The nose of the man who was nought like the nasoes. It is self-tinted, wrinkling, ruddled. His kep is a gorsecone. He am Gascon Titubante of Tegmine—sub—Fagi whose fixtures are mobiling so wobiling befear my remembrandts. She, exhibit next, his Anastashie. She has prayings in lowdelph. Zeehere green egg brooms. What named blautoothdmand is yon who stares? Gugurtha! Gugurtha! He has becco of wild hindigan. Ho, he hath hornhide! And hvis now is for you. Pensee! The most beautiful of woman of the veilchen veilde. She would kidds to my voult of my palace, with obscidian luppas, her aal in her dhove's suckling. Apagemonite! Come not nere! Black! Switch out! (Joyce, 1957)

■ NEOLOGISMS

Helen W. is a slender and alert woman of forty-four who is the mother of four children. She has a history of mental illness for the past ten years. She is cooperative, and speaks in a persuasive and plausible manner. Her facial expression is mobile, and her mood appears somewhat elevated.

The patient is well oriented in all areas. She knows who she is, the day and month, and the fact that she is in a mental hospital. Both her recent and remote memory appear to be unimpaired. It is impossible to examine her for many psychological functions because she cannot be distracted long enough from her delusional stories to make accurate estimates of her judgment. The patient has no insight into her condition.

At the time of the initial interview, the patient believed that she was a professor at the University of Smithsonian in England, and that she was the only woman professor among many men. She said that she had attended many other universities in Europe, and had been accepted as an authority on the planets and the satellites. She placed great emphasis on the fact that she was the only woman professor, and that she was obliged by the University of Law to have relations with any of the male professors who desired it. She believed there was a war on between the Univeristy of Smithsonian and Purdue University for the mastery of her three specialties which are psychiatry, "sexiatry," and "mythiatry."

The following excerpts from an interview with the patient show her frequent use of neologisms: "I am here from a foreign university . . . and you have to have a 'plausity' of all acts of amendment to go through for the children's code . . . and it is no mental disturbance or 'puterience' . . . it is an 'amorition' law . . . there is nothing to disturb me . . . it is like their 'privatilinia' . . . and the children have to have this 'accentuative' law so they don't go into the 'mortite' law of the church."

The patient was in the psychiatric hospital for the next two years. When seen again she was found to be loose and delusional in her thinking, and continued to tell a vague and disjointed story of her professorship at the University of Smithsonian where she was instructing young boys in the science of "texules."

Sometimes the psychotic person will use involved sentences, the meanings of which are well hidden. One psychotic said, "I am the double polytechnic irretrievable." Another commented, "They put the hypnotic idle atrophy on me." And a third said, "I have been hypnotized by the subconscious force of supernature." Still another psychotic exclaimed, "My son has been thrust into the vortex of the educational ecclesiastic of the specifics of the world."

Another speech characteristic of certain psychotics is *echolalia*, or the repetition of words spoken by someone else. When the examiner says to a person, "How old are you?" the answer is parrot-like, "How old are you?" There is an automatic feedback of everything that is said.

The puzzling nature of the communication process in the psychotic is shown in the following interview:

DOCTOR: Who invented the airplane?
PATIENT: I do know.
DOCTOR: You mean, you don't know.
PATIENT: I do know.
DOCTOR: You do know.
PATIENT: Yes, I do.
DOCTOR: If you do know, can you tell me?
PATIENT: If I do know, how can I tell you? I could.
DOCTOR: You could tell me.
PATIENT: Yes, because I do know. I do know, I do know, ah, who invented the airplane.
DOCTOR: Okay, if you do know who invented the airplane, tell me who invented the airplane.
PATIENT: I can.
DOCTOR: You can.
PATIENT: I sure could.

DOCTOR: You sure could. Okay, can you tell me now who invented the airplane?

PATIENT: I do know.

DOCTOR: You do know.

PATIENT: Yes, I know.

DOCTOR: That means that you have the answer. You have the answer to that question.

PATIENT: Yes.

DOCTOR: Yes. Alright, now can you tell me what the answer is?

PATIENT: Who invented the airplane, I do know.

DOCTOR: What you mean to say is that you don't know.

PATIENT: I do know. If I don't know, I, I, I, I wouldn't be able to tell you.

DOCTOR: You're not able to tell me, though, are you?

PATIENT: Yes, I am, for I do know (Laffal and Ameen, 1959).

When psychotic individuals communicate with one another, the result is a strange mixture of sense and nonsense. In the following conversation between two psychotic young men, the communication process manages to maintain itself in spite of the non sequiturs and general lack of contact:

JONES: (laughs loudly, then pauses) I'm McDougal, myself.

SMITH: What do you do for a living, little fellow? Work on a ranch or something?

JONES: No, I'm a civilian seaman. Supposed to be high mucka-muck society.

SMITH: A singing recording machine, huh? I guess a recording machine sings sometimes. If they're adjusted right. Mm-hm. I thought that was it. My towel, mm-hm. We'll be going back to sea in about—eight or nine months though. Soon as we get our—destroyed parts repaired.

JONES: I've got love sickness, secret love.

SMITH: Secret love, huh? (laughs)

JONES: Yeah.

SMITH: I ain't got any secret love.

JONES: I fell in love, but I don't feel any woo—that sits over—looks something like me—walking around over there.

SMITH: My, oh, my only one, my only love is the shark. Keep out of the way of him.

JONES: Don't they know I have a life to live?

SMITH: Do you work at the air base? Hm?

JONES: You know what I think of work, I'm thirty-three in June, do you mind?

SMITH: June?

JONES: Thirty-three years old in June. This stuff goes

out the window after I lived this, uh—leave this hospital. So I can't get my vocal cords back. So I lay off cigarettes. I'm a spatial condition, from outer space myself.

SMITH: (laughs) I'm a real spaceship from across.

JONES: A lot of people talk,—that way, like crazy, but believe it or not by Ripley, take it or leave it—alone—it's in the *Examiner*, it's in the comic section, believe it or not by Ripley, Robert E. Ripley, believe it or not, but we don't have to believe anything unless I feel like it. (pause) Every little rosette—too much alone.

SMITH: Yeah, it could be possible.

JONES: I'm a civilian seaman.

SMITH: Could be possible. I take my bath in the ocean.

JONES: Bathing stinks. You know why? Cause you can't quit when you feel like it. You're in the service.

SMITH: I can quit whenever I feel like quitting. I can get out when I feel like getting out.

JONES: Take me, I'm a civilian, I can quit.

SMITH: Civilian?

JONES: Go my—my way.

SMITH: I guess we have, in port, civilian.

JONES: What do they want with us?

SMITH: Hm?

JONES: What do they want with you and me?

SMITH: What do they want with you and me? How do I know what they want with you? I know what they want with me. I broke the law, so I have to pay for it (Haley, 1959).

The chief signs of personality breakdown, as expressed in writing, are the excessive use of punctuation (quotation marks, exclamation points, capitalization, and underscoring), overproductivity, peculiar and bizarre expressions, and changes in the quality of the handwriting itself. One psychotic wrote furiously on world problems, offering solutions by the dozen and expressing his willingness to act as a mediator between the nations. He delighted in complicated forms of expression and wrote extensively on unintelligible topics.

Some psychotics find a particular satisfaction in rhyming and the play of words. The following letter illustrates the way in which a woman elaborates and intellectualizes a relatively simple idea.

Dear Doctor _____:
I hope the last letter of mine didn't offend you in any way. I couldn't help snickering, laughing and sneering

as I wrote all that stuff. I was immensely involuntarily amused at·my own bumptious presumptiousness and generally (to me) delicious maliciousness.

DISTURBANCES OF NONVERBAL COMMUNICATION

The symbolic actions of the psychotic, in the form of gestures, mannerisms, and body movements, are important signs of personality disorganization. A skilled psychiatrist or psychologist can make clinical inferences about the personality merely by observing the way a person walks, moves about, sits down, and stands up. These motor symptoms become diagnostic in the case of those people who are on the verge of breaking with reality or who have already broken with reality. Some psychotics go through all sorts of weird-looking movements and make peculiar gestures with their hands and arms. To the uninitiated observer, such movements and gestures appear meaningless. Actually, they may be rich with symbolic meaning. Each movement, in its own way, may reveal something of the inner conflict.

An elderly lady stood throughout the day in the corridor of the hospital. Each time the door opened and someone entered the ward, she made a series of complex measuring movements with her hands. For many months she refused to tell anyone what she was doing. Then one day she confided that she was measuring people for their coffins. Another woman held up the three middle fingers of her hand. She explained later that the first outside finger represented the number 7, the middle finger represented herself, and the other outside finger represented the "others." She held up these fingers to "protect" herself from the doctor and nurses. Such symbolic gesturing retains something of the magical practices and beliefs of children and savages.

A psychotic stood against the wall for hours, with his arms raised above his head. One arm was bent over his head with his index finger extended as if pointing. Another woman sat with her eyes tightly shut and would open them only for a moment or two at a time. She explained that when her eyes were open the doctor and nurses saw what she was seeing and that they were therefore seeing through her eyes. To prevent this, she kept her

eyes closed. In another case, a small gray-haired woman in her sixties walked slowly from one building to another. Without warning, she spread out her arms and executed a series of dance steps across the courtyard. When she reached the entrance to her building, she turned around, bowed several times, and blew kisses to an imaginary audience. Another woman, of about the same age, crossed the hospital courtyard carrying a bucket of lettuce. Halfway across, she stopped, placed the bucket on the ground, ceremoniously picked out a leaf of lettuce, and placed it carefully on the ground. After circling the leaf three times, she continued on her way.

It is occasionally possible to make a diagnosis of psychosis merely on the basis of the nonverbal actions of a person. When a person enters the examining room and sits down, with eyes tightly shut, and responds to all questions with a vigorous shake of the head, the seriousness of the personality disorganization is at once apparent. In a similar way, the skilled clinician becomes sensitive to a wide range of more subtle motor manifes-

Figure 10.3 *A drawing by a psychotic patient. (Courtesy of Ciba,* State of Mind.*)*

tations. The underlying psychotic process is often revealed by slight and sometimes almost imperceptible mannerisms, postures, and facial expressions. These minimal motor cues, easily missed by the student or the inexperienced clinician, may contribute in an important way to the diagnosis of psychosis in borderline conditions.

The psychotic disorders include the various forms of schizophrenia, the paranoid conditions, and the three principal affective reactions, namely, manic-depressive psychosis, involutional psychosis, and psychotic depression.

SCHIZOPHRENIA

Of all the psychotic disorders, the schizophrenic reactions make up the largest group. More than a quarter of a million schizophrenic patients are in our mental hospitals, with another hundred thousand or more victims of the disorder not hospitalized. The disorder accounts for 18.8 percent of first admissions to mental hospitals and 49.2 percent of the resident hospital population (NIMH, 1970). These figures reflect both the large number of people involved and the chronicity of the disorder. Schizophrenia is also important because of its resistance to treatment. Fortunately, major advances in the control and treatment of schizophrenia are being made at this time; but the fundamental nature of the condition is not yet understood.

This large category includes a group of disorders manifested by characteristic disturbances of thinking, mood and behavior. Disturbances in thinking are marked by alterations of concept formation which may lead to misinterpretation of reality and sometimes to delusions and hallucinations, which frequently appear psychologically self-protective. Corollary mood changes include ambivalent, constricted and inappropriate emotional responsiveness and loss of empathy with others. Behavior may be withdrawn, regressive and bizarre (DSM-II, 1968).

This class of disorders has been observed and described clinically for the past three hundred years. One of the early brain anatomists wrote a paper in 1672 called "Stupidity and Morosity," in which he pointed out that young people sometimes exhibit signs of mental deterioration (Willis, 1672). Both Pinel and Conolly later described

cases of mental deterioration among adolescents. By the middle of the nineteenth century it was well established that there existed a type of mental disorder that combined emotional and intellectual deterioration, and that this condition was seen frequently among young people. A Belgian physician used the term *demence precoce*, or "early dementia," to describe these cases in 1860 (Morel, 1860). The Latinized term *dementia praecox* came into popularity at the turn of the century when Emil Kraepelin used it in the fifth edition of his *Lehrbuch der Psychiatrie*.

It was Eugen Bleuler (1857–1930), however, who insisted that the condition was not a single disorder but a group of symptoms of varying origin. He believed the main characteristic of the disorder to be a "splitting" or shattering of the person's thinking, and for this reason he coined the term *schizophrenia* in 1911 (Bleuler, 1911). This term is used currently and includes a group of psychotic reactions marked by disturbances in reality relationships and in emotional and intellectual processes. While there are important differences in the symptom pictures of schizophrenic individuals, there is a common core of apathy and indifference, withdrawal, and the splitting of thought processes from their normal emotional tone.

All people are seclusive to some degree and under certain circumstances. They withdraw into themselves and isolate themselves from others, at times even from those they love most. Such isolation becomes necessary from time to time. It is a protective device that insulates people from the often difficult task of maintaining a serene and effective relationship with others. Each person constructs a system of "psychological distances" that determines the degree to which he permits himself to enter into emotional relationships with other people. When the psychological distance is short, people enjoy active and warm relationships with others. When the distance is great, they remain cold and aloof.

Some people are close to nearly everyone. They make friends while waiting for the bus, while making a purchase in a store, or while sitting in the park. Others are close to some people but remain distant toward others. And some people—those who are characteristically seclusive and withdrawn—tend to keep everyone at a distance all the time. It is in this latter, and relatively small, group that a break with reality is likely to occur. Such a personality in itself is no guarantee that a break will take place. But it is the soil from which schizophrenia develops.

It is difficult to make generalizations about the symptoms of the schizophrenic disorders because there are so many different subtypes, each with its own distinctive characteristics. However, certain common features are observed from time to time in all persons with this diagnosis. Emotionally these people are apathetic or indifferent, or they overreact. Their thinking is likely to be bizarre and often regressive and deteriorated. Delusions and hallucinations of all types are common. Speech may show distinctive changes in the form of rambling and circumstantiality, lack of spontaneity, and evasiveness, or there may be gross changes such as stylized speech, neologisms, echolalia, or incoherence.

The schizophrenic thought process, which is one of the most fascinating phenomena in human psychology, has received increasing attention. The schizophrenic reasons in a way quite different from that of normal subjects. He follows a private logic of his own making. The thinking of the schizophrenic person has been described variously as *prelogical, paralogical,* and *paleological.* These terms, which are largely synonymous, suggest the nonlogical nature of the thinking process.

The schizophrenic uses a form of non-Aristotelian logic in his thinking. This type of logic is found among children and primitives as well as psychotic persons. More than two thousand years ago, Aristotle demonstrated that *A* is *A* and cannot be *B*. However, the schizophrenic, along with the dreamer and the primitive man, thinks with a different kind of logic. Among certain primitive men, there is the belief that some human beings are crocodiles. It is not that some human beings act like crocodiles, but they actually *are* crocodiles. On the surface such a belief is absurd. If a man is a man, he cannot be a crocodile. But the logic of the primitive mind as well as the schizophrenic mind is of a different order. This special logic makes it quite possible for a man to be a crocodile. One man was convinced that he was Switzerland. Following the logic of the normal mind, it seems incredible that a human being could entertain such a thought. However, the

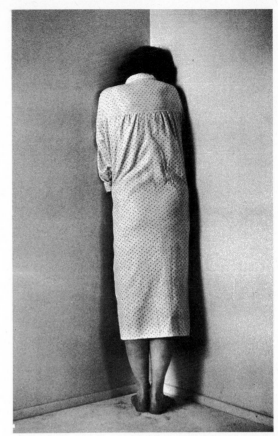

Figure 10.4 *The seclusiveness and withdrawal of the schizophrenic who literally turns her back to the world around her. (Courtesy of Mead Johnson Laboratories.)*

patient's thinking followed the line of "Switzerland loves freedom. I love freedom. I am Switzerland" (Bleuler, 1950).

The clinician who works with the schizophrenic soon learns to adapt himself to the peculiar logic used by the individual. A psychotic may be asked if he hears voices. When the patient assures the examiner that he does not, the skilled clinician does not hesitate to ask what would appear to be a non sequitur, "What do the voices say to you?" The patient is not surprised at such a question, nor is the clinician surprised when the patient replies, "They say all sorts of things."

In the behavioral area, the schizophrenic, more than any other psychotic, betrays himself by his posture, facial expression, mannerisms, and other symbolic movements. A tentative diagnosis of schizophrenia sometimes can be made on the basis of motor behavior alone. In some cases, the limbs can be molded into any position, and they will remain in that position indefinitely. In other cases, the patient mimics the motor movement of other people. These symptoms, while not common ones, are suggestive of schizophrenia, although such behavior also is seen occasionally in certain types of brain syndromes.

Schizophrenia presents a major mental health challenge. In the United States, schizophrenics account for about one-half of the resident patients in the state and county mental hospitals and VA psychiatric hospitals. The incidence of hospitalization of schizophrenic adolescents and children is increasing. It is estimated that at least 2 percent of all Americans born in 1960 will at some point fall victim to schizophrenia. Although the current length of hospitalization has decreased (only about 10 percent of admissions are retained for more than one year as compared to 20 to 40 percent in 1954), the rate of release is somewhat slower for schizophrenia than for the rest of the hospital population. Through intensive rehabilitation programs and improved drug treatments, some progress has been made in combating this disorder, but its exact cause has defied adequate definition.[2]

THE CLASSIFICATION OF SCHIZOPHRENIA

The schizophrenic reactions are classified into eight major types according to the distinguishing symptom pattern. However, there is a considerable degree of overlapping of symptoms and much room for difference of opinion, even among experts. It is not unusual for a schizophrenic person to be diagnosed as one type in one hospital and another type in another hospital. Many cases of schizophrenia present challenging problems of differential diagnosis. The major categories of this psychosis are: (1) simple, (2) hebephrenic, (3) paranoid, (4) catatonic, (5) schizoaffective, (6) undifferentiated, (7) childhood, and (8) residual.

Simple Schizophrenia

The simple type of schizophrenia is one of the most difficult to identify because the person rarely shows the more dramatic symptoms such as disorientation, delusions, hallucinations, or disturbances of language or action. Instead, he shows a gradual waning of interest and activity, usually during adolescence or early adult life. He withdraws from family and friends and seeks to be alone, often remaining in his room and refusing to eat. There is little or no interest in school, recreation, and work. He is inclined to become careless about his personal habits and appearance and is content to indulge in daydreaming.

This type of reaction is characterized by reduction in external attachments and interests and by impoverishment of human relationships. It involves adjustment on a lower psychobiological level of functioning, with an increase in the severity of symptoms over long periods, usually with apparent mental deterioration, in contrast to the schizoid personality in which there is little if any change.

■ **SIMPLE SCHIZOPHRENIA**

Edwin W. is a forty-nine-year-old man who has been in a psychiatric hospital for more than thirty years. He was a physically healthy and mentally alert youngster

---

[2]A number of excellent books dealing with the problems of schizophrenia are available. Among them are *The Lafayette Clinic Studies on Schizophrenia* (Wayne State University Press, 1970), edited by G. Tourney and J. S. Gottlieb; *Theories of Schizophrenia* (Atherton, 1969), edited by A. H. Buss; *Schizophrenia: Research and Theory* (Academic Press, 1968) by W. E. Broen, Jr.; and Eugen Bleuler's classic *Dementia Praecox, or The Group of Schizophrenias* (International Universities, 1950). Excellent comprehensive surveys are found in Leopold Bellak's *Schizophrenia: A Review of the Syndrome* (Logos, 1958); and *The Etiology of Schizophrenia* (Basic Books, 1960), edited by D. D. Jackson. Other general discussions of the condition include *Schizophrenia* (Ronald, 1959), edited by Alfred Auerback; *Chronic Schizophrenia: Explorations in Theory and Treatment* (Free Press, 1960), edited by Lawrence Appleby, J. M. Scher, and John Cumming; and Frank Fish's *Schizophrenia* (Williams and Wilkins, 1962).

until the third year of high school, when he failed Latin. He became discouraged, and refused to return to school for his senior year. He took a job as a bank messenger, but after nine months' employment decided to return to a military academy, where he did well in his academic subjects. He also won several athletic medals. However, he complained that he could not concentrate, and felt that he did not have enough intelligence to go to college. He returned to work, but soon lost his job because he remained in bed until late morning. He refused to mix with his friends, and became exceptionally quiet. He lost interest in everything around him, and would not leave the house unless coaxed by his family. Occasionally he would go to his room and cry. He would shrug his shoulders frequently, saying, "What's the use!" The patient often talked of going away, insisting that his family did not care for him. He was sent to a private sanitarium and later transferred to the state psychiatric hospital. When first seen at the hospital, the patient was well oriented; and his memory was intact. Speech was slow, and the patient would reply to questions only after much prompting. There were no delusions, hallucinations, or other signs of severe mental illness.

During the thirty years of hospitalization, the patient has remained withdrawn and apathetic. His speech is slow and soft, and he speaks in a low monotone. He does not mingle with other patients, and sits by himself most of the time. He is generally well behaved and seldom causes a disturbance on the ward. He shows no interest in his surroundings or in ward activities. Although the patient was well oriented when he first came to the hospital, there has been a certain amount of deterioration over the years. He is no longer certain about the date or his age. When asked how long he has been in the hospital, he replies, "about two or three months." When questioned about how he likes it at the hospital, he replies, "pretty good." He presents the classic picture of the long-term hospitalized simple schizophrenic patient.*

While there is no marked intellectual impairment, the simple schizophrenic gives the impression of being dull mentally. His apathy, indifference, lack of ability to concentrate, and low level of motivation sometimes suggest mental retardation. Psychological testing, however, shows that the person is not mentally retarded, even though he gives that impression. Nevertheless, the simple

schizophrenic is likely to be dull emotionally, to withdraw from social and interpersonal relations, and to be indifferent to social standards of various kinds.

A second problem of differential diagnosis is between the simple schizophrenic and the inadequate personality. Both conditions result in ineffective social, family, and work relations, with the person showing a long history of failure and lack of general adaptive capacity. The key distinguishing factor between these two conditions is the apathy and withdrawal tendencies seen in the schizophrenic. The inadequate personality may appear to try to function effectively, even though he does not seem to be able to do so. The schizophrenic, however, does not try.

Over a period of time the symptoms become worse, and many simple schizophrenics drift into a life of vagrancy, delinquency, and prostitution. Because of the relatively mild nature of the symptoms and the reasonably good contact with reality, these cases usually do not find their way to the psychiatric clinic or the mental hospital. They are more likely to be involved chronically with the courts and with social agencies.

Hebephrenia

The hebephrenic form of schizophrenic reaction was first described in 1871 by a German psychiatrist (Hecker, 1871). The word *hebephrenia* is derived from Greek and means "youthful mind." It was thought originally that the condition developed during the early years of life.

Unlike the simple schizophrenic, the hebephrenic individual shows a severe disintegration of the personality. Disorientation, delusions, hallucinations, symbolic language disturbances, and symbolic actions are seen in their most exaggerated forms. However, the most clearly identifying symptoms in this type of schizophrenia are the silly and inappropriate giggling and smiling, facial grimaces, and bizarre language. There also may be a wide range of mannerisms, gestures, posturings, and attitudinizings. Some of the most dramatic psychotic symptoms are seen in hebephrenia. These people show a rapid deteriora-

*Case 1 of audiotape 6, "Psychotic Disorders: Schizophrenic Reactions I," in *Case Interviews to Accompany The Disorganized Personality.*

Figure 10.5 *The hebephrenic type of schizophrenia. (Roger-Viollet, Paris.)*

tion of intellectual efficiency; and the fragmentation of their thinking and emotional instability, along with the other psychotic symptoms, may be pronounced.

■ HEBEPHRENIA

Wilma F. is a fifty-three-year-old woman who was first admitted to a mental hospital thirty years ago when she became excited, tore off her clothing, and struck her mother. She talked to herself, believed other people were in the room with her, assumed bizarre poses, giggled constantly, and acted in a silly manner. She was given a diagnosis of schizophrenia, hebephrenic type, and was discharged as improved after fifteen months. After leaving the hospital, the patient remained at home and helped with the housework. She had little interest in men until she was in her early thirties when she became promiscuous and lived with a number of different men. She had her first illegitimate child when she was thirty-four, and a second by a different man four years later. While both babies were placed in foster homes by a charitable organization, one of the children has since been admitted to the same psychiatric hospital although neither the mother nor the daughter knows the presence of the other.

When the patient was forty years old, she again became mentally disturbed with a recurrence of her silly behavior and episodes of violence. When seen at the hospital she smiled excessively and inappropriately. She blamed her difficulties on "getting mixed up with the wrong man." There was some indication of delusional thinking, although hallucinations could not be elicited. The most outstanding symptom was her inappropriate laughter, giggling, and meaningless smiling. The patient's condition remained unchanged, and she was still in the hospital after a period of twelve years.*

In the past, prolonged hospitalization was required in cases of hebephrenia. Every state hospital has a number of such patients who were admitted twenty, thirty, and even forty years before. Today, while cases of hebephrenia are seen from time to time, new methods of treatment are able to prevent the chronic regression and deterioration that was so common not many years ago. While we do not understand the special etiology of this type of schizophrenia, important steps have been taken in reducing the severity of its effects.

Paranoid Schizophrenia

The paranoid type of schizophrenia is one of the most commonly seen forms of mental disorder. The condition is marked by delusions and hallucinations, frequently of an accusatory and threatening nature. The person believes that what is happening in the world around him somehow concerns him. He is certain that the radio and television programs make references to him and that other everyday occurrences refer to him directly or indirectly. He is convinced that various forces are operating against him. While the persecutory ideas predominate in the paranoid picture in most cases, there are other forms of paranoid schizophrenia characterized by sexual preoccupation, religious ideas, and somatic complaints. While the delusional system of the paranoid schizophrenic is the central feature of the disorder, it is often contaminated with other symptoms. Frequently a homosexual component is detectable in the delusions and in the implications of the hallucinations. Characteristically, the paranoid schizo-

---

*Case 2 of audiotape 6, "Psychotic Disorders: Schizophrenic Reactions I," in *Case Interviews to Accompany The Disorganized Personality*.

phrenic does not show the regression or deterioration of the hebephrenic type. As a consequence, he sometimes manages to avoid hospitalization and may make a marginal adjustment in the community.

The paranoid schizophrenic, in the early stages of his disorder, reveals himself by evasiveness, suspicion of others, ideas of reference, and other paranoid symptoms. Somewhat less frequently, the early delusional material involves religious ideas or feelings of exaggerated self-importance and grandeur.

The delusions and hallucinations of the paranoid schizophrenic take many forms, ranging from the deceptively plausible to the bizarre. A businessman was sure that his partners were trying to get rid of him and take over the company. A married man believed that his wife and children were plotting to get hold of his property and bank accounts. At the other extreme, and more clearly schizophrenic, is the woman who said, "One of the doctors stole my mind out of my head, and he is going to use it to make a lot of money." Another person wore a rubber suit at home to protect himself from the rays of an "influencing machine" which a spiteful neighbor was directing against him.

A thirty-three-year-old tailor insisted that people had influence over him through "concentration" and "hypnotism." He said that these people, whom he did not know, were trying to force him to do "abnormal" things. He also confided that there were people who had the power to pull his brain out and replace it with an inferior brain. He said that he was suspicious of his fellow workmen and that people in Hollywood were trying to dope him. A city fireman said that a porch light on a nearby house was broadcasting stories about him. A twenty-one-year-old laborer said that "they" were going to lower him into hot acid and make hot iron out of him. He also complained that people were sprinkling powder in his room "to make him weak."

A young single woman was sent to a hospital because she complained that she was being tortured and persecuted and that there were wires around her. She would become extremely angry if her family did not unquestioningly accept her explanations of her behavior. For a month before admission she had heard the voices of three men, especially at night. These men talked about her in such an insulting way that she put cotton in her ears in order to shut out their voices. She also had the idea that electricity was passing through her body, that "they" were experimenting on her with television, and that someone was trying to seduce her by means of electric vibrations.

Another woman said her mother was a "redbird" which meant "a person who drinks and gives people diseases." She blamed her mother for a venereal disease she had contacted from a boarder. She said that her mother put dope in the coffee so that she succumbed to the advances of this man. She believed that her mother studied books in order to become a witch and that she took away her brain power by working on her spinal cord. She said her head had been crushed, that her skull was filled with snakes and wax, and that she was bothered by electricity.

The following delusions are typical of the ideas expressed by paranoid schizophrenics in the psychiatric hospital:

They poured acid down my throat. . . . They want to tie me under a bridge and then steal my furniture. . . . Two men have been trying to get in my bedroom window to keep me from giving the news. . . . They are trying to catch me to throw me in the Irish Sea. . . . An opium smoker doped me by sticking a needle in my heel. . . . The manager of the baseball team tried to give me syphilis by putting germs on my sandwich. . . . The Masons have secret signs to tell what is going on in the world. They have bells that ring messages in code. . . . Some boys injected mercury into my brain to make me do things. . . . They are trying to steal my secrets by using electricity on me. . . . People can control my thoughts and movements. . . . My mother is trying to use my mind. . . . The Italians won't let me have my hair cut.

■ PARANOID SCHIZOPHRENIA

Dorothy L. is a forty-nine-year-old single woman who had a high school education and worked as a switchboard operator for twenty-six years. During that time she took evening college courses in art, interior decorating, and business administration. Her main interest was in collecting antiques. She lived her entire life on a small farm, first with her parents, later with her younger brother and sister, and more recently alone. The father was a passive person who provided well for his family as a farmer. The mother was a borderline psychotic who had paranoid ideas, and a sister had a history of neuroticism.

The patient made a reasonably good early adjustment. The mother died when the patient was thirty-four, and two years later the patient took off suddenly for New Orleans. At the time, she was confused and delusional. However, she returned to her job, where her somewhat bizarre behavior was tolerated for several years. Then, when she was forty, she had a more serious break with reality, and had to be hospitalized for two months.

For the past eight years the patient has been living on the farm with an aged uncle who receives an old-age pension. She is known as a character and an eccentric in the community. She objects to her uncle using the electric lights or the hot water, and she attempts to prevent him from eating the food. For months she carried an old shopping bag with her, never allowing it out of her sight. When her brother finally managed to look into it, he found nothing but old rags in which mice had built a nest. The patient became such a problem in the community by bothering her neighbors with her delusions that it became necessary to place her in a psychiatric hospital.

When admitted to the hospital, the patient was untidy, spoke rapidly, and sat in an almost, statue-like position as she told her story. There was a flight of ideas, with loose associations, neologisms, and bizarre delusions. Her emotional tone was flat and inappropriate. She remained completely detached, even when describing the most vivid persecutory delusions.

The patient told a story of being persecuted by the British and Dutch "confusea," an agency which believes in killing and which has been plotting against her ancestors and members of her family. The story becomes highly involved. She believes that John the Baptist was her great-grandfather, and that Pope Clement and Sister Maria Theresa were her grandparents. She says that she is a direct descendant of the clan of Abel. The patient talks at length about the symbolic significance of words and letters. For example, in the word CATHOLIC, the C means the semicircle where people gather, A stands for the clan of Abel, T means the cross, H stands for the builders of corrals, O for the stones placed in a circle around water, L for women, and I for men.*

The paranoid schizophrenic is inclined to be very verbal about his ideas and beliefs. Some of the "Letters to the Editor" in the newspapers appear to be written by borderline schizophrenics

of this type. Moreover, because of their tendency toward intellectualization, their views not infrequently are taken seriously. In more advanced stages of the disorder, the psychotic elements become clear. The following letters are typical of those received from paranoid schizophrenics:

Dr. _____:
We are getting near God's Holy years AGAIN. So let us servants of God watch our language and meanings Please. Such as vanity, iniquity and swearing. Study the ten commandments Please. God Wants His Earth Straight and Clean AGAIN.
Sincerely,

Dear Dr. _____:
God is Consciousness; Consciousness is Everything the Ultimate Reality. Life is an Evolution of Consciousness. The Divine Plan is the Evolution of Spiritual Consciousness. The Super-Conscious, the Conscious and Subconscious are the 3 departments of the One Consciousness. It is a balance of opposite Polarities on all questions into Ultimate Synthesis. As follows: Religions, Metaphysical Philosophies and Truths, Psychiatry and Occupations, You have the Vegetarian-Meat Eating Polarities. The Pacifism-Militarism Polarities. The Sex Transmutation-Sex Expression Polarities. The Fasting-Naturopathic and the Medical Polarities. Colonization-Individualism Polarities. I call your attention to the Multiplicity of Metaphysical Occult and Progressive Groups in Southern California. The New World Order. The Coming World Government is an ultimate synthesis of Individualism and the Whole. I suggest that you and your World Psychiatrists write a book on New Age Spiritual Development in Southern California: the World Cradle of the New Age.
Respectfully,

The paranoid form of schizophrenia is important as a mental health problem because of its frequency and because it appears in a wide range of forms from very mild to quite severe. While in the milder cases it is possible for the person to make a marginal adjustment in society, the mere presence of such individuals in the community is potentially dangerous. Many accusations and legal actions have been brought against innocent people by borderline paranoid schizophrenics whose psychoses have not been recognized.

---

*Case 3 of audiotape 6, "Psychotic Disorders: Schizophrenia Reactions I," in *Case Interviews to Accompany The Disorganized Personality*.

Catatonia

The catatonic type of schizophrenia was first described in 1868 by a German physician who called the condition "tension insanity" (Kahlbaum, 1874). It was believed to be an organic disease during the nineteenth century. The disorder was attributed to an edema, or swelling, of the brain. The most common symptom is a generalized inhibition of motor activity, although in some cases there is excessive motor activity, grimacing, overtalkativeness, and unpredictable emotional outbursts.

The most classic catatonic symptoms are related to the stupor. They include a combination of mutism, rigidity, and the peculiar quality of muscular tonus called *cerea flexibilitas,* or waxy flexibility. The arm or leg of the patient can be placed in any position, and the limb remains in that position, sometimes for minutes or even hours. While this symptom is already diagnostic of catatonia, it is not necessary to the diagnosis. Most catatonic patients show the symptom only occasionally, and some not at all.

The motor symptoms in catatonia are more important, or at least more easily observed, than the intellectual or the emotional symptoms. The person sits or stands in one position, refusing to talk to anyone and seeming not to pay attention to anything that is said. Sometimes there is a rigidity of the muscles and a general resistance to movement. Occasionally there may be symbolic gesturing, posturizing, and stereotyped movements. Socrates, the Greek philosopher who stood motionless from early morning on one day until sunrise on the next, through an entire night when there was a hard frost, may have been a catatonic.

In spite of the fact that the catatonic seems completely out of touch with the world around him, there is evidence that the person does know what is happening, but simply does not respond to the ordinary stimulation of his environment. People who have been in catatonic stupors and have later described their experiences indicate that they were aware of the world around them but felt unable to respond to it in a meaningful way.

The excited phase of catatonia is somewhat less frequent than the stuporous phase. When it does occur, it is likely to show violence and impulsivity and makes schizophrenia one of the

Figure 10.6 *The catatonic type of schizophrenia. Note the fetallike position. (Photograph by Bill Bridges.)*

most dangerous of the mental disorders. Such people develop attacks of rage in which they become destructive and tear apart everything they can get their hands on. Without warning, these people are capable of attacking other persons in the most aggressive way. The excited phase is marked by a continued restlessness, overactivity, sleeplessness, and episodes of aggressive acting out.

The onset of catatonia is likely to be sudden. An individual who has otherwise appeared to be relatively normal will one day be found in a catatonic stupor. Similarly, catatonic excitement is frequently first observed as a completely unexpected burst of violence. It is likely that a certain number of assaultive acts, and even homocides, have been committed by individuals in outbursts of catatonic excitement.

■ CATATONIA

Harry G. is a twenty-seven-year-old man who developed his mental illness while serving a prison sentence in the Army. He became depressed and unable to sleep, refused food, was uncooperative, expressed paranoid ideas, and had auditory and visual hallucinations. He was transferred from the military prison to an Army hospital, and after a period of treatment he was returned to civilian life and placed in a psychiatric hospital.

The patient was reared in a poor neighborhood, with his parents separating when he was eight years old. He lived with his mother for a short time, and then moved in with the father. The patient ran away at age eleven because of the father's neglect and abusiveness. He returned to his mother and entered public school where he failed repeatedly. He left school at age sixteen to go to work, married at seventeen, and eventually had five children.

The patient was described as preferring to be alone, mixing with others only when he was drinking. He was a combative person who felt everyone was against him. Before being inducted into military service he had numerous arrests for gambling and excessive drinking, disorderly conduct, assault with a knife, and other charges.

When seen at the hospital, the patient was neat and clean in his dress and habits. While he was rather seclusive in his behavior, he caused no difficulties in the ward, and he cooperated readily with nurses, attendants, and examiners. His mood was somewhat depressed, and his emotional level appeared markedly flattened; but there were no abnormalities noted in his thinking. When asked why he was in the hospital, he told a story of having been sent to military prison for striking a non-commissioned officer who tried to take a bottle of cognac away from him. The patient said, "I was always in trouble in the Army, always for just little things, but always in trouble."

The most distinguishing feature in this case was several psychotic episodes in which the patient became mute, would not obey instructions, and sat or stood in one place for hours at a time. He would follow slowly if taken by the hand and led, but he would not move on his own initiative. When questions were put to him, it appeared as if he did not hear. While his eyes were open, he stared straight ahead in an unseeing way. The diagnosis in each instance was catatonic schizophrenia.*

Catatonic schizophrenia tends to be episodic, with the individual having a number of relatively short attacks over a period of years. However, chronic cases of schizophrenia with catatonic components are seen in every large psychiatric hospital.

At the psychological level, the catatonic posture has been explained by psychoanalysts in terms of a regression to the uterine period. This view regards the catatonic stupor as a symbolic representation of the unconscious desire to return to the womb of the mother. It has been suggested also that the catatonic state is comparable to the feigned death reaction which is utilized by lower animals to protect them from terrifying situations. Finally, the catatonic stupor may symbolize death itself, with its implication of an ultimate escape from all care and worry. Such views, however, are unsubstantiated hypotheses.

The evidence for a biochemical basis of catatonic schizophrenia is substantial. It has been shown that animals injected with heavy water (deuterium oxide), or such drugs as bulbocapnine, show motor reactions similar to those seen in human catatonia. Such reactions can also be obtained in the experimental animal by the production of certain types of brain lesions. Another experimental evidence of a possible biochemical basis for catatonia is the fact that the injection of sodium amytal or the inhalation of carbon dioxide and oxygen results in periods of lucidity in these patients. This lucid interval lasts from a few minutes to a few hours, and then the individual reverts to his catatonic stupor.

Schizo-affective type

Some schizophrenic individuals show a considerable degree of emotion. The emotional instability may be so pronounced that they may present difficult management problems. During the course of a single interview such people may show affective changes ranging from laughter to tears.

When this type of emotional instability is combined with delusional ideas, the results are often of a serious nature. Strong emotional attachments are developed particularly by women, and quite

---

*Case 1 of audiotape 7, "Psychotic Disorders: Schizophrenic Reactions II," in *Case Interviews to Accompany The Disorganized Personality.*

unsuspecting men sometimes find themselves the innocent victims of the delusional affections of someone they hardly know or do not know at all.

A young professor had a student in his class who received C's and D's in her quizzes and failed to take the final examination. She came in to see the professor about a make-up examination, which was prepared for her, but she never took it. That was the last the professor heard of her until the following year when he was teaching at another university. One morning he received a collect telegram which read:

Dear _____:

I am a lover thru and thru, and I'm in love with you. I am sitting by the telephone straight and tall, waiting for you to call.

Love,

The professor was completely mystified by the telegram, and thought it might be some kind of poor joke. But when he arrived home that evening, there was a long-distance call from his former student, who was obviously in a highly confused state. She poured out an incoherent story about her engagement being broken off because she had been in his class at the university. The next day the professor received several letters. One read:

Dear _____:

Please come down and get me. I love you. I'll die if you don't marry me. I can't see four good lives going to waste—yours, mine, and the two people to whom we are engaged. My fiance knows about you, and that's why he'll never be happy with me. Everywhere I go everyone knows the story about you and I. I'll never have friends any more, and I have to live here. Won't you please come back and get me because it's you I love and no one else. My whole life will be ruined. Now that I know you were always supposed to marry me, I can't contain myself until I hear from you. Please call and let me talk to you because I love you.

Love,

On the outside of one of the envelopes, the student wrote: "Sealed with a kiss. It's all your fault. Now I'm in love with you." The situation became progressively worse, with the student making telephone calls and sending telegrams and letters both to the professor and to the girl to whom he was engaged. In addition, the student began telephoning the professor's former colleagues at the university, demanding information and making accusations. Finally, it was possible to have the girl committed to a psychiatric hospital; and a completely unjustified scandal and public embarrassment were avoided.

The acute schizo-affective attack is one in which the mental content is predominantly schizophrenic, but with a turmoil of emotion. Sometimes these people become so disturbed they are dangerous to themselves and to others. While such individuals now are kept under control by means of psychoactive drugs, they were for many years among the most violent in the psychiatric hospital.

Undifferentiated Type

Many cases of schizophrenia cannot be easily classified as simple, hebephrenic, paranoid, catatonic, or schizo-affective. When there is such a combination and overlapping of symptoms that the patient cannot be placed in a clear-cut diagnostic category, a diagnosis of undifferentiated schizophrenia is made. This condition, like the schizo-affective type, is a relatively recent addition to the classification of schizophrenia.

The following letter is one of a series received from a chronic undifferentiated schizophrenic. This patient makes a reasonably adequate social adjustment and has never been hospitalized.

Dear Dr. _____:
This material is flying all over the country now to about 20 research men. Federal agent said #1 over his head had me dictate it in simple form—this recorded (also Washington, D.C.) and ask me to see M? Another department better versed on this subject (no time). I do not know if you received another letter. I asked someone else to read first and mail. Now I could not tell you one word that is in #2. My writings are kept by all medical men—no comment—no return on request—after all four pages difficult for me to do over (public stenographer). Twelve copies of that gone out. Please return this copy (have copied if you want). I want a line of encouragement from just one. Why—

opposition and arguments every night with J. My biggest problem "All I want you to do is get whatever you are doing over with. No intuition stuff, I want facts."

■ UNDIFFERENTIATED SCHIZOPHRENIA

Sylvia M. is a forty-five-year-old single woman who was admitted to a psychiatric hospital after a series of complaints by neighbors, the fire department, and the Board of Health. The patient's psychotic condition existed for at least four years, during which time she had been living alone. She hallucinated actively, talked to herself, and screamed at night. Neighbors reported she would scream from the window, "Get out of here, or I'll kill you if you take the children." The patient has never been married and has no children. Her apartment was filthy, with thirty-seven large bags of garbage found in her apartment when she was hospitalized.

The patient was an excellent student in school and graduated from her university with honors in sociology. She was an active and well-liked member of a sorority, and following her graduation she took a position in the field of social work. She enjoyed a secure financial position, and was considered an attractive and well-dressed woman. Several young men wanted to marry her, but her father interfered each time.

Sylvia's mother died soon after the child was born, and the father became an alcoholic. The patient was adopted by relatives, although she did not know of her adoption until her adoptive mother died while the patient was in her late twenties. At that time she had an emotional disturbance which required hospitalization. Upon her recovery she returned home and took care of her father until his death a few years ago. Since that time she has been living alone, showing a steady deterioration of her personality.

When seen at the hospital, the patient appeared somewhat older than her age of forty-five years. She was unkempt and disheveled. When she entered the interview room she was suspicious and looked carefully at the walls and into the corners. She was tense and agitated, frequently rubbing her hands, and sometimes giggling and laughing inappropriately. She commented, "There doesn't seem to be much the matter with me, just my nerves." When asked why she was in the hospital, she replied that she had no idea except that the police brought her. At times she appeared puzzled and bewildered. She was oriented for time, place, and person, although her remote and recent memory were impaired. She showed much delusional material centering on her practice of "standing" as a part of some type of legal action involving her nonexistent children. She admitted that she did not understand it very well but knew that the situation required that she stand up for long intervals, sometimes throughout the night.*

The diagnosis of undifferentiated schizophrenia has been made with increasing frequency since this category was introduced into the official classification system. Since cases of mental disorder, and particularly schizophrenia, are seldom clearcut as textbooks suggest, the problem of differential diagnosis is often a difficult one. Schizophrenics frequently combine features of hebephrenia and catatonia with thinking that is characteristic of paranoid schizophrenia. On one examination a person may show a particular symptom picture which suggests catatonia; at another time the same person may impress the examiner with his paranoid thinking. There may also be hebephrenia or schizo-affective components. It may be difficult, if not impossible, to specify exactly the type of schizophrenia with which one is dealing. For such cases the classification of undifferentiated schizophrenia was introduced.

Childhood Type

There has been an increasing recognition of the fact that the psychotic break with reality sometimes occurs during childhood. Caelius Aurelianus, in ancient Rome, described a case of mania in a child, and the early literature contains other scattered reports of serious personality breakdown in children. By the nineteenth century, the existence of psychotic behavior in children was recognized widely. Benjamin Rush discussed the condition in his textbook on psychiatry (Rush, 1812), and Moreau de Tours published a book in 1888 on the mental disturbances of children. However these early writers attempted to fit the personality disturbances of children into the existing categories of adult mental disturbances. It was not

---

*Case 2 of audiotape 7, "Psychotic Disorders: Schizophrenic Reactions II," in *Case Interviews to Accompany The Disorganized Personality*.

until the 1920s that child psychiatry became established as an important medical specialty (Kanner, 1925).

While less than 1 percent of the first admissions to mental hospitals are under eighteen years of age, the actual incidence of psychosis in childhood is probably higher than the hospital figures show. Some psychotic children are not recognized as such; and, when serious emotional disturbances do occur, parents and relatives are likely to be reluctant to allow institutionalization. Moreover, the facilities for treating psychotic children are limited. Such factors tend to obscure the true incidence of schizophrenia among children.

> This category is for cases in which schizophrenic symptoms appear before puberty. The condition may be manifested by autistic, atypical, and withdrawn behavior; failure to develop identity separate from the mother, and general unevenness, growth immaturity and inadequacy in development (DSM-II, 1968).

While the serious emotional disturbances of childhood often have a schizophrenic-like character, some authorities question the accuracy of the term *childhood schizophrenia*. They feel that the relationship between the childhood personality disorder and the adult form of schizophrenia has not been established adequately. Nor are they convinced that such a relationship can be established. For this reason, some psychologists and psychiatrists prefer the less specific terms of *childhood psychosis* or *infantile autism*. The word "autism" refers to the seclusiveness, withdrawal from reality, and lack of communication seen in children of this type.

One of the distinguishing symptoms of the psychotic child is the apparent unresponsiveness to other people. Other characteristics are the need for close physical contact, interference with speech development, distortion of emotional expression, difficulty in learning, variations in motor behavior, sudden and unexpected releases of violent emotions, and disturbances of the thinking processes.

■ CHILDHOOD SCHIZOPHRENIA

Tommy M. is a twenty-four-year-old patient whose psychotic behavior was first observed when he was about six years old. He was an extremely hyperactive and restless youngster who was easily distracted, and who sometimes refused to talk. When he did speak, he repeated such phrases as, "Tony Macaroni, Tony Macaroni, Tony Macaroni," or began counting without being asked, "One, two, three, vanilla pudding; one, two, three, vanilla pudding."

When Tommy was ten years old, he was sent to a special school. His motor coordination and posture were good, and he was able to use his hands and feet very well. The school reported that his response to music and literature was extraordinary. He loved to listen to stories and could relate parts of them from memory. He was also fond of music, and could reproduce a melody correctly after hearing it once. It was reported that his enunciation and pronunciation of words were perfect, although sometimes he said things that made no sense. On occasions, he used advanced words like "confidentially" and "necessary."

His teacher reported: "This youngster's behavior is his greatest problem. He is definitely disturbed. If one could get him to cooperate, one might really be surprised how intelligent he really is. His behavior improved considerably throughout the year. Earlier in the year he refused to come inside the classroom and ran away. At the end of the school year, this behavior had reversed and he was refusing to leave the classroom."

Tommy was seen by a diagnostic center when he was twelve years old. During his stay at the center, he was observed in many different situations. Negativism was present during all the examinations. He often became restive, twisted and turned in his chair, giggled at the examiner while watching his face very closely, and rambled off into disconnected associations triggered by the question. It was observed that he used words at a much higher level than he was able or willing to define on a vocabulary test.

Tommy was admitted to a psychiatric hospital when he was fourteen years old. At that time he was in poor contact with his surroundings. He withdrew from the examiner, and faced the other way during the initial interview. He showed anxiety in the form of quick nervous movements, but there were no truly bizarre actions. Most of the time he seemed preoccupied in fantasy. His speech was frequently irrelevant and often incoherent. His mood was sometimes inappropriate, with his thought content limited to a few perseverated comments about his father's car, a swimsuit, and a vague story about a relative he liked.

When examined ten years later, the patient was twenty-four years old. He was overactive, paced back and forth, stooped down to pick things off the floor, and gazed at the ceiling. Most of the time he avoided looking at the examiner, although he would do so if a direct command were given. He said he was born in 1953, and that he was ten years old. He said he heard voices, and pointed to the corner of the room where he said some boys were standing.*

What causes childhood psychosis? One theory is that the condition is due to a genetic defect or abnormality. However, autistic children are rarely born to autistic parents. Also, while the rate of autism in brothers and sisters is higher than that in the general population, it is still low for a hereditary disorder.

A different view of autism is that the condition is a psychogenic disturbance based on the child's learned response to the personality characteristics of the parents. It has been observed that the parents of autistic children are often detached, cold, and obsessive. But even if there is a relationship between the personality of the parents and childhood autism, and this relationship is by no means certain, we would be faced with the problem of explaining why one child becomes autistic when the brothers and sisters do not develop the condition.

Another theory of autism is that the condition is due to brain damage. The support for this belief is that a picture identical to childhood autism develops when brain disease occurs in infancy or early childhood. While evidence can be marshalled for each of the major theories, the cause of this psychotic disorder in children is completely unknown.[3]

Residual Type

The residual type of schizophrenia is seen in the person who has had serious schizophrenic disturbances and who has improved enough to return home and to make at least a marginal adjustment in the community. Nevertheless such people continue to show traces of the disorder in their thinking, emotions, and actions. These residual symptoms are not incapacitating and may not interfere seriously with the individual's adjustment to his family, his work, or his social life.

The terms *ambulatory, borderline,* and *pseudoneurotic* schizophrenia have also been used to refer to the many cases of marginal schizophrenia found in every large community. While important steps have been taken in the treatment of schizophrenia, and while an increasing number of these persons are being returned to the community after relatively short periods of hospitalization, there are few "cures" in the sense of the eradication of all evidence of the schizophrenic process. There is a growing belief that one does not cure schizophrenia but merely manages the symptoms. Whether or not this point of view is valid will depend upon further investigations into the cause of the disorder.[4]

ETIOLOGY OF SCHIZOPHRENIA

In his classic monograph on schizophrenia published early in the 1900s, Eugen Bleuler said, "We do not know what the schizophrenic process actually is." Today, nearly three-quarters of a

---

*Case 3 of audiotape 7, "Psychotic Disorders: Schizophrenic Reactions II," in *Case Interviews to Accompany The Disorganized Personality.*

[3]Among the books on psychotic disorders in children are William Goldfarb's *Childhood Schizophrenia* (Harvard University, 1961); A. M. Des Laurier's *Experience of Reality in Childhood Schizophrenia* (International Universities, 1962); Kenneth Soddy's *Clinical Child Psychiatry* (Bailliere Tindall, 1960); and the second edition of Leo Kanner's classic *Child Psychiatry* (Thomas, 1948). Nontechnical books of unusual interest are M. Sechehaye's *Autobiography of a Schizophrenic Girl* (Grune & Stratton, 1951); and Louise Wilson's *This Stranger My Son* (Putnam, 1968).

[4]*Schizophrenia Bulletin,* a publication first issued in 1969, facilitates the dissemination and exchange of information about schizophrenia and provides abstracts of the recent literature on the subject. It is prepared jointly by the Center for Studies of Schizophrenia and the National Clearing House for Mental Health Information and is available from the National Institute of Mental Health, 5454 Wisconsin Avenue, Chevy Chase, Md. 20015.

century later, Bleuler's comment is equally true. The problem of etiology in the schizophrenias is complicated by the fact that this group of disorders includes a variety of conditions. It is unlikely that there is a single cause common to all the schizophrenias. One would hardly expect, on the basis of the symptom picture, to find the same causative factors responsible for such widely divergent clinical types as simple schizophrenia and catatonia. While it is true that the various forms of schizophrenia show withdrawal and disorganization, these characteristics express themselves in widely different ways.

In spite of the apparent differences among the various schizophrenias, efforts have been made to arrive at a common etiology. Theories of causation include (1) heredity, (2) constitution, (3) biological factors, (4) psychological factors, and (5) social factors.

Heredity

The possibility that heredity plays a role in the etiology of schizophrenia was suggested by Emil Kraepelin, who reported an incidence of 53.8 percent of mental disorder in the families of more than a thousand schizophrenic patients. Later studies also revealed a relatively high rate of mental disturbance in the families of schizophrenics.

There are several genetic theories of schizophrenia, ranging from nonspecific influence involving many genes (polygenic) to the belief that schizophrenia is caused by a single gene (monogenic).

One of the problems in schizophrenia is the very wide range of severity of symptoms. There is a gradual shading from normality to severe schizophrenia in terms of apathy, withdrawal, suspiciousness, and degrees of thinking disturbance. There appears to be the same type of grading of characteristics as we find in normal personality traits. A theory of polygenic inheritance, involving multiple gene influences, can account for this great range—from normality to severe schizophrenic disorder.

The most exhaustive study of heredity in schizophrenia was made by Franz Kallmann, who studied 1,087 schizophrenic patients admitted to the Berlin Herzberge Hospital between 1893 and 1902 (Kallmann, 1938). He also studied parents, husbands, and wives of the schizophrenic patients, direct descendants; brothers, sisters, half-brothers, and half-sisters; and nephews and nieces. These patients represented a cross section of the entire North German population. Kallmann concluded that schizophrenia is not inherited directly but rather is transmitted by recessive genes in the form of a predisposition. Individuals with this predisposition to the disorder will develop schizophrenic reactions when placed under sufficient stress. Individuals who are not predisposed develop a different type of defensive reaction.

The rate of schizophrenia in the general population in the United States is 0.85 percent. Kallmann showed that when one sibling had schizophrenia, another sibling had it in 14.3 percent of the cases. When one fraternal twin had the disorder, the other twin had it in 14.5 percent of the cases. However, when one identical twin had schizophrenia, the disorder was found in the other identical twin in 86.2 percent of the cases. Since the morbidity rate for schizophrenia is not 100 percent when both parents are schizophrenic or in the case of identical twins, it is probable that the disorder is not a purely hereditary trait. Table 10.1 shows incidence rates for schizophrenia based on Kallmann's figures.

A study in Finland attempted to trace and diagnose all male twins born in the period 1920–1929. A total of 17 cases were found in which one of two identical twins was diagnosed as schizophrenic at one time and had a surviving co-twin available

Table 10.1 *Incidence rates for schizophrenia*

BLOOD-RELATED	
Identical twins (not separated)	91.1%
Identical twins (separated five years or more)	77.6%
Fraternal twins	14.5%
Brothers and sisters	14.3%
Half-brothers and half-sisters	7.1%
Cousins	2.6%
NONRELATED	
Stepbrothers and stepsisters	2.1%
Marriage partners	1.8%
General population	0.85%

SOURCE: Adapted from figures published at various times by F. J. Kallmann, M.D.

for study. The concordance rate for schizophrenia varied from 6 to 36 percent, depending upon the diagnostic criteria employed. It was concluded that concordance figures are not as significant in schizophrenia as they have been considered to be in the past on the basis of earlier studies (Tienari, 1967).

However, the weight of evidence supports a genetic factor in the causation of schizophrenic illness. Even though there is a wide variation in the concordance rate for identical twins in various studies, there is a significant difference in the concordance rates for identical and fraternal twins. Additional support for the operation of a genetic factor is given by the finding that when neither parent is schizophrenic, the risk of schizophrenia in the brother or sister of a schizophrenic is about 8 or 9 percent. If one of the parents is schizophrenic, the risk is 12 percent. When both parents are schizophrenic, the risk is above 35 percent (Shields, 1968).

Some authorities believe that although genetic factors are responsible for the features of most of the schizophrenias, the disorder can appear without a genetic predisposition in some cases. For example, it has been shown that amphetamine poisoning can result in schizophrenia-like psychoses and that there are schizophrenia-like states associated with some forms of epilepsy (Slater, 1968).

The most reasonable theory of schizophrenia, based on clinical and research findings available at the beginning of the 1970s, is that some type of hereditary background is necessary to produce schizophrenia but that the hereditary predisposition is not sufficient in itself to make the symptoms appear. Some type of physical, psychological, or environmental stress is required to trigger the disorder.

Even if it comes about that genetic factors are of primary importance in schizophrenia, it is still necessary to identify the kinds of environments or stress situations which bring about the schizophrenic disorder in those who are predisposed to it.

Constitution

Constitutional factors also appear to play a role in schizophrenia since there is some evidence that a significant number of these patients have a char-

acteristic physical build. The work of both Kretschmer and Sheldon points in this direction (see Chapter 3). Kretschmer attempted to relate the schizoid personality to the asthenic body build. He believed that the tall and linear body type is associated with the schizoid personality and that when individuals having this body type develop a serious mental disorder, it is most likely to be schizophrenia. Sheldon also emphasized a relationship between body types and schizophrenia.

Since schizophrenia develops in a relatively young age group, the age factor may account for these findings. However, most clinicians who have had long experience with schizophrenic people are struck by what appears to be a distinguishing physical make-up. It is entirely possible that the physical constitution of the person is not a determining factor in the disorder, but that the genetic and/or developmental factors responsible for the schizophrenia are also responsible for the asthenic physique.

Biological Factors

Physical conditions of all kinds have been suggested as the possible cause of schizophrenic reactions. Among the many biological theories advanced have been glandular disorders, endocrine disturbances, brain damage, and toxins. Some physicians even blamed the condition on excessive masturbation, and others felt it was related to decayed teeth, diseased tonsils, and infections in various other parts of the body.

Early in the present century there was an active interest in the pathological changes in schizophrenia. Studies of brain tissue cells in these cases showed alterations of considerable significance. However, the observed changes are not consistent from person to person and consequently do not point to a specific causative factor. More recently, interest has been directed toward biochemical functions.

In the early 1900s both Kraepelin and Jung suggested the presence of an unknown toxic substance (toxin x) in the schizophrenic. This theory of autointoxication received scant interest for many years because of the hypothetical nature of the toxin. However, there has been increasing evidence that there may be toxic substances in the body fluids of schizophrenics.

An Italian investigator in the late nineteenth

century found that the blood of psychotic persons, when injected into experimental animals, caused death. He came to the conclusion that the death was due to toxic substances present in the blood of the patients (Keup, 1954). Other studies established that the blood serum of schizophrenics kills tadpoles, while tadpoles survive in normal serum (Fischer, 1953); that the serum inhibits the germination of plant seed (Macht, 1950); and that it is toxic to certain molds and fungi (Fedoroff, 1956). Experiments have also shown that the injection of blood plasma from certain psychotics produces a disorganizing effect in rats which interferes with their performance.

Rats were trained to climb a vertical rope approximately 5 feet high. They were induced to climb by the incentive of a dish of food on a platform at the top of the rope and by a mild electric shock applied to their feet through a wire grid on the floor of the cage. After intensive training, the rats learned to climb the rope in about 4 seconds after the electrical stimulus was applied. However, there was a highly significant delay in the climbing time of rats injected with plasma from schizophrenic patients. In addition to the delay in climbing time, the animals showed marked changes in their cage behavior. They huddled in the back of the cage and became quiet and withdrawn. Climbing was clumsy, and when the animals reached the feeding platform they refused to eat (Winter and Flataker, 1958).

At Tulane University, plasma from schizophrenics was injected into the veins of normal prison inmates who volunteered for the study. All volunteers receiving plasma developed symptoms which persisted for 15 to 45 minutes. While the reactions were not severe, the subjects described symptoms of personality disturbance. Control subjects receiving plasma from normal donors did not show these symptoms (Heath et al., 1958).

One group of investigators has studied the affect of schizophrenic serum on the web-forming behavior of the orb-weaver spider *Zilla-x-notata* (Bercel, 1960). This test animal has been used for the biological assay of substances that influence central nervous system function. Various stimulants and depressants result in web formations that are characteristic, predictable, and reproducible.

In the web-weaving experiments, spiders were saturated with the serum from normal subjects, from patients with various organic diseases, from psychotic persons other than schizophrenics, and from people with the various types of schizophrenia. Incomplete or rudimentary webs appeared in 66.7 percent of the cases when the serum from catatonic individuals was used. The rudimentary response was found only in catatonic schizophrenia, not in other forms of schizophrenia, other psychotic states, organic disturbances, or normal serum.

Among other findings of the Tulane group has been a special kind of protein or globulin at sites in the forebrain region of schizophrenics. This finding has been used as evidence to support the

Figure 10.7   Left, *the web of the spider* Zilla-x-notata, *after treatment with the blood serum of normal human subjects;* right, *a disorganized web woven by a spider treated with the serum of a schizophrenic patient. (Courtesy of Dr. Nicholas A. Bercel.)*

hypothesis that schizophrenia is an autoimmune disease (one in which the body manufactures an antibody that acts against its own cells). According to this theory, the globulins originating in the blood of schizophrenics impair the normal transmission of messages from one brain cell to another (Heath, 1970).

Another line of biochemical research concerns the urinary constituents in mental illness. One research group found marked differences between the urinary excretion of schizophrenic patients and normal subjects (McGeer et al., 1957). Other studies have indicated that animals injected with extracts do not exhibit similar changes. In some animals, symptoms last for five to eight hours (Meduna and Vaichulis, 1948). Similarly, pathological changes in the electrical brain waves follow injections of urinary extracts from schizophrenic patients, while these changes do not occur with normal extracts (Wada and Gibson, 1959).

An additional area of interest in the neurochemistry of personality disturbances is related to the cerebrospinal fluid. This fluid is formed in part by the action of nerve centers in the brain and in part as a result of an exchange between the blood and the nervous system. Since the cerebrospinal fluid maintains a chemical balance with the blood as well as with other fluids of the central nervous system, the fluid is sensitive to disease processes involving the brain and spinal cord. While significant changes have been observed in connection with neurological diseases, most of the work related to schizophrenia is of a contradictory nature. Even in those cases where there is general agreement on the findings, their significance, in terms of personality disorganization, is generally obscure.

Another possible indication of a biochemical basis for at least some forms of schizophrenia is the demonstration of a characteristic odor in the sweat of schizophrenic patients. This odor has been mentioned from time to time in the literature, but it has now been established that there is a scientific basis for it. The presence of the odor may be due to an inborn error of metabolism.

Further evidence that schizophrenia may be the result of a biochemical defect was provided by a study which showed that an abnormality in the function of the neurohormone *serotonin* may give rise to abnormal behavior by allowing people to dream while awake. Using cats as subjects, a drug was given which prevented the brain from producing serotonin. The cats seemed to hallucinate, attacked other cats, and behaved with a mixture of normality and abnormality seen so frequently in the mentally disordered.

Another theory of schizophrenia is called the "leaky membrane" theory. According to this view, something in the blood of a schizophrenic causes the brain cell membrane to leak chemicals in and out with unusual ease. A leaky membrane could cause chemicals to act abnormally both inside and outside the cell. Such a condition could create dangerous antibodies, distort brain metabolism, and disrupt transmission of the nerve impulse. It has been suggested that the chemical which might be causing membranes to leak is *alpha 2 globulin.*

A major reason for the active interest in the biochemistry of schizophrenia was the discovery that drugs such as mescaline and lysergic acid (LSD-25) are able to release psychotic-like symptoms in normal people (Hoffer et al., 1954). While the behavioral disorganization due to such drugs is readily distinguishable from schizophrenia, there are enough similarities to suggest a relationship. More important, both LSD-25 and mescaline show a structural similarity of the molecules to such naturally occurring neurohormones as noradrenalin and serotonin. The similarity suggests that if LSD-25 and mescaline can produce psychotic-like symptoms, and if these drugs are structurally similar to noradrenalin and serotonin, disturbances of the naturally occurring neurohormones may be related to psychotic behavior.

While it is impossible at this time to demonstrate a specific organic cause for schizophrenia, the evidence suggests such a cause in at least some of the types of schizophrenia. It is certainly no coincidence that schizophrenic individuals show so many nonspecific organic variations. The puzzle has been an intriguing one for many years, and we may now be very close to at least a partial solution. Until that time, the importance of psychological and cultural stress in the development of schizophrenia cannot be neglected.

Psychological Factors

During the first half of the present century, psychological explanations of the schizophrenic disorders rivaled biological explanations in number and variety. The least complicated psychological view is that schizophrenia is a flight from reality, with withdrawal from active and emotional participation in the outside world. More basically, the disorder may be a regression to more primitive forms of adjustment. Evidence for this regression is the narcissism of the schizophrenic, his preoccupation with sexual activities and elimination, and, in some cases, the infantile-like sucking movements made by the patient. Finally, the "fetal posture" assumed by some schizophrenics has been interpreted as a psychological regression to the mother's womb.

In psychoanalytic theory, schizophrenia has been regarded as a condition in which there is a pronounced libidinal and ego regression. In terms of libido, the regression is to the oral sucking stage of psychosexual development, while the ego regression is to an early stage of narcissism. According to this theory, the schizophrenic has difficulty with his social and sexual identifications during the adolescent period, and it is at this time that the regression begins. Such a theory does not preclude the role of constitutional factors or of traumatic experiences during infancy and childhood.

Some of the psychological theories of schizophrenia are not theories at all. Rather, they are observations about the behavior of patients or inferences about their experiences. For example, it is probably true that in schizophrenia there is a disorder of the ego relationship with external reality, as well as a failure in communication, ambivalent interpersonal relationships, and doubt and uncertainty about sexual identity. Similarly, the schizophrenic exhibits an inability to interpret symbols properly. But in each of these instances, a symptom is involved rather than a causative factor.

Social Factors

There has been a continuing interest in the study of the impact of social organization on the incidence of schizophrenia. At one time it was thought that schizophrenia was a mental disorder brought on by the complexities of civilization. More recently it has been observed that schizophrenia occurs in a wide variety of cultural groups, regardless of the level of technological advance. In recent years, such factors as social isolation, social mobility, parent-child relationships, parental personality, family environment, and family interaction have been studied with reference to their possible roles in the etiology of the schizophrenic psychoses (Clausen and Kohn, 1960).

One theory of schizophrenia is that it is the result of a pathological process of personality development which begins relatively early in life. While some authorities believe the disorder to be exclusively a function of social variables, it is more probable that the pathological processes occur only in genetically vulnerable individuals. Another hypothesis is that social isolation is necessary to the development of schizophrenia. There is also evidence that schizophrenic reactions may be associated with social class, since a disproportionate number of hospitalized schizophrenics come from slum areas and lower socioeconomic levels (see Table 10.2).

When all types of schizophrenia are considered, the ecological studies show a decrease in incidence of the disorder from high rates in the center of the city to low rates in the suburbs. There is a gradient from areas of disorganization to areas of stability. Within the schizophrenic group, the catatonic states appear to come primarily from areas in which foreign-born persons and blacks are housed, and in which a great deal of cultural conflict is combined with conditions of poverty. Catatonia is also frequent in areas with large immigrant populations. Paranoid schizophrenics are most heavily concentrated in the rooming-house areas, and the concentration toward the periphery of the city becomes successively lower. This condition also is distributed heavily in the hobo district. The

Table 10.2 *Distribution of normals and schizophrenics by social class*

SOCIAL CLASS	PERCENT OF NORMALS	PERCENT OF SCHIZOPHRENICS
I	3.2	0.7
II	8.4	2.7
III	22.6	9.8
IV	47.4	41.6
V	18.4	45.2

SOURCE: Adapted from A. B. Hollingshead and F. C. Redlich, *Social Class and Mental Illness.* New York: John Wiley & Sons, Inc., 1958.

trend for hebephrenics is similar to that of the paranoids, though less marked. Both types tend to originate in the rooming-house areas in which the primary social group is disorganized and a relatively high degree of isolation is present (Faris and Dunham, 1939).

There is some question about the factors responsible for the ecological distribution of schizophrenia. It may be that there is an increased probability that schizophrenics in the central areas of a city will be referred to psychiatric hospitals or that individuals who are prone to schizophrenia tend to become segregated in the central areas. It is also possible that the critical factor may be social isolation or increased mobility, both of which are increased in the central areas of a large city.

Another cultural theory of the etiology of schizophrenia is that the condition is the result of the experience of each particular child early in life in interaction with significant adults who are themselves in conflict. Studies of the families of schizophrenic patients show a relatively high incidence of emotional disturbance on the part of parents. Many parents are deficient in motivation or helpless and ineffective in their routine activities. Emotional difficulties are not uncommon, and psychosomatic symptoms are verbalized frequently. Disturbances of psychosexual behavior also are common.

In many instances, the mother is considered to be *schizophrenogenic*. That is, her behavior and personality tend to foster schizophrenic reactions on the part of the child. Most emphasis has been placed on the mother-child relationship, particularly during the early months of the child's life. Less attention has been given to the father-child relationship, although interest in this problem has been developing.

In an effort to determine the characteristics of the parents of schizophrenic persons; a study was made of the personality characteristics of mothers and fathers (Jackson et al., 1958). Twenty psychiatrists specializing in the treatment of schizophrenia were asked to describe their conceptions of the mothers and fathers of the patients. Three types of mothers and three types of fathers were described. The three types of mothers were the "puritanical" mother, the "helpless" mother, and the "Machiavellian" mother. The puritanical

mother is an overly controlled, highly moral, and determined woman. The helpless mother is weak, anxious, and confused. The Machiavellian mother tends to be manipulating and uses others in an attempt to attain her way. She is described as devious, hostile, unforgiving, and unethical.

The three types of fathers were described as the "defeated" father, the "autocratic" father, and the "chaotic" father. The defeated father is an uncertain, passive, and self-abasing person. He is awkward and pathetic in his social relationships. The autocratic father is a driving, aloof, and impassive man, who may be quite successful but is not given to warm interpersonal relationships. The chaotic father is an anxious man who is influenced in an exaggerated way by the external and internal forces that play upon him.

TREATMENT AND PROGNOSIS

As a result of the inability to isolate a common cause for the schizophrenias, it has not been possible to develop a specific form of treatment for this group of conditions. The result has been the use of treatment techniques varying as widely as the theories to account for the schizophrenias. It would be no exaggeration to say that almost every physical and psychological method used in treatment in the field of mental disorder has been used at one time or another in the treatment of schizophrenia. The major treatment approaches, however, have involved the various forms of shock therapy, psychosurgery, and the tranquilizing drugs. Specialized forms of psychological treatment have also been developed in an effort to treat these conditions.

In the two decades between 1950 and 1970 the National Institute of Mental Health supported more than 3,000 research projects investigating various aspects of schizophrenia. There were nine research projects with a total expenditure of slightly more than 100,000 dollars in 1948. By 1958, the Institute spent 4.8 million dollars on schizophrenia research, and by 1968 more than 300 research projects were being supported at a total expenditure of more than 12 million dollars. The projects ranged from electron microscopic studies of brain cells to large epidemiologic surveys; from studies of abnormal urinary excretions to disturbances in family communication patterns; and from studies of the effects of tranquilizers on the monkey midbrain to the usefulness of these drugs for various types of patients. The result of this major effort has been a substantial improvement in the care and treatment of schizophrenia. The period of hospitalization has been dramatically shortened.

The prognosis in the schizophrenic disorders varies with the particular type of schizophrenia. It also varies with the age of the person, the duration of the disorder, the type of onset, and the person's psychological history. Generally speaking, the prognosis in the schizophrenias is best in cases of short duration, when the victim is an adolescent or a young adult, when the onset has been sudden, and when the psychological background of the person has been relatively stable and free from schizoid behavior. The prognosis is also better where there is a more or less specific precipitating incident which sets off the condition. In terms of the several types of schizophrenic reactions the best prognosis is in catatonia. The poorest prognosis is in simple schizophrenia and in the chronic forms of paranoid schizophrenia.

THE PARANOID STATES

Some psychotic individuals develop complex delusional systems, but without the disorientation, hallucinations, and disturbances of language and action seen so frequently among schizophrenics. In these cases, called *paranoid reactions*, the delusions tend to be more or less systematized and integrated with the rest of the personality. Moreover, there is little or no intellectual deterioration, and emotional responses are completely consistent with the ideas held. As a result, the delusions of the paranoid person are sometimes so persuasive that the ideas are accepted by others who are not mentally disturbed.

The word *paranoia* was already in use at the time of Hippocrates, with a meaning roughly equivalent to the now obsolete term *insanity*. With the emergence of modern psychopathology in the eighteenth century, the word took on a more specific meaning. It referred primarily to a condition in which the mental faculties appeared to remain intact, though at the same time the individual was the victim of a highly organized delusional system.

In *First Lines of the Practice of Physik,* published in 1777, William Cullen used the term *vesaniae* for these conditions, while Esquirol and other writers in the early part of the nineteenth century preferred the term *monomania*. It was in Germany, however, that the most intensive work was done with this group of disorders.

Kraepelin distinguished between paranoid dementia praecox and paranoia in 1893. While paranoia was a popular diagnosis late in the nineteenth century and early in the present century, it is now of historical interest only. Conditions of this type are included under the paranoid reactions.

The classic symptom picture of the paranoid reaction is one in which there is no loss of intellectual efficiency and in which the person is quite capable of functioning adequately in all areas except those involving his delusional system. This system is usually one that develops slowly over a relatively long period of time. Moreover, the system has a high degree of internal consistency. In fact, if the individual's basic assumptions are granted, the delusional system is likely to have a compelling logic. An interesting aspect of the paranoid reaction is that this logic often makes it possible for a person to convince others of the reasonableness of his ideas. The intensity and apparent sincerity of the individual often sway others, sometimes resulting in strange cults, sects, and movements in religion, philosophy, political science, economics, and similar fields.

■ PARANOID REACTION

Walter P. was a twenty-three-year-old single man when he was admitted to a psychiatric hospital. When he was twenty, his family and friends began to notice a change in his behavior. He became increasingly talkative and developed an idea that he was destined to make the world over. His preoccupation with this project became so great that he quit his job, neglected his health and personal appearance, and refused to speak to members of his family. He became more and more withdrawn and spent his entire time making entries in a series of notebooks in which he outlined, in the most minute detail, his plans for a utopian community. The first notebook bears the title *The Picto-piaist Movement*, and starts with the following paragraph: "An International Society, the members of which stand for the creating of a Modern Utopia, in which that strata of people, with the proper Intellect, Perspective, Nature, and Physique, will form a society where all are Happy, Contented, and Peaceful, just as their Creator meant them to. We will segregate ourselves from the general society of the world until such time when those who are outside our New Movement shall look upon Life in general as we do."

The notebooks contain detailed entries on various locations in different parts of the world where the utopian community might be located. The patient decided finally that the ideal location would be the Galapagos Islands, off the coast of South America. He planned to build a schooner to transport his "disciples" and their supplies down the Ohio and Mississippi Rivers to the Gulf of Mexico, and then to the Islands. The notebooks contain not only detailed drawings of the schooner and long lists of supplies but hundreds of notes on new religious, economic, and social systems. Public buildings are sketched, and several pages are devoted to the specifications for a communal bakery. Every detail was carefully entered, from the cost of elaborate baking equipment to the cost of a dozen muffin cups.

Usually the paranoid individual appears quite normal in his conversation, emotional responsiveness, and actions. It is only in the area of his delusional ideas that he betrays his underlying disturbance. Since he has convinced himself so completely of the reality of his delusion, he cannot tolerate any criticism of his ideas. No matter how much evidence there is to the contrary or how unlikely or impossible his plans and proposals, any questioning results in evasiveness, defensiveness, and irritability. Such people are inclined to make sweeping generalizations and come to far-reaching conclusions based entirely on their delusional ideas rather than on facts or reality. Paranoid persons are potentially dangerous, and the world has more than once suffered at the hands of leaders whose paranoid beliefs went unrecognized until it was too late.

Paranoid people are also characterized by their suspicion of others. They spend their time reading derogatory motives and insidious plans into the actions of everyone around them. They are suspicious of everything that is said or done.

They are troubled with doubt and uncertainty. They ask themselves: "Why did he say that? What is he up to? What is going on here?"

A Chicago woman sued her husband for a divorce because he spied on her with binoculars for most of the nine years of their married life. A Dayton, Ohio, woman hired a plane to follow her husband's car when he left his job at the Wright-Patterson Air Force Base. She thought there was too much mileage on the car, and she wanted to find out where her husband went after he left work.

A forty-year-old married graduate student complained that a professor in one of her classes was behaving in a "peculiar way" toward her. One of the ideas she had developed was that the professor was in love with her and was using various secret and symbolic devices for telling her about how he felt. She was quite sure that, whenever the professor put a diagram on the blackboard, it had some hidden meaning for her and that this meaning was usually sexual. She felt that the diagrams were becoming increasingly suggestive and embarrassing to her.

There is little or no regression in the paranoid reaction, and the fragmented and scattered quality of schizophrenia is not present. The ego is relatively well preserved, with projection being the chief defensive response to stress and conflict. Frequently the paranoid delusions appear suddenly as a reaction to difficult environmental situations or to personal frustration. When this is the case, the disorder may show improvement quite as suddenly when the stress has been relieved. In other cases, the condition persists and follows a chronic course.

The following letter clearly illustrates the nonschizophrenic type of paranoid thinking:

Dear Dr. _____ :
I have a neighbor who owns and operates an ultrasonic machine. The transducer is projected toward us, i.e., we are in the direct beam of its energy! This neighbor has tried at various times to kill us but we have always managed to run from the apartment, thereby getting out of its beam before it affects us too much! Most of the time, he has just turned it on us to give us various feelings (not all of them at once, of course): headaches, fever, extreme fatigue or nervousness, tiredness, irritability, dizziness, nausea, sometimes fainting and a feeling of "impending doom."

There is absolutely nothing in the world we can do about it, or at least there hasn't been so far. That is what makes our case so unique! They could murder us, as they did a neighbor of ours, and even a post mortem would only show an ordinary heart attack. No one can even prove it on our neighbor, because it would only show what an ordinary heart attack would show. His widow knows this fact and so do we. She couldn't even tell the authorities because they would think she was crazy or too unbalanced by her grief.

Really, there is no telling how many more of these machines our neighbor owns throughout the country. He certainly wouldn't stop with one since he has long since recognized his strength and secret treachery. No one has caught him yet and no one is able to except for one thing that I shall write later.

Why is this man doing this? He used to be our neighbor and he hated us for what we are and what we have—those are the only things that we have been able to figure out other than that he has a complex he can't outgrow. He just happened onto this machine and he has followed us around the country with it, moving in just next door with it wherever we have moved to get away from him.

Since there is no obvious law governing machines of this sort, there is nothing we can do to stop him. Can you imagine a flat-foot cop having the knowledge of an ultrasonic machine? There aren't any! It doesn't come under the jurisdiction of the F.B.I. since there is no federal offense committed, nor the F.C.C. because they are only interested in radio waves.

To prove all this in a mechanical way, that this neighbor actually has an ultrasonic machine, and that he projects it on our apartment, we would have to order CUSTOM-BUILT (from a reputable electronics firm) a model GA 1007 sound pressure equipment with built-in calibrator, and with a M-123 microphone, cost around $1350. Who has money like that nowadays to spend on such a thing? WHAT WOULD YOU DO?

Sincerely,

P.S. Call me long distance, reverse the charges. I'll be glad to give you any more information after 5 P.M.

The paranoid patient tells a much more coherent story than does the schizophrenic. His delusions are more highly organized, and he does not have the speech characteristics or mannerisms of the schizophrenic. In the paranoid patient, the delusion of persecution is the most important, and sometimes the only, symptom. In

the schizophrenic, the persecutory delusion is only incidental to a great many other symptoms of personality disorganization. It is often possible to talk to a paranoid patient for some time without setting off his delusional ideas. The schizophrenic, however, has so many symptoms that he is likely to reveal his condition in the very first things he says or does.

Paranoid reactions are much less frequent than schizophrenic reactions, making up only about 0.5 percent of first admissions to mental hospitals (NIMH, 1970). Generally, these patients have a better education and come from somewhat higher socioeconomic groups than other patients. They are usually in good physical condition and show little deterioration when prolonged hospitalization is required.

It sometimes happens that the delusional system of a paranoid person is accepted by someone else, usually a husband or wife or a close relative with whom the patient has been living. When this happens, both individuals share the psychosis by participating in the same delusional system. This relatively rare, but extremely interesting, condition is known as *folie à deux*.

■ FOLIE À DEUX

Ruth and Robert F. are a married couple who developed interlocking delusional systems over a period of years, and who were admitted to the hospital on the same day. The husband is fifty-eight years old, and his wife, who had been married previously, is sixty-five. They have been married thirty years and are childless. The husband, who has worked as a carpenter and a painter, had an eighth grade education; his wife went through the fifth grade.

There is evidence that the wife has been something of a problem throughout her life. At twenty-four she attempted suicide by eating matches. She had the reputation in her family of being a stingy woman who felt that other people were trying to get her money. The early part of the marriage was marked by many quarrels, arguments, and threats of separation. There was a particularly stormy period when the wife was in her early forties, and she became preoccupied with ideas of her husband's infidelity. At that time she accused him of infecting her with syphilis he had contracted in relations with other women. Personal stress was aggravated by an Ohio River flood which destroyed most of the couple's property. The wife became despondent and attempted suicide by drowning. She was sent to a hospital for several weeks where she was diagnosed as having a situational depression.

Several years later, someone broke into the couple's house and stole several hundred dollars' worth of property. This incident caused additonal worry to both husband and wife and increased the wife's belief that there was some sort of plot against them. From that time, the wife's ideas became more and more delusional. The husband was not convinced of the truth of her suspicions until about six months ago, when he began to share her delusions in an active way.

The wife believes that for the past few years people have been laughing at her as she walked along the street, that they whispered to one another that she had syphilis, and that her neighbors were plotting against her and persecuting her. She says that they yell unkind remarks at her, and accuse both her husband and herself of homosexuality.

The wife also believes that members of a gang entered her house while she and her husband were away, and planted microphones and TV cameras in the walls of the bedroom. As a result all their conversations are recorded and broadcast over a nationwide hook-up. Both the husband and wife saw a man who was pretending to be a house-to-house salesman, but who was selling "radar gas machines" to the neighbors. Several of the neighbors bought the machines, and beamed the "death rays" toward the patients' house. The beams penetrated the bedroom and almost choked the woman and her husband. The couple also heard voices coming from a machine in one of the department stores, and from another machine behind closed doors at City Hall where the couple went to lodge complaints against the neighbors who were persecuting them. When the city officials would not take action, the husband threw several heavy iron bolts through the windows of a neighbor's house. It was this action that brought the couple to the attention of the police, and finally brought them to the hospital.

ETIOLOGY OF THE PARANOID REACTIONS

There is very little evidence suggesting a genetic, constitutional, or biological etiology in the paranoid reactions. For this reason, psychological and psychosocial explanations have been emphasized. One possibility is that paranoid reactions are more like neuroses than psychoses, and that the reactions are essentially a matter of the exaggerated use of projection as a defense mechanism when anxiety is aroused by internal or external stress. The use of projection, rather than some other defense, could very well be a matter of early learning. The paranoid person characteristically blames others for his deficiencies, his frustrations, and his failures. Projection makes it possible for the patient not only to blame his environment but also to believe that the people in his environment are persecuting him. It is only a step from blaming someone for your troubles to the belief that people are deliberately and actively attempting to harm you.

Paranoid reactions develop in their most serious form during the age range of forty to fifty-five. One theory suggests that the patient is reacting to his increased feelings of personal insecurity, inadequacy, and inferiority. He begins to realize he is growing old, and he becomes concerned with the real or imagined loss of his abilities and attractiveness. He is faced with the fact that many of his life goals are not going to be attained. He feels he has been a failure and a disappointment both to himself and to others.

Faced with such feelings, the patient begins to look around for a scapegoat. He cannot bear to believe that the fault lies within himself, and he therefore projects the blame to others. He tells himself that other people have been the cause of his disillusionments and difficulties. And the more he tells himself that this is the case, the more he believes it and the more suspicious he becomes of other people. Soon he comes to believe that he is being taken advantage of and, in some cases, persecuted.

Freud advanced the theory that the paranoid reaction is a defense against unconscious homosexual inclinations. Such people, according to this view, are attracted to a member of the same sex, and the fantasy of "I love him" is triggered. However, such a notion is unacceptable to most people, and this thought is changed to "I do not love him, I hate him." Eventually this feeling is projected toward the love object in the form "He hates me, therefore he persecutes me."

While the Freudian theory of the paranoid reaction is an ingenious approach, having a degree of clinical evidence to support it, the theory is unnecessary as a general model for the disorder. It is entirely possible that some paranoid projections are based on an unconscious homosexuality. It is equally probable that other projections have a quite different motivation.

TREATMENT AND PROGNOSIS

The treatment of paranoid reactions is a long and difficult procedure. For the most part, such treatment involves an attempt to shatter the crystallized delusional system by means of medical treatment and a follow-through with psychotherapy in an effort to bring about a personality reorganization. However, it is only with the greatest difficulty that one or the other of these objectives is reached. In some respects, the paranoid reactions are among the most resistant to treatment. Since the underlying personality pattern is likely to be deeply imbedded and tightly organized, the likelihood of improvement in these cases is generally rather poor.

THE AFFECTIVE DISORDERS

In the schizophrenic and paranoid psychoses, the symptoms are primarily disturbances in the intellectual processes of the person. In the affective disorders, the basic symptoms are related to emotional responsiveness. Such conditions are severe disorders of mood, with disturbances of thought and behavior secondary to the emotional turbulence. It will be recalled from Chapter 7 that the cyclothymic personality disorder is one in which there are marked swings in mood but no psychotic symptoms. In the affective reactions, the mood swings range from mild to severe and are accompanied by delusions, hallucinations, disorientation, and other evidences of lack of contact with reality.

The seriousness of the affective disorders is suggested by the fact that approximately 90,000 people are hospitalized for depressive reactions each year. In addition, depression may be a contributing cause of many other apparently physical illnesses.

One of the earliest descriptions of mood disorders is found in the *Praenotiones* and *Prophetica* of Hippocrates. In these ancient medical writings, the symptoms of melancholia are described in detail. Hippocrates in Greece, Galen in Rome, and Avicenna in Arabia all believed that melancholia was caused by a *succus melancholicus*, or melancholy humor, or fluid, which was a waste product of the liver and spleen. This belief persisted as late as the eighteenth century, when an eminent physician—in his *Aphorisms: Concerning the Knowledge and Cure of Diseases*—wrote of melancholy: "This disease arises from that malignancy of the blood and humors, which the ancients called Black Choler" (Boerhaave, 1735).

The term *melancholia* originally conveyed no idea of gloom, dejection, or depression. *Melageholan* meant simply to be mad, or to be out of one's mind. Aristophanes often used the word in this general sense, without any indication of low spirits. In 1621, Sir Robert Burton wrote one of the classics of world literature called *The Anatomy of Melancholy*. This book brought together everything that was known about the subject up to that time.

Hippocrates and other physicians of ancient Greece also described *mania*, a state of pathological elation, excitement, and exaltation. The condition was marked by physical as well as psychological overactivity. It was a serious elevation of mood and an exaggerated feeling of well-being. Later, in Rome, Cicero rejected the term mania and substituted *furor*.

In modern psychopathology, the affective reactions are made up of three major psychotic disturbances: (1) manic-depressive reaction, (2) involutional psychotic reaction, and (3) psychotic depressive reaction.

MANIC-DEPRESSIVE REACTION

It was observed many centuries ago that certain individuals have intense swings in mood, ranging from deep depression to exaggerated feelings of optimism and happiness. Such behavior has been described in the Bible, in the early Greek tragedies, and in ancient medical writings. From the time of Hippocrates, and even before, it had been noticed that a relationship existed between mania and melancholia. But it remained for Alexander Trallianus, in the sixth century, to point out that recurrent episodes of these two extremes of emotional behavior were often seen in the same person.

The importance of this observation was lost during the dark ages of medicine and went unrecognized until the seventeenth century, when it was referred to as *folie maniaco-mélancolique,* or madness with mania and melancholy in the same patient. However, it was not until the work of two French physicians in the nineteenth century that a clear-cut clinical description of the condition was made. One gave the name *folie circulaire* to the disorder (Falret, 1854) and the other referred to the condition as *folie à double forme* (Baillarger, 1853). As a result, the disorder was known in the late 1800s as *circular insanity*, referring to the alternating episodes of emotional excitement and depression. In Germany, the term *cyclothymia* was used to describe those conditions in which mania alternated with depression (Kahlbaum, 1874), and this work led Emil Kraepelin to suggest the name *manic-depressive reaction* to include those conditions in which the mania and melancholia are part of the same disorder. The term appeared for the first time in Kraepelin's monumental textbook of psychiatry (Kraepelin, 1896).

This group of psychotic reactions is marked by severe mood swings, with a tendency to remission and recurrence. In addition to the fundamental emotional alterations, there may be disorientation, delusions, hallucinations, and psychotic disturbances of language and action.

The manic-depressive reactions are exaggerations of the mood swings most people have from time to time. Sometimes people are "on top of the world," and at other times they are "down in the dumps." Yet, most of the time, they cannot say why they feel as they do. Many people travel through life fluctuating between sadness on the one hand and elation on the other. In general, they manage to maintain a balance, without going too far in either direction. Some men and women, for reasons which remain obscure, go too far in one direction or the other. Some go so far, in fact, that they need to be hospitalized. Fortunately most of the attacks are short-lived, and the average stay in the hospital is only a few months. While most of the patients recover completely, they are likely to have future attacks. When seen in the psychiatric hospital, the manic-depressive reaction is designated ordinarily by the predominant symptom of the emotional cycle.

Manic Reaction

The manic, or excited, phase of the manic-depressive psychosis is marked by elation, feelings of well-being, optimism, self-confidence, self-assurance, and generally high spirits. Along with this elevation in mood there is a general increase in psychomotor activity—the person talks a lot and is restless. Thoughts flow freely and are expressed easily and rapidly. As the disorder progresses, there may be delusions and hallucinations, along with such physical symptoms as increased heart rate and blood pressure, heightened muscle tone, and alert expression. Because of the overactivity, sleeplessness and loss of weight are seen from time to time in these patients.

As the manic reaction progresses, the symptoms present three stages of increasing seriousness: (1) hypomania, (2) acute mania, and (3) hyperacute mania. In the stage of *hypomania*, there is a moderate degree of elation and overactivity. The person has an extraordinary sense of self-confidence and faith in his ability to accomplish whatever he undertakes. He seems to have boundless energies and acquires an unusual social facility because of his lack of self-consciousness. Many hypomanics manage to remain outside the mental hospital. In fact, the individual who is mildly hypomanic and does not progress to a stage of more serious symptoms sometimes does unusually well in endeavors where these traits are important.

In the hypomanic stage of elation, people show symptoms which may be the very factors responsible for business or professional success. They become self-confident and somewhat boastful, and they are inclined to be dominating and assertive. They are described as being "dynamic," as a "go-getter," a "ball of fire," or the "life of the party," But in some cases, the pressure of activity leads to overtalkativeness, loud and rapid speech, furious writing, exaggerated gestures, and eccentric dress.

■ HYPOMANIA

Paul J. is a fifty-six-year-old schoolteacher who was admitted to a psychiatric hospital from the county jail after having been picked up at a local hotel where he had been staying. The incident which brought him to the attention of the court was one in which he ran down a hotel corridor in nude pursuit of a chambermaid. He had also stuck toilet paper to the doors of various hotel rooms with toothpaste, and it was reported that he urinated in the wastebaskets from time to time. He became such a problem at the hotel that the police were called, and the police department probated him to the psychiatric hospital.

The patient came to the interview straight from a shower. He did not bother to dry himself off, and his head was dripping with water. His personal habits in grooming since admission have been good, and he has not given any active trouble on the ward. However, he has been verbally overactive, and this has not made him popular with the other patients. For the most part, during the interview, he was difficult to contend with, due to his verbal overactivity. The interview consisted of a continual interrupting in an effort to keep some relevancy to the story. His manner and voice were overbearing and condescending, and his posture varied from slumping in the chair to thumping on the table.

During the interview, the patient said he felt fine, and everything was wonderful. When the physician addressed him as Paul, he became upset and said he would be pleased and honored if he were to be called Willis. When asked why he rushed from his shower, he said that he had to take showers to get massage and heat for his injured spine. He left the shower in a hurry because "there were six lunatics in there having coffee and cigarettes." He said that he came to this city to see a friend. When on the plane on the trip to the city, he met a "professional Southern woman" who had a child with her. He said the child smeared feces from its diaper on his suit, and in the resulting furor the the woman stole his money and ran toward the back of the plane. He said he went after her, and got his money back. At one time he said that everybody with an IQ over 110 is neurotic. He also said, "I'm as nutty as a fruitcake, but as pure as a dove." He said he feels superior to most other people, and he showed a marked contempt for the human race. He was fully oriented for person, place, and time.

The patient has an M.A. degree, and taught for twelve years in high schools and colleges in various parts of the country. He was active in church work and school activities. Under ordinary circumstances, he was well adjusted, thoughtful, kind, and coperative. He was divorced from his wife during one of his personality disturbances when he became angry with her for having him sent to a hospital.*

In the state of *acute mania*, there is a break with reality. People become more irritable, impatient, and overbearing. Speech becomes confused, and patients may say vulgar and vicious things. They have flights of ideas which appear incoherent or nearly incoherent to the listener. They may even become combative and destructive, rush about tearing and breaking things, yelling and shouting, and showing hostility and aggression in every move they make. Some people become lewd and obscene, expose themselves, or make crude sexual advances toward others. Physical and mental activities become so great that patients find little time to sleep or eat. They become partially disoriented and have occasional delusions and hallucinations.

■ MANIC REACTION

Duncan A. is a forty-five-year-old married man who was admitted to a psychiatric hospital after becoming so overactive that it was impossible for him to work or remain at home. The illness was observed about two months before the patient came to the hospital. At that time he was agitated and excited, but refused to seek medical advice. In the months prior to hospitalization the patient talked excessively, and his eating and sleeping habits became irregular. Two weeks prior to admission the patient was sleeping only two to three hours a night, and ate very little. He developed the idea that his wife's first husband, who was dead, was coming back to take her and the children from him. The patient finally became so upset that his wife had him committed to the hospital.†

---

*Case 1 of audiotape 8, "Psychotic Disorders: Affective Reactions," in *Case Interviews to Accompany The Disorganized Personality.*

†Case 2 of audiotape 8, "Psychotic Disorders: Affective Reactions," in *Case Interviews to Accompany The Disorganized Personality.*

When the affective reaction has advanced to *hyperacute mania,* the excitement of the patient becomes so intense that he is likely to be totally disoriented with an outpouring of incoherent speech and a burst of frenzied activity that leaves him physically exhausted. Restless pacing, loud singing, shouting and screaming, gesticulating, and pounding and tearing occur in most cases. The excitement is so intense that it endangers the patient and those who must come in contact with him. Delusions are severe and hallucinations are vivid, with a total lack of insight and control. At one time it was necessary to keep this type of patient in protective restraint for hours or days at a time. Today, thanks to advances in the use of drugs, relatively few manic patients reach the hyperacute stage of the disorder.

Depressive Reaction

In the depressive phase of the manic-depressive reaction, the person feels sad and discouraged. He loses interest in his surroundings, and life seems hopeless. As a result, there is a general reduction in psychomotor activity. Both thought and action are slowed down progressively. As the condition worsens, delusions and hallucinations may be present. In most cases, there are definite bodily symptoms in the form of loss of muscle tone, sadness of facial expression, and a variety of vegetative symptoms such as lowered blood pressure, lack of appetite, constipation, diminished secretion of saliva, and insomnia. Among women there may be interference with the menstrual cycle.

There are times when everyone feels dejected, gloomy, and listless. Life seems to be a burden. People get the "blues" and see only the dark side of things. Many people have personalities slanted consistently in this direction. Depression, unhappiness, the attitude of uncertainty, doubt, and defeat, and thoughts of suicide are common experiences. The depressive phase of the manic-depressive reaction is a severe extension of such symptoms. As the reaction progresses, it passes through three major stages known as (1) simple depression, (2) acute depression, and (3) depressive stupor.

In *simple depression,* there is a general slowing down of physical and mental activity, with a feel-ing of dejection and discouragement. Bodily complaints are frequent, and there is usually loss of appetite and loss of weight. The thinking of the person remains clear, and unless the depression progresses to the next stage, hospitalization is not ordinarily necessary.

In the stage of *acute depression,* the retardation of mental and physical activity is increased, and the feelings of worthlessness and failure become more pronounced. The person may sit alone for hours at a time, refusing to speak to friends or relatives. He sees no hope for recovery, and ideas of suicide are common. It is during this stage of the disorder that the preoccupation with bodily ailments begins to take on a delusional quality. Vague and poorly defined hallucinations also may be present.

When the affective reaction reaches the stage of *depressive stupor,* the patient becomes completely mute and occasionally resistive and negativistic. Such psychotic symptoms as confusion, disorientation, delusions, and hallucinations are seen frequently; and because of the almost complete lack of motor activity, these patients sometimes must be fed artificially. Under the circumstances, there may be a general deterioration in the health of the patient, with increased danger of infection, toxic reactions, and circulatory disturbances.

■ MANIC-DEPRESSIVE REACTION, DEPRESSED TYPE

Pauline B. is a fifty-seven-year-old widow who graduated from high school, attended business school, and had training as a nurse. She has had three commitments to mental hospitals for her depressions. When seen at the hospital on her most recent admission, the patient presented the typical picture of depression. She appeared sad, talked in a somewhat whining voice, and showed psychomotor retardation. She had numerous self-condemnatory ideas, and was preoccupied with thoughts of suicide. Her general attitude was one of hopelessness. She said that life is not worth living, and that she would be better off dead. She had no interest in anything, and there was nothing left to live for. Between her depressive episodes, the patient is regarded as a happy outgoing person, although subject to rather wide swings in her mood.

Mixed Reaction

In an occasional case of the manic-depressive disorder, a mixed reaction in seen, with a combination of elation and depression. In the agitated depression, which is more characteristic of involutional psychosis than manic-depressive disorder, the person paces the floor, wrings his hands, bursts into tears, and shows a picture of depression in a setting of overactivity. Another type of mixed reaction is the manic stupor in which the person remains in a stuporous condition but has a facial expression of elation and exaltation.

Etiology of Manic-depressive Reactions

Our knowledge of the cause of the manic-depressive psychoses is as incomplete as our knowledge of the cause of the schizophrenias. The entire range of causative factors, including heredity, constitution, psychological conflict, and social stress, has been suggested at one time or another to explain manic-depressive conditions. While less current research is being directed toward this condition than toward schizophrenia, there has been a rather persistent feeling that this disorder will be explained eventually in terms of a physical etiology.

One reason for the widespread acceptance of the possibility of ultimately finding a physical cause for the manic-depressive reactions is the genetic evidence. As early as 1896, Kraepelin commented that from 60 to 80 percent of his cases of manic-depressive psychosis had a genetic basis. Since that time, the hereditary factor has become increasingly apparent. In a series of studies of identical twins, it was found that if one fraternal twin was manic-depressive, the other twin was also manic-depressive in 26 percent of the cases. However, when one identical twin had the disorder, the other twin had it in 95.7 percent of the cases. Such a finding is a powerful argument for the importance of heredity in this disorder It has been suggested that the manic-depressive psychosis is due to a specific neurohumoral disturbance which depends upon the mutative effect of a single dominant gene (Kallmann, 1953). See Table 10.3.

It is also possible that the manic-depressive type of psychosis is related to the female sex chromosome and may be caused by one or two defective genes. One investigation of 426 manic-depressives indicated that an ill father almost never had an ill son. Only one such sick father-son pair was observed. But mothers passed the illness to both sons and daughter. More than twice as many mothers as fathers were ill. The evidence suggest an X (female)-linked inheritance of the dominant type (Science News, 1968).

Constitutional factors may also be important in the etiology of the manic-depressive reactions. This theory is based on the assumption that there are inborn constitutional tendencies toward extreme mood swings.

There is a further possibility that there may be a biochemical factor underlying the disorder. Since the manic and depressive episodes usually appear suddenly and often disappear quite as suddenly, the theory of a shift in body chemistry cannot be dismissed. However, no significant differences in biological functions have been re-

Table 10.3 *Hereditary incidence of manic-depressive psychosis**

PARENTS AFFECTED BY THE PSYCHOSIS	INCIDENCE OF THE PSYCHOSIS
Neither parent	7% of siblings of the patient (Rüdin)
One parent	24% of children as a definite illness (Rüdin)
	33.3% of children as a definite illness (Lewis)
	16.7% of children as a mild affective disorder (Lewis)
Both parents	66.7% of children as a definite illness (Lewis)
	33.3% of children as a mild affective disorder (Lewis)

*Occurs in 0.4%, or 1 in 250, of the general population.
SOURCE: Adapted from S. Kraines, *Mental Depressions and Their Treatment,* The Macmillan Company, New York, 1957, p. 61.

ported in patients during their attacks of the disorder. One type of clinical evidence for a biochemical basis for depression is that emotional changes are common during the premenstrual period. Since the manic-depressive reaction is more common among women than among men, this greater frequency in occurrence might be accounted for in terms of the greater cyclical variation in sex gland function. Another theory is that the symptoms of the manic-depressive reaction are produced by disturbances in the thalamic area of the brain, and are related to hereditary susceptibility and hormonal activity.

At the psychological level, mania and melancholia are viewed as being part of the same depressive pattern. That is, the overactivity of the manic is the person's frantic struggle to overcome the underlying depression. Occasionally an elated person will confess to his deep feelings of depression and admit that his overactivity is his way of trying to forget his feelings of inadequacy, inferiority, and unhappiness. Many men and women who are not mentally disturbed use a similar defense. The endless round of plans, duties, parties, luncheons, conferences, club meetings, and similar activities may be an attempt to deny failure and overcome anxiety.

In the depressive reaction, the person gives in to his basic feelings and attempts to insulate himself from the stress of life through the admission that he is inadequate to cope with the world. He becomes self-accusatory, guilt-ridden, and depressed because he has given up the struggle. Such people blame themselves, feel unworthy, and sink deeper and deeper into hopeless resignation.

INVOLUTIONAL PSYCHOTIC REACTION

In the first century A.D., Aretaeus described a special form of depression in which the individual was at the same time in a state of agitation. When the scientific approach to psychopathology once again emerged in the eighteenth and nineteenth centuries, this earlier-described agitated depression began to be associated with women and particularly with the involutional period, or "change of life."

Traditionally the involutional reaction was thought to be limited to the female, and most of the early works on the subject dealt with problems unique to women. In the mid-eighteenth century, a doctoral thesis with the title *De puerperarum Mania et Melancholia* was presented at the University of Göttingen in Germany. In addition to consideration of the mental disturbances associated with pregnancy, confinement, and childbirth, mention was made of emotional disturbances during the menopause.

The concept of the male involution did not appear in the literature until early in the nineteenth century, when the term *climacteric insanity* was used to include the mental disorders of both men and women at this critical period of life. Nevertheless, the notion persisted that the condition was peculiar to women and that it was related to the glandular changes at the time of menopause. This view was held even though attempts to relate the condition to glandular changes in women were generally unsuccessful.

It is now well established that men as well as women go through an involutional period. The condition begins somewhat earlier in women, usually between the ages of forty-five and fifty-five. In men the changes are more gradual and less noticeable, and are likely to occur between fifty-five and sixty-five. The condition accounts for about 4 percent of all first admissions to public mental hospitals and about 12 percent of the first admissions for psychotic disorders (NIMH, 1970).

The involutional reaction starts with a person's feeling sorry for himself, frequent crying spells, and a general restlessness, apprehension, and uneasiness. He becomes sad and anxious and is overwhelmed with vague feelings of impending danger. Such people are indifferent, show a lack in energy and decision, dislike their work and amusements, avoid parties, and become despondent. They have vague fears and anxieties and show many hypochondriacal symptoms. They are irritable and moody, lose their psychological and physical elasticity, and may become self-accusatory. The condition often leads to thoughts of suicide.

The physical complaints include feelings of pressure or emptiness in the head, rush of blood to the head, dizziness, poor sleep and appetite, loss of weight, and coldness of the hands and feet. As the condition becomes more severe, the person may complain of pain and suffering. He begins to pace the floor, wring his hands, pick at his skin, bite his nails, and tear at pieces of paper or cloth.

■ INVOLUTIONAL REACTION

Laura A. is a fifty-year-old woman who was admitted to a psychiatric hospital after complaining at home that she was "losing her mind." For days she made this complaint, spoke of a "visual fog," and said her mind was a "blank." She had involuntary episodes of crying over a period of several months and was sent to a private hospital, where the treatment she received did not alleviate her symptoms.

When seen at the psychiatric hospital, Laura was a short woman who looked many years older than her age. Her eyes were sunken and her long straight hair disheveled. She had the appearance of a sad and somewhat ghostly person who constantly repeated her symptoms in a flat singsong voice. She complained that she "had no head," that her mind was gone, and that a nerve in her forehead was making her "holler." She cried repeatedly, "Help me! Keep me from hollering!" Her moaning and occasional screaming could be stopped temporarily by distracting her, and it was possible with some effort to get her to talk about herself. She was well oriented in all areas, although her thinking was somewhat rambling and egocentric. While her mood was one of dejection, she was restless and disturbed.

The patient was seen on a number of subsequent occasions, and there appeared to be some degree of deterioration. She did not remember the examiner, and she became increasingly hostile and vicious. At the time of her admission to the hospital she had been a rather gentle person in spite of her agitation. The patient was placed on medication, and two weeks later was sitting quietly on the ward in a rather relaxed state. She did not remember talking previously to the examiner, but she repeated the ideas that her mind was gone, her head was no good, and that she was "crazy." She said that she talks too much, walks up and down too much, and "acts like an animal." She concluded by saying there was no hope for her. While these ideas were similar to those expressed when she was admitted to the hospital, they were now expressed in a relatively calm and unemotional way. Several months later the patient was able to leave

the hospital and make a satisfactory adjustment. She returned to work as a secretary, and managed her home efficiently and with growing interest in her activities.*

In some people, the involutional psychotic reaction is marked by delusions of persecution. In these cases, the person blames his frustration in life on others. He uses projection to defend himself against the anxiety generated by the stresses of middle age. It is not unusual for people of this type to compensate for a colorless and unsatisfactory life by constructing elaborate delusions involving action and excitement.

■ INVOLUTIONAL PSYCHOTIC REACTION: PARANOID TYPE

Ruth W. is a fifty-two-year-old single woman who was a quiet, attractive, and well-balanced person throughout most of her life. She had graduated from high school with a B average and had attempted nurse's training school for two years. However, the work was disturbing to her and she gave it up. She was severely disappointed, but she appeared to accept the fact that she was not suited to nursing. She became a secretary and worked efficiently for a number of years. Some weeks before her hospitalization, the patient resigned her position and began to talk about going to Japan to take a position in the embassy. She packed a large number of suitcases in preparation for the trip to Japan where she said she was to meet her husband and children. She insisted that she was married, and that J. Edgar Hoover had been one of the witnesses. In spite of the protestations of her relatives, she looked forward each day to a telegram from Japan. When the telegram did not arrive, the patient became increasingly withdrawn, and very seldom left her room. She developed numerous delusions about her travels throughout the world, and her activities as a secret agent.

The involutional depressive reaction is complicated by a number of physical and psychological factors. On the physical side, there are important glandular changes taking place at this time of life. There is a shift of glandular pattern and a disturbance of body chemistry. Among women, this change is dramatically illustrated

---

*Case 3 of audiotape 8, "Psychotic Disorders: Affective Reactions," in *Case Interviews to Accompany The Disorganized Personality*.

by the menopause, or the end of the menstrual cycle. In the majority of women, there are only mild external physical signs of the inner changes. Under ordinary circumstances a woman might expect occasional physiological signs such as trembling, flushing or blanching of the skin, heightened sensitivity to noises, and a tendency to perspire more readily.

Among males, the middle years of life are marked by a decline in sexual capacity, with its implication of loss of youth. There is also a gradual decline in energy and general physical prowess. Moreover, it is at this time that men ordinarily reach the peak of their earning power and occupational status. For the most part, men have achieved all they can hope to achieve. The "future" to which they have looked forward for so many years suddenly has arrived. The realization that they have not attained what they had hoped to attain is critically disturbing to many men. An overwhelming sense of frustration may develop at the thought that most of the opportunities in life have already passed.

In the woman, the cessation of menstruation and ovarian activity is a dramatic signal that she has reached the midpoint of life. It indicates the end of the childbearing period and is interpreted sometimes as a sign that she will no longer appeal to men as a sex object. Women begin to feel lonely and neglected, believing they have lost their physical attractiveness.

For both men and women, there is a growing awareness that life is passing by with increasing rapidity. Friends and family move away or die. Children grow up and leave the home. The individual who develops an involutional reaction becomes increasingly preoccupied with himself and his problems. He dwells on past failures, evidences of poor health, and the bleakness of the years ahead.

The involutional years are also marked by a realization of the economic problems of the future. Most people are not able to accumulate sufficient savings to allow them to lead a worry-free life during their later years. Some must look forward to help from their children or relatives. Others know they are destined to depend upon inadequate pensions or social security. Many more know that they will become wards of the city or state welfare system. Such an outlook is not designed to give comfort or to lead to optimism and lightheartedness during these critical years.

While many persons with this disorder improve spontaneously, the period of recovery is relatively long, frequently two or three years before the patient comes out of the depression. When physical and psychological treatment measures are combined, the recovery period is speeded in a significant way. When recovery finally does occur, the symptoms are likely to disappear entirely, with the depression being lifted and with increased feelings of happiness and capacity for work.

PSYCHOTIC DEPRESSION

The psychotic depressive reaction is one in which the patient is so severely depressed that he distorts reality and experiences delusions and hallucinations. While this reaction does not always include prominent psychotic symptoms, the depression may be so deep that the patient appears to be in a stupor. It becomes necessary at times to feed him through a tube because he refuses to take nourishment.

The major difference between the neurotic depression and the psychotic depressive reaction is the depth of the depression and the presence of psychotic symptoms. Both conditions may appear as the result of environmental stress, but only the psychotic depressive reaction includes delusions, hallucinations, and disorientation (see Table 10.4).

The psychotic depression differs from the depression of the manic-depressive psychosis in that there is an absence of a history of repeated depressions or of marked mood swings. The difference between these two conditions is illustrated by the occurrence of the two types of depression among twins. In the manic depressive disorders, there is a very high concordance of psychosis among identical twins; in psychotic depression, the concordance is relatively low and approaches the rate for ordinary siblings. This finding suggests that the psychotic depressive reaction is not linked with the genetic factor which appears to operate in the manic-depressive psychosis.

Psychotic depressions, which sometimes follow traumatic events and experiences, often accompany the onset of old age. Such depression

Table 10.4 *Clinical features of neurotic versus psychotic depression*

FEATURE	NEUROTIC DEPRESSION	PSYCHOTIC DEPRESSION
1. Quality of depression	Normal despondency	Abnormal melancholy
2. Variability of depression	Much	Little or none
3. Delusions	Absent	Sometimes present
4. Depersonalization	Absent	Present
5. Anxiety component	Strong	Weak
6. Neurotic components (hysteria, obsessive compulsiveness, etc.)	Strong	Weak
7. Diurnal variation	None	Worse in morning or evening
8. Concentration	Intact	Poor
9. Guilt	None or insincere	Intense remorse
10. Reaction to self	Pity	Pitiless
11. Weight loss	Variable	Invariable
12. Constipation	Variable	Invariable
13. Health	Usually poor	Good except during episode
14. Precipitating event	Clear and strong	Absent or weak
15. Family history of depression	Absent	Present

From L. G. Kiloh and R. F. Garside, "The Independence of Neurotic Depression and Endogenous Depression," *Brit. J. Psychiat.*, **109**, 451–463. 1963.

may be a severe situational reaction to the realization that one is approaching the end of the life span. For men and women who are not prepared philosophically for death, the severe depression may be an attempt to evade the reality that life is drawing to a close.

The problem of depression is being attacked on several fronts, with studies of the biological, psychological, and social factors involved in the etiology, treatment, and prevention. Evidence which suggests a hereditary factor is that psychotic depression is more prevalent among the relatives of people suffering from affective psychoses than among the relatives of those suffering from schizophrenia. There is an obvious need for more systematic studies of the contribution and interaction of genetic and environmental factors in the etiology of the psychoses.

We are moving closer to a biochemical theory of at least some of the depressions. It is a common observation that we are more likely to be depressed when we are tired and worn out physically. Depressions also occur frequently in combination with diseases of the nervous system and other disorders. It is clear also that certain drugs can lift people out of their depression. The evidence suggests that some types of depression, if not all depression, are rooted in the physical condition of the body.

Most research on depression is concentrated on biological factors. Studies are currently testing the hypothesis that many depressions are associated with an absolute or relative lack of chemical substances *(catecholamines)* at important sites in the brain. Other scientists are testing the hypothesis that severe psychotic depressive disorders are associated with abnormalities in central nervous system activation. Recent studies have extended earlier findings that "stress hormone" *(steroid)* metabolism may be abnormally elevated in some depressive disorders, and new findings suggest that other substances, including thyroid hormone and insulin, may be involved.

Intensive studies of patients with severe depressive states have yielded well-substantiated findings. Such studies employed continuous behavioral observations and independently recorded estimations of pituitary-adrenal glandular function by means of determinations of excretion of urinary metabolites of cortisol (16-OHCS). One subgroup of depressed patients showed continually elevated 17-OHCS levels. Another subgroup showed normal levels despite clinical evidence of depression, while a third group manifested elevated 17-OHCS levels only during periods of crisis during the course of the illness (NIMH, 1970).

Preliminary findings based on data from patients who committed suicide subsequent to this project suggest the possibility that 17-OHCS levels, and perhaps other biochemical measures, can be useful in predicting suicidal potential (NIMH, 1970).

The possible etiological significance of disturbed pituitary-adrenal function is being studied by employing drugs which block this system at certain points, while observing various behavioral elements of depression. The efforts to classify depressive states on a biochemical basis might provide a more rational basis for therapy.

Data from recent studies of various antidepressant drugs and from studies of sleep and dreams have opened new avenues of investigation into the comparative effectiveness of various drugs and have also provided specific working hypotheses about causative factors. The effect the depression has upon the central nervous system, hormonal system, electrolyte balance, and metabolism is being increasingly clarified. However, a basic understanding of this family of disorders still presents a major scientific challenge.

SUMMARY

1. The psychotic disorders are among the most serious of the personality disturbances. The major symptoms, which indicate a loss of contact with reality, are *disorientation, delusions, hallucinations, emotional disturbances,* and *disordered verbal* and *nonverbal communication.* The disoriented person may not know who he is or where he is, or he may be confused about time relationships. Delusions are false ideas to which an individual adheres even in the face of logical evidence to the contrary. They may involve any area of thinking, but they are most frequently concerned with ideas of persecution or grandeur, religion, sex, or body changes. Hallucinations are false perceptions in which the person most commonly reports hearing voices or seeing objects which do not exist. Hallucinations may also involve taste, odor, touch, and other sensations.

2. Emotional disturbance is a somewhat less clear symptom of psychosis, since emotional upset occurs in connection with many of the more ordinary difficulties in life. However, when an emotional disturbance is severe, impulsive, or inappropriate, the possibility of psychosis must be considered. The psychotic person may also show disturbances of verbal communication. Because of his lack of contact with reality, he is likely to express himself in highly personal ways, and his language often appears bizarre. Among the more common psychotic disturbances of language are *neologisms,* or new words made up by the patient; *echolalia,* or the repetition of words spoken by someone else; *stylized phrases;* and *non sequiturs.* Similarly, the writing of the psychotic may be marked by an excessive use of punctuation, bizarre expressions, symbolic drawings, and general unintelligibility. In the nonverbal area, the psychotic may engage in symbolic actions in the form of obscure gestures, peculiar mannerisms, odd postures, and stereotyped movements.

3. Psychotic symptoms are seen in different combinations in the principal diagnostic groups, which include the *schizophrenic, affective,* and *paranoid* reactions. The schizophrenic reaction is marked primarily by seclusiveness and withdrawal from reality, although the different types of this disorder show a wide and sometimes con-

fusing range of symptoms. The schizophrenic reactions include the *simple, hebephrenic, catatonic, paranoid, undifferentiated, schizo-affective, childhood,* and *residual* types of the disorder.

4. The paranoid reactions are conditions in which complex delusional systems are developed but without the disorientation, hallucinations, emotional inappropriateness, and disturbances of language and action seen so frequently in schizophrenia. The relatively logical delusions of the paranoid person are most frequently delusions of persecution, but occasionally they involve other areas. There is little or no intellectual deterioration, and the delusional ideas may appear quite persuasive to other people.

5. The affective psychotic reactions are conditions in which the basic symptoms are in the emotional area. Here the disturbances are of mood rather than thinking. The most important disorders of this type are the *manic-depressive, involutional psychotic,* and *psychotic depressive* reactions. The manic-depressive reaction is one in which the person experiences pronounced swings in mood from elation to depression. These swings are so severe that the person is usually required to enter a hospital for treatment. The pattern of the mood swing tends to be irregular, with some patients showing only episodes of elation, others showing only depression, and a few showing both extremes of mood.

6. The involutional psychotic reaction is a depression typical of the middle years of life. At one time it was thought to be due to endocrine changes in connection with the involutional period. Today it is recognized as a complex psychobiologic reaction to a particular period of life. The psychotic depression is a severe reaction in which the person may become completely unresponsive. The condition is sometimes related to traumatic events, especially during the later years of life.

7. The cause of psychotic behavior is not known. Since these conditions are not classified among the brain disorders, the implication is that the etiology is psychological and cultural. There is clinical evidence also that psychological and cultural factors may play a critical role in determining the form of a psychosis and the conditions under which it appears. There is strong evidence, however, to suggest that at least some of the psychotic disorders may be of organic origin. The evidence in support of this possibility includes genetic studies, the persistent finding in certain psychotic disorders of wide variations in biological measures, and the production of psychotic-like states by means of drugs.

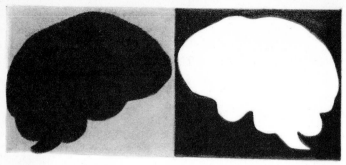

11 THE BRAIN DISORDERS

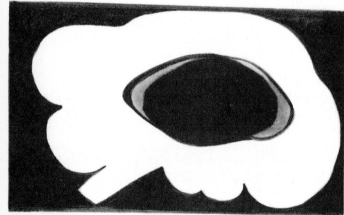

The various forms of personality disorganization discussed to this point have included only conditions having a psychological, or psychogenic, cause. The assumption is that the situational stress reactions, the personality disorders, the psychoneuroses, the psychophysiologic conditions, and the psychoses occur independently of any pathological condition of the organism. In the psychotic disorders, this assumption is probably incorrect since we have seen that there is a growing body of clinical evidence suggesting that at least some of the psychoses appear to be related to biochemical disturbances. Nevertheless, until a specific organic cause can be demonstrated, the conditions discussed thus far must be considered to be largely the result of psychological and cultural stress.

There are other conditions, however, which have a more or less clear-cut organic etiology. Through-

out the history of mental disturbance, it has been recognized that some types of personality disorganization have been related to physical disorders and dysfunctions. The extent to which this relationship has been emphasized has varied from time to time and has depended upon the intellectual climate and the level of scientific sophistication. The interest in organic causes was stressed during the time of Hippocrates and Galen and again during the nineteenth century. As a result of the influence of Sigmund Freud, the first half of the present century saw a turning away from the physical point of view and a preoccupation with psychodynamic relationships. Since the middle of the century there has been a return to an active interest in the possible organic basis of the various forms of disturbances of behavior and personality.

When a personality disturbance arises as a result of a pathological state of the nervous system, the condition is called a *brain syndrome.* As long as the disorder is temporary and reversible, it is an *acute brain syndrome;* when the symptoms become irreversible or long lasting, it is a *chronic brain syndrome.* The conditions of interest to the psychiatrist and the clinical psychologist are: (1) the intoxications, (2) the convulsive disorders, (3) the disorders due to infection, (4) disturbances due to brain tumors, (5) disturbances due to brain injury, and (6) the brain disorders of later life. In addition, there are a number of brain syndromes of indefinite and more obscure origin.

THE INTOXICATIONS

The psychological disturbances resulting from various types of intoxication are important because of their frequency and seriousness. These disorders are conditions in which the organic reaction and the personality disorganization are a result of the toxic action of alcohol, drugs, metals, or gas. They make up 6.4 percent of first admissions to our mental hospitals. The brain disorders resulting from metals and gas are restricted for the most part to industrial poisons.

ALCOHOL INTOXICATIONS

It will be recalled from Chapter 7 that alcohol addiction in itself is not a brain syndrome and is more properly classified as a personality disorder. It is only when the excessive drinking has resulted in temporary or permanent damage to the nervous system that the condition is classified as an organic brain disorder. The five major types of brain disorders associated with alcoholism are: (1) pathological intoxication, (2) delirium tremens, (3) alcoholic hallucinosis, (4) alcoholic deterioration, and (5) Korsakoff's syndrome. Of these, the first two types are acute conditions, the third type may be either acute or chronic, and the fourth and fifth types are chronic disturbances.

Figure 11.1 *The incidence of brain disorders as a percentage of total first admissions to public mental hospitals in the United States. (From data furnished by the National Institute of Mental Health, 1970.)*

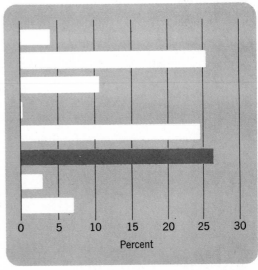

Pathological Intoxication

This acute type of alcoholic brain disorder appears with dramatic suddenness after the ingestion of relatively small amounts of alcohol. In such cases, a bottle of beer or a glass of wine is sometimes enough to throw a susceptible person into a state of violence, confusion, agitation, and excitement. Symptoms include disorientation, hallucinations, and delusions, combined with exaggerated emotional responses. Extremes of anger, rage, and hostility are frequently present, along with anxiety and terror. Occasionally the drinker is plunged into depression, and he sometimes makes an attempt at suicide.

During the outbursts of violence, a person may commit almost any kind of assaultive crime. Physical aggression, heterosexual and homosexual advances, and even homicide are not uncommon. Usually it requires two or three people to subdue this type of alcoholic. The episode of excitement and confusion may last from a few hours to a day or more and is followed ordinarily by a long period of sleep. When the person awakens, he is unable to remember anything of what happened.

Pathological intoxication is the condition to which police officers refer as "crazy drunk." This type of alcoholic suddenly goes berserk and proceeds to break up the room or the bar. The acute and unsuspected nature of the outburst, is seen in the case of a sixteen-year-old boy whose mother gave him a hot whiskey toddy when he caught a head cold. The youngster reacted by going on a neighborhood rampage. He struck his mother and four men who tried to restrain him, bit three other men, and broke a window. Finally quieted in jail, he had no memory of the violent episode. Maurice Utrillo, one of the great modern French painters, also experienced violent episodes following the use of alcohol. At one time he directed his violence against pregnant women, chasing them in the street, pulling their hair, and attempting to kick them in their abdomens. In Detroit, a twenty-six-year-old salesman had a few drinks at a convention and then rushed out and struck four women and two children over the head with a piece of metal pipe. When captured by the police, the man said,

"I'm not a drinking man, but when I drink, I'm mean."

The underlying mechanisms of pathological intoxication are not clear. At the neurophysiological level, it is possible that the victim of this disorder has an unusual sensitivity to alcohol, with an extremely low tolerance. Some experts believe there is a connection between pathological intoxication and earlier brain injury. Psychologically, these people are unstable emotionally, and the small amount of alcohol so disorganizes control that the typical emotional storm is released. The relative infrequency of the condition, combined with its temporary nature, has made careful investigation difficult.

Delirium Tremens

This condition is an acute brain disorder which develops after prolonged periods of heavy drinking. The condition is most likely to appear in patients who have a history of some years of alcoholism, and it is relatively rare before the age of thirty. The disorder was first described in 1813 by a physician who observed an acute congestion of the brain associated with an excess of free fluid (Sutton, 1813). However, since the microscope was not available to him, he was not aware of the changes in the brain cells which are now known to be present.

The disorder, which is an acute alcoholic episode superimposed on chronic alcoholism, is marked by delirium and hallucinations. The first signs of the onset include a lack of appetite, increasing restlessness, irritability, and fitful sleep with disturbing dreams. These symptoms are accompanied by mounting fear and apprehension. As the disorder enters the more serious stage, body temperature goes up, with flushing of the skin and profuse sweating. There is a marked tremor of the hands and tongue and sometimes of the facial muscles as well. Other symptoms include physical weakness, overactive reflexes, and an unsteady gait. There may be convulsions due to excessive loss of body fluids. At one time, death due to concurrent physical disabilities was frequent, but mortality today has been very much reduced.

In the excited phase of delirium tremens, the

psychological symptoms include mental confusion and intense anxiety and fearfulness. Disorientation for time and place is common, although the patient often continues to know who he is. The most dramatic psychological symptoms are the hallucinations. In most cases, they are visual and tactile, with the patient seeing his room alive with insects, vermin, and rodents. The pattern of the wallpaper may be seen as the eyes of rats glaring at the patient; the design of the rug becomes a snake coiled and ready to strike. The patient feels roaches and spiders crawling on his body, and he claws frantically at his skin in a futile effort to rid himself of the horrible creatures. When auditory hallucinations are present, they are likely to be of a threatening nature, often with homosexual content.

An attorney, a victim of delirium tremens and confined in a santitarium, said: "Doctor, they have a most peculiar and curious way of handling their cows here. You see those palm trees and the cows that are tethered in them? That is strange in the first place, but the most curious thing is the way they move the cows to other pastures. They do not take them down and put them into other trees; they dig up the trees and move them bodily with the cows still in them." Another patient, a physician, heard a police siren and then thought he heard officers dragging chains up the stairs to chain him. The patient ran to a second-floor window, leaped out, and fractured his leg. Still another patient saw his image in a mirror, thought it was someone who was after him, and drove his fist through the glass (Nielsen, 1956).

In a study of delirium tremens cases treated at the Detroit Receiving Hospital, the average duration of the episode was three days, although the average hospital stay was more than five days because of other illnesses associated with the condition. On the first day in the hospital, 40 percent of the patients had hallucinations, 58 percent showed marked tremors, and 60 percent suffered from uncontrollable anxiety. All patients showed some degree of confusion and disorientation. On the second and third days in the hospital, a number of the patients showed more pronounced anxiety, confusion, and tremors. However, the other symptoms showed a marked reduction (Krystal, 1959).

■ **DELIRIUM TREMENS**

Martin H. is a thirty-nine-year-old married man who was admitted to a psychiatric hospital as a result of excessive drinking. The patient is a long-term alcoholic who drank continuously but nevertheless managed to make a fairly adequate adjustment. He worked variously as a waiter, bartender, and janitor. About two months prior to his admission to the hospital, the patient began to drink even more heavily than usual. One night, while it was very quiet, the patient jumped up in bed and told his wife he was going to climb on the roof and "give that airplane pilot ten dollars to quit buzzing the house." The next night the patient heard a group of women talking in the house and told his wife he was going to ask them to leave. The wife threatened to leave him after he attempted to beat her when she insisted there was no one else in the house. He agreed then to enter the hospital for treatment. When admitted to the hospital, the patient was experiencing an episode of delirium tremens. He sat in a state of great anxiety, his hands trembling, and he repeated over and over again that he thought he was going to die. He became extremely fearful, thought he saw bugs and small animals in the room, and showed evidence of extreme physical distress.*

The exact nature of delirium tremens is not known, although it appears to be a withdrawal symptom since it occurs most frequently when the individual has been drinking heavily and is suddenly deprived of alcohol. The condition is probably a metabolic disturbance involving impaired carbohydrate metabolism, faulty protein metabolism, disturbed water balance, and vitamin deficiency, particularly of the B complex. The alcohol, by supplying the necessary calories, reduces the person's appetite. Consequently, a vitamin deficiency is established. And since the vitamins of the B complex are of critical importance in the metabolism of the neurons, their continued lack brings about disturbances of the nervous system.

---

*Case 1 of audiotape 10, "Brain Disorders: Intoxications" in *Case Interviews to Accompany The Disorganized Personality*.

Alcoholic Hallucinosis

This condition is one in which the major symptom is the hallucination, although there may be a certain amount of delusional material. In a typical case, the sensory reactions are normal, and there is no confusion, disorientation, or delirium. The person may be well oriented and even able to carry on his daily work. This type of alcoholic hallucination was made famous in *Harvey*, Mary Chase's fantastic play about a genial drunk and his friend, an invisible rabbit.

The principal symptom is the auditory hallucination, in which voices seem to be making insulting, accusatory, and derogatory remarks, often with homosexual overtones. At times the person will respond to the delusions and hallucinations by attacking his supposed tormentors. In many respects, alcoholic hallucinosis resembles paranoid schizophrenia, and the question of differential diagnosis arises frequently. In its acute form, alcoholic hallucinosis lasts from a few days to several weeks and recurs with continued drinking. After a number of years of heavy drinking, the symptoms become irreversible.

■ ALCOHOLIC HALLUCINOSIS

Daniel R. is a fifty-three-year-old man who was admitted to a psychiatric hospital following an episode in which he suddenly became delusional and believed that someone was chasing him. The patient had been living at a community welfare center, and was committed at the request of the Welfare Department. There is little past history because of the absence of friends and relatives. The patient was born in a Southern state, has remained unmarried, and has traveled to various parts of the country. Shortly following admission to the hospital he became more agitated and disturbed, read the Bible at great length, and was preoccupied with religious matters. He was rather vague and detached, but he moved freely among the patients on the ward and responded appropriately when approached.

When asked why he came to the hospital, the patient answered, "On the twenty-fifth of February I saw a word on the wrapper of a lump of sugar. When I looked up the word in the dictionary, I couldn't find it. I asked a man about it, and he showed me a card that had the word *Minnesota* on it. He asked me if I wanted to go there and I said, 'No.'" When questioned about his drinking habits, he was rather indefinite but admitted that he drank heavily from time to time. His conversation was filled with unrelated details, and he had to be interrupted frequently to obtain an adequate history. The most striking feature of the case was the combination of delusional and hallucinatory material. A diagnosis was made of chronic brain syndrome associated with alcoholism. The sudden onset, the paranoid ideas, and the rich combination of delusions and hallucinations suggest alcoholic hallucinosis.*

The mechanism of alcoholic hallucinosis is not clear. The condition presents an interesting paradox since the person is often well oriented and shows few signs of deterioration. At the same time, the hallucinatory experiences have a particularly real and vivid quality. One possibility is that the alcohol releases an underlying schizophrenic-like process which expresses itself in the hallucinatory experience.

Alcoholic Deterioration

Most chronic alcoholics show progressive deterioration over the years. This deterioration, which is probably due to impairment of the nerve cells of the cerebral cortex as a result of a nutritional deficiency, ranges from mild symptoms of personality disorganization to serious states of dementia.

Among the earliest symptoms of alcoholic deterioration is the tendency of the person to act out his more primitive impulses. His inner controls weaken, and he resorts to an infantile and narcissistic pattern in his attempts to satisfy his needs. Gradually, as a result of the realization that his family and friends are critical of his behavior, he becomes hostile and resentful, with increasing feelings of guilt. These feelings reinforce the psychological need for alcohol, which in turn aggravates the metabolic disturbance. As the cells of the brain are altered, the person shows memory impairment, difficulties in attention, loss of judgment, and emotional instability in varying degrees.

---

*Case 2 of audiotape 10, "Brain Disorders: Intoxications," in *Case Interviews to Accompany The Disorganized Personality*.

There may be no psychological symptoms for many years, and no history of hallucinosis or delirium tremens. Yet gradually, physical and psychological symptoms become apparent. The person shows a general irritability and discontent, with increasing anxiety and depression. However, the defenses against these feelings may be strong, and the person hides his depression under a superficial camaraderie and good humor. He is less successful in hiding his forgetfulness, dullness in comprehension, impaired judgment, and poverty of ideas.

Other early symptoms are seen in the ethical and moral behavior of the person. There is an increasing breakdown in standards of behavior and in social inhibitions. Personal appearance is neglected, unconcern is shown for family obligations, and lies are told with greater frequency and less and less guilt. Vulgar speech and lewd actions are not uncommon. In the physical area, the deterioration is shown in tremors and muscular weakness, in stomach, kidney, and liver disorders, and in a characteristic facial expression which has been described as being "flat" and "ironed out."

Alcoholic deterioration is generally seen in men and women who drink steadily over a period of many years, but who avoid acute episodes of heavy drinking. Such people have a history of drinking excessively, but they do not go on binges.

■ ALCOHOLIC DETERIORATION

Edgar T. is a sixty-year-old man who was admitted to a psychiatric hospital with a long history of heavy drinking. The patient has been hospitalized many times because of his excessive drinking, and has been in jail on many occasions for drunkenness. He has never been able to hold a job for any length of time. When seen during the initial interview, the patient was pleasant and cooperative. He admitted drinking heavily since adolescence, at times averaging about a fifth of whiskey a day. When seen at the hospital, the patient was completely disoriented. He did not know the day, month, or year, and thought he was in Kansas City when actually he was in Cincinnati. Although John F. Kennedy was President of the United States at the time of the examination, the patient said the President was Truman and that the President before him was Harding. The clinical picture was typical of the confusion and deterioration associated with organic changes brought on by many years of excessive drinking.*

Korsakoff's Syndrome

This disorder, first described in 1887, is characterized by disorientation, memory impairment, and falsification of memory, in addition to organic symptoms in the form of multiple neuritis. While the syndrome has been associated traditionally with the more severe forms of alcoholism, it is more accurately a vitamin deficiency secondary to alcoholism and is found in other conditions as well. In any case in which a toxic condition results in degeneration of cells in the cerebrum and the peripheral nerves, Korsakoff's syndrome might be expected to develop.

Korsakoff's syndrome in alcoholics is frequently detected when what appeared to be an attack of delirium tremens fails to clear. Instead of recovering within a few days, the person remains confused and disoriented. He fails to recognize friends or relatives, and a serious memory loss is apparent. The physical symptoms of the Korsakoff syndrome are inflammation of the nerves, anesthesia of various areas of the skin, and paralysis. A sign frequently seen in this condition is the wrist drop, in which the patient cannot raise his hand. The major psychological symptoms of the Korsakoff syndrome are memory disturbances, confabulation, or the filling in of memory gaps, delirium, and emotional instability.

The syndrome is a deceptive disorder in many ways. Superficial conversation with the patient may reveal a reasonably clear consciousness. It is only when the patient is carefully questioned that the true extent of the impairment is recognized. As long as the patient limits his conversation to his immediate surroundings and circumstances, he appears to function in a normal manner. But as soon as recall is necessary, he resorts to confabulation.

---

*Case 3 of audiotape 10, "Brain Disorders: Intoxications," in *Case Interviews to Accompany The Disorganized Personality*.

The prognosis in Korsakoff's syndrome is poor, since the removal of the toxic condition does not ordinarily bring about complete recovery. The treatment, which includes massive doses of vitamins and a high-caloric diet, can be expected to bring about only partial restoration of normal psychological function.

■ **KORSAKOFF'S SYNDROME**

Fred D. is a sixty-nine-year-old married man who was admitted to a psychiatric hospital because of his confusion and disorientation. The patient had a history of many years of heavy drinking, although he denied drinking during the past several years. When seen in the admitting ward, the patient was neatly dressed, but there was some deterioration of his personal habits. Although pleasant and sociable with the interviewer and ward personnel, he was definitely confused. He wandered about the ward, investigating objects and trying on other people's clothing. He talked freely, though his speech tended to be rambling and at times incoherent. Most of his spontaneous conversation centered on himself, and there were a number of hypochondriacal complaints. The patient was disoriented for time and place, although he was able to give his name. He could not give his correct address, said his age was ninety-one, and was unable to name the day, the month, or the year. He did not know where he was, although he said he was sent here by his landlord because he had been drinking. He admitted that he had been arrested for fighting and drinking, but said that he had never had an attack of delirium tremens. The patient showed the characteristic symptom picture of Korsakoff's syndrome with disorientation, confusion, and a strong tendency toward confabulation. When asked where he was, he said he was in a brewery. He gave the name of the brewery, but when asked the same question a few minutes later, the patient named another brewery. Similarly, the patient said that he knew the examiner, called him by name, but a little later called him by another name, and gave a different reason for being in the hospital.*

Etiology of the Alcohol Intoxications

There are several approaches to the causes of alcoholism. One is concerned with the physiological effects of alcohol on the body and the tissue of the nervous system. When alcohol is taken into the body, it is absorbed by the walls of the stomach and intestinal tract and enters the bloodstream as alcohol. It is not broken down or altered as in the case of most foods. The absorbed alcohol is then carried to the liver and eventually to the heart, where it is pumped to all parts of the body, including the nervous system.

Of the alcohol taken into the body, only about 10 percent is eliminated through the breath, urine, and perspiration. The other 90 percent remains in the body to be oxidized to form carbon dioxide and water. However, this process of oxidization is slow, with only 5 to 10 grams (about two teaspoons) of alcohol burnt up in an hour. Any excess remains in the blood and tissues until it can be oxidized. The effects of excessive amounts of alcohol in the body are multiple, and many are only vaguely understood. Disturbances of metabolism, endocrine function, and hypothalamic action probably are involved, and a cycle of increased physiological tolerance and tissue need is established.

Of equal importance is the vitamin deficiency caused by excessive alcohol intake. The heavy drinker soon finds that the alcohol supplies all the calories needed by his body, and he becomes disinclined to eat wisely or regularly. The result is a deficiency of increasingly serious degree in important nutrients, particularly vitamins.

The possibility that even social drinking might result in brain damage has been suggested. Research shows that a heavy intake of alcohol causes such changes in the blood and blood vessels that brain cells could be destroyed by oxygen starvation. The effect of this minimal brain damage is cumulative. The outward signs of this type of brain damage are increasing forgetfulness and the progressive loss of ability to work efficiently.

There is also evidence that alcohol damages the brain by causing blood cells to clump. This process slows the rate of blood through the capillaries of the brain. Brain cells are thus killed by oxygen deprivation.

Granting the operation of these physiological factors, it remains to be explained how it happens that one person who drinks heavily becomes an alcoholic in the clinical sense while another heavy drinker does not progress this far. The most

---

*Case 4 of audiotape 10, "Brain Disorders: Intoxications," in *Case Interviews to Accompany The Disorganized Personality*.

generally accepted explanation is that the chronic alcoholic uses his excessive drinking to satisfy some basic and pressing personality need. The nature of this need, according to this view, varies from one alcoholic to another. In one case it is an escape from some intolerable conflict situation, in another it is to forget feelings of inferiority and inadequacy, and in still another it is to prove courage and masculinity.

Another theoretical approach to the etiology of alcoholism is that the disorder represents a developmental defect of the personality as a result of social and envionmental influences. There is some evidence that, as a group, alcoholics tend to have a much greater attachment to the mother than to the father. The mothers are likely to be strong, dominating personalities who are idealized by the patient. The fathers, who are less loved, are also likely to be stern and autocratic. Alcoholics tend to be raised in environments demanding a marked degree of unquestioning obedience. The validity of the developmental theory of alcoholism has not been established and must await further research of both a clinical and a social nature.

Another theory of the etiology of alcoholism is based on the possibility that an inherited metabolic pattern makes certain individuals particularly susceptible to the destructive influences of alcohol. This constitutional-genetic theory, if established, would make it possible to explain the onset of alcoholism in cases where neither developmental nor psychodynamic factors appear to be operative and to explain why so many men and women with damaging developmental and psychodynamic influences do not become alcoholic, even under the most stressful conditions.[1]

DRUG INTOXICATION

As in the case of alcoholism, a differentiation must be made between mere dependence on drugs and the organic brain disorders which sometimes develop as a result of excessive and prolonged use of drugs. Every drug-dependent person runs the risk of brain damage, and many addicts experience acute episodes of brain disorder from time to time. More chronic forms of brain disorder due to drugs are seen relatively infrequently in the psychiatric hospital. When such cases are seen, they are likely to be due to morphine, the barbiturates, and the bromides. Occasional toxic states are observed following the use of drugs in the treatment of various physical illnesses.

Morphinism

The toxic effects of morphine are reflected in the physical and psychological symptoms. Among the physical symptoms are motor disturbances, glandular impairment, nutritional disturbance, and a variety of other difficulties. The motor disturbances include paralysis and tremor. There is also a decrease of the rhythmic movement of the alimentary canal, and an inability to control urine.

Numerous other physical symptoms are seen in morphine intoxication. The nails of the fingers and toes become brittle, the enamel of the teeth softens, and the hair turns gray. Skin eruptions are common, and fever may occur as the result of abscesses caused by the drug injections. Glandular impairment is reflected in partial or complete impotence in men and menstrual problems and sterility in women. There is a decrease in the secretion of saliva and an increase in the secretion of sweat. The glands of the skin are affected, and the skin becomes dry.

The early personality changes in morphine addiction are selfishness and carelessness, with the addict becoming indifferent and forgetful. He shows less and less initiative and finds it difficult to sleep. Later, hallucinations are common symptoms. More permanent psychological symptoms are loss of memory, deadening of sensation, and a breakdown of morale. Morphine addicts often become negligent, lose their sense of conscience, and may engage in various forms of deceitful behavior.

---

[1]Excellent accounts of the toxic disorders are to be found in *Etiology of Chronic Alcoholism* (Blackwell, 1955), edited by Oskar Diethelm; *Alcoholism* (Thomas, 1956), edited by George N. Thompson; R. J. Williams's *Nutrition and Alcoholism* (University of Oklahoma, 1951); and C. B. Courville's *Effects of Alcohol on the Nervous System of Man* (San Lucas, 1955).

■ DRUG INTOXICATION

Richard C. is a fifty-five-year-old divorced man who is the oldest of five brothers. At age five, his harsh and neglectful father died and the mother had to seek employment. The patient stayed with his maternal grandparents, who pampered and overprotected him. When he was nine years old, his mother remarried, and subsequent siblings were favored by the step-father, who was a cold and unaffectionate person. During adolescence, the patient revolted quite actively against parental authority and refused to attend school. He enlisted in the Navy at age fifteen but was released because he was underage. He reenlisted when he became of age, and remained in the Navy for seven years. While in the Navy the patient contracted tuberculosis and was admitted to a Veterans Administration Hospital. At the hospital, he was treated with morphine for his chest pains. His drug addiction dates from this early medical treatment. Since that time, he has had twelve admissions to the Lexington Narcotic Farm. The patient has a very poor work record and has supported himself and obtained money for drugs by gambling, petty theft, confidence games, forged prescriptions, and engaging in homosexual prostitution. For several months prior to his admission to the psychiatric hospital, the patient's narcotic intake increased to the point where the signs of a brain syndrome were becoming pronounced. The patient was unable to walk unassisted, and several times fell down and blacked out.

Barbiturate Intoxication

As with most other drugs, there are wide individual differences in the reaction to the ingestion of the barbiturates. Some patients are able to take these sedative drugs more or less regularly over long periods without signs of intellectual deterioration. Other patients, taking lesser amounts of the drug for shorter periods, become irritable and lethargic. Sometimes paranoid ideas become prominent. Many people show varying degrees of intellectual deterioration, personal inefficiency, and general deterioration.

Because of the widespread use of the barbiturates to induce sleep, it is not unusual to see cases of acute barbiturate poisoning. Depressive individuals not infrequently save their tablets until they feel they have acquired a lethal dose and then take capsules with suicidal intent. Such individuals fall into a deep coma from which they cannot be awakened. An acute poisoning of this type is a medical emergency. In addition to the

coma, the patient shows a weak rapid pulse, along with low blood pressure, shallow respiration, and a rapidly developing cyanosis, or bluish discoloration of the skin. The condition is controlled by washing out the stomach and by administering drugs to counteract the effects of the barbiturate.

Bromide Intoxication

Toxic conditions resulting from the excessive use of bromides are less common today than they were some years ago, mainly because of the substitution of various other less toxic drugs for the bromides. In the nineteenth century, the various salts of bromide were used extensively as sedatives. Soon the anticonvulsive properties of the bromides became apparent, and until the early 1900s the bromides were used widely in cases of convulsive disorder. In spite of the sharp decrease in the use of these drugs, brain disorders resulting from the excessive use of bromides are seen from time to time.

In cases of mild bromide intoxication, the person becomes irritable, complains of fatigue and weakness, and is unable to sleep well. He finds it difficult to concentrate, is drowsy, shows disturbances of attention and memory, and may be confused. These psychological symptoms are accompanied by digestive disturbances, dry skin, coated tongue, tremors of the tongue and fingers, and menstrual disturbances in women.

In the more severe forms of bromide intoxication, the person becomes confused, excited, and fearful and may show delirium with fever. The speech is thick and hesitant, and the face is without expression. Paranoid ideas are seen frequently, and hallucinations sometimes occur. In some cases, symptoms similar to those seen in schizophrenia are observed. The acute mental disturbances may last from a few days to six or eight weeks.

Amphetamine Intoxication

When the stimulating effects of the amphetamine drugs became known, there was a sharp increase in their use. As with most drugs, excessive use results in biochemical imbalances, and in the case of amphetamine and methamphetamine, there may also be some degree of personality disorganization.

These drugs produce feelings of well-being and exhilaration, although these initial reactions are likely to be followed by exhaustion and depression. When used excessively, the drugs result in tension and apprehension, trembling, sleeplessness, and marked loss of appetite. The clinical picture is that of a paranoid psychotic reaction with a minimal disturbance of the intellectual functions. Delusions of persecution and auditory (and sometimes visual) hallucinations are accompanied by such autonomic symptoms as rapid pulse and dilated pupils.[2]

Other Drug Intoxications

Toxic and delirous reactions develop from the use of a number of other drugs. While not seen frequently, toxic-delirious reactions to penicillin have been reported. The sulfonamides, or sulfa drugs, sometimes bring on mental symptoms in the form of headache, dizziness, confusion, and inability to concentrate. Toxic-confusional states have also been observed following the use of isoniazid, a drug used in the treatment of tuberculosis. The first symptoms are neurological and involve muscular twitchings and overactive reflexes. The psychological picture includes disorientation and hallucinations. In a few cases, Korsakoff's syndrome follows the acute stages of the intoxication.

Thiocyanate is a drug used in the treatment of high blood pressure. When the blood thiocyanate level becomes seriously elevated, a toxic confusional state is sometimes produced. Symptoms include disorientation, hallucinations, agitation, slurring of speech, and convulsions in some cases.

Such drugs as cortisone and ACTH produce psychological symptoms as a result of their direct action on the central nervous system. While the exact mechanism of the action is not known, these hormones alter the electrolytic and water patterns of the body. Unlike most drugs, the clinical picture of cortisone and ACTH action is not the usual toxic-confusional state. Patients are inclined to be good-natured and optimistic, with

emotional disturbances varying from depression to elation. Changes in the body image and feelings of depersonalization are not unusual. Similarly, delusions and hallucinations may be present. The psychological picture varies to a considerable extent and appears to be related to the underlying personality structure.

GAS AND METAL INTOXICATION

Personality disorganization resulting from the effects of gas and metal poisons is far less common than similar disorganization resulting from drugs and alcohol. In most cases, gas and metal intoxications are accidental and grow out of the industrial uses of these substances. Even though they are not seen frequently, they do occur from time to time, and the possibility of such conditions must be recognized and their symptoms understood.

Carbon monoxide is one of the most frequent sources of mental confusion. This gas, which is inhaled intentionally in suicidal attempts and accidentally from the exhaust fumes of automobiles, produces an oxygen deficiency in the brain. Acute poisoning by carbon monoxide results in severe intoxication and unconsciousness. Patients pass from the coma to a state of confusion and delirium. In somewhat fewer cases, there may be a clear period for a week or so following the coma, after which the patient may show such symptoms as apathy, indifference, and lack of responsibility. In some cases, neurological symptoms also are present.

Individuals who are exposed to carbon monoxide fumes in relatively small amounts over a long period of time may also develop psychological symptoms. In these cases, depression, agitation, emotional instability, anxiety, memory defect, and confusion may be seen. The psychological symptoms are accompanied by headache, dizziness, gastrointestinal disturbances, muscular pains, and heart palpitation.

The increased use of carbon disulphide in manufacturing processes has resulted in toxic

---

[2]Students interested in brain disorders resulting from drug abuse are referred to Lawrence Kolb's *Drug Addiction* (Thomas, 1962); the second edition of *Narcotics and Narcotic Addiction* (Thomas, 1962) by D. W. Maurer and V. H. Vogel; and P. H. Connell's *Amphetamine Psychosis* (Chapman & Hall, 1958).

conditions marked by insomnia, loss of memory, apathy, excessive fatigue, and unpleasant dreams. Neurological symptoms are also present in the form of loss of touch and pain sensation, irritability of the motor nerves, and muscular weakness.

With reference to the metals, lead poisoning is seen most frequently among children who eat flaked-off paint containing lead. Adults exposed to lead fumes over long periods in connection with their work may also develop symptoms of lead poisoning.

There are two major reactions to lead poisoning: (1) acute delirious episodes and (2) progressive mental deterioration. In the acute delirium, the onset is sudden and the condition is marked by restlessness, confusion, persecutory delusions, visual hallucinations, and violent outbursts. In some cases, convulsions occur. In chronic lead poisoning, the progressive mental deterioration takes the form of apathy, depression, memory disturbances, speech defects, and confabulation suggestive of Korsakoff's syndrome.

Mercury poisoning is most frequently seen among workers who are exposed to the inhalation of volatile mercury over extended periods of time. The psychological symptoms include irritability, feelings of inadequacy, discouragement, and impulsive emotional outbursts. In some cases, there may be apathy and memory difficulties. The neurological signs include coarse tremors and muscular weakness.

The typical symptom picture in manganese poisoning is restlessness, euphoria, and uncontrollable episodes of laughter and crying. Neurological symptoms include disturbances of speech and gait, tremors of the tongue and of the extremities, and weakness of the muscles.

■ LEAD INTOXICATION

Walter F. is a twenty-six-year-old man who developed normally until age two and a half, at which time he had convulsive seizures, vomiting, and lethargy. He was hospitalized for three months and given a diagnosis of lead intoxication from eating paint. When he returned home, the patient did not talk until he was five years old, although prior to the convulsions he had learned to talk and walk and had developed other motor skills usual at that age. For some months, the patient showed sudden periods of crying and extreme fear reactions. The child was not admitted to the public school because of his deficiencies. He remained home where he was somewhat undependable. Generally he enjoyed being with people but often he was hostile and rebellious. He spent most of his time watching television.

When the patient was twenty-two, he had a series of severe seizures and some months later became increasingly moody, irritable, and difficult to manage. Shortly before his hospitalization, he had a severe seizure during which he injured his head and had to be hospitalized. He was restless and confused and complained that nothing looked the same to him. At times he seemed incoherent. When he returned home, he showed wide mood swings, became increasingly belligerent and unmanageable, talked to himself, and showed a pressured speech. Since the family could not manage him, he was admitted to the psychiatric hospital.

At the time of the initial examination, the patient was found to be a somewhat disorganized man who appeared younger than his age. When he came into the examining room, he was suspicious and asked, "Well, what's going to happen now?" During the examination the patient displayed many mannerisms, especially involving his hands. He would stop talking suddenly and scratch the left side of his face, rub the back of his head, stand up, turn around, and rub his buttocks. He was impulsive and unpredictable. For a while he would sit quietly, and then he would get up, pace the floor restlessly, or come close to the examiner and look down in a glowering and challenging way. His gait was awkward, and his face occasionally broke into a frozen, wide-mouthed, toothy smile.

THE CONVULSIVE DISORDERS

Convulsive behavior, or *epilepsy*, is one of the most dramatic symptoms of disturbed brain function. The earliest medical writings contained vivid clinical descriptions of such behavior, and the convulsion has continued to be a subject of great interest to the neurologist, the psychiatrist, and the clinical psychologist. While important steps have been taken in recent years in the control of the surface symptoms of convulsive behavior, its underlying nature remains largely unknown. Moreover, the clinical symptoms must be recognized and understood before the necessary treatment measures can be taken.

Epilepsy is far more common than many people believe. Most estimates are that 2 million or more Americans are victims of the disorder. This would be about one in 100 persons. Since only contagious diseases are reported to local health departments by physicians, it is difficult to obtain comprehensive information about the prevalence of epilepsy. Also, many people with convulsive disorders conceal their condition because of the prejudice and misunderstanding concerning the condition. Only about 50,000 are hospitalized, and of these the majority are in special institutions and residential schools for epileptics. A relatively small number of such patients are admitted to psychiatric hospitals (1.1 percent of first admissions*), since convulsive disorder in itself is essentially a neurological disorder rather than a psychological or psychiatric problem. In some cases the convulsive disturbance occurs with an unrelated personality disorganization, and in other cases the personality disturbance is associated directly with the neurological condition.

Epilepsy costs the nation many millions of dollars each year in patient care, research, and lost earning power. Overall, the economic burden, in both direct and indirect costs, is probably well over one billion dollars a year. Much of this cost is unnecessary. Many of the victims of epilepsy are intelligent people capable of earning a good living. Much greater efforts are needed in education and in placing victims of epilepsy in suitable employment. The epileptic is not so much crippled by his disorder as he is by public prejudice. The word "epilepsy" strikes fear into many people —fear that is rooted in misunderstanding. Prejudice against the person with epilepsy denies him a normal life and forces him to become a burden on his family and society.

There are several important misconceptions concerning convulsive disorder. The first is that epilepsy is inherited. Most experts do not believe this to be the case. However, certain tendencies which make it easier for one person than another to experience convulsive behavior may be inherited.

Another misconception is that convulsive disorder gets worse with age. Generally this is not the case. It is more likely that seizures become less frequent as the person grows older. In some cases the disorder disappears, even without treatment, after a period of years.

A third misunderstanding is that convulsive disorder leads to, or is associated with, mental retardation and mental disorder. Both of these beliefs are false. Convulsive disorder is a neurological condition rather than a psychiatric or psychological one. However, because of the stress of the condition, emotional problems are likely to be somewhat more frequent among patients with convulsive disorders.

A final misconception is that epileptics cannot work normally or do things that most other people do. Actually it has been found that patients have fewer seizures if they lead active, normal lives. Most patients can work, participate in sports, go to school, marry and have children, and drive a car if, through medication, they can completely control their seizures. In some states patients are not permitted to do all these things, but this attitude is an outmoded one and is being altered largely through the efforts of the Epilepsy Foundation of America and other organizations interested in the welfare of patients with convulsive disorders.

Some Facts about Epilepsy

There are more than 2 million epileptic people in the United States.

The total cost of convulsive disorder to the nation probably exceeds a billion dollars.

There are a number of different types of epilepsy.

At least 50 percent of all epileptic persons can gain complete control over their seizures through anticonvulsant drugs.

Another 30 percent can achieve partial control through medication.

Seizures usually become less frequent as the patient grows older.

Most patients can go to school, take part in sports, work, marry, and have children.

Seizures are not necessarily associated with mental illness or mental retardation.*

---

*Mental Health Statistics, Series A, No. 2. National Institute of Mental Health, 1969.

*Epilepsy Foundation of America, 1970.

The convulsive disorders have been classified traditionally as *idiopathic* and *symptomatic*. Idiopathic disorders are disturbances having no apparent etiologic agent to account for them. Such disorders are not accompanied by structural changes in the organism. This type of convulsive disorder has been described variously as *essential, cryptogenic, primary, genetic,* and *hereditary*. Symptomatic convulsive disorders, however, are related directly to an underlying pathological condition of the organism. Conditions responsible for the appearance of symptomatic convulsions include syphilis of the brain, intoxication, head injuries, cerebral arteriosclerosis, and brain tumors. In such cases, in which the convulsive behavior is merely a symptom of some other disorder, the condition is classified under the more basic disturbance, not as a convulsive disorder or epilepsy. This symptomatic type of convulsive disorder has also been called *secondary, acquired,* and *focal* epilepsy.

Convulsive disorder expresses itself in four major forms:

1. *Grand mal* seizures
2. *Petit mal* seizures
3. *Psychomotor*, or temporal-lobe, attacks
4. *Jacksonian* seizures

The first form is characterized by the classic epileptic convulsion; the second by transient losses of consciousness for short periods without convulsions; the third by a variety of nonconvulsive behavior with disturbances of consciousness; and the fourth by localized convulsive behavior.

GRAND MAL SEIZURES

The *grand mal* seizure, the most dramatic, involves violent convulsions of the entire body. In approximately 50 percent of the cases, the convulsions are preceded by sensory or motor changes which the person comes to regard as a warning that an attack is imminent. This *aura* (from the Latin word for breeze, i.e., "the wind before the storm") may involve any of the senses. It appears a few seconds before the convulsion, although sometimes it may be minutes or even hours, in which case it is likely to take the form of irritability, sleeplessness, or headache. In many cases, the aura is a visual experience involving flashes of light, streaks of color, spinning disks, and similar phenomena. In other cases there are noises, melodies, odors, tastes, sensations of warmth or cold, unpleasant body sensations, numbness, tickling, itching, dizziness, nausea, sweating, muscle twitches. One patient suddenly felt the urge to run. Feodor Dostoevski, the Russian novelist, experienced feelings of ecstasy before his attacks. Whatever the aura, it allows the person to sit or lie down in a safe place, and to minimize the chances of injury during the seizure.

The first indication of the convulsion itself is a peculiar and characteristic cry, loud and sharp, due to the muscular contractions of the chest and throat and the involuntary expulsion of air from the lungs. This air, forced suddenly through the partially contracted throat, gives an unmistakable quality to the sound. With the cry, the person ordinarily loses consciousness and falls to the floor. A severe contracture of the entire musculature, called the *tonic phase* of the convulsion, takes place. The body is rigid, the jaws are tightly clenched, and the arms and legs are extended. During this initial phase, which lasts from ten to twenty seconds, there is an interruption of breathing due to the rigidity of the muscles. The pressure on the arteries of the neck and the lack of oxygen result in a temporary *cyanosis* or blueness of the skin.

The tonic phase of the convulsion is followed immediately by the *clonic phase*, in which there is a series of violent alternations of contraction and relaxation of the muscles. The entire body twists and turns in a rhythmic movement, with a powerful pounding of the arms and legs. It is at this time that the person is apt to injure himself. Saliva frequently escapes from the mouth as foam, and the person may lose control of his bladder and bowels. The clonic phrase usually lasts from one to five minutes.

In most *grand mal* seizures, the clonic phase is followed by confusion and disorientation. During this period of clouded consciousness, the person may open his eyes, get up, and attempt to wander about. Occasionally there are outbursts of violent rage and aggressive actions which have been referred to as *epileptic furor*. Whether or not the clonic phrase is followed by a well-defined clouded state, the next part of the syndrome is a deep, stuporous sleep that may last from a few minutes to several hours. When the person awakens, he has no memory for his attack, although he is aware that he had it because of the muscular soreness, aches and pains, and headache.

While the clonic phase of all *grand mal* seizures is similar, considerable individual variation exists with regard to the aura, the pattern of behavior immediately following the convulsion, and the frequency of attacks. The frequency varies from as few as one or two convulsions a year to five or ten a day. In *status epilepticus*, the *grand mal* seizures follow one another in such rapid succession that the convulsion appears to be continuous.

PETIT MAL SEIZURES

The *petit mal* seizure, first described in 1906, is marked by a transitory loss of consciousness which usually lasts only a few seconds. During this time the eyes remain open with a peculiar staring look, and there may be an accompanying pallor. Often there is yawning, jerking of the head, sudden laughter, twitchings of the facial muscles, or rapid fluttering of the eyelids. There is no generalized convulsion, and the person does not fall to the ground. During the lapses of consciousness, the person stops whatever he is doing and starts again a few seconds later where he left off. He may continue a conversation from the exact point where he stopped talking.

Petit mal seizures may be infrequent, or they may occur several hundred times each day. The disorder is seen more often among children, in whom the seizures sometimes disappear spontaneously during adolescence or, in other cases, may be replaced by *grand mal* seizures.

TEMPORAL-LOBE SEIZURES

It has been recognized for many years that there is a type of convulsive disorder in which the convulsion itself is replaced by a rich variety of symptoms including loss of memory, auditory hallucinations, impulsive acting out, and dissociative reaction, but in which consciousness is not lost. Traditionally, this condition has been called

psychomotor epilepsy or an *epileptic equivalent.* Other terms include *psychic seizures, epileptic fugues, epileptic automatisms, and epileptic dream states.*

The clinical relationship of symptoms of this type to convulsive disorder was established on the basis of disturbances of the brain-wave patterns. For many years the brain structures related to the symptoms were unknown. Work performed at the Montreal Neurological Institute established the fact that these symptoms grow out of disturbances of the functions of the temporal lobes and related structures (Penfield and Jasper, 1954). Thus this type of convulsive disorder is called a *temporal-lobe seizure.*

During the attack, victims experience varying degrees of confusion and behave in quite different ways. Some people mumble incoherently, chew and grind their teeth, and gesticulate; others take off their clothing, wander about, or move in an automatic, dreamlike way; still others show rage behavior during which they become assaultive and may commit the most serious crimes of violence. Vincent Van Gogh, the Flemish painter, had recurring periods of confusion which were probably temporal-lobe seizures. During one episode, he cut off his ear, wrapped it in a sack, and gave it to a woman friend as a present. In his final attack, he shot himself in the abdomen.

JACKSONIAN SEIZURES

This disorder, described originally by the noted British neurologist J. Hughlings Jackson, is marked by convulsions which are limited to circumscribed parts of the body, with the convulsive movements involving only an arm, a leg, or the face (Jackson, 1873). The movements follow the same pattern, which differs from patient to patient, and which starts at one point and spreads to neighboring muscle groups. In some cases the convulsive movements begin at the angle of the mouth and spread to the muscles of the eye, face, and neck; in other cases, the movements start between the thumb and index finger and spread to the hand, arm, and shoulder. Or they may start with the large toe and then include the foot, leg, and thigh. Ordinarily there is no loss of consciousness during the attack.

■ CONVULSIVE DISORDER

Edwin F. is a twenty-seven-year-old single man with a history of *grand mal, petit mal*, and psychomotor seizures. The *petit mal* condition was noticed first when the patient was ten years old. Since that time he has shown various other forms of convulsive disorder and has been on continuous medication.

He was referred to a psychiatric hospital when he was twenty-two years old because of uncontrollable seizures involving both legs. The condition cleared spontaneously soon after hospitalization. After six months in the hospital, the patient was discharged. Two months later, he was admitted to the city hospital in a dirty, unshaven, confused state. He appeared to be having auditory hallucinations, and had the delusion that someone was trying to kill him. He was referred to the psychiatric hospital, where a diagnosis was made of chronic brain syndrome associated with a convulsive disorder. Within several days the patient's condition improved, although there was a loss of memory for the entire episode.

The patient was sickly as a child and frequently ran high fevers without apparent cause. He was a feeding problem throughout his early years. When he entered school, he had trouble concentrating and did poor academic work. His teachers described him as a "dreamy" individual. However, intelligence tests showed that he was of well above average intelligence. The first convulsive seizures were noted when he was twelve years old. He was working as a caddy at a golf course, and his companion noticed that he had brief blackout periods. The mother recalled instances in which she had seen him blink his eyes and seem dazed for a few seconds at a time when he was younger. Eventually neurological examinations were undertaken, and a diagnosis of convulsive disorder was established. As he grew older, Eddie showed various behavior problems and adjustment difficulties. On one occasion he ran away from home, on another he stole an automobile, and he had an extremely poor work record. There is also a history of heterosexual promiscuity and homosexual prostitution.

When seen at the hospital, the patient was a neat, pleasant, and cooperative young man who appeared eager to talk about his problems. While there was some irrelevancy, there were no signs of disorientation,

delusions, hallucinations, or other psychopathology. His judgment appeared good, and there was some degree of insight.*

ETIOLOGY OF CONVULSIVE SEIZURES

Efforts to explain the nature of convulsive behavior have ranged from the primitive idea of spirit possession to the current emphasis on psychogenic and physiogenic (particularly bioelectrical) factors. Hippocrates, who took a completely naturalistic view of the disorder, believed it to be caused by a disturbance of the bile. Later, in ancient Rome, Fabricius said it was due to "biliary concretions." In the early nineteenth century, it was believed that convulsions were caused by any condition that forces excessive amounts of blood to the head (Esquirol, 1838). Some physicians attributed epilepsy to such factors as violent exercise, pregnancy, alcoholic overindulgence, masturbation, and suppression of the menses. Another author blamed the seizures on "overfatigue, long walks, carrying heavy loads, or prolonged mental exertion" (Tuke, 1892).

The psychological view of convulsive behavior is that it is a reaction to frustration, or a form of escape from an intolerable situation. It has been shown experimentally that an animal placed in a conflict situation for which there is no solution may react with convulsive behavior. It is also possible that men and women, upon occasion, react in a similar fashion and for similar reasons.

Even if one or another psychogenic theory of convulsive behavior is valid, the underlying neurophysiological mechanism remains to be explained. Most of the earlier explanations emphasized lack of oxygen in the brain, spasms of the cerebral arteries, altered permeability of the cell membranes, a disturbance of water balance, lowered blood sugar, and similar factors. (See Table 11.1.) More recently, attention has been directed to the bioelectrical activity of the brain. This approach looks upon idiopathic convulsive disorder as a result of disturbed cerebral electrical activity. The disorder is, in fact, due to an "elec-

---

*Case 1 of audiotape 11, "Brain Disorders: Miscellaneous Reactions," in *Case Interviews to Accompany The Disorganized Personality.*

Table 11.1 *Biochemical changes during convulsions*

MEASUREMENT	CHANGE DETECTED
Blood-brain barrier	Permeability of the cerebral cell is increased. Inorganic phosphate and potassium ions leak into cerebral venous blood. Venous blood sodium falls slightly. Cerebrospinal fluid acetylcholine, inorganic phosphate, and albumin increase.
Oxygen consumption	Increases with each convulsion.
Brain carbohydrate	Glycogen stores decrease; glucose may or may not decrease.
Blood sugar and lactic acid	Increase in peripheral venous blood, but not in blood flowing from the brain. Lactic acid rises with first convulsion, remains high until end of convulsive activity.
Blood phosphocreatine	Decreases.
Brain ATP	More or less constant; decreases if blood pressure falls.
Brain ammonia	Greatly increased.
Blood urea	Increases, remaining elevated for many hours.
Blood calcium	Increases at first, then falls during a few hours; slowly returns to normal.
Plasma epinephrine	Increases rapidly; falls rapidly after convulsion.
Blood protein	Rises; returns to normal in 1 to 4 hours.
Blood glutamic acid	Increases in the peripheral venous blood, but not in jugular blood.

SOURCE: Adapted from T. L. Sourkes, *Biochemistry of Mental Disease*, Paul B. Hoeber, Inc., New York, 1962, p. 371.

trical storm" in the brain. This disturbance, or *cerebral dysrhythmia,* can be demonstrated objectively by means of the EEG (electroencephalogram).

Electrical disturbances of the brain can be triggered in susceptible people by a wide variety of stimuli. Flashing lights are a common source of stimulation leading to convulsions because of the powerful influence on the brain waves. Two young girls attending a psychedelic show in England had attacks brought on by the flashing strobe lights. Other reports of convulsive seizures have been attributed to high-intensity and high-frequency sounds generated by rock musicians.

One woman experienced a seizure every time she heard the voices of certain radio announcers. To confirm that the seizures were caused by the voices, tapes of programs broadcast by the announcers were obtained, and the patient was studied at the Epilepsy Center at the University of Wisconsin. Each time a tape was played, the woman had a convulsive attack. Medical treatment was continued until the patient could listen to the announcers without signs of a seizure. Scientists at the center suggested that variations in pitch, rhythm, and stress of pronunciation by the announcers may have played a part in bringing on the attacks (Forster, 1968).

There is evidence that heredity plays an important, if not completely clear, role in the etiology of convulsive disorders of the idiopathic type. Among identical, or monozygotic, twins, if one twin has a history of idiopathic convulsive disorder, the other twin is likely to have a similar history. Such concordance of convulsive behavior is seen in between 60 and 90 percent of identical twins but in less than 10 percent of fraternal, or dizygotic, twins (Shields and Slater, 1960).

The most clear-cut etiology is seen in symptomatic convulsive disorders in which an irri-

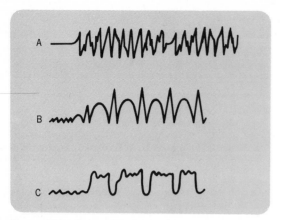

Figure 11.2 *Some EEG abnormalities seen in convulsive disorders. (a) Normal alpha rhythm, (b) three-per-second spike and wave pattern of* petit mal *convulsive disorder, (c) square-topped waves of psychomotor disorder. (Courtesy of Longview State Hospital.)*

tating agent is responsible for the seizures. When this agent is removed by surgical means, the seizures are frequently brought under control. However, in cases of idiopathic disorders, the seizures are likely to be related to a complex interaction of electrical activity of the brain, physical factors determining the convulsive threshold for an individual patient, and psychological factors which may play a role in precipitating the convulsion.

Even in these cases, a genetic predisposing factor may be present. A study of the families of symptomatic, or focal, epilepsy patients reported findings supporting the view of a genetic basis for temporal-lobe epilepsy. The incidence of abnormalities among families of epilepsy-prone patients was significantly higher than in control subjects (Andermann, 1969).

EPILEPSY RESEARCH

While most persons with epilepsy are able to lead normal and productive lives, many still suffer from seizures that do not respond to treatment.

Epilepsy research programs have two aims: (1) to develop more effective treatment methods, and (2) to understand the basic defect so that epilepsy can be "cured" rather than merely controlled.

The National Institute of Neurological Diseases and Stroke sponsors five clinical epilepsy research centers in the United States. One is located at the University of Washington, where studies of the fundamental mechanisms underlying epilepsy are being conducted. Another center, at the University of Wisconsin, is conducting both clinical and basic research studies. A third center at the Brain Research Institute of the University of California at Los Angeles is concentrating on a study of the electrical process underlying the epileptic state in animals and in man. A fourth center at Yale University is conducting a program of research into mechanisms of epilepsy and of phenomena associated with seizure states. In addition, a neuropharmacology research center is supported at the University of Utah. This center is concerned primarily with the study of the action of anticonvulsant drugs.[3]

One of the greatest needs in the field of epilepsy research has been a more appropriate experimental animal for laboratory investigation. While a number of animals have been used over the years, the difficulty has been that none were found in which epileptic seizures occur spontaneously. All seizures in experimental animals had to be induced mechanically. In the late 1960s, scientists discovered that the African baboon *Papio papio* has an epileptic seizure in response to a flickering light stimulus. The reaction of this animal provides a new basis for research into the physiology of light-induced seizures as well as for testing drugs which may be effective in controlling seizures.

It will take the combined efforts of all segments of the community to attack the problem of epilepsy successfully. Physicians must keep abreast of the latest developments. Teachers must be willing to accept and understand children with this disorder and recognize that they should have the benefit of regular schooling. Social agencies must

[3]*Epilepsy Abstracts* is a monthly publication which regularly scans more than 3,000 journals for information about all aspects of convulsive disorder. Articles from the world literature are indexed and abstracted. First published in 1967, it is an important source of current information about epilepsy. Available from the National Institute of Neurological Diseases and Stroke, Bethesda, Md. 20014.

be aware of the special problems associated with the disorder. Employers must be acquainted with the true capabilities of employees who have epilepsy and with the local laws affecting their status. Fortunately, most states now assume the financial risk of on-the-job injury to employees with epilepsy. And, perhaps most important of all, families must be helped to recognize the true nature of the disorder and to feel no shame.[4]

INFECTIOUS DISORDERS

Various types of psychological symptoms are observed in infectious diseases. In the acute phases of infectious diseases, particularly those conditions involving high body temperatures, the most common and prominent symptom is delirium. In the more chronic stages of infectious disease, the symptoms may include depression, irritability, excitement, apathy, stupor, delusions, and hallucinations.

It is quite possible for psychological symptoms and personality changes to be associated with infectious disorders which do not invade the central nervous system. Systemic infections such as typhoid fever and pneumonia are often accompanied by personality disturbances during the period of high fever. However, the intracranial infections involving the brain are of greater interest to the psychologist and the psychiatrist. These conditions are best illustrated by *neurosyphilis,* by the several forms of *encephalitis,* by *meningitis,* and by *brain abscesses.*

NEUROSYPHILIS

It will be recalled that the first mental disorder identified as having a specific organic basis was *dementia paralytica,* later known as *general paresis* or simply *paresis.* This condition, caused by syphilis of the brain, has been one of the most important brain syndromes from the historical point of view and, until the discovery of the antibiotics, from the practical clinical point of view as well. It was not until the 1940s that the control of early syphilitic infection became effective enough to bring about a sharp decrease in mental disorder resulting from this infection.

The symptoms of paresis were described in the medical literature long before syphilis was recognized as the major cause; many factors were thought to be involved in its development. It was not until the middle of the nineteenth century that serious interest turned to the relationship between syphilis and mental disorder. Prior to that time, it had not occurred to physicians that there could be a connection between syphilis, which was thought of as a skin disease, and the symptoms of personality disorganization.

Syphilis is an infectious disease caused by a spiral microorganism, or spirochete. The organism enters the body through minute abrasions in the skin or in the mucous membranes. The infection can be transmitted to the fetus while it is still developing or while it is passing through the birth canal at the time of birth. However, syphilis is never inherited.

The course of syphilis follows four major stages: (1) primary stage, characterized by a sore, or chancre; (2) secondary stage, marked by a coppery rash; (3) tertiary stage, marked by chronic inflammation of cellular tissue; and (4) quaternary stage, or degenerative phase, in which cardiovascular and nervous system lesions appear. This fourth stage ordinarily is reached from five to twenty years after the initial infection, although in many cases the nervous system is affected sooner. The involvement of the nervous system takes place by way of the bloodstream.

The term *neurosyphilis* is used to indicate that the spirochete has attacked some part of the brain or spinal cord. However, only a relatively small number of untreated or poorly treated cases of syphilis develop neurosyphilis. In most cases, some other system of the body is attacked. The reason the microorganism selects the nervous

---

[4]Among the many books about epilepsy and the convulsive disorders are *Psychosocial Function in Epilepsy* (Thomas, 1970) by M. J. Horowitz; *Basic Mechanisms of the Epilepsies* (Little, Brown, 1969) edited by H. H. Jasper et al.; E. A. Rodin's *The Prognosis of Patients with Epilepsy* (Thomas, 1968); *Living with Epileptic Seizures* (Thomas, 1963) by Samuel Livingston; D. B. Tower's *Neurochemistry of Epilepsy* (Thomas, 1960); and the two-volume *Epilepsy and Related Disorders* (Little, Brown, 1960) by W. G. and M. A. Lennox.

system in one patient and a different system in another patient is not clear. It has been suggested that there are two distinct types of organisms, one being *dermatotropic* and attacking the skin, the other being *neurotropic* and attacking the nervous tissue. The problem has been whether these properties belong to the microorganism or whether constitutional factors in the patient determine the manifestation of the disease (Bruetsch, 1955).

The changes in the brain and its membranes are typical in this disease and are seen readily on gross or microscopic examination. The brain as a whole is likely to be shrunken, with the membranes thickened and adherent. The deepened convolutions are filled with a turgid fluid, and the ventricles are usually dilated. Under the microscope, the cells (especially the ganglion cells) show degenerative changes and atrophied fibers.

The neurological symptoms develop gradually. In the early stages of the disease they may not be present, or if they are, they may be so slight as to be undetected during a neurological examination. In other cases, the early stages of the disease may be characterized by pronounced neurological disturbances which appear suddenly. The reason for this wide discrepancy is to be found in the nature of the brain lesion. The microorganism of syphilis attacks the nervous tissue in different areas in different patients.

One of the most important neurological changes in general paresis is the pupillary disturbance. The pupils become unequal in size, and there is a disturbance of the reflexes. This condition, seen in the more advanced stages of general paresis, is found in about 50 percent of the cases. Here the pupil does not respond to light, although it does accommodate to distance.

The speech disturbance in general paresis is rather typical and frequently forms the basis for the initial diagnosis. The speech of these patients becomes indistinct due to slurring and mispronunciation. Even in the earlier stages of the disease, the patient finds it difficult or impossible to repeat such words and phrases as "Methodist Episcopal," "hippopotamus," and "medical superintendent." In attempting to repeat such words, the patient characteristically stumbles, stutters, and omits important syllables. As the disease progresses, speech becomes increasingly unintelligible.

The handwriting of patients with general paresis also shows characteristic changes. In the beginning stages of the disease, the most pronounced change is the unsteadiness of the writing. In later stages of the disorder, the handwriting becomes coarse and heavy, letters are omitted, and the writing is crude and untidy. In the final stages, writing becomes entirely impossible, with the patient able only to scratch a few lines on a sheet of paper. The following letter was written by a paretic patient to a secretary working in the hospital:

Darling Madame:
Goodmoring wonderful madame. How are you today —are you your little best? This is an acquaintence positive and it is positive true that madame is a mighty fine girl. Also, Mary, Beatrice and Bertha girls are positive very nice. And it gives me sincere gratitude to say something about you folks. At the present time I am not doing things the mighties of level evollition, or worth a dam, prosperious assimililation seems to be defiliated—and of simplest reason. I don't know what the hell level vurge thinks this is. Of course I am expecting to get a visit from (very little nice madame), and I have not pass it up, though things seem to be reasumable slow. Just what have you planned for your summer varieties? I have always admired your evolutionize challengency.

Exquisitely yours,

This letter shows many of the characteristic disturbances of verbalization and writing seen in the paretic. The patient was above average in intelligence and had completed two years in high school. The misspellings and bizarre forms found in the letter are a result of the destructive brain processes rather than a lack of education.

The physical changes in the brain also lead to disorders of movement. The patients drag their feet, walk with a shuffling gait, and have trouble keeping their balance. They cannot catch a ball tossed to them, they have trouble buttoning their clothes, and they are unable to thread a needle or tie a knot. In some cases there are mannerisms, such as grimacing, dancing about, ceaseless rubbing and picking, grunting, smacking the lips, chewing, and sighing. Features become flabby and expressionless, and the voice is monotonous or tremulous. The condition in which the spirochetes invade not only the cells of the cortex but also the cells of the spinal cord is known as *tabo-paresis.* Here the disturbance in gait is more pronounced.

The psychological symptoms are as varied as the physical symptoms. Among the first signs of the disorder are loss of memory and judgment. The patients are unable to notice contradictions in their own thinking or in the conversation of others. Emotionally, the brain syphilis patient is quite unstable and unpredictable. His mood changes from one extreme to the other. One moment he is happy and gay; the next he is morose and depressed. A little later he will sulk, and then he will have a temper tantrum. He is easily excited by trivial events and has frequent fits of crying and laughing. Moreover, these patients develop a rich variety of delusions and hallucinations.

The brain syphilis patient usually shows an increasing disregard for propriety, customs, and social niceties. His lack of inhibitions makes him tactless and frequently grossly offensive. He becomes careless of his personal appearance, and his table manners deteriorate to a point where he eats greedily and noisily.

The simple deteriorating or dementing form of general paresis is seen most frequently. The psychological deterioration develops gradually and is marked by memory loss, diminishing insight, increasingly poor judgment, and irresponsibility. In many of these cases, the mood is elevated and appears somewhat hypomanic. There are no pronounced delusions, hallucinations, or excitement.

The expansive type of general paresis is marked by delusions of grandeur and an exalted mood. The patients believe themselves to be multimillionaires, members of royal families, or other prominent and distinguished persons. The grandiosity and impracticality of the paretic is shown in the case of a patient who handed a nurse an order for 25 pounds of tobacco, a dozen bottles of perfume, four accordions, 60 dozen handkerchiefs, a field marshal's uniform, 26 thousand quarts of blueberries, a thousand boxes of ham, a stage, and a carpenter. Another paretic wrote a check for five thousand dollars and gave it to an attendant who brought him a glass of water. Still another patient visited a physician and offered him a million dollars a month to be his personal physician while the patient traveled in Europe.

The depressed type shows the symptoms of persistent melancholy and gloom. In some cases, there is an agitated depression suggestive of the involutional psychosis. A senile form of general paresis has also been identified in which the symptoms appear late in life. Some years ago, these cases were more likely to be diagnosed as senile or arteriosclerotic conditions. More recent advances in the histopathology of the nervous system have indicated that at least some of the psychoses of old age are due to syphilitic infection earlier in life.

Clinical experience suggests that the premorbid personality of the patient determines the type of psychological symptom seen in general paresis. That is, the organic changes in the brain release underlying personality characteristics. A small number of cases of paresis show symptoms of the schizophrenic type. In such cases, the organic brain disturbance releases schizophrenic features of the personality which might otherwise have remained unexpressed.

As a result of widespread public education and new methods of treatment and control, paresis is much less common today than it was not many years ago. The dramatic reduction in the incidence of the disease is shown by psychiatric hospital admission rates. The rate from 1927 to 1931 ranged between 20 and 25 percent of total admissions. By 1969 it was less than one-tenth of 1 percent (NIMH, 1969).

The danger of paresis is always present in cases of syphilis where there has been no treatment or where the treatment has not been adequate. In this connection, there has been a sharp increase in infectious syphilis in recent years, particularly among teen-agers.

■ **PARESIS**

Charles H. is a somewhat obese forty-year-old man who was referred to a psychiatric hospital after mailing a threatening letter to a county judge. When the incident was investigated, it was found that the patient had become an increasing problem in the home. He had been married for nineteen years and apparently got along quite well until he began having recent episodes of agitation and excitement. Between the episodes he was euphoric, expansive, and increasingly grandiose. He told his wife about various schemes and multimillion-dollar deals in which he was involved. The wife knew that his statements had no basis but she passed them off at first as an attempt on his part to impress her and his friends. The letter he sent to the judge was in connection with his belief that the courts were blocking one of his big "deals."

The police, who recognized that Charles was mentally ill, sent him to a hospital where it was found that he was suffering from syphilis of the nervous system. He was placed on penicillin treatment, and although his mental condition improved, he continued to express grandiose ideas. When examined three years after the termination of the treatment, the patient talked about his fortune of several million dollars and his plan for building a series of factories for RCA and a new baseball stadium for the Cincinnati Reds. The patient was neat and clean, his intelligence was in the average range, and he was fully oriented. He showed a clinical picture of early arrested paresis.*

The two major types of brain syphilis are (1) *meningovascular,* involving the membranes and blood vessels of the brain, and (2) *meningo-encephalitic,* involving the brain tissue. In both conditions, localized lesions cause acute psychological disturbances marked by confusion and delirium. There may be clouding of consciousness and disorientation for temporary periods. Emotional changes also take place. In the chronic cases, the psychological symptoms may resemble any of the psychoses.

Juvenile Paresis

This condition was first described in 1877 (Clouston, 1883). It occurs in children and adolescents suffering from congenital syphilis, in which the infection is transmitted through the bloodstream from the mother to the fetus. However, only about 1 percent of cases of congenital syphilis later develop juvenile paresis. The condition usually makes its appearance early in life, with mental retardation a frequent symptom. Convulsions are also seen in many cases.

Ordinarily, the physical signs of congenital syphilis are present. These signs include Hutchinson's teeth, with characteristic notching of the middle incisors; the residue of a previous in-

flammation of the cornea; and nerve deafness. The psychological symptoms of juvenile paresis show wide variation and may simulate schizophrenia and other psychotic conditions.

■ JUVENILE PARESIS

Kaybee J. was admitted to a psychiatric hospital at the age of sixteen following a series of convulsive seizures. From that time he presented a serious management problem. The family had been unable to care for him at home or to understand what he said. When he was taken to the probate court, he attempted to take off his clothes. At the hospital it was necessary to restrain him in bed because he attacked the attendants and tried to bite them. He turned his head from side to side and mumbled unintelligibly. He was incontinent and continually soiled the bed. He did not respond to questions, although he said something about being "crazy." He was completely out of contact with his environment.

After twenty-five years, the patient is practically mute, although he makes sounds when watching television. Sometimes he becomes upset while watching the programs and gets up and fights; otherwise he sits quietly all day long. The patient has exhibited some homosexual characteristics, and attendants find it necessary to watch him at all times. It is impossible to communicate with him. There is no judgment or insight. Occasionally the patient has convulsive seizures.

ENCEPHALITIS

This infectious disease of the brain is an inflammatory-degenerative disorder associated with a number of etiologic factors including a filtrable virus and infections such as measles, mumps, and hepatitis. Epidemic encephalitis, a form of the disease which appeared in Romania in 1915, was first identified in 1917 (Von Economo, 1931). By 1919 the disease had spread throughout Europe and into America. This disorder was also called *encephalitis lethargica,* but since the lethargy is not always present, the condition is known today as *type A encephalitis.* While the acute form of epidemic encephalitis has not been reported since 1925, chronic forms of the disease

---

*Case 2 of audiotape 11, "Brain Disorders: Miscellaneous Reactions," in *Case Interviews to Accompany The Disorganized Personality.*

are still seen in hospitals. The filtrable virus which attacks the brain tissue remains active in the nervous system over a period of years, similar to the action of the microorganism of neurosyphilis.

The symptoms of acute epidemic encephalitis take a wide variety of forms, including neurological and psychological changes. The acute cases are of two types: (1) the *irritative hyperkinetic* and (2) the *hypersomnic-opthalmoplegic*. In the irritative type of the disease, there is restlessness, hyperactivity, and various forms of convulsive seizures. These motor symptoms point to an involvement of the basal ganglia.

■ ENCEPHALITIS

Laura L. is a forty-three-year-old married woman who was admitted to a hospital after making a series of suicidal attempts to stab, choke, and poison herself. The patient has had a long history of irritable and unstable behavior. When she was a year old, she had an attack of infantile encephalitis which was followed by a partial paralysis of one side of her body. At twenty-five, the first symptoms of convulsive disorder appeared. Seven years ago the patient married her husband after a two-month acquaintance. The husband was mentally dull and also had symptoms of a convulsive disorder. The patient neglected her housework throughout the marriage. About a year and a half before admission, the patient and her husband moved in with the husband's mother, and the patient felt that her husband and his mother joined together to ridicule and dominate her. She soon began to stay in bed all day, reading her Bible for periods of five or six hours. When she was rebuked, she made another suicidal attempt, and was referred to the psychiatric hospital.

When first seen at the hospital, the patient was hostile and negativistic, and she required restraint and sedation during the first two days. Occasionally she lashed out with shrieking complaints that she was being punished for reading the Bible. "It's all my husband and his mother, I'm just dirt under their feet. Nobody wants anyone who has been paralyzed." Later the patient became more pleasant, although she was preoccupied with religious topics. At the time of her examination she was cooperative, friendly, and well oriented. She spoke freely about her situation. Her thinking was fairly well organized, although somewhat circumstantial. Speech was intelligible and coherent, with strong paranoid ideas directed toward her husband and her mother-in-law. She said that she once had a vision of Christ who spoke to her. The patient showed a severe lack of practical judgment, a bizarre kind of moralizing, an overreaching of her capacity, and a number of personalized responses showing body preoccupation and feelings of persecution. A diagnosis was made of chronic brain syndrome associated with intracranial infection.

The acute hypersomnic type of encephalitis is characterized by drowsiness and sleepiness. Patients fall into a lethargy and frequently sleep for days or even weeks. In addition, there are numerous neurological signs, particularly disturbances of the ocular apparatus. The chronic hypersomnic type of encephalitis is often associated with *Parkinsonism*, a syndrome in which there is a masklike face, tremors of the hands and fingers, and a propulsive gait. In addition, there may be various other forms of motor disturbances.

The apparent cause of Parkinsonism is the lack of the body chemical *dopamine*, but the administration of plain dopamine is not effective in treating the disorder since this chemical does not cross the walls of the blood vessels to enter the cells of the brain. However, a chemical variant, *L-dopamine*, can penetrate the brain and is then broken down in the brain cells to supply the lacking substance. This chemical has brought about dramatic improvement in many cases of Parkinsonism. In those cases which respond to drug treatment, the frozen facial expression tends to relax, and both gait and posture return toward normal. Speech and writing difficulties become less severe, and restlessness during sleep is relieved.

Among children, there are striking changes in behavior following encephalitis. They become irritable, fussy, quick-tempered, boisterous, and restless. They are not able to play peacefully with other children, nor do they get along well with their parents. Such children become quarrelsome, tease other children, and show streaks of brutality. Teachers find them impudent, disobedient, and unresponsive to discipline. It is not unusual for such children to curse their parents or to strike at them. Moreover, they become neglectful about their personal appearance, lose their sense of modesty, and frequently show tendencies toward exhibitionism. Temper tantrums, attacks of screaming, emotional instability, and excessive moodiness are common symptoms. The children run away from home and are involved in episodes of stealing, vandalism, sexual misbehavior, and other forms of delinquency. For the most part, the changes are in the area of personality and behavior, with little change in intellectual ability.

While epidemic encephalitis is no longer seen in an acute form, there are other forms of encephalitis which do occur from time to time and which are accompanied by psychological and neurological symptoms. There was a Japanese encephalitis epidemic in 1924 during which about 7,000 cases were reported, with a mortality rate of approximately 60 percent. This strain of encephalitis is known as *type B encephalitis*. Residuals of the Japanese type B encephalitis were reported in the 1950s by United States military personnel in Korea and Japan. *St. Louis encephalitis* was identified during the epidemic in that city during the summer of 1933. The disease is marked by headache, irritability, loss of memory, and drowsiness. The mortality rate in the St. Louis epidemic was about 20 percent. Other cases of encephalitis are associated with such diseases as measles, mumps, and infectious mononucleosis (Wechsler, 1963)

Sydenham's chorea is a form of encephalitis in which the infection involves the cortex and the basal ganglia. The condition is regarded as a rheumatic disorder in which there are exudative changes, or discharges, involving the brain rather than the joints or heart. Because of an association with scarlet fever, tonsillitis, endocarditis, and rheumatic conditions, it has been suggested that the microorganism is a streptococcus. The disease, frequently found in children, is somewhat more common among girls than among boys. The primary symptom of Sydenham's chorea is muscular incoordination in which there are involuntary movements of the extremities, with characteristic facial grimaces. Personality changes take the form of emotional instability. These patients become restless, irritable, quarrelsome, and resentful. Defects in concentration, attention, and memory are not uncommon. The children are likely to be tearful and fretful. They are difficult to handle and frequently show various forms of behavior problems. In some cases, there may be episodes of delirium. This form of chorea is likely to last for

several months and often recurs. There is increasing evidence that personality changes of a permanent character follow episodes of this disease in a number of cases (Baker, 1955).

MENINGITIS

Cerebrospinal meningitis is another brain syndrome caused by intracranial infection. The symptoms begin rather abruptly with intense headache, fever, chills, and vomiting. Other symptoms include a painful stiffness of the neck, sensitivity above the spine, restlessness, irritability, disorientation, and, in some cases, convulsions. In subacute cases, there may be only drowsiness and mild confusion. The patient is unable to concentrate, and he is irritable and depressed. Such cases may show complete improvement, or there may be residual symptoms in the form of sensory defects, motor paralyses, and mental retardation. The most common infectious agent in meningitis is the meningococcus, although meningitis may also be caused by a wide range of other microorganisms including streptococci, pneumococci, and tubercle bacilli.

In tuberculous meningitis, the symptoms develop slowly, with an apparently normal person becoming irritable, fatigued, disinclined to engage in activities, and difficult to control. There is usually a mild delirium combined with restless sleep. As the intracranial process becomes more serious, such symptoms as headache, clouding of consciousness, and confusion become more prominent. In the earlier stages of the disease, the patient can remain in touch with his environment for short periods if he is roused. As the condition becomes more serious and the lethargy deepens, the patient sinks into a coma in which he is completely out of touch with his environment. In some cases, adults show various degrees of agitation along with their confusion.

BRAIN ABSCESS

This form of cerebral infection may be caused by various types of microorganisms, including staphylococci, streptococci, pneumococci, *H. influenzae,* and actinomyces. The abscess may be produced directly as a result of injury to the head, or by means of infections of the ear, face, or scalp. It is not unusual to have brain abscesses associated with mastoid and sinus infections. Paranasal sinus infection leads to suppuration (pus formation) in the frontal regions of the brain, while mastoid infections are more likely to spread to the temporal lobe and the mid-portions of the cerebrum, as well as to the cerebellum.

It is also possible for infections in other parts of the body to reach the brain. Lung abscess, bronchial infections, sinus disorders, liver abscess, and amoebic dysentery may result in brain infection. Such infections are also produced by bacterial heart disease, which may interfere with the cerebral blood vessels, resulting in softening or hemorrhaging and the development of a suppurative process.

The physical symptoms of brain abscess include loss of weight, poor appetite, constipation, and fever. There may be headache, vomiting, and optic neuritis as a result of the increased cranial pressure. Paralysis, aphasic disturbances, sensory deficits, and convulsions are also observed. The psychological symptoms include restlessness, irritability, insomnia, disturbances of memory, inability to concentrate, delusions, and hallucinations.

The danger of personality disorganization due to infectious disorders has decreased sharply as a result of the development of antibiotics (such as sulfonamide, penicillin, or streptomycin) and similar drugs. Advances in surgery have also helped to decrease the incidence of psychological disorder associated with infectious disease.

BRAIN TUMORS

Brain tumors are pathological masses of cells which grow in the brain. They exert their effect on behavior and personality either directly through damage to brain centers involving speech, hearing, vision, or other sensorimotor functions, or indirectly through disturbances in blood circulation or increased intracranial pressure of the cerebrospinal fluid. In the latter cases, the brain cells are subjected to degenerative processes as the result of lack of needed nutritional substances,

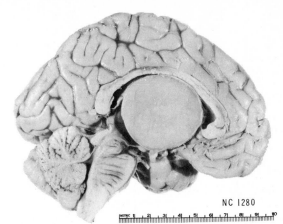

Figure 11.3 *A midsagittal view of the left cerebral hemisphere showing a large cyst of the brain. (Courtesy of Dr. Abraham T. Lu.)*

or the increased pressure brings about a mechanical displacement of the cells. In either case, symptoms of personality disturbance may appear.

The clinical course of a brain tumor ordinarily involves a progressive loss of function—sometimes rapid, in other cases a slow process lasting many months or years. As the brain tumor expands, various types of neurological symptoms become prominent, depending upon the size and location of the growth. Such symptoms as paralysis, visual defects, pathological reflexes, sensory disturbances, and similar difficulties are seen. In the more advanced brain tumors, the most common symptoms are headache, vomiting, and papilledema, or swelling of the optic nerve. These symptoms are frequently associated with apathy and are often followed by blindness, stupor, and death.

Psychological symptoms are very often the first signs of tumors of the brain. In many cases, intellectual and emotional changes occur weeks or months before there is neurological evidence of the brain tumor. Frequently the first sign of this type of disorder is a vague feeling of anxiety which may be an expression of the patient's unconscious realization of the disorder. Many tumors develop in so-called "silent" areas of the brain—areas which do not produce neurological symptoms and which are not critical to the sensory, motor, or association functions of the individual. Such patients show few or no symptoms for long periods of time, often over a span of years. Post-mortem examinations of the brains of individuals who have died of other causes indicate that some people have brain tumors without ever realizing it.

The most common of all brain tumors are the *gliomata*. These tumors, accounting for approximately half of all brain tumors, are tumors of the brain tissue proper. An additional 15 percent of brain tumors are *meningiomata* arising from the coverings of the brain and spinal cord. *Pituitary tumors* make up still another 5 to 10 percent of the cases. Secondary carcinoma, or *metastatic tumors*, account for from 5 to 25 percent of the total, with rare *neoplasms* making up the remainder (Bailey, 1948).

The most frequently seen varieties of gliomata associated with personality changes are (1) astrocytoma, (2) glioblastoma multiforme, and (3) medulloblastoma. The *astrocytoma* is a slow-growing brain tumor which infiltrates the brain. This type of tumor is frequently present in the brain for many months or even years before it is diagnosed. Among children, it is found most frequently in the cerebellum and does not result in personality disorganization until late in the development of the tumor, when the increased intracranial pressure may produce symptoms. As with most tumors of the brain, the type of symptom is determined to a large extent by the location of the tumor. When the astrocytoma is in the temporal lobe, symptoms similar to those seen in temporal-lobe seizures sometimes are observed.

The *glioblastoma multiforme* ordinarily develops late in life and grows rapidly. It is seen most frequently in the frontal lobe or the temporal lobe. In either case, personality disturbances are likely to be present. Because such tumors expand rapidly, the patient finds it difficult to adapt to the changing demands of his environment. Depending upon the location of the tumor, there may be convulsive seizures, visual disturbances, aphasia, and similar symptoms. The third type of gliomata, the *medulloblastoma,* is a common tumor found in childhood and involves the brainstem. The symptoms are usually limited to palsy of the cranial nerves, with some cases showing altered states of consciousness. In such cases, the condition may be mistaken for a schizophrenic stupor.

In the meningiomata, or tumors arising from the meninges of the brain and spinal cord, the early personality changes may be extremely subtle. These tumors develop slowly, and the changes are so slight that the patient adjusts to them without being aware of the organic damage. The neoplasm is often found in the anterior basal part of the skull, a location which allows the tumor to grow to a large size with no clinical symptoms other than the progressive personality change. While such tumors frequently go unrecognized, they can often be treated successfully by surgery when they are discovered.

The nature of the symptoms seen in meningiomata depend upon the location of the tumor, its size, and the level of the patient's adjustment. In the early stages of the growth, psychological defensive measures taken by the personality are frequently sufficient to handle the gradual changes that occur. Later, symptoms become more pronounced. Tumors in the frontal region may result in minimal intellectual impairment. When the meningioma is in the olfactory region, there is a slow but progressive dementia with olfactory disturbances, and sometimes blindness and other visual symptoms.

■ BRAIN TUMOR

Frances S. is a fifty-nine-year-old woman who is cooperative during the examination, but shows little initiative and poor motivation. Her attitude is friendly, and her mood is fairly even. However, she can be brought to a smile or to tears without difficulty. Her thinking is illogical and highly delusional. She is convinced that neighborhood children break into her flat and put rat poison in her food, detergent in the sugar, and furniture polish in the coffee. The patient is disoriented for time and situation, but not for place or person. Her judgment is poor, and insight is lacking. Speech is intelligible and organized, although her delivery is rather jerky. Skull x-rays and the EEG have confirmed the presence of a glioma tumor of moderate size in the frontal area of the brain.

The pituitary tumor is usually characterized by endocrine and visual disturbances, although tumors in the area of the third ventricle may result in personality disturbances. Apathy, sleepiness, difficulty in attention and concentration, confusion, and loss of memory are not uncommon. Some patients become irritable and hyperactive. There also may be delusions and hallucinations.

A metastatic tumor of the brain is one in which the primary site of the disorder is in another part of the body. In most cases, this type of brain tumor occurs in multiples, with as many as fifty or more *neoplasms*, or new growths, scattered through the brain tissue. Significantly, in about 50 percent of the patients, the original tumor tissue in the distant part of the body is clinically latent.

It is difficult to describe a typical clinical picture of a patient with metastatic tumors of the brain because of the widespread nature of the tumor tissue and the consequent variety of symptoms. As one might expect, the overt symptoms depend upon the location and extent of the tumor masses within the brain. If the neoplasms involve motor areas, there are motor symptoms. Similarly, tumors in the sensory areas result in sensory symptoms, and tumors in other areas result in disturbances of functions mediated by the particular brain area.

BRAIN INJURY

As in the case of brain tumors, the physical and psychological symptoms associated with injury to the head vary over a wide range. Since injuries are of differing degrees of severity and involve various parts of the head, the symptoms are of different kinds. They include the acute symptoms immediately following the injury and the chronic symptoms which last for months or years following it. The immediate symptom of any serious head injury is most likely to be a disturbance of consciousness. This disturbance may range from the patient being temporarily dazed to a complete loss of consciousness lasting from minutes to days. Head injury may be accompanied by nausea, vomiting, headache, and dizziness. In some cases there is confusion and disorientation, while in more serious injuries there may be delirium, incoherence, and hallucinations.

Damage to the brain may be the result of tiny hemorrhages over large areas of the brain, or it may involve the rupture of major blood vessels. There may also be an edema, or swelling, of the tissue itself, and in penetrating wounds of the brain there may be direct damage to brain centers. The three major types of cerebral trauma are: (1) cerebral concussion, (2) penetrating craniocerebral injuries, and (3) intracranial vascular accidents.

The cerebral concussion syndrome is one of the most common forms of brain trauma. Many accidents in ordinary everyday living involve nonpenetrating blows to the head. A fall from a ladder, tripping over the curb, striking one's head against an open cupboard door, slipping on the ice, and other common accidents in the home or at work frequently result in a glancing blow to the head. If the blow is severe enough, the underlying brain tissue is affected. The victim may "see stars," lose consciousness, become confused and disoriented, or show other symptoms.

Following the actue period, the patient may experience such symptoms as headache, dizziness, inability to concentrate, and deficient memory. The concussion victim may also show irritability, loss of energy, decreased tolerance for physical stress, and inability to sleep. The symptoms usually clear within a matter of days or weeks.

■ BRAIN CONCUSSION

Joe F. is a fifty-six-year-old man who was admitted to a hospital following a severe concussion. The patient, who had fallen down a flight of steps, became confused and disoriented. Moreover, his speech was incoherent and irrelevant. On his arrival at the hospital, the patient was hesitant and confused. His gait was unsteady, and motor coordination was impaired. The patient's facial expression was generally blank, although occasionally he would attempt to smile. He was only partially oriented, and his judgment was poor. There was just enough insight to make the patient feel despondent about his confusion. He apologized for giving incorrect answers and said that before the accident his mind had been clear.

One example of the concussion syndrome with which most people are familiar is the "punch drunk" boxer. In these cases, the constant battering of the head in the ring, even though the damage during any one fight may be minimal and often unnoticeable, eventually leads to psychological symptoms. The cumulative effect of subtraumatic blows to the head leads to the concussion and the symptoms accompanying it.

In craniocerebral injuries, the damage involves penetration of the skull and brain tissue. Any sudden and severe blow to the head by a sharp object can result in a penetrating wound. The type of symptom seen depends to a large degree upon the location of the wound and the extent of the brain damage. Accidental injuries of the penetrating type are usually associated in civilian life with automobile accidents, plane crashes, train wrecks, and industrial accidents. During war, such injuries are common among civilians and military personnel.

■ CRANIOCEREBRAL INJURY

Josselyn F. is a forty-year-old divorced woman admitted to a psychiatric hospital following an automobile accident in which she received severe head injuries. The patient was a university graduate who spoke French, Spanish, German, and Italian in addition to English. Following an emergency operation, the patient was in a coma for two weeks. When she regained consciousness, she spoke a word salad made up of several foreign languages. The patient was incontinent and soiled herself, and was unable to carry on a conversation. Her responses were slow, and there was spontaneous weeping, with silly and bizarre actions. She was placed in a private hospital for a period of four years, during which time there was slow improvement. Eventually she was sent to the psychiatric hospital, where she was observed to be cooperative and oriented for place, person, and time. However, her memory was impaired severely. The most prominent symptom was the fact that the patient felt that she had been killed four years ago at the time of the accident. She referred constantly to "the time I was killed." The patient showed wide swings in her mood, although she frequently seemed somewhat depressed. Most of the time she attempted to cover her depression by a forced joviality.

The surgical removal of brain tissue is also a form of penetrating injury, even though the operation is performed to correct some other condition such as an abscess or brain tumor. As a result of the improvement of neurosurgical techniques during World War I, there was a rapid expansion of brain surgery during the 1920s. By 1930, it was possible to remove large areas of the brain, including the entire frontal lobe. While the studies of soldiers injured in battle involved difficult problems of the tissue-shattering effect of high-speed projectiles, surgical lobectomy made possible a relatively controlled condition. A number of investigators were quick to take advantage of the opportunity to explore the functions of the

frontal region more extensively. It was found that large amputations of the frontal lobe frequently produce surprisingly little disturbance of function.

The complexity of the dynamics of cerebral trauma is illustrated in a case in which an injury in the frontal region and the consequent formation of scar tissue resulted in serious behavior abnormalities. Following the removal of the frontal lobes, the symptoms disappeared (Hebb and Penfield, 1940). The case shows that bilateral removal of the anterior third of the frontal lobes may have no obvious effect on human intelligence or personality. The absence of gross deterioration, however, does not rule out the possibility of impairment in such areas as learning in social situations, initiative, and the ability to plan and organize.

In 1938, an operation was developed for the removal of the right cerebral hemisphere (Dandy, 1938). In practice, the operation does not involve a complete removal of the right hemisphere since certain key structures near the mid-line of the brain must remain intact if the patient is to remain alive. In such cases, the neurological findings are similar in all patients. There is a paralysis of the left side of the body, but the patient is able to limp about with a cane. Similarly, the left angle of his mouth may be slightly paralyzed, and he cannot see objects over his left shoulder. Occasionally these patients complain of crawling sensations on the left side of the body, and they may experience pain on the left side. However, if the patient is not subjected to painful stimuli, he is not particularly uncomfortable.

The personality effects of the removal of the right hemisphere of the brain are more varied from patient to patient than are the physical results of the operation. Many patients of this type show little or no deterioration on simple intelligence tests. Similarly, personality often remains unaltered. On the other hand, there have been observations in which marked personality changes follow the operation. Some subjects become facetious, irresponsible, and petulant and are given to violent emotional outbursts. Other patients show a tendency to panic and to peevishness.

Observations have also been made on a patient following left temporal lobectomy (Fox and German, 1935). After removal of the left temporal lobe in a right-handed man, the analysis of his speech functions revealed a deficient auditory receptive mechanism and impaired retention of auditory speech memories. The visual mechanism suffered little impairment.

A birth injury is also a craniocerebral trauma, although here the damage ordinarily does not involve a penetration of the skull and brain. During an instrumental delivery or a particularly difficult natural birth, the head of the infant may be compressed or otherwise distorted, resulting in some degree of damage to the brain tissue. However, only the most severe injuries result in neurological or psychological symptoms because of the semifluid consistency of the infant brain and the abundant supply of undifferentiated nerve cells.

Another type of cerebral trauma often accompanied by personality disorganization is the cerebral vascular accident in which various types of damage to the brain tissue results from the narrowing, blocking, or bursting of a blood vessel. When a blood vessel narrows, the flow of blood is diminished, and the brain area supplied by that blood vessel does not receive its proper nourishment. Similarly, the removal of waste material is hampered, and the entire cellular process is disturbed. When a vessel is blocked entirely, the cells supplied by the blood vessel may be destroyed completely.

In acute cerebral thrombosis (stroke), the blood vessel ruptures and the brain area is flooded by the hemorrhaging blood. If the bleeding continues, the patient dies. But in a great many cases, the bleeding is self-limiting or is stopped by medical treatment, and the patient recovers. The damage from such a vascular accident may nevertheless result in a wide range of neurological and psychological symptoms.

The patient may show such neurological signs as paralysis of the facial muscles, the arm, and the leg on the side of the body opposite the site of vascular accident. As a result of the facial paralysis, which also involves the tongue and throat, the patient has difficulty in speaking, eating, and swallowing. Depending upon the extent of the brain damage, he may have difficulty in walking or using his hand and arm.

Because of the lengthening age span and the greater number of older men and women in the population, strokes are the third leading cause of death in the United States, with the incidence increasing sharply with age. Between age 55 and 64 the incidence is 4 per 1,000 population. It rises to 9.4 per 1,000 between ages 65 and 74, to 21 per 1,000 between 78 and 84, and it reaches 50 per 1,000 over age 85 (National Institute of Neurological Diseases and Stroke, 1970).

■ CEREBROVASCULAR ACCIDENT

Edward J. is a sixty-one-year-old divorced man who was admitted to a psychiatric hospital after the third of a series of three "strokes," each approximately one year apart. Before his admission to the hospital the patient several times undressed completely and walked around the house as if there was nothing unusual about his behavior. He became confused in other ways, and was not sure whether it was day or night, morning or afternoon. He talked in a rambling and incoherent manner, suspected that neighbors and relatives were spying on him, and burned his food to a crisp by turning the gas up very high and then forgetting it completely. He was sent to the hospital following an incident in which his sister found him sweeping the front porch in the nude.

When seen at the hospital the patient was quite jovial, and rather sociable in a confused way. His speech was coherent, but often irrelevant. He fidgeted a good deal during the interview and once or twice arose from his chair and roamed around. He attempted to be cooperative, but he would forget instructions given to him. Edward spoke in a spontaneous way but was extremely distractible. He showed a flight of ideas, was unable to remain on one subject and was disoriented for time and place. When asked where he was, he replied, "This is a chemical plant. They do a lot of analyzing here." He knew his name, but not his age. When asked the date, he replied, "It's the sixteenth or seventeenth of October, 1915. At least it was last week." His judgment was impaired, and insight completely lacking.*

The neurological symptoms of the stroke depend upon the area of the brain affected. The damage is generally localized, and the symptoms are similar to those seen in cases of brain tumor. The difference in the clinical picture between the

---

*Case 3 of audiotape 11, "Brain Disorders: Miscellaneous Reactions," in *Case Interviews to Accompany The Disorganized Personality*.

stroke victim and the patient with a tumor is that in the former condition, the symptoms appear abruptly, may improve considerably, and may then appear again with the occurrence of a further stroke. The symptoms seen in the tumor case are likely to be of a more gradual development. When the initial stroke has not been recognized, the subsequent symptoms are sometimes difficult to diagnose.

In massive strokes, the abruptness and severity of the symptoms leave little doubt about their cause. However, many strokes are relatively minor and occur in areas of the brain which do not produce neurological symptoms. In such cases, the only changes noticed are those of a psychological nature. In the later years of life, some individuals experience a degree of personality disorganization as a result of the cumulative effects of small strokes which go unrecognized.

BRAIN DISORDERS OF LATER LIFE

The organic changes of old age are among the most important sources of personality breakdown, even though many people who live to an advanced age manage to keep their emotional balance, their intellectual integrity, and their physical vigor. George Bernard Shaw was intellectually alert until he died at age ninety-four. Bernarr MacFadden, a well-known magazine publisher, made a parachute jump from an airplane into the Hudson River on his eighty-third birthday. Most people are not so fortunate. They succumb to the ravages of psychological conflict and physical deterioration. The realization that life is soon to end, combined with the natural breakdown of the body, may cause varying degrees of personality disorganization.

An increasingly large number of men and women live to a relatively advanced age. In 1900, there were approximately 3 million men and women in this country over sixty-five years of age. By 1950, the number had risen to 10 million. In 1960 it had exceeded 16 million, by 1970 it was more than 20 million, and by the year 2000 there will be about 65 million men and women over age sixty-five (U.S. Bureau of the Census, 1970). This increase in the old-age population has presented, and will continue to present for many years, a mental health problem of very considerable proportions. These disorders account for 15 percent of the first admissions to public mental hospitals in the United States (NIMH, 1969).

The brain syndromes of later life include the *presenile* disorders, the *senile* disorders, and *cerebral arteriosclerosis*. The presenile disorders are those which resemble the disorders of later life but which in fact appear prematurely, while the senile disorders are the typical deteriorative disorders of old age. Cerebral arteriosclerosis is a brain syndrome of later life marked by a hardening of the arteries of the brain.

PRESENILE DISORDERS

The term *presenile* refers to the age period between forty-five and sixty. The two most common presenile disorders are (1) Alzheimer's disease and (2) Pick's disease. In addition, there are several minor presenile disorders.

The first case of Alzheimer's disease was described in 1906 (Alzheimer, 1907). The case was that of a woman who had died at fifty-one years of age following a rapidly progressing dementia. Her brain showed a conspicuous tissue reaction including the development of tangled threadlike structures in many cortical ganglion cells. The physical changes bore a striking similarity to the changes found in the brains of patients of advanced age. The clinical picture of Alzheimer's disease is marked by psychological, neurological, and pathological findings. In the first stages of the disorder, the outstanding symptom is an increasing intellectual deterioration marked by impairment in reasoning, defective perception and comprehension, and disturbance of coordination. Loss of memory for recent events is another early symptom. Speech functions may be involved, with the patient forgetting words, having difficulty in pronunciation, and being unable to comprehend the meaning of what is said to him.

In the second stage of the disease there is a general intellectual impairment with an outstanding memory difficulty. At this time apprehension, confusion, confabulation, and vague delusions begin to be noticed. Sometimes compulsive crying and laughing are seen along with restlessness, aimless wandering, and a tendency to repeat the same acts. As the disorder progresses, behavior becomes less and less purposeful. During this stage of the disease, speech disturbances are prominent. The patient has difficulty articulating his words, speech is slurred, sentences are incomplete, and names are mixed up. Understanding of the speech of others also is disturbed.

In the third stage of Alzheimer's disease, the patients are reduced to a state of severe dementia and a more or less vegetative existence. Speech is limited, and contractures of the extremities are frequent. The course of the disease is progressive, with death from two to ten years after the onset of symptoms. The average duration of the disease is about four years.

While Alzheimer's disease is the most common of the presenile dementias, it is a relatively rare disorder. However, post-mortem examinations performed in psychiatric hospitals suggest that the disorder is more frequent than is generally supposed, with the condition being mistaken for something else at the time of diagnosis. The incidence among women is somewhat greater than among men, and there is some suggestion of a familial trend.

Originally it was thought that Alzheimer's disease was merely a form of precocious senility, but there is evidence today that the disease sometimes occurs very early in life. The possibility of a juvenile form of the disorder has been suggested. While there is a question about the exact nature of these early cases of Alzheimer's disease, the fact that they do occur from time to time suggests the presence of factors other than mere aging. Nevertheless, the average age of onset in the presenile psychosis of the Alzheimer type is about fifty-six years. Since the majority of these cases do occur during the presenile period, aging is probably an important, if not necessary, factor. There is also reason to believe that constitutional predisposition, based on the genetic makeup, is involved in determining the premature pathologic aging of the brain.

■ ALZHEIMER'S DISEASE

Betty L. is a fifty-nine-year-old married woman who was admitted to a psychiatric hospital after becoming so seriously confused that she could not remain at home unattended. The first symptoms were noticed about five years earlier, when the patient was fifty-four. At that time she became forgetful and seemed to be unable to coordinate her thinking and her actions. Gradually the symptoms became worse. She showed an increasing lack of concern for personal hygiene, her memory loss became more severe, and at times she was totally disoriented. Before her illness, the patient was an extremely congenial person who had a large number of friends. She enjoyed people and participated actively in the P.T.A. and other organizations.

At the time of the examination, the patient was found to be depressed, confused, and somewhat agitated. She could not remember where she lived, and she did not know where she was at the time. She said she was sure she had a husband, but did not know where he was. At frequent intervals she commented that she could not talk because she was "so nervous." At one point she exclaimed, "I love my daddy," and then she began to cry. A diagnosis was made of chronic brain syndrome associated with presenile brain disease. Following the death of the patient, an autopsy showed brain changes characteristic of Alzheimer's disease.*

A second major presenile disorder is Pick's disease, a condition marked by progressive dementia, localized cortical signs, and atrophy, or wasting away, of the frontal and temporal lobes of the brain. The condition was first described in 1892 (Pick, 1892). Since that time, the disease has evolved as a distinct clinical and pathological entity. It is a rare condition and is seen much less frequently than Alzheimer's disease. Approximately twice as many women as men suffer from this condition.

The location of the atrophied areas varies from patient to patient, but the most frequent type is that in which the atrophy is of the bilateral frontal lobes. Next in frequency is the bilateral temporal type. The atrophied areas appear shrunken and rough-surfaced and may be of a brownish-yellow color. The wasting process sometimes spreads from the frontal and temporal lobes to involve the parietal lobe, the occipital lobe, and the basal ganglia. The result is a rich variety of neurological and psychological symptoms.

The clinical picture of Pick's disease is characterized by a slowly progressive dementia of the organic type, with symptoms of localized cortical

*Case 1 of audiotape 9, "Brain Disorders: Reactions of Old Age," in *Case Interviews to Accompany The Disorganized Personality*.

lesions. In the early stages of the disorder, there is gradual intellectual impairment, with the patient showing difficulty in thinking and concentration. The most striking symptom is the loss of the abstract attitude, with the concrete attitude remaining intact. Patients are usually able to deal reasonably well with the concrete aspects of reality but are likely to have difficulty in making abstractions, in generalizing, and in synthesizing Neurological disturbances are frequently present during the early stages of the disease. Moreover, there is a narrowing and blunting of the emotional reaction and a disturbance of moral and social values.

The second stage of Pick's disease is marked by increasing intellectual deterioration. In some cases there is refusal to talk, intellectual inertia, loss of initiative and spontaneity, and general psychomotor retardation. In other cases, restlessness, talkativeness, and aimless activity are the outstanding symptoms. It is remarkable that memory may not be much impaired, and the patient usually does not show the delusions, hallucinations, or confabulations seen so frequently in other organic dementias. During this stage, the atrophy of the brain can ordinarily be demonstrated by means of x-ray and other brain-mapping techniques.

In the final stage of Pick's disease the patient sinks into a vegetative existence in which speech may be reduced to the automatic repetition of simple words and paralyses and contractures of the arms and legs occur. Convulsive seizures are also frequent at this time. The disorder lasts from two to fifteen years and is invariably fatal. There is no known treatment for Pick's disease (Robertson et al., 1958).

■ **PICK'S DISEASE**

Margaret J., a sixty-year-old widow and mother of three children, was a completely normal and well-balanced person during her early life and adult years. She graduated from a large state university, was happily married, and engaged in an active social life. Among her three children, one became a professor. The family enjoyed a relatively high socioeconomic status, and the patient and her husband had many friends.

The first symptoms were noticed following the husband's death, when the patient was fifty-one. At that time, she became forgetful, irritable, and confused. There was also occasional difficulty in speaking. These symptoms gradually became more severe, and an x-ray of the skull was made when the patient was fifty-four. The skull film showed atrophy of the prefrontal lobes. As a result of progressive deterioration, it became necessary to hospitalize the patient at age sixty. She was sometimes incontinent and careless about her toilet habits, at times she exhibited herself, and occasionally she attacked other patients.

At the time of the psychiatric examination, the patient was pleasant and friendly, but she could not be examined because of difficulty in communication due to impairment of the speech centers in the brain. She made sounds with the rhythm and intonation of normal speech, yet the material was largely unintelligible on first hearing it. However, when recorded on tape, and played back several times, the thought content became increasingly clear. Following the death of the patient four months after her admission to the hospital, an autopsy revealed brain changes characteristic of Pick's disease.*

There are two major theories of the etiology of Pick's disease. One is based on Pick's original belief that the condition is a variety of senile dementia and is a slowly evolving progressive atrophic process. The other view is that the disorder is due to a specific hereditary degenerative process that is essentially independent of old age (Bagh, 1946). The evidence for the second point of view is that the condition follows a family pattern, that the pathology of the disorder is relatively independent of the ordinary degenerative changes of the senile brain, and that the disease is sometimes found long before the presenile period.

SENILE BRAIN DISEASE

The senile state is a gradually progressive disorder with increasing mental and physical deterioration. The rate of the deterioration varies considerably from patient to patient, with many symptoms of a transitory kind. Restlessness, agitation,

---

*Case 2 of audiotape 9, "Brain Disorders: Reactions of Old Age," in *Case Interviews to Accompany The Disorganized Personality.*

confusion, and similar symptoms may be seen at one time but later may be absent, only to appear once again. Generally, the progress is downward, and unless the psychosis is interrupted by an intercurrent physical disease, patients become more and more deteriorated, helpless, incontinent, and bedridden. Finally, the senile psychotic leads a completely vegetative existence with death occurring from pneumonia, infection from decubital ulcers ("bedsores"), or other terminal diseases.

The line between normal senility and senile brain disorder is a completely arbitrary one and often depends upon the facilities available for caring for the aging patient. The wards of mental hospitals contain many elderly patients who are feeble and confused, but who are not psychotic in the strict sense of the term. If these patients had a place to live and someone to look after them, there would be no reason for them to be in a psychiatric hospital.

The disorder is seen in women about twice as often as in men, with the age of onset ranging from the sixties to the nineties. The onset of the disorder is usually gradual, with an exaggeration of previous personality traits combined with the attitudes characteristic of aging individuals. There is a gradual impairment of efficiency, a general slowing down of psychomotor functions, and an increase in errors of judgment combined with a deterioration of personal habits. The early symptoms come on so gradually that the families of these patients are frequently unaware of the seriousness of the changes.

■ SENILE BRAIN DISEASE

Alice A. is a seventy-eight-year-old widow who was admitted to a psychiatric hospital from a home for the elderly where she had become unmanageable. She was very confused, did not recognize her relatives, and thought her son was her father. Frequently she was excited and noisy and used profane language. At the hospital she had to be led to the examining room, and while she was somewhat agitated, she tried to be cooperative. In spite of her agitation, her facial expression changed little during the interview. Once a question was put to her, she continued to talk but was seldom able to answer intelligently. She rambled

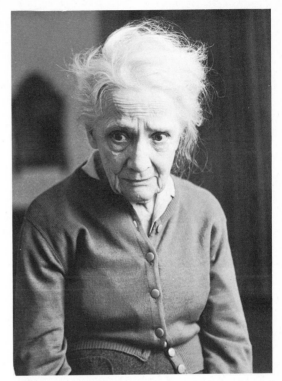

Figure 11.4 *The first signs of senility are loss of memory and confusion. (Courtesy of Knoll Pharmaceutical Co.)*

on and on, frequently mentioning her "daddy." She said her daddy had been at the hospital only a short time before, that he had talked to her, and that he would return soon to take her home. From time to time she interjected a word or phrase in French. She knew her name but was otherwise completely disoriented. Her memory for both remote and recent events was defective, and rational conversation was impossible. There was a total lack of insight.*

At the level of gross anatomy, the brains of senile patients show shrinkage of the cerebral convolutions and the white matter to one degree or another. However, the changes observed in the brains of senile psychotics are sometimes no more pronounced than those seen in the brains of nonpsychotic individuals of the same age.

The microscopic changes in the cerebral cortex are of considerable variety and of a nonspecific

*Case 3 of audiotape 9, "Brain Disorders: Reactions of Old Age," in *Case Interviews to Accompany The Disorganized Personality*.

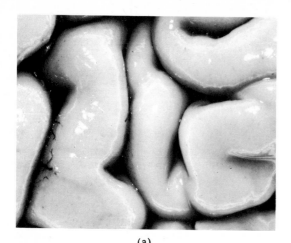

(a)   (b)

Figure 11.5 *Brain atrophy and aging. (a) Convolutions of the frontal lobe of the normal brain of a young adult. (b) Shrunken and atrophied convolutions of the same brain area in an aging patient. (Courtesy of Dr. J. A. N. Corsellis, London.)*

nature. Shrinkage and atrophy of the neurons are frequent, and while there may be a dropping-out of many individual nerve cells, the overall cortical architecture is not affected. A characteristic lesion of the senile brain is the *senile plaque.* These plaques, which are found between the nerve cells and which vary in size and number, consist of masses of granular material, often with a pale center surrounded by a ring of threadlike material. It is not clear how these plaques are developed, and they are found only in the central nervous system of the human species.

One of the major problems in understanding senile psychoses is that the physical changes which are observed in the brains of psychotic patients are by no means consistent. The changes in themselves are often not pronounced enough to account for the presence of the disease. Similar changes are found in the brains of many individuals of advanced age. In some cases, the brains of normal men and women show very marked changes, and yet there are no psychotic symptoms. This fact suggests the possibility of a psychological component in the senile psychosis.

The causes of the senile psychoses have not been fully determined. However, several factors play a role in the causation. Among these critical factors are (1) heredity and constitution, (2) physical changes within the organism, and (3) psychological stress and conflict.

Genetic factors play an important role in the

brain syndromes of later life. Longevity itself is dependent in part upon one's hereditary make-up. It is a common observation that the length of one's life, barring injury, infection, and similar acute conditions, depends upon genetic influence. It is true also that the point at which psychological symptoms begin to express themselves during the later years is dependent to some extent upon heredity. There are many families in which the mental break occurs at about the same time in members of the family over a period of several generations. It is not that the mental disorder of old age is in itself inherited. Rather, the physical conditions which allow the organism to withstand stress are similar due to a similarity in genetic makeup.

While the cellular changes that occur during aging are of major importance in the development of senile disorders, psychological and social factors cannot be ignored. Even under the most ideal psychological and social conditions, many aging men and women develop the symptoms of senility and arteriosclerosis. However, a very large group of people show degenerative signs of aging long before it would appear to be indicated from a physiological point of view. When aging takes place in an adverse social and psychological climate, personality disorganization is precipitated more quickly.

Just as there are objective and predictable physiological changes which occur with increased age, there are also psychological changes which take place. While the functions measured by standard intelligence tests appear to decline as a person grows older, the decline is selective in that some functions fall off more rapidly than others. This apparent decline in intelligence must be interpreted with extreme caution. While it is probably true that certain functions making up the trait of intelligence are increasingly less efficient as one grows older, other factors must be considered. The motivation during psychological testing is certainly not the same for older people as it is for those who are younger. The declining motivation unquestionably plays a role in the apparent loss of intellectual capacity.

Another important variable is related to sensorimotor functions. Men and women in their sixties write much more slowly than subjects thirty years younger. Obviously, any test depending upon writing speed is likely to handicap older people. The factor of speed in other areas is also important. The tempo of living is slower during the later years, and this slowing down of activity is reflected in the test situation.

Finally, the problem of educational level must be taken into account. Most tests of intelligence are heavily weighted with items that depend upon knowledge rather than ability. Since men and women of advanced years are likely to have had less formal education than younger people, the lower scores on intelligence tests might very well reflect a difference in education, rather than a difference in basic ability.

In addition to genetic and psychological influences in the senile psychoses, the cultural milieu in which aging takes place must be considered. It is probable that aging occurs more rapidly in certain environmental settings. An elderly person who is emotionally rejected, financially insecure, and generally unaccepted will probably age more rapidly than one who is emotionally and financially secure. For this reason, the attitude of relatives, the availability of friends, the opportunity for socialization, and similar factors are important in resisting the stresses of later life.

At the community and national level, the general attitude of the group toward the aging individ-

Figure 11.6 *An enlargement of a photomicrograph showing senile plaques present (a) to a slight degree and (b) to a severe degree. (Courtesy of Dr. J. A. N. Corsellis, London.)*

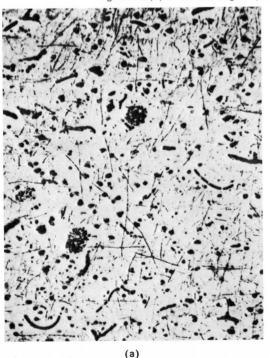

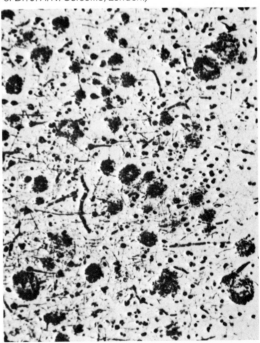

(a)   (b)

ual is of significance. There are some cultures in which the elderly members of the group are held in the very highest esteem. In other cultures, the aged are regarded as unproductive members of the group who must be tolerated until their death. The attitude of the group—the family, the local community, or the larger cultural unit— plays a critical role in determining the onset of senility.

CEREBRAL ARTERIOSCLEROSIS

The essential feature of mental disorder associated with cerebral artiosclerosis, or hardening of the arteries of the brain, is that the psychological changes are dependent upon the cerebral blood vessels. The condition is seen most frequently among the more advanced age groups, but from time to time it is seen during middle age. Arteriosclerosis is found in about 25 percent of people between 40 and 49 years of age, 50 percent of

those between 50 and 59, 75 percent of those between 60 and 69, and 90 percent of those over 70. A small percentage (about 10 percent) attain old age without developing arteriosclerosis, and a smaller percentage (about 3.5 percent) have moderate arteriosclerosis as early as age 20 to 29. Men are affected more frequently than women, the ratio being approximately 3 to 1. The age of onset ranges from the middle forties to the eighties, with the average in the mid-sixties.

The physical basis of arteriosclerosis is the thickening of the walls of the arteries, which leads to difficulty in the diffusion of foodstuffs and oxygen and a resulting destruction of surrounding brain tissue. Except for the external layer of the artery, which may be served by an independent blood supply, the rest of the artery gets its nourishment directly from the blood flowing through it. This nourishment includes minerals, vitamins, proteins, carbohydrates, and fats dissolved or suspended in the blood serum. Fatty deposits in the walls of the arteries lead to a hardening of the

Figure 11.7 *Cerebral vascular changes associated with aging. (a) Blood vessels at the base of the normal brain of a young adult. (b) The same blood vessels—enlarged, thickened, and damaged— in an elderly patient. (Courtesy of Dr. J. A. N. Corsellis, London.)*

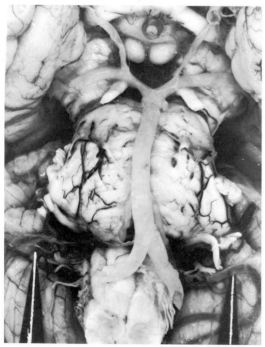

(a)

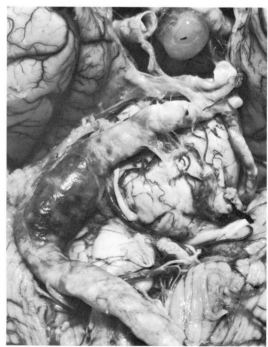

(b)

blood vessels and a loss of resiliency. The result is an interference with the exchange of essential food substances and waste products between the bloodstream and the cells of the brain.

The course of arteriosclerotic psychosis varies from patient to patient. In some cases there is confusion and clouding of consciousness associated with cerebral vascular accidents, which lead to a fatal outcome in a short period. In other cases, there is chronic illness of many years duration. The average duration of this disease in a typical psychiatric hospital is from three to four years. The outcome is usually death.

The first symptoms of psychosis with cerebral arteriosclerosis are likely to be headache, dizziness, vague physical complaints, and more or less prolonged periods of physical and mental letdown. The actual onset of the disorder may be sudden or gradual, with more than 50 percent of the cases showing an acute onset marked by a sudden attack of confusion. There may be clouding of consciousness, loss of contact with surroundings, incoherence, and restlessness.

In cases where the onset is gradual, the symptoms are very similar to those of senile psychosis. There is a gradual intellectual decline, with loss of efficiency and impairment of memory. Irritability, quarrelsome behavior, jealousy, and a general lowering of moral and ethical standards are common. Ideas of mistreatment and persecution are seen frequently, and where there is extensive organic involvement, the patient may show explosive outbursts of weeping or laughter.

While neurological changes are not usually observed in the early stages of arteriosclerotic psychoses, such changes generally put in an appearance as the disorder progresses. Irregular tremors, unsteady gait, paralysis, aphasic disturbances, and convulsive seizures are not uncommon.

There has been a marked rise in admission rates for cerebral arteriosclerosis in recent years.

While part of the increase can be explained by the growing willingness of relatives to hospitalize older people for mental disorder, there also has been an actual increase in the incidence of arteriosclerosis.

Observations of animals confined in zoos have thrown interesting light on the increase in arteriosclerosis. Early in this century, arteriosclerosis occurred in a very small proportion of the animals. More recently, there has been a sharp increase in the disorder among younger animals, particularly those in the more crowded family groups and colonies where increasing social pressure has been the rule. The director of the Penrose Research Laboratory of the Zoological Society of Philadelphia believes that the social pressure is a stress situation which leads to an imbalance in adrenal secretions (Ratcliffe and Cronin, 1958). This endocrine imbalance may result in the earlier and more rapid laying down of fatty deposits in the blood vessels. It is possible that social stress among predisposed humans may result in similar damage to blood vessels.[5]

■ CEREBRAL ARTERIOSCLEROSIS

Elizabeth R. was admitted to a hospital at age seventy-three. The present attack began about five years before her admission, when the patient developed the idea that she was being hypnotized by her relatives. She heard voices, with members of her family cursing her and telling her that she was no good. Other voices hinted that someone wanted to kill her. The patient's husband is blind, and just before her admission to the hospital she tried to pour scalding water over him. She thought he hypnotized her and wanted to kill her. For five months, the patient refused to sit at the same table with her husband. She argued constantly with her family and with neighbors, cursing anyone who came near her. She was afraid that she would be killed and thought that she must kill other people for her protection. She boiled water all day long to break the "spell," and kept the lights on at all times in different places in the house to scare away the evil

---

[5]The physical, psychological, and social problems of aging are discussed in *Human Aging and Behavior* (Academic Press, 1968), edited by G. A. Talland; F. Post's *Persistent Persecutory States of the Elderly* (Pergamon Press, 1966); *Problems of the Aged* (Thomas, 1965), edited by C. B. Vedder and A. S. Lefkowitz; *Behavior, Aging, and the Nervous System* (Thomas, 1965), edited by A. T. Welford and J. E. Birren; J. A. N. Corsellis' *Mental Illness and the Aging Brain* (Oxford University Press, 1962); *Psychopathology of Aging* (Grune & Stratton, 1961), edited by P. H. Hoch and Joseph Zubin; and W. M. Johnson's *The Older Patient* (Hoeber, 1960).

spirits. She believed that when the train whistled near her home, it ordered her to do different things. She grew increasingly destructive and dangerous toward her blind husband, who attempted to quiet her by hitting her with his cane. At the hospital, the patient said: "The electric light catches me every time I walk from room to room. My husband makes money behind my back. He hypnotizes me. My grandfather sent you doctors to see me."

SUMMARY

1. Personality disturbances due to a more or less clear-cut organic cause are called brain disorders, or brain syndromes. The major brain syndromes are (1) the intoxications, (2) the convulsive disorders (epilepsy), (3) disorders due to infection, (4) brain tumors, (5) brain injuries, and (6) brain disorders of old age.

2. The toxic disorders include alcoholism, drug reactions, and gas and metal poisoning. The brain syndromes associated with alcoholism are *pathological intoxication, delirium tremens, alcoholic hallucinosis, alcoholic deterioration,* and *Korsakoff's syndrome.* The first two of these conditions are acute, the third may be either acute or chronic, and the fourth and fifth are chronic. Brain disorders due to drug addiction are seen much less frequently than those due to alcoholism. The most important syndromes due to drugs are *barbital, bromide,* and *amphetamine* intoxication and *morphinism.* Personality disturbances are also seen occasionally as a result of intoxications growing out of the industrial use of certain gases and metals.

3. The convulsive disorders are classified as *idiopathic* and *symptomatic.* The idiopathic conditions are those in which there is no apparent structural change to account for the disturbance. Symptomatic disorders are related to some underlying pathological condition of the organism. The brain syndromes associated with convulsive disorders take the form of *grand mal* and *petit mal* seizures, *psychomotor* or *temporal-lobe* attacks, and *Jacksonian* seizures. *Grand mal* is characterized by violent convulsions, while *petit mal* involves a transitory loss of consciousness which may last only a few seconds. Temporal-lobe seizures show a variety of psychological symptoms, but there is no loss of consciousness. The Jacksonian seizure is one in which the convulsion is limited to an arm, a leg, or part of the face. Both psychological and organic factors are involved in the production of the convulsive disorders.

4. Infectious disease may also result in psychological disturbance, particularly during the acute phases of the illness. The psychological symptoms are often due to the secondary effects of high fever, but in brain syphilis, encephalitis, brain abscess, and similar conditions, the microorganism of the infection makes a direct attack on the tissue of the nervous system. In the case of brain tumors, the effect on behavior and personality may take place directly through damage to brain centers or indirectly through disturbances in blood circulation or the increased intracranial pressure of the cerebrospinal fluid. The nature of the psychological symptoms depends upon the location, size, and rate of development of the tumor.

5. Personality disturbances due to injury to the brain also vary in accordance with the location and extent of the injury. The major types of brain injury are *cerebral concussion, craniocerebral injuries,* and *intracranial vascular accidents.* The concussion is a relatively temporary disturbance due to nonpenetrating blows to the head, with the symptoms usually clearing in a matter of hours, days, or weeks. In craniocerebral injuries, the damage involves penetration of the skull and brain tissue. When psycho-

logical symptoms occur, they are likely to be more severe and long-lasting. The intracranial vascular accident, or stroke, is due to brain damage resulting from the narrowing, blocking, or bursting of a blood vessel. The blood flow is lessened, and the brain area supplied by the blood vessel does not receive its proper nourishment. Brain cells may be destroyed completely, or their normal functioning may be hampered. Depending upon the brain areas affected by the vascular accident, the psychological and neurological symptoms may be mild and temporary or severe and long-lasting.

6. The brain disorders of old age have become increasingly important as a result of the larger number of elderly men and women in the population. The brain syndromes of later life include the *presenile* and *senile* disorders and *cerebral arteriosclerosis*. The presenile disorders are conditions which appear at an age before the changes associated with old age are ordinarily expected. Senile brain disease is a progressive disorder in which there is a gradually increasing mental and physical deterioration. In cerebral arteriosclerosis, or hardening of the arteries of the brain, the involvement of the cerebral blood vessels interferes with the exchange of essential substances between the bloodstream and the brain tissue.

12 MENTAL RETARDATION

The problem of mental retardation is one which, until the middle of the present century, was relatively neglected by specialists in the field of mental health. The condition has been recognized over the centuries, but for various reasons it was not considered of much importance. Fortunately, a new and vigorous interest in mental retardation developed following World War II. The somewhat hopeless attitude which pervaded the thinking of all but a few physicians, psychologists, social workers, and educators gave way to a refreshing optimism. The possibility of preventing many cases of mental retardation and of improving the lot of many more became well established.

Mental retardation in itself is not a personality problem and at first might appear out of place as a topic in a book dealing with abnormal psychology. Certainly there is no implication that mental retardation and personality disturbance are synonymous or necessarily related. There are, however, many parallels, and in some areas there is an important overlap. This overlap is seen most clearly in the relationship between mental retardation and the brain disorders. Also, the lack of intellectual ability frequently results in behavior difficulties which bring the patient into conflict with his family and the community.

The traditional attitude toward mental retardation is expressed in a report by the Children's Bureau of the U.S. Department of Health, Education, and Welfare:

> Before 1940, mental retardation was not of great concern to this nation. Most of the severely damaged infants did not survive, and the general feeling about those who did was that little or nothing could be done for them. A common way of handling the problem was to hide it. Most states were fairly complacent about what they did for this group: chiefly, special classes for school-aged children in a few urban areas, and seventy-five state operated institutions for residential care of those who could not function in the community. (Children's Bureau, 1961)

Among the factors responsible for the increased interest in the mentally retarded following World War II were the emergence of parent organizations in the community, a series of important findings about the biochemistry of certain forms of mental retardation, and the willingness on the part of the federal government to make funds available for research, demonstration programs in education and training, and new medical and psychological treatment techniques. The result of these several influences was a new and theretofore unknown vigor in connection with the plight and problems of the mentally retarded.

Mental retardation today afflicts the lives of an estimated 6 million persons in the United States. Its impact is directly felt by the some 20 million family members who share the burden and problems of care of the retarded, whose inadequate intellectual development impairs their ability to learn and to adapt to the demands of society.

The causes of mental retardation are multiple; they involve both physical and environmental factors operating singly or in subtle interactions. Resolution of this complex problem requires the scientific talent from many disciplines—biological, behavioral, and social—in a concerted effort involving basic and applied research over an age span from conception through maturity. The program of research and research training supported by the National Institute of Mental Health

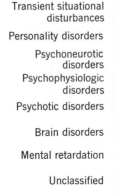

Figure 12.1 *The incidence of mental retardation as a percentage of total first admissions to public mental hospitals in the United States. (From data furnished by the National Institute of Mental Health, 1970.)*

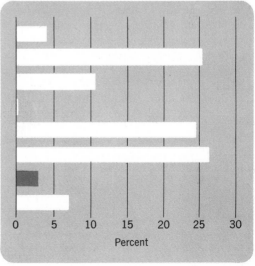

Transient situational disturbances
Personality disorders
Psychoneurotic disorders
Psychophysiologic disorders
Psychotic disorders
Brain disorders
Mental retardation
Unclassified

0   5   10   15   20   25   30
Percent

is an important part of our nation's effort to combat the problem of mental retardation, which ranks as a major health, social, and economic problem.[1]

HISTORICAL BACKGROUND

The history of mental retardation parallels the history of man. Just as some members of early civilizations were victims of mental disturbances, others were mentally retarded. References to such individuals are found in the earliest medical writings, and some of the more easily identified clinical types of mental retardation were depicted in the drawings and other art forms of ancient civilizations. The mentally retarded were regarded variously as persons to be feared, scorned, mistreated, punished, exploited, made fun of, cared for, worshipped, and revered. Attitudes changed with the times, improved with increasing medical knowledge, and reflected community feelings and policies.

In general, the lot of the mentally retarded was somewhat better than that of the mentally disturbed. The fool and the simpleton frequently were objects of amusement and were more likely to arouse pity and compassion than fear or revulsion. As a result, with the possible exception of the grotesque clinical types of mental retardation, the history of the mentally retarded was more tranquil than that of the mentally disturbed.

Those who were clearly fools or simpletons were allowed to wander unmolested through the countryside. Many had the freedom of the castles, and such individuals were often regarded as the "children of God." At one time, a house into which a mentally retarded person was born was considered blessed. There was a common belief that such individuals walked on earth but conversed in heaven.

One of the first serious studies of mental retardation was undertaken in France late in the 1700s when the case of Victor, the "Wild Boy of Aveyron," was investigated (Itard, 1932). This defective boy of eleven or twelve years of age had been living in the woods without contact with other people for a number of years. He had been observed on several occasions, completely naked, seeking berries and roots. He was captured in 1799 by three hunters when he climbed into a tree in an attempt to escape from them. The boy was taken to Paris where he was considered to be an incurable idiot. The attending physician insisted that the boy could be cured, believing the condition due to the boy's lack of contact with people.

Victor was studied over a period of five years, but he did not learn more than a few words. His emotional behavior was crude, and his reaction to the environment was largely in terms of his biological needs. A report to the French Minister of the Interior contained the following:

> . . . One cannot help concluding: First, that by reason of the almost complete apathy of the organs of hearing and speech, the education of this young man is still incomplete and must always remain so; secondly, that by reason of their long inaction the intellectual faculties are developing slowly and painfully, and that this development, which in children growing up in civilized surroundings is the natural fruit of time and circumstances, is here the slow and laborious result of a very active education in which the most powerful methods are used to obtain most insignificant results; thirdly, that the emotional faculties, equally slow in emerging from their long torpor, are subordinated to an utter selfishness and that his puberty, which was very strongly marked and which usually sets up a great emotional expansion, seems only to prove that if there exists in human beings a relation between the needs of the senses and the affections of the heart, this sympathetic agreement is, like the majority of great and generous emotions, the happy fruit of education (Itard, 1824).

In spite of the pessimism expressed in the report, Victor did make progress. When compared with normal adolescents, the boy seemed at a considerable disadvantage. However, compared with his original behavior when captured in the woods, his behavior five years later showed

---

[1]*Mental Retardation Abstracts:* This quarterly publication scans approximately 2,000 technical magazines and professional journals and presents brief abstracts of all articles dealing with any aspect of mental retardation. It is available from the Superintendent of Documents, U.S. Government Printing Office, Washington, D.C. 20402.

marked improvement. Victor's case indicated that while it is too much to expect a mentally retarded child to develop normal intelligence through training, he can nevertheless be made to show striking improvement in his behavior.

In England, the first asylum for the mentally retarded was opened in 1840. Seven years later the first state institution for the retarded in the United States, the Walter E. Fernald State School, was opened in Massachusetts. Similar state schools were opened in New York, Pennsylvania, and Ohio during the next ten years. By 1876, there were twelve schools for training the mentally retarded, and it was in that year that the superintendents of these schools formed the Association of Medical Officers of American Institutions for Idiots and Feebleminded Persons. This organization evolved into the American Association for the Study of the Feebleminded and eventually became the present American Association on Mental Deficiency.

The emphasis on heredity, triggered by the rediscovery of the work of Gregor Mendel in 1900, was also a milestone in the history of mental retardation. During the last two decades of the nineteenth century, there was an active interest in the familial incidence of mental retardation, just as there was an interest in the familial occurrence of genius. In the main, this interest stemmed from the writings of Sir Francis Galton, who dealt extensively with both problems (Galton, 1883).

One of the first important family studies investigated the family pedigree of two mentally retarded sisters and found a high incidence of mental retardation in their descendants (Dugdale, 1877). A few years later, the results of the classic study of the Kallikak family were published (Goddard, 1913). Both studies seemed to support the idea that mental retardation has a genetic basis. Quite apart from the questionable validity of the investigations, they served to stimulate further interest in the problem of mental retardation.

The establishment of the psychological laboratory at the Vineland Training School at Vineland, New Jersey, was of much greater practical importance. This laboratory gained an international reputation and set the pattern for research efforts at various other institutions. In the 1920s and 1930s, there was a further development of

Figure 12.2 *Henry H. Goddard, 1866–1957, American psychologist and pioneer in the field of mental retardation. (Courtesy of the Vineland Training School.)*

services for mentally retarded children. Various clinics, in connection with hospitals and other community agencies, offered diagnostic and consultation services to parents and their retarded children.

World War II also contributed to the history of mental retardation in that retarded men assigned to the Special Training Units were found able to perform valuable and constructive services. It became apparent that many men who earlier would have been rejected as unsuitable because of low intellectual ability could be trained effectively for labor battalions. This realization had a later influence in civilian life, particularly in connection with the use of high-grade retardates in industrial organizations. Following World War II, advances in the field of mental retardation were rapid and extensive. Important progress was made in the understanding of the etiology of mental retardation, early identification and diagnosis of the condition, education and training, prevention and treatment, and research.

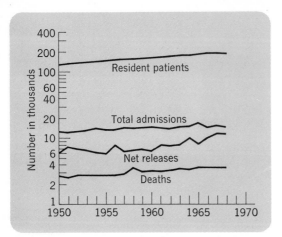

Figure 12.3 *Number of resident patients, total admissions, net releases, and deaths in public institutions for the mentally retarded in the United States, 1950–1968. (Mental Health Statistics, Current Facility Reports, National Institute of Mental Health, 1969.)*

The extent of the problem of mental retardation has not been determined accurately, primarily because of the difficulty in locating cases and the relatively few patients in institutions. During World War II, 4.5 percent of all men examined were rejected because of mental retardation. Slightly more than 700,000 men between 18 and 37 years of age were rejected for this reason from the beginning of selective service until the end of World War II, although this figure included many illiterates who were not in actual fact mentally retarded. It is probable that approximately 3 percent of the population of the United States, or more than 6 million children and adults, can be classified among the mentally retarded. Of this number, less than 200,000 reside in institutions (NIMH, 1970).

TERMINOLOGY AND CLASSIFICATION

In Chapter 2 it was noted that the terminology and classification of mental illness underwent many revisions and alterations over the years and that even today it is stabilized only precariously. The same is true for mental retardation. As late as the early 1960s it was defined in a number of different ways, and the mentally retarded

were classified into a variety of types and levels. The American Association on Mental Deficiency has been making a concerted effort to establish a common terminology and classification, but conflicting systems have been advanced by the World Health Organization, the National Association for Retarded Children, and the American Psychiatric Association.

A variety of labels have been used to designate patients who are mentally retarded. The World Health Organization prefers *mental subnormality,* while the diagnostic manual of the American Psychiatric Association uses *mental deficiency.* Other less common terms are *amentia, hypophrenia,* and *oligophrenia.* The term *feeblemindedness,* once very popular, is no longer used by specialists in this field.

Similarly, there have been many attempts to define mental retardation. A seventeenth-century English definition stated:

> He that shall be said to be an idiot from his birth, is such a person who cannot count or number twenty pence, nor tell who was his father or mother, nor how old he is, so as it may appear that he has no understanding of what shall be for his profit or what for his loss. If he has sufficient understanding to know and understand his letters, and to read by teaching or information, then it seems he is not an idiot (Tuke, 1892).

The English legal definition set forth in the Parliamentary Act of 1929 is that mental retardation is "a condition of arrested or incomplete development of mind existing before the age of eighteen years, whether arising from inherent causes or induced by disease or injury" (Mental Deficiency Commission, 1929). One of Great Britain's most distinguished authorities in the field of mental retardation defined the condition as ". . . a state of incomplete mental development of such a kind and degree that the individual is incapable of adapting himself to the normal environment of his fellows in such a way as to maintain existence independently of supervision, control, or external support" (Tredgold, 1937). A definition of mental retardation proposed by a prominent American authority is as follows: "Mental deficiency is a state of social incompetence obtained at maturity, resulting from developmental arrest of intelligence because of constitutional (hereditary or acquired) origin" (Doll, 1941). The official definition adopted by the American Association on Mental Deficiency is: "Mental retardation refers to sub-average general intellectual functioning which originates during the developmental period and is associated with impairment in adaptive behavior."

There have also been many attempts to classify mental retardation. Some of these have been in terms of the grade or severity of the retardation, others have been directed toward the form of the retardation, while still others have involved the clinical type of retardation. A distinction was made in England as early as the thirteenth century between the "born fool" and the "lunatic." In the case of the former, who was mentally retarded, property reverted permanently to the Crown. However, the property of the lunatic was under the care of the Crown only as long as the individual was mentally disturbed.

One of the first scientific attempts to classify mentally retarded patients was undertaken in France when patients were divided into three degrees of "idiocy" depending upon their ability to use language (Esquirol, 1838). The highest

degree of idiocy was marked by the patient's use of words in short phrases. In the second degree of idiocy, the patient was able to utter only monosyllables or certain cries. The lowest level was marked by the absence of all ability to communicate verbally, even in a most primitive manner.

Today, the classification of mental retardation is approached from several directions, with at least three classification dimensions. The first is *measured intelligence,* the second is *adaptive behavior,* and the third is *etiology.*

MEASURED INTELLIGENCE

The first important attempt to segregate and classify the mentally retarded in terms of measured intelligence occurred during the early part of the present century when the Binet-Simon Test was developed (Binet and Simon, 1916). These investigators introduced the concept of the *mental age,* a measure of intellectual ability in terms of test performance. A child of six who could pass tests at the eight-year level was said to have a

Figure 12.4 *Scenes from a ward in an institution for the retarded. While considerable progress has been made in the care and treatment of the mentally retarded, much remains to be done in many institutions, where scenes like this are not uncommon. (Photograph by Fred Kaplan, Black Star.)*

(a)

(b)

mental age of eight. Such a child would be intellectually advanced. However, the six-year-old who could pass only tests at the four-year level would have a mental age of four and would be mentally retarded. Later, a ratio was established between the mental age and the chronological age. This index was called the *intelligence quotient* (IQ).

In terms of psychological test scores, an IQ of 100 is considered the midpoint of the distribution. It is the theoretical "average intelligence," although for practical purposes the entire range of IQ scores from 90 to 110 is regarded as average. Approximately 50 percent of the population falls into this group. Table 12.1 gives comparable figures for the levels of intelligence used most frequently in clinical psychology.

For many years, the terms *moron, imbecile,* and *idiot* were used to describe the levels of mental retardation. These terms are seldom used now by careful writers, but since the words appear frequently in the earlier literature on mental retardation, it is important to know that the term *idiot* was used for individuals having a mental age of less than three years, or an intelligence quotient of less than 20. The term *imbecile* indicated a mental age of three to seven years, or an intelligence quotient of 20 to 49. A *moron* was a person with a mental age of eight or higher, and an intelligence quotient between 50 and 69.

The *idiot savant* is another category of mental retardation mentioned in the early literature. This term refers to a patient who has some special ability such as an exceptional memory, musical talent, or mechanical facility. A classic example of this type of patient was the "Genius of Earlswood Asylum," whose model ships were masterpieces of construction. In one 10-foot model, he used more than a million tiny wooden pins and pegs. The "genius" wore a Navy uniform, and when his models were admired by visitors to the institution, he would express his pleasure by patting his head and repeating, "Very clever, very clever" (Tredgold and Soddy, 1956).

Actually the *idiot savant* is misnamed since most patients with unusual special abilities are only mildly retarded. The "genius" was admitted to the institution when he was fifteen years old, and his personality and speech defects made him appear more retarded than actually was the case. It is nevertheless true that patients of very limited general intelligence sometimes demonstrate a surprising talent or proficiency.

While the terms *moron, imbecile,* and *idiot* had a wide use for a great many years, they are best avoided since they have an emotional loading which is completely undesirable. Moreover, the labeling of a patient in this way adds little to our understanding of the case. It has the damaging effect of overgeneralizing both physical and psychological characteristics. Individual variations, even among the relatively low levels of mental retardation, are of considerably greater importance than are the similarities.

Among more acceptable terms describing levels of mental retardation, there is little unanimity of opinion. The *Manual on Terminology and Classification in Mental Retardation* places *borderline mental retardation* between IQ 70 and 84, *mild retardation* between 55 and 69, *moderate retardation* between 40 and 54, *severe retardation* between 25 and 39, and *profound retardation* below 25. The National Association for Retarded Children uses the terms *marginally independent* (IQ 50 to 75), *semidependent* (IQ 25 to 50), and *dependent* (IQ 0 to 25).

To add to the confusion, the diagnostic manual of the American Psychiatric Association departs radically from the more usual conception of the levels of mental retardation and designates anyone with an IQ between 70 and 85 as having a *mild mental deficiency,* with emphasis on vocational impairment. Individuals with IQs between 50 and 70 are considered to have a *moderate mental deficiency* and to be in need of special training and guidance. *Severe mental deficiency* is re-

Table 12.1 *The distribution of intelligence*

IQ RANGE	PERCENT OF POPULATION
130 and above	2.2
120–129	6.7
110–119	16.1
90–109	50.0
80–89	16.1
70–79	6.7
69 and below	2.2

SOURCE: Adapted from David Wechsler, *The Measurement of Adult Intelligence* (3d ed.). The Williams & Wilkins Company, Baltimore, 1944, p. 37.

served for the IQ range of 0 to 50, and these patients are judged to be in need of custodial and protective care. This classification is unrealistic in that more than 20 million people, most of whom are making an adequate social, economic, and personal adjustment, are classified technically as mentally retarded. In the present chapter, the terms *mild, moderate,* and *severe* will be used in accordance with the recommendation of the World Health Organization, which considers the IQ range of 50 to 69 as mild retardation, 20 to 49 as moderate, and 0 to 19 as severe.

■ MILD RETARDATION

Stella G. is a fifteen-year-old girl who was referred to a psychiatric clinic when she was suspected of being mentally retarded. She came to the attention of the juvenile court as a result of a series of sex offenses in which she left home and was gone for four days. She was found with a seventeen-year-old boy in the basement of the home of the boy's grandmother. Stella was placed on probation and returned to her parents and school, where she appeared to be making a good adjustment. Several weeks later she left home to visit a girl friend, with her mother's permission, but instead she met the boy with whom she had been involved previously and stayed with him for three days. It was learned later that the young couple spent the time in a wooded area near the patient's home. When the patient was returned home, she covered her face with her hands and was tearful, withdrawn, and completely uncommunicative. Since she refused to eat or to talk to anyone, it was necessary to admit her to a psychiatric hospital.

At the hospital, the patient refused to come to the psychologist's office and it was necessary to examine her in her room. She was found sitting on the edge of the bed with her head and shoulders drooped and her eyes covered with her hands. She was completely withdrawn, seclusive, and uncommunicative, remaining inaccessible for a number of days. Gradually she came out of her seclusiveness, and although she did not mingle with other patients on the ward, she was willing to talk to the staff members. Eventually a complete psychological examination became possible, and it was found that the girl was functioning in the range of mild mental retardation with an intelligence quotient of 65.*

ADAPTIVE BEHAVIOR

It became apparent many years ago that sharp divisions based on psychological test results could not be made among the mentally retarded. Wide differences in social adaptability were observed among patients with identical test scores. Recognition of the shortcomings of a classification based on test scores alone led to an emphasis on classification in terms of the training and educational potential of the patient. Viewed in this way, the mentally retarded population can be divided into three major groups. The first and smallest of these groups is made up of those patients who are *untrainable* and who must remain completely dependent because of their low intellectual level. This group makes up about 5 percent of the total number of mentally retarded patients. The second major group, according to this classification, includes about 20 percent of the total, those individuals who are *trainable* to some extent. These patients constitute the most neglected group at the present time. The third major group, by far the largest, is made up of about 75 percent of the total mental retardates in the country. These individuals are considered to be *educable;* with the aid of special classes they can be expected to reach a reasonable degree of educational achievement and to make an adequate social and economic adjustment in the community.

The classification of mentally retarded people on the basis of intellectual level and trainability is useful where various types of educational and occupational placements must be made. In such placements, people of similar ability level must be grouped together, and a system of psychological classification becomes important. However, it is also possible, and frequently more desirable, to classify mental retardation on the basis of the cause of the disorder.

CLASSIFICATION BY ETIOLOGY

The revised edition of the *Manual on Terminology and Classification in Mental Retardation* lists eight major groups of mental retardation

---

*Case 1 of audiotape 12, "Mental Retardation," in *Case Interviews to Accompany The Disorganized Personality.*

based on probable causes. These eight groups include mental retardation associated with diseases and conditions due to:

1. Infection
2. Intoxication
3. Trauma or physical agent
4. Disorders of metabolism, growth, and nutrition
5. New growths (neoplasms, tumors)
6. Unknown prenatal influence
7. Unknown or uncertain organic cause
8. Uncertain, or presumed psychologic, cause

The first seven of these groups are made up of conditions with definite physical symptoms. The eighth group, by far the largest in terms of number of cases, is made up of the undifferentiated cases.

Retardation Associated with Infection

The first group of clinical types of mental retardation includes those cases in which infection plays a part in the etiology of the condition. An infection of the mother prior to the birth of the child may be transmitted in a direct way to the brain of the fetus. A mother with a syphilitic infection may transmit the disease to the developing fetus by way of the placenta. The child may then develop the characteristic signs of congenital syphilis, including abnormalities of the brain, skeleton, teeth, and eyes, and positive laboratory findings. In a number of these cases, mental retardation is a prominent symptom. Similarly, in mothers who contract *rubella*, or German measles, during the first three months of pregnancy, the infant may show symptoms which include deafness, cataract, malformations of the heart, and mental retardation.

About 50,000 of the 250,000 born each year with birth defects are the result of the action on the prenatal environment of foreign substances such as drugs and attack by the virus of German measles. Following the 1964–1965 rubella epidemic, between 20,000 and 40,000 infants were born mentally retarded or suffered from a variety of serious physical defects (NIAID, 1969).

A variety of other prenatal infectious conditions may lead to mental retardation in the child. These conditions include *cytomegalic inclusion body disease*, in which a maternal virus infects the fetus,

and *toxoplasmosis*, which is an infection due to a protozoan-like organism. In both conditions the infection may be latent in the mother but transmitted to the fetus. As a result, there may be a wide variety of physical symptoms along with mental retardation.

Toxoplasmosis, a disease which can cause severe neurological damage to the developing fetus, has long been a puzzler to medical science because its mode of transmission remained a mystery. Investigators have now detected a human-borne parasite in Puerto Rico which seems to be associated with the infection in children there.

Although 30 percent of American women show evidence of exposure to toxoplasmosis, the rate is twice as high for blacks as for whites, and four times as high for Puerto Ricans, in whom 50 percent of the children under two carry evidence of exposure. The Puerto Rican rate is similar to that in Western Europe, where poorly cooked meat has been demonstrated to be the source of infection. Estimates are that of the 88 percent of congenital toxoplasmosis cases which survive, 85 percent are mentally retarded, and more than 60 percent are spastic (NIMH, 1969). Once the disease carrier is pinned down, work can begin on development of preventive treatment.

A number of illnesses during infancy and childhood may also result in mental retardation; examples are various types of meningoencephalitis and complications of diseases such as measles and chicken pox which can be seriously damaging. It has been estimated that approximately 5 percent of all cases of mental retardation are due to some type of infection of the brain (Sarason, 1959).

■ MODERATE RETARDATION

Flora M. is a slightly obese eleven-year-old girl who was admitted to a psychiatric hospital with a history of mental retardation and emotional disturbance. In school, the girl had been placed in a slow learners' class but was too hyperactive to be continued in that setting. The child talked constantly, and her attention span was very limited.

The child had two convulsions when she was ten months old. These convulsions were associated with a high fever accompanying an infectious disease. When three years old, she vomited a number of times and had another convulsion. Following the convulsion, she regressed from singing songs and making complete sentences to phrases and scattered words. At four years of age, her overactivity became pronounced. From age four to seven, she attended nursery school, where she was easily distracted and did not take part in group activities. She was then placed in a special class for slow learners, but her behavior problems became so serious that it was necessary to discontinue the training. She also presented increasingly difficult problems in management at home. The parents, who found it easier to accept their daughter as emotionally disturbed than as retarded, agreed to have her hospitalized. The psychological examination showed her to have an IQ of 45.*

Retardation Associated with Intoxication

The second classification of mental retardation by etiology is associated with various forms of intoxication. In a few cases, the retardation may be related to maternal toxemias of pregnancy or to maternal intoxications due to carbon monoxide, lead, arsenic, quinine, and other substances. Postnatal accidental poisoning of infants and children by lead, insecticide, salicylates, and other toxic substances may also result in permanent brain damage and mental retardation.

Kernicterus is a brain disorder resulting from a toxic condition during the first few days following birth. The term refers to the yellow staining of certain nuclear masses of the brain, including the basal ganglia and the hypothalamic nuclei. Pathologists observed this pigmentation for many years before it was identified as bilirubin, a pigment found characteristically in the body fluids and other tissues of the normal newborn infant in cases of jaundice.

The early signs of kernicterus take the form of feeding difficulties, drowsiness, instability of body temperature, and a rather high-pitched cry. Later, there may be rigidity of the musculature. In the most serious cases, the symptoms increase in severity and lead to death. While symptoms may persist in survivors, the infant often appears normal for some months on superficial examination. Later, there may be deafness and mental retardation. Fortunately there has been a steady decline in the incidence of kernicterus over the years as a result of early detection and the use of fluid transfusions.

A brain disorder sometimes follows inoculation with antitetanus serum or the use of smallpox, rabies, and typhoid vaccines. The nervous system reactions ordinarily involve the peripheral nerves, but in a few cases they may affect the brain. In these relatively rare cases, there are signs of disturbances of brain function in the form of coma, stupor, and convulsions. The neurological impairment sometimes results in behavior disorders and mental retardation.

Retardation Associated with Trauma

The third classification of mental retardation by etiology is associated with physical damage in the form of injuries prior to birth, at the time of birth, or immediately following birth. Prenatal injury is a rare condition but does occur from time to time. Perhaps the best example of this is in connection with x-ray irradiation of the uterus. When pregnant women are exposed to large amounts of irradiation, the incidence of defective offspring is significant. The type and degree of damage depends to some extent upon the developmental stage of the fetus. When the uterus is irradiated during the first three months of pregnancy, the incidence of mental retardation in the offspring is significantly high.

A more important type of damage associated with mental retardation is birth injury. Difficulties during labor may result in damage to the infant's brain. Severe injuries of this type are likely to be reflected in symptoms present immediately following birth. The symptoms include respiratory difficulties, convulsions, and the inability to make normal sucking movements. Less severe brain damage may not be immediately apparent and may be expressed later in infancy or early childhood in a variety of ways. It is difficult to delineate a model for the behavior of brain-injured children because the extent and location of the injury vary from one child to another. As a result, a wide range of symptoms is possible. In some children, there is a general mental retardation; in others, the re-

---

*Case 2 of audiotape 12, "Mental Retardation," in *Case Interviews to Accompany The Disorganized Personality.*

tardation is limited to a more specific disability. Similarly, the severity of the symptoms varies from case to case.

One of the main causes of nervous system damage results during pregnancy from compression of the umbilical cord, which supplies blood carrying oxygen and nutritional substances from the mother to the fetus. Cord compression produces a condition called *asphyxia,* which means oxygen deprivation and consequent suffocation of the tissues. Studies of the rhesus monkey show that the severity and type of damage caused by asphyxia depend upon when during pregnancy the injury occurs.

The earlier the asphyxia occurs, the less vulnerable the fetus and the longer the period of oxygen deprivation it can withstand. Fetuses at three and one-half months (pregnancy in the rhesus lasts six months) can withstand oxygen deprivation twice as long as a full-term monkey infant. Moreover, the earlier in pregnancy the asphyxia is introduced, the less the overall damage to the brain and, particularly, the less the damage to the higher parts of the brain.

■ MENTAL RETARDATION ASSOCIATED WITH BIRTH INJURY

Edward F. is a fifty-four-year-old man who is mentally retarded as a result of a birth injury. He was nearly four years old before he walked or talked, and he remained in school only a few months. He was cared for by his parents until he was about eighteen, at which time they could no longer handle him because of his interest in girls. He was sent to a relative in a rural area, where he remained for a number of years working on the farm and causing no trouble. When the family moved to the city, the patient's interest in girls was revived. He spent much of his time looking at pictures of women's underclothing and he had a considerable collection of such pictures from newspapers and magazines. At the time of his examination, the patient was found to be a neat, cooperative, and somewhat fearful man. Throughout most of the interview he picked at his handkerchief or leaned far forward over the desk with his arms folded. His movements were generally slow, and he repeated such phrases as "I like to work on a farm," and "I would like to go back home and work on the farm some more." The patient was quite unstable emotionally, and at one time when he told how another patient threw something at him on the ward, he burst into a flood of tears. At an-

other time, the patient said he liked to laugh and "cut up." He then broke into somewhat grotesque and smothered laughter. The psychological examination showed an IQ of 60.

The risk of hemorrhage of the brain is also present at the time of birth. In normal births, this risk is minimal. However, in cases of abnormal position of the fetus, breech extraction, the use of forceps, and other obstetrical procedures, the possibility of bleeding in the brain is increased. In premature infants, where the blood vessels are immature, a considerable additional risk is involved.

Of the 300,000 babies born prematurely in the United States each year, 45,000 are dead within the first month of life. Many of those infants who survive show mental retardation, allergies, and a variety of physical disorders and disabilities. Brain damage is the cause of the mental retardation in about 5 percent of institutionalized cases.

Cerebral palsy is a motor disability associated with organic brain damage or malformation. It is not a single disease, but a condition characterized by a multitude of causes and resultant degrees of impairment. Frequently the exact cause is unknown. The condition is discussed in the literature under such names as *spastic paralysis, cerebral diplegia, spastic diplegia, birth-injury palsy,* and *Little's disease.*

While the identifying symptoms are motor, there may be a real or apparent mental retardation in a substantial number of cases. Most instances of intellectual deficiency are seen among the *spastics,* or cases with paralysis and uncoordinated reflexes. This type of cerebral palsy is designated frequently by the extent of the paralysis. In *monoplegia,* the paralysis involves a single limb of the body; in *hemiplegia,* the paralysis is of one side of the body; in *triplegia,* three limbs are paralyzed; and in *paraplegia,* only the legs are involved. *Diplegia* refers to the paralysis of both legs and both arms, with the legs more seriously affected, while in *quadraplegia* all four limbs are involved, with the arms more seriously paralyzed. Cerebral palsy afflicts an estimated 600,000 Americans. Its cause and cure thus remain one of the most puzzling problems in medical research.

The damage from cerebral palsy can be limited to motor difficulties affecting a few fingers or can extend throughout the body. It can be tragically obvious in the hemiplegic baby with spastic paralysis or strangely elusive, impairing development several years later. The condition is neither contagious nor progressive. The brain lesions which produce the damage have been shown to be associated with physiological events surrounding pregnancy and birth, events which until recently were little understood.

Prognosis for treatment and recovery ranges from excellent to extremely poor. Braces to support weak muscles, exercise to stimulate development, and special coaching for patients handicapped by complications like deafness, blindness, and speech disorders have enabled some children to reach a level of functioning close to normal. Even those afflicted with amost total motor involvement and mental retardation have been helped to make some progress.

Although research to improve rehabilitation methods can make many victims more productive, the hope for the future rests with scientists working to uncover, prevent, and remedy the complications which cause the crippling damage in the first place.

Another important discovery is that it is long-term *partial* oxygen deprivation during gestation rather than sudden total deprivation that produces the types of cerebral palsy seen in humans. Experiments on animals which induced acute total asphyxia produced a pattern of neuropathology which bore little resemblance to the various well-recognized patterns seen in humans who are afflicted with cerebral palsy or mental retardation caused by brain damage at birth. In cases of partial asphyxia, the resulting damage appeared as forms of pathology seen in the brains of humans damaged during pregnancy of the mother or at birth.

Cerebral palsy, because of its severity, its varied associated disabilities, and lack of understanding by the public, presents peculiar and important problems for rehabilitation and research. Attitudes of employers, of parents, and of the clients themselves are being investigated, as are the special testing and training methods which are necessary for the diagnosis and treatment of the different motor and speech deficiencies involved. Because of the dependency of such people on family help, a central problem is the training of the

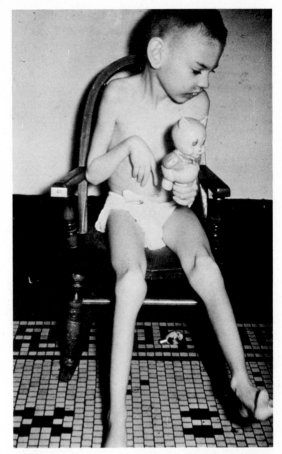

Figure 12.5 *A mentally retarded child showing the symptoms of spastic paralysis. (Courtesy of the Columbus State Hospital.)*

cerebral palsied toward independent living and eventual competitive employment.

In cases of *athetosis,* which is marked by involuntary movements due to inadequate voluntary control of the muscles, the damage is at the level of the basal ganglia, with little or no involvement of the higher brain centers. This situation is also true where *ataxia,* or impairment in the ability to maintain and regulate postural and intentional activity, is the central symptom. The lesion in this condition is ordinarily in the cerebellum.

Estimates of the incidence of mental retardation among cerebral palsy patients range from slightly below 30 percent to close to 80 percent. The lack of agreement among the various studies is due to the great difficulty in administering conventional psychological tests to patients with severe motor disability and speech disturbances. There is the further problem of the type of brain injury of the patients being examined. It is virtually impossible to match groups in terms of extent and location of the brain damage. The social and emotional environment of the members of the cerebral palsy group under investigation also has an effect on the apparent amount of retardation.

Table 12.2 indicates the distribution of the intelligence level of 143 cases studied as part of a cerebral palsy project sponsored by the New Jersey State Crippled Children's Commission. When the borderline and mentally retarded patients were considered as a group, it was found that 29 percent were in the borderline classification, 27 percent were mildly retarded, 22 percent were moderately retarded, and 21 percent were severely retarded (McIntire, 1938).

In a few cases, mental retardation may be associated with anoxemia, or lack of oxygen, at the time of birth or after birth as a result of anesthetic accidents. Since brain cells are extremely sensitive to changes in the oxygen supply, damage may take place when that supply is shut off or falls below normal levels. In some cases, mental retardation results from accidental brain injuries received during infancy or later in life. Many children sustain minor head injuries as a result of falling from chairs, tables, and cribs. Usually no permanent damage results, although occasionally when the injury is associated with a fractured skull or prolonged unconsciousness due to concussion, it may be followed by an intellectual defect in the child. Later in life, accidental brain injuries, disorders of the blood vessels of the brain, and asphyxia may sometimes result in mental retardation.

Retardation Associated with Disorders of Metabolism, Growth, and Nutrition

Some of the most carefully studied clinical types of mental retardation are associated with disorders of metabolism, growth, and nutrition. Millions of young children in developing countries experience some degree of mental retardation because of inadequate nutrition. This phenomenon is also observed in some sections of the United States. Since the problem is complicated by social and psychological factors, the role of dietary deficiencies in man is not easy to assess. However, a relatively short period of undernutrition in animals results in smaller brain size at maturity, even if the animals are maintained on a good diet after weaning (Scrimshaw and Gordon, 1968).

Disorders of metabolism—the physical and chemical process by which body cells are built up and broken down, and by which energy is made available for their functioning—are also factors in the causation of mental retardation. The most important disturbance of fat metabolism is *infantile cerebral lipoidosis,* or *Tay-Sachs's disease.* This disorder, which is transmitted as a single recessive gene, is one in which the infant usually appears normal at birth, with the clinical signs appearing between the ages of one month and one year. Such a child then becomes apathetic, shows muscular weakness, is unable to hold his head steady or maintain his posture, and loses his ability to grasp objects. Ordinarily there is a visual deterioration leading to blindness, and death occurs within a few years. Because it is a disease of infancy and involves blindness, an hereditary factor, and mental retardation, the condition is also known as *infantile amaurotic family idiocy.*

Phenylketonuria is the most important disturbance of protein metabolism associated with mental retardation. This disorder, which is also transmitted as a simple recessive trait, is one in which the patient is unable to metabolize the amino acid phenylalanine. The result is an accumulation of phenylalanine, most of which is excreted in the urine. Children with this clinical disorder show a number of characteristic physical symp-

Table 12.2 *Distribution of intelligence in 143 cases of cerebral palsy*

CLASSIFICATION	PERCENT
Gifted	None
Superior	7
High average	12
Average	29
Dull normal	13
Borderline	8
Mentally retarded	18
Unclassified	13

SOURCE: Adapted from S. B. Sarason, *Psychological Problems in Mental Deficiency,* Harper & Row, Publishers, Incorporated, New York, 1959, p. 169.

toms along with various degrees of mental retardation. Most cases show severe retardation. The discovery of this condition in 1934 was an important breakthrough in demonstrating the relationship between biochemical disturbance and mental retardation. It was found that the condition accounts for between 0.5 and 1 percent of the institutionalized cases of mental retardation and that the disorder is genetically determined and clearly differentiated from other forms of mental retardation (Fölling, 1934).

Other disorders of protein metabolism include *hepatolenticular degeneration,* or *Wilson's disease,* and *porphyria.* The former condition is transmitted as a simple recessive trait and involves an increased copper concentration in the tissue which damages the liver, brain, and other organs. Because of the damage to the nervous system, mental retardation may accompany this disorder involving the excretion of porphyrins in the urine. This disorder is also inherited, and it is transmitted as a dominant trait. While the disorder usually involves adults and results in personality disturbances, in some instances it occurs in children and produces mental retardation.

An example of a disorder of carbohydrate metabolism is *galactosemia,* in which there is an accumulation of galactose in the bloodstream. An infant who is symptom-free at birth begins to show the signs of this disorder when placed on the usual milk diet. The child loses his appetite, and there is jaundice and vomiting with progressive evidence of malnutirition. The high level of galactose in the blood is associated frequently with low blood-sugar levels (hypoglycemia), which may cause convulsions. The major symptoms of galactosemia are cataract, enlargement of the liver, and mental retardation. Severe and prolonged hypoglycemia in childhood has also been confirmed as a cause of cerebral palsy and mental retardation.

Studies of hypoglycemic children who are sensitive to the amino acid *leucine,* found in most proteins, have shown that this variety of the disease clusters in families and that the condition often improves spontaneously after three to six years of age. This finding makes it possible for physicians to counsel families in which the disease tends to occur.

Another condition in the group of disorders of metabolism, growth, and nutrition is *hypothyroidism,* in which there is decrease in, or absence of, the thyroid hormone *thyroxin.* Congenital *hypothyroidism* may be due to iodine deficiency in the mother during pregnancy, or to an absence or underdevelopment of the thyroid gland. It may also be due to a genetically determined enzyme defect which results in a defective synthesis of thyroxine by the infant.

Traditionally, this disorder has been known as *cretinism.* The origin of the word *cretin* is uncertain. It has been suggested that it is derived from *chrétien,* the French word for Christian, in keeping with the once popular notion that the cretin is especially blessed by heaven. Other authorities

Figure 12.6 *Hypothyroidism, the type of mental retardation sometimes referred to as "cretinism." (Courtesy of the Columbus State School.)*

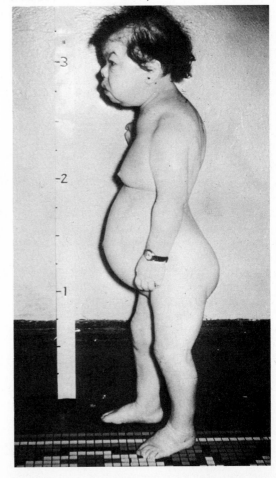

derive the term from *cretina,* which means stupid or silly. Another view is that the term is derived from *cretine,* the word for alluvial soil—the sandy and muddy sediment deposited by streams and rivers—since it was believed at one time that an alluvial region was related to the cause of the disorder.

The symptoms of the disorder have been recognized for many centuries. Such ancient writers as Juvenal and Pliny referred to the condition, although the term first appeared in a will executed during the fifteenth century in which the testator provided for the safekeeping of the patient. Felix Plater referred to Swiss cretins as early as 1500. The first systematic treatise on this condition was published in 1792.

In 1841, a Swiss physician established a small institution for these patients near Interlaken. At the time, various theories were advanced to account for the disorder. Some physicians blamed the "confined air" of the lower valleys, others thought it might be related to glacier water, while still others believed it had something to do with the mineral content of the water. By the middle of the nineteenth century, a relationship between cretinism and goiter (a thyroid disorder) had been established.

The hypothyroid infant is rarely recognized at birth, but the symptoms become apparent during the early months. The older child is ordinarily dwarfed, with the features being coarse and heavy. There is a general appearance of dullness and apathy. In most cases there is a swollen abdomen which, when combined with other distinguishing features, gives the child a characteristic appearance. Mental retardation in the untreated is a constant symptom. Fortunately, these cases are identified relatively easily, and the necessary endocrine therapy can be initiated. At one time, institutions for the mentally retarded had many cases of this type. Relatively few such cases are admitted to the hospitals today.

Another condition in this group, notable for its unusual clinical features rather than for its frequency among the mentally retarded, is *gargoylism,* or *Hurler's disease.* This disorder is marked by a defect in the metabolism and connective tissue and by abnormal deposits in various tissues of the body, particularly the brain, cornea, liver, heart, lungs, and spleen. The patient may resemble a gargoyle in physical appear-

ance. There is a large head with a protruding forehead, bushy eyebrows, and a flattened nose. The features are coarse and heavy, and the head is completely out of proportion to the stunted body. The mental retardation ranges from mild to severe and is usually present by the time the child is two years old. There are two forms of gargoylism, both of an hereditary nature. One form is due to an ordinary recessive gene, while the other is a sex-linked recessive trait.

Mental retardation has been found to be three times as frequent in children of mothers who had *acetonuria* (an excess of acetone bodies in the urine) in the last third of their pregnancies in comparison with children of acetone-free pregnancies. This finding is related to earlier surveys which showed that diabetes accompanied by acetonuria during pregnancy is associated with evidence of subnormal intellectual and neurological function in children, while nonacetonuric diabetes during pregnancy is not. The finding supports the theory that acetonuria indicates episodes when the nutritional supply of a pregnant mother is insufficient for the fetus, since a fetus usually triples its weight in the last trimester of pregnancy and is then most in need of nutrients. Although only 1 percent of pregnant women are believed to have diabetes, 3 to 5 percent of pregnant women may have acetonuria alone (NIMH, 1969).

Retardation Associated with Tumors

The fifth group of clinical types of mental retardation consists of conditions associated with neoplasms, or tumors. One such disorder is *neurofibromatosis,* or *Von Recklinghausen's disease,* a condition characterized by *cafe au lait,* or coffee-colored, skin patches of varying sizes. Skin tumors may also be present. While normal intelligence is found in most victims of neurofibromatosis, some show mental retardation of varying degrees of severity. The disease follows a dominant hereditary pattern with variable expressivity. As a result, some patients show incomplete forms of the disease.

Tuberous sclerosis, or *epiloia,* is another neoplastic disease transmitted by a dominant gene with variable expression. This disorder is characterized by numerous nodules and tumors throughout the brain and other parts of the body. A butter-

(a)

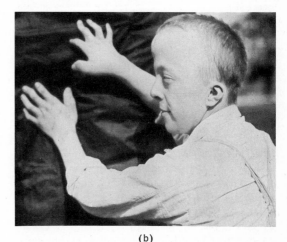

(b)

Figure 12.7 *Scaphocephaly. (a) The front view of a patient with a cranial developmental defect. (b) A close-up side view of the head of the same patient. (Courtesy of the Columbus State School.)*

fly-shaped rash develops on the face and spreads over a wider and wider area. The condition may be accompanied by the development of convulsions and by retarded mental development. Mental disorder occasionally occurs in patients who survive to adulthood. Many patients, however, are normal in every respect except for the skin lesions.

Retardation Associated with Unknown Prenatal Influence

The sixth clinical classification is made up of a number of medical conditions associated with mental retardation and ascribed to unknown prenatal causation. The most common of these conditions includes the various forms of congenital cerebral defects and Mongolism.

The congenital cerebral defects of unknown cause include *anencephaly,* in which there is a complete absence of the cerebrum, cerebellum, and flat bones of the skull. Other conditions involve malformations of the surface of the brain, and include *macrogyria,* in which the gyri (convolutions) are few and broad while the sulci (fissures) are short, shallow, and wide, and *microgyria,* in which the brain is small and the normal

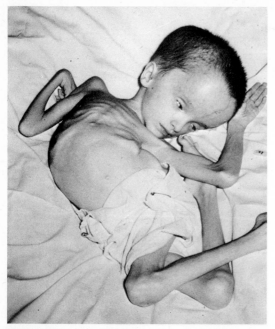

Figure 12.8 *Mental retardation associated with hydrocephalus, showing typical paralysis and wasting of the limbs. (Courtesy of the Columbus State School.)*

convolutions are replaced by a large number of small close-set convolutions separated by shallow grooves. Another congenital disorder is *porencephaly,* in which there are large funnel-shaped cavities in the brain communicating with the ventricles. While congenital porencephaly is a developmental disturbance, acquired porencephaly can be due to hemorrhagic or inflammatory lesions which form a cystic cavity.

In addition to the inborn cerebral defects, there are a number of conditions in which there are associated defects of the skull. These conditions include *craniostenosis, congenital hydrocephalus, hypertelorism, macrocephaly,* and *microcephaly.*

Distortions of the skull due to craniostenosis most commonly take the form of a steeple-shaped skull (*acrocephaly* or *oxycephaly*) or a long narrow "boat-shaped" head (*scaphocephaly*). In acrocephaly, there is a high narrow forehead which slopes to a high point. This condition, which is probably determined genetically, is due to a premature closing of some of the bones of the skull. Some degree of mental retardation is usually, though not always, seen in these cases. When retardation does occur, it is probably present from

birth. Similarly, scaphocephaly may be associated with mild to severe mental retardation. The shape of the head in scaphocephaly is also due to a premature closing of skull bones which causes the head to grow in the forward and backward directions rather than sideways.

In *congenital hydrocephalus,* there is an increased amount of cerebrospinal fluid. The condition may be present at birth, or the head may begin to enlarge soon after birth. The most frequent cause is an obstruction in the cerebrospinal fluid pathways, although there may also be a failure in the absorption mechanism. Whatever the cause, as the fluid accumulates, the skull enlarges and the brain becomes compressed due to the expansion. In the more serious cases, the patients show paralysis, convulsions, and other serious physical symptoms. However, the severity of both physical and mental symptoms varies, with mental retardation (if present) ranging from mild to severe.

Another form of inborn cranial defect is *hypertelorism,* or *Grieg's disease.* This disorder is due to an abnormal development involving the sphenoid bone at the base of the skull. As a result, the distance between the eyes is increased, giving the patient a characteristic appearance. In extreme cases, the eyes appear to be at the side of the head rather than in the normal frontal position. Mental retardation is sometimes associated with this condition.

Macrocephaly is a relatively rare condition in which there is an increase in the size and weight of the brain due to an abnormal growth of supportive tissue. While the enlargement of the skull may be noticed at birth, the major growth occurs later. In most cases the patient is severely retarded. The opposite condition is *microcephaly,* in which the skull is abnormally small. Primary microcephaly is transmitted as a single recessive gene and presents a typical clinical picture. The face and lower part of the head remain relatively normal, while the small skull recedes to a point. The most important diagnostic sign is the discrepancy between the normal face and the relatively small skull. Mental retardation usually ranges from moderate to severe. Secondary microcephaly refers to a significant decrease in cranial volume due to any mechanism interfering with the growth of the brain.

Mongolism has been one of the most intriguing

clinical types of mental retardation. The mongoloid patient is likely to be somewhat smaller than average, with a characteristically round face having sloping eyebrows and eyelids, which give a somewhat Oriental appearance. It was this appearance which originally suggested the term "mongolism." The tongue of the mongoloid frequently has characteristic transverse fissures, and in some severe cases the tongue tends to protrude from the rather small mouth. The teeth may be small and misshapen. The skin is frequently lacking in elasticity, and circulation may be poor due to associated congenital heart disease. The hands and feet also tend to show characteristic signs. The little finger may be short, and there may be only one crease in the finger rather than the usual two. Similarly, the cleft between the first and second toes is sometimes unusually large. The palms frequently have a characteristic appearance, with the two main skin creases replaced by a single crease. The fingerprints may have loops rather than the usual whorls.

The mental retardation associated with mongolism ranges from moderate to severe, although a few scattered cases of mild retardation have been reported. There appears to be a relationship between the severity of the physical symptoms and the degree of retardation.

Until recently, the cause of mongolism was unknown. Various theories were advanced, including advanced age of the mother at the time of the birth of the child, glandular imbalance, biochemical disturbances, infectious disease, and toxic conditions. However, in each of these cases it was possible to demonstrate the presence of mongolism when these suggested factors did not appear to be operative. One consistent finding was that there were no reported cases of mongolism in only one of a pair of identical twins. All such cases appeared to be concordant for this disorder. The concordance rate for fraternal twins, however, was only 4 percent, or the rate of the disorder in ordinary siblings (Penrose, 1954).

The first major breakthrough in our knowledge

Figure 12.9 *Microcephaly. (a) A front view of a thirty-year-old patient. (b) A close-up side view of the head of the same patient. (Courtesy of the Columbus State School.)*

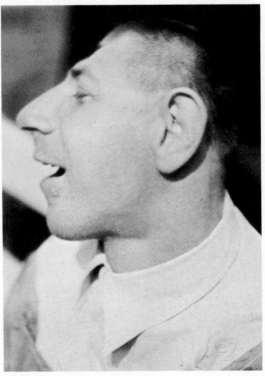

(a)   (b)

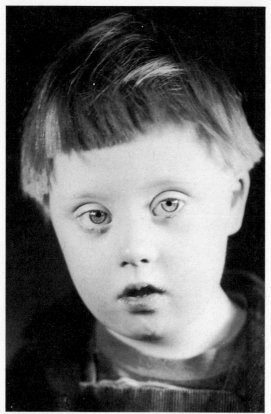

Figure 12.10 *Mental retardation associated with mongolism. (Courtesy of Dr. Clemens E. Benda.)*

of the etiology of mongolism occurred in 1959 with the discovery of an extra chromosome in the cells of mongoloid individuals (Lejeune et al., 1959). Instead of a normal pair of chromosomes, there are three chromosomes. Since chromosomes are numbered in a standard way, it has been possible to identify chromosome 21 as the one which appears in triple number rather than the usual pair. This tripling, called *trisomy,* results in a total of forty-seven chromosomes in the cell rather than the normal number of forty-six. Whenever this extra chromosome is present in the cell, the clinical symptoms of mongolism are observed in the individual.

A new use to which some of the government funds earmarked for mental retardation are being put is in the area of cytogenetic and biochemical laboratory services. Projects include chromosome analysis and diagnosis of various medical con-

ditions which may be genetic and result in mental retardation. On the basis of these analyses, counseling is being offered to parents seeking advice on genetic questions. Biochemical laboratories also do continuing monitoring of patients with metabolic diseases. Training in medical genetics is an important aspect of many of these projects.

Retardation Associated with Unknown Organic Cause

The seventh group of clinical types of mental retardation is made up of a series of conditions which are due to unknown or uncertain cause and in which neurological and physical symptoms are prominent. These symptoms may be any one of a number of types, with most of the conditions presumed to be of a genetic nature. The conditions, which are relatively infrequent, involve diffuse sclerosis of the brain and cerebellar degeneration.

Retardation Associated with Presumed Psychologic Cause

The eighth classification is made up of conditions in which there is an apparent absence of organic disease or pathology to account for the retarded functioning. Such cases make up the overwhelming majority of all mental retardation. These are the cultural-familial cases, which have been variously designated as primary, genetic, hereditary, familial, and constitutional. The group also includes mental retardation associated with environmental deprivation, emotional disturbances, infantile autism, and early childhood psychotic states.

■ FAMILIAL RETARDATION

Johnny and Bobby W. are mentally retarded brothers of fourteen and sixteen years of age. The boys live with their mother and father and nine brothers and sisters. The entire family lives in two dirty and dreary tenement rooms in a poor neighborhood. The front room has a double bed, a rollaway bed, chairs, a chest of drawers, and a television set. The second room is a kitchen in which food is left on the table, dishes remain unwashed, and the stove is dirty and crusted with food. Both the father and mother are mentally dull and filled with frustration and hopelessness. The boys came to the attention of the police when neighbors complained of their activities in the neighborhood.

Bobby has a rather pleasant, although somewhat vacant, expression. During his examination he talked steadily in an apparent effort to impress the examiner. He works irregularly at a car wash in the neighborhood, where he is regarded as a good worker and is able to follow orders to a limited extent. His IQ is 50.

Johnny, his fourteen-year-old brother, appears more seriously retarded. During the examination, Johnny was able to tell how many ears and legs he had, but he did not know how many fingers he had. He did not know how many pennies are in a nickel, or how many days in the week. He was unable to count nine blocks placed in front of him. He complained constantly about his treatment by other boys and repeated over and over again that he wanted to go home. From time to time he buried his face in his hands and cried. The impression was that of a mentally retarded and emotionally regressed boy. His IQ is 40.*

It is probable that the familial type of mental retardation is due to a combination of genetic and environmental factors. The analogy here is a hand in a bridge game. On one deal the cards combine to form a very fine hand; at another time, the hand is a "bust." Similarly, the combination of hereditary and developmental factors produces a superior intellect in one child and an inferior intellect in another. In both the poor bridge hand and the inferior intellectual functioning, the difficulty is the result of a normal variation.

Since most cases of mental retardation do not show biological abnormalities as measured by presently available diagnostic techniques, there has been a persistent interest in the possible role of early emotional deprivation and disturbed parent-child relationships in the development of the condition. Those who hold to this point of view look upon such deprivation as being analogous to a vitamin or endocrine deficiency. Emotionally deprived children are considered to be oversensitive to psychological stress in the same way that the patient with vitamin deficiency is oversusceptible to infection. To support this position, there is evidence that maternal deprivation results in a retarded rate of development, greater susceptibility to disease, and less adaptability in later life (Bowlby, 1952).

In a classic study of the influence of the environment on level of intellectual functioning, infants from an orphanage were placed individually in wards of an institution for the mentally retarded. The babies ranged in age from seven to thirty months, and they were placed in wards where minimally retarded older girls were allowed to play with the babies and give them attention. A control group of infants remained in the orphanage. Later, when these children were retested, those placed in the institution, where development was stimulated, increased approximately 27 IQ points; infants remaining in the orphanage dropped 26 points (Skeels and Dye, 1939). While the experiment was open to criticism, the dramatic findings led to further interest in the possibility of raising intellectual level by manipulating the sociopsychological environment.

In a more carefully controlled study undertaken at the Institute for Research on Exceptional Children at the University of Illinois, 81 children between the ages of three and six with IQ scores between 45 and 80 were studied for the effects of environmental stimulation. Two training groups, one in the community and one in an institution, were evaluated along with comparable preschool children in communties and institutions who did not receive preschool training. It was found that the children in the training group who received preschool training increased from an average IQ of 61 to 71 on a standard intelligence test. The mentally retarded children who did not receive preschool training dropped from an average of 57 to 50 on the same test. More important, 25 percent of the children in the training group were able to be paroled from the institution, whereas none of the children without training was paroled (Kirk, 1958).

The term "deprivation dwarfism" has been used to refer to a combination of mental retardation and stunted physical growth related to unhappy home conditions. Removing children from such homes can result in a spurt of physical and psychological growth. If the intellectual level reaches the normal range, the apparent retardation was an example of "pseudo-retardation" rather than true mental retardation. The symptoms, which are often no-

---

*Cases 3 and 4 of audiotape 12, "Mental Retardation," in *Case Interviews to Accompany The Disorganized Personality*.

ticed by age two, include extreme shyness, inability to control temper, insatiable hunger and thirst, and a craving for bizarre foods. Such children are most likely to be found in home situations where there is a history of alcoholism, sexual incompatibility, illness, beatings, unemployment, and unwanted pregnancies.

The reason for the physical retardation is not known. One theory is that continuous anxiety results in a digestive system that is less able to absorb food. Another view is that the growth hormone of the pituitary gland is involved in some way. The exact way in which mental state and growth are related, and how an emotional problem becomes a physical one, is not known.

The effects of early childhood deprivation are seen in a study of two groups of infants, each diagnosed as retarded but without brain damage. The two groups were raised separately and differently. One group was given early mothering and care and was reared in good foster homes. Members of this group became educated, are employed in various occupations and professions, and are raising normal families. The other group, left to custodial and nonstimulating institutional care, are for the most part wards of the state thirty years later (Brown, 1969).

While emotional deprivation and other sociocultural factors unquestionably influence the level of intellectual expression, they probably do not influence the basic level of intellectual capacity. Social and psychological factors often operate to prevent the full realization of a child's intellectual capacity. That capacity, however, has rather definite limits. The problem of true mental retardation involves the limits of capacity rather than the limits of the expression of the capacity. According to this view, no matter how low the expressed ability of the child, he is not truly mentally retarded if this level can be raised to the borderline range of normal intelligence or higher.[2]

IDENTIFICATION AND DIAGNOSIS

The problem of early identification and diagnosis of mental retardation is of very great importance. In some types of mental retardation, the identification of the physical condition underlying the disorder must be made at the time of birth or very shortly thereafter if treatment is to be effective.

An important breakthrough in the identification of an organic condition underlying mental retardation has been the early detection of phenylketonuria, a condition in which there is a pathologically large amount of phenylpyruvic acid in the urine. Unless this condition is detected during the early months of infancy and adequately treated by special diet, permanent brain damage may occur. The first step in early detection was the use of a diaper test. Later, the development of a relatively simple blood test made even earlier diagnosis possible. A number of other conditions, including hypothyroidism, galactosemia, and various maternal blood sensitivities, also require early identification if they are to be treated successfully.

The problem of early identification and diagnosis is complicated by the fact that relatively few cases of mental retardation are based upon early demonstrable pathology of the nervous system or disturbances of biochemistry. The larger group of mental retardates is made up of individuals who appear to be constitutionally defective. While a complex kind of genetic influence may be suspected, direct evidence of the role of heredity is rarely available. Such cases do not lend themselves readily to early identification.

A report of the Joint Expert Committee of the World Health Organization states:

> Although some forms of mental subnormality, usually those of severe grade, are recognizable at birth, the majority of cases look much like normal children and are first distinguished by their slowness of develop-

---

[2]Books dealing with the various clinical forms of mental retardation are the second edition of C. H. Carter's *Handbook of Mental Retardation Syndromes* (Thomas, 1970); the revised edition of C. E. Benda's *Down's Syndrome: Mongolism and Its Management* (Grune & Stratton, 1969); *Cerebral Palsy and Related Disorders* (Blakiston, 1960) by Eric Denhoff and I. P. Robinault; and *Cerebral Palsy in Childhood and Adolescence* (Williams and Wilkins, 1961), edited by J. L. Henderson.

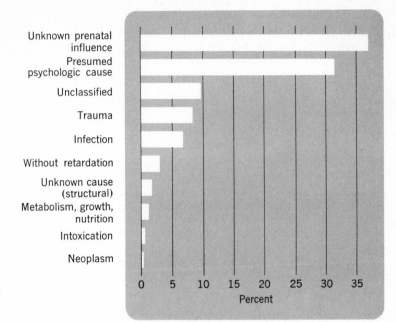

Figure 12.11 *The distribution of mental retardation in terms of causal factors. (From data furnished by the National Institute of Mental Health, 1963. Data of this nature is hard to come by, but it is most unlikely that the distribution has changed much since 1963.)*

ment. During the period of infancy, only cases of fairly gross handicap are likely to be diagnosed. In the preschool years, however, it becomes possible to discover a good deal of moderate subnormality and some mild cases. Others are not suspected until they are of school age (WHO, 1954).

The identification of mental retardation during infancy is ordinarily limited to those infants who have characteristic physical symptoms or biochemical abnormalities. When children enter school, a number of mentally retarded are identified because of their inability to keep up with the class or because of persistent problems of discipline. Adolescence presents another opportunity for identification since disciplinary problems and acting-out of conflict reflect the youngster's inability to exercise behavior controls. (See Table 12.3.)

The diagnosis of mental retardation is not merely a matter of giving an intelligence test and ascertaining the intellectual level. The diagnosis must also include medical, psychological, educational, and social evaluations. Moreover, diagnosis is a continuing matter. The child suspected of being retarded mentally must be observed carefully, in all phases of his behavior,

over a period of time and under a wide variety of circumstances. It was pointed out in Chapter 10 that cases of simple schizophrenia are sometimes mistaken for mental retardation. Similarly, certain organic conditions are accompanied by a behavioral picture suggesting mental retardation.

The recognition of the importance of early identification and diagnosis of mental retardation is reflected in the development of a variety of community services. A number of institutions for the mentally retarded operate preadmission or outpatient clinics where diagnostic services are available. These clinics have been developed in part because of the long waiting lists for admission to hospitals for the retarded and the need for careful selection of patients. Where such outpatient services are available, the family of the mental retardate may be offered expert diagnostic and advisory services involving medical, psychological, and social matters. Unfortunately, many institutions for mental retardation are located away from urban centers or are seriously understaffed, making adequate outpatient services impracticable or impossible.

Another type of identification and diagnostic service is the community clinic, usually spon-

Table 12.3 *Developmental characteristics of the mentally retarded*

DEGREES OF MENTAL RE- TARDATION	PRESCHOOL-AGE (0–5) MATURATION AND DEVELOPMENT	SCHOOL-AGE (6–20) TRAINING AND EDUCATION	ADULT (21 AND OVER) SOCIAL AND VOCATIONAL CAPABILITIES
Profound (IQ below 20)	Gross retardation; minimal capacity for functioning in sensorimotor areas; needs nursing care.	Some motor development present; cannot profit from training in self-help; needs total care.	Some motor and speech development; totally incapable of self-maintenance; must have complete care and supervision.
Severe (IQ 20–35)	Poor motor development; speech is minimal; generally unable to profit from training in self-help; little or no communication skill.	Can talk or learn to communicate; can be trained in elemental health habits; cannot learn functional academic skills; profits from systematic habit training.	Can contribute partially to self-support under complete supervision; can develop self-protection skills to a minimal useful level in controlled environment.
Moderate (IQ 36–52)	Can talk or learn to communicate; poor social awareness; fair motor development; may profit from self-help; can be managed with moderate supervision.	Can learn functional academic skills to approximately 4th-grade level by late teens if given special education.	Capable of maintaining himself in unskilled or semi-skilled occupations, needs supervision and guidance when under mild social or economic stress.
Mild (IQ 53–68)	Can develop social and communication skills; minimal retardation in the sensorimotor areas; is rarely distinguished from normal until later age.	Can learn academic skills to approximately 6th-grade level by late teens. Cannot learn general high school subjects. Needs special education particularly at secondary school age levels.	Capable of social and vocational adequacy with proper education and training. Frequently needs supervision and guidance under serious social or economic stress.

SOURCE: Adapted from *Health, Education and Welfare Indicators*, U.S. Department of Health, Education, and Welfare, June, 1962, p. vi.

sored locally and supported by state and federal government funds. These clinics, which serve a limited area or an entire region, have been increasing at a rapid rate. In 1950 there was not one specialized full-time clinic for the mentally retarded in the United States. By 1970, there were over 100 clinics of this type in operation.

The clinical team, which travels from community to community offering expert services on scheduled days, also helps to identify individuals with mental health problems. While the effectiveness of the traveling team is limited in many ways, the program does make services available to many communities which otherwise would be without them.

The White House Conference in 1960 recommended that community facilities for diagnosis and identification be available to anyone suspected of a mental handicap, and that integrated diagnostic study involving all necessary professional skills be provided. It was also recommended that services for adequate identification and treatment be planned, organized, and distributed to be available as early as possible, as continuously as possible, with as little dislocation as possible, and with as much social restoration as possible, and that these services be integrated at the local level with all the available health, education, and welfare services. The conference also recommended that schools provide multidiscipline services for identification of mental handicaps at the start of a child's school experience, with evaluation throughout his education.

These recommendations served as guidelines for local, state, and federal government programs and had been implemented to some degree by 1970. Most programs, however, were faced with a serious lack of funds and qualified personnel.[3]

EDUCATION AND TRAINING

The education and training of the mentally retarded poses a problem of major proportions, particularly at the level of the local community. More than 90 percent of the retarded remain in the community and must be provided for by local agencies. Depending upon the financial and psychological resources of the patient's family, the community must assume a greater or lesser share of responsibility for care, education, training, and rehabilitation. Even under the most favorable family circumstances, the community must contribute in various ways to the job of training and educating the retarded. Whether the mentally retarded patient becomes a community problem or a community asset depends in large measure upon the availability of community services and a constructive community attitude.

The education and training possibilities in the field of mental retardation are much greater than most authorities realized until recently. The U.S. Office of Education reported that in 1922 there were 23,000 mentally retarded children in special classes. By 1970, this figure had increased to over a quarter of a million.

Most of the growth of school programs for retarded children who are educable has occurred in recent years. The special classes, for children in the IQ range of 50 to 75, are staffed ideally by teachers with training in dealing with the mentally retarded. These classes involve programs of study tailored to the slower intellectual development of the students. While important strides have been taken by state officials and the local boards of education in the improvement and expansion of special school programs for the retarded, much remains to be done.

Whether a mentally retarded child is educable depends upon a number of factors. Ordinarily such a child is educable if he shows a rate of intellectual development which is from one-half to three-fourths that expected of a normal child of the same age. He is also considered educable if he can be expected to acquire fourth- or fifth-grade achievement in academic subject matter, even if he does not begin his formal reading until he is nine to twelve years old. The educable mentally retarded child is able to develop adequate communication skills for ordinary situations, to develop social adequacy, and in most cases to develop occupational skills which result in economic independence later in life.

The methods used for educating the mentally retarded at the elementary level include various types of special classes and the special school. The special class may be homogeneous, with a narrow range of chronological and mental ages, or heterogeneous, with a wide range. The homogeneous class is more likely to be found in a large school system, while the heterogeneous class is more typical of the small school system. In the case of the special school, the children are transported from various areas to a center for the mentally retarded.

A variety of methods are used at the secondary level. In the integrated special class, the pupil spends part of each day in the special class with an adjusted program and part of each day in regular classes in industrial arts, home economics, physical education, music, arts and crafts, and other activity courses. In some cities there is an adjusted regular class program in which the retarded are placed in the slow sections of regular classes, so that more individual attention may be given to them. In a few large cities there are special occupational high schools offering apprenticeship training and preparation for a variety of semiskilled jobs.

Special programs for the moderately retarded, or "trainable," children (as opposed to mildly re-

---

[3]*Mental Retardation* is a bimonthly magazine containing relatively nontechnical articles and news items about developments and programs in the field of retardation. It is available from the American Association on Mental Deficiency, P. O. Box 96, Willimantic, Conn. 06226.

tarded, or "educable," children) have also been introduced in some school systems. However, because of additional problems, programs for trainable children have not developed as rapidly as programs for the educable, even taking into account the fewer numbers of trainable children.

The eventual effectiveness of trainable children was demonstrated dramatically by a study of pupils who had attended New York City classes for children with IQs of between 40 and 50 (Saenger, 1957). It was found that only 26 percent were subsequently institutionalized, 27 percent of those residing in the community were working for pay at the time the study was made, and another 9 percent had worked for pay at one time or another.

In addition to special classes and schools, other programs for education and training have been developed. The day-care center meets the needs of the child who is too young or too retarded to be included in other community programs. When such children remain at home, they place a heavy burden on other family members, particularly where the financial pressure is such that both parents must work. Even under favorable family circumstances, isolation in the home does not provide the stimulation which has been found helpful in so many cases. The day-care center is also of considerable help to the parents because it gives some relief from the often difficult task of caring for the retarded child, makes it possible to spend more time with nonretarded children in the family, allows the mother to work if necessary, and contributes to a generally healthier family and social life.

The sheltered workshop is another phase of education and training for the mentally retarded. Among the educable group, many adolescents and young adults need special work experience in a controlled environment before they can be placed on jobs in the open community. The sheltered workshop gives such individuals the opportunity to develop their work skills to a point where they can get a job. In the case of the trainable group, the sheltered workshop offers an opportunity for continuing work supervision. In most instances, members of this group do not become eligible for outside placement.

The Office of Vocational Rehabilitation of the U.S. Department of Health, Education, and Welfare makes grants available to states for the purpose of extending and improving services for the vocational rehabilitation of the mentally retarded. Work projects, vocational training centers, counselor training, counseling services, purchase of equipment, and similar programs have been made available.

The parents of mentally retarded children are faced with very special problems quite unknown to the parents of children with average intelligence. The physical and emotional needs of mentally retarded children and their problems of social adjustment place heavy demands on the parents. Even when parents have strong emotional resources, special problems are likely to arise for which there is no ready solution. Moreover, as the child grows older, there are matters of physical health, schooling, and, in the more serious cases, placement which must be considered carefully. For these reasons, parent-counseling services have been made available in a number of communities.

Through counseling, parents can be brought to understand the importance and implications of diagnostic findings, planning can be facilitated for the immediate and long-range care of the child, plans can be worked out for education and training, and, often most important, the parents can be helped to accept the retarded child and to handle their own emotional problems in this connection.

For mentally retarded children who live at home, community-sponsored educational and training programs must be supplemented by home training services. Most parents are not sufficiently knowledgeable to cope with the complex psychological and social problems posed by a retarded child. They need specialized training, advice, guidance, and frequently emotional support in order to meet the needs of the child. For this reason, various local, state, and federal agencies offer an increasing number of services to parents in order to raise the level of home training.

There are many ways in which state vocational rehabilitation agencies have been organizing and developing their services for the mentally retarded. Of prime importance has been the growing reliance on counselors and other vocational rehabilitation staff who work only with retarded individuals. This specialized staff, whose numbers have increased as programs and facilities have expanded, may be assigned to local vocational rehabilitation offices, schools, institutions, sheltered workshops, or other facilities serving the mentally retarded. By concentrating their attention, these counselors attempt to develop rehabilitation plans based on the special problems of the retarded and to be broadly responsive to the needs of both the retarded individual and his family.

Specialized vocational rehabilitation staffs have been particularly effective in developing cooperative vocational rehabilitation–school programs that help the retarded make a satisfying transition from school to work. These cooperative school programs are found in many communities throughout the country and have greatly strengthened both special education and vocational rehabilitation efforts with the retarded. The cooperative program structure varies greatly from state to state. In some states, program administration is statewide; in others there are individual arrangements with individual school districts. Some programs function only to serve the mentally retarded, and others include youth with all kinds of disabilities. In some states, only vocational rehabilitation and special education are involved, while in others vocational education is included.

Most cooperative arrangements have resulted in vocationally oriented curricula within the schools. All of them, however, provide for a comprehensive evaluation of the retarded young person's vocational rehabilitation potential; the provision of personal adjustment and prevocational training; counseling; on-the-job training and work experience; job placement; and follow-up and related vocational rehabilitation case services.

The number of retarded young people enrolled in cooperative vocational rehabilitation work-study programs is increasing steadily as new programs are developed. These cooperative programs have reduced the school dropout rate of retarded youngsters and have provided continuous service to youngsters during the school years when they are best able to benefit from them.

Recent research efforts have resulted in a variety of community-based projects that involve community resources in training the retarded and easing their transition into the wider community. For example, the San Francisco Aid for Retarded Children, Inc., worked with retarded adults who had little or no employment background. It was found that 40 percent of the group could be trained and placed in outside employment. A number of work-study programs for retarded adolescents have been sponsored by state divisions of Vocational Rehabilitation jointly with local school boards, parent organizations, private schools, and state departments of education. In these projects which also included severely retarded adolescents, 40 percent have been placed in outside jobs.

The Bourbon County Schools work-study project, one of several in Appalachia, was established in Kentucky, a state with one of the highest school dropout rates in the nation. The retarded subjects were children of impoverished parents; the majority were from homes of tenant farmers or farm laborers with earnings well below the poverty level. Despite the massive handicaps of cultural deprivation and mental retardation among the youngsters studied, this project, over its three-year term, reported a dropout rate of only 5 percent. Moreover, 88 percent of the sample of youngsters served have been trained and placed in jobs, thus contributing not only to their own independence, but also to the economic welfare of their parents and the community at large.

TREATMENT AND PREVENTION

The treatment of mental retardation parallels and overlaps that of personality disturbance and mental disorder. Tranquilizing drugs are as applicable to the disturbed mentally retarded as they are to the disturbed normal or the anxious neurotic. Similarly, the psychological treatment of individuals and groups applies to the mentally retarded as well as to the emotionally ill. While physical and psychological treatment are discussed in Chapters 14 and 15, there are some treatment procedures which are more or less unique to several of the clinical types of mental retardation. Because of the specialized nature of these treatment methods, they will be discussed briefly here.

The prevention of mental retardation is closely bound to the treatment of the underlying cause.

In fact, prevention is a matter of early detection so that the necessary treatment measures can be instituted before serious brain damage occurs. The most effective treatment programs are in connection with relatively few of the clinical types of mental retardation. When the intellectual deficiency is associated with biochemical disorders, early detection often makes it possible to adopt treatment measures which may completely prevent mental retardation.

The U.S. Children's Bureau and the National Institutes of Health initiated a jointly sponsored phenylketonuria-prevention program in which the blood specimens of all newborn infants were tested as part of regular hospital routine. It was emphasized that if only two babies afflicted with phenylketonuria were found in the course of the tests, the financial saving due to the avoidance of life-long severe mental retardation would equal the cost of testing the 400,000 babies in the program. In one year, at least twenty-five affected infants were located and placed on a low phenylalanine diet before brain damage or mental retardation took place as a result of the phenylketonuria. Assuming that these children would have died in an institution between age thirty-five and forty, and that the average cost to the state would have been approximately 2,000 dollars per year for each of these children, the detection program involved a potential saving to the states of almost 2 million dollars. This saving does not include the value of potential earnings and productivity of the twenty-five children.

There is also growing interest in metabolic diseases other than PKU that lead to mental retardation. The Children's Bureau is supporting a study of the clinical application of screening tests to detect *galactosemia, maple syrup urine disease,* and *histidinemia.* Support is also being given by the bureau to conduct studies of new approaches to broader screening methods, for example, a battery of automated tests for screening metabolic diseases. In addition, field trials are being conducted of a simple method to determine elevations of ten different amino acids for detection of metabolic disorders.

Increasing attention is also being paid to lead poisoning. Lead is still an ingredient in many paints, and many children become mentally retarded or suffer other damage from eating lead paint that has flaked off walls and woodwork in old, dilapidated housing. Programs of prevention, casefinding, follow-up of cases, and other measures have been initiated to cope with this problem.

Endocrine therapy is also available for the treatment of selected mental retardates, primarily cases of hypothyroidism. At one time the hypothyroid was an important clinical type in institutions for the mentally retarded. Today, thanks to the increased knowledge of endocrinology and the development of hormone therapy, few cases of hypothyroidism enter hospitals for the mentally retarded.

The tranquilizing drugs, which are discussed in detail in Chapter 14 are designed to control behavior rather than to improve intellectual functioning. However, the child who can be made more tranquil is better able to make use of his resources, and for this reason his functioning is improved. While the tranquilizers do not make him more intelligent, they may control disturbing behavioral symptoms and thereby make it possible for the retarded patient to function more effectively. In this sense, the drugs may be of value in the treatment of some of the mentally retarded. Surgery can also prove useful in certain cases of mental retardation, especially when the retardation is associated with hydrocephaly, craniostenosis, or brain tumors.

The most common form of mental retardation, the familial type, ordinarily cannot be prevented, nor is specific organic treatment indicated. The treatment in these cases is more likely to be social and psychological than medical. Even though there is no possibility of correcting the low mental capacity in these cases, the patient can be helped in various ways to realize his fullest potential.

While the problem of psychological treatment is discussed at length in Chapter 15, it should be noted here that this form of treatment has assumed an important place in the field of mental retardation since the middle 1950s. Prior to that time, psychological treatment was used very little with retarded patients. It was assumed quite generally that average or higher intellectual ability was needed in order to profit from this treatment approach. Leading authorities in the field emphasized that the mentally retarded group was not amenable to the approach. Similarly, several widely publicized studies seemed to indicate that treatment success was related in a positive way to level of intelligence. However, the developing interest in other problems related to mental retardation encouraged a number of psychologists and psychiatrists to take another look at the possibility of utilizing psychological treatment with the retarded. It is now well established that psychotherapy, particularly on a group basis, and behavior therapy can be beneficial in selected cases of mental retardation.

Greater emphasis is being placed on study and research in genetics and on genetic counseling to decrease and prevent the hereditary forms of mental retardation. Programs for early diagnosis and treatment are being made available through public health services and hospital laboratories in order to prevent some of the biochemical forms of mental deficiency. Finally, special attention is being paid to the care and treatment of mentally retarded children in deprived groups, and particularly to preventing socially determined mental retardation through the improvement of the economic, social, educational, and nutritional situation.

RESEARCH APPROACH

As in other fields of mental health, future advances in connection with the mentally retarded will depend upon more research. The recognition of this fact has led to a sharply increased emphasis on research in prevention, diagnosis, treatment, education, and care. Most of the research has been directed toward medical problems, because local, state, and federal funds in this area have been more readily available. However, there has been an increasing trend toward research in the behavioral fields. This research directs itself more especially to problems of a psychological and psychosocial nature.

The complexity of mental retardation requires multidisciplinary research approaches. It is encouraging to observe that not only are the obvious combinations (such as biochemists working with psychopharmacologists) becoming more and more common, but less expected combinations, such as behavioral scientists working closely with clinical and basic scientists, are beginning

to be seen. The Mental Retardation Research Centers which are funded by Congress under Public Law 88-164 are serving to facilitate this kind of interdisciplinary effort.

Research in mental retardation utilizes a vast array of techniques, from classical observation and description to the most advanced and sophisticated electronic recording and statistical methods. Since for some kinds of work it is neither feasible nor desirable to use human subjects, a number of investigators are attempting to develop appropriate animal models for research use.

Evidence from work with a variety of animal species, supplemented by scattered tests in humans, indicates that protein and calories deprivation may inhibit mental and social development. In animal studies, these effects seem to depend upon fairly acute nutritional deprivation of the type only seen in grossly malnourished children. Several studies have been organized in South and Central America, where malnutrition is widespread, thereby providing a natural test area for the relationships between nutritional deprivation and intellectual and social development.

The largest of these studies is being undertaken in the Guatemala Highlands by the Institute for Nutrition of Central America and Panama, under a contract with the Pan American Health Organization. This study involves matching pairs of rural, isolated villages on a number of factors, and then providing a protein-rich food supplement to one village in each pair. The other village will also receive medical care (but no diet supplement), with provisions to match social inputs that might positively influence intellectual development. Continuous data monitoring measures intellectual development up through age six.

Another study, conducted by Harvard University and the National Institute of Nutrition at Bogota, is investigating the development of pairs of siblings living in urban ghettos in Bogota, Columbia. These pairs of children, all under the age of three years, include one acutely malnourished and one adequately nourished child, both of whom are receiving supplemented diets throughout the study. This design permits control of genetic variables and, to a considerable degree, the social and environmental factors surrounding malnutrition. Tests also are being used to follow the emotional development of the children.

In Mexico, investigators are focusing on nutrition of the mother and the infant. They are making controlled studies of breast milk consumption, because premature weaning without adequate food substituted is increasingly recognized as a probable factor in impaired development of the central nervous system and in possible behavior deficits in deprived children. Another project, in Chile, is studying children who have been hospitalized with acute malnutrition at a very early age, often as young as six to eight months. The behavioral patterns of these children following nutritional rehabilitation are being monitored. An interesting part of this project has been the development of a method of cerebral transillumination which provides clear indications of the amount of fluid within the cranial cavity, thereby indicating the relative reduction in brain size as a result of nutritional deprivation.

In the area of learning, investigators are conducting a variety of analyses of the learning process as it operates among the mentally retarded, with a view toward identifying techniques which may facilitate that process. Such variables as attention span, capacity for retention, distortions of perception, and visual discrimination are being scrutinized to increase the retardate's ability to absorb and profit from his experiences, and to facilitate his intellectual and social development. A specific goal of this work is to develop improved teaching methods. Automated teaching techniques are being used in several studies, focusing on programmed learning to develop reading and other skills.

A report of the American Association on Mental Deficiency Project on Technical Planning in Mental Retardation stated the research objective in the following words:

> Our goal should be to promote expanded programs of research in all areas related to mental defect and retardation. Progress in methods of prevention, treatment, diagnosis, education and training, and rehabilitation, depends upon research. Much past research has been unitary and sporadic. The research leadership in universities, hospitals, clinics, and in the larger grant agencies should give more attention to planning in the total research effort so that basic and applied research, research in the medical and behavioral sciences, and research in what appears to be neglected areas receive the relative consideration and stimulation they deserve.

The greatest impetus to research has been the availability of federal funds through the National Institute of Mental Health and the National Institute of Neurological Diseases and Blindness, as well as other government agencies. These funds go to hospitals, medical schools, universities, and private laboratories.

Private agencies have also been important in fostering research in the field of mental retardation. A long-term study of the biochemical aspects of mental retardation is being carried out at the California Institute of Technology under a Ford Foundation grant. Research centers have been established at the Johns Hopkins University and the Massachusetts General Hospital with funds furnished by the Joseph P. Kennedy, Jr., Foundation.

The federal government has recommended that research be undertaken in the following areas:

1. The nature of intellectual skills required to permit the mentally retarded to function independently in the several sectors of our society.

2. Differential abilities in the mentally retarded, for better understanding of individual differences beyond the unitary IQ index.

3. Development of guidelines for grouping children according to their learning characteristics.

4. Assessment of the cumulative effects of continuous developmental programs.

5. Factors contributing to an unfavorable stereotype of the mentally retarded in public and professional groups, for action programs to modify this stereotype.

The recommendation has also been made that a uniform method of recording and reporting data be developed and adopted to facilitate research in mental retardation, and that financial support of promising programs of research and training of research personnel in the field of mental handicaps be multiplied many times.[4]

SUMMARY

1. Mental retardation was a relatively neglected subject until the middle of this century, when there was a renewed interest in the problem. While mental retardation is not a personality disturbance, there are so many related emotional problems that the condition can be treated as a part of abnormal psychology. Also, the early history of mental retardation paralleled the history of mental illness, even though the mentally retarded were somewhat better understood and treated more humanely.

2. Some key points in the history of mental retardation were the study of the case of Victor, the "Wild Boy of Aveyron," the opening of special institutions for the retarded during the nineteenth century, and the emphasis on family studies of retardation triggered by the publication of Mendel's work on inheritance. More recent attention has centered on new developments in biochemistry and on social and psychological advances in education, training, and treatment.

3. Terminology in the field of mental retardation has been confusing because of lack of agreement on definitions and classifications. The most important bases of classification are *measured intelligence, adaptive behavior,* and *etiology.* Measured intelligence is a matter of test scores, while adaptive behavior involves educability and trainability. Classification in terms of etiology, or causal factors, includes conditions due to infection, intoxication, brain injury, and disorders of metabolism. Additional conditions are due to unknown prenatal influences, uncertain organic causes, and presumed psychologic causes. Most cases of mental retardation fall in the last-named group.

4. It is important to identify and diagnose mental retardation early because it is only in this way that effective treatment can be undertaken. However, the problem is complicated by the fact that very few cases show early pathology of the nervous system or biochemical disturbances. In order to arrive at the earliest possible identification and diagnosis, a variety of community services have been developed for these purposes.

5. Since more than 90 percent of the mentally retarded remain in the community, the problem of education and training is an important one. The retarded can be divided into three groups: the *educable,* the *trainable,* and the *untrainable.* The first group is the largest and includes those children and adults who can learn to become self-supporting individuals. They must learn at a relatively slow pace, and special schools and classes are required for them. Those in the trainable group can also learn, but they must live and work in a sheltered environment. The untrainable group is the smallest and is made up of those individuals who must be taken care of throughout their lifetimes.

---

[4]Recommended books dealing with research in the field of mental retardation are *Behavioral Research in Mental Retardation* (University of Oregon, 1968), edited by H. J. Prehm et al.; *Handbook of Mental Deficiency: Psychological Theory and Research* (McGraw-Hill, 1963), edited by N. R. Ellis; and *Mental Retardation: A Review of Research* (University of Chicago Press, 1964), edited by H. A. Stevens and R. Heber.

6. The treatment of mental retardation, which includes *drugs, surgery,* and *psychological treatment,* is determined by the cause of the particular disturbance. When the retardation is identified early enough, it is sometimes possible to lessen the severity of the retardation or to prevent it entirely by appropriate physical treatment. Once the retardation has established itself, treatment measures are limited to training, education, and behavior therapy. While these methods do little to alter the underlying retardation, they make it possible for the patient to realize his full potential and to make a better adjustment in terms of his work, his social life, and his personal life.

7. The research approach to mental retardation makes use of a variety of techniques and concerns itself with a wide range of problems. Considerable emphasis is being placed on the role of malnutrition as a contributing cause of retardation. Research in the area of learning ability is directed toward discovering effective methods for modifying the behavior of retarded individuals to facilitate their social and intellectual development.

13 PSYCHODIAGNOSIS

To gain a full understanding of the field of abnormal psychology, it is necessary to consider the problems of diagnosis and treatment as well as those of historical development, causation, and the description of the clinical syndromes. This chapter, and the two chapters following, deal with the practical matters of how the clinical psychologist and the psychiatrist go about uncovering and identifying the various forms of personality disturbance, and how such conditions are treated once they have been recognized and classified.

The word *diagnosis,* used widely in medicine and increasingly in psychology, social work, and remedial education, means identification of a disease or disorder and recognition of its relationship to other conditions. In medicine, the diagnosis is made on the basis of physical signs and symptoms. Body temperature, pulse rate, blood pressure, blood cell count, skin color, reflexes, pain, nausea, and similar symptoms combine to form the diagnostic picture of physical illnesses. In the same way, psychological signs combine to give the characteristic picture of the different psychological disorders. Psychodiagnosis is the specialized technique in which psychological methods are used to reveal the nature and extent of psychological damage. As such, psychodiagnostic procedures are used in a variety of situations, from the identification of the problem child in public school to the classification of the seriously disturbed person in the psychiatric hospital.

Accurate diagnosis has important practical significance because treatment must be directed toward specific and identifiable diagnostic categories. In general medicine, penicillin is remarkably effective in certain types of pneumonia (pneumococcal) but useless in other types (viral). Similarly, attempts must be made to identify specific subgroups of psychological disturbances which are responsive to one type of therapy but not another.

At the same time, the inadequacy of current diagnostic techniques has been demonstrated repeatedly. In one study of patients admitted to the psychiatric ward of a general hospital, only 34 percent of the patients (most with chronic and severe illnesses) could be given an adequate diagnosis within the categories provided by the Diagnostic Manual of the American Psychiatric Association (Pinsker, 1968).

A different type of evidence indicating the uncertainty of diagnosis in psychiatric conditions was a cross-cultural study comparing the diagnoses of psychotic patients from essentially similar populations in outpatient clinics in the United States and the Netherlands. Americans classified patients as "schizophrenic" thirteen times more often than did their Dutch colleagues. The questions raised are: Is schizophrenia really that much more prevalent in the United States? Are the criteria for diagnosis different in the two countries? Or do we require more knowledge to define the specific nature of the disorder called schizophrenia?

Table 13.1 illustrates the problem of obtaining reliable psychiatric diagnoses by listing six clinical categories along with the percentage of agreement among psychiatrists.

THE CLINICAL APPROACH

The clinical approach, in contrast to psychological testing and to the measurement of physiological variables, is one in which the individual is studied as a unique whole. In the diagnosis of personality disorganization, the clinical approach is used by psychologists as well as psychiatrists. The major clinical techniques employed in psychodiagnosis are (1) the case history, (2) the diagnostic interview, and (3) the analysis of expressive behavior.

THE CASE HISTORY

The case history is the starting point for the clinical evaluation. The history brings together all available information about the individual under study. It serves not only to orient the psychologist and the psychiatrist to the total situation, but also in many cases to yield important clues which determine the direction of the diagnostic interview. The major areas covered in the case history include:

1. Identifying information, such as name, address, age, religion, occupation, and marital status
2. A statement of the problem
3. The reason for referral
4. Family history and background, including information on grandparents, parents, and brothers and sisters
5. Health and medical history, including child-

Table 13.1 *Extent to which psychiatrists agreed on diagnosis for six clinical categories*

CATEGORY	PERCENT AGREEMENT
Personality trait disturbance	38
Involutional melancholia	40
Schizophrenic reaction	53
Sociopath	54
Anxiety reaction	55
Neurotic depression	63

From A. T. Beck et al., "Reliability of Psychiatric Diagnoses. 2: A Study of Consistency of Clinical Judgments and Ratings," *Amer. J. Psychiat.*, **119**: 351–357, 1962.

hood diseases, accidents and injuries, and surgical operations

6. School and educational background, including level attained, past failures, and special difficulties
7. Personal and social adjustment as a child, as an adolescent, and as an adult
8. Work and occupational record, including jobs held, wages, and adjustment to the work situation
9. Marital history and adjustment, including courtship, family climate, and relationship to marital partner and children
10. Personality description

The effectiveness of the case history depends upon the care with which it has been prepared and the accuracy of the information it contains. Some clinics and hospitals are fortunate in having a social service department with trained social workers who have the skill and time to collect and organize large amounts of background data. In such agencies, the clinician is furnished with the complete case history. However, in many settings, the case history material is prepared by untrained workers. In other agencies and institutions, the clinical psychologist or the psychiatrist must rely upon the diagnostic interview for background information. Here taking the history is not merely a means of collecting information; it is a method for establishing contact with the troubled individual and creating a workable interpersonal relationship.

THE DIAGNOSTIC INTERVIEW

The second major clinical technique used in psychodiagnosis is the personal interview. In this approach, the clinician sees the person, talks to him, asks him questions, and observes his reactions and behavior. In many instances, the diagnostic interview requires as much as an hour or longer, although some cases are so clear-cut in their symptom pictures that a diagnosis can be made in a very few minutes. Where a particularly difficult problem of differential diagnosis exists, more than one diagnostic interview may be required.

The diagnostic value of the personal interview depends to a large extent upon the skill and experience of the clinician. Signs and symptoms are meaningless unless the observer is able to appreciate their significance. The student who aspires to a career in clinical psychology, psychiatry, psychiatric nursing, or psychiatric social work must realize that there is no adequate substitute for personal contact. No amount of reading of textbooks, case histories, or psychological reports can take the place of direct experience with men, women, and children who show the various forms of personality disorganization.

Through repeated and intensive contact with people who are having problems, the student interviewer gradually emerges into a clinician. With each new case the clinical frame of reference becomes enlarged, and the pattern seen today becomes a standard of comparison for tomorrow. In this way, clinical judgment develops and becomes increasingly sensitive. Much of psychodiagnosis remains more an art than a science, however one might wish it to be otherwise.

Even so, the diagnostic interview does have its objective guideposts in the form of the behavior characteristics of the individual being studied. From the moment the individual walks through the door of the clinician's office, he is telling the psychologists something about himself. One person enters the office with complete possession and self-confidence, another enters shyly and with embarrassment, still another appears suspicious, and others are hostile, depressed, anxious, or agitated. Such signs are noted automatically by the clinician, even before the first words have been exchanged.

Throughout the diagnostic interview, the individual reveals himself in the tone of his voice, his posture, the expression of his face, the gestures he uses, the movements of his limbs, and similar actions. All this is quite apart from the answers to questions or the story related by the patient. What the person says may be of considerably less importance than how he looks and acts. The diagnostic interview in the hands of a skilled clinician is probably the most important single factor in understanding and classifying the disorganized personality.

EXPRESSIVE BEHAVIOR

An important aspect of the diagnosis of personality disturbance is the analysis of expressive behavior. The way in which a person writes, walks, talks, and draws sometimes reveals more about his problems, conflicts, and disturbances than hours of interviews and tests. Posture, gesture, motor attitudes, and muscular movements reflect underlying psychological states to a very considerable extent.

It has been recognized for many centuries that a person reveals something of his personality in his body movements. In Proverbs 6:12–13, the Bible says, "A naughty person, a wicked man, walketh with a froward mouth. He winketh with his eyes, he speaketh with his feet, he teacheth with his fingers. . . ." Movement is a language of personality that comes to be known to every clinician who works in the area of psychological diagnosis.

Symbolic Movement

The postures, gestures, gait, and physical attitudes of the person with an emotional disturbance are important clues to the inner dynamics of the disorder. Such movements sometimes have a symbolic meaning and may be of significance for treatment. While movements often are expressions of immediate emotional states, they may also be reactions to former life experiences. Freud believed that such movements represent the reappearance in consciousness of repressed fantasies and memories. Today there is widespread interest in the conscious and unconscious significance of the way people stand, walk, sit, and move. Behavior of this type has been called "body language" (Fast, 1970).

A study of postural behavior during psychoanalytic treatment showed that such behavior is motivated by underlying psychological processes. It was found that the postural pattern may become temporarily or permanently altered as psychological changes occur during treatment. These movements and positions resemble the primitive actions and physical attitudes of infants. It is as if the emotional regression associated with phases of the treatment provokes regressive postures.

In the case of one individual, the arms were kept rigid and close to the body, a posture which soon was revealed as related to attempts to control thoughts of childhood autoerotic practices. The expression of hostility and aggression was accompanied by the involuntary clenching of the fists. Anxiety and insecurity were revealed by an excessive amount of restless turning and shifting of position (Deutsch, 1947).

In the mentally retarded, as well as in psychotics, the rockings, suckings, head-bangings, and bizarre rhythmic movements may be related to primitive erotic needs. Sometimes the movements are mere expressions of pleasure; occasionally they are more overtly sexual.

Language

There is also a close and revealing relationship between the form and content of speech and the unconscious life of the individual. Freudian psychology emphasizes the relationship between unintended forms of verbal expression and unconscious dynamics. It is also possible that metaphors and idioms which are used today in an abstract way once may have had a concrete and even magical meaning. These meanings may still be alive in the unconscious of the individuals who use them.

As early as 1916, it was suggested that mental disorder should be studied in terms of speech behavior and that a significant relationship exists between language structure and personality structure (Southard, 1922). Another psychiatrist insisted that the structure of language in behavior disorders might well be investigated with the same detailed care that is used in the study of cell structure (Whitehorn and Zipf, 1943). While we have a great distance to go in this direction, there has been a constantly growing interest in the language of emotionally disturbed individuals. The three major diagnostic approaches based on language are the analysis of (1) tone and quality of the voice, (2) syntax, or grammatical constructions, and (3) semantics, or meaning.

Handwriting

Handwriting is another form of expressive behavior. The assumption is made that if there are no physical or physiological barriers, a person's

(a)

(b)

(c)

(d)

(e)

Figure 13.1 *Paintings of a cat by an artist who developed a mental illness. In the early part of the century one of the best-known British artists was Louis Wain, an eccentric bachelor who lived surrounded by the cats that he used as models for his popular drawings. In the early 1920s Wain had a schizophrenic breakdown with intermittent relapses until his death in 1936. Note the progressive increase in detail and the increasingly abstract treatment. There is a preoccupation with detail and a compulsive filling in of space. Both of these characteristics are likely to be found in drawings by schizophrenic individuals. (World Health Organization, Guttman-Maclay Collection.)*

handwriting will reveal his characteristic tension systems. Handwriting is certainly one of the languages used by the unconscious to make itself understood, and many clinicians, particularly those trained in Europe, feel that the analysis of handwriting can be useful in the description and diagnosis of personality disturbances.

Various types of handwriting disturbances have been suggested in the different clinical conditions. In brain disorders, the organic disturbance of the brain causes an impairment of the perceptual and motor control necessary in writing. The patient with syphilis of the brain shows coordinative difficulties, with rapid and careless writing, irregular tremors, frequent blotting, and omission of letters and words. In the affective psychoses, the depressed individual is believed to exhibit a slow and deliberate style of writing, with a tendency to run downward in words and lines and a shrinking of capital letters. The manic on the other hand, is more likely to be inconsistent in the overall dimensions of his writing, as well as in the direction and slant of his writing. Letters and words may be large and expanded, and the background may be involved in some cases.

Art Productions

A variety of art forms have been used as an aid to psychodiagnosis. Drawings, brush painting, finger painting, clay modeling, and sculpture are expressive media through which the unconscious needs and conflicts of individuals with disorganized personalities are revealed to the psychologist and the psychiatrist.

At the form level, the art productions of the mentally disordered may show lack of integration, distortions and disproportions, stereotypy and perseveration, the compulsive filling in of space, lack of symmetry, and similar features which are seldom found in the drawings of those who are not mentally disturbed. The content may reflect the underlying nature of the pathological process. Among psychotics, there may be a representation of delusional ideas or hallucinatory experiences. Drawings may stress sexual or religious themes, or the material may be symbolic or allegorical. Paranoid individuals may depict ambitious projects, making use of plans, maps, and complex designs. Sexual themes, hidden or overt, are not uncommon and sometimes are indicative of disturbances of psychosexual development.[1]

[1]For supplementary reading in the general area of psychodiagnosis the student is referred to the appropriate sections of any one of a number of excellent surveys of clinical psychology, such as the *Handbook of Clinical Psychology* (McGraw-Hill, 1965), edited by B. B. Wolman; *Clinical Psychology: An Introduction to Research and Practice* (Appleton Century Crofts, 1962) by N. D. Sundberg and L. E. Tyler; and Molly Harrower's *The Practice of Clinical Psychology* (Thomas, 1961).

PSYCHOLOGICAL TESTING

The use of psychological tests in psychodiagnosis is a specialty practiced largely by the clinical psychologist. Psychiatrists ordinarily do not have the time, inclination, or training to make use of the many specialized testing techniques available to the mental health clinician. Yet one of the country's best-known psychiatrists said, "The practice of psychiatry without the assistance of modern psychological testing is as old-fashioned and out-of-date as would be the practice of orthopedics without the X-ray" (Menninger et al., 1947).

While few clinicians would disagree with this view, there has been a growing dissatisfaction with the conventional and established psychological tests. Even the best of the clinical tests have been questioned as to their standardization, reliability, and validity. Such tests are particularly vulnerable to criticism on the basis of inadequate standardization with minority groups.

The most useful psychodiagnostic tests can be grouped under three major headings: (1) tests to measure intelligence, or general ability, and its deficiencies, (2) tests to detect brain damage, and (3) tests to evaluate personality, either in its totality or in terms of isolated traits or trait systems.

EVALUATION OF INTELLIGENCE

The cornerstone of psychodiagnostic testing is the evaluation of intellectual functioning. The degree of organization of the factors contributing to intelligence, as well as the level of organization, are diagnostic reference points of considerable value to the clinician. While there is no generally acceptable definition of intelligence, most definitions emphasize the degree of integration of present patterns of behavior and the ability to modify these patterns as a result of new experience.

The intelligence of an individual is of importance in psychodiagnosis in a number of ways. At first glance, it might appear that intelligence has a bearing only on the question of whether or not a person is mentally retarded. The determination of intellectual level in such cases is certainly of critical importance and may very well mean the difference between an individual's being institutionalized or permitted to make an effort to adjust to a society which is intellectually superior to him. However, the measurement of intelligence for such purposes is only one limited aspect of the usefulness of the evaluation of intelligence in psychodiagnosis.

Through the measurement of intellectual functioning, the clinician is able to study the ways in which personality disorganization has interfered with intellectual activity. Since different forms of psychopathology affect intelligence in different ways, it is helpful diagnostically to have a clear picture of the present level of general ability even though that present level is not an accurate reflection of true ability. Such factors as apathy, hostility, lack of interest, poor motivation, inattention, impairment of memory, and organic deficit operate to mask the real ability of the individual.

The job of the clinician is not only to measure present ability but also to estimate potential ability and to judge accurately the reasons for any discrepancy between present intellectual functioning and actual level of ability. The measurement of intelligence is also important in psychodiagnosis because it permits the clinician to make observations under a relatively standard set of conditions. By noting the reactions to the various questions and tasks required by the clinical test of intelligence, the psychologist is able to observe such characteristics as determination, perseverance, tolerance for frustration, ability to maintain attention, emotional stability, reaction to stress, and similar personality components.

Whatever the purpose of the evaluation of intelligence—diagnosing mental retardation, studying the effects of personality disorganization on intellectual functioning, or using the test situation as a means of gaining insight into personality characteristics—the psychologist has available to him a variety of techniques for accomplishing his purpose.[2]

---

[2]Books dealing with some of the more general problems of diagnostic testing include the R. R. Holt revision of *Diagnostic Psychological Testing* (International Universities Press, 1968), edited by David Rapaport and others; Joseph Gilbert's *Clinical Psychological Tests in Psychiatric and Medical Practice* (Thomas, 1969); and *Psychological Techniques in Diagnosis and Evaluation* (Pergamon, 1960) by T. C. Kahn and M. B. Giffen.

(a)   (b)   (c)

Figure 13.2 *Pioneers in the development of individual tests of intelligence. (a) Alfred Binet 1856–1911, French physician who developed the first widely used individual test of intelligence. (National Library of Medicine, Washington, D.C.) (b) Lewis Terman, 1877–1956, Stanford University psychologist whose 1916 revision of the Binet test established it as the most widely used individual test of intelligence. (Courtesy of Stanford University.) (c) David Wechsler, 1896–   , American psychologist who developed the Wechsler-Bellevue, WAIS, and WISC tests of intelligence. (Courtesy of Dr. Wechsler.)*

EVALUATION OF BRAIN DAMAGE

For many years psychologists have been interested in the use of psychological tests to detect organic change in the brains of patients with personality disturbances. Where organic changes are pronounced, various neurological, x-ray, and electronic techniques are useful. But these physical methods are often insensitive to the early and more subtle changes in the nervous system, particularly in the brain. Because of the need for recognizing these early changes, an increasing amount of attention has been directed to tests for organicity.

In every case referred to the clinical psychologist for a diagnostic work-up, the possibility exists of underlying destructive processes in the nervous system. In many cases, this possibility is remote and can be ruled out without much difficulty. But in other cases, special methods must be used to determine the possible presence of such damage.

There have been two major lines of development related to the psychological study of brain damage. One has its roots in the interest in localized damage from injuries and accidents, brain tumors and similar processes, and surgical removal of brain tissue. The interest in this type of damage goes back many years and ranges from early clinical reports of accidental brain injury to current attempts to evaluate psychological changes accompanying advanced forms of neurosurgery.

The second line of development has grown out of early studies of psychotics. It was observed that these individuals often scored well below their expected levels on tests of intelligence. This deficiency in test performance was so general that it was assumed that a special process, called *deterioration,* was involved. For many years attempts were made to isolate and measure this deterioration factor. Today it is recognized that the only true deterioration occurs in certain diffuse organic conditions such as alcoholism, cerebral arteriosclerosis, and brain infections.

The major psychological approaches to the evaluation of organic brain damage are through the use of (1) tests of abstract thinking, (2) tests of deterioration, and (3) tests of perceptual-motor functioning.

Tests of Abstract Thinking

Some of the earliest methods of studying the psychological effects of brain damage grew out of observations during World War I. Soldiers

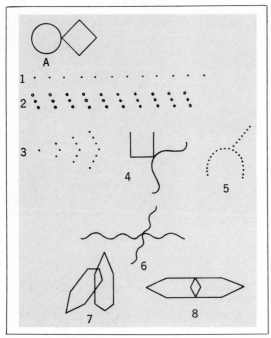

Figure 13.3 *The Bender-Gestalt test figures. (Courtesy of Dr. Lauretta Bender, and the American Orthopsychiatric Association.)*

with severe injuries to the brain sometimes were found to be able to respond to the world around them only in a limited way. The primary impairment appeared to be an inability to think in abstract terms. The thinking of the patients seemed limited to a concrete attitude.

Tests of Deterioration

Following the introduction of the Stanford-Binet test of intelligence in 1916, there was considerable interest in the frequent discrepancy seen between a mental patient's test score and his real level of ability. In many cases, patients obtained scores well below what might be expected on the basis of educational background, occupational level, and other factors. The measure of this discrepancy came to be regarded as an index of the amount of deterioration that had taken place as a result of the mental illness.

While some of the early work on deterioration included a consideration of organicity, the original concept of deterioration had a much broader connotation. The early emphasis was less on detecting organic changes than on meas-

uring the degree of breakdown in psychological functions from whatever cause.

The first important studies of deterioration were based on an analysis of the Stanford-Binet scores of psychiatric patients. In an effort to arrive at an objective way of approaching the problem, the score on the vocabulary test was used as an estimate of the intelligence of the individual prior to his illness, and the total score as an indication of present functioning. The discrepancy between these two scores was considered to be a measure of deterioration. The vocabulary score was used as an estimate of original intellectual level because vocabulary is probably the best single index of verbal intelligence and is highly resistant to change, even in the face of severe psychological breakdown. The words used and the grammatical forms remain relatively constant in spite of loss of memory, disorientation, delusions, hallucinations, and other symptoms of serious personality disorganization.

Perceptual-motor Tests

One of the most widely used clinical tests of organicity is the Bender-Gestalt Test. Lauretta Bender, a psychiatrist at Bellevue Hospital in New York City, became interested in using a series of simple designs, borrowed from the work of the German school of Gestalt psychology, to study the perceptual processes of people with personality disorders. As early as 1932, she began to study the visual-motor patterns produced by the mentally retarded and by schizophrenics (Bender, 1938). Soon she became interested in the use of the method in organic diseases of the brain. Similar studies were made of visual-motor gestalt production following head trauma. Since that time, the test has been used for a variety of purposes, including the measurement of intelligence, personality disturbance, brain injury and organicity, and the effects of therapy (Hutt and Briskin, 1960).

The administration of the test is not difficult. The patient is seated at a table and given a sheet of paper and a pencil with an eraser. He is then told that he is to copy nine designs that will be shown to him one at a time. The first design is shown, and after the patient has copied it, he is shown the second drawing, and so on until the entire series has been copied.

One of the major difficulties in the use of the Bender-Gestalt Test in diagnosis has been the lack of a widely acceptable quantitative scoring system. While Lauretta Bender suggested such a system originally, and while there have been several more recent attempts to develop a quantitative approach, most clinicians rely upon their clinical insight and intuition in making interpretations. Particular attention is paid to the qualitative aspects of the deviations made in copying the designs.

Among the more important general deviations in the Bender-Gestalt designs are oversimplification, displacement, fragmentation, distortion,

Figure 13.4 *Bender-Gestalt deviations. Drawings (compare with Figure 13.3) by people suffering from (a) alcoholism, (b) cerebral arteriosclerosis, (c) psychotic depression, (d) schizophrenia.*

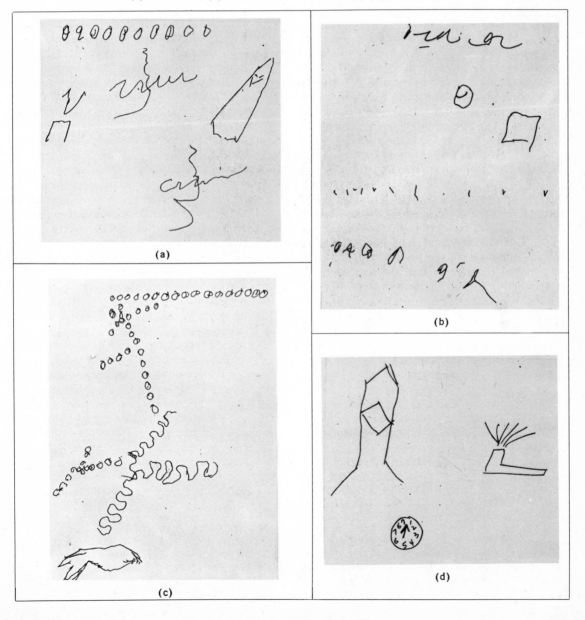

rotation, elaboration, and in the most serious cases, complete destruction of the gestalt, or pattern, of the design. In addition, each individual design lends itself to special analysis because of its unique characteristics. While psychotics sometimes show disturbed functioning on this test, the principal value of the method is considered to be in the diagnosis of organicity.

In order to improve the sensitivity of the Bender-Gestalt Test to organic brain damage, patients are sometimes required to recall the designs after having copied them. After the figures have been copied, the cards and the patient's drawings are removed, and he is given a new sheet of paper and told to draw as many of the figures as he can remember. The idea is that perceptual patterns break down relatively quickly in damaged brain fields, and that organicity will be reflected by the impairment of visual memory.[3]

EVALUATION OF PERSONALITY

Diagnostic work in the field of emotional disturbance requires, in most cases, a detailed study of the personality structure and dynamics of the person under observation. It is not enough to know the level of intelligence, the degree of the discrepancy between present intellectual functioning and actual ability, and whether organic factors might be playing a role in the person's symptoms. It is often more important to have an accurate picture of the overall personality of the individual and to have some clues about the underlying forces which have shaped the personality.

The psychologist has many tests and techniques available for the study of personality. However, these methods are not equally valuable to the clinician. Some are more suited for studying personality traits, while others are designed to reveal unconscious motivation. The major approaches to the study of personality are the *objective approach* and the *projective approach*.

The Objective Approach

The objective approach to personality study employs traditional psychological methods: (1) personality characteristics are inferred from direct observation of behavior; (2) personality traits are plotted in terms of a rating scale; and (3) the individual is asked by means of questionnaires and inventories to describe his own personality.

The clinical psychologist uses direct observation in an almost automatic way in his diagnostic work. Each time he is with an individual he is making a series of clinical judgments based on his appearance, what he says, his emotional state, and similar aspects of behavior open to observation. The validity of such observation is in direct relationship to the skill and experience of the practitioner; it is an invaluable aid to the sophisticated clinician but may be of little value to the layman or the naive interviewer.

In order to increase the effectiveness of the direct interview, the clinician sometimes uses the method of controlled observation, in which the individual is observed for predetermined periods of time or under specified conditions. In this way, it becomes possible to describe, study, and compare samples of behavior. In terms of objectivity, it is a step beyond the general clinical impression obtained as a result of relatively uncontrolled direct observation.

Since the effectiveness of clinical observation is so dependent upon the skill of the observer—his ability to sense what is important, as well as to describe it—specialized types of rating scales have been developed to make observation more objective and to permit less skilled observers such as nurses, aides, and others who have contact with disturbed individuals to participate in the evaluation of personality. The accurate observation and recording of behavior on the ward of a psychiatric hospital is of the greatest importance. Such observation and recording make possible a more objective evaluation of the changes in be-

---

[3]The specialized problems of diagnostic testing with patients with brain damage are discussed in *Neuropsychological Testing in Organic Brain Dysfunction* (Thomas, 1969), edited by W. L. Smith and M. J. Philippus; Bessie Burgmeister's *Psychological Techniques in Neurological Diagnosis* (Hoeber, 1962); and *Psychological Evaluation of the Cerebral Palsied Person* (Thomas, 1962) by R. M. Allen and T. W. Jefferson.

havior and furnish a method by means of which the effectiveness of the forms of treatment can be measured.

A number of rating scales and behavior charts have been developed to facilitate the observation and recording of the behavior of emotionally disturbed people. These scales and charts can be used to check an individual's behavior against his diagnosis, or they can be used to assist in the initial formulation of the diagnosis.

Another approach to diagnosis is the personality questionnaire or inventory. The first important test of this type was developed during World War I for use in military service. As a result of the increasing knowledge of psychological and psychiatric disorders, it became desirable to devise a method for screening out the more obviously unstable and disturbed recruits.

While a dozen or more tests of this type are available, and while some have been found useful in guidance and personnel work, most of them offer little that is useful to the clinician interested in psychodiagnosis. The single possible exception is the Minnesota Multiphasic Personality Inventory (MMPI), which appeared in 1943 (Hathaway, 1945). This test is made up of more than 500 statements which the subject is required to designate as being "true," "false," or "cannot say," insofar as the statement applies to the subject himself. The responses are scored, and the results are recorded in nine clinical diagnostic categories. However, the MMPI was designed to reflect components of the personality rather than to facilitate diagnostic classification. Because of the deceptive simplicity of this test in yielding diagnoses, the MMPI must be used with great caution by inexperienced clinicians. In the hands of an expert in the field, the MMPI becomes a valuable tool in both personality evaluation and research.

The Projective Approach

Personality diagnosis by means of the projective approach involves the revelation of the uniqueness of personality through responses to relatively unstructured materials and situations. The projective test creates an ambiguous situation in which the individual is encouraged to express himself in such a way that he will reveal unconsciously the basic structure and dynamics of his personality. The essential nature of the projective test is reflected in many clinical questions used in personality evaluation. Children are sometimes asked the question, "What kind of animal would you like to be?" The answer to this question frequently throws light on the type of personality with which the clinical staff is dealing. Consider the youngster who said he would like to be a germ. Asked why, he replied, "I'd be so small, nobody would bother me." In another case, a delinquent boy said he would like to be an alligator "because alligators can go under the water and eat people." When asked what kind of an animal he would not want to be, he replied promptly, "A leopard." The reason he gave was that leopards "eat people too fast." Very little clinical acumen is needed to sense the basic personality differences between these two boys.

Since each person responds to the world around him in a characteristic way, the nature of his response becomes a clue to his personality. Projective techniques make use of this fact by presenting the subject with more or less ambiguous stimuli in the form of inkblots, pictures, incomplete stories or sentences, isolated words, mosaics, finger paints, clay, blocks, and similar materials. The subject is required to respond to the material in any way that seems appropriate. Skilled clinical psychologists are able to make many valid inferences about a person's general behavior from the analysis of responses to projective material.

The clinical psychologist has strong convictions about the usefulness of projective techniques on the basis of his ability to predict from projective material to actual behavior, and on the basis of the comparison of projective material with material obtained from other clinical sources, such as the case history, the clinical interview, and nonprojective tests. While such validation is clinical and qualitative rather than quantitative, it is persuasive enough to make the projective method the most widely used and respected approach to personality diagnosis. There is no doubt that projective techniques in the hands of a skilled clinical psychologist are capable of giving clinical insights that could otherwise be obtained only after long and costly personality exploration.

Word-association Tests

The word-association test is a projective method in which the individual being studied is presented with a word and required to respond with the first word that comes to his mind. While nineteenth-century psychologists such as Sir Francis Galton and Wilhelm Wundt used word associations, they were interested primarily in reaction time. The use of the method in personality investigation did not develop until Sigmund Freud and his colleagues pointed out the relationship which exists between a person's word associations and his inner needs and conflicts.

Among the psychoanalysts, Carl G. Jung was interested as early as 1904 in using word association as a method for uncovering the emotional complexes hidden deep in the personality (Jung, 1919). He presented a standard list of 100 words to his patients. Through an analysis of the kinds of responses, Jung often was able to get clues to the nature of the hidden conflicts. While the Jung list of words was used widely in clinics in Europe, a list developed in the United States in 1910 had the advantage of being standardized on a large number of normal subjects and mental patients (Kent and Rosanoff, 1910). Frequency tables of responses made possible a frame of reference for the interpretation of a subject's responses. A third word-association test of importance was developed in 1946 (Rapaport et al., 1945–1946). This list of 60 words was based on psychoanalytic theory and was designed to explore the areas of aggression and sexuality, with emphasis on the oral, anal, and phallic levels of psychosexual development.

The responses to word-association tests are analyzed on two levels: (1) the *formal* level and (2) the *content* level. The formal analysis includes a study of reaction time and the various forms taken by the response. The content analysis refers to the study of the symbolic meaning of the words.

A record of the reaction time makes it possible to study emotional blocking in addition to the more obvious analysis of the response words themselves. If a person takes longer than a few seconds to respond to a stimulus word, there is the possibility of an unconscious reason for the delay. Such delays may be related to the fact that the word touches off painful associations, is un-

comfortably close to repressed experiences, or threatens to bring into consciousness material that is anxiety-provoking or guilt-laden. In addition to reaction time, the formal analysis deals with the various forms taken by the response. Some people, as an expression of resistance or as a defense against anxiety, repeat the stimulus word (Table—*Table*). Others simply modify the stimulus word and respond with a derivative form (Dark—*Darkness*). Still others give "clang" associations, or responses based on the sound of the stimulus word and not on its meaning (Hand —*Land*). Particles of speech may also be used as responses, with the individual responding with a pronoun, auxiliary verb, or an adverb.

While the formal analysis of word associations is a valuable method for determining resistance, emotional blocking, anxiety and guilt, and other evidences of conflict, it does not reveal the nature of the conflict. To obtain insight into this phase of the problem, the clinical psychologist relies on the analysis of content. Here, the meaning of the response word is studied for whatever light it might throw on the unconscious conflicts and motivations of the subject. If the word "bed" is presented to the individual and he responds promptly with the word "room," he has not given a clue to any deeper problems. But the person who responds to "bed" with the word "disgust" is making a highly personal association that might be of clinical significance.

A young woman who responded to the word "man" with the rather unusual word "shoe" later revealed a repressed incident during childhood when she was returning home from school and a man who was parked near the schoolyard enticed her into his car. When this man began making improper advances, the girl struggled free and jumped out. In her haste, she lost one of her shoes. The youngster did not tell her parents, and the traumatic incident of childhood was repressed. The word-association test uncovered a hidden source of shame and guilt that unconsciously had been bothering the young woman for nearly twenty years.

Some clinicians object to the word-association test because they feel that it yields limited information on the personality as a whole and requires a long time to give, considering the relatively small amount of clinically significant data so often obtained. As a result, the test is not used widely in modern psychodiagnosis. In some respects the test has been underrated, because it can be a valuable tool in cases where the individual is severely inhibited and finds it difficult to talk easily about himself.

Sentence-completion Tests

The sentence-completion test is a projective method in which a person is presented with a series of partial sentences and required to complete the meaning. Originally the method was used in Germany as a nonprojective test of intellectual ability. The first serious attempts to use the method in personality exploration were begun in the 1930s, and one of the earliest tests of this type was published in 1940 (Rohde, 1957). Several attempts were then made to devise sentence-completion tests for various assessment programs during World War II. One test was used as a projective technique in the Office of Strategic Services, and another was used for evaluating the adjustment of men in an Army Air Force convalescent hospital.

A sentence-completion test designed specifically to assist in psychodiagnosis is made up of a series of partially completed sentences beginning with simple statements related to insight and orientation. The remaining sentences in the test are concerned with ten major areas important in psychodiagnosis: depressive tendencies, hostility and aggression, sexual preoccupation, religous feeling, psychosomatic complaints, autistic tendencies, relation to parents, paranoid tendencies, fear and anxiety, and guilt feelings.

Many individuals with serious personality disturbances have a degree of insight into the disturbed nature of their thinking and behavior. The following sentence completions were selected from diagnostic examinations at a psychiatric hospital.

I am here because I am mentally ill.
I think that my mind is gone.
I am here because I am mentally disturbed.
I think that my mind is not right.
I am here because I am insane.

Fear and anxiety are shown clearly in such sentence completions as:

I am afraid of most everything and everyone.
The thoughts that I have are very frightening.
I feel tense all the time.
I worry every minute of my life.

Guilt feelings are expressed in other sentence completions:

I am sorry that I ever drank alcohol.
I feel guilty about always trying to get even.
I am ashamed of killing my first husband.
I think that hell is where I'm going.
I am ashamed of my dirty mind.

Feelings of inadequacy and inferiority are seen in such completions as:

My father was a better man than I am.
They are saying that I am a failure and a joke.
I am sorry that I failed.
Somebody is trying to make something out of me.

The sentence-completion test is also sensitive to feelings of hostility and aggression:

My thoughts are mostly of getting even with people.
I am irritated by the good for nothing, stinking city of Cincinnati, and its dirt.
I fly off the handle all the time.
My greatest fear is that I will cut my mother's head off.
I worry that I might hurt myself in some way.

Attitudes toward sexuality are expressed in many ways:

My sex life is something I have become afraid of.
Sexual thoughts aren't good.
I think that sex is dirty.
Sex relations are improper. They disgust me!
My sex life had a dull start but it promises to liven up in the future.

Suspicion and paranoid trends are quite apparent in such sentence completions as:

The thing that makes me mad is somebody trying to make me out a fool.
Somebody is trying to get me sick.
Somebody wants me to be ruined out of sheer envy and jealousy.
My greatest fear is what my enemies will try to do to me.
I worry about being followed by suspicious characters.

In addition to providing clues to personality traits and attitudes, the pattern of the sentence-

Figure 13.5 *Figure drawings by a normal well-adjusted young adult. (a) Drawing of a woman; (b) drawing of a man.*

completion test sometimes suggests a clinical diagnosis. The following sentence completions were made by a thirty-four-year-old woman recently admitted to a hospital. A diagnosis of schizophrenic reaction, paranoid type, could be made with a high degree of confidence on the basis of these few samples of her thinking:

> *My name is* Jesus Christ.
> *I am here because* I forgave you.
> *My parents* I adore and I love, and I put them in jail.
> *My enemies* are my right hand and my left hand.
> *Somebody is trying* to embalm me while I am alive.

The secret, symbolic, and bizarre thinking of the schizophrenic also is shown in the sentence completions of another woman:

> *The date* is today.
> *I am here because* of W.
> *I think that my mind* G.
> *The thoughts that I have* SP.
> *My parents* W.
> *My body.* MP BWHS AMD.
> *I feel anxious* OWT UNH.
> *My greatest fear is* NOMF.

Figure Drawings

In the figure-drawing test, the individual being studied is given a pencil and a sheet of paper and asked to draw a person. He is assured that drawing ability is not important, and he is encouraged to make the effort. If the first drawing is that of a man, the individual is given another sheet of paper and told to draw a woman. If the first drawing is a woman, he is then told to draw a man. These two drawings become the basis for the personality study (Machover, 1949). The interpretation of such figure drawings depends upon a consideration of three aspects: (1) the general overall impression given by the drawings, (2) the analysis of the structural features of the drawings, and (3) the analysis of the content of the drawings.

Each set of figure drawings gives an immediate first impression. Some convey action, while others seem quite static; some appear hostile and aggressive, others being passive and submissive. Or the general impression may be one of tenseness, rigidity, constriction, or expansiveness. This first impression is conveyed to the interpreter by such factors as the posture of the figures, the expression of the face, or the carrying angle of the limbs.

The structural analysis of figure drawings concerns itself with such factors as the size of the figures, their placement on the page, the pressure of the lines, the use of shading, and the amount of detail used in drawing the figures and the background.

The content analysis of figure drawings provides a rich source of clinical information in some cases. This form of analysis takes into consideration the parts of the body emphasized and the clothing and accessories included in the drawings. Some of the most important diagnostic insights come from the study of the parts of the body emphasized by the person being examined.

Self-image Test

The self-image test requires the subject to describe himself in a variety of ways. In one version of the test, the person is told to write down as many true statements as possible beginning with the words "I am." In another version, he is asked to tell who he is in twenty different ways. In either case, he projects his personality through the manner in which he perceives himself. The clinical psychologist analyzes the responses to these questions and attempts to get significant clues about unconscious motivation and inner conflicts.

Many people describe themselves in terms of the roles they play in life. Sometimes these roles are occupational, as in the case of the man who wrote:

> I am a man.
> I am a carpenter.

> I am a die setter.
> I am a farmer.
> I am a bricklayer.

Or the roles may be personal, emphasizing family relationships:

> I am Elizabeth R.
> I am a mother.
> I am the mother of four children.
> I am the grandmother of three children.
> I am the daughter of Mary B.

The child-adult ambivalence of adolescence is shown in the self-descriptions of a young man who wrote:

> I am Claude F.
> I am a boy.
> I am a man.
> I am a 17-year-old boy.

The following self-description of a thirty-one-

Figure 13.6 *Human figure drawings by a disturbed adolescent involved in a series of sex delinquencies. (Psychiatric Clinic, Hamilton County Juvenile Court.)*

(a)   (b)

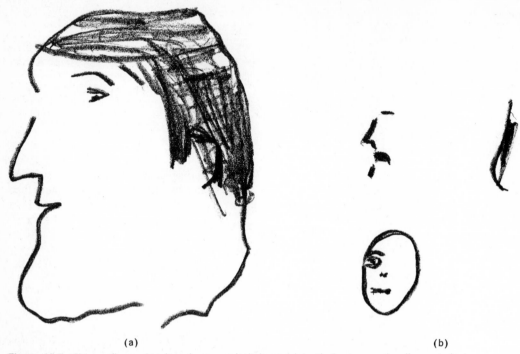

(a)   (b)

Figure 13.7 *Human figure drawings by a narcissistic and latently homosexual college student. (a) The head of the male figure is a self-portrait. (b) The subject became nauseated when he attempted to draw the female figure.*

year-old woman suggests the regressive thinking of the schizophrenic:

> I am a woman.
> I am a girl.
> I am a child.
> I am a baby.

Chronic brain syndrome patients may have great difficulty in describing themselves, and sometimes fall back on repetitive and stereotyped phrases:

> I am a boy.
> I am a boy.
> I am a boy.
> I am a father.
> I am a father.
> I am a father.

In some organic cases, the patient simply repeats his name over and over again.

> I am Harry S.
> I am Harry S.
> I am Harry S.

A patient with a chronic brain syndrome due to alcoholism perceived himself with striking clarity when he wrote:

> I am one fool.
> I am one fool.
> I am one fool.

Thematic Apperception Test

The Thematic Apperception Test (TAT) requires the subject to make up a story about a series of pictures which are presented to him one at a time. The idea for this type of test was introduced as early as 1907, when a group of adolescents and young adults were asked to write stories suggested by pictures. The stories were then analyzed in terms of such factors as unity, length, details, imaginative quality, use of the first person, and relative emphasis on religious, moral, and social elements.

The TAT was developed in 1935 at the Harvard

Psychological Clinic (Murray and Morgan, 1938). The test consists of twenty cards, nineteen of which contain a picture, while one card is blank. There are thirty cards in the series, but separate groups of cards are used for boys, for girls, for males over age fourteen, and for females over fourteen. The test cards are coded in such a way that the clinician can put together the appropriate group.

The pictures are handed, one at a time, to the subject, who is asked to make up a story about each one, and to imagine a scene on the blank card. He is asked to explain what is happening, what led up the situation, what the characters are thinking and feeling, and what the outcome is likely to be. When all the stories have been told, the examiner may inquire further using direct questions, free association, or special cards to bring out further details. Depending upon the length of the stories and the extent of the examiner's inquiries, the test may require several hours to administer and is sometimes given over two sessions.

The interpretation of TAT material is ordinarily made on a subjective basis by the clinician, with little reference to formal scoring. However, several systems of interpretation have been advanced. One of the most important emphasizes the analysis of the *needs* of the central figure of the story and the *press* of the environment. The needs are the internal motivating forces of the central character or characters, while the press is the personal and impersonal forces of the external world which operate to influence the hero's behavior. Other systems of interpretation analyze such factors as the context of the situation, the directing sets, the expression of emotion, defense mechanisms, evidence of conflict and frustration, feelings of guilt and anxiety, and level of aspiration.

The stories produced in response to the TAT are derived from books, movies, and television programs; events experienced by friends or relatives; personal experiences; and conscious and unconscious fantasies. While material derived from the latter two sources would appear to be most important clinically, it is also necessary to know what kind of stories and incidents from other sources have been retained by the person being studied.

The following story was given as a response to card 1, which shows a young boy who appears to be sitting at a table and looking at a violin:

> He's sitting there because he broke his fiddle. He is acting real mad about it. He must have been playing or something like that, and he broke it. He is just sitting at the table looking at it. I guess it was his. He is mad. One of his friends may have broken it, and he is going to call his mother and tell her what happened. I guess his mother will straighten things out. Maybe she will buy him a new one.

Even the most superficial analysis of this story reveals at least five themes. First there is the idea of the "broken fiddle," suggesting hostility and aggression. Second, the person telling the story says twice that the boy is "mad" about it, emphasizing feelings of anger. The third theme is a paranoid one derived from the statement that "one of his friends may have broken it." Maternal de-

Figure 13.8 *Henry A. Murray, 1893– , Harvard University psychiatrist who developed the Thematic Apperception Test. (Courtesy of Dr. Murray.)*

Figure 13.9 *Card 12F of the Thematic Apperception Test. The subject is required to make up a story based on this and other pictures in the series. (Courtesy of Dr. Henry A. Murray and the Harvard University Press.)*

pendency is suggested by the fact that the boy is going to "call his mother." The fifth theme is optimism and is expressed by the fact that the mother probably will "straighten things out" and "buy him a new one."

There have been several modifications of the TAT. One has been the inclusion of other racial types in the faces and figures in the pictures to permit nonwhites to identify with the situations portrayed. In the Thompson modification, eighteen of the original TAT cards were redrawn to depict blacks (Thompson, 1949). Another modification is a series of ten cards for use with children. The pictures center on feeding conflicts, sibling rivalry, toilet training, and similar situations common to children. This modification is known as the Children's Apperception Test (CAT) (Bellak, 1954).

Since the TAT is time consuming in terms of both administration and interpretation, efforts have been made to develop a shorter form for clinical use. One procedure has been for the clinician to select arbitrarily only those cards

which he feels might be helpful in revealing something of the dynamics of the subject's personality. A more objective approach to a short form of the TAT is one in which subjects must select the TAT pictures they like best and those they like least. These cards are then used for the test. It has been found that by using only ten cards selected in this manner, it is possible to identify 80 to 90 percent of the significant material yielded when all cards are used (Bentley, 1951). While most clinicians use a short form of the TAT for preliminary screening, the complete test is used for more comprehensive personality studies.

Rorschach Test

The most highly developed, and the most widely used, of the projective methods of psychodiagnosis is the Rorschach test. This test requires the person to find meaning in a standard series of ten inkblots. The idea for using inkblots as a psychological test had its origins in the "cloud pictures" of a German psychologist who used inkblots to study the process of imagination during the latter part of the nineteenth century (Stern, 1914). Hermann Rorschach (1884–1922), a Swiss psychiatrist, extended the use of inkblot interpretation to the problems of psychoanalysis and mental disorder in 1911. After experimenting with a wide variety of blots made with black and colored inks, he developed a series of ten inkblots to be used as stimuli. Five of the cards are in shades of gray, two combine color with the black and white, and three are in color. He published the results of his studies in 1921, along with a detailed description of the administration, scoring, and interpretation of the test (Rorschach, 1942).

Rorschach developed a psychodiagnostic technique of considerable sensitivity. It evaluates the emotional life of the individual, estimates his intellectual level, and throws light on the unconscious components of the personality.

The subject is handed one card at a time and required to describe what the inkblot looks like to him. He may hold the card in any way he wishes and make as many responses as he can. A normal adult of average intelligence gives two or three responses to each inkblot for a total of twenty to thirty association responses for the entire test.

The responses are taken down verbatim by the clinician. After the subject has responded to the ten inkblots, the clinician conducts an *inquiry,* which is a close questioning of the person to obtain more detailed information on each of the responses. The inquiry is necessary because the scoring of the Rorschach test requires a knowledge not only of the response itself but also of the part of the inkblot that stimulated the response and of a number of other factors determining the response. Such information can come only from asking the person how he arrived at his particular response.

There are three major categories in the scoring of the Rorschach test. The first is the *location,* or where the response is seen; the second is the *determinants,* or how and why it is seen; and the third is the *content,* or what is seen. Additional scoring categories include the originality of the response, the degree of organization of the responses, and the order in which the responses are made.

The interpretation of the Rorschach test also takes place at the level of *symbolic analysis.* In this approach, interpretation is based on the possible hidden meaning of the responses. This form of analysis is more subjective than formal analysis and depends to a large degree upon the clinical intuition and experience of the psychologist making the interpretation.

Feelings of aggression and hostility are frequently reflected in the responses to the Rorschach cards. The following responses were given to card 1 by a thirty-two-year-old woman diagnosed as having a chronic brain syndrome with convulsive disorder.

1. It looks like a chicken, cut up and broken in two.
2. A butterfly, squashed and flattened out.
3. A person torn loose, as if he was in a car wreck.
4. The cover on an ironing board, scorched and wrinkled.

The use of such terms as "cut up," "broken in two," "squashed," "flattened out," "torn loose," and "scorched" suggests the turbulent and aggressive nature of this woman's psychological life.

Extensive clinical experience with the Rorschach test has shown that some types of personality disturbances have more or less characteristic test patterns. Organic brain patients are likely to give few responses, with a decrease in movement and in popular responses, an increase in animal responses, and a lengthened reaction time. Such people also tend to have a relatively low number of good percepts, and few space and shading responses. It is not unusual to find blocking, color naming, and perseveration in the records of these individuals.

Schizophrenic records are characterized by peculiar and unusual responses, often to the point of being bizarre. The form quality is poor, and there may be more than the expected number of color responses. Unusual details and white spaces may be emphasized, human responses are avoided, and sex responses are common.

Figure 13.10 *Hermann Rorschach, 1884–1922, Swiss psychiatrist who developed the inkblot test for studying the personality. (Courtesy of Hans Huber Verlag.)*

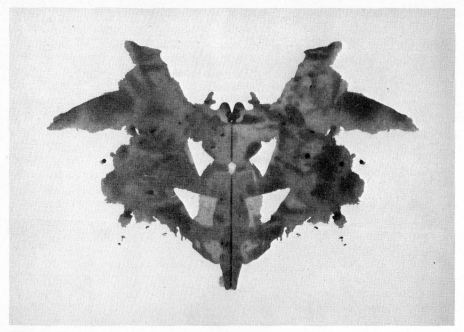

Figure 13.11   *The first in the series of ten inkblots presented to a subject during the Rorschach test. The patient is required to describe whatever the inkblot suggests to him. (Reprinted with the permission of Hans Huber Verlag, Bern, Switzerland.)*

Depressive states are marked by a high percentage of well-perceived responses but a low total number of responses. There is also likely to be an increase in animal and common responses. Failure to respond, rejection of the cards, and preoccupation with the shading and dark aspects of the blots are characteristic of the depressed patient.

While the Rorschach technique is easily administered, analysis and interpretation are quite different matters. They depend not only upon experience in previously giving the test, but even more so on clinical experience and a thorough knowledge of the psychodynamics of human behavior. In the hands of a skilled clinician, the test can be extremely revealing. But in the hands of overly enthusiastic or poorly trained Rorschach "experts," the analysis of the personality can become nothing more than a recital of professional clichés.

In spite of the great mass of work with this technique, there is little quantitative validation of the patterns which are claimed to be characteristic of the various personality disturbances. Some psychologists reject the test completely. While the Rorschach test is certainly a means of obtaining insight into personality, the remarkable results obtained depend not only on the instrument but perhaps even more on the clinical sensitivity of the investigator.[4]

---

[4]There are many important books dealing with specific psychodiagnostic techniques. A representative sampling of books of this type includes *Clinical Psychological Assessment of the Human Figure Drawing* (Thomas, 1969) by M. McElhaney; Emmanuel Hammer's *The Clinical Application of Projective Drawings* (Thomas, 1958); *The Clinical Use of the Revised Bender-Gestalt Test* (Grune & Stratton, 1960) by Max L. Hutt and Gerald J. Briskin; *The Rorschach Technique: An Introductory Manual* (Harcourt, Brace, 1962) by Bruno Klopfer and Helen H. Davidson; M. I. Stein's *The Thematic Apperception Test* (Addison-Wesley, 1955); and William E. Henry's *The Analysis of Fantasy: The Thematic Apperception Technique in the Study of Personality* (Wiley, 1956).

ELECTROPHYSIOLOGY

Recent developments in the field of electrophysiology—that branch of physiology dealing with the electric phenomena of the body—are opening new avenues to the diagnosis of personality disturbances and behavior disorders. New techniques involving complex electrical recording of physiological changes make it possible to evaluate quite precisely the nature of an individual's reactions even when circumstances prevent him from verbally communicating his experience.

The most important electrophysiological technique in psychodiagnosis is the measurement of brain waves (electroencephalography). Other approaches of this general type are the recording of the electrical resistance of the skin (electrodermal response), neuromuscular responses (electromyography), and eye movements and pupillary reactions (electrooculography).

ELECTROENCEPHALOGRAPHY

One of the most intriguing approaches to diagnosis has been through the measurement of spontaneous electrical changes in the brain. It was recognized early in the present century that all living tissues, including brain cells, possess electrical properties which can be studied in terms of the familiar units of electrical measurement. However, the early studies attracted scant attention because electrical phenomena associated with nervous activity were little understood, and because the electrical potentials were so minute that their details could not be measured adequately.

Electroencephalography (EEG) as a diagnostic approach began with the work of Hans Berger, a German investigator who became interested in the early observations on the spontaneous electrical activity of the brain and began a series of investigations in his own laboratory. After several years of study, he published his classic report on human brain electrical potential (Berger, 1929).

Berger demonstrated the presence of more or less continuous rhythmic fluctuation of potential recorded from electrodes attached to the scalp. He showed that these electrical potential changes arose from the brain tissue and were not due to cir-

culatory pulsations, muscle activity, or other extraneous factors. He found that the electrical activity of the brain is modified by sleep, anesthesia, and various forms of sensory stimulation; that the patterns of activity vary with age in young children; and that certain pathological clinical conditions produce abnormal electrical recordings. The range of brain potential frequencies, called the *cortical frequency spectrum,* can be divided into three major bands. The first band (delta rhythm) is that of slow frequencies from less than 1 cycle per second to 8 cycles per second. The second band (alpha rhythm) consists of the medium, or "normal," frequencies which range from 8 to 12 cycles per second. The third band (beta rhythm) is made up of rapid frequencies from 12 to 40 or more cycles per second. Some of these rhythms stand out clearly in a record and can be identified without particular difficulty. Other rhythms are more complex, and the only way their existence can be detected is by the manner in which they alter the shape of the visible waves. In addition, there are harmonics, or multiples, of the lower frequencies.

The EEG patterns are influenced by such factors as cell metabolism, the electrical properties of the

Figure 13.12 *Hans Berger, German neurophysiologist and discoverer of the electrical rhythms of the brain. (National Library of Medicine.)*

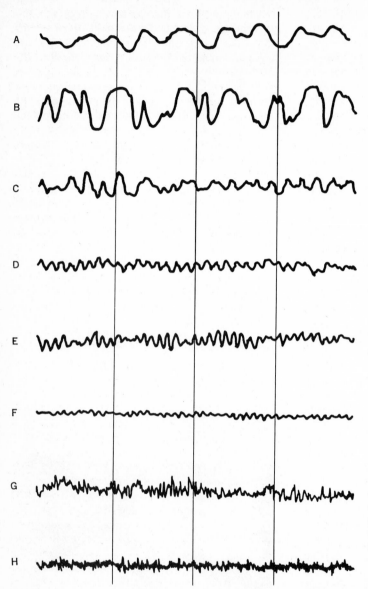

Figure 13.13 *The cortical frequency spectrum.* A, *two-per-second brain waves;* B, *two to four per second;* C, *four to five per second;* D, *eight per second;* E, *nine to ten per second (Alpha rhythm);* F, *eleven per second;* G, *fourteen-to-sixteen-per second waves with superimposed fast activity;* H, *thirty to forty per second. (From E. M. Bridge,* Epilepsy and Convulsive Disorders in Children, *New York, McGraw-Hill, 1949, p. 534.)*

cell membrane, the character of the surrounding fluid medium, and electrical impulses along, but independent of, the neural pathways. To account for the patterning of the EEG record, a "pacemaking" system has been postulated. This system is believed to control the rhythm and regularity of the brain waves.

The usefulness of the EEG is somewhat limited

because the recordings are ordinarily taken from the intact skull. As a result of this restriction on electrode placement, only those characteristics involving the cortex or subjacent white matter of the upper and side surfaces of the cerebral hemispheres can be detected. Characteristics determined by the subcortical nuclei, cerebellum, and undersurface of the brain are less readily accessible. To meet this problem several variations of EEG technique have been developed. One variation is the recording of electrical activity from the surface of the exposed brain. In the investigation of action current from the area of the hypothalamus, the signals are picked up by means of electrodes attached to the base of the brain.

The diagnostic value of the abnormal EEG is most clear-cut in the detection of brain damage and epilepsy, with some of the behavioral disorders ranking next. Psychotic reactions have been associated with EEG abnormality, but not in any consistent or conspicuous way. The psychoneuroses are even less definite in their correlation with EEG changes. It is also interesting to note that about 15 percent of the normal population shows EEG abnormalities.

The importance of the EEG in epilepsy lies in the fact that identifiable types of electrical discharge patterns have been associated with the major forms of convulsive disorder. In the case of *grand mal* seizures, there is a gradual buildup of high-voltage fast waves that reach their most exaggerated form during the clonic phase of the convulsion. The *petit mal* type of epilepsy is associated with a wave and spike formation with a frequency of three per second. Finally high-voltage square-topped waves are seen in many cases of temporal-lobe epilepsy.

An important aspect of the EEG in epilepsy is that frequently there are indications of the disturbance in the EEG record between attacks. That is, even though the patient does not show the disorder clinically at the time, the EEG tracing reveals the underlying electrical pattern associated with the disorder. Obviously, this fact is of considerable value both in diagnosing and in the evaluation of treatment procedures.

However, the EEG is by no means an infallible technique. In some cases of overt convulsive conditions, the EEG tracing is questionable or even negative. And in many cases where there has never been clinical evidence of convulsive behavior, the EEG reveals patterns suggestive of convulsive disorder. Such contradictions are evidence of the early stage of development in the field. It is probable that some of the secrets of convulsive disorder, as well as other brain disorders, will

one day be revealed as a result of the refinement of present-day methods of the electronic exploration of the brain.

EEG research has also contributed to our knowledge of the lower brain structures. It was observed many years ago that there are characteristic EEG wave patterns ranging from those obtained during sleep to those obtained during states of extreme activity such as those associated with convulsions. Deep sleep is characterized by large waves of a low frequency. In lighter sleep the frequencies are somewhat higher but not as high as when the subject is awake. Similarly, states of relaxed wakefulness have lower frequencies than states of alerted wakefulness. Fast waves are characteristic of highly alerted states. These differences, observed clinically for many years, now are related to the ascending reticular activating system. Lesions of the system result in lowered alertness in the form of lethargy and drowsiness, while electrical stimulation of the system results in increased arousal.

Some of the most recent and exciting work in the field of brain waves has been the development of the technique of *EEG activation*. This method is used in cases of suspected convulsive disorders, brain tumors, psychomotor (or temporal-lobe) epilepsy, and similar conditions. Through the use of activating procedures, it is sometimes possible to detect pathological brain wave patterns which might otherwise be overlooked. Among the methods used for EEG activation are photic stimulation, hyperventilation, gas inhalation, and various drugs. Photic activation is carried out by means of a powerful light, a diffusing screen, and a system for varying the duration and frequency of the flashes presented to the subject's eyes. One of the significant discoveries has been that it is possible to pace, or drive, the brain rhythms by lights flashing in the range of two to twenty or more flashes per second.

Different emotional states are marked by quantitative differences in the photically activated EEG. Significant differences between the sexes have been observed in the driving response, with females showing a greater response at all frequencies. Response ratios are significantly higher in anxiety states than in depressions, with control subjects and paranoid schizophrenics in an inter-

Figure 13.14 *An EEG examination of a young patient with suspected brain damage. (a) An electrode being pasted to the patient's scalp. (b) Electrodes in place. (c) The electrode wires are plugged into the EEG apparatus. (d) The patient relaxes in bed during the examination. (e) Eight pens make a graphic record of the electrical signals from the eight scalp electrodes. (f) A thirty-second sample of the patient's brain waves. (EEG Laboratory, Longview State Hospital.)*

mediate range. Other forms of EEG activation also show characteristic patterns under varying conditions and with the different clinical groups.

ELECTRODERMAL RESPONSE

The electrodermal response, also known as the *galvanic skin response* (GSR) and the *psychogalvanic response* (PGR), is a reaction which involves changes in the electrical resistance of the skin as a result of emotional states. Fear, anxiety, anger, and other emotions are accompanied by a moistening of the skin, which causes changes in electrical resistance. It is often possible to detect underlying emotional conflicts through the analysis of the graphic record of these electrical changes. The first studies of this type took place early in the present century in connection with emotional changes during the administration of word-association tests designed to detect unconscious "complexes." Since that time there has been a continuing interest in electrodermal changes in the various clinical conditions. Schizophrenics, for example, tend to show a significantly lower electrodermal response than normals (Martin et al., 1960).

There are a number of difficulties in using the electrodermal response as a diagnostic method. A major problem is in establishing the conditions under which the recordings are made. Since skin resistance is highly sensitive, variations occur as a result of many internal and external stimuli which are difficult to control. Another problem is the difficulty of making a meaningful analysis of the highly complex recorded data.

ELECTROMYOGRAPHY

The measurement of the electrical activity of the muscles of the body by means of the electromyograph (EMG) has been of considerable interest for many years. Its primary use has been in the diagnosis of conditions showing tremors, impairment of muscle movements, and other neurological problems. It has also been used to evaluate the general level of muscular tension.

The EMG studies have indicated that states of generally increased muscular activity and tension appear to be relatively constant in individual subjects, that high muscle tension is associated with depressed moods, that disturbed individuals as a group appear to have a considerable amount of neuromuscular hypertension as compared to control groups, and that overall muscular tension decreases as these people improve. By feeding EMG signals into an averaging computer it has been possible to make increasingly more sensitive diagnostic evaluations (Caine and Lader, 1969).

While the electromyograph is used primarily in the study of neurological disorders, the measurement of muscular tension also has diagnostic implications for personality disturbances. Just as changes in the electrical resistance of the skin give a continuous reading of the emotional state of the individual, the tension in the muscles of the body also indicates emotional conflict by signaling an increase in tension when hidden conflicts are touched upon during diagnostic interviews and treatment sessions.

ELECTROOCULOGRAPHY

Considerable interest has developed in the measurement of changes in the size of the pupil of the eye as an indication of personality problems. It is known that the size of the pupil grows larger when the individual looks at something which interests him. Various emotional states affect the size of the pupil in various ways. Attempts are being made to correlate pupillary responses to emotional conflict by presenting the individual with pictures of situations which the clinician suspects might be related to the individual's disorder, and then studying the pupillary response to the pictures. Even though the individual is not consciously aware of his feeling, the pupillary response could be an indication of unconscious attitudes.

The major disadvantage of electrooculography, as well as other electrophysiological diagnostic techniques, is the relatively elaborate instrumentation required to make the necessary observations. For this reason, with the exception of the EEG, electrophysiological diagnostic methods have limited use in everyday diagnostic procedures. The importance of the electrophysiological diagnostic approach lies in the future when the information will be fed into a computer for storage and analysis.[5]

COMPUTER-ASSISTED DIAGNOSIS

Recent advances in computer technology have opened vast new possibilities in low-cost, sensitive, reliable analysis of diagnostic information. Computer analysis can be equally valuable in the clinical approach, psychological testing, and electrophysiology.

A number of projects are engaged in programming computers with clinical observation data. Members of mental health clinical teams are being trained to make observations of a person on specially designed forms and on a continuing basis. These observations are similar to those made in connection with behavior rating scales and other procedures for recording the everyday behavior of people during their routine activities. However, instead of forming the basis for relatively crude ratings and comparisons, the information is fed into a computer. It is then analyzed, and a computer readout is furnished on the person's behavior. Present behavior is compared with previously established norms, and the report also indicates the extent and direction of any changes which have taken place.

The best example of computer analysis of psychological test information is in connection with the MMPI personality evaluation scale. It will be recalled that in this test a person is required to answer many questions about his attitudes, feelings, and behavior. A graph is then drawn indicating the relative weight of items pointing to such clinical symptoms as depression, hypochondria, paranoid thinking, and so on. A narrative report is then ordinarily written by the clinician to describe the patient. Projects are now under way, however, in which the data are programmed into a computer, which furnishes a readout describing the personality pattern of the person. (Fowler and Miller, 1969).

The computer has also taken an important place in the electrophysiological approach to psychodiagnosis. The value of the computer is illustrated dramatically in connection with the analysis of EEG records. One of the shortcomings of the EEG as a diagnostic tool has been the necessity of relying on the visual inspection of brain wave tracings by EEG experts. Not only has there been a shortage of qualified personnel in this field, but the complexity of the tracing has led to a relatively low level of reliability in interpretation. Only those conditions associated with marked changes in the EEG record have been identified with any degree of certainty. Moreover, EEG interpretation has been time consuming and unavailable to large numbers of people who live away from the metropolitan medical centers where EEG facilities are located. The computer is now bringing EEG analysis to patients no matter where they live. EEG information obtained in a local clinic can be relayed over ordinary telephone lines to data banks located hundreds or thousands of miles away, and a reply in the form of a complete and detailed EEG analysis can be in the hands of the patient's physician in a matter of minutes.

The Missouri State Division of Mental Health uses computerized diagnostic aids to identify high-risk patients more likely than others to escape, contemplate suicide, or engage in assaultive behavior. A statewide computer system also identifies low-risk patients in these same categories, thereby aiding personnel in decisions to relax control and allow patients more freedom. Results have indicated that computers are able to make a significant contribution to the clinical decision-making process (Roche Report, 1971).

While these techniques are still in the development stage, it can be expected that very rapid progress will take place during the 1970s. Computer diagnosis, already important in other phases of medicine and public health, could very well become one of the most significant technological developments in mental health during this decade.

---

[5]Students interested in electrophysiological measurement in diagnosis and research are referred to *Hans Berger on the Electroencephalogram of Man* (Elsevier, 1969), edited by Pierre Gloor.

MENTAL STATUS REPORT

PATIENT NO. 3
EXAMINING DOCTOR NO. 2
DATE OF EXAMINATION NOVEMBER 14, 1967

THE PATIENT IS A 42 YEAR OLD FEMALE WHO LOOKS HER AGE, APPEARS TO BE IN NORMAL PHYSICAL HEALTH, AND IS UNREMARKABLE IN BODY BUILD. SHE HAS NO PHYSICAL DEFORMITY. THE PATIENT'S POSTURE AND GAIT ARE UNREMARKABLE. THE FACIAL EXPRESSION OF THE PATIENT IS FRIGHTENED AND HER DRESS IS METICULOUS. OTHER BODY MOVEMENTS INCLUDE SLIGHT TREMOR.

HER GENERAL BEHAVIOR IS SLIGHTLY HISTRIONIC, MODERATELY OBSESSIVE, AND SLIGHTLY WITHDRAWN.

THE AFFECT IS ONE OF MODERATE ANXIETY, SLIGHT PERPLEXITY, SLIGHT FRIGHT, AND MODERATE DEPRESSION. THERE IS ASSOCIATED MARKED PESSIMISM ABOUT THE FUTURE, MODERATE SELF-REPROACH, MARKED NARROWNESS OF INTERESTS, MARKED INDECISION, MODERATE FEELINGS OF GUILT, AND SLIGHT SUICIDAL PRE-OCCUPATION. THERE ARE DIURNAL MOOD VARIATION SYMPTOMS WHICH ARE MILDLY WORSE IN THE MORNING.

THE PATIENT'S SLEEP PATTERN IS DISTURBED SEVERELY IN THE EARLY PART OF THE NIGHT, MODERATELY IN THE MIDDLE PART OF THE NIGHT, AND MILDLY IN THE LATTER PART OF THE NIGHT. THERE IS SOME LOSS OF APPETITE, MODERATE LOSS OF ENERGY, AND MILD LOSS OF WEIGHT. THE PATIENT HAS COMPLAINTS OF SEVERE DISTURBANCE IN SEXUAL ACTIVITY IN THE DIRECTION OF HYPOACTIVITY. SHE IS MODERATELY CONCERNED WITH CURRENT HEALTH. THERE ARE SPECIFIC SYMPTOMS OF MILD HEADACHES AND MODERATE CARDIOVASCULAR DISORDER. THERE IS MILD RETARDATION AND MODERATE OBSESSIONS/RUMINATIONS APPARENT IN THE THOUGHT PROCESS. CONTENT INCLUDES MODERATE PHOBIAS.

PERCEPTION IS NORMAL.

SENSORIUM IS CLEAR.

THERE IS FULL ORIENTATION.

ATTENTION-CONCENTRATION IS MILDLY IMPAIRED. MEMORY SHOWS MILD GENERAL IMPAIRMENT FOR RECENT EVENTS AND MILD GENERAL IMPAIRMENT FOR REMOTE EVENTS. INTELLIGENCE OF THE PATIENT IS ASSESSED AS ABOVE AVERAGE AND HER INSIGHT IS CONSIDERED TO BE ADEQUATE. JUDGEMENT IS NORMAL. THE PATIENT HAS MODERATE INFERIORITY FEELINGS.

THE PATIENT DISPLAYS LACK OF RESPONSIBILITY TO A MODERATE DEGREE IN FAMILY MATTERS AND TO A MODERATE DEGREE IN SOCIAL MATTERS.

HAMILTON RATING SCALE

ITEM	SCORE
1.DEPRESSED MOOD	2
2.GUILT-FEELINGS	2
3.SUICIDE	2
4.INSOMNIA EARLY	2
5.INSOMNIA MIDDLE	1
6.INSOMNIA LATE	1
7.ENERGY	3
8.RETARDATION	1
9.AGITATION	0
10.ANXIETY PSYCHIC	3
11.ANXIETY SOMATIC	1
12.APPETITE, ETC.	1
13.SOMATIC GENERAL	2
14.GENITAL SYMPTOMS	2
15.HYPOCHONDRIASIS	0
16.LOSS OF WEIGHT	1
17.INSIGHT	0
18.DIURNAL VARIATION AM	1
TOTAL	24

ACUTE SCHIZOPHRENIA

ITEM	SCORE
ITEMS 1,2,3 OF SCALE REQUIRE DATA FROM OTHER SOURCES.	
4.AFFECTIVE SYMPTOMS	0
5.COGNITIVE SYMPTOMS	1
6.PERCEPTUAL SYMPTOMS	0
7.POVERTY OF SPEECH	0
8.DELUSIONAL SYMPTOMS	0
TOTAL	01

WING RATING SCALE

ITEM	SCORE
1.FLATNESS OF AFFECT	1
2.POVERTY OF SPEECH	1
3.INCOHERENCE	1
4.COHERENT DELUSIONS	1
TOTAL	04

(a)

MENTAL STATUS REPORT

PATIENT NO. 4
EXAMINING DOCTOR NO. 4
DATE OF EXAMINATION DECEMBER 11, 1967

THE PATIENT IS A 42 YEAR OLD FEMALE WHO LOOKS HER AGE, APPEARS TO BE IN EXCELLENT PHYSICAL HEALTH, AND IS UNREMARKABLE IN BODY BUILD. SHE HAS NO PHYSICAL DEFORMITY. THE PATIENT'S FACIAL EXPRESSION, POSTURE, GAIT AND BODY MOVEMENTS ARE UNREMARKABLE. HER DRESS IS METICULOUS.

HER GENERAL BEHAVIOR IS UNREMARKABLE.

THE AFFECT IS ONE OF MILD ANXIETY. THERE ARE DIURNAL MOOD VARIATION SYMPTOMS WHICH ARE MILDLY WORSE IN THE EVENING. THERE IS NO DISTURBANCE OF SLEEP PATTERN. THERE IS NO LOSS OF APPETITE, NO LOSS OF ENERGY, AND NO LOSS OF WEIGHT. THE PATIENT HAS COMPLAINTS OF MILD DISTURBANCE IN SEXUAL ACTIVITY IN THE DIRECTION OF HYPOACTIVITY.

SHE IS NOT OVERLY CONCERNED WITH CURRENT HEALTH. THERE IS MILD OBSESSIONS/RUMINATIONS APPARENT IN THE THOUGHT PROCESS.

PERCEPTION IS NORMAL.

THE PATIENT IS DISTURBED TO A MILD DEGREE BY DEPERSONALIZATION EXPERIENCES.

SENSORIUM IS CLEAR.

THERE IS FULL ORIENTATION.

MEMORY IS NORMAL. INTELLIGENCE OF THE PATIENT IS ASSESSED AS AVERAGE AND HER INSIGHT IS CONSIDERED TO BE ADEQUATE. JUDGMENT IS NORMAL. THE PATIENT HAS MILD INFERIORITY FEELINGS.

THE PATIENT IS AWARE OF AND MEETS HER RESPONSIBILITIES.

HAMILTON RATING SCALE

ITEM	SCORE
1.DEPRESSED MOOD	0
2.GUILT-FEELINGS	0
3.SUICIDE	0
4.INSOMNIA EARLY	0
5.INSOMNIA MIDDLE	0
6.INSOMNIA LATE	0
7.ENERGY	0
8.RETARDATION	0
9.AGITATION	0
10.ANXIETY PSYCHIC	1
11.ANXIETY SOMATIC	0
12.APPETITE, ETC.	0
13.SOMATIC GENERAL	0
14.GENITAL SYMPTOMS	0
15.HYPOCHONDRIASIS	0
16.LOSS OF WEIGHT	0
17.INSIGHT	0
18.DIURNAL VARIATION PM	1
TOTAL	02

ACUTE SCHIZOPHRENIA

ITEM	SCORE
ITEMS 1,2,3 OF SCALE REQUIRE DATA FROM OTHER SOURCES.	
4.AFFECTIVE SYMPTOMS	0
5.COGNITIVE SYMPTOMS	0
6.PERCEPTUAL SYMPTOMS	0
7.POVERTY OF SPEECH	0
8.DELUSIONAL SYMPTOMS	0
TOTAL	00

WING RATING SCALE

ITEM	SCORE
1.FLATNESS OF AFFECT	1
2.POVERTY OF SPEECH	1
3.INCOHERENCE	1
4.COHERENT DELUSIONS	1
TOTAL	04

(b)

Figure 13.15 (a) A computerized diagnostic write-out on a depressed patient before drug treatment. (b) The diagnostic write-out on the same patient after treatment.

SUMMARY

1. Psychodiagnosis refers to the identification of personality problems, behavior disturbances, and mental disorder. The method is a part of the clinical approach, which studies the individual as a unique whole. The principle clinical techniques used in psychodiagnosis are the *case history,* the *interview,* and the *psychological test.* Other diagnostic procedures involve *electrophysiological measurements* and *computer-assisted evaluation.*

2. The case history includes the background information necessary for the diagnostician to understand the development of the disturbance and the setting in which it occurred. The interview makes it possible to observe behavior in a relatively standardized situation. It permits the psychologist to evaluate the individual in terms of general appearance, manner, voice, gestures, expressed attitudes, and similar characteristics. The third clinical technique, the psychological test, is used to measure *intelligence,* to detect *brain damage,* and to evaluate *personality.*

3. While intelligence tests may be used either with groups or with individuals, individual tests are used almost exclusively in psychodiagnosis. In addition to providing an index of mental ability, intelligence tests contribute to the evaluation of personality and the detection of organic damage of the brain. More specialized tests of brain damage have been developed to measure abstract thinking, deterioration, and perceptual-motor organization.

4. Psychodiagnosis in the area of personality is accomplished by means of the *objective approach* and the *projective approach.* The objective approach involves the direct observation of behavior, the use of rating scales to measure personality traits, and inventories and questionnaires by means of which the individual describes his own personality. The projective approach uses relatively ambiguous and unstructured situations to which the person must respond. The tests include word associations, inkblots, sentence completions, figure drawings, and the telling of stories suggested by pictures.

5. The diagnostic approach to personality disorganization also makes use of a variety of electrophysiological techniques. These methods include the recording of brain wave patterns (electroencephalography), skin resistance (electrodermal response), neuromuscular tension (electromyography), and eye movements and pupillary reactions (electrooculography). Another advanced development in diagnosis is the use of the electronic computer in the description of the individual and his behavior, and in the analysis of pertinent information about him.

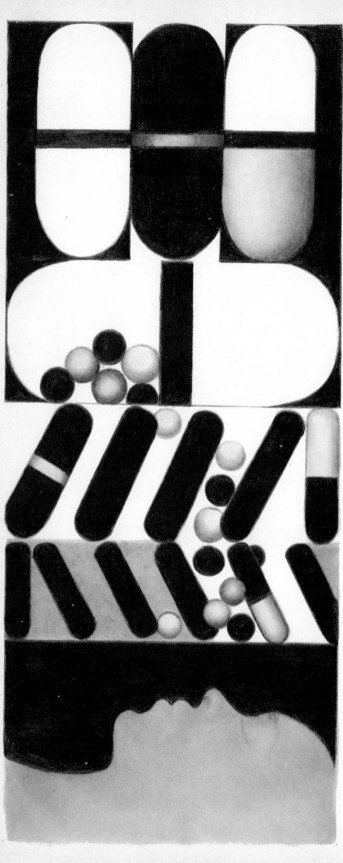

14 MEDICAL TREATMENT OF MENTAL DISORDER

Modern medical treatment of personality disturbance was anticipated many centuries ago by the use of drugs and medicants, primitive surgical procedures, and other techniques designed to alter or influence the mind through the body. Today, physical treatment methods form the basis for *neuropsychiatric,* or medical therapy. The major methods of medical treatment are:

1. Drug therapy
2. Sleep therapy
3. Shock therapy
4. Surgical therapy

DRUG THERAPY

The use of drugs is one of the oldest forms of treatment for mental disorder. The medical literature of ancient Greece contains many references to *hellebore,* a drug obtained from a species of plants. Physicians of the time were quite familiar with the emetic, or vomiting-producing, action of white hellebore and the purgative effects of black hellebore. When Melampus used this drug to cure the daughters of Proetus in Greek mythology, it was known as *melampodium.* In a letter to Hippocrates, Democritus wrote, "Hellebore, when given to the sane, pours darkness over the mind; but for the insane, it is very profitable." Later, in ancient Rome, Pliny discussed the use of hellebore in his work *Natural History.*

Since those early times, drugs of many kinds have been used to treat people with disturbed personalities. Some of the drugs have been effective; others have been of little or no use. Occasionally the drugs have had destructive, rather than therapeutic, effects. The most widely used drugs in modern chemotherapy are sedatives, tranquilizers, antidepressants, and anticonvulsants.

SEDATIVES

The beneficial effects of rest and sleep, and the need to control the agitated and sometimes violent person, were apparent to the earliest physicians. As a result, drugs that quiet, calm, soothe, and even depress the individual have been used widely throughout the history of medicine. Such drugs are therapeutic in the sense that they help the body to reconstitute itself physically. It is not unusual for tense and agitated people to wear themselves down. Rest and sleep, induced by sedative drugs, break the physical pattern and permit a reorganization of energies. Sedatives also make the disturbed individual more amenable to management and to other forms of treatment.

The sleep-producing effect of poppy seed (opium) was well known to the ancient Greeks. It was a common observation that both mania (elation) and melancholia (depression) responded favorably to the drug. Until the nineteenth century, the opiates were the most widely used drugs in the treatment of the behavior disorders. Unfortunately, these sedative drugs have many disadvantages, including their addictive quality and the depth of the sleep produced. The other sedative drugs made their appearance during the middle and latter part of the nineteenth century. Anesthetic drugs, including ether and chloroform, were also developed at that time for use during surgery.

A few of the compounds tested as anesthetics were found to produce longer periods of sleep than were necessary or desirable for surgical use. It was out of these longer-acting anesthetics that the sedatives were developed.

The first drug which had a satisfactory sedative effect was *chloral hydrate.* While the compound had been known since 1832, it was not until the 1860s that its sedative effects were discovered. Similarly, the *bromides* were first introduced into medical treatment in the early 1800s, but it was the latter half of the century before they were used for their sedative action. The use of the bromides as sedatives was limited because of their slow penetration to the brain and their toxic side effects. Since bromides are essentially motor depressants, they have also been used for the control of convulsive seizures.

Paraldehyde, a drug discovered in the 1820s but not introduced as a sedative until 1881, proved to be a safe and effective agent for producing sleep and to be free from the depressing effects on the heart produced by chloral hydrate and the toxic side effects of the bromides. Its major disadvantage, a persistent odor given to the breath, was an important factor in limiting its use. However, it was prescribed for many years in cases of mania and dementia, in the control of restlessness accompanying paresis, and in the treatment of alcoholic patients with delirium tremens.

The *barbiturate* drugs were introduced in 1903 and soon replaced most of the earlier sedatives in clinical practice. Since that time, a wide range of barbiturates has been developed. These drugs have little or no undesirable taste or odor and produce sedative and hypnotic effects ranging from mild drowsiness to deep anesthesia. The principal disadvantage is that they are likely to be habit-forming. Table 14.1 lists the ways in which they affect the brain.

The more recently developed *nonbarbiturate sedatives* have the advantage of being relatively free of the danger of addiction, and there is less

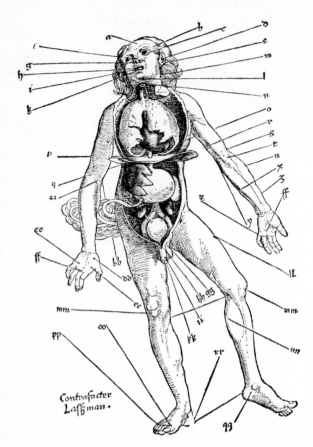

Figure 14.1 Bloodletting Chart. *A woodcut by Johannes Wechtlin, showing the recommended spots for venesection. The artist based his illustration, which first appeared in 1517, on the dissection of an executed criminal. (Philadelphia Museum of Art.)*

drowsiness, haziness, and fatigue on the following day. While the newer drugs are not as effective as the barbiturates, they are used when milder degrees of sedation are required.[1]

TRANQUILIZERS

The tranquilizing drugs are among the most effective of those used in the treatment of mental disorder. Developed for the most part since 1950, these drugs are neither sedative nor narcotic in the ordinary sense. In many cases they induce a detached serenity without loss of consciousness and without noticeable impairment of the intellectual ability.

The introduction of tranquilizing drugs had an important impact on the treatment of emotional disturbances. Through their calming and relaxing effects, disturbed individuals frequently become more cooperative and communicative. The need for more radical treatment is reduced, mechanical restraints in psychiatric hospitals are seldom needed, and patients are likely to be more receptive to various other forms of individual and group therapy. Moreover, the tranquilizing drugs can be administered to an entire ward by one or two relatively untrained attendants.

---

[1]*Psychopharmacology Bulletin* is a publication designed to facilitate the exchange of information among scientists in the field. The emphasis is on rapid and informal reporting of work which has not yet appeared in the scientific literature. It is available from the International Reference Center for Information on Psychotropic Drugs (NIMH), 5454 Wisconsin Avenue, Chevy Chase, Md. 20015.

The effect of the tranquilizing drugs on restraint measures in mental hospitals was pointed out before a Senate Appropriation Subcommittee when the Commissioner for Research for the New York State Department of Mental Health testified:

> One fact has stood out as fairly well proved, and that is that these drugs will allow us to carry out a more humane kind of treatment. Restraint and seclusion, which is something that we try to minimize at all times, has been recorded for years, and it has stood at a fairly stable index figure. It was an irreducible minimum. Within six months [after tranquilizers were introduced], restraint and seclusion figures for the Department as a whole dropped about 20 percent. In some places they were cut in half (Brill, 1955).

It is possible to classify the tranquilizing drugs into two classes: (1) the major tranquilizers and (2) the minor tranquilizers. The drugs in the first group, which are used to control the symptoms of disturbed psychotics, produce a characteristic kind of emotional calmness with relatively little sedative effect. They are not habit-forming, and dependence rarely develops. The incidence of motor symptoms and other side reactions is rather high, however, and the use of the major tranquilizers entails certain risks. While they are able to control the symptoms in many cases, the drugs do not get rid of the causes of the disorders.

The minor tranquilizers also have a calming and relaxing effect, but to a lesser degree than that produced by the major tranquilizers. These drugs do not cause the motor symptoms characteristic of the major tranquilizers, and side reactions are relatively infrequent and easily controlled. Some of the minor tranquilizers tend to be habit-forming. Drugs in this group are more effective in the treatment of psychoneurotic disorders than in the treatment of disturbed psychotics.

The Major Tranquilizers

The major tranquilizers can be divided on a pharmacological basis into the *phenothiazine group* and the *rauwolfia group. Chlorpromazine,* a phenothiazine, and *reserpine,* a rauwolfia alkaloid, are of historical importance because they were the first tranquilizers to be developed. They were discovered independently and were made available about the same time in the early 1950s. The clinical usefulness of these two drugs set the stage for a decade of lively interest in the development of newer and more effective psychoactive drugs of all types.

Chlorpromazine was synthesized in France in 1952 during a search for a compound which would potentiate, or enhance, the effects of conventional anesthetic drugs. It was used first as a chemical treatment at the University of Paris to control

Table 14.1   *The action of barbiturates on the brain*

BRAIN AREA	FUNCTION OF BRAIN AREA	EFFECT
Neocortex	Discriminative aspects of consciousness	Depression
Thalamus	Transmission of alerting impulses to cortex; modulation of action of reticular formation	Stimulation
Hypothalamus	Regulation of autonomic functions, correlating them with motor activities	Depression
Reticular formation	Alerting of behavior and/or EEG	Depression
Limbic system	Correlates emotional and intellectual aspects of consciousness	Depression
Respiratory nuclei	Initiation and regulation of respiration	Depression
Neurohormonal depots	Regulation of affective behavior	No effect

SOURCE: Adapted from *Tranquilizers, Barbiturates and the Brain.* Courtesy of Harold E. Himwich, M.D., and the Wallace Laboratories.

Figure 14.2 The Physician Curing Fantasy. *An anonymous engraved French broadsheet of the seventeenth century which satirizes medical theories of physical treatment fashionable in the seventeenth century. (Philadelphia Museum of Art.)*

agitation and excitement. The unique effects of the drug as a tranquilizer soon became apparent (Delay and Deniker, 1952).

Chlorpromazine is given orally or by means of intramuscular injection. While small doses produce drowsiness and reduction of motor activity, the individual is easily aroused and is able to pay attention, follow instructions, and respond normally. Even when large doses are given, there is little evidence that the higher mental functions are impaired, as they are in the case of sedatives and central nervous system depressants. Clinical observation, as well as psychological tests, shows relatively normal functioning of the brain as reflected by memory, judgment, information, and intelligence.

The most common side effects of the drug are drowsiness and psychomotor retardation. Dryness of the mucous membranes, skin disorder, and, less

frequently, jaundice as a result of liver dysfunction have also been reported. As the amount of the drug is increased, the patient may show the typical signs of Parkinsonism, including rigidity, the masked face, drooling, and the pill-rolling tremor. This syndrome can ordinarily be relieved through the use of drugs effective in the treatment of Parkinsonism.

The exact way in which chlorpromazine influences behavior is not known. It is probable that the psychological effects depend upon changes in the diencephalic region of the brain. The drug appears to stabilize the autonomic nervous system and may have an effect on general metabolism through the lowering of cellular oxygen requirements. Also, the drug may influence the endocrine system as well as the hypothalamus and the reticular substance.

The *rauwolfia* group of major tranquilizers

was developed from the plant *rauwolfia serpentina,* named after Leonhard Rauwolf, a German physician and botanist of the sixteenth century. Popularly known as mandrake, or snakeroot, because of the long and snakelike appearance of its ground root, the plant thrives in India, Burma, Ceylon, and other tropical countries. The root was used medically in ancient Rome, where Pliny referred to its sleep-producing effects. However, in larger doses the drug leads to wild excitement. The phrase "shrieking like mandrakes" grew out of the knowledge of the effects of this plant. Shakespeare's Banquo may have been referring to mandrake when he asked, "Or have we eaten of the insane root that takes the reason prisoner?" (*Macbeth,* I, iii).

Snakeroot has been used for many centuries in the folk medicine of India as a sedative, a laxative, and a fever-reducing drug. It has been sold in bazaars as a cure for snake bite, for the toxemia of pregnancy, for putting restless children to sleep, and for mental disorder of various kinds. Mahatma Gandhi is said to have used rauwolfia to sustain himself during his program of passive resistance.

The first scientific interest in rauwolfia was in connection with its ability to lower blood pressure. This action was demonstrated clinically in 1931. However, the crystalline alkaloid having tranquilizing effects was first isolated in 1952 by a research team in Switzerland. The alkaloid, called reserpine, has had a wide application in the treatment of mental disorder. The clinical usefulness of reserpine extends in a number of directions. Its greatest effectiveness is in connection with neurotic reactions, particularly those showing tension and anxiety in which there are palpitations, elevated blood pressure, and rapid heart rate. In the psychotic reactions, reserpine is sometimes effective in acute cases of schizophrenia in younger individuals, where the delusions and hallucinations may be decreased or eliminated. There may be an improvement in communication and social relations, and individual and group psychological treatment may be facilitated. The drug

Table 14.2 *Major classes of psychoactive drugs (Adapted from* Psychopharmacology Bulletin, *vol. 5, no. 4, 1969, p. 4.)*

Major tranquilizers:	Examples:
Phenothiazine derivatives	Chlorpromazine, thioridazine
Butyrophenanes	Haloperidol
Thioxanthines	Thiothixene, chlorprothixene
Minor tranquilizers	
Substituted diols	Meprobamate, tybamate
Benzodiazepines	Chlordiazepoxide, diazepam, oxazepam
Miscellaneous	Hydroxyzine, buclizine
Antidepressants:	
Tricyclics	Imipramine, amitriptyline
MAO inhibitors	Isocarboxazid, phenelzine
Others	Combination of amitriptyline and perphenazine
Stimulants:	
Amphetamines	Dextroamphetamine, methamphetamine
Others	Methylphenidate
Sedatives:	
Barbiturates—long- and intermediate-acting	Phenobarbital, butabarbital
Others	Bromisovalum
Hypnotics:	
Barbiturates—short-acting	Pentobarbital, secobarbital
Nonbarbiturates	Glutethimide, ethchlorvynol

is relatively ineffective in the various depressive reactions.

The side effects of reserpine include a wide range of symptoms. Many people experience a nasal stuffiness, lowered blood pressure, and gastrointestinal symptoms. Others show drowsiness, fatigue, dizziness, muscular aches and cramps, eye symptoms, and menstrual irregularities. Serious depression is observed in some cases. These side effects may be controlled in part or completely by reducing the dosage. There are few problems of tolerance, addiction, or withdrawal.

The action of reserpine appears to be chiefly in the region of the hypothalamus and in the lower brain centers concerned with heart action, blood pressure, and sleep and arousal. The drug inhibits these centers and provides protection against stimuli coming from peripheral and cortical areas. The frequent result is a tranquilizing and calming effect, along with an enhanced sense of well-being. While the precise action of reserpine is not known, the drug depletes the brain of its serotonin, the powerful neurohormone which is related to the transmission of nerve impulses. See Table 14.3 for effects of tranquilizers on the brain.

The calming effects of the tranquilizers are shown in their action on the rhesus monkey. The normal active rhesus monkey is a timid and antagonistic animal which is distrustful of man and constantly seeks to escape. Such animals can be handled safely only by persons wearing heavy gloves. However, after an injection of a tranquilizer, the same monkey may become almost playful. He may roll on his back in a friendly attitude and respond by grasping the hand of the investigator with no effort to resist. It is even possible to remove the chain which ordinarily is needed to restrict the monkey's activity. Since the animal is no longer afraid, he makes no effort to escape. The facial expression shows curiosity and calmness.

In comparing chlorpromazine and reserpine, the former acts more rapidly and is more effective in schizophrenia. States of acute excitement respond well to either drug, while depressions do not respond to chlorpromazine and may be made

Table 14.3 *The effects of tranquilizing drugs on brain areas*

BRAIN AREA	FUNCTION OF BRAIN AREA	PHENOTHIAZINES	RAUWOLFIA DERIVATIVES
Neocortex	Discriminative aspects of consciousness	No effect	No effect
Thalamus	Transmission of alerting impulses to cortex. Modulation of action of reticular formation	Stimulation	No effect
Hypothalamus	Regulation of autonomic functions	Depression of sympathetic mechanisms	Depression of sympathetic mechanisms; parasympathetic mechanisms stimulated
Neurohormonal depots	Regulation of affective behavior	Blocking effect	Depleting effect
Reticular formation	Alerts behavior and/or EEG	Depression	Stimulation
Limbic system	Correlates intellectual and emotional aspects of consciousness	Stimulation	Stimulation

SOURCE: Adapted from *Tranquilizers, Barbiturates and the Brain.* Courtesy of Harold E. Himwich, M.D., and the Wallace Laboratories.

more severe through the use of reserpine. Some people respond better to one drug, while other individuals having similar symptoms will respond better to the other drug. Sometimes a better response is shown to a combination of chlorpromazine and reserpine than to one drug alone.

The Minor Tranquilizers

The minor tranquilizers can be classified on a pharmacological basis into the *propanediol carbamate* group and the *diphenyl methane* group. There is also a miscellaneous group of more or less unrelated drugs. As in the case of the major tranquilizers, new compounds have been added at a rapid rate, and the classification has undergone continuing revision.

The best-known example of a tranquilizer derived from propanediol carbamate is meprobamate (Miltown). This drug, first reported in 1950, is of low toxicity and shows few side effects. It acts primarily on the subcortical centers and produces a state of muscular relaxation. While the drug does not affect the autonomic nervous system, it is effective in relieving fear, tension, and anxiety. It also reduces hostility and aggression, and in some cases it has been used to control convulsive seizures.

ANTIDEPRESSANTS

The dramatic results obtained with the tranquilizing drugs in the late 1950s were responsible for a sharp step-up in the investigation of other psychoactive drugs. Since the tranquilizers are not useful in cases of depression and since these conditions are widespread in the population, major research was turned in this direction. The result was the development of new antidepressant drugs and the further development of older drugs known to have antidepressive properties.

The antidepressant drugs may be classified into *stimulants* and *suppressants*. The stimulants may have a *direct action,* a *bimodal action,* in which the direct stimulation is supplemented by a slower and cumulative indirect effect, or a predominantly *indirect action*. These three types of stimulating drugs are used for the most part in

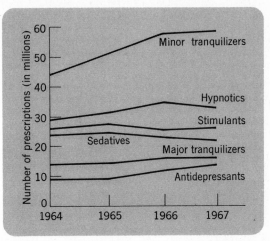

Figure 14.3 *The number of prescriptions for the major classes of psychoactive drugs filled in United States stores, 1964–1967. (Adapted from* Psychopharmacology Bulletin, *vol. 5, no. 4, 1969, p. 9.)*

the treatment of depression in which there is a slowing down of thinking and movement. The suppressant drugs are used in the agitated forms of depression.

Direct Stimulants

The direct stimulants have a brief and rapid action on the central nervous system in which the effect may wear off in a matter of hours. Sometimes there is a letdown feeling following the use of these drugs. The stimulants of this type tend to raise the blood pressure and to reduce the appetite. While they are relatively nontoxic, they are occasionally habit-forming, and patients sometimes develop a dependency upon them.

One of the first direct stimulants used as an antidepressant was *amphetamine sulphate* (Benzedrine). In 1935 this drug was found to be effective in the treatment of narcolepsy, a condition characterized by untimely and involuntary episodes of sleep. Further use of the drug indicated that it elevates the mood, lessens depression, and increases cheerfulness. In most patients, there are decreased feelings of fatigue and a greater interest in work. Patients lose their shyness and gain self-confidence. In larger amounts, the drug leads to an increase in speech production, facetiousness, and uncontrollable laughter. The stream of mental activity is accelerated, and thought content is enriched. However, when the drug is withdrawn, there are likely to be symptoms of weakness, depression, gastrointestinal disturbances, and trembling.

In psychiatric treatment, the drug has been used for the relief of fatigue, for apathetic neurotics, and for depressed psychotics. The drug is more successful in treating milder cases of depression than deep depression. It does not have therapeutic value in schizophrenia, and in fact sometimes releases violent outbursts when given to patients of this type.

Because of the stimulating effects of amphetamine sulfate, the drug has been used by students cramming for their examinations, by motorists and truck drivers on long trips, and by others who need to remain awake and full of energy. There was such a general abuse of the drug that it became necessary to place legal restrictions on its sale. Its addictive nature and undesirable side effects were so serious that the drug was replaced by other amphetamines. The amphetamine derivatives are also addictive and must be used in a carefully controlled manner.

Indirect Stimulants

The indirect stimulants used in depression have the common characteristic of inhibiting the action of the enzyme monoamine oxidase (MAO). While there may be a slight direct stimulating effect on the central nervous system, the action of the MAO-inhibitors is quite slow, and some days or weeks may be required before the effects become apparent. This prolonged action is maintained and there are no letdowns in mood. The drugs are used in cases of nonagitated depression, depression which has not responded to other forms of therapy, and some forms of schizophrenia with depressive features.

The method of treatment with the indirect stimulants of the MAO-inhibitor type is somewhat different from that of other antidepressive drugs. The MAO-inhibitors are usually administered in relatively large doses at the beginning of the treatment. Since these drugs are more toxic than other antidepressants, there must be continued medical supervision. As soon as a favorable response is shown, the amount of the drug is ad-

justed to a maintenance level just below the appearance of side reactions. Once this maintenance level is attained, there is little need for further adjustment of the dosage.

Among the MAO-inhibitors, iproniazid (Marsilid) has been studied most intensively. This drug was introduced in 1951 to treat tuberculosis. Since the side effects included a marked elevation in mood, the drug was tried with depressed patients. The early results were dramatic, but it was found that the drug was toxic and that its use led to a number of troublesome symptoms. As a result, iproniazid was replaced by MAO-inhibitors with less toxic side reactions. Among these other MAO-inhibitors was isocarboxazid, which was as efficient as iproniazid but whose side effects were less frequent and less dangerous.

Although the MAO-inhibitors are valuable in the treatment of a variety of depressive conditions of the psychotic type, neurotically depressed people are often faced with disturbing autonomic side reactions. The exact mode of action of the MAO-inhibitors is unknown. The drugs appear to be related to the functions of the neurohormones such as serotonin, noradrenalin, and similar substances involved in the control of the transmission of nerve impulses in the central nervous system (Hartmann, 1969).

Bimodal Stimulants

The bimodal stimulants are those having a dual action. In addition to a direct stimulation of the central nervous system, there is a slower-acting effect as a result of the inhibition of monoamine oxidase. The bimodal stimulants are used for the rapid but sustained action needed in the nonagitated neurotic and psychotic depressions and in the depressed forms of schizophrenia.

Suppressants

The central nervous system suppressants are used primarily in the treatment of depressions accompanied by pacing, restlessness, and agitation. Such depressions are relatively common during the climacterium, or change of life, and are seen frequently among involutional psychotics. The suppressants calm the disturbed individual and improve his mood.

Table 14.4 *Effects of amphetamine sulphate*

1. STIMULATION OF MENTAL RESPONSE

a. Major effects. Acceleration of the stream of mental activity and increase in content of thought; increase in coordinate mental activity and general efficiency; increase in perception and alertness; increase in initiative; increase in attention and meticulousness; decrease in confusion; decrease in sleep requirement and insomnia; decrease in fatigue; decrease in reticence and improved performance on psychometric tests.

b. Paradoxic effects. Retardation of the stream of mental activity; incapability to concentrate; forgetfulness; dullness, increase in fatigue, malaise, and drowsiness; decrease in perception and alertness; decrease in attention; confusion; transitory delirium; tactile and other somatic hallucinations, paraesthesias and anaesthesias, heart consciousness, and generalized sensations of warmth.

2. STIMULATION OF SPEECH FUNCTION

a. Major effects. Increase in speech activity, disappearance of mutism, talkativeness to the point of loquaciousness; increase in accessibility with willingness to discuss personal problems, ventilation of conflicts, and elaboration of delusions and hallucinations; increase in coherent and relevant speech.

b. Paradoxic effects. Decrease in speech activity, decrease in logical progression of thought with increase in incoherent and irrelevant speech.

3. STIMULATION OF MOTOR FUNCTION

a. Major effects. Increase in motor activity; increase in coordinate physical activity with increase in physical efficiency; tremulousness, restlessness, extreme hyperkinesis; and aggravation of convulsive seizures.

b. Paradoxic effects. Decrease in motor activity with decrease in physical efficiency.

4. STIMULATION OF AFFECTIVE FUNCTION

a. Major effects. Elevation of mood with cheerfulness, a feeling of well-being, exhilaration, euphoria, elation; uncontrollable laughter; facetiousness; a state of ready irritability and increased irritation; increase in drive, urge, and spontaneity; decrease in shyness; increase in confidence; hair-trigger-like reactions with sudden changeability of mood; agitation, impatience, impulsiveness, and self-assertiveness approaching aggressiveness in some; aggravation of assaultiveness; homicidal tendencies in mentally ill persons.

b. Paradoxic effects. Lowering of mood with depression or melancholy; uncontrollable crying; aggravation of suicidal tendencies; resentfulness; surliness; anxiety; increase in worry.

SOURCE: Adapted from E. C. Reifenstein and E. Davidoff, "The Psychological Effects of Benzedrine Sulphate." *Amer. J. Psychol.* **42:**56, 1939.

ANTIEXCITEMENT DRUGS

The most recent development in the drug treatment of affective disorders is the use of *lithium carbonate*, a drug which inhibits the formation of an important chemical regulator (cyclic adenosine 3,5-monophosphate) of virtually all hormone activity. Controlled clinical studies indicate that lithium carbonate is effective in the treatment of mania, especially those patients showing a cyclic history (Sikes and Sikes, 1970). The principal objection to lithium carbonate has been a relatively high degree of toxicity, although this danger has diminished as experience with the drug has increased.

As with all forms of treatment, the evaluation of the effectiveness of mood-influencing drugs presents a number of practical difficulties. While excellent results have been reported in many cases, a question remains as to the fundamental value of this class of drugs. In a study of approximately one thousand clinical reports of the use of a wide range of antidepressant drugs, it was concluded that in well-designed studies the differences between the effectiveness of antidepressant drugs and placebos are not impressive. This same study found that the method used in drug research is of more significance to the outcome of a clinical trial than is the drug being studied (Smith et al., 1969).

ANTICONVULSANTS

Drugs of various kinds have been used to control the several types of convulsive behavior, including *grand mal, petit mal,* temporal-lobe (or psychomotor), and Jacksonian seizures. Because of the serious and disabling nature of *grand mal* attacks, the early emphasis was placed on controlling them.

The first important anticonvulsant drugs were the *bromides*, whose early sedative role we have already discussed. While bromine was discovered in 1826, it was not until the middle of the century that reports were published on the use of the bromides in convulsive disorders. In spite of their known physical and mental side effects, the drugs were used widely as anticonvulsive agents At the National Hospital for Paralysis, Epilepsy and Allied Diseases in London, about half a million doses were administered each year during the late nineteenth century (Tuke, 1892).

Of all various bromine salts (potassium, ammonium, and sodium), sodium bromide came to be preferred because it is less irritating and less disagreeable in taste. Bromide acts as a motor depressant, raising the threshold of motor-neuron discharge and thus inhibiting the convulsive seizures. The drug depresses the entire central nervous system with the exception of the medulla. Heavy doses of bromide are usually necessary in treating convulsive seizures, and since the body eliminates the drug slowly, there is an ever-present danger of bromide intoxication.

The bromides remained the only major anticonvulsant treatment until the barbiturates were discovered early in the present century. In 1903, it was found that these drugs have sedative effects (Fischer and von Mering, 1903), but their anticonvulsant properties were not clearly recognized until 1912, when *phenylethyl-barbituric acid*

(phenobarbital) was given to patients and the seizures disappeared entirely in milder cases and became less severe in the more serious cases (Hauptman, 1912). From that time, the drug took its place with the bromides as an important form of treatment for convulsive disorders.

As in the case of other anticonvulsant drugs, treatment must be continued indefinitely. There is always the danger of barbiturate intoxication marked by unsteadiness, somnolence, slow breathing, increased heart rate, slowing of peristalsis, and a drop in body temperature. Acute episodes of barbital intoxication are characterized by deep coma, disorientation, and euphoria, although irritability, agitation, and depression are seen occasionally.

A third major anticonvulsive drug, *sodium diphenyl hydantoinate* (Dilantin sodium), was introduced in 1937 (Putnam and Merritt, 1937). This drug, which was found to be more effective than the barbiturates in the control of seizures, has less of a sedative effect. It does have toxic properties, which produce instability of gait, tremor, gastric upset, skin eruptions, and swelling of the gums. Since the severity of the reaction occasionally is prohibitory, anticonvulsants of lower toxicity are used in the treatment of some cases.

A limiting factor of the drug is that it is useful only in *grand mal* seizures. *Petit mal* may be aggravated by the drug. However, in addition to its anticonvulsant properties, the drug sometimes brings about improvement in behavior in the form of increased cooperation, alertness, and a better general attitude. While part of this improvement in conduct can be explained in terms of reduction in the number of convulsive seizures, the drug appears capable of producing distinct personality changes in nonepileptic psychotics. The drug has also been used successfully in the treatment of the behavior problems of children (Goldberg and Kurland, 1970).

In addition to the classic anticonvulsive drugs such as the bromides, the barbiturates, and sodium hydantoinate, a number of other drugs have been developed to control *grand mal* seizures. *Methyl hydantoin* (Mesantoin) is related to sodium hydantoinate, but has the advantage of having fewer side effects. Another drug used in controlling convulsive behavior of the *grand mal* type is *primidione* (Mysoline), a compound related chemically to the barbiturates but acting over a much broader range. Early in the 1950s, a powerful new anticonvulsive drug, *phenylacetyl urea* (Phenurone), was demonstrated clinically. It contains the phenyl radical which appears to be one of the important factors in the anticonvulsant activity of some of the most effective drugs.

The *vital dyes,* which are substances used for staining living tissues, have also been used as anticonvulsants. Both neutral red and brilliant vital red have been tested on experimental animals and on epileptics. Threshold convulsive doses of camphorated oil and other convulsants were given to experimental animals, and each animal was then given two or three intravenous injections of brilliant vital red until the skin and mucosa became conspicously red. When convulsant drugs were given again, convulsions did not occur in most cases. Following the animal experimentation, investigators used the dye successfully with people having convulsive disorders.

There are indications that some of the future anticonvulsive drugs may be chemicals of the enzyme class. The development of an enzyme attack on convulsive disorders began in 1943 when it was found that glutamic acid is linked to the metabolism of acetylcholine, the neurohormone which had previously been shown to be related to convulsions (Nachmansohn and Machado, 1943). The possibility of using enzymes in the treatment of such behavior is significant because they may directly attack the cause of the disorder, while other chemicals merely check the convulsions which are a symptom of the condition.

While the major emphasis in anticonvulsive drugs has been the control of *grand mal* seizures, other drugs have been developed to treat *petit mal* and psychomotor seizures. The first important drug in the treatment of *petit mal* was *trimethadione* (Tridione). This drug was first reported in Germany in 1938, and its anticonvulsive influence on experimental animals was demonstrated in 1944. The effectiveness of the drug in the control of *petit mal* attacks was shown the following year. Since that time, other drugs (Milontin, Paradione) have been found to be effective in *petit mal* disorders. The control of psychomotor seizures is less well established, although some of the drugs used in the treatment of *grand*

mal attacks also alleviate psychomotor symptoms in selected cases.

The many anticonvulsant drugs now available make possible a relatively high degree of control of epileptic seizures. These drugs, if used regularly, can control 80 percent of the cases of epilepsy. In about 50 percent of the cases there is complete control, while in the remaining 30 percent the frequency of seizures is reduced markedly (NIMH, 1969).

OTHER DRUG TREATMENTS

In addition to the more widely used drug treatments discussed up to this point, there are several other drug therapies of a more experimental, and sometimes controversial, nature. One such approach is the drug treatment of narcotic addiction; another is the use of LSD and other hallucinogens, or hallucination-producing drugs; and there has been an increasing interest in improving the molecular balance of the brain.

Methadone Therapy

Drug dependence has been an unusually difficult condition to treat. Even under the most favorable circumstances, the rate of relapse has been disappointingly high. One of the most promising treatments has been *methadone*, a pain-killing synthetic drug which does not produce the pleasant effects—the "high"—of heroin and other opiates. As a result, drug addicts given methadone lose their desire for narcotics. A three-year study of methadone at the Rockefeller University Hospital in New York and the Beth Israel Medical Center showed that nearly three hundred addicts lost their habit and none returned to heroin.

The controversial side of the treatment is that methadone is itself addictive, and the patient must be maintained indefinitely on this drug. But methadone does not have the toxic effects of heroin; when an addict has become stabilized on methadone, he feels alert, physically well, and able to live a normal life. Also, the physical dependence on methadone is less severe than on heroin or other opium derivatives. While the exact mechanism by which methadone works is not known, it apparently involves tolerance and cross-tolerance. Since the methadone presumably works on the same brain centers as heroin, it induces a cross-tolerance to heroin and blocks its effect.

Treatment with Hallucinogenic Drugs

LSD and related hallucinogenic drugs have been used with varying success in the treatment of a number of personality disturbances. Early enthusiasm for the effectiveness of LSD with alcoholics was not supported, with more recent studies indicating that the long-term gains with this form of treatment are negligible (Bowen et al., 1970). However, an LSD derivative (methysergide) has been used successfully in the treatment of schizophrenic children. These autistic, or withdrawn, children showed increased alertness, vigor, and purposeful activity after receiving the hallucinogenic drug (Fish et al., 1969).

Molecular Balance Treatment

There is growing interest in the possibility of preventing mental disorder by providing an optimal concentration of chemical substances normally present in the human body. The method has been used for a number of years in a rather unsystematic way. Today it is being proposed as a treatment approach comparable in its effectiveness to drug therapy, shock therapy, and psychological treatment.

It was noted in Chapter 12 that children suffering from mental retardation associated with phenylketonuria are treated by using a diet containing a smaller than normal amount of the amino acid *phenylalanine*. Patients on a normal diet have in their tissues an abnormally high concentration of phenylalanine and some of its reaction products. A decrease in the amount of phenylalanine results in an approximation of the normal concentration and leads to a decrease or disappearance of the symptoms.

There are many other examples of the importance of an optimal molecular balance in the brain. LSD, mescaline, and other hallucinogens cause profound psychological changes. The inhalation of fumes and gases also affects consciousness through alterations of the molecular arrangement of the brain. Low concentration of vitamins may also be associated with mental disorder. There is also evidence that psychological functions and behavior are affected by changes in the concentration in the brain of other substances that are normally present. Such observations have led a number of molecular biologists to suggest that the controlled correction of the molecular imbalance of the brain and nervous system may well be an important future development.

Psychopharmacology has become one of the most productive areas in research into the treatment of personality disturbances. Many new drugs effective in the treatment of mental disorder have been developed. Advances have also been made in the development of a standard animal screening technique which can be used to identify chemical compounds with properties similar to those chemicals having demonstrated treatment value. And the search continues for the development of good animal models of human psychiatric disorders on which chemical compounds can be tested.[2]

SLEEP THERAPY

The curative and restorative value of sleep has been known for many centuries. The ancient Egyptians knew of its efficacy in the treatment of both

---

[2]Good introductions to chemotherapy are provided by Richard Mathison's nontechnical book *The Eternal Search: The Story of Man and His Drugs* (Putnam, 1958); Nathan Kline's *Psychopharmacology Frontiers* (Little, Brown, 1959); and O. A. Battista's *Mental Drugs: Chemistry's Challenge to Psychotherapy* (Chilton, 1960). More technical discussions of drug therapy are found in *A Symposium on Drugs and Sensory Functions* (Little, Brown, 1969), edited by Andrew Herxheimer; *Antipsychotic, Antianxiety, and Antidepressant Drugs* (Veterans Administration, 1966) by E. M. Caffey and others; *Depression and Antidepressant Drugs* (Massachusetts Department of Mental Health, 1960), edited by D. M. Rogers; *Tranquilizing and Antidepressive Drugs* (Thomas, 1962) by W. M. Benson and B. C. Schiele; and *Chemotherapy in Emotional Disorders* (Blakiston, 1960) by F. F. Flach and P. F. Regan III.

Figure 14.4 *A patient being given a short-acting intravenous barbiturate in connection with prolonged sleep therapy. (Courtesy of Eli Lilly and Company.)*

physical and mental disorders. References to sleep and mental disorder are also found in the writings of early Greek and Roman physicians. And in 1700, Herman Boerhaave recommended sleep in the treatment of melancholia.

The earliest articles on modern sleep therapy were published late in the nineteenth century. They discussed problems of bromide sleep treatment in mental disorder and reported recoveries following the use of massive doses of bromide for acutely excited people. However, wide acceptance of sleep therapy had to wait for the work of a Swiss psychiatrist who treated schizophrenics by means of this method in 1922 (Klaesi, 1922). His patients at the Burgholzli Hospital in Zurich were put to sleep for eight to ten days. The method was called *prolonged narcosis.*

The treatment was based on the theory that inflammatory processes can be cured by local anesthesia through a breaking of the vicious cycle between stimulus and increased blood supply. Klaesi reasoned that there may be a similar cycle in mental disorder in which emotional excitement causes motor restlessness, which in turn leads to further excitation. Central anesthesia, in the form of prolonged narcosis, was his means of breaking this cycle. Through mixtures of barbiturates and other drugs, he brought about a quieting effect which was used to facilitate the treatment. Interviews by the psychiatrist took place during the twilight state between the periods of sleep.

Various techniques have been used to bring

about prolonged narcosis. Some neuropsychiatrists use two drugs. The first, injected early in the morning, is a slow-acting drug which brings on a continuous state of drowsiness. The second drug is given whenever necessary to keep the person asleep. People are kept asleep for twenty to twenty-two hours per day, and their pulse, blood pressure, and respiration are checked periodically. They are awakened for periods of ten to fifteen minutes to drink fluids and to eliminate. The usual cycle of night and day is ignored, and treatment takes place in a darkened room. Excellent results have been obtained in transient situational conditions accompanied by high levels of tension or agitation, and in the anxiety neuroses.

ELECTRONARCOSIS

Electronarcosis is a form of sleep therapy in which the individual is made unconscious by an electric current. One of the earliest experiments of this kind was carried out in 1902, when a narcosis-like state was produced in rabbits and dogs by applying an electrical current to the central nervous system (Leduc, 1902). One electrode was placed on the head and the other at the end of the spine of the animal. When the current was applied, the animal fell on its side, and respiration stopped. The current then was decreased to a level at which respiration resumed, and the animal remained motionless as long as the current was maintained. The animal could not be aroused even by strong stimuli. As soon as the current was interrupted, the animal awoke without any apparent ill effects.

Later, the investigator tried the procedure on himself. At the beginning of the application of the current, unpleasant sensations were experienced at the site of the electrodes. These sensations ceased on further increase of the current. The first sign of central nervous system involvement was an inability to speak. Soon afterwards, he was unable to move, although he remained conscious. During the application of the strongest current he heard what was said, but perception was dreamlike, and painful stimuli were felt as though they were applied to an extremity deeply asleep.

As a result of more recent studies, a relatively standardized method of electronarcosis has been developed. The current is maintained at an initial level for thirty seconds, during which time the body becomes rigid. The heart stops beating for a few seconds, and there is no breathing until the current is lowered and the body relaxes. Consciousness is lost immediately, and the individual remains asleep until the current once again is turned off.

Prolonged sleep therapy has been used widely in Russia, and an instrument called an *electrosone* was developed to induce electronarcosis. One pair of electrodes is placed over the eyes, and the other set is fitted behind the ears. A low-voltage current is sent through the sleep centers of the brain making it possible to achieve deep sleep in a few moments. The patient awakens refreshed and invigorated. This instrument has been used with varying degrees of success in the treatment of insomnia, hypertension, and a variety of psychiatric disorders. Experiments are being carried out in the United States with equipment patterned after the electrosone.

While prolonged narcosis was used originally in cases of excited, sleepless, and unmanageable individuals, the method has since been used in other types of mental disorder. Cases of anxiety, depression, or agitation appear to be most suitable for prolonged narcosis. In general, the treatment is more effective in the affective reactions than in the schizophrenias.

Explanations of the therapeutic effects of prolonged narcosis have centered on biochemical changes, neurophysiological processes, and psychodynamic relationships. The biochemical explanation emphasizes improved cellular oxidation and the facilitation of metabolic changes. The neurophysiologic theory regards sleep as a stage in internal inhibition, permitting the cortical cells to recover their normal state. The psychodynamic explanation emphasizes the feeling of being utterly defenseless and completely dependent on nurses and doctors. It has been suggested that the nature of the treatment and the atmosphere in which it is carried out may create an infantile and regressive state from which the treated person experiences emotional rebirth.

THE SHOCK THERAPIES

Shock therapy is a specialized form of treatment in which deep comas and/or convulsions are induced artificially. The therapeutic advantages of the method grow out of the metabolic, neuroelectrical, and biochemical changes associated with the drastic and fundamental physiological reorganization forced on the individual by shock-inducing drugs, gas, or electrical current.

INSULIN SHOCK

The first controlled shock therapy in the treatment of mental disorder was insulin shock. Insulin had been used in neuropsychiatry for the purpose of stimulating the appetites of patients so they would gain weight and strength, and there had been some interest in insulin for the symptomatic relief of excitement. However, the use of insulin to induce *hypoglycemia,* or lowered blood sugar, was first reported in 1933 by the Austrian physician, Manfred Sakel (1900-1957).

Sakel stumbled on the insulin-shock treatment by accident. His work on morphine addiction led him to believe that adrenalin was a factor in bringing about the withdrawal symptoms which are characteristic of addiction. He decided to use insulin as an adrenalin antagonist. Occasionally a person being treated slipped into a hypoglycemic reaction, and Sakel observed a decrease in psychotic symptoms. As a result of these findings, he began to use the method in the treatment of schizophrenia and other psychoses (Sakel, 1938).

In insulin-shock therapy, the patient is given intramuscular injections of insulin while fasting during the early morning hours. As a result of the lowering of the blood sugar level, the characteristic signs of hypoglycemia put in their appearance several hours after the injection. There is weakness, hunger, progressive sleepiness, considerable perspiration, and occasional periods of excitement. As the somnolence deepens and the individual goes into the typical shock state, there are transitory spasms of the extremities, muscular twitching, body tremors, heavy breathing, and various forms of mumbling and muttering. The shock reaction leads to a deep coma, and occasionally there are convulsions. Spontaneous awakening ordinarily follows the convulsive behavior. Unless a convulsion takes place, the coma is terminated after several minutes to an hour by giving sugar water by mouth. In an emergency, when quick arousal is desired, an intravenous injection of glucose is given.

Upon awakening, there may be a short phase of psychomotor excitement followed by one of confusion. Speech is at first unintelligible, although the individual understands questions and replies by nodding or shaking his head. Later, he may resemble a person under the influence of alcohol. He will talk in an unconcerned and playful manner for a short while, after which his thoughts become more orderly.

The following observations were made by a physician who received insulin-shock therapy during an attack of schizophrenia:

> I heard very distinctly the voices of the doctor and sister. I do not now remember what they were saying. I saw the doctor's and sister's faces. The doctor asked me repeatedly if I was awake and slapped me lightly on the left cheek, as he usually does when I am recovering from a coma. I could not speak and I felt very helpless and confused mentally. The next recollection I have is of the nurse's white worried face with its distended arteries and forehead vein looking down at me and asking me if I was alright. He asked me this question two or three times but I could not answer him. He felt my pulse and arranged my bed clothes rapidly—very rapidly—it seemed to me, two or three

> times. I was conscious of a tremendous effort I seemed to be making to avoid slipping into a land which was different from that of the nurse's, as being a land or "life" of no movement. The nurse seemed to me to be making also a terrific effort to help me, to bring me back to *his* life. I felt fully conscious of this intensive and combined effort and strove or seemed to strive with all my powers to drag myself back from this abyss of "no movement." I do not recollect moving my limbs, on the contrary I seemed to be paralyzed in my voluntary movements. After a long struggle in which at times I thought that I could not make the effort any longer—I found that I could speak, and I felt an overwhelming sense of gratitude to the nurse whom I hailed as my "saviour." I had an intolerable thirst and also felt very hungry. I asked the nurse for sweet drinks and he brought me a glass of tea and sandwiches of which I ate three or four. I insisted on the nurse having a sandwich, which he did to please me. I also insisted that he should have a drink, but he replied that he would have one later. Sister came in then and I discussed the question of glucose and its relation to obesity. . . (Mayer-Gross, 1959).

The most frequently seen complications arising out of insulin-shock therapy include prolonged coma, in which there may be acute damage of the brain cells, fractures due to the violent convulsion, respiratory disorders, and more rarely, but more dangerous, cardiovascular involvement.

Among the factors important in predicting the probable effectiveness of insulin therapy with a given person are age, sex, and heredity, the type of mental disorder, the nature of the onset, the duration of the condition, the presence of previous attacks, and the constitutional makeup of the individual. The exact effectiveness of the treatment has never been determined because of the lack of standardization of treatment, control groups, and uniform reporting. While some cases seem to show a permanent cure, others relapse after initial improvement and require additional series of shock treatments.

There have been numerous theories to account for the beneficial effects of insulin shock. There is a possibility that insulin corrects disturbances of oxidation which produce an accumulation of incompletely oxidized products of metabolism in the nerve cells. Insulin treatment also produces a state of increased excitability of the autonomic centers. This increased excitability is linked with endocrine changes which may lead to a more normal biochemical balance within the body.

METRAZOL CONVULSIVE THERAPY

The convulsive treatment of mental disorder was introduced in 1934 by Ladislaus von Meduna (1896—   ), then superintendent of the Royal State Mental Hospital in Budapest (Meduna, 1936). Basing his work on his theory that there is a fundamental antagonism between convulsive disorders and schizophrenia, he set about deliberately to induce convulsions in his schizophrenics.

Paracelsus had used camphor for this purpose in the sixteenth century, and by the eighteenth century the drug was in common use. Meduna also began his work with camphor, but he found that the absorption rate was slow and that it was necessary for the person to walk about in order to bring on the desired reaction. Moreover the time of the convulsion was unpredictable, and the reaction was difficult to control. As a result, Meduna turned to the use of intravenous metrazol, a quick-acting drug that is rapidly absorbed by the body.

The typical reaction to metrazol injection is like that of a *grand mal* convulsive seizure, but it is of an extremely violent nature and a shorter duration. Following the convulsion, which begins ten to twenty seconds after the injection, the patient passes into a short coma, during which the quality of respiration improves, color becomes more nearly normal, and relaxation occurs. There is then a gradual clearing of consciousness, with increased muscular coordination.

A psychiatrist who volunteered to undergo a single metrazol convulsion described his feelings in the following words:

> After the injection, I felt my body and limbs tending to lie straight in the bed and my head turning to a central position. Then very rapidly something seemed to move in my arms and thorax and to pass up to the base of my neck, where it stopped and increased in intensity. This sensation was not painful but felt very queer and circumscribed halfway between thought and sensation, like the ideas in delirium. Unconsciousness developed very quickly, but otherwise its onset felt like the coming of normal sleep and was not resisted (Gillespie, 1939).

As in the case of insulin shock, the effectiveness of metrazol convulsive therapy is difficult to evaluate. Both short-term and long-term improvements have been observed, although many individuals require additional convulsive treatment to maintain their gains. An important objection to the treatment has been the complications which include fractures and dislocations, intense fear prior to the injection, and unpleasant sensations when the convulsion does not occur.

One of the most generally accepted theories of metrazol treatment is that the beneficial effects are due to a lack of oxygen, which reduces brain metabolism. Autonomic changes and endocrine changes also appear to be important in this connection. The behavioral changes following convulsive therapy have been described in terms of a fundamental death threat, release of aggression, loss of newer habits and release of older habits, satisfaction of a need for punishment, and the restructuring of the ego system.

ELECTROSHOCK THERAPY

The use of electricity in medical treatment took place many centuries before electrical energy was isolated. Scribonius Largus, in ancient Rome, was the author of a formulary in which he recommended applications of live electric eels for chronic headache. Both Pliny and Dioscorides referred to similar remedies.

William Gilbert, physician to Queen Elizabeth, used the word *electricity* in 1600 in a work titled *Tractatus de Magnete*. While there were scattered electrophysical experiments, the use of electricity in medicine was relatively unimportant until the early eighteenth century. Beginning in 1744, the Royal Academy of Science in France published a yearly report on electrotherapy. The belief in the therapeutic benefits of electricity was widespread and led to the treatment of a great variety of ills. Electrotherapy included spark treatments, electric baths, vibrators, shocks with the Leyden jar, electrical percussion instruments, static breezes, and combinations of medicinal substances with electricity. An early book on electrotherapy described how people were seated on wooden stools and electrified by means of a large revolving frictional glass globe. The physician then drew sparks from the individual. The beneficial results of the treatment were believed to be due to the driving of excess blood from the af-

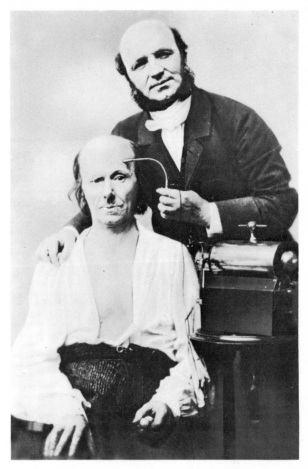

Figure 14.5 *Duchenne of Boulogne treating a patient by means of electricity in the late nineteenth century. (Bettmann Archive.)*

fected tissue. It is more likely that the effects were psychological.

Richard Lovett used electricity successfully in the treatment of mental disorder as early as 1756, only ten years after the first electrical condenser was developed by Pieter Van Musschenbroek. The principal form of treatment involved giving mild electric shocks in the treatment of paralysis and epilepsy. The method was also used in cases of hysteria and melancholia.

During the nineteenth century there was an increased interest in the medical application of electricity. It was suggested that all diseases should be treated by this method before they were considered incurable. Numerous experiments were undertaken to study the effects of electricity in various mental disturbances. One investigation was for the purpose of "awakening the energy of idiotic persons" (Tuke, 1892). Other studies were made of the influence of electricity on the nervous system. It was concluded that mental disorders of recent origin, and especially the functional disorders, could benefit from electrical treatment. Jean Martin Charcot and others, in the latter part of the nineteenth century, made medical history by applying weak galvanic currents in the treatment of hysterical conditions.

The modern technique of electroshock therapy (EST) involves the production of a convulsion by passing an electric current through the brain. The Italian investigators Ugo Cerletti and L. Bini are credited with the first important developments of this technique, although there were prior electroshock experiments in South America. Cerletti reported in 1937 that he had passed an electric current through the head of a dog and

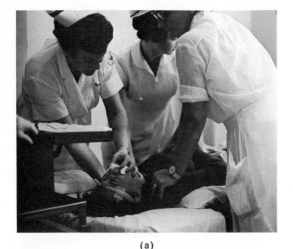

(a)

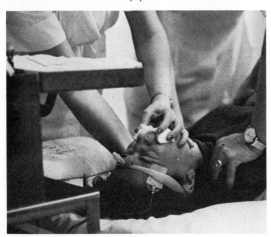

(b)

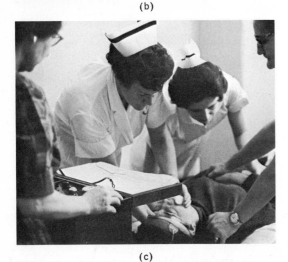

(c)

produced a typical convulsive seizure without apparent damage to the brain. Later experiments established the usefulness of the method in the treatment of mental disorder (Cerletti and Bini, 1938).

The conventional equipment in electroshock treatment uses 60-cycle alternating current, since this current brings about the necessary stimulation of the brain with a minimum of tissue damage. The individual is placed on a comfortable bed with a pillow under his head. The convulsion is then induced by electrodes placed on the head. When the current is turned on, the body becomes rigid and breathing stops for a few seconds. Recovery is rapid, and men and women treated in offices and clinics may be dressed and ready to leave within half an hour after their arrival.

The treatment is frightening to many people. It may be followed by periods of increased restlessness and agitation and states of excitement and uncooperativeness. The individual often appears confused and experiences a temporary loss of memory. A man who was treated by EST gave the following account of his experience:

The next morning at six o'clock I was told to stay in bed. There would be no breakfast this morning, because I was getting shock treatment. I already knew quite a bit about shock treatment. I had helped them give it to other patients many times. I worked in the dormitory, helping to lift the unconscious patients into bed from the wagon, covering the bandage gag that prevented the patient from biting his tongue or chipping his teeth, tying a man in bed if necessary, and occasionally holding the patient down in bed when things got really rough. It wasn't easy work and in a way I was glad not to be doing it this morning.

At nine o'clock the doctor came on the ward. The doctor was a good friend of mine and it was a nice feeling to know that someone was doing his best to help me. But at this moment I was none too happy. I hoped that I'd be the first on the list to get treatment. Yet I was glad to see another patient wheeled out first. I was scared and there was no getting around it. I wondered if I was going to burn, and if I did burn, whether I'd smell. But by this time there was an awful

Figure 14.6 *Electroshock therapy. A soft pad is placed between the patient's teeth to prevent possible biting of the tongue during the convulsion. (Longview State Hospital.)*

cry down the hall and I knew that the first patient's shock treatment had begun.

Soon a man was pushed into the dormitory and lifted into bed while another man on another wagon was pushed into the visiting room where the shock was administered. They had a system. Fifteen patients could be given shock treatment in an hour, easily.

Now it was my turn. I climbed up on the high wagon and stretched out. Three sand bags in the form of a pyramid stuck into the small of my back to expand my chest. Many of the men squirmed and fidgeted and fooled with the sand bags trying to make themselves comfortable. But you were never on the wagon long. A counterpane was pulled up to my neck and a small straw pillow, though covered with a clean towel, was wet with the sweat of the men who had gone before. I was wheeled out into the hall to wait my turn. There was another scream and a gurgling coughing groan, and the patient ahead of me was moved out down the hall and into the dormitory, with arms and legs and head flopping around. Before I realized it I was zooming down the hall. Mac was pushing me, and Mac was in a hurry.

The wagon bumped over the thick rubber matting that formed a hollow rectangle for the wagon to fill. The doctor was looking down, smiling. "Hello there, young fellow." "Good morning, Sir." Sarge was rubbing some sticky stuff on my head beside my ears. I had seen tubes of the stuff in the office, "electrode jelly." After all you had to make a good contact—to burn. I was mighty scared and there was no use kidding about it. Mac held my right arm and pressed hard with the elbow just inside my shoulder muscle. Sarge had the other arm. Another attendant climbed up on the wagon and lay across my knees gripping the side of the wagon with hands and toes. The three attendants would hold me down during my convulsion. The theory was: The more severe the convulsion, the better the results. I heard the doctor give the pretty blonde nurse a set of numbers, and I knew that she was setting the dials. "God, don't let her give me an overdose." Mac's face was about eight inches above my own. I looked up into Mac's eyes. Mac wasn't smiling a bit. I stared up into Mac's eyes and slowly said over and over to myself, "Mac, you big Irish lug, take care of me now." Very deliberately, very slowly a black shade came up over my eyes. I woke up sometime later feeling completely refreshed, not tired or logy, or drugged with sleep, just ready for a big day (Alper, 1948).

EST is most useful in the affective reactions. The treatment is given several times a week in cases of ordinary acute depression, but in cases of great disturbance and agitation or depression of suicidal proportions, it may be given daily or even twice daily. The frequency of treatment is decreased as clinical improvement is shown. A course of treatment ranges from five to twenty or more electroshocks.

EST has several advantages over other convulsive methods. One advantage is that the brain stimulation can be limited to where it is needed, that is, the motor area of the frontal lobe. Convulsant drugs are more likely to cause a generalized excitation of the entire brain. Another advantage of EST is that toxins are not introduced into the blood circulation. There is an immediate loss of consciousness and the person being treated is relatively free from the fright and anxiety associated with other forms of shock treatment. There is less psychomotor excitement following the treatment, and the muscular convulsions are less violent, with fewer chances for injury. The method is simple, and there is a minimal expense involved. Finally, there are no prolonged aftereffects such as headache, nausea, and similar symptoms. EST is not indicated in cases with brain pathology and spinal disorders, or in most cases of pregnancy, metabolic disturbance, or cardiac pathology. The treatment is not without certain risks in the form of bone fractures from the convulsions and possible brain damage.

While it is not known how electroshock therapy achieves its results, the EST brings about changes of carbon-dioxide and oxygen tension and equilibrium, disturbance of acid base balance, and the formation of intermediary products of metabolism. The entire autonomic system is affected by these changes. EST also lowers the blood–brain barrier and makes possible a more ready passing of chemical substances from the circulating blood into the brain and cerebrospinal fluid.

The effectiveness of EST as a treatment method is indicated by the fact that while insulin and metrazol therapy are relatively little used today, electroshock is still used to treat resistant cases of depression. EST has helped to lift some very severe depressions.

ANOXIC SHOCK THERAPY

A number of attempts have been made to alter the personality of mentally disturbed individuals by means of shock induced by gas of various kinds. Among the gases used in the treatment of mental disorder have been ether, oxygen, nitrogen, hydrogen, nitrous oxide, and carbon dioxide.

The anesthetic properties of ether were first discovered in 1846, and etherization as a treatment for mental disorder was widely advocated for a number of years. It was considered valuable in acute excitements and depressive agitations and was used in the treatment of hysterical conversion symptoms. The inhalation of oxygen, nitrogen, and hydrogen was also advocated for the treatment of various personality disturbances.

Nitrous oxide, commonly called "laughing gas," was introduced in 1928 as a treatment in mental disorder (Zador, 1928). When this gas is used, consciousness returns rapidly after the termination of the inhalation. Within a minute or so, the individual is able to answer questions and engage in conversation. While there is no confusion,

Figure 14.7 *Early brain surgery. From a painting attributed to Hieronymous Bosch. Galleria del Prado, Madrid. (Photo Viollet, Paris.)*

he is aware of having lost consciousness. He may declare, "I must have been asleep," or he may ask how long he has been unconscious. Most people have dreams, but they are not always able to recall them. If the dreams are remembered, they are likely to be quite vivid and to offer material for the evaluation of the person's emotional condition.

Carbon dioxide therapy, another form of anoxic shock, was first reported by A. S. Loevenhart and his associates in 1929. In this early work, a mixture of 40 percent carbon dioxide and 60 percent oxygen was used with psychotics. The inhalation of the mixture has the effect of rousing individuals from catatonic-like stupors. After a person has inhaled the mixture for two or three minutes, he may become more normal in his responses and in his activities. He may talk freely, coherently, and intelligently during a period of fifteen or twenty minutes.

A man who received this form of treatment described his experience in the following words:

> When I went under, I found myself in a dark mysterious void. Shadows were all around me, but there was some kind of illumination. Spearheads of red circular dots were coming from the ends of the vision to a dark shape in the center, my eyes were led by the dots to the shape. I myself was led on one of the spearheads to the center shape. Then as I reached it the scene changed—probably in a flash—and I was in a cave. Along the walls, standing side by side, were monstrous red devils, with horned heads bent toward me. They made no effort to grab me—they just stood there inanimately, as if they knew that merely the sight of them was enough. I saw no legs—they probably were covered by their robes of scarlet. They had no facial characteristics of any kind—nose, mouth, eyes, etc., all there was, was the shapes of their heads and horns. Some kind of illumination was present besides their bright red shapes, and that seemed to flicker like fires. There was another flash, and this scene changed into something like a shadowy void (Meduna, 1950).

The therapeutic effect of carbon dioxide therapy is probably related to the electrophysiological action of the carbon dioxide on the neurons, to changes in the endocrine system, and to the increase in cerebral oxygenation. Carbon dioxide produces an increased supply of oxygen to the brain due to dilation of the arteries. It also produces aburpt changes in the acidity-alkalinity ratio of the blood and the brain tissue.

PSYCHOSURGERY

The origins of the surgical treatment of mental disorder are lost in the early history of primitive man. There is ample evidence that various types of *trephination*, or opening of the head, occurred in a number of primitive civilizations. Several collections of ancient skulls reveal various methods by which trephining was carried out. Many of these skulls suggest that the operations were performed for the relief of symptoms rather than as a part of a magic ritual or religious ceremony.

In ancient Greece and Rome, the head was sometimes opened to let out the vapors and humors thought to be responsible for disturbed behavior. Later, at the medical center at Salerno in the twelfth century, Roger Frugardi recommended opening of the skull in cases of mania and melancholia to permit the poisons and other noxious material to escape to the outside. A similar recommendation was made in the seventh century by Marcus Aurelius Severinus. But most of the attempts to alleviate personality disturbances by this method have developed since the late nineteenth century.

The beginning of modern psychosurgery can be traced to the work of the Swiss psychiatrist Gottlieb Burckhardt. Prompted by earlier observations of other workers on changes in the behavior of dogs following the removal of frontal brain areas, Burckhardt operated on the brains of several psychotics in 1891. Four operations were performed on one patient. The first of these consisted of the removal of a tiny amount of cortex from the parietal area. Several other brain areas also were operated on, and finally the patient became quiet and docile (Burckhardt, 1890–1891).

The modern era of psychosurgery began with experimental work in the United States. Brain operations on two now famous chimpanzees, Becky and Lucy, showed that surgical interference with the frontal brain areas did away with anxiety and frustration. Before the removal of the frontal lobes, the animals would race about, scream, shake the bars of their cages, defecate and urinate, and otherwise show symptoms of anger and excitement in the face of experimentally induced frustration. Following the removal of the frontal lobes, the same animals became

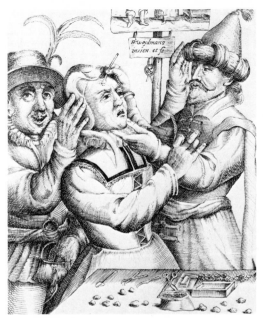

Figure 14.8 Operation for Stones in the Head. *An early seventeenth-century engraving by H. Weydmans. A popular saying of the time (and still current) was: "He has stones (or rocks) in his head." Charlatans of the sixteenth and seventeenth centuries took advantage of the superstition of a physical cause for dementia by making superficial incisions in the scalp in pretending to effect a cure. It was not uncommon to extract small stones supplied by a confederate. (Philadelphia Museum of Art.)*

indifferent and showed a lack of concern. They were no longer frustrated by their inability to solve difficult problems put to them. After a few desultory attempts they would give up without any of the symptoms of agitation shown before the operation (Fulton and Jacobsen, 1935).

Egas Moniz (1874–1955), a distinguished Portuguese psychiatrist, heard a report of this work at the Second International Neurological Congress in London in 1935. It occurred to him that if this indifference to frustration could be brought about in experimental animals, it might be possible to relieve human reactions to frustration in the same way. He reasoned that certain mental disorders might be due to maladaptive cell complexes in the frontal areas of the brain. The problem was to develop a technique for destroying or isolating the cell complexes in

Site of
operation

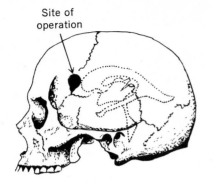

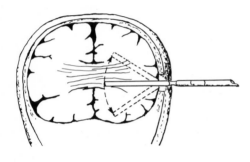

Figure 14.9 *The operation of prefrontal lobotomy. The figure at the top shows the approximate location of the hole drilled in the skull on each side of the forehead. The figure in the middle is a front view of the head in cross-section, showing how the surgical knife is moved upward and downward to cut the pathways in the brain. (Courtesy of* Scientific American.*)*

lobotomy. Such surgical procedures came to be known as *psychosurgery*.

When psychosurgery was first introduced, it was used in cases where shock therapy had been unsuccessful. It was found that while the surgical approach could not improve cases of intellectual deterioration, such symptoms as fear, worry, elation, refusal of food, lack of cooperation, destructiveness, and disorientation could be relieved. In addition, delusions, ideas of reference, apathy, and auditory hallucinations sometimes disappeared after the operation. The best results were eventually obtained in the agitated depressive form of involutional psychosis. Psychosurgery has also been used with children, but the results have been less favorable than with adults.

As in the case of the shock therapies, the mechanisms are not clear by means of which the several forms of psychosurgery result in changes in behavior and subjective experience. In the case of the operative techniques which are directed toward the highly localized destruction of small areas of tissue, the results can usually be explained in terms of the conventional functions associated with that area. When the psychosurgical operation has damaged more extensive brain areas and when more complicated brain functions are involved, the explanation of observed changes is considerably more difficult.

When there is an interference with the neural pathways between the thalamus and the frontal cortex, there may be significant reduction in the emotional component of the mental disturbance. Freeman and Watts, speaking of prefrontal

order to force the brain to reorganize itself in a more normal way.

Moniz returned to Portugal and interested a neurosurgeon, Almeida Lima, in working with him to perfect a brain operation which would meet his requirements. Moniz and Lima decided that the best procedure would be one that would cut the association tracts connecting the prefrontal brain areas with the centers in the thalamus. The operation of *bilateral prefrontal leucotomy* was developed to achieve this result. Later, in the United States, Walter Freeman and James Watts modified the technique and called it *prefrontal*

Figure 14.10 *Some of the leaders in the development of medical and surgical treatment methods for mental illness. (a) Ladislaus J. Meduna, 1896– , Hungarian psychiatrist who was a pioneer in the development of convulsive therapy for the treatment of schizophrenia. (Courtesy of Dr. Meduna.) (b) Jean Delay, 1907– , French psychiatrist who was the first to use tranquilizing drugs in the treatment of mental illness. (Courtesy of Dr. Delay.) (c) Egas Moniz, 1874–1955, Portuguese neurosurgeon who developed modern psychosurgery, (Courtesy of Dr. Almeida Lima and the Centro de Estudos Egas Moniz, Lisbon, Portugal.) (d) Walter Freeman, 1895– , American neurosurgeon who introduced psychosurgery to the United States, (Courtesy of Dr. Freeman.)*

(a)

(b)

(c)

(d)

lobotomy, suggested that the "sting" of the disorder is drawn when the emotional nucleus is removed. There may also be a reduction in the association pathways which limits the spread of stimuli going to different cortical areas. This reduction in pathways could bring about an extensive neural reorganization, possibly with therapeutic implications.

There is a further possibility that the psychosurgical operations force a reintegration of present stimuli with past memories and earlier responses. Moreover, some critics of psychosurgery have suggested that the therapeutic changes come about merely as a result of suggestion and/or the extra care and attention made available during the preoperative period. At the psychodynamic level, the threatening nature of the brain surgery may alert the emergency reserves of the organism, and the improvement may be a response to the unconscious death threat. The state of our knowledge does not permit us to say which, if any, of these explanations is related to the improvement seen in many people.[3]

SUMMARY

1. The medical treatment of mental disorder has been carried out by means of *drugs, sleep, shock,* and *surgery.* One of the oldest physical treatments—as well as the one most emphasized in modern neuropsychiatric therapy—is the use of drugs. The most widely used drugs are the *sedatives, tranquilizers, antidepressants,* and *anticonvulsants.*

2. Sedatives are used for their calming and relaxing effects and their ability to control overactivity. The first sedatives were the opiates and the bromides. The early part of the present century saw the introduction of the barbiturate drugs, while the nonbarbiturate sedatives have been developed since World War II. The tranquilizing drugs, also a relatively recent development, have a calming and relaxing effect but are neither sedatives nor narcotics in the ordinary sense. They bring about a tranquil state in which the individual does not lose consciousness and in which there is little or no impairment of intellectual functioning.

3. The major tranquilizers are drugs used for the control of symptoms in psychotic conditions; the minor tranquilizers are more frequently used to relieve anxiety and tension states in essentially normal individuals. The major tranquilizers are not habit-forming, but some of them have serious side effects. Side effects are not a problem with the minor tranquilizers, but these drugs tend to be habit-forming.

4. The antidepressant drugs are used to get rid of the symptoms of depression. These drugs include the *direct, indirect,* and *bimodal stimulants* and the *suppressants.* The *direct stimulants* act on the central nervous system and are of relatively short action. The *indirect stimulants* which inhibit the action of the enzyme system have a rather slow initial antidepressant effect but a relatively stable long-range action. The *biomodal stimulants* have both a rapid direct action on the central nervous system and a sustained slower effect as a result of the inhibition of the enzyme system.

---

[3]Important books covering the entire range of medical treatment include *The Great Physiodynamic Therapies in Psychiatry* (Hoeber, 1956), edited by A. M. Sackler and others; the third edition of *An Introduction to Physical Methods of Treatment in Psychiatry* (Livingstone, 1954) by W. Sargant and E. Slater; and the third edition of *Somatic Treatments in Psychiatry: Pharmacotherapy; Convulsive, Insulin, Surgical, Other Methods* (Grune & Stratton, 1961) by Lothar B. Kalinowsky and Paul H. Hoch.

The central nervous system suppressants are drugs used in the treatment of depressions accompanied by restlessness and agitation.

5. Chemotherapy also includes anticonvulsant drugs for the control of *grand mal*, or major, convulsive seizures; *petit mal*, or transient loss of consciousness; *psychomotor attacks*, or convulsive equivalents marked by a wide range of symptoms; and other less common forms of convulsive behavior. All psychoactive drugs involve problems such as the side effects, the action of drugs in combination, habit formation, individual tolerance, and similar matters.

6. Sleep therapy as a form of treatment has a long history. In prolonged narcosis, the sleep is induced by drugs. More recently, electric sleep has been induced by an electrical stimulation of the sleep centers in the brain. The method is used most frequently in cases of sleepless, excited, and unmanageable patients. It is used also in some of the more benign affective reactions.

7. The major shock therapies include *insulin shock, convulsive therapy,* and *electroshock*. Most of these forms of therapy have been discarded, with the exception of electroshock, which is still used in cases of depressions which are resistant to drug treatment.

8. The use of psychosurgery in the treatment of mental disorder reached its greatest popularity in the years immediately preceding World War II. In the basic operation, called *prefrontal lobotomy*, incisions are made in the frontal lobes of the brain, cutting a substantial part of the fibers connecting the frontal areas and the thalamus. The result is a reduction in the level of anxiety.

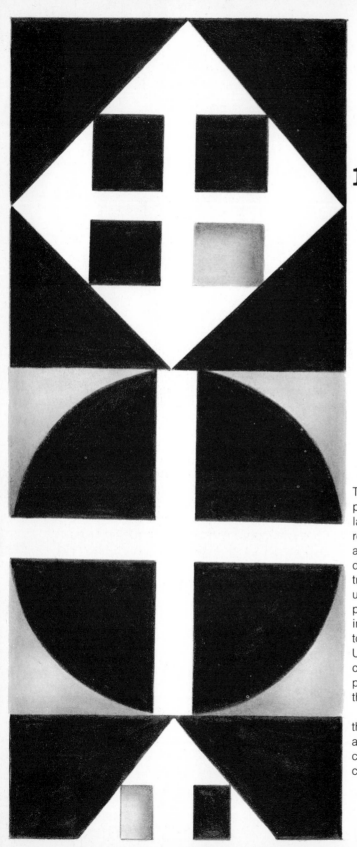

15 PSYCHOLOGICAL TREATMENT

The psychological approach to the treatment of personality disturbances and mental disorder is largely a product of the twentieth century; yet the roots of psychological treatment reach back to antiquity. The explanation for this seeming paradox is the fact that psychological methods of treatment were used for centuries without any real understanding of what was happening. Reason, persuasion, suggestion, sympathetic understanding, even fear and terror were used in the effort to "cure" the victims of personality derangements. Until the early part of the present century, physicians were using, on a completely intuitive basis, psychological methods that had been applied throughout recorded history.

The temple priests of ancient Egypt and Greece, the medicine men of the primitive tribes of Africa and South America, the mesmerists of eighteenth-century France, and the nineteenth-century physicians who relied upon reason and persuasion to influence disturbed people—all were making use of forms of psychological treatment. While the methods frequently were effective, the underlying explanations were naive or nonexistent.

It remained for Sigmund Freud, starting around 1890, to develop a comprehensive and systematic theory and method of psychological treatment. This system, which came to be known as *psychoanalysis,* had a dramatic impact during the first half of the century on the theory and practice of treating personality disturbances. At the same time a number of other forces were at work, with the result that a wide range of nonmedical techniques were developed to treat the disorganized personality. These methods, including psychoanalysis, are known collectively as *psychotherapy.*

In the years following World War II, many psychotherapists became increasingly disenchanted with traditional psychotherapy. Most of the conventional methods were, they thought, needlessly time consuming and open to challenge in terms of results as well. This rather widespread dissatisfaction led to a new emphasis upon personality disturbance and disorganization as a *learned* reaction. The treatment of such conditions, according to this view, must be in terms of the principles of unlearning and relearning. This theoretic approach is called *behavior theory,* while the treatment method has become known as *behavior therapy.*

Some psychologists and psychiatrists use the term psychotherapy to include all forms of psychological treatment, which, they reason, involves an influencing process with common elements. While these common elements do exist, the differences between conventional psychotherapy and behavior therapy are sufficiently pronounced to consider these two treatment approaches separately. One major difference is that conventional psychotherapy assumes that the symptoms of a personality disturbance are expressions of deeper problems which must be treated if the individual is to show improvement. Behavior therapy takes the position that the symptom itself is the disorder, and that the goal of treatment is the removal of the symptom. Another difference is that conventional psychotherapy places major emphasis upon the role of insight or self-understanding in the treatment process, while behavior therapy does not require this type of understanding on the part of the person being treated.

INDIVIDUAL PSYCHOTHERAPY

Psychotherapy is undertaken for a variety of reasons. Ordinarily, the individual comes to the psychotherapist for relief of disturbing symptoms. But behind this surface need is the implied need to be happy, to increase his efficiency, and to improve his social adaptation. At a different level, psychotherapy is designed to strengthen feelings of self-esteem and security, to increase self-acceptance, to assist in the integration of intellectual and emotional activities, and to direct them toward more positive goals.

Every psychotherapeutic relationship includes a number of factors common to all types of therapy and independent of theoretical considerations. There is always a troubled person and there is always a therapist. They meet in a special kind of setting, and an interpersonal relationship is established. This relationship has a beginning, a middle, and an ending. The key to psychotherapy is to be found in the psychological dynamics of the person being treated and the therapist and in their relationship during the course of the treatment.

There are many different techniques of psychotherapy, and various attempts have been made to group and classify them in meaningful ways. All psychotherapy can be divided into *individual* therapy and *group* therapy, but within these two there are wide and important differences.

A useful approach to the classification of psychotherapy is in terms of the objectives of the treatment. One type of therapy is designed to give intellectual and emotional support to the individual, a second type attempts to reeducate him in terms of his attitudes toward the world and toward himself, while a third type attempts to effect deep and fundamental alterations in the basic personality structure of the individual. These three types of therapy have been called *supportive, reeducative,* and *reconstructive* psychotherapy.

SUPPORTIVE PSYCHOTHERAPY

In supportive therapy the therapist is interested in the greatest possible improvement in the shortest possible time. The aim of the treatment is to remove symptoms so that the person can live a relatively normal, symptom-free life. No special efforts are made to alter his attitudes, to get at the underlying causes of the trouble, or to bring about important personality changes.

The supportive approach is used widely by psychiatrists, clinical psychologists, psychiatric social workers, and other trained therapists. Sometimes it is used as the only approach, but more often it is combined with reeducative or reconstructive techniques. The supportive approach is used also by untrained professionals such as nurses, teachers, physicians, lawyers, and clergymen, and by friends and relatives. The approach is often used in an intuitive, unconscious, and uncontrolled way, in contrast to the methods of the trained psychotherapist who uses the supportive technique as part of a planned treatment program.

The technique of *reassurance* is one of the most frequently used methods in supportive psychotherapy, even though there is a tendency on the part of some psychotherapists to depreciate its importance or even its desirability. However, it is unlikely that a psychotherapeutic relationship could exist without the troubled person feeling reassured in some way. The mere presence of the therapist is reassuring.

The therapist reassures and gives emotional support in many ways. It is helpful to anyone with a disability, physical or emotional, to be told that there are others with similar problems, that he can be helped, and that he will improve. Direct verbal reassurance of this type is used to some degree in all forms of psychological treatment. The physician who is calm, soothing, and optimistic in the face of even the most serious illness is using the psychotherapeutic technique of reassurance though he may not do so deliberately or consciously.

Direct reassurance is used from time to time to control episodes of acute anxiety. Reassurance by the psychotherapist is a means by which the ego defense mechanisms of the individual may be strengthened temporarily. There are times when the person in therapy needs to be reassured. Sometimes anxiety becomes overwhelming, and reassurance is one of the ways in which this anxiety can be alleviated.

Few trained psychotherapists would limit themselves to the use of reassurance in their work, although the method used alone is helpful in some of the more superficial emotional disturbances. In other cases, where a person is seeking approval for the evasion of responsibilities, indiscriminate reassurance may do more harm than good.

Supportive therapy is also facilitated through the use of *suggestion*. This technique has been used for many centuries in general medicine and more recently in psychological medicine. Faith in the physician and in the medicine he prescribes has been an important, if not the most important, factor in cures from the time of primitive man. There is an old saying that "Whoever has faith in his physician can be cured by a drink of water." Physicians have known the truth of this statement for centuries and have used the principle with great effectiveness. The efficacy of the modern *placebo,* a "medicine" without intrinsic therapeutic value, depends largely upon the use of suggestion. A person may get well because the physician says he should get well, or because the physician tells him the medicine will make him well.

Many psychotherapists object to the use of suggestion in treatment because they feel that the method does not get at the causes of the disorder, that the effects are likely to be temporary, and that the use of suggestion may cause the person being treated to lose faith in the therapist. It has even been said that suggestion therapy contains an element of trickery. Nevertheless, suggestion is a fundamental part of all psychotherapy and is used unconsciously even by the most bitter opponents of suggestion therapy. Psychotherapy without the element of suggestion is impossible. In any case, some people can be helped substantially by the treatment of symptoms, and others are actually better off if the treatment does not take place at a deep level. Suggestion is a powerful and a frequently valid psychotherapeutic technique.

In the early 1900s, *persuasion* was used as a supportive technique in psychotherapy. Efforts were made to persuade the person to give up his unhealthy emotional habits and replace them with healthy ones. In this type of therapy, he was ordered to bed and put on a special diet preliminary to personal talks by the physician. The therapist would explain the functional nature of the disturbance and the importance of changed attitudes and positive thinking based on an improved philosophy of life.

Persuasion, as a therapeutic tool, places emphasis on the proper mental attitude toward life, the necessity for facing adversity, the desirability of accepting oneself as one is, and the tolerance of one's limitations. Many inspirational techniques are of this kind. While carefully planned persuasion might be helpful in selected cases, pressure and coercion are ordinarily of little real value. Authoritative measures, such as threats, prohibitions, exhortations, and reproaches, are likely to be ineffective and are frequently damaging. Some therapists use persuasive techniques when the people they are treating show uncontrolled emotionality or endanger their own lives or the lives of others, in cases of dependent personalities who refuse to face life's situations, and in immature and acting-out types.

Another form of supportive therapy is *emotional catharsis,* or the release of tension through an emotional outpouring. The mere ventilation of difficulty through "talking things out" has therapeutic value. Through the discussion of a person's problems, it is sometimes possible to arrive at a point where he no longer reacts to his difficulties in an emotional way. The repeated verbalizations desensitize the individual and make the experiences less anxiety-provoking.

Most people have had occasion to observe the therapeutic effect of "getting something off one's chest." When there is a serious conflict or difficulty, it helps to talk to someone about it. The mere verbalizing of the difficulty, and the sharing of it with someone who is sympathetic, seem to ease the situation to some degree. Also, the more the matter is discussed, the less threatening it appears. Even if talking about the difficulty does not bring one closer to a solution, it seems to lessen the tension and anxiety associated with the problem.

In *milieu therapy,* another supportive technique,

the treatment is through the removal or modification of environmental stress. The approach may concern itself with financial problems, housing, work, recreation, or family and marital difficulties. The assumption is that the troubled person's problems have grown out of difficult and unpleasant circumstances, and that he can be returned to normal personality adjustment through making the environment less stressful. Milieu therapy is effective in some cases but is of little use when the conflicts are within the individual. Also, there are people who seem to have a need for a disorganized life, and when organization is imposed upon them, they fail to respond in the expected manner.

The simple *externalization of interests* is another supportive technique. The redirection of interest toward the outside world, in the form of arts, crafts, music, games, sports, recreation, and hobbies, is an example of this form of support. Occupational therapy, recreational therapy, and music therapy are methods of directing the interests of people into constructive channels for therapeutic purposes. While the approach is a somewhat superficial one, it is nonetheless valuable in many cases, particularly when combined with other approaches.

Supportive therapy is indicated for people who have strong inner resources and when there has been satisfactory previous adjustment. It is valuable when the problem is dependent upon situational, or environmental, conditions. Supportive therapy is also used when the individual is unable to tolerate the anxieties associated with deeper forms of therapy. Similarly, when a person is poorly motivated, supportive therapy might be used with the modest goal of enabling him to live with his neurotic defenses. This form of treatment is also used when the intellectual level is relatively low, when time and resources are limited, in cases of extreme character rigidity, and in cases in which the symptoms are dangerous to the individual or to others.

Supportive therapy may last from a very few sessions to several hundred, with meetings from one to three times each week. The primary goal of this type of therapy is to strengthen the existing defenses of the individual. The material covered during the interview is ordinarily limited to the immediate symptoms the person feels and experiences and to the difficulties he faces in the environment.[1]

REEDUCATIVE PSYCHOTHERAPY

The second major form of psychotherapy is reeducative psychotherapy. As in the case of supportive psychotherapy, there are a number of different techniques of reeducative psychotherapy. The principal approaches of this method are *directive* and *nondirective.*

The *directive* approach is based on an authoritarian relationship between the therapist and the person being treated. To one degree or another the therapist actively manipulates the life of the patient. He may make suggestions, advise, furnish information, give counsel, and regulate the person's daily activities. The key feature of this form of treatment is that the therapist takes an active and authoritative role in it.

A number of criticisms have been leveled against directive therapy. Too often the solution to the difficulty is the therapist's solution rather than the person's own; that is, the therapist is likely to impose his own goals and sense of values on the person he is treating. There is the additional objection that directive therapy keeps the individual on a dependency level and repeats the disciplinary atmosphere of the parent-child relationship. As a result, the individual finds himself unable to become free of his authoritarian conscience. Since many neurotic reactions are due to an oversevere superego, such therapy can do more harm than good.

It is argued also that directive therapy interferes with self-sufficiency and gives the person little opportunity to develop ego strength. He simply incorporates the ideas and attitudes of the therapist, and while he may behave in a more desirable way, the underlying self-structure is not altered. In spite of these criticisms, some of which are valid, the fact remains that the majority

of psychotherapeutic approaches are directive to one degree or another.

In the *nondirective* approach, the individual is largely responsible for his own cure. The therapist does not impose his views on him. Rather, during the course of the therapy, the person being treated arrives at a solution which is his own. The therapy assumes that each individual has an inner potential for growth and maturity, that he can achieve insight in the relationship, and that he can make constructive use of it. There is a basic reliance on the individual himself for the content and the direction of the treatment process. The therapist makes no effort to guide him or to clarify his attitudes. No patterns or values are imposed on him, and no efforts are made to interpret his behavior for him. Instead, emphasis is placed on his expression of feeling. The therapist accepts feelings in a tolerant, nonjudgmental way and reflects them in such a way that the individual can become fully aware of his own attitudes.

In the nondirective therapeutic process the individual comes for help, and the helping situation is defined for him. The therapist encourages free expression of feeling in regard to the problem and accepts, recognizes, and clarifies these negative feelings. When negative feelings have been quite fully expressed, they are followed by the first expressions of the positive impulses which may make for later growth. The therapist accepts and recognizes these positive feelings in the same manner in which he accepted and recognized the earlier negative feelings.

Insight, in the form of understanding and accepting oneself, is the next important aspect of the therapeutic process. As insight develops, there is a process of clarification of possible decisions and courses of action. There is also the initiation of significant positive behavior. As insight develops further, there is a more complete and more accurate self-understanding, and the individual gains courage to see more deeply into his motives and his actions. The result is increasingly integrated positive action and a

---

[1] *Psychotherapy and Psychosomatics:* This bimonthly journal is published in Switzerland by the International Federation for Medical Psychotherapy. Articles are written in English, German, and French, with translated summaries. The journal is available from Albert J. Phiebig, Inc., P. O. Box 352, White Plains, N.Y. 10620.

feeling of decreasing need for help. Finally, there is a growing recognition by the person being treated that the relationship must end.

Nondirective therapy is a more difficult procedure than directive therapy, even though the role of the therapist in nondirective therapy seems less important. In the nature of things, people are inclined to be free with their advice and suggestions. Psychotherapists are no exception, unless they have received specialized training in the nondirective approach.

Nondirective therapy was originally used with maladjusted college students, in cases of marital adjustment problems, in vocational counseling, in parent-child relationships, and in the mild personality disturbances and neurotic reactions. However, as therapists gained additional experience with the nondirective approach, the technique was extended to other groups. Those least likely to respond favorably to the nondirective approach are psychotics, people with low intelligence, excessively dependent persons, and those who find it difficult to verbalize their feelings.

RECONSTRUCTIVE PSYCHOTHERAPY

The third major type of psychotherapy is reconstructive therapy. This approach is directed toward a fundamental reorganization of the basic personality structure and dynamics of the person in treatment. It may include some of the techniques of supportive therapy and of reeducative therapy, but reconstructive therapy goes much farther. It is concerned with the deep and unconscious levels of personality and designed to bring about basic and profound changes in personality. The major forms of reconstructive therapy are (1) Freudian psychoanalysis, (2) non-Freudian depth therapy, (3) psychoanalytically oriented therapy, and (4) psychotherapy with psychotics.

The method of *psychoanalysis*, as a technique of psychotherapy, began to take form in 1886 when Sigmund Freud became associated with Josef Breuer, a physician who had been using hypnosis in the treatment of neurotics. Breuer's method was to let the person talk while under hypnosis and say what was troubling him. He

Figure 15.1 *Carl R. Rogers, 1902–   , psychologist who made major contributions to the development of the nondirective method of psychotherapy. (Courtesy of Dr. Rogers.)*

observed that hypnotized people talked freely and often displayed considerable emotion. Moreover, they seemed to feel better when they awakened.

Freud was impressed with Breuer's method, and he began to use the same technique. No suggestions were given. The hypnotic state was used merely to allow the individual to ventilate his problems. Because of the emotion released during the session, the method was called *catharsis*. In 1893, Freud and Breuer published their first paper on hysteria, and in 1895 they published their classic book *Studies on Hysteria*. These publications established psychoanalysis as a theory as well as a method of treatment.

Freudian psychoanalysis is a long-term psychological treatment that may last for two or three years or longer, with meetings from three to five times a week. The therapist maintains a passive and nondirective role, but interpretation is common as therapy progresses. The basic tech-

Figure 15.2 *Sigmund Freud, 1856–1939, Austrian physician who developed the psychoanalytic form of psychotherapy. (Collection Viollet, Paris.)*

nique used in Freudian psychoanalysis is *free association*. This method is one in which the person being treated is made to relax comfortably on a couch and to speak whatever comes to mind. He is encouraged to speak freely and to continue whether or not what he says makes sense, is "proper," or is painful to talk about. He is told that everything he says and thinks is important to the treatment process.

Freud explained the free-association technique to people who consulted him by saying:

Before I can say anything to you, I must know a great deal about you; please tell me what you know about yourself. . . . One thing more, before you begin. Your talk with me must differ in one respect from an ordinary conversation. Whereas usually you rightly try to keep the threads of your story together and to exclude all intruding associations and side-issues, so as not to wander too far from the point, here you must proceed differently. You will notice that as you relate things various ideas will occur to you which you feel inclined to put aside with certain criticisms and objections. You will be tempted to say to yourself: "This or that has no connection here, . . . or it is nonsensical, so it cannot be necessary to mention it." Never give in to these objections, but mention it even if you feel a disinclination against it, or indeed just because of this. Later on you will perceive and learn to understand the reason for this injunction, which is really the only one you have to follow. So say whatever goes through your mind. Act as if you were sitting at the window of a railway train and describing to some one behind you the changing views you see outside. Finally, never forget that you have promised absolute honesty, and never leave anything unsaid because for any reason it is unpleasant to say it (Freud, 1924).

Through the analysis of material produced by means of free association, the therapist begins to get clues about the possible underlying causes of the personality difficulty. The type of material produced through free association varies with the individual. Rigid personalities are likely to produce relatively controlled material, particularly in the early phases of therapy. More flexible personalities produce a wide range of varied, and often chaotic, material.

The following material is an example of free association in therapy:

I can see myself as a little girl—sort of a visual image —standing between Father and Mother. I am thinking "Which one will like me?" Mother is looking at Father, very upset; she's all taken up with his flirtation. Father is looking away, watching the New York girl sitting on the beach. This whole thing is at the beach, and the same beach where I played in the sand when Mother almost drowned. Father and Mother are both completely taken up and neither notices me. The whole thing is so vivid that I can see it, but I don't know if it's a real memory. I think I just concocted it out of different scraps of memory. The New York woman is like a snake in the garden of Eden. If I attract her and make her like me, that would make me feel satisfied. Father would be real mad and Mother would too. You know, while I'm telling you this, I can actually see it going on, sort of like a movie; I can actually see my mother's face getting angrier and angrier. The reason why Mother gets so angry about it is that if I take the New York woman away from Father, he will come back to Mother and become more threatening to her. He will do something terrible to Mother if I take Mother's rival away. I never thought of that before.

I wonder if that has something to do with my sex problem (Janis, 1958).

The ability to free-associate is a skill most people need to acquire. It takes practice to be able to verbalize freely and spontaneously the thoughts that come to mind. Some people find free association relatively easy, while others find it extremely difficult.

The analysis of dreams is another technique used in Freudian psychoanalysis. The therapist encourages people in treatment to keep a record of their dreams and to bring them to therapy sessions for discussion and analysis. Through the analysis of the dreams, the therapist is able to explain symbolic behavior and to redirect unacceptable impulses. Ordinarily the person describes the dream as he remembers it, and the therapist then asks for spontaneous associations. In this way, the therapist is able gradually to discover the hidden meaning of the dream.

While the psychoanalyst engages in a certain amount of explanation and interpretation, he must remain objective and impersonal. He does not argue or persuade, nor does he praise and condemn. Neither does he advise. By his encouragement of free association, the psychoanalyst attempts to explore the unconscious content of his patient's mind. Through reliving childhood experiences, and with the assistance of the therapist, the person's mental and emotional life is reorganized in a more positive and constructive way.

In psychoanalytic therapy, the individual may become emotionally attached to the therapist, and there may be a reenactment of the child-parent relationship. The therapist uses this relationship to illustrate unconscious fantasies and ego resistances, and in this way the person being treated becomes aware of the existence of infantile attitudes. The therapist tracks down early identifications and shows the person how these early experiences have affected his emotional life. The cure is effected when the emotional attachment to the therapist is understood and accepted, when the dream content has changed, and when the amnesia for past significant experiences has been overcome.

There is a very real question about the extent to which psychoanalytic therapy is effective because of its unique theoretical concepts and method. It is much more likely that the success of psychoanalysis as a form of treatment is due to certain basic elements found in many other types of psychotherapy. These basic elements include the presence of a sympathetic, noncritical, and accepting listener; desensitization or deconditioning through constant repetition; the relearning of attitudes; and the instituting of more positive modes of behavior.

In *psychoanalytically oriented therapy*, the techniques and theories of psychoanalysis are used to varying degrees, but wide variations are seen from therapist to therapist. The therapy may last from several sessions to several hundred, with meetings one to three times each week. Dream material is used, and the therapist may call for projective psychological tests. The therapeutic sessions deal with present situations and relation-

Figure 15.3 *Franz Alexander, 1891–1964, American psychoanalyst and former director of the Chicago Psychoanalytic Institute. (Courtesy of Dr. Alexander.)*

ships and utilize unconscious material only when the progress of therapy seems to require it. The face-to-face interview is used in most instances, although the couch may be used at times. The psychoanalytically oriented therapist may take advantage of such treatment adjuncts as play therapy, art therapy, group therapy, and hypnosis.

The approach of *non-Freudian depth therapy* is similar in many ways to orthodox psychoanalysis, but with some modification. The treatment sessions may be two to four times a week for two or more years. The couch is used sometimes, but more frequently the therapy is conducted by means of a face-to-face interview. Also, the therapeutic sessions are more likely to be focused on current situations, interpersonal relationships, and other sources of conflict. Free association is used to some degree but not exclusively. The attitude of the therapist may range from nondirectiveness to a moderate degree of directiveness.

Psychotherapy with psychotics is a special form

Figure 15.4 *Theodor Reik, 1888–1970, prominent lay analyst and founder of the National Psychological Association for Psychoanalysis. (Courtesy of Dr. Reik.)*

of reconstructive therapy. By the very nature of the problem, the therapist must aim at profound changes in the personality of the disturbed person. For many years, it was felt that little value could be derived from using psychotherapy with individuals out of contact with reality. While a few psychotics were treated by means of psychotherapy, the procedure usually was undertaken very early in the psychotic process or after the acute phases of the psychosis had subsided. It is recognized now that special psychotherapeutic techniques are valuable even in the acute and disorganized psychotic episodes.

The fundamental aim of psychotherapy with psychotics is to bring about a more realistic integration of the ego. Sometimes it is necessary to reinstitute neurotic patterns of behavior, but neurotic defenses are ordinarily more desirable than psychotic defenses. In the manic-depressive reactions, psychotherapy is most effective at the beginning of the mood cycle when the elation or depression first appears. The best therapeutic results are seen in hypomania and simple depression. Reasonably good results are also possible in involutional psychotic reactions and psychotic depressive reactions, either early in the process or in conjunction with electroshock therapy. Schizophrenia has been particularly resistant to psychotherapy because of the weakness of the ego, the fear of relationships with other people, and the attitude of apathy, detachment, hostility, and aggression. As a result, the schizophrenic has been considered a relatively poor risk for psychotherapy.

The most important advance in the use of psychotherapy with psychotics, and particularly with schizophrenics, has been the method of *direct analytic therapy* (Rosen, 1953). This approach is one in which the therapist unmasks the symptoms presented by the psychotic individual and confronts him with the unconscious meaning of his disturbed behavior at every possible opportunity. It is an heroic type of psychotherapy and places extraordinary demands upon the psychotherapist, who makes an effort to enter the very heart of the psychosis. He attempts to speak the language of the psychotic and to adapt himself to the basic processes of the psychotic state. In this way, he seeks to make contact with the disturbed person. His interpretations are less important than the "getting through" to the individual. Direct analytic therapy has been described as "speaking directly to the patient's unconscious."[2]

GROUP PSYCHOTHERAPY

Group psychotherapy is a method of treatment in which a number of people are treated at one time, or in which group dynamics are used in the treatment of one person. While new as a controlled method, group therapy is old in a more general sense. The technique has been used for centuries by religious leaders and philosophers. Ancient priest-physicians used group methods to control and lessen the anxiety of their followers. In these various instances, there was an intuitive realization of the importance of the group approach.

Today there are a number of different types of group psychotherapy. The most common approach has been the conventional therapeutic group. Other group treatment methods are role-playing, family therapy, encounter groups, and resocialization.

THE CONVENTIONAL THERAPEUTIC GROUP

In this group, the pattern of treatment is similar to that of individual psychotherapy. The therapist meets with the group, rapport must be established, group members ventilate their conflicts, transference relationships are built up between the therapist and group members and between group members themselves, resistance is encountered and must be overcome, interpretations are made,

Figure 15.5 *John Rosen, 1902–   , psychiatrist who developed direct analysis as a form of psychotherapy for psychotic patients.*

insight is achieved, constructive action is taken, and eventually the therapy is terminated.

While many of the same dynamic processes are found in both individual and group psychotherapy, the emphasis may be different. Since the relationship between the group member and his therapist is not as intense as in individual psychotherapy, transference is not likely to be as strong. On the other hand, the presence of other group members may make it possible for the group member to express feelings more freely than would be the case in individual therapy. The group setting

---

[2]The student who wishes to do additional reading in the field of psychotherapy might begin with Elizabeth Ogg's short and nontechnical *Psychotherapy: A Helping Process* (Public Affairs Pamphlet No. 329, 1962). Another good starting point is *Modern Therapy of Personality Disorders* (Brown, 1966) by J. H. Masserman. An unusual and valuable book is Bernard Steinzor's *The Healing Partnership* (Harper & Row, 1969).

The student who wishes to pursue the subject more seriously might then turn to *Six Approaches to Psychotherapy* (Dryden, 1955), edited by J. L. McCary and D. E. Sheer; *Contemporary Psychotherapies* (Free Press, 1961), edited by Morris Stein; Robert A. Harper's *Psychoanalysis and Psychotherapy: Thirty-six Systems* (Prentice-Hall, 1959); and *Psychotherapy and the Modification of Abnormal Behavior* (McGraw-Hill, 1971) by Hans Strupp.

Figure 15.6 *Group therapy. (Department of Psychology, Longview State Hospital.)*

makes it easier for a person to progress more rapidly because of the greater realization that he is not alone in his difficulties. Also, the group member may improve because he alters his behavior to conform to the expectations of other group members.

Rapport and the early ventilation of material are likely to be facilitated in the group setting. Emotional release may not be as intense, and interpretation by the therapist ordinarily is more general. Finally, insight tends to be somewhat more superficial than in individual psychotherapy. While the group setting may facilitate psychotherapy, it does not lead to personality changes as fundamental as those achieved through individual therapy.

In the formation of a therapeutic group, age differences must not be too great, and social background should be somewhat similar. Mixed groups of men and women are permissible, but this type of group encourages acting out of unacceptable behavior. The main problem is to achieve group balance. There must be sufficient variety to the group so that members are able to observe different defense mechanisms and reaction patterns. Obviously, a group made up entirely of depressives, of withdrawn schizophrenics, or of anxiety neurotics would not be well balanced.

People are selected and prepared for group psychotherapy in several ways. In institutional settings, an individual may be assigned to a therapeutic group without previous interview or preparation. It is more desirable for the therapist to see the person in an individual interview, to get some idea of his problems, and to offer group therapy as a way of solving these problems. A third procedure, which is used more in private practice and community clinics, is to start with individual psychotherapy and later to switch to a therapeutic group.

There are some people who ordinarily do not do well in group psychotherapy just as they do not respond favorably to individual treatment. Those with low intelligence, acute depressions, antisocial personality reactions, and marked paranoid tendencies are relatively poor choices for the group approach. Similarly, aggressive homosexuals and others who show poor control of their behavior respond unfavorably to group methods.

The group therapist may play any one of a number of roles, depending upon the particular type of therapy. In a highly nondirective type of therapy, the therapist plays a minimum role. At the other extreme, in didactic group therapy, he takes the entire responsibility for the presentation. Generally, the therapist participates by structuring the situation, making comments, focusing upon important problems, encouraging group interaction, clarifying group interrelations, and interpreting signs of resistance by members of the group.

When the therapist assumes a passive and nondirective approach, the group members lead the discussion and determine the direction to be followed. The therapist is present but remains inactive except when an impasse is reached or when the material needs interpretation. In an active and semidirectional approach, the therapist selects the most appropriate topic for discussion from topics suggested by the members. The discussion then takes place with contributions from the group. The therapist maintains a major role, stimulating the participants and guiding their discussions. Relevant material is stressed and developed, and irrelevant material is rejected.

In addition to the group therapist, there is ordinarily a recorder who may or may not participate actively in the therapeutic process. His purpose is to observe the members of the group and to record as much of the verbal and nonverbal behavior as possible. The recorder usually confers with the therapist immediately following the meetings, and the data are analyzed and plans are made for future sessions.

Tape recorders have limited usefulness in group sessions because they do not record such important data as facial expression, posture, and gestures. Videotape recordings are better suited to recording group sessions, but camera placement presents a problem if all group participants are to be adequately monitored.

The human recorder, who sometimes moves on to become a group therapist, must have sufficient training in psychology to know what is happening to individuals and to the group and sufficient self-discipline to focus constantly on the group process. He must be on guard against a therapeutic or personal relationship with the members of the group, and he must be careful not to assume a supervisory or competitive role with the psychotherapist. While the recorder may play the role of a cotherapist under certain circumstances, he functions most frequently as a nonparticipating observer.

ROLE-PLAYING

A more specialized form of group treatment is *role-playing,* the most developed example of which is *psychodrama* (Moreno, 1953). In this treatment method, people are encouraged to act out their conflicts and difficulties in a controlled setting. In clinics and hospitals, the psychodrama includes patients, physicians, nurses, and even visitors to the sessions. A simple situation is selected, such as a family quarrel or a problem with a fellow employee at work, and the individual is encouraged to express himself by playing a role. Other group members participate spontaneously as they are needed to facilitate the situation being enacted. The therapist might assume the role of a parent or an employer. A nurse becomes a wife, mother, sister, or girl friend. Throughout the psychodrama, the therapist and his assistants encourage the individual to verbalize his conflicts and to try out various methods for dealing with them. The hostile person practices being less aggressive in his relations with others; the withdrawn person is helped to take a more active part in group activities.

FAMILY THERAPY

Family therapy is another approach to group treatment. It was not unusual in the past for group therapy to include other members of the family in individual psychotherapy, but the idea of treating the family as a unit and on a group basis is relatively new. This form of group psychotherapy grew out of the work with disturbed children, where it became clear that if one member of a family is emotionally disturbed, it is likely that other members also need treatment.

In the late 1950s the National Institute of Mental Health pioneered the use of family therapy as an approach to understanding disturbed families and in the treatment of family members. This work has continued, with particular emphasis on the nature of family dynamics and structure as well as the techniques, process, and outcome of family therapy.

One investigator selected fifty families with adolescent schizophrenic members and provided treatment for the whole family in the home. In the great majority of cases it was possible to avoid hospitalizing the schizophrenic member of the family. Hospitalization was necesary in only two of the fifty cases, and then only for a brief period of time. Ordinarily about half of these individuals would have been hospitalized. Clinical and social improvement was reflected in the adolescent member's return to school and a more effective functioning of the family as a whole.

There is evidence that improvement may not require a trained therapist. Psychology students were employed by one investigator as "companion counselors." Under supervision the students visited the schizophrenic children in their homes four or five times a week. In addition a remedial teacher helped the children who were retarded in school. Nine schizophrenic children were in the pilot project for a period of three months, and none needed to be hospitalized. As additional children were included in the study, it became apparent that schizophrenic children can remain in the home and function reasonably well with the help of minimally trained personnel.

The treatment of entire families makes possible a more positive and realistic attitude toward the problems of the troubled individual. The family members come to recognize the common character of their difficulties, and this recognition reduces the sense of uniqueness and builds healthier relationships between the group members. As the members of the family gain insight into the individual's difficulties and their own reactions, they are able to deal more effectively with their personal problems. In this way, the goals of therapy with the disturbed person are enhanced.

RESOCIALIZATION

Resocialization, a form of group treatment in the broadest sense, is also capable of bringing about constructive changes in the behavior of people with mental disorders. An example of this treatment approach is a National Institute of Mental Health project in which patients were moved to a residential unit designed to simulate family living conditions. A common area for both men and women provided an opportunity for resocialization, or relearning forgotten or neglected interpersonal behavior. Daily small-group sessions provided the focus for treatment. Although the average length of hospitalization prior to the project was more than seventeen years, thirty-four percent of those in the pilot project responded to the new program with moderate to marked improvement; eleven percent improved enough to be discharged.

In another project, approximately five hundred chronically institutionalized schizophrenics underwent a resocialization program. Among this group were some two hundred who had recovered from the acute phases of the disorder but continued to exhibit some degree of crippling social deterioration which prevented their return to their families and communities. A three-phase program provided intensive remotivation and resocialization. Initially, these people were moved to a special hospital unit for a daily schedule of activities. Emphasis was placed on meaningful cooperative relationships with other troubled people and with staff members. Other family members were encouraged to participate, even at the earliest stages of the program. As the disturbed individuals improved, they were moved to smaller units on the hospital grounds where they received more individual therapy. Attention was focused on assisting them to overcome socially undesirable behavior. The final phase was to prepare them to return to their homes by showing them how to take advantage of the community's educational, work, recreational, and social resources (NIMH, 1969).

Intensified programs of resocialization can be effective even with chronic schizophrenics. Those hospitalized continuously for more than five years were transferred to a newly remodeled and refurbished ward. Even the most chronic cases proved able to participate in all group activities on a full-day schedule. They conducted their own ward government and appointed their own committees, which acted in liaison with the professional staff. Vocational testing and guidance was provided, leading initially to in-hospital and later to community job placement. Of the original group of thirty schizophrenics, all of whom had been hospitalized for five or more years, twenty percent became ready for discharge or were approaching that point at the time of the report.

Resocialization has also been achieved through a comprehensive program of vocational rehabilitation. One project led to a thirteen percent discharge rate among nearly eight hundred chronic schizophrenics, eighty-five percent of whom had been hospitalized continuously for more than two years. The program centered on the assignment of each person to some of a variety of rehabilitation projects. The projects included sheltered workshops and specific jobs within the hospital complex as well as sheltered and competitive

Figure 15.7 Dance in a Madhouse. *A lithograph by George Bellows, New York, 1917. (Philadelphia Museum of Art.)*

jobs in the community. When a person demonstrated his ability to hold a job in the community, he was eligible for a discharge to a halfway house or to live with his family.

ENCOUNTER GROUPS

This highly controversial type of group therapeutic experience attained an almost cultish vogue by 1970. Referred to variously as T-groups (training groups), sensitivity training, and leadership training, the essence of the group experience is the relatively intimate encounter, or close interaction with others and the working out of personal and interpersonal problems with the assistance of a "trainer" or group leader and other members of the group.

The encounter group movement got under way in the late 1940s when a small group of social psychologists undertook a summer project to train a group of community leaders to deal with interracial problems. Research assistants sat in on the meetings to record the interactions of the participants for later study and analysis. The group members themselves asked for permission to sit in on the later meetings at which the interactions were to be examined. The encounter group was born out of the strong emotional reactions experienced by the group members when confronted with the information about their own behavior.

Despite a persistent effort on the part of some advocates of the encounter group to divorce it from therapy, the group experience is unquestionably a therapeutic one. Herein lies its power and effectiveness, but here also is its greatest danger. In spite of the very considerable interest in encounter groups of all kinds, there has been a justifiable uneasiness over such groups on the part of some psychiatrists and psychologists. While many behavioral scientists find merit in the theory of the encounter group, the principal objections center on the all too frequent lack of qualifications of the "trainers" or group leaders, and the invasion of the rights of the participants.

As one critic put it in an editorial published by the American Psychiatric Association:

Today we are witnessing a proliferation of sensitivity training programs aimed at persons in educational, industrial, and community settings. Variations of sensitivity programs have been established that purport to train community development leaders, promote international relations, secure labor-management harmony, increase marital happiness, and resolve other thorny problems via the T-group method of enhancing interpersonal communications. That so much has been promised by sensitivity training and so little delivered by means of evaluation and research findings sug-

Figure 15.8 *A nude encounter group. (J. M. Vincent.)*

gests that psychiatrists should be increasingly aware and distressed about these programs.

Of primary concern to psychiatrists, many of whom have seen the "casualties" of insensitive sensitivity training programs and "trainers," should be the outright invasion of individual privacy such programs tend to promote. Sensitivity training appears to have been so effectively oversold to an unaware public, clamoring for psychiatric and psychological insights, that it is not uncommon for teachers, business representatives, high government officials, and others to be required, as a function of their jobs, to participate in these sessions. As a consequence, these participants involuntarily and unknowingly may be subjected to personal onslaught in a pseudo-psychotherapeutic situation characterized by inappropriate transferences and unrelenting group pressures to "reveal themselves," while unprotected by the ethical safeguards which are inherent in a professional therapeutic en-

counter. For some participants the results have been traumatic indeed!" (English, 1969)

The effectiveness of the encounter group as a method of treatment has yet to be demonstrated. It is too early to tell whether the encounter movement will become an accepted addition to psychological treatment techniques or whether it will be merely another fad promoted by incompetents, cultists, and charlatans.[3]

THE IMPORTANCE OF GROUP THERAPY

In group therapy the group members receive emotional support through the group relationship, while at the same time experiencing a degree of

---

[3]*The Journal of Applied Behavioral Science,* first published in 1965, is recommended to students who are interested in following developments in the field of T-groups and sensitivity training. This publication is available from the NTL Institute for Applied Behavioral Science, 1201 Sixteenth St., N.W., Washington, D.C. 20036.

emotional release. Pent-up aggression is expressed, with a consequent reduction of guilt feelings. Moreover, the group situation provides for an increased acceptance of the self and of others. Group members come to tolerate their own deficiencies and inadequacies and to sympathize with the weaknesses of other members. The group also provides an opportunity to test various forms of social reality. For people who have been institutionalized, the group becomes a stepping-stone toward learning how to handle the puzzling and difficult problems of interpersonal relations in the family and community. Finally, the group experience leads directly to an increased tolerance for frustration on the part of group members.

Group treatment is the only way in which psychological help can be brought to people in large psychiatric hospitals on a scale approximate to the need. Staff shortages of psychiatrists, clinical psychologists, psychiatric social workers, and psychiatric nurses are such that individual therapy in a public mental hospital is virtually impossible. Fortunately, there is a marked trend in hospitals in the United States toward a wider use of group methods of treatment.

In addition to the more formally organized group treatment programs, various group activities in the psychiatric hospital have a therapeutic effect. Recreational programs, occupations carried on in groups, ward activities, and even going to the dining room can be a part of the treatment process. Spontaneous and informal group activities are important factors in bringing about an eventual psychological readjustment and a return to the community.[4]

SPECIAL TECHNIQUES IN PSYCHOTHERAPY

In addition to the various types of psychotherapy, several specialized techniques are used from time to time in psychological treatment, depending upon the thereoretical persuasion and technical skill of the therapist. Two examples of these are hypnotherapy and drug-facilitated psychotherapy.

HYPNOTHERAPY

The earliest important use of hypnosis in modern psychotherapy took place in the early 1880s when Josef Breuer used the method in Vienna. A young woman showed a variety of hysterical symptoms including paralysis of both legs and an arm, disturbances of vision and hearing, difficulties in speaking, and personality dissociation. The symptoms disappeared when she recalled, under hypnosis, early life experiences of a disturbing kind which were related to the long illness and death of her father.

Today, hypnosis has become a powerful tool in the hands of the skilled psychotherapist. There are at least four different ways in which hyp-

---

[4]The problems and methods of group treatment are presented in I. D. Yalom's *The Theory and Practice of Group Psychotherapy* (Basic Books, 1970); *Psychotherapy through the Group Process* (Atherton Press, 1967), edited by D. S. Whitaker and M. A. Lieberman; and *Group Psychotherapy and Group Function* (Basic Books, 1963), edited by M. Rosenbaum and M. Berger; and *Group Psychotherapy* (Free Press, 1962) by Hugh Mullan and Max Rosenbaum.

Students interested in the treatment of entire families are referred to *Intensive Family Therapy* (Hoeber, 1970), edited by Ivan Boszormenyi-Nagy and J. L. Framo; N. W. Ackerman's *Treating the Troubled Family* (Basic Books, 1966); *Family Therapy and Disturbed Families* (Science and Behavior Books, 1969), edited by G. H. Zuk and Ivan Boszormenyi-Nagi; and *Psychotherapy for the Whole Family* (Springer, 1965) by A. S. Friedman et al.

Students interested in the encounter group as a form of behavior modification should turn to *Using Sensitivity Training and the Laboratory Method* (Association Press, 1968) by R. L. Batchelder and J. M. Hardy; *Personal and Organizational Change through Group Methods* (Wiley, 1965) by E. H. Schein and W. G. Bennis; and *T-Group Theory and Laboratory Method* (Wiley, 1964), edited by L. P. Bradford et al. A nontechnical account of truth labs, sensitivity training, sensory awareness, marathon therapy, and similar innovations is *Turning On* (Macmillan, 1969) by Rasa Gustaitis.

nosis may be applied therapeutically: (1) direct suggestion that a symptom will disappear, (2) suggestion directed toward the attitudes underlying symptoms, (3) abreaction of traumatic experiences, and (4) hypnoanalysis.

The oldest and most widely used technique of hypnotherapy is direct suggestion for the removal of symptoms. With this method, suggestions are made to the individual under hypnosis that his symptoms will disappear. This is the least complex therapeutic application of hypnosis, and there are few functional disturbances that have not been treated successfully in this way. Even symptoms of known organic origin can be alleviated by direct suggestion under certain favorable conditions. The scope of direct suggestion is almost unlimited, and if the individual responds at all to this type of treatment, the response is usually prompt and the improvement rapid. However, since the method is often used merely as a suppressive form of therapy to remove symptoms, the therapeutic goal may be achieved without his gaining insight into the emotional roots of his difficulty. Accordingly, the possiblity of relapse, or the formation of substitute symptoms, is always present.

A somewhat more advanced method is direct suggestion used to alter attitudes underlying symptoms. This method was developed by workers who were embarrassed by the complete absence of a rationale in classical hypnotherapy. The historical significance of this approach lies in the fact that it reflected the growing awareness of the importance of giving the person some understanding of his difficulty. The course of treatment is usually longer for this method, because specific etiological factors underlying the symptoms must be established before the suggestion for cure can be formulated. Since this technique provides the individual with a degree of understanding of his problem, it is a more substantial method of hypnotherapy and capable of providing more lasting results.

The third method of hypnotherapy, the abreaction, or release, of emotional experiences through reliving them, has been found particularly suitable in the traumatic neuroses of war. In such cases, the individual is hypnotized and encouraged to "relive" his fearsome battle experiences. The disturbing incidents are worked through repeatedly until he can accept the fact that the original trauma is no longer a threat to him. The technique is based on the psychological principles of desensitization and deconditioning. It was used to advantage during World War I with soldiers showing hysterical symptoms. The method brought about a quick cure in some cases of conversion reaction. While the abreactive method was also used in World War II, the hypnotic state was usually brought about by the use of drugs rather than by the verbal methods of hypnosis.

The major advantage of the abreactive technique over direct suggestion to remove symptoms or to alter attitudes is that it is an expressive rather than suppressive method. The method is brief, often yields good clinical results, and can be used by therapists who have not had intensive training in the methods and theories of dynamic psychotherapy. In the hands of a therapist well grounded in the problems of psychodynamics, the abreactive method can be an effective adjunct to reconstructive psychotherapy.

The term *hypnoanalysis* has been used to describe a variety of therapeutic techniques ranging from classical abreaction to modified psychoanalytic treatment carried out with the patient in hypnosis. More precisely, the term is used to describe all the dynamically oriented forms of hypnotherapy that combine the techniques of hypnosis with those of depth therapy. The person treated by hypnoanalysis is given a training period for a week or two during which he is taught to enter the hypnotic state rapidly and he is without effort. He learns to verbalize under hypnosis, to recall under hypnosis and in the posthypnotic state, and to develop posthypnotic amnesia. Following the training period, the person being treated may be seen daily, with ordinary free association used until resistance is encountered. Hypnosis is then induced, and free association is continued in this state. Some therapists, however, prefer to conduct the entire series of therapeutic sessions under hypnosis.

One of the most valuable techniques used in hypnoanalysis is *age regression*. By means of this method a person can be taken back to earlier periods in his life so that events can be recalled more readily. To induce regression the individual is placed in a deep trance and slowly disoriented as to time and place. The specific age period to which regression is desired may be suggested to the subject, or he may be asked to select a significant period. Forgotten memories and experiences not readily available to him as an adult may then be recaptured and brought to the surface of consciousness.

An example of the type of material produced during regression under hypnosis is the following verbatim response during a hypnoanalytic session. It was suggested to a man that he was a tiny baby. He said:

I remember—about eight—no six months old maybe. A very little baby. I have a bottle with a nipple on it. I was . . . yes. My mother giving me one. My father is sitting there. His eyes have green in them but they are not shining. Six or seven months old. Old enough to hold a spoon. My mother is feeding me. I'm all sloppy, all slopped up. I like spilling everything all around, get a kick out of getting all dirty, everything smeared all over my face. She . . . then I am looking at the sky. The sun is shining. There is nothing wrong with me. The wind is blowing. I feel myself moving, moving. I guess somebody is pushing me. Once in awhile I look at—wires or something. They must be wires to telephone poles. There is a little jar—and a bump —bump. It feels nice. Things are rolling by. I am not watching anything in particular. I know! I'm in the carriage. Sometimes I can see—people, looking over the carriage, looking at me. I can't make them out. The sky is all lit up. The people looking at me and the sky bright behind them. I can see the shape of their heads and their hats but I can't make them out. They seem different. I'm on my back looking up at them, that's why I can't make them out. They're not clear. They're all blurred up, far away. A woman's hat . . . a man's hat. . . . I can't see their faces; can't tell who they are. They're looking at me (Lindner, 1944).

The stimulation and interpretation of dreams during hypnosis also play a part in hypnoanalysis. As in psychoanalysis, dreams indicate the character of repressed material, the nature of transference, the manifold disguises that resistances assume, and the stages of therapeutic progress. Dreams may be stimulated by suggestion under hypnosis, or they may be posthypnotically induced. A further use of hypnotic dreaming is in the recovery of dreams which have been forgotten, as well as specific portions of dreams which have been repressed or subjected to extensive elaboration.

Hypnotherapy is used widely in the Soviet Union in treating a number of conditions. The major uses are in connection with the neuroses, alcoholism, somatic disease, dermatology, childbirth, and other problems in obstetrics and gynecology (Hoskovec, 1967).

One of the advantages of the use of hypnosis in psychotherapy is that treatment sometimes can be speeded with a saving in time and cost. Whether or not hypnosis is used as an adjunct to therapy depends to a large extent upon the particular orientation and theoretical persuasion of the therapist. Those therapists who are reluctant to use hypnosis are inclined to view it as an artificial situation in which undesirable attitudes of dependency are established in the patient.[5]

DRUG-FACILITATED PSYCHOTHERAPY

Psychological treatment is sometimes facilitated by drugs used to release unconscious material. Variously designated by such terms as *narcotherapy, narcoanalysis,* and *narcosynthesis,* this method may occasionally be quicker and more effective than the more conventional methods of deep analysis. The principal drugs are pentothal, mescaline, lysergic acid, and phenethylamine. Each of these acts to release psychological material which the therapist may be able to use to advantage in the treatment.

Pentothal sodium was first used during World War II for uncovering the relationships between specific incidents in combat and the symptoms of neurotic conversion reactions. In the following case, a twenty-three-year-old sergeant was sent overseas and assigned to an Air Force com-

---

[5]Among the more important books dealing with hypnotherapy are Lewis Wolberg's *Hypnoanalysis* (Grune & Stratton, 1945); *Hypnotherapy* (International Universities Press, 1947) by Margaret Brenman and M. M. Gill; John Watkins' *Hypnotherapy of War Neuroses* (Ronald Press, 1949); *Hypnosis in Modern Medicine* (Thomas, 1953), edited by Jerome Schneck; *Shapes of Sanity* (Thomas, 1960) by Ainslie Meares; and William S. Kroger's *Clinical and Experimental Hypnosis in Medicine, Dentistry and Psychology* (Lippincott, 1963).

bat unit. The second mission was an extremely difficult one, and the sergeant lost two of his friends. He developed nightmares and dreams of combat, and was sent to a hospital in a depressed and restless state. He complained of a peculiar black spot before his eyes in the shape of a plane. He was extremely anxious about his future and was terror-stricken at the thought of future missions. During one drug-induced treatment session he said in an excited way:

I am going over Bremen. We're knocked out of formation. We lost an engine going over France and one engine over the target when the fighters hit us. I am no good—throw me out. I can't see. We're still over Bremen. Something happened. Something in front of my eyes. He's going to crack. He's going to crash into us. (Who?) An ME 109. Get the hell out! Just get out of his way. George, you'd better come back and take over for me. (Where are you going?) Getting the hell out of here. I'm no good. I can't see a thing. I can see a little now. They're coming in again. There he goes, George. There go the pieces. Flames. There's more of them. Wish I could focus my eyes. That's flak. Something just blew. The whole tunnel's apart. They blew all the plexiglass out. My God! My eyes are leaving. (Don't you have your goggles on?) Yes! I'll get them on as soon as I clear my eyes. We'll never make it back today. Won't get to London after all, George. There's one coming after you, George. He just peeled off. They're coming in low—watch me, Gus. Fred, look out—there are ten of them lined up. Oh my God! My eyes are okay now. I can see as good as ever. I thought I was going blind. That first was too much for me. I suppose I'm going to be grounded now. My hands are okay, George. Doc said I'd be grounded for three weeks. Here's your ship—it's all shot to hell but we got her back. Hope we don't have to go over that place again. Three times is too much. You know, George, my eyes never cleared up. I see spots and think they're fighters but when I aim at them they're gone. I don't trust them anymore. I am no damned good now. Sure, I know the guns. I can't pick out fighters. What the hell good am I? You're a swell bunch of fellows or you're crazy. Okay. Good night (Grinker and Spiegel, 1945).

During the 1950s, there was a sharply increased interest in drugs which induce artificial psychoses. These psychomimetic drugs, or hallucinogens, also have found a place in psychotherapy. The two most commonly used drugs of this type are *mescaline* and *lysergic acid,* or LSD-25. Mescaline induces a violent emotional upheaval,

while LSD-25 is used for bringing repressed material to consciousness and for increasing insight into underlying psychodynamics.

A twenty-six-year-old man was given mescaline as a part of his treatment (Denber, 1956). Eight minutes after the injection, he exclaimed: "I am suffocating. I see purple flashes. I didn't know that I was going." He arose, staggered around the room, and then fell to his hands and knees, clutching at his throat. Thirteen minutes after the injection he was in an acute panic state. He gesticulated wildly and shouted: "I wanna do something right but I can't. They're killing me. What have I done wrong with my life?" He clutched his throat and screamed, "I hate everybody. What is all this? Oh, my God, he'll kill me." He was asked to explain his actions and statements, but there was no reply. An hour after the injection he was asked to describe his feelings. "It's indescribable horror. It comes and it goes. Horrors, horrors, horrors."

When LSD-25 is used in therapy, the sessions last for several hours or more, since it takes the drug from fifteen minutes to two hours to become effective. The treatment sessions are held from twice a week to once a month, with conventional psychotherapy carried out between drug sessions. During LSD-25 therapy, the individual remains oriented and does not lose contact with reality. Under ordinary circumstances, there is little or no loss of memory for the events of the treatment session. Unconscious material is more easily produced, and there may be a recapturing of both recent and childhood memories, an increased identification with other people, the production of fantasies, and the appearance of insight.

Phenethylamine is a drug which is similar in effects to amphetamine sulphate but does not cause the serious side reactions. The characteristic psychological picture following the use of this drug includes elation, a decrease in inhibition, a livelier interest, and a longer attention span. Following the injection of the drug, there may be feelings of light-headedness and relaxation. Some people remark that they are "floating on air."

When phenethylamine is used in therapy, there may be a stimulation of emotionally charged material including painful memories, intimately per-

Table 15.1 *Some differences between Freudian psychotherapy and behavior therapy*

FREUDIAN PSYCHOTHERAPY	BEHAVIOR THERAPY
1. Derived from clinical observations.	Derived from experimental studies.
2. Considers symptoms the visible signs of unconscious causes.	Considers symptoms as unadaptive conditioned responses.
3. Regards symptoms as evidence of repression.	Regards symptoms as evidence of faulty learning.
4. Believes that symptoms are determined by defense mechanisms.	Believes that symptoms are determined by individual differences in conditionability and by accidental environmental circumstances.
5. The treatment of neurotic disorders must concern itself with the past history of the individual.	Treatment is concerned with present behavior; the historical development of symptoms is largely irrelevant.
6. Cures are brought about by dealing with underlying unconscious processes, not by treating the symptom itself.	Cures result from treating the symptom itself through getting rid of unadaptive conditioning responses and establishing desirable responses.
7. The interpretation of symptoms, dreams, and actions is an important part of treatment.	Interpretation is irrelevant.
8. Treating symptoms is believed to lead to the elaboration of new symptoms.	Symptomatic treatment, properly carried out, leads to permanent recovery.
9. Transference relations are necessary for the cure of neurotic disorders.	Transference is not essential for the cure of neurotic disorders.

Adapted from H. J. Eysenck, "Learning Theory and Behaviour Therapy." J. *Ment. Sci.*, **105**, 61–75, 1959.

sonal fantasies, and delusional ideas. The paranoid person who is evasive and vague may verbalize his delusions with accompanying emotional reactions and increased psychomotor activity. Paradoxically, the excited manic individual sometimes appears more calm, with the push of speech, overtalkativeness, and overactivity being lessened. Catatonic schizophrenics occasionally become more accessible. The rich responses sometimes made available to the therapist are of considerable value in both diagnosis and treatment.

Drug-facilitated therapy has a number of advantages. It lowers ego defenses and permits an increased expression of repressed material. It also encourages the externalization of repressed emotions, aids in recapturing early memories, stirs up rich fantasies, and makes possible a more effective rapport with the therapist.[6]

BEHAVIOR THERAPY

The term *behavior therapy*, first used in the 1950s (Skinner and Lindsley, 1953), refers to those methods of psychological treatment which make de-

[6]The use of drugs in connection with psychological treatment is discussed in detail in *Hallucinogenic Drugs and Their Psychotherapeutic Use* (Thomas, 1963), edited by R. Crochet; and *The Use of LSD in Psychotherapy and Alcoholism* (Bobbs-Merrill, 1967), edited by H. A. Abramson.

liberate use of learning theory and techniques to bring about a modification of the patient's behavior. Major emphasis is placed on getting rid of the disturbing symptom rather than on achieving insight.

This system, which has emerged as a workable alternative to traditional forms of psychotherapy, has its historical foundations in the work of Ivan Pavlov in Russia and E. L. Thorndike in the United States—pioneers in the behavioral sciences who devoted themselves to the laboratory study of the problems of learning. *Classical conditioning* grew out of Pavlov's work, and *instrumental,* or *operant, conditioning* emerged from Thorndike's research. Most of the methods of behavior therapy are based on one or the other, or a combination, of these fundamental learning models.

TREATMENT BY CLASSICAL CONDITIONING

In classical conditioning, a stimulus which ordinarily does not result in a response is substituted for the normal stimulus which *does* elicit the response. For example, food will normally cause an animal to salivate, but the sound of a bell will not bring about this response. However, by carefully manipulating the conditions, a bell alone can make an animal salivate.

How is this accomplished? Pavlov found the answer. By repeatedly pairing a normal stimulus (unconditioned stimulus) with a second stimulus (conditioned stimulus), the second stimulus alone will eventually elicit the response. We say that the animal has learned to respond to a new situation. The animal has been *conditioned*.

This classical conditioning model is one way in which people learn new patterns of behavior. It does not require understanding on the part of the individual, nor does it require his permission or cooperation. It is a form of neurological programming that determines the conditions under which a given type of behavior will appear.

An example of classical conditioning in therapy is the *conditioned aversion* treatment of chronic alcoholism. When this treatment was introduced in 1940, the usual procedure was to admit the alcoholic individual to a hospital where he was given massive doses of vitamins. The conditioned aversion to liquor was brought about by having

the person being treated sit comfortably in front of a table filled with bottles of liquor. The procedure was explained to him, and he was told that he would develop such a dislike for liquor that he would never want to drink again. He was then given a glass of water containing emetine and a hypodermic injection of emetine hydrochloride. These drugs are nauseants, making the person vomit when alcohol is taken into the body. At first the patient was urged to pour a drink, look at it, smell it, and taste it. However, he was not allowed to swallow it. In this way, the conditioning was extended to the sight, smell, and taste of liquor. Later, the patient was encouraged to drink until vomiting occurred each time. The treatment usually required about eight sessions, with the patient returning after three to six months for a reinforcement treatment (Voegtlin, 1940).

The conditioned aversion treatment used with alcoholics today is often carried out with the drug *tetraethylthiuramdisulphide*, or Antabuse. A strong and unpleasant physical reaction occurs in anyone who drinks alcoholic beverages after taking the drug. There is a flushed feeling in the face, increased pulse rate, difficulty in breathing, and a splitting headache. The drug is eliminated slowly, and as long as it is in the body, a drink of alcohol brings on the typical reaction. Antabuse therapy, which is a form of continuous conditioning, is based on the fact that the drug increases the conversion of ethyl alcohol to acetaldehyde, with the increase of this otherwise normal metabolite causing the discomforting symptoms.

TREATMENT BY OPERANT CONDITIONING

Operant conditioning is a method of behavior modification in which the individual's own behavior influences the learning process. Behavior that is considered by the therapist to be positive and desirable is reinforced by means of rewards; undesirable behavior is not rewarded. In some cases, undesirable behavior leads to punishment (negative reinforcement). Through methods such as these, the behavior of the person being treated is gradually shaped in positive directions.

When behavior is modified by operant methods, the emphasis is placed on the successive reinforcement of small segments of response which approximate the behavior to be learned. Once the desired behavior has been established, its control and continuation depend upon how often and how much the behavior is reinforced.

Most operant conditioning used in behavior therapy makes use of reward learning. The rewards used to reinforce desirable behavior include words and gestures indicating approval, candy, money, or other items and privileges which have a positive reinforcing effect.

It is possible to alter a person's behavior in the direction of more normal actions by means of carefully selected rewards and schedules of reinforcement. Clinical improvement is indicated by the increase in the number of favorable responses over a period of time.

In one of the early attempts to use reward learning in the treatment of psychotics, the injections of insulin were given to raise their hunger level. They were then given a series of simple problems to solve. When they were successful, they were rewarded with candy. Later, the problems became more difficult. As the successes continued, the insulin was discontinued, and the reward became associated with the therapist. Social rewards for desirable behavior eventually took the place of the candy. When the behavior of the experimental group of psychotics was compared with a control group, those treated by operant conditioning showed a significant improvement in their behavior (Peters and Jenkins, 1954).

In another experiment using reward learning as a treatment measure, a group of chronic schizophrenics was treated three times a week for fifteen weeks in sessions lasting twenty to thirty minutes each. The members of the group were encouraged to speak and to operate a series of levers on a problem-solving apparatus, individually and in cooperation with one another. Correct performance was rewarded with candy and cigarettes even though it was necessary to place the candy in the mouths of some of the most deteriorated members of the group. The food

Figure 15.9 *B. F. Skinner, 1904–   , American psychologist who has made major contributions to the theoretical foundations of behavior therapy. (Baris of Boston.)*

reinforcement was followed by verbal reinforcements such as "good" or "very good." Every response which gradually moved the individual toward speaking and constructive movement was reinforced. Eventually these individuals were able to talk about what they were doing and to work cooperatively with one another. Six months after the treatment had ended, the gains in behavior were maintained (King, Armitage, and Tilton, 1960).[7]

In the Behavior Research Laboratory of the Harvard Medical School, psychotic subjects enter a small experimental room in which there is a chair and a panel on one wall (Lindsley, 1960). The panel has a plunger that can be pulled, and there is a small aperture through which rein-

---

[7]*Behavior Research and Therapy* is an international multidisciplinary journal devoted to the application of modern learning theories, to the control of maladaptive behavior, and to the improvement of learning efficacy. Published quarterly, it is available from the Pergamon Press, Maxwell House, Fairview Park, Elmsford, N.Y. 10523.

forcing rewards can be presented to the subject. When the subject pulls the plunger, the reward, or reinforcement, is presented to him. Work at the laboratory has indicated that the special characteristics of the behavior of chronic psychotics can be studied effectively by this method.

In an experiment with autistic children, the youngsters learned to manipulate various devices. The first was a simple electrical switch; for operating it the child was rewarded with food. Gradually more complex performances were built up with such reinforcers as candy, music, the opportunity to play a pinball machine, and permission to look through a picture viewer. In a later phase of the experiment, coins were used as reinforcers, and the children could use the coins to operate devices which presented cartoons; to get a trained animal to perform; to play with an electric organ, a motor-driven rocking horse, an electric train, and a television set and even to obtain a life jacket and to go swimming. The children eventually learned to save the coins and use them only when certain stimuli indicated that the coins would be effective in "purchasing" one of the rewards. While the children exhibited essentially normal behavior for periods of several hours, they remained autistic outside the controlled environment of the laboratory (Ferster, 1961).

In another study, six schizophrenic children ranging in age from three to eight years who had shown little or no social interaction with other children were trained to operate a lever to obtain coins which served as reinforcers (Ferster and Skinner, 1957). These coins were then used to get candy and crackers from vending machines. Each child worked alone for thirty minutes a day in the experimental room until his typical pattern of behavior was obtained. The children were then paired on the basis of length of hospitalization, and both members of the pair were placed together in a room for all of the following sessions.

At first either child of the pair was able to operate the coin lever at any time during the session. Then in order to obtain coins the children were required to alternate, to take turns in using the coin lever. Next, a new lever had to be operated before the coin lever was operated, and again the two children were required to take turns on the new lever. Finally, one child was required to op-

erate the new lever so that the other could obtain coins, and vice versa. The study showed that it is possible to shape cooperative responses in early childhood schizophrenia in an average of twenty-three training sessions.

The operant conditioning of motor behavior is shown in the work with an eighteen-year-old youth who remained mute and would not move, except to open his mouth, blink his eyes, and move his arms, head, and shoulders slightly. The experimenter chose as the response to be rewarded a specific movement of the right arm; a warm sugar-milk solution was the primary reinforcement. Each time the patient made the proper arm movement, the sugar-milk solution was injected into his mouth, and he swallowed it. By the fourth conditioning period, the arm movement response became well differentiated: the youth gave an average of three responses per minute as compared with less than one per minute during the first conditioning session. The three responses per minute allowed just enough time for the milk to be injected and swallowed, which means that the response rate was about as high and consistent as it could be. During the entire previous life of this individual, very little had been learned. However, in the four operant conditioning sessions, considerable learning took place in view of his almost vegetative nature (Fuller, 1949).

The practical extension of operant conditioning methods has been demonstrated by a program of operant control to reduce the frequency of disruptive activities in the ward of a mental hospital. It was possible to reduce the incidence of delusional talk by refusing to pay attention to it, to control violence by reinforcing nonviolent behavior, and to get people to eat who previously refused to eat without help. Since most of the hospitalized individuals liked to keep their clothing neat and clean, the nurses deliberately spilled food on the clothing of anyone who insisted on being spoon-fed. As a result of avoidance conditioning, the patients eventually returned to self-feeding (Ayllon and Sommer, 1960).

Another form of operant conditioning was used in an experiment in which hard-to-manage adolescent delinquents were gradually involved in treatment. The therapist began by working with the boys as experimental subjects rather than patients. He paid them for participating in the project. At first each boy was allowed to arrive at any time during the day that suited him. When he did arrive, his presence was reinforced by fruit, sandwiches, or soft drinks.

He was then paid to talk into a tape recorder. Later he was allowed to help build electronic equipment, to listen to music, to take driving lessons, or to participate in other desirable activities. When the treatment session was over, a time convenient to the boy was set for the following day. In the beginning, the experimenter was not concerned about the early or late arrival of the youngster. Gradually, as attendance became more regular, the boy was paid more for arriving at the correct time. After fifteen to thirty meetings, the boys arrived on time and at the experimenter's convenience, and the reinforcement was shifted from the payment to the interpersonal relationship between the experimenter and the subject. Gradually, through the controlled use of operant shaping procedures, the boys' hostility and suspicion were overcome and they became able to accept treatment in the usual manner (Slack, 1960).

An important development in behavior therapy has been the application of operant conditioning to verbal behavior. Some of the earliest research in the field of verbal conditioning was a series of experiments in which subjects were instructed to say words individually and not to use sentences, phrases, or number. Plural nouns were reinforced by the verbal responses "mmm-hmm" and "uh-huh," a visual stimulus in the form of a flash of red light, and a low tone as an auditory stimulus. The use of all three forms of stimuli resulted in a significant increase in the number of plural noun responses (Tessel, 1955).

In an experiment using schizophrenic and neurotic subjects it was found that while the neurotic subjects could be conditioned verbally, the schizophrenic subjects could not. The reinforced response was any personal pronoun the subject uttered, and the reinforcing stimulus was "good" (Cohen and Cohen, 1960). However, in another verbal conditioning study, the amount of delusional speech was controlled in a psychotic who had been in a psychiatric hospital twenty years. When nondelusional speech was used the experimenter smiled, nodded his head, or responded verbally. Whenever the subject spoke in a delusional way, the experimenter responded by turning away, looking at the floor, or gazing out the window. The nondelusional responses increased during the experiment, but the delusional material reappeared when the reinforcing stimuli were discontinued (Rickard et al., 1960). Other investigators found it possible to reinstate verbal behavior in psychotics who had been mute for many years. When all approximations to speech responses were reinforced, there were marked increases in verbalization (Isaacs et al., 1960).

Research in verbal conditioning has a special pertinence for psychotherapy, and controlled laboratory situations have been designed in an attempt to create analogs of psychotherapy. In this research, selective verbal reinforcement is used to create desirable responses on the part of the patient-subject. Verbal reinforcement includes the use of such words as "fine," "good," "O.K.," and similar expressions. Nonverbal reinforcement takes the form of nodding the head, smiling, and leaning forward in an attitude of interest. Sometimes the rewarding reinforcement for undesirable behavior is in the life situation of the individual, and it then becomes necessary to eliminate the reinforcement if behavior is to be modified and socially improved.

A young woman developed a case of neurodermatitis in which itching and constant scratching persisted for two years despite medical treatment. Following the appearance of the skin disorder, the girl began to receive more attention from her father, who had previously shown a preference for her brother, and from other members of the family. The treatment consisted of advising the family to ignore the ailment. The girl's fiance, who had been applying an ointment to the patient's skin, was asked to refrain from doing it, because it was considered to be a positive reinforcement of the symptoms. When all reinforcement by the family was omitted, the scratching decreased over a period of two months and the skin disorder disappeared at the end of three months. Four years later the young woman was happily married and employed, and there had been no recurrence of the symptoms (Walton, 1960).

The withholding of reinforcement, or reward, has also been used to treat tantrum behavior in children. A child who had been ill for an extended period became so accustomed to having his parents in the room with him that after he recovered he went into a tantrum whenever his parents attempted to leave the room. They were forced to spend hours at a time with him to prevent his crying and screaming. Being present in the room was a positive reinforcer of the tantrum behavior. The parents were advised to leave the bedroom and not reenter it in spite of the child's outcries. Not surprisingly, the tantrum behavior disappeared in a very short time (Williams, 1959).

In aversive conditioning, the behavior therapist attempts to bring about the desired behavioral changes through the use of negative (unpleasant) reinforcers. Instead of receiving rewards for desirable behavior, aversive therapy employs forms of punishment for expressions of undesirable behavior.

In one approach, a tape recorder presented a series of verbal descriptions of homosexually erotic situations. The patient (a male in this case) received an aversive-conditioning electric shock immediately after each deviant scene was played. Descriptions of heterosexually erotic situations, recorded by a seductive female voice, were presented from time to time, after which no shock followed. Patients were treated every day for the first week, and then at less frequent intervals. When necessary, booster treatments were given from time to time to reinforce the original treatment sessions (Feingold, 1968).

SELF-CONFRONTATION

This form of behavior modification uses closed-circuit television or videotape as a means of allowing the patient to see himself as others see him. The impact of the experience leads some patients to alter their behavior in more positive and acceptable directions. That this should be so is not surprising. Observe how people walking along a downtown street look at themselves in mirrors and tend to straighten up and hold their heads higher. The self-consciousness experienced by most people when they are being photographed is another everyday indication of the emotional importance of our "body image."

An early attempt to study the effects of self-confrontation made use of instantaneous disk recordings. The immediate playback of recordings of psychotic speech was found, in some cases, to have a dramatic impact on the behavior of the patient. Schizophrenics who seemed completely out of contact suddenly became serious and attentive as they listened to their own psychotic speech. Full-length mirrors were also used to confront patients with their own images (Kisker, 1940). The sound film made it possible both to see and hear oneself, but the procedure was expensive and time consuming. With the advent of videotape recording and the possibility of immediate playback, there was a very great increase in the use of self-confrontation techniques in clinical research and treatment.

In one self-confrontation study, alcoholics were shown pictures of themselves taken while under the influence of a small amount of alcohol. The pictures were obtained while the patients were talking about personal matters with a psychiatrist. Different patterns of coping behavior were observed. When the patients later viewed themselves on the screen, they expressed considerable dissatisfaction with how they looked and how they acted (Paredes et al., 1969).

Videotapes are also used in group treatment. The patients and doctors interact under the eye of the camera for the first part of the session. The members of the group then watch the recorded replay. One patient may see a revealing gesture that he had never noticed before. Another patient may catch the double level of love and anger during a verbal exchange. The tape stops from time to time to permit comments on what is being seen. One patient said, "I look like I didn't mean a word I was saying." Another patient commented, "I never knew I looked so pretty." A major advantage of the technique is that it is extremely difficult to remain indifferent to self-confrontation of this type.

The effectiveness of the self-confrontation method was demonstrated in a study comparing brief psychotherapy, counseling, and videotape feedback as methods of behavior modification. Over a two-year period the videotape confrontation resulted in the greatest improvement (Kaswan and Love, 1969).

SUMMARY

1. The psychological approach to the treatment of personality disturbances and behavior disorders takes two principal forms: *psychotherapy* and *behavior therapy*. In addition, a number of specialized techniques are used to influence thinking, feelings, and behavior.

2. The term "psychotherapy" is a very general one and includes a wide range of techniques. All psychotherapy, however, involves an individual and a therapist, a therapeutic setting, and an interpersonal relationship. This form of treatment can be carried out with individuals or with groups. While the dynamics of group therapy are roughly similar to those of individual psychotherapy, the approach permits the use of such additional techniques as psychodrama and the treatment of entire families.

3. The major types of psychotherapy are *supportive, reeducative,* and *reconstructive.* Supportive psychotherapy is designed primarily to strengthen the existing defenses of the person being treated and to make him better able to face his problems. The specialized techniques of supportive treatment include reassurance, suggestion, persuasion, emotional catharsis, modification of environmental stress, and redirection of the individual's interests.

4. Reeducative psychotherapy attempts to modify behavior through a process of relearning. The two principal reeducative approaches are *directive* and *nondirective.* The directive approach is one in which the therapist takes the major responsibility for the treatment and its results. The method tends to be authoritarian. In nondirective therapy the individual is largely responsible for his own improvement.

5. Reconstructive therapy, which seeks to bring about a fundamental reorganization of basic personality patterns, is directed toward the unconscious levels of the personality. The best examples of reconstructive therapy are *Freudian psychoanalysis, non-Freudian depth therapy, psychoanalytically oriented therapy,* and *direct analytic therapy.* Freudian psychoanalysis uses free association and the analysis of dreams as its principal techniques. The treatment attempts to uncover critical experiences of early life and to show the relation of these experiences to the patient's present difficulties. Non-Freudian depth therapy and psychoanalytically oriented therapy evolved from orthodox Freudian psychoanalysis but introduced important modifications in theory and technique. Direct analytic therapy is a specialized form of depth therapy used primarily in the treatment of psychotics.

6. Among the specialized techniques used in psychological treatment are *hypnotherapy* and *drug-facilitated therapy.* Hypnotherapy may involve prolonged hypnosis, the direct suggestion that a symptom will disappear, or suggestion directed toward the change of attitudes underlying a symptom. The approach also may utilize the abreaction of traumatic experiences or the more complex techniques of hypnoanalysis. In drug-facilitated psychotherapy the use of drugs is most frequently directed toward the release of unconscious material.

7. The behavior therapy approach emphasizes learning and relearning as a method of treatment. The changes in thinking, feelings, and behavior are brought about by means of two well-established conditioning procedures: *classical conditioning* and *operant,* or *instrumental, conditioning.* Most types of behavior therapy make use of operant conditioning, which modifies attitudes and behavior through reinforcers. Positive re-

inforcers are rewards of various kinds given to the individual for showing improved behavior. Negative reinforcers are pain-inducing or anxiety-provoking events made to accompany unacceptable behavior. The pattern, or schedule, of reinforcement is an important part of behavior therapy.

OTHER AUDIOTAPES

Sensory Hypnoanalysis
Milton V. Kline gives a twenty-six-minute talk on a specialized form of hypnotherapy. Recorded in 1968. Sound Seminar 75464, *McGraw-Hill Book Company.*

Behavior Therapy at the Crossroads: Problems and Prospects
Durand F. Jacobs presents a thirty-minute overview of the application of psychological techniques based on learning principles and methods to correct maladaptive and unadaptive behavior. Traces the development of these techniques from the work of Pavlov and Skinner to present applications to human behavior problems. Recorded in 1968. Sound Seminar 75434, *McGraw-Hill Book Company.*

16 EXPERIMENTAL AND INNOVATIVE PSYCHOPATHOLOGY

The story of the disorganized personality would not be complete without considering some of the experimental and innovative approaches to the problem of psychological disturbances. The research approach, which began in the nineteenth century, was influenced by several lines of scientific interest, including investigations in the field of hypnosis, the measurement of individual differences, and the exploration of the brain and its function by means of experimental surgery, electrical stimulation, and drugs. Other scientists, working in the laboratory, attacked such problems as somatic reactivity, perception, and the higher mental processes.

By the beginning of the present century, the research approach to personality disorganization was well established. The first psychological laboratory in a mental hospital in the United States was founded in 1892 at McLean Hospital in Massachusetts (Cowles, 1895), and Emil Kraepelin emphasized the importance of psychological experimentation in connection with mental disorder by insisting that psychological theories must be based on laboratory findings (Kraepelin, 1896). He made use of the word-association technique and investigated changes in reaction time resulting from such conditions as fatigue, hunger, and intoxication.

Many of the early research studies in psychopathology were open to objections of a most serious kind. Too little attention was given to the selection of subjects; standardization of criteria for clinical change was neglected; properly matched control groups were seldom used; and follow-up studies were often lacking. Fortunately, the clinical psychologist and the psychiatrist have become increasingly skillful and sophisticated in research methodology.

The field of experimental psychopathology has been given additional impetus by its recognition as an area of specialization in our universities. In the early 1900s, a number of colleges and universities emphasized the research approach to mental disorder in a variety of courses. It was not until after World War II, however, that specific training in this field was made available. Universities now offer courses in experimental psychopathology, and several schools confer the doctorate in this field of specialization. Similarly, an increasing emphasis on research in the training of psychiatric residents in medical schools has contributed to the establishment of an experimental psychopathology.

Important advances in our knowledge of mental health and mental disorder have grown out of the activity in the field of experimental psychopathology. While research alone cannot supply all the answers, it does clarify many difficult problems, provide new leads, suggest new techniques, and guide the clinician in his day-to-day work with individuals who consult him about their personality disturbances.

It is not easy to classify the wide range of research approaches to psychopathology. A basic feature of research is that problems often do not fit into neat categories. There is much overlapping, and there are many new directions. In this chapter, therefore, the classification is neither inclusive nor systematic. Rather, several of the larger areas of research have been selected as examples of the range of experimental work being directed toward mental disorder.[1]

BRAIN-BEHAVIOR RESEARCH

An important avenue of research in experimental psychopathology has been the investigation of the relationship between behavior and the functions of the brain. The understanding of this relationship is of practical importance because the impairment of brain function underlies many forms of neurological and mental disorder. Moreover, the activity of the brain is critically involved with the control of human behavior, and further knowledge in this field is basic to man's future development as an individual and as a social being.

Interest in this subject reaches far back into the history of anatomy. From the time of Hippocrates, physicians made clinical observations on behavior disturbances associated with diseased and accidentally damaged brains. However, it was not until the latter part of the nineteenth century that knowledge of the nervous system, surgical techniques, and the use of electricity were sufficiently advanced to allow controlled observations and experimentation. Since that time there has been a persistent and increasing interest in the relationship between brain function and behavior. While many scientific disciplines contribute to our knowledge of the brain, the science of experimental psychopathology has profited particularly from studies of brain damage and stimulation.

---

[1]Some of the more important books in the general field of experimental psychopathology are B. A. Maher's *Introduction to Research in Psychopathology* (McGraw-Hill, 1970); *Research in Psychopathology* (Van Nostrand, 1963), edited by H. C. Quay; *Experimental Foundations of Clinical Psychology* (Basic Books, 1962), edited by Arthur J. Bachrach; *Handbook of Abnormal Psychology: An Experimental Approach* (Pitman, 1960), edited by H. J. Eysenck; *Lectures on Experimental Psychiatry* (University of Pittsburgh Press, 1961), edited by Henry W. Brosin; and *Aspects of Psychiatric Research* (Oxford University, 1962), edited by Derek Richter and others.

Figure 16.1 *Wilder Penfield, 1891– , world-renowned brain surgeon at the Montreal Neurological Institute and McGill University. (Courtesy of Roche Laboratories Medical Image.)*

The interest in brain-behavior research is exemplified by the establishment in 1960 of the International Brain Research Organization (IBRO). The broad purposes of the IBRO are to provide leadership in interdisciplinary brain research throughout the world, to serve as a clearinghouse for information in the field, to plan symposia and international study groups on various aspects of cerebral physiology, and to provide the framework for fellowships to enable specialists to do collaborative research on the brain.

BRAIN STIMULATION

Research in brain stimulation differs from experimental damage in that the stimulation studies involve the intact brain and are applicable to the human subject. This approach developed following the discovery of electricity and the refinement of experimental techniques by means of

which electrical current could be applied to living tissue without damaging or destroying it. As a result, research workers obtained a tool of the greatest importance in brain research.

The studies of brain stimulation grew out of the early nineteenth-century interest in the localization of mental functioning. Frances Gall, in 1813, proposed an extreme form of brain localization embodied in his theory of phrenology (Gall and Spurzheim, 1809). One of the first authorities to take exception to this point of view was a French scientist, who held that mental functions are not highly localized but depend upon the interaction of large cerebral areas (Flourens, 1824). A spirited controversy grew around these two positions. However, it was agreed that most of the sensory and motor functions are relatively well localized. For many years, the controversy remained on a theoretical level. It was not until late in the century, when more precise techniques for stimulating the brain were developed, that controlled observations on man became possible.

Early studies demonstrated that when specific brain areas are electrically stimulated, movements of the arms and legs on the opposite side of the body take place. The work suggested that the motor functions of the brain are relatively localized. Additional observations were made by the American neurosurgeon Harvey Cushing, early in the present century (Cushing and Eisenhardt, 1938). Not until the 1950s was it shown that the generally accepted clear-cut distinction between sensory and motor areas of the cortex could not be supported. Stimulation of areas of the brain traditionally regarded as sensory can result in movement as well as sensation. Similarly, sensory representation in the motor cortex is now well established (Field, 1960).

Another line of brain stimulation research has involved the relationship between subcortical structures and emotional expression. As early as 1892, the emotional responses of dogs whose brain hemispheres had been removed were observed (Goltz, 1892). In 1925, the classic work on "sham rage" in the decorticated animal was published (Cannon and Britten, 1925). However, the most important work on the relation of electrical stimulation of lower brain centers to emotional behavior showed that stimulation of the hypothalamus results in a rage reaction and that the reaction stops when the stimulus is discontinued (Hess, 1954).

Electrical stimulation of the brain has also established the fact that the autonomic functions of the body are represented in the cortex. Certain parts of the cortex yield somatic as well as visceral responses. When the cortical motor area related to the hand is stimulated, there may also be sweating of the palm of the hand. In a similar way, stimulation of the cortical area related to eye movement sometimes results in pupillary changes and tear formation (Kennard, 1947).

Some of the most provocative studies in electrical brain stimulation have been carried out at the Montreal Neurological Institute under the direction of Wilder Penfield and his associates (Penfield and Roberts, 1959). Penfield, a brain surgeon, has been particularly interested in the surgical treatment of convulsive disorders. However, in the course of his operations he discovered some interesting facts about brain localization. One of the most remarkable discoveries was that the stimulation of certain brain areas is able to elicit past memories.

The first "evoked memories" were reported when Penfield produced recollections on the part of his patients by stimulating the temporal-lobe cortex. The patients appeared to experience, both in visual and in auditory form, past events in their lives. The same recollections occasionally could be reproduced at a later time by stimulating the same spot or adjacent areas on the cortex. In other cases, the repeated stimulation of the same area produced a different recollection or none at all. Penfield suggested that the electrical stimulation of the temporal cortex reactivated brain patterns which were a part of the original experience (Penfield, 1952).

In one case, a thirty-seven-year-old man received a head injury while serving in the Canadian Merchant Marine. Convulsive attacks began three months later and continued for six years until the time of his operation. He appeared confused and would say things not appropriate to the situation. Sometimes he would say, "It is caught," or "It shows." Later the patient would have no memory for his seizures. When the brain was stimulated during the operation, the patient described a feeling that interfered with his speech. In another case, when the upper surface of the right temporal lobe was being stimulated, the patient cried out, "Yes, Doctor! Yes, Doctor!

Figure 16.2 *The exposed human brain, showing points stimulated electrically during experimental studies at the Montreal Neurological Institute. (Courtesy of Dr. Wilder Penfield.)*

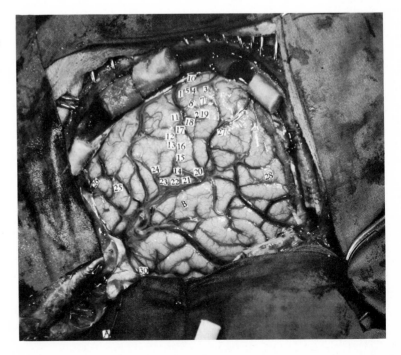

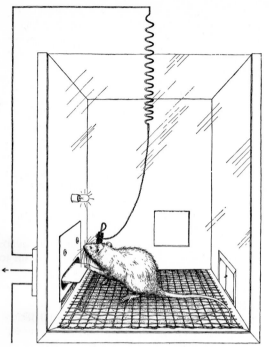

Figure 16.3 *A self-stimulation circuit. When the rat presses the foot treadle, a mild electric shock is delivered to the animal's brain. (Courtesy of* Scientific American.)

Now I hear people laughing—my friends—in South Africa." The patient had recently come from his home in South Africa, and when the stimulation was completed, he said that it had seemed to him that he was actually with his cousins at their home, where he and two young ladies were laughing together (Penfield and Roberts, 1959).

One of the extensions of this type of research has been electrical stimulation and recording through implanted electrodes in the brain of unanesthetized and free-moving animals. As a result, it has been possible to develop operant conditioning techniques for allowing experimental animals to stimulate their own brains. In the self-stimulation experiments, the animal has a pair of tiny silver electrodes implanted in his brain. He can stimulate his hypothalamus electrically by touching a lever on one wall of the cage. Each

time the lever is pressed, the animal receives a pleasurable electrical stimulation. The lever then must be released and touched again if the animal is to receive an additional stimulus.

In ordinary random behavior, without current, animals press the lever from ten to fifty times per hour. When stimulating current is received, the pedal may be pressed from 500 to 7,000 times per hour. Animals allowed to stimulate freely for long periods of time continue the self-stimulation until they are exhausted. When the self-stimulated shock is delivered to the hypothalamus, some animals press the lever to receive the shock continuously for as long as forty-eight hours without satiation. However, when the shock is delivered to other brain structures, there is a decreasing rate of lever pressing within four to eight hours (Olds, 1955).

The self-stimulation studies are of considerable theoretical interest. While it is not clear why self-stimulation has such a strong rewarding effect, the positive feedback, or pleasurable experience, reinforces the need to continue the behavior. Experiments in this area may eventually clarify some of the problems of compulsive disorders. It is also possible that episodes of psychotic agitation may involve an excessive amount of positive feedback which subserves positive reinforcement mechanisms. Self-stimulation experiments also provide information concerning the neuroanatomical systems related to motivated behavior. Finally, the self-stimulation technique in animals has been used to evaluate the effects of various drugs used in neuropsychiatry (Olds and Travis, 1960).[2]

BIOMEDICAL MONITORING

The research interest in both spontaneous and experimentally induced somatic reactions has taken a variety of directions. One interest has been the relation between emotional responses and autonomic activity. Work in this area, which began in the late 1800s, gained momentum in the 1920s when the importance of bodily changes as emer-

[2]*The Journal of Psychiatric Research* is a quarterly publication carrying clinical and research articles with biological, psychological, and sociological orientations. The papers are of a technical nature, and the journal is recommended primarily for advanced students. It is available from the Pergamon Press, Elmsford, N.Y. 10523.

gency functions in emotional states was demonstrated (Cannon, 1929). A second line of interest has been the recording and evaluation of electrical changes in brain tissue. Finally, there has been continuing attention to the relation of muscle action potential to tension and anxiety.

Radio biotelemetry is the most advanced type of physiological monitoring. The method, made possible by the invention of the transistor in 1948, is one in which a tiny transmitter capsule is attached to the body or swallowed by the individual under observation. Signals transmitted from the capsule are picked up by means of a radio receiving antenna. Free-ranging humans or lower animals can be studied under a wide variety of conditions without interfering with normal activity. Stress patterns at home and at work can be monitored continuously.

The relevance of radio biotelemetry to psychopathology is indicated by some of the variables which have been monitored: body movement, breathing patterns, blood pressure, heart rate, electrical resistance of the skin, body temperature, and brain wave patterns.

Telestimulation is an advanced technique that has been combined with biotelemetric monitoring. A pocket-size radio device has been developed that will warn epileptics of an impending seizure. The changes in brain wave activity can be monitored by tiny scalp electrodes hidden in the hair. These electrodes are connected to a small transmitter carried in a pocket or attached to a belt. The brain waves that are picked up are radioed continuously to a computer programmed to detect dangerous changes and to transmit warning signals back to the patient. Once the warning signal has been received, the patient can quickly find a place to rest or can take extra medication (Ordon, 1970).[3]

MIND-ALTERING DRUGS

One of the most challenging problems in experimental psychopathology has been the attempt to develop laboratory models of mental disorders in man. In spite of the fact that no specific organic basis has been found for most of these conditions, many research workers and clinicians feel that at least some of the forms of mental disorder will be explained ultimately in terms of biochemical disturbance. The result has been a considerable amount of research directed toward the mind-altering, or *psychedelic*, drugs.

Various terms have been used to describe these drugs and to distinguish them from narcotics and other physiologically addictive drugs. The term *hallucinogenic* refers to the ability of the mind-altering drug to induce, or to generate, hallucinations. These drugs have also been called *psychotomimetic* drugs because the effects sometimes resemble, or mimic, the symptoms seen in psychotic states.

Hallucinogens are chemicals that produce transient psychotic-like states in normal people. They make it possible to induce hallucinations, delusions, dissociations, and feelings of unreality under relatively standardized conditions. The value of the investigation of these psychotomimetic substances is that if it can be discovered why known chemical compounds cause changes in behavior, there may be clues to the chemical structure and processes of natural substances in the body which may be related to mental disorder.

The use of drugs to induce hallucinations and other symptoms of mental disturbance has been a common practice for many centuries. The Oracle at Delphi probably induced her prophetic visions with belladonna. The drug *datura stramonium*, known during the Middle Ages as "the sorcerers' herb," induced a pathological condition known until the eighteenth century as *daturism*. Christopher Dosta, in 1602, described the effects of the drug:

He who swallows the powdered seeds of *datura* remains for a long time in the condition of a madman, laughing, weeping, but sometimes chatting with another person and replying to him as if he were in his right senses, although he is not so, as he does not recognize those who speak to him, and does not remember his own discourse when he recovers his reason.

---

[3]*Brain Research* is an international journal devoted to fundamental research in the brain sciences. It contains original research papers, short communications, and book reviews. Published monthly, it is available from American Elsevier, New York, N.Y. 10017

In the late nineteenth century, Emil Kraepelin experimented with the psychopathological effects of intoxicating drugs in an effort to produce artificial psychoses. He hoped that histological examinations would then indicate the pathoanatomical substrate in some of the mental disorders. Kraepelin's work met with limited success because of the general lack of knowledge of drug action at that time.

While the modern field of psychopharmacology was established in the early 1930s with the publication of *Phantastica: Narcotics and Stimulating Drugs* (Lewin, 1931), it was not until the 1950s that intensive work was begun on experimentally induced mental disorders. Since that time, interest has focused for the most part on marijuana (cannabis), mescaline (peyote), and LSD (lysergic acid diethylamide).

MARIJUANA

Marijuana is a name given in the United States and Latin America to a preparation made from the hemp plant (*cannabis sativa*). This plant grows wild in most countries and is used throughout the world as an intoxicant. In 1950 the United Nations estimated that cannabis preparations were used by more than two hundred million people, most of them in Asia and Africa.

The strength of the hemp plant as an intoxicant varies depending upon the climate, the method of cultivation, and the manner of preparing it. Cannabis preparations have many names in other parts of the world. In Morocco it is called *kif*, in South Africa it is *dagga*. In India there are three grades of the drug: *bhang* is inexpensive and of relatively low strength; *ganja* is several times stronger; and *charas*, the strongest of all, is the unadulterated resin obtained from the plant or dried flower. Charas is about five to eight times stronger than the marijuana used in the United States. The term *hashish* is used in literature to refer to any form of the cannabis drug, although technically it is a powdered and sifted form of charas.

The principal active ingredient in marijuana is THC (tetrahydrocannabinol). In low dosage, this compound induces behavior that is similar to alcoholic intoxication; in high dosages the drug frequently results in hallucinations. Nearly a hundred derivatives of THC have been synthesized and studied for their drug effects on behavior.

Of all the illegal drugs currently in use in our society, marijuana has generated the most popular concern. Next to alcohol it is the most widely abused drug. Its use was originally concentrated in limited sectors of of the population, but it has now come to include large numbers of junior high school to college-age youth. Nationwide college surveys indicate that approximately 20 percent of college students have used marijuana one or more times, and that roughly 8 percent have used LSD or other hallucinogenic drugs. Information from one university showed a dramatic rise in the use of marijuana from 21 percent of students in 1967 to 57 percent in 1968 to 70 percent in 1969 (NIMH, 1969).

An interesting finding experimentally, and one which has been observed frequently among marijuana smokers, is that many people do not become "high" on their first exposure to marijuana even if they smoke it properly. The high effect comes with continued use of the drug. One possibility is that getting high depends upon some type of drug sensitization. Another possibility is that the repeated use of marijuana reduces psychological inhibitions and permits the experience of becoming high.

One study of the effects of marijuana included nine healthy male volunteers, age twenty-one to twenty-six, all of whom had smoked tobacco cigarettes but had never tried marijuana. Eight chronic users of marijuana also participated in the study. The age range for the users was the same as for nonusers.

All of the subjects were volunteers, and had psychiatric interviews during which they were told that they might be asked to smoke marijuana. They were driven home following the experiment, and they agreed not to engage in any unusual activity or operate machinery until the next day. They also agreed to report for follow-up interviews six months after the experiment. They were protected from legal repercussions through agreements with the Federal Bureau of Narcotics, the office of the attorney general of the state in which the experiments took place, and the state Bureau of Drug Abuse and Control.

The marijuana was supplied by the Federal Bureau of Narcotics. The marijuana assayed at 0.9 percent THC, which is considered "good, average" marijuana. The low dose used in the study was 0.5 gram, and the high dose was 2.0 grams. The marijuana was administered in the form of cigarettes, with each subject smoking two cigarettes in succession. Placebo cigarettes consisted of chopped outer coverings of mature stalks of male hemp plant containing no THC.

The physiological measures used in this study were heart rate, breathing rate, pupil size, blood sugar level, and the condition of the blood vessels of the eyes. Psychological tests were also given. At the end of the psychological tests each subject was left in a room with a tape recorder and told to describe an interesting or dramatic experience in his life. After exactly five minutes, he was interrupted and asked how long he had been in the room. In this way an estimate of the ability to judge time was obtained.

It was found that the maximum effects were present fifteen minutes after smoking the marijuana. These effects diminished after thirty to sixty minutes and disappeared after three hours. While all of the chronic users became "high" on the high dose of marijuana, only one naive subject had this same type of reaction on the high dose.

There were three outstanding findings. Most subjects receiving marijuana in either high or low doses recognized that they were getting a drug; most subjects receiving placebos recognized that they were receiving placebos; and most subjects called their high dose a low dose.

In the naive subjects, the marijuana in both low and high doses was followed by the increased heart rate fifteen minutes after smoking. The high doses caused a greater increase in the chronic users than in the naive subjects. There was no change in the breathing rate in the naive group although the chronic users showed a small increase which was not considered clinically significant. There was no change in pupil size in any of the subjects. There was significant reddening of the blood vessels of the eyes in one of the nine subjects receiving the placebo, three of nine receiving the high dose. The reddening occurred in all of the chronic users receiving the high dose. There was no change in blood sugar levels.

On the psychological tests, the performance of naive subjects was impaired at fifteen and ninety minutes after smoking, but chronic users started with good performance and improved slightly after smoking marijuana (Weil, Zinberg and Nelsen, 1968).

There has been sharp disagreement, even among well-informed scientists, regarding the degree of the threat posed by marijuana. Adequate data, particularly on the implications of low-dosage, long-term social usage, are generally lacking.

One area of concern has been the relation between the use of marijuana and crime. This relationship was suggested as early as the year 1300 when Marco Polo reported that the drug was used to give courage for committing assassinations and other crimes. In fact, the word *assassin* comes from an Arabic word meaning hashish-eaters.

In the 1930s in the United States it was generally believed that the use of marijuana led to serious crime. The Commissioner of Public Safety in New Orleans wrote that some of the homes for boys were "full of children who had become habituated to the use of cannabis and fortified themselves with the drug to shoot down police, bank clerks, and casual bystanders" (Gomila, 1938).

More recent evidence suggests that while there is an increase in petty crime among marijuana users, there is no corresponding increase in major crimes. The panel on drug abuse at the 1962 White House Conference on Narcotic and Drug Abuse stated, "Although marijuana has long held the reputation of inciting individuals to commit sexual offenses and other anti-social acts, evidence is inadequate to substantiate this."

Another point of considerable concern is the possible relationship between marijuana use and heroin addiction. The Mayor's Committee report (New York City, 1944) supported the view that there is no significant relationship between marijuana and other drugs. The report stated, "The instances are extremely rare where the habit of marijuana smoking is associated with addiction to these other narcotics." This finding has been widely challenged in more recent years.

Much of the controversy over marijuana's possible effects arises out of overinterpretation or misinterpretation of what little data are presently available. However, the absence of reliable evidence of the harmfulness of a substance does not demonstrate its harmlessness. Frequently, it requires relatively long-term chronic use of a substance before its public health implications are apparent. Cigarette smoking provides an obvious and apt example.

MESCALINE

The use of mescaline as an hallucinogen had its beginnings in the tribal and religious ceremonies of the Mexican Indians. The drug is obtained from the sacred cactus, or peyote plant, which has been known for centuries for its psychological effects. Mescaline, the active principle of peyote, was isolated chemically in 1898. At that time its ability to produce visual color hallucinations was observed. Later studies indicated that mescaline produces a psychotic state resembling schizophrenia.

Peyote is usually taken in the form of an alcoholic extract or combined with chloroform. The main action of the drug is that of a cerebral stimulant. With moderate doses, the first experience is that of a mild sensation of gastric distension which later produces a slight nausea and dizziness. However, this sensation is relatively pleasant and is accompanied by an exhilarated feeling. Visual acuity becomes exaggerated, objects stand out with special clearness, lassitude is felt, and characteristic visual hallucinations appear.

The hallucinations are relatively simple at first and consist of colored figures which arrange themselves into bizarre tapestry-like formations. Gradually more complicated visions of faces, forms, and landscapes emerge. The images change frequently and are brilliantly colored. With larger doses of peyote, the complexity of hallucinations increases. Sounds heard in the room become associated with visual images. The stroke of a clock may cause an "explosion of color." The various notes of the piano produce characteristic colors.

Weston LaBarre, an anthropologist, described at some length the use of peyote among Indian tribes. After all-night ceremonies, the men lounge about and tell of their visions and experiences. These reports, of a highly personal nature, are psychologically revealing. Another tribal use of peyote is for the treatment of various ailments, including mental disorder.

Heinrich Klüver, a University of Chicago psychologist, swallowed powdered mescal buttons and described his experiences. The visions, which were localized at reading distance, could not be influenced voluntarily. The observation of the phenomena was accompanied by pleasant feelings. There was an unwillingness to be intellectually active, accompanied by a distortion of time. Klüver's body and organs seemed most of the time to be nonexistent or detached from himself. Even the sound of his voice had an unreal quality.

In an investigation of mescaline psychosis experimentally induced in a group of healthy adults, the symptoms resembled very closely those of the schizophrenic, the manic-depressive, and the acute toxic confusional and delusional reactive types. In addition, the mescaline produced specific symptoms peculiar to itself in the form of vegetative changes, synesthesia, or "colored hearing," and peculiar qualities of visual experience. Schizothymic subjects showed schizophrenic symptoms, while cyclothymics developed hypomanic and manic reactions.

In describing mescaline intoxication, one subject reported:

There came over me a feeling of bodily lightness. When I walked, my limbs had no weight. If the toe of my shoe touched the wall, there was no hard contact. This sensation of weightlessness persisted throughout the whole of the time that I was under the influence of the drug. But after its first onset, I quickly became accustomed to it. It seemed inevitable and natural, and I did not notice it again until I was beginning to emerge into the everyday world.

Another subject reported:

To my great surprise, I realized that I had no head. In its place, there was a sheet of ground-glass, such as is used in a camera as a screen. Where my ear was, was an insoluble mystery. I could not find it so long as with open eyes I followed and controlled the movements of my searching hand. I was quite unconscious of the position of any part of my body.

In his book *The Doors of Perception,* Aldous Huxley described his experiences after taking a mescaline pill. He took the drug at eleven o'clock in the morning, and the effects began half an hour later and lasted for about eight hours. He describes one of his experiences in the following way:

That chair, shall I ever forget it? Where the shadows fell on the canvas upholstery, stripes of an incandescent so intensely bright that it was hard to believe that they could be made of anything but blue fire. For what seemed an immensely long time I gazed without knowing, even wishing to know, what it was that confronted me. At any other time I would have seen a chair barred with alternate light and shade. Today the percept had swallowed up the concept. I was so completely absorbed in looking, so thunderstruck by what I actually saw, that I could not be aware of anything else. Garden furniture, laths, sunlight, shadow—these were no more than names and notions, mere verbalizations, for utilitarian or scientific purposes, after the event. The event was this succession of azure furnace-doors separated by gulfs of unfathomable gentian. It was expressly wonderful, wonderful to the point, almost, of being terrifying. And suddenly I had an inkling of what it must feel like to be mad.

The importance of mescaline in psychiatric research is based not only on the similarity of the drug reaction to psychotic symptoms, but also on the fact that the chemical formula of mescaline is similar to that of adrenalin. Because of this similarity, as well as the similarity in symptoms, one of the hypotheses in the early 1950s was that an *M-substance* (mescaline-like) might

be the cause of schizophrenia. Such an hypothesis had been suggested earlier by several investigators, but the search for this hypothetical substance did not get under way seriously until the work of Abram Hoffer in 1954. This investigator believed that *adrenochrome,* a metabolite of adrenalin, was responsible for psychotic symptoms such as overactivity, depression, hallucinations, and loss of insight. Later, similar claims were made for other oxidation products of adrenalin including *adrenoxine* and *adrenolutin.*

LSD

Another psychosis-producing drug is *lysergic acid diethylamide,* or LSD-25. This drug is derived from ergot, a substance which has been associated with mental illness since the Middle Ages. The hallucinogenic effects of LSD-25 were first observed by Albert Hoffman, a research chemist in Switzerland. Hoffman was working with the drug in 1943 when he accidentally sucked a small quantity through a glass tube. Less than an hour later, he became confused and muddled in his thinking and developed visual and auditory hallucinations. Hoffman did not understand what was happening, and he was so frightened that he left his laboratory and started home on his bicycle. Although he lived only a short distance away, he said later that the ride was like a nightmare. It seemed as if he rode a thousand miles. When Hoffman recovered, he deliberately measured out a quantity of the chemical, and took it again. This time the experience was even more severe.

Figure 16.4 *Changes in web construction following administration of mescaline to spiders. Left, geometric uniformity of a normal web. Right, erratically shaped web produced under the influence of mescaline. (Courtesy of the Schering Corporation.)*

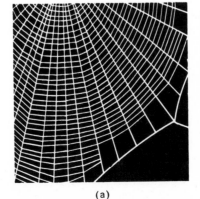
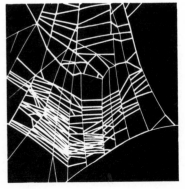

(a)   (b)

He developed all the signs of schizophrenia. As a result, the psychosis-producing nature of the drug was established.

In a study in which two graduate students in psychology volunteered to take LSD-25, the first symptoms of personality disorganization were noticed in the area of mood. The subjects began to smile more often, and then they started to giggle. Everything suddenly seemed humorous. Finally they became hilarious and roared with laughter. Sometimes they laughed at what others said and sometimes apparently at their own thoughts. Their mood was completely inappropriate to the situation. A careful medical check was kept on each subject during the experiment. Every fifteen minutes a physician recorded blood pressure and heart action. While minor changes in the functioning of the body took place, they were of relatively little importance.

After a period of several hours, the subjects in the experiment were confused in their thinking. The inappropriate laughter was gone, except for occasional silly giggling. A little later, the subjects became suspicious. One crouched on a bed in the corner of the room and looked fearfully at anyone who came near him. Later he said that he thought he might be killed. At the height of the confused thinking, hallucinations were experienced. The subjects heard voices and saw strange figures in the room. One student reported seeing human shapes and animal forms in the wood grain on the doors.

The first volunteer described his experience, which lasted more than five hours, in the following way:

> The pervading feeling was that there was a gulf between me and the rest of the environment. It seemed that it would be impossible for me to communicate with those across this gulf because I could not establish any common points of reference. Also, within this state there were hallucinations and a sense of timelessness, all unusual, none of which had any real emotional tone to them.

The second volunteer retained symptoms of his mental disturbance for more than thirteen hours. When it came to an end, he wrote:

> I had very little by way of visual hallucinations, but what I consider the important thing was that I felt dissociated, plagued, pounded, weighed-down—all

these are inadequate to describe the horrible state I was in. Perhaps the central thing was suspicion and fear that you would find out about me, or perhaps think things that were not true. On and on this went, and as was no doubt obvious, I decided to do as little as possible so I wouldn't make any mistakes.

As in the case of mescaline, there is a question about whether the symptoms seen as a result of LSD-25 are in fact similar to schizophrenia. Certainly the outward signs of LSD-25 intoxication bear a strong resemblance to the behavior of some schizophrenic patients. Such a superficial resemblance, however, does not mean that the underlying biodynamics are necessarily the same. It is well known that certain states of alcoholism, particularly in alcoholic hallucinosis, are highly similar to paranoid schizophrenia. It may be that the alcohol in one case, and the LSD-25 in the other, act merely to release the schizophrenic potential within a given patient.

Few drugs have had so profound an effect on American culture in so short a time as LSD. Its use, never great in terms of the percentage of the population who have tried it, has helped to create an entire subculture—the drug-based "hippie" groups. Unlike other illegal drugs, LSD first became popular among middle-class professionals and artists. At the same time, its profound psychological effects generated an initial optimism among scientific investigators about its potential usefulness for creating a model of psychosis and a psychotherapeutic adjunct. These views have tempered with time.

With respect to possible biological effects of LSD, there have been conflicting reports of chromosomal damage, with uncertainty expressed as to the ultimate significance of these findings. An underlying concern has been that chromosomal changes found by some investigators have also been observed in survivors of the atomic bombing of Hiroshima and might be related to an increased probability of developing leukemia-like disorders.

In 1970 the National Institute of Mental Health was the only legal supplier of LSD for research purposes in the country. The Institute has supported research projects investigating the value of this drug as a therapeutic agent in the treatment of alcoholism and schizophrenia, as well as basic research into the mechanism of action and total biological activity of hallucinogenic drugs. Scientists working with LSD have also been studying the possible adverse biological effects of LSD use, in particular the genetic consequences. Several investigators have reported chromosomal aberrations from their studies with LSD. Others have been unable to replicate these results. Since there have been few before-and-after studies in man on the biological effects of LSD, and since the current data are contradictory, there is no clear evidence at this time of chromosomal damage in humans resulting from LSD usage. However, on the basis of presumptive evidence and animal studies, it seems clear that the use of LSD should be avoided particularly by women in the child-bearing years. The information currently available about the biological hazards of LSD and other hallucinogenic drugs is incomplete and requires much additional research.

ABNORMAL BEHAVIOR IN ANIMALS

It is not generally known that a wide range of behavior disorders observed in man are also found in lower animals. While it is always dangerous to make analogies from the behavior of lower animals to that of man, the weight of the clinical evidence indicates that there are indeed very impressive parallels between disorganized behavior in man and lower animals.

Animals characteristically react to severe stress with behavior disturbances. Following a serious flooding of a coastal area of Great Britain, veterinarians reported that many house pets shared a decrease in appetite, depression, a tendency to hide in dark corners and under furniture, and a refusal to venture outside. Spontaneous recovery occurred in many mild cases within a few days. Other animals required treatment with sedatives (Mitchell, 1953). Similar cases were seen in Great Britain during World War II. Cats retreated into cupboards and other dark places, refusing to emerge and rushing back into hiding if forcibly removed. As a result of the nightly bombing and gunfire over several months, treatment was futile, and the animals did not recover (Joshua, 1968).

Neurotic-like behavior also occurs in animals. The following description of the behavior of a female dachshund reported by a veterinarian in Austria shows a clear relationship between symptoms and events in the environment:

> This dog would vomit if left alone in the house, when laborers were working in it, if furniture was moved, or if suitcases were packed. Also if something suddenly occurred (in or outside the apartment) that diverted the interest of the owner and his wife so that the dog was not the center of attraction as it was accustomed to being, it would fall onto its side and extend its limbs and twist its neck as though experiencing a fit. The symptoms began after the dog had been exposed at the age of 1½ years to a series of family arguments, during which time suitcases frequently were packed. The convulsive-like behavior disappeared at once if everybody left the room; the dog would then get up and follow (Brunner, 1968).

Animals also show depressed behavior. One dog, a Doberman pinscher, first showed the symptoms after the death of a tomcat with which the dog grew up and shared sleeping quarters. It refused to eat and was no longer playful; it would wait at the front door, search the room, and appear generally listless. A German boxer became depressed following the death of its owner, with whom the dog had lived continuously for nine years. Its appetite failed, it lost weight, paced the room during the night, was listless and apathetic,

Figure 16.5 *Because it is depressed, this unhappy and lonely infant monkey clutches itself for comfort and security. (University of Wisconsin Regional Primate Research Center.)*

and showed no guarding behavior when strangers knocked at the door. Treatment with tranquilizers was unsuccessful, and the boxer died two months later from uncertain causes (Brunner, 1968).

Homosexual behavior has been observed in many animals. Monkeys and apes form homosexual pairs for various periods, with the same individuals taking up heterosexual relations later on (Meyer-Holzapsel, 1968). An observation of considerable interest is that male ducks can be made homosexual by rearing them together in groups of five to ten individuals for a period of at least seventy-five days. Male ducks reared in this way form homosexual pairs when liberated upon a lake in spite of the presence of many females. Female ducks, however, never become homosexual if reared under the same conditions as the males (Schultz, 1965).

Disorganized behavior on a collective basis also occurs in animals. The behavior of a herd of horses or cattle can reach panic proportions as the result of the agitation of a single animal. Sometimes the action is motivated by a noise or lightning, or the cause may be vague or not apparent. In either case, the agitation leads to a wild flight. The other horses show the same behavior through what appears to be a contagious imitation. Similar collective symptoms have been observed in cattle at pasture when the entire herd shows foot stamping, pacing, agitation, and mad running (Chertok and Fontaine, 1965).

EXPERIMENTAL BEHAVIOR BREAKDOWN

One of the continuing interests of research workers in experimental psychopathology has been the attempt to create laboratory analogs of behavior disorders in animals. Most of the work has been directed toward inducing "experimental neuroses" by means of conditioning and other learning techniques. Studies have also been undertaken to determine how drugs and other chemicals bring about pathological behavior in animals.

Conditioning Techniques

Beginning early in the present century with the experiments of the Russian neurophysiologist Ivan Pavlov, there has been a persistent interest in the use of classical conditioning to produce experimental behavior breakdown. A second research approach has been the induction of experimental behavior disorders in animals by means of drugs in an attempt to simulate disturbances found in man. The value of being able to produce behavior disturbances in the laboratory is that a careful study can be made of the exact conditions under which such behavior develops. It becomes possible to analyze conditions which interfere with the development of the disorder and to test treatment measures designed to get rid of the disorder once it has been established.

In his classic studies of the influence of the central nervous system on the digestive glands, Pavlov trained dogs to stand quietly in a special frame while gastric juice or saliva was collected. Small portions of food were presented to the dog, and the amount of salivary secretion was measured. Pavlov also found that he could train his dogs to secrete saliva in anticipation of food when certain signals were given before the actual feeding.

During one of the experiments, an unexpected observation led to the development of Pavlov's interest in behavior disorders. A dog was shown a circle marked on a card and was trained to salivate in expectation of food given after each display of the card. Through conditioning, an excitatory reflex was established. This same dog was also trained not to salivate if the card was marked with an ellipse rather than a circle. Through conditioning, an inhibitory reflex was established. When these two responses were well established, the ellipse was gradually made more and more like a circle. When the dog could no longer differentiate between the circle and the ellipse, the resulting conflict precipitated a behavior disturbance. The dog became restless and uncooperative, refused to eat, and howled and struggled in his harness. Pavlov described the behavior of the animal in the following way:

The hitherto quiet dog began to squeal in its stand, kept wriggling about, tore off with its teeth the apparatus for mechanical stimulation of the skin, and bit through the tubes connecting the animal's room with the observer, a behavior which never happened be-

(a)

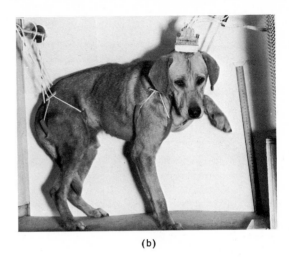

(b)

Figure 16.6 *Brain stimulation conditioning studies at the Center for Brain Research, University of Rochester. (a) Electrode connector assembly fixed to the skull of an experimental animal. (b) A characteristic conditioned response in the form of the lifting of a foreleg. (Courtesy of Dr. Robert W. Doty.)*

fore. On being taken into the experimental room the dog now barked violently, which was also contrary to its usual custom; in short, it presented all the symptoms of a condition of acute neurosis (Pavlov, 1941).

Pavlov used the term *experimental neurosis* to describe the behavior of his dogs, since the animals showed objective symptoms similar in many respects to those seen in neurotic men and women. He found that experimental behavior disorders in animals could be produced under three conditions: (1) when extremely powerful stimuli which overstrain the excitatory processes of the animal are used as conditioned stimuli in place of weaker stimuli which ordinarily produce the animal's activity, (2) when the animal is required to utilize excessively strong inhibitions so that the inhibitory processes are overtaxed, and (3) when a conflict is produced by means of presenting

conditioned positive and negative stimuli in rapid sequence.

Some of the most extensive work on the development of experimental neuroses in animals by means of conditioning has been carried out at the Pavlovian Laboratory at Johns Hopkins University. The case of Nick is a classic study. The experimental work with this dog was begun in 1932, and observations of the animal's behavior continued until he was accidentally killed in a fight with another dog in 1944.

Nick was trained to differentiate between two tones, one of which was reinforced by food while the other was not. After the experiment had continued for a few months, the two tones, one excitatory and the other inhibitory, were brought closer together in pitch until it became increasingly difficult to distinguish the pitch of the two tones. The dog became extremely agitated and refused

Figure 16.7 *W. Horsley Gantt, 1893–   , distinguished research scientist in the field of experimental psychiatry and founder and director of the Pavlovian Laboratory at Johns Hopkins University. (Courtesy of Roche Laboratories, Medical Image.)*

to eat the food that was offered when the tone was sounded. During this period, the dog showed such symptoms as extreme restlessness, panting, rapid heart rate, and attempts to escape from the experimental room.

Experiments with Nick were discontinued in 1934, and he was brought to the experimental room only occasionally for observation. In spite of prolonged rest, the dog showed an exaggeration of the previous symptoms and developed various additional symptoms including asthmatic-like breathing and abnormal sexual reactions. The symptoms appeared only when he was brought into the experimental room or when some element of the experimental environment was presented to him (Gantt, 1944).

Another center for research in conditioning was established at Cornell University in 1926, where work was begun with experimental behavior dis-

orders in sheep. The sheep were taken from the fold to the laboratory and placed on a platform where they were fastened to a beam overhead by loops of cord around their bodies. While the animals were in this position, food was given at the beginning and end of each experiment. As a result of this feeding procedures, after a few days the animals ran forward and tugged on their rope as they were led from the fold to the laboratory, climbed on the platform on their own accord, and remained standing quietly for several hours.

The experiments began by determining a threshold intensity of an electric shock sufficient to evoke the bending of the foreleg. No sign of nervousness or stubborness was observed in this connection. The experimenters then sought to secure a delayed conditioned reaction to the ticking of a metronome. When this training was speeded up by increasing the number of tests per day, the animals became restive and nervous. Whereas they formerly stood quietly on the platform between the tests, they now became extremely restless. Also, the animals no longer appeared willing to go to the laboratory. They had formerly run to the laboratory, pulling the attendants along with them, but now they tried to run away. They had to be dragged or pushed to the place of the experiment and then lifted to the platform (Liddell, 1952).

In a different conditioning procedure, cats were trained to respond to a signal, such as a flash of light or the sound of a bell, by opening a box to secure food. The animals were then trained to step on a switch which would operate the feeding signals any time they wished. During the training, the cats remained friendly, entered the training cage willingly, and operated the switch efficiently. Later in the experiment, the animals were permitted to work the switch and to reach for the food, but from time to time there was an unexpected air blast or electric shock. The cats never knew when this painful and unpleasant experience would result from the switch. At times there would be food without the painful and unpleasant stimulus, while at other times the animals would have to cope with this stimulus. As a result, an intense conflict was established, and disorganized patterns of behavior appeared. The animals would crouch, tremble, breathe rapidly, and develop a pounding pulse and an increase in blood pressure. The symptoms were similar to those seen in human anxiety reactions.

In an extension of the experiments, animals lost some of their fear and anxiety when they were fed small amounts of dilute alcohol solution. When mildly intoxicated, the animals would once again return to their feeding on signal, in spite of the threat of the air blast or electric shock. The cats associated the smell or taste of alcohol with their loss of fear and soon came to prefer the alcohol solution to plain milk. As soon as the effects of the alcohol wore off, the animals returned to their state of fear and anxiety. A type of experimental alcohol addiction had thus been established (Masserman, 1943).

In another laboratory, an electrode was attached to the tail of a cat and another electrode to the tail of a mouse. The mouse was then put with the cat, and since the cat was very hungry it pounced on the mouse. Upon contact, the electrical circuit was closed, and the cat received an electric shock. After only one experience of this type, a neurotic reaction appeared in the cat. It dropped the mouse from its mouth and ran away in an attempt to hide. Before the experiment, a mouse was the strongest food stimulus for the cat, but afterward, the mouse was able to remain close to the cat and even to climb over its back and head.

The movements of the cat were inhibited whenever the mouse was nearby. However, the electrocardiogram of the cat showed a speeded-up heart rate and other changes. The sight of a mouse brought about these changes in the cat even a month after the traumatic experience (Kurtsin, 1968).

Behavior disorders have also been produced in monkeys by first training them to give various responses to obtain food. When these responses were well established, a toy snake was presented in the food box. The animals reacted to the conflict between hunger and fear by developing various behavior deviations. Some of the animals retreated, some showed apprehensiveness, patterns for securing food were altered, and there were disturbances in feeding. Gastrointestinal dysfunctions were observed, and there were motor disturbances, sexual deviations, phobias, changes in social behavior, and altered relationships with the experimenter.

The behavior disturbances in the monkeys were sufficiently progressive and persistent to interfere seriously with their health and well-being. For as long as a year after the experiment, their behavior remained essentially unchanged in spite of the fact that the environment was made as pleasant and nontraumatic as possible. Medication and special diet were necessary to keep some

Figure 16.8 *The conditioning frame used to study experimental behavior disorders in animals at the Cornell University Behavior Farm Laboratory. (Courtesy of* Scientific American.*)*

of the animals alive while encouragement of the individual animal was sufficient treatment in other cases. In more dependent animals, a form of group therapy was observed whereby action of the less dependent animals encouraged the others, and this pattern led to relatively symptom-free re-adaptation. The animals which adapted well to general laboratory routine, which learned efficiently, and which explored various substitute maneuvers in their initial efforts to resolve conflicts subsequently showed a greater resistance to stress situations. Also, these animals responded more readily to therapy (Masserman and Pechtel, 1953).

Another pioneer in the study of experimental behavior disorders in animals used a modified Lashley jumping apparatus in training rats to discriminate between two circles differing in brightness and background. The rats were trained so that when they jumped at a door with a black circle, the door would open and they would be rewarded with food. However, if the rat jumped at the door with a white circle, the door would not open, and the animal would strike against the closed door and fall into a basket beneath the apparatus. Repetitions of this experience made it possible for the rats to learn quickly that they must always jump to the door with the black circle, and not to the door with the white circle.

After the jumping pattern was well established, conflict was introduced into the situation. In one experiment, only one door was presented to the animal, and this door contained the white circle to which the animal had learned not to jump. However, the experimenter forced jumping by directing a blast of air toward the animal. Some animals jumped but attempted to avoid the door, and others remained passively on the platform. A number of rats showed marked behavior disturbances. They jumped to the floor, ran in circles, made tic-like movements with their heads, pounded the floor with their forepaws, and finally went into a catatonic-like state in which they could be molded into any position by the experimenter (Maier, 1939).

This work led to a controversy about whether the critical factor was the conflict or the sound of the air blast. The investigator insisted it was the conflict, since he found such seizures occurring nine times more frequently when air blast was used with conflict than when air blast was used alone. Other investigators, however, emphasized the importance of the auditory stimulation.

It is now clear that the auditory stimulation plays a critical role in the development of seizures in rats. It had been observed as early as the 1920s that when rats in the laboratory heard the sound of jingling keys, they sometimes raced about frantically, running and jumping until they were exhausted. However, the phenomenon was not subjected to careful study until Maier's work in 1938, when it was found that not only the hiss of air, but also the high-pitched tones of a Galton whistle, the ringing of a bell, or the sound of a buzzer could bring on the convulsive pattern. Generally, high frequencies are more effective than low frequencies and continuous sound more effective than interrupted sound, but exceptions are frequent.

There are a number of advantages to the audiogenic method of inducing abnormal behavior in animals. It requires neither complex apparatus nor highly experienced investigators, and the time element is minimized considerably. Not only can a number of animals be tested in a single experimental session, but group testing has little or no effect upon the appearance of the disorganized and convulsive states. Finally, the situation can be easily reproduced in any laboratory, and the technique can be demonstrated before large groups of observers.

The maze method has also been used to induce experimental behavior disorders in animals. In a series of studies of rats in a spatial maze, behavior disorders were observed which were similar to those induced in the conditional response experiments. The rats were trained to run a relatively simple maze which was readily learned by the animals. When, however, an attempt was made to teach the same animals a modified sequence, the disruption of behavior appeared even though no punishment was used (Carmichael, 1938).

An experimental behavior disorder was also observed in a cat learning to run a difficult maze. The cat had been a docile subject, entering the maze willingly and learning rapidly. In 230 trials he had reached an accuracy level of 90 percent correct choices. The stress of the difficult learning situation finally became too much for the animal. On the next trial, a dramatic change in behavior was observed. The animal hesitated much longer than usual at the choice point, finally jumped into another alley, and then raced to the front of the maze. During the remainder of the trial, he worked slowly and whimpered continually. He began to resist entering the maze, attempted to escape from it, refused to work at times, meowed loudly, and urinated at maze points where he had to choose which turn to take. There was a progressive increase in emotional disturbance and in the number of errors. The cat regressed to an incorrect-response pattern typical of the earlier phases of training (Karn, 1938). In a similar study of maze learning, disorganized behavior was observed in a dog. The activity of the animal was characterized by rapid movements in the maze, head-turning, pronounced trembling, and whining. Here the behavior appeared before it was possible to determine the extent of learning which had taken place (Karn and Malamud, 1939).

The objection to the concept of the experimental neurosis in these cases is that it is dangerous to make an analogy between the behavior of lower animals and the behavior of man. The mere labeling of disturbed animal behavior as an experimental neurosis does not necessarily make the behavior comparable to a neurosis in man. Despite this reservation, some of the behavior disorders in lower animals bear a close resemblance to the behavior disorders of man.

Drugs and Chemical Studies

Experimental behavior disorders have also been induced in animals by means of drugs and other chemicals. The drug most frequently used has been *bulbocapnine*, an alkaloid extracted from the plant bulbs of *corydalis cava*. While bulbocapnine was used as early as 1904 to produce a state of catalepsy, or muscular rigidity, in the cat, the most important point in the development of bulbocapnine research was reached in 1920 (DeJong, 1945). Injection of bulbocapnine in small doses in mammals produces catalepsy, organic and vegetative disorders, and other elements of a cata-

tonic-like syndrome. Larger doses lead to typical convulsive seizures.

These results are obtained only in mammals with a fully developed cerebral cortex. In animals with an incompletely developed cortex, such as birds, only a partial and unstable catalepsy can be obtained. In animals lacking a cortex, such as fish and reptiles, bulbocapnine produces convulsions. These findings suggest that cortical factors may be important in the development of the catatonic syndrome in human subjects.

Experimental catalepsy has also been induced in animals by means of various other substances, including toxins, the breakdown products of mescaline and adrenalin, insulin, nicotine, and deuterium, or heavy water. Subcutaneous injections of the *B. coli* toxin produce pathological sleep, a catatonic syndrome characterized by negativism and aggression, or vegetative disorders. It is also possible to bring about a state of stupor in animals by means of injecting them with insulin.

Studies on the behavior of animals in which an opiate addiction has been experimentally induced show that the drug-influenced behavior survives morphine abstinence for weeks. This fact suggests a similarity to the sustained drug-influenced behavior of human addicts. Differences among rat strains have been identified, and animals can be classified as addiction-prone and addiction-resistant. This finding suggests that inherent physiological characteristics seemingly genetically transmitted—play a part in the animal's proneness to addiction.[4]

NEW DIRECTIONS IN TREATMENT

It was pointed out in Chapter 15 that there has been a continuing and growing dissatisfaction among psychologists and psychiatrists with psychological treatment techniques. This dissatisfaction has been primarily in terms of the lack of significant changes in behavior even after intensive therapy. It has not been clear whether

---

[4]A book of unusual interest dealing with disorganized behavior in animals is *Abnormal Behavior in Animals* (Saunders, 1968), edited by M. W. Fox. An earlier important book is W. H. Gantt's *Experimental Basis for Neurotic Behavior* (Hoeber, 1944).

the poor results have been due to unknown factors involving the therapist, the patient, the therapeutic relationship, or some combination of these factors. For this reason, a number of studies have been directed toward these variables. There has been a continuing research interest in the personality characteristics of the therapist, the type of individual most likely to respond to therapy, and the conditions of the therapist-patient relationship.

Because psychological treatment has not been as effective as most therapists would wish, a wide range of innovative approaches have been used. For example, the conventional therapy group has been extended to include unusual and controversial procedures. Group therapy in the nude is one of the procedures which make it difficult to distinguish between sensationalism and science.

The general decline in conventional psychotherapy as a treatment method has resulted in a marked shift in interest in the direction of behavior modification techniques. The behavior therapy approach, based as it is on a theory of conditioning, does not require the personal relationship between patient and therapist that is so much a part of conventional psychotherapy. As a result, the behavior therapy approach lends itself to automation.

Various electronic devices have been used to reinforce desired responses. Audiotapes and videotapes have been combined with delivery systems which automatically produce a reward when appropriate responses are made. In this way, behavior can be systematically shaped and modified in line with the goals of treatment in a particular case.

Some of the most exciting and controversial research in the field of psychological treatment is the use of a computer to simulate (play the role of) the therapist. Computers have been programmed to carry on a simple treatment dialog which is similar to the probing questions asked by a therapist during the early sessions of treatment. The person being treated types out his questions and answers, and these are transmitted to the computer by means of teletype. The computer then sends back a typewritten reply.

The typewritten dialog between the person being treated and the computer is so realistic that trained psychiatrists who read the material without knowing how it was obtained agree that it is an adequate interview. Since it is without emotions, the computer does not become distracted and may be better able than a human interviewer to probe into the background, the feelings, and the attitudes of the person being treated.

The following material is a part of a typewritten exchange between a computer and a subject.

COMPUTER: I would like to know more about your background, especially about your family life.
PERSON: My father and mother did not get along well.
COMPUTER: Tell me something else you think is important about your father.
PERSON: He was hard to live with because he was so domineering.
COMPUTER: Are you like your father?
PERSON: No, I am not.
COMPUTER: In some way though you must be like your father.
PERSON: He liked to fish and I do too.
COMPUTER: Did you admire him when you were young?
PERSON: I don't think so.
COMPUTER: Why not?
PERSON: Because he was too weak a person.
COMPUTER: I see. Now tell me something else about him.
PERSON: Well, he was very opinionated.
COMPUTER: Was there much friction between you and him when you were growing up?
PERSON: Yes. We fought all the time.
COMPUTER: Perhaps you were afraid of him.
PERSON: I certainly was. He used to really blow up.
COMPUTER: Perhaps you are still fearful of older men.
PERSON: Let's talk about something else.
COMPUTER: O.K. Go ahead. I will try to follow what you have to say about it (Colby and Enea, 1967).

How is this feat accomplished? Through a complex method of programming, the computer is able to recognize several hundred key words and phrases—for example, "my mother," "my father," "I worry," "I hate." The computer then selects a response from a group of replies that are appropriate to the key word or phrase that has been recognized. The computer also stores and keeps a record of key topics. When the subject types a sentence that is not related to the key words, the computer is programmed to bring the person back to the critical topic. While the computer is limited to relatively simple questioning, clarifying, and rephrasing, the potential for more extensive probing, and even interpretation, exists.

It is not possible to say at this time how far computer technology will take us in the treatment of psychological disorders. Critics of the method are concerned about the lack of human contact, absence of emotional relationship, and general coldness of the approach. There is evidence, however, that the human relationship is not of primary importance in modifying human behavior. If this is indeed the case, there would seem to be no technological reason why a very highly sophisticated form of computer-based therapy could not be developed. The advantages in terms of economics and bringing treatment services to very large numbers of people who now receive minimal services would be incalculable.[5]

SUMMARY

1. While the experimental approach to the problems of abnormal psychology reaches back at least to the beginning of the present century, there has been a new emphasis on experimental and innovative approaches to the problems of mental disorder. This research approach had its beginnings in the study of individual differences, the action of drugs, interest in the relationship between brain functions and behavior, the behavior disturbances of animals, and some of the more traditional problems of experimental psychology.

2. The brain-behavior relationship remains an area of innovative investigation. Studies of the effects of brain stimulation continue to interest psychologists and psychiatrists because such studies throw new light on brain functions. The most advanced areas of brain-behavior research deal with the electronic monitoring of the nervous system under stress and other conditions related to psychological disturbance.

3. The mind-altering drugs have been a source of research interest because behavior influenced by them often resembles the behavior of disturbed individuals. Included in this group—referred to as *hallucinogens* and *psychotomimetic* drugs—are marijuana (cannabis), mescaline (peyote), and LSD (lysergic acid diethylamide). While the possible damaging effects of these drugs have not been clarified, the experimental psychopathologist finds them a source of very great interest because they make it possible to simulate mental disorder in the laboratory.

4. The study of animals, both in their natural state and under laboratory conditions, also makes possible a relatively controlled investigation of disturbed behavior. While it is recognized that one cannot always generalize from the behavior of lower animals to that of man, most psychologists and psychiatrists recognize a number of very striking parallels between some forms of disturbed behavior in lower animals and behavior observed in man. Most interest has been centered on the use of conditioning techniques to induce disturbed behavior in animals and on the use of drugs and other chemical means to interfere with the animal's normal behavior. Through the development of animal models of abnormal behavior, researchers can study possible causes of disorder and test the effectiveness of treatment methods.

---

[5]The research approach applied to psychological treatment is developed in *Methods of Research in Psychotherapy* (Appleton, 1966) by L. A. Gottschalk and A. A. Auerbach; *The Investigation of Psychotherapy* (Wiley, 1966), edited by A. P. Goldstein and S. J. Dean; and *Psychotherapy Research: Selected Readings* (Rand McNally 1966), edited by Gary Stollak et al.

5. Interest in new approaches to psychological treatment has persisted because of a general dissatisfaction with the effectiveness of currently available techniques. Supportive, reeducative, and reconstructive forms of individual psychotherapy have generally been disappointing except in very highly selected cases. The result has been the exploration of a number of new types of group experience as forms of treatment. The most innovative approach is the use of the computer as a supplement to treatment. While this use is now limited to the gathering of relatively simple information about the patient, there is a definite possibility that we are on the threshold of an entirely new field of computer-assisted treatment.

GLOSSARY

This glossary is designed primarily to help the student understand the textbook and related readings. Synonyms and descriptive phrases frequently are substituted for definitions. The student who is interested in more exact and complete definitions is referred to the third edition of the *Psychiatric Dictionary* (Oxford University Press, 1960); *Blakiston's Gould Medical Dictionary* (McGraw-Hill, 1972); and *A Comprehensive Dictionary of Psychological and Psychoanalytical Terms* (David McKay Company, Inc., 1958).

Ablation: Surgical removal of part of the body.

Abortion: Expulsion of the embryo from the uterus during the first three months of pregnancy.

Abreaction: Release of emotion by reliving a traumatic experience.

Abscess: Area of pus resulting from disintegration of tissue.

Acetylcholine: Chemical mediator in the transmission of the nerve impulse; neurohormone.

Achondroplasia: Abnormal development of the bones resulting in dwarfism.

Acrocephaly: Distortion of the skull giving the head a steeple-shaped appearance; oxycephaly.

Acrophobia: Fear of heights.

ACTH: Adrenocorticotropic hormone.

Acute mania: Second stage in the development of the manic reaction.

Addison's disease: Syndrome resulting from an underproduction of adrenocortical hormones.

Ademine: Basic chemical unit of the DNA molecule.

Adenoma: Nonmalignant tumor of glandular origin.

Adrenal cortex: External portion of the adrenal gland.

Adrenal glands Endocrine glands located adjacent to the kidneys.

Adrenal medulla: Inside core of the adrenal gland.

Adrenalin: Hormone of the adrenal medulla having a stimulating effect on the sympathetic nervous system; epinephrine.

Adrenochrome: Breakdown product of noradrenalin; hallucinogenic substance.

Adrenocorticotrophic hormone: Secretion of the anterior pituitary gland which stimulates the adrenal cortex.

Adrenolutin: Breakdown product of noradrenalin; hallucinogenic substance.

Adrenolytic: Having the ability to offset the action of substances which stimulate the sympathetic nervous system.

Adrenosterone: Secretion of the adrenal cortex; related to sexual development.

ADS: Antidiuretic chemical secreted by the posterior pituitary gland.

Affect: Feeling or emotional tone.

Affective disorder Personality disturbance marked by extremes in mood.

Affective incontinence: Lack of emotional restraint.

Afferent nerves: Peripheral nerves which carry impulses from receptors to the central nervous system; sensory nerves.

Aftercare movement: Program of assistance for mental patients following their release from the hospital.

Age regression: Technique in hypnosis by means of which a patient is taken back to an earlier period in life.

Agnosia: Inability to recognize persons or objects.

Agoraphobia: Fear of open places.

Aichmophobia: Fear of pointed objects.

Alarm reaction: First stage of the general adaptation syndrome.

Alcoholic hallucinosis: Brain syndrome due to alcoholism and characterized by delusions and hallucinations, often of a persecutory nature.

Alkalosis: Abnormally alkaline condition of the blood.

Alpha-2-globulin: Chemical suspected of influencing cell membranes and causing other chemicals to act abnormally both inside and outside the cell.

Alpha waves: Ten-per-second brain waves.

Alzheimer's disease: Presenile brain disorder.

Ambivalent: Having contradictory feelings or attitudes.

Amebic dysentery: Form of inflammation of the intestines.

Amenorrhea: Decrease or complete cessation of menstruation.

Amentia: Mental retardation.

Amitriptyline: Antidepressive drug.

Amnesia: Loss of memory.

Amok: Personality disturbance characterized by sudden outbursts of aggression; reported among the Malays.

Amphetamine sulphate: Antidepressant drug; Benzedrine.

Anal stage: Level of psychosexual development.

Analeptic drug: Restorative drug, facilitating respiration and wakefulness.

Analytical psychology: Theory of personality advanced by Carl G. Jung.

Androgen: Male sex hormone.

Anemia: Decrease in red blood cells leading to a deficiency in the oxygen-carrying capacity of the blood.

Anencephaly: Complete absence of the cerebrum, cerebellum, and flat bones of the skull.

Anesthesia: Loss of sensitivity to stimuli.

Angina syndrome: Pain in the region of the heart.

Animism: Belief that the world is controlled by supernatural beings.

Anomaly: Obvious deviation from type.

Anorexia nervosa: Psychogenic loss of appetite.

Anoxemia: Deficiency of oxygen in the blood and tissues.

Anoxic shock therapy: Physical treatment based on shock induced by gas of various kinds.

Anticholinergic drug: Drug which inhibits action of parasympathetic branch of autonomic nervous system.

Anti-insulin hormone: Secretion of the anterior pituitary gland influencing the insulin-producing tissue of the pancreas.

Antimetabolite: Chemical compound shaped to resemble a neurohormone but having minor structural differences.

Anxiety: Psychophysiologic reaction to threat.

Apathy Absence of emotional response.

Aphasia: Inability to understand or use language meaningfully.

Aphonia: Inability to speak above a whisper.

Aplasia: Absence or impaired development of an organ or part of the body.

Apnoea: Breathing difficulty.

Apraxia: Loss of ability to perform purposeful movement in the absence of paralysis or sensory disturbance.

Archetype: Original model or type.

Arctic hysteria: Personality disturbance observed among the natives of Northern Siberia; marked by a high degree of suggestibility.

Argyll Robertson pupil: Neurological sign in which the pupil of the eye reacts to accommodation but not to light; sign of brain syphilis and other diseases.

Arteriosclerosis: Hardening of the arteries.

Ascorbic acid: Vitamin C.

Asthenic: Weak.

Asthenic type: Tall and thin body type described by Kretschmer.

Astrocytoma: Form of brain tumor.

Ataractic drug: Tranquilizing drug.

Ataraxia: State of detached serenity without loss of consciousness produced by tranquilizing drugs.

Ataxia: Impairment of muscular coordination.

Athetosis: Involuntary movements of the limbs due to inadequate control of the muscles.

Athletic type: Muscular type described by Kretschmer.

Atrophy: Wasting or shrinking of body tissues.

Audiogenic seizure: Sound-induced convulsive seizure.

Aura: Characteristic warning experience preceding a convulsive seizure.

Autokinetic effect: Apparent movement of a fixed point of light in a darkened room.

Automatic writing: Writing without conscious control.

Autonomic: Self-governing; relatively independent.

Autonomic nervous system: Vegetative nervous system.

Avitaminosis: Vitamin deficiency.

Babinski reflex: Neurological sign in certain organic disorders of the nervous system.

Barbital: Sedative drug.

Basal ganglion: Mass of gray matter in the subcortex.

Basal metabolic rate: Minimum rate at which heat is produced by a person at rest; a measure of vital functioning.

Benign: Relatively mild.

Benzedrine: Synthetic stimulant to the central nervous system.

Berger rhythm: Brain wave.

Beta rhythm: Brain wave; shallower and faster than the alpha rhythm.

Bhang: See *Marijuana*.

Bibliotherapy: Use of reading for cure of psychological disorders.

Bimodal stimulant: Drug having a direct stimulating action on the central nervous system and a slower-acting effect as a result of the inhibition of monoamine oxidase.

Binet test: Comprehensive scale of intelligence.

Biotelemetry: Recording biological functions of animals or humans by means of radio signals and similar means.

Biotin: Vitamin H.

Biovular twins: Fraternal twins; dizygotic twins.

Birth trauma: Shock of birth.

Birth-injury palsy: See *Cerebral palsy*.

Bisexual: Having the characteristics of both sexes.

BMR: See *Basal metabolic rate*.

Body image: Mental image one has of his own body.

Bromide: Sedative and anticonvulsant drug.

Bufotenine: Naturally occurring structural analogue of serotonin; hallucinogenic substance.

Bulbocapnine: Plant alkaloid used to induce experimental catatonia.

Bulimia: Excessive appetite.

Cannabis indica: Indian hemp.

Carbonic anhydrase: Enzyme.

Cardiazol: Metrazol.

Cardiovascular: Pertaining to the heart and blood vessels.

Carotene: Vitamin A.

Castration anxiety: Fear of genital injury.

Catalepsy: Characterized by muscular rigidity.

Catecholamines: Chemical substances suspected of playing a role in certain types of depressions.

Cathexis: Channeling and fixation of libido.

Cerea flexibilitas: Waxy flexibility sometimes seen in catatonic schizophrenia.

Cerebellum: Brain structure related to the control of movement and body coordination.

Cerebral diplegia: See *Cerebral palsy*.

Cerebral dysrhythmia: Abnormal rhythm of the brain waves.

Cerebral injection: Form of psychosurgery in which the frontal lobes are injected with alcohol, procaine, or other solutions.

Cerebral palsy: Motor disability associated with organic brain damage or malformation.

Cerebral topectomy: Form of psychosurgery in which a thin slice of cortical tissue is cut from each of the frontal lobes.

Cerebrotonia: Personality type inclined toward intellectual pursuits; associated with the ectomorph body type described by Sheldon.

Cerebrum: Largest and most recently developed part of the human brain; the two-lobed structure growing as an extension of the brainstem.

Ceruloplasmin: Copper protein in the serum of the body.

CFF: Critical flicker frequency.

Chloral hydrate: Sedative drug.

Chlorpromazine: Tranquilizer of the phenothiazine group.

Choleric: Angry and irritable.

Cholesterol: Unsaturated alcohol of the class of sterols; constituent of all animal fats and oils.

Cholinergic drug: Drug which stimulates the parasympathetic nervous system.

Cholinesterase: Enzyme.

Chorea: Neurological condition marked by incoordinate movements of the head and extremities.

Choroid plexus: Pertaining to a system of delicate blood vessels in the brain.

Circumstantial: Irrelevant.

Claustrophobia: Fear of closed places.

Climacterium: Change of life; the menopause.

Clonic phase: Second phase of the *grand mal* convulsion; involuntary contractions and relaxations of the musculature.

Cocaine: Drug obtained from the leaves of the coca plant.

Coconscious: Not conscious but capable of becoming conscious.

Colitis: Inflammation of the colon.

Collective unconscious: That part of the unconscious which is inherited; racial unconscious.

Colloidal gold curve: Biochemical index used in the detection of syphilis and other infectious disorders.

Coma: Stupor.

Compensation: Defense mechanism; attempt to overcome inferiority.

Complex: Group of emotionally toned ideas that have been repressed.

Compulsion: Unwelcome repetitive action.

Conceptual quotient: Index of intellectual efficiency and mental deterioration.

Concordance: Similarity of characteristics in twins.

Concussion: Neurological disturbance produced by a severe blow to the head or spinal column; associated with such symptoms as shock, unconsciousness, and paralysis.

Condensation: Telescoping images in a dream.

Confabulation: Filling in memory gaps.

Congenital: Existing from birth.

Conjunctival hyperemia: Condition in which the eyes have a "bloodshot" appearance.

Constitution: Total biological make-up of an individual.

Content analysis: Analysis of projective test responses in terms of their symbolic meanings.

Conversion reaction: Neurotic condition in which anxiety is converted into physical symptoms.

Convolution: Irregular fold of the outer surface of the brain.

Convulsion: Pathological muscular contraction.

Coprophilia: Sexual attraction to excretory processes and products.

Cortex: Outer or surface layer of the brain or other organ.

Cortical frequency spectrum: Range of electrical waves produced by the brain.

Cortical undercutting: Form of psychosurgery in which brain tissue is cut at the junction of the gray and white matter in the prefrontal cortex.

Corticosterone: Hormone of the adrenal cortex.

Corticotropin: Anterior pituitary hormone which regulates the activity of the adrenal cortex.

Cortin: Substance containing several hormones and extracted from the adrenal cortex.

Cortisone: Hormone produced by the adrenal cortex.

Co-twin control: Method of studying the hereditary factor in mental illness of twins.

Countertransference: Emotional attachment of the therapist to the patient.

Covert: Concealed or disguised.

CQ: Conceptual quotient.

Cranial anomaly: Abnormal structure of the bones of the head.

Craniostenosis: Premature closing of the cranial sutures.

Cretinism: Mental and physical retardation resulting from thyroid insufficiency during fetal life or early infancy.

Cryptogenic: Of unknown origin.

Curare: Drug which paralyzes motor nerves.

CVA: Cerebrovascular accident; a "stroke."

Cyanocobalamin: Vitamin B_{12}.

Cyanosis: Bluish discoloration of the skin due to lack of oxygen.

Cyclazocine: Drug used in treatment of heroin addiction.

Cycloid: Pertaining to relatively marked fluctuations of mood.

Cyclothymia: Personality pattern marked by alternating periods of elation and depression.

Cyclothymic: Showing marked mood swings.

Cytomegalic inclusion body disease: Infectious condition in which a maternal virus infects the fetus; may be associated with mental retardation.

Cytosine: Basic chemical unit of the DNA molecule.

Death instinct: Tendency of the id to strive toward death and destruction; thanatos.

Decarboxylation: Metabolic breakdown process.

Decerebration: Removal of the cerebrum.

Decortication: Removal of the cortex, or parts of it.

Defense mechanism: Technique used by an individual to avoid what is unpleasant or anxiety-provoking.

Dehydrated: Lacking in water.

Delahara: Personality disturbance similar to Amok; observed in the Philippines.

Delirium tremens: Acute delirium precipitated by alcohol and associated with anxiety, tremors, hallucinations, and delusions.

Delta wave: Slow EEG wave seen during sleep and brain pathology.

Delusion: Belief contrary to reality and held in spite of evidence and common sense.

Dementia: Impairment of mental functioning.

Dementia paralytica: See *Paresis*.

Demerol: Narcotic derived from morphine.

Demography: Analysis of population variables.

Demonology: View that mental illness is caused by possession by the Devil.

Depersonalization: Loss of sense of reality or identity.

Depth therapy: Reconstructive psychotherapy.

Dermatotropic: Influencing or involving the skin.

Desoxycorticosterone: Hormone produced by the adrenal cortex which acts on mineral metabolism.

Deterioration: Progressive impairment of function.

Deterioration index: Measure of intellectual deterioration.

Deuterium oxide: Heavy water.

Diabetes mellitus: Physical disorder characterized by an excess of sugar in the blood and other organs; associated with a disturbed insulin production.

Diagnosis: Identification of a disease or disorder.

Diencephalon: Thalamus and hypothalamus; part of the fore-brain.

Diplegia: Paralysis of legs and arms, with the legs more seriously affected.

Direct analytic therapy: Form of depth psychotherapy used with psychotic patients.

Directive psychotherapy: Psychological treatment in which the therapist actively manipulates the life of the patient; an authoritarian approach.

Disengagement: Defense mechanism based on noninvolvement.

Disorientation: Confusion about time, place, and person.

Displacement: Shifting of emotional emphasis.

Dissociation: Splitting of consciousness into two or more semi-independent parts.

Diurnal: Daily.

Dizygotic twins: Fraternal twins; biovular twins.

DNA (deoxyribonucleic acid): Protein molecule which carries genetic information.

Dramatization: Changing abstract ideas into concrete images in dreams.

Dream work: Process by which the instinctual urges of the id are transformed into a dream.

Duodenum: First part of the small intestine.

Dysfunction: Abnormal functioning.

Dyskinesia: Disturbance of voluntary muscular reaction.

Dysmegalopsia: Hallucination in which the body is felt to be unsymmetrical.

Dysmenorrhea: Painful menstruation.

Dysplasia: Disharmony between different regions of the body.

Dysplastic type: Atypical body type associated with glandular disturbances.

Dystrophy: Impaired growth.

Echolalia: Repetition of the exact words spoken by someone else.

Echopraxia: Automatic imitation of another's movements.

Echul: Personality disturbance of a sexual nature seen among the Dieguefio Indians.

Ecology: Study of the distribution of mental patients in the environment.

ECT: Electroconvulsive therapy.

Ectomorph: Fragile linear body type described by Sheldon.

Edema: Excessive accumulation of fluid in the tissue.

EEG: Electroencephalogram; brain waves.

EEG activation: Technique for enhancing the EEG response by drugs or other means.

Efficiency index: Measure of intellectual deterioration.

Effort syndrome: Neurotic heart disorder marked by fatigue, breathing difficulties, trembling, fainting, giddiness, and fear of effort.

Ego: Self, person, or individual, as distinguished from others.

Egocentric: Self-centered.

EKG: Electrocardiogram.

Elaboration: Altering a dream in retelling it.

Electra complex: Repressed desire of a female for incestuous relations with her father.

Electrocardiogram: Graphic record of the electric potential which accompanies the heartbeat.

Electroencephalography: Recording the electrical waves of the brain.

Electromyography: Measurement of muscle action potential.

Electronarcosis: Electric sleep.

Electro-oculography: Recording eye movements and pupillary reactions.

Electroshock therapy: Treatment of a behavior disorder by electric shock to the brain.

Electrosome: Instrument used to apply electric current to the brain to induce sleep for treatment purposes.

Embolism: Stoppage of a blood vessel by a clot or obstruction.

Embryo: Organism in the earliest phase of its prenatal development.

Emetic: Drug which induces vomiting.

EMG: Electromyogram.

Emotional catharsis: Emotional release through the reliving of a traumatic experience.

Encephalitis: Inflammation of the brain tissue.

Encephalitis lethargica: Brain disorder associated with sleepiness.

Encephalopathy: Brain disease.

Encounter group: Therapeutic-like group interaction in which personal and interpersonal problems are worked out with the assistance of a group leader and other members of the group.

Endocrine gland: Ductless gland.

Endogenous: Arising from within the body.

Endomorph: Round and fat body type described by Sheldon.

Enuresis: Involuntary discharge of urine; bedwetting.

Enzootic ataxia: Behavior disorder in sheep due to copper deficiency.

Enzyme: Organic substance capable of producing other substances by catalytic action.

Eonism: Transvestism.

Epidemiology: Location and statistical study of psychiatric cases in a hospital or community.

Epilepsy: Group of nervous diseases marked primarily by convulsions.

Epileptic furor: Condition of excitement following a *grand mal* convulsion or substituting for it.

Epileptiform seizure: Convulsion resembling those of epilepsy.

Epiloia: Inherited neoplastic disease sometimes associated with mental retardation; tuberous sclerosis.

Epinephrine: See *Adrenalin*.

Ergasias: Reaction types of personality disturbance in the system of Adolf Meyer.

Ergotamine: Naturally occurring structural analogue of serotonin; an hallucinogenic substance.

Erogenous: Pertaining to sexual, libidinal, or erotic behavior or feeling.

Erotic: Pertaining to sex sensations or their stimuli.

Erythrocyte: Red blood cell.

Escape mechanism: Defense mechanism.

Essential epilepsy: See *Idiopathic epilepsy*.

Essential hypertension: High blood pressure.

EST: Electroshock therapy.

Estrogen: Any female sex hormone.

Estrone: Female sex hormone produced by the ovaries from the fetal period until menopause.

Ethnic: Pertaining to groups of people believed to be biologically related.

Etiology: Study of causes or origins of a disease.

Eukadol: Narcotic derived from morphine.

Euphoria: Exaggerated feeling of well-being.

Evoked memories: Memories produced by stimulation of the cortex of the temporal lobe.

Exhibitionism: Exhibiting one's sex organs to other people.

Existentialism: Philosophical approach based on the importance of personal freedom, personal decision, and personal commitment.

Exogenous: Originating outside the body or outside the nervous system.

Experimental neurosis: Experimental behavior disorder induced in animals by means of conflict.

Extirpation: Complete removal or surgical destruction of a part of the body.

Familial: Pertaining to the family; hereditary.

Family-care system: Treatment of the mentally ill through placement with private families.

Fantasy: Daydream.

Fetishism: Sexual deviation in which articles of clothing or parts of the body become a substitute for the love object.

Fetus: Human embryo after the sixth to eighth week of pregnancy.

Field-dependent: Dependent upon visual field cues in space orientation experiments.

Field-independent: Dependent upon body cues in space orientation experiments.

Filtrable: Capable of passing through a filter.

Fissure: Furrow or groove on the surface of the brain.

Fistula: Abnormal outlet from an internal organ to the outside of the body.

Fixation: Arrest of psychosexual development.

Flaccid: Limp; without normal tonus.

Flagellation: Whipping.

Focal: Localized.

Focused ultrasound: Form of psychosurgery by means of high-frequency sound waves directed into the brain.

Folie à deux: Shared psychosis; usually of husbands and wives or close relatives.

Forebrain: Uppermost portion of the brain; cerebrum and diencephalon.

Formboard: Performance test of intelligence.

Freidreich's ataxia: Neurological disorder.

Frigidity: Absence of sexual feeling in women.

Frustration: Psychological state resulting from the blocking of goal-directed activity.

Frustration tolerance: Level of one's ability to accept frustration.

Fugue: Relatively long period of amnesia in which the patient usually leaves home.

Functional: Psychological; psychogenic.

Funkenstein test: Blood pressure reaction to an intramuscular injection of methacholine (Mecholyl).

GABA: Gamma amino butyric acid; chemical mediator in the transmission of the nerve impulse; neurohormone.

Galactosemia: Condition marked by an accumulation of galactos in the bloodstream; may be associated with mental retardation.

Galvanic skin response: Electrical skin resistance.

Ganglion: Nerve center.

Ganglion cells: Group of nerve cells usually located outside the brain and spinal cord.

Gargoylism: Disorder marked by a defect in the metabolism of connective tissue substance, may be associated with mental retardation.

G.A.S.: General adaptation syndrome.

Gastritis: Stomach distress.

Genetic code: Chemical pattern in the DNA molecule which determines the physical structure of the organism.

Genital: Pertaining to the sex organs.

Glaucoma: Increased intraocular pressure; hardening of the eyeballs.

Glia cells: Supporting cells in the nervous system.

Glioma: Intrinsic tumor of the brain tissue.

Glutamic acid: Enzyme having anticonvulsive properties.

Gonadotrophic hormone: Secretion of the pituitary gland influencing the sex glands.

Gonads: Sex glands.

Grand mal: Major convulsive seizure.

Grantham lobotomy: Form of psychosurgery in which a needle electrode is inserted in the frontal area of the brain and tissue is destroyed through electrocoagulation.

Graphology: Analysis of handwriting characteristics.

Grieg's disease: See *Hypertelorism.*

GSR: Galvanic skin response.

Guamine: Basic chemical unit of the DNA molecule.

Gynandromorphy: Bisexuality of the physique.

Gyrus: Convolution of the brain.

Habitus: Body build.

Hallucination: Perception without an appropriate external stimulus.

Hallucinogen: Chemical substance capable of producing hallucinations.

Harmaline: Chemical substance capable of producing hallucinations.

Harmine: Naturally occurring structural analogue of serotonin; hallucinogenic substance.

Hasheesh: See *Marijuana.*

Hemiplegia: Paralysis of one side of the body.

Hepatolenticular degeneration: See *Wilson's disease.*

Hermaphrodite: Individual with both male and female sex organs.

Heroin: Narcotic derived from morphine.

Heterosexual: Pertaining to relations with members of the opposite sex.

Hindbrain: Lower brain structures including the pons, medulla, and cerebellum.

Hirsutism: Hairiness.

Histamine: Chemical mediator in the transmission of the nerve impulse; neurohormone.

Histidine: Amino acid source of histamine.

Homeostasis: Maintaining a balance or equilibrium in bodily processes.

Homosexual: Pertaining to erotic relationships between members of the same sex.

Hormone: Chemical substance secreted by the endocrine glands.

Humanism: Psychological approach in which human interests, values, and dignity predominate.

Hurler's disease: See *Gargoylism.*

Hutchinson's teeth: Notched or pegged teeth seen in congenital syphilis.

Hydrocephalus: Increased volume and pressure of cerebrospinal fluid in the ventricles of the brain.

Hydroxytryptamine: An intermediate product in certain metabolic processes.

Hyperemesis gravidarum: Nausea and vomiting of early pregnancy.

Hyperemia: Increased amount of blood in part of the body.

Hyperinsulinism: Overproduction of insulin.

Hyperkinesis: Excessive muscular action.

Hyperopia: Farsightedness.

Hypersomnic: Pertaining to excessive sleepiness.

Hypertelorism: Congenital cerebral defect characterized by an abnormal development of the skull; Grieg's disease.

Hypertension: High blood pressure.

Hyperthyroidism: Overactivity of the thyroid glands.

Hyperventilation syndrome: Combination of physical symptoms brought on by overbreathing.

Hypnoanalysis: Combination of the techniques of hypnosis with those of depth therapy.

Hypnosis: Sleep-like condition of heightened suggestibility.

Hypoadrenocorticism: Underproduction of adrenocortical hormones.

Hypochondria: Obsessive preoccupation with one's health.

Hypoglycemia: Lowered blood sugar.

Hypokinesis: Lethargy; underactivity.

Hypomania: Earliest stage in the development of the manic reaction.

Hypophrenia: Mental retardation.

Hypophysis: Endocrine gland located at the base of the brain; pituitary gland.

Hypoplasia: Underdevelopment of part of the body.

Hypotensive action: Ability to lower blood pressure.

Hypothalamus: Group of nuclei at the base of the brain involved in the regulation of various body processes.

Hypothyroidism: Thyroid underactivity.

Hysteria: Neurotic condition marked by an involuntary loss or disorder of function caused by psychological conflict.

Id: Deepest level of the unconscious; the source of instinctual impulses seeking immediate gratification of primitive needs.

Identification: Defense mechanism by means of which an individual affiliates himself with another person, group, or movement.

Ideomotor: Pertaining to a motor response elicited by an idea.

Idiopathic epilepsy: Convulsive disorder without known or specific organic cause; essential epilepsy.

Idiot savant: Form of mental retardation in which the patient exhibits a special ability or exceptional talent.

Imipramine: Antidepressive drug.

Impotence: Inability of the male to perform the sexual act.

Imu: Personality disturbance similar to Lata; observed among the Ainu women of Japan.

Incest: Sex relations between close relatives of opposite sexes.

Incoherence: Disconnected and unrelated thoughts.

Individual psychology: Theory of personality advanced by Alfred Adler.

Infantile amaurotic family idiocy: See *Tay-Sach's disease.*

Infantile autism: Childhood psychosis.

Infantile cerebral lipoidosis: See *Tay-Sach's disease.*

Infantilism: Extreme immaturity and dependency.

Inkblot test: See *Rorschach test.*

Insight: Understanding; seeing meaningful relationships.

Insulin: Hormone produced by tissue imbedded within the pancreatic mass; related to sugar metabolism.

Insulin shock therapy: Physical treatment based on the induction of hypoglycemia or lowered blood sugar.

Intentional tremor: Tremor which appears when some specific movement is about to be performed.

Interaction chronograph: Instrument that gives a continuous recording of a number of interview interaction variables.

Interpersonal theory: View that personality disturbance is determined by social behavior and interpersonal situations rather than by constitutional factors.

Intrapsychic: Taking place within the mind or self.

Intrapsychic censor: Process by means of which unconscious strivings are kept out of consciousness.

Introjection: Absorption of the personality of another person into oneself; defense mechanism.

Iproniazid: MAO-inhibitor type of antidepressant; Marsilid.

IQ: Intelligence quotient.

Isocarboxazid: MAO-inhibitor type of antidepressant.

Izoniazid: Energizing drug; antidepressant.

Jacksonian seizure: Convulsive disorder in which the muscular contraction is limited to the arm, leg, or face.

Juramentado: Personality disturbance of an aggressive nature observed among the Mohammedan Moros.

Juvenile paresis: Syphilis of the brain and associated psychological symptoms in children and adolescents.

Kent-Rosanoff test: Standardized word-association test.

Kernicterus: Brain disorder resulting from a toxic condition during the first few days following birth; may be associated with mental retardation.

Ketogenic diet: Diet rich in fats; used to control convulsive disorders.

Kimilue: Personality disturbance of a sexual nature observed among the Diegueno Indians.

Kleptomania: Compulsive urge to steal.

Korsakoff's syndrome: Brain disorder associated with alcoholism.

Lapsus linguae: Slip of the tongue.

Lata: Personality disturbance marked by extreme passivity and suggestibility; observed among the Malays.

Latency period: Stage in psychosexual development.

Latent: Inactive, dormant, hidden.

Latent dream: Deeper symbolic level of a dream.

Leptosomic type: Tall and thin body type described by Kretschmer; asthenic type.

Lesbianism: Homosexuality in women.

Lesion: Injury or wound.

Lethargy: Morbid drowsiness; inaction and apathy.

Leucotomy: Form of psychosurgery.

Libido: Constructive or destructive psychic energy.

Life instinct: Tendency of the id to strive toward integration of living substance into larger wholes; Eros.

Life style: Behavior pattern adopted early in life as a means of overcoming feelings of inferiority.

Lilliputian hallucination: Hallucination involving tiny figures of people or animals.

Limbic lobe: Ringlike convolution around the base of the cerebral hemisphere; visceral brain.

Lithium carbonate: Drug used in the treatment of psychological depression.

Little's disease: See *Cerebral palsy*.

Lobectomy: Removal of a lobe.

LSD-25: Lysergic acid diethylamide; hallucinogenic drug derived from ergot.

Lues: Syphilis.

Lysergic acid: Naturally occurring structural analogue of serotonin; hallucinogenic substance.

MA: Mental age.

Macrocephaly: Large-headedness.

Macrogyria: Condition in which the gyri and convolutions of the brain are few and broad while the sulci and fissures are short, shallow, and wide.

Macropsia: Hallucination in which the patient perceives his body or parts of his body as being unnaturally large.

Malnutrition: Deficiency in calories, proteins, and vitamins.

Mania: Overactivity, excitement, and violence.

Manifest dream: Dream as the dreamer remembers it.

MAO: Monoamine oxidase; enzyme.

Marijuana: Drug obtained from the hemp plant.

Masochism: Sexual pleasure derived from physical or psychological pain and suffering.

Medulla: Bulblike structure at the top of the spinal cord forming the lowest part of the brain.

Medulloblastoma: Form of brain tumor.

Melancholia: Depression.

Menarche: Age of onset of menstruation.

Meninges: Membranes of the brain and spinal cord.

Meningioma: Tumor arising from the membranes covering the brain.

Meningoencephalitis: Inflammation of the brain and its membranes.

Meningovascular: Involving the membranes of the brain and the cerebral blood vessels.

Menopause: Natural end of the menstrual cycle; "change of life"; climacteric.

Mental age: Level of intellectual development in terms of the average of a particular age group; MA.

Meprobamate: Tranquilizing drug derived from propanediol carbamate.

Mescaline: Hallucinogenic drug obtained from the cactus plant.

Mesmerism: Animal magnetism; hypnotism.

Mesomorph: Square muscular body type described by Sheldon.

Metabolism: Building up and breaking down of body cells.

Metastatic: Pertaining to the transfer of a disease from a primary source to a distant one.

Metastatic tumor: Tumor arising at a location in the body other than the primary source.

Methadone: Substitute drug used in treatment of heroin addiction.

Methyl hydantoin: Anticonvulsant drug; Mesantoin.

Metrazol: Drug used in convulsive therapy.

Microcephaly: Small-headedness.

Microgyria: Condition in which the normal convolutions of the brain are replaced by a large number of small close-set convolutions separated by shallow grooves.

Micropsia: Hallucination in which the patient feels his body or parts of his body to be unusually small.

Midbrain: Part of brain which developed from the middle of the primitive brain; mesencephalon.

Migraine: Severe form of familial headache.

Milieu therapy: Supportive type of psychological treatment based on the removal or modification of environmental stress.

Misala: Personality disturbance similar to Amok; observed among African tribes.

Mongolism: Form of mental retardation in which the patient has the facial characteristics of a member of the Mongolian race; associated with a disturbance of the chromosomes.

Monoamine oxidase: Enzyme; MAO.

Monomania: Nineteenth-century term for mental illness marked by highly organized delusions.

Monoplegia: Paralysis involving a single limb of the body.

Monozygotic twins: Uniovular twins; identical twins.

Moral insanity: Nineteenth-century term for character disorder.

Morphine: Narcotic drug derived from opium.

Mutism: Inability to speak.

Myopia: Nearsightedness.

Myxedema: Adult hypothyroidism.

Naloxone: Drug which counteracts effects of opiates.

Narcissism: Self-love.

Narcoanalysis: See *Narcotherapy.*

Narcolepsy: Neurotic attacks of sleep.

Narcosynthesis: See *Narcotherapy.*

Narcotherapy: Use of drugs to facilitate the release of unconscious material.

Natural areas: Areas which develop during the growth of a city.

Naturalism: View that illness is the result of natural causes.

Necrophilia: Sexual attraction to death and dead bodies.

Negative transference: Hostile and antagonistic feelings which the patient develops toward the psychotherapist.

Negativism: Resistance; contrary behavior.

Neologism: Made-up word having a private meaning for the mental patient.

Neoplasm: Tumor.

Neurasthenia: Neurotic reaction characterized by weakness, fatigue, and lack of physical vitality.

Neuritis: Inflammation of a nerve.

Neurocirculatory asthenia: See *Effort syndrome.*

Neurodermatosis: Skin disorders occurring in cases of emotional instability.

Neurofibromatosis: Neoplastic disorder associated in some cases with mental retardation.

Neurohormone: Chemical mediator in the transmission of the nerve impulse.

Neurotropic: Influencing or involving the nervous tissue.

Niacin: See *Nicotinic acid.*

Nicotinamide: See *Nicotinic acid.*

Nicotinic acid: Vitamin of the vitamin B complex; niacin, nicotinamide.

Nondirective psychotherapy: Psychological treatment in which the patient is largely responsible for the solution to his problems; a client-centered approach.

Noradrenalin: Chemical mediator in the transmission of the nerve impulse; neurohormone; norepinephrine.

Norepinephrine: See *Noradrenalin.*

Nosology: Pertaining to classification.

Nucleotides: Chemical subunits of the DNA molecule.

Object love: Love directed toward other persons and things.

Obsession: Unwelcome recurring idea.

Occlusion: Closing of an artery.

Oculogyric: Referring to movements of the eyes.

Oedipal relationship: Erotic attachment of the young child to the parent of the opposite sex.

Olfactory brain: Limbic lobe; visceral brain.

Oligophrenia: Mental retardation.

Open-door policy: Program of unlocked hospital wards.

Ophthalmoplegic: Pertaining to a paralysis of the ocular muscles.

Overt: Open to objective observation.

Oxycephaly: Distortion of the skull giving the head a steeple-shaped appearance; acrocephaly.

Paleocortex: Limbic lobe; visceral brain.

Paleological thinking: Nonlogical nature of the thinking process of the schizophrenic patient.

Palsy: Paralysis.

Pantothenic acid: Calcium pantothenate; vitamin involved in the metabolism of fat, protein, and carbohydrate.

Papilledema: Edema or swelling of the optic nerve.

Paralogical thinking: See *Paleological thinking.*

Paralysis agitans: Shaking palsy; Parkinson's disease.

Paranasal: Located near the nasal cavities.

Paranoid: Characterized by suspiciousness.

Paraplegia: Paralysis involving only the legs.

Parasympathetic system: Segment of the autonomic nervous system.

Parataxic distortions: Disturbances of social perception.

Paresis: Brain disorder due to syphilis.

Parkinsonism: Neurological disorder characterized by rigidity, tremors, and impaired motor function.

Passive-aggressive: Characterized by rebellion through inaction and stubbornness.

Passive-dependent: Characterized by passivity and dependency.

Pathogenic: Causing disease or disorder.

Pathological: Abnormal, diseased, or disordered.

Pathological intoxication: Acute brain disorder characterized by a violent reaction to relatively small quantities of alcohol.

Pedophilia: Sexual inclinations directed toward children.

Pellagra: Physical disorder due to lack of nicotinic acid.

Pepsin: Protein-splitting enzyme.

Peptic ulcer: Lesion of the mucous lining of the stomach or duodenum.

Perceptual defense: Selective blocking of the input of anxiety-producing stimuli.

Performance test: Nonverbal psychological test.

Periodontal: Pertaining to the area of the teeth and gums.

Peristalsis: Rhythmic contraction of smooth muscles of gastrointestinal tract.

Pernicious anemia: Physical symptom complex related to vitamin B_{12} deficiency.

Personal unconscious: That part of the unconscious which develops as a result of individual experience.

Petit mal: Convulsive disorder characterized by brief losses of consciousness.

PGR: Psychogalvanic response.

Phallic period: Stage in psychosexual development.

Phallus: Male sex organ.

Penethylamine: Stimulating drug used in narcotherapy; Pervitin.

Phenothiazine: Chemical base of certain tranquilizing drugs.

Phenyl acetyl urea: Anticonvulsant drug; Phenurone.

Phenylethyl barbituric acid: Anticonvulsant drug; phenobarbital.

Phenylketonuria: Disturbance of protein metabolism frequently associated with mental retardation.

Phlegmatic: Cold and self-possessed.

Phobia: Pathological fear.

Photic activation: Technique for exaggerating the EEG by light stimulation.

Photophobia: Sensitivity to light.

Phrenology: Theory that character traits are localized in specific regions of the brain.

Pibloktoq: Personality disturbance marked by sudden episodes of excitement; observed among the Eskimos.

Pick's disease: Presenile brain disorder.

Pituitary: Endocrine gland located at the base of the brain; hypophysis.

Pleasure principle: Pertaining to the need for instinctual urges to be gratified immediately either directly or through fantasy.

Polymorphous perversion: Pertaining to the theory that the sex drive in the child has no predetermined outlet and leads to behavior that would be deviant or perverse in an adult.

Polynucleotide: Enzyme.

Porencephaly: Congenital disorder in which there are funnel-shaped cavities in the brain communicating with the ventricles.

Porphyria: Metabolic disorder involving the excretion of porphyrins in the urine; transmitted as a dominant trait; may be associated with mental retardation.

Preconscious: Not conscious but capable of becoming conscious.

Prefrontal lobotomy: Form of psychosurgery.

Prelogical thinking: Nonlogical nature of the thinking process of the schizophrenic patient.

Premenstrual tension: Emotional reaction in women prior to the onset of the menstrual cycle.

Presenile: Pertaining to premature aging.

Primal scene: Childhood memory of an early sexual experience, often related to parental sexual relations.

Prodromal: Early or warning signs of disease.

Progesterone: Female sex hormone produced by the ovaries during the active reproduction years.

Prognosis: Predicted outcome of a disorder.

Projection: Placing blame elsewhere; defense mechanism.

Projective test: Personality test based on responses to relatively unstructured materials and situations.

Prolonged narcosis: Sleep therapy.

Prostigmine: Chemical related to acetylcholine; stimulates the parasympathetic system.

Pseudocyesis: False pregnancy.

Pseudoneurotic schizophrenia: Marginal type of schizophrenia having strong neurotic components.

Pseudoretardation: Clinical condition which gives the appearance of mental retardation but in which the patient is not retarded.

Psychasthenia: Neurotic reaction characterized by obsessions, compulsions, and phobias.

Psyche: Human mind.

Psychiatry: Medical specialty dealing with the diagnosis and treatment of mental illness.

Psychoactive drugs: Drugs which affect the psychological functions of the individual.

Psychoanalysis: Freudian theory of personality and technique for treating personality disturbances.

Psychobiology: Psychiatric approach advanced by Adolf Meyer.

Psychodrama: Psychological treatment based upon the deliberate acting out of conflict situations.

Psychogalvanic response: Electrical skin resistance.

Psychogenic: Having a psychological origin.

Psychomotor: Motor behavior associated with psychological processes.

Psychomotor seizure: Convulsive disorder characterized by a wide range of behavior disturbances of a dissociative nature.

Psychosis: Severe mental illness.

Psychosurgery: Brain surgery used to treat mental illness.

Psychotherapy: Treatment of emotional and behavior disturbances by psychological methods.

Psychotomimetic: Resembling a psychosis.

Psychotropic: Capable of influencing the mind.

Puerile: Childish.

Pupillometry: Measurement of pupillary changes as an indication of emotional reactions.

Purposive accident: Unconsciously motivated accident.

Pyknic type: Stout and compact body type described by Kretschmer.

Pyromania: Compulsive urge to set fires.

Quadriplegia: Paralysis of all four limbs of the body.

Quaternary stage: Stage in the development of syphilis.

Racial unconscious: That part of the unconscious which is inherited; collective unconscious.

Radio surgery: Form of psychosurgery in which proton rays are beamed into the brain tissue.

Rapport: Emotional acceptance of the therapist by the patient, and of the patient by the therapist.

Rationalization: Giving reasons and making excuses; defense mechanism.

Reaction formation: Denying a conflict; defense mechanism.

Reactive depression: Neurotic depressive reaction.

Reality principle: Pertaining to the necessity for instinctual urges to be adjusted to the demands of the environment.

Recall reaction: Third phase of the disaster syndrome.

Recoil reaction: Second phase of the disaster syndrome.

Reconstructive psychotherapy: Psychological treatment directed toward a fundamental reorganization of the basic personality structure and dynamics of the patient.

Regression: Return to behavior used at an earlier period in life; defense mechanism.

Remission: Period of improvement in the course of mental illness.

Repetition compulsion: Need to repeat a behavior pattern over and over in an effort to reduce anxiety.

Repression: Unconscious tendency to exclude painful material from consciousness; defense mechanism.

Reserpine: Tranquilizing drug derived from the plant *rauwolfia serpentina*.

Resistance: Reluctance on the part of the patient in psychotherapy to produce significant material because of its anxiety-provoking nature.

Reticular activating system: See *Reticular formation*.

Reticular formation: Lower brain structure related to arousal, alertness, and consciousness.

Rhinencephalon: Visceral brain; limbic lobe.

Riboflavin: Vitamin B$_2$.

Ribonuclease: First enzyme to be artificially synthesized.

RNA (ribonucleic acid): Chemical molecule involved in the transmission of genetic information.

Rorschach test: Projective personality test in which the subject is required to respond to a series of inkblots.

Rubella: Measles.

Sadism: Sexual satisfaction from giving pain to others.

Sanguine: Hopeful and confident.

Scaphocephaly: Distortion of the skull giving the head a long and narrow appearance.

Scatter: Irregularity of test performance on intelligence scales.

Schizoid: Seclusive, withdrawn, and unsociable; schizophrenic-like.

Schizophrenogenic: Contributing to the development of schizophrenia.

Scotophilia: Erotic satisfaction obtained from observing others; voyeurism.

Secondary gains: Secondary advantages derived from a neurotic symptom.

Secondary ventilation: Discharge of deeper levels of emotion-laden material during psychotherapy.

Self-confrontation: Treatment technique in which the individual observes his own deviant behavior by videotape or other means.

Self-stimulation: Technique by means of which animals are able to stimulate their brains electrically.

Senile: Pertaining to old age.

Senile plaque: Type of cell structure characteristic of the aging brain.

Sensory isolation: Experimental reduction of sensory cues.

Sequelae: Aftereffects of an injury or disorder.

Serotonin: Chemical mediator in the transmission of the nerve impulse; neurohormone.

Shock reaction: First phase of the disaster syndrome.

Sibling: Brother or sister born of the same parents.

Sibling rivalry: Rivalry between brothers and sisters.

Sodium diphenyl hydantoinate: Anticonvulsant drug; Dilantin sodium.

Soldier's heart: See *Effort syndrome*.

Somatic: Pertaining to the body.

Somatotonia: Temperament expressed through exertion, exercise, and physical self-expression; associated with the mesomorph body type of Sheldon.

Somnambulism: Sleepwalking.

Somniloquy: Sleeptalking.

Spastic diplegia: See *Cerebral palsy*.

Spastic paralysis: See *Cerebral palsy*.

Spirochete: Organism of syphilis.

Stage of exhaustion: Third stage of the general adaptation syndrome.

Stage of resistance: Second stage of the general adaptation syndrome.

Status epilepticus: Succession of convulsive seizures without intervening recovery of consciousness.

Stigmatization: Psychogenic skin eruptions having religious significance.

Still reaction: Protective device used by certain animals when in danger; "playing dead."

Stress: Force applied to a system; physical and psychological pressures exerted on the body and personality.

Structural analogue: See *Antimetabolite*.

Sturge-Weber syndrome: Condition in which an excessive growth of blood vessels in the skin causes a large birthmark on the face and neck.

Subcortical: Below the cerebral cortex.

Subcutaneous: Under the skin.

Sublimation: Gratification of primitive impulses in a socially approved manner; defense mechanism.

Substitution: Defense mechanism; adopting realistic goals in place of unrealistic ones.

Substrate: Underlayer.

Sulci: Shallow grooves on the surface of the brain.

Superego: That part of the personality structure which incorporates parental standards; conscience.

Supportive psychotherapy: Psychological treatment designed to remove symptoms by reinforcing existing personality defenses.

Surrogate mother: Substitute mother.

Sympathetic system: Segment of the autonomic nervous system.

Symptomatic: Pertaining to a specific symptom.

Syndrome: Group of symptoms which combine to form a particular disease or condition.

Systemic: Pertaining to a system of the body.

T-group: Training group; a form of encounter group.

Tabo-paresis: Form of syphilis of the nervous system involving the brain and spinal cord.

Tachycardia: Rapid heart rate.

Tarantism: Dancing mania.

Taraxein: Protein fraction related to ceruloplasmin; reported in schizophrenics.

TAT: Thematic Apperception Test; projective test of personality using a series of pictures.

Tay-Sach's disease: Hereditary disorder of fat metabolism; may be associated with mental retardation.

Telestimulation: Stimulation of the nervous system of a subject by means of radio or similar means.

Temporal lobe seizure: See *Psychomotor seizure.*

Tertiary stage: Stage in the development of syphilis.

Testosterone: Principal male sex hormone.

Thalamotomy: Form of psychosurgery in which electrodes are introduced into the thalamic region of the brain.

Thalamus: Lower brain structure serving as a sensory relay center.

THC (tetrahydrocannabinol): Active chemical ingredient in marijuana.

Therapy: Treatment.

Thermocoagulation: Form of psychosurgery in which brain centers are destroyed by electricity.

Thiamine: Vitamin B_1.

Thiocyanate: Drug used to control high blood pressure.

Thrombosis: Bloodclotting.

Thymine: Basic chemical unit of the DNA molecule.

Thyroid glands: Pair of endocrine glands on each side of the neck below the larynx.

Thyrotrophic hormone: Secretion of the anterior pituitary gland influencing the thyroid glands.

Thyroxine: Thyroid gland hormone.

Tic: Involuntary jerking of a small muscle group.

Tigretier: Form of dancing mania observed in Africa.

Tonic phase: First phase of the *grand mal* convulsion; characterized by a contraction of the musculature.

Toxemia: Condition in which the blood contains toxic or poisonous substances.

Toxin: Poisonous substance.

Toxoplasmosis: Infection due to a protozoan-like organism; may be associated with mental retardation.

Transference: Process in psychotherapy in which the therapist assumes the role of a substitute parent; an emotional bond between the patient and therapist which is a reliving of childhood experiences.

Transference neurosis: Intense transference relationship which develops during depth therapy.

Transorbital lobotomy: Form of psychosurgery in which the brain is entered through the thin bony structure behind the eye.

Transplacental: Transmitted by way of the placenta.

Transvestism: Wearing the clothing of members of the opposite sex.

Trauma: Shock or injury.

Tremor: Rhythmic and involuntary muscle movements.

Trephination: Cutting a small opening in the skull.

Trimester: Three-month period, usually with reference to pregnancy.

Trimethadione: Drug used to treat *petit mal* convulsions; Tridione.

Triplegia: Paralysis of three limbs of the body.

Tropenkohler: Personality disturbance similar to Amok; observed among African natives.

Tryptamine: Intermediate product in certain metabolic processes.

TTD: Tetraethylthiuram-disulphide; drug used in the conditioned aversion treatment of alcoholism; Antabuse.

Tuberous sclerosis: Inherited neoplastic disease sometimes associated with mental retardation; epiloia.

Tunnel vision: Progressive restriction of the visual field.

Type-token ration: Relation of the number of different words used in a speech sample to the total number of words used.

Tyrosine: Amino acid found in protein substances.

Ultrasonic: Pertaining to sound waves of higher frequency than can be heard by the human ear.

Unconscious: Below the threshold of consciousness; nonconscious.

Uniovular twins: Identical twins; monozygotic twins.

Urethra: Duct that discharges urine from the bladder.

Urticaria: Hives; itching eruptions on the skin.

Uterus: Structure in which the embryo of mammals develops within the mother's body.

Vagus nerve: Tenth cranial nerve; pneumogastric nerve.

Vandalism: Malicious destruction of property.

Vasomotor: Pertaining to the expansion and contraction of the blood vessels.

Vasomotor rhinitis: Congestion of the nasal mucous membrane and the conjunctivae of the eyes.

Venesection: Bloodletting.

Ventricle: Small cavity within the heart or the brain.

Verbigeration: Meaningless and sterotyped repetition of words or phrases.

Vertigo: Dizziness.

Vesania: Eighteenth-century term for all mental disorders.

Vicarious: Pertaining to a substitute.

Virilism: Development by a female of the secondary sex characteristics of a male.

Visceral: Pertaining to the internal organs.

Visceral brain: Ringlike convolution around the base of the cerebral hemisphere; limbic lobe.

Viscerotonia: Relaxed, sociable, and convivial temperament, associated with the endomorph body type described by Sheldon.

Vital dye: Substance used for staining living tissues.

Vitamin A: Carotene.

Vitamin B₁: Thiamine.

Vitamin B₂: Riboflavin.

Vitamin B₆: Group of vitamins including pyridoxine, pyridoxol, and pyridoxamine.

Vitamin B₁₂: Cyanocobalamin.

Vitamin C: Ascorbic acid.

Vitamin H: Biotin.

Von Recklinghausen's disease: Neoplastic disorder associated in some cases with mental retardation; neurofibromatosis.

Voyeurism: Erotic satisfaction obtained from observing others; scotophilia.

WAIS: Wechsler Adult Intelligence Scale.

Wassermann test: Test of the blood or cerebrospinal fluid for the detection of syphilis.

Wechsler tests: Series of comprehensive tests of intelligence.

Wilson's disease: Inherited disorder of protein metabolism which may be associated with mental retardation.

WISC: Wechsler Intelligence Scale for Children.

Withdrawal symptoms: Physical and psychological symptoms associated with the attempt to stop the use of certain drugs.

Witigo: Personality disturbance in which the victim believes he is turning into a cannibal; observed among Canadian Indian tribes.

XYY variant: Genetic deviation in which there are two Y (male) chromosomes rather than one, which is more common.

Zoophilia: Sexual inclinations directed toward animals; bestiality.

Zygote: Fertilized egg.

REFERENCES

Aberle, D. F. Arctic hysteria and latah in Mongolia. *Ann. N.Y. Acad. Sci.,* 1952, **2,** 291.

Abramson, H. A. (ed.) *Neuropharmacology.* New York: Josiah Macy, Jr., Foundation, 1960.

Action for mental health: The final report of the joint commission on mental illness and health. New York: Basic Books, Inc., Publishers, 1961.

Alanen, Y. *The mothers of schizophrenic patients.* Copenhagen: Munksgaard, 1958.

Alexander, F. The neurotic character. *Int. J. Psycho-Anal.,* 1930, **11,** 292.

Alexander, F., & Saul, L. J. Respiration and personality—a preliminary report: Part I. Description of the curves. *Psychosom. Med.,* 1940, **2,** 110.

Alper, Thelma. An electric shock patient tells his story. *J. Abnorm. Soc. Psych.,* 1948, **43,** 201.

Alvarez, W. C. *Nervousness, indigestion and pain.* New York: Paul B. Hoeber, Inc., 1943.

Alzheimer, A. Uber eine eigenartige Erkrankung der Hirnrinde. *Centralbl. Nervenheit. Psychiat.,* 1907, **18,** 177.

American Psychiatric Association, 1968. Meeting of the American Psychiatric Association, Boston, Mass., 1968.

American Psychiatric Association, 1970. Joint Information Service.

Ames, Frances. A clinical and metabolic study of acute intoxication with *cannabis sativa* and its role in the model psychoses. *J. ment. Sci.,* 1958, **104,** 991.

Andermann, Eva. Cited in the hearings before a subcommittee of the Committee on Appropriations, House of Representatives, 91st Congress, First Session, Part 3, p. #136, 1969.

Anderson, V. V. *Psychiatry in industry.* New York: Harper & Brothers, 1929.

Annual Report, 1969. Office of School Buildings, New York City.

Ashby, W. A. A report on the current status of an attempt to correlate abnormality of distribution of one brain enzyme with mental dysfunction. *J. nerv. ment. Dis.,* 1950, **112,** 425.

Ayllon, T., & Sommer, R. A directive or a permissive approach? *Ment. Hosp.,* 1960, **11,** 45.

Bagh, K. von. Klinische und pathol-anat. Studien an 30 Fällen von umshriebener Atrophie der Grosshirnde (Picksche Krankheit). *Ann. med. int. Fenniae,* 1946, 132.

Bailey, P. *Intracranial tumors.* (2d ed.) Springfield, Ill.: Charles C Thomas, Publisher, 1948.

Baillarger, J. De la mélancholie avec stupeur. *Ann. méd.-psychol.,* 1853, **5,** 251.

Baker, A. B. (ed.) *Clinical neurology.* New York: Paul B. Hoeber, Inc., 1955.

Bales, R. F. *Interactional process analysis.* Reading, Mass.: Addison-Wesley Publishing Company, Inc., 1950.

Bartholow, R. Experimental investigations into the functions of the human brain. *Amer. J. med. Sci.* (new series), 1874, **67,** 305.

Barton, W. E. *Wall street journal,* Jan. 28, 1970.

Bauer, J. *Constitution and disease.* (2d ed.) New York: Grune & Stratton, Inc., 1947.

Beaglehole, E. Culture and psychosis in New Zealand. *J. Polynesian Soc.,* 1939, **48,** 144.

Beard, G. M. *A practical treatise on nervous exhaustion (neurasthenia): its symptoms, nature, sequences, and treatment,* New York: Wood, 1880.

Beaumont, W. *Experiments and observations on the gastric juice and the physiology of digestion.* Boston: 1929. Reprinted.

Bellak, L. *The TAT and CAT in clinical use.* New York: Grune & Stratton, Inc., 1954.

Bender, Lauretta. *A visual motor gestalt test and its clinical use.* New York: American Orthopsychiatric Association, 1938.

Benedict, Ruth. *Patterns of culture.* Boston: Houghton Mifflin Company, 1934.

Bennetts, H. W., & Chapman, F. E. Copper deficiency in sheep in Western Australia: A preliminary account of the etiology of enzootic ataxia of lambs and an anemia of ewes. *Australian vet. J.,* 1937, **13,** 138.

Bentley, Harriet Q. The development of a short form thematic apperception test based upon subject's self selections. Unpublished doctoral dissertation. University of Cincinnati, 1951.

Bercel, N. A. A study of the influence of schizophrenic serum on the behavior of the spider *Zilla-x-notata. Arch. gen. Psychiat.,* 1960, **2,** 189.

Berger, A. S., & Simel, P. J. Effect of hypnosis on intraocular pressure in normal and glaucomatous subjects. *Psychosom. Med.,* 1958, **20,** 321.

Berger, H. Ueber das Elektrenkephalogramm des Menschen. *Arch. Psychiat.,* 1929, **87,** 527.

Berkowitz, L. (ed.) *Roots of aggression.* New York: Atherton Press, Inc., 1970.

Bernard, C. *Introduction to the study of experimental medicine.* New York: Dover Publications, Inc., 1957.

Bernheim, H. *Suggestive therapeutics: A treatise on the nature and uses of hypnotism.* New York: G. P. Putnam's Sons, 1889.

Bexton, W. H., et al. Effects of decreased variation in the sensory environment. *Canadian J. Psychol.,* 1954, **8,** 70.

Binet, A., & Simon, T. *The development of intelligence in children.* Baltimore: The Williams & Wilkins Company, 1916.

Bleuler, E. *Dementia Praecox oder die gruppe der Schizophrenien.* In G. Aschaffenburg (ed.), *Handbuch der Psychiatrie.* Leipzig: 1911.

Bleuler, E. *Dementia praecox or the group of schizophrenias.* New York: International Universities Press, Inc., 1950.

Block, H. S. Army clinical psychiatry in the combat zone: 1967–1968. *Amer. J. Psychiat.,* 1969, **126,** 294.

Bluestone, H., & McGahee, C. L. Reaction to extreme stress: Impending death by execution. *Amer. J. Psychiat.,* 1962, **119,** 393.

Boerhaave, H. *Aphorisms: Concerning the knowledge and cure of diseases.* London: 1735.

Bogoch, S. Fractionation and quantitative analysis of cerebrospinal fluid constituents with reference to neuropsychiatric disorders. *Amer. J. Psychiat.,* 1958, **114,** 1028.

Bogoras, W. *The Chukchee.* Jessup Expedition Report, 1904–1909. New York: American Museum of Natural History.

Bourneville, M. *Science et miracle: Louise Lateau, ou la stigmatisée Belge.* Paris: 1878.

Bowen, W. T., et al. Lysergic acid diethylamide as a variable in the hospital treatment of alcoholism: A follow-up. *J. Nerv. Ment. Dis.,* 1970, **150,** 111.

Bowlby, J. *Maternal care and mental health.* Geneva: World Health Organization, 1952.

Brady, J. V. Ulcers in "executive" monkeys. *Scient. American,* 1958, **199,** 95.

Braid, J. *Neurypnology, or the rationale of nervous sleep.* London: 1843.

Braude, J. M. The sex offender and the court. *Fed. Probation,* 1950, **14,** 17.

Brigham, A. *Remarks on the influence of mental cultivation upon health.* Edinburgh: 1835.

Brill, A. A. Pibloktoq or hysteria among Peary's Eskimos, *J. nerv. ment. Dis.,* 1913, **40,** 514.

Brill, H. U.S. Senate Appropriations Subcommittee Hearing, Washington, D.C., 1955.

Bronson, W. *The earth shook, the sky burned.* Garden City, N.Y.: Doubleday & Company, Inc., 1959. P. 25.

Bronson, F. H., & Desjardins, Claude. Aggression in adult mice: Modification by neonatal injections of gonadal hormones. *Science,* 1968, **161,** 705.

Brown, W. T., et al. Ulcerative colitis and the personality. *Amer. J. Psychiat.,* 1938, **95,** 407.

Bruch, Hilda. *The importance of overweight.* New York: W. W. Norton & Company, Inc., 1957.

Bruetsch, W. L. Neurosyphilis: Symptomatology and pathology. In A. B. Baker (ed.), *Clinical neurology.* New York: Paul B. Hoeber, Inc., 1955.

Brunner, F. The application of behavior studies in small animal practice. Chapter 22 in *Abnormal behavior in animals,* M. W. Fox (ed.). Philadelphia: W. B. Saunders Company, 1968.

Burckhardt, G. Ueber Rinden-excisionen, als Beitrag zur Operativen Therapie der Psychosen. *Allg. Z. Psychiat.,* 1890–1891, **47,** 463.

Burton, R. *The anatomy of melancholy.* Oxford: Printed for Henry Cripps, 1651.

Caine, D. B., & Lader, M. H. Electromyographic studies of tremor using an averaging computer. *Electroenceph. Clin. Neurophysiol.,* 1969, **26,** 86.

Cameron, D. E. Psychic driving. *Amer. J. Psychiat.,* 1956, **112,** 502.

Cannon, W. B. *Bodily changes in fear, hunger, pain and rage.* (2d ed.) New York: D. Appleton-Century Company, Inc., 1929.

Cannon, W. B. *The wisdom of the body.* New York: W. W. Norton & Company, Inc., 1932.

Cannon, W. B., & Britton, S. W. Studies on the conditions of activity in endocrine glands. XV. Pseudo-affective medulliadrenal secretion. *Amer. J. Physiol.,* 1925, **72,** 283.

Cantril, H. *The invasion from Mars.* Princeton, N.J.: Princeton University Press, 1940.

Carmichael, L. Learning which modifies an animal's subsequent capacity for learning. *J. genet. Psychol.,* 1938, **52,** 159.

Carothers, J. C. A study of mental derangement in Africans and an attempt to explain its peculiarities, more especially in relation to the African attitude to life. *Psychiatry,* 1948, **11,** 47.

Cavan, Ruth S. *Suicide.* Chicago: University of Chicago Press, 1928.

Cerletti, U., & Bini, L. L'Elettroshock. *Arch. Psicol. Neurol. Psichiat.,* 1938, **19,** 266.

Chapman, A. H. Psychogenic urinary retention in women. *Psychosom. Med.,* 1959, **21,** 119.

Chapple, E. D., & Arensburg, C. M. Measuring human relations: An introduction to the study of the interaction of individuals. *Gen. Psychol. Monogr.,* 1940, **22,** 3.

Charcot, J. M. Hypnotism in the hysterical. In D. H. Tuke (ed.) *A dictionary of psychological medicine.* New York: McGraw-Hill Book Company, 1892.

Chertok, L., & Fontaine, M. Introduction à une clinique psychosomatique veterinaire. In *Psychiatrie Animale.* Paris, 1965.

Chess, Stella, & Thomas, Alexander (eds.). *Annual progress in child psychiatry and child development.* New York: Brunner/Mazel, 1968.

Children's Bureau, U.S. Department of Health, Education, and Welfare. *Clinic programs for mentally retarded children.* Washington, D.C.: Government Printing Office, 1961.

Clark, R. E. Psychoses, income and occupational prestige. *Amer. J. Sociol.,* 1949, **54,** 433.

Clausen, J. A., & Kohn, M. L. Social relations and schizophrenia: A research report and a prospective. In D. D. Jackson (ed.), *The etiology of schizophrenia.* New York: Basic Books, Inc., Publishers, 1960.

Clausen, J. A., & Yarrow, M. R. The impact of mental illness on the family. *J. soc. Issues,* 1955, 11. (Entire issue.)

Clouston, T. S. *Clinical lectures on mental diseases.* London: 1883.

Cohen, E., and Cohen, B. D. Verbal reinforcement in schizophrenia. *J. abnorm. soc. Psychol.,* 1960, **60,** 443.

Colbert, E., & Chamberlin, E. *Chicago and the great conflagration.* New York: Vent, 1871.

Colby, K. N., & Enea, H. Heuristic methods for computer understanding of natural language in the context-restricted on-line dialogue. *Mathematical Biosciences,* 1967, **1,** 1.

Conolly, J. *An inquiry concerning the indications of insanity.* London: 1830.

Cooper, J. M. The Cree witiko psychosis. *Primitive Man,* 1933, **6,** 20.

Cotton, H. A. *The defective, delinquent and insane: The relation of focal infections to their causation, treatment and prevention.* Princeton, N.J.: Princeton University Press, 1921.

Cowles, E. The advancement of psychiatry in America. *Amer. J. Insanity,* 1895, **52,** 364.

Cranswick, E. H. Tracer iodine studies on thyroid activity and thyroid responsiveness in schizophrenia. *Amer. J. Psychiat.,* 1955, **112,** 170.

Cumming, Elaine, & Henry, W. E. Growing old: The process of disengagement, New York: Basic Books, Inc., 1961.

Curran, D., & Mallinson, P. Recent progress in psychiatry; psychopathic personality. *J. ment. Sci.,* 1944, **90,** 266.

Cushing, H., & Eisenhardt, L. *The meningiomas.* Springfield, Ill.: Charles C Thomas, Publisher, 1938.

Dandy, W. E. Removal of right cerebral hemisphere for certain tumors with hemiplegia. *J. Amer. med. Ass.,* 1938, **90,** 823.

Darrah, L. W. Cited in The difficulty of being normal. *J. nerv. Dis.,* 1939, **90,** 730.

Davis, J. M. Personality, perceptual defense, and stereoscopic perception. *J. abnorm. soc. Psychol.,* 1959, **58,** 398.

Davis, Katherine B. *Factors in the sex life of twenty-two hundred women.* New York: Harper & Brothers, 1929.

DeJong, H. H. *Experimental catatonia and its implications for human pathology.* Baltimore: The Williams & Wilkins Company, 1945.

Delay, J., & Deniker, P. Le traitement des psychoses par une méthode neurolytique derivee de l'hibernotherapie (le 4560 R.P. utilisé seul en cure prolongée et continué). *C. R. Congr. Médicins Alienistes Neurol.,* 1952, 1.

Denber, H. C. B. Studies on mescaline. *J. nerv. ment. Dis.,* 1956, **124,** 75.

Deutsch, F. Analysis of postural behavior. *Psychoanal. Quart.,* 1947, **16,** 195.

Di Giovanni, A. *Clinical commentaries deduced from the morphology of the human body.* London: Eyre & Spottiswoode (Publishers), Ltd., 1919.

Dittes, J. E. Galvanic skin response as a measure of patient's reaction to therapists' permissiveness. *J. abnorm. soc. Psychol.,* 1957, **55,** 295.

Dohan, F. C. *Roche Report: Frontiers of Hospital Psychiatry,* 1968, **5,** 3.

Doll, E. A. The essentials of an inclusive concept of mental deficiency. *Amer. J. ment. Defic.,* 1941, **46,** 214.

Dongier, M., et al. Psychophysiological studies in thyroid function. *Psychosom. Med.,* 1956, **118,** 310.

Draper, G., et al. *Human constitution in clinical medicine.* New York: Paul B. Hoeber, Inc., 1944.

Dublin, L. I., & Spiegelman, M. The longevity of American physicians, 1938–1942. *J. Amer. med. Ass.,* 1947, **134,** 1211.

DiCara, L. V., & Miller, N. E., Instrumental learning of vasomotor responses by animals. *Science,* 1968, **159,** 1485.

DSM-II. *Diagnostic and statistical manual of mental disorders* (2d ed.) Washington, D.C.: American Psychiatric Association, 1968.

DuBois, Cora. *The people of Alor.* Minneapolis: University of Minnesota Press, 1944.

Dugdale, R. L. *The Jukes.* (3d ed.) New York: G. P. Putnam's Sons, 1877.

Dunbar, F. *Emotions and bodily changes.* (3d ed.) New York: Columbia University Press, 1946.

Dunham, H. W. Current status of ecological research in mental disorder. *Soc. Forces,* 1947, **25,** 321.

Eaton, J. W., & Weil, R. J. *Culture and mental disorders: A comparative study of the Hutterites and other populations.* Chicago: The Free Press of Glencoe, Ill., 1955.

Eichler, R. M., & Lirtzman, S. Religious background of patients in a mental hygiene setting. *J. nerv. ment. Dis.,* 1956, **124,** 514.

Einstein, A. *Essays in science.* New York: Philosophical Library, Inc., 1954.

Eisendrath, R. M. The role of grief and fear in the death of kidney transplant patients. *Amer. J. Psychiat.,* 1969, **126,** 381.

Ekstein, E. Ueber kriegsamenorrhoe. *Zbl. gynäk.,* 1919, **43,** 609.

Elliotson, J. *Numerous cases of surgical operations without pain.* London: 1843.

Ellis, H. *Studies in the psychology of sex.* New York: Random House, Inc., 1942.

Engel, G. L. Studies of ulcerative colitis, III. The nature of the psychologic processes. *Amer. J. Med.,* 1955, **19,** 231.

English, J. T. Sensitivity training: Promise and performance. *Amer. J. Psychiat.,* 1969, **126,** 142.

Enos, W. F., et al. Coronary disease among United States soldiers killed in action in Korea. *J. Amer. med. Ass.,* 1953, **152,** 1090.

Esdaile, J. *Mesmerism in India and its practical application in surgery and medicine.* Hartford, England: S. Andrus, 1850.

Esquirol, J. E. D. *Des maladies mentales considerée sous les rapports médical, hygiénique et médico-légal.* Paris: J.-B. Baillière, et fils, 1838.

Estabrooks, G. H. *The Jukes in 1915.* Washington, D.C.: Carnegie Institution of Washington, 1916.

Eysenck, H. J., & Prell, D. The inheritance of neuroticism: An experimental study. *J. ment. Sci.,* 1951, **97,** 441.

Eysenck, S. B. G. An experimental study of psychogalvanic reflex responses of normal, neurotic and psychotic subjects. *J. psychosom. Res.,* 1956, **1,** 258.

Falret, J. De la folie circulaire. *Bull. Acad. Med.* Paris, 1854, **19,** 382.

Faris, R. E. L., & Dunham, H. W. *Mental disorder in urban areas.* Chicago: University of Chicago Press, 1939.

Fast, J. *Body language.* Philadelphia: M. Evans & Company, Inc., 1970.

Fawcett, J. A., & Bunney, W. E., Jr. *Arch. gen. Psychiat.,* 1965, **13**(3), 232–238.

Fedoroff, S. Toxicity of schizophrenics' blood serum in tissue culture. *J. Lab. Clin. Med.,* 1956, **48,** 55.

Feingold, L. An automated technique for aversive conditioning in sexual deviation. In Rubin, R., & Franks, C. M. (eds.), *Advances in behavior therapy.* New York: Academic Press, 1968. Pp. 25–30.

Feinsilver, D. Communication in families of schizophrenic patients. *Arch. gen. Psychiat.,* 1970, **22**(2), 143.

Ferenczi, S. *Further contributions to the theory and technique of psychoanalysis.* London: The Hogarth Press, Ltd., 1926.

Ferraro, A., & Jervis, G. A. Experimental disseminated encephalopathy in the monkey. *Arch. neurol. Psychiat.,* 1940, **43,** 195.

Ferrier, D. *The function of the brain.* London: Smith, Elder, 1876.

Ferster, C. B. Positive reinforcement and behavioral deficits of autistic children. *Child Develpm.,* 1961, **32,** 437.

Ferster, C. B., & Skinner, B. F. *Schedules of reinforcement.* New York: Appleton Century Crofts, 1957.

Field, J. (ed.) Neurophysiology. In *Handbook of physiology.* Washington, D.C.: American Physiology Society, 1960, Sec. 1.

Field, M. J. Mental disorder in rural Ghana. *J. ment. Sci.,* 1958, **104,** 1043.

Field, M. J. *Search for security: An ethnopsychiatric study of rural Ghana.* Evanston, Ill.: Northwestern University Press, 1960.

Fischer, E., & von Mering, J. Ueber eine Neue Classe von Schlafmitteln. *Ther. Gegenw.,* 1903, **5,** 77.

Fischer, R. Stress and the toxicity of schizophrenic serum. *Science,* 1953, **118,** 409.

Fish, B., et al. Schizophrenic children treated with methysergide. *Dis. Nerv. Syst.,* 1969, **30,** 534.

Flarsheim, A. Ego mechanisms in three pulmonary tuberculosis patients. *Psychosom. Med.,* 1958, **20,** 475.

Flourens, P. *Experimental researches on the properties and functions of the nervous system in the vertebrate animal.* Paris: Crevot, 1824.

Fodor, Nandor. *The search for the beloved.* New York: Thomas Nelson & Sons, 1949.

Folling, A. Uber Ausscheidung von Phenylbrenz-traubensäure in den Harn als Stoffwechselanomalie in Verbindung mit Imbezilität. *Z. Physiol. Chem.,* 1934, **227,** 169.

Forster, F. M. *Med. World News,* May 17, 1968.

Fortune, R. F. *The sorcerers of Dobu.* New York: E. P. Dutton & Co., Inc., 1932.

Foster, Elizabeth. *Chidren of the mist.* New York: The Macmillan Company, 1961.

Fowler, R. D., Jr., & Miller, M. L. Computer interpretation of the MMPI. *Arch. gen. Psychiat.,* 1969, **21,** 502.

Fox, J. C., & German, W. J. Observations following left (dominant) temporal lobectomy. *Arch. neurol. Psychiat.,* 1935, **33,** 791.

France, S. *On the horrible vice of drunkenness.* 1531.

Franz, S. I. The reeducation of an aphasic. *J. philos. psychol. sci. Methods,* 1905, **2,** 589.

French, T. M., & Alexander, F. Psychogenic factors in bronchial asthma. *Psychosom, Med.,* Monogr. No. 4, 1941.

Freud, S. Analysis of a phobia in a five-year-old boy. In A. Strachey & J. Strachey (eds.), *Collected papers.* New York: Basic Books, Inc., Publishers, 1959.

Freud, S. *Collected papers.* London: The Hogarth Press, Ltd., 1924.

Freud, S. The defense neuro-psychoses. In *Collected papers,* 1896. London: The Hogarth Press, Ltd., 1924–1950.

Freud, S. The predisposition to obsessional neuroses. In Joan Riviere (ed.), *Collected papers.* New York: Basic Books, Inc., Publishers, 1959.

Friedman, P., & Linn, L. Some psychiatric notes on the *Andrea Doria* disaster. *Amer. J. Psychiat.,* 1957, **114,** 426.

Fritsch, G., & Hitzig, E. Ueber die Elektrische Ergbarkeit des Grosshirns. *Arch. Anat. Physiol. wissensch. Med.,* 1870, **3,** 300.

Fromm, E. *Man for himself.* New York: Holt, Rinehart and Winston, Inc., 1947.

Frumkin, R. M. Occupation and major mental disorders. In A. M. Rose (ed.), *Mental health and mental disorder.* New York: W. W. Norton & Company, Inc., 1955, ch. 8.

Fuller, P. R. Operant conditioning of a vegetative human organism. *Amer. J. Psychol.,* 1949, **62,** 587.

Fulton, J. F., & Jacobsen, C. E. *The functions of the frontal lobes, a comparative study in monkeys, chimpanzees, and man.* London: Abstracts of the Second International Neurological Congress, 1935.

Gall, F. J. *Sur les fonctions du cerveau.* Paris: J.-B. Baillière et fils, 1825, 6 vols.

Gall, F. J., & Spurzheim, J. G. *Récherches sur le systeme nerveux.* Paris: 1809.

Galton, F. *Hereditary genius: An inquiry into its laws and consequences.* New York: D. Appleton & Company, Inc., 1883.

Galton, F. *Inquiries into human faculty and its development.* London: Macmillan & Co., Ltd., 1883.

Gantt, W. H. *Experimental basis for neurotic behavior.* New York: Paul B. Hoeber, Inc., 1944.

Garma, A. On the pathogenesis of peptic ulcer. *Int. J. Psychoanal.,* 1950, **31,** 53.

Geist, H. Psychological aspects of rheumatoid arthritis. *Proceedings of the 77th annual convention of the American Psychological Association,* 1969, **4,** 769–770.

Geocaris, K. The patient as listener: A new dimension in the structure of psychotherapy. *Arch. gen. Psychiat.,* 1960, **2,** 81.

Gerard, D. L., & Siegel, J. The family background of schizophrenia. *Psychiat. Quart.,* 1950, **24,** 47.

Gide, A. *Corydon.* New York: Farrar, Straus & Cudahy, Inc., 1950.

Gide, A. *The secret drama of my life.* Paris: Boar's Head Books, 1951. Pp. 40–41.

Gillespie, J. E. O. N. Cardiazol convulsions: The subjective aspect. *Lancet,* 1939, **1,** 391.

Gillespie, W. H. A contribution to the study of fetishism. *Int. J. Psychoanal.,* 1940, **21,** 401.

Glickstein, M., & Sperry, R. W. Intermanual somesthetic transfer in split-brain rhesus monkeys. *J. comp. physiol. Psychol.,* 1960, **53,** 322.

Glueck, S., & Glueck, Eleanor. *Delinquents in the making: Paths to prevention.* New York: Harper & Row, Publishers, 1952.

Glueck, S., & Glueck, Eleanor. *Unravelling juvenile delinquency.* Cambridge, Mass.: Published for the Commonwealth Fund by Harvard University Press, 1950.

Goddard, H. H. *The Kallikak family.* New York: The Macmillan Company, 1913.

Goitein, P. L. Potential prostitute: Role of anorexia in defense against prostitution desires. *J. crim. Psychopath.,* 1942, **3,** 359.

Goldberg, J. B., & Kurland, A. A. Dilantin treatment of hospitalized cultural-familial retardates. *J. Clin. Pharmacol.,* 1970, **10,** 24.

Goldhamer, H., & Marshall, A. W. *Psychosis and civilization.* Glencoe, Ill.: The Free Press, 1953.

Goltz, F. L. Der Hund ohne Grosshirn. *Arch. gen. Physiol.,* 1892, **51,** 570.

Gomila, F. R. "Present status of the marijuana vice in the United States", in *Marihuana: America's new drug problem.* Philadelphia: J. B. Lippincott Company, 1938.

Gottschalk, L. A., et al. Verbal behavior analysis: Some content and form variables in speech relevant to personality adjustment. *Arch. neurol. Psychiat.,* 1957, **7,** 300.

Graves, R. J. Palpitation of the heart with enlargement of the thyroid gland. *London med. surg. J.,* 1835, **7,** 516.

Gregory, I. Studies of parental deprivations in psychiatric patients. *Amer. J. Psychiat.,* 1958, **115,** 432.

Griesinger, W. *Pathologie und Therapie der Psychischen Krankheiten.* Stuttgart: 1845.

Grimm, Elaine R. Psychological investigation of habitual abortion. *Psychosom. Med.,* 1962, **24,** 369.

Grinker, R., & Spiegel, J. *Men under stress.* New York: McGraw-Hill Book Company, 1945. Adapted from pp. 400–401.

Groddeck, G. *The book of the it: Psychoanalytic letters to a friend. Nerv. ment. Dis. Monogr.,* 1928.

Gull, W. W. Anorexia nervosa. *Clin. Soc. Trans.,* 1874, **7,** 22.

Gurin, G., et al. *Americans view their mental health: A nationwide interview survey.* New York: Basic Books, Inc., Publishers, 1960.

Hadley, E. E., et al. Military psychiatry. *Psychiatry,* 1944, **7,** 379.

Haley, J. An interactional description of schizophrenia. *Psychiatry,* 1959, **22,** 321.

Hall, J. K., et al. (eds.) *One hundred years of American psychiatry.* New York: Columbia University Press, 1944.

Hare, H. *Swinburne: A biographical approach.* London: H. F. & G. Witherby, Ltd., 1949.

Harlow, H. F. Primary affectional patterns in primates. *Amer. J. Orthopsychiat.,* 1960, **30,** 676.

Harlow, H. F., & Woolsey, C. N. (eds.) *Biological and biochemical bases of behavior.* Madison, Wis.: The University of Wisconsin Press, 1958.

Hartmann, E. Anti-depressants and sleep; Clinical and theoreti-

cal implications. Chap. 23 in Kales, A. (ed.), *Sleep: Physiology and pathology.* Philadelphia: J. B. Lippincott Co., 1969.

Hathaway, S. R., & McKinley, J. C. *Minnesota multiphasic personality inventory: Manual.* New York: Psychological Corporation, 1951.

Hauptman, A. Luminal bei Epilepsie. *München med. Wschr.,* 1907–1909, 1912, 54.

Havemann, E. Who's normal? Nobody, but we all keep trying. *Life,* Aug. 8, 1960, **49,** 78.

Heath, R. G., et al. Behavioral changes in non-psychotic volunteers following administration of taraxein, the substance obtained from the serum of schizophrenic patients. *Amer. J. Psychiat.,* 1958, **114,** 917.

Heath, R. G. Perspectives for biological psychiatry. *Biol. Psychiat.,* 1970, **2,** 81.

Hebb, D. O., & Penfield, W. Human behavior after extensive bilateral removal from the frontal lobes. *Arch. neurol. Psychiat.,* 1940, **43,** 421.

Hecker, E. Die Hebephrenic. *Arch. path. Anat., Physiol.,* 1871, 52.

Henderson, D. K. *Psychopathic states.* New York: W. W. Norton & Company, Inc., 1939.

Henry, G. W. *All the sexes: A study of masculinity and femininity.* New York: Holt, Rinehart and Winston, Inc., 1955. Pp. 4–8.

Henry, J., & Henry, Zunia. *Doll play of Pilaga Indian children.* New York: American Orthopsychiatric Association, 1944. Research Monographs, No. 4.

Hermann, J. B., & Barbour, H. G. Catatonia produced by introduction of heavy water into the cerebrospinal fluid. *Science,* 1937, **86,** 244.

Hess, W. R. *Diencephalon autonomic and extrapyramidal functions.* London: William Heinemann, Ltd., 1954.

Hirning, J. C. Indecent exposure and other sex offenses. *J. clin. Psychopath. Psychother.,* 1945, **7,** 105.

Hoenig, J., & Sreenivasan, U. Mental hospital admissions in Mysore State, India. *J. ment. Sci.,* 1959, **105,** 124.

Hoffer, A. Adrenalin metabolites and schizophrenia. *Dis. nerv. Syst.,* 1960, **21,** 79.

Hoffer, A., et al. Schizophrenia: A new approach. *J. ment. Sci.,* 1954, **100,** 29.

Hoffman, F. J. *Freudianism and the literary mind.* Baton Rouge, La.: Louisiana State University Press, 1945. P. 208.

Hollingshead, A. B., & Redlich, F. C. *Social class and mental illness: A community study.* New York: John Wiley & Sons, Inc., 1958.

Hollingshead, A. B., et al. Social mobility and mental illness. *Amer. sociol. Rev.,* 1954, **19,** 577.

Hood, A. N. Personal experiences in the great earthquake. *Living Age,* May, 1909, **261,** 355.

Horney, Karen. *Neurosis and human growth.* New York: W. W. Norton & Company, Inc., 1950.

Hoskovec, J. A review of some major work in Soviet hypnotherapy. *Int. J. clin. exp. Hypn.,* 1967, **15,** 1.

Hunt, J. M., & Guilford, J. P. Fluctuation of an ambiguous figure in dementia praecox and in manic-depressive patients. *J. abnorm. soc. Psychol.,* 1933, **27,** 443.

Hurst, E. W. The effects of the injection of normal brain emulsion into rabbits. *J. Hyg.,* 1932, **32,** 33.

Hutt, M. L., & Briskin, G. J. *The clinical use of the revised Bender-Gestalt test.* New York: Grune & Stratton, Inc., 1960.

Huxley, A. *The doors of perception.* London: Chatto and Windus, Ltd., 1954.

Hyde, R. W., & Kingsley, L. K. Studies in medical sociology: I. The relation of mental disorders to the community socio-economic level. *New England J. Med.,* 1944, **231,** 543.

Hyde, R. W., & Kingsley, L. K. Studies in medical sociology: II. The relation of mental disorders to population density. *New England J. Med.,* 1944, **231,** 571.

Hynek, R. M. *Konnersreuth; a medical and psychological study of the case of Teresa Neumann.* (Trans. and adapted by L. C. Sheppard.) London: Burns, Oates & Washburne, Ltd., 1932.

Innes, G., et al. Emotion and blood pressure. *J. ment. Sci.,* 1959, **105,** 840.

Isaacs, W., et al. Application of operant conditioning to reinstate verbal behavior in psychotics. *J. speech hear. Disord.,* 1960, **25,** 8.

Israel, S. L. *Diagnosis and treatment of menstrual disorders and sterility.* (4th ed.) New York: Paul B. Hoeber, Inc., 1959.

Itard, J. M. G. *The wild boy of Aveyron.* New York: Appleton-Century-Crofts, Inc., 1932.

Itard, J. M. G. *Rapports et mémories sur le sauvage de l'Aveyron: L'idiotié et la surd-mutité.* Paris: Bibliothèque d'Education Spéciale, 1824.

Jackson, D. D., et al. Psychiatrists' conceptions of the schizophrenic parent. *Arch. neurol. Psychiat.,* 1958, **79,** 448.

Jackson, J. H. On the anatomical, physiological, and pathological investigation of the epilepsies. *West Riding Lunatic Asylum med. Rep.,* 1873, **3,** 315.

Jaco, E. G. *The social epidemiology of mental disorders: A psychiatric survey of Texas.* New York: Russell Sage Foundation, 1960.

James, W. *Varieties of religious experience.* London: Longmans, Green & Co., Ltd., 1938.

Janet, P. *Psychological healing.* New York: The Macmillan Company, 1925, 2 vols.

Janis, I. L. *Psychological stress: Psychoanalytic and behavioral studies of surgical patients.* New York: John Wiley & Sons, Inc., 1958. P. 67.

Jelliffe, S. E. *The technique of psychoanalysis.* New York: Nervous and Mental Diseases Publishing Co., 1914.

Jellinek, E. M. Recent trends in alcoholism and alcohol consumption. *Quart. J. Stud. Alcohol,* 1947, **8,** 23.

Jenkins, R. L., & Brown, A. W. The geographical distribution of mental deficiency in the Chicago area. *Proc. Amer. Ass. Stud. ment. Def.,* 1935, **40,** 291.

Jodrey, Louise H., & Smith, J. A. Releasable histamine levels and histamine tolerance in the tissues of 291 psychotic patients. *Amer. J. Psychiat.,* 1959, **115,** 801.

Joshua, Joan. Abnormal Behavior in Cats. Chapter 23 in *Abnormal Behavior in Animals,* M. W. Fox (ed.). Philadelphia: W. B. Saunders Company, 1968.

Jowett, B. (trans.) *The dialogues of Plato.* New York: Random House, Inc., 1953.

Joyce, J. *Finnegans wake.* Cambridge, Mass.: Harvard University Press, 1957.

Jung, C. G. *The structure and dynamics of the psyche.* New York: Pantheon Books, a division of Random House, Inc., 1960. Pp. 395–399.

Jung, C. G. *Studies in word-association.* (Trans. by M. D. Eder.) New York: Moffat, Yard, 1919.

Kahlbaum, K. *Die Katatonie oder das Spannungsirresein.* Berlin: 1874.

Kallmann, F. J. *The genetics of schizophrenia.* Locust Valley, N.Y.: J. J. Augustin Publisher, 1938.

Kallmann, F. J. *Heredity in health and mental disorder.* New York: W. W. Norton & Company, Inc., 1953.

Kanner, L. *Child psychiatry.* Springfield, Ill.: Charles C Thomas, Publisher, 1925.

Kanner, L. *Child Psychiatry.* (3d ed.) Springfield, Ill.: Charles C Thomas, Publisher, 1957.

Kaplan, D. M., & Mason, E. A. Maternal reactions to premature birth viewed as an acute emotional disorder. *Amer. J. Orthopsychiat.,* 1960, **30,** 539.

Karn, H. W. A case of experimentally induced neurosis in the cat. *J. exp. Psychol.,* 1938, **22,** 589.

Karn, H. W., & Malamud, H. R. The behavior of dogs on the double alternation problem in the temporal maze. *J. comp. Psychol.,* 1939, **27,** 461.

Kaswan, J., & Love, L. R. Confrontation as a method of psychological intervention. *J. nerv. ment. Dis.,* 1969, **148,** 224.

Katchadourian, H. A., and Churchill, C. W. Social class and mental illness in urban Lebanon. *Soc. Psychiat.,* 1969, **4**(2), 49–55.

Katz, J., et al. Psychoendocrine aspects of cancer of the breast. *Psychosom. Med.,* 1970, **32,** 1.

Kazansky, V. I. *Cancer.* Moscow: Foreign Languages Publishing House, 1955.

Kennard, Margaret. Autonomic interrelations with the somatic nervous system. *Psychosom. Med.,* 1947, **9,** 29.

Kennedy, F., et al. Psychiatric study of William Heirens. *J. crim. Law Criminol.,* 1947, **38,** 325.

Kent, Grace H., & Rosanoff, A. J. A study of association in insanity, *Amer. J. Insanity,* 1910, **67,** 37.

Kerckhoff, A. C., & Back, K. W. *The June bug: A study of hysterical contagion.* New York: Appleton Century Crofts, 1968.

Keup, W. Biochemie der Schizophrenia. *Mschr. Psychiat. Neurol.,* 1954, **128,** 56.

Kimball, C. P. Psychological responses to the experience of open heart surgery. *Amer. J. Psychiat.,* 1969, **126,** 348.

King, G. F.; Armitage, S. G.; & Tilton, J. R. Therapeutic approach to schizophrenics of extreme pathology: an operant-interpersonal method. *J. abnor. soc. Psychol.,* 1960, **61**(2), 276–286.

Kinsey, A. C., et al. *Sexual behavior in the human female.* Philadelphia: W. B. Saunders Company, 1953.

Kinsey, A. C., et al. *Sexual behavior in the human male.* Philadelphia: W. B. Saunders Company, 1948. Pp. 610–666.

Kirk, S. A. *Early education of the mentally retarded.* Urbana, Ill.: The University of Illinois Press, 1958.

Kisker, G. W. Neuropathological and psychological implications of bilateral prefrontal lobotomy. *J. nerv. ment. Dis.,* 1944, **99,** 1.

Kisker, G. W. Self-confrontation in schizophrenia: Preliminary report. Columbus, Ohio, Columbus State Hospital Clinical Reports, 1940.

Kisker, G. W. *Sentence completion D-scale.* Cincinnati, Ohio: Longview State Hospital, 1958.

Klaesi, J. Dauernarkose Mittels Somnifen bei Schizophrenen. *Z. ges. neurol. Psychiat.,* 1922, **74,** 557.

Klein, Henriette, et al. *Anxiety in pregnancy and childbirth.* New York: Paul B. Hoeber, Inc., 1950.

Klüver, H. *Mescal.* London: George Routledge & Sons, Ltd., 1928.

Klüver, H., & Bucy, P. Psychic blindness and other symptoms following bilateral temporal lobectomy in rhesus monkeys. *Amer. J. Physiol.,* 1937, **119,** 352.

Knapp, H. K., et al. Personality variations in bronchial asthma. *Psychosom. Med.,* 1957, **19,** 443.

Knowlton, W. M. Electricity in the treatment of insanity. Paper presented to Amer. Med.-Psychol. Ass., Milwaukee, Wis., 1901.

Koch, J. A. L. *Die Psychopathischen Minderwertigkeiten.* Ravensburg, Germany: Maier, 1891.

Kopeloff, N. *Bacteriology in neuropsychiatry.* Springfield, Ill.: Charles C Thomas, Publisher, 1941.

Kopeloff, L. M., et al. Recurrent convulsive seizures in animals produced by immunologic and chemical means. *Amer. J. Psychiat.,* 1942, **98,** 881.

Kraepelin, E. *Lehrbuch der Psychiatrie.* (5th ed.) Leipzig, Germany: Barth, 1896.

Kraepelin, E. *Psychiatrie.* Leipzig, Germany: Barth, 1915.

Kretschmer, E. *Physique and character.* London: Kegan Paul, Trench, Trubner & Co., Ltd., 1925.

Kroeber, A. L. Totem and taboo: An ethnologic psychoanalysis. *Amer. Anthrop.,* 1920, **22,** 48.

Kroger, W. S., & Freed, S. C. *Psychosomatic gynecology.* Chicago: The Free Press of Glencoe, Ill., 1956.

Krystal, H. The physiological basis of the treatment of delirium tremens. *Amer. J. Psychiat.,* 1959, **115,** 137.

Kurtsin, I. T. Pavlov's concept of experimental neurosis and abnormal behavior in animals. Chap. 6 in *Abnormal behavior in animals,* M. W. Fox (ed.). Philadelphia: W. B. Saunders Company, 1968.

LaBarba, R. C. Experimental and environmental problems in cancer. *Psychosom. Med.,* 1970, **32,** 259–276.

LaBarre, W. *The peyote cult.* New Haven, Conn.: Yale University Press, 1938.

Laffal, J., & Ameen, L. Hypotheses of opposite speech. *J. abnorm. soc. Psychol.,* 1959, **58,** 267.

Lamberd, W. G. The treatment of homosexuality as a monosymptomatic phobia. *Amer. J. Psychiat.,* 1969, **126,** 94.

Landis, C., & Page, J. D. *Modern society and mental disease.* New York: Holt, Rinehart and Winston, Inc., 1939.

Landis, C., & DeWick, H. N. The electrical phenomena of the skin. *Psychol. Bull.,* 1929, **26,** 64.

Lantz, H. R. Population density and psychiatric diagnosis. *Sociol. soc. Res.,* 1953, **37,** 322.

Laubscher, B. J. F. *Sex, custom and psychopathology; a study of South African pagan natives.* New York: Robert M. McBride Co., Inc., 1938.

Laughlin, H. T. *The neuroses in clinical practice.* Philadelphia: W. B. Saunders Company, 1956. Pp. 39–40.

Leduc, S. Production du sommeil et de l'anesthesie generale et locale par le courant electrique. *C. R. Acad. Paris,* 1902, **135,** 119.

Leighton, A. H. *My name is legion.* Volume 1. *The Stirling County studies in psychiatric disorder and sociocultural environment.* New York: Basic Books, Inc., Publishers, 1961.

Lejeune, J., et al. Étude des chromosomes somatiques de neuf enfants mongoliens. *C. R. Acad. Sci.,* 1959, **248,** 1721.

Lemere, F. What happens to alcoholics? *Amer. J. Psychiat.,* 1953, **109,** 674.

Lemkau, P., et al. Mental hygiene problems in an urban district: Second paper. *Ment. Hyg., N.Y.,* 1942, **26,** 100.

Leshan, L. L., & Worthington, R. E. Personality in cancer. *Brit. J. Med. Psychol.,* 1956, **29,** 49.

Lesser, L. I., et al. Anorexia nervosa in children. *Amer. J. Orthopsychiat.,* 1960, **30,** 572.

Lewin, L. *Phantastica: Narcotic and stimulating drugs: Their Use and abuse.* London: Kegan Paul, Trench, Trubner & Co., Ltd., 1931.

Lewis, N. D. C., & Engle, B. (eds.) *Wartime psychiatry.* New York: Oxford Book Company, Inc., 1954.

Lewis, T. *Soldier's heart and effort syndrome.* London: Shaw & Sons, Ltd., 1940.

Liddell, H. S. Experimental induction of psychoneuroses by conditioned reflex with stress. In *The biology of mental health and disease.* New York: Milbank Memorial Fund, 1952, chap. 29.

Lidz, T. Schizophrenia and the family. *Psychiatry,* 1958, **21,** 21.

Lieberman, M. A. Psychological effects of institutionalization. *J. geront.,* 1968, **23,** 343.

Lin, T. A study of the incidence of mental disorder in Chinese and other cultures. *Psychiatry,* 1953, **16,** 313.

Lindner, R. M. *Rebel without a cause: The hypnoanalysis of a criminal psychopath.* New York: Grune & Stratton, Inc., 1944. P. 217.

Lindsley, O. R. Characteristics of the behavior of chronic psychotics as revealed by free-operant conditioning methods. *Dis. Nerv. Syst.,* 1960, **21,** 66.

Loewi, O. Uber Humorale Ubertragbarkeit der Herznervenwirkung. *Pflüg. Arch. ges. Physiol.,* 1921, **189,** 239.

Logan, L., et al. *A study of the effect of catastrophe on social disorganization.* Chevy Chase, Md.: Operations Research Office, 1952.

Lombroso, C. *Crime: Its causes and remedies.* (trans. by H. Horton.) Boston: Little, Brown and Company, 1911.

Lord, W. *A night to remember.* New York: Holt, Rinehart and Winston, Inc., 1955.

MacDonnell, M. F., & Flynn, J. P. Attack elicited by stimulation of the thalamus and adjacent structures of cats. *Behaviour,* 1968, **31,** 185.

Machover, K. *Personality projection in the drawings of the human figure.* Springfield, Ill.: Charles C Thomas, Publisher, 1949.

Macht, D. I. Influence of some drugs and of emotions on blood coagulation *J. Amer. med. Ass.,* 1952, **148,** 265.

Macht, D. I. Pharmacologic reactions of normal and psychotic blood serums. *Sth. Med. J.,* 1950, **43,** 1049.

MacWilliam, J. A. Some applications of physiology to medicine; blood pressure and heart action in sleep and dreams; their relation to haemorrhages, angina, and sudden death. *British med. J.,* 1923, **2,** 1196.

Maier, N. R. F. *Studies of abnormal behavior in the rat: The neurotic pattern and an analysis of the situation which produces it.* New York: Harper & Brothers, 1939.

Malinowski, B. *Sex and repression in savage society.* New York: Harcourt, Brace & World, Inc., 1927.

Malzberg, B. Important statistical data about mental illness. In Arieti, S. (ed.), *American Handbook of psychiatry.* New York: Basic Books, Inc., Publishers, 1959. Pp. 161–174.

Malzberg, B. New data relative to incidence of mental disease among Jews. *Ment. Hyg., N. Y.,* 1936, **20,** 280.

Malzberg, B. Important statistical data about mental illness. In Arieti, S. (ed.), *American Handbook of psychiatry.* New York: Basic Books, Inc., Publishers, 1959, Pp. 161–174.

Martin, B., et al. Verbal and GSR responses in experimental interviews as a function of three degrees of therapist communication. *J. abnorm. soc. Psychol.,* 1960, **60,** 234.

Masserman, J. H. *Behavior and neurosis: An experimental psychoanalytic approach to psychobiologic principles.* Chicago: University of Chicago Press, 1943.

Masserman, J. H., & Pechtel, C. Conflict-engendered neurotic and psychotic behavior in monkeys. *J. nerv. ment. Dis.,* 1953, **118,** 408.

Maudsley, H. *The pathology of mind.* (3d ed.) London: Macmillan & Co., Ltd., 1879.

Maxwell, W. *De medicina magnetica.* London: 1679.

Mayer-Gross, W. Model psychoses, their history, relevancy and limitations. *Amer. J. Psychiat.,* 1959, **115,** 673.

McCarthy, R. G. (ed.) *Drinking and intoxication.* New York: The Free Press of Glencoe, Inc., 1959.

McCord, W., & McCord, Joan. *Origins of crime; a new evaluation of the Cambridge-Somerville youth study.* New York: Columbia University Press, 1959.

McGeer, P. L., et al. Aromatic metabolism in schizophrenia. I. Statistical evidence for Aromaturia. *J. nerv. ment. Dis.,* 1957, **125,** 166.

McGinnies, E. Emotionality and perceptual defense. *Psychol. Rev.,* 1949, **56,** 244.

McIntire, J. T. The incidence of feeblemindedness in the cerebral palsied. *Proc. Amer. Ass. ment. Def.,* 1938, **43,** 44.

McNish, R. *Anatomy of drunkenness.* Edinburgh: 1835.

Meduna, L. J. *Carbon dioxide therapy.* Springfield, Ill.: Charles C Thomas, Publisher, 1950. P. 31.

Meduna, L. J. *Die Konvulsionstherapie der Schizophrenie.* Halle: Marhold, 1936.

Meduna, L. J., & Viachulis, J. A. Hyperglycemic factor in urine of so-called schizophrenics. *Dis. nerv. System,* 1948, **9,** 248.

Meerloo, J. A. M. Fear and the flu. *New Leader,* Jan. 6, 1958.

Menninger, K. *The human mind.* New York: Alfred A. Knopf, Inc., 1930.

Menninger, K., et al. The new role of psychological testing in psychiatry. *Amer. J. Psychiat.,* 1947, **103,** 473.

Menninger, W. C. The inter-relationships of mental disorders and diabetes mellitus. *J. ment. Sci.,* 1935, **81,** 332.

Mental Deficiency Commission, 1920 Report. London: H. M. Stationery Office, 1929.

Mercier, C. Diet as a factor in the causation of mental disease. *J. ment. Sci.,* 1916, **62,** 505.

Merzbach, A. Mental changes associated with avitaminosis. *Harefuah,* 1941, **20,** 22.

Mesmer, F. A. *Mémoire sur la découverte du magnétisme animal.* Paris: 1781.

Mettler, Cecilia C., & Mettler, F. A. *History of medicine.* New York: McGraw-Hill Book Company, 1947. P. 159.

Meyer, A. *Psychobiology.* Springfield, Ill.: Charles C Thomas, Publisher, 1957.

Meyer-Holzapsel, Monica. *Abnormal Behavior in Zoo Animals.* Chapter 25 in *Abnormal Behavior in Animals,* M. W. Fox (ed.) Philadelphia: W. B. Saunders Company, 1968.

Miller, N. E., & DiCara, L. V. Instrumental learning of vasomotor responses by rats. *Science,* 1968, **159,** 1485.

Mitchell, J. R. A Psychosis Among Cats. *Vet. Rec.* 1953, **65,** 254.

Mittleman, B., & Wolff, H. G. Emotions and skin temperature: Observations on patients during psychotherapeutic (psychoanalytic) interviews. *Psychosom. Med.,* 1943, **5,** 211.

Moloney, J. C. Psychiatric observations in Okinawa Shima. *Psychiatry,* 1945, **8,** 391.

Moore, H. E. Some emotional concomitance of disaster. *Ment. Hyg.,* N.Y., 1958, **42,** 45.

Morel, B. *Traité des maladies mentales.* Paris: 1860.

Moreno, J. L. *Who shall survive? Foundations of sociometry, group psychotherapy and sociodrama.* (2d ed.) New York: Beacon House, Inc., 1953.

Mowrer, O. H., et al. *Psychotherapy: theory and research.* New York: The Ronald Press Company, 1953.

Murray, H. A., & Morgan, C. D. *Explorations in personality.* New York: Oxford Book Company, Inc., 1938.

Musgrave, W. E. Tropical neurasthenia, tropical hysteria and some special tropical hysteria-like neuro-psychoses. *Arch. Neur. Psychiat.,* 1921, **5,** 398.

Mutrux, S., & Glasson, B. Study of cholinesterase of blood and cerebrospinal fluid in various psychiatric syndromes. *Mschr. Psychiat. Neurol.,* 1947, **114,** 20.

Myers, J. K., & Roberts, B. H. *Family and class dynamics in mental illness.* New York: John Wiley & Sons, Inc., 1959. P. 180.

Näätähän, E. K., & Jänkälä, E. O. Effect of psychic stress on cells of the pituitary body and suprarenal glands of rats. *Ann. med. exp. biol. Fenniae,* 1954, **32,** 410.

Nachmansohn, D., & Machado, A. L. Effect of glutamic acid on the formation of acetylcholine. *J. Biol. Chem.,* 1943, **150,** 485.

Neuhaus, E. C. A personality study of asthmatic and cardiac children. *Psychosom. Med.,* 1958, **20,** 181.

New York City, 1944. *The marihuana problem in the city of New York.* The Mayor's Committee on marihuana. Lancaster, Pa.: Cattell Press.

New York Times, Jan. 21, 1968, p. 11C.

New York Times, Feb. 16, 1970.

Newsweek, June 3, 1968, p. 68.

Neilsen, J. M. The neurology of alcoholism. In G. N. Thompson (ed.), *Alcoholism.* Springfield, Ill.: Charles C Thomas, Publisher, 1956, chap. 6.

NIAID, 1969. Special report. National Institute of Allergy and Infectious Diseases. Bethesda, Maryland.

NIMH, 1969. Budgetary Hearings for the National Institute of Mental Health before a Subcommittee of the Committee on Appropriations, Ninetieth Congress, Second Session. Washington, D.C., 1968.

NIMH, 1968. Budgetary Hearings for the National Institute of Mental Health before a Subcommittee of the Committee on Appropriations. Eighty-ninth Congress, Second Session, Washington, D.C., 1967.

NIMH, 1970. Budgetary Hearings for the National Institute of Mental Health before a Subcommittee of the Committee on Appropriations, Ninety-first Congress, First Session. Washington, D. C., 1969.

NINDS, 1970. National Institute of Neurological Diseases and Stroke, Bethesda, Maryland.

Obermayer, M. E. *Psychocutaneous medicine.* Springfield, Ill.: Charles C Thomas, Publisher, 1955.

Ocko, F. H. Unusual psychiatric manifestations of neurological disease. *Bull. N. Y. Acad. Med.,* 1959, **35,** 269.

Odegaard, O. *Emigration and insanity.* Copenhagen: Munksgaard, 1932.

Odegaard, O. Marriage and mental disease: Study of social psychopathology. *J. ment. Sci.,* 1946, **92,** 35.

Oleck, H. L. Legal aspects of premenstrual tension. *Int. Record Med.,* 1953, **166,** 492.

Olds, J. Reward from brain stimulation in the rat. *Science,* 1955, **122,** 878.

Olds, J., & Travis, R. P. Effects of chlorpromazine, meprobamate, pentobarbital, and morphine on self-stimulation. In L. Uhr & J. G. Miller (eds.), *Drugs and behavior.* New York: John Wiley & Sons, Inc., 1960, chap. 15.

Opler, M. K. *Culture, psychiatry and human values.* Springfield, Ill.: Charles C Thomas, Publisher, 1956.

Parfitt, D. N., & Gall, C. M. Psychogenic amnesia; the refusal to remember. *J. ment. Sci.,* 1944, **90,** 511.

Park, R. E., & Burgess, E. W. *The city.* Chicago: University of Chicago Press, 1921.

Paredes, A., et al. A clinical study of alcoholics using audio-visual self-image feedback. *J. nerv. ment. Dis.,* 1969, **148,** 449.

Partridge, G. C. Current conceptions of psychopathic personality. *Amer. J. Psychiat.,* 1930, **10,** 54.

Pauling, Linus. Orthomolecular psychiatry. *Science,* 1968, **160,** 265.

Pavlov, I. P. *Lectures on conditioned reflexes.* Vol. 2. *Conditioned reflexes and psychiatry.* London: Lawrence and Wishart, Ltd., 1941.

Pavlov, I. P. *Lectures on conditioned reflexes.* (Trans. by W. H. Gantt.) New York: International Publishers Company, Inc., 1928.

Penfield, W. The interpretative cortex. *Science,* 1959, **129,** 1719.

Penfield, W. Memory mechanisms. *Arch. Neurol. Psychiat.,* 1952, **67,** 178.

Penfield, W., & Jasper, H. *Epilepsy and the functional anatomy of the brain.* Boston: Little, Brown and Company, 1954.

Penfield, W., & Roberts, L. *Speech and brain mechanisms.* Princeton, N. J.: Princeton University Press, 1959.

Penrose, L. S. Observation on the etiology of mongolism. *Lancet,* 1954, **2,** 505.

Perceval, J. T. The parliamentary inquiry and popular notions concerning the treatment of lunatics. *J. Psychol. Med. Ment. Path.,* 1860, **13,** 45.

Perry, S. E., et al. *The child and his family in disaster: A study of the 1953 Vicksburg tornado.* Committee on Disaster Studies, Disaster Study No. 5. Washington, D. C.: National Academy of Sciences—National Research Council, 1956.

Peters, H. N., & Jenkins, R. L. Improvement of chronic schizophrenic patients with guided problem-solving, motivated by hunger. *Psychiat. Quart. Suppl.,* 1954, **28,** 84.

Pick, A. Ueber die Beziehungen der senilen Hirnatrophie zur Aphasia. *Prag. med. Wschr.,* 1892, **17,** 165.

Pincus, G., & Hoagland, H. Adrenal cortical responses to stress in normal men and in those with personality disorders. *Amer. J. Psychiat.,* 1950, **106,** 641.

Pinel, P. *A treatise on insanity.* Paris: 1798.

Pinsker, H. The irrelevancy of psychiatric diagnosis. Paper read at the American Psychiatric meeting (Detroit), May, 1967.

Pound, E. The Pisan cantos. In *The cantos of . . . . .* Norfolk, Conn.: New Directions, 1948. P. 43.

Price, A. D., & Deabler, H. L. Diagnosis of organicity by means of spiral after-effect. *J. consult. Psychol.,* 1955, **19,** 299.

Prichard, J. C. *A treatise on insanity.* London: 1839.

Prince, M. *The dissociation of a personality.* London: Longmans, Green & Co., Ltd., 1905.

Protell, M. R. *Roche report: Frontiers of hospital psychiatry,* 1968.

Putnam, T. J., & Merritt, H. H. Experimental determination of the anticonvulsant properties of some phenyl derivatives. *Science,* 1937, **85,** 525.

Quackenbos, J. D. *Hypnotic therapeutics.* New York: Harper & Brothers, 1908. P. 41.

Rank, O. *The trauma of birth.* New York: Harcourt, Brace and Company, Inc., 1929.

Rapaport, D., et al. *Diagnostic psychological testing.* Chicago: The Year Book Publishers, Inc., 1945–1946. 2 vols.

Ratcliffe, H. L., & Cronin, M. T. Changing frequency of arteriosclerosis in mammals and birds in the Philadelphia Zoological Garden. *Circulation,* 1958, **18,** 41.

Reckless, W. C. *Vice in Chicago.* Chicago: University of Chicago Press, 1933.

Reed, C. A. L. Diagnostic methods and pathologic constants in idiopathic epilepsy. *J. Amer. med. Ass.,* 1916, **66,** 336.

Reichard, S., & Tillman, C. Patterns of parent-child relationships in schizophrenia. *Psychiatry,* 1950, **13,** 247.

Rennie, T. A. C., et al. Urban life and mental health. *Amer. J. Psychiat.,* 1957, **113,** 831.

Ricciuti, H. N. Comparison of critical flicker frequency in psychotics, psychoneurotics, and normals. *Amer. Psychologist,* 1948, **3,** 276.

Richter, C. P. On the phenomenon of sudden death in animals and man. *Psychosom. Med.,* 1957, **19,** 191.

Rickard, H. C., et al. Verbal manipulation in a psychotherapeutic relationship. *J. clin. Psychol.,* 1960, **16,** 364.

Riley, J. W., Jr., et al. The motivational pattern of drinking. *Quart. J. Stud. Alcohol,* 1948, **9,** 353.

Ripley, H. S., & Wolff, H. G. Life situations, emotions, and glaucoma. *Psychosom. Med.,* 1950, **12,** 215.

Roberts, B. H., & Meyers, J. K. Religion, national origin and mental illness. *Amer. J. Psychiat.,* 1954, **110,** 759.

Roberts, E. Some aspects of the biochemistry and physiology of gamma amino butyric acid in the central nervous system. *Amer. J. Orthopsychiat.,* 1960, **30,** 15.

Robertson, E. E., et al. The clinical differentiation of Pick's disease. *J. ment. Sci.,* 1958, **104,** 1000.

Roche report: Frontiers of hospital psychiatry, Sept. 1, 1968. P. 21.

Rohde, Amanda R. *The sentence completion method.* New York: The Ronald Press Company, 1957.

Rorschach, H. *Psychodiagnostics: A diagnostic test based on perception.* New York: Grune & Stratton, Inc., 1942.

Rosanoff, A. J., et al. Criminality and delinquency in twins. *J. crim. Law Criminol.,* 1934, **24,** 923.

Rose, A. M. (ed.) *Mental health and mental disorder.* New York: W. W. Norton & Company, Inc., 1955.

Rose, A. M., & Stub, H. R. Summary of the incidence of mental disorders. In A. M. Rose (ed.), *Mental health and mental disorder.* New York: W. W. Norton & Company, Inc., 1955.

Rosen, J. N. *Direct analysis.* New York: Grune & Stratton, Inc., 1953.

Rosenow, E. C. Bacteriologic, etiologic and serologic studies in epilepsy and schizophrenia. *Postgrad. Med.,* 1947, **2,** 346.

Rosenthal, D. *Genetic theory and abnormal behavior.* New York: McGraw-Hill Book Company, 1970.

Ross, M., & Mendelsohn, F. Homosexuality in college: A preliminary report of data obtained from one hundred thirty-three students seen in a university student health center and a review of pertinent literature. *Amer. med. Ass. Arch. Neurol. Psychiat.,* 1958, **80,** 253–263.

Roth, P. *Portnoy's complaint.* New York: Random House, Inc., 1969.

Roth, W. F., Jr., & Luton, F. H. The mental health program in Tennessee. *Amer. J. Psychiat.,* 1943, **9,** 662.

Rowntree, L. G. Effects on mammals of administration of excessive quantities of water. *J. Pharmacol.,* 1926, **29,** 135.

Rüdin, E. *Zur Verebung und Neuentstehung der Dementia Praecox.* Berlin: Springer-Verlag OHG, 1916.

Rush, B. *Medical inquiries and observations upon diseases of the mind.* Philadelphia: 1812.

Rylander, G. *Mental changes after excision of cerebral tissue. Acta Neurol. Psychiat.,* Suppl. 25. Copenhagen: Einar and Munksgaard, 1943.

Saenger, G. *The adjustment of severely retarded adults in the community.* Albany, N.Y.: New York State Interdepartmental Health Resources Board, 1957.

Sakel, M. *The pharmacological shock treatment of schizophrenia.* New York: Nervous and Mental Diseases Publishing Co., 1938.

Sala, S. L., & Salerno, E. Psychological factors in obstetrics and gynecology: Spontaneous emotional abortion. *Bol. Soc. Obst. Ginec.* Buenos Aires, 1945, **24,** 243.

Sanger, M. D. The psyche and dermatitis. *State of Mind,* 1959, **3,** (2).

Sarason, S. B. *Psychological problems in mental deficiency.* New York: Harper & Row, Publishers, Incorporated, 1959. P. 204.

Scheflen, Norma. Semantic conditioning and anxiety. *Dissert. Abstr.,* 1958, **19,** 369.

Schlaegel, T. F., Jr. *Psychosomatic ophthalmology.* Baltimore: The Williams and Wilkins Company, 1957.

Schoenberg, M. J. Remarks on psychosomatic factors in glaucomatous hypertension. *J. clin. Psychopath.,* 1945, **6,** 451.

Schroeder, W. W., & Beegle, J. A. Suicide: An instance of high rural rates. In A. M. Rose (ed.), *Mental Health and mental disorder.* New York: W. W. Norton & Company, Inc., 1955, ch. 27.

Schutz, F. Homosexual ltat und Pragung, *Psychol. Forsch.,* 1965, **28,** 439.

Seabury, D. *What makes us seem so queer?* New York: McGraw-Hill Book Company, 1934.

Seligman, C. G. Temperament, conflict and psychosis in a stone-age population. *Brit. J. med. Psychol.,* 1929, **9,** 187.

Selye, H. *The story of the adaptation syndrome.* Montreal: Acta, 1952.

Sexton, M. C. The autokinetic test: Its value in psychiatric diagnosis and prognosis. *Amer. J. Psychiat.,* 1945, **102,** 399.

Shaw, C. R., et al. *Delinquency areas.* Chicago: University of Chicago Press, 1929.

Sheldon, W. H. *Varieties of human physique.* New York: Harper & Brothers, 1940.

Sherrington, C. S. *Proc. royal Soc.,* London, 1897.

Shields, J., & Slater, E. Heredity and psychological abnormality. In H. J. Eysenck (ed.), *Handbook of abnormal psychology.* London: Sir Isaac Pitman & Sons, Ltd., 1960.

Shields, J. Summary of the genetic evidence. In David Rosenthal & S. S. Kety (eds.), *The transmission of schizophrenia.* New York: Pergamon Press, 1968.

Shurley, J. T. Profound experimental sensory isolation. *Amer. J. Psychiat.,* 1960, **117,** 539.

Siemes, F. Hiroshima—August 6, 1945. *Bull. Atomic Scientists,* 1946, **1,** 2.

Sikes, J. C., & Sikes, S. C. Lithium carbonate treatment in psychiatry. *Dis. Nerv. Syst.,* 1970, **31,** 52.

Silver, L. B.; Dublin, Christina C.; & Lourie, R. S. Does violence breed violence? Contributions from a study of the child abuse syndrome. *Amer. J. Psychiat.,* 1969, **126**(3), 404–407.

Skeels, H. M., & Dye, H. N. A study of the effects of differential stimulation on mentally retarded children. *Proc. Addresses Amer. Ass. ment. Def.,* 1939, **44,** 114.

SKF Psychiatric Reporter, 1968, **37,** 10.

Skinner, B. F., & Lindsley, O. R. Studies in behavior therapy. Status report I, Naval research contract N5, Ori-7662, 1953.

Slack, C. W. Experimenter-subject psychotherapy. *Ment. Hyg.,* 1960, **44,** 238.

Slater, E. A review of earlier evidence on genetic factors in schizophrenia. In David Roset Rosenthal & S. S. Kety (eds.), *The transmission of schizophrenia.* New York: Pergamon Press, 1968.

Smith, P. B. A Sunday with mescaline. *Bull. Menninger Clin.,* 1959, **23,** 20.

Smith, A.; Traganza, E.; & Harrison, G. Studies on the effectiveness of antidepressant drugs. *Psychopharmacology Bulletin* (Special Issue), March, 1969.

Snyder, C. R. Culture and sobriety: A study of drinking patterns and socio-cultural factors related to sobriety among Jews. *Quart. J. Stud. Alcohol.,* 1955, **16,** 101.

Southard, E. E., & Jarrett, M. C. *The kingdom of evils.* New York: The Macmillan Company, 1922.

Spencer, S. J. G. Homosexuality among Oxford undergraduates. *J. ment. Sci.,* 1959, **105,** 393.

Speransky, A. D. *A basis for the theory of medicine.* Moscow: I.C.P.S., 1935.

Squier, R., & Dunbar, F. Emotional factors in the course of pregnancy. *Psychosom. Med.,* 1946, **8,** 161.

Srole, L., et al. *Mental health in the metropolis: The midtown Manhattan study.* Vol. I. New York: McGraw-Hill Book Company, 1962.

Stein, A., et al. Changes in hydrochloric acid secretion in a patient with a gastric fistula during intensive psychotherapy. *Psychosom. Med.,* 1962, **24,** 427.

Stekel, W. *Sadism and masochism.* (Trans. by L. Brink.) Vol. 2. New York: Liveright Publishing Corporation, 1929. P. 175.

Stern, L. *Kulturkreis und Form der geistigen Erkrankung.* Halle: Carl Marhold, 1913.

Stern, W. *The psychological methods of testing intelligence.* (Trans. by G. M. Whipple.) Baltimore: Warwick and York Incorporated, 1914.

Stock, M. B. *Science News,* 1967, **91,** 307.

Stockings, G. T. A clinical study of the mescaline psychosis with special reference to the mechanism of the genesis of schizophrenia and other psychotic states. *J. ment. Sci.,* 1940, **86,** 29.

Stoll, W. Lysergsäure-diäthylamid, ein Phantastikum aus der Mutter-korngruppe. *Schweiz. Arch. Neurol. Psychiat.,* 1947, **60,** 1.

Straub, L. R., et al. Disturbances of bladder function associated with emotional states. *J. Amer. med. Ass.,* 1949, **141,** 1139.

Sullivan, H. S. *The interpersonal theory of psychiatry.* New York: W. W. Norton & Company, Inc., 1953.

Suter, C., et al. Sound-induced seizures in animals. *Neurology,* 1958, **8,** Suppl. 1, 117.

Sutton, T. *Tracts on delirium tremens.* London: 1813.

Sweetser, W. *Mental hygiene.* New York: Langley, 1843.

Swinburne, A. C. *Selected poems of . . . .* New York: Dodd, Mead & Company, Inc., 1928.

Szasz, T. S. Some observations on the relationship between psychiatry and the law. *Amer. med. Ass. Arch. Neurol. Psychiat.,* 1956, **75,** 297.

Tedeschi, C. G. I1 trauma cerebrale di minima intesita, singolo e repetuto. *Minerva Chir.,* 1949, **4,** 141.

Tessel, C. Anxiety and the conditioning of verbal behavior. *J. abnorm. soc. Psychol.,* 1955, **51,** 496.

Thompson, C. E. *Manual for the thematic apperception test: Thompson modification.* Cambridge, Mass.: Harvard University Press, 1949.

Thorndike, L. *The history of magic and experimental science.* New York: Columbia University Press, 1923–1956.

Tienari, Pekka. Concordance and discordance for schizophrenia in twins. Proceedings of the Fourth World Congress of Psychiatry, 1967, **2,** 1082.

Tietze, C., et al. Personality disorder and spatial mobility. *Amer. J. Soc.,* 1942, **48,** 29.

Time, Sept. 25, 1950, **56,** 54.

Tinbergen, N. *Social behavior in animals.* London: Methuen & Co., Ltd., 1953.

Titchener, J. L., & Levine, M. *Surgery as a human experience: The psychodynamics of Surgical practice.* New York: Oxford University Press, 1960.

Toffelmier, G., & Luomala, K. Dreams and dream interpretation of the Diegueno Indians of Southern California. *Psychoanal. Quart.,* 1936, **2,** 195.

Tooth, G. *Studies in mental illness in the Gold Coast.* London: Colonial Research Publication No. 6, 1950.

Touraine, G. A., & Draper, G. Migrainous patient; constitutional study. *J. nerv. ment. Dis.,* 1934, **80,** 1.

Tredgold, A. F. *A textbook of mental deficiency.* (6th ed.) Baltimore: William Wood & Company, 1937. P. 4.

Tredgold, R. F., & Soddy, L. (eds.) *A text-book of mental deficiency.* (9th ed.) Baltimore: The Williams & Wilkins Company, 1956.

Treuting, T. F., & Ripley, H. S. Life situations, emotions and bronchial asthma. *J. nerv. ment. Dis.,* 1948, **108,** 380.

Tryon, R. C. Genetic differences in maze-learning ability in rats. *Yearb. nat. soc. Stud. Educ.,* 1940, **39,** 111.

Tucker, W. B., & Lessa, W. A. Man: A constitutional investigation. *Quart. Rev. Biol.,* 1940, **15,** 265.

Tuke, D. H. *A dictionary of psychological medicine.* New York: McGraw-Hill Book Company, 1892. 2 vols.

Tuke, W. H. Cited by D. H. Tuke, *Chapters in the history of the insane in the British Isles.* London: Kegan Paul, 1882.

Uchimara, Y., et al. Imu among the Ainu. *Japan. J. Neuropsychiat.,* 1938, **42**(1).

USPHS, 1970. Special report. United States Public Health Service, Washington, D.C.

U.S. Strategic Bombing Survey, 1945. *The effect of bombing on health and medical care in Germany.* Washington, D.C.: Government Printing Office.

U.S. Strategic Bombing Survey, 1946. *The effects of atomic bombs on Hiroshima and Nagasaki.* Washington, D.C.: Government Printing Office.

U.S. Strategic Bombing Survey, 1947. *The effects of strategic bombing on German morale.* (2 vols.) Washington, D.C.: Government Printing Office.

Van Loon, F. G. H. Amok and lattah. *J. abnorm. soc. Psychol.,* 1927, **4,** 434.

Voegtlin, W. L. Treatment of alcoholism by establishing a conditioned reflex. *Amer. J. med. Sci.,* 1940, **199,** 802.

Von Economo, C. *Encephalitis lethargica: Its sequelae and treatment.* (Trans. by K. O. Newman.) Fair Lawn, N.J.: Oxford University Press, 1931.

Voth, A. C. An experimental study of mental patients through the autokinetic phenomenon. *Amer. J. Psychiat.,* 1947, **103,** 793.

Wada, J., & Gibson, W. C. Behavioral and EEG changes induced by injection of schizophrenic urine extract. *Amer. med. Ass. Arch. Neurol. Psychiat.,* 1959, **81,** 747.

Wallace, A. F. C. *Tornado in Worcester.* Washington, D.C.: National Academy of Sciences—National Research Council, 1956, Publ. No. 362.

Walshe, W. H. *The nature and treatment of cancer.* London: Taylor and Walton, 1846.

Watson, J. B., & Rayner, R. Conditional emotional reactions. *J. exp. Psychol.,* 1920, **3,** 1.

Wechsler, I. S. *Clinical neurology.* (9th ed.) Philadelphia: W. B. Saunders Company, 1963.

Wedge, B. M. Occurrence of psychoses among Okinawans in Hawaii. *Amer. J. Psychiat.,* 1952, **109,** 255.

Weil, A. T.; Zinberg, N. E.; & Nelsen, J. M. Clinical and psychological effects of marihuana in man. *Science,* 1968, **162,** 1234.

Weiss, E., & English, O. S. *Psychosomatic medicine.* Philadelphia; W. B. Saunders Company, 1943. Pp. 613–614.

Welch, B. L., & Welch, A. S. Sustained effects of brief daily stress (fighting) upon brain and adrenal catecholamines and adrenal spleen and heart weights of mice. *Proc. Nat. Acad. Sci.,* 1969, **64,** 100.

Whitehorn, J. C., & Zipf, G. K. Schizophrenic language. *Arch. Neurol. Psychiat.,* 1943, **49,** 831.

Williams, C. D. The elimination of tantrum behavior by extinction procedures. *J. abnorm. soc. Psychol.,* 1959, **59,** 269.

Willis, T. *Stupidity and morosity.* London: 1672.

Winder, C. L. Some psychological studies of schizophrenics. In D. D. Jackson (ed.), *The etiology of schizophrenia.* New York: Basic Books, Inc., Publishers, 1960, chap. 8.

Winter, C. A., & Flataker, L. Effect of blood plasma from psychotic patients upon performance of trained rats. *Arch. neurol. Psychiat.,* 1958, **80,** 441.

Witkin, H. A., et al. *Personality through perception: An experimental and clinical study.* New York: Harper & Brothers, 1954.

Wittenborn, J. R. *Psychiatric rating scales.* New York: The Psychological Corporation, 1955.

Wolff, H. G., & Wolff, S. *Human gastric function: An experimental study of a man and his stomach.* Fair Lawn, N.J.: Oxford University Press, 1943.

Wooley, D. W., & Shaw, E. Some neurophysiological aspects of serotonin. *British med. J.,* 1954, **2,** 122.

WHO, 1951. Expert Committee on Mental Health. Report on the 1st Session of the Alcoholism Committee, World Health Organization, Geneva, Switzerland.

World Health Organization, 1954. *The mentally subnormal child.* Technical Report Series, No. 75. Geneva, Switzerland: World Health Organization.

WHO, 1961. Special report. World Health Organization, Geneva, Switzerland.

Yap, P. M. The latah reaction: Its pathodynamics and nosological position. *J. ment. Sci.,* 1952, **98,** 515.

Yap, P. M. Mental diseases peculiar to certain cultures: A survey of comparative psychiatry. *J. ment. Sci.,* 1951, **97,** 313.

Zador, J. Der Lachgas (NO)-Rausch in seiner Bedeutung für Psychiatrie und Neurologie. *Arch. Psychiat.,* 1928, **84,** 1.

NAME INDEX

SUBJECT INDEX